A Companion to Nazi Germany

WILEY BLACKWELL COMPANIONS TO WORLD HISTORY

This series provides sophisticated and authoritative overviews of the scholarship that has shaped our current understanding of Europe's past. Each volume comprises between 25 and 40 concise essays written by individual scholars within their area of specialization. The aim of each contribution is to synthesize the current state of scholarship from a variety of historical perspectives and to provide a statement on where the field is heading.

The essays are written in a clear, provocative, and lively manner, designed for an international audience of scholars, students, and general readers. The Blackwell Companions to European History series is a cornerstone of the overarching Companions to History series, covering British, American, and World History.

A COMPANION TO NAZI GERMANY

Edited by

Shelley Baranowski,
Armin Nolzen,
and
Claus-Christian W. Szejnmann

WILEY Blackwell

Registered Office(s)
John Wiley & Sons, Inc., 111 River Street, Hoboken, NJ 07030, USA
John Wiley & Sons Ltd, The Atrium, Southern Gate, Chichester, West Sussex, PO19 8SQ, UK

Editorial Office
101 Station Landing, Medford, MA 02155, USA

For details of our global editorial offices, customer services, and more information about Wiley products visit us at www.wiley.com.

Wiley also publishes its books in a variety of electronic formats and by print-on-demand. Some content that appears in standard print versions of this book may not be available in other formats.

Library of Congress Cataloging-in-Publication data applied for

[Hardback] 9781118936887

Cover Image: © Everett Historical/Shutterstock
Cover Design: Wiley

Set in 10/12pt Galliard by SPi Global, Pondicherry, India

Printed in Great Britain by TJ International Ltd, Padstow, Cornwall

10 9 8 7 6 5 4 3 2 1

Contents

Notes on Contributors

Aleida Assmann was Professor of English Literature and Literary Theory at the University of Konstanz, Germany (1993–2014), and holds guest professorships at various universities (Princeton, Yale, Chicago, and Vienna). Her main areas of research are the history of media and cultural memory, with special emphasis on Holocaust and trauma. Publications in English are *Memory in a Global Age: Discourses, Practices and Trajectories* (ed. with Sebastian Conrad, 2010), *Cultural Memory and Western Civilization: Functions, Media, Archives* (2012), and *Introduction to Cultural Studies: Topics, Concepts, Issues* (2012).

Shelley Baranowski is Distinguished Professor of History Emerita at the University of Akron, Ohio. Her most recent books include *Nazi Empire: German Colonialism and Imperialism from Bismarck to Hitler* (2011) and *Strength through Joy: Consumerism and Mass Tourism in the Third Reich* (2004). Her current book project is a study of mass violence among the Axis empires.

Frank Becker is Professor of Modern and Contemporary History at the University of Duisburg-Essen. He received his doctorate in history at the University of Münster in 1992, where he received his habilitation in 1998. In 2003, he was Visiting Scholar at the German Historical Institute London and, in 2006, Visiting Professor at Vienna University. His publications include *Bilder von Krieg und Nation: Die Einigungskriege in der bürgerlichen Öffentlichkeit Deutschlands (1864–1913)* (2001), *Den Sport gestalten: Carl Diems Leben (1882–1962)* (2013), and *Zivilisten und Soldaten. Entgrenzte Gewalt in der Geschichte* (ed., 2015).

Marc Buggeln is a research assistant at the Humboldt-University in Berlin. He received his PhD from the University of Bremen in 2008 with a study on the satellite camp system of the Neuengamme concentration camp. This study won the Herbert-Steiner-Preis in 2009 and the translation funding prize Geisteswissenschaften International in 2011. He is a member of the editorial board of *HSozKult*. Currently he is working on a history of public finance in West Germany.

David Clarke is Senior Lecturer in German at the University of Bath. He has published research on German literature and film, with a particular focus on the German Democratic Republic and cultural memory. His most recent research addresses the politics of memory in relation to human rights abuses in the German Democratic Republic. He is co-author, with Ute Wölfel, of *Remembering the German Democratic Republic: Divided Memory in a United Germany* (2011).

Charles E. Closmann is an associate professor of history at the University of North Florida. His research interests include the environmental history of water pollution in Nazi Germany and the relationship between war and the environment. His current project concerns the history of militarized landscapes in Florida.

Debórah Dwork is the Rose Professor of Holocaust History and the founding director of the Strassler Center for Holocaust and Genocide Studies, Clark University. She is a leading authority on university education in this field, as well as her area of scholarship: Holocaust history. One of the first historians to record Holocaust survivors' oral histories and to use their narratives as a scholarly source, Dwork's books include *Children With A Star* (1991) and, with Robert Jan Van Pelt, *Auschwitz*, (1270–1996) and *Flight from the Reich* (2009).

Jörg Echternkamp is Associate Professor for Modern History at Martin Luther University, Halle-Wittenberg, and Research Director at the Centre for Military History and Social Sciences, Potsdam. He held the Alfred Grosser chair at Sciences Po, Paris, in 2012–2013. Key publications are *Soldaten im Nachkrieg* (2014), *Germany and the Second World War, Volume 9/1–2: German Wartime Society 1939–1945* (ed., 2008–2014), *Der Aufstieg des deutschen Nationalismus* (1998), and *Experience and Memory: The Second World War in Europe* (2010).

Geoff Eley is Karl Pohrt Distinguished University Professor of Contemporary History at the University of Michigan, Ann Arbor. His most recent works include *Forging Democracy: The History of the Left in Europe, 1850–2000* (2002), *A Crooked Line: From Cultural History to the History of Society* (2005), and *Nazism as Fascism: Violence, Ideology, and the Ground of Consent in Germany, 1930–1945* (2013). He is currently writing a general history of Europe in the twentieth century.

Manfred Gailus, DPhil, is apl. Professor of Modern German History at the Centre for Research on Antisemitism at the Technical University of Berlin. His major research interests are the social, political, cultural, and religious history of the nineteenth and twentieth centuries, especially the history of nationalism, Protestantism, and National Socialism. His main publications are *Protestantismus und Nationalsozialismus: Studien zur nationalsozialistischen Durchdringung des protestantischen Sozialmilieus in Berlin* (2001), *Nationalprotestantische Mentalitäten: Konturen, Entwicklungslinien und Umbrüche eines Weltbildes* (ed. with Hartmut Lehmann, 2005), *Mir aber zerriss es das Herz: Der stille Widerstand der Elisabeth Schmitz* (2010), *Täter und Komplizen in Theologie und Kirchen 1933–1945* (ed., 2015), and *Friedrich Weißler: Ein Jurist und bekennender Christ im Widerstand gegen Hitler* (2017).

Stephen G. Gross is an assistant professor at New York University in the Department of History and the Center for European and Mediterranean Studies. His first book, *Export Empire: German Soft Power in Southeastern Europe, 1890–1945* (2015), explores the relationship between imperialism, economic development, and cultural exchange from the perspective of non-state actors. His research has been supported by the Fulbright Fellowship, the DAAD (Deutscher Akademischer Austauschdienst), and the Institute for New Economic Thinking, and he has published articles on political economy in *Central European History*, *Contemporary European History*, and *German Politics and Society*, among other journals. He is currently working on his second book, which will examine German energy policy in a European and global context, from 1945 to the present.

Michael Grüttner, is apl. Professor for Contemporary History at the Technische Universität Berlin. His research interests are the social history of the nineteenth and twentieth centuries, the history of National Socialism, and the history of universities. Among his publications are *Studenten im Dritten Reich* (1995), *Biographisches Lexikon zur nationalsozialistischen Wissenschaftspolitik* (2004), *Universities under Dictatorship* (co-ed. with John Connelly, 2005), *Die Berliner Universität zwischen den Weltkriegen 1918–1945* (in cooperation with Christoph Jahr et al., 2012), and *Das Dritte Reich 1933–1939* (2014).

Jens-Uwe Guettel holds a *Staatsexamen* degree in History and English from the Freie Universität Berlin and a PhD in History from Yale University. He is Associate Professor of History and Germanic Languages and Literatures at the Pennsylvania State University and is currently working on a book project on radical democracy and reform in the German Empire before 1914. Recent publications include *German Expansionism, Imperial Liberalism, and the United States, 1776–1945* (2012), 'The US Frontier as Rationale for the Nazi East? Settler Colonialism and Genocide in Nazi-occupied Eastern Europe and the American West', *Journal of Genocide Research*, vol. 15, no. 4 (2013), and 'The Myth of the Pro-colonialist SPD: German Social Democracy and Imperialism before the First World War', *Central European History*, vol. 45, no. 3 (2012).

Elizabeth Harvey is Professor of History at the University of Nottingham. She is the author of *Youth and the Welfare State in Weimar Germany* (1993) and *Women and the Nazi East: Agents and Witnesses of Germanization* (2003). She co-edited, with Lynn Abrams, *Gender Relations in German History* (1996) and, with Johanna Gehmacher and Sophia Kemlein, *Zwischen Kriegen: Nationen, Nationalismen und Geschlechterverhältnisse in Mittel- und Osteuropa 1918–1939* (2004). She co-edited, with Johanna Gehmacher, a special issue on political travel for *Österreichische Zeitschrift für Geschichtswissenschaften* (2011) and co-edited, with Maiken Umbach, a special issue on photography and twentieth-century German history for *Central European History* (2015). Her current research interests include the history of photography and photojournalism and the history of private life under National Socialism. She is currently working on a project on gender and forced labour under Nazism.

Isabel Heinemann is Assistant Professor of Modern and Contemporary History at Münster University, Germany. Her main fields of interest are National Socialist racial policies and the history of the US American family in the twentieth century. Among her publications are '*Rasse, Siedlung, deutsches Blut*': *Das Rasse- und Siedlungshauptamt der SS und die rassenpolitische Neuordnung Europas* (2nd edn, 2003), *Inventing the Modern American Family: Family Values and Social Change in 20th Century United States* (2012), and 'Defining "(Un)wanted Population Addition": Anthropology, Racist Ideology, and Mass Murder in the Occupied East', in *Racial Science in Hitler's New Europe 1938–1945* (ed. Anton Weiss-Wendt and Rory Yeomans, 2013).

Konrad H. Jarausch is Lurcy Professor of European Civilization and Senior Fellow of the Zentrum für Zeithistorische Forschung in Potsdam/Germany. He has written and/or edited over 40 books on German and European history, among them, most recently, *Out of Ashes: A New History of Europe in the 20th Century* (2015).

Sven Keller is a research fellow (2009–2012) at the University of Augsburg, since 2012 a research fellow at the Institute of Contemporary History, Munich, and since 2015 also curator of the Dokumentation Obersalzberg. Recent publications are *Volksgemeinschaft am Ende: Gesellschaft und Gewalt 1944/45* (2013), *Dr. Oetker und der Nationalsozialismus: Geschichte eines Familienunternehmens 1933–1945* (with Jürgen Finger und Andreas Wirsching; 2013), and *Tagebuch einer jungen Nationalsozialistin: Die Aufzeichnungen Wolfhilde von König 1939–1946* (ed., 2015).

Thomas Kühne (PhD, University of Tübingen) is the Strassler Professor of Holocaust History at Clark University. His research inquires into the cultural history of war and genocide. His most recent book is *The Rise and Fall of Comradeship: Hitler's Soldiers, Male Bonding and Mass Violence in the 20th Century* (2017). His awards include fellowships from the Guggenheim Memorial Foundation, the Institute for Advanced Study, Princeton, and the German Bundestag Research Prize.

Andrea Löw is Deputy Director of the Centre for Holocaust Studies, Institute of Contemporary History, Munich. Her research is on the Holocaust, especially on ghettos. Some of her publications are *Alltag im Holocaust: Jüdisches Leben im Großdeutschen Reich 1941–1945* (ed., with Doris L. Bergen and Anna Hájková, 2013), *Das Warschauer Getto: Alltag und Widerstand im Angesicht der Vernichtung* (together with Markus Roth, 2013), and *Juden im Getto Litzmannstadt: Lebensbedingungen, Selbstwahrnehmung, Verhalten* (2nd edn, 2010).

Wendy Lower is the John K. Roth Professor of History and Director of the Mgrublian Center for Human Rights, Claremont McKenna College. Her most recent study, *Hitler's Furies: German Women in the Nazi Killing Fields* (2013), was a finalist for the National Book Award and the National Jewish Book Award. She is the author of *Nazi Empire Building and the Holocaust in Ukraine* (2005), and editor of *The Diary of Samuel Golfard and the Holocaust in Galicia* (2011).

Lars Lüdicke, DPhil, is an historian and publisher. His major research interests are modern history with a special focus on the history of Germany in its international context, politics, and constitutional and social history. His main publications are *Griff nach der Weltherrschaft: Die Außenpolitik des Dritten Reiches 1933–1945* (2009), *Constantin von Neurath: Eine politische Biographie* (2014), and *Hitlers Weltanschauung: Von 'Mein Kampf' bis zum 'Nero-Befehl'* (2016).

Daniel Mühlenfeld, MA, is working on a PhD thesis dealing with the Reich Ministry for People's Enlightenment and Propaganda. Recently he has published essays on Nazi propaganda and the 'people's community': 'Die Vergesellschaftung von "Volksgemeinschaft" in der sozialen Interaktion: Handlungs- und rollentheoretische Überlegungen zu einer Gesellschaftsgeschichte des Nationalsozialismus', *Zeitschrift für Geschichtswissenschaft*, vol. 61 (2013); 'Vom Nutzen und Nachteil der "Volksgemeinschaft" für die Zeitgeschichte. Neuere Debatten und Forschungen zur gesellschaftlichen Verfasstheit des "Dritten Reiches"', *Sozialwissenschaftliche Literaturrundschau*, vol. 36 (2013) ; 'Between State and Party: Position and Function of the Gau Propaganda Leader in National Socialist Leadership', *German History*, vol. 28 (2010); and 'Was heißt und zu welchem Ende studiert man NS-Propaganda? Neuere Forschungen zur Geschichte von Medien, Kommunikation und Kultur während des "Dritten Reiches"', *Archiv für Sozialgeschichte*, vol. 49 (2009).

Armin Nolzen, MA, is a member of the editorial board of *Beiträge zur Geschichte des Nationalsozialismus* (www.beitraege-ns.de). He is currently working on a history of the NSDAP, 1919–1945. Among his publications are 'Charismatic Legitimation and Bureaucratic Rule: The NSDAP in the Third Reich, 1933–1945', *German History*, vol. 23 (2005), and 'The NSDAP, the War, and German Society', in *Germany and the Second World War*, vol 9. pt. 1: *German Wartime Society 1939–1945: Politicization, Disintegration, and the Struggle for Survival* (2008), edited by Jörg Echternkamp, translated by Derry Cook-Radmore. His major research interests are the societal history of the Nazi regime, the comparative history of fascist movements, socialization research, and the Frankfurt School.

Richard Overy is Professor of History at the University of Exeter, UK. He has published more than 30 books on the European dictatorships, the Second World War, and the history of air power, including *Why the Allies Won* (1995), *Russia's War* (1998), and *Chronicle of the Third Reich* (2010). His book *The Dictators: Hitler's Germany and Stalin's Russia* (2004) was winner of the Wolfson Prize; his book *The Bombing War: Europe 1939–1945* (2013) won a Cundill Award for Historical Literature in 2014. He is a Fellow of the British Academy.

Kiran Klaus Patel is Jean Monnet professor of European and global history at Maastricht University. He is a member of the historians' committee researching the history of the Reich Ministry of Labour during the Nazi regime. Key publications include *Soldiers of Labor: Labor Service in Nazi Germany and New Deal America, 1933–1945* (2005), *The New Deal: A Global History* (2016), and Special Section of *Journal of Contemporary History* (ed. with Sven Reichardt), 'The Dark Sides of Transnationalism: Social Engineering and Nazism, 1930s–1940s' (2016).

Thomas Pegelow Kaplan is the Leon Levine Distinguished Professor and Director of the Center for Judaic, Holocaust, and Peace Studies at Appalachian State University in North Carolina. His research focuses on histories of violence, language, and culture of Nazi Germany and the 1960s global youth revolts. He is the author of *The Language of Nazi Genocide: Linguistic Violence and the Struggle of Germans of Jewish Ancestry* (2009) and numerous chapters and articles.

Lisa Pine is Reader in History at London South Bank University. Her research interests include the social history of Nazi Germany and the Holocaust. Her main publications are *Life and Times in Nazi Germany* (2016), *Education in Nazi Germany* (2010), *Hitler's 'National Community': Society and Culture in Nazi Germany* (2007), and *Nazi Family Policy, 1933–1945* (1997). She teaches courses on modern and contemporary history.

Dieter Pohl is Professor of Contemporary History at the Alpen Adria University in Klagenfurt, Austria. He also serves as a member of the executive board of the European Holocaust Research Infrastructure and several other advisory boards. Among his publications are *Verfolgung und Massenmord in der NS-Zeit* (2003), *Die Herrschaft der Wehrmacht: Deutsche Militärbesatzung und einheimische Bevölkerung in der Sowjetunion 1941–1944* (2008), *Zwangsarbeit in Hitlers Europa* (co-ed., 2013), *Die Verfolgung und Ermordung der europäischen Juden durch das national-sozialistische Deutschland 1933–1945* (co-editor, since 2007; to date 9 vols.).

Karl Heinrich Pohl teaches history and history didactics at the University of Kiel. His academic interests are history of the bourgeoisie, labour history, regional and local history as well as history didactics of museums and memorial sites. His recent publications are *Gustav Stresemann, Biografie eines Grenzgängers* (2015), *Historische Museen und Gedenkstätten in Norddeutschland* (ed., 2015), and *Der kritische Museumsführer: Neun Historische Museen im Fokus* (2013).

Kim Christian Priemel is Associate Professor of Contemporary European History at the University of Oslo. His major publications are *The Betrayal: The Nuremberg Trials and German Divergence* (2016) and *Flick: Eine Konzerngeschichte vom Kaiserreich bis zur Bundesrepublik* (2007).

Alexandra Przyrembel is Professor of Modern European History at the University of Hagen. She is especially interested in the global history of capitalism, the history of knowledge, and the history of emotions. She has co-edited, with Rebekka Habermas, *Von Käfern, Märkten und Menschen: Wissen und Kolonialismus in der Moderne* (2013), and authored *Verbote und Geheimnisse: Das Tabu und die Genese* *der europäischen Moderne (1784–1913)* (2011), 'Ambivalente Gefühle: Sexualität und Antisemitismus im Nationalsozialismus', *Geschichte und Gesellschaft*, vol. 39 (2013), and '*Rassenschande': Reinheitsmythos und Vernichtungslegitimation im Nationalsozialismus* (2003).

Thomas Schaarschmidt is Head of Department at the Centre for Contemporary History Potsdam (ZZF). In 2007 he edited *Die NS-Gaue: Regionale Mittelinstanzen im zentralistischen Führerstaat* together with Jürgen John and Horst Möller. Previously he was based at Leipzig University. He has published on international relations and on the idea of regionality in Nazi and Communist Germany. His current research project deals with political and social mobilization in Nazi Berlin.

Detlef Schmiechen-Ackermann is Professor of Modern History at Leibnitz University, Hanover. His most recent major publications are *Der Ort der 'Volksgemeinschaft' in der deutschen Gesellschaftsgeschichte* (ed., 2018), '*Volksgemeinschaft': Mythos, wirkungsmächtige soziale Verheißung oder soziale Realität im 'Dritten Reich'? Zwischenbilanz einer kontroversen Debatte* (ed., 2012), *Grenzziehungen – Grenzerfahrungen – Grenzüberschreitungen: Die innerdeutsche Grenze 1945–1990* (ed., 2011), *Geschichte Niedersachsens: Volume 5: Von der Weimarer Republik bis zur Wiedervereinigung* (2010), and *Diktaturen im Vergleich* (2010; 3rd. edn).

Astrid Schwabe teaches history and history didactics at the European University of Flensburg (Germany). After her MA in Cultural Studies she pursued a doctorate at the Institute for Regional Contemporary History of Schleswig-Holstein. Her academic interests are contemporary regional history and public history, in particular teaching and learning history through digital media. Her publications include *Historisches Lernen im World Wide Web* (2012), *Filme erzählen Geschichte* (2010), and *Schleswig-Holstein und der Nationalsozialismus* (2nd edn, 2006).

Alexa Stiller is a research associate in the Department of History at the University of Berne, Switzerland. Her PhD thesis was on the Nazis' Germanization policy in the annexed territories of Poland, France, and Slovenia. She has published several articles on Nazi Germanization policy, the Holocaust, and the Nuremberg trials. Her major publications are *Reassessing the Nuremberg Military Tribunals: Transitional Justice, Trial Narratives, and Historiography* (2012) and *NMT: Die Nürnberger Militärtribunale zwischen Geschichte, Gerechtigkeit und Rechtschöpfung* (2013).

Pamela E. Swett is Professor of History at McMaster University in Canada. She has published articles and books on daily life and its intersections with political and commercial developments in Weimar and National Socialist Germany, including *Selling under the Swastika: Advertising and Commercial Culture in Nazi Germany* (2014) and *Neighbors and Enemies: The Culture of Radicalism in late Weimar Berlin* (2004).

Claus-Christian W. Szejnmann is Professor of Modern History at Loughborough University. His major publications are *Heimat, Region, and Empire: Spatial*

Identities under National Socialism (ed. with M. Umbach, 2012), *Rethinking History, Dictatorship and War: New Approaches and Interpretations* (ed., 2009), *Ordinary People as Mass Murderers: Perpetrators in Comparative Perspective* (ed. with O. Jensen, 2006), *Vom Traum zum Alptraum: Sachsen in der Weimarer Republik* (2000), and *Nazism in Central Germany: The Brownshirts in "Red" Saxony* (1999).

Benjamin Ziemann is Professor of Modern German History at the University of Sheffield, UK. His many publications include *Contested Commemorations: Republican War Veterans and Weimar Political Culture* (2013), *Encounters with Modernity: The Catholic Church in West Germany, 1945–1975* (2014), *Understanding the Imaginary War: Culture, Thought and Nuclear Conflict, 1945–90* (ed. with Matthew Grant, 2016), and *Reading Primary Sources: The Interpretation of Texts from Nineteenth- and Twentieth-Century History* (ed. with Miriam Dobson, 2008).

Introduction

SHELLEY BARANOWSKI, ARMIN NOLZEN, AND
CLAUS-CHRISTIAN W. SZEJNMANN

0.1 Overview

During its brief lifetime, National Socialist Germany became one of the most, if not the most, destructive regimes in history (Burleigh and Wippermann 1991; Evans 2003, 2005, 2008). Its imperialism, which at minimum aspired to dominate Europe, entailed the massive expulsions of racial 'inferiors' from territories that the Nazi leadership slated for colonial settlement, the ruthless exploitation of agricultural land, natural resources, and labour, and the persecution and murder of many groups, including the total extermination of the Jews (Hilberg 1961; Friedländer 1997, 2007; Mazower 2009). As the most extreme outcome of European continental and global rivalries since the sixteenth century, the Nazi regime succumbed only after a long and ruinous war that ended European hegemony and reshaped a global order dominated by the United States and the Soviet Union for nearly a half a century. The scale of Nazi violence, the extent of its racial 'purification', and especially its eliminationist antisemitism continue to disturb us to this day.

Since the end of the Second World War, historians have continually debated the causes of National Socialism's rise to and consolidation of power and the Nazi regime's motivations for territorial expansion and genocide (Kershaw 2015). Was Nazism the result of Germany's pathological development since (variously) the Reformation, the failed revolutions of 1848, the Bismarckian unification in 1871, or the defeat in the First World War, or was it the most extreme outcome of European modernity? Was Nazism the expression of lower middle-class resentment directed especially against the working class, or was it in fact a 'catch-all' protest party that cut across class, religious, and regional lines? To what degree was Nazism anti-Marxist or anti-capitalist? To what extent did the Third Reich rule by terror?

A Companion to Nazi Germany, First Edition. Edited by Shelley Baranowski,
Armin Nolzen, and Claus-Christian W. Szejnmann.
© 2018 John Wiley & Sons Ltd. Published 2018 by John Wiley & Sons Ltd.

Or was popular consent at least as important in sustaining Nazism as repression? To what extent did Germans share Nazism's ideology and objectives, including eliminationist antisemitism? And what exactly was Nazi ideology and how did it relate to and engage with contemporary traditions and ideas? Also, did Hitler and the Nazi leadership plan the 'Final Solution' far in advance or did the extermination of the Jews evolve from 'cumulative radicalization' (Mommsen 1997), the exigencies of war, or the complex interplay between initiatives on the ground and at the top?

Over the last two decades, approaches and themes in the scholarship about Nazism as well as public engagement and the readiness to confront the past have changed dramatically due to developments such as the 'cultural turn' and comparative history, generational shifts, the end of the Cold War, German unification, and the increasing influence of the media and the digital revolution. In the meantime, the burgeoning scholarship on the Holocaust since the end of the Cold War, including 'perpetrator studies' (Hilberg 1993; Herbert 2000; Longerich 2012), recent explorations on Nazism and colonialism, and newer work on the impact of the Nazi 'people's community' (*Volksgemeinschaft*; see Steber and Gotto 2014), is raising new questions about the way the Third Reich operated and about the relationship between the Nazi regime and the German people. Nowadays, it seems highly questionable to consider this relationship a dichotomy between 'authority' (*Herrschaft*) and 'society' (*Gesellschaft*). There is now a 'societal turn', which understands Nazi Germany as a type of a modern genocidal regime in which politics, the economy, law, art, and education intersected and to which more or less all groups in society – civil service, technical elites, middle classes, workers, women, and youths – heavily contributed (Kühne 2010; Stargardt 2015). The central focus on Hitler is greatly diminished, and whilst we do not wish to downplay aspects of terror during the regime (Wachsmann 2015), accommodation, activism, and consent were the most common patterns of behaviour, and resistance to Nazism was a rare exception (Gellately 2002; Fritzsche 2008; Rohrkrämer 2013). The focus of this volume will be on covering Nazi society as a whole, showing the interrelations between high politics, mass culture, daily life and collective and individual behaviour. Its main concern is to show how Nazism was able to infiltrate and mobilize German society as a whole and the extent to which 'ordinary Germans' contributed.

Coming to terms with Nazism shaped both Germanys after the Second World War and continues to influence united Germany since 1990. Issues such as memories, reparations, and pedagogy, and the work of memorial sites and museums have gained in importance and make the topic of continuing relevance today (Reichel, Schmid, and Steinbach 2009). This is because much of the Western world sees the Holocaust and Nazism as a moral 'ground zero' in the past and as the ultimate example of evil, which serve as a lesson and moral standard for the present and the future. However, the days when it seemed the preserve of historians and politicians to engage with Nazism are long gone. Journalists, writers, artists, filmmakers, and also the wider public have often made crucial contributions and shaped debates and approaches, while companies, cities, and public services are commissioning (or resisting!) studies about their particular role during the Third Reich.

Seventy years after the end of the Third Reich, traditional periodization has lost relevance, and contextualizing Nazism and the Third Reich is much broader than before. This volume makes an effort to shed light on continuities and discontinuities by going beyond the years that mark the start and the end of the Nazi dictatorship, 1933 and 1945, for example, by exploring what happened to Nazi perpetrators after 1945 in both Germanys. Today many scholars question whether it makes sense to see the Holocaust as a unique event, or rather as the most extreme example of genocide that has become a horrific feature of modern humankind. These questions will be addressed more thoroughly by a separate Blackwell companion to the Holocaust which will be edited by Simone Gigliotti and Hilary Earl (2018). One thing seems certain: Nazism and the Third Reich occupy an undiminishing importance and relevance in today's societies. It is time to take stock of exciting and path-breaking new developments and approaches. Whilst this volume cannot and does not claim to cover all of them, its contributions nevertheless seek to take stock of, reflect on, and suggest new avenues for research and engagement on some of the major issues surrounding the topic.

0.2   Contents

The *Companion to Nazi Germany* begins with the Nazi Party's emergence in the 1920s, continues through its rise to power in the early 1930s to the defeat of the Third Reich in 1945, and concludes with its complex repercussions in the post-war era. Each chapter assesses the relevant historiographical debates and raises questions that will stimulate new research. The chapters are grouped under five thematic topics: (I) Theories, Background, and Contexts; (II) Structures of Nazi Rule; (III) Economy and Culture; (IV) Race, Imperialism, and Genocide; and (V) Legacies of Nazism. Although it is difficult to avoid overlap among the sections – the most obvious case being the theme of race – we have grouped the chapters according to their primary emphasis.

0.2.1   *Theories, Background, and Contexts*

This section has two objectives: first, to assess the historiography of Nazism, and second, to explore the prehistory of the Nazi regime from the First World War to 1933. Thus, Geoff Eley's 'How Do We Explain the Rise of Nazism? Theory and Historiography' begins by surveying the debates from the 1920s to the present: fascism, totalitarianism, the German 'deviation' from the West (*Sonderweg*), and the discussion about continuities and/or discontinuities from earlier periods in German history to the Third Reich. After surveying the social histories of the rise of Nazism and the dynamics of the Nazi appeal, Eley argues that carefully distinguishing between the political and economic sources of Weimar's delegitimization allows us to appreciate in a fresh way the significance of the republic's last four years. Konrad Jarausch's 'Organic Modernity: National Socialism as Alternative Modernism' zeroes in on one of the most persistent historical debates, the relationship between National Socialism and the modern era. Rather than see Nazism and modernity as opposites or as an example of 'reactionary modernism', as Jeffrey

Herf (1984) argued, Jarausch provides the rubric of 'organic modernity', Nazism's attempt to create a 'racial utopia' that would eliminate the social polarization inherent in the democratic and communist variants of modernity.

As for the contexts of Nazism's emergence, Benjamin Ziemann's 'The First World War and National Socialism' opens by acknowledging the significance of the war and the German defeat to the emergence of Nazism, which recent scholarship has emphasized. Yet by examining public political performances and symbols, he underscores the limited impact of the German right despite its putschism, emphasizing instead the ability of the republican state and pro-republican groups to create a democratic polity for a time. It was not until the mid-1920s that the right began to realign as the Nazi Party reformed and ultimately assumed leadership, especially as the Weimar economy weakened. Similar to Ziemann's recognition of the contingencies of the Nazi rise to power, Shelley Baranowski's 'The Collapse of the Weimar Parliamentary System' notes that historians of Germany no longer accept that the Weimar Republic was congenitally flawed from its beginnings. Instead, piecing together recent trends in the scholarship, she suggests that the breakdown of the parliamentary system after 1929 arose from a perfect storm, which combined the increasing reluctance of the First World War allies to exert leverage over Germany (unlike during the hyperinflation and putschism of 1923), the anti-republican radicalization and fragmentation of the German right, and the mushrooming popular support for National Socialism. Alternatively, Claus-Christian Szejnmann's 'National Socialist Ideology' looks at how Nazi ideology was intrinsically interwoven with German traditions and the emotions and expectations of many of its people. He argues against brushing aside Nazi ideology as 'mere propaganda' or narrowly focusing on its violent antisemitic core. Instead, he takes seriously the attempts by the Nazis to *persuade* Germans on a variety of pressing concerns during a historically unique crisis by engaging with society and its diverse culture and traditions, by being shaped by it and contributing to it themselves – including the emergence of a powerful anti-capitalist *Zeitgeist* – and by negotiating shared visions as well as differences and conflicts. Szejnmann thus helps to explain the Nazis' increasing popularity during the Weimar Republic, the binding force and dynamic nature of the 'people's community', and Nazism's ability to penetrate and mobilize society so comprehensively during the racist dictatorship.

0.2.2 Structures of Nazi Rule

Since the 1960s, the scholarship has moved away from exclusively top-down approaches. Yet it is appropriate to begin our examination of the Third Reich in power with a section on the party itself and its efforts to transform the German state and impose its ideological imperatives. Beginning with the Nazi Party organization, Armin Nolzen's 'The NSDAP After 1933: Members, Positions, Technologies, Interactions' evaluates the history of the NSDAP (*Nationalsozialistische Deutsche Arbeiterpartei*) between 1933 and 1945 by examining its members, positions, technologies, and interactions. With its rapid membership growth, the party developed into four distinct organizational units: the party itself, its divisions, affiliates, and sponsored organizations. Through a process of ongoing differentiation, each of these units separated from one another after 1933. Simultaneously the NSDAP transformed its positions and cadre politics into a hierarchy, which advanced six technologies to pursue its 'people management' (*Menschenführung*): institutionalization, education, mobilization, violence, social work, and policing. Through those technologies, the NSDAP overcame its inner conflicts. Jens-Uwe Guettel's 'Work(ers) Under the Swastika' argues that the Nazi regime's repression of organized labour in the months immediately following its assumption to power was critical to bringing its other ideological goals to fruition (see also Mason 1993). To be sure, Guettel points out that despite the size of the working-class parties and organizations, workers themselves did not compose a unified bloc and their positions towards the Nazi regime varied from acceptance to begrudged accommodation. Nevertheless, having noted the declining interest in labour history in recent years, he forcefully argues for the reintroduction of labour as indispensable category of analysis (see also Wildt and Buggeln 2014). Detlef Schmiechen-Ackermann's 'Resistance' shows how in the historiography about the Third Reich various kinds of 'Widerstand' against Hitler have competed with a narrow interpretation that associated with it the aim to destroy Nazism. In response, he identifies several periods and types of resistance: communist resistance, socialist resistance, dissent and nonconformity on the basis of religious convictions, military opposition, Jewish resistance, youth resistance, and resistance behind barbed wires. The numerous types of resistance, nonconformity, and dissent stress the need for a broad definition of 'Widerstand' which also allows for terminological diversification. Above all, Schmiechen-Ackermann argues that after 1933 accommodation and collaboration were the normal patterns of public behaviour, while 'resistance' aiming to overthrow the Nazi regime was pursued only by a minority.

In turn, Thomas Schaarschmidt's 'Centre and Periphery' describes the establishment of the Nazi state beginning with its destruction of federalism, which had been a key principle of the German constitution since the Reich's founding in 1871. After Hitler came to power, it took just two years to establish a highly centralized state in which regional institutions were supposed to be little more than administrations working on behalf of central authorities. Nevertheless, the improvised character of the Nazi state provoked new power arrangements on the intermediate level which helped to mobilize social and material resources for Hitler's military objectives. In this context, regional party leaders became key players. Since they were invested with new powers during the war, they became crucial for the interaction of the central, intermediate, and local levels in Nazi Germany. Thomas Pegelow Kaplan's 'Information Policies and Linguistic Violence' describes the efforts of the Nazi propaganda ministry under Joseph Goebbels to redirect the resources of the state to fight Nazism's enemies. Noting that historians have either overemphasized or minimized the power of Nazi propaganda, he focuses instead on the 'linguistic violence' that Nazi information agencies deployed, which permeated everyday discourse. Using the Reich 'Crystal Night' (*Kristallnacht*) pogrom as an example, Pegelow Kaplan argues that 'linguistic violence' targeted racial 'enemies' and in turn spawned actual violence. Although 'enemies' carved out some space to contest their persecution, the agencies associated with the propaganda ministry were crucial to reconstructing the language to exclude and punish those whom the regime assaulted.

Kiran Klaus Patel, in 'Education, Schooling, and Camps', stresses the continuities with earlier periods in Nazi educational thinking and practice. He points out the inconsistencies and conflicts in the Nazi educational system and emphasizes the active role of ordinary citizens. While some Germans opposed the Third Reich's educational efforts and others were excluded from its remit, many actively embraced its educational agenda. This held true for Germans of both sexes. Self-mobilization was therefore often more important than top-down ideologization, and individual educational institutions were often less influential than the fact that Germans were increasingly part of a society shaped by Nazi values. Michael Grüttner's 'Research and Scholarship' shows that National Socialism indeed was an anti-intellectual movement that restricted academic freedom. Yet Nazism was not anti-science, as has been claimed for a long time; rather it tried to use science for its own purposes. The Nazi regime developed an instrumental attitude towards science with different consequences for various academic disciplines. Whereas the Third Reich supported the natural and engineering sciences, the humanities stagnated and theology feared for its existence. Nevertheless, scholars and scientists in numerous fields willingly participated in the regime's repression, racial cleansing, imperialism, and genocide. To a certain degree, they were motivated by a particular Nazi morality which Thomas Kühne discusses in his chapter. Its components – race as the law of nature, a code of honour, an ethic of hardness, and the dictatorship of the community over the individual – were to replace Judaeo-Christian and Western moralities. Yet the Nazi regime did not succeed in replacing the older moralities. Instead, the murderous violence of the Third Reich arose from the competition between Nazi morality and its predecessors.

Finally, Richard Overy and Sven Keller shift our attention to Germany internally as the prospect of defeat loomed. Both contributions converge on the question as to why Germans held firm until the war's end. Overy's 'The German Home Front Under the Bombs' focuses on a central problem for the dictatorship in keeping together a wartime consensus and ensuring that there was no repeat of the crisis in 1918, particularly once heavy bombing of German working-class districts began. After examining social and economic experiences, the impact of Allied bombing, and the regime's effort to uphold a consensus, Overy concludes that most clung to the hope that ultimately Germany would prevail. Similarly, Sven Keller's 'Total Defeat: War, Society, and Violence in the Last Year of National Socialism' surveys four topics to demonstrate the recent scholarly attention to the final years of the Third Reich: the impact of military setbacks, the nature of Nazi rule and internal crises, Nazi violence, and finally the impact of defeat. In response to the question about why the Germans 'stuck it out' (*durchhalten*), Keller argues that the Nazi regime remained sufficiently stable to ensure its survival until the Allies defeated it.

0.2.3   *Economy and Culture*

This section shifts our attention to the complex reception, relationships, and negotiations between the Nazi regime, the drivers of the German economy, German cultural institutions, and German society at large. Consistent with recent scholarship, one of the most prominent themes of the chapters here challenge once hard-and-fast distinctions between support for the regime and opposition to it, inasmuch as the lines between them were murky, variable, circumstantial, and dependent on personal or group commitments and interests. If many Germans had reservations about the regime, those did not suffice to produce sustained opposition. Some of the chapters in this section deal with ambiguities in the broader society and in the interior lives of Germans; ambiguities which reveal both the limits of opposition to the Nazi regime and the durability of identities that pre-existed National Socialism. Yet they also underscore the subtle ways in which Germans aligned themselves at least partially to Nazi values and objectives.

Stephen Gross's 'The Nazi Economy' capitalizes on the rediscovery of Franz Neumann's pioneering work of 1942, and in particular devotes attention to four issues relevant to the relationship between the Nazi state and the German economy: imperialism, crises in foreign trade, the guidance of private industry, and 'Aryanization' (*Arisierung*). After assessing the numerous debates about the economy, Gross emphasizes the complex mix between coercion and collaboration that linked the state and German corporations forged by the Depression, war, and imperialism. Likewise, Kim Christian Priemel's chapter, 'National Socialism and German Business', deals with corporations but specifically challenges the long-standing controversy as to whether in the Third Reich politics dominated the economy or vice versa. Therefore, he highlights how negotiations between the Nazi government and corporations shaped economic policies and business strategies and demanded compromises on both sides. Although big business did not bring the Nazis to power, Priemel argues, entrepreneurs and managers supported the regime's most central objectives. Expanding the discussion from production to consumption, Pamela Swett's 'Individual Consumers and Consumption in Nazi Germany' analyses various aspects of consumer culture in Nazi Germany ranging from the regime's 'people's products' to privately marketed consumer goods. She argues that the enticements to 'Aryan' Germans to consume reflected trends begun before 1933 and seen elsewhere in Europe. Swett maintains that despite the Nazi regime's calls for a *Volksgemeinschaft*, which would eliminate social conflict, class difference continued to shape individuals' identities as consumers and corporate efforts to sell goods and services. Pre-existing social structures and international trends proved at least as strong as Nazi appeals to a 'people's community'.

Shifting our attention to the diverse components of culture in the Third Reich, Elizabeth Harvey examines how gender was implicated in the regime's racially defined order of exclusion, inclusion, and subordination. She focuses especially on practices of persecution and exclusion in Germany after 1933, models of activism and comradeship within the Nazi movement, and conquest and territorial expansion in the Second World War. From its beginnings, Nazism championed virility and male 'comradeship' and presupposed the subordination of women. Yet Harvey notes that the opportunities for women's participation expanded during the Third Reich, which made women complicit in its racist practices and imperialism. Manfred Gailus's 'Religion' analyses the complex history of Protestants and Catholics during the Third Reich. Religious revival and an avoidance of open opposition to antisemitic policies characterized both major churches, although bitter internal divisions characterized Protestants more than Catholics. Inconsistency characterized the religious policy of the NSDAP and the Nazi state. Gailus argues that in the long run, despite the hopes of both churches for a 're-christianization' of society, the Nazi regime aimed at superseding the 'old belief' (Christianity) with a 'new belief', the Nazi quasi-religious and racial 'German Belief' (*Deutschglaube*). Lisa Pine's chapter, 'Family and Private Life', deals with the inherent racism implemented by the Nazi regime to redress both the 'crisis of the family' and the decline in the nation's birth rate. She examines a series of measures and incentives designed to achieve the goal of increasing the birth rate. In the process, she explores the blatantly sinister side of Nazi family and population policy, including the sterilization law of July 1933 and legal measures to prevent marriages between Jews and 'Aryans' and marriages between healthy 'Aryans' and those deemed 'unfit' for marriage due to physical or mental illness.

The topics of sport, cinema and the arts, emotions, and the environment further expand this volume's attention to the diverse expressions of culture. Frank Becker's chapter on sports describes its integration into the National Socialist concept of the *Volksgemeinschaft*. Sports were to embody the National Socialist idea of humankind, which was oriented towards action and deed. They were to procure health, strength, and beauty for the 'German body' (*Volkskörper*) in the following ways: to provide statistical data and facilitate biopolitical interventions; to allow the practical experience of 'racial identity' (*Rassenidentität*) through body-centred actions; to put the *Volksgemeinschaft* on display during mass performances; to toughen the people for work and war, and to provide a perceptual foil for warfare using sport's competitive character. To accomplish these tasks, the valuation of sports greatly increased in the German educational system, as well as in National Socialist mass organizations. The traditional German system of sports clubs and associations was aligned to the Nazi Party's structure (*gleichgeschaltet*). Yet Nazi organizations that promoted sports engaged in a process of negotiation that had the effect of integrating even self-described nonconformists. Daniel Mühlenfeld's chapter on cinema, art, and music, aspects of culture that several institutions (from the propaganda ministry to the German Labour Front) sought to shape, offers a threefold examination of cultural policy in the Third Reich, the role of artists, and popular reception. He argues that although the Nazi vision of culture lacked a coherent agenda other than the negative identification of what was 'Jewish' or 'degenerate', popular reception was critical to Nazism's paramount consideration, the prevention of social unrest. Thus, the need for entertainment and escapism increasingly defined the regime's support of the arts, especially that projected by the radio and cinema. Alexandra Przyrembel applies the insights of a relatively new field of study, the history of emotions, to enable a better understanding of the popular acceptance of National Socialism, one that broadens the current discussion about the extent and limits of the *Volksgemeinschaft*. The two 'emotional regimes' that she uses as examples, the 'positive' emotions of love and caring in the case of women and ambivalent or negative feelings towards Jews as reflected in court cases, became 'spaces of communication' that eased their acceptance of National Socialism, especially its racial politics. Finally, Charles Closmann's chapter analyses the contradictions in the Nazi regime's seemingly 'positive' environmental policy of sustainability and preservation. At the outset of Nazi rule, some high-ranking Nazi leaders supported sustainability and an array of ecological initiatives, and overall its record was comparable to that of the Weimar and Federal Republics. In fact, the Reich Nature Protection Law of 1935 allowed unprecedented power to expropriate land to preserve natural monuments and resources without compensation. Nevertheless the regime's work creation programmes, the centrality of autarky and expansionism, and total war triumphed over sustainable forestry, clean water, the fertility of the soil, and biodynamic farming.

0.2.4 Race, Imperialism, and Genocide

In the 1980s and 1990s, historians shifted away from debating the class bases of Nazism and redirected their attention to Nazi ideology, especially its racism and antisemitism. Part of this was driven by an attempt to explain the participation of 'ordinary' Germans in the Nazi regime's crimes. These trends, together with the collapse of the Soviet bloc and the reunification of Germany between 1989 and 1991, significantly expanded the archival sources available for studying the war itself and increased the desire among scholars to overcome the once dominant (and narrow) focus on the Nazi regime before the war.

Dieter Pohl's chapter covers the uses of terror before and during the Second World War. He emphasizes first that the Nazi regime aimed at intimidating and destroying its real and potential opponents. Though distinct from systematic racial violence like the crimes against Jews, Roma, the mentally ill, or the mass deportations of Poles and Slovenes, terror was also inherent in racial persecution. Pohl analyses four phases of terror beginning with the *Machtergreifung* (seizure of power) of 1933/34, which revealed the typical pattern of acquiring and sustaining power in an authoritarian dictatorship. Second, he describes the deployment of terror within the camp system, in addition to the camps' political and economic functions and development over time and space. Third, he describes terror in the process of conquering foreign countries during the campaigns in 1939 and 1941, which was closely connected to warfare but also included the systematic killing of the intelligentsia in Poland and the Soviet Union. Fourth, he addresses the policies of suppression and 'reprisal' in occupied territories. Alternatively, Debórah Dwork's 'Flight and Exile' focuses on those who struggled to escape Nazi terror. She pushes beyond the usual concentration on flight from a particular country to a particular destination. Instead she focuses on the escape, especially of Jews, to a variety of destinations from the entirety of Nazi-occupied Europe. Arguing that the experiences of refugees have mostly escaped the attention of Holocaust historians, Dwork suggests that the history of flight and exile expands the history of the Holocaust into a previously underexplored area. Although fortunate to have escaped the cataclysm, being uprooted and in many cases only partially integrated into their receiving nations, many refugees continued to lead difficult lives.

This section then moves to the preparations for war and the conduct of the war itself. In his account, 'Germany and the Outside World', Lars Lüdicke discusses the menacing underpinnings of Nazi foreign policy. On 30 January 1933, the German Reich was considerably demilitarized and multinationally embedded in and dependent on the 'outside world' – and thus was further away from being ready for war than other European Great Powers. And yet, only six and a half years later, on 1 September 1939, Hitler was able to unleash a long-lasting global 'racial war' (*Rassenkrieg*) towards victory or downfall. Within six years the Reich was armed and several crucial barriers were broken. That the other European powers failed to cooperate against the initially weak Nazi state between 1933 and 1939 cannot be explained from the perspective of national history, but only in terms of a 'history of facilitation' derived from multipolar interaction and by taking the strategies of the 'outside world' into account. For his part, Jörg Echternkamp focuses on German 'militarism' and Nazi preparations for war, starting soon after Hitler's seizure of power in 1933. Because military conflicts of the future were likely to involve total war, these preparations had to mobilize society as extensively as possible. As Echternkamp shows, the Wehrmacht benefited heavily from that process because it increased its manpower by universal conscription and the paramilitaries of the NSDAP, especially the Hitler Youth. At the beginning of the war, the Wehrmacht mobilized some 4 556 000 men following the almost unchecked build-up and expansion of the army, navy, and air force. Of those, 750 000 made up the active force (22 600 officers and some 150 000 NCOs) and 3.8 million served as their replacements. The mobilization of personnel, rearmament, and the nation ideologically 'ready to defend itself' turned the 100 000-strong army of the Weimar Republic into a 'military community' which numbered some 10 million conscripts in total among the 18 million German soldiers who fought in the Second World War.

We then turn our attention to three chapters that demonstrate the recent interest in the Nazi regime's racial agendas. Isabel Heinemann evaluates National Socialist race theories and racial policies, their preconditions, practices, and outcomes. She asks first whether the deeply rooted belief in different categories of 'racial worth' (*Rassewert*) and 'racial degradation' (*Entartung*) helps to explain the internal functioning of the Nazi regime and the unbroken loyalty of perpetrators, bystanders, and collaborators until the very end. Second, she analyses to what degree Nazi racism differed from race theories and policies common in the Western countries during the first half of the twentieth century. Heinemann concludes that 'race' needs to be considered as the central integrating principle of the Nazi state, one that incorporates other basic tenets, including the economic exploitation of the occupied countries. Marc Buggeln and Alexa Stiller deal with populations subject to Nazi rule. Buggeln's 'Unfree and Forced Labour' addresses modern dictatorships' inherent tendency to limit or even abolish free employment relationships that predominate in democratic capitalist states. For him, it comes as no surprise that from 1933 the Nazi regime introduced various forms of compulsory and forced labour. Yet it was not until the beginning of the war that the Nazi authorities established an almost Europe-wide network of forced labour based on deportation, hunger, violence, and finally mass murder. Civilian forced labourers, prisoners of war, and concentration camp detainees were coerced into working under disastrous conditions to keep the German war economy running. Foreign forced labourers deported to Germany usually were, in material terms, better off than in their home countries, but they often faced a hostile environment. Stiller's 'Ethnic Germans' turns our attention to *Volksdeutsche* ('ethnic Germans') living in Nazi-occupied countries. The alleged homogeneity of these groups, she argues, was in fact a political construction of the Nazis. The Nazi regime made *Volkstum* (ethnicity) policy a guide for imposing a uniform identity on Germans outside the Reich. Its support for 'ethnic Germans' in Europe was the reverse side of its policy towards Jews and other 'undesired' populations. 'Ethnic Germans' were targets of, witnesses to, and perpetrators of Nazi mass violence during the Second World War.

The conditions that subject populations endured in German-occupied Europe were horrendous, especially in the East where the Third Reich imagined its enlarged imperium. Forced labour, hunger and starvation, repression, and mass executions were routine. Yet the Holocaust – the extermination of the Jews – reached another level of horror. Antisemitism was central to the Nazis' conspiratorial interpretations of the past and present, and eliminating the Jews was crucial to creating the *Volksgemeinschaft* and expanding Germany's *Lebensraum* ('living space'). Therefore, this section concludes with two essays that illuminate both the current debate and the experiences of the initiators of the Holocaust and their victims. Andrea Löw focuses on the Nazi practice of ghettoization with which the Nazi regime continued its policies of the spatial segregation of 'ordinary Germans' and their 'objective enemies'. The majority of Jews persecuted by the Nazis were forced to live in ghettos for periods of varying duration. Some ghettos existed for several years, others only for a few weeks or even days. Particularly in the larger ghettos, social structures developed and the ghetto dwellers tried to organize their lives. They tried to fight constant hunger and disease and even established some kind of cultural life and education for their children. The different Jewish reactions to ghettoization and persecution are at the centre of Löw's interest. Wendy Lower's 'Holocaust Studies: The Spatial Turn' indicates that the widening geographical scope for studying the 'Final Solution' has become the most important recent development in Holocaust Studies. She closely examines four topics that have recently occupied the attention of Holocaust scholars – decision making and proximity to sites of mass murder, biography with its attention to individual agency, collaboration, which has incorporated the participation of thousands of non-German actors and sources, which multiplied especially with the collapse of the Soviet bloc. As a consequence, Lower sees the potential for the further development of a European-wide research agenda, which pushes historians to become 'transnational comparativists', who explore more deeply the complexities of the Nazi system, the relationships between occupiers and occupied, and the further incorporation of non-Jews and non-Germans into the categories of victim and perpetrator.

0.2.5 Legacies of Nazism

The catastrophic defeat, division, and occupation of Germany after 1945 and the Allies' determination to punish Germans for Nazism's manifold atrocities left Germans to cope with untold suffering and bitterness. Thus, coming to terms with the recent past was wrenching for both post-war Germanys despite the striking differences in their interpretations of the Third Reich. Aleida Assmann analyses distinct phases of remembering and forgetting in the 70 years of the Federal Republic of Germany's post-war history that evolved due to historical change, the construction of new social frames, the introduction of new values, and the rise of new actors. In these various phases we may discern a larger pattern of transformation that can be described as a shift from 'mastering the past' to 'preserving the past'. This transformation in memory involves another important shift from a 'finishing line' to a 'dividing line'. The past is no longer overcome by bracketing, silencing, or forgetting it, but by remembering it. David Clarke outlines the official politics of memory in the German Democratic Republic (GDR) in relation to National Socialism, and discusses the relationship between this official memory and the ways in which ordinary GDR citizens interpreted Germany's history. He concludes by examining the controversy surrounding the anti-fascist legacy of the GDR in post-unification Germany. Last but not least, Karl Heinrich Pohl and Astrid Schwabe address the topic of presenting and teaching the past since 1945 by emphasizing the remembrance of the Holocaust in different countries and in a global context. They conclude by noting that in recent decades a plethora of new research and presentation approaches to the Holocaust has emerged that indicates a dynamic international interest and a paradigm shift.

We noted at the outset of this introduction that National Socialism has not lost its relevance in today's societies. In the course of producing this volume, looking to the history of the Third Reich has become even more pressing with the emergence of radical nationalist movements, especially in Europe (including the Russian Federation) and the United States – movements that threaten the underpinnings of the post-Second World War political order, the neoliberal global economy, and even the ecological future of the planet. Not surprisingly, many have looked to the rise of fascism in the 1920s and 1930s for parallels that help us to understand the present. Historical analogies can be crude, misleading, and insensitive to the peculiarities of time and context. Yet, without denying the dangers in too-facile analogies, examining the fascist and National Socialist past can raise probing questions about the present.

References

Burleigh, Michael and Wippermann, Wolfgang. 1991. *The Racial State: Germany, 1933–1945*. Cambridge: Cambridge University Press.

Evans, Richard. 2003. *The Coming of the Third Reich*. London: Penguin.

Evans, Richard. 2005. *The Third Reich in Power*. London: Penguin.

Evans, Richard. 2008. *The Third Reich at War*. London: Penguin.

Friedländer, Saul. 1997. *Nazi Germany and the Jews, Volume 1: The Years of Persecution, 1933–1939*. New York: HarperCollins.

Friedländer, Saul. 2007. *Nazi Germany and the Jews, Volume 2: The Years of Extermination, 1939–1945*. New York: HarperCollins.

Fritzsche, Peter. 2008. *Life and Death in the Third Reich*. Cambridge, MA: Harvard University Press.

Gellately, Robert. 2002. *Backing Hitler: Consent and Coercion in Nazi Germany*. Oxford: Oxford University Press.

Herbert, Ulrich, ed. 2000. *Nazi Socialist Extermination Policies: Contemporary German Perspectives and Controversies*. New York: Berghahn.

Herf, Jeffrey. 1984. *Reactionary Modernism: Technology, Culture, and Politics in Weimar and the Third Reich*. Cambridge: Cambridge University Press.

Hilberg, Raul. 1961. *The Destruction of the European Jews*. New Haven, CT: Yale University Press.

Hilberg, Raul. 1993. *Perpetrators, Victims, Bystanders: The Jewish Catastrophe, 1933–1945*. New York: Harper Perennial.

Kershaw, Ian. 2015. *The Nazi Dictatorship: Problems and Perspectives of Interpretation*, 4e. London and New York: Bloomsbury.

Kühne, Thomas. 2010. *Belonging and Genocide. Hitler's Community, 1918–1945*. New Haven, CT and London: Yale University Press.

Longerich, Peter. 2012. *Heinrich Himmler*. Oxford: Oxford University Press.

Mason, Timothy. 1993. *Social Policy in the Third Reich. The Working Class and the 'National Community'*. Providence, RI and Oxford: Berg.

Mazower, Mark. 2009. *Hitler's Empire: Nazi Rule in Occupied Europe*. London: Penguin.

Mommsen, Hans. 1997. 'Cumulative Radicalisation and Progressive Self-destruction as Structural Determinants of the Nazi Dictatorship.' *In Stalinism and Nazism: Dictatorships in Comparison*, edited by Ian Kershaw and Moshe Lewin, 75–87. Cambridge: Cambridge University Press.

Reichel, Peter, Schmid, Harald, and Steinbach, Peter. 2009. *Der Nationalsozialismus: Die zweite Geschichte. Überwindung – Deutung – Erinnerung*. Munich: C.H. Beck.

Rohkrämer, Thomas. 2013. *Die fatale Attraktion des Nationalsozialismus. Zur Popularität eines Unrechtsregimes*. Paderborn: Ferdinand Schöningh.

Stargardt, Nicholas. 2015. *The German War: A Nation Under Arms, 1939–1945*. New York: Basic Books.

Steber, Martina and Gotto, Bernhard, eds. 2014. *Visions of Community in Nazi Germany: Social Engineering and Private Lives*. Oxford: Oxford University Press.

Wachsmann, Nicholas. 2015. *KL: A History of the Nazi Concentration Camps*. New York: Farrar, Straus and Giroux.

Wildt, Michael and Buggeln, Marc, eds. 2014. *Arbeit im Nationalsozialismus*. Munich: De Gruyter Oldenbourg.

PART I

Theories, Background, and Contexts

CHAPTER ONE

How Do We Explain the Rise of Nazism? Theory and Historiography

GEOFF ELEY

What are the contexts for understanding the rise of Nazism? Immediately after 1945, Nazism's origins were sought straightforwardly in the far regions of the deeper German past: 'Nazi Germany [was] seen as the culmination of German history, the logical endpoint of a malign potential nurtured in that culture for centuries' (Caplan 2008, 4). This characterized most of the public commentary after the war's end, from the reportage and reflections of journalists and academics through the moralizing of critics and clergymen to the rhetoric of politicians and the popular common sense. Without some grappling with those deeper origins, it seemed, the disastrous turn in German history would never be explained. The Nazis were thought to have drawn upon beliefs deemed characteristic of German culture stretching back through the nineteenth century to the Lutheran Reformation, and even the Middle Ages. Only by relating Nazism's appeal to a set of deep-seated and pervasive dispositions – militarism, deference to authority, veneration of the state, weakness of liberalism – could it be rendered intelligible. If such traditions of thought set Germany sharply apart from the liberal-democratic West, then perhaps Nazi success could begin to make sense.

An origins narrative had already emerged from the war itself. A prime instance was A.J.P. Taylor's *Course of German History* (completed in September 1944), initially commissioned by Britain's Political Warfare Executive for the advice of the future occupying administration of Germany. Expanding an essay on the Weimar Republic into a full-scale account of what we now call the long nineteenth century, Taylor related German national character to the geopolitical determinism of

A Companion to Nazi Germany, First Edition. Edited by Shelley Baranowski, Armin Nolzen, and Claus-Christian W. Szejnmann.

Germany's central European location: 'it was no more a mistake for the German people to end up with Hitler than it is an accident when a river flows into the sea' (Taylor 1961, vii). Likewise, having published as a medievalist in 1938, Geoffrey Barraclough produced three books in rapid succession after the war, each placing the twentieth century in the strongest possible relationship to earlier times (Barraclough 1938, 1946a, 1946b, 1950). In *The Roots of National Socialism, 1783–1933* (1941), to cite a third example, Rohan D'Olier Butler, a British civil servant and official historian, presented Nazism as merely the political climax of a long-seeded intellectual tradition. 'The exaltation of the heroic leader'; 'the racial myth'; antisemitism; 'the concept of the all-significant totalitarian state'; 'the community of the folk'; 'the full program of economic autarky'; 'the tradition of militarism'; the idea of 'the dynamic originality of German culture in contrast to the superficial civilization of the West'; 'the polemic against reason'; 'the supernatural mission of German culture'; 'living-space'; 'Pan-Germanism'; 'law as folk-law'; 'the abasement of the individual before the state' – each of these was taken to be distinctively German, descending by linear continuity from the late eighteenth century. As Butler put it: 'The Nazis said that might is right; Spengler said it; Bernhardi said it; Nietzsche said it; Treitschke had said as much; so had Haller before him; so had Novalis' (Butler 1941, 277–278).

This reflex of explanation marked the immediate post-war decades. *Because* Germany produced Nazism, ipso facto its history was singular, with peculiarities deeply embedded in the German past. Germany's 'path to modernity' had been distorted or stalled. The intellectual outlook of Germans broke radically from the West – not only from the Enlightenment and its values, but also in a romantic-nationalist counter-reaction against the French Revolution. If the deeper conditions for Germany's difference were found in earlier periods, from the Reformation and Thirty Years War to the rise of Brandenburg-Prussia, then the main crucible remained the nineteenth century. Wars against Napoleon; Stein–Hardenberg era; Holy Alliance and Metternichian reaction; failure of the 1848 revolutions; Bismarck's 'revolution from above' and policy of 'blood and iron'; creation of the unified Prusso-German state – these became the markers of Germany's divergence from Britain and France. 'Authoritarian', 'militarist', bureaucratic', 'Prussian' were the adjectives commonly in use. Well into the 1960s, this was the default understanding of Nazism's place in the longer arc of Germany's past. An imposing 1955 UNESCO anthology, *The Third Reich*, was one key reference point, William Shirer's *The Rise and Fall of the Third Reich* (1960) another (Vermeil 1955; Shirer 1960).[1]

There was a stronger socio-political version of this deep-historical account. Until the new start after 1945, it ran, the ground had yet to be laid for a viable German liberalism, whether via constitutional restraints on royal and aristocratic power, the growth of parliamentary government and civil liberties, or the political culture of an active and responsible citizenry. In contrast with Britain and France, where liberalism wrested power from monarchy and aristocracy through violent revolution, liberalism in Germany lacked comparable success. Germany's tragedy, Max Weber liked to say, was that, unlike the Stuarts and Bourbons, no Hohenzollern had ever had his head chopped off: standing before a decisive breakthrough in the 1848 Revolution (Taylor's 'turning-point' where German history 'failed to turn'), German liberals failed the test (Taylor 1961, 69). Weber explained this sociologically: neither as forthrightly liberal nor indeed as fully 'bourgeois' as its British counterparts, the German bourgeoisie proved incapable of developing the political culture that Germany's 'modernizing' capitalist economy required. In his concise rendition of Weber's views, Anthony Giddens (1972, 16–17) puts it like this: 'in Germany, the liberal bourgeoisie did not engineer a "successful" revolution. Germany achieved political unification as a consequence of Bismarck's promotion of an aggressively expansionist policy; and industrialization was effected within a social structure in which power still devolved upon traditionally established elite groups.'

In failing to conquer the past, Germany became vulnerable to the future: with the authoritarianism of 'pre-industrial traditions' still intact, the conflicts of a rapidly 'modernizing' society became harder to absorb. When that same authoritarianism outlasted even the German Revolution of 1918–1919, the old elites felt disastrously empowered in undermining Weimar's new democratic order. In Edgar Feuchtwanger's words (1973, 21), 'the very class which should have been the buttress of liberalism and stability [the educated bourgeoisie] became a prey to extremism', supporting democracy's right-wing enemies instead. German liberalism's apparent weakness was derived from a sociology of deference and accommodation (a so-called feudalization of the bourgeoisie), which bolstered the precedence of pre-industrial elites. The failed Revolution of 1848 became the pivotal event – or non-event – for the longer term future. No one put this more clearly than Theodor Hamerow (1966, vii), the classic historian of German unification: 'The penalty for the mistakes of 1848 was paid not in 1849, but in 1918, in 1933, and in 1945.'

Through the 1960s, for Marxists and liberals alike, this perspective proved remarkably resilient. No less disparaging than Weber, Karl Marx bequeathed an indictment of the German bourgeoisie to later generations of adherents, from the pre-1914 SPD (Social Democratic Party) to the Weimar Republic's wider left-wing intelligentsia.[2] It was shared by an assortment of younger historians open to Marxism – a disconnected network of talented outsiders fleeing Nazism in the 1930s, including Eckart Kehr, Hans Rosenberg, Georg W.F. Hallgarten, Alfred Vagts, Gustav Mayer, and Veit Valentin – who were later adopted by the critical West German historians discussed below.[3] Post-1945 Marxist philosophers and sociologists took the same view of German bourgeois deficiencies, from Georg Lukács (1980, excerpted 1966) to Leo Kofler (1979) and Ernst Bloch (2009). 'Just as England is the eternally "finished" country in Europe', Kofler pronounced (1979, 537, 739), 'so Germany is the one eternally stuck halfway.' And: 'The historical chain of failures on the part of the bourgeoisie in Germany is the cause of "Prussianism" pure and simple.' Isaac Deutscher (1972, 169) was especially blunt:

since the Reformation the tragedy of Germany [is] that it has not advanced with the times, and that Germany has never fought through its own revolution. The French had their great revolution. The English carried theirs through in the seventeenth century and then experienced a long process of reform, democratization, and progress. Germany has in many respects remained fixed in the sixteenth century and at the catastrophe of the Thirty Years War. Every revolution has failed.[4]

By the early 1970s, two prevailing versions had coalesced.[5] On the one hand, a strong typification of the 'German case' for purposes of comparison – as an authoritarian syndrome of pre-industrial traditions and arrested liberalism – became central to social science literatures on political development, especially when dealing directly with fascism and its origins: why were Germany and Italy hospitable to fascism, and not Britain or France? Classic exemplars included Alexander Gerschenkron (1943, 1962), Ralf Dahrendorf (1967), and above all Barrington Moore, Jr (1966).[6] While valorizing the bourgeoisie very differently, orthodox Marxist-Leninist historiography in the German Democratic Republic (GDR) produced accounts quite congruent.[7] Key historians (Krieger 1957; Walker 1971) extended the argument towards the patterning of social life and deep-rooted cultural traits, covering everything from family structure and child-rearing practices to cultures of provincialism and what Fritz Stern (1972) called 'vulgar idealism', or unpolitical veneration of *Kultur*, *Bildung*, and the cultivated life. The imprint of two essays by Talcott Parsons from the 1940s (1964a, 1964b) was unmistakable.[8] German history acquired a meta-narrative of marked divergence from political development in Britain, France, and United States.

'Germany' stood for the authoritarian path of modern political development – for 'dictatorship' as against 'democracy', in Moore's famous typology, for misdevelopment and failed modernization, for illiberalism and what went wrong. Nazism's possibility became inscribed in this stark contrast between 'Germany' and 'the West' – in the disjunction between economic modernity and political backwardness, or the grand contradiction of a dynamic economy housed inside an unreformed political framework. The persistence in Germany of 'authoritarian and anti-democratic structures in state and society' prevented democratizing change, enabling pre-industrial elites to entrench their dominance (Bracher 1969, 1339).[9] Lacking the consensus-building mechanisms of a modern parliamentary system, permanent structural instability undermined the German polity. Elites became used to fabricating and exploiting political crises, right up to the wager on Nazism in 1933. The Nazis' success presupposed this continuity of pre-industrial and authoritarian attitudes at the polity's centre, linked to a powerful bloc of dominant socio-economic interests consistently obstructing any liberalizing change.

Meanwhile, on the other hand, a new West German grouping of social-science historians shaped an especially strong thesis of German exceptionalism or the *Sonderweg* ('special path'). From the early 1970s, Hans-Ulrich Wehler anchored Nazism's origins to the deep sociology of German backwardness outlined above. He located Germany's peculiar authoritarianism inside the core structures of the pre-1914 imperial state – monarchy, army, aristocratic privilege, Prussian predominance, more ambivalently the bureaucracy, in general the institutionally secured primacy of pre-industrial elites – whose recalcitrance always impeded reform. In the political system, this obstructionism required a ruling cluster of interests – the 'alliance of iron and rye', or the political bloc of heavy industry and big agriculture originally forged by Bismarck in the 1870s. The resulting politics described a space where over the longer term Nazism could succeed: 'The fatal consequences of the government politics through which the political predominance of the pre-industrial elites was to be preserved in the period of high industrialization were revealed quite clearly between 1914 and 1929, when these structures came apart. By that time, the politics had helped create the dangerous conditions which smoothed the way for National Socialism' (Wehler 1988, 269). The practitioners of that politics held back the growth of liberal-democratic institutions before 1914, while surviving the 1918 Revolution to fight another day. They destabilized the Weimar Republic and helped decisively in hoisting the Nazis into power.

Nazi success came only contingently from capitalism's immediate crisis after 1929, in other words. Far more crucial were these 'historical handicaps from the time of the authoritarian state' (Winkler 1983). If Germany alone produced fascism out of the world economic crisis, this came from a deeper lying backwardness: 'Prussian militarism … Junker cliques … statolatry of clergy and professoriat … preponderance of heavy industry in the political decision-making process' (Wehler 1983, 53). Nazism came from a blockage of modernization: 'In Germany it was not "bourgeois dominance" based in successful industrial capitalism that tipped over into fascism', Wehler insisted, but precisely its opposite, 'a deficit of civility [*Bürgerlichkeit*], of bourgeois parliamentarism, and of firmly anchored bourgeois political culture that opened the way to the abyss' (Wehler 1983, 53). Germany's *Sonderweg* consisted in these structures of backwardness and misdevelopment:

> The reasons why democracy was liquidated in Germany in the course of the world economic crisis and not in the other developed societies have less to do with the course of the crisis itself than with the different pre-industrial histories of these countries. The conditions for the rise of fascism have at least as much to do with feudalism and absolutism as with capitalism. (Winkler 1978, 83)

Or, in Jürgen Kocka's version (Kocka 1980, 11): 'Whoever does not want to talk about pre-industrial, pre-capitalist, and pre-bourgeois traditions should keep quiet about fascism.'[10]

Two other lines of thought intersected with these views. Each also went back to the 1920s and 1930s. The *first* line of inquiry connects closely with the structural argument about development and backwardness. In Barrington Moore's rendition (1966), the societal dominance of different types of modernizing coalitions, based on specific configurations of landowning and urban-bourgeois social interests and their links to popular forces ('lord and peasant in the making of the modern world'), explained contrary developmental trajectories of 'dictatorship' versus 'democracy'. In this comparative framework, Germany's vulnerability to Nazism came from patterns of partial, uneven, and failed modernization leaving pre-industrial elites intact and throwing unreformed political institutions and 'traditional' social structures into contradiction with the 'modern' economy. The resulting tensions then impacted intermediate strata between dominant classes and workers, namely, the lower middle class or petty bourgeoisie. German industrialization was especially disruptive for two broad sectors of population – small-scale traditional owners and producers known as the *Mittelstand*, and new categories of white-collar officialdom and employees proliferating inside the industrial economy or the 'new *Mittelstand*'. Research into the social support for fascist movements has consistently emphasized exactly these groups: a large 'traditional' sector of agricultural smallholding, handicrafts, carting, shopkeeping, and other small-scale trading; and the 'modern' white-collar sector of salaried employees, lower grade civil servants, junior managerial and technical personnel, teachers, clerical workers, and lower professions. In its multiple dimensions (structural, material, cultural, psychological), the complicated ambivalence of these groupings towards the modernizing process left them prey to protest movements of the radical right like Nazism.[11]

Critics already saw fascist support like this in the 1920s. For liberal historian Luigi Salvatorelli (1923), it expressed 'the class struggle of the petty bourgeoisie, squeezed between capitalism and the proletariat, as the third party between the two conflicting sides' (Roberts 1980, 337). Historians and sociologists, non-Marxists and Marxists alike, shared this view. Under pressure of an extreme socio-economic crisis, with left-wing insurgencies threatening the political order, both Nazis and Italian fascists found ready reservoirs of mass support in the social anger of the lower middle class. Atomization and insecurity had also become endemic to this group's experience of modern urban living under capitalism: absent social solidarities or a collective culture comparable to the labour movement's associational world, those circumstances dramatically worsened under the Depression, exposing them to the Nazis' authoritarian-populist appeal. Key sociologies of the 1950s reinforced this analysis. Nazism was 'a manifestation of the risks inherent in mass society, demonstrating that [the latter] could be the nursery of irrational ideologies, demagogy, and totalitarianism, as well as democracy and pluralism' (Caplan 2008, 5).[12] Within this framework, the lower middle class were structural casualties of modernization. Losers in the march of technological progress and in 'extreme revolt against the modern industrial world', they sought refuge in rhetorics of 'utopian anti-modernism' (Turner 1975, 133–134). Perhaps the sharpest formula for the resulting politics, with its ascription of Nazi support, was Seymour Martin Lipset's 'extremism of the middle' or 'radicalism of the center'.[13]

A *second* classic line of inquiry concerned Nazism's relationship to German capitalism. If the main lineage was Marxist, going back to the 1930s, an interest in Nazi links to powerful interests of the economy remained much wider.[14] By the 1970s, the driving question was less the sensational 'Who paid Hitler?' (Thyssen 1941) than a more searching analysis of the Nazis' role in resolving the political crisis of 1930–1933 in a manner congenial to ruling interests in the economy. Research focused on the operative alignments across capital's various factions and industry's associated political thinking, whether as corporately organized lobbying or via the parties. The intricacies of industry's political manoeuvring and varying impact on government could then be better assessed.[15] An approach developed for pre-1914 political history, focused on the heavy industrial–agrarian alliance and its blocking of reform, was now projected forward into the Weimar years, often by the same historians. Locating anti-democratic rigidities in this continuity of ruling elites, the new work presented Weimar politics as the adversarial representation of organized interests.[16] That politics was again placed in a wider social field, mobilizing old and new *Mittelstand* as described above (e.g. Winkler 1974). This decisively boosted interest in social history, fixing attention on the interrelations among economy, politics, and social structure.

By the early 1980s, impressive scholarship accumulated around Nazism as a movement. Local and regional studies were a main focus, with pioneering monographs by William Sheridan Allen (1984) on Northeim and Jeremy Noakes (1971) on the surrounding area of Lower Saxony; in West Germany itself, Martin Broszat (Director of the Munich Institut für Zeitgeschichte, 1972–1989) presided over the Bavaria Project, with six volumes (1977–1983) on that region's ordinary life in the Nazi era.[17] Just as important were systematic sociologies of the Nazi Party (NSDAP) and its electorate, equivalent work on the SA (*Sturmabteilung*, Stormtroopers), the beginnings of research on the youth and women's auxiliaries, analyses of the movement's varying strength across localities of different types, and accounts of its appeal to varying social groups and constituencies. After Dietrich Orlow's solid organizational history of the NSDAP (1969, 1973), Michael Kater dissected the social character of its rank-and-file membership and leaders (1983), with similar studies following on the SA (Jamin 1984; Bessel 1984; Fischer 1983; Reiche 1986). Thomas Childers (1983), Richard Hamilton (1982), and Jürgen Falter (1991) analysed the Nazi electorate. A cross-section through this scholarship appeared in a volume edited by Childers (1986) on the diversity of mobilizations helping compose the Nazi Party's overall constituency.

These literatures continue expanding our knowledge of Nazism as a movement. Among regional and city-based studies, Anthony McElligott on Altona (1998), Claus-Christian Szejnmann on Saxony (1999), Oded Heilbronner on southern Baden (1998), and Pamela Swett on Berlin (2004) especially stand out. Yet interest has mainly shifted elsewhere – either to the regime years of the Third Reich itself and especially the period of the war, emphasizing the racial state and Holocaust, or else away from Nazism altogether to other aspects of Weimar. For histories of the Nazi *movement*, we seem to have reached provisional equilibrium. Two monographs showing this best are Peter Fritzsche's *Rehearsals for Fascism* (1990) and Rudy Koshar's study of Marburg (1986): each showed the party's local strengths growing not in the vacuum of cultural despair and social atomization, but precisely from the solidities of bourgeois sociality and political cohesion. Shifting focus from both the Depression's economic privations and nationalist anger about Versailles, Fritzsche embeds Nazism's distinctiveness in a larger story of patriotic concentration: 'The twenty-year period beginning in 1914 was characterized by the steady advance of a broad populist revolution that was animated by war, drew strength from the Revolution of 1918, menaced the Weimar Republic, and finally culminated in the rise of the Nazis' (Fritzsche 1998, jacket description). A new Right learned how to appropriate and redeploy the potentials of the democratic breach of 1918: 'Better than anyone else, the Nazis twisted together ideas from the political Left and Right, crossing nationalism with social reform, antisemitism with democracy, fear of the future with hope for a new beginning. This radical rebelliousness destroyed old authoritarian structures as much as it attacked liberal principles' (Fritzsche 1998, jacket description).

Fritzsche's first book (1990) came at the apex of the intensely accumulating social history of the rise of the Nazis, just as his later synthesis (1998) stands for a remarkably solid consensus about the Nazi regime's breadth of popular legitimacy. While sanctioned coercively by the violence of 1933–1934 and still needing elaborate ideological work, the new regime presumed a reliable reservoir of popu-lar conformity and acquiescence.[18] Here, Fritzsche explains Nazism's success by *moving away* from the movement itself to examine the far broader coalescence of right-wing patriotism around avowedly anti-democratic and authoritarian goals. In appealing to the German right's hyper-nationalism and anti-socialist hatreds, the Nazis 'gave sharp political definitions to imprecisely held affinities and frustrated expectations' (Fritzsche 2008b, 71). They built on 'a vaguely "national-socialist" consensus' (lower case) that was already apparent by 1924–1925, while adding their own 'compelling vision of the nation as a solidaristic racial entity that had little in common with the deferential hierarchies of the Second Reich' (Fritzsche 2008b, 72). As Fritzsche argues, 'their program was consistent with the transfor-mation of the political landscape in Germany since 1918, and they effectively expressed the basic "national" and "social" inclinations of the majority of Protestant voters':

> Much as local elites such as landowners, merchants, and clergymen worked with the National Socialists and in due course legitimized them, Nazi success rested on a broader populist uprising that had challenged and undercut the power of conserva-tives throughout the 1920s. Thus the National Socialist seizure of power in 1933 was the triumph of a 'right-wing Jacobinism' in which a variety of working-class and middle-class groups sought a political voice and policies of change in the name of the German nation. (Fritzsche 2008b, 71, 72)[19]

With Fritzsche's work we can think differently about Nazi sociology. As Nazi members and voters came disproportionately from those categories, evidence still supports the 'petty bourgeois thesis'. But more striking was the heterogeneous breadth. In contrast with the parties of the left, the NSDAP continuously grew its social appeal: in 1928–1932, combined SPD-KPD votes fell from 40.4% to 35.9%, contracting around an historic working-class core even as half the wage-dependent population cast their votes elsewhere. If the left found it ever harder to break through the 'sociological, ideological, religious, and, not least, sex barriers' defin-ing the 'historic working class' in Germany, then the Nazis broadened their base in multiple directions (Mason 1993, 52).[20] They proved adept at tapping popular hopes and resentments, promising all and nothing in the same breath. However cynical and opportunist (often it was neither), this eclecticism was a major accom-plishment. In rallying such disparate support before 1933, the NSDAP was a pop-ular political formation without precedent in the German polity. It not only subsumed the right's long-standing organizational fragmentation. It also united a broadly based ensemble of subordinate classes, centred on the Protestant peasantry and petty bourgeoisie (old and new), reaching deep into the wage-earning popula-tion.[21] It did so on the terrain of ideology.

This return to the salience of Nazi ideology, after the long hiatus of social history's dominance, decisively shifted the historiographical ground. Fritzsche's reading of Nazi political success is an especially strong indication. So, too, is the continuing impact of *The Racial State* (Burleigh and Wippermann 1991), along with seminal writings of Detlev Peukert (1993) and the arrival of gender history into the discussion (Bridenthal, Grossmann, and Kaplan 1984), which together focused attention on eugenicist and biopolitical thinking, biological politics, and the 'scientification of the social', not only in the Third Reich itself but also for the Weimar antecedents. New scholarship on the 'SS state' reaches back to the 1920s in the same way, most powerfully in Michael Wildt's work (2009). While more obliquely related to the rise of Nazism, work on 'political religion' illuminates how its appeal was shaped (Steigmann-Gall 2003; Bärsch 1998). Each of these areas requires attention once we accept Fritzsche's case for the wider coalescence of a 'vaguely "national-socialist" consensus.' Finally, the oeuvre of Tim Mason (1995a, 1995b), though mostly concentrated on the 'regime' rather than the 'movement', remains a rich source of challenging questions, especially with respect to gender and the pre-1933 dynamics between Nazism and the working class.

Mason's classic essay, 'The Primacy of Politics: Politics and Economics in National Socialist Germany' (1966), written at the very outset of serious scholarship, brings us to a final point: in the rise of Nazism the crisis of 1929–1933 remains ultimately decisive (Mason 1995a, 53-76). Structurally speaking, the context was longer. The fragility of parliamentary process went back to the conjuncture of war and revolution in 1917–1923, with the left's unprecedented gains (reformist and revolutionary) and earlier radicalizing of the right. As Fritzsche reminds us, by the mid-1920s the disunity of the latter and its damaged popular credibility opened the space for still more radical speculations. The crisis of 1918–1919 was resolved via public accommodations for labour: unions acquired new corporative legitimacy; socialists gained commanding local government presence; the SPD acquired central space on the national stage, with still greater militancy on the communist left. For the right, parliamentary methods seemed to have exhausted their potential by 1929–1930, securing neither the political representation of dominant classes in the state nor sufficient mobilizing of consent in elections. This was how Nazism prospered: the political cohesion of the dominant classes and their leading economic fractions could no longer be organized successfully inside existing parliamentary negotiations and party government, while the popular legitimacy of the same constitutional framework passed simultaneously into crisis. These destructively intersecting crises destabilized national politics with ever-increasing intensity after March 1930, opening a space where exceptional remedies could be taken seriously. By the summer of 1932 at the latest, the Nazis were the credible mass movement making an 'extra-systemic solution' feasible. In what remains the most incisive formulation, this is how David Abraham (1986, 277) described the resulting dilemma:

> Could no bourgeois political force organize the political unity of the dominant economic fractions out of the diversity and fractiousness of their economic interests? Was no political unity possible and no mass political support available within the Republic, despite the single-mindedness of the dominant classes' anti-socialism? Were the maintenance of capitalist economic relations and political democracy so antithetical in *this* conjuncture that abandonment and undermining of the Republic were self-evident necessities for the dominant classes?[22]

In *this* Weimar crisis, adjustments within the given constitutional arrangements looked increasingly untenable. More radical options beyond those boundaries were available.

By his patient unscrambling of 'politics and economics', Tim Mason enabled the more subtle and satisfying treatment of Nazism's relationship to the crisis of German capitalism as it persisted into the 1930s. As Fritzsche and others have shown, Nazism's rise presumed an earlier crisis in the *political* stabilities of Weimar democracy, requiring primary attention to a broader right-wing coalescence of the years 1918–1925. That process in its turn was shaped by the impact of the wartime conjuncture and its revolutionary denouement. Neither can be understood without searching ideological analysis. Each will require careful assessment of earlier developments before 1914. But reaching ever further back into the nineteenth century (even beyond), in contrast, is less likely to help and may easily confuse. The best understanding of the rise of Nazism will involve keeping these two problems in tension: what were the conditions of possibility for Nazism's successful emergence as a complex political formation in the years 1925–1933? And: what kind of crisis brought it to power? If the first question has now been exhaustively treated, on foundations solidly assembled in the 1970s and 1980s, then the second remains frozen on that very same ground. To make the rise of Nazism really intelligible, it is in the early 1930s – with the immediate fascism-producing crisis – that future research should begin.

Notes

1   Half a century later, Shirer's book remains a bestseller.
2   In 1848, the German bourgeoisie was 'inclined from the outset to treachery against the people and compromise with the crowned representatives of the old society … making a bargaining-counter of its own wishes, without initiative, without faith in itself, without faith in the people, without a world-historical function; an accursed old man, who found himself compelled to lead and mislead the first youthful impulses of a robust people in his own senile interests – sans teeth, sans eyes, sans taste, sans everything …' (Marx 1973, 192–194).
3   Mainly marginalized by the German academic establishment of the 1920s, these individuals received variable recognition in exile. Their works were systematically republished in the 1960s and 1970s at Hans-Ulrich Wehler's instigation. See Wehler (1980). Most influential was Hans Rosenberg, who taught in the United States at Brooklyn College and University of California, Berkeley. See especially Rosenberg (1958).
4   See also Poulantzas (1973, 168–184); Grebing (1974).
5   For comprehensive critique, see Blackbourn and Eley (1984).
6   The nine collaborative volumes of *Studies in Political Development* sponsored by the US SSRC Committee on Comparative Politics and published by Princeton University Press (1963–1978) was a prime source for the interpretive syndrome. Veblen (1966) was another idiosyncratic but influential version.
7   See Bleiber (1977), along with Richard J. Evans's review in *Social History* (1979); also Poulantzas (1973, 1974).
8   Also Dahrendorf (1967, 404): 'The social basis of German authoritarianism, thus of the resistance of German society to modernity and liberalism, consisted in a structural syndrome that held people to social ties in which they had found themselves without their doing and that prevented them from full participation.'

9   Also Fraenkel (1964, 27): the key question was 'why … Germany has found it so difficult to understand the parliamentary system of government, to come to terms with it, and apply it successfully'.

10   Kocka was turning on its head a famous anti-capitalist aphorism of Max Horkheimer: 'Whoever does not want to talk about fascism should keep quiet about capitalism.'

11   The classic statement of this view was Winkler (1972a); also Winkler (1976a, 1972b). More generally, Leppert-Fögen (1974).

12   See Riesman (1950), Arendt (1951), Nisbet (1953), Kornhauser (1959), Ortega y Gasset (1932), Lederer (1940), Neumann (1942). In general, Giner (1976), Halebsky (1976).

13   See Lipset (1963, 127–179), chapter 5, 'Fascism' – Left, Right, and Center'. Lipset uses neither of the cited phrases per se. He was also sceptical about the 'mass society' thesis (1963, 144).

14   Neumann (1942), Schweitzer (1964), Hallgarten (1955). The 1935 Comintern resolution defined fascism as 'the open, teroristic dictatorship of the most reactionary, most chauvinist, and most imperialist elements of finance capital'. But for wider Marxist thinking, see Beetham (1984).

15   The case for Nazi reliance on big business, in line with the 1935 Comintern formula, was carried mainly by GDR historians, for example, Czichon (1967), a work easily discredited by its errors. A main critic was Henry Ashby Turner in key articles of 1968–1972, later folded into Turner (1985).

16   See Mommsen, Petzina, and Weisbrod (1974), the proceedings of a week-long conference in June 1973, with 57 contributions in a thousand pages.

17   Also Pridham (1973).

18   Fritzsche's more recent book, *Life and Death in the Third Reich* (2008a), further elaborates his argument.

19   'Right-wing Jacobinism' was a concept borrowed from Eley (1986, 270).

20   Also Childers (1976), Fischer (1996), Mühlberger (2003), Szejnmann (1999, 205–239).

21   This distinction of the NSDAP – in finally becoming 'the long-sought party of middle-class concentration' going back to the 1890s (Childers 1983, 262) – coexisted with its character as a 'people's party'. Earlier debates over the latter now seem settled. See Mergel (2011, 434–435). More generally, Winkler (1976b), Falter (1990).

22   See also the penultimate section of Abraham's final chapter, 'Toward the Extra-Systemic Solution' (1986, 302–308).

References

Abraham, David. 1986. *The Collapse of the Weimar Republic: Political Economy and Crisis*, 2nd edn. New York: Holmes & Meier.

Allen, William Sheridan. 1984. *The Nazi Seizure of Power: The Experience of a Single German Town, 1922–1945*. New York: Franklin Watts. Original edition 1965.

Arendt, Hannah. 1951. *The Origins of Totalitarianism*. New York: Harcourt Brace Jovanovich.

Bärsch, Claus-Ekkehard. 1998. *Die politische Religion des Nationalsozialismus: Die religiöse Dimension des NS-Ideologie in den Schriften von Dietrich Eckart, Joseph Goebbels, Adolf Rosenberg und Adolf Hitler*. Munich: Wilhelm Fink Verlag.

Barraclough, Geoffrey. 1938. *Medieval Germany: Essays by German Historians*. Oxford: Blackwell.

Barraclough, Geoffrey. 1946a. *The Origins of Modern Germany*. Oxford: Blackwell.

Barraclough, Geoffrey. 1946b. *Factors in German History*. Oxford: Blackwell.

Barraclough, Geoffrey. 1950. *The Medieval Empire: Idea and Reality.* London: Historical Association.

Beetham, David, ed. 1984. *Marxists in Face of Fascism: Writings by Marxists on Fascism from the Interwar Period.* New York: Barnes & Noble.

Bessel, Richard. 1984. *Political Violence and the Rise of Nazism: The Storm Troopers in Eastern Germany 1925–1934.* New Haven, CT: Yale University Press.

Blackbourn, David and Eley, Geoff. 1984. *The Peculiarities of German History: Bourgeois Sdociety and Politics in Nineteenth-Century Germany.* Oxford: Oxford University Press.

Bleiber, Helmut, ed. 1977. *Bourgeoisie und bürgerliche Umwalzung in Deutschland 1789–1871.* Berlin: Akadamie Verlag.

Bloch, Ernst. 2009. *The Heritage of Our Times*, German edn. Cambridge: Polity Press.

Bracher, Karl Dietrich. 1969. 'The Nazi Takeover.' *The History of the Twentieth Century*, 48. London: Purnell.

Bridenthal, Renate, Grossmann, Atina and Kaplan, Marion, eds. 1984. *When Biology Became Destiny: Women in Weimar and Nazi Germany.* New York: Monthly Review Press.

Broszat, Martin et al., eds. 1977–1983. *Bayern in der NS-Zeit.* 6 vols. Munich: Oldenbourg.

Burleigh, Michael and Wippermann, Wolfgang. 1991. *The Racial State: Germany, 1933–1945.* Cambridge: Cambridge University Press.

Butler, Rohan D'Olier. 1941. *The Roots of National Socialism, 1783–1933.* London: Faber & Faber.

Caplan, Jane. 2008. 'Introduction.' In *Nazi Germany. The Shorter Oxford History of Germany*, edited by Jane Caplan, 1–25. Oxford: Oxford University Press.

Childers, Thomas. 1976. 'The Social Bases of the National Socialist Vote.' *Journal of Contemporary History* 11, 17–42.

Childers, Thomas. 1983. *The Nazi Voter: The Social Foundations of Fascism in Germany, 1919–1933.* Chapel Hill: University of North Carolina Press.

Childers Thomas, ed. 1986. *The Formation of the Nazi Constituency 1919–1933.* London: Croom Helm.

Czichon, Eberhard. 1967. *Wer verhalf Hitler zur Macht? Zum Anteil der deutschen Industrie an der Zerstörung der Weimarer Republik.* Cologne: Pahl-Rugenstein.

Dahrendorf, Ralf. 1967. *Society and Democracy in Germany.* London: Weidenfeld & Nicolson.

Deutscher, Isaac. 1972. *Marxism in Our Time.* London: Cape.

Eley, Geoff. 1986. 'What Produces Fascism: Pre-Industrial Traditions or a Crisis of the Capitalist State?' In *From Unification to Nazism: Reinterpreting the German Past*, 254–282. London: Allen & Unwin.

Evans, Richard J. 1979. Review. *Social History* 4(3), 535–540.

Falter, Jürgen W. 1990. 'The First German *Volkspartei*: The Social Foundatons of the NSDAP.' In *Elections, Parties, and Political Traditions. Social Foundations of German Parties and Party Systems, 1867–1987*, edited by Karl Rohe, 53–81. New York: Berg.

Falter, Jürgen. 1991. *Hitlers Wähler.* Munich: C.H. Beck.

Feuchtwanger, Edgar J. 1973. 'Introduction.' In *Upheaval and Continuity: A Century of German History*, edited by Edgar J. Feuchtwanger, 11–27. London: Oswald Wolff.

Fischer, Conan. 1983. *Stormtroopers: A Social, Economic, and Ideological Analysis 1929–35.* London: George Allen and Unwin.

Fischer, Conan, ed. 1996. *The Rise of National Socialism and the Working Classes in Germany.* Providence: Berghahn Books.

Fraenkel, Ernst. 1964. 'Historical Handicaps of German Parliamentarism.' In *The Road to Dictatorship, Germany 1918–1933*, edited by Theodor Eschenburg, 25–38. London: Oswald Wolff.

Fritzsche, Peter. 1990. *Rehearsals for Fascism: Populism and Political Mobilization in Weimar Germany*. New York: Oxford University Press.

Fritzsche, Peter. 1998. *Germans into Nazis*. Cambridge, MA: Harvard University Press.

Fritzsche, Peter. 2008a. *Life and Death in the Third Reich*. Cambridge, MA: Harvard University Press.

Fritzsche, Peter. 2008b. 'The NSDAP 1919–1934: From Fringe Politics to the Seizure of Power.' In *Nazi Germany. The Shorter Oxford History of Germany*, edited by Jane Caplan, 48–72. Oxford: Oxford University Press.

Gerschenkron, Alexander. 1943. *Bread and Democracy in Germany*. Berkeley: University of California Press.

Gerschenkron, Alexander. 1962. *Economic Backwardness in Historical Perspective*. Cambridge, MA: Harvard University Press.

Giddens, Anthony. 1972. *Politics and Sociology in the Thought of Max Weber*. London: Macmillan.

Giner, Salvador. 1976. *Mass Society*. London: Martin Robertson.

Grebing, Helga. 1974. *Aktuelle Theorien über Faschismus und Konservatismus: Eine Kritik*. Frankfurt am Main: Kohlhammer.

Halebsky, Sandor. 1976. *Mass Society and Political Conflict: Towards a Reconstruction of Theory*. Cambridge: Cambridge University Press.

Hallgarten, George W.F. 1955. *Hitler, Reichswehr und Industrie: Zur Geschichte der Jahre 1918–1933*. Frankfurt am Main: Europäische Verlagsantalt.

Hamerow, Theodor S. 1966. *Restoration, Revolution, Reaction: Economics and Politics in Germany, 1815–1871*. Princeton: Princeton University Press.

Hamilton, Richard F. 1982. *Who Voted for Hitler?* Princeton: Princeton University Press.

Heilbronner, Oded. 1998. *Catholicism, Political Culture, and the Countryside: A Social History of the Nazi Party in South Germany*. Ann Arbor: University of Michigan Press.

Jamin, Mathilde. 1984. *Zwischen den Klassen: Zur Sozialstruktur der SA-Führerschaft*. Wuppertal: Peter Hammer Verlag.

Kater, Michael. 1983. *The Nazi Party: A Social Profile of Members and Leaders, 1919–1945*. Cambridge, MA: Harvard University Press.

Kocka, Jürgen. 1980. 'Ursachen des Nationalsozialismus.' *Aus Politik und Zeitgeschichte*, 21, 9–13.

Kofler, Leo. 1979. *Zur Geschichte der bürgerlichen Gesellschaft. Versuch einer vestehenden Deutung der Neuzeit*. Berlin: Luchterhand. First published 1948.

Kornhauser, Willia.. 1959. *The Politics of Mass Society*. Glencoe, IL: Free Press.

Koshar, Rudy. 1986. *Social Life, Local Politics, and Nazism: Marburg, 1880–1935*. Chapel Hill: University of North Carolina Press.

Krieger, Leonard. 1957. *The German Idea of Freedom*. Chicago: University of Chicago Press.

Lederer, Emil. 1940. *State of the Masses: The Threat of the Classless Society*. New York: W.W. Norton.

Leppert-Fögen, Annette. 1974. *Die deklassierte Klasse. Studien zur Geschichte und Ideologie des Kleinbürgertums*. Frankfurt am Main: Fischer Taschenbuch Verlag.

Lipset, Seymour Martin. 1963. *Political Man: The Social Bases of Politics*. Garden City, NY: Anchor Books.

Lukács, Georg. 1980. *The Destruction of Reason*. London: Merlin. German edn 1954.

Lukács, Georg. 1966. *Von Nietzsche zu Hitler oder Der Irrationalismus und die deutsche Politik*. Frankfurt am Main: Fischer.

Marx, Karl. 1973. 'The Bourgeoisie and the Counter-Revolution', *Neue Rheinische Zeitung*, 14 December 1848. In Karl Marx, *The Revolutions of 1848*, edited by David Fernbach, 186–213. Harmondsworth: Penguin.

Mason, Tim. 1993. *Social Policy in the Third Reich: The Working Class and the 'National Community*. Providence, RI: Berg.

Mason Tim. 1995a. 'The Primacy of Politics: Politics and Economics in National Socialist Germany.' In *Nazism, Fascism, and the Working Class: Essays by Tim Mason*, edited by Jane Caplan, 53–76. Cambridge: Cambridge University Press. First published 1966.

Mason Tim. 1995b. *Nazism, Fascism, and the Working Class: Essays by Tim Mason*, edited by Jane Caplan. Cambridge: Cambridge University Press.

McElligott, Anthony. 1998. *Contested City: Municipal Politics and the Rise of Nazism in Altona, 1917–1937*. Ann Arbor: University of Michigan Press.

Mergel, Thomas. 2011. 'Dictatorship and Democracy, 1918–1939.' In *The Oxford Handbook of Modern German History*, edited by Helmut Walser Smith, 434–435. Oxford: Oxford University Press.

Mommsen, Hans, Petzina Dietmar, and Weisbrod, Bernd, eds. 1974. *Industrielles System und politische Entwicklung in der Weimarer Republik*. Düsseldorf: Droste Verlag.

Moore, Jr, Barrington. 1966. *Social Origins of Dictatorship and Democracy: Lord and Peasant in the Making of the Modern World*. Boston, MA: Beacon Press.

Mühlberger, Detlef. 2003. *The Social Bases of Nazism, 1919–1933*. Cambridge: Cambridge University Press.

Neumann, Franz. 1942. *Behemoth: The Theory and Practice of National Socialism, 1933–1944*. Oxford: Oxford University Press.

Neumann, Sigmund. 1942. *Permanent Revolution*. New York: Harper & Row.

Nisbet, Robert. 1953. *The Quest for Community*. New York: Oxford University Press.

Noakes, Jeremy. 1971. *The Nazi Party in Lower Saxony, 1921–1933*. Oxford: Oxford University Press.

Orlow, Dietrich. 1969, 1973. *The History of the Nazi Party, 1919–1945*. 2 vols. Pittsburgh: University of Pittsburgh Press.

Ortega y Gasset, José. 1932. *The Revolt of the Masses*. London: George Allen & Unwin. Originally published in Spanish, 1930.

Parsons, Talcott. 1964a. 'Democracy and Social Structure in Pre-Nazi Germany.' In *Essays in Sociological Theory*, 104–123. New York: Free Press.

Parsons, Talcott. 1964b. 'Some Sociological Aspects of Fascist Movements.' In *Essays in Sociological Theory*, 124–141. New York: Free Press.

Peukert, Detlev J.K. 1993. 'The Genesis of the "Final Solution" from the Spirit of Science.' In *Reevaluating the Third Reich*, edited by Thomas Childers and Jane Caplan, 234–252. New York: Holmes & Meier.

Poulantzas, Nicos. 1973. *Political Power and Social Classes*. London: New Left Books.

Poulantzas, Nicos. 1974. *Fascism and Dictatorship*. London: New Left Books.

Pridham, Geoffrey. 1973. *Hitler's Rise to Power: The History of the NSDAP in Bavaria, 1923–1933*. London: Hart-Davis MacGibbon.

Reiche, Eric G. 1986. *The Development of the SA in Nürnberg, 1922–1934*. Cambridge: Cambridge University Press.

Riesman, David. 1950. *The Lonely Crowd: A Study of the Changing American Character*. New Haven, CT: Yale University Press.

Roberts, David D. 1980. 'Petty-Bourgeois Fascism in Italy: Form and Content.' In *Who Were the Fascists? Social Roots of European Fascism*, edited by Stein Ugelvik Larsen, Bernd Hagtvet, and Jan Petter Myklebust, 337–347. Bergen: Universitetsforlaget.

Rosenberg, Hans. 1958. *Bureaucracy, Aristocracy, and Autocracy: The Prussian Experience, 1660–1815*. Boston, MA: Beacon Press.

Salvatorelli, Luigi. 1923. *Nazionalfascismo*. Turin: P. Gobetti.

Schweitzer, Arthur. 1964. *Big Business in the Third Reich*. Bloomington: Indiana Universiy Press.

Shirer, William L. 1960. *The Rise and Fall of the Third Reich.* London: Heinemann, Secker & Warburg.

Steigmann-Gall, Richard. 2003. *The Holy Reich: Nazi Conceptions of Christianity, 1919–1945.* Cambridge: Cambridge University Press.

Stern, Fritz. 1972. 'The Political Consequences of the Unpolitical German.' In *The Failure of Illiberalism: Essays on the Political Culture of Modern Germany*, 3–25. London: George Allen & Unwin.

Swett, Pamela E. 2004. *Neighbors and Enemies: The Culture of Radicalism in Berlin, 1929–1933.* Cambridge: Cambridge University Press.

Szejnmann, Claus-Christian W. 1999. *Nazism in Central Germany: The Brownshirts in 'Red Saxony.* New York: Berghahn Books.

Taylor, A.J.P. 1961. *The Course of German History.* London: Methuen.

Thyssen, Fritz (Friedrich). 1941. *I Paid Hitler.* New York: Farrar & Rinehart.

Turner, Henry Ashby. 1975. 'Fascism and Modernization.' In *Reappraisals of Fascism*, edited by Henry Ashby Turner, 133–134. New York: New Viewpoints.

Turner, Henry Ashby. 1985. *German Big Business and the Rise of Hitler.* New York: Oxford University Press.

Veblen, Thorsten. 1966. *Imperial Germany and the Industrial Revolution.* Ann Arbor: University of Michigan Press. First published 1915.

Vermeil, Edmond, ed. (International Council for Philosophy and Humanistic Studies and UNESCO). 1955. *The Third Reich.* London: Weidenfeld & Nicolson.

Walker, Mack. 1971. *German Home Towns: Community, State, and General Estate, 1648–1871.* Ithaca, NY: Cornell University Press.

Wehler, Hans-Ulrich. 1980. *Historische Sozialwissenschaft und Geschichtsschreibung.* Göttingen: Vandenhoeck & Ruprecht.

Wehler, Hans-Ulrich. 1983. '30 Januar 1933 – ein halbes Jahrhundert danach.' *Aus Politik und Zeitgeschichte*, 29 January.

Wehler, Hans Ulrich. 1988. 'Industrielles Wachstum und früher deutscher Imperialismus.' In *Aus der Geschichte lernen? Essays*, 256–271. Munich: C.H. Beck.

Wildt, Michael, 2009. *An Uncompromising Generation: The Nazi Leadership of the Reich Security Main Office.* Madison: University of Wisconsin Press.

Winkler, Heinrich August. 1972a. *Mittelstand, Demokratie und Nationalsozialismus: Die politische Entwicklung von Handwerk und Kleinhandel in der Weimarer Republik.* Cologne: Kiepenheuer & Witsch.

Winkler, Heinrich August. 1972b. 'Extremismus der Mitte: sozialgeschichtliche Aspekte der nationalsozialistischen Machtergreifung.' *Vierteljahreshefte für Zeitgeschichte* 20, 175–191.

Winkler, Heinrich August. 1974. 'Vom Protest zur Panik: Der gewerbliche Mittelstand in der Weimarer Republic.' In *Industrielles System und politische Entwicklung in der Weimarer Republik*, edited by Hans Mommsen, Dietmar Petzina, and Bernd Weisbrod, 778–791. Düsseldorf: Droste Verlag.

Winkler, Heinrich August. 1976a. 'From Social Protectionism to National Socialism: The German Small-Business Movement in Comparative Perspective.' *Journal of Modern History* 48, 1–18.

Winkler, Heinrich August. 1976b. 'Mittelstandsbewegung oder Volkspartei? Zur sozialen Basis der NSDAP.' In *Faschismus als soziale Bewegung: Deutschland und Italien im Vergleich*, edited by Wolfgang Schieder, 97–118. Hamburg: Hoffmann and Campe.

Winkler, Heinrich August. 1978. 'Die "neue Linke" und der deutsche Faschismus. Zur Kritik neomarxistischer Theorien über den Nationalsozialismus.' In *Revolution, Staat, Faschismus: Zur Revision des Historischen Materialismus*, 65–117. Göttingen: Vandenhoeck & Ruprecht.

Winkler, Heinrich August. 1983. 'Wie konnte es zum 30 Januar 1933 kommen?' *Aus Politik und Zeitgeschichte*, 29 January, abstract.

Further Reading

Allen, William Sheridan. 1984. *The Nazi Seizure of Power: The Experience of a Single German Town, 1922–1945*, 2nd edn. New York: Franklin Watts.
Still the most vivid account of the rise of the Nazis in a single town. Originally published in 1965; revised and updated for the second 1984 edition.
Bridenthal, Renate, Grossmann, Atina, and Kaplan, Marion, eds. 1984. *When Biology Became Destiny: Women in Weimar and Nazi Germany*. New York: Monthly Review Press.
A watershed collection of path-breaking essays that established gender as a central category of historical analysis and understanding for Nazism.
Caplan, Jane, ed. 2008. *Nazi Germany. The Shorter Oxford History of Germany*. Oxford: Oxford University Press.
An excellent anthology of authoritative introductory essays.
Eley, Geoff. 2013. *Nazism as Fascism: Violence, Ideology, and the Ground of Consent in Germany, 1930–1945*. London: Routledge.
Interconnected interpretive essays that critically survey the historiography of Nazism to build arguments about the processes that made Germans into Nazis.
Evans, Richard J. 2005. *The Coming of the Third Reich*. London: Penguin.
A tour de force of general history that places the rise of the NSDAP and the seizure of power in the general social and political history of early twentieth-century Germany.
Fritzsche, Peter. 1998. *Germans into Nazis*. Cambridge, MA: Harvard University Press.
A critical synthetic account that presents both a coherent narrative for the political history of the Weimar years and a strong argument about the bases of Nazi success.
Kershaw, Ian. 2015. *The Nazi Dictatorship: Problems and Perpectives of Interpretation*, 4th edn. London: Bloomsbury Academic.
The best and most comprehensive of the critical guides to the interpretative debates shaping historical writing on the rise of Nazism and the character of the Third Reich.
Mason Tim. 1995. *Nazism, Fascism, and the Working Class: Essays by Tim Mason*, edited by Jane Caplan. Cambridge: Cambridge University Press.
Empirically rich and analytically sophisticated essays by the premier social historian of Nazism of his generation.
Peukert, Detlev J.K. 1992. *The Weimar Republic: The Crisis of Classical Modernity*. New York: Hill and Wang.
A brilliantly original set of commentaries on the Weimar Republic that set the agenda for the past several decades of historiography on the subject.
Wildt, Michael. 2009. *An Uncompromising Generation: The Nazi Leadership of the Reich Security Main Office*. Madison: University of Wisconsin Press.
A vital study of the socio-cultural formation of the higher SS leadership in the political and ideological conflicts of the 1920s and 1930s.

CHAPTER TWO

Organic Modernity: National Socialism as Alternative Modernism

KONRAD H. JARAUSCH

On 2 July 1936 Heinrich Himmler celebrated the thousand year anniversary of King Henry the Fowler's death with other Nazi leaders in the ancient cathedral of Quedlingburg. The subsequent transformation of the Romanesque *Dom* from a Christian place of worship into a neopagan cult space for the SS sought to provide the Third Reich with historical legitimacy by linking the Nazi dictatorship to its grand medieval predecessors. Reconstructing crumbling castles and building new *Ordensburgen*, the National Socialists set out to train the racial elite of the future in such a heroic and inspiring environment. Historians were quick to seize this interest in order to sponsor their research in *Burgenforschung*, justified by providing historical grounding for an upstart mass movement. This National Socialist preoccupation with medieval trappings was a typical expression of the reactionary mythologizing of the Third Reich (Link 2014).

But on 28 May 1938 Adolf Hitler also laid the cornerstone for the construction of a huge industrial complex, designed to motorize Germany by producing a 'people's car' (*Volkswagen*). The Austrian designer Ferdinand Porsche had won a competition for the development of a cheap but durable automobile for 1000 Marks with his unusual rear-engine design. Outflanking established manufacturers, he raised the necessary capital by gaining the sponsorship of the German Labour Front which made the *Volkswagen* a prestige object for its membership. In order to use the most up-to-date methods, Porsche twice visited the Ford plants in Dearborn, Michigan, copying their assembly line facilities. He subsequently built the largest European car factory in the fields near Fallersleben and the *Mittellandkanal*. Though the war transformed the KdF ('Beetle') prototypes quickly into jeeps, the gigantism of the VW project showed a contrasting, modernizing face of the Nazi dictatorship (Mommsen and Grieger 1996).

A Companion to Nazi Germany, First Edition. Edited by Shelley Baranowski, Armin Nolzen, and Claus-Christian W. Szejnmann.
© 2018 John Wiley & Sons Ltd. Published 2018 by John Wiley & Sons Ltd.

Ever since, historians have debated whether the Third Reich was a reactionary effort to go back to the past or a modernist attempt to shape the future. While contemporary opponents considered National Socialism a right-wing movement, Ralf Dahrendorf (1967) and David Schoenbaum (1980) stressed its unintentional modernizing effects. Liberal intellectuals who considered modernity as synonymous with democracy vigorously denounced the reactionary features of Hitler's rule. But social historians like Michael Prinz and Rainer Zitelmann (1994) countered that the Nazi *Volksgemeinschaft* ('people's community') was a thoroughly modern project, while Detlev Peukert (1992) pointed to its destructive side. Exploring the up-to-date style of popular culture in the Third Reich, cultural historians like Peter Fritzsche (1996, 1; Betts 2002) claimed in turn: 'The Nazis were modernists because they made the acknowledgement of the radical instability of twentieth century life the premise of relentless experimentation.'

This controversy about the relationship of the Third Reich to modernism has reached a dead end because it fails to address the sociological concept of multiple modernities. Instead of emphasizing a single normative process of democratic modernization, the macrosociologist Shmuel N. Eisenstadt (2003; Preyer 2013) has recognized the existence of competing visions of modernity. When historicized and adapted to the rival ideologies coming out of the First World War, this perspective suggests that the liberal consensus of modernization fractured into competing communist and capitalist versions, contrasting Lenin's programme of revolutionary transformation of Russia with Wilson's more moderate vision of democratic development. Out of the post-war crisis of Italy, Mussolini fashioned a third alternative of fascism that spread to Germany during the chaos of the Weimar Republic under the name of National Socialism. In this triangular conflict between modernities, the Nazis occupied a special place (Jarausch 2015).

A plural perspective of competing modernities raises the question of what connected the Nazi version to and distinguished it from its rivals? Clearly as a political mass movement that employed the most recent technology, National Socialism resembled communism and liberalism. But in terms of ideological content, the Hitler dictatorship rejected the Enlightenment values of its competitors. Jeffrey Herf (1984) has tried to resolve this paradox by coining the term 'reactionary modernism', which simply juxtaposes both aspects of the Third Reich as one concept. This suggestion is helpful in recognizing the tension between the different facets of National Socialism, but it does not go far enough in specifying *how* the Nazis themselves sought to reconcile their contradictory aims. To characterize the peculiar nature of this strange mixture between past and future, the following remarks will suggest a more precise concept of 'organic modernity'.

2.1 Reactionary Aspects

Ample evidence of the rejection of modernity points, indeed, to the reactionary character of the Third Reich, defined by a series of deep resentments. Chief among them was an attack on the entire 'system' of the Weimar Republic as representation of democracy that was dividing and enfeebling Germany. To the Nazis, democratic government was strongly associated with the loss of the First World War for which they held republican leaders, the 'November criminals', responsible. Hitler and his followers despised the internal fragmentation of representative politics, denouncing the lobbying of interest groups and the compromises of parliament. At the same time, they were furious about the external weakness which forced Germany to accept the 'shameful peace' of Versailles and to cooperate with its erstwhile Western enemies. Finally, they also denounced the crises periodically produced by unrestrained capitalism (Fritzsche 1998; Szejnmann 2013).

At the same time, National Socialists also developed a burning hatred of communism as a rival alternative to decaying democracy. Already the basic assumptions of Marxist egalitarianism that would level societal distinctions ran counter to the Nazi sense of social order and hierarchy. Moreover, the shocking tales of Baltic Germans, describing the atrocities of the Bolshevik Revolution and the Civil War, made many Hitler supporters shudder, since they threatened the culture and lifestyle of the middle class. The prominence of Jewish leaders like Leon Trotsky or Rosa Luxemburg seemed to confirm the un-German character of socialist radicalism. The Communist Party also appeared to be their chief competitor for the working-class vote due to its mastery of the techniques of mass politics such as rallies and propaganda (Waddington 2007). Finally, the Soviet Union, populated by 'inferior Slavs', loomed as an international danger from the East.

Hitler and many other National Socialist leaders also personally loathed the so-called decadence of cultural modernism as expressed by the Weimar avant-garde. They feared a whole series of styles and contents derived from the Moloch of hectic urbanism that seemed to dissolve middle-class taste and propriety. For instance, the book-burning ceremonies of the spring of 1933 were a symbolic effort to stamp out the corrosive influence of progressive intellectuals. At the same time, the infamous Munich exhibition of degenerate art issued a warning against experimental styles such as expressionism which were undermining conventions of representation. Similar campaigns targeted the powerful rhythms of popular music as an outgrowth of 'Negroid racial inferiority' (Mosse and Jones 1984; Goggin 1991). In the cultural realm, the Nazi movement rested on a massive backlash against experimentation in style and content that assaulted hallowed traditions.

Many of the resentments against modernity combined in a racial antisemitism that went far beyond the traditional religious prejudice among Catholics or Lutherans against the so-called killers of Christ (Confino 2014). The post-emancipation hatred of Jews drew upon quasi-scientific definitions that made race an inescapable biological trait, allegedly poisoning the German body politic. Since Judaeophobia served as a screen for projecting multiple fears, Nazis saw no contradiction in being anti-capitalist and anti-communist at the same time. Although Jews in Central Europe amounted to hardly more than 1% of the population, their over-representation in certain pursuits like law, medicine, finance, and publishing aroused resentment among their Aryan competitors during the Great Depression. While radical antisemitism was crucial for the original core of Nazi activists, it failed to disturb the majority of the electorate, since much of the population shared a milder form of social prejudice (Katz 1980).

These selected examples clearly indicate that National Socialism was a move-ment which placed itself on the political right and was considered by opponents as reactionary. The culmination of such 'antis' as anti-liberalism, anti-communism, anti-modernism, and anti- Semitism was not just an exaggeration of an otherwise sensible quest but rather the essence of its ideology and appeal. From a moderniza-tion perspective, National Socialism can be seen as an articulation of a deep unease with the pace of social change during the first third of the twentieth century. It did not help that many new technical, economic, societal, and cultural trends were associated with upheavals like war or depression that threatened ever larger num-bers of people (Jäckel 1981). Since conservative efforts to preserve tradition appeared to be failing, the National Socialists embarked upon a more radical and in many ways utopian search for a past that had never existed.

In contrast to these phobias, the Nazis also developed a positive vision of the past that, though rather hazy in detail, had considerable appeal. One central tenet was the 'blood and soil' agrarianism advocated by the theoretician Walter Darré. Ignoring the growing mechanization of agribusiness, this romanticized invocation of the Middle Ages celebrated the strength of an armed peasantry of *Wehrbauern* as key to the health of a nation. Physical toil on the land would cure the neurasthenia of the cities and reinvigorate the Aryan race by cleansing it of degenerate tendencies (Bramwell 1985). To stop speculation in land, a complicated inheritance law (*Reichserbhofgesetz*) sought to save the family farm by preventing its mortgaging and subdivision. Moreover, a compulsory service law required grade-school graduates to do farm labour in order to counteract the flight to the cities, provide peasants with cheap manpower, and teach the young the value of working in fields and stables.

Another retro-fantasy of the Nazis was the propagation of Norse mythology that provided proof of the superiority of the Aryan race. Lacking the Roman herit-age of written records and imposing stone buildings, they had to resort to a legacy of runes and oral sagas in order to fashion an imposing prehistory. They therefore celebrated the victory of Arminius over the Legions in the Teuteburg Forest which had kept Rome from extending its influence beyond the *limes*. Invoking the Saxon tradition, the Nazis also tried to revive the Germanic deities like Odin, Freya, or Thor so as to create a combative neopaganism that would replace the enfeebling influence of Christianity. Though largely lost in the myths of prehistory, the Vikings became a favourite role model due to their daring seamanship and fighting ferocity (Hare 2015). This murky realm of oral tradition, celebrated in Wagnerian operas, served as inspiration for a return to a militant past.

Similarly, the quest for 'living space', inspired by a simplistic reading of geo-politics, suggested a reactionary utopia with murderous consequences. Originally coined by geographers, the notion of *Lebensraum* rested on a pre-industrial under-standing of national strength that equated the possession of territory with a healthy race, nourished by the soil. In order to stop population loss by emigration, rightist ideologues argued that Germany's overcrowding ought to be relieved by conquer-ing additional lands. Since the overseas colonies had been lost in the First World War, the Nazis advocated eastward expansion so as to gain space for agrarian settle-ments, spreading into the fertile regions of the Ukraine and extending all the way to the sunny Crimea. Though the ethnic cleansing of the resident populations required war, *völkisch* propagandists hoped thereby to reconsolidate the fragmented German speakers into an empire in the East (Mazower 2008).

A final positive appeal that was derived from misplaced Germanic traditions was the leadership principle of subordination to a charismatic *Führer* or leader. Frustrated with the bickering of Weimar parliamentarianism, the Nazis proposed a political alternative that would provide unquestioned authority and clear direction. They found it in a medieval custom of free men electing a leader for the purpose of war, a *Herzog*, whom they would be prepared to follow without question. This alternative version of 'Germanic democracy' claimed to anoint a Führer from among the *Volk* whose orders, flowing downward through a cadre of intermediaries, were always to be obeyed. By proclaiming National Socialism a movement rather than a party, Hitler claimed the mantle of such leadership and sought to create a mythical bond by acting for the people (Kershaw 1998). Ignoring the complexity of modern society, this carefully staged leadership cult justified the Nazi dictatorship.

Combined with the rejection of the present, these positive retro-utopias reinforce the impression of the basically reactionary character of National Socialism. The ideological trappings of agrarianism, Nordic style, living-space fantasies, and leadership cult were not efforts to recover actual history, but rhetorical devices to cite a mythological past in order to inspire a heroic present. In contrast to appealing to controversial leaders like the Kaiser, Bismarck, or Frederick the Great, these references invoked much earlier figures like Barbarossa whose actual existence was shrouded in mystery and who could therefore be instrumentalized for radical aims. These mythical imaginaries created a deadly mixture of racism, expansionism, and dictatorial control that would propel the Third Reich into the Second World War and devastate the entire European continent (Rich 1973). Not really trying to preserve the past, the Nazis abused it to remake the future.

2.2 Modern Dimensions

In contrast to such reactionary features, National Socialism also had many traits that mark the movement as undeniably modern. The vehemence of the rejection of modernism signalled that Hitler's dictatorship was itself part of the cauldron of modernity, since it demonstrated an effort to escape its negative concomitants by making use of its positive potential. The Nazi leadership was enamoured of modern technology, exemplified by automobiles and airplanes, and sought to use the most up-to-date equipment such as loudspeakers, radio, and film in order to propagandize its aims while relying on recent inventions in weapons' development. Moreover, the entire biopolitical project of cleansing and toughening up the *Volkskörper* was an enormous social engineering enterprise, typical of modernity (Fritzsche 1996; Betts 2002; Smelser 1990). In spite of its reactionary rhetoric, National Socialism took great pains to appear actionist, youthful, and future-oriented.

Ignoring Germanic mythologizing, the Nazi leadership embraced modern technology both for its heady experience and for its instrumental capacity to further their aims. While still struggling as an artist, Hitler himself possessed a permanent pass to the Deutsche Museum where he could marvel at the astonishing inventions of German engineers. The entire Nazi leadership loved to ride in open roadsters during parades in order to receive the accolades of the crowd, and to experience the intoxication of speed on the newly built superhighways of the *Autobahn*. The Third Reich was especially proud of the successes of the 'silver arrows' of Mercedes or Auto Union in racing for the world drivers' championship against Ferrari or British brands (Nixon 1986). The Nazis were similarly enthusiastic about airplanes, which Hitler used during his election campaigns not just for their speedy transport, but also for their aura of technological modernity.

Under the deft direction of Joseph Goebbels, the Nazis employed the most up-to-date media devices in order to propagandize their aims or entertain the masses. The loudspeaker was an essential aid in magnifying Hitler's magnetic voice so that it could reach thousands during a mass rally. Similarly, the Third Reich subsidized the development of a cheap radio, the *Volksempfänger*, in order to enable the Führer to speak to millions of listeners in their home or in public places. Nazi journalists produced dramatic newsreels, shown before feature films in cinemas, which gave viewers the illusion of being present during important political occasions or sporting events which were presented as German triumphs. Finally, by controlling the UFA film company Goebbels could also shape its shallow escapist fare like the Hans Moser comedies or more devious propaganda portrayals like the antisemitic movie *Jud Süss* (Ross 2008).

Before and during the Second World War the Nazi military also proved quite innovative in developing modern weapons which were superior to those of its enemies. Overcoming Prussian traditionalists in the cavalry, the Wehrmacht created highly manoeuvrable tanks, the *Panzer*, connected by radio, which could quickly attack en masse. At the same time, the Luftwaffe created lethal dive bombers, the infamous Junkers Stukas, that wreaked havoc with enemy infantry. When the Allies produced more numerous and effective weapons during the middle of the war, Hitler pushed for the development of 'miracle weapons' that were once again more technically advanced. These included especially Werner von Braun's V-2 rockets, targeted on Great Britain, as well as the first jet-engine fighter planes of Heinkel. Fortunately, the effort to create nuclear bombs did not make enough headway in order to become operational (Tooze 2006).

The Nazis succeeded in mobilizing engineers by extolling 'German technology' and reorganizing the technical professions. Since most technicians were employed by industry, they were particularly hard hit in the Great Depression, with over one third losing their jobs. Hence many engineers were receptive to the promises of the National Socialist League of German Technology, led by Fritz Todt, to improve their lot by public works and rapid rearmament. Nazi engineers also fulfilled a long-held wish to create Chambers of Technology in order to raise their professional esteem and control the labour market. Though obliterating the distinction between academic and semi-academic engineers, these measures revived hope and made many technicians join the Nazi cause (Guse 2011; Allen 1996). By seizing the opportunities offered by the Third Reich's recovery and imperialism, they became embroiled in designing the machinery of the Holocaust.

On a more general level, National Socialism was a mass dictatorship that was 'itself a transnational formation of modernity that emerged in response to the global processes that swept through the twentieth century'. Proposed by Paul Corner and Jie-Hyun Lim (2016), this perspective goes beyond the totalitarian emphasis on 'dictatorship from above' which stresses repression from the top. Instead it highlights the importance of popular mobilization that creates a 'dictatorship from below', because in an age of mass politics dictatorship required the complicity of the oppressed. In a mass dictatorship, coercion and consent, domination and hegemony, forced mobilization and self-mobilization were no longer polar opposites but rather complementary processes. In the Third Reich, the charismatic nature of Hitler's rule combined ruthless repression by the party and SS with acclamation and consent by the majority of the German population.

On the one hand, the Nazi system developed an elaborate repertoire of instruments of domination according to the traits of totalitarianism theory. Traditional authoritarian dictatorships like Franco's rule in Spain rested heavily on the military, the church, and the bureaucracy, relying on age-old habits of deference. In contrast, the more modern Third Reich cemented its ascendancy through an elaborate ruling ideology, promoted by a mass party that was directed by an unquestioned leader. Moreover, it used systematic terror against enemies, had a monopoly of the means of violence, employed sophisticated propaganda, and subordinated the economy to political aims. Not only the methods of dominating German society but also the efforts to establish total control by eliminating any potential opposition were themselves rather modern. Hence there was little doubt about the fundamentally repressive character of the regime (Friedrich and Brzezinski 1956; Broszat 1981).

On the other hand, the Third Reich incessantly strove for mass mobilization in order to create an image of overwhelming popular consent. For instance, the compulsory membership in Nazi auxiliary organizations such as the Stormtroopers, Hitler Youth, teachers' league, people's welfare, air-defence volunteers, and so on sought to structure all social activities. Moreover, periodic campaigns such as collecting clothing for the poor during winter or eating one meal of simple vegetable stew per week were supposed to demonstrate the equality of the ethnic community. At the same time, uniformed Nazi formations engaged in endless street demonstrations and torchlight marches which culminated in the impressive Nuremberg party rallies where hundreds of thousands of followers cheered their charismatic leader. Such voluntary participation was rewarded with minor posts, medals, 'Strength through Joy' tickets, and the like (Baranowski 2004; Gellately 2001).

Both vectors of Nazi dictatorship combined in unleashing unprecedented levels of violence, directed against internal and external enemies. Since their movement was a product of the civil war atmosphere of the early Weimar Republic, National Socialists had little compunction in vilifying their opponents linguistically as well as harming them physically (Pegelow Kaplan 2009). They were only too eager to adopt the innovation of the concentration camp to incarcerate whomever they considered undesirable. At the same time, they used martial language and paramilitary training to prepare young men for the next, hopefully more successful war, which would avenge the defeat of 1918. The massive rearmament programme that brought the country to the brink of insolvency was a logical outgrowth of this social Darwinist thinking. The result was a paradoxical situation of reassurance to their supporters and terror to their domestic and foreign foes (Merkl 1975).

Jeffery Herf's (1984, 1–17) concept 'reactionary modernism' is an effort to deal with this paradoxical evidence of an anti-modern reaction that was profoundly modern at the same time. In effect, this approach restates the paradox noted already by the Scandinavian-American sociologist Thorstein Veblen (1915) during the First World War: in terms of its economic development Germany seemed highly modern, but in terms of the democratic governance it remained autocratic. By examining the neo-romantic ideas of Spengler, Jünger, or Sombart, Herf captures the deep longing for a utopian past that would heal the manifold problems accompanying rapid social change. At the same time, his engagement of the cultural ambitions of German engineers deals with the modernizing aspects of advancing technology in the service of national strength. This paradoxical assessment is no doubt correct, but it does not go far enough.

2.3   Biological Politics

The Nazis' anti-modernism was quintessentially modern because it attempted a gigantic social engineering project that sought to make Germany capable of competing on a world stage. Earlier efforts at rooting out religious heretics or establishing mercantilist control over subjects pale in comparison to the systematic nature and ruthless implementation of Hitler's quest to create political unity and racial superiority. Inspired by the sense of national community during the First World War, the National Socialists sought to unite the *Volksgemeinschaft* by excluding all potentially divisive enemies and gathering members of the ethnic diaspora in one greater Reich. At the same time, they embarked upon a racist effort to purify and strengthen the *Volkskörper* by purging foreign elements and facilitating Aryan reproduction (Burleigh 2000). The aim of this enormous enterprise was the creation of a superior master race that would rule Europe in the future.

One important goal of National Socialist (NS) efforts was to strengthen the mythical unity of the nation by fashioning a true community of the people, a real *Volksgemeinschaft*. Hitler and many of his close followers longed to revive the political 'truce within the castle' of the First World War or the comradeship in the trenches in order to fashion a national purpose beyond all divisions. This national community would level social distinctions and abolish class warfare in a common cause. Moreover, the *Volksgemeinschaft* was supposed to transcend those ideological and religious cleavages that had hampered joint efforts in the past. Such a sense of shared fate would also overcome ancient regional differences and submerge local allegiances into a greater national cause. While the left decried this rhetoric as 'socialism of the fools', autobiographies show that many Germans bought into the notion of a people's community as a worthy goal (Schmiechen-Ackermann 2012).

Beyond symbolic gestures, the effort to strengthen the national community involved a series of positive measures, amplified by propaganda. For instance, the Nazis amalgamated public support for the poor and single mothers in a huge National Socialist People's Welfare organization that soon outstripped church charity (Hammerschmidt 1999). At the same time, they tried to stop the century-old emigration of surplus population by providing jobs through public works and rearmament. The *Anschluss* of Austria, the incorporation of the Sudetenland, and the effort to reattach Danzig, Memel, and Alsace-Lorraine to Germany were also foreign policy initiatives that sought to join German-speaking territories to the Reich. Finally, Hitler tasked Himmler with the 'strengthening of Germandom' in 1939 by bringing members of the ethnic diaspora from the East home into the fold and consolidating them into a coherent settlement area in the Warthegau (Koehl 1957).

The Nazi vision of a homogenous *Volksgemeinschaft* also implied a series of negative initiatives to exclude political enemies, those considered racially inferior as well as disliked foreigners. Immediately after the seizure of power the SA (*Sturmabteilung* / Stormtroopers) and the police rounded up prominent political opponents, including hard-line communists, moderate social democrats, and some members of liberal parties and held them in detention in order to eliminate potential rivals. Due to rampant antisemitism the Jews became a special target of intimidation, discrimination, and physical violence in order to make them emigrate. All members of the resistance who fell into the Gestapo's claws were imprisoned in the rapidly expanding system of the concentration camps (Johnson 2000). And finally, the NS government had deported several tens of thousands of undesirable nationals, mostly Poles, from the German Reich even before it unleashed the Second World War.

The core of this project of social engineering was a decidedly modern concept of biopolitics, understood as 'the biologization of the social'. In a leap from the individual to the collective, this science-based racism set out to improve the *Volkskörper*, the physical body of the nation, in order to make it fit to survive international competition. In many ways, this approach represented the progressive medicalization of society through an expansion of public health concerns which also infected democratic societies. But in the particular context of the Third Reich, this eugenic project was connected to a purportedly scientific racism which set out to strengthen the racial composition of the Aryan nation by a series of state interventions. Seen from this perspective, 'Nazism does not appear as a bizarre and inexplicable eruption, but as a product of the ongoing and ubiquitous biopolitical project of modernity' (Dickinson 2004).

A central instrument of this eugenic policy was the effort to strengthen the body of the nation through positive and negative measures. Thinking in racial terms, the Nazi leadership was obsessed with improving public health through mandatory clinics and preventive medicine, carrying Weimar's social medicalization even further. Part of this approach was encouragement of active participation in sport through propagating images of a healthy Aryan body without make-up or other beauty aids. Believing that national power rested on a growing population, Hitler and his followers were similarly concerned with the faltering of demographic growth that was levelling off after the completion of the population transition. The Nazis therefore not only created numerous incentives for encouraging reproduction, but also instituted support programmes such as *Lebensborn* in order to help unwed mothers to bring up healthy, racially pure children (Timm 2010).

Negative eugenic measures were even more drastic, since they ranged all the way from discrimination to mass murder. In order to improve the racial stock, the infamous Nuremberg Laws prohibited sex between Aryans and other races, most notably Jews, requiring proof of racial purity going back for two generations in order to allow marriages. At the same time, Nazi doctors implemented a mass sterilization programme in order to keep people who were 'hereditarily ill' from reproducing. Moreover, the T4 programme silently killed over 100 000 handicapped inmates of charitable institutions by lethal injection or poison gas, ignoring the pleas of their families. Finally, this biopolitical thinking led to the genocide of Jews, as well as the mass murder of Slavs, Roma, and homosexuals (Burleigh 1991; Aly 1994). While democracies also engaged in sterilization, the Nazis were far more systematic and ruthless in implementing their eugenic fantasies.

Another important aspect of biopolitics was the creation of a 'new man' through the radical reassertion of gender roles as basis for a racial struggle for international supremacy. Themselves a product of the camaraderie of the trenches and the post-war militias, the Nazis celebrated manliness of strength and authority in contrast to Weimar effeminacy and decadence. The National Socialist image of a man was that of a fearless soldier, capable of fighting courageously for the fatherland. The Hitler Youth tried to mould men that would be 'quick as greyhounds, tough as shoe leather and hard as Krupp steel' through paramilitary exercises, parades, and indoctrination. Such heroic men would be capable of defending hearth and home, ready 'to die for Germany' if need be (Baird 1990). While this male ideal implied the restoration of patriarchy, its racial radicalism went beyond tradition, anticipating a global struggle for national survival (Mosse 1996).

The female counterpart was the praise of motherhood as fulfilment of personal life as well as crucial service for the national community. Panicked by the drastic decline in the birth rate during the Weimar Republic, the Nazi leadership emphasized the restoration of fertility as public duty. In order to create space for procreation, the Third Reich limited female access to higher education and pushed women back into the home with the 'double earner' provision that prohibited both spouses working in public jobs (Stephenson 2001). In order to reduce infant mortality, the Nazi Women's League instituted courses in homemaking, schooling lower class women in modern methods of home economics. Moreover, the leadership created symbolic forms of recognition such as the 'mother's honour cross', bestowed upon women who raised four or more children. In spite of its traditional style, the rabid natalism of this policy was quite modern (Loroff 2011).

Much of this biopolitical effort was science based, combining state-of-the-art research with a murderous project of racial hegemony. 'The frightening truth is that the Nazis supported many kinds of science, left politics (as we often think about it) out of most, and transformed but did not abandon ethics' (Proctor 2000, 337). In technology, German engineers were leaders in developing such things as television, tape recording, or rockets and jet planes. In medicine, the cancer and tobacco research was world class, even if the concentration camp experiments show a shocking lack of human compassion. Other scholarly efforts were even more questionable, because in areas such as racial science, Jewish research, or ethnic history they pursued irrational Nazi aims (Steinweis 2006). It is this peculiar mixture of highly developed scientific study with a hegemonic project based on a lethal set of racist prejudices which describes their particular modernity.

2.4   The Organic Alternative

In contrast to the communist or liberal competitors' faith in progress (Furet 1999; Jarausch 2015, 102–180, 261–286), the Nazis' emphatic rejections of negative aspects of modernity have made their incoherent and irrational ideology look rather reactionary. In many ways, National Socialism was a grab-bag of resentments against the consequences of rapid socio-economic changes such as the economic crises, burgeoning metropolis, emancipation of women, shallowness of popular culture and the like. Nazi ideologues rejected liberalism as responsible for German defeat, political fragmentation, and mass unemployment, pronouncing democracy incapable of solving problems of the future. They took communism more seriously as a rival philosophy due to its techniques of mobilizing the masses but denounced its mechanical levelling as destruction of culture. In their racist fantasies, Jews were responsible for biological decline and cultural decadence, implying that Germany could only return to health if it were purged of their noxious presence (Bialas and Fritze 2014).

But since they sensed that there was ultimately no escape from the modern world, the National Socialists also tried to develop an alternative, more positive version of modernity centred on the national community. Instead of sinking into parliamentary strife, the nation should willingly follow a strong leader, leaving behind the petty egotisms. Instead of engaging in class warfare, the *Volksgemeinschaft* should come together in a common quest for greatness to dominate the European continent. Instead of seeking private profit, citizens should work together for the common wealth. Instead of losing valuable population to emigration, the country should set out to conquer new living space in the East (Bajohr and Wildt 2009). In order to achieve such ambitious aims, the Nazis were willing to use the latest advances of scientific research and technological development. By being used for their ethnic utopia, such instruments would not have *de*structive but rather *con*structive results.

Going beyond mere instrumentalization of modern methods, the Nazis' biopolitical project of social engineering suggests the need for a new concept that might be called 'organic modernity'. According to the third edition of Webster's Unabridged Dictionary (Babcock Gove 1968, 1590), the adjective 'organic' when applied to society interprets it as 'having the characteristics of a living plant or animal'. Nazi ideology sought just such an approach which would avoid the pitfalls of democratic or communist modernity and instead create a racial utopia which would heal the *Volkskörper* of its many contemporary diseases. The fantasy of 'blood and soil' painted an attractive picture of fighting farmers, drawing strength from living on the land. Inspired by *völkisch* life reformers of the turn of the century, the National Socialist approach to modernity envisaged a more natural existence that would strengthen the nation physically and mentally for the coming struggle against the liberal or socialist rivals for political supremacy (Williams 2007).

Captivating though it was for many supporters, this organic vision of modernity exacted a frightful price in human suffering. The Nazi concept of the national community excluded political enemies on the left, robbing them of their human rights and forcing them to emigrate or to go underground. Hitler's dreams of ethnic settlement in the East unleashed the Second World War which claimed 55 million victims, one fifth of them Germans themselves. The racial drive to purify the physical body of the nation authorized an unprecedented genocide of Jews and other victims that has come to represent the ultimate embodiment of human evil. Even if they attracted support from fascist sympathizers and local auxiliaries, these confused ideas ultimately discredited themselves due to their exclusiveness and violence. Instead of offering a constructive alternative, the Nazi dream of organic community revealed the destructive side of modernity (Jarausch 2015, 341–368).

Like its Soviet counterpart, further research on Nazi modernity has to address a number of unresolved conceptual and historiographical issues. The basic challenge is a more critical engagement of the elusive concepts of modern, modernity, modernization, and modernism in order to grapple with their shifting implications. Comparing the transformative projects of the ideological rivals, moreover, needs to distinguish between what they had in common as mass politics and where their aims clashed with each other. Exploring the illiberal dimensions of modernization also requires disentangling the positive hopes for progress from the negative experiences of suffering, engendered by such social engineering. While the liberal, communist, and fascist blueprints often borrowed methods from each other, they differed starkly in the degree of violent repression or peaceful persuasion employed (David-Fox 2006). Finally, such a notion of competing modernities ought to open up interpretative horizons beyond Europe to their global implications.

References

Allen, Michael. 1996. 'The Puzzle of Nazi Modernism: Modern Technology and Ideological Consensus in an SS Factory at Auschwitz.' *Technology and Culture* 37, 527–571.

Aly, Götz. 1994. *Cleansing the Fatherland: Nazi Medicine and Racial Hygiene*. Baltimore, MD: The Johns Hopkins University Press.

Babcock Gove, Philip, ed. 1968. *Webster's Third New International Dictionary of the English Language Unabridged*. Springfield, MA: G. & C. Merriam Co.

Baird, Jay W. 1990. *To Die for Germany: Heroes in the Nazi Pantheon*. New York: Wiley.

Bajohr, Frank and Wildt, Michael, eds. 2009. *Volksgemeinschaft: Neue Forschungen zur Gesellschaft des Nationalsozialismus*. Frankfurt: Fischer Verlag.

Baranowski, Shelley. 2004. *Strength through Joy: Consumerism and Mass Tourism in the Third Reich*. Cambridge: Cambridge University Press.

Betts, Paul. 2002. 'The New Fascination with Fascism: The Case of Nazi Modernism.' *Journal of Contemporary History* 37, 541–558.

Bialas, Wolfgang and Fritze, Lothar, eds. 2014. *Nazi Ideology and Ethics*. Cambridge: Cambridge Scholars Publishing.

Bramwell, Anna. 1985. *Blood and Soil: Richard Walter Darré and Hitler's 'Green Party'*. Bourne End: Kensal Press.

Broszat, Martin. 1981. *The Hitler State: The Foundation and Development of the Internal Structure of the Third Reich*. London: Longman.

Burleigh, Michael. 1991. *The Racial State: Germany 1933–1945*. Cambridge: Cambridge University Press.

Burleigh, Michael. 2000. *The Third Reich: A New History*. London: Palgrave Macmillan.

Confino, Alon. 2014. *A World without Jews: The Nazi Imagination from Persecution to Genocide*. New Haven, CT: Yale University Press.

Corner, Paul and Lim, Jie-Hyun, eds. 2016, *Handbook of Mass Dictatorship*. London: Palgrave Macmillan.

Dahrendorf, Ralf. 1967. *Society and Democracy in Germany*. Garden City, NJ: Doubleday.

David-Fox, Michael. 2006. 'Multiple Modernities versus Neo-Traditionalism: On Recent Debates in Russian and Soviet History.' *Jahrbücher der Geschichte Osteuropas* 54, 535–555.

Dickinson, Edward Ross. 2004. 'Biopolitics, Fascism, Democracy: Some Reflections on our Discourse about "Modernity".' *Central European History* 37, 1–48.

Eisenstadt, Shmuel N. 2003. *Comparative Civilizations and Multiple Modernities*. Leiden: Brill.

Friedrich, Carl and Brzezinski, Zbigniew K. 1956. *Totalitarian Dictatorship and Autocracy*. Cambridge, MA: Harvard University Press.

Fritzsche, Peter. 1996. 'Nazi Modern.' *Modernism/Modernity* 3, 1–22.

Fritzsche, Peter. 1998. *Germans into Nazis*. Cambridge, MA: Harvard University Press.

Furet, François. 1999. *The Passing of an Illusion: The Idea of Communism in the Twentieth Century*. Chicago: University of Chicago Press.

Gellately, Robert. 2001. *Consent and Coercion in Nazi Germany*. Oxford: Oxford University Press.

Goggin, Mary-Margaret. 1991. '"Decent" versus "Degenerate" Art: The National Socialist Case.' *Art Journal* 50, 84–92.

Guse, John C. 2011. '*Volksgemeinschaft* Engineers: The Nazi "Voyages of Technology".' *Central European History* 44, 447–477.

Hammerschmidt, Peter. 1999. *Die Wohlfahrtsverbände im NS-Staat: Die NSV und die konfessionellen Verbände Caritas und Innere Mission im Gefüge der Wohlfahrtspflege des Nationalsozialismus*. Opladen: Leske + Budrich.

Hare, J. Laurence. 2015. *Excavating Nations: Archaeology, Museums, and the German–Danish Borderlands*. Toronto: University of Toronto Press.

Herf, Jeffrey. 1984. *Reactionary Modernism: Technology, Culture, and Politics in Weimar and the Third Reich*. Cambridge: Cambridge University Press.

Jäckel, Eberhard. 1981. *Hitler's World View: A Blueprint for Power*. Cambridge, MA: Harvard University Press.

Jarausch, Konrad H. 2015. *Out of Ashes: A New History of Europe in the 20th Century*. Princeton, NJ: Princeton University Press.

Johnson, Eric A. 2000. *Nazi Terror: The Gestapo, Jews and Ordinary Germans*. London: John Murray.

Katz, Jacob. 1980. *From Prejudice to Destruction: Anti-Semitism, 1700–1933*. Cambridge, MA: Harvard University Press.

Kershaw, Ian. 1998. *Hitler 1889–1936: Hubris*. London: Allen Lane.

Koehl, Robert L. 1957. *RKFDV: German Resettlement and Population Policy 1939–1945: A History of the Reichskommission for the Strengthening of Germandom*. Cambridge, MA: Harvard University Press.

Link, Fabian. 2014. *Burgen und Burgenforschung im Nazionalsozialismus: Wissenschaft und Weltanschauung 1933–1945*. Cologne: Böhlau.

Loroff, Nicole. 2011. 'Gender and Sexuality in Nazi Germany.' *Constellations* 3, 49–61.

Mazower, Mark. 2008. *Hitler's Empire: Nazi Rule in Occupied Europe*. London: Allen Lane.

Merkl, Peter H. 1975. *Political Violence under the Swastika: 581 Early Nazis*. Princeton, NJ: Princeton University Press.

Mommsen, Hans and Grieger, Manfred. 1996. *Das Volkswagenwerk und seine Arbeiter im Dritten Reich*. Düsseldorf: Econ.

Mosse, George L. 1996. *The Image of Man: The Creation of Modern Masculinity*. New York: Oxford University Press.

Mosse, George L. and Jones, James W. 1984. 'Bookburning and the Betrayal of German Intellectuals.' *New German Critique* 31, 143–55.

Nixon, Chris. 1986. *Racing the Silver Arrows: Mercedes-Benz versus Auto Union 1934–1939*. London: Osprey.

Pegelow Kaplan, Thomas. 2009. *The Language of Nazi Genocide: Linguistic Violence and the Struggle of Germans of Jewish Ancestry*. New York: Cambridge University Press.

Peukert, Detlev. 1992. *The Weimar Republic: The Crisis of Classical Modernity*. New York: Hill & Wang.

Preyer, Gerhard. 2013. 'The Perspective of Multiple Modernities: On Shmuel N. Eisenstadt's Sociology.' *Theory and Society: Journal of Political and Moral Theory* 30, 187–225.

Prinz, Michael and Zitelmann, Rainer, eds. 1994. *Nationalsozialismus und Modernisierung*. Darmstadt: Wissenschaftliche Buchgesellschaft.

Proctor, Robert. 2000. 'Nazi Science and Nazi Medical Ethics: Some Myths and Misconceptions.' *Perspectives in Biology and Medicine* 43, 335–436.

Rich, Norman. 1973. *Hitler's War Aims*. 2 vols. New York: W.W. Norton.

Ross, Corey. 2008. *Media and the Making of Modern Germany: Mass Communications, Society, and Politics from the Empire to the Third Reich*. Oxford: Oxford University Press.

Schmiechen-Ackermann, Detlef, ed. 2012. '*Volksgemeinschaft*': *Mythos, wirkungsmächtige soziale Verheißung oder soziale Realität im 'Dritten Reich'? Zwischenbilanz einer kontroversen Debatte*. Paderborn: Schöningh.

Schoenbaum, David. 1980. *Hitler's Social Revolution: Class and Status in Nazi Germany, 1933–1939*. New York: W.W. Norton.

Smelser, Ronald. 1990. 'How "Modern" Were the Nazis? DAF Social Planning and the Modernization Question.' *German Studies Review* 13, 285–302.

Steinweis, Alan. 2006. *Studying the Jew: Scholarly Antisemitism in Nazi Germany*. Cambridge, MA: Harvard University Press.

Stephenson, Jill. 2001. *Women in Nazi Germany*. Harlow, UK: Routledge.

Szejnmann, Claus-Christian W. 2013. 'Nazi Economic Thought and Rhetoric during the Weimar Republic: Capitalism and its Discontents.' *Politics, Religion and Theology* 14, 355–376.

Timm, Annette. 2010. *The Politics of Fertility in Twentieth Century Berlin*. New York: Cambridge University Press.

Tooze, Adam. 2006. *Wages of Destruction: The Making and Breaking of the Nazi Economy*. London: Penguin.

Veblen, Thorstein. 1915. *Imperial Germany and the Industrial Revolution*. New York: Macmillan.

Waddington, Lorna L. 2007. 'The Anti-Komintern and Nazi Anti-Bolshevik Propaganda in the 1930s.' *Journal of Contemporary History* 42, 573–594.

Williams, John A. 2007. *Turning to Nature in Germany: Hiking, Nudism and Conservation, 1900–1940*. Stanford: Stanford University Press.

CHAPTER THREE

The First World War and National Socialism

Benjamin Ziemann

National Socialism had important roots in the political culture of late Imperial Germany. From the 1880s, some of the core ingredients of National Socialist ideology and its political style were articulated in German politics. Radical nationalist pressure groups such as the Pan-German League, founded in 1891, developed the ideology of *völkisch* nationalism that situated the essence of belonging to Germany in a collective ethnic and biological identity. *Völkisch* nationalism also construed the Jews as a racial entity and as the epitome of everything that endangered the German nation. The populist political rhetoric and performative style of Nazi agitation also had precursors in Wilhelmine Germany. Despite these roots and precursors in the politics of late nineteenth-century Germany, National Socialism was in many ways a distinctive post-war phenomenon. The First Word War was a transformative period in German and European history more generally. As the war reshaped social identities and realigned political collectives, it worked as a catalyst that brought crucial features of the fascist political paradigm together: the belief in the need to purify and remake the German nation through the exclusion of 'alien' groups; the glorification of war and violence as the basis of national collective identity, and unfettered aggression in the international arena as a means to returning the German nation to the status of a Great Power (Traverso 2003).

Yet while there is widespread agreement on the crucial significance of the First World War for the development of National Socialism as a mass movement, there is a need to distinguish between different layers and arenas of political rhetoric and mobilization. It is also prudent to avoid a deterministic perspective that sees the Great War as a direct precursor of the Nazi seizure of power in 1933 or even the Holocaust. Historian Omer Bartov, for instance, has described the Holocaust as 'the almost perfect reenactment of the Great War' and its 'imagery of hell'

A Companion to Nazi Germany, First Edition. Edited by Shelley Baranowski, Armin Nolzen, and Claus-Christian W. Szejnmann.
© 2018 John Wiley & Sons Ltd. Published 2018 by John Wiley & Sons Ltd.

(Bartov 1996, 48–49). According to Bartov, the main difference was that the Holocaust saw a complete disjunction between perpetrators on the one side and victims on the other. Core elements of the Holocaust, however, such as 'barbed wire, the machine guns, the charred bodies, the gas, the uniforms' had already been crucial features of front-line fighting in the First World War (Bartov 1996, 48–49). It would be misleading, however, to overestimate the significance of such rather formal, technical analogies. Connections between the First World War and the Second, between war and National Socialism, have to be established at the level of patterns of social action and with regard to popular mythologies.

The first section below discusses the radicalization of right-wing nationalism and antisemitism in the context of war and defeat. The second will analyse different aspects of what historian George L. Mosse (1990) has called in a seminal interpretation the 'brutalization' of German politics in the post-war period, that is, the increasing propensity for the use of violence in the political arena. The third section examines the prominent place the First World War had in the collective mythology and the heroic narratives of the Nazi Party (NSDAP) and its sub-organizations such as the SA (*Sturmabteilung*) or Stormtroopers. These narratives tapped into the notion of a generation that was fundamentally shaped by the experiences of war and defeat. Yet again, it would be wrong to assume a direct causal link between the experience of the war and the formation of a generation of Nazi activists (Donson 2010). Since the turn of the century, the semantics of youth and generational conflict had become an important element of German culture. In this context, 'generation' is best understood as an imaginary marker of group identity and as a form of social self-description rather than as a social collective that was generated by shared experiences. Generation formation was never coherent or even complete in the sense that all members of a certain age cohort were shaped in similar ways, as will be seen when we discuss the notion of the 'front-line generation'.

3.1   Radical Nationalism and Antisemitism Through War and Defeat

The beginning of the war in August 1914 was a moment of national reconciliation among the Germans. On 4 August 1914, Kaiser Wilhelm II claimed in front of party representatives that he would not any longer know parties, but only Germans. Thus, he announced the *Burgfrieden* or 'fortress peace' that aimed to suspend domestic strife and accepted the socialist Social Democratic Party into the fabric of national politics. Exaggerated figures of the large scores of male youths who volunteered for the army epitomized the sense of national enthusiasm that marked Germany's entry into the war. Painstaking research has dispelled the myth that most Germans greeted the beginning of the war in August 1914 with jubilation. Socialist working-class people and peasant farmers in remote villages were among those who either resented the war or reacted with a mixture of initial despair and – as the conscripts left for the front – determination. Yet regardless of the reality on the ground, the public perception of national unity and strength was a crucial reference point for subsequent nationalist politics (Verhey 2000).

In the context of the *Burgfrieden*, the notion of a *Volksgemeinschaft* or people's community also gained increasing currency. Occasionally used in political discourse since the 1880s, the term was now widely employed by intellectuals of different political leanings to depict the newly found sense of national unity. Implying a strong state and government independent of the parties, the vision of a *Volksgemeinschaft* appealed to many people across the liberal–conservative spectrum (Verhey 2000). Widespread talk about the people's community did not imply that it would immediately shape up as a structural reality. But it created a new horizon of expectations and fostered a new emotional regime of nationalism, which, in turn, created its own exclusionary effects. Siegfried Jacobsohn, the left-liberal editor of the intellectual journal *Schaubühne*, realized as much when he noted, upon the news of German mobilization on 1 August 1914, 'We will not only mobilize men, but also higher [i.e. patriotic] feelings, and we will bash everybody's hat who does not appear to have got plenty of those' (cited in Ziemann 2011, 380).

The first to be at the receiving end of such exclusionary practices were the Jews. The overwhelming majority of the about 600 000 German Jews strongly supported the national war effort. Many male Jewish citizens volunteered for the army, thus tapping into the notion of the *Burgfrieden* and believing that any discrimination they had faced in the past could be left behind. Yet both on the front line and on the home front, Jews were soon confronted with increasing suspicion and resentment. Amidst the heightened expectations for conformity that the war had triggered, even the extended national commitment of the Jewish community was not considered to be sufficient. This spiral of expectations created an even more aggressive exclusionary backlash once the German war effort suffered its first severe setbacks in 1916. It is more than coincidence that the Prussian War Ministry issued its infamous 'Jew count' – a decree that ordered all commanders to compile the number of Jews serving in their units – in October 1916, after the battle of Verdun had exhausted manpower resources but had failed to produce a major breakthrough as had been expected (Ziemann 2011, 384).

It is certainly misleading to posit a direct continuity from the exclusionary drive behind the 'Jew count' in 1916 to the Holocaust (see Ziemann 2011, 385). Yet there is no doubt that the agitation of antisemitic associations such as the *Reichshammerbund* radicalized during the war. Perhaps even more important than the relentless activity of such radical-nationalist pressure groups was the incremental shift from an antisemitism of words and rhetoric to an antisemitism of the deed. Indicative of this shift, that started during the war, is the slow build-up of the number of violent incidents during the war in which Jewish businesses and individuals were targeted, had their shop windows smashed, or were insulted and injured (Bergmann and Wetzel 2002). Up till the armistice in November 1918, the number of such incidents was still relatively small. But they foreshadowed an important element of National Socialist antisemitism. The Nazis no longer sought to exclude Jews from the German nation only in texts and speeches. Right from the start, they used speech acts mainly to incite immediate violent action against specific Jewish communities (Niewyk 1990). Thus, they were part and parcel of the increasing tide of direct antisemitic violence and pogrom action that swept across provincial Germany throughout the 1920s and early 1930s (Wildt 2011). At any rate, antisemitism remained what it had been prior to 1914: a projection of the alleged inferiorities of the Jews on the side of the antisemites, but not a turn against anything that could be accurately described as 'semitism' – which is why it is wrong to hyphenate the term 'antisemitism'.

Raising the bar for expectations of national unity, the world war radicalized antisemitic thought and action when these expectations did not materialize. Yet even more important than the war was German defeat in November 1918. Only a few months earlier, nationalist circles had still invested high hopes in a German victory that would bring significant annexations. They could draw comfort from the fact that the Bolsheviki had been forced to sign the Treaty of Brest-Litovsk in March 1918 – which forced Russia to cede large territories to Germany and to make the Ukraine independent – and that German troops had broken the stalemate of the Western Front and made major advances in their spring offensive. In October 1918, when the German Army Supreme Command all of a sudden asked the civilian government to negotiate an armistice, and its terms were known to the German public, disappointed expectations turned into deep resentment. Nationalist circles tried to identify scapegoats, and the Jews were the first they turned to. The 'stab-in-the-back' legend, which identified betrayal by civilians as the reason for German defeat, had many different forms and permutations. But in its radical versions, it basically expressed vitriolic hatred against the Jews and a Manichaean world-view that ascribed everything that was wanting about Germany's post-war situation to the Jews. A vivid iconographic expression of this perception is a drawing that frigate captain Bogislav von Selchow added to his diary in November 1918. It shows a Jewish woman, clearly indexed by her large nose, driving a spear into the back of a German soldier with an immaculate uniform and an Iron Cross on his chest. With snakes instead of hair and a fiery gaze, the woman is depicted as Medusa, one of the Gorgons of ancient Greek mythology, a monster that would turn anyone into stone who would look into her eyes (Epkenhans 1996, 175). Images like these were later a staple of Nazi propaganda, indicating that resentment against the fact and terms of German defeat were crucial perceptions that directly fed into the Nazi appeal to the masses.

Right from the beginning, the Nazis tried to shore up resentment against the terms of the Treaty of Versailles in which the Entente powers stipulated that Germany should lose 14% of its territory and pay reparations to the Allies, based on the so-called war guilt clause in article 231. Yet the Nazis were not alone in their campaign against the Treaty. When the terms of the Treaty were made public in May 1919, large sections of the German public were united in their outright rejection, including not only the extreme right, but also moderate conservatives, liberals, and moderate Social Democrats (Voelker 2002). Agitation against the Treaty of Versailles remained a staple of Nazi rhetoric, which turned it into an indictment against the pro-republican parties and politicians, whom the Nazis accused of pursuing a treasonous 'politics of fulfilment' vis-à-vis the Allies. It is important to note, however, that such a radical rhetoric did not garner widespread support even by the late 1920s. In 1929, the German government agreed to the Young Plan, which actually reduced Germany's annual reparation payments. The Nazis joined other radical nationalist organizations in their demand for a plebiscite on the Young Plan.

But when the referendum was held in December 1929, only 5.8 million Germans or a mere 14% of the electorate supported it (Schwabe 2014, 875). Ten years after the Treaty of Versailles had been approved by the German parliament, the Nazis had to acknowledge that only a small minority of Germans supported radical measures against it.

Defeat in November 1918 provided a crucial legacy for National Socialist thinking also in another respect. It taught the leadership of the Nazi Party the important lesson that *Durchhalten* or 'holding out' in a total war required material compensation for broad sections of the population. This line of reasoning stood in a certain contradiction to the 'stab-in the-back' legend that attributed defeat and revolution in 1918 solely to the evil-doing of Jewish communists. In contrast to this myth, many of those generals and party bureaucrats who organized Germany's economic preparation for another war, from 1933, acknowledged that the revolution had been prepared by the mass strike in January 1918, and by the legitimate discontent over food shortages and other deprivations that it brought into the open. The total war of 1914–1918 had made extreme demands on the working class, something for which it had to be compensated if that wager was to be repeated in a future war. Thus, fear of another November 1918 informed much of Nazi social and economic policy from the mid-1930s (Mason 1971). At a time when mass unemployment had given way to severe labour shortages, the Party made strenuous efforts to pre-empt any potential working-class discontent through high levels of consumer goods production and specific social benefits for German 'Aryan' workers. Such an emphasis, however, impacted on armaments production, leading to a series of improvised compromises prior to 1939. During the Second World War, these contradictions were only 'solved' through the large-scale reliance on forced labour and the brutal exploitation of the occupied territories (Mason 1993).

3.2   Brutalization: Violence as a Legacy of the Great War

One of the core characteristics of National Socialists was their readiness to use physical violence against their political opponents and those allegedly racially inferior groups who seemed to endanger the substance of the German *Volk*. War, not as an ultimately limited confrontation between diplomats, armies, and states, but conceived of as an existential struggle for the remaking of the *Volk* as a social organism, stood at the very heart of the Nazi vision of politics. For the Nazis, war was not just a violent confrontation, it was a form of societal politics or social engineering, a notion that deeply shaped the German conduct of war at the Eastern Front from 1939 onwards (Geyer 1986). Which ideas and practices informed and nurtured this perception of mass violence as a way to rebuild and maintain a hierarchical social order? Some strands of recent scholarship have suggested taking the colonial practices of late Imperial Germany as the point of departure.

The German nation, unified in 1871, had acquired a formal empire of overseas colonies only belatedly, from the 1880s, and the significance of the colonies as places for settlement and sources of economic revenue remained fairly limited. Yet the German military was repeatedly involved in brutal wars against indigenous people. The first of them, fought from 1904 to 1908 in German South West

Africa – nowadays Namibia – quickly escalated into a wholesale genocide against the two main tribes, the Herero and Nama. While still en route to the colony on a steamer in June 1904, General Lothar von Trotha issued his infamous kill order that gave German troops licence to shoot all natives even if they were only suspected of taking part in rebellious acts or of treason. Trotha, who had been called in to secure German victory, clearly pursued the vision of a racial hierarchy between the colonizers and their indigenous subjects, a hierarchy that could only be maintained through violence. In the process, up to 80% of the Herero and Nama were killed (Zimmerer 2004). Yet is the undisputed fact of this colonial genocide sufficient to suggest lines of continuity from 'Windhuk to Auschwitz', that is, from the administrative centre of German South West Africa to the killing sites of the Holocaust in occupied Poland (Zimmerer 2004)? After intensive debate, most historians disagree with this view. They point out that racial purification, not instrumental domination, was the ultimate aim of the Holocaust, and that any direct lines of continuity, such as through the deployment of military personnel in both theatres of war, can be discarded (Gerwarth and Malinowski 2009). One might add to this critique that there are only very few examples in the speeches of leading Nazis such as Hitler or Himmler suggesting that they conceived of the war in the East in terms of a colonial enterprise parallel to the British Empire.

Thus, it is preferable to follow the established view that the Nazi propensity to apply violence against political enemies and to place it at the heart of their vision for a remaking of society is situated in the experiences of the First World War and the post-war crisis. One particularly powerful formulation of this view was offered by the late George L. Mosse in his comparative analysis of the glorification of the Great War in Western Europe. Mosse highlighted the 'brutalization of German politics' in the wake of the war. Germany was the one country in which the view that war was 'a means of personal and national regeneration' had gained widespread currency, and prompted the Nazis and other right-wing groups to turn with ruthless energy against 'internal foes'. Thus, the unleashing of aggression and the establishing of a hegemonic, soldierly masculinity at the front line spilled over into the post-war period (Mosse 1990, 159–181, quotes 159–160). Such a reversal of the civilizing process had potentially affected all belligerent nations, as Mosse acknowledged. Yet Great Britain and France as 'victorious nations' were able to quickly absorb the aftershocks of violence and to keep brutalization in check (Mosse 1990, 159).

George Mosse's notion of a 'brutalization' of German politics is still a helpful framework to understand the connections between the front-line experience and the emergence of National Socialism as a major political player in the Weimar Republic. But there is a need to avoid undue generalizations and to describe the connections between wartime aggression and fascist violence in a tangible and detailed fashion. It would be wrong, for instance, to assume that a majority, let alone all German front-line soldiers, had been brutalized by the war experience. For instance, before 1914, Germany had already had a substantial social labour movement. After 1918, Social Democratic war veterans gathered in their own veterans' associations such as the *Reichsbund* of war disabled and dependents. From 1924, the *Reichsbanner Schwarz-Rot-Gold*, a league of mostly socialist war veterans, combined a socialist reading of the front-line experience with a principled affirmation of the Weimar Republic. At least until the mid-1920s, both associations clearly outnumbered the combined membership of all radical-nationalist veterans' and combat leagues. And, to be sure, both *Reichsbund* and *Reichsbanner* members strictly advocated moderately pacifist values, thus demonstrating that not only had they remained unaffected by any brutalization, but also actively tried to curb some of its effects in the public arena (Ziemann 2013).

It is also worthwhile considering the example of the Führer of the Nazi movement. In August 1914, Adolf Hitler volunteered for service in the Bavarian contingent of the German army, and subsequently served in the 16th Bavarian Reserve Infantry Regiment 'List'. After the war, in many of his speeches and also in his book *Mein Kampf* (1940), in which he detailed his political struggles in the form of a *Bildungsroman* or novel of self-formation, Hitler presented himself as a battle-hardened war veteran who had been upset about the increasing war-weariness of the home front and who was hence devastated when the news of German defeat reached him in a hospital in November 1918. However, careful scrutiny of the surviving record has established that hardly any details of his post-war testimony match the reality. Hitler served as a dispatch-runner who was charged with delivering instructions to the companies of the Regiment List. In practice, he saw battle action only once and spent most of his time safely behind the front line with the officers of the regimental staff, which increasingly became his ersatz family. There is no reliable evidence to suggest that Hitler was politically or ideologically radicalized by his wartime service, something that can be said for the majority of the enlisted men in the Regiment List (Weber 2010). In that respect, soldiers of the regiment were very similar to other units which were recruited from predominantly Catholic and rural southern Bavaria. Most soldiers from this region tried to cope with the strains of industrialized warfare through traditional stabilizing patterns such as their Catholic piety (Ziemann 2007). As a driving force behind euthanasia and the Holocaust, Hitler may have been the most brutal of all veterans of the First World War. But he was certainly not brutalized by his military service.

Brutalization, however, certainly played a role among the Stormtroopers of the *Sturmabteilung* (SA), the paramilitary combat league of the Nazi Party. Here it is necessary to distinguish between the leadership corps of the Stormtroopers and ordinary rank-and-file members. Slightly more than half of the leadership corps of the SA – everyone of the rank of *Sturmführer*, the equivalent of an army lieutenant, or higher – was a member of the core of the front-line generation, that is, the age cohort born between 1890 and 1900. From a sample of those men in the three highest ranks within the SA, from *Standartenführer* to *Gruppenführer*, almost three quarters had served in the immediate front line during the war, towards the end of the war mostly in the rank of an officer, and 85% of them had received a war decoration. But it was not only the professional expertise in the organization and application of violence that had prepared these men for participation in the fascist combat league. To military defeat and revolution in 1918, events that they interpreted as a national tragedy and personal humiliation, they responded by extending their military service into the post-war period. Almost half of the higher SA leadership corps had been active Freikorps members in 1918/1919. These units were mobilized by the government of the Weimar Republic to quell the second phase of the revolution. They cracked down with brutal violence on communist uprisings in Berlin, Munich, and other parts of the Reich, or fought against the Bolsheviki in the newly founded Baltic states of Latvia and Estonia. Another 40% of the higher SA leaders had also served in other right-wing combat leagues before they joined the Stormtroopers. Their professional experience in the military helped these men advance through the ranks of the SA. The Imperial Army and its alleged glory was generally an undisputed role model for those who joined the National Socialist combat league (Reichardt 2010, 245–246; in more detail: Reichardt 2002, 348–384).

The leadership corps of the SA is thus a prime example for the brutalization of German politics in the wake of the First World War. Yet for the large number of the rank-and-file Stormtroopers a direct transmission from wartime violence to fascist mobilization does not apply. It was only in 1931 that the SA turned into a mass movement that attracted more than 100 000 members. At this point, 77% of them were younger than 30 years, and hence had not served in the military during the war (Reichardt 2010, 245–246). However, that does not mean that members of the war youth generation – those born between 1900 and 1910 – were not also profoundly shaped by the war. Both elementary school instruction and voluntary youth service during the war had been geared towards bellicose nationalistic mobilization. Pupils followed the advances of the German army on maps in their classrooms, and a rhetoric of nationalist participation raised hopes of victory and embedded enemy images in the collective mindset of both middle-class and working-class youth (Donson 2010).

These more widely shared experiences shaped the group culture of the SA mass movement of the early 1930s, which was largely made up of members of the war youth generation. Here, the war had a prominent place as an imaginary space, filled with fantasies of adventurous battles and driven by the notion of male camaraderie. The mass culture of the early 1930s supported such a highly romanticized reading of the war experience. Popular war movies and the widely sold dime novels presented heroic narratives of the German front-line soldier and his almost superhuman struggle against treacherous enemies (Krassnitzer 2002). These imaginations and representations of trench warfare were not only idealistic projections that made up for the economic misery of the early 1930s, but were also deeply relevant for the political activism of the Stormtroopers, or, more precisely, for the violence that they enacted against their political enemies on the left. Acts of collective violence against socialist working-class organizations and their members were part and parcel of the everyday practice of the SA and provided an important cohesive factor of its group culture. When they targeted social democrats and communists as a group, the Stormtroopers relied on a notion of camaraderie that was modelled along the lines of the idealized front-line community of the wartime army (Reichardt 2007; also Reichardt 2002, 100–199). In this respect, fascist political violence during the 1920s and early 1930s shared a crucial context with the atrocities that Wehrmacht soldiers committed during the Second World War, particularly at the Eastern Front. Both in the *Sturmabteilungen* as well as among Wehrmacht soldiers, the cultural practice of male bonding in small groups provided a morality that strengthened ties among the in-group. Masculine comradeship allowed SA men and Wehrmacht soldiers to disregard the plight of those outsiders who were targeted as victims of fascist violence. The community of (para-) military men was thus an important building block of the wider national community (Kühne 2010).

The notion of the war youth generation is not only helpful to understand the propensity and capacity for violence among the Stormtroopers of the SA, many of whom had a working-class background, but it also applies to those mostly academically trained members of the Nazi elite who were in charge of the planning and implementation of the terror against political enemies of the Third Reich and of the genocide against the Jews. From a representative sample of 221 members of the leadership corps of the Reich Main Security Office (RSHA), slightly more than three quarters were born after 1900. Attending secondary school during the First World War, they were infused with the jingoistic culture and patriotic instruction that was prevalent at the time. Many of them joined the Freikorps in early 1919 even though they had no prior military training. During their university studies in the 1920s, the political radicalization of these young academics was to a large extent an attempt to use the idealized world of the front-line soldiers as an intellectual framework for their fight against the Weimar Republic. These desk-perpetrators of the most horrendous Nazi atrocities understood themselves as the 'generation of the unbound': their *völkisch* radicalism and their will to purge Germany of its alleged enemies was not reined in by any moral concerns, since they imagined themselves as political soldiers who were in charge of purifying the nation (Wildt 2002, 41–142).

While the notion of the war youth generation is one important element in explaining the formation of a constituency of committed Nazi activists both among the leadership corps and among rank-and-file members, it would be wrong to apply this concept in a mechanical and uniform form (see Donson 2010). Nationalistic pedagogy and economic deprivation during the war did not shape all German youth who were born between 1900 and 1910 in equal fashion. And even among those who had actually been ardent victory watchers and authors of patriotic war poems during the war, we find future socialists and pacifists such as the playwright Bertolt Brecht and Gustav Heinemann – born in 1899 – who served as President of the Federal Republic from 1969 to 1974 (see Donson 2010, 88). Wartime experiences had certainly fostered a mentality which predisposed many middle-class youth to idealize the seemingly well-ordered and stable world of the military, and to long for the glory and honour that the German front-line soldiers seemed to encapsulate. Yet the war created only a predisposition, not a causality that unfolded with necessity. And even among those who transformed their wartime patriotism into National Socialist activism, this was rarely ever a direct and immediate conversion.

Hardly anyone is better placed to drive home this argument than the key architect of the Nazi genocide, Heinrich Himmler (1900–1945). Born into a Protestant lower middle-class family – his father was a low-ranking civil servant in Bavaria – Himmler experienced the First World War both as an exciting opportunity and as a major disappointment. He greeted the beginning of the war with 'jubilant patriotism', and was captivated by the excitement of the military mobilization. When Army Reserve units prepared trenches and dugouts for train-ing purposes in the town where he and his family spent their 1915 summer holi-days, he was excited and jotted down sketches in his diary. When his older brother Gebhard joined the *Landsturm* in July 1915, Heinrich could only note with envy: 'If only I were old enough, I'd be out there like a shot' (Longerich 2012, 11–26, quotes 21). Eventually, his father was successful in securing early admission to military training for Heinrich. Yet when training commenced in the barracks of a regiment in Regensburg in December 1917, Heinrich was immediately homesick and showed signs of physical weakness. This tension between the ideal of a strong soldier and his inability to match this ideal was subsequently a driving force in Himmler's political career. His hope to see battlefield action during the war, how-ever, did not materialize. At the end of the war, his political orientation was neither fixed nor profoundly radicalized. Shortly before he was discharged from the army in December 1918, Heinrich Himmler sympathized with the Bavarian People's Party, a conservative Catholic group that has just broken away from the Centre Party. He joined the Nazi Party only in 1923 (Longerich 2012, 23–26).

3.3   Mythologies of the War Experience

As we have seen in the previous section, the 'brutalization' of Germany's political culture in the aftermath of the Great War played a crucial role in enabling the for-mation of a mass constituency of Nazi activists who were ready to use violence against their opponents. However, 'brutalization' did not directly affect the front-line generation through their exposure to wartime violence, as George Mosse had assumed. Quite the contrary: the reintegration of the demobilized war veterans into German society worked rather smoothly, and in the immediate post-war period, socialist and moderate pacifist readings of the front-line experience were actually prevalent among the veterans (Bessel 1993; Ziemann 2013). Thus, 'bru-talization' worked rather indirectly. Wartime mobilization and propaganda had opened up an imaginary space that was populated with dramatized enemy images and feverish expectations of German victories and heroic deeds. During and after the war, the war youth generation of those born between 1900 and 1910 tapped most eagerly into these imaginations and used them as guidelines for their own personal and political endeavours.

This is only one example of the relevance of the mythologies of the war experi-ence for the formation of the Nazi constituency. At all levels of German society during the Weimar Republic, private conversations and public rhetoric tried to inject meaning into the death of the fallen soldiers. Set in stone, local war memori-als tried to translate these meanings into a physical, tangible reality. Throughout the Weimar Republic, the meaning of mass death was as contested as the most appropriate forms to honour their legacy (Ziemann 2013). In the nationalist camp, two main mythological narratives of the meaning of mass death were employed: Langemarck and Verdun. Both myths transformed the events on one battlefield into a wider tale of fighting and dying for the German nation. The Langemarck myth built on the battles in Flanders in September 1914, during which many reserve regiments were virtually wiped out while advancing through open fields. The myth turned these events into a heroic sacrifice of young war volunteers, who had only formed a small fraction of the actual combatants. Langemarck was the tale of young students, the elite of the nation, who gave their lives in a brief moment of idealistic hopefulness. The myth of Verdun, on the other hand, had a much more aggressive ring to it. Here the key notion was not sacrifice, but survival, not advancement, but *durchhalten* ('holding out') amidst a landscape of war that was dominated by machinery. With its symbolism of the battle-hardened soldier, his face black with soot under his steel helmet, Verdun was the quintessential fascist mythology of the 'new man' who had been galvanized in the battles of materiel (Hüppauf 1986). The Verdun myth was much more relevant for Nazi propaganda as it demonstrated the need to persevere and to employ extreme willpower against a world of adversaries. In addition, it was in line with the populist appeal of Nazi propaganda that tried to amalgamate support from all social strata, whereas the Langemarck myth was presented as the sacrifice of the German student elite. Yet it is a testament to the flexibility of the ideological practices of the Nazi Party that, despite these reservations, the Hitler Youth, from the mid-1920s, started incorporating Langemarck into its core set of mythological narratives of the war experience (Weinrich 2012, 245–312).

The flexibility and populist nature of Nazi ideology is best exemplified by the appropriation of the symbol of the 'unknown soldier'. The Western Allies had pioneered this symbol in 1920 with the burial of an 'unknown soldier' in Paris and London respectively. Here, this symbol encapsulated the dignity and equality of the citizenship that had served the nation during the war – even though the French authorities went to great lengths to make sure that no corpse of a black colonial soldier was among those that were chosen for the selection of the 'unknown soldier'. Precisely because this symbol was perceived as democratic and intrinsic to the Western Allies, in Germany initially only Social Democratic war veterans supported its use. Yet Hitler, who was well aware of the ways in which France and the United Kingdom used this symbol, had no problem in adopting it for his own political purposes. From 1929, Goebbels and other leading Nazis referred to Hitler as the German 'unknown soldier'. Starting with the electoral breakthrough to a mass party in 1930, Hitler frequently used the cipher of the 'unknown soldier' to develop his own populist interpretation of radical nationalism and to mark a decisive break with the Wilhelmine understanding of it. In Hitler's view, the real challenge for nationalist politics was to overcome the deep cleavages in society and politics. And that could only be achieved through a sense of duty and commitment, not by a member of the bourgeoisie, but by someone who was intrinsically connected to the fate of the German people and to their suffering in the post-war period. No one other than a 'nameless individual' like the 'humble front-line soldier in the nameless army of twelve million people' could accomplish that. In Hitler's rendering of the 'unknown soldier', he had not died in service of his nation, but lived on to fight for a rebirth of Germany amidst the crippling effects that the Treaty of Versailles had on society and the economy (Ziemann 2013, 194).

3.4   Conclusion

Like fascist movements in many other European belligerent nations, from Belgium, France, and Italy to Austria, Hungary, and Romania, National Socialism was distinctively characterized as a post-war phenomenon. While its ideology and aspects of its political performance had important precursors in Wilhelmine Germany prior to 1914, the Nazi Party itself was contextualized in the political upheaval and counter-revolutionary activism of first Munich and then Bavaria in the immediate post-war period. However, that does not mean that National Socialism was a direct and immediate outcome of war and defeat. A short comparison with Italy is helpful to drive home this point. Here, Benito Mussolini, the founder and driving force of the fascist movement and its party, the *Partito Nazionale Fascista* (PNF), established a clear and deliberate sense of the links between the battle in the trenches and the need to rebuild the Italian nation and to cleanse it of the allegedly corrupting influence of liberalism and parliamentary rule. For this project, he coined the notion of a *trincerocrazia* or 'trenchocracy', a political system in which front-line soldiers who had battled for the nation were actually in charge. In the same vein, the fascist newspaper *Gerarchia* declared in 1922: 'Fascism is a child of the war. Its core does consist of former front-line soldiers (but real ones!)' (Reichardt 2002, 366–367). This rhetoric was matched by the actual political development, as the large majority of the early PNF members were war veterans, and a considerable number of the *squadristi*, the Fascist paramilitary organization, had been members of the *arditi*, the shock-troop units of the Italian army during the Great War. Thus, there was a direct link between wartime mobilization and the organization of early Fascism in Italy that was not in place during the early years of the NSDAP, from its founding in 1919 to the failed Hitler putsch in November 1923.

The link between the First World War and the formation of National Socialism is more indirect in another sense, too. Recent historiography on Weimar Germany has corrected the older view that the Republic was doomed to fail from the start, under the impact of defeat, economic upheaval, and political instability. Instead, historians have established the considerable political traction of pro-republican groups and the ability of the republican state to develop a meaningful and persuasive public rhetoric, performative display of symbols, and state pageantry (Ziemann 2010). National Socialist mobilization took place against the backdrop of these relatively successful attempts to construct a democratic polity, and have to be interpreted as initially quite desperate efforts to realign and unite the German right for the purpose of the outright destruction of this polity. It is a somewhat ironic fact that the key period for the formation of this radical-nationalist constituency took place during the mid-1920s, the allegedly quite stable period of the Weimar Republic, when the Steel Helmet and other right-wing combat leagues developed a radical populist rhetoric and realigned voters in the Protestant regions of Germany (Fritzsche 1990). Once the economic crisis kicked in from 1930 onwards, the Nazis could successfully absorb this potential into their own political appeal.

References

Bartov, Omer. 1996. *Murder in Our Midst: The Holocaust, Industrial Killing, and Representation.* New York and Oxford: Oxford University Press.

Bergmann, Werner and Wetzel, Juliane. 2002, 'Antisemitismus im Ersten und Zweiten Weltkrieg. Ein Forschungsüberblick.' In *Erster Weltkrieg - Zweiter Weltkrieg: Ein Vergleich. Krieg, Kriegserlebnis, Kriegserfahrung in Deutschland,* edited by Bruno Thoß and Hans-Erich Volkmann, 437–469. Paderborn: Schöningh.

Bessel, Richard. 1993. *Germany after the First World War.* Oxford: Clarendon Press.

Donson, Andrew. 2010. *Youth in the Fatherless Land: War Pedagogy, Nationalism, and Authority, 1914–1918,* Cambridge, MA and London: Harvard University Press.

Epkenhans, Michael. 1996. '"Wir als deutsches Volk sind doch nicht klein zu kriegen ..." Aus den Tagebüchern des Fregattenkapitäns Bogislav von Selchow 1918/19.' *Militärgeschichtliche Mitteilungen* 55, 165–224.

Fritzsche, Peter. 1990. *Rehearsals for Fascism: Populism and Political Mobilisation in Weimar Germany.* New York and Oxford: Oxford University Press.

Gerwarth, Robert and Malinowski, Stefan. 2009. 'Hannah Arendt's Ghosts: Reflections on the Disputable Path from Windhoek to Auschwitz.' *Central European History* 42, 279–300.

Geyer, Michael. 1986. 'Krieg als Gesellschaftspolitik. Anmerkungen zu neueren Arbeiten über das Dritte Reich im Zweiten Weltkrieg.' *Archiv für Sozialgeschichte* 26, 557–601.

Hitler, Adolf. 1940. *Mein Kampf.* Munich: Zentralverlag der NSDAP. First published 1925 and 1926.

Hüppauf, Bernd. 1986. 'Langemarck, Verdun and the Myth of a NEW MAN in Germany after the First World War.' *War & Society* 6, 70–103.

Krassnitzer, Patrick. 2002. 'Die Geburt des Nationalsozialismus im Schützengraben. Formen der Brutalisierung in den Autobiographien von nationalsozialistischen Frontsoldaten.' In *Der verlorene Frieden. Politik und Kriegskultur nach 1918,* edited by Jost Dülffer and Gerd Krumeich, 119–148. Essen: Klartext.

Kühne, Thomas. 2010. *Belonging and Genocide. Hitler's Community, 1918–1945.* New Haven, CT and London: Yale University Press.

Longerich, Peter. 2012. *Heinrich Himmler.* Oxford: Oxford University Press.

Mason, Timothy. 1971, 'The Legacy of 1918 for National Socialism.' In *German Democracy and the Triumph of Hitler,* edited by Anthony Nicholls and Erich Matthias, 15–39. London: Allen & Unwin.

Mason, Timothy. 1993. *Social Policy in the Third Reich. The Working Class and the 'National Community'.* Providence, RI and Oxford: Berg.

Mosse, George L. 1990. *Fallen Soldiers: Reshaping the Memory of the World Wars.* New York and Oxford: Oxford University Press.

Niewyk, Donald L. 1990. 'Solving the "Jewish Problem". Continuity and Change in German Antisemitism, 1871–1945.' *Leo Baeck Institute Yearbook* 35, 335–370.

Reichardt, Sven. 2002. *Faschistische Kampfbünde. Gewalt und Gemeinschaft im italienischen Squadrismus und in der deutschen SA.* Cologne: Böhlau.

Reichardt, Sven. 2007, 'Fascist Marches in Italy and Germany: Squadre and SA before the Seizure of Power.' In *The Street as Stage. Protest Marches and Public Rallies since the Nineteenth Century,* edited by Matthias Reiss, 169–188. Oxford: Oxford University Press.

Reichardt, Sven. 2010. 'Die SA im "Nachkriegs-Krieg".' In *Nationalsozialismus und Erster Weltkrieg,* edited by Gerd Krumeich, 243–259. Essen: Klartext.

Schwabe, Klaus. 2014. 'World War I and the Rise of Hitler.' *Diplomatic History* 38, 864–879.

Traverso, Enzo. 2003. *The Origins of Nazi Violence*. New York and London: New Press.

Verhey, Jeffrey. 2000. *The Spirit of 1914: Militarism, Myth and Mobilization in Germany*. Cambridge: Cambridge University Press.

Voelker, Judith. 2002. '"Unerträglich, unerfüllbar und deshalb unannehmbar". Kollektiver Protest gegen Versailles im Rheinland in den Monaten Mai und Juni 1919.' In *Der verlorene Frieden: Politik und Kriegskultur nach 1918*, edited by Jost Dülffer and Gerd Krumeich, 229–241. Essen: Klartext.

Weber, Thomas. 2010. *Hitler's First War. Adolf Hitler, the Men of the List Regiment, and the First World War*. Oxford: Oxford University Press.

Weinrich, Arndt. 2012 *Der Weltkrieg als Erzieher: Jugend zwischen Weimarer Republik und Nationalsozialismus*. Essen: Klartext.

Wildt, Michael. 2002. *Generation des Unbedingten: Das Führungskorps des Reichssicherheitshauptamtes*. Hamburg: Hamburger Edition.

Wildt, Michael. 2011. *Hitler's Volksgemeinschaft and the Dynamics of Racial Exklusion: Violence against Jews in Provincial Germany, 1919–1939*. New York: Berghahn Books.

Ziemann, Benjamin. 2007. *War Experiences in Rural Germany, 1914–1923*. Oxford and New York: Berg.

Ziemann, Benjamin. 2010. 'Weimar was Weimar. Politics, Culture and the Emplotment of the German Republic.' *German History* 28, 542–571.

Ziemann, Benjamin. 2011. 'Germany 1914–1918. Total War as a Catalyst of Change.' In *The Oxford Handbook of Modern German History*, edited by Helmut Walser Smith, 378–399. Oxford: Oxford University Press.

Ziemann, Benjamin. 2013. *Contested Commemorations. Republican War Veterans and Weimar Political Culture*. Cambridge: Cambridge University Press.

Zimmerer, Jürgen, 2004. 'Colonial Genocide and the Holocaust. Towards an Archaelogy of Genocide.' In *Genocide and Settler Society: Frontier Violence and Stolen Indigenous Children in Australian History*, edited by A. Dirk Moses. 49–76. New York: Berghahn Books.

Further Reading

Alcalde, Ángel. 2017. *War Veterans and Fascism in Interwar Europe*, Cambridge: Cambridge University Press.
Best comparative analysis of the construction of the fascist war veteran.

Bessel, Richard. 2004. *Nazism and War*. New York: Random House.
Excellent short survey on the role of war in the formation of Nazi policy and political practice from 1918 to 1945.

Kühne, Thomas. 2010. *Belonging and Genocide. Hitler's Community, 1918–1945*. New Haven, CT and London: Yale University Press.
Pathbreaking study that connects mythologies and rituals of male bonding in the military with the wider Nazi project of a national community.

Mason, Timothy. 1971, 'The Legacy of 1918 for National Socialism.' In *German Democracy and the Triumph of Hitler*, edited by Anthony Nicholls and Erich Matthias, 15–39. London: Allen & Unwin.
Seminal article that established how the popular groundswell of dissatisfaction with the war in late 1918 influenced Nazi thinking on the need to provide sufficient food and material resources for the civilian population during another war effort.

Schwabe, Klaus. 2014. 'World War I and the Rise of Hitler.' *Diplomatic History* 38, 864–879.

Short summary of the significance of the Versailles peace settlement on Hitler's thinking and Nazi mobilization.

Stibbe, Matthew. 2010. *Germany 1914–1933. Politics, Society and Culture*. Harlow, UK: Longman.

The very best short survey on Germany from the First World War to 1933, with an extensive discussion of the impact of the war on German politics.

Wildt, Michael. 2009. *Generation of the Unbound: The Leadership Corps of the Reich Security Main Office*. Madison: University of Wisconsin Press.

Path-breaking study of the leadership corps of a central decision-making body for the Nazi terror, with pertinent reflections on the role of the war experience on shaping the mindset of these SS functionaries.

CHAPTER FOUR

The Collapse of the Weimar Parliamentary System

SHELLEY BARANOWSKI

Until the mid-1980s, historians customarily viewed the Weimar Republic as a chronic and crisis-ridden failure, the poster child of Germany's 'deviation' from the liberal democratic West. Since then, scholars have come to recognize Weimar's possibilities and contingencies, and not just its flaws. They began by de-emphasizing the power of 'premodern' aristocratic elites, who according to previous accounts survived the Revolution of 1918 to impede democratization and elevate Hitler into power (Blackborn and Eley 1984). Or, by focusing on social policy and the Weimar welfare state, they redefined the republic as a 'classically modern' rupture from the previous century (Peukert 1987). Most recently, historians have explored diverse issues, such as mass culture, mass consumption, the extension of women's suffrage and constitutional guarantees of social rights, and the debates over citizenship that ensued in light of the post-First World War border changes. They also focus on the rituals, practices, and symbols of popular politics to acknowledge the strength of popular commitment to the republic, as well as the conflicts that arose from competing social and political visions (Weitz 2007; Brown 2009; Canning, Barndt, and McGuire 2010; Ziemann 2013). Even the term 'crisis', which has so characterized Weimar, has undergone a re-examination. Instead of being synonymous with Weimar's congenital weaknesses, 'crisis' for contemporaries expressed the openness to future possibilities and the desire of Germans to promote change (Follmer and Graf 2005; Graf 2008). In brief, Weimar is no longer the sad reflection of Germany's long-term 'misdevelopment' or the tragic way station to the Third Reich. In fact, as Anthony McElligott suggests, we should not study Weimar as a self-contained period at all. Rather, Weimar's central debate, the nature of political authority, emerged first during the First World War. It continued

A Companion to Nazi Germany, First Edition. Edited by Shelley Baranowski, Armin Nolzen, and Claus-Christian W. Szejnmann.
© 2018 John Wiley & Sons Ltd. Published 2018 by John Wiley & Sons Ltd.

without resolution under the Republic, leaving it to the 'unbounded authority' of the Nazis to end it in 1936 (McElligott 2014).

Still, the critical question remains: how did the National Socialists take power and in short order transform a liberal democracy with a progressive constitution into a murderous dictatorship? Three interlocking issues, which converged beginning in 1928 during what appeared to be the height of the republic's era of stabilization, provide an explanation: (1) the delegitimation of American-dominated liberal capitalism, which boosted authoritarian, autarkic, and imperialist remedies to economic collapse and political instability and the elites who advocated them; (2) the fragmentation and radicalization of Germany's Protestant, non-socialist electoral constituencies, which undermined the liberal and conservative bourgeois parties that had been accustomed to governing; and (3) the mass support of National Socialism that transformed it into the only party on the right with a credible claim to lead a right-wing coalition. To be sure, the division of the Weimar electorate into splinter parties, the impact of economic hardship on Germany's contested relationships with its wartime enemies, and the social bases and ideology of the Nazi Party and its electorate have hardly escaped the attention of historians past or present. Yet recent international history, as well as newer scholarship on the conflicts within the German right and on Nazi populism, force us to recognize that Weimar's demise arose from the specific constellations of its final five years rather than from long-term failures and inherent flaws.

4.1   The Irony of German Weakness: The Defeat of Putschism, and American Economic Intervention

In October and November 1918, Germany's appeal for an armistice in the face of its military collapse and that of its allies, popular war weariness, and the impact of wartime privations on the home front sparked the German Revolution and the abdication of Kaiser Wilhelm II. The Weimar Republic emerged from a shaky compromise between the military, civil service, and industrialists on the one side and the Majority Socialists on the other, who, after Wilhelm's flight, headed the interim Council of People's Deputies until an election could produce a new national assembly. The Socialists agreed to preserve the military and its officer corps and set aside their goal of socializing the economy. In return, their adversaries accepted a Western-style liberal democracy, the protection of workers through collective bargaining and binding arbitration, and an eight-hour workday. Because both sides feared a repeat of the Bolshevik Revolution, the Council dissolved the populist workers' and soldiers' councils and violently suppressed wildcat strikes and the uprisings of radical leftists who had broken with the Social Democratic Party (SPD); actions that relied on the military and the paramilitary Freikorps to carry out. That cooperation extended to fighting the Bolsheviks in the Baltic region in order to retain Germany's gains from its wartime occupation and the Treaty of Brest-Litovsk (Stibbe 2010, 67–83; Hagen 2012, 227–240; Kolb and Schumann 2013, 166–178).

The national elections in January 1919 to elect a constitution-writing national assembly seemingly endorsed the Majority Socialists' reformist path, inasmuch as the Socialists and their allies in the Reichstag, the Centre Party and the Progressives (renamed the Democratic Party or DDP), won an outright majority. The constitution that the national assembly enacted guaranteed equal voting rights for all citizens, full legal equality between men and women, ministerial responsibility to the Reichstag, civil liberties, and extensive social welfare provisions. Nevertheless, the constitution also reflected the compromises that limited the revolution, beginning with the retention of the imperial nomenclature of the 'German Reich' rather than 'republic' as the formal name of post-war Germany. In addition, it codified substantial presidential powers to balance those assigned to parliament, and it carried over proportional representation from the Second Empire. Both would, over the long term, contribute to the fracturing of Weimar's last years (Stibbe 2010, 71; Kolb and Schumann 2013, 179–185). Moreover, the ruling 'Weimar coalition' had to swallow a bitter pill in June 1919 by signing the massively unpopular Versailles Treaty, which imposed significant territorial losses and the occupation of the Rhineland, the reduction of the armed forces, the sacrifice of Germany's overseas empire, and the assignment of an as yet unspecified reparations bill. The government's decision to sign the treaty to escape the threat of an Entente invasion, cost the coalition dearly in the national elections of June 1920, and indeed the Versailles *Diktat* thereafter became the means through which the republic's enemies vented their hostility (Lorenz 2008). The loss of the coalition's majority produced a political landscape polarized between the parties of the right furious at continued working-class uprisings and an extreme left angry at the government's suppression of those same uprisings. Until the mid-1920s, political conflict and economic instability threatened the republic's survival.

The German Communist Party (KPD) continued to press for a proletarian overthrow of capitalism altogether in repeated strikes and revolts. Although violently put down by counter-revolutionaries in the spring of 1919, Marxist 'councils' launched revolutions in Bavaria, the Ruhr, and Saxony. In 1920, the national government dispatched the military again to suppress workers in the Ruhr who had formed a 'red army' of revolution. In 1923, the national government dismissed the KPD-led governments of Saxony and Thuringia, in addition to stifling scattered leftist insurrections elsewhere. Yet the right, embodied in party-political terms in the post-war successor to the National Liberals, the German Peoples' Party (DVP) and the German National Peoples' Party (DNVP), was the bigger threat despite having acceded to the republic to forestall a more radical revolution. Although its populist base was heterogeneous, ranging from veterans and embittered university students to peasants, rural school teachers, small business proprietors, and some workers, business, military, civil service, landowning, and clerical elites gave the right more influence (Weitz 2007, 92; Pyta 1996). Thus despite its earlier compromises in the immediate aftermath of war and revolution, the right covertly and overtly abetted putschism and assassinations, most notably those of the finance minister Matthias Erzberger and the foreign minister Walther Rathenau.

Yet with due acknowledgement of the severity of early Weimar upheavals, the republic survived two serious right-wing coup attempts, the Kapp Putsch of 1920 being the first of them. For a time, the putschists occupied Berlin, forcing the government to flee to Dresden and then to Stuttgart. Yet the right collapsed in the face of a trade-union organized general strike and the fear that the French, who occupied the Rhineland, would intervene further (Könnemann and Schulze 2002, introduction; Mommsen 1996, 81–84). Similar considerations undermined the second coup attempt three years later. In January 1923, French and Belgian troops occupied the Ruhr believing that the Weimar government was deliberately inflating its currency to default on its reparations. In addition to confiscating coal and industrial goods as payment in kind, the French covertly promoted the separation of the Ruhr and the Rhineland from Germany, provoking a government-subsidized campaign of passive resistance in response (Fischer 2002). Inflation that soared to unimaginable heights and the Weimar government's decision in November 1923 under its new chancellor Gustav Stresemann to halt the resistance spawned the Hitler-led Munich Putsch, the goal of which was to oust the government in Berlin. Yet here too, fears of continued social unrest and further territorial dismemberment, divisions among the conspirators, and the lack of support from the Bavarian government and the military undermined the coup. Unlike Italy where Italian elites turned to Mussolini in 1922 to destroy the left and the liberal state without fear of foreign intervention, German elites had less room to manoeuvre. To be sure, France won a pyrrhic victory in forcing the German government to halt passive resistance. Its British and American allies refused to back the occupation, and its own economy suffered as a result. Yet Germany's weakness had proven sufficiently obvious to underscore the irony of its position. Its vulnerability to the victors of the First World War saved the republic.

As Zara Steiner and Adam Tooze have argued, a permanent solution to the Ruhr disaster lay in the intersection of American economic power and the desire of Weimar's premier statesman, Gustav Stresemann, to use the United States as a counterweight to the British and French, briefly as chancellor in a 'grand coalition' extending from the SPD to the DVP (August to November 1923) and subsequently as Weimar's foreign minister until his death in 1929. Believing that putschism was economically ruinous and politically counter-productive, Stresemann exploited American fears of a French dismemberment of Germany by laying the groundwork for stabilization through the Dawes Plan and by improving Franco-German relations as the way to modify the post-war peace settlement (Steiner 2007, 240–250; Tooze 2006, 3–7; 2015, 447–461). The Dawes Plan forced a French withdrawal from the Ruhr, lengthened the term for payment of reparations, underwrote the stabilization the Reichsmark, and provided transfer protection if scheduled payments threatened the stability of the mark and international currency markets. The settlement opened the door to American loans and investment, which despite Weimar's persistent structural weaknesses stimulated a modest recovery between 1924 and 1929 that returned Germany's gross national product and per capita income to 1913 levels (James 1997). The second of Stresemann's achievements, the Locarno Treaties of 1925, required that Germany permanently accept its post-war western boundaries. Yet Germany's gains were significant. The signatories did not challenge the Treaty of Rapallo, which Walther Rathenau had concluded with the Soviet Union in 1922. In addition to allowing the Reichswehr, the newly formed and smaller armed forces permitted by Versailles, to test new weaponry under cover in the USSR, Rapallo spared Germany a Franco-Soviet encirclement. Moreover, Stresemann was not forced to concede the finality of

Germany's eastern borders. Finally, France renounced support for Rhenish separatism and the signatories granted Germany admission to the League of Nations. If membership in the League did not restore Germany's pre-war overseas empire, Germany's presence prevented the victorious empires from exercising full sovereignty over its mandates (Mommsen 1996, 204–206; Steiner 2007, 387–410; Pederson 2015, 4055–4259).

To be sure, hostility to the republic hardly disappeared among the far left and certainly not among the right, which condemned Stresemann's foreign policy as spineless. Hitler received a prison term for his role in the Munich Putsch, but the brevity of his sentence betrayed the sympathy he attracted and the conservatism of the Weimar judiciary. If the Nazi Party subsequently followed the 'legal' route to power by competing in national and regional elections, neither its hatred of the Weimar 'system' nor the violence that its Stormtroopers unleashed against the Party's 'enemies' subsided. In 1925 the election to the Reich presidency in 1925 of Paul von Hindenburg, the 'hero' of the iconic First World War victory at Tannenberg, exposed a yearning for a charismatic figure who embodied the *Volk* 'community', an image that Hindenburg himself assiduously cultivated. Like the DNVP and the DVP, each of which claimed a diverse populist base to offset their socially privileged leaderships, Hindenburg personified the plebiscitary ambitions of post-war German conservative nationalism (Pyta 2007). Finally, antisemitic violence, a regular occurrence before stabilization, hardly disappeared, even if the bourgeois parties formally disassociated themselves from it (Walter 1999). Regardless, the republic retained striking reserves of popular support that pro-republican organizations, holidays, and symbols illustrated. Those organizations, whose numbers exceeded those of the right-wing Stahlhelm, included Social Democratic veterans' associations that advocated pacifism and international solidarity (Ziemann 2013). Even the most obdurate anti-republican party, the DNVP, capitalized on its gains in the 1924 national election to enter the government, albeit briefly, in 1925 and then again in 1927. Aside from the KPD and later the National Socialists, communication and negotiation across party lines among deputies allowed the Reichstag to function (Mergel 2012). The 1928 national elections yielded a broad-based 'grand coalition' headed by the Social Democrat Hermann Müller, which extended from the DVP on the right to the SPD on the left, seeming testimony to Weimar's durability.

4.2   Fragmentation and Radicalization on the Right

As the grand coalition attempted to govern, tremors in the global economy undermined the foundations upon which stabilization rested. Shifting American priorities, the Wall Street crash, and the collapse of liberal capitalism converged with mounting domestic dissatisfaction to create a suitable climate for the resurgence of Weimar's most determined enemies. In 1928, well before the collapse of the New York Stock Exchange, the flow of American capital into Germany began to slow as domestic interest rates rose. At home, the new ruling coalition faced major internal conflicts over the construction of battle cruisers and the renegotiation of reparations as the Dawes Plan had originally stipulated. It also confronted the assault of

industrialists against the costs of the Weimar welfare state, especially unemployment insurance and collective bargaining agreements reinforced by binding arbitration. The Ruhr lockout in November 1928, the protests of employers in the iron
industry against a court decision favourable to its workers, signalled a return to the
management–labour conflicts of earlier in the decade, in which employers tangled
bitterly over wages and productivity (Borchardt 1991; McElligott 2014, 80–81;
Abraham 1986, 220–270). Resistance proved even more tenacious in agriculture,
Germany's weakest sector. Having faced high indebtedness and increased taxation
since stabilization, the collapse of global commodity prices, and in the view of
many agriculturalists the unwillingness of successive Weimar cabinets to provide
sufficient protection against foreign imports, middling farmers resorted to extra-
parliamentary means to vent their anger. In late 1928, the peasant-based 'Rural
People Movement', which formed first in Schleswig-Holstein and then extended
further east, staged boycotts, strikes, and bomb attacks against banks and government offices. Despite having benefited disproportionately from profligate 'Eastern
Aid' (Osthilfe) programmes to shore up the primary sector, large estate owners,
especially in the eastern Prussian provinces, mobilized as well against Weimar's
alleged bias in favour of low food prices for urban consumers (Heberle 1970;
Baranowski 1995, 118–126).

In 1928, the same national elections that produced the grand coalition severely
punished the two Protestant bourgeois parties, the DVP and the DNVP, that had
participated in ruling coalitions. Peasants and small producers, who had not
already changed their party allegiance (Winkler 1972), migrated in droves to special interest parties who catered to their demands. Although suffering significant
losses, the DVP could at least participate in the governing coalition thanks to
Stresemann's significance as foreign minister (Steiner 2007, 459). The DNVP's
decline, on the other hand, was devastating. Its share of the electorate dropped
from 20% to 14% from the previous elections in 1924, shrinking its relatively
accommodationist Reichstag delegation and motivating its provincial organizations to remove the party's old-line Prussian leader Kuno von Westarp and replace
him with the Pan-German media magnate Alfred Hugenberg. Rejecting all cooperation with the Weimar 'system', Hugenberg aimed to mobilize an authoritarian
nationalist and racist extra-parliamentary coalition against the republic, which
would include the National Socialists (Jones 2009; Mergel 2002, 422–427). Even
the Centre Party, the electorate of which remained relatively stable, moved sharply
to the right. Once a mainstay of the Weimar coalition, the Centre chose as its new
national chairman the monsignor Ludwig Kaas to strengthen the party's ties to the
Catholic Church, press for an authoritarian state, and, following the wishes of its
middle-class constituencies, minimize the influence of the party's labour wing
(Mommsen 1996, 261–262).

Developments emanating from across the Atlantic exacerbated anti-republican
sentiment in two ways. The decline of American lending damaged the German
economy which had come to depend on it, while American trade and reparations
policy encouraged radical nationalist solutions to bolster Germany's position in
Europe. The withdrawal of American loans before and after the Wall Street crash
weakened corporations that invested in modernization, as well as regional and

municipal governments that borrowed to expand their infrastructure and under-write social programmes. Moreover, American protectionism, namely the Hawley-Smoot tariff of 1930 which raised import duties to unprecedented levels, deprived German manufacturers of their most important market, which had been crucial to Stresemann's strategy of linking Germany's fortunes to American economic power. To be sure, the renegotiation of reparations anticipated in the Dawes agreement and codified six years later in the Young Plan modestly benefited Germany in that it reduced annual annuity payouts and lengthened the term of amortization. In removing transfer protection, which foreign commissioners had overseen, the Young Plan restored Germany's sovereignty over the management of its finances and laid the groundwork for the final Allied withdrawal from the Rhineland in 1930. The Reichstag approved the agreement with a comfortable majority. Yet despite the dismal failure of the referendum against the Young Plan organized by the Pan-Germans, the Stahlhelm, the Nazis, and other right-wing pressure groups, the Plan was a mixed blessing. The very termination of transfer protection made Berlin totally responsible for fulfilling its terms, and the annual annuity payments were greater than the Müller cabinet had expected (Tooze 2006, 13–14; Ritschl 2002, 128–141). Disappointment with the Young Plan and the mounting economic crisis provoked the right into a full-throttle assault against the Weimar welfare state and into increasing demands for unilateralism. Even on Constitution Day of 1930, a holiday that normally gave expression to popular support for the republic, right-wing voices collectively expressed their aggressive nationalism in response to the return of full sovereignty to the Rhineland (McElligott 2014, 54–61). Quite apart from Stresemann's sudden death just days before the Wall Street crash, which removed the republic's principal champion of multilateral diplomacy to restore Germany as a great power, the grand coalition survived only as long as the Young Plan negotiations required the appearance of stability. Following the Reichstag's favourable vote, the coalition acrimoniously dissolved after failing to agree on a budget (Mommsen 1996, 281–282).

The fall of the last government capable of mustering a majority led, to all intents and purposes, to a three-year presidential dictatorship in which President Hindenburg appointed the chancellor. That in turn allowed his appointee to rule by decree under the terms of Article 48, a prime example of the clash between presidential and parliamentary power embedded in the Weimar constitution (Weitz 2007, 122). Under such conditions, the most a chancellor could expect was the toleration of the Reichstag parties, not a supporting majority. The first appointee, the conservative leader of the Centre Party's Reichstag delegation, Heinrich Brüning, introduced extensive austerity measures, tightening credit, imposing higher taxes, and cutting public spending, especially wages and salaries. The degree of Brüning's commitment to parliamentary democracy (or the lack of it) remains a topic of debate, but there is little doubt that his economic and foreign policies favoured the advocates of authoritarianism at home and muscularity abroad (Steiner 2007, 640–641; Kolb and Schumann 2013, 263; Jones 2016). By using budgetary savings, Brüning expected to eliminate Germany's foreign debt and leave nothing for reparations, thus terminating its most vexing problem. In addition to forging ahead with the construction of two battle cruisers, the Brüning cabinet's foreign minister, Julius Curtius, pursued an Austro-German customs union and bilateral trade agreements with other Central and Southeastern European nations to accomplish a long-standing nationalist ambition, a German-dominated *Mitteleuropa*. Although the outcry against the Austro-German union curtailed that project, the Hoover administration's tepid response to the Brüning government's unilateralism, as well as its decision in 1931 to impose a moratorium on reparations without consulting the British and French, meant that Germany was now free from the pressure that had earlier contained aggressive nationalism (Tooze 2015, 487–490; Mommsen 1996, 356–398).

Nevertheless, Hindenburg's presidential dictatorship could not solve its most acute problem, the lack of popular legitimacy. In a highly mobilized, well-educated advanced industrial society, even an authoritarian regime required popular support. Neither Brüning nor his successors, the Catholic nobleman Franz von Papen and the general Kurt von Schleicher could cobble together a majority to alter the constitution. In fact, Brüning's decision to call national elections in the autumn of 1930 redounded to the benefit of the Nazis, who won 18% of the vote and 107 seats in the Reichstag. The KPD increased its parliamentary contingent to 77 seats. The SPD, whose influence the government wanted to eliminate, remained the largest party. Of the *Bürgerbloc* parties of the stabilization era, only the Centre's electorate remained relatively stable as the DNVP and the DVP continued to lose out to splinter parties. The results of two additional federal elections in 1932, the first in July and the second in November, gave even less comfort to the right. Both underscored the utter lack of representation in Papen's 'cabinet of barons'. The first more than doubled the Nazi share of the electorate to 37.3% while it increased the size of the KPD's parliamentary contingent. Despite losing votes in the November election, owing to Hitler's inability to obtain the chancellorship for himself, the Nazis still retained 196 Reichstag seats while the Communist total climbed to 108. Again, only the Centre retained a stable electorate. As chancellor, Papen contributed his share to dismantling the Weimar 'system' by removing the SPD-dominated government of Prussia, but the continuous use of Article 48 in the absence of parliamentary backing provided an insecure foundation for governing. Thus, given the ideological common ground that existed between the traditional right and the Nazis – anti-Marxism, anti-republicanism, antisemitism, and a German imperium on the continent – the Nazis offered a mass base sufficient to create a system-changing coalition. Still, the party's populism, its vehement attacks on 'reactionaries', and Hitler's insistence on becoming chancellor presented a major stumbling block.

4.3   Why the Nazis?

Recent scholarship has argued that bitter divisions within the nationalist right, exacerbated by the decline of electoral support for the DVP and DNVP, enabled Hitler's accession to power. The right's weakness and disunity, not the power of conservative elites to forge an 'alliance' with the National Socialists, as Fritz Fischer and Hans-Ulrich Wehler and others once suggested, worked to Nazism's benefit (Jones 2014; Beck 2008). Indeed, the last cabinet prior to Hitler's assumption as chancellor, that of Kurt von Schleicher, desperately sought to compensate for the right's electoral shortcomings by forging a broad coalition that included the Nazis and the Centre, and by dangling the prospect of job creation programmes, the toleration of the SPD and the trade unions (Turner 2008). Such plans amounted to a fantasy. The resistance of industrialists against overtures to the trade unions, agrarian elites infuriated by Schleicher's refusal to impose quotas against foreign agricultural imports and his proposed withdrawal of subsidies from big agriculture, the enmity of his predecessor Franz von Papen, and Hitler's refusal to accept the status of junior partner in such a coalition proved fatal. If Schleicher was shrewd enough to see that mass support was crucial to keeping his government in power, the right's deep divisions undermined his solutions. Yet the story of Hitler's accession in 1933 is incomplete if we focus solely on conservative disunity and fecklessness. Despite possessing strengths that no right-wing government could do without, the Nazi Party could not achieve a majority on its own. Ultimately, it needed highly placed conservative elites with access to the Reich president to reach its goal.

We can begin with the Nazi Party's strengths that enhanced its bargaining position among the disparate collection of parties, paramilitary and combat organizations, and economic interest groups that composed the right. After Hitler's dismal failure in the Munich Putsch and his subsequent, if brief, imprisonment, the Nazi Party seemed a spent force. Yet following Hitler's release in 1925, the party evolved into a formidable nationwide organization geared to building a sufficient mass following that would leverage it into power by constitutional means. Unlike the DNVP and DVP, which despite their populist claims remained convocations of notables (*Honoratiorenpolitik*) who presumed their fitness for leadership, Nazi activists appeared at the pubs, football fields, and countless voluntary associations to win support. Thus they lent substance to the party's claim to realize a true 'people's community' (*Volksgemeinschaft*) that would unite and strengthen a divided nation (Rohrkrämer 2014; Fritzsche 2014). Although Nazism's electoral centre of gravity became strongest in the Protestant small towns and rural regions of northern and eastern Germany, its backing cut across generational, gender, class, regional, and religious lines to a degree that only the Centre Party could remotely approach. It even showed some success in attracting workers, especially agricultural labourers and workers in smaller, non-union firms who had few ties to the organized left (Falter 1990; Kolb and Schumann 2013, 267–73). Among urban workers, particularly those with strong ties to the parties of the left, the party faced tough competition. To be sure, Nazis and Communists who lived in the same working-class neighbourhoods shared a common language of nationalism, masculinized paramilitary violence, and anti-bourgeois revolution, but although each side infiltrated the other, the extent to which allegiances shifted can be hard to pin down (Brown 2009).

Hitler's leadership was essential to the Nazi Party's appeal. His charisma in the Weberian sense of the term (Kershaw 1987) contributed to his increasing popular standing as a strong leader in a time of crisis, a 'man of the people' who distinguished himself from the *faux* populism of other leaders on the right. His modest background, which he made no bones about expressing, contrasted sharply with the *bildungsbürgerlich* or aristocratic origins of his rivals. He embodied the party's paradoxical promise to unify the Volk 'community' and transcend Germany's deep social, religious, and regional divisions while simultaneously appealing to the aspirations of many Germans for upward mobility and individual achievement (Föllmer 2013, 19–100). Nazism's anti-Marxism, anti-republicanism, antisemitism, and vehement hatred of Versailles became staples of its campaign rallies. Yet in addition to its persistent attacks on bourgeois 'reactionaries', the party excelled in its ability to speak to the impact of the economic crisis on ordinary Germans. It successfully articulated populist rage against the failures of global 'plutocratic' and 'Jewish' liberal capitalism while offering autarky, national etatism, and 'socialism' (defined as equality of opportunity) as remedies for those willing to work for the *Volksgemeinschaft* (Szejnmann 2013). It hardly hurt the Nazis that they had not served in national governments before 1933 and thus assumed no responsibility for the failures of bourgeois cabinets. Despite the obstructionism of Nazis and Communists in the Reichstag that contributed to undermining parliament's effectiveness, it made little difference to a public that had by 1930 lost all respect for the behind-the-scenes deal making of 'parliamentarism' (Mergel 2012, 473–485).

Schleicher's political demise allowed Hitler to leverage his party's mass base and overcome the resistance of key conservatives to his chancellorship. Until Schleicher's tenure, the conservative nationalist Alfred Hugenberg, who was most responsible, ironically, for radicalizing the DNVP after 1928, had grown increasingly leery of Hitler. The Führer's intransigence and independence on three previous attempts to unite the right, the Young Plan referendum in 1929, the Harzburg rally in 1931 to call for the dissolution of the Brüning government, and the bitterly contested presidential campaign of 1932 infuriated the DNVP leader. Yet the traditional right had manoeuvred itself into a trap with no escape, a dilemma that Hugenberg's own conduct especially made evident. Although opposed to a Hitler chancellorship, he refused to support Schleicher's return to 'parliamentarism', thus enabling the outcome he sought to avoid (Jones 1992, 2016, 176–313). The Nazi Party may have lost two million voters and 34 seats in the November 1932 elections, but it still maintained the Reichstag's largest delegation. It was the only party on the right upon which an authoritarian solution could be constructed.

The institutional rupture between parliament and the chancellor, the divisions among powerful interests, and the disconnect between unrepresentative governments and popular legitimacy allowed a small coterie of conservative leaders close to President Hindenburg, with the toleration of leading industrialists, agrarians, and generals, to coalesce around a Hitler chancellorship. They concluded that a Hitler-led government of 'national concentration' was the only way to achieve the right's goals of rearmament, imperialism, and authoritarianism while avoiding a civil war (Eley 2013, 207; Abraham 1986, 271–318). Having decided between 1928 and 1930 during the emerging global economic crisis that compromise with the Socialists was intolerable and weakening the Reichstag was preferable, they had no answer to the fecklessness of governments since 1930 other than to include the Nazis and their popular following. Even if the relationship between conservative elites and Nazis did not amount to a cohesive alliance as scholars once suggested, their convergence on critical issues before and after the 'seizure' of power laid the foundations of a murderous dictatorship. Hindenburg and Papen may well have believed that the Nazis' losses in November would make Hitler more cooperative, especially because conservative appointments outnumbered the Nazis in the new government. Yet conservatives were only too willing to grant powers to the Nazis to eliminate common enemies. They acceded to Hitler's demand to dissolve the Reichstag immediately and hold new elections. They gave the Prussian and Reich interior ministries to Hermann Göring and Wilhelm Frick respectively, which gave the Nazis substantial police powers to use against the left, Jews, and other 'community aliens'. They endorsed the raft of 'emergency decrees' following the Reichstag Fire, and enabling legislation unbounded by restrictions on its duration that granted Hitler dictatorial powers. Although subjected to Nazi attacks on the bourgeois conventions of well-ordered government, denounced as over-entitled 'reactionaries' by Nazi propagandists, and assaulted by SA men, conservatives could mount no coherent or effective alternative defence (Mommsen 1996, 490–544; Pyta 1996; Winkler 2005, 521–616; Beck 2008, 146–292).

4.4 Conclusion

Until 1928, the Weimar Republic survived as a parliamentary democracy despite its tumultuous beginnings and the tenacity of anti-republican opposition. Far from being the conduit between Imperial Germany and the Third Reich or destined to fail from the beginning, Weimar's difficulties, inflation included, differed little from those of other European nations after the First World War. Relatively speaking, Weimar's economy remained the strongest in Europe, not least because little of the fighting occurred on German soil, and its neighbours depended on it for coking coal (Marks 2013, 658). And Weimar democracy was hardly unique in succumbing to authoritarianism, even if the fascist regime that followed it exceeded the extremes of other fascisms. Further research that draws on comparative, international, and transnational approaches would more clearly highlight the similarities and differences among nations after World War I as they wrestled with common problems.

What recent scholarship does underscore, however, is that Allied leverage, particularly in the conflict over reparations, weakened over time enough to revitalize and radicalize the German right's campaign against the republic. In 1923 French soldiers occupied the Rhineland and the Ruhr, in the latter case to force Germany to pay its reparations. The ruinous consequences of hyperinflation, separatism in the Rhineland, and right-wing putschism increased fears that more territorial losses would follow if stability were not restored. American concern regarding French ambitions after the collapse of German resistance to the Ruhr occupation brought a meeting of the minds between the United States and Stresemann. American financial intervention subsequently helped to stabilize the Reichsmark and weaken the anti-republican right. Yet between 1928 and 1933 political and economic constellations changed. Disappointment with the terms of the Young Plan, the fall of the Socialist-led grand coalition, the final withdrawal of Allied forces from the Rhineland, and the global economic collapse directly and indirectly enabled the right to assert its agendas of rearmanent, a German *Mitteleuropa*, the disempowerment of the

Reichstag, and the dismantling the Weimar welfare state. In contrast to its behaviour during the early years of the republic, the right pursued its agenda by electoral means but its failures resulted in increasingly desperate attempts at coalition building as the bourgeois parties disintegrated. Beginning with Chancellor Brüning, Germany signalled that unilateralism and bilateralism not multilateral negotiation would define German foreign policy. As the tepid response of the Hoover administration to the proposed Austro-German customs union made clear, and the Hoover moratorium on reparations payments confirmed, the leverage that had once constrained Germany was no longer present. Because the strategies of conservative elites only benefited the Nazis, the most extreme exponent of the right's objectives, the consequences would be disastrous.

References

Abraham, David. 1986. *The Collapse of the Weimar Republic: Political Economy and Crisis*, 2nd edn. New York: Holmes & Meier.

Baranowski, Shelley. 1995. *The Sanctity of Rural Life: Nobility, Protestantism, and Nazism in Weimar Prussia*. New York: Oxford University Press.

Beck, Hermann. 2008. *The Fateful Alliance: German Conservatives and Nazis in 1933: The Machtergreifung in a New Light*. New York and Oxford: Berghahn Books.

Blackbourn, David, and Eley, Geoff. 1984. *The Peculiarities of German History: Bourgeois Society and Politics in Nineteenth-Century Germany*. Oxford: Oxford University Press.

Borchardt, Knut. 1991. *Perspectives on Modern German Economic History and Policy*. Cambridge: Cambridge University Press.

Brown, Timothy S. 2009. *Weimar Radicals. Nazis and Communists between Authenticity and Performance*. New York and Oxford: Berghahn Books.

Canning, Kathleen, Barndt, Kersten, and McGuire, Kristin, eds 2010. *Weimar Publics/Weimar Subject: Rethinking the Political Culture of Germany in the 1920s*. New York and Oxford: Berghahn Books.

Eley, Geoff. 2013. *Nazism as Fascism: Violence, Ideology, and the Ground of Consent in Germany 1930–1945*. London and New York: Routledge.

Falter, Jürgen. 1990. *Hitlers Wähler*. Munich: C.H. Beck.

Fischer, Conan. 2002. *The Ruhr Crisis 1922–1924*. Oxford: Oxford University Press.

Follmer, Moritz. 2013. *Individuality and Modernity in Berlin: Self and Society from Weimar to the Wall*. Cambridge: Cambridge University Press.

Follmer, Moritz and Graf, Rüdiger, eds. 2005. *Die 'Krise' der Weimarer Republik. Zur Kritik eines Deutungsmuster*. Frankfurt am Main: Campus.

Fritzsche, Peter. 2014. 'Die Idee des Volkes und der Aufstieg der Nazis.' In *Attraktion der NS-Bewegung*, edited by Gudrun Brockhaus, 3581–3893. Essen: Klartext. Electronic edition.

Graf, Rüdiger. 2008. *Die Zukunft der Weimarer Republik. Krisen und Zukunftsaneignungen in Deutschland 1918–1933*. Oldenburg: De Gruyter.

Hagen, William W. 2012. *German History in Modern Times: Four Lives of the Nation*. Cambridge: Cambridge University Press.

Heberle, Rudolf. 1970. *From Democracy to Nazism: A Regional Case Study on Political Parties in Germany*. New York: Fertig.

James, Harold. 1997. *The German Slump: Politics and Economics 1924–1936*. Oxford: Clarendon Press.

Jones, Larry Eugene. 1992. '"The Greatest Stupidity of My Life": Alfred Hugenberg and the Formation of the Hitler Cabinet, January 1933.' *Journal of Contemporary History* 27, 63–87.

Jones, Larry Eugene. 2009. 'German Conservatism at the Crossroads: Count Kuno von Western and the Struggle for Control of the DNVP, 1928–30.' *Contemporary European History* 18, 147–177.

Jones, Larry Eugene, ed. 2014. *The German Right in the Weimar Republic: Studies in the History of German Conservatism, Nationalism, and Antisemitism*. New York and Oxford: Berghahn Books.

Jones, Larry Eugene. 2016. *Hitler versus Hindenburg: The 1932 Elections and the End of the Weimar Republic*. Cambridge: Cambridge University Press.

Kershaw, Ian. 1987. *The 'Hitler Myth:' Image and Reality in the Third Reich*. Oxford: Clarendon Press.

Kolb, Eberhard and Schumann, Dirk. 2013. *Die Weimarer Republic*, 8th edn. Munich: Oldenbourg.

Könnemann, Erwin and Schulze, Gerhard eds. 2002. *Der Kapp-Lüttwitz-Ludendorff Putsch*. Munich: Olzog.

Lorenz, Thomas. 2008. *'Die Weltgeschichte ist das Weltgericht!' Der Versailles Vertrag in Diskurs und Zeitgeist der Weimarer Republik*. Frankfurt and New York: Campus.

Marks, Sally. 2013. 'Mistakes and Myths: The Allies, Germany, and the Versailles Treaty.' *Journal of Modern History* 85(3), 632–659.

McElligott, Anthony. 2014. *Rethinking the Weimar Republic. Authority and Authoritarianism 1916–1936*. London: Bloomsbury.

Mergel, Thomas. 2012. *Parlamentarische Kultur in der Weimarer Republik: Politische Kommunikation, symbolische Politik und Öffentlichkeit im Reichstag*. Düsseldorf: Droste.

Mommsen. Hans. 1996. *The Rise and Fall of Weimar Democracy*. Chapel Hill, NC and London: University of North Carolina Press.

Pedersen, Susan. 2015. *The Guardians: The League of Nations and the Crisis of Empire*. Oxford: Oxford University Press.

Peukert, Detlev J.K. 1987. *Die Weimarer Republik. Krisenjahre der Klassischen Moderne*. Frankfurt am Main: Suhrkamp.

Pyta, Wolfram. 1996. *Dorfgemeinschaft und Parteipolitik 1918–1933: Die Verschränkung von Milieu und Parteien in den protestantischen Landgebieten Deutschlands in der Weimarer Republik*. Düsseldorf: Droste.

Pyta, Wolfram. 2007. *Hindenburg: Herrschaft zwischen Hohenzollern und Hitler*. Munich: Siedler.

Ritschl, Albrecht. 2002. *Deutschlands Krise und Konjunktur, 1924–1934: Binnenkonjunktur, Auslandsverschuldung und Reparationsproblem zwischen Dawes Plan und Transfersperre*. Berlin: Akademie Verlag.

Rohrkrämer, Thomas. 2014. 'Die fatale Attraktion des Nationalsozialismus in der Weimarer Republik.' In *Attraktion der NS-Bewegung*, edited by Gudrun Brockhaus, 1746–2130. Essen: Klartext. Electronic edition.

Steiner, Zara. 2007. *The Lights That Failed: European International History 1919–1933*. Oxford: Oxford University Press.

Stibbe, Matthew. 2010. *Germany 1914–1933: Politics, Society and Culture*. Harlow, UK: Longman.

Szejnmann, Claus-Christian. 2103. 'Nazi Economic Thought and Rhetoric During the Weimar Republic: Capitalism and Its Discontents.' *Politics, Religion and Ideology* 14(3), 355–376.

Tooze, Adam. 2006. *The Wages of Destruction: The Making and Unmaking of the Nazi Economy*. London: Allen Lane.

Tooze, Adam. 2015. *The Deluge: The Great War and the Remaking of Global Order, 1916–1931*. New York: Penguin.

Turner, Henry Ashby. 2008. 'The Myth of Chancellor von Schleicher's *Querfront* Strategy.' *Central European History* 41(4), 673–681.

Walter, Dirk. 1999. *Antisemitische Kriminalität und Gewalt: Judenfeindschaft in der Weimarer Republik*. Bonn: Dietz.

Weitz, Eric D. 2007. *Weimar Germany: Promise and Tragedy*. Princeton, NJ: Princeton University Press.

Winkler, Heinrich-August. 1972. *Mittelstand, Demokratie und Nationalsozialismus: Die politische Entwicklung von Handwerk und Kleinhandel in der Weimarer Republik*. Cologne: Kiepenhauer & Witsch.

Winkler, Heinrich-August. 2005. *Die Geschichte der Ersten Deutschen Demokratie*, 4th edn. Munich: C.H. Beck.

Ziemann, Benjamin. 2013. *Contested Commemoration: Republican War Veterans and Weimar Political Culture*. Cambridge: Cambridge University Press.

Further Reading

Brockhaus, Gudrun, ed. 2014. *Attraktion der NS-Bewegung*. Essen: Klartext.
An anthology that exemplifies the state of the scholarship on the appeal of Nazism.

Canning, Kathleen, Barndt, Kerstin, and McGuire, Kristin, eds. 2010. *Weimar Publics/ Weimar Subjects. Rethinking the Political Culture of Germany in the 1920s*. New York and Oxford: Berghahn Books.
A selection of essays that cover range of topics in the current Weimar scholarship.

Jones, Larry Eugene, ed. 2013. *The German Right in the Weimar Republic: Studies in the History of German Conservatism, Nationalism, and Antisemitism*. New York and Oxford: Berghahn Books.
This collection of essays highlights current debates on German conservatism.

Kolb, Eberhard and Schumann, Dirk. 2013. *Die Weimarer Republik*, 8th edn. Munich: Oldenbourg.
A recent update of a long indispensable analysis of the numerous debates on Weimar.

McElligott, Anthony. 2014. *Rethinking the Weimar Republic: Authority and Authoritarianism 1916–1936*. London: Bloomsbury.
An excellent survey of Weimar through a single overarching theme.

Steiner, Zara. 2007. *The Lights That Failed: European International History 1919–1933*. Oxford: Oxford University Press.
An impressive scholarly achievement that illuminates the international context with which Weimar engaged.

Stibbe, Matthew. 2010. *Germany 1914–1933: Politics, Society and Culture*. Harlow, UK: Longman.
An excellent English-language survey of the debates on Germany from the outbreak of the First World War to the beginnings of the Nazi state.

Tooze, Adam. 2015. *The Deluge: The Great War and the Remaking of Global Order, 1916–1931*. New York: Penguin.
An international history that emphasizes the weaknesses of the American state and its implications.

Weitz, Eric D. 2007. *Weimar Germany: Promise and Tragedy*. Princeton, NJ: Princeton University Press.
An excellent synthesis of Weimar's potential and the sources of its downfall.

CHAPTER FIVE

National Socialist Ideology

CLAUS-CHRISTIAN W. SZEJNMANN

The inter-war period is often referred to as the 'Age of Extremes'. Many contemporaries were shaped by the horrendous experience of the First World War and its repercussions and felt anxious about rapid changes taking place in a world without certainties. This created unstable societies leading to various political-economic systems, including Bolshevism, fascism, National Socialism, and Francoism. Today we know that Hitler, Stalin, Mussolini, and Franco, despite establishing brutal dictatorships that practised persecution and mass murder – and, in the case of Nazi Germany, also genocide – depended on the support, mass participation, and (self)-mobilization of many people. In Germany, many 'ordinary' men and women saw National Socialism as the answer to their problems and were mobilized by its vision. This challenges our historical understanding and our faith in human nature.

This chapter focuses on the belief system of the Nazis and its relationship with German society. In post-1918 Germany, the dramatically politicized culture offered unique opportunities for political participation and collective action. At a time when many contemporaries diagnosed a society facing a profound crisis, a plethora of values, views, and visions for a better future circulated. During the new age of the masses, every proponent of alternative ideologies with real ambition to win mass support had to explain the ills in society and project a vision for a better future that resonated with contemporaries. Coming to power, and then staying in power, required legitimacy. The Nazis, like communists and other extremists, expressed a powerful critique of the contemporary world they lived in and promised to create something that functioned better than the existing liberal system, which seemed outdated and bankrupt. Instead, they proposed to create societies that were fairer and more just.

Our focus will be mainly, but not exclusively, on the period during the Nazi rise to power until 1933. This is when National Socialist ideology emerged and evolved, and set the foundation and direction for what happened during the dictatorship. This chapter reflects on a complex historiography which has seen dramatic shifts in

A Companion to Nazi Germany, First Edition. Edited by Shelley Baranowski,
Armin Nolzen, and Claus-Christian W. Szejnmann.
© 2018 John Wiley & Sons Ltd. Published 2018 by John Wiley & Sons Ltd.

interpretations and approaches as well as heated controversies. At the heart of the debate is often the relationship between Nazi ideology and German society, which seems to boil down to one key question: to what extent did racist-genocidal values resonate among Germans? However, this contribution is as much about how experts have tried to make sense of Nazi ideology as it is about drawing attention to existing gaps.

5.1 Historiography

Contemporary commentators expressed a view about National Socialism and its ideology that changed little for many decades. Whilst during the 1920s many recognized that the Nazi movement was dangerous and coined the phrase 'Hitler, that is war!' (Wippermann 2001, 18), many were dismissive about its ideology: Theodor Heuss stated that Nazi ideology lacked substance and coherence (Wippermann 2001, 11) whilst Thomas Mann described it as 'primitive popular vulgarity' (Mann 1994, 154). However, no other interpretation exerted such a long-term influence as Hermann Rauschning's book *Germany's Revolution of Destruction* (1939), which reduced Nazi ideology to little more than nihilistic and demagogic propaganda designed to deceive the population.

After 1945 there was a clear focus on the evil and irrational Hitler and his henchmen to explain Nazism and genocide: in the Anglo-Saxon countries there was a widespread belief that Hitler had exploited sinister traditions to mould a generation of brutal killers; at the Nuremberg trials only the Gestapo and the SS were classified as 'criminal organizations', and German perpetrators hid behind the motive of self-survival: apparently they would have risked their own lives if they had not followed orders. Ultimately this shifted the blame onto Hitler, who was dead (Szejnmann 2008, 25–29). While debates about Nazi ideology centred on the evilness of Hitler's apparent 'master plan' from the early 1920s, some 'intentionalists' increasingly highlighted a more serious and logical consistency behind his thinking and acting. Most importantly, Eberhard Jäckel concluded in his path-breaking study *Hitler's World View* (1969) that Hitler indeed had a consistent ideology that centred on antisemitism and foreign policy. This was fiercely questioned by the 'structuralists' led by Martin Broszat and Hans Mommsen, who insisted that Nazi ideology was little more than a propagandistic toy. Even on race – together with aggressive expansionism the only authentic component – the Nazis were contradictory as the road to Auschwitz was not straight but 'twisted'. Structuralists described a population that did not believe in the regime's ideological message and that was marked by resignation and compliance rather than enthusiasm. In short, the social history dominant of the 1970s was characterized by a split between 'ideology' and 'social context' (Eley 2013, 18).

Starting in the 1980s, major shifts in interpretation took place due to the 'cultural turn' in the discipline, leading to the growth of four key areas: women's history and gender analysis, everyday life history (*Alltagsgeschichte*), race hygiene, and the recognition of the centrality of the Holocaust. The shift of focus to the broader context and societal settings of Nazi ideas brought ideology back to the centre of discussion (Eley 2013, 18 f.). Most importantly, a growing number of experts (Burleigh and Wippermann 1991; Schmuhl 1987) emphasized that Nazi racism was not based on the crazy ideas of some fanatics but 'was deeply embedded in the philosophy and institutional structure of German biomedical sciences' (Eley 2013, 20). The once prominent interpretation that Nazism was an 'alien' ideology and movement that had seduced Germans made way to the dramatic recognition that it had grown from within society, that it had enjoyed considerable support for many of its visions and policies, and that many 'ordinary' men and women participated in its perpetration. These developments also heralded the replacement of class analysis by race as an explanatory concept of Nazism and the Third Reich. Whilst social historians had been looking at forms of inequality and hierarchy within the class structure of society in order to understand behaviour, they (and indeed most scholars working on Nazism at that time) had ignored Nazism's two most crucial aspects: the regime's popularity and endurance, and the policies of biological racism and genocide (for an honest reflection, see Mason 1993, 282). This cemented the model of the 'racial state' which was dominated by biological rather than social categories (Eley 2013, 21), and overcame the claim that workers were immune to Nazism (Schneider 1999; Schmiechen-Ackermann 1998; Fischer 1996).

However, did all this actually mean, as Daniel Goldhagen famously claimed in the mid-1990s, that it was not the Nazis but the German people who were ultimately the driving force behind the Holocaust due to their deep-rooted and eliminationist antisemitism (Goldhagen 1996)? This raised uncomfortable questions about the extent of perpetration and focused attention on antisemitism: how important was the latter in explaining the Holocaust and the motivation of perpetrators? Ensuing research suggests that the Nazi elite's extreme racism was central in explaining their motivation and behaviour: they committed crimes due to ideological conviction. However, even among the core Nazis the topic of race is complex: (i) there were substantial differences in racial thinking between Nazi ideologues (Stone 2016; Smelser and Zitelmann 1993); (ii) whilst the racial thinking of key planners and executioners of the Holocaust made genocide possible, genocide depended on cumulative radicalization (Wildt 2003, 866); (iii) substantial differences amongst the Nazi elite created uncertain policies towards Jewish *Mischlinge*, Jews living in mixed marriages, and mixed marriages between Germans and 'racially inferiors' (Meyer 1999; Kundrus 2009).

The extent and depth of antisemitism among the wider population is much more contentious. Scholars have argued that during the Weimar Republic a new antisemitism emerged based on racial ideology, which established itself as the predominant form of discourse on the 'Jewish question'. However, it remains controversial whether in the course of the 1920s antisemitism had become a 'mass phenomenon' (Hecht 2003) or whether it was, above all, part of the fundamental conviction of the political right (Walter 1999) (for two opposing views on the Third Reich, see Bajohr and Pohl 2006 and Longerich 2006). Most experts today find it difficult to square National Socialism's racist core ideology with mass mobilization before 1933. Richard Evans argued:

> The men who joined paramilitary associations like the Nazis' brownshirted Storm Divisions (SA) often had only the vaguest idea of Nazi ideology. For many of them, violence became a way of life, almost a substitute for ideology … These were

extreme views [i.e. racial struggle for world leadership and living space in which degenerates and enemies were eliminated; CS], and it is not surprising that they failed to exert much attraction for the great majority of Germans for most of the Weimar Republic. ... Nevertheless, the rapid rise in support of the Nazis ... would not have been possible had many Germans not shared at least some of their ideological commitments, even if only in a very watered-down form ... Many people supported the Nazis either because they discounted some of their more extreme views, or because they were ignorant of them, or because they despaired of the alternatives. (Evans 2008, 44, 46)

This mirrors the widespread interpretation that genocidal antisemitism and the conquest of territory in the East were not important nor suitable for the mass mobilization; and that the Nazi success in coming to power 'was based not least on the vagueness of its programme, which sought to be all things to all voters' (Evans 2008, 28). What then explains Nazi success if not ideology? Hans-Ulrich Wehler lists the following factors: 'the cult of the leader, Hitler's charismatic impact, the return to national greatness, radical revision of the Versailles order, "Volksgemeinschaft" and national ascent to overcome the crisis' (Wehler 2003, 580). These are all broad phenomena in society – plus Hitler (we come back to this apparent separation between them and ideology). Furthermore, the tendency to emphasize manipulation over ideology continues to play an important role. A special issue commemorating 75 years of Hitler's seizure of power by *Der Spiegel* magazine emphasized Hitler's focus on propaganda and Goebbels' propaganda skills, claiming: 'The NSDAP of the Weimar Republic ... was basically a propaganda movement' (Sontheimer 2008). However, theories of seduction and manipulation raise various issues. To start with, voters lose their autonomy and are thus not taken seriously – this proved extremely convenient for East and West Germany to legitimize a new and unblemished start after 1945. Also, anyone who looks at the Nazi message in the context of propaganda should be aware that this is not the same as analysing its ideology. For the Nazis, propaganda was a means to an end – in other words, a strategy to realize a vision for society – and it is only in the latter that we find their ideology. Finally, it does not take seriously the Nazis' willingness and ability to engage and persuade with arguments and ideas. This is not meant to downplay the central role of violence, 'recklessness', and 'organisational dynamism' (Mommsen 2000, 112 f.), and the emergence of a kind of new post-First World War lifestyle among extremists like Hitler and Gregor Strasser for whom in 1918 the war never ended, but instead human history became reduced to the principles of struggle and war (Hartmann et al. 2016, 45).

5.2   Nazi Ideology 'from below'

Within the Nazi movement there were wide-ranging and lively discussions about political visions and objectives that mirrored diverse and sometimes contradictory opinions on various topics. Nazis delivered countless speeches and published a substantial body of political thought in the form of books, articles, and programmes. According to Barbara Miller Lane and Leila J. Rupp, the ideas of various Nazi leaders were distinctive, shifted over time, and formed 'a doctrine in the process of rapid development into which new ideas were continually introduced' (1978, xi). The diversity of the Nazi movement becomes evident when looking at its range of publications. By the early 1930s, the Nazis were publishing at least 120 newspapers (Deutsches Institut für Zeitungskunde 1932, 27), specialized publications for party activists (teachers, workers, etc.), and publications with a specific local purpose such as *Häuserblockzeitungen* (newspapers for housing blocks) or factory newspapers. True, the Nazis only published an extremely small fraction of contemporary newspapers and non-daily papers and magazines, which were dominated by the political right. However, with the exception of the three NSDAP flagship newspapers – the Munich headquarters' *Völkischer Beobachter*, Joseph Goebbels' Berlin paper *Der Angriff*, and Julius Streicher's notorious antisemitic paper *Der Stürmer* – most of the other Nazi publications are hardly known. There were similarities but also considerable differences between these publications. Some Nazi newspapers were written mainly for farmers, workers, or middle-class people; some editors pushed more nationalist or socialist messages; and all editors had to respond to their specific local and regional political, economic, and cultural environment (see images of newspaper covers and accompanying commentary).

Berliner Arbeiter-Zeitung, 28.7.1929

Coburger National-Zeitung, 1.10.1930 (© Institut für Zeitungsforschung, Dortmund)

Niedersachsen Stürmer, 24.1.1931

Der Märkische Adler, Nr. 1, 1928 (© Universitätsbibliothek der Humboldt-Universität zu Berlin, Historische Sammlungen: Fa 60136/6:F4

Comment: At first glance, the four newspaper front pages illustrated indicate very little about the NSDAP. Most local and regional NSDAP newspaper covers include images that literally blend into the local milieu, such as the eagle on *Der Märkische Adler*, the hammer and sickle on the *Berliner Arbeiter-Zeitung*, the castle on the *Coburger National-Zeitung*, and the horse rider and the plain countryside with a traditional farmhouse on the cover of the *Niedersachsen Stürmer*. Similarly, the names of the papers often refer to a region or a town in the title, whilst the reference to the NSDAP was often reserved for the subtitle.

Existing knowledge about National Socialist ideology is largely based on the writings and speeches of well-known Nazi leaders such as Hitler, Goebbels, Himmler, and Rosenberg (Hitler 1980, 1992–2003; *Die Tagebücher Goebbels* 1998–2006; Piper 2015; Longerich 2012; Kershaw 1998). Even though there remain uncertainties and disagreements about various aspects of Hitler's ideology – a lack of sources means that Hitler's activities during the post-revolutionary period remain clouded in mystery; and whilst we have a good idea about what Hitler read and who influenced his ideas, here too remain uncertainties (Hartmann et al. 2016, 56ff.; Töppel 2016; Weber 2010; Hamann 1999) – most scholars agree on Hitler's core view: human development was based on an eternal social Darwinist struggle; the exclusion and then elimination of the Jews as they threatened the 'racial hygiene' of the Aryan 'master race'; the acquisition of *Lebensraum* in the East. In broad terms, Hitler's ideology comprised of four central ideas: 'The idea of race, the idea of space, the idea of violence, and finally the idea of dictatorship' (Hartmann et al. 2016, 45).

What is often lost sight of is that the Nazi movement was an extremely dynamic movement comprising of much more than the core Nazi leadership. Within it, communication flowed in all directions: top-down, bottom-up, and horizontally (for the external side, see the next section). Scholarship about district leaders – their background, motivation, and views (Stelbrink 2003; Arbogast 1998) – or literally thousands of speeches of lesser known party activists is hardly picked up except in the most specialized literature. The situation is similar in relation to NSDAP publications and internal party correspondence that contains countless contributions from 'normal' party members to local officials and regional and national representatives about many aspects of their movement – including its aims and visions and how to translate these into practice – and broader issues in society. In short, we lack a comprehensive and comparative analysis of all the material discussed above that reflects the considerable diversity of Nazi ideology, and that locates it in the broader context of society. Similarly, there have been no systematic attempts to synergize the rich findings of how the Nazis operated beyond their Munich headquarters in local and regional settings, and with what effect (Szejnmann 2003, 2014a).

5.3   Was There a Core Set of Beliefs?

According to the traditional view, Hitler handled ideology within the Nazi movement pragmatically, following the dictum that the broader the 'ideological church' of Nazism, the more supporters could be won over (Tyrell 1993, 34). This worked because Hitler stood above these ideological differences, as ultimate loyalty was to the Führer. This thesis convinces in many ways, but the pitfall is again that it shifts all the focus and ownership onto Hitler. Indeed, whilst most scholars agree that National Socialism from 1921 onwards was always the Hitler movement – later the NSDAP proclaimed during election campaigns: 'Our Programme is called Hitler' – even this 'world-historical individual' (Wehler 2003, 551) depended on interaction with his party and the wider society. For this reason, most scholars have been at pains to point out that Nazism was not just Hitlerism.

Once more, this raises fundamental questions about the nature of Nazi ideology. Thomas Klepsch, in a little-known book from 1990, argued that there was indeed a coherent Nazi ideology that worked internally and interacted with the wider society (Klepsch 1990, esp. 244–249; summarized in Ziemann and Szejnmann 2013, 329–330). Its core was expressed in the 1920 party programme, Hitler's *Mein Kampf*, and the draft programme of the Strasser brothers. Other aspects were added thereafter. In the economic sphere, the visions of a national, corporate idealist economic system and the claim that increasing unemployment and cutbacks in social welfare were felt to be 'the result of an economy that was deformed by the "Slavery of Interest", reparation payments, class war and selfishness' – and very recently, Chris Szejnmann emphasized the importance of anti-capitalism as a central component of Nazi ideology and as key explanation for Nazi success during the world economic crisis (Szejnmann 2013, 2014b; also see section 5.4 below). In the political sphere, the Führer principle replaced the idea of a Germanic Führer democracy. In foreign affairs, there was a belief that national strength was regained by internal unity and rearmament, and that a powerful Germany would expand towards the East. Finally, in the sociocultural sphere, the Nazis harboured gender-specific ideas: boys were supposed to receive a paramilitary education, while girls were prepared early on for their anticipated role as mothers. According to Klepsch, these segments were linked up and united into one ideology by two delusions (*Wahnvorstellungen*) that provided Nazi ideology with a 'centre of gravity:' the patho-logical anxiety about the Bolshevist Soviet Union, and the pathological hatred of Jews. Overall then, Klepsch described Nazi ideology as a 'pulsating structure' (*pulsierendes Gebilde*) that had an insane core, and whose periphery consisted of ideological segments that could be varied according to specific needs. As a result, the Nazis were able to react with flexibility at the periphery without losing their ideological cohesion.

More recently, Lutz Raphael described the emergence of a diverse Nazi world-view that left room for opposing views and legitimate controversies (Raphael 2006; also see 2014). According to him, key elements of the world-view of the Nazi elite around Hitler were never presented to the public as a fixed canon. Instead there was often reference to 'National Socialist thoughts' and related keywords such as '*Volksgemeinschaft*', 'Reich', 'Führer', or 'race' which were vague and widely used in pre-1933 society. In fact, the closeness and openness of Nazi ideology towards other ideas and concepts, some of which had little to do with racist antisemitism (for example its pseudo-religious cult of the nation or militarism), was a specific strength and contributed to its easy transmission. This was helped by the Nazis' incorporation of diffuse desires and expectations for a radical change or a new beginning after the disappointments and difficulties of the post-war years. Once liberal-democratic and Marxist ideas were excluded from public discourse at the beginning of the dictatorship (and then demonized as ideological enemies), a broad field of opinions could be articulated – as long as they did not challenge the core elements of Nazi ideology. In short, Raphael described the emergence of a heterogeneous Nazi world-view from 1933 that was marked by a weakly controlled plurality that left room for opposing views and legitimate controversies.

5.4 Towards a Social and Cultural History of Nazi ideology

An understanding of Nazi ideology as a 'pulsating structure' is a helpful way of locating its place in wider culture and society. The 'cultural turn' over the last 30 years has increasingly made historians look at the 'ideological traffic between "Germans" and "Nazis"' (Fritzsche 2008, 7) and shared dispositions in culture and mentalities. This reflects the general trend that the reduction of ideology to intellectual history is disappearing and that intellectual history has become more closely linked to cultural and social history. In the face of this, it became obvious that the narrow view of Nazi ideology comprised of the NSDAP's 25-point pro-gramme and Hitler's *Mein Kampf* had to be overcome by a radical broadening and deepening of the perspective. For example, numerous studies about the rise of the Nazis have emphasized the cohesion of the nationalist milieu around a set of core beliefs that coexisted with many disagreements and organizational divisions (Rohkrämer 2007; Szejnmann 1999, 2000; Pyta 1996). Of course, it is essential that the scholarship continues to emphasize progressive and pluralistic areas of German society and resists the trap of the inevitability of Nazism's rise to power (Canning, Barndt, and McGuire 2013; McElligott 2009). Naturally, we have significant knowledge about the embeddedness, or not, of Nazi ideology in some areas of German culture and society. Scholarship about the relationship between the *völkisch* movement, 'Conservative Revolution', and Nazism has charted complex intellectual and organizational networks that were unified by a commitment to inequality (Breuer 2011) and that were seeking radical answers in response to what they perceived as a comprehensive cultural crisis (Kellogg 2005; Schmitz and Vollnhals 2005). Overall, however, more research is needed to locate Nazism more fully in the various spheres of culture and society. What role did it play in various networks and belief systems? What exactly were the commonalities and differences? How did Nazi ideology itself spread into broader circles and affected individuals? What is the importance of time, place, gender, age, and language?

In the following, we want to show the potentials of research focusing on the construction of semantics, mechanisms of popularization, and cultural multiplication factors. In a pioneering work attempting to grasp the precise meaning of the constituent parts of the semantics of Nazi ideology, Klaus Holz analysed Hitler's first major antisemitic speech from 13 August 1920 (Holz 2010). He showed how Hitler constructed utopias which made him suggest the exclusion and persecution of the Jews. Hitler's antisemitic semantics interpreted modern societies, situated individuals in it, constructed collective identities, and suggested a future vision for society (Holz 2010, 362). Derek Hastings (2010) analysed the complex evolution of the Nazi movement in Munich and demonstrated the existence of a Catholic–Nazi synthesis that peaked in 1923. He argued that Nazism was transformed in the mid-1920s from a political movement that was closely intertwined with a distinctive Catholic tradition in the Bavarian capital and championed the principle of Positive Christianity. It was initially formulated and publicized as the official Nazi antidote to the 'Jewish-materialistic spirit', becoming a political religion in its own right that was based on the messianic Hitler cult with national ambitions and a much broader appeal. Finally, Chris Szejnmann's work on the role of anti-capitalism in Nazi ideology and its broader appeal shows the way the Nazis benefited during the world economic slump from a powerful anti-capitalist *Zeitgeist* based on economic and moral-ethical considerations (2013, 2014b). Nazi economic thought and rhetoric were central to the Nazi rise to power and provided the party with a crucial legitimacy and authenticity to succeed against what many regarded as the broken liberal economic system. For this to work, it was crucial that the core economic visions expressed by the Nazis early on – demanding state control but allowing private initiatives that benefited the common good; championing autarky and withdrawal from international cooperation in favour of nationalist policies – turned into widely accepted economic views during the slump. But why did contemporaries open themselves up to this? The analysis of Nazi ideology and rhetoric in the context of contemporary culture, and how this again was influenced by historical developments, led to new insights. The key was the Nazis' active engagement with a society that shared widespread anti-capitalist sentiments during the specific crisis conditions of the slump from the late 1920s. The Nazis' appeal depended less on fighting the enemy or presenting a clearly defined party programme than on persuading 'the other' by using commonly used language and metaphors that often hid different meanings (also Brown 2009).

Recent research emphasizes the importance of the concept of the *Volksgemeinschaft* ('people's community') and its roots among the nationalist right, the liberals, and the left in Weimar Germany in helping to explain how the Nazis benefited from deep-rooted sentiments and longings (Wildt 2009, 2014). This refers to the Nazi vision of overcoming class divisions and forming one harmonious *Volkskörper* (people's body) that restores Germany's greatness. It projected an egalitarian utopia for society whilst describing a plan of action: everything had to be subject to the 'common good' instead of serving the 'self-interest'. This was not only a key vision that helped it win mass support during the Weimar Republic, but it is also essential in explaining growing and enduring mass support and (self-)mobilization amongst Germans during the Third Reich (Schmiechen-Ackermann 2012; Steber and Gotto 2014; Wildt 2008).

Why did the concept of *Volksgemeinschaft*, but also anti-capitalism, work so powerfully in favour of Nazism? During the extreme crisis from the late 1920s onwards, the longing for *Volksgemeinschaft* and the sentiment that the liberal capital economic system was devastating for Germany unleashed unprecedented activity and energy among Nazi supporters and mobilized large parts of the nation. The underlying driver for this was the longing to overcome alienation in modernity through both revolution and restoration. Even though the *Volksgemeinschaft* and anti-capitalism were complex and multilayered phenomena with diverse meanings, an increasing number of contemporaries identified the Nazis as their leading proponents. The Nazis benefited from a general rhetoric and dynamic that was directed against the existing system, and the uncertainty whether the existing international liberal capitalist system would survive the crisis at all. The Nazis proclaimed that society required a 'moral recovery' in which 'work', 'performance', and 'responsibility' became core ideals and where everyone strived to work for the 'common good'. This vision was contrasted with individualist-liberalism that centred on selfishness and profit, and which had destroyed deep-seated human morals and values. This vision, including the words and slogans they used, struck a deep emotional resonance in society.

Clearly, when discussing the NS (National Socialist) *Volksgemeinschaft* or anti-capitalism, one should avoid talking about something 'real' – social and economic reality and Nazi propaganda talk must be differentiated. At the same time, one should not simply dismiss this but should take seriously these phenomena as integrative parts of Nazi ideology before and after 1933. Finally, and crucially, from the end of the 1920s, Nazi activists often did not discuss their vision within a coherent and complex racial theory. The 'decoupling' of the different parts meant that Nazi semantics took on the function of a door-opener since not all contemporaries understood the racially loaded terms and their NS interpretation (Szejnmann 2013, 2014b). Arguably, 'National Socialist terminology was … characterized by a polyvalence of meaning which permitted a richness of ideological variants and pre-conditioned its flexibility. To contemporaries, ideology indeed appeared as a net of concepts and metaphors which was superimposed on everyday life and became increasingly impossible to escape' (Steber 2014, 27). Peter Fritzsche argued: 'Germans became Nazis because they wanted to become Nazis and because the Nazis spoke so well to their interests and inclinations' (Fritzsche 1998, 8). What then was so appealing about the Nazis? Not their racial prejudices, but their vision of a new nation that corresponded to a populist ethnic nationalism and individual desires for social mobility, both ensuring national well-being (Fritzsche 1998, 9, 209). The key then is that the Nazis coupled their attack against the system with a positive vision of renewal: to build a German society that not only worked better but was also substantially fairer. In this sense, the world economic crisis fed the widespread hope for fundamental renewal (Graf 2008) – and some argued that this unique world-historical epochal break demanded decisive action to realize a better future. This was a society which was still strongly influenced by Christian language and metaphors of existential dualism of good and bad, light and darkness, catastrophic present and redemptive future. In this situation, the transition from ideology to utopia was fluent, and for broad sections of society the realization of utopia seemed possible (Hardtwig 2003, 6–8).

5.5 Conclusions

Why does Nazi ideology before 1933 matter? The simple answer is that it helps us to explain why the Nazis managed to become so popular in the first place; why, under a democracy, large sections of society trusted this violent and racist movement not only to run their country but also to bring about major change; and why during a totalitarian racist dictatorship they were able to penetrate and mobilize society so comprehensively through top-down ideologization and self-mobilization.

Nazi ideology understood in a broad context was intrinsically linked to and interwoven with German society and the emotions and motivations, conscious and unconscious, of many of its people. This helps us to understand the binding force and dynamic nature of the Nazi national community, and the connection the Nazis made with 'German traditions and national expectations in a historically unique constellation of German and European history' (Bialas 2014, 16); and most profoundly, and in relation to the unfolding of racial persecution, murder, and genocide against minority groups, how the shift was possible from humanism and Christian charity and welfare ethics, to *völkisch* racism and the formation of biological-moral attitudes (Bialas 2014, 11). Geoff Eley has commented:

> Whereas the ideas themselves were important, Nazi ideology was as much to be found embedded and embodied in social practices and social relations as it was inside people's heads: in what they did as well as what they thought, in their relationships and their actions, and in the structured circumstances – small scale, material, quotidian – where they did them. (Eley 2013, 102)

The Nazis postulated a radical vision that provided them with a legitimacy and authenticity in their struggle to succeed the existing liberal system. Many of their views had deep historical and ideological roots in German society, tapped into widespread values, beliefs, and emotions, and were fundamentally built around a vision and promise that was projected into the future. While extreme antisemitism and social Darwinist expansion were key drivers for Nazi leaders and core activists, this was not necessarily the case for its broader constituency. During the world economic crisis the Nazis benefited from an 'anti-system' rallying cry that condemned the divisions, unfairness, and failures of the existing system and questioned its future viability. Most importantly, in the fierce battle between ideologies after the First World War they presented their vision of the *Volksgemeinschaft* – 'German socialism' based on work and performance and subject to the principle of 'common good before selfishness' – as the only viable alternative to (i) international 'selfish' capitalism that looked broken and decadent, (ii) 'Marxist international socialism', and (iii) the class divisions and class struggle inherent in both. The Nazis seemed to offer a new solution to the inherent tensions in modern capitalism between the well-being of and rewards for the individual and the whole society by meeting demands for radical change *and* longing for continuity and restoration. According to Claudia Koonz:

> Nazism fulfilled the functions we associate with ideology. It supplied answers to life's imponderables, provided meaning in the face of contingency, and explained the way the world works. It also defined good and evil, condemning self-interest as immoral and enshrining altruism as virtuous. Binding ethnic comrades (*Volksgenossen*) to their ancestors and descendents, Nazi ideals embedded the individual within the collective well-being of the nation. (Koonz 2005, 2)

We should take seriously the attempts by the Nazis to *persuade* Germans: how they interacted with society and its culture; how they were shaped by it and contributed to it themselves; how they negotiated themselves through shared visions and values and differences and conflicts. Key to this was the way they used commonly shared slogans and metaphors – including those originally shaped by Marxists, proponents of national etatism, and that of the Catholic Church – which they reloaded with their own values and meanings (Szejnmann 2013). Nevertheless, while by 1932 many Germans were mobilized by the Nazi vision – including many who fully understood the Nazi concept of a biological-utilitarian *Volksgemeinschaft* and 'social justice' based on notions of *inequality* – the core constituency of organized labour and Catholicism clung to their traditional values and world-views. However, the undercurrent values and visions in German society and their trajectory made a shift towards Nazism during the Third Reich possible.

If the ongoing trend to historicize National Socialism has made experts look beyond the stigma of 'irrational' and 'evil' into analysing broad societal connections, other developments are significantly changing our perspective too: in particular, the trend to view historical developments in a broader international context. Long gone is the time when Nazi ideology was seen as the culmination of exclusively German intellectual traditions. Today we know that its ideology draws on beliefs and ideas from many countries (e.g. Kellogg 2005); Nazism is increasingly viewed as part of imperialist expansion and empire building (Baranowski 2011); and many experts see the Nazi Holocaust no longer as a unique historical event but as an example of an extreme genocide with parallels in other countries in the modern era. Hence Mark Mazower recently observed: 'National Socialism … fits into the mainstream not only of German but also of European history far more comfortably than most people like to admit' (Mazower 2008, xii).

References

Arbogast, Christine. 1998. *Herrschaftsinstancen der württembergischen NSDAP. Funktion, Sozialprofil und Lebenswege einer regionalen NS-Elite 1920–1960*. Munich: De Gruyter Oldenbourg.

Bajohr, Frank and Pohl, Dieter. 2006. *Massenmord und schlechtes Gewissen: Die deutsche Bevölkerung, die NS-Führung und der Holocaust*. Frankfurt am Main: Fischer.

Baranowski, Shelley. 2011. *Nazi Empire: German Colonialism and Imperialism from Bismarck to Hitler*. Cambridge: Cambridge University Press.

Bialas, Wolfgang. 2014. *Moralische Ordnungen des Nationalsozialismus*. Göttingen: Vandenhoeck & Ruprecht.

Breuer, Stefan. 2011. *Ordnungen der Ungleichheit: Die deutsche Rechte im Widerstreit ihrer Ideen 1871–1945*. Darmstadt: Wissenschaftliche Buchgesellschaft.

Brown, Timothy S. 2009. *Weimar Radicals: Nazis and Communists between Authenticity and Performance*. New York: Berghahn Books.

Burleigh, Michael and Wippermann, Wolfgang. 1991. *The Racial State*. Cambridge: Cambridge University Press.

Canning, Kathleen, Barndt Kerstin, and McGuire, Kristin, eds. 2013. *Weimar Publics / Weimar Subjects: Rethinking the Political Culture or Germany in the 1920s*. New York: Berghahn Books.

Deutsches Institut für Zeitungskunde. 1932. *Handbuch der Deutschen Tagespresse*, 4th edn. Berlin: Deutsches Institut für Zeitungskunde.

Die Tagebücher von Joseph Goebbels. Aufzeichnungen 1923–1941. 1998–2006, edited by Elke Fröhlich. 9 vols. Munich: K.G. Saur.

Eley, Geoff. 2013. *Nazism as Fascism: Violence, Ideology, and the Ground of Consent in Germany 1930–1945*. London: Routledge.

Evans, Richard J. 2008. 'The Emergence of Nazi Ideology.' In *Nazi Germany*, edited by Jane Caplan, 26–47. Oxford: Oxford University Press.

Fischer, Conan, ed. 1996. *The Rise of National Socialism and the Working Classes in Weimar Germany*. Oxford: Berghahn Books.

Fritzsche, Peter. 1998. *Germans into Nazis*. Cambridge, MA: Harvard University Press.

Fritzsche, Peter. 2008. *Life and Death in the Third Reich*. Cambridge, MA: Harvard University Press.

Goldhagen, Daniel J. 1996. *Hitler's Willing Executioners: Ordinary Germans and the Holocaust*. London: Little, Brown.

Graf, Rüdiger. 2008. *Die Zukunft der Weimarer Republik: Krisen und Zukunftsaneignungen in Deutschland 1918–1933*. Munich: Oldenbourg.

Hamann, Brigitte. 1999. *Hitler's Vienna: A Portrait of the Tyrant as a Young Man*. Oxford: Oxford University Press.

Hardtwig, Wolfgang 2003. 'Einleitung: Utopie und politische Herrschaft im Europa der Zwischenkriegszeit.' In *Utopie und politische Herrschaft im Europa der Zwischenkriegszeit*, edited by Wolfgang Hardtwig, 1–12. Munich: Oldenbourg.

Hartmann, Christian, et al. 2016. *Hitler, Mein Kampf: Eine kritische Edition*. Vol. 1. Munich and Berlin: Institut für Zeitgeschichte.

Hastings, Derek. 2010. *Catholicism and the Roots of Nazism: Religious Identity and National Socialism*. Oxford: Oxford University Press.

Hecht, Cornelia. 2003. *Deutsche Juden und Antisemitismus in der Weimarer Republik*. Bonn: Dietz.

Hitler, Adolf. 1980. *Sämtliche Aufzeichnungen 1905–1924*. Edited by Eberhard Jäckel and Axel Kuhn. Stuttgart: Deutsche Verlags-Anstalt.

Hitler, Adolf. 1992–2003. *Reden, Schriften, Anordnungen, Februar 1925 bis Januar 1933*. Edited by Institut für Zeitgeschichte, 6 vols (in 13 partial vols). Munich: K.G. Saur.

Holz, Klaus. 2010. *Nationaler Antisemitismus: Wissenssoziologie einer Weltanschauung*, new edn. Hamburg: Hamburger Edition.

Jäckel, Eberhard. 1969. *Hitlers Weltanschauung: Entwurf einer Herrschaft*. Tübingen: Rainer Wunderlich Verlag [Translated as Eberhard Jäckel. 1981. *Hitler's World View. A Blueprint for Power*. Cambridge, MA: Harvard University Press.]

Kellogg, Michael. 2005. *The Russian Roots of Nazism: White Émigrés and the Making of National Socialism 1917–1945*. Cambridge: Cambridge University Press.

Kershaw, Ian. 1998. *Hitler. 1989–1936: Hubris*. London: Penguin.

Klepsch, Thomas. 1990. *Nationalsozialistische Ideologie: Eine Beschreibung ihrer Struktur vor 1933*. Münster: Lit.

Koonz, Claudia. 2005. *The Nazi Conscience*. Cambridge, MA: Harvard University Press.

Kundrus, Birthe. 2009. 'Regime der Differenz. Volkstumspolitische Inklusionen und Exklusionen im Warthegau und im Generalgouvernement 1939–1944.' In *Volksgemeinschaft. Neue Forschungen zur Gesellschaft des Nationalsozialismus*, edited by Frank Bajohr and Michael Wildt. 105–123. Frankfurt am Main: Fischer.

Longerich, Peter. 2006. *'Davon haben wir nichts gewusst!' Die Deutschen und die Judenverfolgung 1933–1945*. Munich: Pantheon.

Longerich, Peter. 2012. *Heinrich Himmler*. Oxford: Oxford University Press.

Mann, Thomas. 1994. 'An Appeal to Reason (1930).' In *The Weimar Republic Sourcebook*, edited by Anton Kaes, Martin Jay, and Edward Dimendberg. 150–159. Berkeley: University of California Press.

Mason, Timothy W. 1993. *Social Policy in the Third Reich: The Working Class and the 'National Community'*. Oxford: Oxford University Press.

Mazower, Mark. 2008. *Hitler's Empire: Nazi Rule in Occupied Europe*. London: Penguin.

McElligott, Anthony ed. 2009. *Weimar Germany*. Oxford: Oxford University Press.

Meyer, Beate. 1999. *'Jüdische Mischlinge': Rassenpolitik und Verfolgungserfahrungen 1933–1945*. Hamburg: Dölling & Galitz.

Miller Lane, Barbara and Rupp, Leila J., eds. 1978. *Nazi Ideology before 1933: A Documentation*. Manchester: Manchester University Press.

Mommsen, Hans. 2000. 'The Nazi Regime: Revolution or Counterrevolution?' In *The Problem of Revolution in Germany, 1789–1989*, edited by Reinhard Rürup, 209–128. Oxford: Berg.

Piper, Ernst. 2015. *Alfred Rosenberg: Hitlers Chefideologe*. Munich: Allitera Verlag.

Pyta, Wolfram. 1996. *Dorfgemeinschaft und Parteipolitik 1918–1933: Die Verschränkung von Milieu und Parteien in den protestantischen Landgebieten Deutschlands in der Weimarer Republik*. Düsseldorf: Droste.

Raphael, Lutz. 2006. 'Die Nationalsozialistische Weltanschauung. Profil, Verbreitungsformen und Nachleben.' In *Kriegsende 1945. Befreiung oder Niederlage für die Deutschen? Gedanken über die Hintergründe des Rechtsextremismus in der Bundesrepublik Deutschland*, edited by Günter Gehl, 27–42. Weimar: Bertuch Verlag Gmbh.

Raphael, Lutz. 2014. 'Pluralities of National Socialist Ideology: New Perspectives on the Production and Diffusion of National Socialist Weltanschauung.' In *Visions of Community in Nazi Germany: Social Engineering and Private Lives*, edited by Martina Steber and Bernhard Gotto, 73–86. Oxford: Oxford University Press.

Rauschning, Hermann. 1939. *Germany's Revolution of Destruction*. London: William Heinemann.

Rohkrämer, Thomas. 2007. *A Single Communal Faith?: The German Right from Conservatism to National Socialism*. Oxford: Berghahn Books.

Schmiechen-Ackermann, Detlef. 1998. *Nationalsozialismus und Arbeitermilieus: Der nationalsozialistische Angriff auf die proletarischen Wohnquartiere und die Reaktion in den sozialistischen Vereinen*. Bonn: Dietz.

Schmiechen-Ackermann, Detlef, ed. 2012. *'Volksgemeinschaft': Mythos, wirkungsmächtige soziale Verheißung oder soziale Realität im 'Dritten Reich'?: Zwischenbilanz einer kontroversen Debatte* Paderborn: Schoeningh.

Schmitz, Walter and Vollnhals, Clemens, eds. 2005. *Völkische Bewegung, Konservative Revolution, Nationalsozialismus: Aspeckte einer politisierten Kultur*. Dresden: W.E.B. Universitätsverlag.

Schmuhl, Hans-Walter. 1987. *Rassenhygiene, Nationalsozialismus, Euthanasie: Von der Verhüttung zur Vernichtung 'lebensunwerten Lebens', 1890–1945*. Göttingen: Vandenhoeck & Ruprecht.

Schneider, Michael. 1999. *Unterm Hakenkreuz. Arbeiter und Arbeiterbewegung 1933 bis 1939*. Bonn: Dietz.

Smelser, Ronald and Zitelmann, Rainer, eds. 1993. *The Nazi Elite*. London: Palgrave.

Sontheimer, Michael. 2008. 'Verwirrte Empfindungen'. In *Hitler's Machtergreifung. 30. Januar 1933: Der Anfang vom Untergang. Spiegel Spezial Geschichte*, 29 January. http://www.spiegel.de/spiegel/spiegelspecialgeschichte/d-55573714.html (accessed 7 September 2016).

Steber, Martina. 2014. 'Regions and National Socialist Ideology: Reflections on Contained Plurality.' In *Heimat, Region, and Empire. Spatial Identities under National Socialism*, edited by Claus-Christian W. Szejnmann and Maiken Umbach, 25–42. Basingstoke, UK: Palgrave Macmillan.

Steber, Martina and Gotto, Bernhard, eds. 2014. *Visions of Community in Nazi Germany: Social Engineering and Private Lives*. Oxford: Oxford University Press.

Stelbrink, Wolfgang. 2003. *Die Kreisleiter der NSDAP in Westfalen-Lippe: Versuch einer Kollektivbiographie mit biographischem Anhang*. Münster: Nordrhein-Westfälisches Staatsarchiv.

Stone, Dan 2016. 'Nazi Race Ideologues.' *Patterns of Prejudice* 50(4–5), 445–457.

Szejnmann, Claus-Christian W. 1999. *Nazism in Central Germany: The Brownshirts in 'Red' Saxony*. Oxford: Berghahn Books.

Szejnmann, Claus-Christian W. 2000. *Vom Traum zum Alptraum. Sachsen während der Weimarer Republik*. Dresden: Gustav Kiepenheuer.

Szejnmann, Claus-Christian W. 2003. 'Verwässerung oder Systemstabilisierung? Nationalsozialismus in Regionen des Deutschen.' *Neue Politische Literatur* 48, 208–250.

Szejnmann, Claus-Christian W. 2008. 'Perpetrators of the Holocaust: A Historiography.' In *Ordinary People as Mass Murderers. Perpetrators in Comparative Perspectives*, edited by Olaf Jensen and Claus-Christian W. Szejnmann, 25–54. Basingstoke, UK: Palgrave Macmillan.

Szejnmann, Claus-Christian W. 2013. 'Nazi Economic Thought and Rhetoric During the Weimar Republic: Capitalism and its Discontents.' *Politics, Religion & Ideology* 14, 355–376.

Szejnmann, Claus-Christian W. 2014a. 'Regionalgeschichte und die Erforschung des Nationalsozialismus. Forschungsstand und Forschungsperspektiven.' In *Sachsen und der Nationalsozialismus*, edited by Günther Heydemann, Jan Erik Schulte, and Francesca Weil, 21–40. Göttingen: Vandenhoeck & Ruprecht.

Szejnmann, Claus-Christian W. 2014b. 'Semantik der Kapitalismuskritik in Deutschland nach dem Ersten Weltkrieg.' In *Wirtschaftskrisen als Wendepunkte: Ursachen, Folgen und historische Einordnungen vom Mittelalter bis zur Gegenwart*, edited by Stephan Lehnstaedt and Dariusz Adamczyk, 77–99. Osnabrück: Fibre-Verlag.

Töppel, Roman. 2016. '"Volk und Rasse". Hitlers Quellen auf der Spur.' *Vierteljahreshefte für Zeitgeschichte* 64, 1–35.

Tyrell, Albrecht. 1993. 'Gottfried Feder: The Failed Policy-maker.' In *The Nazi Elite*, edited by Ronald Smelser and Rainer Zitelmann, 28–38. London: Palgrave.

Walter, Dirk. 1999. *Antisemitische Kriminalität und Gewalt. Jugendfeindlichkeit in der Weimarer Republik*. Bonn.

Weber, Thomas. 2010. *Hitler's First War: Adolf Hitler, the Men of the List Regiment, and the First World War*. Oxford: Oxford University Press.

Wehler, Hans-Ulrich. 2003. *Deutsche Gesellschaftsgeschichte. Volume 4: Vom Beginn des Ersten Weltkriegs bis zur Gründung der beiden deutschen Staaten, 1914–1949*. Munich: C.H. Beck.

Wildt, Michael. 2003. *Generation des Unbedingten. Das Führungskorps des Reichssicherheitshauptamtes*. Hamburg: Hamburger Edition.

Wildt, Michael. 2008. *Geschichte des Nationalsozialismus*. Göttingen: Vandenhoeck & Ruprecht.

Wildt, Michael. 2009. 'Die Ungleichheit des Volkes. "Volksgemeinschaft" in der politischen Kommunikation der Weimarer Republik.' In *Volksgemeinschaft: Neue Forschungen zur Gesellschaft des Nationalsozialismus*, edited by Frank Bajohr and Michael Wildt, 24–40. Frankfurt am Main: Fischer.

Wildt, Michael. 2014. 'Volksgemeinschaft. A Modern Perspective on National Socialist Society.' In *Visions of Community in Nazi Germany. Social Engineering & Private Lives*, edited by Martina Steber and Bernhard Gotto, 43–59. Oxford: Oxford University Press.

Wippermann, Wolfgang. 2001. 'Ideologie.' In *Enzyklopädie des Nationalsozialismus*, edited by Wolfgang Benz and Hermann Graml, 11–21. Munich: Deutscher Taschenbuch-Verlag.

Ziemann, Benjamin and Szejnmann, Claus-Christian W. 2013. '"Machtergreifung". The Nazi Seizure of Power in 1933.' *Politics, Religion & Ideology* 14, 321–337.

Further Reading

Bialas, Wolfgang and Fritze, Lothar, eds. 2014. *Nazi Ideologie und Ethics*. Cambridge: Cambridge Scholars Publishing.

Brustein, William. 1996. *The Logic of Evil: The Social Origins of the Nazi Party, 1925–1933*. New Haven, CT: Yale University Press.

Dennis, David. 2012. *Inhumanities: Nazi interpretations of Western Culture*. Cambridge: Cambridge University Press.

Evans, Richard J. 2003. *The Coming of the Third Reich*. London: Penguin.

Hartmann, Christian and Plöckinger, Othmar, eds. 2017. *Hitler. Mein Kampf: Eine Kritische Edition*. Munich: Institut Für Zeitgeschichte.

Irdachi, Constantin, ed. 2010. *Comparative Fascist Studies: New Perspectives*. London: Routledge.

Müller, Jan-Werner. 2011. *Contesting Democracy: Political Ideas in Twentieth-Century Europe*. New Haven, CT: Yale University Press.

Raphael, Lutz. 2014. 'Pluralities of National Socialist Ideology: New Perspectives on the Production and Diffusion of National Socialist Weltanschauung.' In *Visions of Community in Nazi Germany: Social Engineering and Private Lives*, edited by Martina Steber and Bernhard Gotto, 73–86. Oxford: Oxford University Press.

Schönhoven, Klaus and Vogel, Hans-Jochen, eds. 1998. *Frühe Warnungen vor dem Nationalsozialismus: Ein historisches Lesebuch*. Bonn: Dietz.

Weindling, Peter. 1989. *Health, Race and German Politics between National Unification and Nazism 1870–1945*. Cambridge: Cambridge University Press.

Zitelmann, Rainer. 1989. *Adolf Hitler. Eine politische Biographie*. Göttingen: Muster-Schmidt.

PART II

Structures of Nazi Rule

CHAPTER SIX

The NSDAP After 1933: Members, Positions, Technologies, Interactions

ARMIN NOLZEN

6.1 Introduction

At any rate '*Organisation*' remained an honest and honoured word within the LTI, indeed it underwent a further refinement which had not existed prior to 1933, except perhaps in occasional and isolated technical contexts. The will to totality entailed an excess of organization, right down to the *Pimpfe*, no, right down to the cats: I was not allowed to make any more contributions to the Society for the Prevention of Cruelty to Cats because there was no room *in Das deutsche Katzenwesen* [The German Feline] – this really was the name of the society's newsletter, which had become a Party organ – for those mongrel creatures which resided with Jews: Later they took our pets away from us, cats, dogs, even canaries, and killed them, not just in isolated cases and out of individual malice, but officially and systematically …. (Klemperer 2006, 94; in general, see Nowojski 2004)

When Victor Klemperer, a professor of French literature at Dresden University who was removed from his position in spring 1933 because he was Jewish, wrote his famous *Lingua Tertii Imperii* (LTI) immediately after the Second World War, he still was enraged about a small detail of Nazi persecution. Klemperer complained about the systematic killing of pets living with Jews, and he saw that as a result of the Nazi regime's intrinsic 'will to totality'. For him, the National Socialist German Workers' Party (*Nationalsozialistische Deutsche Arbeiterpartei*, NSDAP) was the driving force behind that will. This, at least, can be gathered from his mentioning of the word *Pimpfe*, which alluded to the members of the Hitler Youth (*Hitlerjugend*, HJ). By referring to the NSDAP's 'excess of organization' especially after 1933, Klemperer made a pivotal point. He reminded us how

A Companion to Nazi Germany, First Edition. Edited by Shelley Baranowski, Armin Nolzen, and Claus-Christian W. Szejnmann.

important organization was for the Third Reich in general. The following synthesis of the NSDAP's historical development after 1933 adheres strictly to the party's 'organization'. Using the work of the German sociologist Niklas Luhmann (1976, 2000), it evaluates organization as a specific type of a social system based on decision. Organizations, as Luhmann argues, reproduce themselves self-referentially on the basis of their own operational logic, and decisions as communications are the key elements in this process (Seidl and Becker 2006; Seidl and Mormann 2014). By understanding the NSDAP as a social system of a type of 'organization', it is, therefore, necessary to analyse its decisions according to its own operational routines.

6.2   Membership Growth, Means of Motivation

The NSDAP's decisions on membership formed its first and most important organizational routine. When Adolf Hitler became Reich Chancellor on 30 January 1933, the NSDAP had nearly 850 000 members. They drew from all social strata, were overwhelmingly Protestant, more than 90% male, and generally between the ages of 21 and 40 (Kater 1983, 19–71; Kupfer 2006, 53–108). Moreover, the Nazi electorate, which reached the peak of its success in the Reichstag election of 31 July 1932, when it gained 13.8 million votes, crossed class lines and also corresponded to the age structure of the population (Falter 1991, 364–375; 2013). The party stronghold lay in Protestant rural areas, but it did well in heavily Catholic and industrial towns. The increased votes among Catholic and female voters, however, remained comparatively modest.

After the seizure of power (*Machtergreifung*), hundreds of thousands of new members flocked to the Nazi Party, the structure of which soon changed fundamentally (Orlow 1973; Grill 1983; Pätzold and Weißbecker 2009). The party immediately restricted membership retroactively from 1 May 1933 because the flood of new applications overwhelmed the responsible offices (Lükemann 1963, 30–32). At the same time, the Nazi paramilitary organizations and auxiliary associations swallowed up the existing associations and federations. Scholars generally refer to this process as alignment (*Gleichschaltung*), the model for which was the violence of 2 May 1933 when activists of the National Socialist Factory Cell Organization (*Nationalsozialistische Betriebszellenorganisation*, NSBO), the Stormtroopers (*Sturmabteilung*, SA), and the Protective Squads (*Schutzstaffel*, SS) destroyed the trade unions (Kratzenberg 1987; Siemens 2017). This alignment also depended on local initiatives by groups that had previously remained aloof from Nazism, who now adapted their associations and federations to the Nazi Party in an unparalleled act of voluntary mobilization from below (Allen 1984; Bergerson 2004; Imhoof 2013). In any case, the Nazi paramilitary organizations and auxiliary associations continued to accept new members, reaching several million in number, but who were no longer required to belong to the party. Finally, each of these organizations built its own apparatus to integrate the new members. The vertical official channels that arose were now only integrated into the Nazi Party through personal unions. Thus, the paramilitary organizations and auxiliary associations were formally independent of the Nazi Party.

Table 6.1 Members of the NSDAP and its organizations, as at 1 September 1939.

Nazi Party	5 310 000
Divisions	
Stormtroopers	1 329 448
Protective Squads	235 526
National Socialist Motor Corps	350 000
(*Nationalsozialistisches Kraftfahrkorps*, NSKK)	
Hitler Youth and League of German Girls	8 700 000
(*Hitlerjugend*, HJ, and *Bund Deutscher Mädel*, BDM)	
National Socialist Women's Groups	2 300 000
(*Nationalsozialistische Frauenschaft*, NSF)	
National Socialist German Students' League	39 339
(*Nationalsozialistischer Deutscher Studentenbund*, NSDStB)	
National Socialist University Teachers' League	7 200
(*Nationalsozialistischer Deutscher Dozentenbund*, NSDozB)	
Affiliations	
German Labour Front	22 127 793
(*Deutsche Arbeitsfront*, DAF)	
National Socialist Doctors' Alliance	30 000
(*Nationalsozialistischer Deutscher Ärztebund*, NSDÄB)	
National Socialist League of Legal Officials	104 171
(*Nationalsozialistischer Rechtswahrerbund*, NSRB)	
National Socialist Teachers' Alliance	300 000
(*Nationalsozialistischer Lehrerbund*, NSLB)	
National Socialist People's Welfare Organization	14 187 834
(*Nationalsozialistische Volkswohlfahrt*, NSV)	
National Socialist War Victims' Welfare	1 600 000
(*Nationalsozialistische Kriegsopferversorgung*, NSKOV)	
Reich League of German Civil Servants	1 700 000
(*Reichsbund der Deutschen Beamten*, RDB)	
National Socialist League of German Engineers	140 000
(*Nationalsozialistischer Bund Deutscher Technik*, NSBDT)	
Sponsored Organizations	
German Women's Enterprise	6 300 000
(*Deutsches Frauenwerk*, DFW)	
National Socialist Reich League for Physical Exercise	3 613 000
(*Nationalsozialistischer Reichsbund für Leibesübungen*, NSRL)	
National Socialist Air Corps	230 000
(*Nationalsozialistisches Fliegerkorps*, NSFK)	
National Socialist League of Alumni	75 000
(*Nationalsozialistischer Altherrenbund*, NSAhB)	
Reich Colonial League	1 200 000
(*Reichskolonialbund*, RKolB)	
Reich Veterans' League	2 307 250
(*Reichskriegerbund*, RKrB)	
Reich League of Ex-career Military	130 000
(*Reichstreubund ehemaliger Berufssoldaten*, RTrB)	

Source: Nolzen (2008, 116–117); corrected by Kramer (2011, 48–49) and Grüttner (2014, 109).

Until 1 September 1939, four sub-areas developed within the NSDAP: the Nazi Party, itself which had grown to 5.5 million party comrades (*Parteigenossen*); its divisions (*Gliederungen*); its affiliations (*angeschlossene Verbände*); and its sponsored organizations (*betreute Verbände*) (see Table 6.1). The largest division in quantitative terms were the HJ and the League of German Girls (*Bund Deutscher Mädel*, BDM), to which 8.7 million girls and boys between the ages of 10 and 18 belonged, followed by the National Socialist Women's Groups (*Nationalsozialistische Frauenschaft*, NSF), with more than 2.3 million female members. The largest of the affiliations was the German Labour Front (*Deutsche Arbeitsfront*, DAF), which encompassed nearly 22 million people. Among the sponsored organizations, the German Women's Enterprise (*Deutsches Frauenwerk*, DFW) was the largest with 6.3 million female members. Second was the National Socialist Reich League for Physical Exercise (*Nationalsozialistischer Reichsbund für Leibesübungen*, NSRL) with 3.6 million members (Bernett 1983, 2008), but its apparatus differed because it was based not on individual but on organizational membership (see Ahrne and Brunsson 2011). Institutionally, the NSDAP's organizations were almost completely independent of one another. The only exceptions were the NSF and the DFW (Arbogast 1998, 85–97; Michel 2007). The Nazi Party, its divisions, affiliations, and sponsored organizations represented a veritable network, which, it has been estimated, encompassed more than two thirds of all 'Aryan' Germans by 1 September 1939.

Research on the members of these organizations, however, is rare (Falter 2016 is an exception), and this is an effect of a widespread apologetic turn soon after 1945. During denazification, the German population played down their former membership and party engagement to exonerate themselves, and historical research has followed this trend for a long time (see Herwig 2014). It was primarily interested in the different motives for joining party organizations and did not pay adequate attention to membership procedures and mechanisms of integration. Therefore, it is necessary to change perspective and evaluate the members' actions and their motives for staying within these organizations. Combining empirical research and organizational sociology (Kühl 2013, 17–86; 2016, 44–113), we can distinguish between six different kinds of membership motivation in the NSDAP (see Table 6.2).

Each of the NSDAP's organizations used these six means and mechanisms to motivate its members, but to a different degree. Money was predominantly used within the party (Kater 1983, 190–228), the DAF (Hachtmann 2012, 531–55), and the National Socialist People's Welfare Organization (*Nationalsozialistische Volkswohlfahrt*, NSV) (Hammerschmidt 1999, 366–418), which paid its functionaries different remunerations and expense allowances and employed its members. Coercion as a means and positive and negative sanctions as its main mechanism served, for example, to integrate male and female youths into the HJ and the BDM (Buddrus 2003, 368–494; Kollmeier 2007, 91–197). Identification with the goal was most significant in organizations that concentrated on one purpose, such as the National Socialist Doctors' Alliance (*Nationalsozialistischer Deutscher Ärztebund*, NSDÄB) (Kater 1989) and the National Socialist War Victims' Welfare (*Nationalsozialistische Kriegsopferversorgung*, NSKOV) (Diehl 1987). Activities

Table 6.2   Means and mechanisms of membership motivation in the NSDAP.

Means	Mechanisms of motivation
Money	Remuneration and expense allowance
Coercion	Positive and negative sanction
Identification with the goal	Flexible expectations and fictive consenting
Attractiveness of activities	Careers and cognitions
Comradeship	Common experience and shared values
Reputation	Distinctions and informal influence

attracted most of the members of the National Socialist Motor Corps (*Nationalsozialistisches Kraftfahrkorps*, NSKK), and the National Socialist League of Legal Officials (*Nationalsozialistischer Rechtswahrerbund*, NSRB), which also enabled careers and cognitions (Feiten 1981; Sunnus 1990; Hochstetter 2005). With comradeship, the paramilitary organizations strove to create a common experience and shared values (Reichardt 2009, 406–475; Hein 2012, 191–255). And reputation was guaranteed to all members holding positions within the party and its affiliations, which were not remunerated. In contrast to average members, they had plenty of opportunities to implement distinctions and to exercise informal influence over non-members.

6.3   Positions, Functionaries

The social systems of 'organizations', however, not only decide on membership procedures, but also on positions (*Stellen*), functionaries, and their careers (Luhmann 1976, 137–155; Luhmann 2000, 231–239). After its re-founding in 1925, the NSDAP had neither succeeded in establishing a clear hierarchy, nor created an order of positions to administer inner party affairs (Noakes 1971, 1981, 2004). This changed with its membership growth after 1933. On the one hand, the NSDAP's apparatus expanded by the creation of millions of new positions. On the other hand, a process of centralization began after Hitler appointed Rudolf Hess as Deputy Führer (*Stellvertreter des Führers*) on 19 April 1933 (Pätzold and Weißbecker 1999). With that, Hess was authorized to issue 'political instructions' (*politische Weisungen*) to the entire NSDAP (Longerich 1992). In all financial affairs, Reich Treasurer Franz Xaver Schwarz held the same power position (Lükemann 1963) (see Table 6.3). The first recipients of Hess's and Schwarz's political and financial instructions were the Reich leaders (*Reichsleiter*) of the NSDAP. They were responsible for special tasks within the Nazi Party, its divisions, affiliations, and sponsored organizations (Reibel 2008).

On the next organizational level of the Nazi Party, the regional leaders (*Gauleiter*) were subordinate to Hess's and Schwarz's directives directly (Hüttenberger 1969; Priamus 2011). The *Gauleiter*, however, were the superiors of the district leaders (*Kreisleiter*) (Roth 1997; Lehmann 2007), who in turn were the superiors of the local leaders (*Ortsgruppenleiter*) (Reibel 2002). The regional, district, and local leaders were called 'bearers of sovereignty' (*Hoheitsträger*). On

Table 6.3 Offices and leaders of the NSDAP's Reich executive (Reichsleitung).

Reich Treasurer	Deputy *Führer*
Franz Xaver Schwarz	Rudolf Hess
The *Führer's* Chancellery	Main Office for Civil Servants
Philipp Bouhler	Hermann Neef
Reich Propaganda Office	Main Office for Education
Joseph Goebbels	Fritz Wächtler
Reich Press Chief	Office for Racial Policy
Otto Dietrich	Walter Groß
Reich Leader for the Press	Main Office for People's Health
Max Amann	Leonardo Conti
Reichsführer SS	Reich Students Leader
Heinrich Himmler	Gustav Adolf Scheel
Supreme SA Leader	Reich University Teachers Leader
Viktor Lutze	Walther Schultze
Leader of the NSKK	Reich Sport Leader
Adolf Hühnlein	Hans von Tschammer und Osten
Reich Youth Leader	Reich Organizational Leader
Baldur von Schirach	Robert Ley
Supreme Party Court	Main Organization Office
Walter Buch	Fritz Mehnert
Commissioner for Supervision	Main Indoctrination Office
Alfred Rosenberg	Friedrich Schmidt
Foreign Policy Office	Main Personnel Office
Alfred Rosenberg	Otto Marrenbach
Reich Office for Legal Affairs	Reich Women's Leader
Hans Frank	Gertrud Scholtz-Klink
Reich Office for Agrarian Policy	Main Office for People's Welfare
Richard Walther Darré	Erich Hilgenfeldt
Main Office for Municipal Policy	Main Office for War Victims
Karl Fiehler	Hanns Oberlindober
Colonial Policy Office	Main Office for Technical Affairs
Franz Ritter von Epp	Fritz Todt

Source: Mehnert (1936) and Frei (1993, 244–247).

the basis of the 'leadership principle' (*Führerprinzip*), Hess's political and Schwarz's financial instructions applied to the entire top-down structure of the NSDAP. At each descending level of the Nazi Party were officials who were subordinate to the *Hoheitsträger* in disciplinary terms although technically answerable to the *Reichsleiter*. There were, for example, specialized branches for the treasury, education, propaganda, and for the tasks completed by the divisions, and the affiliated and sponsored organizations. The party embraced more than half a million of functionaries, the political leaders (*Politische Leiter*) (Table 6.4). Below the Reich executive, it consisted of honorary officials almost exclusively so that

Table 6.4 The Nazi Party's political leaders by position and date of joining, as at 1 January 1935.

Position	Joiners before 14 September 1930 %	Joiners between 15 September 1930 and 30 January 1933 %	Joiners after 30 January 1933 %	Total
Gau leader	30 (100)	–	–	30
Gau office leader	507 (63.8)	253 (31.9)	34 (4.3)	794
Other *Gau* officials	947 (30.0)	1.705 (54.0)	504 (16.0)	3.156
Gau (subtotal)	1.484 (37.3)	1.958 (49.2)	538 (13.5)	3.980
Kreis leader	575 (69.5)	250 (30.2)	2 (0.3)	827
Kreis office leader	3.340 (23.4)	7.091 (49.7)	3.843 (26.9)	14.274
Other *Kreis* officals	1.392 (11.1)	4.849 (38.9)	6.236 (50.0)	12.477
Kreis (subtotal)	5.307 (19.2)	12.190 (44.2)	10.081 (36.6)	27.578
Local branch leader	4.852 (23.4)	10.996 (53.1)	4.876 (23.5)	20.724
Cell leader	4.775 (8.7)	26.540 (48.3)	23.661 (43.0)	54.976
Block leader	6.723 (3.3)	52.119 (25.5)	145.517 (71.2)	204.359
Local branch office leader	10.057 (8.8)	42.232 (37.0)	61.827 (54.2)	114.116
other local branch officials	3.734 (4.9)	20.337 (26.4)	52.858 (68.7)	76.929
Local branches (subtotal)	30.141(6.4)	152.224 (32.3)	288.739 (61.3)	471.104
Political leaders (total)	36.932 (7.3)	166.372 (33.1)	299.358 (59.6)	502.662

Source: Reichsorganisationsleiter (1935, 1939, vol. III, 52, 54, 58, 60, 84, 86, 92, 94, 112, 114).

more than 98% of its political leaders were not remunerated. The same is true for most of the divisions' and affiliations' functionaries. The affiliations' officials were called Prevailers (*Walter*) (Table 6.5). The high percentage of NSDAP honorary officials shows a certain degree of self-mobilization within its organizations (Müller-Botsch 2009). But it has also to be emphasized that up to 95% of the NSDAP members remained without an office. These rank-and-file members only paid their regular dues.

Other than a few examples (Kater 1983; Benz 2009; Wegehaupt 2012), the NSDAP's cadre politics have not been thoroughly analysed. This is surprising, because soon after 1933 it became increasingly important. Regarding the political leaders, we know at least the main conditions necessary for advancing to higher positions: ideological fanaticism, unconditional loyalty to superiors, readiness to exercise violence, permanent activism, and membership in the party before 1933. The NSDAP's positions normally required cognitive competences from its functionaries, such as accounting and billing, working with files, organizing, addressing an audience, and so forth. The offices of the Deputy Führer, the Reich Treasurer, and the Reich Organizational Leader (Nolzen 2011) fixed the general criteria for

Table 6.5 Leading officials (*Führende*) of the Nazi Party's affiliations, the NSF, the NSDStB, and the Reich Food Estate (Reichsnährstand, RNSt), as at 1 January 1935.

Organization	Leading officials (total)	Political leaders from that (%)	Total	Prevailers from that (%)	
				Party comrades from that (%)	Non-Party comrades from that (%)
NSF	50.731	13.079 (25.8)	37.652 (74.2)	2.871 (5.7)	34.781 (68.5)
NSDStB	1.690	268 (15.9)	1.422 (84.1)	410 (24.3)	1.012 (59.8)
DAF	819.943	50.935 (6.2)	768.108 (93.8)	120.088 (14.7)	648.020 (79.1)
RDB	53.868	13.859 (25.7)	40.009 (74.3)	19.538 (36.4)	20.426 (37.9)
NSLB	32.491	5.560 (17.1)	26.931 (82.9)	13.119 (40.4)	13.812 (42.5)
BNSDJ	4.838	1.025 (21.2)	3.813 (78.8)	2.179 (45.0)	1.634 (33.8)
NSBDT	2.584	788 (30.5)	1.796 (69.5)	1.051 (40.7)	745 (28.8)
RNSt	101.852	13.915 (13.7)	87.937 (86.3)	26.260 (25.8)	61.677 (60.5)
NSDÄB	2.497	1.193 (47.8)	1.304 (52.2)	818 (32.8)	486 (19.4)
NSV	322.075	31.936 (9.9)	290.139 (90.1)	85.352 (26.5)	204.787 (63.6)
NSKOV	84.246	7.329 (8.7)	76.917 (91.3)	12.831 (15.2)	64.086 (76.1)
Total	1.475.915	139.887 (9.5)	1.336.028 (90.5)	284.562 (19.3)	1.051.466 (71.2)

Source: Calculated on the basis of Reichsorganisationsleiter (1935, 1939 II, 10, and III, 14–15).

a party career, and the Supreme Party Court sanctioned political leaders who violated party norms or showed deviant behaviour (McKale 1974). The *Hoheitsträger* decided on nominations and advancement within the party by evaluating the daily performance of their staff officials. And the other offices of the Reich executive board controlled personnel policies in their areas of jurisdiction.

In general, the development of the NSDAP's personnel policies can be divided into four phases. From 1933 to autumn 1935, an uncontrolled growth of positions and usurpation of offices took place that the hierarchy could not control. Between autumn 1935 and spring 1941, the Deputy Führer, the Reich Treasurer, and the Reich Organizational Leader tried to implement a target-orientated cadre politics, which was quite successful. But at the beginning of the war against the Soviet Union in summer 1941, the NSDAP suffered an immediate loss of both paid and voluntary functionaries because of their conscription in the Wehrmacht. Thus, it centralized its horizontal staffs and closed down some offices which were not necessary for warfare (*nicht kriegsnotwendig*). From the summer of 1943 to the end of the war the NSDAP lost more than 50% of the functionaries that had held office before 1939/1940. In this fourth phase, the Party Chancellery (*Parteikanzlei*) under the leadership of Martin Bormann, who in the meantime replaced Hess as Deputy Führer (Lang 1979), tried to mobilize members who had previously not held an office (Nolzen 2008, 172–180). The Party Chancellery succeeded and soon monopolized the NSDAP's personnel policies.

6.4   Technologies, Decision Programmes

After the Nazi Party's re-founding in 1925, its organizations developed six different technologies (Luhmann and Schorr 2000, 127–251), which were aimed at 'people management' (*Menschenführung*) (Rebentisch and Teppe 1986): institutionalization, education, mobilization, violence, social work, and policing (see Nolzen 2014). These six technologies cannot be sharply distinguished from one another. The term 'technology' encompasses an analysis of intent and strategy, tactical manoeuvres, organizational mechanisms, routines and practices, and refers strictly to the level of 'organization'. Therefore, the main task of interpretation is not to focus on individual or collective behaviour but to identify significant patterns of operations within a unique organizational system. The Nazi Party, its divisions, affiliations, and sponsored organizations used these six technologies, differing only in intensity and scope. By doing so, the NSDAP implemented specific decision programmes (Luhmann 2000, 256–278) to fulfil its tasks of *Menschenführung* within and without its apparatuses. With these six technologies, a dominating decision programme emerged (Table 6.6).

Institutionalization primarily refers to the different mechanisms for integrating new members into the NSDAP by establishing norms and an ongoing process of textualization. The norms encompassed membership regulations, for example, the introduction of the 'Aryan paragraph' (*Arierparagraph*) to remove or prevent members suspected of 'Jewish descent' (*jüdische Abstammung*) (Meyer 1999, 252–259), behavioural rules for party comrades, and the standard operating procedures in the NSDAP's organizations. It was thus necessary to textualize their

Table 6.6 The NSDAP's technologies and dominating decision programmes.

Technologies	Dominating decision programmes
Institutionalization	Establishing norms and textualization
Education	Teaching and learning
Mobilization	Organizational planning and reform
Violence	Stigmatization and repression
Social work	Welfare and medical care
Policing	Surveillance and 'political judgements'

daily work through files, card indexes, certificates, reports, printed collections of decrees, and so on (Unger 1974, 83–104, 221–261; Buddrus 2003, 250–304). To educate its members, the NSDAP established programmes for technical and ideological teaching and learning (see Kraas 2004; Schmerbach 2008; Harten 2014). Organizational planning and inner reform underwrote mobilization. To act violently, the NSDAP established routines of stigmatization and repression (Wildt 2007). Social work expanded throughout the Second World War, because the affiliations provided welfare and medical care after Allied bombing raids (Süß 2003; Mouton 2007). Finally, the party's cell and block leaders policed German society (Schmiechen-Ackermann 2000; Meyer 2002, 73–104); they used many instruments of day-to-day-surveillance and drew up 'political judgements' (*politische Beurteilungen*) of those who tried to gain benefits or promote their careers (Thieler 2014). With its technologies and decision programmes, the NSDAP guaranteed its own organizational reproduction.

6.5 Interactions, Issues

In social systems of 'organizations', technologies and decision programmes are embedded in operative routines which require physical presence. These interactions are fluid because communication changes rapidly when a new individual shows up or when the participants become silent (Luhmann 1995, 405–436; Kieserling 1999, 15–32). To be able to reproduce themselves, interactions need issues. In its propaganda campaigns, however, the NSDAP, from 1928/1929, politicized all issues to attract voters and to win elections (Ohr 1997, 142–232; Sneeringer 2002). The following overview, therefore, is only heuristic because it is nearly impossible to identify all the NSDAP's interactions with dominating issues. In Nazi interactions, the fluctuation of issues was generally high. But is has to be emphasized that for stabilizing interactions, issues were more important than collective performance. By focusing on specific issues, cognitive schemes emerged, which were internalized by individuals and served as a precondition for their future actions (Table 6.7). The most striking examples for that are the celebrations and gatherings which evoked specific images of 'leadership' (*Führung*) and 'people's community' (*Volksgemeinschaft*) (Behrenbeck 1996; Freitag 1997). These images later guided the participants' actions. For each individual, being present at the NSDAP's celebrations and gatherings made a difference (in general, see Brockhaus 1997).

Table 6.7   The NSDAP's main interactions and its dominating issues.

Interactions	Dominating issues
Conferences and staff meetings	Information and implementation
Instructions and camps	Militarization and morale
Celebrations and gatherings	'Leadership' and 'people's community'
Denunciations and pogroms	Purity and danger
Counselling and physical examinations	'Socialism of the deed' and 'People's health'
Inspections and summonses	Deviance and conformity

The same is true for conferences and staff meetings with which the NSDAP tried to maintain the flow of information and implement political and financial directives (Nolzen 2005). Instructions and camps concentrated on military exercise and morale (in general, Kühne 2006). With denunciations and pogroms, the NSDAP propagated the 'racial purity' (*Rassenreinheit*) of the German 'people's body' (*Volkskörper*) (Uhle 1999; Schulle 2001). Counselling and physical examinations were integral parts of the 'socialism of the deed' (*Sozialismus der Tat*) and the 'people's health' (*Volksgesundheit*) (Fiebrandt 2014). Talks about deviance and conformity accompanied inspections and summonses. The level of 'organization' framed these interactions and issues, which had some specific consequences (see Kieserling 1999, 359–387). First, the NSDAP tended to pressure its members to refrain from interactions with non-members. Second, repeated face-to-face contacts between the members of the NSDAP's organizations occurred. Third, those who belonged to the party and its affiliated associations participated in common interests, mentalities, and patterns of action. Fourth, members could observe alienation of others from the NSDAP. Fifth, activism was visible. Sixth, people recognized themselves as members of the NSDAP's organizations and, from that, a multitude of personal conflicts resulted because those organizations competed against each other in different ways. Seventh, interactions with non-members relied either on propaganda or on violence. Thus, the NSDAP turned out to be a 'greedy institution' (Coser 1974; Fleck 2013), which claimed unconditional loyalty to its leaders and principles.

6.6   Conclusion

Soon after its seizure of power in 1933, the NSDAP differentiated a whole network of organizations which separated themselves from one another by different patterns of membership regulation and motivation. This directly resulted from the unprecedented growth of membership which, at that time, the NSDAP's hierarchy could not control. Until 1936/1937, Himmler's SS separated almost completely from the NSDAP (Nolzen 2009), and the HJ, DAF, and NSV underwent a similar development (Buddrus 2003; Hachtmann 2012; Hansen 1991). The ongoing process of differentiating within the NSDAP arose from the relations between organizations and their members, or, in terms of systems theory, from relations between the system and its environment (Luhmann 2000, 88–122). On the one hand, there were the NSDAP's organizations, but on the other there were persons who decided either to join as members, or to remain with the associations that voluntarily aligned. There was a kind of Nazi revolution in 1933, but it did not derive from violence on the streets or efforts to overthrow the hated Weimar Republic. The real revolution arose from the two million voluntary member applications to the Nazi Party between February and April 1933, because this flood changed its structures fundamentally. This also sheds a new light on the discussion of the 'cumulative radicalization' (Mommsen 1997) that took place in the Third Reich. Clearly, it did not emerge from the Nazi regime's structural components alone, but also from individual decisions which were highly contingent.

With Hess's appointment as Deputy Führer and the establishment of the *Reichsleitung* in late 1933, the NSDAP's organizational structures got consolidated. Together with the offices of the Reich Treasurer, the Reich Organizational Leader, and the Supreme Party Court, Hess and his staff were able to centralize the NSDAP and establish a working hierarchy between the Reich leadership and the regional *Gaue*. These offices monopolized decisions (see Luhmann 2000, 222–255) about positions and functionaries. Because of the 'leadership principle', they did not decide directly about the NSDAP's personnel, but set the premises that guided cadre politics. They fixed regulations to nominate only political leaders who joined the Nazi Party before 1933, strove to dissolve the personal unions between state and party offices, and established behavioural norms and sanctions. One of the most important tasks of the NSDAP's cadre politics, however, lay in the rearrangement of positions, both horizontally and vertically. It is not easy to assess the effects of that permanent organizational restructuring. In general, historical research tends to label the NSDAP an amorphous body characterized by organizational chaos (paradigmatic is Bollmus 2006). By doing so, most authors neglect the NSDAP's organizational logics and do not pay adequate attention to its inner dynamics.

In order to reproduce themselves, the NSDAP's organizations after 1933 relied on technologies and decision programmes. Its six technologies – institutionalization, education, mobilization, violence, social work, and policing – derived from imitation. The Bolsheviks, the Catholic hierarchy, and the Prussian military were the main role models (see Dröge 2015). All of the NSDAP's decision programmes were implemented as standard operating procedures. Additionally, the technologies and decision programmes served as organizational memory. Each social system of an 'organization' needs to memorize its past decisions in order to draw up new ones (Walsh and Ungson 1991). Technologies structure the ways in which operations shall take place, and decision programmes fix organizational means and ends. In the NSDAP, an official and an unofficial organizational memory emerged after 1933. Decision programmes and their textualization in files, statistics, card indexes, decrees, and so on were the official part, and technologies and their materialization in the functionaries' experiences and cognitions were the unofficial part of that organizational memory.

Because of its rapid growth in membership after 1933, the number of interactions taking place in the NSDAP multiplied. As a consequence, more and more interactions in the Third Reich were framed by its organizations. The same was true for issues so that the NSDAP monopolized agenda setting throughout the

Third Reich. With the number of interactions and issues increasing, the importance of individuals and the conflicts between them expanded as well (Kieserling 1999, 257–302). The NSDAP, however, did not disintegrate in a constant struggle of all against all (*Kampf aller gegen alle*) as most scholars assume. Instead of this, a latent interdependence between interactions and issues at the one hand and conflicts and problem solving on the other hand emerged. At the level of interaction, mechanisms of conflict management arose. Mediation, repression, and avoiding communication were its main tasks. The semantics of 'comradeship' and 'community' also played an important role for dealing with inner conflicts.

This brings us back to Klemperer's observation regarding the assumed Nazi 'will to totality' materializing in 'total organization' through the NSDAP. This will to totality was only one side of the coin. It has to be emphasized that within broad segments of the German population there also existed a 'will to align' or to anticipatory obedience, which after 1933 enabled the NSDAP's operations of 'people management'. To understand this correlation, historical research has to focus to the NSDAP's organizational mechanisms. This has to be done by changing one's perspective from individuals to the level of 'organization'. Historiography about the Nazi regime in general is concentrated too much on individuals and their interactions, on Nazi ideology and its manifestations. This is all well and good, but one has to consider that after 1933 the NSDAP and its organizations framed most interactions. This framing, however, affected interactions – for example, when people acted violently against 'objective enemies' (*objektive Gegner*). The NSDAP's violence did not result from spontaneous acts, but was organized in a deliberate manner. By recognizing organizational framing, ideology as a driving force for action can be deconstructed into the different means of membership motivation. Consequently, it is necessary to analyse the Third Reich as a 'society of organizations' (Perrow 1991). This term refers not only to organization, but to organization in a specific society, and to interactions in specific organizations. Thus, three different levels have to be considered simultaneously: society, organization, and interactions.

References

Ahrne, Göran and Brunsson, Nils. 2011. *Meta–organizations*. Cheltenham, UK: Edward Elgar.

Allen, William Sheridan. 1984. *The Nazi Seizure of Power: The Experience of a Single German Town 1922–1945*, rev. edn. New York: F. Watts.

Arbogast, Christine. 1998. *Herrschaftsinstanzen der württembergischen NSDAP: Funktion, Sozialprofil und Lebenswege einer regionalen NS–Elite, 1920–1960*. Munich: Oldenbourg.

Behrenbeck, Sabine. 1996. *Der Kult um die toten Helden: Nationalsozialistische Mythen, Riten und Symbole*. Vierow bei Greifswald: SH Verlag.

Benz, Wolfgang, ed. 2009. *Wie wurde man Parteigenosse? Die NSDAP und ihre Mitglieder*. Frankfurt am Main: Fischer Taschenbuch Verlag.

Bergerson, Andrew Stuart. 2004. *Ordinary Germans in Extraordinary Times: The Nazi Revolution in Hildesheim*. Bloomington: Indiana University Press.

Bernett, Hajo. 1983. *Der Weg des Sports in die nationalsozialistische Diktatur: Die Entstehung des Deutschen (Nationalsozialistischen) Reichsbundes für Leibesübungen*. Schorndorf: Hofmann.

Bernett, Hajo, ed. 2008. *Nationalsozialistische Leibeserziehung: Dokumentation ihrer Theorie und Organisation*, 2nd edn, by Hans Joachim Teichler, and Berno Bahro revised and enlarged edition. Schorndorf: Hofmann.

Bollmus, Reinhard. 2006. *Das Amt Rosenberg und seine Gegner: Studien zum Machtkampf im nationalsozialistischen Herrschaftssystem*, 2nd edn with a bibliographical essay by Stephan Lehnstaedt. Munich: Oldenbourg.

Brockhaus, Gudrun. 1997. *Schauder und Idylle: Faschismus als Erlebnisangebot*. Munich: Kunstmann.

Buddrus, Michael. 2003. *Totale Erziehung für den totalen Krieg. Hitlerjugend und nationalsozialistische Jugendpolitik*. Munich: K.G. Saur.

Coser, Lewis A. 1974. *Greedy Institutions: Patterns of Undivided Commitment*. New York: Free Press.

Diehl, James M. 1987. 'Victors or Victims? Disabled Veterans in the Third Reich.' *Journal of Modern History* 59, 705–736. doi: 10.1086.243283.

Dröge, Martin. 2015. *Männlichkeit und 'Volksgemeinschaft.' Der westfälische Landeshauptmann Karl Friedrich Kolbow (1899–1945): Biographie eines NS-Täters*. Paderborn: Schöningh.

Falter, Jürgen W. 1991. *Hitlers Wähler*. Munich: C.H. Beck.

Falter, Jürgen W. 2013. *Zur Soziographie des Nationalsozialismus: Studien zu den Wählern und Mitgliedern der NSDAP*. Cologne: Gesis.

Falter, Jürgen W., ed. 2016. *Junge Kämpfer, alte Opportunisten: Die Mitglieder der NSDAP 1919–1945*. Frankfurt am Main and New York: Campus.

Feiten, Willi. 1981. *Der Nationalsozialistische Lehrerbund. Entwicklung und Organisation: Ein Beitrag zum Aufbau und zur Organisationsstruktur des nationalsozialistischen Herrschaftssystems*. Weinheim and Basle: Juventa.

Fiebrandt, Maria. 2014. *Auslese für die Siedlergesellschaft: Die Einbeziehung Volksdeutscher in die NS–Erbgesundheitspolitik im Kontext der Umsiedlungen 1939–1945*. Göttingen: Vandenhoeck & Ruprecht.

Fleck, Christian. 2013. 'Lewis A. Coser – A Stranger within More than One Gate.' *Czech Sociological Revue* 49, 951–968.

Frei, Norbert. 1993. *National Socialist Rule in Germany. The Führer State 1933–1945*. Oxford and Cambridge: Blackwell.

Freitag, Werner, ed. 1997. *Das Dritte Reich im Fest: Führermythos, Feierlaune und Verweigerung in Westfalen 1933–1945*. Bielefeld: Verlag für Regionalgeschichte.

Grill, Johnpeter H. 1983. 'The Nazi Movement in Baden 1920–1945.' PhD thesis, University of North Carolina Chapel Hill.

Grüttner, Michael. 2014. *Das Dritte Reich 1933–1939*. Stuttgart: Klett-Cotta.

Hachtmann, Rüdiger. 2012. *Das Wirtschaftsimperium der Deutschen Arbeitsfront 1933–1945*. Göttingen: Wallstein.

Hammerschmidt, Peter. 1999. *Die Wohlfahrtsverbände im NS–Staat: Die NSV und die konfessionellen Verbände Caritas und Innere Mission im Gefüge der Wohlfahrtspflege des Nationalsozialismus*. Opladen: Leske + Budrich.

Hansen, Eckhard. 1991. *Wohlfahrtspolitik im NS–Staat: Motivation, Konflikte und Machtstrukturen im 'Sozialismus der Tat' des Dritten Reiches*. Augsburg: Maro.

Harten, Hans-Christian. 2014. *Himmlers Lehrer: Die Weltanschauliche Schulung in der SS 1933–1945*. Paderborn: Schöningh.

Hein, Bastian. 2012. *Elite für Volk und Führer? Die Allgemeine SS und ihre Mitglieder 1925–1945*. Munich: Oldenbourg.

Herwig, Malte. 2014. *Post War Lies: Germany and Hitler's Long Shadow*, translated by Jamie Lee Searle and Shaun Whiteside. London: Scribe.

Hochstetter, Dorothee. 2005. *Motorisierung und 'Volksgemeinschaft.' Das Nationalsozialistische Kraftfahrkorps (NSKK) 1931–1945*. Munich: Oldenbourg.

Hüttenberger, Peter. 1969. *Die Gauleiter: Studie zum Wandel des Machtgefüges in der NSDAP*. Stuttgart: DVA.

Imhoof, David M. 2013. *Becoming a Nazi Town: Culture and Politics in Göttingen between the World Wars*. Ann Arbor: University of Michigan Press.

Kater, Michael H. 1983. *The Nazi Party: A Social Profile of Members and Leaders, 1919–1945*. Cambridge: Cambridge University Press.

Kater, Michael H. 1989. *Doctors Under Hitler*. Chapel Hill: University of North Carolina Press.

Kieserling, André. 1999. *Kommunikation unter Anwesenden: Studien über Interaktionssysteme*. Frankfurt am Main: Suhrkamp.

Klemperer, Victor. 2006. *The Language of the Third Reich: LTI, Lingua Tertii Imperii: A Philologist's Notebook*, translated by Martin Brady. London: Athlone Press.

Kollmeier, Kathrin. 2007. *Ordnung und Ausgrenzung: Die Disziplinarpolitik der Hitler–Jugend*. Göttingen: Vandenhoeck & Ruprecht.

Kraas, Andreas. 2004. *Lehrerlager 1932–1945: Politische Funktion und pädagogische Gestaltung*. Bad Heilbrunn: Klinkhardt.

Kramer, Nicole. 2011. *Volksgenossinnen an der Heimatfront: Mobilisierung, Verhalten, Erinnerung*. Göttingen: Vandenhoeck & Ruprecht.

Kratzenberg, Volker. 1987. *Arbeiter auf dem Weg zu Hitler? Die Nationalsozialistische Betriebszellen–Organisation. Ihre Entstehung, ihre Programmatik, ihr Scheitern. 1927–1934*. Frankfurt am Main: Peter Lang.

Kühl, Stefan. 2013. *Organizations: A Systems approach*. Farnham, UK: Gower.

Kühl, Stefan. 2016. *Ordinary Organizations: Why Normal Men Carried Out the Holocaust*, translated by Jessica Spengler. Cambridge: Polity Press.

Kühne, Thomas. 2006. *Kameradschaft. Die Soldaten des nationalsozialistischen Krieges und das 20. Jahrhundert*. Göttingen: Vandenhoeck&Ruprecht.

Kupfer, Torsten. 2006. *Generation und Radikalisierung: Die Mitglieder der NSDAP im Kreis Bernburg 1921–1945*. Berlin: Author.

Lang, Jochen von. 1979. *The Secretary. Martin Bormann: The Man Who Manipulated Hitler*. New York: Random House.

Lehmann, Sebastian. 2007. *Kreisleiter der NSDAP in Schleswig–Holstein: Lebensläufe und Herrschaftspraxis einer regionalen Machtelite*. Bielefeld: Verlag für Regionalgeschichte.

Longerich, Peter. 1992. *Hitlers Stellvertreter: Führung der Partei und Kontrolle des Staatsapparates durch den Stab Heß und die Partei–Kanzlei Bormann*. Munich: K.G. Saur.

Luhmann, Niklas. 1976. *Funktionen und Folgen formaler Organisation*, 3rd edn. Berlin: Duncker & Humblot.

Luhmann, Niklas. 1995. *Social Systems*, translated by John Bednarz Jr. with Dirk Baecker. Stanford: Stanford University Press.

Luhmann, Niklas. 2000. *Organisation und Entscheidung*. Opladen and Wiesbaden: Westdeutscher Verlag.

Luhmann, Niklas and Schorr, Karl-Eberhard. 2000. *Problems of Reflection in the System of Education*, translated by Rebecca A. Neuwirth. New York: Waxmann.

Lükemann, Ulf. 1963. 'Der Reichsschatzmeister der NSDAP: Ein Beitrag zur inneren Parteistruktur.' PhD thesis, Free University of Berlin.

McKale, Donald M. 1974. *The Nazi Party Courts: Hitler's Management of Conflict in his Movement, 1921–1945*. Lawrence: University Press of Kansas.

Mehnert, Fritz. 1936: 'Die Organisation der NSDAP und ihrer angeschlossenen Verbände.' In *Der Schulungsbrief. Das zentrale Monatsblatt der NSDAP und DAF*, edited by the

Reichsorganisationsleiter der NSDAP in Zusammenarbeit mit der DAF, iii, 329–370. Berlin: Zentralverlag der DAF.

Meyer, Beate. 1999. *'Jüdische Mischlinge.' Rassenpolitik und Verfolgungserfahrung 1933–1945.* Hamburg: Christians.

Meyer, Beate. 2002. *'Goldfasane' und 'Nazissen.' Die NSDAP im ehemals 'roten' Stadtteil Hamburg–Eimsbüttel.* Hamburg: Galerie Morgenland.

Michel, Anette. 2007. '"Führerinnen" im Dritten Reich: Die Gaufrauenschaftsleiterinnen der NSDAP.' In *'Volksgenossinnen.' Frauen in der NS–Volksgemeinschaft*, edited by Sybille Steinbacher, 115–137. Göttingen: Wallstein.

Mommsen, Hans. 1997. 'Cumulative Radicalization and Progressive Self-Destruction as Structural Determinants of the Nazi Dictatorship.' In *Stalinism and Nazism: Dictatorships in Comparison*, edited by Ian Kershaw and Moshe Lewin, 75–87. Cambridge: Cambridge University Press.

Mouton, Michelle. 2007. *From Nurturing the Nation to Purifying the Volk: Weimar and Nazi Family Policy, 1918–1945.* Cambridge: Cambridge University Press.

Müller-Botsch, Christine. 2009. *'Den richtigen Mann an die richtige Stelle.' Biographien und politisches Handeln von unteren NSDAP–Funktionären.* Frankfurt am Main and New York: Campus.

Noakes, Jeremy. 1971. *The Nazi Party in Lower Saxony 1924–1933.* London: Oxford University Press.

Noakes, Jeremy. 1981. 'The Nazi Party and the Third Reich: The Myth and Reality of the One–Party State.' In *Government, Party and People in Nazi Germany*, edited by Jeremy Noakes, 11–33, 2nd edn. Exeter: Exeter University Press.

Noakes, Jeremy. 2004. 'Leaders of the People? The Nazi Party and German Society.' *Journal of Contemporary History* 39, 189–212. doi: 10.1177.0022009404042128.

Nolzen, Armin. 2005. 'Charismatic Legitimation and Bureaucratic Rule. The NSDAP in the Third Reich, 1933–1945.' *German History* 23, 494–518. doi: 10.1093/0266355405gh355oa.

Nolzen, Armin. 2008. 'The NSDAP, the War, and German Society.' In *Germany and the Second World War*, vol. 9, pt. 1: *German Wartime Society 1939–1945: Politicization, Disintegration, and the Struggle for Survival*, edited for the Militärgeschichtliches Forschungsamt Potsdam, Germany by Jörg Echternkamp. Translation editor Derry Cook-Radmore, 111–206. Oxford: Clarendon Press.

Nolzen, Armin. 2009. '"… eine Art von Freimaurerei in der Partei"? Die SS als Gliederung der NSDAP, 1933–1945.' In *Die SS, Himmler und die Wewelsburg*, edited by Jan-Erik Schulte, 23–44. Paderborn: Schöningh.

Nolzen, Armin. 2011. 'Die Reichsorganisationsleitung als Verwaltungsbehörde der NSDAP. Kompetenzen, Strukturen und administrative Praktiken nach 1933.' In *Der prekäre Staat. Herrschen und Verwalten im Nationalsozialismus*, edited by Sven Reichardt and Wolfgang Seibel, 121–166. Frankfurt am Main and New York: Campus.

Nolzen, Armin. 2014. 'The Nazi Party's Operational Codes after 1933.' In *Visions of Community in Nazi Germany: Social Engineering and Private Lives*, edited by Bernhard Gotto and Martina Steber, 87–100, Oxford: Oxford University Press.

Nowojski, Walter. 2004. *Victor Klemperer (1881–1960). Romanist – Chronist der Vorhölle.* Berlin: Hentrich & Hentrich.

Ohr, Dieter. 1997. *Nationalsozialistische Propaganda und Weimarer Wahlen: Empirische Analysen zur Wirkung von NSDAP–Versammlungen.* Opladen: Westdeutscher Verlag.

Orlow, Dietrich. 1973. *The History of the Nazi Party*, vol. 2. Newton Abbot, UK: David & Charles.

Pätzold, Kurt and Weißbecker, Manfred. 1999. *Rudolf Heß: Der Mann an Hitlers Seite.* Leipzig: Militzke.

Pätzold, Kurt and Weißbecker, Manfred. 2009. *Geschichte der NSDAP 1920 bis 1945*, 3rd edn. Cologne: PapyRossa.

Perrow, Charles. 1991. 'A Society of Organizations.' *Theory and Society* 20, 725–672. doi: 10.1007/BF00678095.

Priamus, Heinz–Jürgen. 2011. *Meyer: Zwischen Kaisertreue und NS–Täterschaft. Biographische Konturen eines deutschen Bürgers*. Essen: Klartext.

Rebentisch, Dieter and Teppe, Karl. 1986. 'Einleitung.' In *Verwaltung contra Menschenführung im Staat Hitlers. Studien zum politisch-administrativen System*, edited by Dieter Rebentisch and Karl Teppe, 7–32. Göttingen: Vandenhoeck & Ruprecht.

Reibel, Carl-Wilhelm. 2002. *Das Fundament der Diktatur: Die NSDAP–Ortsgruppen 1932–1945*. Paderborn: Schöningh.

Reibel, Carl–Wilhelm. 2008. 'Die Parteizentrale der NSDAP in München. Administrative Lenkung und Sicherung der Diktatur.' In *München und der Nationalsozialismus. Menschen, Orte, Strukturen*, edited by Stefanie Hajak and Jürgen Zarusky, 87–121. Berlin: Metropol.

Reichardt, Sven. 2009. *Faschistische Kampfbünde: Gewalt und Gemeinschaft im italienischen Squadrismus und in der deutschen SA*. 2nd, rev. edn. Cologne, Weimar, and Vienna: Böhlau.

Reichsorganisationsleiter der NSDAP, ed. 1935.1939. *Parteistatistik der NSDAP. Stand: 1. Januar 1935 (ohne Saarland)*. 4 vols. Munich: Franz Eher Nachf.

Roth, Claudia. 1997. *Parteikreis und Kreisleiter der NSDAP unter besonderer Berücksichtigung Bayerns*. Munich: C.H. Beck.

Schmerbach, Folker. 2008. *Das 'Gemeinschaftslager Hanns Kerrl' für Referendare in Jüterbog 1933–1939*. Tübingen: Mohr Siebeck.

Schmiechen-Ackermann, Detlef. 2000. 'Der "Blockwart". Die unteren Parteifunktionäre im nationalsozialistischen Terror– und Überwachungsapparat.' *Vierteljahrshefte für Zeitgeschichte* 48, 575–602.

Schulle, Diana. 2001. *Das Reichssippenamt: Eine Institution nationalsozialistischer Rassenpolitik*. Berlin: Logos.

Seidl, David and Becker, Kai Helge, eds. 2006. *Niklas Luhmann and Organization Studies*. Copenhagen: Liber and Copenhagen Business School Press.

Seidl, David and Mormann, Hannah. 2014. 'Niklas Luhmann as Organization Theorist.' In *The Oxford Handbook of Sociology, Social Theory, and Organization Studies. Contemporary Currents*, edited by Paul S. Adler, Paul du Gay, Glenn Morgan, and Michael Reed, 125–157. Oxford: Oxford University Press.

Siemens, Daniel. 2017. *Stormtroopers: A New History of Hitler's Brownshirts*. New Haven, CT: Yale University Press.

Sneeringer, Julia. 2002. *Winning Women's Votes: Politics and Propaganda in Weimar Germany*. Chapel Hill: University of North Carolina Press.

Sunnus, Michael. 1990. *Der NS–Rechtswahrerbund (1928–1945): Zur Geschichte der nationalsozialistischen Juristenorganisation*. Frankfurt am Main: Peter Lang.

Süß, Winfried. 2003. *Der 'Volkskörper' im Krieg: Gesundheitspolitik, Gesundheitsverhältnisse und Krankenmord im nationalsozialistischen Deutschland 1939–1945*. Munich: Oldenbourg.

Thieler, Kerstin. 2014. *'Volksgemeinschaft' unter Vorbehalt. Gesinnungskontrolle und politische Mobilisierung in der Herrschaftspraxis der NSDAP–Kreisleitung Göttingen*. Göttingen: Wallstein.

Uhle, Roger. 1999. 'Neues Volk und reine Rasse. Walter Gross und das Rassenpolitische Amt der NSDAP (RPA) 1934–1945.' PhD thesis, University of Aachen.

Unger, Aryeh L. 1974. *The Totalitarian Party: Party and People in Nazi Germany and Soviet Russia*. Cambridge: Cambridge University Press.

Walsh, James P. and Ungson, Gerardo Rivera. 1991. 'Organizational Memory.' *The Academy of Management Review* 16, 57–91. doi: 10.5465/AMR.1991.427899.

Wegehaupt, Philipp. 2012. '*Wir grüßen den Haß!.' Die ideologische Schulung und Ausrichtung der NSDAP-Funktionäre im Dritten Reich.* Berlin: Metropol.

Wildt, Michael. 2007. *Volksgemeinschaft als Selbstermächtigung: Gewalt gegen Juden in der deutschen Provinz 1919 bis 1939.* Hamburg: Hamburger Edition.

Further Reading

Falter, Jürgen W., ed. 2016. *Junge Kämpfer, alte Opportunisten: Die Mitglieder der NSDAP 1919–1945.* Frankfurt am Main and New York: Campus.

A path-breaking quantitative social history of the Nazi Party strongly differentiating between regions and richly accompanied by tables.

Grill, Johnpeter H. 1983. 'The Nazi Movement in Baden 1920–1945.' PhD thesis, University of North Carolina Chapel Hill.

This study is still indispensable to understanding the NSDAP's organizational development at the regional level.

Kühl, Stefan. 2016. *Ordinary Organizations: Why Normal Men Carried Out the Holocaust,* translated by Jessica Spengler. Cambridge: Polity Press.

Provocative, stimulating, and insisting on the level of organization for analysing the police batallions' killings in the General Government of 1941–1942.

Orlow, Dietrich. 1969, 1973. *The History of the Nazi Party.* 2 vols. Newton Abbot, UK: David & Charles.

The unique complete history of the Nazi Party. Since 2007, it is also available as a single-volume paperback by Enigma Publishers.

Siemens, Daniel. 2017. *Stormtroopers: A New History of Hitler's Brownshirts.* New Haven, CT: Yale University Press.

The first complete history of the Stormtroopers, unique in its cultural historical approach.

CHAPTER SEVEN

Work(ers) Under the Swastika

JENS-UWE GUETTEL

This chapter argues that it is impossible to write the history of labour and labourers under the swastika as a simple story of heroic resistance. At the same time, the following analysis also shows that compared to other social groups (or 'classes') in Germany, dissent within this particular social group was high, despite the fact that after the destruction of organized labour in spring and summer of 1933 the room for manoeuvre for individuals became extremely limited. Yet between 1933 and 1945, and even though their autonomy was severely restricted, hundreds of thousands of workers nonetheless attempted to defend their personal interests and continued to voice their dissent.

The chapter also discusses the most important issues and trends in studies on the German labour movement and National Socialism from 1945 to the present. It evaluates numerous scholarly debates, among them discussions over the (non-) existence of the German working class, and questions of its integration, participation, and/or resistance against the National Socialist (NS) regime.

7.1 Destruction, Integration, and Resistance: Labour in Germany, 1933–1945

On 23 March 1933, Otto Wels, the chairman of the Social Democratic Party of Germany (SPD), was the last German politician to publicly criticize Adolf Hitler and the National Socialists for more than 12 years. On the day that the German rump parliament (the Communist Party had already been banned and many of its members arrested) voted for the Enabling Act, Wels made clear what voting for this decree actually meant: 'Never before, since there has been a German Reichstag, has the control of public affairs by the elected representatives of the people been

A Companion to Nazi Germany, First Edition. Edited by Shelley Baranowski, Armin Nolzen, and Claus-Christian W. Szejnmann.

diminished to such an extent as is happening now, and is supposed to happen even more through the new Enabling Act ....' Because only the SPD representatives rejected this decree, the act was passed and provided Hitler with dictatorial powers (Wels 1933).

The new National Socialist government saw the labour movement as both its main political enemy and a key demographic to be won over. Just over a month after the passage of the Enabling Act the regime renamed the traditional day of celebration of the international labour movement to 'the Day of National Labour'. Yet right after having offered this carrot, it pulled out the stick. On 2 May 1933, it banned labour unions while Stormtroopers (*Sturmabteilung*, SA) demolished union offices and arrested union leaders, many of whom ended up in the concentration camps the regime had created in the wake of the Reichstag Fire Decree of February 1933. These camps were almost exclusively filled with political opponents of the regime, first and foremost Communists and Social Democrats.

The events of spring 1933 show that the regime's first task was to eliminate working-class organizations. By 1934 almost all of Germany's most long-standing democratic institutions – labour unions, the SPD, other working-class associations and clubs – had either been destroyed or rendered politically impotent. At the same time, the organization that replaced the labour unions on 10 May 1933, Robert Ley's *Deutsche Arbeitsfront* (German Labour Front, DAF), demonstrated that in the new National Socialist Germany 'work' itself was deemed very important even if working-class organizations should not exist: Ley therefore did not want his organization to be a 'workers' front' but a 'work front'. The regime needed 'work both as economic substance' and as a tool of mobilization for educational and other purposes – among them, ultimately, the extermination of Jews and other unwanted groups. Workers' interests were not a major concern for the new rulers, while the 'destruction of the struggle of the classes', that is, the demolition of the political and socio-cultural ways in which workers traditionally expressed themselves, was. The regime's initial focus on silencing workers does not mean that the Nazis were completely successful in destroying working-class culture(s), milieus, and institutions. However, we cannot doubt that this particular aspect of 'synchronization' (*Gleichschaltung*) shifted German socio-political dynamics in fateful and terrible ways (Hachtmann 2014, 87; Buggeln and Wildt 2014).

The new regime's early and well thought out persecution measures were more than adequate to stifle any well-organized opposition. After 30 January 1933, working-class organizations realized too late that no ordinary government handover had happened. This fact became abundantly clear after the Reichstag Fire Decree, when the first wave of arrests, public intimidations, and humiliations (verbal as well as physical) began. Ultimately, even during its first five months in power, the new regime thus fooled Communists, Social Democrats, and labour union activists twice. Initially, labour activists believed that 30 January 1933 merely marked a more or less 'normal' change in government. Then, during and after the first wave of persecution, they assumed that the Nazis' oppressive measures would parallel Bismarck's Anti-Socialist Laws, which had banned all public socialist activities, but left working-class neighbourhoods alone. As a result, the first resistance activities of the labour movement (both Social Democratic and Communist) vis-à-vis the NS regime consisted of creating safe houses for activists who had gone underground and establishing hideaways for printing presses and other materials needed for political agitation. However, in April and May 1933, coordinated raids of whole districts and working-class housing blocks by police, the Gestapo, fire brigades, and other emergency services frustrated these efforts. It quickly became apparent that the lessons learned from the German Empire's Anti-Socialist Laws did not help under Nazi rule. By late spring and early summer 1933, the new regime had therefore 'created an atmosphere of insecurity and helplessness even in working-class strongholds that had until recently seemed to be safe'. The reports that the Sopade, the émigré organization of the outlawed Social Democratic Party based in Prague, received from Germany between 1933 and 1935 make clear that while the regime had largely failed to convert former Communists and Social Democrats, large-scale resistance had become impossible by the summer of 1933 (Peukert 1987, 104, 109).

At the same time, the story of German workers and working-class milieus is not just about failed and thwarted resistance. Even before 1933, German workers had never been a homogeneous socio-political and/or cultural group, and they had never unanimously voted either Social Democratic or Communist during the Weimar years – and neither had they before 1914–1918. For example, up until the March 1933 elections, especially in the Catholic regions of Germany, many workers continued to vote for the Centre Party. At the same time, around 25% of Germany's workers voted for the Nazi Party (NSDAP) in 1932 – although this group was likely composed of those who had never voted either SPD or Communist in the first place. As a result, even during the initial waves of persecution in early 1933, neither the regime's suppression nor the responses to it by the diverse regional working-class milieus, institutions, and associations were homogeneous. For example, if before January 1933 a socialist organization had been active in combating the Nazis, the new regime's actions against it were usually swift. Yet, other groups and institutions were often not bothered immediately and some remained unscathed until 1945. The Association for Worker Singers (DAS), for instance, actively engaged with the NS government in order to secure its continued existence. Ultimately, both the regime's actions between 1933 and 1936 (after 1936, its measures became increasingly radical) and the reactions to them ran the gamut from acceptance, resignation, and conformity to outright resistance. Regional factors clearly played a role as well: while there are records of resistance activities among and within, for example, former workers' sports clubs in Berlin, Bremen, and other major German cities, there exist few sources for such activities in Bavaria or Saxony. It therefore comes as no surprise that Social Democratic underground reports from Germany during the early years of the NS regime reveal that once the Nazis had firmly entrenched themselves, workers took advantage of the opportunities offered by Germany's new leaders. Most importantly, they accepted jobs created by the rearmament-fuelled economic boom. The Sopade reports indicate that, once employed again after years of being out of work (full employment was reached around 1937), workers were not inclined to risk this improvement of their and their families' living conditions because of politics. A complicated picture thus emerges: workers certainly did not resist the Nazis as a group or 'class'. At the same time, working-class areas and institutions definitely offered more significant resistance – ranging from 'mere' refusals to use the 'Hitler greeting' all the way to active underground work – than other regions or demographics (Schmiechen-Ackermann 1997, 123–127; Peukert 1987, 101; Brustein and Falter 1995; Zollitsch 1990; Lüdtke 1989; Fischer 1996; Pyta 1989; Mallmann 1996; see also Häberlen 2013, 378–379; Swett 2007).

While the NS regime contained large-scale working-class resistance, it still sought to win over workers through propaganda and 'education' measures as well as through offers of state-sponsored vacation and leisure-time opportunities, which were underwritten by the various sub-organizations of the DAF, most importantly by the 'Strength through Joy' association (KdF). Workers took advantage of these opportunities, but it is difficult to gauge their effectiveness and success. As Shelley Baranowski (2004) has shown, the popularity of KdF trips among workers, even former Communists and Social Democrats, clearly 'weakened what possibilities existed for a coherent and effective opposition. In the midst of a sullen and generally pervasive hostility among workers toward Nazism in general, the regime's social policy yielded positive results.' At the same time, 'tourists knew that KdF trips were under surveillance ...' and 'the manner of selection ... virtually guaranteed nationalistic responses'. Despite these ambiguities during the second half of the 1930s, one behavioural development among workers nevertheless became apparent: after 1936, workers began to use the labour shortages arising from full employment to negotiate wage raises individually. Alternatively, and worse from the regime's perspective, workers started slacking off, calling in sick, or engaging in other forms of absenteeism. It is tempting to view these developments, which even included local strikes, as a new form of resistance of 'the working class' against the regime, but this was by and large not the case, despite certain exceptions. Most of the time, workers and employees merely took advantage of the opportunities that full employment offered them. These developments were not to the regime's liking, as they hampered Germany's production capacity. Yet these occurrences also demonstrated that especially younger workers were willing to accept the conditions that the regime created, as after 1936 individual instead of collective bargaining could improve one's personal financial situation. While not in the regime's interest, these developments weakened the traditional principle of working-class solidarity. The experiences of a younger generation of workers, who lacked self-acquired knowledge of the pre-Nazi Weimar years, may thus have contributed to the decline of distinct working-class milieus, which after 1945 did not re-emerge to the extent they had existed before the 'seizure of power' (Baranowski 2004, 196, 197; Peukert 1987, 113).

All these developments suggest that the Nazi years represented an important break in the history of organized labour in Germany as the Third Reich abruptly ended Weimar-era socialist or, more specifically, Social Democratic welfare and labour policies, among them, most significantly, the principle of collective bargaining. The language used by Adolf Hitler and Robert Ley when talking about work and workers makes abundantly clear that the history of the labour movement and organized labour's more than half a century old struggle for the improvement of workers' social and economic conditions were not the bench marks of the new

National Socialist regime. Instead, the model was the front-line comradery of the trenches of the Great War. Wistful memories of the First World War thus replaced socialist and Social Democratic language and content. As Hitler put it: 'We have to carry the momentous shared social experience [*Gemeinschaftserlebnis*] of the Great War into our great community [*Lebensgemeinschaft*] … This is the ultimate purpose of the Labor Front' (Hachtmann 2014). The terminology used by NS leaders described workers as an army-like body of people – 'soldiers of work', in Hitler's words – that could be deployed according to the Führer's interests and according to the necessities of rearmament and the war economy (Hachtmann 2014). This militarization of German labour thus rhetorically turned entrepreneurs – 'the leaders of business' – into 'officers of the economy'. In turn, the DAF's own 'workshop chairmen' (*Betriebsobmänner*) were sometimes termed 'staff sergeants'. Robert Ley and the DAF also often reappropriated older socialist terms, for example the suffix '-*gemeinschaft*', meaning 'collective' or 'community', in order to add it to other phrases, among them '*Frontgemeinschaft*' or '*Betriebsgemeinschaft*'. On the one hand, these idioms suggested that warfare and work were communal experiences shared and supported at all cost by the whole *Volksgemeinschaft* ('people's community'). At the same time, the intended militarization of labour also completely reframed the meaning of these terms, thereby infusing them with a strong sense of social Darwinist competition. Tellingly, Robert Ley thus defined the new National Socialist meaning of the word 'community' by using the phrase 'community means selection' (Hachtmann 1989; Hachtmann 2006; Hachtmann 2012, 123; Hitler and Ley cited in Hachtmann 2014, 89, 90; Brustein and Falter 1995; Zollitsch 1990; Lüdtke 1989; Fischer et al. 1996; Mallmann 1996; Buggeln and Wildt 2014, xvii–xviii).

Despite the DAF's focus on competition and selection, after 1933 many workers nevertheless experienced a rise in their standard of living because of higher wages, especially once full employment had been reached in 1936. To be sure, this development was an improvement only when set in relation to the depths of the Great Depression, but this did not make it less real for contemporaries. Still, the average hourly wage in 1936 was 22.8% and in 1943 still 8% lower than in the pre-crisis year 1929. Simultaneously, the share of the national income of the lower half of the income scale dropped by 7% from 1928 to 1936; at the same time, the richest 1% of all Germans increased their share of the total German income by 5%. These developments show that, at least on a strictly economic level, the NS regime did not break down class barriers, better the living conditions of German workers, or fulfil old Social Democratic demands. Instead, as indicated and foreshadowed by Robert Ley's and the DAF's rhetoric, work was supposed to integrate workers into a strictly hierarchically and racially defined 'people's community', which could be utilized for the purpose of war – a war that would only be over once the preconditions for the racial and spatial reordering of Germany and Europe had been created (Hachtmann 1989; 2006; 2012, 123; Hitler cited in Hachtmann 2014, 89; Brustein and Falter 1995; Zollitsch 1990; Lüdtke 1989; Fischer et al. 1996; Mallmann 1996; Buggeln and Wildt 2014, xvii–xviii).

Once we switch our focus from the six years of peace to the war years between 1939 and 1945, it becomes clear how successful the regime had been at suppressing organized resistance in working-class milieus by 1939. Moreover, the decreasing importance of the German Labour Front after 1939 indicates that the regime was well aware of this development. While Robert Ley's DAF remained an integral component of the Nazi regime throughout the war, at least in the newly conquered territories (beginning with the Sudetenland in 1938), Ley was largely unsuccessful at carving out spheres of control for his institution. Following the annexation of the Sudetenland, DAF planners envisioned social uplift opportunities for German workers willing to move to the new territories. However, the army, the SS and industrialists ignored these plans. After the invasion of the Soviet Union had begun, Ley attempted to involve himself in the exploitation of the soon-to-be acquired Eastern Empire (*Ostreich*). To be clear, Ley did not have any qualms about Nazi Germany's envisioned eastward expansion. Yet ultimately only Heinrich Himmler shared the intensity of Hitler's obsession with obtaining living space in Eastern Europe. As a result, the SS had sidestepped the DAF even before the invasion. During a conference on 30 October 1941, Ley was thus flabbergasted to learn about the magnitude of the annexations envisioned by Hitler and Himmler (Guettel 2013).

Beginning with the invasion of Poland, the regime added another dimension of work to its arsenal: slave labour. As historian Ulrich Herbert (2000, 193) notes: 'The National Socialist "deployment of foreigners" between 1939 and 1945 was the largest use of foreign forced labor since the end of slavery in the nineteenth century.' By 1944, around 7.6 million foreigners 'officially reported as working in the territory of the Reich, largely brought there by force for work deployment' (Herbert 2000, 195). However, Ley's Labour Front was not in control of these measures. Instead, Fritz Sauckel, who worked under Hermann Göring in the Four-Year-Plan Office and eventually held the title of 'General Plenipotentiary for Work Deployment', had been charged with this task. All of these developments illustrate the DAF's decreasing importance after 1939 while simultaneously highlighting the fact that during the Second World War the regime was not nearly as worried about 'the fiery red glow' of German working-class resistance as it had been in 1933 (Herbert 2000, 196). The lack of widespread opposition thus has to be taken at least in part as a sign of the Nazis' overall success in silencing and partially co-opting even working-class milieus. Indeed, especially during the war years, workers in the so-called *Altreich* largely followed the regime's requests to participate (*mitmachen*). At the same time, they also perceived these demands as mandatory rather than voluntary (Herbert 2000; Rauh-Kühne 1997, 145–165; Buggeln and Wildt 2014, ix–xxxviii; Eley 2013, 102; Schneider 2014, 1341).

After 1941, under the cover of the war against the Soviet Union the regime also began to use labour for extermination: Jews died en masse not only in death camps and from the systematic and continuous massacres of the *Einsatzgruppen* behind the Eastern Front, but also in slave-labour powered factories adjacent to the death camps. At the same time the forced infrastructural work in the newly conquered eastern territories was deadly as well. As a result, during the war years the regime's 'offerings' to Germans and German workers in the *Altreich* also included direct and indirect profits from the spoils of war as well as the regime's slave labour system. Germans accepted these offerings – among them, most importantly, the continued easy availability of basic food items, at least compared to the First World War. Did this behaviour turn German workers into 'satisfied robbers', or the Nazi regime into a 'courtesy dictatorship', as Götz Aly (2005) has argued? Many scholars have disagreed. They point out that the disproportionately high percentage of workers among those who because of 'political offenses' were caught in the wheels of the National Socialist terror suggests that such a judgement blurs the lines between accepting the prevailing situation and actively supporting the Nazis' crimes and genocide (Schneider 2014, 1341).

The regime wanted workers to support Nazi policies, and it also wanted them to willingly participate in bringing about NS-based socio-political changes, among them increasing the birth rate and generating acceptance for a new, racialized nationalism. During the war, the regime further stepped up its 'participation anticipations', which after September 1939 began to include drastic changes at all social and cultural levels. While workers did not cease to exist as a social class between 1933 and 1945, after 1933 an increasingly state-sponsored process of *Entklassung* (de-classing) left its mark on working-class lives and milieus. True, this process was not new, as often the Third Reich merely maintained socio-economic developments that had begun as early as 1914: both the state-sponsored integration of working-class institutions during the Great War as well as the post-1918 democratization of German society had already chipped away at the meaningfulness of 'class consciousness' among German workers. The Nazis continued these developments with a clear goal in mind: the creation of an ideologically and racially homogeneous *Volksgemeinschaft*. While this ideological goal conflicted with other, more immediate aims of the regime, among them satisfying Germany's old social and business elites and increasing rearmament as quickly and efficiently as possible, between 1933 and 1939 the regime's propaganda measures nevertheless attempted to actively bring about an *Entklassung* of workers. Moreover, after September 1939 the challenges of war further amplified a general sense of community across all social classes. Ultimately, all of these attempts and developments brought about lasting socio-economic and socio-cultural changes: after 1945 the rebuilding of political structures tried to evoke the old social frameworks of Weimar: in the western Trizone, the SPD was therefore re-founded as a working-class party, and the CDU and FDP as conservative and bourgeois parties. At the same time, the acceptance of the principles of wage autonomy and collective bargaining across the political spectrum (a big difference compared to employers' attitudes during the Weimar years) indicates that real differences existed between the Weimar years or the German Empire and the ways workers understood themselves and were understood after 1945 in West Germany (Schneider 2014, 1346, 1348; Geyer 2002).

7.2   Scholarship on Organized Labour, the Demise of the Weimar Republic, and National Socialism since 1945

After 1945, especially in West Germany, few scholars were interested in labour and work under the Nazis. Instead, conservative resistance fighters such as Carl Goerdeler or Claus von Staufenberg were among the preferred research topics.

This trend began to change in the early 1960s with the publication of the first studies of Fritz Fischer and Hans-Ulrich Wehler. During this decade, various narratives
on the 'seizure of power' of the NSDAP and on the regime's early years in power
were established. One focused on the resistance of workers and their institutions
against the threat of the Nazis (Heinrich August Winkler, Gerhard A. Ritter) while
another attempted to highlight the labour movement's responsibility for the rise of
the Nazis. The latter perspective ultimately placed the blame for the demise of the
Weimar Republic and the ascent of the National Socialists squarely on the shoul-
ders of the biggest German working-class institution, the SPD. This interpretation
tied the 'seizure of power' in January 1933 to pre-1933 developments, and, most
importantly, emphasized the many shortcomings and failures of the Social
Democrats during the 'German Revolution' in November 1918 and afterwards.
To be sure, this criticism emanated at least as much from contemporaneous sources
from across the political spectrum in Weimar Germany as from subsequent historical analyses. Yet after 1945 historians linked this critique of the SPD to Weimar's
collapse. This perspective accused the party of having 'sold out' the interests of the
German working class in 1918/1919 by working with Germany's 'old elites'
(especially the army leadership), which in turn caused an unbridgeable enmity
between Social Democrats and Communists that 10 years later undermined working-class resistance against the Nazis (Schorske 1955; Roth 1963). As a result, the
SPD was directly implicated in the destruction of the republic that it had helped to
create. Current versions of this perspective attempt to link the SPD in other ways
to the rise of the National Socialists. Götz Aly (2011) thus recently contended that
the SPD's focus on the collective, the good of the many versus the good of the few,
created a mindset that the NSDAP could racially charge and successfully utilize.
Ultimately, Aly characterizes the Nazi regime as having fulfilled older Social
Democratic demands. Along similar lines, others have posited that, even before
1914, the SPD accepted the existence of a 'Jewish problem'. As a result, the SPD
added to (rather than combated) antisemitism in Germany, therefore helping to
make the Nazis' exterminatory antisemitic attitudes palatable for a broad public. In
many ways, these views are extremes, and much of the recent scholarship does not
support their arguments. A number of prominent historians, among them Hans-
Ulrich Wehler and Adam Tooze, have thus, for example, rejected Aly's contention
that the Nazis actually redistributed wealth from top to bottom (Fischer 2007).

The post-1945 debate about Germany's left before and up to the Nazi takeover
has therefore been composed of at least two sides. Criticism of the SPD's role during the early years of the Weimar Republic has thus in fact come from both the
right and the left. At the same time, this criticism coexisted with accounts that
stressed the achievements of organized labour and Social Democracy under the
German Empire before 1918 as well as during the Weimar years. Until the late
1970s, the conception that Germany's pre-1933 working-class institutions (and
their remnants after 1933) had been strong and thus resistant to National Socialist
temptations was particularly widespread among scholars embracing the latter
perspective. Their studies also took for granted that a culturally and politically
homogeneous working class had indeed existed in Germany prior to 1933. During
the early 1980s this perspective unravelled. As a result, works on working-class

institutions and their fate during the Nazi years became less frequent, while the number of both broader assessments and as well as microstudies on specific regions and milieus increased. Since 1990, scholars' diminished focus on institutions, among them KPD (*Kommunistische Partei Deutschlands*, German Communist Party)-related resistance organizations as well as the exiled SPD (Sopade), may also reflect the declining importance of political parties in German public and cultural life since reunification: estimates of both SPD and CDU membership have steadily decreased in the past three decades (Herbert 1989, 321; Ritter 1959; Mason 1995; Wehler 1971).

The recent literature thus displays a number of trends. Studies have moved away from old concepts of the 'working class'. Instead, new works on the labour movement during the Third Reich often reconceptualize and question the existence of homogeneous working-class milieus. As a result, a multifaceted picture has emerged that includes Catholic and often decidedly non-socialist or non-communist workers as well as Social Democrats, Communists, and labour union activists. The most recent studies have also begun to look more closely into National Socialist perceptions of 'work' and 'labour' – for example, the relationship between whom the regime deemed fit to work and the euthanasia measures undertaken against even racially acceptable 'Aryan' tuberculosis patients. While structuralist historians such as Timothy Mason and Detlev Peukert focused on problems that the Nazis created by maintaining an industrial-capitalist system while simultaneously dismantling all institutions that represented workers' interests, newer works scrutinize the function of 'labour' and 'work' within the regime. This tendency of the recent scholarship also reflects historians' renewed interest in National Socialist ideology (Rauh-Kühne 1997, 145–165; Wolters 2008; Eley 2013, 102; Bernhard 2016).

As a result, during the past two decades the historiography on the relationship between the labour movement and National Socialism largely abandoned institutional perspectives. Instead, detailed studies on voting patterns and microstudies of specific socio-cultural milieus have advanced the field (Brustein and Falter 1995; Swett 2007; Häberlen 2013). This trend runs counter to developments in the broader study of late nineteenth- and early twentieth-century German history, in which scholars have chosen different methodological vantage points, among them global and transnational perspectives as an alternative to the traditional nation-state paradigm. These broad approaches, for instance Sebastian Conrad's *Globalisierung und Nation im Deutschen Kaiserreich* (2006) and Andrew Zimmerman's *Alabama in Africa; Booker T. Washington, the German Empire, and the Globalization of the New South* (2010), challenge us to view late nineteenth- and early twentieth-century German history not merely from within the country, but also as part of larger, global socio-economic and socio-cultural developments. While these two studies are not directly relevant to the history of the Third Reich, they nevertheless demonstrate the cultural and economic importance of 'work' and 'labour' to Germany's transnational interconnectedness. To a degree, historians of Weimar and Nazi Germany have followed suit. Adam Tooze's *The Wages of Destruction* (2007) locates the Second World War and the Nazis' frenzied and genocidal quest for living space within the framework of an increasingly Americanized global economy, while Timothy Snyder's controversial *Bloodlands* (2010) traces the geography of mass murder and genocide across Eastern European borders. However, because these works integrate the development of Nazism and of the National Socialist state into more extensive *longue durée* and spatial perspectives, they tend to concentrate almost exclusively on the nationalist camp while at the same time wanting 'to write the socialist camp out of the bigger historical picture' (Ziemann and Szejnmann 2013, 326). Placing greater emphasis on the German left and the labour movement would make it easier to produce more nuanced analyses of individual and collective agency under the regime. Simultaneously, it would also make possible more precise delineations of the Third Reich's socio-economic and socio-cultural structures, which could, for example, complicate Timothy Snyder's attempt to resurrect an intentionalist perspective on the regime's expansionist and genocidal policies after 1939 (Schneider 2014, 1337–1343).

Scholars interested in the history of labour and workers under the Nazi regime should accept the challenge posed by the recent transnational and global histories: it will be beneficial for the field as a whole if historians begin to link the many important regional and milieu studies with their focus on the realities of labour under the swastika to larger perspectives, especially given labour history's relative marginalization after 1990. Reintroducing labour as one of the main analytical categories in NS-related research could assist scholars in connecting local and global developments. Important recent studies on *Zwangsarbeit* (slave labour) during the war years thus demonstrate the multifaceted and regionalized nature of this phenomenon. *Zwangsarbeit* within the *Altreich* (i.e. within Germany's pre-1938 borders) differed from forced-labour conditions in the occupied territories. Yet the situation in occupied Poland, for example, was different from that in Yugoslavia or Belgium. In turn, these differing local conditions were nevertheless connected to the regime's larger needs and its often incongruous attempts at realizing NS ideology. The barely touched issue of female labour within Germany, which in contradiction to NS ideological tenets increased after 1939, is another case in point. As a result, our knowledge of the subject of labour – forced, free, female, etc. – under the NS regime would benefit from larger European and transatlantic analytical frameworks that not only focus on the 'inner German' tensions between NS ideology and the regime's socio-economic needs, but also scrutinize how developments in Germany compared and corresponded to changes in the economic and socio-cultural situation of male and female workers in other industrialized countries between 1933 and 1945.

7.3 Conclusion

Did the NS regime's successful suppression of organized labour destroy 'the German working class?' No, because 'the German working class' as a homogeneous politically conscious group never existed in the first place. However, German workers constituted their own social group both before and after 1933. While the regime's *Volksgemeinschaft*-focused propaganda measures attempted to remove the bourgeois stigma from being a manual labourer, the Third Reich neither promised nor wanted to abolish class barriers. At the same time, Nazi policing and repression were largely successful in preventing free and unchecked communication between workers. After the 'seizure of power' it therefore became increasingly difficult and dangerous to come together to actively oppose the regime. In spite of these conditions, even during the regime's final years workers dissented en masse in the form of absenteeism and slacking-off. In addition, hundreds of thousands of German workers at least temporarily participated in political resistance activities. At the same time, these activities existed side by side with expressions of consent, and/or unpolitical 'getting by' attitudes. After 1945, working-class culture(s), institutions, and milieus were re-established, yet not with the same depth and cohesion that they had possessed before 1933. This development may have been partially the result of the NS regime's suppression, coercion, and integration measures, but the structural changes of the post-war German economy (especially in West Germany) are certainly causal factors as well. As a result, measuring the Nazi regime's lasting effect on work and labourers in Germany is as challenging as determining the regime's long-term bearing on other aspects of German society. In retrospect, the social and economic changes brought about by the NS regime between 1933 and 1945 can and should be evaluated against the backdrop of the larger socio-economic trends in the middle decades of the twentieth century.

Yet any attempt to write the history of labour under the National Socialist regime has to also acknowledge the caesuras of 1933 and 1945, as these dates had real importance for contemporaries. The National Socialists' actions against workers and their institutions were swift, and they brutally changed the lives of many German workers unexpectedly and radically within a couple of weeks in the spring of 1933 – and only Germany's total defeat in 1945 put an end to these profound alterations. From its beginnings in January 1933, the NS regime was well aware that before it could turn its attention to other ideological goals (among them, of course, also the eventual annihilation of German and European Jews), it had to destroy the ability of Germany's workers to organize themselves politically. In turn, the destruction of the labour movement endeared the new regime to Germany's nationalist and conservative business elites, thus further ensuring their cooperation. In addition, beginning with the annexation of Austria, Heinrich Himmler and Reinhard Heydrich were able to deploy SS manpower to the annexed territories because they required fewer forces at home. The obliteration of all working-class institutions with even the slightest political relevance was thus the necessary precondition for many other actions the NS regime took after the 'seizure of power'. In consequence, it was the main guarantee that German society truly 'worked' in the National Socialist sense of the term (Ziemann and Szejnman 2013, 326; Schneider 2014, 1337–1343; Buggeln and Wildt 2014, ix–xxxviii).

References

Aly, Götz. 2005. *Hitlers Volksstaat: Raub, Rassenkrieg und Nationaler Sozialismus*. Frankfurt am Main: Fischer Taschenbuch Verlag.

Aly, Götz. 2011. *Warum die Deutschen? Warum die Juden? Gleichheit, Neid und Rassenhass, 1800–1933*. Frankfurt am Main: S. Fischer.

Baranowski, Shelley. 2004. *Strength Through Joy: Consumerism and Mass Tourism in the Third Reich*. Cambridge: Cambridge University Press.

Bernhard, Patrick. 2016. '"In the Shadow of 'Euthanasia'": A New Study on the Murder of Tuberculosis Patients during National Socialism.' https://zzf-pdm.academia.edu/PatrickBernhard (accessed 25 January 2016).

Brustein, W. and Falter, J.W. 1995. 'Who Joined the Nazi Party? Assessing Theories of the Social Origins of Nazism.' *Zeitgeschichte* 3–4, 83–108.

Buggeln, Marc and Wildt, Michael. 2014. 'Arbeit im Nationalsozialismus.' In *Arbeit Im Nationalsozialismus*, edited by Marc Buggeln and Michael Wildt. Munich: De Gruyter.

Conrad, Sebastian. 2006. *Globalisierung und Nation im Deutschen Kaiserreich*. Munich: C.H. Beck.

Eley, Geoff. 2013. *Nazism as Fascism: Violence, Ideology, and the Ground of Consent in Germany, 1930–1945*. Abingdon, UK: Routledge.

Fischer, Conan et al., eds. 1996. *The Rise of National Socialism and the Working Classes in Weimar Germany*. Providence, RI and Oxford: Berghahn Books.

Fischer, Lars. 2007. *The Socialist Response to Antisemitism in Imperial Germany*. Cambridge: Cambridge University Press.

Geyer, Michael. 2002. '"There is a Land Where Everything is Pure: Its Name is Land of Death": Some Observations on Catastrophic Nationalism.' In *Sacrifice and National Belonging in Twentieth-Century Germany*, edited by Marcus Funck, Greg Eghigian, and Matthew Paul Berg. Arlington: Texas A&M University Press.

Guettel, Jens-Uwe. 2013. 'The US Frontier as Rationale for the Nazi East? Settler Colonialism and Genocide in Nazi-occupied Eastern Europe and the American West.' *Journal of Genocide Research* 15(4), 401–419.

Häberlen, Joachim C. 2013. 'Scope for Agency and Political Options: The German Working-Class Movement and the Rise of Nazism.' *Politics, Religion & Ideology* 14(3), 377–394.

Hachtmann, Rüdiger. 1989. *Industriearbeit Im 'Dritten Reich': Untersuchungen zu den Lohn- Und Arbeitsbedingungen in Deutschland 1933–1945*. Göttingen: Vandenhoeck & Ruprecht.

Hachtmann, Rüdiger. 2006. *Ein Koloß auf tönernen Füßen: Das Gutachten des Wirtschaftsprüfers Karl Eicke über die Deutsche Arbeitsfront vom 31. Juli 1936*. Munich: Oldenbourg.

Hachtmann, Rüdiger. 2012. '"Volksgemeinschaftliche Dienstleister"? Anmerkungen zu Selbstverständnis und Funktion der Deutschen Arbeitsfront und der NS-Gemeinschaft "Kraft Durch Freude".' In *'Volksgemeinschaft:' Mythos, wirkungsmächtige soziale Verheißung oder soziale Realität im 'Dritten Reich?'* edited by Detlef Schmiechen-Ackermann. Paderborn: Schöningh.

Hachtmann, Rüdiger. 2014. 'Arbeit und Arbeitsfront: Ideologie und Praxis.' In *Arbeit Im Nationalsozialismus*, edited by Marc Buggeln and Michael Wildt. Munich: De Gruyter Oldenbourg.

Herbert, Ulrich. 1989.' "Arbeiterschaft im 'Dritten Reich." Zwischenbilanz und offene Fragen.' *Geschichte und Gesellschaft* 15(3).

Lüdtke, Alf. 1989. 'What happened to the "Fiery Red Glow?" Workers' Experiences and German Fascism.' In *The History of Everyday Life: Reconstructing Social Experiences and Ways of Life*, edited by Alf Lüdtke. Princeton, NJ: Princeton University Press.

Mallmann, Klaus-Michael. 1996. *Kommunisten in der Weimarer Republik: Sozialgeschichte einer revolutionären Bewegung*. Darmstadt: Wissenschaftliche Buchgesellschaft.

Mason, Timothy W. 1995. *Nazism, Fascism and the Working Class*. Cambridge: Cambridge University Press.

Peukert, Detlev. 1987. *Inside Nazi Germany: Conformity, Opposition, and Racism in Everyday Life*. New Haven, CT: Yale University Press.

Pyta, Wolfram. 1989. *Gegen Hitler und für die Republik: Die Auseinandersetzung der deutschen Sozialdemokratie mit der NSDAP in der Weimarer Republik*. Düsseldorf: Droste.

Rauh-Kühne, Cornelia. 1997. 'Anpassung und Widerstand? Kritische Bemerkungen zur Erforschung des Katholischen Milieus.' In *Anpassung, Verweigerung, Widerstand. Soziale Milieus, politische Kultur und der Widerstand gegen den Nationalsozialismus in Deutschland im regionalen Vergleich*, edited by Detlef Schmiechen-Ackermann. Berlin: Gedenkstätte Deutscher Widerstand.

Ritter, Gerhard A. 1959. *Die Arbeiterbewegung im Wilhelminischen Reich: Die Sozialdemokratische Partei und die Freien Gewerkschaften 1890–1900*. Berlin: Colloquium Verlag.

Roth, Guenther. 1963. *The Social Democrats in Imperial Germany: A Study in Working-Class Isolation and National Integration*. Totowa, NJ: Bedminster Press.

Schmiechen-Ackermann, Detlef. 1997. 'Sozialistische Milieuvereine nach 1933. Strategien der Anpassung und der Verweigerung am Beispiel der Arbeitersportler und Arbeitersänger.' In *Anpassung, Verweigerung, Widerstand. Soziale Milieus, politische Kultur und der Widerstand gegen den Nationalsozialismus in Deutschland im regionalen Vergleich*, edited by Detlef Schmiechen-Ackermann. Berlin: Gedenkstätte Deutscher Widerstand.

Schneider, Michael. 2014. *In der Kriegsgesellschaft: Arbeiter und Arbeiterbewegung 1939 bis 1945*, edited by Gerhard A. Ritter. Bonn: Dietz.

Schorske, Carl. 1955. *German Social Democracy, 1905–1917: The Development of the Great Schism*. Cambridge, MA: Harvard University Press.

Snyder, Timothy. 2010. *Bloodlands: Europe between Hitler and Stalin*. New York: Basic Books.

Swett, Pamela. 2007. *Neighbors and Enemies: The Culture of Radicalism in Berlin, 1929–1933*. Cambridge: Cambridge University Press.

Tooze, Adam. 2007. *The Wages of Destruction: The Making and Breaking of the Nazi Economy*. New York: Viking.

Wehler, Hans-Ulrich. 1971. *Sozialdemokratie und Nationalstaat: Nationalitätenfragen in Deutschland 1840–1914*. Göttingen: Vandenhoeck & Ruprecht.

Wels, Otto. 1933. 'Rede am 23. März 1933.' http://www.spd.de/linkableblob/5698/data/geschichte_rede_otto_wels.pdf (accessed 18 October 2015).

Wolters, Christine. 2008. 'Der Umgang mit therapieverweigernden Tuberkulosekranken im Nationalsozialismus.' *Das Gesundheitswesen* 70(7).

Ziemann, Benjamin and Szejnmann., Claus-Christian W. 2013. '"Machtergreifung". The Nazi Seizure of Power in 1933.' *Politics, Religion & Ideology* 14(3), 321–337.

Zimmerman, Andrew. 2010. *Alabama in Africa: Booker T. Washington, the German Empire, and the Globalization of the New South*. Princeton, NJ: Princeton University Press.

Zollitsch, Wolfgang. 1990. *Arbeiter zwischen Weltwirtschaftskrise und Nationalsozialismus: Ein Beitrag zur Sozialgeschichte der Jahre 1928 bis 1936*. Göttingen: Vandenhoeck & Ruprecht.

Further Reading

Baranowski, Shelley. 2004. *Strength Through Joy: Consumerism and Mass Tourism in the Third Reich*. Cambridge: Cambridge University Press.

Buggeln, Marc and Wildt, Michael. 2014. 'Arbeit im Nationalsozialismus.' In *Arbeit Im Nationalsozialismus*, edited by Marc Buggeln and Michael Wildt. Munich: De Gruyter Oldenbourg.

Geyer, Michael. 2002. '"There is a Land Where Everything is Pure: Its Name is Land of Death': Some Observations on Catastrophic Nationalism.' In *Sacrifice and National Belonging in Twentieth-Century Germany*, edited by Marcus Funck, Greg Eghigian, and Matthew Paul Berg. Arlington: Texas A&M University Press.

Herbert, Ulrich. 1989. 'Arbeiterschaft im "Dritten Reich": Zwischenbilanz und offene Fragen.' *Geschichte und Gesellschaft* 15(3).

Herbert, Ulrich. 2000. 'Forced Laborers in the Third Reich: An Overview.' *International Labor and Working-Class History* 58, 192–218.

Lüdtke, Alf. 1989. 'What happened to the "Fiery Red Glow?" Workers' Experiences and German Fascism.' In *The History of Everyday Life. Reconstructing Social Experiences and Ways of Life*, edited by Alf Lüdtke. Princeton, NJ: Princeton University Press.

Mason, Timothy W. 1995. *Nazism, Fascism and the Working Class*. Cambridge: Cambridge University Press.

Schneider, Michael. 1999. *Unterm Hakenkreuz: Arbeiter und Arbeiterbewegung 1933 bis 1939*, edited by Gerhard A. Ritter. Bonn: Dietz.

Schneider, Michael. 2014. *In der Kriegsgesellschaft: Arbeiter und Arbeiterbewegung 1939 bis 1945*, edited by Gerhard A. Ritter. Bonn: Dietz.

Peukert, Detlev. 1982. *Volksgenossen und Gemeinschaftsfremde: Anpassung, Ausmerze und Aufbegehren unter dem Nationalsozialismus*. Frankfurt am Main: Bund-Verlag.

Winkler, Dörte. 1985. *Frauenarbeit im 'Dritten Reich'*. Hamburg: Hoffmann und Campe.

CHAPTER EIGHT

Resistance

DETLEF SCHMIECHEN-ACKERMANN

8.1 *Widerstand* – An Ambiguous Term and Concept with Different Meanings

During the late 1960s and 1970s the term '*Widerstand*' became more and more important in political debates in Germany. Simultaneously, the meaning of the term varied: *Widerstand* could mean passive resistance against conditions of 'power' or 'rule' which were understood as being unfair. This attitude of protest intended to take a firm stand against authorities, the government, or the political system. Michel Foucault defined 'resistance' as the opposite of 'power', and Pierre Bourdieu described 'resistance' as a collective protest movement in the public sphere.

In the historiography about the Third Reich a broad definition of various kinds of *Widerstand* against Hitler competed with a narrow interpretation that associated it with the aim to destroy Nazism. Then, in 1982, Detlev Peukert suggested a model of four principal types of politically deviant behaviour: nonconformity, refusal, protest, and resistance (Peukert 1982, 97). Martin Broszat suggested the term '*Resistenz*' to characterize patterns of social behaviour which tended to limit the power of the regime in everyday life or to repel requirements of Nazi politics (Broszat 1981, 697–699; see also Wildt 2007a, 121–122). However, this 'low-level' description of resistance did not gain much support (Mallmann and Paul 1993).

As a result of these debates, a broad as well as a narrow definition could be useful depending on the specific cognitive interest. To discuss the diversity of protest against and nonconformity to Nazi rule, we will use a broad definition of *Widerstand* here. This broad understanding of 'resistance' is usually sub-classified (Kenkmann 2008, 144–149) in 'nonconformity' (occasional violations of Nazi codes of behaviour and attitudes, mostly in a private sphere and informal social relationships), 'refusal' (to deny obedience to only some aspects of Nazi rule, but in the public sphere and with the intention to criticize the politics of the regime), and 'protest' (more fundamental rejection of Nazi politics in the public sphere). The most elaborate kind of 'resistance' (broad definition) is organized political resistance (narrow definition). To focus on the circumstances of clandestine underground activities and the chances of success for these political resistance organizations, the branding as 'resistance in the narrow sense' is helpful. All types of nonconformist behaviour will be discussed as 'resistance' in a superordinate concept. 'Resistance' as resolute action to overthrow the regime will be marked as 'resistance in the narrow sense' (Benz 2014, 10–12).

8.2   Periods and Types of Resistance in Nazi Germany

The first battle of the German resistance against Hitler was lost when the president of the German Reich, Paul von Hindenburg, handed over power to Adolf Hitler as leader of the Nazi movement on 30 January 1933. Political radicalization characterized the final years of the Weimar Republic, which saw a steady rise in armed hostilities in the streets of bigger (and even smaller) German cities. The Stormtroopers of the Nazi *Sturmabteilung* (SA) demonstrated their rising power by marching through the streets of working-class districts, disturbing political meetings of their enemies, and looking for violent confrontations with Social Democrats and Communists. They tried to occupy the 'social terrain' of urban quarters (Schmiechen-Ackermann 1998, 108–435).

Savage and unregulated terror carried out by local branches of the SA and the efforts of NSDAP (*Nationalsozialistische Deutsche Arbeiterpartei*, Nazi Party) officials to secure their power marked the first months after Hitler had been appointed Reich chancellor. By the middle of March 1933, many political opponents, among them more than 10 000 communists, had been arrested (Roth 2016, 14–30) and were held in 'protective custody' (*Schutzhaft*) (an euphemistic term for political imprisonment). They were held in concentration camps like Dachau, Oranienburg, and Moringen, but also in many improvised local camps. Not coincidently, the exodus of opponents of the Nazis into political exile (to France, Great Britain, the United States, Russia, Czechoslovakia, Scandinavia, and other places) began. Until 1939 the number of political refugees from Germany and Austria totalled at least 25 000, perhaps even 40 000 persons (Schmiechen-Ackermann 2015).

Parts of the German Labour Movement, which went underground, dominated the initial phase of organized resistance inside Germany. This *Arbeiterwiderstand* was relatively extensive in 1933/1934, but its failure to challenge the Nazi regime became manifest from the middle of the 1930s (Peukert 1986). The secret state police (*Geheime Staatspolizei* or simply Gestapo) was in the long run very efficient in destroying it. In 1937 the vast majority of Communist, Socialist, and Social Democratic resistance fighters were exiled, imprisoned, or dead. Since the Third Reich had consolidated its power, the remaining political opponents and some small groups that continued to struggle against Hitler, who reached the peak of his popularity around 1937/1938, found themselves in a disadvantageous position. Between the 'Reich Crystal Night' (*Reichspogromnacht*) in November 1938 and the attack on the Soviet Union in 1941, the forms and types of resistance changed too: from the hopeless attempt at mass resistance to clandestine individual actions and conspiracies of small elite groups, especially in the Wehrmacht. During the first phase of the Second World War, when the German armies ran from victory to victory, the framework for successful resistance was very unfavourable (Roth 2016, 240–260). These conditions changed after the huge counter-offensive of the Red Army, which led to the disastrous defeat of the 6th Army at Stalingrad. Ordinary Germans perceived this as a turning point of the war, triggering a shift in sentiment. Many Germans who earlier inscribed themselves in the racial project of the Aryan *Volksgemeinschaft* ('people's community') (Wildt 2007b; Schmiechen-Ackermann 2012; Von Reeken and Thießen 2013; Steber, and Gotto 2014) now characterized themselves as a desperate *Schicksalsgemeinschaft* ('community of destiny'). While belief in the 'Hitler myth' (Kershaw 2003) diminished progressively, conditions for successful resistance improved a little. New Communist underground groups were formed (Mehringer 1997, 167–180) and elitist conspiratorial circles discussed how to get rid of Hitler (Mehringer 1997, 180–233).

8.3   The Wide Range of Resistance and Nonconformity in Nazi Germany: Organizations, Social Milieus, and Individuals

Many different forms of nonconformity, opposition, and resistance arose in working-class and middle-class milieus (for a broad outline, see Steinbach and Tuchel 1994; Mehringer 1997; Benz 2014). Resistance (in the broad definition) could arise out of organizations, which were banned and dissolved in 1933, but also out of social networks which were organized in an informal way. And, sometimes, even single persons tried to challenge the Nazi dictatorship. During the early years of the Third Reich, resistance activities in the tradition of the labour movement were most extensive, but nevertheless impotent (Schneider 1999, 783–1078).

8.3.1   Communist Resistance

Communist Party leaders called upon their followers to form small groups, hold clandestine meetings, distribute leaflets, and agitate against National Socialism. In autumn 1933, probably around 60 000 Communists still paid membership fees to illegal Communist Party cells (Mehringer 1997, 84). It was not only members of the banned *Kommunistische Partei Deutschlands* (German Communist Party, KPD) who organized themselves in that way, but also small circles of the former communist clubs for youth, sports, and culture, and of the paramilitary *Rotfrontkämpferbund*. Generous estimations calculate that up to half of the membership of the KPD (around 300 000 in 1932) took part in these forms of 'mass resistance' (Kenkmann 2008, 152; Mehringer 1997, 84). But the human loss, or 'blood tariff' (*Blutzoll*), of this political strategy was enormous. One significant reason for the collapse of this tactic of mass resistance was that too many communists had been well known to the political police even before 1933. During March 1933, around 11 000 communists were held in prisons, early concentration camps, and 'wild camps', where Stormtrooper (SA) units detained and maltreated their political enemies. In June 1933, 17 of 28 district leaders of the illegal KPD had been imprisoned (Benz 2014, 18). But the party leadership, which in June was partitioned into a steering committee operating inside the Reich and a foreign party executive in Moscow, did not adjust its strategy until August 1935. In these first years of the Nazi dictatorship, many illegal regional party organizations were dismantled and their leading cadres captured, only to be restored and dismantled again. As consequence of this tactic, communist 'resistance' in general was limited to maintaining political cohesion and party activities in a hopeless struggle to survive as a political organization (Weber 1984, 86). The decreasing numbers of detentions reflected the breakdown of mass resistance: in 1935 the Gestapo arrested around 15 000 communists, in 1936 11 000, in 1937 8000, and in 1938 3800 (Weber 1984, 93). While inside Germany consent to Nazi politics was steadily growing and conditions for resistance activities were deteriorating, the political struggle against Hitler shifted more and more to the exiles (Amsterdam, Paris, Prague, and especially Moscow). Yet in addition to the destruction of most clandestine circles, the Hitler–Stalin Pact meant great uncertainty for communist opponents inside and outside the Third Reich.

Some remaining resistance circles operated from 1939 to 1944 in Leipzig, Hamburg, Berlin, Magdeburg, and Mannheim. These regional resistance groups had in common the desire to remain independent from the foreign party executive in Moscow. Usually these regional underground organizations had a specific profile. While communist propaganda after 1945 claimed that the foreign party executive should have led these resistance circles in Germany, this can be verified only in one case: in January 1942, Wilhelm Knöchel (a member of the KPD Central Committee) travelled from Amsterdam to Düsseldorf, Essen, Wuppertal, and Berlin and formed a clandestine KPD organization in the Rhine-Ruhr district that distributed the underground newspapers *Der Friedenskämpfer*, *Freiheit*, and *Ruhr-Echo*. More than 200 fellow combatants were arrested. Wilhelm Knöchel was executed in 1944 and approximately 50 others were murdered in concentration camps or committed suicide (Mehringer 1997, 176–717).

Not all German communists agreed with the Stalinist KPD leadership that Social Democrats were political enemies along with the National Socialists. Therefore some groups left the KPD even before 1933 and organized their own resistance circles after Hitler came to power. They named themselves *Kommunistische Partei Deutschlands/Opposition* (KPO). It is estimated that up to 3000 followers took part in clandestine circles inside the Reich or in the activities of the exile headquarters, which operated from Strassburg. By 1937, the Gestapo had destroyed most of the KPO underground circles (Weber 1984, 94; Mehringer 1997, 86–88). German adherents of Leon Trotsky and anarcho-syndicalists formed small resistance circles too, but did not become very important (Weber 1984, 95; Mehringer 1997, 94–96).

In total, the death toll from communist resistance was enormous. Several thousand communists were sentenced to death by the *Volksgerichtshof*, the *Sondergerichte*, and other courts, or were murdered in concentration camps or during the 'wild terror' of the SA in 1933. Four members of the Politbüro of the illegal KPD became victims of Nazi terror: John Scheer in 1934, Konrad Blenkle in 1943, and

Ernst Schneller and Ernst Thälmann in 1944. In addition to the casualties of the Third Reich, German communists suffered from the Stalinist terror too. More leading German communists became victims of Stalinism than of Nazism. Five members and two candidates of the foreign party executive (the most prominent was Heinz Neumann) were murdered during the Stalinist 'cleansings' whilst in exile in Moscow (Weber 1984, 95).

8.3.2   Rote Kapelle

Another group, which cooperated partially with communist resistance organizations, and named the *Rote Kapelle* ('Red Orchestra') by the Gestapo, conducted spy activities on behalf of the Soviet Union in different European countries (Coppi, Danyel, and Tuchel 1994). Key figures of this huge, but loose, network in Berlin, which connected intellectuals, artists, workers, clerks, and military personal, were the German air force officer Harro Schulze-Boysen, the economist Arvid Harnack, and the writer Adam Kuckhoff. Approximately 100 men and 50 women met in several private circles and discussion groups. Many participants had become friends in the youth movement of the Weimar years. Some shared communist or social democratic political beliefs, others Christian or liberal conceptions. Schulze-Boysen and Kuckhoff had been influenced by national-revolutionary ideas and were looking for a synthesis of nationalism and socialism. They were convinced that National Socialism did not provide this 'third way' at all, and therefore they became strong critics of the Hitler regime (Mehringer 1997, 169–173). They had contacts with the communist underground in Berlin, and, indeed, Harro Schulze-Boysen decided in March 1941 to inform a staff member of the Soviet intelligence service in Berlin about the military preparations for the attack on the Soviet Union. But the manifold resistance activities were not restricted to communist propaganda and espionage. The Harnack/Schulze-Boysen group (to use a more precise term) distributed illegal leaflets and connected enemies of the Nazi regime in informal social gatherings. This resistance network distinguished itself as a movement that encompassed members of different social and generational backgrounds and political beliefs. In August 1942, the Gestapo was able to decode a radio message of the Soviet intelligence service in which the names and addresses of Schulze-Boysen and Kuckhoff were mentioned. During the weeks that followed, the Gestapo succeeded in destroying nearly the entire network. Approximately 130 persons were arrested, of whom 79 were brought to trial at the *Reichskriegsgericht* and 13 at the *Volksgerichtshof*. Thirty men and 19 women were executed, among them Harro Schulze-Boysen, his wife Libertas Schulze-Boysen, Adam Kuckhoff, and Arvid and Mildred Harnack. Five members of the group were murdered without trial, four others committed suicide (Coppi, Danyel, and Tuchel 1994).

8.3.3   Social Democratic and Socialist Resistance

During the final years of the Weimar Republic, the party executive of the *Sozialdemokratische Partei Deutschlands* (Social Democratic Party, SPD) fought against Hitler with all lawful means, but it would not call up its followers – especially the SPD-dominated paramilitary formation *Reichsbanner Schwarz-Rot-Gold* – for an uprising against Hitler. As a consequence of this strictly legal orientation, 94 Social Democratic members of the Reichstag voted 'no' in the parliamentary debate (23 March 1933) on the *Ermächtigungsgesetz* (Enabling Act), which conceded Hitler extensive powers at the expense of the parliament. SPD chairman Otto Wels declared emotionally: 'It is possible to take our freedom and lives, but not our honour.' And indeed, the Nazis had already arrested or forced into exile 26 of the 120 elected SPD members of the Reichstag. In May 1933 a larger portion of the party funds was confiscated and in June 1933 all political parties except the NSDAP were prohibited. Many prominent Social Democratic politicians (e.g. Kurt Schumacher and Ernst Reuter) were arrested, others died under Gestapo arrest (like Rudolf Hilferding, in 1941) or in concentration camps (like Heinrich Jasper in Bergen-Belsen in 1945). The party chairman, Otto Wels, went into exile in Prague in spring 1933 (and fled in 1938 to Paris, where he died a year later).

In the last years of the Weimar Republic the core group of the socialist milieu had consisted of 200 000 officials, but including numerous social democratic clubs for sports, culture, and youth, it incorporated approximately five million persons. In both Reichstag elections of 1932, the SPD received more than seven million votes. How did these Social Democratic officials, members, voters, and sympathizers behave after Hitler came to power? Up to 6000 officials went into exile (Schmiechen-Ackermann 2015, 581), some thousands were arrested or murdered through Nazi terror, and a vast majority withdrew from public life into the private sphere and tried not to become conspicuous as potential political enemies. There are also examples of socialists who adjusted to or supported the Nazi regime outright. Attempts to maintain nonconformist political opinions and to meet with old friends in informal circles (e.g. in pubs, allotments, card game circles) were very widespread. Members of former socialist sports and culture organizations joined new, innocuous middle-class clubs to conserve their social cohesion (Mehringer 1997, 69–72; Schmiechen–Ackermann 1998, 436–643). Only a very few people were willing to go further. For Hanover and Leipzig (both cities were regional foci of social democratic resistance) it is estimated that perhaps 3–4% of the former SPD membership participated actively in resistance circles (Schmid 1994a, 57; 1994b, 304).

The exiled executive board of the SPD (also known as the Sopade) reconstituted itself in Prague in May 1933 and in January 1934 published the Prague Manifesto of the Social Democratic Party in Exile (*Prager Manifest der Sopade*) (Schneider 1999, 890–895). A dozen 'border secretariats' (*Grenzsekretariate*), external support bases designed to monitor conditions in Germany, were set up in Copenhagen, Brussels, and Saarbrücken. They had to establish contacts and to develop communication lines to supply social democratic resistance circles with leaflets and underground newspapers (Mehringer 1997, 72–73). But not all Social Democrats who resisted against the Nazi regime accepted the leadership of the Sopade. A significant proportion of party members had waited for the signal of uprising in January 1933, which the SPD executive board did not give. Therefore, these mostly leftist activists (for example, the Rechberg group in the Mannheim-Heidelberg region; the *Kampstaffeln* in Leipzig; the *Rote Kämpfer* and *Roter Stoßtrupp*, both operating from Berlin) now formed a new organization. The biggest resistance group of leftist social democrats formed in Hanover, reaching out to several towns nearby. The *Sozialistische Front* produced and distributed their own leaflets (with up to 1000 copies) and organized approximately 700 members in clandestine circles. The first arrests proceeded in February 1935, and by summer 1936 the Gestapo had crushed the whole organization. The intellectual head of the group, journalist Werner Blumenberg, escaped to Amsterdam at the last moment. More than 200 participants were sentenced to several years of imprisonment (Schmid 1994b; Mehringer 1997, 74–75).

Even before 1933, other socialists had distanced themselves from the political course of the SPD executive committee and looked for a third position between SPD and KPD (Foitzik 1986; Benz 2014, 29–31). The *Sozialistische Arbeiterpartei Deutschlands* (SAP or SAPD), founded in 1931, was committed to a policy of *Einheitsfront* ('united front') against Hitler. The SAP cooperated with the KPO, but not with the Stalinist executive committee of the KPD. When Hitler came to power, the new socialistic party had 17 000 members. It is estimated that approximately 5000 followers joined resistance activities, including the later West German chancellor Willy Brandt and Otto Brenner, who became very important for the trade union movement after 1945. Important SAP bases were Berlin, Dresden, Breslau, Mannheim, and Hanover. A foreign headquarters was established in Paris in 1933. Until 1937 most of the resistance fighters operating inside the Reich were arrested by the Gestapo and very few groups endured until 1939 (Von zur Mühlen 1984, 62–65; Benz 2014, 29; Döscher-Gebauer and Schmid 2015). A second group established itself around the programmatic document *Neu Beginnen* ('new beginnings'), which was published in Karlsbad in autumn 1933 (Schneider 1999, 8987–890). Many members of this 'Leninistic organization' lived in Berlin, but a wide-ranging network included several German cities. Prominent leaders were Walter and Ernst Loewenheim, Richard K. Löwenthal, Ossip K. Flechtheim, and Fritz Erler. Many followers were arrested in 1935 and 1936, and by 1938 the network had largely been destroyed (Mehringer 1997, 88–91; Benz 2014, 29–30).

The elitist but strongly socialist party International Socialists Fighting League (*Internationaler Sozialistischer Kampfbund*, ISK) carried out the most spectacular and sophisticated resistance activities. During the night in crowded areas of German cities, members of this group stamped anti-Hitler slogans on the pavement, using chemical preparations that made the lettering visible only in daylight. When Hitler inaugurated the first section of the newly built autobahn near Frankfurt in May 1935, ISK resistance fighters painted the slogan 'Nieder mit Hitler' ('Down with Hitler') overnight on bridges and on the motorway. Although the ISK was not very numerous (perhaps a few hundred persons), the organization established six effective districts in Germany (mainly in Berlin, Hamburg, Hanover, Cologne, Frankfurt, and Munich). ISK's uncontested leader Willi Eichler moved to Paris in November 1933 to establish a foreign headquarters there, which was transferred to London in 1938. Fritz Eberhard led resistance activities inside the Reich (Mehringer 1997, 91–92; Benz 2014, 30–31). After his escape at the end of 1937, Erna Blencke took over for some weeks. It is noteworthy that many persons who had been involved in ISK resistance activities remained unrecognized when the Gestapo shut down the underground network between 1936 and 1938 (Döscher-Gebauer and Schmiechen-Ackermann 2015). Willi Eichler, Fritz Eberhard, Erna Blencke, and other ISK members (Alfred Kubel, Helmut Kalbitzer, Ludwig Gehm) played important roles in the SPD after 1945.

In the spring of 1933, the Nazis dissolved the socialist trade unions and the union headquarters, which had been important meeting points for organized workers for over a century. The *Deutsche Arbeitsfront* (German Labour Front) replaced the formerly independent trade unions. A considerable number of trade unionists gave up political activities and retired to the private sphere. Others continued to meet in nonconformist circles and to maintain their political beliefs among private contacts (Mehringer 1997, 96–100). Special forms of resistance in a significant trade unionist tradition were rare, but railway workers, seafarers, and inland navigation operators performed essential functions for the communication between exiled organizations and resistance groups inside the Reich. Some prominent functionaries constituted a network for continuous contacts, but their activities did not have a significant impact. Others participated in cross-milieu resistance circles, like Wilhelm Leuschner, who was executed after the failure of the attempted coup of 20 July 1944 (Benz 2014, 27–29).

8.3.4   Georg Elser

Resistance is very often – but not necessarily – based on collective action. The most prominent example of a lone fighter with working-class background is Georg Elser. Motivated by his sense of decency, honesty, and ethics, Elser decided to murder the tyrant Hitler in November 1939. Very talented as craftsman, he built a bomb and placed it in a column of the *Bürgerbräukeller* (a large beer hall) in Munich, where the Nazis were to commemorate their attempted coup of 1923. Because of bad weather Hitler had to change his plans. Instead of flying back to Berlin, he took the train and left the assembly early. The bomb exploded exactly at that place where Hitler had given his speech – but some minutes after he had left. Eight persons were killed and 63 injured. Georg Elser was captured when he tried to escape to Switzerland. He was arrested and without trial confined to Sachsenhausen, later to Dachau, where he was murdered on 9 April 1945 by an SS officer (Steinbach and Tuchel 2010; Benz 2014, 42–45).

8.3.5   Resistance, Dissent, and Nonconformity on the Basis of Religious Convictions

The political behaviour of the Roman Catholic Church towards National Socialism was ambivalent. Initially Hitler solicited support and signed the *Konkordat* (a state contract between the Vatican and the Hitler government) in July 1933, which guaranteed the institutional and economic existence of the Roman Catholic church in Germany. The Centre Party (*Zentrumspartei*) and the Bavarian People's Party (*Bayerische Volkspartei*), two political parties closely connected to Catholicism, had agreed to the Enabling Act. Despite this, they were liquidated, and soon later other activities of Catholic clubs were restricted. Catholic social milieus fluctuated between ideological rejection and adjustment to the new regime. Some historians (e.g. Blessing 1988) argue that relatively few Catholics voted for the NSDAP, and generally kept a critical distance (*Resistenz*) from Nazi politics during the Third Reich. Others reject that opinion and emphasize that the majority of Catholics soon adjusted to Hitler's politics (Rauh-Kühne 1991; Schmiechen-Ackermann 1999, 333–409). The Catholic clergy and laity remained largely quiescent despite sporadic resistance (Denzler 1984, 141; Van Norden 1994).

Compared to the Catholic electorate, the NSDAP received a much bigger share from the Protestant middle class in late Weimar elections. The church hierarchy and the Protestant laity welcomed Hitler's accession in 1933 as a 'national recovery'. But soon conflicts arose, when the ecclesio-political fraction, the 'German Christians' (*Deutsche Christen*) tried to seize power in the Protestant church, a movement openly supported by Hitler. In response, the Confessing Church (*Bekennende Kirche*), founded in May 1934 in Wuppertal-Barmen, opposed the German Christians. Under the intellectual leadership of Martin Niemöller, the Confessing Church generally was not generally hostile to National Socialism, but rejected its political influence in questions of religious doctrine (Van Norden 1994, 73–80; Mehringer 1997, 118–121; Benz 2014, 32–33; as case study, see Schmiechen-Ackermann 1999, 197–332). When Hitler recognized that the 'church struggle' could negatively impact his plans to mobilize German society in preparation for war, he postponed a decision regarding the Protestant church conflict until after the war.

Public protest or resistance activities (in the narrow sense) against Hitler and National Socialism involved only a few isolated individuals (Van Norden 1984, 126; Benz 2014, 345). Some clergymen and church members of both confessions demonstrated political courage and many of them paid with their lives or at minimum suffered long imprisonment. Here are four prominent examples: Bernhard Lichtenberg, dean of the Catholic Saint Hedwig's cathedral in Berlin, held public prayers for persecuted Jews in 1938 and protested against the murder of disabled people in 1941. He died in prison in 1943 (Benz 2014, 35). Pastor Paul Schneider resisted all attempts to dilute the Christian faith with Nazi ideas. When he was interrogated and arrested several times in 1937, a conflict escalated within his parish of Dickenschied in the Rhine Province, with local Nazis and the NSDAP *Kreisleiter* (district leaders). After his release, Schneider returned to his province, defying the order not to return home. Arrested once again and imprisoned in Buchenwald, he refused to perform the Nazi salute and as the 'preacher of Buchenwald' held prayer meetings. He was murdered in July 1939 (Benz 2014, 38–39). From 1938 the Protestant theologian Dietrich Bonhoeffer stayed in constant contact with exponents of the military opposition, especially Wilhelm Canaris, Hans Oster, and Klaus von Dohnanyi. He accompanied Helmuth von Moltke on several official journeys for the military counter-intelligence to Scandinavia, which were to provide his British partner, the Anglican bishop George Bell, with secret information about the German resistance (Benz 2014, 41). When his connections to the military opposition were revealed, Bonhoeffer was arrested in April 1943 and murdered in concentration camp Flossenbürg on 9 April 1945. Finally, Gertrud Luckner, who worked for the Catholic social association Caritas in Freiburg, assisted persecuted Jews by providing them with fake passports to escape to

Switzerland. She was detained by the Gestapo in March 1943 and held in the women's concentration camp Ravensbrück (Benz 2014, 35–36).

The small religious community of Jehovah's Witnesses (with roughly 25 000 members in Germany) was prohibited in 1933. It is estimated that 50% of this community continued their forbidden religious proselytizing (Mehringer 1997, 102–107). Often, they were subjected to National Socialist persecution because they refused the Nazi salute and military service. Up to 10 000 Jehovah's Witnesses were arrested. About 2000 were held in concentration camps and approximately 1200 were killed. Two hundred and fifty Jehovah's Witnesses were sentenced to death because they refused military service (Garbe 1993). This religious sect suffered the highest percentage of casualties among all groups persecuted on the basis of religious convictions. Other small religious communities, for example the Church of Jesus Christ of Latter-Day Saints or Mormons, tended towards conformity interrupted with occasional resistance.

8.3.6   Other Forms of Resistance, Dissent, and Nonconformity in Middle-class Milieus

The *Weiße Rose* ('White Rose') group is often labelled as 'resistance of students'. This categorization is appropriate, if we consider that Munich university was a very important location of their resistance activities, which several students at this university carried out. Hans and Sophie Scholl, Willi Graf, Christoph Probst, and Alexander Schmorell, all of them between 21 and 25 years old, formed the core group of this resistance circle. But the critical discussions in this loose network would not have taken place without their teacher Kurt Huber, a professor of philosophy and musicology. Other artists and intellectuals participated too. In June 1942, the *Weiße Rose* began to produce and distribute leaflets which highlighted the criminal nature of the Nazi rule and persuaded readers to resist the regime. When Hans and Sophie Scholl threw leaflets into the atrium of Munich university in February 1943, a caretaker detained them and delivered them to the Gestapo. Four days later the *Volksgerichtshof* sentenced the Scholl siblings and Christoph Probst to death and executed them on the same day. During the following weeks the Gestapo investigated the circle's connections. In a second *Volksgerichtshof* trial, Willi Graf, Kurt Huber, and Alexander Schmorell were sentenced to death. Eleven other participants received jail terms (Scholl 2013; Bald 2009; Mehringer 1997, 182–187; Benz 2014, 48–49). The commemoration of this intellectual middle-class resistance circle strongly influenced West Germany's confrontation with the National Socialist past in the post-war years (Steinbach 1988, 3).

The formula 'sporadic resistance in the midst of dominant adjustment', which characterized working-class and confessional milieus, was even truer for bourgeois milieus outside the military sector. Only a few gathered the courage to resist in a significant way. Some remarkable groups should be mentioned as *pars pro toto*. Operating from Hamburg and Berlin, a circle of young liberals gathered around two leading figures, the businessman Hans Robinsohn and the judge Ernst Strassmann, who exchanged republican ideas and information on the Nazi regime (Sassin 1993; Benz 2014, 69–72). Several conservative and liberal dissidents crowded round the former Lord Mayor of Leipzig, Carl Goerdeler, and met like-minded people in the *Mittwochsgesellschaft* in Berlin, a private circle for scientific discussions. Some diplomats chose the apartment of Hanna Solf, widow of the former German ambassador in Tokyo, as a meeting point. In addition, Freiburg professors and clergymen came together in the so-called Freiburg Circle (*Freiburger Kreis*) to discuss how Christians should behave towards an unchristian regime (Benz 2014, 77–84). Several monarchists with critical views of the Nazi regime gathered in Bavaria around the lawyer Adolf von Harnier (Mehringer 1997, 141–144). Even among those with National Socialist or folkish ideas, an anti-Hitler-organization developed, the *Schwarze Front* ('black front') under the leadership of Otto Strasser who led this group from exile in Vienna and later in Prague. When the military defeat of the Third Reich became evident, responsible citizens in many places tried to end the fighting and organize an orderly surrender to the Allied armies. In Bavaria, a military unit founded the *Freiheitsaktion Bayern*, but SS and Wehrmacht units arrested and executed their followers. In several cases, resistance led to murderous acts of revenge, committed by Nazi fanatics in the last days of war (Mehringer 1997, 243–246).

The most important, mostly middle- and upper-class circle of dissidents and resistance fighters was the Kreisau Circle (*Kreisauer Kreis*) named for its meeting point, the feudal estate of count Helmuth James Graf von Moltke in Kreisau, Lower Silesia. Since 1938, important participants who met at Kreisau castle and occasionally in Munich or Berlin included count Yorck von Wartenburg, Moltke who served under the Supreme Command of the German Armed Forces in Berlin, the jurist Adam von Trott zu Solz, and Hans Bernd von Haeften, both of whom served in the Ministry of Foreign Affairs. The discussion group included professors like Adolf Reichwein, theologians like Eugen Gerstenmaier, Hans Poelchau, and Alfred Delp, and Social Democrats like Julius Leber, Carlo Mierendorff, and Theodor Haubach. The *Kreisauer Kreis* brought together nobleman and commoners, Protestants and Catholics, conservatives, liberals, and socialists. Approximately 20 people were involved in the core group, with several others kept in loose contact. The Kreisau meeting in May 1942 arrived at its 'fundamental declaration' – its views about a fundamental rearrangement of German society after Hitler – according to the values of humanity, Christian ethics, and justice. The Kreisau group did not plan an uprising, but prepared itself for political leadership after the breakdown of National Socialism. In January 1944, the Gestapo arrested Count Moltke and detained him in Sachsenhausen. After the assassination attempt against Hitler on 20 July 1944, the tight connections between the Kreisau Circle and the conspirators in the military became obvious. Moltke, Yorck, Trott, Hans Bernd von Haeften, Delp, Haubach, Leber, and Reichwein were sentenced to death and executed (Mehringer 1997, 190–197; Benz 2014, 72–77).

8.3.7 Military Opposition and the Uprising of 20 July 1944

The vast majority of the military high command welcomed Hitler's seizure of power in January 1933, and only a very few senior officers objected to the murders of the Night of the Long Knives on 30 June 1934 and the suppression of the SA.

Nonconformity and opposition in military circles arose only at the turn of the year 1937/1938, when several high-ranking officers became alarmed about Hitler's aggressive foreign policy. Among them were the generals Ludwig Beck, Erwin von Witzleben, Franz Halder, and Walther von Brauchitsch, as well as admiral Wilhelm Canaris and his chief of staff Hans Oster. Two competing tendencies existed: one group developed plans for an assassination plot and military coup, and a second limited itself to discouraging Hitler's war plans (Benz 2014, 86–88).

At the request of Hitler, Ludwig Beck resigned from active service as chief of the general staff in August 1938, and Franz Halder became his successor. Several conspirators developed concrete plans to kill Hitler and overthrow the regime when Hitler threatened Czechoslovakia with war in autumn 1938. Some under the leadership of Lieutenant Colonel Hans Oster plotted the assassination of Hitler, but the impact of appeasement politics, especially the diplomatic results of the Munich conference, made these considerations obsolete. The murder of the tyrant had to be postponed. The dissidents in the armed forces kept in touch with civilian opponents of the regime. Until its exposure in April 1943, the agency for counter-intelligence in the Armed Forces High Command (Canaris, Oster) represented the most important military resistance circle. From 1941 three other centres of resistance developed: in the staff of the Commander of the Reserve Army in Berlin around colonel Claus Schenk Graf zu Stauffenberg (Mehringer 1997, 205–210, 216–218), in the agency of the military commander in occupied France (around general Carl-Heinrich von Stülpnagel), and on the Eastern Front (around general staff officer Henning von Tresckow; Mehringer 1997, 197–205). Several assassination attempts had been prepared in 1943 and in spring 1944, but all failed or were cancelled at the last moment (Hoffmann 1985, 69–326; Benz 2014, 90–91).

Stauffenberg was the only person in the inner circle of military resistance who had direct access to Hitler. When he was called to the headquarters *Wolfsschanze* ('wolf's lair') near Rastenburg in East Prussia to submit a report to the Führer, the conspirators decided to act immediately. Tresckow stated that success would no longer be decisive, but the resistance had to undertake the attempt out of 'great responsibility to the world and to history'. On 20 July, Stauffenberg joined the meeting with Hitler and placed his briefcase with a bomb under a huge map table. Then he left the room on a pretext. The bomb exploded and Stauffenberg was convinced that Hitler was dead. Minutes later he left by plane to Berlin where he arrived in the afternoon and reported the allegedly successful elimination of Hitler. Immediately thereafter in Berlin, but also in Vienna, Prague, and Paris, 'operation Valkyrie' (which meant to arrest leading Nazis in important places) was triggered. But Hitler had survived the bomb explosion with only slight injuries and issued instructions by telephone and spoke on the radio. Because he received great support, the uprising failed. Around 11 p.m., troops loyal to Hitler seized the *Bendlerblock*, where the agency of the Commander of the Reserve Army was located. A few minutes after midnight Claus Schenk Graf zu Stauffenberg, Friedrich Olbricht, Albrecht Ritter Mertz von Quirnheim, and Werner von Haeften were executed in the courtyard of the *Bendlerblock*. Ludwig Beck committed suicide in his office, Henning von Tresckow at the front (Mehringer 1997, 218–226). Several trials before the *Volksgerichtshof* against the military insurgents and the civilian dissidents associated with them usually ended with death sentences. Relatives of the leading figures of the plot were arrested as guilty by association (*Sippenhaft*). In total, the regime killed more than 200 (the exact number is unknown) resistance fighters and dissidents after 20 July (Hoffmann 1985, 327–622; Ueberschär 2006). If the assassination attempt on Hitler had succeeded, a substantial number of the victims of the last months of the war might have been saved. Perceptions of the assassination attempt of 20 July 1944 in post-war West Germany were contradictory, ranging from initial defamation to respect (Steinbach 2004; Tuchel 2014).

8.3.8   Jewish Resistance and 'Silent Heroes'

Generally, it is very difficult for a small and persecuted section of the population to develop sustained resistance activities. Therefore, we encounter 'Jewish resistance' in Germany in the form of self-assertion, rather than as an offensive attack on the Nazi regime (Benz 2014, 51–52). Nevertheless, some authors seek to prove that persecuted Jews in Germany and all over Europe did not go 'as lambs to the slaughter', but resisted in many ways (Kwiet and Eschwege 1986; Lustiger 2004).

A 1993 exhibition in Berlin (Löhken and Vathke 1993) highlighted three Jewish resistance circles: 'Not going along, but hurrying away' was the motto of a small group (in the beginning, 11, and later up to 40 persons) of Jewish youngsters, who assembled round their teacher Jizchak Schwersenz to form the *Chug Chaluzi* ('circle of pioneers') organization. From the day of the *Fabrikaktion* deportations of 27 February 1943, when the Gestapo captured Jews at their working places, they lived underground, met to practise their religion, and prepared for new tasks in Israel. The *Chug Chaluzi* survived successfully in Berlin until May 1945. Their leader Jizchak Schwersenz fled to Switzerland in February 1944 (Benz 2014, 54). *Die Gemeinschaft für Frieden und Aufbau* ('community for peace and development') consisted of Jews and non-Jews, who from autumn 1943 organized hiding places for Jews in Luckenwalde near Berlin. This small group was discovered and dismantled in October 1944, and their leader Werner Scharff was murdered in Sachsenhausen (Benz 2014, 53–54). Until the exhibition mentioned above included it as 'Jewish resistance', the *Gruppe Baum* (Baum Group) was included with the 'communist resistance'. In several interconnected circles, approximately 100 young Jewish and communist members gathered under the leadership of the electrician Herbert Baum. These resistance fighters carried out a spectacular action when they committed an arson attack on the anti-communist propaganda exhibition 'Soviet Paradise' (*Das Sowjetparadies*) in May 1942 in Berlin. The impact on the exhibition was very limited, but the consequences were disastrous. Within four days of the assault the Gestapo had arrested members of the group. Herbert Baum and Walter Bernecker did not survive the Gestapo arrest. Twenty-two other participants were executed after they had been sentenced to death by the *Sondergericht Berlin* and the *Volksgerichtshof*. Only a few members of this group survived. Moreover, in retaliation (*Vergeltungsaktion*), the Gestapo arbitrarily detained 500 Berlin Jews, executing half of them and imprisoning the other half (Lange 2015, 167–169).

Many Jews who had to face deportation tried to escape by going underground. It is estimated that up to 7000 Jews in Berlin – for instance, the entertainer Hans

Rosenthal – and 12 000 in the Reich as a whole chose that option (Kosmala 2007; Benz 2014, 55–64). Surviving illegally, without papers and without food, meant relying on the support of non-Jewish friends, neighbours, and benefactors. A programme to honour those non-Jewish helpers as 'unsung heroes' which the Senate of Berlin promoted between 1958 and 1966 (Riffel 2007) had nearly been forgotten, when in the 1990s new research began to explore the activities of thousands of *Stille Helden* ('silent heroes'). Numerous cases of *Rettungswiderstand* (Lustiger 2011) are now recorded in an exhibition and learning site in Berlin-Mitte.

8.3.9   Youth Resistance and Women's Resistance

In addition to adult men and women, members of youth organizations and young adults displayed nonconformist behaviour, participated in protests, and joined resistance circles. The spectrum of juvenile resistance covers a wide range of social milieus and subcultures, from the *Wandervogel*, the bourgeois youth movement, to the anglophile *Swings*, and religious beliefs and political opinions from Catholicism to communism – as described previously (Benz 2014, 45–51; Lange 2015). A specific phenomenon of the war period were working-class teenage gangs (*wilde Cliquen*), which arose in many urban spaces. In the Rhine-Ruhr region they called themselves *Edelweißpiraten*, *Navajos*, or *Kittelbachpiraten*, in Munich *Blasen*, and in Leipzig and Halle *Meuten*. They lived a nonconformist lifestyle and rejected the Hitler Youth (*Hitlerjugend*). Because they avoided all the duties the Nazi state imposed them, the Gestapo recognized them as dangerous political enemies. In their self-assessment, these teenage gangs were not politically motivated, but in the face of the dictatorship they tried only to live the life they wanted.

Women were also involved in resistance activities in many ways. They supported the male-dominated political resistance groups (this is the very traditional view in the topic), but they also hid Jews or prepared young Jewish girls for emigration (Geyken 2014). Particular attention has been given to the courageous protest of hundreds of 'Aryan' women (and a few men too) in front of a Jewish detention building in the Rosenstraße, Berlin-Mitte. Their husbands, sons, and relatives had been held even though they were in so-called 'mixed marriages' (*Mischehen*) with one 'Aryan' and one Jewish partner and therefore should have exempted from deportations. After verification of their status, nearly all the detained were released. Nathan Stolzfus's argument that the protests forced the Gestapo to release the detained (Stoltzfus 1999) has been challenged by Wolf Gruner who argues the regime did not then intend to deport Jewish partners in mixed marriages (Gruner 2005).

8.3.10   Resistance Behind Barbed Wire

Detained and observed persons had only limited opportunities for resistance at their disposal. Nevertheless, in Gestapo reports from March to September 1944, resistance activities of at least 2700 forced labourers and Russian prisoners of war were mentioned for 38 cities (Mehringer 1997, 242). Considering the enormous number of foreign slave workers, the Nazi regime was very concerned about the possibility of a big uprising. But organized riots did not occur. Concentration camp inmates were in an even more difficult position. 'Resistance' meant, in this context, forms of self-assertion and organized help for fellow prisoners (Mehringer 1997, 246–252).

8.3.11   Desertion and the National Committee for a Free Germany

For decades after 1945, conscientious objection and desertion were considered controversial types of 'resistance'. Now, they are respected widely as a courageous form of defiance (Benz 2014, 104–107). Approximately 35 000 soldiers were condemned for desertion during the Second World War. The military jurisdiction imposed 22 000 capital punishments and 15 000 deserters were executed (Benz 2014, 104–107). Although the Soviet government supported the *Nationalkomitee Freies Deutschland* (National Committee for a Free Germany, NKFD), it belongs to the history of German resistance (Benz 2014, 102). Down to the present day, the perception of this organization in Germany is controversial. Founded by exiled communists and German prisoners of war in July 1943, the NKFD tried to convince members of the Wehrmacht that they should fight against Hitler and not against the Red Army. A *Bund Deutscher Offiziere* ('federation of German officers') was established, which soon was merged with the NKFD. The success of its propaganda remained relatively limited. Since Stalin recognized that a military victory over the German armed forces was probable, he increasingly lost interest in this organization (Mehringer 1997, 252–258).

8.4   Conclusion

The numerous types of resistance, nonconformity, and dissent stress the need for a broad definition of *Widerstand* which also allows for terminological diversification. It is necessary to reserve *Widerstand* for political opposition that aimed to end Nazi rule with or without violence. The history of the research field underscores a major scholarly challenge, which has not yet been realized: the contextualization of consent, terror, and resistance in a broad and multi-perspective history of society (*Gesellschaftsgeschichte*) in Nazi Germany. Above all, we have to recognize that after 1933 accommodation and collaboration were the normal patterns of public behaviour (Rohkrämer 2013; Schmiechen-Ackermann 2012), while 'resistance' remained only an exceptional option for a few opponents of the Hitler regime.

References

Bald, Detlef. 2009. *Die 'Weiße Rose': Von der Front in den Widerstand*, 2nd edn. Berlin: Aufbau.
Benz, Wolfgang. 2014. *Der deutsche Widerstand gegen Hitler*. Munich: C.H. Beck.
Blessing, Werner. 1988. '"Deutschland in Not, wir im Glauben ..." Kirche und Kirchenvolk in einer katholischen Region 1933–1949.' In *Von Stalingrad zur Währungsreform*, edited by Martin Broszat, Klaus-Dietmar Henke, and Hans Woller, 3–111. Munich: Oldenbourg.
Broszat, Martin. 1981. 'Resistenz und Widerstand: Eine Zwischenbilanz des Forschungsprojekts.' In *Bayern in der NS-Zeit, Volume 4: Herrschaft und Gesellschaft im Konflikt,* Teil C, edited by

Martin Broszat, Elke Fröhlich, and Anton Grossmann, 691–709. Munich and Vienna: Oldenbourg.

Coppi, Hans, Danyel, Jürgen, and Tuchel, Johannes. 1994. *Die Rote Kapelle im Widerstand gegen den Nationalsozialismus*. Berlin: Edition Hentrich.

Denzler, Georg. 1984. *Anpassung oder Widerstand? Katholische Kirche und Drittes Reich*. Munich and Zurich: Piper.

Döscher-Gebauer, Susanne and Schmid, Hans-Dieter. 2015. 'Die Sozialistische Arbeiterpartei (SAP) in der Illegalität.' In *Linkssozialistischer Widerstand gegen die nationalsozialistische Diktatur in Hannover*, edited by Susanne Döscher-Gebauer, Hans-Dieter Schmid, and Detlef Schmiechen-Ackermann, 13–74. Peine: Hahnsche Buchhandlung.

Döscher-Gebauer, Susanne and Schmiechen-Ackermann, Detlef. 2015. 'Die Widerstandtätigkeit des Internatuionalen Sozialstichen Kampfbundes (ISK) gegen den Nationalsozialismus in Hannover.' In *Linkssozialistischer Widerstand gegen die nationalsozialistische Diktatur in Hannover*, edited by Susanne Döscher-Gebauer, Hans-Dieter Schmid, and Detlef Schmiechen-Ackermann, 75–157. Peine: Hahnsche Buchhandlung.

Foitzik, Jan. 1986. *Zwischen den Fronten: Zur Politik, Organisation und Funktion linker politischer Kleinorganisationen im Widerstand 1933 bis 1939/40 unter besonderer Berücksichtigung des Exils*. Bonn: Verlag Neue Gesellschaft.

Garbe, Detlef. 1993. *Zwischen Widerstand und Martyrium: Die Zeugen Jehovas im 'Dritten Reich'*, 4th edn. Munich: Oldenbourg.

Geyken, Frauke. 2014. *Wir standen nicht abseits: Frauen im Widerstand gegen Hitler*. Munich: C.H. Beck.

Gruner, Wolf. 2005. *Widerstand in der Rosenstraße: Die Fabrik-Aktion und die Verfolgung der 'Mischehen' 1943*. Frankfurt am Main: Fischer.

Hoffmann, Peter. 1985. *Widerstand, Staatsstreich, Attentat: Der Kampf der Opposition gegen Hitler*, 4th edn. Munich and Zurich: Piper.

Kenkmann, Alfons. 2008. 'Zwischen Nonkonformität und Widerstand: Abweichendes Verhalten unter nationalsozialistischer Herrschaft.' In *Das 'Dritte Reich': Eine Einführung*, edited by Dietmar Süß and Winfried Süß, 143–162. Munich: Pantheon.

Kershaw, Ian. 2003. *Der Hitler-Mythos: Führerkult und Volksmeinung*, 2nd edn. Munich: dtv.

Kosmala, Beate. 2007. 'Stille Helden.' *Aus Politik und Zeitgeschichte*, 14–15, 29–34.

Kwiet, Konrad and Eschwege, Helmut. 1986. *Selbstbehauptung und Widerstand: Deutsche Juden im Kampf um Existenz und Menschenwürde 1933–1945*, 2nd edn. Hamburg: Christians.

Lange, Sachsa. 2015. *Meuten, Swings Edelweißpiraten: Jugendkultur und Opposition im Nationalsozialismus*. Mainz: Ventil Verlag.

Löhken, Wilfried and Vathke, Werner, eds. 1993. *Juden im Widerstand: Drei Gruppen zwischen Überlebenskampf und politischer Aktion. Berlin 1939–1945*. Berlin: Hentrich.

Lustiger, Arno. 2004. *Zum Kampf auf Leben und Tod! Vom Widerstand der Juden in Europa 1933–1945*, 2nd edn. Erfstadt: Area.

Lustiger, Arno. 2011. *Rettungswiderstand: Über die Judenretter in Europa während der NS-Zeit*. Göttingen: Wallstein.

Mallmann, Klaus-Michael and Paul, Gerhard. 1993. 'Resistenz oder loyale Widerwilligkeit? Anmerkungen zu einem umstrittenen Begriff.' *Zeitschrift für Geschichtswissenschaft* 41, 99–116.

Mehringer, Hartmut. 1997. *Widerstand und Emigration: Das NS-Regime und seine Gegner*. Munich: dtv.

Peukert, Detlev. 1982. *Volksgenossen und Gemeinschaftsfremde: Anpassung, Ausmerze und Aufbegehren unter dem Nationalsozialismus*. Cologne: Bund-Verlag.

Peukert, Detlev J.K. 1986. 'Der deutsche Arbeiterwiderstand 1933 bis 1945.' In *Der deutsche Widerstand 1933–1945*, edited by Klaus-Jürgen Müller, 157–181. Paderborn.: Schöningh.

Rauh-Kühne, Cornelia. 1991. *Katholisches Milieu und Kleinstadtgesellschaft: Ettlingen 1918–1939.* Sigmaringen: Jan Thorbecke.

Riffel, Dennis. 2007. *Unbesungene Helden: Die Ehrungsinitiative des Berliner Senats 1958 bis 1966.* Berlin: Metropol.

Rohkrämer, Thomas. 2013. *Die fatale Attraktion des Nationalsozialismus: Zur Popularität eines Unrechtsregimes.* Paderborn: Schöningh.

Roth, Markus. 2016. *'Ihr wißt, wollt es aber nicht wissen.' Verfolgung, Terror und Widerstand im Dritten Reich.* Munich: C.H. Beck.

Sassin, Horst R. 1993. *Liberale im Widerstand: Die Robinsohn-Strassmann-Gruppe 1934–1942.* Hamburg: Christians.

Schmid, Hans- Dieter. 1994a. 'Der organisierte Widerstand der Sozialdemokraten in Leipzig 1933–1935.' In *Zwei Städte unter dem Hakenkreuz,* edited by Hans-Dieter Schmid, 26–70. Leipzig: Leipziger Universitätsverlag.

Schmid, Hans- Dieter. 1994b. 'Sozialistische Front.' In *Lexikon des deutschen Widerstandes,* edited by Wolfgang Benz and Walter H. Pehle, 302–306. Frankfurt: S. Fischer.

Schmiechen-Ackermann, Detlef. 1998. *Nationalsozialismus und Arbeitermilieus: Der nationalsozialistische Angriff auf die proletarischen Wohnquartiere und die Reaktion in den sozialistischen Vereinen.* Bonn: Dietz.

Schmiechen-Ackermann, Detlef. 1999. *Kooperation und Abgrenzung: Bürgerliche Gruppen, evangelische Kirchengemeinden und katholisches Sozialmilieu in der Auseinandersetzung mit dem Nationalsozialismus in Hannover.* Hanover: Hahnsche Buchhandlung.

Schmiechen-Ackermann, Detlef, ed. 2012. *'Volksgemeinschaft': Mythos, wirkungsmächtige soziale Verheißung oder soziale Realität im 'Dritten Reich'?. Zwischenbilanz einer kontroversen Debatte.* Paderborn: Schöningh.

Schmiechen-Ackermann, Detlef. 2015. 'Rassismus, politische Verfolgung und Migration: Ausgrenzung und Austreibung unerwünschter Gruppen aus dem nationalsozialistischen Deutschland.' In *Handbuch Staat und Migration in Deutschland seit dem 17. Jahrhundert,* edited by Jochen Oltmer, 573–642. Berlin and Boston: De Gruyter.

Schneider, Michael. 1999. *Unterm Hakenkreuz: Arbeiter und Arbeiterbewegung 1933 bis 1939.* Bonn: Dietz.

Scholl, Inge. 2013. *Die weiße Rose,* 15th edn. Frankfurt am Main: Fischer.

Steber, Martina and Gotto, Bernhard. 2014. *Visions of Community in Nazi Germany: Social Engineering and Private Lives.* Oxford: Oxford University Press.

Steinbach, Peter. 1988. 'Widerstandsforschung im politischen Spannungsfeld.' *Aus Politik und Zeitgeschichte* B 28/88, 3–21.

Steinbach, Peter. 2004. 'Der 20. Juli 1944 – mehr als ein Tag der Besinnung und Verpflichtung.' *Aus Politik und Zeitgeschichte* B 27, 28, 5–10.

Steinbach, Peter and Tuchel, Johannes, eds. 1994. *Widerstand gegen den Nationalsozialismus.* Berlin: Akademie.

Steinbach, Peter and Tuchel, Johannes. 2010. *Georg Elser: Der Hitler-Attentäter.* Berlin: be.bra.

Stoltzfus, Nathan. 1999. *Widerstand des Herzens: Der Aufstand der Berliner Frauen in der Rosenstraße 1943.* Munich and Vienna: dtv.

Tuchel, Johannes. 2014. 'Zwischen Diffamierung und Anerkennung: Zum Umgang mit dem 20. Juli 1944 in der frühen Bundesrepublik.' *Aus Politik und Zeitgeschichte* 27, 18–24.

Ueberschär, Gerd R. 2006. *Stauffenberg und das Attentat vom 20: Juli 1944. Darstellung, Biographien, Dokumente.* Frankfurt am Main: Fischer.

Van Norden, Günther. 1984. 'Christen im Widerstand.' In *Widerstand und Verweigerung in Deutschland 1933 bis 1945,* edited by Richard Löwenthal and Patrick von zur Mühlen, 111–128. Berlin/Bonn: Dietz.

Van Norden, Günther. 1994. 'Widersetzlichkeit von Kirchen und Christen.' In *Lexikon des deutschen Widerstandes*, edited by Wolfgang Benz and Walter H. Pehle, 68–82. Frankfurt: Fischer.

Von Reeken, Dietmar and Thießen, Malte. 2013. *'Volksgemeinschaft' als soziale Praxis: Neue Forschungen zur NS-Gesellschaft vor Ort*. Paderborn: Schöningh.

Von zur Mühlen, Patrick. 1984. 'Sozialdemokraten gegen Hitler.' In *Widerstand und Verweigerung in Deutschland 1933 bis 1945*, edited by Richard Löwenthal and Patrick von zur Mühlen, 57–75. Berlin and Bonn: Dietz.

Weber, Hermann. 1984. *Die KPD in der Illegalität. In Widerstand und Verweigerung in Deutschland 1933 bis 1945*, edited by Richard Löwenthal and Patrick von zur Mühlen, 83–101. Berlin, Bonn: Dietz.

Wildt, Michael. 2007a. 'Das "Bayern-Projekt", die Alltagsforschung und die "Volksgemeinschaft".' In *Martin Broszat, Der 'Staat Hitlers' und die Historisierung des Nationalsozialismus*, edited by Norbert Frei, 119–129. Göttingen: Wallstein.

Wildt, Michael. 2007b. *Volksgemeinschaft als Selbstermächtigung: Gewalt gegen Juden in der deutschen Provinz 1919 bis 1939*. Hamburg: Hamburger Edition.

CHAPTER NINE

Centre and Periphery

THOMAS SCHAARSCHMIDT

9.1 Towards a Centralized Dictatorship

For decades the Third Reich was typically described as a highly centralized state with a political hierarchy reaching from Adolf Hitler at the top down to remote areas of Germany and, later on, to various parts of occupied Europe. Even if we include the other prominent figures of Nazi rule, such as Heinrich Himmler, Hermann Göring, or Albert Speer, the Nazi state seems to embody a highly centralized government. Although they competed with each other, the Nazi state's central institutions – the SS (*Schutzstaffel*), the Four Year Plan organization, and the Ministry for Armaments – worked in a similar centralized manner (Hüttenberger 1976, 429). While substantial research has focused on the polycratic structure of Nazi Germany, the relationship and interaction between different levels of the political system are often neglected.

As modern Germany was a densely populated country with many large cities, such as Munich, Hamburg, Cologne, Nuremberg, Frankfurt, Breslau, Leipzig, and Königsberg, the juxtaposition of 'centre' and 'periphery' might be misleading. Although Berlin became the uncontested capital of Germany, the rest of the country could hardly be described as 'periphery' in the sense that spatial distance from Berlin went hand in hand with decreasing importance. In the context of the Nazi state, the terms 'centre' and 'periphery' are even more confusing when attention is focused on Berlin where institutions and leading figures at the centralized, intermediate, and local government levels worked hand in hand (Kreutzmüller 2012, 121).

Although the centralization of power accelerated after the First World War, the German regions outside Berlin were anything but backwaters. They became even less peripheral after 1938 when Nazi Germany began annexing new territories in Austria, Czechoslovakia, Poland, and France. For example, Saxony and Silesia, which had been portrayed as contested border regions in the early Nazi years, had

A Companion to Nazi Germany, First Edition. Edited by Shelley Baranowski,
Armin Nolzen, and Claus-Christian W. Szejnmann.
© 2018 John Wiley & Sons Ltd. Published 2018 by John Wiley & Sons Ltd.

to change their image when the Sudetenland, the western part of Czechoslovakia, and large areas of Poland were incorporated into the German sphere of influence.

Federalism had been a key German constitutional principle since the founding of the Reich in 1871. Nevertheless, the German state's internal structure differed across regions. While some territories were governed by monarchs and preserved substantial sovereign rights, the Kingdom of Prussia, which covered two thirds of the Reich, retained its own administrative sub-structure of provinces, administrative regions (*Regierungsbezirke*) and districts. Since the First World War had triggered a wave of centralizing measures, the November revolution of 1918 and the immediate deposal of the emperor and his fellow monarchs changed the fabric of the German state. Although the German Reich remained a federal state, several measures tipped the balance towards a stronger central authority. During the 15 years of the Weimar Republic, debates on overall *Reichsreform* never came to a close. These efforts started with Hugo Preuß's plea for a unified federal state (*unitarischer Bundesstaat*) in 1918 and sparked a barrage of complaints against over-centralization and the utter destruction of federalism (John 2001). In the end, the central government's interventions in Bavaria (1919), Saxony and Thuringia (1923), as well as the presidential cabinets during the last years of the Weimar Republic and the dismissal of the democratically elected government in Prussia on 20 July 1932, substantially weakened the federal principles of the constitution.

However, the attitude of leading National Socialists and other ultra-nationalist parties towards federalism and centralization was ambiguous. On the one hand, many Nazis portrayed themselves as the vanguard of a strong and unified centralized state. Yet on the other hand, they used the federal structure of the Weimar Republic to build political strongholds on the regional level (John 2001, 317). After Nazi politicians were appointed ministers in the governments of Thuringia and Brunswick in 1930, only two years later and several months prior to Hitler's nomination as Chancellor, regional party leaders became heads of government in Anhalt, Mecklenburg-Schwerin, Oldenburg, and Thuringia.

The organizational division of the NSDAP (*Nationalsozialistische Deutsche Arbeiterpartei*, Nazi Party) into regional (*Gaue*), district (*Kreise*), and local branches (*Ortsgruppen*) was based on its pragmatic objective to organize election campaigns and to gain votes. Therefore, the NSDAP's *Gau* structure roughly mirrored the constituencies necessary for victory in general elections. Nevertheless, rallying the party faithful and mobilizing new voters inevitably went hand in hand with raising expectations of the local population and getting involved with regional politics, interests, and conflicts. Many party functionaries were well-established members of the regional and local society and remained aware of their fellow citizens' desires and expectations. Although the brown and black uniforms of NSDAP, SA (*Sturmabteilung*, Stormtroopers), and SS members conveyed the impression of complete unity, their social ties on the regional and local level have to be taken into account. These proved to be particularly useful when it came to spreading Nazi ideas into all walks of life.

Nevertheless, most measures Hitler's government launched after 1933 spurned higher levels of centralization. The complete political takeover in all parts of the country immediately after the general elections of 5 March 1933, as well as the

'Preliminary Law to Align the Regional Authorities with the Reich' (*Gleichschaltungsgesetz*) on 31 March 1933, the establishment of federal governors (*Reichsstatthalter*) in all German territories on 7 April 1933, and the 'Law on Re-Structuring the Reich' (*Gesetz zum Neuaufbau des Reiches*) on 30 January 1934, sounded the death knell of traditional federalism. According to the German legal theorist Carl Schmitt's commentary, the laws 'liberated' German federalism from all remnants of sovereignty. That is to say, the administrative territorial structure survived but it became part of the unified and centralized *Führerstaat* (Schmitt 1933, 12; John 2007, 37–38).

As far as administrative authority mirrored regional party structures, the NSDAP's *Gauleiters* were appointed as federal governors. With the exception of Prussia, where *Gauleiters* were appointed to the position of provincial presidents (*Oberpräsidenten*), the federal governors in other territories didn't become leaders or members of the regional administration, but remained representatives of the central government tasked with controlling politics at the regional level. Theoretically this difference didn't matter, as the appointment of federal governors established administrative lines of command from the Reich's Ministry of Interior (*Reichsministerium des Innern*) down to regional and local authorities.

At the same time, an increasing number of administrative tasks, such as the police and the judiciary, came under the direct control of central ministries and party agencies. Therefore, some federal governors started complaining that their authority was dissipating (Hüttenberger 1969, 114). As a consequence, on 30 January 1935 the second 'Law on Federal Governors' (*Reichsstatthaltergesetz*) paved the way for the appointment of federal governors to head of regional governments. Compared to the initiatives of Wilhelm Frick and the Ministry of Interior for a *Reichsreform*, the law of 1935 appeared to be the final attempt to preserve a minimum of direct control at the regional level (Rebentisch 1989, 236). However, even this proposal failed, as only a few federal governors and *Gauleiters* seized the opportunity to become prime minister (Mommsen 2000, 231).

Although Frick's attempts to enact thoroughgoing structural reform stalled, the policy of alignment (*Gleichschaltung*) proved highly successful for implementing Nazi politics. In a mere two years the *Länder* and Prussian provinces were transformed into obedient subdivisions of the Reich under the guidance of devoted party figures ready to mobilize the material and social resources of the German territories for the imperialistic and racist aspirations of the central leadership. As it turned out, the lack of clear-cut structures, and the vagueness of the federal governors' authority, presented excellent conditions for the creation of flexible and pragmatic power arrangements on the regional level. These arrangements fitted perfectly into the fabric of the Nazi political system and contributed to its dynamic character (Rebentisch 1989, 537).

Since the NSDAP came to power, political initiatives of party activists at the regional and local levels played a major role in shaping Nazi politics. In some cases, central measures appeared to be reacting to local developments which threatened to get out of control and, therefore, had to be contained and harnessed. When, on 10 May 1933, the German Students' Organization, under the guidance of the National Socialist German Students' League (*Nationalsozialistischer Deutscher*

Studentenbund, NSDStB), burned so-called un-German authors' books in Berlin's Opera Square, they were imitating similar events that had taken place in other German cities in the preceding two months. Immediately after general elections on 5 March, local SA and SS members completed the destruction of the Social Democratic Party and Communist Party infrastructures by looting their buildings and burning their books and party symbols. Furthermore, local and regional branches of the Hitler Youth (*Hitlerjugend*, HJ) started 'cleansing' school libraries by burning books in school yards and public squares (Treß 2008, 14–20). The students' campaign against the 'un-German spirit', which began on 13 April and extended to the events in Berlin in May, was an attempt to coordinate local and regional initiatives.

The Nuremberg Laws were another example of how initiatives from above and below interacted. In this perspective, their proclamation in September 1935 appears as an initiative by central authorities to regain control after a major wave of antisemitism swept several regions of the Reich. After the central boycott of Jewish shops on 1 April 1933, local and regional party activists, many of them in close cooperation with Julius Streicher's *Stürmer* newspaper, started new campaigns against Jewish businesses by attacking shop owners and their non-Jewish customers (Wildt 2007, 194; Ahlheim 2011, 295–299). By mid-1935, Jewish men and their non-Jewish girlfriends were being denounced for committing 'race defile' (*Rassenschande*) and betraying the 'Aryan race'. Local party activists and members of the SA and SS humiliated them by marching them through crowded streets in processions of disgrace (*Prangerumzüge*) similar to those directed against opposition politicians, rabbis, and other Jews in the first months of the Nazi regime. After attempts to stem the tide of antisemitic aggression from below in August 1935, the government took the initiative by codifying the racial segregation of 'Aryans' and Jews through the Nuremberg Laws (Wildt 2007, 282).

The interplay of local and regional party activists on the one hand, and central authorities on the other, often provoked irritation and conflict (Faludi 2013). Nevertheless, it proved to be essential for the emergence, practice, and radicalization of Nazi politics (Gruner 2002). The evolution of a new political fabric that allowed institutions and activists at different levels of the Nazi state to compete and cooperate suited the mobilization of resources more effectively than a political system in which federal governors, *Gauleiters*, and both regional and provincial governments would have been little more than subdivisions of the Reich Ministry of the Interior.

9.2   The Formation of New Regional Authorities

The first initiatives for establishing new political arrangements at the regional level emerged as early as 1935, several years before the annexation of Austria and the establishment of *Reichsgaue* began shifting the balance of central and regional institutions (Hüttenberger 1969, 157–8). Initially the efforts of the *Gauleiters* and federal governors to regain control over centralized branches of regional administrations dovetailed, to some degree, with the Reich's Interior Ministry intention to establish a 'unity of administration on the intermediate level' (*Einheit der*

Verwaltung in der Mittelinstanz) to resist other central administrations' claims (Ruck 2011, 92). However, the 'men on the spot' were also concerned with changes to public administrations as well as party institutions.

Although Rudolf Hess, the Deputy Führer (*Stellvertreter des Führers*) in the NSDAP, and his chief of staff Martin Bormann repeatedly stressed the fundamental distinction between party and state, centralization measures, like the appointment of *Gauleiters* to the position of federal governors, tended to strengthen the already existent entanglement. In their capacity as federal governors or provincial presidents they were subordinated to the Reich's Interior Ministry, but as *Gauleiters* they had been appointed by Adolf Hitler personally and, therefore, insisted on being members of the inner circle and considered equal to ministers and leading party officials (*Reichsleiter*) in Berlin (Ruck 1996, 109–10). From a constitutional point of view these two standpoints were not compatible (Mommsen 2000, 231). In practice, combining party and state functions in one hand offered essential prerequisites for the development of new power structures in the German regions (Ruck 2011, 97).

In principle, almost all regional authorities were subdivisions of central institutions. This applied to the federal governors and *Gauleiters*, as well as the provincial presidents and sub-provincial presidents (*Regierungspräsidenten*) in Prussia, the various party offices, the regional staffs of old and new bureaucracies, as for example, the armaments inspections of the military districts, the regional commissions (*Rüstungskommissionen*) of Albert Speer's Ministry for Armaments and Military Production (*Reichsministerium für Rüstung und Kriegsproduktion*), the regional branches of the SS and police, as well as the regional authorities for industry (*Landeswirtschaftsämter*) and agriculture (*Landesernährungsämter* and *Landesbauernführer*), for the recruitment and employment of labour (*Landesarbeitsämter* and *Generalbevollmächtigter für den Arbeitseinsatz*), and for infrastructure (*Landesplanungsgemeinschaften*). While central party institutions, such as the departments for propaganda and party finance, held direct control over regional party offices, some *Gauleiters* began extending their influence by controlling regional administrations and by horizontal and vertical networking.

Taking the large array of regional institutions into account, the new authorities established by the *Gauleiters* were just one player amongst many others. The *Gauleiters*' success depended on the ability to coordinate, integrate, network, and cooperate with other institutions. In most cases, cooperative initiatives were sparked by important national issues, such as the mobilization for the Four Year Plan, the 'Aryanization' (*Arisierung*) of Jewish property, or the challenges associated with the consequences that aerial warfare had for society and economy. Although regional-level institutions were similar in almost every *Gau*, regional party leaders' initiatives followed no general guidelines and, therefore, the outcome varied from one place to another. Even the institutions that served as cornerstones of new regional power clusters differed. For example, in Thuringia, Fritz Sauckel decided for the *Reichsstatthalter* office while his Saxon counterpart Martin Mutschmann chose the State Chancellery, the office of the Saxon prime minister, as his personal power base (John 2002, 43; Wagner 2004, 365–68).

Regional cultural traditions that were associated with local identities were particularly tempting as a means of appealing to, and controlling, the local population. The concept of *Heimat* as a mystic rallying ground of the nation became extremely popular in reaction to the defeat in the First World War and the deepening social and political rifts following the November 1918 revolution. The ultra-nationalistic idea of 'blood and soil' (*Blut und Boden*) stressed the importance of being embedded in local culture originating from one's own place of belonging. For decades, the tribalist idea of *Heimat* was represented by homeland associations (*Heimatvereine*) and their regional umbrella organizations (Steber 2010, 162, 277, 311). While central Nazi institutions such as Alfred Rosenberg's National Socialist Culture Association (*Nationalsozialistische Kulturgemeinde*) lacked efficient regional and local substructures, the new local political elites were in a far better position to establish links with existing cultural associations and their leading figures.

While these efforts were supposed to help integrate the population into the new social framework of the Nazi 'people's community' (*Volksgemeinschaft*), simultaneously other leading political figures portrayed themselves as representatives of regional traditions and interests (Kißener and Scholtyseck 1997, 22–26; Steber 2010, 358–359, 367). In some cases, this claim was instrumental to fending off competing territorial claims, as in the Bavarian part of Swabia, but regional affiliations were never directed against decisions made by central authorities. As long as regional political elites promoted a popular culture based on the principles of 'blood and soil', which contributed to closer social integration and the political education of the local population, they were acting in accordance with the central leadership's intentions (Steber 2010, 324–326; Dahm 1996, 221–224).

The proclamation of the Four Year Plan (*Vierjahresplan*) in September 1936 offered an important incentive for regional leaders to consolidate their influence over regional administrations and party institutions. The ambitious objective of preparing Germany for war in a short, four-year period was echoed by a whole range of regional initiatives. When Hermann Göring, the head of the Four Year Plan authority, appealed to the *Gauleiters* for help in November 1936, some of them responded by establishing new administrations to mobilize their regions' material and social resources.

In a few weeks, the Thuringian Nazi leadership under the guidance of Sauckel set up a new party main office (*Gauhauptamt*) to coordinate all measures necessary to prepare Germany for war. Göring's decision to employ the Nazi party and regional leaders to push the Four Year Plan through effectively advanced their personal ambitions in a number of ways. First, the new party institution Sauckel intended to establish strengthened his regional power base as he insisted on heading the new organization himself. Second, it offered an opportunity to enforce his control over the administrative region of Erfurt, which belonged to the Thuringian party organization but was part of the Prussian state (John 2002, 44).

While in Bavaria a Central Office for the Implementation of the Four Year Plan was created in the regional Ministry of Commerce and Trade, the *Gauleiter* of Bavarian Swabia, Karl Wahl, founded the Swabian Research Association, as well as the Regional Office for the Four Year Plan, with similar functions as their Thuringian counterpart (Gotto 2006a, 158). In Saxony, a propaganda campaign for regional pride and self-esteem, which had already started in early 1936, was turned into a regional cultural organization, the so-called *Heimatwerk Sachsen*, which was presented as Saxony's contribution to the Four Year Plan. Other than the initiatives in Thuringia and Swabia, it focused on political education and social mobilization (Schaarschmidt 2007, 134–135). By reminding the Saxons of their past military, economic, and cultural achievements, it sought to rouse their pride and, consequently, their readiness 'to work towards the *Führer*' (Schaarschmidt 2004). Although the *Gauleiters* claimed that their initiatives proceeded in accordance with the central authority of the Four Year Plan, Göring turned against the new regional organizations. In February 1937, he declared them to be rather detrimental to his national efforts and demanded they be liquidated as soon as possible (Hartmannsgruber 2005, 115–117). While in some regions the new institutions became redundant and vanished, in others they continued to flourish and strengthen the *Gauleiters'* regional position. In Saxony the *Heimatwerk* remained an integral part of the *Gauleiters'* power structures until the last days of the war.

At the same time the expropriation of Jewish German property under the pretext of 'Aryanization' offered tempting opportunities for regional and local party chiefs to assert their authority (Bajohr 2015, 452–453). In some regions the second wave of antisemitic boycotts and pogroms in June 1935 paved the way for a wholesale confiscation and transfer of Jewish property. For example, the small territory of Schaumburg had almost completed expropriation of Jewish property before 'Aryanization' at the national level had even begun (Werner 2010, 557). Already in the early stages of the Nazi regime, when its anti-Jewish policy focused on restriction and segregation, Thuringian *Gauleiter* Sauckel had taken the lead by initiating legal proceedings against the Jewish weapons manufacturer Simson located in Suhl. Within three years he had forced the owners into emigration and transformed the highly profitable company into the Wilhelm Gustloff Foundation, which he placed under his personal control (Gibas 2006, 34).

Other regional leaders such as Streicher, the Frankonian party chief and editor of the antisemitic *Stürmer* weekly, and *Gauleiter* Adolf Wagner, his influential counterpart in Munich, followed Sauckel's example (Drecoll 2009, 47–54, 66). The administration for 'Aryanization' that Wagner had established in November 1938 became a highly efficient instrument for the plunder of Jews living in Munich and Upper Bavaria, advancing the *Gauleiter's* interests as well as those of central authorities in Berlin. In Frankonia a substantial proportion of the 'Aryanization' proceeds were channelled into bank accounts of the regional party organization, a clear violation of the NSDAP's system of party finance (Hüttenberger 1969, 126–127). The investigations into Streicher's corrupt practices finally led to his dismissal in 1941 (Drecoll 2009, 77–83). Although the embezzlement of funds threatened to damage the Party's reputation, Streicher's antisemitic propaganda and the ruthless 'Aryanization' of Jewish property in Frankonia went hand in hand with the central government's policy to drive German Jews from the country.

In the final years before the outbreak of the Second World War, the growing influence of regional authorities made itself felt when the Reich Interior Ministry, the Central Party Office in Munich, and the *Gauleiters* negotiated over the appointment of new sub-provincial presidents in Prussia. Increasingly, Frick's vision of government by an administrative elite of efficient and performance-oriented public servants collided with the *Gauleiters*' interest in placing loyal supporters in important positions. As early as April 1937, Frick complained to Hess that the *Gauleiters*' growing impact on regional personnel policy threatened to bring about a new kind of 'particularism' (*Gaupartikularismus*) at the expense of national unity (Schrulle 2008, 75–76).

In order to regain influence over the new regional power arrangements, Frick supported the concept of coherent regional structures labelled as *Reichsgaue*. While similar plans had been drafted by other regional party leaders (Wagner 2004, 36–57), the term *Reichsgau* was first used in the 'Law on Greater Hamburg' (*Groß-Hamburg-Gesetz*) in January 1937. On the one hand, it emphasized the Hanseatic city's independent status in the new Nazi order, while on the other, the claim was supported by a new form of regional government according to which *Gauleiter* Karl Kaufmann, the federal governor of Hamburg, tightly controlled all departments of the city's administration (Lohalm 2005, 125–134). According to Wilhelm Stuckart, Frick's secretary of state (*Staatssekretär*), strengthening the position of the *Gauleiter-Reichsstatthalter* was the only means of checking the influence of other central authorities, both old and new, on regional ministries and administrations (Gebel 2000, 104).

From March 1938, the concept of *Reichsgau* became the dominant pattern for the internal structure of territories annexed to Germany. According to the Laws for Austria (*Ostmarkgesetz*) and Sudetenland (*Sudetengaugesetz*) of April 1939, the *Gauleiters* and federal governors were equipped with comprehensive powers to control even the regional offices of central authorities. Although the Reich Interior Ministry claimed that it intended to establish a kind of regional self-government (*Gauselbstverwaltung*), the new regional powers in the *Reichsgaue* derived all their influence from acting on behalf of the political leadership on the national level. Accordingly, they hardly represented a new kind of federalism. When Konrad Henlein was appointed *Reichsstatthalter* of Sudetenland, it quickly became clear that several central authorities disliked Frick's plans and thwarted Henlein's ambitions as much as possible. Similar to the territories annexed during the war, Henlein's power depended largely on his ability to establish good relations with the regional representatives of the SS, the military, the Four Year Plan administration, and other institutions (Gebel 2000, 106–110).

Compared to Kaufmann in Hamburg, or Henlein in Sudetenland, most of the *Gauleiter-Reichsstatthalter* who headed the *Reichsgaue* in occupied and annexed territories during the Second World War, such as Arthur Greiser in the *Warthegau*, Albert Forster in Danzig-West Prussia, Erich Koch in extended East Prussia, and Fritz Bracht in Upper Silesia, proved to be far more successful in establishing new power relations. As the conquered provinces were inhabited by other nationalities and Jews, their primary tasks consisted of extensive ethnic cleansing according to Nazi racial ideals and the implementation of completely new administrative structures staffed by German civil servants. In order to cope with these extraordinary challenges, the central political leadership bestowed more and more power on the leading men in the new *Reichsgaue* (Epstein 2010, 148–9). Although in principle this transfer of power coincided with Frick's ideas of Nazi statehood, it very soon turned against the Interior Ministry's interests (Podranski 2008, 99).

By combining the authority of regional party chief and federal governor, the heads of the new *Reichsgaue* extended their control of regional propaganda offices, the judiciary, regional finance, church politics, and the forced employment of the non-German workforce (Pohl 2007, 401). Their high-handed recruitment of personnel for the new administrations in annexed territories in particular went contrary to Frick's intentions when he propagated the idea of the *Reichsgau* (Meindl 2004, 111). While Danzig's Forster remained at loggerheads with Himmler's claim on dominating racial politics in the occupied territories, Arthur Greiser established close links with the SS and police (Pohl 2007, 402–403). In the end, Greiser became Himmler's representative for the strengthening of Germandom in Wartheland (*Beauftragter des Reichskommissars für die Festigung des deutschen Volkstums*) and acted in concert with regional SS and police chiefs (*Höherer SS- und Polizeiführer*). This symbiotic relationship made Wartheland a deadly laboratory for racial and antisemitic experiments, or, as Greiser declared, 'the parade ground of practical National Socialism' (Epstein 2010, 124).

9.3   The Nazi Political System Under Pressure of War

Despite significant differences, the *Gauleiters* of the Eastern *Reichsgaue* used to portray their provinces as *Mustergaue*, that is, role models for the other regions in Germany and their relationship with central authorities (Kaczmarek 2007, 353). At that time, even in Kaufmann's *Reichsgau* of Hamburg, the implementation of a consistent governing structure was little more than a vision. At least in some regions the federal governors or provincial presidents had been successful in gaining more influence on regional decision making and establishing new institutions that served to help unify party and state functions.

When German forces attacked Poland in September 1939, the already existing differences between the *Gaue* in the *Altreich* became even greater. Immediately after the outbreak of war, the Ministerial Council for the Reich's Defence (*Ministerrat für die Reichsverteidigung*) appointed 15 *Gauleiters* to Reich defence commissioners (*Reichsverteidigungskommissare*), one for each military district (*Wehrkreis*). They became the civilian counterparts to the regional military commanders and were responsible for the organization of civil defence as well as the mobilization of social and material resources for war. In order to fulfil these expectations, the decree of 1 September 1939 empowered them to give instructions to most civil administrations in their *Gau*. Although the decree stressed that the Reich defence commissioners acted under the supervision of the Reich's Interior Ministry and on behalf of central authorities, their new powers strengthened their position in the complex fabric of the Nazi dictatorship (John 2007, 44).

With a few exceptions, the military districts didn't follow *Gau* boundaries and, therefore, extended into more than one *Gau*. As a result, the remaining 19 *Gauleiters* were subordinated to their equals, now in the position of Reich defence commissioners. In some cases they were appointed as deputies, in others they were only represented in the new Reich Defence Committees (*Reichsverteidigungsausschüsse*).

In these advisory boards they sat side by side with provincial presidents, sub-provincial presidents, regional minister presidents, SS leaders, trustees of labor (*Treuhänder der Arbeit*), and other *Gauleiters*. The new regional committees offered the prospect of coordinating diverging interests and mitigating the detrimental effects of polycratic competition on the central level (Gotto 2006b, 38). However, their practical value varied from one district to another. In some territories they proved to be highly efficient, in others they were widely neglected as the newly appointed Reich defence commissioners preferred to govern without regard for other regional authorities (Schaarschmidt 2014, 109).

Compared to the new *Reichsgaue* on the Eastern frontier, the relationship between central and regional authorities in the *Altreich* didn't change significantly during the first years of the Second World War. Although the *Gauleiters* gained some new powers, these were counterbalanced by centralizing trends in the armaments industry. In 1939 they were appointed commissioners for the evacuation of the civilian population from endangered territories in border regions and, in 1940, to Regional Housing Commissioners (*Gauwohnungskommissare*). However, neither housing nor evacuation were critical issues in the early years of the war (Strehle 2013, 163–164; Harlander 1995, 210).

After the Wehrmacht attacked the Soviet Union in June 1941, the comprehensive mobilization of all available resources for war became of utmost importance. Although central authorities in Berlin took the lead, in most cases they depended on the support of regional authorities. Almost immediately after his own appointment to General Commissioner for Labour Supply (*Generalbevollmächtigter für den Arbeitseinsatz*) in March 1942, the Thuringian *Gauleiter* Sauckel made all his fellow *Gauleiters* regional representatives of his new labour administration (Hüttenberger 1969, 166–168). In doing so, Sauckel intended to employ the new regional power arrangements as substructures of his newly created central authority.

While this process could be interpreted as an intentional devolution of power, Joseph Goebbels strove for centralization when he established the National Socialist Organization for Folklore (*NS-Volkskulturwerk*) in May 1942. Goebbels wanted to control the array of regional cultural organizations (*Gauheimatwerke*) that flourished under the protection of several *Gauleiters*. As they largely consisted of amateurs, they were beyond the Reich chamber of culture's (*Reichskulturkammer*) reach. Paradoxically, because Goebbels's new umbrella organization depended on the cooperation of existing regional institutions, the outcome of his initiative was quite similar to Sauckel's decision to rely on the *Gaue*. In the end, the propaganda minister had to eat humble pie and accept the *Gauleiters'* choice as representatives of his new organization (Schaarschmidt 2004, 233–235).

At the same time, when Sauckel bestowed new powers on regional authorities, Speer, Fritz Todt's successor as Minister for Armaments, tried to use the coordinating and mobilizing capabilities of regional institutions without losing control of the mobilization process. In order to reduce the *Gauleiters'* growing influence over the economy, Speer established regional armaments commissions for each military district, which involved a wide range of civilian and military institutions and interests. Even obstinate *Gauleiters* who used to ignore Speer's instructions had to accept the decisions of the armaments commissions chaired by respected personalities who were appointed by the minister himself (Werner 2013, 219–224). In the long run, the commissions proved efficient instruments for mitigating regional conflicts and gaining support for the complete adjustment of the economy to the necessities of total warfare.

During the second half of the war, attempts to centralize authority stood in contrast to measures that strengthened regional and local authorities. In November 1942, the conflicts caused by the appointment of only a number of *Gauleiters* to Reich defence commissioners in 1939 were settled by adjusting the military districts to the smaller *Gau* territories. In this context, the whole economic administration, with the important exception of the armament industry, was adapted to the territories of the Gaue (John 2007, 45). When, in August 1944, the armaments commissions were adapted to the *Gau* structure as well, Speer's primary objective was to counter the effects of Goebbels's appointing the *Gauleiters* to his regional representatives as Reich Commissioner for Total Warfare (*Reichsbevollmächtigter für den totalen Kriegseinsatz*) and to check their ambitions to recruiting the workforce of armament factories for the Wehrmacht (Werner 2013, 230–231).

After the battle of Stalingrad, German cities and military and industrial installations were increasingly bombed by Allied air forces, and the tremendous losses inflicted upon the German army could not be replaced by the mobilization of new resources. At least the official campaign for a more efficient administration (*Vereinfachung der Verwaltung*) offered some prospect of directing the workforce of useless bureaucracies into the ranks of the Wehrmacht. For several *Gauleiters*, the call for administrative reform offered a suitable pretext to resume their efforts for new power arrangements on the regional level. In occupied territories where *Gauleiters* governed either as federal governors (e.g. Greiser in the *Warthegau*), general commissioners (e.g. Hinrich Lohse in the *Reichskommissariat Ostland*), chiefs of civil administration (e.g. Siegfried Uiberreither in Lower Styria), or high commissioners (e.g. Franz Hofer in the *Operationszone Alpenvorland*) as well as in many territories of the *Altreich*, regional party chiefs tried to concentrate all portfolios in a small number of authorities and merge party and state structures to an even greater extent than before the war.

Authorities on the intermediate level (*Regierungsbezirke*) between districts, larger cities, and the *Gau*, were either made redundant, as in most Prussian provinces, or were abolished completely, as in Saxony, even though the central government tried to restrict initiatives from below. In some Prussian regions the administrations of sub-provincial presidents were transformed into offices of newly centralized *Gau* authorities (Schrulle 2008, 445–446). By early 1943, few ministries existed on the regional level. In a number of cases some ministries had been fused with the regional state chancelleries, while in others there remained but one regional authority. In Saxony, *Gauleiter* Mutschmann seized the opportunity to implement his long-term plan for a 'Gau government' under the roof of the state chancellery. He even proceeded with his project despite Hitler's opposition. Taking into consideration that as early as 1936 leading public servants of the Saxon state chancellery had issued instructions to the regional party organization, it appears that Mutschmann sought to create a single political authority under his personal control to deal with administrative and party matters alike (Schaarschmidt 2007, 138–140).

The growing influence of regional party leaders, which Franz Neumann described in his supplement to *Behemoth* in 1944 (Neumann 2009, 535–537), largely depended on the NSDAP's new role in coping with the massive damage caused by Allied air raids (Süß 2011, 230). In their double function as party chief and regional Reich defence commissioners, *Gauleiters* were responsible for controlling the chaos caused by air raids while continuing to mobilize German society to continue fighting until the very end. While local party leaders were supposed to care for the urgent needs of evacuees and those made homeless, the *Gauleiters* set up regional operation staffs (*Gaueinsatzstäbe*) to coordinate the efforts of all relevant offices and institutions to provide help to the needy, repair damage, and restore order (Nolzen 2008, 169–170). Even when central lines of command failed in the last months of the war, many regional power arrangements and structures continued to exert influence until Allied forces finally put an end to Nazi rule.

9.4   Conclusions

Although the radicalization of Nazi politics on the regional level didn't change the final outcome of the war, it demonstrated that some kind of multilevel governance had been established after the old federal order was removed by Hitler's seizure of power. Despite earlier plans to establish a centralized political system with clear-cut lines of command, regulations regarding the exercise of authority at the intermediate level were far less clear than those imposed upon local government by the German Municipal Code of 1935 (*Deutsche Gemeindeordnung*). Hitler's aversion to a cohesive *Reichsreform* opened the floor for new political and administrative arrangements involving conflicting interests on the regional level. Although Frick, Himmler, and others repeatedly complained that regional party chiefs aspired to create a kind of new federalism, the eventual outcome was quite different. As the *Gauleiters'* authority depended almost completely on their appointment by Hitler, they always acted on behalf of the Reich. Even when they insisted on the uniqueness and importance of 'their' region, their actions represented the interests of the central leadership.

As no master plan existed for how institutions and leading figures on the different levels of the Nazi state should interact, a large variety of arrangements emerged in a permanent process of bargaining. Some regional authorities were particularly successful in establishing personal networks on the regional level, as well as between leading personalities at the central, regional, and local levels. The outcome depended on initiatives from below, conflicts of interests between key actors, the economic and military importance of territories, and diverging borderlines between *Länder*, provinces, military districts, and *Gaue*. The fluidity of power arrangements that resulted from a fundamental preference for informal and improvised means makes it particularly difficult to determine the relationship between the centre and periphery in the Nazi state.

References

Ahlheim, Hannah. 2011. '*Deutsche, kauft nicht bei Juden!*': *Antisemitismus und politischer Boykott in Deutschland 1924 bis 1935*. Göttingen: Wallstein.

Bajohr, Frank. 2015. 'Die Profiteursgesellschaft des "Dritten Reiches".' In *München und der Nationalsozialismus. Katalog des NS-Dokumentationszentrums München*, edited by Winfried Nerdinger, 450–456. Munich: C.H. Beck.

Dahm, Volker. 1996. 'Kulturpolitischer Zentralismus und landschaftlich-lokale Kulturpflege im Dritten Reich.' In *Nationalsozialismus in der Region: Beiträge zur regionalen und lokalen Forschung und zum internationalen Vergleich*, edited by Horst Möller, Andreas Wirsching, and Walter Ziegler, 123–138. Munich: Oldenbourg.

Drecoll, Axel. 2009. *Der Fiskus als Verfolger: Die steuerliche Diskriminierung der Juden in Bayern 1933–1941/42*. Munich: Oldenbourg.

Epstein, Catherine. 2010. *Model Nazi: Arthur Greiser and the Occupation of Western Poland*. Oxford: Oxford University Press.

Faludi, Christian, ed. 2013. *Die 'Juni-Aktion' 1938: Eine Dokumentation zur Radikalisierung der Judenverfolgung*. Frankfurt am Main and New York: Campus.

Gebel, Ralf. 2000. '*Heim ins Reich!*' *Konrad Henlein und der Reichsgau Sudetenland (1938–1945)*. Munich: Oldenbourg.

Gibas, Monika, ed. 2006. *Arisierung in Thüringen: Entrechtung, Enteignung und Vernichtung der jüdischen Bürger Thüringens 1933–1945*. Erfurt: Landeszentrale für politische Bildung.

Gotto, Bernhard. 2006a. *Nationalsozialistische Kommunalpolitik: Administrative Normalität und Systemstabilisierung durch die Augsburger Stadtverwaltung 1933–1945*. Munich: Oldenbourg.

Gotto, Bernhard. 2006b. 'Polykratische Selbststabilisierung: Mittel- und Unterinstanzen in der NS-Diktatur.' In *Hitlers Kommissare: Sondergewalten in der nationalsozialistischen Diktatur*, edited by Rüdiger Hachtmann and Winfried Süß, 28–50. Göttingen: Wallstein.

Gruner, Wolf. 2002. *Öffentliche Wohlfahrt und Judenverfolgung: Wechselwirkungen lokaler und zentraler Politik im NS-Staat (1933–1942)*. Munich: Oldenbourg.

Harlander, Tilman. 1995. *Zwischen Heimstätte und Wohnmaschine: Wohnungsbau und Wohnungspolitik in der Zeit des Nationalsozialismus*. Basle: Birkhäuser.

Hartmannsgruber, Friedrich, ed. 2005. *Akten der Reichskanzlei. Die Regierung Hitler*. Vol. 5. Munich: Oldenbourg.

Hüttenberger, Peter. 1969. *Die Gauleiter: Studie zum Wandel des Machtgefüges in der NSDAP*. Stuttgart: Deutsche Verlagsanstalt.

Hüttenberger, Peter. 1976. 'Nationalsozialistische Polykratie.' *Geschichte und Gesellschaft* 2, 417–442.

John, Jürgen. 2001. '"Unitarischer Bundesstaat", "Reichsreform" und "Reichs-Neugliederung" in der Weimarer Republik.' In *'Mitteldeutschland': Begriff – Geschichte – Konstrukt*, edited by Jürgen John, 297–375. Rudolstadt: Hain.

John, Jürgen. 2002. 'Der NS-Gau Thüringen 1933 bis 1945: Grundzüge einer Struktur- und Funktionsgeschichte.' In *Klassikerstadt und Nationalsozialismus: Kultur und Politik in Weimar 1933 bis 1945*, edited by Justus Ulbricht, 25–52. Weimar: Stadtmuseum.

John, Jürgen. 2007. 'Die Gaue im NS-System.' In *Die NS-Gaue: Regionale Mittelinstanzen im zentralistischen 'Führerstaat'*, edited by Jürgen John, Horst Möller, and Thomas Schaarschmidt, 22–55. Munich: Oldenbourg.

Kaczmarek, Ryszard. 2007. 'Zwischen Altreich und Besatzungsgebiet: Der Gau Oberschlesien 1939/41–1945.' In *Die NS-Gaue: Regionale Mittelinstanzen im zentralistischen 'Führerstaat'*, edited by Jürgen John, Horst Möller, and Thomas Schaarschmidt, 348–360. Munich: Oldenbourg.

Kißener, Michael and Scholtyseck, Joachim. 1997. 'Nationalsozialismus in der Provinz: Zur Einführung.' In *Die Führer der Provinz: NS-Biographien aus Baden und Württemberg*, edited by Michael Kißener and Joachim Scholtyseck, 11–29. Constance: Universitätsverlag.

Kreutzmüller, Christoph. 2012. *Ausverkauf: Die Vernichtung der jüdischen Gewerbetätigkeit in Berlin 1930–1945*. Berlin: Metropol.

Lohalm, Uwe. 2005. '"Modell Hamburg": Vom Stadtstaat zum Reichsgau.' In *Hamburg im 'Dritten Reich'*, edited by Axel Schildt, 122–153. Göttingen: Wallstein.

Meindl, Ralf. 2004. 'Die Politik des ostpreußischen Gauleiters Erich Koch in den annektierten polnischen Gebieten als Ausdruck nationalsozialistischer Zielvorstellungen'. In *Deutschland und Polen in schweren Zeiten 1933–1990: Alte Konflikte – neue Sichtweisen*, edited by Czesław Madajczyk, 101–115. Poznan: Instytut Historii UAM.

Mommsen, Hans. 2000. 'Reichsreform und Regionalgewalten: Das Phantom der Mittelinstanz 1933–1945.' In *Zentralismus und Föderalismus im 19. und 20. Jahrhundert: Deutschland und Italien im Vergleich*, edited by Oliver Janz, Perangelo Schiera, and Hannes Siegrist, 227–237. Berlin: Duncker & Humblot.

Neumann, Franz. 2009. *Behemoth: The Struggle and Practice of National Socialism, 1933–1944*. Chicago: Ivan R. Dee.

Nolzen, Armin. 2008. 'The NSDAP, the War, and German Society.' In *Germany and the Second World War*, vol. 9, pt. 1: *German Wartime Society 1939–1945: Politicization, Disintegration, and the Struggle for Survival*, edited for the Militärgeschichtliches Forschungsamt Potsdam, Germany by Jörg Echternkamp. Translation editor Derry Cook-Radmore, 111–206. Oxford: Clarendon Press.

Podranski, Thomas. 2008. 'Gauleiter als regionale Politikakteure in den eingegliederten Ostgebieten des Deutschen Reiches.' *Zeitschrift für Genozidforschung* 9, 95–130.

Pohl, Dieter. 2007. 'Die Reichsgaue Danzig-Westpreußen und Wartheland: Koloniale Verwaltung oder Modell für die zukünftige Gauverwaltung?' In *Die NS-Gaue: Regionale Mittelinstanzen im zentralistischen 'Führerstaat'*, edited by Jürgen John, Horst Möller, and Thomas Schaarschmidt, 395–405. Munich: Oldenbourg.

Rebentisch, Dieter. 1989. *Führerstaat und Verwaltung im Zweiten Weltkrieg: Verfassungsentwicklung und Verwaltungspolitik 1939–1945*. Stuttgart: Steiner.

Ruck, Michael. 1996. 'Zentralismus und Regionalgewalten im Herrschaftsgefüge des NS-Staates' In *Nationalsozialismus in der Region: Beiträge zur regionalen und lokalen Forschung und zum internationalen Vergleich*, edited by Horst Möller, Andreas Wirsching, and Walter Ziegler, 99–122. Munich: Oldenbourg.

Ruck, Michael. 2011. 'Partikularismus und Mobilisierung: Traditionelle und totalitäre Regionalgewalten im Herrschaftsgefüge des NS-Regimes.' In *Der prekäre Staat: Herrschen und Verwalten im Nationalsozialismus*, edited by Sven Reichardt and Wolfgang Seibel, 75–120. Frankfurt am Main and New York: Campus.

Schaarschmidt, Thomas. 2004. *Regionalkultur und Diktatur: Sächsische Heimatbewegung und Heimat-Propaganda im Dritten Reich und in der SBZ/DDR*. Cologne, Weimar, and Vienna: Böhlau.

Schaarschmidt, Thomas. 2007. 'Die regionale Ebene im zentralistischen "Führerstaat": Das Beispiel des NS-Gaus Sachsen.' In *Länder, Gaue und Bezirke: Mitteldeutschland im 20. Jahrhundert*, edited by Michael Richter, Thomas Schaarschmidt, and Mike Schmeitzner, 125–140. Halle: Mitteldeutscher Verlag.

Schaarschmidt, Thomas. 2014. 'Mobilizing German Society for War: The National Socialist Gaue.' In *Visions of Community in Nazi Germany: Social Engineering and Private Lives*, edited by Martina Steber and Bernhard Gotto, 101–115. Oxford. Oxford University Press.

Schmitt, Carl. 1933. *Das Recht der nationalen Revolution*. Berlin: Carl Heymanns.

Schrulle, Hedwig. 2008. *Verwaltung in Diktatur und Demokratie: Die Bezirksregierungen Münster und Minden/Detmold von 1930 bis 1960*. Paderborn: Schöningh.

Steber, Martina. 2010. *Ethnische Gewissheiten: Die Ordnung des Regionalen im bayerischen Schwaben vom Kaiserreich bis zum NS-Regime*. Göttingen: Vandenhoeck & Ruprecht.

Strehle, Markus. 2013. 'Die Kriegsausrichtung des NS-Gaus Thüringen.' In *Mobilisierung im Nationalsozialismus: Institutionen und Regionen in der Kriegswirtschaft und der Verwaltung des 'Dritten Reiches' 1936 bis 1945*, edited by Oliver Werner, 159–179. Paderborn: Schöningh.

Süß, Dietmar. 2011. *Tod aus der Luft: Kriegsgesellschaft und Luftkrieg in Deutschland und England*. Munich: Siedler.

Treß, Werner. 2008. 'Phasen und Akteure der Bücherverbrennungen in Deutschland 1933.' In *Orte der Bücherverbrennungen in Deutschland*, edited by Julius H. Schoeps and Werner Treß, 9–28. Hildesheim: Georg Olms.

Wagner, Andreas. 2004. *'Machtergreifung' in Sachsen: NSDAP und staatliche Verwaltung 1930–1935*. Cologne, Weimar, and Vienna: Böhlau.

Werner, Frank. 2010. 'Die kleinen Wächter der "Volksgemeinschaft": Denunzianten, Boykotteure und Gewaltakteure aus Schaumburg.' In *Schaumburger Nationalsozialisten: Täter, Komplizen, Profiteure*, edited by Frank Werner, 521–583. Bielefeld: Verlag für Regionalgeschichte.

Werner, Oliver. 2013. 'Garanten der Mobilisierung: Die Rüstungskommissionen des Speer-Ministeriums im "totalen Krieg".' In *Mobilisierung im Nationalsozialismus: Institutionen und Regionen in der Kriegswirtschaft und der Verwaltung des 'Dritten Reiches' 1936 bis 1945*, edited by Oliver Werner, 217–233. Paderborn: Schöningh.

Wildt, Michael. 2007. *Volksgemeinschaft als Selbstermächtigung: Gewalt gegen Juden in der deutschen Provinz 1919 bis 1939*. Hamburg: Hamburger Edition.

Further Reading

Gotto, Bernhard. 2006. *Nationalsozialistische Kommunalpolitik: Administrative Normalität und Systemstabilisierung durch die Augsburger Stadtverwaltung 1933–1945*. Munich: Oldenbourg.

This study analyses the municipal administration of Augsburg as an example of local government in Nazi Germany.

Gruner, Wolf. 2002. *Öffentliche Wohlfahrt und Judenverfolgung: Wechselwirkungen lokaler und zentraler Politik im NS-Staat (1933–1942)*. Munich: Oldenbourg.

Gruner's book explains how administrations on different levels of the political system cooperated in excluding German Jews from social welfare.

Hachtmann, Rüdiger and Süß, Winfried, eds. 2006. *Hitlers Kommissare: Sondergewalten in der nationalsozialistischen Diktatur*. Göttingen: Wallstein.

The contributions to this volume explore how new administrations set up in Nazi Germany interacted with existing bureaucracies.

Hüttenberger, Peter. 1969. *Die Gauleiter: Studie zum Wandel des Machtgefüges in der NSDAP*. Stuttgart: Deutsche Verlagsanstalt.

This was the first coherent study on regional power structures in Nazi Germany.

John, Jürgen, Möller, Horst, and Schaarschmidt, Thomas, eds. 2007. *Die NS-Gaue: Regionale Mittelinstanzen im zentralistischen 'Führerstaat'*. Munich: Oldenbourg.

This volume offers insights into the functioning of institutions on the *Gau* level and their relevance for the perseverance of the Nazi state.

Möller, Horst, Wirsching, Andreas, and Ziegler, Walter, eds. 1996. *Nationalsozialismus in der Region: Beiträge zur regionalen und lokalen Forschung und zum internationalen Vergleich*. Munich: Oldenbourg.

The contributions to this volume are focused on the impact of regional institutions on the fabric of Nazi politics.

Richter, Michael, Schaarschmidt, Thomas, and Schmeitzner, Mike, eds. 2007. *Länder, Gaue und Bezirke: Mitteldeutschland im 20. Jahrhundert*. Halle: Mitteldeutscher Verlag.

This book explores different forms of multilevel politics in Germany ranging from federalism to the *Führerstaat*.

Schildt, Axel, ed. 2005. *Hamburg im 'Dritten Reich'*. Göttingen: Wallstein.

This volume gives a profound impression how one of the largest German cities became a cornerstone of Nazi rule in Germany.

Werner, Oliver, ed. 2013. *Mobilisierung im Nationalsozialismus: Institutionen und Regionen in der Kriegswirtschaft und der Verwaltung des 'Dritten Reiches' 1936 bis 1945*. Paderborn: Schöningh.

This volume covers a wide range of civil and military institutions whose contribution was essential for Nazi war policies.

CHAPTER TEN

Information Policies and Linguistic Violence

THOMAS PEGELOW KAPLAN

10.1 Introduction

Beginning with the growth of the Nazi movement, scholars, journalists, and political observers have been analysing the National Socialists' use of language and media control. Most of them resorted to notions of 'propaganda' to shed light on these phenomena, elevating the term to a paradigmatic concept. By now, the scholarly literature has become massive with, literally, thousands of works devoted to the topic.

Mass society theory dominated much of the early investigations of Nazi propaganda (Bussemer 2008). Based on the premise that support by alienated individuals in modern society had to be created communicatively, these approaches focused on the use of the mass media by political parties such as the Hitler movement. Communication scholars like Emil Dovifat embraced simplistic dichotomies of elitist speakers and submissive recipients. Dovifat's (1937) notion of '*Volk*'s speech', allegedly practised by Hitler, even overlapped with Nazi doctrine. Neo-Marxist philosophers such as Theodor Adorno, by contrast, were highly critical of propaganda and its uses by the Nazi state. Adorno (1982) asserted that fascist propaganda built on the socio-psychological pressures of capitalist societies by offering powerful myths, which robbed the masses of their autonomy. For all their differences, these adherents to mass society theory strikingly overlapped in their support for models of top-down manipulation and assertion of Nazi propaganda's successes in manipulating the population.

The far-reaching consensus on the extensive impact of Nazi propaganda continued during the post-war heyday of theories of totalitarianism. These theories explicitly strengthened the use of propaganda as an analytical concept by assigning

A Companion to Nazi Germany, First Edition. Edited by Shelley Baranowski, Armin Nolzen, and Claus-Christian W. Szejnmann.

it a central role in the examination of the totalitarian state's monopoly hold on all means of communication. Ernest K. Bramsted (1965) argued that the Goebbels-led 'propaganda system' translated into the 'wholesale indoctrination of the masses' that 'imbued millions with ... hatred of the Jews' and was outright 'murderous'. Like Bramsted, a broad array of studies presented Goebbels as the central figure and the Nazi 'propagandist "par excellence"' (Boelcke 1970).

In the early 1980s, historians shattered the image of an all-powerful Nazi prop-aganda machine. Their empirically oriented works revealed a 'growing failure' long before the final war year's 'collapse of confidence' (Welch 1983). Their work also removed chief propagandists like Goebbels from the centre of analysis. In reaching consensus on the shortcomings, historians caught up with the empirical-quantita-tive approaches of American communication scholars, who had long advocated a model of weak media impact. Some, especially Ian Kershaw (1983a), began to downplay the impact of Nazi messages in maximalist ways, arguing that the pre-war socio-economic exclusion of Jews resulted from the regime's 'terror and legal discrimination' and could hardly be linked to its antisemitic propaganda.

The return of a critical emphasis on racial ideology in Holocaust Studies during the 1990s also reintroduced models of strong media impact. Jeffrey Herf (2006) argued that wartime antisemitic propaganda was 'integral to Nazi motivation'. He limited, however, those firmly impacted by it to the Nazi leadership and the 'com-munity of anti-Semitic intellectuals'. During the last two decades, scholars in com-munication and media studies, political science, and history have also developed more wide-ranging notions of propaganda. An expanded focus on propaganda of post-1945 socialist countries and Western democracies has led to a shift to broader analyses of communication technologies, eschewing crude notions of manipulation (Diesener and Gries 1996). Especially in the new field of information policy stud-ies, scholars have, furthermore, discarded concepts of propaganda altogether. Communication studies scholar Sandra Braman defines this interdisciplinary academic field as focusing on 'laws, regulations, and doctrinal positions – and other decision making and practices with society-wide constitutive effects – involving information creation, processing, flows, access and, use' (2011). Information policies are thus directly tied to national governments and governing bodies of international organizations. Yet, the fields of analysis also extend to non-govern-mental knowledge production, legal systems, and cultural practices (Braman 2006).

Broader approaches to information policies shed new light on questions of lan-guage, power, and violence in the workings of the Nazi state. Unlike readings of propaganda as 'discursive systems' in the form of superseding intellectual discourses (Bussemer 2008), these approaches allow for analyses of Nazi-authorized dis-courses and their imposition of racialized categories on the population. These phe-nomena amounted to discursive processes of isolating and creating victim populations that constituted a form of linguistic violence (Pegelow Kaplan 2009). These processes inflicted linguistic injuries by means of removing self-control from individuals and groups and denying them the determination of their own concepts of the self. These social categories excluded hundreds of thousands of people by reconstituting them as lying outside the boundaries of national life. In this sense, discourses were 'productive' and cannot simply be equated with notions like spirit

(Sarasin 2003). This linguistic violence created the very targets of Nazi policies. It both made possible and interacted with the regime's brutal physical onslaughts during the 1930s and culminated in the genocide of European Jewry during the war.

The Nazi regime's language remained, however, a site of disorder and contradiction. Nazi propagandists never controlled the complex meanings and multifaceted languages of Germanness and Jewishness. Consequently, the population received and responded to Nazi languages of exclusion in a myriad of ways. Many Germans of Jewish ancestry repeatedly aimed at defying racial categories imposed on them by engaging in practices of 'discursive contestation' (Pegelow Kaplan 2009). These kinds of contestation denote interventions in the discourses on Germanness and Jewishness. Such interventions cited the contradictory terms, submitted them to 'subversive repetitions', and tried to bring about a 'rupture' in the official guidelines on race (Sarasin 2003). Men and women engaged in these practices attempted, however slightly, to shift the imagined boundaries between Germanness and Jewishness in ways that would allow them to undermine the Nazis' attempted imposition of racialized concepts of Jewishness. In contrast to claims based on mass society and totalitarian propaganda theories, this Nazi language did not simply manipulate Germans of Jewish ancestry. Still, it was also not as inconsequential as readings by Kershaw suggested. As Walter Tausk (2000) forcefully expressed before his 1941 deportation and murder in the Kovno ghetto, these racial categories were 'not "only words"'.

10.2 Structures and Forms of Nazi Information Policies and Linguistic Violence, 1933–1939

In late January 1933, the establishment of the Hitler-led coalition government put the vast resources of a modern nation-state at the disposal of the Nazi Party. No longer limited by Weimar government-imposed restrictions such as speaking bans, the Hitler movement enlisted the power of the state to fight its real and imagined enemies. At the same time, the Nazis also built on their Weimar-era information creation. Hannah Ahlheim (2011) has demonstrated continuities in the Nazis' local antisemitic boycotts and language control from the mid-1920s to the mid-1930s, including early successes in creating linguistic separations and new urban 'Jewish' and 'German topographies'. In 1933, the Nazi leadership stepped up not only its linguistic violence, but also the movement's physical violence. Units of the Stormtroopers (*Sturmabteilung*, SA) imprisoned and often tortured some 100 000 Germans – especially Communists, Social Democrats, and union members, including journalists (Sarkowicz 2010).

Party leaders seized the long-anticipated opportunity to establish new political agencies at the level of the state to expand their power. Named Minister for Public Enlightenment and Propaganda in March 1933, Joseph Goebbels recruited his staff at the party's Reich Propaganda Directorate to set up one of the Hitler government's 'most original institutional creation[s]' (Evans 2004). Until 1933, the reach of Goebbels's propagandists had hardly extended to the non-Nazi print media, while their attempts to gain access to the country's broadcasting networks had largely failed. Consequently, the new ministry's press and broadcasting departments eagerly endeavoured to direct the nation's newspapers and radio stations.

In early 1933, Germany was still a nation of newspaper readers. Most of the country's 3400 daily papers were only distributed locally or regionally. Despite the influence of media magnates like Alfred Hugenberg, the head of the German National People's Party, and the rise of the mass and *Generalanzeiger* press, the papers' ownership structures remained complex. Weimar-era parties owned an array of publications – the Social Democrats ran 135 newspapers, for example. As a result, the new regime's information control efforts that targeted the close to 17 million daily newspaper copies faced considerable obstacles. Germany's broadcasting networks with its roughly four million participants, by contrast, proved much easier to direct. Since the Weimar governments had already overseen the establishment of a state-regulated system, in which most of the country's regional broadcasting companies had to join the Reich Radio Company (*Reichsrundfunkgesellschaft*, RRG) under the control of the Reich Ministry of Posts, Goebbels's men could move swiftly (Dussel 1999). Appointed as the RRG's new director of broadcasting, Eugen Hadamovsky set out to centralize the broadcasting system, including the programme content.

In the realms of the press, broadcasting, and – initially to a lesser extent – newsreels, the emerging dictatorship's information policies were developed and implemented by several, often competing, institutions whose staff played a noticeable role as initiators of change and perpetrators of linguistic violence. In the realm of press control, first, Department IV of Goebbels's new ministry integrated the domestic section of the former United Press Office of the Reich government and State Department and targeted the press at home and abroad. Second, Nazi activists took control of the influential, semi-official news agency *Wolff's Telegraphisches Bureau* (WTB). Appointed to the position of WTB editor-in-chief in June 1933, Nazi journalist Alfred-Ingmar Berndt oversaw this agency's gradual integration into the newly formed German News Agency (*Deutsches Nachrichtenbüro*, DNB) that streamlined the information for newspapers, broadcasters, and newsreel producers. Third, the Reich Press Office of the Nazi Party headed by Otto Dietrich controlled the editors of the Nazi Party press. Dietrich gradually expanded his office's influence to non-Nazi papers.

Finally, Goebbels's men established a Reich Chamber of Culture (*Reichskulturkammer*, RCC) in another unprecedented attempt to systematically 'organize the entire life of a nation' (Welch 1993). Brought about by a September 1933 law, the RCC was a key vehicle in the 'coordination' (*Gleichschaltung*) of cultural institutions and offered various means to control the flow of information of the country's media. Presided over by Goebbels, it consisted of seven individual chambers, including one devoted to the press. These chambers were charged with the regulation of the professional conduct in their particular fields. Membership was a precondition to practise one's profession.

Setting out to control the country's press, radio, and newsreels, the staff of these new agencies of the emerging Nazi state created, processed, and restricted information and established still elusive, yet consequential discursive guidelines. These guidelines altered language use at the widest societal level, helping to create a political culture in which mass violence against racialized minorities became possible. For their projects, Goebbels's and Dietrich's men depended on an array of pseudo-legal measures of Hitler's cabinet. For one, their information policies relied on Hitler-solicited presidential emergency decrees such as the one of 4 February 1933 that allowed for the prohibition of periodicals whose content 'threaten[ed] public safety'. By early October, officials of the Reich Ministry of Public Enlightenment and Propaganda (*Reichsministerium für Volksaufklärung und Propaganda*, RMVP) had succeeded with a legal initiative of their own. The new Editors' Law formalized the legal control and transferred editors' obligations from their newspapers' publishers to the Nazi state. The law stipulated that editors had to leave out anything that was 'suitable to weaken … the will of the community of the German *Volk*'. Violations of these vague provisions could lead to the termination of employment or imprisonment (Schmidt-Leonhardt 1935).

In their expanding control of the press, the head of the RMVP's press department and his subordinates increasingly made use of directives and post-publication censorship which, by 1935, had formed elaborate sets of discursive guidelines. For this purpose, officials increasingly relied on the once largely independent Berlin press conference of the capital's journalists. Restructured as an agency of the government in July 1933, it evolved into the 'centre' of the RMVP's 'guidance system' (Abel 1968). At the almost-daily conference, press department staff gave out 'directives for the use of language' that mixed 'concrete instructions', prohibitions, and ministerial announcements. In the most extensive project to date, a research team at Dortmund's Institute for Newspaper Research has located and edited many of the department-issued directives, putting their number at 1500 in 1935 and 3750 in 1938 (Toepser-Ziegert and Bohrmann 1984–2001).

Moreover, the National Socialist Party Correspondence (NSK), published by the Nazi Party's Reich Press Office under the leadership of Otto Dietrich, provided party and non-party journalists with another flurry of statements and admonitions that formed additional layers of discursive guidelines. The NSK's impact increased with Dietrich's growing authority in press and information policy matters. It came to a head in November 1937, when Hitler appointed Dietrich as Press Chief of the Reich government and RMVP state secretary, which weakened Goebbels's control of the press (Figure 10.1).

Racial policies and instructions on how to portray the 'German' and 'Jewish questions' ranked among the RMVP and NSK directives' most prominent themes. The directives took on the shape of discursive regularities that circulated specific sets of racialized categories, statements, and symbols, but also regimented and spelled out what not to print. In their autumn 1935 campaign, RMVP press officials, for example, continued to elevate language projects to separate Germanness and Jewishness in support of the recently promulgated Nuremberg Laws. The DNB's key 16 September 1935 commentary on these laws – turned into the guiding directive – explicitly distinguished between 'German *Volk*' and 'Jewish *Volk*'.[1] To mark the separation, the commentary exclusively circulated phrases like 'Jewry in Germany' and avoided assimilationist terms such as 'German Jews', which had still figured more prominently in the press of the early 1930s. NSK texts also

Figure 10.1   Adolf Hitler, Joseph Goebbels, and Otto Dietrich, c.1935 (INTERFOTO/ Alamy Stock Photo).

reiterated that the official term 'Jew' was not yet 'purely racial'. Instead, everyday language still endowed it with 'religious' attributes. Negating this practice, NSK and DNB materials stated that Jewry was 'not only a religion', but a population that was 'becoming a *Volk*'. The officials' directives brought the language of separation to new heights, rearticulating it as part of the proclaimed legalized 'solution' to the 'Jewish Question'.[2]

While emphasizing these solutions, RMVP officials also conjured up a stream of violent imagery that was to underpin the ways in which Germans should talk and think about things Jewish. Turning repeatedly to the threat of 'Judeo-Bolshevism', autumn 1935 ministerial and party directives depicted Jews as 'wirepullers' who controlled the 'Bolshevist International' that was engaged in 'mass murder' and the 'rape of peoples'. In ascribing 'rape' to allegedly Jewish practices connected to the 'fateful consequences' of 'race mixing', these statements provided the larger context in which journalists and readers should make sense of the Nuremberg Laws and their broader reality.[3]

This intensifying linguistic violence of official Nazi categories interacted with the physical violence of SA units and other Nazi formations. It directed their targeting of journalists in the press, radio, and film, including members of German-Jewish media outlets. Already in March 1933, SA men had ransacked the headquarters of the Central Organization of German Citizens of the Jewish Faith in Berlin and arrested German-Jewish journalists. Even if the initial street violence did not become a permanent reality, it left many non-Nazi journalists in a state of fear. As Margret Boveri (1965) of the Nazi-assailed *Berliner Tageblatt* noted, the crackdown on newspapers had a tremendous effect on the press corps. It demonstrated that the emerging dictatorship would hardly limit its wrath to leftist and German-Jewish publications. In turn, the physical violence increased the authority of the Hitler state's expanding information control.

10.3   A Case Study in Nazi Information Policies and Linguistic Violence: The 1938 November Pogroms

In the self-perception of the Nazi leadership, the use of information and the control of the mass media were pivotal parts of its dictatorial rule and policy implementations. Alfred-Ingemar Berndt, who took over the RMVP's Department IV in April 1936, boasted in July 1944 how he had turned the department into a 'powerful instrument' of Nazi press policies.[4] Yet, upon closer scrutiny, even the regime's high-profile propaganda campaigns revealed striking contradictions and shortcomings in their impact. The Nazis' use of the mass media in the antisemitic onslaughts during the November 1938 pogroms, often referred to as '*Kristallnacht*', illustrates these phenomena.

The pogroms of mid-November 1938 outmatched all previous manifestations of the regime's antisemitic violence. Initiated by Joseph Goebbels during a party meeting in Munich and personally sanctioned by Hitler, SA and SS units destroyed hundreds of synagogues and thousands of Jewish stores throughout the Reich. Nazi activists killed at least 91 Jews and deported more than 26 000 German-Jewish men to concentration camps. Within hours of Herschel Grynszpan's shooting of Ernst Eduard vom Rath in the Parisian embassy on 7 November, press officials issued their directives. They detailed how to cover the assassination of the German diplomat by the Hanover-born son of Jewish immigrant parents. The officials' measures became part of a larger campaign that amounted to another large-scale attempt to turn ever more Gentiles against the country's Jewish communities and advance the physical and linguistic separation between 'Germans' and 'Jews' (Longerich 2006; Pegelow Kaplan 2009). In a flurry of post-pogrom activities, Goebbels and Dietrich's men urged the nation's media to cover the 'Jewish question' at length. During the 17 November Reich press conference, Alfred-Ingemar Berndt gave out the main directives for the 'information campaign'. It had to thoroughly inform the public 'what the Jews ha[d] done to Germany' (Toepser-Ziegert and Bohrmann 1984–2001).

On the one hand, RMVP directives reproduced the anti-Jewish discursive regularities that had saturated the regime's earlier antisemitic campaigns. They reiterated Jews' 'affinity' for Bolshevism based on a shared emphasis on destruction. Jews re-emerged as the driving force behind capitalism and the anti-German 'atrocity propaganda' abroad. Indeed, the two phenomena of capitalism and Bolshevism once again appeared as deeply intertwined. Jewish bankers on Wall Street, the 1938 directives reiterated, were the financiers of the Bolshevik Revolution. The directives culminated in the image of 'world Jewry' as trying to involve Germany in an international conflict that the country was not yet able to win (Toepser-Ziegert and Bohrmann 1984–2001).

This Nazi depiction of Jewish aggression coincided with a corresponding construct of Germanness that transformed the horrific anti-Jewish violence of the *Kristallnacht* pogroms into imagery of German self-control. The post-pogrom directives described Germans as subject to an 'enormous indignation' that had given rise to a 'spontaneous answer' to vom Rath's murder. RMVP directives forbade any front-page coverage and references to German arsonists. 'Synagogues self-ignited', officials stated at the 10 November press conference (Toepser-Ziegert and Bohrmann 1984–2001).

On the other hand, ministry officials adopted an ever blunter rhetoric. Guidelines signalled the 'beginning of a new German attitude towards the Jewish Question'. The directives communicated the idea that Germans demanded a solution to this 'question'. Dietrich's Nazi Party press officials reiterated a switch in Germans' previous 'kindness' towards Jews to 'ruthlessness'. More directly, their National Socialist Party Correspondence embraced Protestant reformer Martin Luther's 1543 call to destroy Jewish synagogues. The NSK's special 18 November issue entitled '*Judas*' Account of Blame in Germany' was replete with this imagery.[5] Claims that the Dietrich-controlled NSK, as Herbert Obenaus (2000) maintained, simply 'went its own way', however, overstate the case. Goebbels's men rather tried to catch up and outperform Dietrich's party staff. Faced with the special NSK issue with its violent imagery, RMVP officials readily made it part of their guidelines.

While NSK authors demanded that journalists write in ways that adhered to the 'separation between the racially alien Jewry and the German *Volk*' in a 'clear' and 'final' form,[6] the Goebbels ministry-endorsed journal *Deutsche Presse* (*DP*) required every German to develop a 'heightened perception for racial terms'. Writing in *DP*'s first post-pogrom issue, Franz Rose urged journalists to place the phrase 'German Jews' in 'quotation marks, treating the phrase ironically'. Not to do so would help Jews 'retain their disguise as … "sham Germans"' (Rose 1938). A closer look at RMVP press directives of this period reveals the absence of terms like 'German Jews'. Instead, the directives consistently employed phrases like 'Jews in Germany' or 'world Jewry' that expressed the separation between Germanness and Jewishness (Toepser-Ziegert and Bohrmann 1984–2001).

Assessing the impact of the 1938 campaign, Peter Longerich (2006) has argued that the press 'predominantly adhered' to the guidelines. Even the editors of the *Frankfurter Zeitung* (*FZ*), a former bastion of liberalism, had largely muted its counter-discourses. Internal *FZ* correspondence reveals the editors' almost frantic quest to capture the correct new '*Sprachregelung* for the … Jewish Question'.[7] The paper did not only start to publish long NSK texts. Articles by the *FZ*'s own editors such as Friedrich Sieburg also became saturated with Nazi imagery of Jews as involved in a 'downright campaign against Germany'.[8]

Yet, even at this time of heightened linguistic violence, the emerging discursive guidelines were hardly as consistent and their impact on media outlets barely as devoid of contradictions as scholars have suggested. Ministry-endorsed DNB texts still talked about 'German Jews' (without quotation marks), undermining the attempts to bring about a 'stringent' linguistic separation. Even the *Völkischer Beobachter* (*VB*), the main Nazi daily, increased the employment of embattled phrases like 'German Jews', even attributing them to Goebbels.[9] These occurrences seemingly proved Rose (1938)'s point about the 'nearly ineradicable mistake' of reprinting terms from the era of assimilation. The ministry repeatedly reprimanded the *VB* for its violation of directives (Toepser-Ziegert and Bohrmann 1984–2001).

While ostensibly peripheral, inconsistencies in the discursive guidelines and subsequent press coverage provided perceptive readers and listeners with discursive strategies and potential ruptures that they could employ in their daily struggles. In his diary reflections, Celle-based engineer Karl Dürkefälden (1985) noted that the press's information flow after the pogrom was so 'general that one did not become aware of anything'. Yet, Dürkefälden likewise revealed the campaigns' contradictions. If anything, he stressed, 'Germans have shot much more frequently at Jews' than vice versa. Based on its country-wide November mood reports, the Social Democratic Party in exile concluded that the regime's antisemitic messaging remained 'ineffectiv[e]', but, undercutting its claims, also admitted that non-Jews believed in the often-repeated statements of 'agitating Jews abroad' (Sopade 1980).

Still, many Germans of Jewish ancestry continued to draw on the Nazi press, radio, and film in attempts to turn the language of the Nazified media against the racial state. In his post-pogrom correspondence with the Reich Agency for Kinship Research, the office in charge of determining racial descent in cases of doubt, Felix Krueger deliberately referenced the *Völkischer Beobachter*'s lingo. Construed as Jewish *Mischling*, the psychology professor cited *VB*-circulated images of alleged Jewish physical differences. 'We six siblings,' he reasoned, 'had all blond ... hair; we all are or were blue-eyed.' They were, thus, 'of purely Aryan, namely predominantly German, the rest Polish descent'.[10] Many Germans of imagined or real Jewish ancestry acted in a similar manner despite and because of the radicalization in the linguistic violence that the regime directed against racialized groups in its 1938 information policies, prompting continued outburst of physical brutalities.

10.4   Nazi Information Policies at War, 1939–1945

During the second half of the 1930s, the Nazi regime embarked on systematic preparations for a future war. These preparations also extended to the Nazi state and party propagandists. In February 1939, the propaganda ministry leadership tightened the control of the privately owned newsreel programmes by authorizing Fritz Hippler to establish the *Deutsche Wochenschau* Central Office at the RMVP. Hippler's office allowed for an easier control and even intervention in the production of programmes (Bartels 2004). The Wehrmacht, too, strengthened its information policies. In April 1939, its Supreme Command (OKW) created the German army's first central military propaganda office, the *Wehrmachtpropaganda-Abteilung*. Commanded by General Hasso von Wedel, this department took control over the rising number of propaganda units in all branches of the armed forces, including new propaganda companies (*Propaganda-Kompanien*) and their cameramen and newspaper and radio journalists (Uziel 2008).

With the outbreak of the war, the goals and tasks of the regime's information policies underwent a distinct shift from consolidating dictatorial rule and mass support to securing popular participation in the war effort and belief in victory.

The propagandists' projects of linguistic separation and violence continued, but they evolved – on an unprecedented scale – beyond a metaphorical 'verbal brutality' (Klemperer 2000). This form of violence prefigured the 'Jewish enemy', prescribing and accompanying the action of the perpetrators in the killing fields of Eastern Europe and on the home front.

On an organizational level, the outbreak of war in September 1939 accelerated the restructuring of the creation and employment of information. From the early days of the war until late April 1945, Goebbels convened a daily morning meeting at the propaganda ministry, often misdubbed 'ministerial conference', that served him as a platform to articulate new campaigns for the media. The meetings brought together government and party representatives with liaison officers from the *Wehrmachtpropaganda-Abteilung* (Boelcke 1970).

The meetings with the propaganda minister were followed by a gathering headed by press chief of the Reich government Otto Dietrich that, as of November 1940, issued yet another set of daily guides (*Tagesparolen*). Targeting the domestic press, Dietrich's guides were presented as a summary of the growing array of directives, but repeatedly challenged Goebbels's instructions. RMVP's press officials opened the midday press conferences in Berlin with Dietrich's daily guides, dictating them to the attending journalists. The RMVP's restructured domestic press department also continued to issue directives of its own that increased from a monthly average of 385 at the beginning of the war to 880 during its height. Scholars have estimated that officials issued roughly 60 000 directives and daily guides in total (Toepser-Ziegert and Bohrmann 1984–2001). In conjunction with the German News Agency texts, these directives formed an extensive grid of discursive guidelines. In addition, the Foreign Office held its own conference for the foreign press (Welch 1993).

Finally, RMVP press officials and the regional Reich Propaganda Offices, in cooperation with specifically assigned Wehrmacht officers, introduced new rules of exclusion by practising pre-publication censorship as of late August 1939. Their counterparts at the ministry's broadcasting department likewise curtailed the work of regional broadcasting. The department's 'Radio Command' (*Rundfunkkommandostelle*), established days before the outbreak of the war, repeatedly removed programmes and added mandatory political broadcasts (Dussell 2002). Even before the introduction of a unity programme, the Reich programme of the *Großdeutscher Rundfunk*, in June 1940, there was barely any room for regionally specific broadcasts. Pushed by politically reliable officials like Hans Fritzsche, who took over the broadcasting department in late 1942, Goebbels, however, refrained from introducing a rigid pre-broadcast censorship to allow for flexible responses to the often rapidly changing military developments (Bonacker 2007).

The research literature has long emphasized the rivalries between Goebbels's ministry, Dietrich's press control apparatus, the Wehrmacht, and the Foreign Ministry (Abel 1968). In the polycratic Nazi state at war, scholars have argued, Hitler left these rivalries in place to secure his position as the highest authority, who could be appealed to and intervene as needed. Even if the competition between these propaganda agencies was palpable, it was hardly detrimental to the wartime exercise of linguistic violence. Often prompted by Goebbels, who coordinated with Hitler, state and party propagandists spearheaded self-styled media 'offensives' in support of the German military's invasions. This dynamic reached new heights with the attack on the Soviet Union in June 1941. The regime's enforced brutalizing language interacted with escalating physical assaults, critically preceding and accompanying the ensuing genocide. Indeed, linguistic violence became a crucial part of the Hitler state's serial genocides and racial war of annihilation.

At the 5 July 1941 meeting at his ministry, Goebbels urged the attendees to portray the German attack as the 'unmasking' of a 'system where Jews, capitalists and bolsheviks work hand in glove' to create 'a quite inconceivable degree of human depravity' (Boelcke 1970). Goebbels's men increasingly relied on imaged-based media such as *Die Deutsche Wochenschau*, created on ministerial orders in November 1940 as the country's sole wartime newsreel (Bartels 2004). The *Wochenschau* of 10 July 1941 captured the minister's directive in its depiction of the recent German occupation of Lvov. Shot by a Wehrmacht propaganda company, the employed footage had been censored by OKW propaganda officers and then passed on to the RMVP (Uziel 2008) (Figure 10.2). While the newsreel narrator spoke of 'Jewish agents of the GPU', the Soviet Union's state political directorate, who had just 'bestially slaughtered thousands of defenceless Ukrainian nationalists', the parallel shift from images of arriving troops and cheering civilians to rows of mutilated corpses had a more far-reaching impact on *Wochenschau* audiences. The newsreel continued with the alleged perpetrators in the form of

Figure 10.2 Still frame from the *Deutsche Wochenschau* of 10 July 1941, which depicts two alleged "Jewish agents." The frame also reveals a Wehrmacht soldier in the background, compounding the power of the camera (Bundesarchiv Filmarchiv/Transit Film GmbH).

Figure 10.3   Still from the *Deutsche Wochenschau* of 10 July 1941, framing putative
Jewish residents of Lemberg in the visual language of antisemitism (Bundesarchiv
Filmarchiv/Transit Film GmbH).

close-ups of male faces, which the voice-over identified as 'Jewish murderous rabble [*Mordgesindel*]' and 'horrifying selection of Lemberg Soviet types ..., mainly
Jews, ... allies of Churchill' (Figure 10.3).[11]

These images belonged to fields of visuality that most viewers would have been
able to place in line with long-established antisemitic imagery prominently recircu-
lated in Fritz Hippler's 1940 antisemitic film *Der Ewige Jude*. The *Wochenschau*
imagery also evoked an increased sense of authenticity among many audiences,
even if it hardly constituted a realistic representation (Bartels 2004). There was no
indication that members of Wehrmacht Battalion 800 had further mutilated the
corpses before the filming or that this unit and local militias had engaged in genocidal killings of Lvov's Jewish population (Heer 2001).

These visual images of alleged Jewish criminals represented another layer of
racialized impositions on persecuted populations that interacted with the linguistic
violence of racist terminology, spurning on perpetrators in the killing fields and
audiences at home. This early July 1941 newsreel reflected the Hitler regime's
discursive restrictions that suppressed any direct portrayals of the Germans' genocide of European Jewry. It also captured other shifts in the wartime guidelines. As
RMVP press department's deputy head Erich Fischer stressed in the ongoing campaign in September 1941, 'the Jews' had drafted 'extermination plans' directed
against Germany and taken steps to implement them as the driving force behind
not only Bolshevism but also Anglo-American 'plutocracy'.[12]

The research literature continues to grapple with questions of reception and
impact of these campaigns. Scholars have analysed the production side and confirmed the renewed shift to more entertainment and non-militaristic music in the
programmes of the *Großdeutscher Rundfunk* since the summer of 1941 (Dussel
2002). They have interpreted this change as evidence of a war-weary population's

increasing lack of interest in political commentary. These changes in the heavily controlled field of radio broadcasting also reveal a striking level of pragmatism on the part of Nazi propagandists, especially after Stalingrad and the Goebbels-announced turn to 'total war' in early 1943.

A more direct focus on popular perceptions has revealed more complex insights into the impact of the regime's information policies. Surviving letters to radio programmes, newspapers, or individual officials reveal substantial support for Nazi messages, especially during the period of military victories from 1939 until 1941. Max Bonacker (2007) has shown that the broadcasts of Hans Fritzsche's *Politische Zeitungs- und Rundfunkschau*, an integral part of the campaigns against 'Judeo-Bolshevism', enjoyed considerable popularity, resulting in tens of thousands of mostly positive letters. Historians have cited detailed reports by Nazi agencies such as regional Reich propaganda offices and the Security Service of the SS (*Sicherheitsdienst der SS*, SD), the SS's Secret Service, to make their case for popular support of campaigns. The SD report on the impact of 'propaganda, press and radio' in early July 1941 stressed the 'profound effect' of the 'realistic coverage of the atrocities of the Bolsheviks' on audiences, 'especially … in the case of the murders of the Ukrainians in Lvov' (Kulka and Jäckel 2010).

In sharp contrast, historians like Peter Longerich and Ian Kershaw have pointed to the blatant shortcomings of Nazi information policies, even in 1941. Beginning in late summer, SD reports, they argue, hardly revealed this level of popular support and future *Wochenschauen* very rarely revisited the persecution of Jews, which could even be seen as a reflection of 'resistance' in the population against the regime's anti-Jewish policies (Longerich 2006). Analysing reports from wartime Bavaria, Kershaw (1983b) detected 'blatant self-interest', 'widespread passivity', and 'emotionless acceptance' of the anti-Jewish policies, further revealing the ineffectiveness of the RMVP's antisemitic messages.

Audience- and perception-centred research faces considerable obstacles. Source-dominated models suffer from limitations of the remaining evidence. Letters to Nazi media outlets were highly self-selective. Repressive laws and policing prevented many from sending critical remarks in the first place. Reports by Nazi agencies are also highly problematic and often self-serving. The revival of communication studies' active-audience perspectives, including refined uses-and-gratification approaches, holds the greatest promise for future research and reveals the need for a middle ground between stark notions of success and failure. 'Positive' uses of the media and its language included practices of discursive contestation, in which Germans of alleged Jewish ancestry drew on Nazi language in their ongoing claims to 'German blood' – like Maria Zahn and her son Dieter, whom the Nazi state reclassified from designated Jew to *Mischling* as late as early February 1945, which helped him to avoid deportation and, quite literally, death.[13]

Despite its limitations, the regime's wartime information control continued with its inherently related campaigns to strengthen the German resolve to carry on and reveal a 'deadly' Jewish 'threat'. Beginning in 1943 and peaking in 1944–1945, Nazi propagandists brought these campaigns to a last, feverish pitch. They intensified their linguistic violence, which still guided many in the ways of seeing their crumbling worlds. Many 'Germans of all walks of life' demonstrated a veritable obsession with the Jews at this time (Friedländer 2007). In numerous campaigns, from Katyn in April 1943 to the Red Army's murder of civilians in the East Prussian village of Nemmersdorf in November 1944, Nazi media directives and the evolving discursive guidelines conjured up images of 'Jewish revenge' that had progressed from the stage of planning to the actual execution, allegedly targeting millions of Germans for slave labour in Russia or outright murder. Reduced in numbers due to the demands of 'total war', the remaining information control personnel disseminated this imagery as a symbol of 'Judeo-Bolshevik' mass murder and Jewry's 'Satanic will to ... destroy'.[14] During the regime's final days, when the production of newspapers and newsreels had largely ended, the role of the spoken word and radio, including the military's broadcasting stations, only rose in importance (Sarkowicz 2010), partaking in the final stages of linguistic onslaught. The precise role of Nazi information control, language, and its violence during this period, however, still has to be explored in future studies.

10.5 Conclusion

Dating back to the time of Nazi rule, scholars have produced studies of the Hitler state's control of the country's media that have largely relied on concepts of propaganda. Many early works overemphasized the importance of institutional approaches and drew on simplistic models of top-down manipulation. All along, the study of Nazi propaganda has fallen short of even reaching a consensus on a definition of this core concept. While taking a middle ground position between those works that overstate the power of Nazi control and more recent studies that highlight its failures, this chapter offers a rethinking of the phenomenon based on the concept of information policies as a form of linguistic violence. The essay draws on discourse analysis and works in the recently established subfield of information policy studies that has informed a new cohort of historians (Sarasin 2003; Zimmermann 2007). The chapter's approach offers ways to analyse the often complex processes with which the regime created the targets of its racial policies and in which members of victimized populations engaged in practices of discursive contestation to defy racial categories imposed on them.

Broader conceptualizations of information policies and linguistic violence also shed new light on the caesura of 1945 and post-fascist approaches to media regulations. On the one hand, the Allied victory brought the Hitler state and its propaganda to an end. Many of its protagonists died in the war, some – like Goebbels – committed suicide, and others – like Dietrich – served prison terms. Still others, including communication scholar Emil Dovifat, remade themselves and enjoyed remarkable post-war careers. On the other hand, information control policies also continued in East and West Germany (Diesener and Gries 1996; Bytwerk 2004). Within weeks of the end of hostilities, American occupation authorities, for example, established the Information Control Division (ICD) as the foremost agency in media supervision in the US zone. A rebuilt German press was a centrepiece in the ICD's approach to denazification. ICD officials combined post-publication scrutiny, reprimands, and press campaigns, paradoxically replicating the tools of Nazi information policies. Despite the ICD's efforts, Nazi language control had a more lasting impact. In late 1946, the Bavarian ICD press chief Ernest Langendorf fumed that the practices of the newly licensed *Passauer Neue Presse* (PNP) were akin to '*Völkischer Beobachter* journalism par excellence'.[15] By circulating and imposing racial categories, news outlets with regional cultural capital like the PNP continued, even if at a reduced level, the Nazi media's linguistic violence in early post-genocidal German society.

Notes

1 'Ausr[ichtung] Herrn Reifenberg', 16 September 1935, Bundesarchiv Koblenz [BAK], ZSG 102/1.
2 *Nationalsozialistische Pressekorrespondenz* [NSK], 16 September 1935, p. 4d and 10 September 1935, p. 2.
3 *Deutsches Nachrichtenbüro* [DNB], 11 September 1935, p. 17; NSK, 18 September 1935, pp. 6–7.
4 Alfred-Ingemar Berndt to Heinrich Himmler, National Archives [NA], College Park, RG 242, A3343, series SSO, reel O 62.
5 NSK, 18 November 1938, pp. 14, 17.
6 Ibid., p. 18.
7 'Ausrichtung Politik', 11 November 1938, BAK, ZSG 102/13.
8 *Frankfurter Zeitung*, 24 November 1938, first morning edition, p. 9.
9 *Völkischer Beobachter*, 12 November 1938, p. 3.
10 Krueger to Saxon Education Ministry, 4 January 1938, USHMM Archives, RG-14.011M, roll 20, p. 212.
11 *Deutsche Wochenschau*, no. 566, 10 July 1941, DW 566/1941, Bundesarchiv-Filmarchiv.
12 'Aus der Pressekonferenz', 26 September 1941, BAK, ZSG 102/34, p. 87.
13 Dieter Zahn, interview by author, tape recording, Leipzig, Germany, 4 August 2001.
14 DNB, 12 November 1944, p. D; NSK, 13 November 1944, p. 30.
15 Langendorf to Kapfinger, 16 December 1946, NA, RG 260, 390/48/7–8/7–3, box 23.

References

Abel, Karl-Dietrich. 1968. *Presselenkung im NS-Staat*. Berlin: Colloquium Verlag.
Adorno, Theodor W. 1982, 'Freudian Theory and the Pattern of Fascist Propaganda.' In *The Essential Frankfurt School Reader*, edited by Andrew Arato and Eike Gebhardt, 118–137. New York: Continuum.
Ahlheim, Hannah. 2011. '*Deutsche, kauft nicht bei Juden!' Antisemitismus und politischer Boykott in Deutschland 1924 bis 1935*. Göttingen: Wallstein.
Bartels, Ulrike. 2004. *Die Wochenschau im Dritten Reich*. Frankfurt am Main: Peter Lang.
Boelcke, Willi A., ed. 1970. *The Secret Conferences of Dr. Goebbels: The Nazi Propaganda War, 1939–43*. New York: Dutton.
Bonacker, Max. 2007. *Goebbels' Mann beim Radio: Der NS-Propagandist Hans Fritzsche (1900–1953)*. Munich: R. Oldenbourg.
Boveri, Margret. 1965. *Wir lügen alle: Eine Hauptstadtzeitung unter Hitler*. Olten: Walter.
Braman, Sandra. 2006. *Change of State: Information, Policy, and Power*. Cambridge, MA: MIT Press.
Braman, Sandra. 2011. 'Defining Information Policy.' *Journal of Information Policy* 1(1), 1–5.

Bramsted, Ernest Kohn. 1965. *Goebbels and National Socialist Propaganda, 1925–1945*. East Lansing: Michigan State University Press.

Bussemer, Thymian. 2008. *Propaganda: Konzepte und Theorien*, 2nd edn. Wiesbaden: Verlag für Sozialwissenschaften.

Bytwerk, Randall L. 2004. *Bending Spines: The Propagandas of Nazi Germany and the German Democratic Republic*. East Lansing: Michigan State University Press.

Diesener, Gerald and Gries, Rainer, eds. 1996. *Propaganda in Deutschland: Zur Geschichte der politischen Massenbeeinflussung im 20. Jahrhundert*. Darmstadt: Primus.

Dovifat, Emil. 1937. *Rede und Redner*. Leipzig: Bibliographisches Institut.

Dürkefälden, Karl. 1985. *'Schreiben, wie es wirklich war': Aufzeichnungen Karl Dürkefäldens aus den Jahren 1933–1945*. Hanover: Fackelträger.

Dussel, Konrad. 1999. *Deutsche Rundfunkgeschichte: Eine Einführung*. Konstanz: UVK-Medien.

Dussel, Konrad. 2002. *Hörfunk in Deutschland: Politik, Programm, Publikum (1923–1960)*. Potsdam: Verlag für Berlin-Brandenburg.

Evans, Richard J. 2004. *The Coming of the Third Reich*. New York: Penguin.

Friedländer, Saul. 2007. *Nazi Germany and the Jews 1939–1945: The Years of Extermination*. New York: HarperCollins.

Heer, Hannes. 2001. 'Einübung in den Holocaust: *Lemberg* Juni/Juli 1941.' *Zeitschrift für Geschichtswissenschaft* 49(5), 409–427.

Herf, Jeffrey. 2006. *The Jewish Enemy: Nazi Propaganda During World War II and the Holocaust*. Cambridge, MA: Harvard University Press.

Kershaw, Ian. 1983a. 'How Effective Was Nazi Propaganda?' In *Nazi Propaganda: The Power and the Limitations*, edited by David Welch, 180–205. London: Croom Helm.

Kershaw, Ian. 1983b. *Popular Opinion and Political Dissent in the Third Reich, Bavaria 1933–1945*. Oxford: Clarendon Press.

Klemperer, Viktor. 2000. *The Language of the Third Reich: LTI*. London: Athlone Press.

Kulka, Otto Dov and Jäckel, Eberhard. 2010. *The Jews in the Secret Nazi Reports on Popular Opinion in Germany, 1933–1945*. New Haven, CT: Yale University Press.

Longerich, Peter. 2006. *'Davon haben wir nichts gewusst!': Die Deutschen und die Judenverfolgung 1933-1945*. Munich: Siedler.

Obenaus, Herbert. 2000. 'The Germans: "An Antisemitic People". The Press Campaign after 9 November 1938.' In *Probing the Depths of Anti-Semitism*, edited by David Bankier. New York: Berghahn Books.

Pegelow Kaplan, Thomas. 2009. *The Language of Nazi Genocide: Linguistic Violence and the Struggle of Germans of Jewish Ancestry*. New York: Cambridge University Press.

Rose, Franz. 1938. '"Polnischer Jude" oder "Jude polnischer Staatsangehörigkeit".' *Deutsche Presse* 28, 454–455.

Sarasin, Philipp. 2003. *Geschichtswissenschaft und Diskursanalyse*. Frankfurt am Main: Suhrkamp.

Sarkowicz, Hans. 2010. '"Nur nicht langweilig werden ..." Das Radio im Dienste der nationalsozialistischen Propaganda.' In *Medien im Nationalsozialismus*, edited by Bernd Heidenreich and Sönke Neitzel, 205–234. Paderborn: Schöningh.

Schmidt-Leonhardt, Hans. 1935. 'Einheit von nationaler Staatsführung und nationaler Geistesführung.' *Deutsche Presse* 25, 654–655.

Sopade (Sozialdemokratische Partei Deutschlands). 1980. *Deutschland-Berichte der Sozialdemokratischen Partei Deutschlands, 1934–1940*. Salzhausen: Nettelbeck.

Tausk, Walter, 2000. *Breslauer Tagebuch 1933–1940*, 4th edn. Berlin: Aufbau Verlag.

Toepser-Ziegert, Gabriele and Bohrmann, Hans, eds. 1984–2001. *NS-Presseanweisungen der Vorkriegszeit*. 19 vols. Munich: Saur.

Uziel, Daniel. 2008. *The Propaganda Warriors: The Wehrmacht and the Consolidation of the German Home Front.* Oxford: Peter Lang.

Welch, David, ed. 1983. *Nazi Propaganda: The Power and the Limitations.* London: Croom Helm.

Welch, David. 1993. *The Third Reich: Politics and Propaganda.* London: Routledge.

Zimmermann, Clemens. 2007. *Medien im Nationalsozialismus: Deutschland 1933–1945, Italien 1922–1943, Spanien 1936–1951.* Vienna: Böhlau.

Further Reading

Heidenreich, Bernd and Neitzel, Sönke, eds. 2010. *Medien im Nationalsozialismus.* Paderborn: Schöningh.
Essays by experts on the latest research on Nazi propaganda, including biographies of activists, and works on film, press, and radio supervision.

Longerich, Peter. 2015. *Goebbels: A Biography.* New York: Random House.
Latest biography of the Nazi propaganda minister that brings together a multitude of sources, including his complete diaries, and uses the genre to dismantle the claim of Nazi propaganda's omnipotence.

Pegelow Kaplan, Thomas. 2009. *The Language of Nazi Genocide: Linguistic Violence and the Struggle of Germans of Jewish Ancestry.* New York: Cambridge University Press.
Offers a conceptualization of the linguistic violence of Nazi discourses; the ways in which perpetrators constructed their perceived enemies; how Nazi agencies communicated to the public; and how Germans of Jewish ancestry contested these changes in their struggle for survival.

Welch, David. 2002. *The Third Reich: Politics and Propaganda*, 2nd edn. London: Routledge.
Readable survey of the Nazi Party and state propaganda apparatus and main policies. Includes appendix with translations of key Nazi propaganda documents.

CHAPTER ELEVEN

Education, Schooling, and Camps

KIRAN KLAUS PATEL

11.1 Introduction

The scenic city of Reichenberg in the recently annexed Sudetenland provided the venue for one of Hitler's most notorious speeches in December 1938. Addressing the topic of the nation's youth, the Führer pontificated:

> This youth does not learn anything but to think German and act German. The boy and the girl enter our organization at the age of ten, … then four years later they move on from the Jungvolk to the Hitler Youth, where we keep them for another four years. And then we definitely do not give them back into the hands of those who created our old class and status barriers; instead, we immediately take them into the Party, into the Labour Front, the SA or the SS, the NSKK, and so on. … And so they will never be free again as long as they live. (Applause) And they are happy with it.'[1]

Education – in a broad sense – was a central concern for the Nazis, and Hitler's speech lends important insights into the Nazis' approach. Creating a new man in a new society with a new moral system was their overt goal. Practice on the ground, however, only partly followed these ideas that in principle addressed all age groups. For this reason, this chapter departs from the older research tradition that has mainly focused on the regime's intentions, frequently interpreting education in the Third Reich as vile indoctrination, engineered by a ruthless leadership that managed to seduce its people (for a recent overview, see Bair 2011). Instead, it emphasizes the continuities in educational thinking and practice to earlier periods, and brings out the inconsistencies and conflicts within the Third Reich. It also stresses the active role of ordinary citizens. While some Germans opposed the

A Companion to Nazi Germany, First Edition. Edited by Shelley Baranowski, Armin Nolzen, and Claus-Christian W. Szejnmann.
© 2018 John Wiley & Sons Ltd. Published 2018 by John Wiley & Sons Ltd.

regime's educational efforts and others were excluded from its remit, many actively embraced the Third Reich's educational agenda. This held true for Germans of both sexes. Self-mobilization was therefore often more influential than top-down ideologization, and specific educational institutions were often less important than the fact that Germans were increasingly part of a society shaped by Nazi values.

11.2   Continuities with Earlier Ideas and the Nazi Approach

Nazism did not present a coherent educational theory or ideology, and owed a lot to earlier pedagogical ideas and practices. The ultimate purpose of education was to help refashion values and identities and to form a *Volksgemeinschaft* ('people's community') built on racism and particularly on antisemitism, and on discipline, aggression, and a feeling of superiority. This approach was to be imported into schooling as the instruction given at schools, but also into all other areas and dimensions of education (for example Benze 1936). Education in the Third Reich celebrated the needs of the 'people's community', to which any individual striving should be subjugated. It centred around a pedagogy of practical, shared experience (*Erlebnis*) instead of abstraction, self-study, and individualism. Any form of resistance had to be broken, and dissenters were to be excluded, along with those not deemed fit for the 'people's community'. To maximize its impact, the Nazis sought to separate citizens from their normal social environment and diminish the role of traditional institutions of socialization and education such as the family and the church. Contempt for intellectualism went hand in hand with a fascination with physical prowess; formal education, in contrast, was associated with obsolete bourgeois culture, Jewishness, and the 'old', corrupt order of the Weimar Republic. Instead, the Nazis praised bold leadership and unconditional obedience, even if these concepts tended to contradict each other. Other ideological tensions remained unresolved, too. Their biological determinism always qualified the role education could play. The role of women, as a final example, was both enhanced but in some ways also suffocated in a highly racialized version of the traditional female caregiver model. Nazi education, in sum, remained fraught with contradictions and unclarities.

Moreover, many Nazi ideas continued and radicalized forms of education and schooling that were well established in Germany prior to 1933 (and elsewhere). Militarism and nationalism had already left a deep mark on pedagogical thinking and practice during the Kaiserreich. Biological determinism and racism had antecedents in thinkers such as Arthur de Gobineau and Houston Stewart Chamberlain. When it came to leadership cult, anti-liberal ideas of community, and the aesthetic exaltation of actual experience, the Nazis built on ongoing policies and practices, too. From the available spectrum of options, they increasingly opted for and escalated the most radical solutions, while suppressing other strands of the debate. This was obviously the case for humanity, rationality, pedagogical autonomy, and those parts of *Reformpädagogik* with strong links to the women's and labour movements. Nazi education did not stand out for its originality, but for the radical ways in which it recombined existing elements of education, and for the ruthlessness with which it tried to put its ideas into practice (Horn 2011).

As a consequence, the Nazis destabilized the boundaries between education – defined by a sequence of institutions; as a specific form of interaction between educators and the educated; and a clearly circumscribed phase in life – and other dimensions of society. Education was supposed to pervade all aspects of the Third Reich and be 'total', with exposure to training and schooling continuous and complemented by mechanisms controlling the performance of individuals. Simultaneously, the role of traditional education institutions was qualified by an alphabet soup of new organizations, including seemingly harmless organizations such as the National Socialist Motor Corps (*Nationalsozialistisches Kraftfahrkorps*, NSKK), as a formation ostensibly simply seeking to improve its members' motoring skills (Hochstetter 2005). In this sense, Hitler's Reichenberg speech summarizes Nazi education's capacious and often impalpable quality.

The educational system that the regime inherited in 1933 was sophisticated and highly differentiated. Building on Germany's long-standing federal tradition, the various states were more important than the Reich, thus producing a great deal of heterogeneity in norms and practices. Besides state actors of all sorts, education in Germany granted an important role to civil society. Denominational schools loomed large; in Prussia, Germany's biggest state, there were some 29 000 Protestant and 16 000 Roman Catholic schools alone. Weimar Germany also proved a fertile ground for experimental, left-leaning state schools; in fact, the country 'stood at the forefront of the progressive education movement', as one scholar put it. The Nazis planned to change all that (Lamberti 2002, 246).

The leaders of the Third Reich were acutely aware of the challenges to their attempts to reshape German society in their image. In principle, Nazi education addressed all age groups. Pupils, students, teachers, but also professional groups such as prospective doctors had to undergo special ideological courses. All Nazi mass organizations – many of which focused on a wide range of adult age groups – had an explicit educational dimension, too. Its sub-organizations for women turned the *Volksgemeinschaft* into a learning objective. The SS (*Schutzstaffel*), as another example, disposed of an elaborate pedagogical programme, employing several thousand teachers between 1933 and 1945. Despite some conflicts, the military leadership closed ranks with Nazi ideologists. Army commander-in-chief Walther von Brauchitsch welcomed an ideological strengthening of the Wehrmacht, but also wanted the army to exercise a greater 'military-ideological influence' on Germany's educational system. Despite such broad aspirations, the regime concentrated its efforts primarily on the young generation, since it was seen as an embodiment of the future and represented the most malleable and accessible segment of the population (quoted in Förster 2008, 520; see also, e.g., Harten 2014, 499–517; Kramer 2011, 31–102).

11.3   Exclusion and Positive Inclusion in Nazi Education

Their scepticism vis-à-vis the Weimar Republic's educational system led the Nazis to a twofold strategy. For one, they aimed at overhauling the existing state education system. Exclusion (*Ausmerze*) and terror were central in this endeavour. Only the 'racially' positive segment of the population was to be educated, while all 'inferiors' were to be 'weeded out'. Jewish, left-leaning, and other 'unreliable' teachers were purged from the profession in 1933/1934. The same holds true for other educators, for instance university professors, resulting in a large exodus and an opening of new career perspectives for candidates who conformed to the regime's expectations. Denominational schools had no future: the Nazis exerted pressure on parents to enrol their children in state schools, and started to convert Protestant and Catholic schools. For some Nazis, such as the party's chief ideologue Alfred Rosenberg, the churches belonged to the regime's main enemies. Under eugenic, racist, and productivist aspects, the 'sterilization law' of July 1933 allowed schools to transfer 'disabled children' from the regular *Volksschule* – which some 90% of all children attended – to special *Hilfsschulen*. Many *Hilfsschule* teachers tolerated or actively contributed to the Reich's sterilization policy and accepted some of their pupils being moved to special institutions for severely handicapped children, where the Nazis practised euthanasia. Jewish children were pushed out of the regular school system and forced to attend private Jewish schools. After a period of discrimination, this policy was formalized with a decree in November 1938, days after the *Pogromnacht*. In view of the deportations, the Nazis ended any kind of schooling for Jewish pupils in the Reich in 1942. And these are but a few examples; over the years, the regime also expanded and radicalized its policies of discrimination, exclusion, and persecution in many other ways (Fölling 1995; Link 2011; Kremer 2011; Wegner 2002).

Proactive measures came on top in these efforts to revamp the existing education system. The Nazis created a variety of elite education agencies, as *Ausmerze* (exclusion) was to be complemented by *Auslese* (positive selection). National Political Institutes of Education (*Nationalpolitische Erziehungsanstalten, Napolas*, from 1933), *Ordensburgen* for future party leaders (from 1936), and the Adolf Hitler schools (*Adolf-Hitler-Schulen*, similar to the *Napolas*, but more focused on the Nazi Party itself and launched in 1937) all served this purpose. While continuing to transmit established knowledge and skill, the regime introduced new school subjects soon after its rise to power. Prussia put *Vererbungslehre* und *Rassenkunde* (genetics and race science) on the curriculum of its schools in September 1933. The whole Reich followed suit in January 1935. The National Socialist Teachers' Alliance (*Nationalsozialistischer Lehrerbund*, NSLB) trained teachers in racial science and a Nazi approach to subjects ranging from arithmetic over history and physics down to zoology. Administratively, the Nazis sought to centralize education, especially with the creation of the Reich Ministry of Science, Education, and National Culture in May 1934, with the fanatic and sophisticated Bernhard Rust at the helm. Publishers were quick to identify business opportunities in supplying refashioned textbooks for the new political order. The 1941–1942 school year saw the introduction of the tuition-fee free *Hauptschule*, mainly geared to giving high-potential pupils in rural areas access to education beyond the level of the *Volksschule*; selection here did not consider the parents' wishes. All these measures aimed at increasing control of existing institutions and reconstructing them along Nazi lines (Pine 2010, 41–66; Link 2011; Nagel 2012).

In another strategy, the Nazis tried to create a parallel universe of ideologized institutions to compensate for the fact that, in 1933, the classic educational system did not allow itself to be instantly and completely transformed into an instrument serving the new regime's interests. Many of these organizations had been set up prior to 1933 under the auspices of the party, for instance the Hitler Youth and the SA (*Sturmabteilung*, Stormtroopers). After the takeover of power, they frequently gained in importance and tried to monopolize action in their respective field. The Hitler Youth (*Hitlerjugend*, HJ) is a good example. At the end of the Weimar Republic it had some 40 000 members – as compared to roughly two million in the various sports associations, one million in Catholic youth organizations, 600 000 in their Protestant equivalents, 550 000 in youth organizations of the political left, and some 70 000 in the *bündisch* youth (Kock 1997, 49). After most rivals had been banned or co-opted into the Hitler Youth in 1933, membership became more and more compulsory during the second half of the 1930s (Kollmeier 2007, 45–52; Buddrus 2003). Besides enhancing the role of Nazi organizations that had already existed prior to 1933, other institutions were newly created – such as the system of *Ordensburgen* for future leaders set up under Robert Ley, Reich organizational leader (*Reichsorganisationsleiter*) of the Nazi Party and head of the almighty German Labour Front. In a third case, existing organizations were fundamentally reorganized along Nazi lines, as in the case of the Reich Labour Service (*Reichsarbeitsdienst*, RAD). It was this rugged landscape of organizations that Hitler referred to in Reichenberg, and his speech reveals that even some five years after the takeover of power, the Führer viewed the role of traditional educational institutions with scepticism (Scholtz 1985; Patel 2005).

The educational establishments mentioned so far mainly targeted adolescents and (young) adults. The Nazi cosmos of institutions kicked in much earlier, however. It commenced with special guidance for the parents of newborns and continued with kindergartens and day care centres (*Horte*) run by the National Socialist People's Welfare Organization (*Nationalsozialistische Volkswohlfahrt*, NSV). From about 1000 in 1935, the number of NSV kindergartens leapt to 15 000 in 1941. Another aspect was the temporary relocation of children to the countryside (*Kinderlandverschickung*), also under the auspices of the NSV. Several hundred thousand children were part of this scheme already prior to 1940 (subsequently the bombing of German cities added urgency to the matter), and they travelled to the countryside often without their parents, either to relatives, peasant families, or special homes. In these cases, too, the idea was to indoctrinate them with Nazi ideas and to create a complete Nazi *Lebenswelt* (life-world), with specific symbols, procedures, values, and experiences (Kock 1997, 69–75).

'Education' could mean very different things in these organizations: vocational training, schooling, or physical and character training. Most of these Nazi educational establishments were, indeed, active in all these areas, even if not all primarily or exclusively served pedagogical purposes. The SA, for instance, also had paramilitary functions and the RAD combined education with a job creation scheme in the first years after 1933. In comparison to classical educational institutions, many Nazi organizations saw a reversal of priorities. In fact, in *Mein Kampf* Hitler had given academic schooling the lowest priority in contrast to 'breeding hale and healthy bodies' and the 'development of the character' (Hartmann et al. 2016, vol. 2, 1041, 1043; my translation). This also implies that ideologization was less central than often assumed. Instead, physical exercise and tests of courage were couched in social Darwinist and racist language; leisure time was not seen as free time, but was meant to deepen educational efforts – as well as to screen their results. For all its inhumanity and brutality, the Nazis' approach to education was sometimes slightly more subtle – and more effective – than a superficial reading of its total pretences might suggest (Keim 1991; Giesecke 1993, 17–29).

11.4   The Pivotal Function of Camps

Most of these newly created Nazi organizations shared an important feature that acquired a paradigmatic role for education during the Third Reich. They opted for the camp (*Lager*) as their pedagogical format. Rudolf Benze, one of the regime's most influential educators, argued that the camp allowed for the 'deep capture of the whole person' (Benze 1943, 72), and another author raved in 1937 that the camp was on its 'triumphal march' in Germany (Mertens 1937, 3). For the Nazis, the camp had a pivotal function, in that it described the regime's most radical utopia in its inclusive as well as exclusive dimensions.

But what were these camps all about? They were characterized by a specific form of accommodation – provisional, quickly available, cheap, and mobile. A growing number of organizations opted for wooden barracks, particularly of the kind first developed in the *Reichsarbeitsdienst*. Alongside the uniformization of buildings, there was a tendency to standardize camp arrangements. Often, they were located in remote areas so as to separate their residents from their normal social environment. Geographical isolation was meant to maximize pedagogical effects; moreover, the barracks were designed to reduce unobserved niches and retreats, instead allowing for disciplining control. One official source bragged that such camps left 'no private sphere, no area able to escape the law of the community' (Krüger 1937, 99). Moreover, there was a clear separation between 'inside' and 'outside', with architectural devices borrowed from the military, such as gateways, fences, and watch-towers. Besides emulating military models and attempting to imbue German youth with military values, the camp was intended to deindividualize. The group was the decisive level of action, and hence the space was not structured for the needs of the individual – the parade ground and mass sleeping quarters made this abundantly clear (Patel 2006).

The Nazis praised these institutions as cradles of the *Volksgemeinschaft*, key in creating a 'new man'. Camp life was hailed as conveying the 'experience of nature' (Riecke 1936, 359). These seemingly harmless words stood for Nazism's blood-and-soil ideology with its racism and its ideal of physical toughness, but also its fantasies of re-agrarization and a specific gender concept. In most organizations, separate camp systems were created for each sex, with this gendered agenda turning caregiving, sport, and housework into important dimensions for women, whereas physical exercise and paramilitary training loomed larger in the educational package for men. Particularly for the latter, militarization and war preparation became more and more important. Simultaneously, the Wehrmacht had an elaborate system of 'ideological warfare' that often built on models and practices developed in other parts of the educational system (Förster 2008).

Obviously, Nazi Germany also created a very different set of camps, built to persecute and exterminate those excluded from the 'people's community'. Concentration camps (*Konzentrationslager*, KZ) and a whole host of other incarceration institutions, for instance the so-called *Arbeitserziehungslager* and the *Jugendschutzlager* (Schwarz 1990, 82–86), shared some of the elements of spatial design and even the educational rhetoric of the camps for *Volksgenossen*, although of course life inside them was dramatically different. This also explains why one and the same location in many instances served first as concentration camp and was then converted to a camp for true 'Aryans', and vice versa – despite all ideologically loaded distinction between the two forms. This indifference towards the form of accommodation reveals Nazism's utopian ambition to refashion the individual and society in all their facets, and shows its instrumental rationality and the inhumanity of its policies (Patel 2006).

11.5   Actors and Their Room for Manoeuvre

Who were the main actors in the field of education and schooling during the Third Reich? As on many other issues, Hitler himself was involved and had the highest power of decision making, but most of the time he took little interest in actual policy. Bernhard Rust, the responsible minister, saw his role frequently challenged. With Alfred Rosenberg, he crossed swords on school functions and the role of universities; with propaganda minister Joseph Goebbels, for instance, on the affiliation of professors with the Reich chamber of culture (*Reichskulturkammer*), as the professional organization of all German creative artists under Goebbels's aegis. While both Rosenberg and Goebbels often opposed Rust, they also hated each other heartily. Moreover, there was the structural antagonism between newly created Nazi institutions and the system of education and training inherited from earlier times. A duplication of competences frequently led to fierce in-fighting between rival institutions. In part, Hitler intentionally created overlapping powers to increase his own scope of action; in part, these clashes reflected the Nazis' distrust of the existing educational system. Moreover, it would be wrong to see these struggles merely as a challenge to Nazi goals and as a source of inefficiency. In some cases, they resulted in a division of labour – for instance between Rust's ministry and the Hitler Youth. And quite generally, such rivalries mobilized and radicalized policies, thus furthering the general aims of the Third Reich. Having said this, these dynamics also make it difficult to extract a specific 'Nazi position' – simply because the Nazis were of many minds; because of continuities with earlier pedagogical practices; and since there was no clear-cut distinction between the Nazi regime and Germany society at large (Nagel 2012, 123–149).

Nazi education policies targeted the sexes in different ways. Elite education focused on boys and men: *Ordensburgen* only accepted male candidates (with women reduced to auxiliary roles, for instance in the kitchen and the laundry), and of the 32 *Napolas* that existed in 1941, only three were for girls. An act from 1933 limited the number of female students at German universities to a quota of 10% of all those eligible to study. And in *Mein Kampf*, Hitler declared that 'the unshakeable goal of female education must be the future mother' (Hartmann et al. 2016, vol. 2, 1057; my translation).

Still, women were no passive victims of the regime. In important ways, even the Führer lagged behind the processes the Third Reich unleashed. The League of German Girls (*Bund Deutscher Mädel*, BDM), for instance, gave girls more independence from parents and other traditional forces than many had previously enjoyed. Despite an emphasis on (future) motherhood, the regime opened up a whole host of new public roles for women. The BDM and the RAD for women, for instance, where thousands of leadership roles had to be filled, created attractive career paths. The restrictive quota at universities fell victim to the needs of war preparation; in fact, almost half of all students during the academic year 1943–1944 were female (Reese 2006; Harvey 2003; Grüttner 1995, 109–126).

11.6   Organizing Nazi Education

The chart shown in Figure 11.1, from Rudolf Benze's 1941 *Erziehung im Großdeutschen Reich*, seems to summarize the system of Nazi education. Benze's chart, however, has to be read with caution. First, all these changes in Germany's educational system were driven more by the will to power than by a grand, explicit pedagogical theory. Education during the Third Reich can only partially be

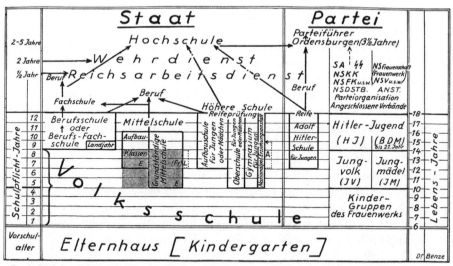

E = Englisch beginnt (Pflichtsprache), (Fr) = Französisch beginnt (Wahlsprache), A = Aufbauzüge einiger Nationalpolitischer Erziehungsanstalten.

Durch die Anordnung des Führers, die ostmärkische Hauptschule (vgl. S. 40) als gehobene Pflichtschule an Stelle der Mittelschule für das ganze Reich einzuführen, wird der Aufbau eine gewisse Änderung erfahren. Der voraussichtliche Bereich der Hauptschule ist durch Rasterung gekennzeichnet. Die zukünftige Gestaltung der beiden Oberklassen der bisherigen Mittelschule ist noch nicht entschieden.

Figure 11.1   'Der Aufbau der Erziehung im Grobdeutschen Reich' [The Structure of Education in the Greater German Reich]. From Rudolf Benze's 1941 *Erziehung im Großdeutschen Reich*, p. 16.

explained by Hitler's ideas. He always remained the highest source of legitimation, but his dispersed remarks did not provide much guidance for concrete policy choices. The role of professional educationalists should not be overestimated either. Many of them offered their services to the regime, and some organizations did occasionally cite authors such as Ernst Krieck, Rudolf Benze, and Alfred Baeumler. All three came to hold important administrative jobs during the Third Reich. Still, their intellectual contributions frequently represented retroactive examination and legitimation of Nazi organizations, and not genuinely new ideas (Giesecke 1993; Keim 1995, vol. 1, 9–72; Hermann and Oelkers 1988).

Second, Benze did not mention the institutions created for those excluded from the *Volksgemeinschaft* – let alone the consequences that such debarment could entail. Seemingly harmless institutions like the RAD monitored their members closely, and all these organizations had highly racialized conditions of access. Sometimes, it was only through enquiries by an educational institution that a person was targeted as an 'alien to the community' due to Jewish ancestry or for other reasons. If an 'Aryan certificate' was not produced, the path from the institutions for 'people's comrades' (*Volksgenossen*) could quickly lead to the camps of terrorization and extermination.[2]

Third, Benze insinuated completeness where, in fact, there were also other organizations and the regime's grasp always remained incomplete. For instance, he left out adult education and social work. Moreover, there were important changes over the course of the 12 years of the Third Reich that his chart did not capture. Benze wilfully painted a distorted picture of a well-organized and all-encompassing educational system. Many organizations that were supposed to take in all eligible young Germans of a certain age cohort were never actually able to do so, simply because they lacked the size and administrative capacity. From 1935 onwards, for instance, the RAD became compulsory for both men and women – but only on paper. In fact, only about two thirds of the relevant male age group were drafted in 1935, and for women the quota was much lower (Patel 2005, 143–148). The continuous system of immersion in organizations imbued with Nazism that Hitler described in Reichenberg was the Nazi ideal – one that often remained far from reality. Having said this, statistical evidence suggests that in the wartime Wehrmacht, the quota of those who had passed through the various Nazi organizations was quite high (Rass 2003, 121–134).

Still, practices on the ground remained very mixed. Fights over competences between rival organizations created overlap and loopholes, reducing the regime's pedagogical reach. Moreover, the Third Reich never fully prioritized its educational system over other goals. The number of Adolf Hitler schools, for instance, always remained much smaller than originally planned. No single age group of *Ordensjunker* went through the elaborate, multi-year education planned for this future elite of the Third Reich. Despite all promises of social mobility, pupils from middle-class families were clearly over-represented in the elite Adolf Hitler and *Napola* schools. Societal processes lagged seriously behind the regime's egalitarian rhetoric. Measured by its own standards, Nazi education was full of shortcomings (Feller and Feller 2001, 21–64, 102–107; Schneider, Stillke, and Leineweber 1996, 37–38).

11.7 'Total' Pretence Versus Practice on the Ground

It is therefore key to distinguish between 'total' pretences and educational practice on the ground. The Nazis themselves claimed to have closed that gap. A publication from 1938, for instance, argued that the RAD had harmonized 'educational intention and reality' (Petersen 1938, 13). This, obviously, was nothing more than a propaganda lie. In all Nazi educational organizations, there was a yawning gap between self-proclaimed goals on the one hand and everyday practice on the other. Despite the pressure they faced, denominational schools survived. Of the 45 000 Protestant and Catholic schools operating in Prussia in 1931, for instance, 34 000 still existed in 1938. The transformation of religious instruction along Nazi lines failed, too – or at least it was postponed until after the 'final victory' (Müller-Rolli 1999, 109–117). The *Hauptschule* never developed into an important educational branch; one scholar has called it a 'ruin' of Nazi school policy (Ottweiler 1985, 250). In general, education and schooling in institutions inherited by the Nazis often remained more traditional than the regime liked to claim.

In the newly created 'Nazi' institutions, things often looked little better. Their hasty expansion led to many administrative problems. The changing overriding priorities of the regime came on top: 'education' had a different status during the first years of the regime, when it often helped to keep the unemployed busy, in comparison to a later period of full employment and on to the war years, when the fight over groups exempted from work or war for educational purposes was often very fierce.

During the war, some of the most utopian elements of educating the 'Aryans' tended to be cut back. The *Ordensburg* Vogelsang dropped its original mission in 1939; the RAD discontinued most of its explicitly educational work in the course of the war, and as early in the war as spring 1940, 95% of all full-time (*hauptamtliche*) Hitler Youth leaders were serving in the Wehrmacht. The system of state schooling was simplified and shortened, and even the pupils at the elite Adolf Hitler schools graduated earlier. Describing the situation in 1941, one of these pupils enthused: 'The Führer needs us at the front' (quoted in Feller and Feller 2001, 54). Military service was now praised as the ultimate form of education (elaborating on an old trope in German and Western thinking), thus inflating the realm of pedagogy and reducing the remit of schooling in the narrow sense. Simultaneously, the protean landscape of 'education' camps were converted into camps for forced labour and KZ inmates (Patel 2006). Particularly after 1942, many resources originally reserved for the *Auslese* among the *Volksgenossen* and Nazi education policies *within* the Reich were redirected to war, terror, and the Holocaust.

This does not mean that the Nazis completely gave up their ideas. A few branches of their educational system in Germany expanded, most notably the *Kinderlandverschickung*. Between September 1940 and autumn 1944, some 850 000 children were sent to camps set up for this purpose. Together with those put in foster families and sent to the countryside with their mothers, more than two million children were relocated by the regime. Particularly for those accommodated in camps, the regime's grasp tightened massively (Kock 1997, 134–143).

Moreover, Hitler's empire beyond the *Altreich* turned into a laboratory for some of Nazi's most radical fantasies. To the West, for instance, Alsace was to be Germanized. Soon after the French capitulation in summer 1940, schools had to adopt the curriculum of the state of Baden and use Nazi textbooks. German was to become the exclusive mother tongue in the region, while Jews, French from other parts of the country, and other 'undesirables' were expelled. Children were encouraged to join the ranks of the BDM and the Hitler Youth. Since it became impossible to register at a secondary school without such affiliation, this amounted to an obligation even before compulsory membership was formally introduced in 1942. The Nazi institutional machinery was working at full swing (Vlossak 2010, 253–266; Finger 2016).

To the East, policies were often even more radical. Children in Poland, Yugoslavia, and other countries that were deemed fit to be 'Germanized' were deported to Germany and raised in special homes. Some 50 000 children (the exact figures are not clear) were kidnapped for this end and exposed to Nazi education (Hopfer 2010; Heinemann 2003, 508–533). Non-German academics at the *Reichsuniversitäten* in Prague and Strasbourg were kicked out or sent to concentration camps, with German scientists taking over. Vis-à-vis non-Germans, the regime's approach to schooling and education was chiefly a racialized policy of exclusion.

11.8   Embracing the Nazi Agenda

And there is a second reason why the inconsistencies and shortcomings of Nazi educational planning should not be overemphasized: why Nazi education really mattered. Besides the massive impact of its exclusionary and violent side, it proved to be quite alluring for a large number of Germans. Even if many individual institutions remained far from realizing their ambitious goals, continuous involvement in this host of institutions had a cumulative effect, just as Hitler had argued in his Reichenberg speech. Moreover, many Germans found the regime's education attractive. At the level of pedagogic methods, rote learning, bovine repetition, and flogging did exist. But there were also attempts to create an interactive and attractive mode of schooling for *Volksgenossen*. Nazi education frequently struck a chord because it integrated some of the more innovative elements of earlier pedagogic debates, for instance by focusing on joint experience, peer leadership, and a close link between theoretical and practical knowledge – which for instance implied that in mathematics, children learned algebra with examples from missile ballistics or by calculating the costs for society of supporting an 'unworthy, feeble-minded' person. Many Germans did not mind – or even found this inspiring (Link 2011; Langewiesche and Tenorth 1989).

At the level of content, Nazi ideas, with their Manichaean division between good and evil, their appeal to the emotions, and their cult of dynamism and commitment, had a particular affinity to adolescent behaviour. Many young Germans were not lured into Nazism, but actively embraced the values and belief system the regime tried to create. Most ideas identified with Nazism had deep roots in

German and European practices. For a lot of Germans, the regime's inner inconsistencies and deficits were but an incentive to work even harder to realize the
utopian *Volksgemeinschaft*. Recent research on a whole host of organizations and
issues – from schools to universities, from the Hitler Youth through the RAD to
the SS – has demonstrated that active self-mobilization for the goals of the
regime was often more important than passive top-down education and indoctrination (see, e.g., Reeken and Thießen 2013; Steber and Gotto 2014; Bajohr
and Wildt 2009).

Moreover, Nazi education offered a broad variety of incentives for those willing
to play by the rules – be it as pupils in a *Napola*, as BDM leaders in the East, or as
an 'Aryan' university professor on a chair from which a Jewish ex-colleague had
been expelled. Equally importantly, schooling and education were increasingly
imbedded in a *Lebenswelt* shaped by Nazi values and forms of interaction. Recent
research has stressed the continuous efforts to create a new, Nazi form of ethics,
co-produced by the regime's leaders and normal Germans. Everyday life was highly
politically charged. Children were encouraged to denounce their parents if they
showed signs of opposition, and swastikas, uniforms, medals, and songs created a
Nazi habitat (Gross 2010; Bialas 2014; Fritzsche 2008).

New opportunities were linked to permanent performance, probation, and
unobtrusiveness, as another factor explaining why many Germans actively opted
into the Nazi framework of thinking and action. Even the apparently most elect of
the regime, like SS members or *Napola* recruits, were made aware that their privileged status was precarious, and tied to permanent testing. No one could be sure
they might not fail on the basis of ultimately vague criteria of performance.
Contemporary estimates put the proportion of 'inferiors' among the German
population at 10–30%, thus revealing the importance and the mobilizing potential
of this ambivalence (Schneider, Stillke, and Leineweber 1996, 47–91; Bock 1986,
458). Being a good *Volksgenosse* meant permanently proving oneself worthy. All
these factors together help to explain why so many Germans, particularly among
the young who had passed through the whole Nazi educational system, supported
the regime until 1944/1945 (Römer 2012).

All the same, not everybody was entranced by the regime's pedagogic efforts.
One of the pamphlets of the student resistance group *Weiße Rose* ('White Rose')
argued that

> during the most fruitful years of our education, Hitler Youth, SA, SS have tried to
> make us uniform, to revolutionize us, and to narcotize us. "Ideological training"
> (*weltanschauliche Schulung*) was the name of the contemptuous method that suffo-
> cated the percolating independence of thinking and judgment in a haze of empty
> phrases. A selection of leaders ... grooms its future party barons to godless, brazen,
> and unscrupulous exploiters and cutthroats. (Siefken 1994, 32)

During the Third Reich, it remained possible to see the dark sides of the regime's
education. It would be wrong to think that all Germans embraced Nazi ideas – even
if a great many did.

11.9 Long-term Effects

The long-term effects of schooling, education, and camp life under the swastika are difficult to summarize. Writing in 1957, German sociologist Helmut Schelsky diagnosed a 'sceptical generation' (Schelsky 1957). According to Schelsky, those born during the 1920s and 1930s, and hence exposed to Nazi education during their childhood, often drew radical conclusions from the defeat in 1945. Their personal biographies made them sceptical of grand utopian designs and instead turned them into pragmatic, sober supporters of post-war democratic Germany. There was, however, a strong autobiographical dimension to Schelsky's work. Only half a generation older than the group he analysed, he himself had been quite fascinated by Nazism only a few years earlier. And while some of his findings might be true for many West Germans, East Germans frequently embraced a new ideology, qualifying the idea of an anti-utopian turn resulting from the Nazi experience (Bude 1995; Ahbe 2007). Moreover, Schelsky should not make us overlook important continuities. The year 1968 in West Germany, for instance, cannot be explained without factoring in the younger generation's revolt against the authoritarian behaviour of their parents that had roots in Nazism and longer trends in German education. Newer research on the generation that experienced the war as children has stressed the regime's education – along with the effects of the war itself – as central factors of their socialization, and it is well known that the traumas of victims were often passed on to the following generations (e.g. Bar-On 1995; Quindeau, Einert and Teuber 2012).

In many ways, Hitler was wrong when he argued in Reichenberg that German youth would 'never be free again during their whole lives'. A mere six-and-a-half years later, the Reich lay in ashes. In the intervening years, Nazi education had never lived up to its 'total' pretences. Still, it cast a dark shadow on the lives of millions, and its legacy lingered long after 1945.

Acknowledgements

I would like to thank Elizabeth Harvey, Felix Römer, and the editors of this volume for their comments on an earlier version of this text.

Notes

1 Author's own translation from the transcript in Deutsches Rundfunkarchiv Frankfurt, 2590330, Hitler's Speech in Reichenberg, 2 December 1938. The version published in the Nazi daily *Völkischer Beobachter* on 4 December 1938 that is normally quoted omitted the last sentence.

2 See, for example, the case of RAD-Oberfeldmeister G.: Bundesarchiv Berlin, R 77/2, especially letter 'Reichsstelle für Sippenforschung to Reichsarbeitsführer Konstantin Hierl', 18 October 1935.

References

Ahbe, Thomas. 2007. 'Deutsche Generationen nach 1945.' *Aus Politik und Zeitgeschichte* 15, 38–46.

Bair, Jeanette. 2011. 'Nationalsozialismus als Gegenstand bildungshistorischer Forschung.' In *Erziehungsverhältnisse im Nationalsozialismus: Totaler Anspruch und Erziehungswirklichkeit*, edited by Klaus-Peter Horn and Jörg-W. Link, 13–26. Bad Heilbrunn: Klinkhardt Verlag.

Bajohr, Frank and Wildt, Michael, eds. 2009. *Volksgemeinschaft: Neue Forschungen zur Gesellschaft des Nationalsozialismus*. Frankfurt am Main: Fischer.

Bar-On, Dan. 1995. *Fear and Hope: Three Generations of the Holocaust*. Cambridge, MA: Harvard University Press.

Benze, Rudolf. 1936. *Nationalpolitische Erziehung im Dritten Reich*. Berlin: Junker & Dünnhaupt.

Benze, Rudolf. 1941. *Erziehung im Großdeutschen Reich: Eine Überschau über ihre Ziele, Wege und Einrichtungen*, 2nd edn. Frankfurt am Main: Moritz Diesterweg.

Benze, Rudolf. 1943. *Erziehung im Großdeutschen Reich: Eine Überschau über ihre Ziele, Wege und Einrichtungen*, 3rd edn. Frankfurt am Main: Moritz Diesterweg.

Bialas, Wolfgang. 2014. *Moralische Ordnungen des Nationalsozialismus*. Göttingen: Vandenhoeck & Ruprecht.

Bock, Gisela. 1986. *Zwangssterilisation im Nationalsozialismus: Studien zur Rassenpolitik und Frauenpolitik*. Opladen: Westdeutscher Verlag.

Buddrus, Michael. 2003. *Totale Erziehung für den totalen Krieg: Hitlerjugend und nationalsozialistische Jugendpolitik*. Munich: Saur.

Bude, Heinz. 1995. *Das Altern einer Generation: Die Jahrgänge 1938 bis 1948*. Frankfurt am Main: Suhrkamp.

Feller, Barbara and Feller, Wolfgang. 2001. *Die Adolf-Hitler-Schulen: Pädagogische Provinz versus Ideologische Zuchtanstalt*. Weinheim: Juventa.

Finger, Jürgen. 2016. *Eigensinn im Einheitsstaat: NS-Schulpolitik in Württemberg, Baden und im Elsass 1933–1945*. Baden-Baden: Nomos.

Fölling, Werner. 1995. *Zwischen deutscher und jüdischer Identität: Deutsch-jüdische Familien und die Erziehung ihrer Kinder an einer jüdischen Reformschule im 'Dritten Reich'*. Opladen: Leske + Budrich.

Förster, Jürgen. 2008. 'Ideological Warfare in Germany, 1919 to 1945.' In *Germany and the Second World War*, vol. 9, pt. 1: *German Wartime Society 1939–1945: Politicization, Disintegration, and the Struggle for Survival*, edited for the Militärgeschichtliches Forschungsamt Potsdam, by Jörg Echternkamp. Translation editor Derry Cook-Radmore, 485–647. Oxford: Clarendon Press.

Fritzsche, Peter. 2008. *Life and Death in the Third Reich*. Cambridge, MA: Belknap Press.

Giesecke, Hermann. 1993. *Hitlers Pädagogen: Theorie und Praxis nationalsozialistischer Erziehung*. Weinheim: Juventa.

Gross, Raphael. 2010. *Anständig geblieben: Nationalsozialistische Moral*. Frankfurt am Main: Fischer.

Grüttner, Michael. 1995. *Studenten im Dritten Reich*. Paderborn: Schöningh.

Harten, Hans-Christian. 2014. *Himmlers Lehrer: Die Weltanschauliche Schulung in der SS 1933–1945*. Paderborn: Schöningh.

Hartmann, Christian et al., eds. 2016. *Hitler, Mein Kampf. Eine kritische Edition*. 2 vols. Munich: Oldenbourg.

Harvey, Elizabeth. 2003. *Women and the Nazi East: Agents and Witnesses of Germanization*. New Haven, CT: Yale University Press.

Heinemann, Isabel. 2003. '*Rasse Siedlung, deutsches Blut': Das Rasse- und Siedlungshauptamt der SS und die rassenpolitische Neuordnung Europas.* Göttingen: Wallstein.

Hermann, Ulrich and Oelkers, Jürgen, eds. 1988. *Pädagogik und Nationalsozialismus.* Weinheim: Beltz.

Hochstetter, Dorothee. 2005. *Motorisierung und 'Volksgemeinschaft': Das Nationalsozialistische Kraftfahrkorps (NSKK) 1931–1945.* Munich: Oldenbourg.

Hopfer, Ines. 2010. *Geraubte Identität: Die gewaltsame 'Eindeutschung' von polnischen Kindern in der NS-Zeit.* Vienna, Cologne, and Weimar: Böhlau.

Horn, Klaus-Peter. 2011. '"Immer bleibt deshalb eine Kindheit im Faschismus eine Kindheit" – Erziehung in der frühen Kindheit.' In *Erziehungsverhältnisse im Nationalsozialismus: Totaler Anspruch und Erziehungswirklichkeit*, edited by Klaus-Peter Horn and Jörg-W. Link, 29–56. Bad Heilbrunn: Klinkhardt Verlag.

Keim, Wolfgang, ed. 1991. *Pädagogen und Pädagogik im Nationalsozialismus: Ein unerledigtes Problem der Erziehungswissenschaft.* Frankfurt am Main: Peter Lang.

Keim, Wolfgang. 1995. *Erziehung unter der Nazi-Diktatur.* Vol. 1. Darmstadt: Primus.

Kock, Gerhard. 1997. '*Der Führer sorgt für unsere Kinder': Die Kinderlandverschickung im Zweiten Weltkrieg.* Paderborn: Schöningh.

Kollmeier, Kathrin. 2007. *Ordnung und Ausgrenzung: Die Disziplinarpolitik der Hitler-Jugend.* Göttingen: Vandenhoeck & Ruprecht.

Kramer, Nicole. 2011. *Volksgenossinnen an der Heimatfront: Mobilisierung, Verhalten, Erinnerung.* Göttingen: Vandenhoeck & Ruprecht.

Kremer, Gabriele. 2011. 'Die Sonderschule im Nationalsozialismus: das Beispiel Hilfsschule.' In *Erziehungsverhältnisse im Nationalsozialismus: Totaler Anspruch und Erziehungswirklichkeit*, edited by Klaus-Peter Horn and Jörg-W. Link, 163–184. Bad Heilbrunn: Klinkhardt Verlag.

Krüger, Alfred. 1937. 'Arbeit und Gemeinschaft: Zur Entwicklung der Arbeitsdienstidee.' *Deutschlands Erneuerung* 21, 96–100.

Lamberti, Marjorie. 2002. *The Politics of Education: Teachers and School Reform in Weimar Germany.* New York: Berghahn Books.

Langewiesche, Dieter and Tenorth, Heinz-Elmar, eds. 1989. *Handbuch der deutschen Bildungsgeschichte, Volume 5: 1918–1945: Die Weimarer Republik und die nationalsozialistische Diktatur.* Munich: C.H. Beck.

Link, Jörg-W. 2011. '"Erziehungsstätte des deutschen Volkes": Die Volksschule im Nationalsozialismus.' In *Erziehungsverhältnisse im Nationalsozialismus: Totaler Anspruch und Erziehungswirklichkeit*, edited by Klaus-Peter Horn and Jörg-W. Link, 79–106. Bad Heilbrunn: Klinkhardt Verlag.

Mertens, Adolf. 1937. *Schulungslager und Lagererziehung.* Dortmund: Crüwell.

Müller-Rolli, Sebastian. 1999. *Evangelische Schulpolitik in Deutschland, 1918–1959.* Göttingen: Vandenhoeck & Ruprecht.

Nagel, Anne C. 2012. *Hitlers Bildungsreformer: Das Reichsministerium für Wissenschaft, Erziehung und Volksbildung 1934–1945.* Frankfurt am Main: Fischer.

Ottweiler, Ottwilm. 1985. 'Die nationalsozialistische Schulpolitik im Bereich des Volksschulwesens.' In *'Die Formung des Volksgenossen': Der 'Erziehungsstaat' des Dritten Reiches*, edited by Ulrich Herrmann, 235–252. Weinheim: Beltz Verlag.

Patel, Kiran Klaus. 2005. *Soldiers of Labor: Labor Service in Nazi Germany and New Deal America, 1933–1945.* Cambridge: Cambridge University Press.

Patel, Kiran Klaus. 2006. '"Auslese" und "Ausmerze." Das Janusgesicht der nationalsozialistischen Lager.' *Zeitschrift für Geschichtswissenschaft* 54, 339–365.

Petersen, Hellmut. 1938. *Die Erziehung der deutschen Jungmannschaft im Reichsarbeitsdienst.* Berlin: Junker & Dünnhaupt.

Pine, Lisa. 2010. *Education in Nazi Germany.* Oxford: Berg.

Quindeau, Ilka, Einert, Katrin, and Teuber, Nadine. 2012. 'Kindheiten im Nationalsozialismus und Zweiten Weltkrieg: Das Zusammenwirken von NS-Erziehung und Bombenangriffen.' *BIOS. Zeitschrift für Biographieforschung, Oral History und Lebensverlaufsananlysen* 25, 87–117.

Rass, Christoph. 2003. '*Menschenmaterial': Deutsche Soldaten an der Ostfront: Innenansichten einer Infanteriedivision 1939–1945.* Paderborn: Schöningh.

Reeken, Dietmar von and Thießen, Malte, eds. 2013. *'Volksgemeinschaft' als soziale Praxis: Neue Forschungen zur NS-Gesellschaft vor Ort.* Paderborn: Schöningh.

Reese, Dagmar, 2006. *Growing up Female in Nazi Germany.* Ann Arbor: University of Michigan Press.

Riecke, Heinz. 1936. 'Gehalt und Gestalt des Arbeitslagers.' *Deutsches Volkstum* 4, 353–359.

Römer, Felix. 2012. *Kameraden: Die Wehrmacht von innen.* Munich: Piper.

Schelsky, Helmut. 1957. *Die skeptische Generation: Eine Soziologie der deutschen Jugend.* Düsseldorf: Eugen Diederichs.

Schneider, Christian, Stillke, Cordelia, and Leineweber, Bernd. 1996. *Das Erbe der Napola: Versuch einer Generationengeschichte des Nationalsozialismus.* Hamburg: Hamburger Edition.

Scholtz, Harald. 1985. *Erziehung und Unterricht unterm Hakenkreuz.* Göttingen: Vandenhoeck & Ruprecht.

Schwarz, Gudrun. 1990. *Die nationalsozialistischen Lager.* Frankfurt am Main and New York: Campus.

Siefken, Hinrich, ed. 1994. *Die Weiße Rose und ihre Flugblätter: Dokumente, Texte, Lebensbilder, Erläuterungen.* Manchester: Manchester University Press.

Steber, Martina and Gotto, Bernhard, eds. 2014. *Visions of Community in Nazi Germany: Social Engineering and Private Lives.* Oxford: Oxford University Press.

Vlossak, Elizabeth. 2010. *Marianne or Germania? Nationalizing Women in Alsace, 1870–1946.* Oxford: Oxford University Press.

Wegner, Gregory Paul. 2002. *Anti-Semitism and Schooling under the Third Reich.* New York: RoutledgeFalmer.

Further Reading

Horn, Klaus-Peter and Link, Jörg-W., eds. 2011. *Erziehungsverhältnisse im Nationalsozialismus: Totaler Anspruch und Erziehungswirklichkeit.* Bad Heilbrunn: Klinkhardt Verlag.
An indispensable overview with many contributions by leading scholars in the field.

Keim, Wolfgang. 1995–1997. *Erziehung unter der Nazi-Diktatur.* 2 vols. Darmstadt: Primus Verlag.
A detailed survey of Nazi education with its various facets.

Lamberti, Marjorie. 2002. *The Politics of Education: Teachers and School Reform in Weimar Germany.* New York: Berghahn Books.
A study on the complex and ferocious debates about school education in Weimar Germany.

Langewiesche, Dieter and Tenorth, Heinz-Elmar, eds. 1989. *Handbuch der deutschen Bildungsgeschichte, Volume 5: 1918–1945: Die Weimarer Republik und die nationalsozialistische Diktatur.* Munich: C.H. Beck.
Slightly dated, still with a lot of very useful information.

Pine, Lisa. 2010. *Education in Nazi Germany.* Oxford: Berg.
A short introduction to the topic in English with a focus on school education.

Schmidtke, Adrian. 2007. *Körperformationen: Fotoanalysen zur Formierung und Disziplinierung des Körpers in der Erziehung des Nationalsozialismus.* Münster: Waxmann.
An innovative contribution analysing contemporary photographs. Inspired by Foucault, the author stresses the importance given to the body by Nazism, but also the variety of its visual representations.

Scholtz, Harald. 1985. *Erziehung und Unterricht unterm Hakenkreuz.* Göttingen: Vandenhoeck & Ruprecht.
An older survey which remains useful.
Stargardt, Nicholas. 2005. *Witnesses of War: Children's Lives under the Nazis.* London: Cape.
An indispensable book to understand the situation of children during the Second World War and how they experienced Nazi education.
Steber, Martina and Gotto, Bernhard, eds. 2014. *Visions of Community in Nazi Germany: Social Engineering and Private Lives.* Oxford: Oxford University Press.
A recent, impressive collection on the debate about *Volksgemeinschaft* in Nazi Germany and the voluntarist turn in research.
Sünker, Heinz and Otto, Hans-Uwe, eds. 1997. *Education and Fascism: Political Identity and Social Education in Nazi Germany.* Abingdon, UK: Routledge.
Probably the best introduction to this topic available in English.

CHAPTER TWELVE

Research and Scholarship*

MICHAEL GRÜTTNER

12.1 Introduction

Historical research on scholarship during the Third Reich began relatively late. In the 1980s large books on the history of individual universities were still being published, with the claim that they had remained almost unaffected in substance by National Socialism. This changed, however, from the 1990s when important academic institutions such as the Max Planck Society and the German Research Foundation (*Deutsche Forschungsgemeinschaft*) started to have their own history as it related to the Nazi period investigated by independent scholars. Meanwhile, extended publications have been released on most universities. These studies have debunked the claim held for a long time that National Socialism had been anti-science. The Nazi state had, in fact, an instrumental attitude towards science, resulting in different consequences for different academic disciplines.

12.2 The German Science and Research Landscape in 1932–1933

The German science and research system reached its peak in the first third of the twentieth century in terms of its international reputation. Particularly in Imperial Germany, universities and non-university institutions were expanded considerably. The German language evolved into an internationally leading scientific language. Among scientists who received Nobel prizes for physics, chemistry, and medicine, nearly a third were German. Without including industrial research, the German research system in the early 1930s was based on five pillars: (i) universities, (ii) techni-

* Translated by Christine Brocks.

A Companion to Nazi Germany, First Edition. Edited by Shelley Baranowski,
Armin Nolzen, and Claus-Christian W. Szejnmann.
© 2018 John Wiley & Sons Ltd. Published 2018 by John Wiley & Sons Ltd.

cal colleges, (iii) the Kaiser-Wilhelm Society (the predecessor of the Max Planck Society), (iv) the German Research Foundation, and (v) academies of science. The 23 universities played the most important role in this research and science landscape. All of them were state funded and, by today's standards, rather small institutions. In 1932 the average German university had 260 teaching staff and 4300 students, and in addition research assistants who were quite important in natural scientific and medical disciplines.

The structure of the German university had not changed much since the nineteenth century. The most important requirement to qualify for a university professorship was the 'habilitation', that is, the second large academic book after the doctoral thesis. After being habilitated the academic was appointed *Privatdozent* and obliged to regularly offer lectures and seminars without receiving a fixed income. These unsalaried lecturers could expect to be appointed as extraordinary professors without the status of a civil servant (*nichtbeamtete außerordentliche Professoren*) a couple of years after their habilitation. This, however, did not change their insecure status. *Privatdozenten* and extraordinary professors were candidates for a full professorship. Full professors were at the core of the teaching body. They dominated all important committees and decided on appointments and habilitations (Grüttner 2005).

The 10 technical colleges (*Technische Hochschulen*) had a similar structure, but were usually smaller. In 1932, an average technical university had a teaching staff of 160, responsible for roughly 2000 students. Whereas universities usually offered a wide range of disciplines, from theology to law and humanities to medicine and natural sciences, technical colleges focused on training engineers, architects, and natural scientists (Dinçkal, Dipper, and Mares 2010).

The most distinguished research institution apart from the universities was the Kaiser-Wilhelm Society (*Kaiser-Wilhelm-Gesellschaft*, KWG), founded in 1911. This institution was to enable outstanding scientists to focus on research unburdened by any teaching and exam duties. The Kaiser-Wilhelm Society was a rather loose association of 34 institutes and other research facilities (1931). It comprised institutions for research in medicine, humanities, and the law; its emphasis, however, was on natural sciences. The Kaiser-Wilhelm Society was funded by both state and private funds (Heim, Sachse, and Walker 2009).

The German Research Foundation was founded in 1920 as 'Emergency Association of German Science' in the wake of the crisis of the post-war era. Before 1933, it considered itself a self-governing body of German scholarship with the task of financially supporting research, particularly at universities. In so doing, the 'international standing of German science' jeopardized by the war and its repercussions should be maintained (Walker et al. 2013).

Since the nineteenth century the five Academies of Sciences in Prussia, Bavaria, Saxony, Göttingen, and Heidelberg had lost much of their previous importance. However, they remained significant for the formation of an academic elite and were still relevant centres of interdisciplinary communication and networking. The academies also sponsored various long-term projects of several decades' duration, particularly in the humanities (vom Bruch et al. 2014). These five pillars of the German research system remained under Nazi rule, but they were given a new structure, new leading personnel, and new objectives.

12.3   Research and Science

In early 1933, no one in the NSDAP (*Nationalsozialistische Deutsche Arbeiterpartei*, Nazi Party) felt responsible for research and scholarship. An association of National Socialist scholars did not exist at this point. Most ministries for education in the German single states were taken over by former teachers such as Bernhard Rust in Prussia and Hans Schemm in Bavaria, who were not familiar with the academic world of the universities. The Nazi Students' League (*Nationalsozialistischer Deutscher Studentenbund*, NSDStB) took advantage of this vacuum, and launched a 'National Socialist university revolution' on its own initiative in 1933–1934. Due to the vehement attacks on 'reactionary' professors, the 'seizure of power' at German universities appeared as a generational conflict temporarily overturning traditional hierarchies: 'With the same boldness as once SA-men in the streets, we look around in the lecture hall today and decide whether or not a professor is allowed to stay. The criterion will be: this man can no longer be a professor because he does not understand us ... We young ones control the university and can do as we like,' a Leipzig student functionary declared in June 1933 (Grüttner 1995, 74). It was only from 1934–1935 that the student functionaries lost influence again.

Scholarship was a policy field Hitler scarcely interfered in, because he was not interested. Even when he had to take crucial decisions, he often reacted indifferently (Grüttner 2000, 557–558). It seems that he primarily intervened and made decisions in situations when different state and party offices got wound up in internal conflicts and could not find a way out. The most important institutions of Nazi science and higher education policy were established between 1934 and 1936: the Reich Ministry of Education, the Higher Education Commission of the Nazi Party, the Nazi Lecturers' League, and the science section in the office of Alfred Rosenberg, the party ideologist. None of these institutions had considerable political influence. The Education Minister (Nagel 2012) Bernhard Rust, in particular, suffered from an unfavourable reputation. At the 1943 rectors' conference he was ridiculed as a 'wayward custodian of science' (Heiber 1992, 315). The Higher Education Commission of the Nazi Party (*Hochschulkommission der NSDAP*), founded in 1934, was supposed to counterbalance the Ministry of Education. Initially the Commission gained significant influence, particularly in medical faculties. But in the end, it could not withstand the pressure due to the in-fighting between different offices of the regime and closed down. From 1935 it was replaced by the Nazi Lecturers' League (*Nationalsozialistischer Deutscher Dozentenbund*). Hardly better regarded than the Ministry of Education, the league had little to offer in terms of science policy concepts. However, when it came to personnel decisions – especially when professors were appointed – the functionaries of the Nazi Lecturers' League had enormous influence (Nagel 2008). Alfred Rosenberg's science section, initially headed by the philosopher Alfred Baeumler, was effectively a one-man operation for years. It was expanded, gradually, only from 1938 and focused on humanities.

Other protagonists such as the Four Year Plan Office (*Vierjahresplan-Behörde*) and the Wehrmacht were interested only in certain subsections of research. Within the Wehrmacht it was the Ministry of Aviation and the Army Weapons Agency

(*Heereswaffenamt*) that influenced science policy. The head of the research department in the *Heereswaffenamt*, Erich Schumann, also held a leading position in the Education Ministry between 1934 and 1937. In 1937, the Education Ministry and the *Heereswaffenamt* established the Reich Research Council (*Reichsforschungsrat*), a cooperation to secure research funding for armament and autarky (Flachowsky 2008). As was common in the Third Reich, the responsibilities of these different institutions were not clearly delineated. Inevitably, various state and party authorities involved in research and science policy competed fiercely for power, in some cases even during the war years. In March 1943, Heinrich Härtle, a politician working at the Rosenberg office, complained that 'disorganization and departmental conflicts ... were even worse on the field of science politics than elsewhere' (Grüttner 2000, 562).

Thus, there was no central control of research and scholarship during the Third Reich. Instead, a fragmentation of science policy is nearer the mark: independently and competing against each other, the different power centres of the Nazi state tried to establish their scientific empire. The science office in the Education Ministry dominated research funding; in 1936, it took over control of the German Research Foundation and played a key role in the Reich Research Council founded in 1937. The Nazi Lecturers' League consolidated its position as some kind of control authority for personnel decisions, being able to support, hamper, or destroy academic careers. Alfred Rosenberg, on the other hand, focused on founding a party university, the so-called *Hohe Schule*, which never progressed beyond planning stage even though it was officially supported by Hitler himself.

Agreement among Nazi science politicians could always be reached when policy measures clearly resulted from ingrained enemy images such as the expulsion of Jewish or politically unwelcome professors and students as well as the abolishment of democratic structures in favour of the 'leadership principle' (*Führerprinzip*). This was accompanied by a personnel policy focusing on political attitudes and 'race' apart from professional achievements. Every important personnel decision from 1933 was based on the political vetting of the candidates. Anyone who did not seem to be at least loyal to the regime had no chance of succeeding.

All Nazi power centres of science policy shared the view that scholarship had to be for the benefit of the *Volksgemeinschaft* ('people's community'). This instrumental attitude towards research and science is illustrated by an article published in the SS newspaper *Das Schwarze Korps* ('The Black Corps') in 1936:

> The dead knowledge junk of the liberalist century is neither for the benefit of the people nor of the state, and we are no longer willing to tolerate the arrogance of some paid civil servants who, with reference to the autonomy of scholarship, demand to continue to pursue stuff that does not interest the people and is of no use for them. (Grüttner 2009, 45)

12.4 Expansion

During the decades after the Second World War, German historiography mainly held the view that National Socialism was an anti-science system. Contrary to this assumption, though, state expenditures for research and scholarship rose considerably during the Nazi dictatorship (Grüttner 2000, 577). Despite strong anti-intellectual resentments, the regime depended on scientific knowledge and utilized it for its own purposes. In fact, the German research system expanded after the Nazi seizure of power: some already existing institutions were enlarged, others were newly established. One of these new facilities was the Reich Institute for History of the New Germany (*Reichsinstitut für Geschichte des neuen Deutschlands*) founded in 1935. Headed by Nazi historian Walter Frank, the institute focused on a trenchantly anti-Semitic historiography. Also, various party organizations established their own research facilities in the years after the seizure of power, such as the Institute for Labour Studies of the German Labour Front (*Arbeitswissenschaftliches Institut der Deutschen Arbeitsfront*) and the SS research foundation Ancestral Heritage (*Ahnenerbe*). Whereas the *Ahnenerbe* initially focused on disciplines such as prehistory and ethnology, which were of special interest to Heinrich Himmler for ideological reasons, during the war it was responsible for medical experiments on humans, where the death of those tested was anticipated and accepted (Reitzenstein 2014).

Natural and technical sciences could expect particularly generous state funding. The Kaiser-Wilhelm Society was one of the main beneficiaries. Its budget increased from 5.1 million Reichsmarks in 1932 to 14.5 million Reichsmarks (Hachtmann 2007). Aviation research was another expanding field that benefited from almost unlimited financial funding given by Hermann Göring's Reich Ministry of Aviation. The most important newly established institution, the German Aviation Research Institute (*Deutsche Forschungsanstalt für Luftfahrt*), cost more than 48 million Reichsmarks in investments until 1939. Other already existing institutions such as the German Laboratory for Aviation (*Deutsche Versuchsanstalt für Luftfahrt*) could multiply their budget after 1933. By the end of the war more than 10 000 people worked in German aviation research (Trischler 1992, 275).

In the course of the Four Year Plan that, according to Hitler's demand, was supposed to 'prepare Germany for war within four years', several new research facilities emerged. In 1938, the Reich Office for Economic Development (*Reichsamt für Wirtschaftsausbau*) headed by Carl Krauch was set up as part of the Four Year Plan Office. With its substantial budget, it supported several research projects. Between 1938 and 1944, it brought 38 institutes of the Four Year Plan Office into being. Most of these facilities were affiliated to already existing research institutions and conducted research projects on behalf of the Four Year Plan Office in the context of the autarky policy. They predominantly worked on developing substitute materials for natural resources, which were in short supply in Germany (Flachowsky 2015).

The expansion of the German research system after 1938 was partly the result of the aggressive Nazi policy of conquest. After the annexation of Austria in spring 1938, nine more universities and colleges were added to the German higher education system. In 1939, the incorporation of the German university in Prague and of the technical colleges of Gdansk, Prague, and Brno followed. This process was completed in 1941 with the founding of the two short-lived 'Reich universities' (*Reichsuniversitäten*) in Poznan and Strasbourg, which were to drive forward the Germanization (*Germanisierung*) of Western Poland and Alsace by scholarly means. Finally, the German occupiers made several attempts to make use of existing scientific institutes, libraries, and collections in the occupied territories for their own purposes.

12.5   Cleansing German Scholarship

Unlike in fascist Italy, the 'cleansing' of German scholarship started immediately after the Nazi seizure of power. Jews and 'non-Aryans' in particular became victims of this policy, and, to a lesser degree, scholars who were found inacceptable by the Nazi regime on political grounds. Jews had played an important role in the German higher education system before 1933. At Prussian universities, roughly 9% of the teaching staff was Jewish in 1924, and at the most important German university, in Berlin, it was as much as 18%. At the same time, however, Jews were highly discriminated against compared to their Protestant and Catholic colleagues when it came to appointments to a chair. Only 17% of Jewish lecturers who taught at Berlin university between 1871 and 1933 achieved the position of a full professor, compared to 45% Protestants and 67% Catholics (Grüttner et al. 2012, 173–174).

The 'cleansing' of German universities lasted several years and was by and large completed in 1938. About 19% of the teaching staff was dismissed in the course of that time. Twice as high was the figure for the – albeit very small – group of female lecturers (Grüttner and Kinas 2007). Technical colleges were less affected by dismissals than universities (Hartshorne 1937, 95). The Kaiser-Wilhelm Society, in contrast, lost almost a third of its academic members and 10 out of 35 institute directors (Rürup 2008, 106).

Who were the victims of this policy? At the universities, roughly four fifths of all dismissals were motivated by anti-Semitism – that is, the victims were Jews, scholars with a Jewish background, or lecturers married to a 'non-Aryan' spouse. The remaining fifth was a rather heterogeneous group comprising supporters of left-wing parties, worshippers of the Confessing Church (*Bekennende Kirche*), Catholic opponents of National Socialism, liberals, dissident conservatives, and homosexuals (Grüttner and Kinas 2007).

Since most of the scholars affected were dismissed during the first three years of Nazi dictatorship, they were forced at an early stage to find a new career outside of Germany. More than 60% of dismissed university lecturers emigrated. Thus, the number of Holocaust victims among the scholars expelled from German universities fortunately remained relatively small. About 4% of them died in camps, were executed as enemies of the regime, or fell victim to Nazi violence in some other way. Others indirectly became victims of National Socialist policy by taking their own lives after their dismissal, or in view of the imminent dismissal. This second group of victims likewise comprised about 4% of the dismissed scholars (Grüttner and Kinas 2007, 143).

In 1938, the Nazi regime embarked on the phase of territorial expansion, initially with the annexation of Austria, the invasion of Czechoslovakia, and finally the Second World War. Universities and other research facilities, which from 1938 onwards were incorporated into the German science and research system, suffered a similar 'cleansing' as the academic world in Germany.In some cases, measures taken were much more radical than in Germany. In Austria, the university of Vienna was affected in particular. According to recent research, 42% of its teaching staff were dismissed (Huber 2015, 669).

As a result, Germany lost a lot of scholarly expertise due to the mass dismissals. This loss was even more significant than the sheer numbers of dismissed scholars indicate. Studies on the history of physics, biology, and chemistry show that among emigrated scientists high achievers were disproportionally represented (Fischer 1991, 541–542; Deichmann 1996, 26; 2001, 138–139). Including those scientists who received a Nobel prize only after their emigration, a total of 24 Nobel laureates fled the Nazi regime in Germany and Austria (Möller 1984, 70).

Aside from the victims of expulsion, the beneficiaries should also be mentioned. For many lecturers, who were not full professors or civil servants and had insecure career prospects in 1932/1933, the mass dismissals offered a second chance, and many of them were more than willing to take it. It was due not least to this situation that a unified reaction of the German universities against mass dismissals was unrealistic. Max Planck, who spoke up for several threatened colleagues, had no illusions about the situation in July 1933. When Otto Hahn suggested bringing together the largest possible number of prominent professors to protest against the treatment of Jewish colleagues, Planck answered: 'if today 30 professors stand up and criticize the government for its actions, tomorrow 150 persons will declare their loyalty to Hitler because they want the positions' (Grüttner and Kinas 2007, 150).

Analysing the dismissals with regard to the Second World War, it is fair to say that the Nazis ultimately strengthened the scientific-military potential of the Allies by expelling several outstanding academics, and in so doing contributed to the defeat of the Axis Powers. The majority of emigrants who left Germany after 1933 moved to Great Britain and the United States, thus to countries on which Hitler Germany declared war in 1939 and 1941. It was the physicists Albert Einstein, Leo Szilard, and Eduard Teller who, after they had fled Germany, initiated building the atomic bomb by pointing out the military potential of nuclear energy to the American president. Driven by the nightmarish fear that Hitler could have the atomic bomb first, many other emigrants in leading positions contributed to the research project that finally led to the development of the first atomic bomb (Rhodes 1986).

12.6 Scholars and Nazism

By 1933, German university teachers were a small group consisting of only 6000–7000 people. Most of them had a Protestant background and nearly all were male. In 1932/1933, women comprised a very small minority of the teaching staff at about 1.2% (Grüttner 2012, 139). The majority of German professors disapproved of the Weimar Republic or were at least sceptical and distanced. They saw the first German democracy predominantly as the 'shameful result of a lost war', as the jurist Wolfgang Kunkel phrased it in retrospect (Kunkel 1966, 107). Politically they were leaning towards the German National People's Party (*Deutschnationale Volkspartei*, DNVP) and the German People's Party (*Deutsche Volkspartei*, DVP).

Unlike the students, who had mainly sided with National Socialism even before 1933, there were only a few Nazi Party members among the teaching staff of German universities before the seizure of power.

This changed after the Nazis came into power. It was mainly the generational background and the academic status that determined the reaction of different groups of people at the university towards National Socialism. As a rule of thumb, the lower the academic status and the younger the people were, the earlier and more intensely they followed Nazism. This means, conversely, that the older and more established they were, the more distanced they remained towards the Nazi Party (Höpfner 1999, 14–16). This was for several reasons. First, the Nazis successfully presented themselves as the party of youth crusading against the 'failure' of the older generation. Also, the younger scholars belonged to a generation of academics who had swung to the right during their studies in the Weimar Republic. And finally, it was precisely the junior scholars who benefited from the Nazi cleansing policy. On the other hand, for the established university teachers, the full professors, the Nazi seizure of power meant a significant loss of their traditional position in favour of the state bureaucracy and the party.

However, during the following years many established full professors also sided with the regime. First and foremost, the foreign policy successes of Nazi Germany drove them into the arms of National Socialism, even those who had initially been cautious and sceptical. In 1938, after the annexation of Austria and the successful solution of the 'Sudeten crisis', the Nazis and their allies had achieved nearly everything the traditional elites had dreamt of since 1919. The previously liberal conservative professor Percy Ernst Schramm wrote in October 1938: '80 million – without bloodshed. Neither Bismarck nor the Maid of Orleans was capable of doing that, only someone who combines the skills and talents of both. One is too moved to go straight back to work …. 1938 is the great year of our lives, no other will ever elevate us like this again' (Grolle 1989, 33).

When the Second World War started, the university teachers – like the German population overall – initially reacted very cautiously. In contrast to 1914, there was little enthusiasm for war at the universities in 1939. Given the evident risks and dangers of this war, a feeling of apprehension dominated. For the chemist Adolf Butenandt (later Nobel laureate and president of the Max Planck Society), the news about the war came as a shock. 'Horror-stricken,' he thought about 'what might be coming' in a letter to his parents. All the greater was the enthusiasm after the first major successes of the Wehrmacht, in particular after the victory over France in spring 1940. Whereas Butenandt still wavered 'between rejoicing and waiting' and hoped for a swift end of the war (Schieder and Trunk 2004, 44–45), others were freer in giving vent to their emotions: 'What a twist of Providence', the Erlangen theologian Hermann Strathmann rejoiced in late May 1940. In 1931, Strathmann had published an acute criticism of National Socialism from a conservative-Christian perspective; in 1940 he described the events as 'of almost mythic greatness'. The 'greatest political hopes of the Germans come true … And we see the *Führer* as a God sent to achieve this task' (Strathmann 1940, 172).

Overall, the atmosphere of military victories led a larger number of professors, who initially had been rather critical of the regime, to lean towards National

Socialism. However, this did not equate to an unconditional identification with the Nazi state. Party organizations interfering in internal university affairs had a particularly deterrent effect. During the second half of the war, when the influence of the Nazi Lecturers' League significantly decreased, university professors could more freely mention their unease with this policy. At the Salzburg rectors' conference in August 1943, the Freiburg university rector Wilhelm Süss, member of the Nazi Party since 1937, almost openly attacked the functionaries of the Nazi League of Lecturers as 'gravediggers of science', who had expelled many able scholars from German universities with their 'one-sided' political assessments. 'How often have the professional achievements of colleagues been overlooked in favour of the political assessment! Had these judges had a sufficient relation to productive academic work or at least true appreciation of scholarly achievements, they would have been more reluctant to give a negative verdict' (Grüttner 2009, 44).

The anti-intellectual attitude of the regime and the related devaluation of academic professions added to the disappointment. The Reich Education Ministry commented critically in a circular decree from 1938 that 'universities and scholarship were publicly often still seen as matters that can be fundamentally and invariably criticized and belittled. This depreciation targets the general value of the university, science and academic studies rather than actual academic achievements. It is not least due to this lack of public recognition that academic professions attract less young people than other career paths' (Grüttner 2000, 575).

12.7 Scholarship: Changes after 1933

Scholars who wanted to be successful under the changed political circumstances had to prove their usefulness to the 'people's community'. They had, in general, two options: as an ideologist or as an expert. During the first years of the Nazi regime the ideological permeation of scholarship took priority. In all disciplines Nazi academics established groups with the objective of building the new National Socialist scholarship. This development did not only apply to the humanities but also reached far into the natural sciences. In particular, 'German Physics', a group of Nazi physicists headed by the Nobel laureates Johannes Stark and Philipp Lenard, earned short-term fame (Beyerchen 1977).

In the following years academics were still considered to be mainly producers of ideology, yet this tendency lost its impact from 1936 onwards. In the context of the autarky policy and the research on armament, the expertise of scientists became more and more important instead.

It soon became evident that groups such as 'German Physics' met with little resonance among scholars. However, most natural scientists and technicians had no problem in contributing as experts to the Four Year Plan and its autarky research and to projects of the armaments research. Even before 1933, it was unquestioned that scholarship among other tasks had to serve the 'national interest'. Accordingly, even those scholars who were no Nazis were more than willing to support what was perceived as 'Germany's new rise' after 1933. This was due not only to a fundamental nationalistic attitude of many scholars; career interests also played a role: the wish to receive more funding or more staff for their own research projects and to increase the reputation of scholarship. Later, during the war, there was also the expectation of being exempted from military service due to research projects being 'essential to the war effort'.

Whereas technical and natural scientific disciplines were funded by the Nazi regime with large sums of money, the humanities stagnated or even shrank both at universities (Grüttner 2000) and within the Kaiser-Wilhelm Society (Hachtmann 2007). In 1940, the National Socialist pedagogue Ernst Krieck expressed the widespread belief 'that the humanities will perish' (Grüttner 2000, 579).

Adapting to the ideology of Nazi dictatorship was contradictory to the traditional guideline of separating scholarship and party politics. And still, the majority of university teachers of the arts faculties was leaning towards the Nazi regime in one way or another. We can distinguish between six different forms of adaptation:

1. Adaptation through suppressing. This mildest variation of adaptation included attitudes such as omitting sensitive topics, not mentioning names of emigrants and other non-persons, quoting Jewish colleagues rarely or not at all.
2. Politicization according to the sandwich principle. Adaptation was limited to some occasional political statements in prefaces, introductions, and conclusions that did not interfere with the content of the academic work.
3. Terminological adaption to the language of the regime by borrowing Nazi terms and including them in academic publications.
4. Adaptation outside the science and research system by joining the Nazi Party or writing newspaper articles while maintaining traditional methods and standards in academic publications at the same time. Such an attitude met the expectations of the regime and simultaneously followed the principle of separating scholarship and politics.
5. Adaptation as paradigm shift by adopting the Nazi racial ideology.
6. Actively supporting the aggressive politics of the regime. This included those parts of the research on the East (*Ostforschung*) and research on the West (*Westforschung*) that were geared to support the Nazi policy of expansion by providing scholarly input or aimed at justifying the war and discrediting the enemy. Humanities scholars also participated in the looting of libraries, museums, and archives in Nazi-occupied territories.

Substantial changes took place in medical research from 1933. Implementing eugenics or 'racial hygiene' (*Rassenhygiene*) as a new paradigm played an important role in this context. Eugenics was based on the assumption that 'natural selection', analysed by Charles Darwin for animals and plants, was overridden in civilized societies by modern medicine and social politics. Contrary to the principle of 'natural selection', eugenicists argued, people with 'inferior genetic traits' reproduced disproportionately. Eugenics as a new science saw its objective being to counter the anticipated degeneration of humankind. The Nazis adopted the basic principles of eugenics at an early stage and by 1933 had already established the statutory basis for forced sterilizations of people with 'genetic illnesses'. Many medical university professors were very enthusiastic about the possibility of improving the genetic pool of the German people by these means. From 1934, eugenic sterilizations and abortions became daily routine in several university hospitals. At the same time, investigating the heritability of certain illnesses evolved into a focus of medical research during the Third Reich. Other research priorities, such as cancer research, did not have a direct connection to Nazi ideology. During the war, many university professors worked for the Wehrmacht as advisory physicians (Eckart 2011).

After implementing the dictatorship in spring 1933, jurisprudence was needed to reinterpret the existing legal system according to Nazi ideology (Grimm 1985). Several bills were issued in 1933 to abolish parliamentary democracy, to establish the dictatorship, and to deprive the Jewish minority of their rights. However, key codifications such as the German Civil and Criminal Code (*Bürgerliches Gesetzbuch, Strafgesetzbuch*) remained in effect, apart from some minor amendments. A fundamental rewriting of these bodies of laws was planned but attempts to establish a Nazi 'People's law code' came to nothing. Jurists closely aligned with the regime thus faced the task of adapting the existing body of laws to the requirements of the regime by reinterpreting them according to National Socialism (Rüthers 1968). The 'Kiel School' proved to be particularly keen in this respect – a group of young scholars who dominated the faculty of law at the university of Kiel since 1933–1934, after the majority of law professors had been dismissed. Other jurists remained more cautious about the political requests of the regime, as the Reich Security Head Office of the SS criticized in 1939: 'Experts rate the situation of the German jurisprudence as very serious … The professorate currently teaching comprises a disproportionate number of older scholars. Many are politically biased and trapped in liberalistic thoughts so that they are not likely to contribute to a renewal of the law' (Boberach 1984, vol. 2, 127).

In theology, it was mainly the Protestants who responded with great enthusiasm to the Nazi seizure of power. As early as 1933, numerous Protestant theologians joined the NSDAP or the 'German Christians' (*Deutsche Christen*, DC) who strove for a synthesis of National Socialism and Christianity. Catholic theologians, on the other hand, were less enthusiastic. Members of the Nazi Party were the exception among the teaching body of the Catholic theologian faculties. Both Protestants and Catholics faced a new situation when opponents of Christianity gained the upper hand in leading Nazi circles. In 1938, relevant state and party offices agreed in general on gradually abolishing theological faculties (Wolgast 1993). Even before the start of the war, four Catholic theologian faculties (in Munich, Innsbruck, Salzburg, and Graz) were closed. The war prevented this policy from being continued. Now, the Nazis wanted to avoid everything possible that jeopardized the loyalty of the Christian population. However, it was decided in 1940 to not fill vacant chairs in order to facilitate the liquidation of the theologian faculties after the war. Most of these departments did indeed remain in place, but were gradually phased out during the war. The number of students shrank even more quickly than the size of the teaching body. Many faculties had more lecturers than students in the final stage of the Third Reich (Grüttner 1995, 130).

12.8   Scholarship and Nazi Crimes

Scholars contributed to Nazi crimes in different ways. Some scientists, in particular physicians, exploited the situation of the concentration camp inmates being deprived of their human rights and used them as guinea pigs for scientific experiments on humans, in some cases in the full knowledge that the person tested would not survive (Eckart 2011). Such lethal experiments on humans were conducted in almost all the larger concentration camps. Most of them had military objectives and were ordered by the SS and certain units of the Wehrmacht. Sometimes scientists themselves took the initiative, for instance the hygienist Wolfgang Rose, who in 1943 requested permission from the SS to test a new vaccination against typhus in the Buchenwald concentration camp.

Much about these experiments was revealed in the Nuremberg Doctors' Trial in 1946–1947. However, the knowledge about these experiments has been externalized by labelling the involved scholars as 'pseudo-scientists'. Proper scholars, so it seemed, were not at all capable of committing crimes. If they did so, it must have been 'pseudo-science'. These exculpatory attempts effectively concealed the fact that most of these 'pseudo-scientists' held common academic qualifications such as doctorates and habilitations. The scholars who conducted those experiments differed from others not in terms of their academic qualification but because they were willing to ignore moral rules which until then had set boundaries for medical research. Crossing these boundaries was the consequence of an ideology making conceivable the extermination of human beings who were regarded as 'inferior' if this might benefit the *Volksgemeinschaft*. Scientific motives also played a role in this. Or, to put it another way, experiments on humans were conducted not least because in so doing some research questions – for instance, the potency of certain drugs – could be tested in the most effective and efficient manner whereas animal test results can never be completely transferable to humans. In this manner, scientific ambitions and Nazi extermination policy formed a symbiosis that resulted in some of the most atrocious episodes in the history of German science.

The best known example of scholarly research in the context of the Nazi extermination policy is the 'Master Plan East' (*Generalplan Ost*) drafted under the leadership of the agronomist SS-Oberführer Konrad Meyer and on behalf of Heinrich Himmler – some kind of 'master plan of the criminal *Volkstum* policy of the SS in Eastern Europe' (Heinemann 2006, 63). This was, in effect, the attempt to realize Hitler's demands for a ruthless Germanization of new 'living space' (*Lebensraum*) in the East by scholarly means. According to this plan, almost five million Germans were to be resettled in western parts of the Soviet Union within 25 years. The local Slav and Jewish population was to be expelled, enslaved, or killed. Due to the rapidly changing war situation, the *Generalplan Ost* could only partially be realized.

The involvement of psychiatrists and physicians in planning and executing the Nazi "euthanasia" programme is well known. The decision in favour of pursuing such a policy was made by the political leadership of the Nazi state. During the planning stage, several physicians were included in the preparations, among them the professors Werner Heyde (Würzburg), Max de Crinis (Berlin), Carl Schneider

(Heidelberg), and Berthold Kihn (Jena), all of them full professors of psychiatry at various German universities. During the following years they acted as reviewers and experts in context of the "euthanasia" killing operation (like other full professors from Bonn, Kiel, Königsberg, Wroclaw) and decided on the life and death of tens of thousands of psychiatric patients (Schmuhl 1992, 191–192).

Scientists as experts and reviewers were also involved in Nazi extermination policies towards Jews and Romani people and decided indirectly on life and death (although they were not always aware of that). The workforce capacity of the anthropological institutes was to a large extent employed to compile certificates of descent in order to assess the 'racial origin' of persons with 'dubious Aryan ancestry'. These certificates were usually issued by request of the Reich Office of Genealogy (*Reichssippenamt*) and were often close to 'charlatanism' (Müller-Hill 1998), in particular when only photographs of the fathers were used to decide on the descent of a person. Certificates from after 1941/1942 that categorized the assessed person as Jewish equalled the death penalty. The Research Institute for Eugenics and Population Biology at the Reich Health Office (*Rassenhygienische und bevölkerungsbiologische Forschungsstelle im Reichsgesundheitsamt*), founded in 1936 and headed by the psychiatrist Robert Ritter, played an important role in persecuting and deporting Romani people (Zimmermann 1996). Ritter's research institute was eager to give advice to the criminal police and other state and party authorities which were responsible for 'gypsy problems'. The institution classified more than 23 000 Romani people as 'full gypsies', 'gypsies of mixed ancestry', and 'non-gypsies'. The decision as to who was to be deported to Auschwitz was mainly based on these classifications.

References

Beyerchen, Alan D. 1977. *Scientists under Hitler: Politics and the Physics Community in the Third Reich*. New Haven, CT: Yale University Press.

Boberach, Heinz, ed. 1984. *Meldungen aus dem Reich: Die geheimen Lageberichte des Sicherheitsdienstes der SS 1938–1945*. 17 vols. Herrsching: Pawlak.

Bruch, Rüdiger vom et al., eds. 2014. *Wissenschaftsakademien im Zeitalter der Ideologien: Politische Umbrüche – wissenschaftliche Herausforderungen – institutionelle Anpassungen*. Stuttgart: Wissenschaftliche Verlagsgesellschaft.

Deichmann, Ute. 1996. *Biologists Under Hitler*. Cambridge, MA: Harvard University Press.

Deichmann, Ute. 2001. *Flüchten, Mitmachen, Vergessen: Chemiker und Biochemiker in der NS-Zeit*. Weinheim: Wiley-VCH.

Dinçkal, Noyan, Dipper, Christof, and Mares, Detlev, eds. 2010. *Selbstmobilisierung der Wissenschaft: Technische Hochschulen im 'Dritten Reich'*. Darmstadt: Wissenschaftliche Buchgesellschaft.

Eckart, Wolfgang U. 2011. 'Medizinische Forschung.' In *Medizin und Nationalsozialismus: Bilanz und Perspektiven der Forschung*, by Robert Jütte et al., 106–178. Göttingen: Wallstein.

Fischer, Klaus. 1991. 'Die Emigration von Wissenschaftlern nach 1933.' *Vierteljahrshefte für Zeitgeschichte* 39, 535–549.

Flachowsky, Sören. 2008. *Von der Notgemeinschaft zum Reichsforschungsrat: Wissenschaftspolitik im Kontext von Autarkie, Aufrüstung und Krieg*. Stuttgart: Steiner.

Flachowsky, Sören. 2015. 'Das Reichsamt für Wirtschaftsausbau als Forschungsbehörde im NS-System: Überlegungen zur neuen Staatlichkeit des Nationalsozialismus.' *Technikgeschichte* 82, 185–224. doi: 10.5771/0040-117X-2015-3-185.

Grimm, Dieter. 1985. 'Die "Neue Rechtswissenschaft": Über Funktion und Formation nationalsozialistischer Jurisprudenz.' In *Wissenschaft im Dritten Reich*, edited by Peter Lundgreen, 31–54. Frankfurt am Main: Suhrkamp.

Grolle, Joist. 1989. *Der Hamburger Percy Ernst Schramm – ein Historiker auf der Suche nach Wirklichkeit.* Hamburg: Verein für Hamburgische Geschichte.

Grüttner, Michael. 1995. *Studenten im Dritten Reich.* Paderborn: Schöningh.

Grüttner, Michael. 2000. 'Wissenschaftspolitik im Nationalsozialismus.' In *Geschichte der Kaiser-Wilhelm-Gesellschaft im Nationalsozialismus*, edited by Doris Kaufmann, vol. 2, 557–585. Göttingen: Wallstein.

Grüttner, Michael. 2005. 'German Universities under the Swastika.' In *Universities Under Dictatorship*, edited by John Connelly and Michael Grüttner, 75–111. University Park, PA: Pennsylvania State University Press.

Grüttner, Michael. 2009. 'Universität und Wissenschaft in der nationalsozialistischen Diktatur.' In *Philosophie im Nationalsozialismus*, edited by Hans-Jörg Sandkühler, 31–55. Hamburg: Meiner.

Grüttner, Michael et al. 2012. *Die Berliner Universität zwischen den Weltkriegen 1918–1945.* Geschichte der Universität Unter den Linden, vol. 2. Berlin: Akademie.

Grüttner, Michael and Kinas, Sven. 2007. 'Die Vertreibung von Wissenschaftlern aus den deutschen Universitäten 1933–1945.' *Vierteljahrshefte für Zeitgeschichte* 55, 123–186. doi: 10.1524/vfzg.2007.55.1.123.

Hachtmann, Rüdiger. 2007. *Wissenschaftsmanagement im 'Dritten Reich': Geschichte der Generalverwaltung der Kaiser-Wilhelm-Gesellschaft.* 2 vols. Göttingen: Wallstein.

Hartshorne, Edward Yarnall. 1937. *The German Universities and National Socialism.* Cambridge, MA: Harvard University Press.

Heiber, Helmut. 1992. *Universität unterm Hakenkreuz, Part II: Die Kapitulation der Hohen Schulen.* Vol. 1. Munich: Saur.

Heim, Susanne, Sachse, Carola, and Walker, Mark. 2009. *The Kaiser Wilhelm Society under National Socialism.* Cambridge: Cambridge University Press.

Heinemann, Isabel. 2006. 'Wissenschaft und Homogenisierungsplanungen für Osteuropa: Konrad Meyer, der "Generalplan Ost" und die Deutsche Forschungsgemeinschaft.' In *Wissenschaft – Planung – Vertreibung: Neuordnungskonzepte und Umsiedlungspolitik im 20. Jahrhundert*, edited by Isabel Heinemann and Patrick Wagner, 45–72. Stuttgart: Steiner.

Höpfner, Hans-Paul. 1999. *Die Universität Bonn im Dritten Reich.* Bonn: Bouvier.

Huber, Andreas. 2015. 'Die Hochschullehrerschaft der 1930er und 1940er Jahre: Sozialstruktur und Karrierewege vor dem Hintergrund politischer Zäsuren.' In *Universität – Politik – Gesellschaft*, edited by Mitchell G. Ash and Josef Ehmer, 649–696. Göttingen: Vienna University Press and Vandenhoeck & Ruprecht.

Kunkel, Wolfgang. 1966. 'Der Professor im Dritten Reich.' In *Die deutsche Universität im Dritten Reich: Eine Vortragsreihe der Universität München*, 103–133. Munich: Piper.

Möller, Horst. 1984. *Exodus der Kultur: Schriftsteller, Wissenschaftler und Künstler in der Emigration nach 1933.* Munich: C.H. Beck.

Müller-Hill, Benno. 1998. *Murderous Science: Elimination by Scientific Selection of Jews, Gypsies, and Others in Germany 1933–1945.* New York: Cold Spring Harbor Laboratory Press.

Nagel, Anne C. 2008. '"Er ist der Schrecken überhaupt der Hochschule": Der Nationalsozialistische Deutsche Dozentenbund in der Wissenschaftspolitik des Dritten Reiches.' In *Universitäten und Studenten im Dritten Reich*, edited by Joachim Scholtyseck and Christoph Studt, 115–132. Berlin: LIT.

Nagel, Anne C. 2012. *Hitlers Bildungsreformer: Das Reichsministerium für Wissenschaft, Erziehung und Volksbildung 1934–1945*. Frankfurt am Main: Fischer.

Reitzenstein, Julien. 2014. *Himmlers Forscher: Wehrwissenschaft und Medizinverbrechen im 'Ahnenerbe' der SS*. Paderborn: Schöningh.

Rhodes, Richard. 1986. *The Making of the Atomic Bomb*. New York: Simon & Schuster.

Rürup, Reinhard. 2008. *Schicksale und Karrieren: Gedenkbuch für die von den Nationalsozialisten aus der Kaiser-Wilhelm-Gesellschaft vertriebenen Forscherinnen und Forscher*. Göttingen: Wallstein.

Rüthers, Bernd. 1968. *Die unbegrenzte Auslegung. Zum Wandel der Privatrechtsordnung im Nationalsozialismus*. Tübingen: Mohr.

Schieder, Wolfgang and Trunk, Achim, eds. 2004. *Adolf Butenandt und die Kaiser-Wilhelm-Gesellschaft: Wissenschaft, Industrie und Politik im 'Dritten Reich'*. Göttingen: Wallstein.

Schmuhl, Hans-Walter. 1992. *Rassenhygiene, Nationalsozialismus, Euthanasie: Von der Verhütung zur Vernichtung 'lebensunwerten Lebens' 1890–1945*, 2nd edn. Göttingen: Vandenhoeck & Ruprecht.

Strathmann, Hermann D. 1940. 'Welch eine Wendung durch Gottes Führung!' *Theologische Blätter* 19, 172.

Trischler, Helmuth. 1992. *Luft- und Raumfahrtforschung in Deutschland 1900–1970*. Frankfurt am Main and New York: Campus.

Walker, Mark et al., eds. 2013. *The German Research Foundation 1920–1970: Funding Poised between Science and Politics*. Stuttgart: Steiner.

Wolgast, Eike. 1993. 'Nationalsozialistische Hochschulpolitik und die theologischen Fakultäten.' In *Theologische Fakultäten im Nationalsozialismus*, edited by Leonore Siegele-Wenschkewitz and Carsten Nicolaisen, 45–79. Göttingen: Vandenhoeck & Ruprecht.

Zimmermann, Michael. 1996. *Rassenutopie und Genozid: Die nationalsozialistische 'Lösung der Zigeunerfrage'*. Hamburg: Christians.

Further Reading

Beyerchen, Alan D. 1977. *Scientists under Hitler: Politics and the Physics Community in the Third Reich*. New Haven, CT: Yale University Press.
Seminal and often quoted ground-breaking study.
Deichmann, Ute. 1996. *Biologists Under Hitler*. Cambridge, MA: Harvard University Press.
Complex study on the history of a single academic discipline.
Grüttner, Michael. 2005. 'German Universities under the Swastika.' In *Universities Under Dictatorship*, edited by John Connelly and Michael Grüttner, 75–111. University Park, PA: Pennsylvania State University Press.
A general overview on university changes after 1933.
Heim, Susanne, Sachse, Carola, and Walker, Mark, eds. 2009. *The Kaiser Wilhelm Society under National Socialism*. Cambridge: Cambridge University Press.
Provides a good overview on the history of the most important German research institutions beside the universities.
Neufeld, Michael J. 1995. *The Rocket and the Reich: Peenemünde and the Coming of the Ballistic Missile Era*. New York: Free Press.
Evaluating Nazi Germany's most innovative and consequential military research project.
Remy, Steven P. 2002. *The Heidelberg Myth: The Nazification and Denazification of a German University*. Cambridge, MA: Harvard University Press.
A case study on the Nazification of a university which throughout the Weimar Republic was considered as being relatively liberal.

Walker, Mark. 1989. *German National Socialism and the Quest for Nuclear Power, 1939–49*.
  Cambridge: Cambridge University Press.
Explains why the Nazis were not capable of constructing the atomic bomb.
Walker, Mark et al., eds. 2013. *The German Research Foundation 1920–1970: Funding
  Poised between Science and Politics*. Stuttgart: Steiner.
Provides a detailed history of the most important German institution for funding scholarly
research.

CHAPTER THIRTEEN

Nazi Morality

THOMAS KÜHNE

'Good and ill have not changed since yesteryear, nor are they one thing among Elves and another among Men,' says Aragorn in J.R.R. Tolkien's *The Lord of the Rings* (1965, 33) when asked by Eomar how one 'shall judge what to do' in a world that 'is all grown strange'. Aragorn articulates a popular illusion – that morality, the collection of ideas about good and evil, is independent of time and space and the same for all humans and societies. Based on assumptions like this, historians have often judged the Nazi crimes against humanity as the ultimate collapse of morality. The Holocaust was the culmination of an effort to 'delegitimize the ethical motivations of social action' and to neutralize 'the impact of primeval moral drives', stated Zygmunt Bauman (1989, 178, 188). Similarly, Hans Mommsen (2002, 22) called attention to the Nazis' 'loss of any moral ties'. Assessments like these reflect a long tradition of demonizing the Nazis. Put on trial, Nazi perpetrators appeared as 'animal-like sadists' (Cramer 2011, 92) and 'monsters', 'devils', or as 'beasts' who by definition lack any kind of human morality (Pendas 2006, 263). Such demonizing of the Nazis allowed post-war societies to distance themselves from what had happened as if they 'had not been responsible for it' (Walser 1965, 189).

13.1 Historicizing Morality

The demonization of the Nazis has been criticized for a long time, starting with Hannah Arendt's formula about the 'banality of evil' (1965) and Stanley Milgram's experiment on obedience and conformity (1963), both of which pointed to the 'ordinariness', and 'normalcy' of the Nazi mindset. Its *moral* fabric, however, was still assessed in a Manichaean way in the 1980s – as if the Nazis simply had

A Companion to Nazi Germany, First Edition. Edited by Shelley Baranowski, Armin Nolzen, and Claus-Christian W. Szejnmann.

abandoned or perverted morality altogether, whether serving as anonymous bureaucrats or acting as mere subjects of obedience and conformity. Only recently have scholars acknowledged that the Nazi crimes arose from a morality of their own, building upon what Émile Durkheim suggested as early as 1900. Instead of conceiving morality as given by God or rooted in eternal natural laws, morality must be analysed as a 'social fact'; that is, subject to human agency (Powell 2012, 43; Durkheim 1982). In this fashion, Peter Haas (1988, 2–3) argued that the Nazis did not expose 'the banality of evil but the human ability to redefine evil ….' Nazi society had a strict, almost puritanical code of moral standards', and it was this 'system of values that drove the Holocaust'. As Claudia Koonz (2003) explained, the Nazi 'ethnic conscience' demanded that charity, kindness, and pity be restricted to the Aryan community, the *Volk*, repudiating Judaeo-Christian traditions of mercy towards the weak and the Enlightenment principles of universalism, individualism, and egalitarianism. Other scholars have illuminated the social Darwinist, eugenicist, and racist roots and elements of the Nazis' 'evolutionary ethics' (Weikart 2009; Bialas 2014a, 2014b; Gross 2010).

Expanding on these studies, I shall first examine four basic features of the Nazi morality: racism, honour, hardness, and community. While this morality indeed abandoned universal morals and thus may be addressed as 'particularistic' (Tugendhat 2001), it was by no means original but built upon amorphous moral discourses that had emerged in Western societies, including Germany, since the nineteenth century. Nazi morality was a hybrid, I argue. Second, this chapter explores the social relevance and subjective appropriation of the Nazi morality. While it could translate directly into genocidal action, the tension between traditional, especially (Judaeo-) Christian and Enlightenment moral standards and the new Nazi morality must be accounted for when it comes to explain the social dynamics of Nazi violence.

13.2   Building the Nazi Morality

Nazi morality aimed to undo the Judaeo-Christian and Enlightenment idea of universalistic ethics. To be sure, these traditions, including the post-1945 human rights movement, have never been as universalistic as they claimed to be. Often, they demand assimilation and adaptation, although covertly; they adhere to European ideas about the self, scientific truth, liberal democracy, and Western civilization. Its universality is limited to those who subscribe to its rules and values (Todorov 1993; Mutua 2002). But moral universalism at least claims to apply to all human beings. The Christian call for pity for the suffering other endorses a limitless concept of humanity.

By contrast, Nazi particularism limited subjects and objects of moral acts rigidly to one group, the *Volk* or *Volksgemeinschaft* ('people's community') – and not to any *Volk* or *Volksgemeinschaft* but only to the racially purified and ideologically united, Nazified Aryan *Volksgemeinschaft*. 'Our ethics,' declared Heinrich Himmler in a secret speech in January 1939, 'comply solely with the needs of our people. Good is what is useful for the people, evil is what damages our people' (Ackermann 1970, 141). Himmler's infamous Posen speech to SS generals in October 1943 presented the Nazi morality in a nutshell. Ideas such as those of Herder who had embraced a plurality of nations based on mutual respect (and envisioned a Europe led by Slavic nations instead of Central or West Europeans) could only be mocked, in Himmler's view:

> It is basically wrong for us to project our whole harmless soul and heart, all our good nature, our idealism, onto foreign peoples. ... The SS man follows only one principle: we must be honest, decent, loyal, and comradely to members of our own blood, and to no one else. ... It is a sin against our own blood to worry about them and give them ideals, so that our sons and grandchildren will have a harder time with them. (Internationaler Militärgerichtshof 1948, 122–123)

13.2.1 Race and the Laws of Nature

The ideological background to this rigid dichotomy had been expounded in scientific and pseudo-scientific treatments since the nineteenth century and popularized by Hitler's *Mein Kampf* and Nazi propaganda. One of its core pieces was deadly antisemitism – the phantasm of a grand Jewish plan to destroy the superior biological substance of the German people. The other core idea was social Darwinism, the idea that all peoples and races are irreconcilably different and engaged in a life-and-death struggle. Only the fittest would survive, and fitness was tied to racial purity. Racial purity equalled moral goodness. Racial mixing, on the other hand, signified evil, degeneration, and (in the long run) extinction. The conception of history as a fateful and perpetual biologically determined struggle for racial dominance left no choice other than to dominate or perish. In Christian theology, defying divine providence was evil, while for Nazism disdain for the racial law of nature was evil. Nazism defined moral goodness as reversing the process of degeneration by implementing race-breeding eugenics, which included sterilization or euthanasia of those who carried sick genes, prohibited further interbreeding, and guaranteed purification of the Aryan race (Weikart 2009, 17–84; 2004).

Aggressive negative eugenics, euthanasia, and genocide, the destruction of all those whose 'blood' was considered hereditarily sick, evil, or both was morally good as it obeyed the eternal laws of nature. Pity, empathy, or mercy towards them was morally bad, the Nazis declared, echoing the eugenicist consensus of many doctors in inter-war Europe and America. In Nazi medical ethics, the health of the people – the German *Volk* – came first, and the health of individuals second, and only those individuals who belonged to the *Volk* were to be cured. The Nazi doctor who, like Josef Mengele, experimented with, and tortured, peoples of 'inferior races', was not just absolved from guilt but actually did good (Lifton 1986; Bialas 2014a, 199–232). The same ethics applied to the persecution of the Jews. Nazi propaganda, policies, and legislation had spread its essence since 1933, denouncing 'false humanity' and 'exaggerated pity' as a crime against the German *Volk* (Fritzsche 2008, 93). The so-called Criminal Orders that the regime issued to the Wehrmacht on the eve of Operation Barbarossa translated this morality into a maxim of warfare by offering amnesty in advance to German soldiers who mistreated, abused, or killed enemy civilians or prisoners of war in the East. Any soldier who did so did good, not evil (Megargee 2006, 19–41; Mineau 2004).

13.2.2   The Code of Honour

Taking up the Western colonial discourse on miscegenation, the Nazis branded violations of the laws against interracial sexual relations as *Rassenschande*. In English, the term is often understood as 'racial defilement' in order to address the suggestion of poisoning or staining that was implied. Literally, however, the term translates as 'racial shame' or racial 'disgrace'. The language of honour at work here – shame or disgrace as the antonyms of honour – was important. German women who were found guilty of having sexual relations with Jewish men or, during the war, with foreign enforced labourers, often had their heads shaved and were paraded through the streets or displayed in their home town's marketplace carrying a placard that said 'I have dishonoured German women', or 'I have been a dishonourable German woman', or 'I have myself excluded [*sic*] from the *Volksgemeinschaft*' (Gellately 1990, 236–238; Przyrembel 2003). They were not simply locked up; first, they were publicly humiliated – that is, symbolically ousted – and only then physically excluded from the community. In a culture of honour, the gazing and controlling eye of the community sets itself up as the highest moral authority and threatens the deviating individual with public shame, exposure, disgrace, and exclusion. Honour is the key word in a moral system that devalues the self and its moral dialogue with God or the Super-Ego as the highest authority and assigns this role to the community or the society, in the way Ruth Benedict in her book (1948) juxtaposed Japanese shame culture and Western guilt culture. A society that 'relies on men's developing a conscience is a guilt culture by definition', Benedict said. The question of morals is here a case for introspection. Guilt is experienced individually. Shame, by contrast, is grounded in the fear of exclusion, exposure, and disgrace, which the community allots to the individual who does not submit to its rules. Shame culture trains one to be inconspicuous, to conform, to join in (Benedict 1948, 222–224).

However, unlike Benedict's assumption, both guilt and shame, or conscience and honour, work in most societies simultaneously, although in varying proportions. Initially an aristocratic concept, honour was, in a way, democratized in modern societies and appropriated by other groups (Bowman 2006). It remained a concept to secure social distinction, to defend against inferiors the privileged identity of an exclusive social group (Simmel 1992, 598–605). Honour is successful in doing so by dictating a set of norms for those who want to belong. Whereas the modern concept of human dignity pertains to the self regardless of his or her social identity and thus promotes the idea 'of inalienable human rights', in a world of honour, 'the individual discovers his true identity in his roles'. In fact, the individual '*is* the social symbols emblazoned on his escutcheon (Berger 1974, 89–91). In this way, the SS motto equalled honour and loyalty: 'My Honour Is Loyalty'. Loyalty to the Führer, to the dictate of racial purity, to the Nazi ideology informed a morality that, together with values such as duty and obedience, relieved the individual of personal responsibility and protected the uniformed community from the contingency of personal choices (Staub 1989, 145–149; Gross 2010, 71–75).

The code of honour demands force against those who challenge or wrong the group. By taking revenge, the honourable group reassures itself of its identity.

In 1914, the German emperor went to war in order to secure the honour of the German nation, and in the same fashion Hitler understood his war as an obligatory response to the disgrace of Germany in 1918/1919 (Scheff 1994, 75–124; Offer 1995). During the Wehrmacht's war of annihilation, the resistance of allegedly inferior, subjugated peoples, especially of partisans and hidden fighters, defied the honour of their superiors. 'Soldiers on the Eastern front are not only fighters according to the rules of war, they are also the bearers of an inexorable folk concept and the avengers of all the bestialities inflicted on the German nation and its kindred peoples. So soldiers must show understanding for the necessity of tough but just atonement to be extracted from the sub-human Jewish race,' declared Field Marshall von Reichenau on 12 October 1941. The code of honour required that communal force be exerted against the entire collective of wrong-doers, not just individuals. The entire village of a partisan was to be destroyed, not just the partisan; or the entire Jewish 'race', not only individual Jews (Kühne 2010, 98–114, 109).

Which community honour nourishes is historically contingent. In premodern times it was the nobility; in the nineteenth century the educated middle class tied its status to the exclusive right of duelling. Gendered notions of honour obliged men to exhibit manliness and women to observe chastity, as illuminated in Theodor Fontane's novel *Effi Briest* of 1896 (Fontane 2001; Frevert 1995, 169–187). The Nazi concept of honour, by contrast, aimed at racial exclusiveness and racial consciousness, not at gender or class distinctions. In Nazi Germany, adultery did not question a man's or a woman's honour as long as the adulterer was Aryan. If they were not, both women and men lost their honour. No one-way road led from the German nineteenth-century honour cult of duelling to the Nazis' particularistic morality. Yet Norbert Elias (1996, 44–119) was right when he examined the fascination with honour and its violent exertion on the German educated middle class as one of the roots of the Nazi mindset. Honour informs particularistic, unequal, and certainly anti-universal moral thinking. In a world of honour, 'good' is what is good for a rigidly exclusive and clearly defined community; 'bad' is what questions it.

13.2.3   The Ethic of Hardness

Military thinking had always suggested Manichaean divisions of the world into friends and foes and thus justified the killing of the latter. But only the belligerent discourse and the 'conduct code of the cool persona' (Lethen 2002, 33) that emerged in Germany from industrialized killing and anonymous death in the First World War laid the groundwork for a morality of mercilessness. Former Stormtrooper Ernst Jünger (1928, 140; 1922, 32, 74) still admitted to his 'guilt' feelings when looking at the corpses after battle, but only to boast about having 'overcome' such qualms to enjoying killing in war. Emotional 'steeling' – that is, immunizing oneself against the Christian morals of guilt and pity – allowed for a belligerent ethic that adored male hardness; it was not the fear of being killed that needed to be overcome, but the moral restraints against doing the killing.

The Nazis went a decisive step further. They demanded the complete absence of pity for their war against civilians and fellow citizens. Dachau camp commander Theodor Eicke's SS (*Schutzstaffel*) training manual demanded that guards should learn to treat prisoners as brutally as possible, although with discipline and control. 'Tolerance means weakness. This means, whenever the interests of the Fatherland are at stake, only ruthless measures are appropriate' (Orth 2000, 130; Dillon 2015). The 'morals of ruthlessness' (Kolnai 1938, 290) did not include giving carte blanche to sadists. He who murdered out of 'hate, blindness, or ambition' gave free rein to his personal pathology. The SS did not appreciate such selfishness when only the community counted (Grimm 1938, 29, 35, 37). 'We as the master race [*Herrenvolk*],' said Himmler in 1938, 'must be hard without being cruel. The master race must be able to eliminate people who harm the community unhampered by Christian mercifulness but it also must remain decent and never torture anyone' (Himmler 1974, 32). Consequently, in his Posen speech, he praised the SS for 'enduring' the murder of the Jews and yet, except for a few cases of 'human weakness', remaining 'decent' and becoming 'hard', thus embodying the SS concept of 'honour' (Internationaler Militärgerichtshof 1948, 145). One of those few cases was SS officer Max Täubner, whom the SS expelled in spring 1943 for displaying blatant cruelty during anti-Jewish 'actions' (Büchler 2003). The sadistic murderer showed the same type of 'human weakness' as a member of the 'master race' who surrendered to pity for racially inferior people. They had failed to sacrifice themselves to the community. The self, a core piece of modern Western ethics, was – next to the racial enemy – the second adversary of the 'we' of the Aryan *Volk*, according to Nazi ethics. The greedy and corrupt egoistic self could count on no more mercy than the Jews. He was 'fated to die', Himmler said in Posen (Internationaler Militärgerichtshof 1948, 146).

13.2.4   *The Dictatorship of the Community*

Nazi morality appreciated individuality, or 'personality', only as an engine of the community, embodied by the charismatic leader who mobilized and united a group of people (Lutz 1936; Bialas 2014a, 56–59). Individuals were valued only in so far as they sacrificed themselves for the *Volk* and for the preservation of their race. As Hitler stated in *Mein Kampf*, 'egotism' was an expression of a 'primitive' state of human development, most visibly represented by the Jews (Hitler 1934, vol. 1, 291–295).

To be sure, most societies grant a certain priority to collective over individual interests. But as the Hungarian-Austrian émigré Aurel Kolnai said in his 1938 account of the ideological fabric of the Third Reich, the difference between the Nazis' communal morality and the Western standard was not simply one 'in the degree of importance attached to community'. It was the 'disagreement on the very nature of community'. Western moral thinking pretends that 'true community can be based only on personality, which is the irreducible core of human existence'. Since the late nineteenth century, however, nationalist thinking, radicalized by the Nazis, understood the *Volk* as a primordial, organic, and naturally grown, if not biologically determined, entity (Mosse 1964). The community – the *Volk* – had its 'own needs and interests justified in themselves, which are emphatically prior to the moral importance of the actual claims not only of any single individual but of the many – e.g. the "majority" as well,' argued Kolnai (1938, 64–66).

The Third Reich essentially redefined morality as the dissolution of the self for the sake of the community and launched an obsessive search for its egoistic enemies. In the Nazi view, the *Volk* was threatened not only by 'racial aliens' such as Jews or Slavs but also by 'community aliens' (*Gemeinschaftsfremde*) such as homosexuals, whores, alcoholics, tramps, beggars, and many others. Nazi propagandists, jurists, doctors, and pedagogues never tired of identifying all kinds of selfish 'community pests' such as the 'coward', the 'shirker', the 'grind', the 'trouble-maker', the 'griper', the 'peacock', the 'uncontrolled', the 'schemer', and the 'loner' (Kühne 2010, 41; Koonz 2003).

To rid Germans of 'egoism' and imbue them with the spirit of community, the Nazi state forced teenagers and adults into a sophisticated training programme. Comradeship was its core virtue. Take Sebastian Haffner's experience as an example. Raised in a liberal Berlin civil service family, he was the perfect subject for the Nazis' re-education programme. In the training camp that he had to join in 1933, everything had to be done together, day and night, with no space or time for the individual to retreat. 'If someone committed a sin against comradeship' by acting superior, showing off, or exhibiting 'more individuality than was permissible, a night-time court in the barracks would judge and condemn him to corporeal punishment'. Comradeship 'actively decomposed' both 'individuality and civilization', observed Haffner when analysing his comrades' ostentatious displays of rudeness, misogyny, profanity, rowdyism – in sum, contempt for civilian manners and morals. Haffner clearly saw, however, that the training in comradeship by decomposing one morality gave birth to another. Comradeship, he wrote, 'relieves men of responsibility for their own actions, before themselves, before God, before their conscience. They do what all their comrades do. … Their comrades are their conscience and give absolution for everything' (Haffner 2002, 257–291).

As was true for the other elements of the Nazi morality, the Nazis did not invent comradeship either. Mythically inflated by the collective memory of the Great War, comradeship merged Christian ideals of brotherly love and the belligerent dichotomy between 'us' and 'them'. In its Christian interpretation, comradeship in war re-enacted Saint John's Gospel 15:13: 'Greater love has no one than this: to lay down one's life for one's friends'. It epitomized the human face of the soldier amidst the inhumanity of war. As comrade, the soldier shared tenderness and empathy with his buddies and would give his own life for them. But this solidarity and altruism was rigidly limited to the in-group, the squad, the platoon, the army – the 'us', which came when defined against the Other – the egoist within the group, the racial enemy outside, or the adversary in battle. Thus, comradeship suited the Nazis' morality well because the profane myth of comradeship transcended the ideological and class divisions of civilian life. It embodied the ideal of a united *Volksgemeinschaft*, no longer burdened by ideological and economic conflicts, the 'egoisms' of a liberal society. In the Nazi version, comradeship replaced the strong emphasis of traditional comradeship on horizontal solidarity among peers through vertical loyalty to the Führer (Kühne 2006, 27–110).

13.3 Practising Moralities

Haffner wrote his reminiscence in 1939 when he was trying to adjust to his London exile – a few months before the Nazi war on Europe started. He had left Germany with his Jewish fiancée and was disgusted at his fellow citizens' acceptance of a culture of violence. Haffner argued that a 'germ' – the germ of comradeship – had infected the 'whole nation' and lured it into a 'despicable and inhuman' condition where 'the sense of responsibility for oneself' was gone. His sombre diagnosis anticipated what would come: the broad social support by major parts of the German people for the Nazi genocidal project. And yet Haffner's assessment exaggerated the unity of Nazi society and underestimated the diversity of ideological, emotional, and moral attitudes that would last until the regime broke down in 1945. The Nazi morality levelled the ground for the Holocaust and other crimes against humanity, but it did so in a more complex way than Haffner thought.

13.3.1 The No-Pity Standard

Doubtless, the Nazis' particularistic, racist, and communal morality facilitated the murderous choices of Nazi perpetrators at their desks, in the occupied territories, on the killing fields, and in the concentration, labour, and death camps. Nazi eliminationist antisemitism, in the way Daniel Goldhagen (1996) has described it, drove killers such as the German police officer who said, after the execution of 200 Jews in Memel in late June 1941, 'Good heavens, damn it, one generation has to go through this so that our children will have a better life' (Rüter and de Mildt 1976, 61). And this morality still informed ordinary German soldiers, who in American or British captivity justified the murder of the Jews as necessary and only regretted that their country had started it before the war was won (Neitzel and Welzer 2012).

These perpetrators and bystanders may have not have been immune to feeling pity for their victims but they knew had to suppress such sentiments. After joining an execution of Jews in the Lemberg area in the General Government in July 1941, SS officer Felix Landau noted in his diary that this left him 'completely unmoved. No pity, no nothing'. He had internalized the ethic of hardness almost perfectly and was proud of it. If there was still a little confusion, it was not because of the Jews but because of his having remembered a moment in his own life when he had almost been executed (Klee, Dressen, and Riess 1991, 96). Women too absorbed the no-pity standard, craving acceptance as fully fledged members of the *Volksgemeinschaft*. Encountering Jewish ghettos in occupied Poland in 1940, Melitta Maschmann, leader of the *Bund Deutscher Mädel* (League of German Girls, BDM), was shocked by the 'wretchedness of the children. … But I clenched my teeth' and switched off my '"private feelings" quickly and utterly'. At an early point in her engagement in the Warthegau, a peer had blasted her for displaying pity for the Poles, and so she had learned to 'suppress my private feelings if they conflicted with political necessity' – the conquest of *Lebensraum* in the East (Maschmann 1964, 65, 68, 70, 82, 106).

Landau and Maschmann are just two examples of Germans who adopted the no-pity standard of Nazi morality. Yet generalizing diagnoses, such as those of

Haffner or Goldhagen, are wrong. At no point did all Germans fall under the sole influence of Nazi morality. Even SS men like Felix Landau and female collaborators such as Melitta Maschmann adhered to elements of traditional morality as they absorbed the Nazi version. Landau's pride in sensing 'no pity' was soaked in cynicism and the ethics of obedience that switched off the moral agency he was once raised to accept. Before the execution near Lemberg started, he remarked, 'Fine, so I'll just play executioner and then gravedigger, why not? Isn't it strange, you love battle and then have to shoot defenseless people' (Klee, Dressen, and Riess 1991, 96).

13.3.2   Competing Moralities

Nazi leaders were aware of the persistence of liberal, conservative, and socialist ideologies and the moral diversity that pervaded society. Parts of this society may have adopted the Nazi morality, but only a few managed to shake off the old moralities altogether. Others refused to allow the no-pity standard to take them over and command their actions. Probably the majority of Germans oscillated between the two moralities. German soldiers, police officers, and SS men, male and female camp guards in the East and all over Europe, and not least Germans at home could switch from one morality to the other, but it was not possible (or only for a few people) to abandon the ethics of mercy and empathy altogether. Instead, it was this morality that haunted perpetrators and bystanders, if only in their nightmares. However, neither these nightmares nor the moral tensions sufficed to slow down, let alone halt, the Nazi machine of destruction. Instead, this machine gained momentum, even after 1943 when the collapse of the Third Reich loomed. Why?

The answer is twofold. On the one hand, a kind of job share, or functional differentiation, between people who observed and acted upon different moralities made sure that the diversity of mindsets did not undermine – but in fact enhanced – the cohesion of the genocidal society. On the other hand, the moral dilemma faced by Germans who could not decide which morality, the universal one or the particularistic one, they should honour, and in which situation, was eventually trumped by a mixture of apathy, cynicism, and fatalism that worked in the same direction: it powered the machine of destruction.

The infamous Police Battalion 101 embodies in a nutshell the moral diversity of Nazi society. When the unit was ordered to murder the Jews of Polish Jozefow in 1942, a minority eagerly agreed, while the commander allowed another minority to back out. The majority acted as ordered, though reluctantly and haunted by pangs of conscience. Other units acted similarly. The Nazi machine of annihilation was surprisingly tolerant towards men who shied away from murder – who, in other words, did not follow the Nazi morality (Browning 1992). They were given other jobs or simply allowed to stand by, or they were sent home. As long as they stayed with the group, and most of them did, they had to swallow being labelled 'weaklings' or 'kids'. They were placed at the bottom of an informal hierarchy that was led by those who demonstrated 'hardness'. The 'weaklings', however, did not claim to be 'too good' to kill, but 'too weak'. In other words, they did not question the morality of the genocidal community but instead interpreted their own constitution – their adherence to the morals of pity – as deviant. They presented themselves as exceptions to the rule of the genocide and thus confirmed the rule as such. This was the price they paid for remaining with their units. By reassuring the community, they avoided being ousted (Kühne 2010, 55–94).

The diversity of mindsets within the *Volksgemeinschaft* did not jeopardize the unity of its criminal actions. Dictatorships like the Third Reich do not integrate society by homogenizing it. The opposite was the case. 'Integration proceeds by maintaining difference, so that even those who are against the regime – critics of Nazis' Jewish policies or committed Social Democrats – have a social arena where they exchange their thoughts and find intellectual brethren. ... the mode of social integration ... was difference, not homogenization' (Neitzel and Welzer 2012, 29). The niches of discontent, however, supported integration in the way relief valves do in a pressure vessel; and also, as I have shown elsewhere (Kühne 2010), the genocidal *Volksgemeinschaft* became real by including even those in a silent majority who inwardly opposed it. Take Wilm Hosenfeld as an example. Hosenfeld was the Wehrmacht captain who in 1944 helped the Jewish pianist Władysław Szpilman to hide and survive in the ruins of Warsaw. The Nazis' annihilation pro-gramme about which Hosenfeld gathered solid intelligence appalled him, and thus he helped Jews and Poles from early on. He was shaken to the core by the 'horrible blood guilt', as he put it, that would now burden the entire German people, as well as by the passivity he noticed everywhere. 'What cowards we are ... that we let this all happen' (Hosenfeld 2004, 286, 302–304, 626–628, 641). He understood the mechanism that made bystanders complicit in evil. Bystanders had choices: they could intervene on behalf of the victims, or at least frown upon the perpetrators' actions and question the perpetrators' inhuman morality. By doing nothing, they demonstrated approval, even if they didn't mean it. And the perpetrators appreci-ated the bystanders' approval. They felt encouraged (Staub 1989, 87). Hosenfeld knew that his uniform – and even more so, his remaining on duty as a German soldier – made him complicit. He felt guilty – unimpressed by, yet caught up in, the Nazi morality in a grand community of crime.

13.3.3   The Community of Crime

Hosenfeld was not alone; he repeatedly met soldiers and officers who also were 'fraught with compassion and embarrassment', felt 'ashamed of being a German', and saw their 'honour as a German officer' disgraced (Hosenfeld 2004, 630, 635, 653). To them, the code of honour included, contrary to the Nazi morality, respect for international laws and age-old traditions such as *ius in bello* that prohibited the killing of civilians (Walzer 1977). Shame, as articulated by these soldiers, was no longer shame before their comrades or the German *Volksgemeinschaft*. It was shame before the watching world – shame generated by universalistic morality. But none of these dissenters felt able to revolt against the *Volksgemeinschaft*. Instead, they knew that by not revolting they had entangled themselves in a grand community of crime from which there was no escape because they would be held responsible for the nation's crimes. 'Although the dreams of ruling the world are gone', there was no reason to quit, a soldier wrote in a letter in June 1943, for 'it is true, we have to win the war if we don't want to put ourselves at the mercy of the Jews' (Buchbender and Sterz 1983, 117).

Erik H. Erikson has called Hitler a 'gang leader, who kept the boys together by demanding their admiration, by creating terror, and by shrewdly involving them in crimes from which there was no way back' (Erikson 1963, 337). The 'mafia principle' united the hard-core group of fanatical, eliminationist antisemites and included murderers, occasional doubters, more serious dissenters, and unwilling yet submissive collaborators. The Nazi morality drove the dynamic of violence not by overruling traditional morality but by engendering tensions between the two and pangs of conscience felt by those who had joined despite their feelings of guilt. Uniting people in a collective crime works best if people are aware that they are participating in the crime and thus separating themselves from the rest of the world. In March 1943, Goebbels agreed with Göring that 'on the Jewish question … we are so committed that there is no escape for us at all. And,' noted Goebbels in his diary, 'that is good. Experience shows that a movement and a *Volk* that have burned their bridges fight much more unconditionally than those who still have the chance of retreat' (Goebbels 1993, 454).

The fear of revenge of the Jews, the Slavs, and other enemies eventually expanded to the home front and united the racially purified *Volksgemeinschaft* in a community of fate (*Schicksalsgemeinschaft*) that had forfeited its moral choices. Some of its members were haunted by guilt and resorted to cynical fatalism, the abandonment of any morality. Others remained convinced of having done the right thing, just at the wrong time. To be sure, on the front lines and on the home front, remnants and reconstructions of altruism and solidarity that did not propel the dynamic of destruction ensured the physical survival of Germans, in some cases even of Jews and other 'racial aliens'. The help from German fellow citizens that allowed the German Jewish literature professor Victor Klemperer to survive the Holocaust is only the most prominent example. But these helpers were rare. More Germans tried to save some part of traditional morality by wearing a mask, the mask of conformity. But, more often than not, it was not the masked self but the mask that determined the choices the soldiers made and the actions they performed, whether they laughed at sexist jokes or terrorized enemy civilians. As one soldier said, 'It is as if you build a husk around your Self', and yet within that husk 'you are absorbed by the crowd around you; you are only a piece of a relentless entity that soaks you up and foists its shape on you. You become barbarous and numb. You are no longer yourself' (Mersmann 1995, 34).

13.4 Conclusion

The Nazi morality aimed at overthrowing the Judaeo-Christian, Western tradition of universal ethics that demand charity for all human beings, not only those of one's own race or nation. Nazi morality also carried on with core features of this moral tradition; it just limited virtues such as a pity, solidarity, empathy rigidly to the acknowledged members of the racially and ideologically purified *Volksgemeinschaft*. At the same time, it demanded the subjugation of the self on behalf of the community, thus radicalizing traditional moral precepts such as the concept of honour and loyalty. But even the racially privileged members of the Aryan *Volksgemeinschaft* never adopted this morality completely. That morality itself was a hybrid, and its social appropriation remained a hybrid as well, broken, incomplete, challenged. What eventually propelled the violent dynamic and served the cohesion of the 'people's community' was not the unambiguous appropriation of the racist Nazi morality by Germans but the conflict, the tension between the two moralities that brewed in them.

Scholarly interest in the Nazi morality has emerged only recently and is still *in statu nascendi*. Its focus so far has been the theoretical and ideological fabric of this morality. This chapter has attempted to go a step further and to demonstrate the societal workings of the Nazi morality with a focus on those Germans who operated and propelled the dynamic of the Nazi violence outside of Germany, most of all on the killing fields of the East. Future research will reveal more nuances in the hybridity of Nazi morality by inquiring into and comparing different regional, institutional, and ideological settings as they operated in Nazi Europe.

References

Ackermann, Josef. 1970. *Heinrich Himmler als Ideologe*. Göttingen: Musterschmidt.

Arendt, Hannah. 1965. *Eichmann in Jerusalem: A Report on the Banality of Evil*. New York: Viking.

Baumann, Zygmunt, 1989. *Modernity and the Holocaust*. Ithaca, NY: Cornell University Press.

Benedict, Ruth, 1948. *The Chrysanthemum and the Sword: Patterns of Japanese Culture*. Boston, MA: Houghton Mifflin.

Berger, Peter, Berger, Brigitte, and Kellner, Hansfried. 1974. *The Homeless Mind: Modernization and Consciousness*. New York: Vintage.

Bialas, Wolfgang. 2014a. *Moralische Ordnungen des Nationalsozialismus*. Göttingen: Vandenhoeck & Ruprecht.

Bialas, Wolfgang. 2014b. 'Nazi Ethics: Perpetrators with a Clear Conscience.' *Dapim* 27, 3–25.

Bowman, James. 2006. *Honor: A History*. New York: Encounter Books.

Browning, Christopher. 1992. *Ordinary Men: Reserve Police Battalion 101 and the Final Solution in Poland*. New York: HarperCollins.

Buchbender, Ortwin and Sterz, Reinhold, eds. 1983. *Das andere Gesicht des Krieges: Deutsche Feldpostbriefe 1939–1945*. 2nd edn. Munich: C.H. Beck.

Büchler, Yehoshua R. 2003. '"Unworthy Behavior": The Case of SS Officer Max Täubner.' *Holocaust and Genocide Studies* 17, 409–423.

Cramer, John. 2011. 'Der erste Bergen-Belsen-Prozess 1945 und seine Rezeption durch die deutsche Öffentlichkeit.' In *NS-Prozesse und deutsche Öffentlichkeit: Besatzungszeit, frühe Bundesrepublik und DDR*, edited by Jörg Osterloh and Clemens Vollnhals, 75–92. Göttingen: Vandenhoeck & Ruprecht.

Dillon, Christopher, 2015. *Dachau and the SS: A Schooling in Violence*. Oxford: Oxford University Press.

Durkheim, Émile, 1982. *The Rules of the Sociological Method and Selected Texts on Sociology and Its Method*. Edited by Steven Lukes. New York: Free Press.

Elias, Norbert. 1996. *The Germans: Power Struggle and the Development of Habitus in the Nineteenth and Twentieth Centuries*. New York: Columbia University Press.

Erikson, Erik H. 1963. *Childhood and Society*, 2nd edn. New York: W.W. Norton.

Fontane, Theodor. 2001. *Effi Briest*. New York: Penguin Classics. First published in German 1896.

Frevert, Ute. 1995. *'Mann und Weib, und Weib und Mann': Geschlechter-Differenzen in der Moderne*. Munich: C.H. Beck.

Fritzsche, Peter. 2008. *Life and Death in the Third Reich*. Cambridge, MA: Harvard University Press.

Gellately, Robert. 1990. *The Gestapo and German Society: Enforcing Racial Policy 1933–1945*. Oxford: Clarendon Press.

Goebbels, Joseph. 1993. *Die Tagebücher*. Edited by Elke Fröhlich, part II, vol. 7. Munich.

Goldhagen, Daniel J. 1996. *Hitler's Willing Executioners: Ordinary Germans and the Holocaust*. New York: Knopf.

Grimm, Friedrich. 1938. *Politischer Mord und Heldenverehrung*. Berlin: Deutscher Rechtverlag.

Gross, Raphael. 2010. *Anständig geblieben: Nationalsozialistische Moral*. Frankfurt: Fischer.

Haas, Peter. 1988. *Morality After Auschwitz: The Radical Challenge of the Nazi Ethics*. Philadelphia, PA: Fortress Press.

Haffner, Sebastian. 2002. *Defying Hitler: A Memoir*. New York: Picador.

Himmler, Heinrich. 1974. *Geheimreden 1933 bis 1945 und andere Ansprachen*. Edited by Bradley F. Smith and Agnes F. Peterson. Frankfurt: Propyläen.

Hitler, Adolf. 1934. *Mein Kampf, Volume 1: Eine Abrechnung; Volume 2: Die nationalsozialistische Bewegung*. Munich: Zentralverlag der NSDAP.

Hosenfeld, Wilm. 2004. *'Ich versuche jeden zu retten': Das Leben eines deutschen Offiziers in Briefen und Tagebüchern*. Edited by Thomas Vogel. Munich: Deutsche Verlagsanstalt.

Internationaler Militärgerichtshof 1948. *Der Prozess gegen die Hauptkriegsverbrecher vor dem Internationalen Militärgerichtshof. Nürnberg 14. November 1945 – 1. Oktober 1946*. Vol. 29. Nuremberg: Internationaler Militärgerichtshof.

Jünger, Ernst. 1922. *Der Kampf als inneres Erlebnis*. Berlin: Mittler.

Jünger, Ernst. 1928. *Das Wäldchen 125: Eine Chronik aus den Grabenkämpfen 1918*, 3rd edn. Berlin: Mittler.

Klee, Ernst, Dressen, Willi, and Riess, Volker, eds. 1991. *'The Good Old Days': The Holocaust as Seen by Its Perpetrators and Bystanders*. New York: Konecky & Konecky.

Kolnai, Aurel. 1938. *The War Against the West*. New York: Viking.

Koonz, Claudia. 2003. *The Nazi Conscience*. Cambridge, MA: Belknap Press.

Kühne, Thomas. 2006. *Kameradschaft: Die Soldaten des nationalsozialistischen Krieges und das 20. Jahrhundert*. Göttingen: Vandenhoeck & Ruprecht.

Kühne, Thomas. 2010. *Belonging and Genocide: Hitler's Community, 1918–1945*. New Haven, CT: Yale University Press.

Lethen, Helmut. 2002. *Cool Conduct: The Culture of Distance in Weimar Germany*. Berkeley: University of California Press.

Lifton, Robert J. 1986. *The Nazi Doctors: Medical Killing and the Psychology of Genocide*. New York: Basic Books.

Lutz, Günther. 1936. 'Das Gemeinschaftserlebnis in der Kriegsliteratur.' PhD thesis, University of Greifswald.

Maschmann, Melitta. 1964. *Account Rendered: A Dossier on my Former Self*. London: Abelard-Schuman.

Megargee, Geoffrey P. 2006. *War of Annihilation: Combat and Genocide on the Eastern Front, 1941*. Lanham, MD: Rowman & Littlefield.

Mersmann, Birke. 1995.*'Was bleibt vom Heldentum?': Weiterleben nach dem Krieg*. Berlin: Reimer.

Milgram, Stanley. 1963. 'Behavioral Study of Obedience.' *Journal of Abnormal and Social Psychology* 67, 371–378.

Mineau, Andre. 2004. *Operation Barbarossa: Ideology and Ethics Against Human Dignity.* Amsterdam: Rodopi.

Mommsen, Hans. 2002. 'Kameraderie und Karrieren: Der Verlust der politischen und moralischen Kontrollinstanzen ließ die Gewalt im Nationalsozialismus eskalieren.' *Frankfurter Rundschau*, 30 March, 22.

Mosse, George L. 1964. *The Crisis of German Ideology: Intellectual Origins of the Third Reich.* New York: Grosset & Dunlap.

Mutua, Makau. 2002. *Human Rights: A Political and Cultural Critique.* Philadelphia: University of Pennsylvania Press.

Neitzel, Sönke and Welzer, Harald. 2012. *Soldaten. On Fighting, Killing, and Dying. The Secret World War II Transcripts of German POWs.* New York: Knopf.

Offer, Avner. 1995. 'Going to War in 1914: a Matter of Honor?' *Politics and Society* 23/2, 213–241.

Orth, Karin. 2000. Die *Konzentrationslager-SS: Sozialstrukturelle Analysen und biographische Studien.* Göttingen: Wallstein.

Pendas, Devin. 2006. *The Frankfurt Auschwitz Trial, 1963–1965: Genocide, History, and the Limits of the Law.* New York: Cambridge University Press.

Powell, Christopher J. 2012. 'Genocidal Moralities. A Critique.' In *New Directions in Genocide Research*, edited by Adam Jones, 37–54. London: Routledge.

Przyrembel, Alexandra. 2003. *Rassenschande': Reinheitsmythos und Vernichtungslegitimation im Nationalsozialismus.* Göttingen: Vandenhoeck & Ruprecht.

Rüter, Christiaan F. and de Mildt, Dick W., eds. 1976. *Justiz und NS-Verbrechen: Sammlung deutscher Strafurteile wegen nationalsozialistischer Tötungsverbrechen.* Vol. 15. Amsterdam: Amsterdam University Press.

Scheff, Thomas J., 1994. *Bloody Revenge: Emotions, Nationalism, and War.* Boulder, CO: Westview Press.

Simmel, Georg. 1992. *Soziologie: Untersuchungen über die Formen der Vergesellschaftung.* Frankfurt: Suhrkamp. First published 1908.

Staub, Ervin. 1989. *The Roots of Evil: The Origins of Genocide and Other Group Violence.* Cambridge: Cambridge University Press.

Todorov, Tzvetan. 1993. *On Human Diversity: Nationalism, Racism, and Exoticism in French Thought.* Cambridge, MA: Harvard University Press.

Tolkien, J.R.R. 1965. *The Two Towers. Being the Second Part of The Lord of the Rings.* New York: Ballantine.

Tugendhat, Ernst. 2001. 'Partikularismus und Individualismus.' In *Aufsätze 1992–2000.* Frankfurt: Suhrkamp.

Walser, Martin. 1965. 'Unser Auschwitz.' *Kursbuch* 1, 189–200.

Walzer, Michael. 1977. *Just and Unjust Wars: A Moral Argument with Historical Illustrations.* New York: Basic Books.

Weikart, Richard. 2004. *From Darwin to Hitler: Evolutionary Ethics, Eugenics, and Racism.* New York: Palgrave Macmillan.

Weikart, Richard. 2009. *Hitler's Ethic: The Nazi Pursuit of Evolutionary Progress.* New York: Palgrave Macmillan.

Further Reading

Fellman, Marc Lee. 2009. *Moral Complexity and the Holocaust.* Lanham, MD: University Press of America.

Haas, Peter. 1988. *Morality After Auschwitz: The Radical Challenge of the Nazi Ethics.* Philadelphia, PA: Fortress Press.
Pioneering work.

Hosenfeld, Wilm. 2004. 'Ich versuche jeden zu retten': Das Leben eines deutschen Offiziers in Briefen und Tagebüchern. Edited by Thomas Vogel. Munich: Deutsche Verlagsanstalt.
The best exemplary diary- and letter-based documentation of the moral and emotional struggles of an ordinary German soldier.

Klee, Ernst, Dressen, Willi, and Riess, Volker, eds. 1991. 'The Good Old Days': The Holocaust as Seen by Its Perpetrators and Bystanders. New York: Konecky & Konecky.
Still the most illustrative collection of primary sources on the mindsets of Nazi perpetrators.

Koonz, Claudia. 2003. The Nazi Conscience. Cambridge, MA: Belknap Press.
Authoritative account of the public discourse on Nazi morality through 1939.

Kühne, Thomas. 2010. Belonging and Genocide: Hitler's Community, 1918–1945. New Haven, CT: Yale University Press.
Probes into the subjective appropriation and the social impact of the Nazi morality.

Roth, John, ed. 1999. Ethics after the Holocaust: Perspectives, Critiques, and Responses. St. Paul, MN: Paragon House.
Documentation of a lively scholarly debate on pros and cons of acknowledging the morality of Nazism.

Weikart, Richard. 2009. Hitler's Ethic: The Nazi Pursuit of Evolutionary Progress. New York: Palgrave Macmillan.
Empirically rich study of a major aspect of Nazi morality.

Welzer, Harald. 2004. 'Mass Murder and Moral Code: Some Thoughts on an Easily Misunderstood Project.' History of the Human Sciences 17, 15–32.

Zimmermann, Rolf. 2005. Philosophie nach Auschwitz: Eine Neubestimmung von Moral in Politik und Gesellschaft. Reinbek: Rowohlt Taschenbuch Verlag.

CHAPTER FOURTEEN

The German Home Front Under the Bombs

RICHARD OVERY

The experience of the German home front during the Second World War has been a difficult subject for historians to confront for a number of reasons. The home front was the arena in which the German people either endorsed or failed to prevent the mass deportation of Germany's Jews. Germans on the home front also continued to work and organize the German war effort right up to the very end, confirming for many commentators, then and now, their deeply embedded identification with the regime. Both these factors make it difficult to argue the case that ordinary Germans were also victims in the war, particularly victims of the sustained bombing campaign that killed and seriously injured around three quarters of a million people and reduced Germany's urban infrastructure to rubble (Niven 2006; Stargardt 2015).

One result of these dilemmas has been the relative neglect of the history of the German home front during the Second World War in favour of extensive historical literature on the armed forces, the German security system, and the Holocaust. Yet the German home front invites a number of important historical questions. What was daily life like, in terms of living standards, patterns of work, and the regular demands of the war effort? What were popular attitudes to the war and the racism of the regime and how is it possible to assess them in a dictatorship that closely monitored the public sphere? How did the German civilian population cope with sustained bombing of the urban area for more than four years? And finally, what kept the German population working and fighting to the end despite the evidence of imminent defeat and catastrophic losses of civilian lives and the civilian milieu? The differing answers that historians have supplied to these issues shape the structure of this chapter, while at the same time they suggest areas where further research is needed.

A Companion to Nazi Germany, First Edition. Edited by Shelley Baranowski, Armin Nolzen, and Claus-Christian W. Szejnmann.
© 2018 John Wiley & Sons Ltd. Published 2018 by John Wiley & Sons Ltd.

14.1   Life and Work on the Home Front

For long after the end of the war in 1945 it was argued that the German population, for at least the first three years of the conflict, and probably beyond, experienced a home front in which few demands were made on them to restrict civilian living standards, change work patterns, or help fund the war through forced or voluntary saving. The home front, so it was argued, lived under a 'peacelike war economy', partly because the regime was keen not to impose too heavy a burden on the home front, partly because the military strategy of the regime was based on the idea of a series of short, limited wars or *Blitzkriege* (Klein 1959; Milward 1965). Under this argument, German war production remained low, German civilian living standards were little different from peacetime, and the imposition of a 'total war' mentality and the sacrifices to support it only came into force in 1944. In particular, it was argued that German women did not shoulder the same burdens of war work as women in Britain and the United States but instead lived on generous military welfare payments that obviated their need for paid work (Rupp 1978; Hancock 1994).

This is an argument that rested heavily on the findings of the United States Strategic Bombing Survey reports on the German wartime economy. Detailed historical research over the past 25 years has dismantled almost all of this original perception of the German home front. German civilian society was profoundly affected by the outbreak of major war from September 1939 onwards (Müller 2000; Tooze 2006). The War Economy decree published on 4 September created the framework for the progressive intervention of the state in every area of civilian life. Among the most important changes was the introduction of a comprehensive rationing system that limited civilian access to the entire range of major foodstuffs and placed limits on what luxury goods could be sold. Controls over the purchase of clothing forced millions of civilians to make do with what they already possessed. Households suspected of hoarding clothing were subject to inspections, and surplus shoes, coats, and suits were confiscated for redistribution or, later, to compensate other households for losses due to bombing (Overy 1994). Over the course of the first wartime years, German consumers, chiefly those in the cities, adjusted to a monotonous diet, long queues for food, and few opportunities to purchase any major consumer items. The difference from the First World War was the insistence that sacrifices should be equally shared, and rationing ensured that a basic minimum (*Existenzminimum*) should be guaranteed in order to avoid any danger of social protest at home.

Consumer shortages had been typical before 1939 as the regime diverted the productive economy to serve the programme of remilitarization, and they were intensified during the war. State pressure to limit the growth of consumption was evident in the fiscal policies adopted after 1939, with increases in income tax, particularly for higher earners, indirect taxes, and intense propaganda to persuade ordinary Germans to save rather than spend. The money saved in the private finance sector was then taken by the state as credit to fund the war effort, a system of 'noiseless finance' (Boelcke 1985). There were exceptions to the stringent control of living standards and consumption. In the countryside, it was possible for farmers to eat well, though the black market was heavily penalized. The richer classes could also enjoy higher standards, though they had to be careful not to do so too obtrusively. The chief beneficiaries of unequal distribution were the National Socialist elite, who were able to draw on special stocks held in warehouses on their behalf, much of it looted from conquered territories. The opportunity to benefit from foreign conquest was also shared by the soldiers and officials who undertook it. Looting was characteristic of the behaviour of German soldiers right from the start of the war in Poland; looted goods were sent back home in thousands of packages to help the soldiers' families. It has been argued that one of the chief purposes of German warfare after 1939 was to seize goods and food that could not be supplied at home. The German people became, in Götz Aly's words, 'Hitler's beneficiaries', as German occupiers spread like locusts over the European New Order (Aly 2006). In most cases, however, the loot was small-scale and temporary, no substitute for the bleak living standards at home. Most of the food seized in the occupied areas was used to feed German armies, or was sent back to help the state fulfil the basic food rations (Corni and Gies 1997; Collingham 2011).

The establishment of the war economy also required stricter discipline over the workforce and its rapid restructuring to meet military requirements. Civilian industry was either curtailed or transformed into production for the vast armed forces. The large quantity of artisan employment declined 50% by 1943, while the transfer of the workforce into jobs serving military contracts raised the percentage of the total working in war and war-related industries from 22% in May 1939 to 56% by May 1941, making clear that the idea of a 'peacelike war economy' in these early years bears little relation to the historical reality. The same can be said of the argument about female participation in the war effort. The large increases in female employment in Britain and the United States appeared to contrast with the almost static employment figures for women in Germany. This situation, it was argued, was the result of National Socialist insistence that the woman's place was at home raising children and supporting her soldier-husband. The statistics, however, have been shown to be very misleading (Overy 1988; Hancock 1994; Stephenson 2005). German women already made up a large proportion of the German workforce in 1939 because of the pressure of labour shortages. By 1945, women comprised more than half of the workforce, while in Britain and the United States the figure peaked at just over one third. Moreover, many women in civilian sectors were redeployed within the same firms to work on war contracts. Women were also recruited in large numbers into welfare, first aid, and civil defence roles while an estimated three million married women with children were employed on part-time or home work. Later in the war, the impact of bombing and evacuation from the cities made it difficult to maintain full female employment and millions of forced female workers from the East were brought in to meet war industry requirements (Herbert 1985; Mommsen 2005).

14.2   The Home Front and the War

One of the least examined questions about the German home front during the war has been the issue of popular attitudes to the course of the war and wartime hardships. Public opinion and everyday life in wartime has become a mainstay of historical writing on the Second World War, but it has been limited in the case of Germany by the nature of the regime and the absence of any public sphere independent of the restrictions imposed by the Nazi Party and the security services. Most historians have relied on the reports produced by the Reich Security Service (*Sicherheitsdienst*, SD) which have survived wartime destruction and were published in a full edition of 17 volumes by Hans Boberach (1984). The reports have to be treated cautiously because they were produced by security agents for the leadership of the security apparatus. Many of them, however, give candid accounts of evidence of popular dissent or grumbling, of wartime rumours and wartime anxieties. The regime had an evident vested interest in taking the pulse of popular opinion in order to refine public propaganda and to be able to anticipate possible social issues. As such, the SD reports remain an essential guide to the ups and downs of home morale across the whole war period (Steinert 1977).

Nevertheless, Germans were not free to express their views in wartime and ran great risks if they did so. Anyone found guilty of undermining the military and economic war effort faced severe punishment; expressions of defeatism later in the war could result in summary execution (Dams and Stolle 2008). But evidence shows that for minor infractions, even listening to foreign broadcasts (a practice that Eric Johnson's oral history project on German wartime behaviour has shown to be widespread), the Gestapo would often let people off with a reprimand or a fine since they were too short of personnel to pursue every case (Gellately 1990; Johnson and Reuband 2005, 292). The number of cases remained relatively small, suggesting that by the war period the regime had successfully established a consensual dictatorship in which the great majority of Germans were content to endorse the system and, above all, to trust in Hitler (Kershaw 1987; Gellately 2001). As a view of the home front, this is largely speculation. Demonstrations of enthusiasm, public displays of support, or membership of party organizations or national associations for welfare or civil defence could as easily be the product of opportunism, ambition, political prudence, or fear. There is no doubt that at moments of triumph, such as the defeat of France in 1940, or the early victories in the Soviet Union, there was widespread popular support for what German forces had achieved, but here too separating support for the regime and its goals from a more straightforward patriotic enthusiasm is difficult. In 1940 and autumn 1941 it seems more likely that popular displays of nationalist solidarity reflected hopes that the war would very soon be over, an ambiguity masked by the apparent wave of spontaneous celebration (Stargardt 2015). The aim of the regime was to use the war to cement the idea of the 'people's community' (*Volksgemeinschaft*) more firmly; the propaganda continually stressed shared sacrifices and the need for strenuous activity. As the war crisis deepened, the 'people's community' was transformed in party discourse into the 'community of fate' (*Schicksalsgemeinschaft*), in an effort to link all Germans in a final apocalyptic struggle for their survival (Gregor 2000; Longerich 2015).

Much recent research on the attitude of the German population has focused more on the extent to which ordinary Germans steered a way between all the conflicting pressures of external conflict and internal surveillance and coercion. But the priority for many families, in which for a great many the woman was now the head of the household, was simply to survive. There was, as Hester Vaizey has put it, limited 'room for maneuver' for the average family in protecting the private sphere, but not much. Women assumed more and more responsibility for work and welfare and were seldom independent of the scrutiny of state and party, on which many families came to depend as conditions on the home front deteriorated (Vaizey 2010; Ginsborg 2014). Survival also depended crucially on circumstances and geography. Civilians in small towns and villages did not experience the same difficulty in getting access to food or coping with bombing and evacuation; in city areas, middle-class Germans usually survived better than working-class communities clustered in the vulnerable city centres. Moreover, as the German population became more mobile during the war, so tensions flared up between different groups of the civilian population. Jill Stephenson, in her study of Württemberg during the war, has highlighted the friction and conflicts between townspeople, villagers, and evacuees over access to food and willingness to work (Stephenson 2006). Townspeople looked down on the peasantry, while country communities regarded townspeople as potentially criminal, lazy, or dirty. Occasionally the conflicts resulted in open demonstrations of protest which local authorities regarded at times as an inevitable result of the massive disruptions caused by wartime exigencies rather than manifestations of political protest (Torrie 2010; Glienke 2011).

For most of the wartime period, protest was, in reality, very limited, though this did not stop the regime from constantly worrying about the possibility of a repeat of 1917–1918 and the alleged 'stab in the back' by the home front. The Western Allies also shared this view that mass popular protest might be possible and targeted working-class residential areas with the bombs in the hope of accelerating the collapse of social cohesion (Overy 2012). The regime monitored the ups and downs of home morale very carefully and adjusted policies, particularly on food, welfare entitlement, and work conditions to make sure that the spectre of home front disaffection in the First World War would not materialize in the crisis years of the Second (Fritzsche 2008). This concern also took the form of diverting popular attention to the enemy within in order to deflect criticism of the regime or the Party. These enemies included communists, 'asocials' (habitual criminals, the workshy), defeatists and traitors, and, above all, the Jews. The identification of the excluded 'other' was designed in part to encourage a sense of inclusion and belonging among the rest of the population. There has always been debate about how much the home front population knew about the deportation and murder of the Jews, but a wave of new research on popular perception of the persecution at both a national and local level has made clear beyond any further doubt that knowledge, though often partial – even speculative – was widespread (Longerich 2006).

Whether that knowledge really did encourage ordinary Germans to identify with the regime's priorities and to commit themselves more fully to the struggle for Germany's future is more questionable, but scapegoats were useful for home front propaganda. It is striking that in the aftermath of the failed July Plot of 1944, in which a small coterie of senior army officers tried to eliminate Hitler and take over the state, there was genuine popular shock and outrage against the evidence of treason at the heart of the system (Noakes 1992). Rather than encourage wider popular social protest, the failed plot made protest in the final year of war less likely. A letter sent to the SD in November 1944 claimed that 90% of the population was still inspired by a 'glowing patriotism'. But the writer continued that in any 'honest and secret plebiscite', not even half the people would think of themselves as National Socialist, but they would never say so (Steinert 1977, 284-5). Intelligence smuggled out to London from the underground Social Democrat movement in 1944 made it clear that the opponents of the regime did not want to be tarred once again with the brush of wartime betrayal, but preferred to wait until German forces had been beaten in the field (Overy 2015).

14.3   Bombing and the Home Front

All aspects of economic and social life, and the morale of the German population, were profoundly affected during the war by the experience of Allied bombing (Beck 1986). It is important to understand the sheer scale of the air campaign. The first small raids began in May 1940 and the last raids took place in late April 1945. During those five years the Allies dropped on Germany 23 times the amount of tonnage dropped on British targets by the German Air Force, a gross total of 1.6 million tons. A high proportion of the bombs dropped by the Royal Air Force were incendiaries, designed to cause maximum damage to the urban residential environment (Friedrich 2008). That damage was exceptional: 39% of the urban built-up area was destroyed with permanent loss of 2.1 million housing units (Hewitt 1983, 263). The losses also included large numbers of public buildings, schools, hospitals, and churches. The human casualties have been the subject of a great deal of historical debate. The official figure arrived at in the Federal Republic in the 1950s was 625 000 (Sperling 1956). More recent research has resulted in estimates of a much lower figure of total dead (including (POWs, foreign workers, and German uniformed personnel), between 353 000 and 420 000, in both cases covering the area of Greater Germany established after the *Anschluss* and the defeat of Poland (Groehler 1990: Overy 2013). Bombing also compelled the urban population to abandon the cities. By September 1944 there were 5.6 million evacuees; by the end of the war 8.9 million. Not all were escaping the bombing, but the figures indicate an exceptional level of geographical mobility in the last year of war.

The bombing made the German home front very different from that of the First World War because it created a permanent link between the home population and the reality of the war rather than isolating the domestic front from the fighting front. Though the principal targets were industrial cities and their populations, most of the country was affected in one way or another, not least because half of British bombs fell on rural areas or urban suburbs, while more remote regions in the north and east of the country became the destination for millions of evacuees and for the dispersal and decentralization of industry. The regime was able to take advantage of the 'civilianization' of warfare by mobilizing the home population for its own defence through programmes of air raid precautions, welfare provision, and voluntary self-help groups. The extensive network of civil defence kept the population in a permanent state of alert or anxiety, while providing the regime with a means to monitor compliance with the war effort through compulsory blackout regulations, firefighting, and shelter provision (Wiggam 2011). Before the war 15 million Germans had signed up for the Reich Air Defence League (*Reichsluftschutzbund*) and by the height of the bombing the figure reached 22 million, a quarter of the population. Members were given preliminary instruction in civil defence, coping with incendiaries, and basic first aid at one of the 3400 civil defence schools set up in Germany (Overy 2013, 414).

The formal civil defence system of wardens, responsible for each apartment block or row of houses, involved regular monitoring of the locality to ensure that householders had access to a cellar or gas-proof room, kept supplies of water and sand for incendiary bombs, and had cleared out combustible materials from attics and lofts. The legislation on air raid protection, first published in May 1937, established three categories: self-protection, which was the responsibility of each household; extended self-protection, under whose terms citizens were responsible for safeguarding local public buildings and offices; and work air protection, the responsibility of the industrial workforce and management (Lemke 2005). The entire air defence and civil defence system was the responsibility of the German Air Force, working in collaboration with local police officials and the Reich Defence Commissars, who were usually local party regional chiefs, or *Gauleiter*. Over the course of the war responsibility shifted away from the air force in favour of local administrators and party officials. The increased weight of bombing in spring 1942 alerted the regime more fully to the social dangers of the bombing campaign. Joseph Goebbels, Minister of Popular Enlightenment and Propaganda, was given commissarial responsibility for coordinating civil defence measures on a national level; a year later Hitler agreed to the establishment of an Inter-Ministerial Committee for Air Protection with Goebbels as its head. In this way, the efforts to maintain morale by propaganda were married to efforts to sustain morale through civil defence and welfare measures (Süss 2006).

For historians, the critical question is the link between home front morale and the experience of bombing. Why did the years of destruction and killing not result in a collapse of war-willingness and more widespread protest against the war? Historians have found a number of ways to answer this question. The efforts of the local and party authorities to provide immediate emergency aid and welfare benefited both the recipients and those who supplied it by creating a compact between regime and people, though one very dependent on the capacity of the regime to fulfil its promises of assistance and compensation. One of the first things was to ensure adequate access to secure shelter. Although this had been an obligation under the 'self-protection' legislation, authorities had been very slow to enforce it and overconfident that bombing would not be a serious threat, certainly in areas thought to be too distant for Allied aircraft. Hitler authorized an 'Immediate Programme' (*Sofortsprogramm*) on 10 October 1940 for construction of emergency bunkers above and below ground, but by 1943 this programme provided shelter for only 3.87% of the population in 76 threatened cities. Instead, households had to rely on the domestic shelter of cellars, basements, or reinforced rooms, which collectively could accommodate 11.6 million people (Overy 2013, 425). The shelters, it has been argued, became a site for the affirmation of the nature of the regime, with close control over entry, strict regulations for behaviour, and the exclusion of Jews and foreign workers in favour of members of the national community (Süss 2011).

The most pressing priorities were welfare and rehabilitation. The distribution of emergency rations, clothes, and household goods, as well as much of the task of emergency billeting, fell on the National Socialist People's Welfare organization (NSV) which had more than 15 million members, a great many of them women volunteers. The bombed out were taken to emergency centres where they were given vouchers for clothes, shoes, soap, and washing powder. They would also be issued with new ration cards if they had been lost or burnt, though the rationing system by the middle years of the war was so complicated that bomb victims found themselves queuing for hours to obtain new ones (Glienke 2011; Süss 2014). Rehabilitation was essential in order to keep workers in or around the factory areas and to encourage an early return to work. Substantial though the urban damage was, it proved possible in the first three years of bombing to organize rapid repair or temporary rebuilding. In many cases homes lacked roof tiles, window glass, or doors, and these could easily be replaced. Special repair units composed of older craft workers were set up, which moved from one bombed area to another, using cardboard or wood to cover over windows, and substitute roofing instead of tiles. The homes were not comfortable or attractive, but millions of those temporarily driven out by the bombs preferred to return to familiar surroundings than move to a distant suburban or rural destination.

The regime had also made a pledge early in the war, long before the bombing became a serious menace, to pay compensation for any war damage, a further way of cementing regime and population on the home front. The system for compensation was complex and grew more so as the war went on. Householders were advised to keep lists of their possessions, even to take photographs of the most valuable. After bombing, they were required to fill out claim forms for all losses, but the process soon became subject to widespread abuse as householders made exaggerated lists of what had been lost and its value. Officials were forced to work on the basis that most claims were overstatements and to provide compensation in line with the obvious needs of the family. By late 1943, payments nationally were running at 700 million Reichsmarks a month, while total claims of 31.7 billion Reichsmarks had been filed, of which 11.6 billion had already been paid (Overy 2013, 434). One of the ways in which physical compensation in the form of clothes and household goods could be made was by buying up or seizing resources in the occupied areas. Warehouses filled up in Germany with clothes, shoes, and furnishings from France, the Low Countries, and Czechoslovakia. More important were the claims made on Jewish possessions and apartments as a result of the bombing. The legislation applying to welfare and compensation did not apply to Germany's Jewish population. From as early as the late autumn of 1940 some local authorities began to evict Jews in order to use their homes for bombed-out 'Aryans'; in Cologne in 1941 the city's Jews were rounded up and made to live in rough barracks while their apartments were distributed to the bombed out. When mass deportation began later in the year, Jewish goods were either seized for future use, or auctioned off at city markets. In Hamburg, for example, auctions of sequestered goods raised 7 million Reichsmarks by the time of the firestorm, in July 1943 (Bajohr 2002, 278–280). The expropriation of Jewish goods in occupied Western Europe also served the interests of the home population. A total of 775 trainloads of goods were sent back to the Reich to help German bomb victims (Torrie 2010, 135–137).

The regime was also at pains to ensure that the workforce would not be disadvantaged by loss of earnings or temporary unemployment, though much argument ensued between employers, the Reich Labour Front, and the government over how compensation should be calculated. The resentment at what was seen as inequitable demands across different forms of employment built on early resentment during the war against state wage policy (Werner 1983). The issue remained incompletely resolved, but in many cases workers found themselves having to undertake post-bombing emergency work or additional hours in the factory to make up for lost time. As the war went on, conditions for the workforce deteriorated. They were compelled to work until the last moment before being allowed down to the factory bunkers (though foreign workers were only allowed in if there was room – otherwise they made do with slit trenches). By the end of 1944 almost a million workers had been moved from their home towns to follow industries dispersed to other parts of the Reich. However, for many German workers conditions changed once large numbers of prisoners of war (POWs) and forced foreign labour came into the German workforce from 1942 onwards (Mommsen 2005). German skilled workers were given supervisory tasks, higher pay, and better conditions compared with the non-German workforce. The unequal access to shelter was reflected in the high number of POWs and foreign workers killed – an estimated 32 000. Thousands of camp prisoners and foreign workers were used to clear up the immediate effects of the bombs, often at considerable risk. Bombing also had the effect of reducing the available number of female workers in 1943–1945 as women left the cities and found themselves without work in the evacuation destination, or forced to help with the welfare and schooling of the evacuated communities (Stephenson 2006).

The detailed reality of the home front under the bombs has been supplied by a large number of city histories that have appeared in the last 25 years. Piecing the story together, it is evident that for all the hardships and inconveniences, losses and physical exhaustion, German urban society and economy kept going under the bombs, partly because options and choices were limited, partly because of fear of the consequences of defeat, partly because the state and the Party managed to provide a sufficient margin of the necessary welfare, compensation, food, and shelter to allow city life to continue. The priority of the regime was to avoid any hint of a 'stab in the back' through a combination of propaganda dedicated to the themes of sacrifice and community and solid evidence that people would continue to be fed and housed.

14.4   The Hard Logic of Total War

Historians have long been aware that explaining how the regime and people sustained the war effort through to the end of 1943 is a different question from the last stage of the war when 'total war' became not only the watchword of the regime but also a harsh reality under the endless rain of bombs, falling food stocks, mass evacuation, and mounting domestic terror. Sustaining the home front under these conditions was a more complex social and political question as defeat loomed and home front confidence in the capacity of the dictatorship to resolve the crisis became more muted. Much of the recent literature on the German home front has concentrated on explaining how the system continued to the bitter end (Kershaw 2011; Bessel 2009).

It is nevertheless remarkable that during the course of 1944, when bombing intensified, the workforce continued to turn up regularly for work. Reich statistical surveys of hours lost during 1944 show that for most war industrial sectors absenteeism accounted for between 14% and 23% of hours that should have been worked, but only between 4% and 10% was attributable to the effects of bombing (Overy 2013, 463). The rest resulted from illness, exhaustion, the hunt for rations, or personal loss. The changed nature of the workforce also made it easier to coerce non-German workers, and their absenteeism rates were very low by comparison. In the end, however, bombing did undermine the capacity of the workforce to continue working, with mass evacuation, the destruction of transport and communications, and the loss of energy supply (Mierzejewski 1988).

Other conditions on the home front also deteriorated, but again with little indication that this might lead to a serious social crisis for the regime. Ralf Blank (2015), in his study of the Ruhr-Rhineland in the last months of the war, has talked of the 'erosion of the *Volksgemeinschaft*' in the conditions of desperation imposed by the heaviest and most remorseless bombing of the war, but this did not constitute a crisis like that of the autumn of 1918. The changing political balance explains some of this. Heinrich Himmler, head of the SS, became Minister of the Interior in August 1943, and the SS continued to intrude more openly into the running of the war economy and the organization of civil defence. In February 1944 Himmler announced that 'no German city will be abandoned' as a result of bombing, and for those inclined to defeatism or made desperate by the circumstances they faced, the SS, security services and the military police were given a more or less free hand to conduct brief 'kangaroo courts' to pass sentence on anyone slacking, looting, or maligning either Hitler or the regime, and by the end could simply hang or shoot anyone who was caught in their net, non-German and German alike, without any process of law. At the same time, the looming military defeats on all fronts in 1944 brought the army closer to home. This made desertion easier, though the penalty for those caught was usually execution, but it also meant that the home population was now much closer to the whole military machine and more conscious than ever of the dangers of echoing the end of the previous war (Hansen 2014).

The evidence from secret police reports and surviving diaries also shows the extent to which sections of the German population still clung to the hope that

the tide of war might be reversed. Great expectations were aroused by the promise in German propaganda from 1943 that new, secret weapons were at hand that
would turn the ride of war. They were delayed so long that Goebbels was forced
to tone the message down, but once the assault with 'Vengeance Weapons'
began, people's expectations rose once more (Steinert 1977; Kirwin 1985). The
state of morale in 1944 was in many ways no more or less volatile than earlier in
the war. Once it became clear that the 'V-Weapons' were not going to bring an
end to the bombing or turn the tide, disillusionment set in, only for hopes to
revive that Hitler might have yet other unexpected surprises. Whatever the nature
of the wartime consensus by this stage of the conflict, the Faustian pact made by
the German people with Hitler and the dictatorship was all that was left.
Thousands of ethnic Germans were murdered by the regime in the last months
and it was a very visible final reckoning as bodies swung on lamp-posts and trees.
Fear almost certainly held the crumbling war effort together as much as a visceral
patriotism.

The growing research interest in the German home front and the modalities of
the bombing war have not provided a final answer to all aspects of the German
wartime experience. The work on particular regions has shown how important it is
to recognize differences in the wartime experience both between different parts of
Germany and between different social groups, or between the experience of women
and men in mass mobilization, work, and daily life. Nick Stargardt's new study of
the German people during the war has opened up fresh paths in the approach
to understanding the relationship between regime and people not as a linear
or generic relationship, but as one based on a variety of nuanced explanations
(Stargardt 2015).

There is also more to be said about the way Germans from the period can
be viewed as victims or not. The more that is known about the bombing war,
the more evident is the deliberate targeting of civilians as such rather than seeing civilian casualties as the accidental 'collateral damage' from bombs aimed
at factories or rail lines. This requires historians to walk a fine line between
seeing German civilians on the home front as victims and seeing them as consensual supporters of a regime that produced millions of victims through genocide, terror, and war (Kettenacker 2003). This is a debate that rests more on
philosophical grounds than historical. Killing German civilians deliberately
from the air is widely regarded as an immoral use of military force that cannot
be justified simply because the enemy has been guilty of immoral acts (Bloxham
2006). On the other hand, failing to acknowledge the horrors that were
inflicted on cities such as Hamburg, Kassel, Pforzheim, or Dresden makes the
suffering of ordinary Germans, chiefly women, children, and the elderly, not
only appear justified but historically unimportant. Rather than ascribe the
labels of 'perpetrator' or 'victim' in this context, historians have an opportunity to explain this aspect of the past rather than to judge it. The German
home front was neither monolithically National Socialist, nor united in sullen
acquiescence or resistance, but was a social, economic, and cultural environment in which the demands of total war dominated, willy-nilly, the daily lives
of the German people.

References

Aly, Götz. 2006. *Hitlers Volksstaat: Raub, Rassenkrieg und Nationaler Sozialismus*. Frankfurt am Main: Fischer.

Bajohr, Frank. 2002. *'Aryanisation in Hamburg': The Economic Exclusion of Jews and the Confiscation of their Property in Nazi Germany*. New York: Berghahn Books.

Beck, Earl. 1986. *Under the Bombs: The German Home Front, 1942–1945*. Lexington: University of Kentucky Press.

Bessel, Richard. 2009. *Germany, 1945: From War to Peace*. New York: Simon & Schuster.

Blank, Ralf. 2015. *Bitter Ends: Die letzten Monate des Zweiten Weltkriegs im Ruhrgebiet 1944/45*. Essen: Klartext.

Bloxham, Donald. 2006. 'Dresden as a War Crime.' In *Firestorm: The Bombing of Dresden, 1945*, edited by Paul Addison and Jeremy Crang, 180–208. London: Pimlico.

Boberach, Hans, ed. 1984. *Meldungen aus dem Reich: Die geheimen Lageberichte des Sicherheitsdienstes der SS 1938–1945*. Herrsching: Pawlak Verlag.

Boelcke, Willi. 1985. *Die Kosten von Hitlers Krieg*. Paderborn: Schöningh.

Collingham, Lizzie. 2011. *The Taste of War: World War Two and the Battle for Food*. London: Allen Lane.

Corni, Gustavo and Gies, Horst. 1997. *Brot-Butter-Kanonen: Die Ernährungswirtschaft in Deutschland unter der Diktatur Hitlers*. Berlin: Akademie Verlag.

Dams, Carsten and Stolle, Michael. 2008. *Die Gestapo: Herrschaft und Terror im Dritten Reich*. Munich: C.H. Beck.

Friedrich, Jörg. 2008. *The Fire: The Bombing of Germany 1940–1945*. New York: Columbia University Press.

Fritzsche, Peter. 2008. *Life and Death in the Third Reich*. Cambridge, MA: Harvard University Press.

Gellately, Robert. 1990. *The Gestapo and German Society: Enforcing Racial Policy 1933–1945*. Oxford: Oxford University Press.

Gellately, Robert. 2001. *Backing Hitler: Consent and Coercion in Nazi Germany*. Oxford: Oxford University Press.

Ginsborg, Paul. 2014. *Family Politics: Domestic Life, Devastation and Survival 1900–1950*. New Haven, CT: Yale University Press.

Glienke, Stephan. 2011. 'The Allied Air War and German Society.' In *Bombing, States and Peoples in Western Europe, 1940–1945*, edited by Claudia Baldoli, Andrew Knapp, and Richard Overy, 184–205. London: Continuum.

Gregor, Neil. 2000. 'A *'Schicksalsgemeinshaft'*? Allied Bombing, Civilian Morale and Social Dissolution in Nuremberg, 1942–45.' *The Historical Journal* 43, 1041–1070.

Groehler, Olaf. 1990. *Bombenkrieg gegen Deutschland*. Berlin: Akademie Verlag.

Hancock, Eleanor. 1994. 'Employment in Wartime: The Experience of German Women during the Second World War.' *War & Society* 12, 43–68.

Hansen, Randall. 2014. *Disobeying Hitler: German Resistance in the Last Year of WWII*. London: Faber & Faber.

Herbert, Ulrich. 1985. *Fremdarbeiter: Politik und Praxis des 'Ausländer-Einsatzes' in der Kriegswirtschaft des Dritten Reiches*. Bonn: Dietz.

Hewitt, Kenneth. 1983. 'Place Annihilation: Area Bombing and the Fate of Urban Places.' *Annals of the Association of American Geographers* 73, 257–284.

Johnson, Eric and Reuband, Karl-Heinz. 2005. *What We Knew: Terror, Mass Murder and Everyday Life in Nazi Germany*. London: John Murray.

Kershaw, Ian. 1987. *The 'Hitler Myth': Image and Reality in the Third Reich*. Oxford: Oxford University Press.

Kershaw, Ian. 2011. *The End: Germany 1944–1945*. New Haven, CT: Yale University Press.

Kettenacker, Lothar, ed. 2003. *Ein Volk von Opfern? Die neue Debatte um den Bombenkrieg 1940–1945*. Berlin: Rowohlt.

Kirwin, G. 1985. 'Allied Bombing and Nazi Domestic Propaganda.' *European History Quarterly* 15, 341–362.

Klein, Burton. 1959. *Germany's Preparations for War*. Cambridge, MA: Harvard University Press.

Lemke, Bernd. 2005. *Luftschutz in Grossbritannien und Deutschland 1923–1939*. Munich: Oldenbourg.

Longerich, Peter. 2006. *'Davon haben wir nichts bewusst!': Die Deutschen und die Judenverfolgung 1933–1945*. Munich: Siedler.

Longerich, Peter. 2015. *Goebbels: A Biography*. London: Bodley Head.

Mierzejewski, Alfred. 1988. *The Collapse of the German War Economy: Allied Air Power and the German National Railway*. Chapel Hill, NC: University of North Carolina Press.

Milward, Alan. 1965. *The German Economy at War*. London: University of London Press.

Mommsen, Hans. 2005. 'The Impact of Compulsory Labor on German Society at War.' In *A World at Total War: Global Conflict and the Politics of Destruction, 1937–1945*, edited by Roger Chickering, Stig Förster, and Bernd Greiner, 177–188. Cambridge: Cambridge University Press.

Müller, Rolf-Dieter. 2000. 'The Mobilization of the German Economy for Hitler's War Aims.' In *Germany and the Second World War: Volume V/1*, edited by Bernhard Kroener, Rolf-Dieter Müller, and Hans Umbreit, 405–786. Oxford: Oxford University Press.

Niven, Bill, ed. 2006. *Germans as Victims: Remembering the Past in Contemporary Germany*. Basingstoke, UK: Palgrave Macmillan.

Noakes, Jeremy. 1992. 'Germany.' In *The Civilian in War: The Home Front in Europe, Japan and the USA in World War II*, edited by Jeremy Noakes, 35–61. Exeter: University of Exeter Press.

Overy, Richard. 1988. 'Mobilisation for Total War in Germany 1939–1941.' *English Historical Review* 103, 613–639.

Overy, Richard. 1994. *War and Economy in the Third Reich*. Oxford: Oxford University Press.

Overy, Richard. 2012. 'The 'Weak Link'? Bomber Command and the German Working Class 1940-1945.' *Labour History Review* 70, 11–34.

Overy, Richard. 2013. *The Bombing War: Europe 1939–1945*. London: Allen Lane.

Overy, Richard. 2015. 'Making and Breaking Morale: British Political Warfare and Bomber Command in the Second World War.' *Twentieth Century British History* 26, 370–399.

Rupp. Leila. 1978. *Mobilizing Women for War*. Princeton, NJ: Princeton University Press.

Sperling, Hans. 1956. 'Deutsche Bevölkerungsbilanz des 2. Weltkrieges.' *Wirtschaft und Statistik* 8, 493–500.

Stargardt, Nick. 2015. *Germany at War*. London: Vintage.

Steinert, Marlis. 1977. *Hitler's War and the Germans: Public Mood and Attitude during the Second World War*. Athens, OH: Ohio University Press.

Stephenson, Jill. 2005. 'The Home Front in "Total War": Women in Germany and Britain in the Second World War.' In *A World at Total War: Global Conflict and the Politics of Destruction, 1937–1945*, edited by Roger Chickering, Stig Förster, and Bernd Greiner, 207–232. Cambridge: Cambridge University Press.

Stephenson, Jill. 2006. *Hitler's Home Front: Württemberg under the Nazis*. London: Continuum.

Süss, Dietmar. 2006. 'Steuerung durch Information? Joseph Goebbels als "Kommissar der Heimatfront" und die Reichsinspektion für die zivilen Luftschutz.' In *Hitlers Kommissare:*

Sondergewalten in der nationalsozialistischen Diktatur, edited by Rüdiger Hachtmann and Winifried Süss, 183–206. Göttingen: Wallstein.

Süss, Dietmar. 2011. 'Wartime Societies and Shelter Politics in National Socialist German and Britain.' In *Bombing, States and Peoples in Western Europe, 1940–1945*, edited by Claudia Baldoli, Andrew Knapp, and Richard Overy, 23–42. London: Continuum.

Süss, Dietmar. 2014. *Death from the Skies*. Oxford: Oxford University Press.

Tooze, Adam. 2006. *The Wages of Destruction*. London: Allen Lane.

Torrie, Julia. 2010. *'For their own Good': Civilian Evacuations in Germany and France, 1939–1945*. New York: Berghahn Books.

Vaizey, Hester. 2010. *Surviving Hitler's War: Family Life in Germany 1939–1948*. Basingstoke UK: Palgrave Macmillan.

Werner, Wolfgang. 1983. *'Bleib übrig:' Deutsche Arbeiter in der nationalsozialistischen Kriegswirtschaft*. Düsseldorf: Schwann.

Wiggam, Marc. 2011. 'The Blackout and the Idea of Community in Britain and Germany.' In *Bombing, States and Peoples in Western Europe, 1940–1945*, edited by Clauudia Baldoli, Andrew Knapp, and Richard Overy, 43–58. London: Continuum.

Further Reading

Bessel, Richard. 2009. *Germany 1945: From War to Peace*. New York: Simon & Schuster.
One of the best available analyses of the collapse of the German home front at the end of the Second World War.

Evans, Richard. 2008. *The Third Reich at War*. London: Allen Lane.
The third volume of a magisterial history of the Third Reich which focuses particularly on the wartime behaviour of the German population.

Gellately, Robert. 2001. *Backing Hitler: Consent and Coercion in Nazi Germany*. Oxford: Oxford University Press.
One of the few major studies of what bound the German people to the dictatorship, even during the war.

Hamerow, Theodore. 1997. *On the Road to the Wolf's Lair: German Resistance to Hitler*. Cambridge, MA: Harvard University Press.
A thoughtful and original study of the main resistance groups in the Second World War.

Kershaw, Ian. 2011. *The End: Germany 1944–1945*. New Haven, CT: Yale University Press.
A powerful analysis of the relationship between the German people and the regime as the war effort collapsed in crisis.

Overy, Richard. 1994. *War and Economy in the Third Reich*. Oxford: Oxford University Press.
The first publication in English to challenge extensively the prevailing view of the Germans' 'easy war' between 1939 and 1945.

Overy, Richard. 2013. *The Bombing War: Europe 1939–1945*. London: Allen Lane.
An account of the bombing that includes a discussion of the impact on the German home front.

Stargardt, Nick. 2015. *Germany at War: A Nation under Arms 1939–45*. London: Vintage.
Based on an impressive range of contemporary diaries and letters, this is the best guide to what ordinary Germans were thinking during the war.

Stephenson, Jill. 2006. *Hitler's Home Front*. London: Continuum.
One of the few detailed studies of a German region during the war, this is a pioneering study of German social reality during the war.

Süss, Dietmar. 2014. *Death from the Skies: How the British and Germans Survived Bombing in World War II*. Oxford: Oxford University Press.
An excellent comparative analysis of German and British society under the wartime bombing.
Tooze, Adam. 2006. *The Wages of Destruction: The Making and Breaking of the Nazi Economy*. London: Allen Lane.
A major revisionist account of the German economy and its place in the German preparation and conduct of the war.

CHAPTER FIFTEEN

Total Defeat: War, Society, and Violence in the Last Year of National Socialism

SVEN KELLER

In the afternoon of 30 April 1945, Hitler killed himself. His dominion had shrivelled to a small area around the Reichskanzlei in Berlin. What had transpired during the weeks before in the *Führerbunker* became the subject of the first historiographic study on the end of the Nazi regime: Hugh Trevor-Roper's widely praised *The Last Days of Hitler* (Trevor-Roper 1947). Decades later, there was a resurgence of fascination with the morbid setting (Fest 2002; Joachimsthaler 2004; Frank 2005), and the scenery became iconographic with the movie *Downfall* in 2004.

In between, and for much of the post-1945 period, the last year of the Third Reich has received little scholarly attention. Other questions were paramount: How had the Nazi seizure of power been possible? Did Hitler's intentions shape the Nazis' genocidal policy, or was he a 'weak dictator' (Mommsen 1971, 702), well-nigh driven by the structural dynamics of polycratic rule and 'cumulative radicalization' (Mommsen 1976)? The final phase of Nazi rule more often than not served only as an epilogue. Until Klaus-Dietmar Henke's weighty and substantial book on the American conquest of Germany (Henke 1995), empirical research on the second half of the war remained sparse; even though interest has been perceptibly growing since then, even as late as 2002 the period was still being counted among the striking 'blind spots of research on contemporary history' (Müller 2002, 320).

Starting out with the crises during the summer of 1944, we will follow the main lines of current research that have gained momentum during the last 20 years. Questions and methods supplied by recent approaches of social and cultural history are now being applied to the final phase of the Second Word War and the Nazi regime, which now can be recognized as a distinct period of the 'Third Reich'. First, military historians have started to transcend the mere history of campaigns

A Companion to Nazi Germany, First Edition. Edited by Shelley Baranowski,
Armin Nolzen, and Claus-Christian W. Szejnmann.
© 2018 John Wiley & Sons Ltd. Published 2018 by John Wiley & Sons Ltd.

and operations and discuss the regime's reaction to the mounting military draw-backs; furthermore, they apply the approaches of modern military history to the Wehrmacht, a body of several millions of men by 1944/1945. Second, historians have started to look beyond the paradigm of polycracy, and into the development of National Socialist rule in the face of military and internal crises. Third, the impact of 'total war' and impending defeat on German society has become perhaps the main focus, stimulated by the debate on the *Volksgemeinschaft* ('people's community'), shading into practically all of the other fields of interest. Why did the Germans not capitulate? Why did they – soldiers and civilians alike – hold out and keep on fighting? This leads to the fourth topic: for the first time, the National Socialist violence and atrocities committed during the last months of the war became issues in their own right. Fifth and finally, the question arises as to what extent total defeat and the violence suffered by the Germans themselves influenced their post-war attitudes.

15.1   Military Setbacks

The developments on the war fronts constituted the basic conditions of the Nazi regime during the last year of its existence. The final phase of the war began with a series of military catastrophes in summer 1944. By the beginning of that year, large parts of Europe were still firmly under German control. After the reverses on the Eastern front in 1943, namely at Stalingrad and Kursk, Hitler's eyes were firmly fixed on the West. The dictator had convinced himself that the war would be decided there, and all would depend on the outcome of the long-expected invasion of Allied troops in France. That was soon put aside, however, when Operation Overlord succeeded, and Allied troops landed in Normandy and cut through France at breath-taking speed. In September 1944, enemy troops crossed the border of the German Reich for the first time, near the old imperial city of Aachen.

Still, the developments in the East proved even more disastrous. When the Red Army started its offensive at the end of July, Army Group Centre (*Heeresgruppe Mitte*) collapsed on a length of almost 700 miles. In the three summer months of 1944 alone the Wehrmacht suffered more casualties than the war in the East had claimed during the three years before. Over half a million German soldiers died, resulting in the biggest military catastrophe in German history: the Soviet Operation Bagration, with its enormous territorial gains, hastened German defeat, led to the first liberation of concentration camps in the East, and had considerable consequences for European post-war order. The Battle of the Bulge, Germany's winter offensive in the West, was nothing but a last gasp; it delayed the inevitable for a few weeks at best.

At the beginning of 1945, the enemy armies had lined up at Germany's eastern and western borders. In mid-January, the final battle and the occupation of the German Reich began. During the following months, more and more of German territory was occupied by Allied forces, until, by the end of April, Germany was split into two ever shrinking pockets in the north and the south.

Until the mid-1990s, military historians concentrated on questions of war policies, strategy, and operations. In 1995, many contributions to a voluminous anthology on the end of the Second World War and the early post war period still focused on the classic topics of military and political history (Volkmann 1995). Such methodologically conservative approaches survive to today and continue to have scholarly merit, as indicated by two examples. First, Anthony Beevor's study of the fall of Berlin (Beevor 2002) offers a detailed account of the military operations on both the German and the Soviet side, the reasoning of leaders and commanders, and the darker sides of the Soviet conquest of the German capital, notably the behaviour of Soviet soldiers. Beevor cites a great many memoirs, which sometimes render his narrative rather episodic. Cultural or social questions, however, are clearly not at the centre of this author's interest. Second, the tenth and last volume of the monumental *Das Deutsche Reich und der Zweite Weltkrieg* series (translated into English under the title *Germany and the Second World War*) was published in 2008 (Müller 2008). In great detail, the first part retraces the fighting on the Western and Eastern fronts, and in the air and on the sea, while the second tends to questions of wartime economy and occupation policy.

Since the mid-1990s, however, more and more military historians have started to reflect on the last stage of the war beyond occupation policy, tactics, and operations. In 2002, an anthology witnessed the growing interest in the end of the war (Hillmann and Zimmermann 2002) and assembled papers on a wide range of topics of modern military history. Many of those new approaches centred on one major question: Why did the Wehrmacht fight to the end in 1945?

At first, this newly dominating line of research focused on the role of Hitler and the failure of Wehrmacht command: while the German military leadership's perception of the war in the East and West had been quite realistic, the generals drew no consequences; in the absence of strategic concepts (Schwendemann 1999; Wegner 1999), they denied reality, retreated into wishful thinking, and waged war purely on the grounds of psychological and ideological hopes (Messerschmidt 1995; Schwendemann 1999; Wegner 1999). The difference between the end of the First World War in 1918, when Germany broke down and sued for peace, and 1945, when it didn't, was striking, and Hitler seemed to have made the difference (Wegner 2000). Why did the dictator never take – or even tolerate – any initiative to conclude the war, despite the odds against him, and against all expectations among Allied intelligence experts? Bernd Wegner pointed out that the dictator had not been detached from reality nor a fantasist who believed in miracles. In fact, he argued, Hitler had harboured few illusions when it came to the military realities of the last war years. Fully aware of the crisis and the probable outcome, he nonetheless refused to capitulate. Instead, he followed a 'choreography of doom', resorting to topoi of glorious demises deeply rooted in German culture since the Prussian wars of liberation in 1813–1815. By setting a splendid example for future generations to follow, losing the war became the way to win it. This outlook was by no means limited to Hitler: '"Collective death" as a deliberate gambit to ascertain immortality was at the heart of the Nazi politics of self-destruction [and] a politics of the funeral pyre, in which the mortal enemies of Nazism, the Reich, and Germandom would go down with the defeated in a cataclysm of destruction – not as an end, but as a beginning of future war' (Geyer 2006, 53–55). This argument has drawn much attention in research; however: loss of reality and realism, the hope of final victory, and the strategy of doom do not necessarily exclude each other. All of it combined may have guided Hitler's perceptions and actions in the end (Keller 2013, 191–216).

Meanwhile, the focus has shifted away from Hitler and the military leadership to 'ordinary' soldiers and why so many of them held out in the face of defeat, while the Wehrmacht as a fighting body suffered from ever rising losses, lacked personnel and armaments, and was sufficiently demotorized that it could no longer oppose the Allied troops effectively. In his extensive study on the Wehrmacht during the last months of the war, Andreas Kunz analyses the structural changes that strengthened the party's influence and the role of the Waffen-SS (also see Keller 2014a), and offers insight into the wide variety of individual behaviour of soldiers, many of whom continued to follow orders and kept up the fight (Kunz 2005).

John Zimmermann inquired into the question why the Wehrmacht and its soldiers upheld their resistance on the Western front (Zimmermann 2009, 2012). Großadmiral Karl Dönitz's cover story, which styled the perpetuated fight in the East as a necessity to save soldiers and civilians fleeing from the Red Army, has long been refuted (Kraus 1995; Hillmann 2002; Schwendemann 2002), and Zimmermann overcomes stereotypes of duty, order, and obedience for the Western theatre. Instead, he emphasizes not only the potentially deadly regime of discipline and punishment, but also the commendations, awards, and promotions in place until the very end. He also points out that even in the West there was no strict dichotomy between fighting soldiers and defeatist civilians.

Stephen G. Fritz's book on the 'Endkampf' (final battle) in the region of Franconia (Fritz 2004) provides insights into military operations and a clear regional focus. He offers a thick description of the fighting on the ground, and his splendid narration takes both sides of the front line into account by including American sources. Fritz also attends to the German civilians who found themselves caught in between, and the violence committed by retreating German troops and die-hard Nazi fanatics, thus building a bridge to the experience of the German population in the area.

Nonetheless, we still understand only partly why many ordinary German soldiers fought on, while some others didn't. While many of the mechanisms and dynamics inside the fighting organization have been identified, what we know is still impressionistic: a broader systematization might reveal more about how those factors played together.

15.2   Nazi Rule and Internal Crises

While the military situation deteriorated in summer of 1944, the situation at home looked equally bleak to the Nazi leadership. On 20 July, Claus Schenck Graf von Stauffenberg carried out his bomb attack on Hitler. Even though the conspirator's attempt on the dictator's life and the subsequent coup failed, it had considerable consequences for the regime's assessment of internal stability. It increased an already virulent perception of internal instability that had grown since Stalingrad, and became even more acute after Mussolini's downfall in summer 1943 and Italy's successive change of alliances.

Using the then popular polycracy paradigm, during the 1980s and 1990s historians addressed the regime's reaction to those crises by identifying the characteristics of and changes in the political system and institutional structures during the last year of National Socialist rule. In his empirically based and voluminous study of administration during the Second World War, Klaus Rebentisch devoted a mere 30 pages to the last 12 months, dubbing the period the 'Disintegration of the Führer State' (Rebentisch 1989, 499). He identified a permanent state of emergency during that time, and interpreted it as the product of an increasingly dysfunctional polycratic system, where state administration, party functionaries, special commissioners, and plenipotentiaries effectively paralysed the regime. Newly created governmental boards like the Reich Defence Council had been stillborn, attempts by Nazi leaders like Goebbels to concentrate power as 'Plenipotentiary for Total War' remained ineffective, and the Reich Defence Commissioners – de facto the *Gauleiters* as regional party leaders – added to the omnipresent conflicts of competence.

Eleanor Hancock (Hancock 1991), looking into much the same topic as Rebentisch, adopted a more personalized approach and ascribed the structural changes during the second half of the war to four eminent National Socialist leaders and their respective organizations: Goebbels and the propaganda apparatus (Longerich 1987; Fröhlich 1990); Bormann and the NSDAP (*Nationalsozialistische Deutsche Arbeiterpartei*, Nazi Party); Himmler and the SS (*Schutzstaffel*); and Speer and the munitions and armaments complex (Schwendemann 2003; Scherner and Streb 2006). Hancock's arguments on the intrinsic ideological rationality of each of their concepts of 'total war' may not always be convincing, but she touches on an important point: ideology and deeply rooted convictions were long neglected as factors guiding individual decisions during the last months of the war.

At any rate, Rebentisch's and Hancock's studies both show that the NSDAP, its leaders, and National Socialist ideology gained in significance during the last year of Nazi rule, leading to further 'partification' and 'Nazification' in all areas. This process, however, is no longer seen as paralysing and ultimately responsible for the regime's downfall. Instead of emphasizing polycratic failure, the strengthening of the party, the ideological recollection and the inner radicalization are now recognized as important stabilizing factors of the regime after the failure of the July 1944 attempt on Hitler's life.

Following Hans Mommsen, recent research stresses the tight interrelation between the catastrophic course of the war and the internal development of the Nazi regime. He observed that in its agony, it turned 'back to its roots' (Mommsen 1999, 2001), assuming that in the end the Nazi regime exposed its very nature once again. Recalling the crises that the party had overcome before 1933, the regime emphasized the importance of the 'iron will', strove for total mobilization of the people, and radicalized its racial murder policy. In the end, it was ideology that kept the regime going.

The key in this strategy of ideologization and mobilization was the party, reaching its peak in power during the war years – more precisely, in the regime's final months (Nolzen 2008). Notably, in total war the NSDAP expanded its influence in all relevant fields of policy: military, administration, social control, and racial prose-cution. Instead of becoming a polycratic menace, the party became the single most important factor in stabilizing the home front.

Ian Kershaw's comprehensive study of the last 10 months of the Third Reich underlines the importance of the structural changes in the system of rule (Kershaw 2011). The bottom line for Kershaw, however, is that Hitler's charisma (as illustrated in his monumental biography of the dictator) remains the primary explanation for the regime's persistence in 1944/1945. Other factors, Kershaw argues, 'were ulti-mately subordinate to the way the charismatic Führer regime was structured', which, even after the dictator's death, became 'charismatic rule without charisma' (Kershaw 2011, 400).

This bottom line, as paradoxical as it is intriguing, partly explains why the Nazi regime did not collapse. However, charisma requires presence, and Hitler rarely appeared in public during the last years of the war. While the persistence or cha-risma can be assumed among the leaders of the party and in the military, in the end it falls short if it is used to explain why so many Germans, civilians and soldiers alike, held out, and why many of them even kept on murdering.

The durability of the party and, in general, its ongoing effectiveness at all hier-archical levels proves to be a decisive element. Party functionaries controlled new organizations like the *Volkssturm* militia (Yelton 2002), and the *Gauleiters* expanded their competences as regional party potentates and now served as Reich Defence Commissioners (Teppe 1986; Blank 2001). Even though this can be read as an indicator pointing to an increasing decentralization and disintegra-tion of central power during the last months, it also enhanced the regime's flex-ibility and assertiveness in an increasingly fragmented scenario. While decentralization was the result of the deteriorating military situation, at the same time it could strengthen National Socialist rule and the regime's grip on the situ-ation regionally.

With almost 9 million Germans being party members and with a close-knit network of local functionaries, the party mobilized and disciplined the populace, according to the parameters of Nazi ideology. What party functionaries called *Menschenführung* ('leading the people') can hardly be overestimated as a stabiliz-ing factor. This epitomizes the close interconnection between the Nazi system of rule and German society during the last stage of the war – a connection crucial to explaining both the regime's surprising stability and capacity to act until the very end, and the perseverance of Germans until the end.

15.3   Total War and the *Volksgemeinschaft*

At first, however, the history of German society in 1944/1945 was mainly addressed as a history of breakdown and dissolution. In 1990, scholars at the Munich Institute of Contemporary History postulated a continuous period of catastrophe experienced by many Germans between Stalingrad and the West German currency reform in 1948 (Broszat, Henke, and Woller 1989) and, against this background, stressed the manifold social and mental continuities that spanned the political caesura of German capitulation on 8 May. The focus then was not so much on the final phase of the war, but rather the conditions of post-war 'ruins society' (Teppe 1995). This perspective argued against the popular and exonerating notion of a 'zero hour' and disputed a sharp division between the Third Reich and the liberal-democratic, economically successful Federal Republic.

At the same time however, other scholars became genuinely interested in the changes in German society after Stalingrad: How did Germans react to the psychological and physical strains of 'total war', the havoc the Allied bombing raids wrought, the military setbacks, and, finally, the military occupation of Reich territory? The dominating perspective was still that of social disintegration, finding the spirit and the attitude of the population changing from 1943 onwards, when the 'high-handed, chauvinist "Volksgemeinschaft"' had turned into an 'emergency community of the exhausted' of largely apathetic Germans fed up with the war (Frei 1990, 296).

At first, it was mainly the large, devastated cities of the Reich that sparked the interest. By the end of 1944, Allied bombing raids had utterly destroyed the city of Cologne. Human gregariousness had turned into a 'society in catastrophe' (Rusinek 1989a, 1989b), and the population among the ruins was down to a quarter compared to before the war. The chaotic circumstances and food shortages led to social atomization and increased criminality, while the regime's police forces literally waged war against groups of escaped foreign forced labourers in hiding. The Gestapo lost all inhibitions in an almost apocalyptic scenario. Similarly, in Hamburg National Socialist rule and social cohesion gradually eroded after the devastating bombing raids of Operation Gomorrah in July/August of 1943 (Bajohr 1998). In smaller, more provincial towns the situation was different: in 1944/1945 they were often undestroyed when the Allied troops approached. Here, the retreat of National Socialist rule and the process of a readjusting society were quite different from the major urban centres (Münkler 2005).

Since then, the perspective on German society during the last year of the war has gradually overcome its early constrictions, and the inquiry of a wider variety of topics has helped scholars to discern not only elements of disintegration but also stabilizing factors. While it is clearly true that the regime's integrative potential abated in many areas and many Germans had utterly lost the enthusiasm they may have felt earlier, National Socialist society remained sufficiently – and surprisingly – stable until total defeat.

The two parts of volume 9 of the monumental *Germany and the Second World War* series (Echternkamp 2008b, 2014), first published in German in 2004 and 2005, departed from the perspective of classic military history the series was otherwise bound to. Its contributions represented the wide variety of aspects researchers were now tackling, striving to improve our understanding of National Socialist society during the war. Its concept of 'war as a state of society' stresses the impossibility of separating one from the other (Echternkamp 2008a) and elaborates on the consequences the war had on National Socialist rule, social practice, individual experience, and the experience of violence in particular, both by the affected and by the agents. Besides Nolzen's aforementioned article on the NSDAP, other notable contributions address air warfare, its effects on German society, and the regime's attempts to mitigate those effects (Blank 2008), or the transformations of National

Socialist propaganda, which turned to a motif of 'strength through fear' when its former persuasiveness started to fail (Kallis 2005, 2008). Even though the volume chronologically spans the entire war, most of the contributions explicitly attend to the last year, and address how the regime reacted to crises and countered destabilizing developments in National Socialist society.

But how successful was the regime in this endeavour? Given the loss of social cohesion asserted in early studies, did National Socialism really fail during wartime due to declining support? This is the conclusion that Jill Stephenson reaches in her book *Hitler's Home Front* (Stephenson 2006). But can the dissent from certain aspects of National Socialism that she finds in rural Württemberg really be taken as evidence for broader dissidence? Stephenson enumerates a great many examples where the rural population opposed the futile defence of their towns and villages, and, in fact, this is not exceptional. But at the same time, Stephenson underexposes indications of compliance and collusion (which, of course, often do not emerge quite as prominently in postwar sources as episodes of heroic resistance do). The regime and its violence appear to be something external, imposed on uninvolved and unwilling Württembergers. But in the end, the crucial question remains: Why then, did Nazi rule remain stable in Württemberg up to the very end, just as it did in other rural areas and in the Reich?

As much as one may be reluctant to use the term 'success' in this context, the regime succeeded in marshalling enough support to survive until the very end – a war fought until total defeat was necessary to overcome National Socialism. The much-cited 'inner front' was stable enough to prevent serious opposition or insurrection. Even as the regime's nerve centre in Berlin started to fail, the regime remained capable of acting through a great number of individual protagonists who had internalized the National Socialist ideology and world-view.

At the core of this frame of reference was the *Volksgemeinschaft*. Whatever the factual condition of German society during the last year, as an ideological concept it remained a powerful guiding principle. The 'people's community' concept of society was the lesson the Nazis had distilled from their perception of Germany's defeat in the First World War: to prevent a second 1918 and defeat in a new war (which Hitler expected as inevitable), the *Volksgemeinschaft* was to reinforce the home front and guarantee inner stability. Its rules of inclusion and exclusion defined 'the enemies of the people' along racial and political lines. They were designed to strengthen the *Volk* in order to prevent treason and breakdown. In this perspective, the *Volksgemeinschaft* was a conceptual counter-model to 1918, conceived as a guarantee against defeat itself. Thus, for many, it did not lose its appeal during the last stage of the war. On the contrary, it only furthered radicalism. On the verge of defeat once again, many clung to the *Volksgemeinschaft* as a model of orientation and direction to the end. The National Socialist world-view had become part of individual identities, and the more desperate the situation, the harder it became to question one's own bearings and convictions. Taking such social dynamics into account is necessary to explain the functioning and the stability of the regime at the end, and it is essential to understand the excessive violence during the last months of the war (Keller 2014b).

15.4   Nazi Violence

Violence is without doubt the single key characteristic of National Socialism, and it culminated during its last year (Wolfrum, Arendes, and Zedler 2006). For quite some time, historians tended to neglect its significance (Bessel 2014), and yet it seems obvious that violence was the pivotal reaction of the regime and convinced Nazis to imminent defeat, to a widespread expectation of prosecution or death, to chaos and the breakdown of society that occurred during the Allied conquest of Germany (Keller 2013). In a menacing and desperate situation, fanatics often chose not to fight the enemy armies, but turned against the 'enemies within' once more. Although not necessarily directed to do so by the regime, individual perpetrators all over the ever-shrinking German sphere of control followed the long-established ideological rules established by the *Volksgemeinschaft* ideology in a last stand against defeat.

Even *Volksgenossen*, members of mainstream Nazi society, were shot or hanged in rising numbers. Whoever did not want to continue the fight, whoever wanted to save his or hers village and home from further destruction, whoever broke down under the strains of a long-lost war was stigmatized as defeatist and a *Volksverräter* ('traitor of the people') and had to fear the regime's brutal revenge. Many of National Socialism's old political foes, long since subdued, were killed, while party veterans settled old scores and the Gestapo 'secured' the hinterland behind the front, killing anyone who was deemed dangerous to the defensive efforts and the home front. Undoubtedly, this ability to spawn violence up to the very last moment and threaten those willing to capitulate was key to the regime's ability to keep up the fight. Even in the last year, however, most victims by far were not war-weary *Volksgenossen*, but the so-called racial enemies of the *Volksgemeinschaft*: foreign slave labourers, prisoners of war, and concentration camp inmates. Those groups attracted little interest in historical research until the mid-1990s (Herbert 1985).

Recently, several studies have expanded our knowledge, for example on the fate of thousands of prison inmates: the Gestapo killed many of its prisoners in numerous mass shootings on Reich territory itself, with an estimated number of victims of over 10 000, most of them foreign forced labourers (Paul 2000; Schmid 2000). When the regular prisons run by the justice department were evacuated upon enemy approach, a similar fate awaited many of their foreign inmates(Wachsmann 2004). Which individuals were killed, evacuated, or even freed illustrates how the mechanisms of selection and murder followed racial rules: just as evacuation guidelines required, and regardless of their crimes, foreign inmates ran a much higher risk of being killed because they were presumed to be a security threat and dangerous to the German population.

This also applied to the inmates of the concentration camps: in December 1944, 714 000 women and men were still incarcerated. In summer 1944, when Allied troops started their approach towards the camps, inmates were at first evacuated in a fairly orderly manner. This changed in mid-January 1945, when the Allied advance gained speed and camps were vacated hastily and without proper preparation (Orth 2002): at least a third of the prisoners perished during the infamous death marches. Beginning with the evacuation of Auschwitz (Strzelecki 1995), hundreds of thousands of inmates were herded towards camps in the Reich, with those too weak or too ill to march on being killed along the way.

The intentions and policies behind the death marches are contradictory and hard to pin down (Zámečník 1985; Bauer 1994). There has been much debate whether the 'final solution to the Jewish question' did in fact end with the shut-down of the extermination facilities at Auschwitz in November 1944 (Bridgman 1990), or whether the marches were a continuation of the Holocaust, with liquidation, not evacuation, being their underlying goal (Bauer 1989; Krakowski 1984). Did an order not to let any prisoner fall into enemy hands exist – or was it even necessary? Did the guards not know on their own what was expected of them?

When Daniel Goldhagen put forward his much-debated thesis of a German 'eliminationist antisemitism', he based his argumentation in part on the death marches, which he interpreted as a last effort to complete the genocide (Goldhagen 1996). His premise that only Jews had been selected for the marches is wrong, however: Jews represented about a third to a half of the prisoners on the marches, and lagging inmates, Jews and non-Jews alike, were killed because they were seen as dangerous. Hence, Daniel Blatman has repeatedly argued that these murders should be viewed separately from the Holocaust (Blatman 1998, 2000, 2005). In 2011, he presented the most comprehensive study on the death marches to date, once again stressing that the death march killings were different from the Holocaust, because they no longer 'adopt[ed] diverse attitudes to different groups of victims' (Blatman 2011, 416).

In the meantime, several studies and edited volumes have investigated single camps like Neuengamme (Garbe and Lange 2005; Hertz-Eichenrode 2000), the Gardelegen massacre (Gring 2004), Ravensbrück (Erpel 2005), and Buchenwald (Greiser 2008). In many cities, concentration camp inmates clearing debris had been publicly present at least since 1944 (Fings 2005); in the countryside, the death marches confronted the population in a most conspicuous way with the National Socialist crimes. The regime no longer cared about secrecy: civilians had to supply the carts and food for the marchers who spend the nights in barns or in the open, and they had to dispatch the corpses of those killed and starved. People could stand at the roadside and watch the columns of dragging humans – and many openly satisfied their curiosity.

All the while, Germans typically did not commiserate. If there were those who felt appalled by the violence or pitied the victims, they did not normally act: attempts to help, however small, seem to have been rare occurrences. The marchers signified the critical situation and the approaching fronts. Even their haggard, devitalized shape seemed to evoke fear: since 1933, concentration camp inmates had been presented to the population as dangerous and threatening social aliens, and now they became a memento of the horrendous acts committed against them, and the retribution to be expected. They became harbingers of chaos and collapse – and unlike the enemy troops, they still could be successfully fought and removed. Confronted with imminent defeat and fearing punishment for its crimes, the *Volksgemeinschaft* closed ranks one last time against its internal foes, indifferent to the suffering of others and too preoccupied with its own fate. It was not just the violence directed by the regime at defeatist Germans that stabilized the regime to the last, but also the violence committed through the *Volksgemeinschaft*: to the very end, its violently upheld racist social order provided a target for a perverted form of anti-chaos reflex (Keller 2013, 291–304).

15.5   The Impact of Defeat

The end of war in 1945 was violent. The victims of National Socialism suffered the most, but it also brought violence to many ordinary Germans. Allied bombing, the final fight on the ground, and the violence of the regime's die-hard protagonists threatened the *Volk* itself. This experience contributed immensely to the awareness that, this time, defeat was nothing like that in 1918 when German troops still stood deep in French territory. Now, it was total defeat. Germany ceased to exist, and the Allies took control. Everywhere, towns and villages lay in ruins. In the East, Germans were expelled and millions uprooted. German guilt was as glaring as it was unthinkable. All of this disposed Germans to abhor further warmongering or National Socialist underground activities. Konrad Jarausch argues that this resulted in the fundamental reversal of German mentalities that rendered possible what he clearly conceives as West Germany's story of success – demilitarization and liberalization (Jarausch 2006).

Richard Bessel, too, has looked at the aftermath of the war, but puts a more intimate focus on the year 1945. In an excellent and inspiring close-up, he creates a portrait of the year, depicting both sides of unconditional surrender. He demonstrates how a surprising transformation from war to peace became possible – even though many Germans remained passive and apathetic. His outlook is not overly optimistic; he does not overlook the fact that the great disorder and the necessities of survival after the capitulation 'allowed [Germans] to leave the Third Reich behind without having to confront their own role in it' (Bessel 2010, 338).

His comment raises the question of German responsibility for the totality and the violence of defeat. Much light has been shed on the question why the Germans kept fighting, and recent research has stressed the regime's long-lasting functional integrity despite social breakdown and administrative decentralization. What seemed to be a history of downfall and growing dysfunctionality discloses stabilizing factors and ideological persistence that allowed the regime to fight and kill until total defeat. Questions do remain: apart from National Socialist ideology, how did other personal convictions and models of order like nationalism, militarism, or patriotism (Stargardt 2010) contribute to this stability? We still know little about the much-cited apathy of Germans, or how the wartime reconfiguration of German society – which had, for example, become decidedly female – affected the final phase of the war. When and how did convinced Nazis realize defeat, how did they make sense of it, and how did they react? Future research will enhance our understanding of the Nazi regime's stability, its ideological effectiveness, and, to a surprising degree, its social cohesion to the very end.

References

Bajohr, Frank. 1998. 'Hamburg – Der Zerfall der "Volksgemeinschaft".' In *Kriegsende in Europa: Vom Beginn des deutschen Machtzerfalls bis zur Stabilisierung der Nachkriegsordnung 1944–1948*, edited by Ulrich Herbert and Axel Schildt, 318–336. Essen: Klartext.

Bauer, Yehuda. 1989. 'The Death Marches, January–May 1945.' In *The Nazi Holocaust, Volume 9: The End of the Holocaust*, edited by Michael R. Marrus, 491–511. Westport, CT: Meckler.

Bauer, Yehuda. 1994. *Jews for Sale? Nazi–Jewish Negotiations 1933–1945*. New Haven, CT: Yale University Press.

Beevor, Antony. 2002. *The Fall of Berlin, 1945*. New York: Viking.

Bessel, Richard. 2010. *Germany 1945: From War to Peace*. New York: Simon & Schuster.

Bessel, Richard. 2014. 'The End of the Volksgemeinschaft.' In *Visions of Community in Nazi Germany: Social Engineering and Private Lives*, edited by Martina Steber and Bernhard Gotto 2014, 281–294. Oxford: Oxford University Press.

Blank, Ralf. 2001. 'Albert Hoffmann als Reichsverteidigungskommissar im Gau Westfalen-Süd, 1943–1945: Eine biographische Skizze.' In *'Bürokratien': Initiative und Effizienz*, edited by Wolf Gruner and Armin Nolzen, 189–210. Berlin: Assoziation A.

Blank, Ralf. 2008. 'Wartime Daily Life and the Air War on the Home Front.' In *Germany and the Second World War, vol. IX/part 1: German Wartime Society 1939–1945: Politicization, Disintegration, and the Struggle for Survival*, edited by Jörg Echternkamp, 370–476. Oxford; New York: Clarendon Press; Oxford University Press.

Blatman, Daniel. 1998. 'Die Todesmärsche – Entscheidungsträger, Mörder und Opfer.' In *Die nationalsozialistischen Konzentrationslager: Entwicklung und Struktur*. Vol. 2, edited by Ulrich Herbert, Karin Orth, and Christoph Dieckmann, 1063–1092. Göttingen: Wallstein.

Blatman, Daniel. 2000. 'The Death Marches, January–May 1945: Who Was Responsible for What?' *Yad Vashem Studies* 28, 155–201.

Blatman, Daniel. 2005. 'Rückzug, Evakuierung und Todesmärsche 1944–1945.' In *Der Ort des Terrors: Geschichte der nationalsozialistischen Konzentrationslager, Volume 1: Die Organisation des Terrors*, edited by Wolfgang Benz and Barbara Distel, 296–312. Munich: C.H. Beck.

Blatman, Daniel. 2011. *Die Todesmärsche 1944/45: Das letzte Kapitel des nationalsozialistischen Massenmords*. Reinbek bei Hamburg: Rowohlt.

Bridgman, Jon. 1990. *The End of the Holocaust: The Liberation of the Camps*. London: Batsford.

Broszat, Martin, Henke, Klaus-Dietmar, and Woller, Hans, eds. 1989. *Von Stalingrad zur Währungsreform: Zur Sozialgeschichte des Umbruchs in Deutschland*. Munich: Oldenbourg.

Echternkamp, Jörg. 2008a. 'At War, Abroad and at Home: The Essential Features of German Society in the Second World War.' In *Germany and the Second World War, vol. IX/part 1: German Wartime Society 1939–1945: Politicization, Disintegration, and the Struggle for Survival*, edited by Jörg Echternkamp, 1–101. Oxford; New York: Clarendon Press; Oxford University Press.

Echternkamp, Jörg, ed. 2008b. *Germany and the Second World War, vol. IX/part 1: German Wartime Society 1939–1945: Politicization, Disintegration, and the Struggle for Survival*. Oxford; New York: Clarendon Press; Oxford University Press.

Echternkamp, Jörg, ed. 2014. *Germany and the Second World War, vol. IX/part 2: German Wartime Society 1939–1945: Exploitation, Interpretations, Exclusion*. Germany and the Second World War. Oxford, New York: Clarendon Press; Oxford University Press.

Erpel, Simone. 2005. *Zwischen Vernichtung und Befreiung: Das Frauen-Konzentrationslager Ravensbrück in der letzten Kriegsphase*. Berlin: Metropol.

Fest, Joachim. 2002. *Der Untergang: Hitler und das Ende des Dritten Reiches. Eine historische Skizze.* Berlin: Alexander Fest.

Fings, Karola. 2005. *Krieg, Gesellschaft und KZ: Himmlers SS-Baubrigaden.* Sammlung Schöningh zur Geschichte und Gegenwart. Paderborn: Schöningh.

Frank, Mario. 2005. *Der Tod im Führerbunker: Hitlers letzte Tage.* 1. Aufl. Munich: Siedler.

Frei, Norbert. 1990. 'Der totale Krieg und die Deutschen.' In *Der nationalsozialistische Krieg,* edited by Norbert Frei and Hermann Kling, 283–301. Frankfurt am Main: Campus.

Fritz, Stephen G. 2004. *Endkampf: Soldiers, Civilians, and the Death of the Third Reich.* Lexington: University Press of Kentucky.

Fröhlich, Elke. 1990. 'Hitler und Goebbels im Krisenjahr 1944: Aus den Tagebüchern des Reichspropagandaministers.' *Vierteljahrshefte für Zeitgeschichte* 38, 195–224.

Garbe, Detlef and Lange, Carmen, eds. 2005. *Häftlinge zwischen Vernichtung und Befreiung: Die Auflösung des KZ Neuengamme und seiner Aussenlager durch die SS im Frühjahr 1945.* Bremen: Edition Temmen.

Geyer, Michael. 2006. 'Endkampf 1918 and 1945: German Nationalism, Annihilation, and Self-Destruction.' In *No Man's Land of Violence: Extreme Wars in the 20th Century,* edited by Alf Lüdtke and Bernd Weisbrod, 35–68. Göttinger Gespräche zur Geschichtswissenschaft 24. Göttingen: Wallstein.

Goldhagen, Daniel Jonah. 1996. *Hitler's Willing Executioners: Ordinary Germans and the Holocaust.* New York: Knopf.

Greiser, Katrin. 2008. *Die Todesmärsche von Buchenwald: Räumung, Befreiung und Spuren der Erinnerung.* Göttingen: Wallstein.

Gring, Diana. 2004. 'Das Massaker von Gardelegen.' *Dachauer Hefte* 20, 112–126.

Hancock, Eleanor. 1991. *The National Socialist Leadership and Total War.* New York: St. Martin's Press.

Henke, Klaus-Dietmar. 1995. *Die amerikanische Besetzung Deutschlands.* Quellen und Darstellungen zur Zeitgeschichte 27. Munich: Oldenbourg.

Herbert, Ulrich. 1985. *Fremdarbeiter: Politik und Praxis des 'Ausländer-Einsatzes' in der Kriegswirtschaft des Dritten Reiches.* Berlin and Bonn: Dietz.

Hertz-Eichenrode, Katharina, ed. 2000. *Ein KZ wird geräumt: Häftlinge zwischen Vernichtung und Befreiung. Die Auflösung des KZ Neuengamme und seiner Außenlager durch die SS im Frühjahr 1945. Katalog zur Wanderausstellung.* 2 vols. Bremen: Temmen.

Hillmann, Jörg. 2002. 'Die Reichsregierung in Flensburg.' In *Kriegsende 1945 in Deutschland,* edited by Jörg Hillmann and John Zimmermann, 35–65. Beiträge zur Militärgeschichte 55. Munich: Oldenbourg.

Hillmann, Jörg and Zimmermann, John, eds. 2002. *Kriegsende 1945 in Deutschland.* Beiträge zur Militärgeschichte 55. Munich: Oldenbourg.

Jarausch, Konrad H. 2006. *Recivilizing Germans, 1945–1995.* Oxford: Oxford University Press.

Joachimsthaler, Anton. 2004. *Hitlers Ende: Legenden und Dokumente.* Munich: Herbig.

Kallis, Aristotle A. 2005. *Nazi Propaganda and the Second World War.* Basingstoke, UK: Palgrave Macmillan.

Kallis, Aristotle A. 2008. 'The Decline of Interpretative Power: National Socialist Propaganda during the War.' In *Germany and the Second World War, vol. IX/part 1: German Wartime Society 1939–1945: Politicization, Disintegration, and the Struggle for Survival,* edited by Jörg Echternkamp, 204–52. Oxford; New York: Clarendon Press; Oxford University Press.

Keller, Sven. 2013. *Volksgemeinschaft am Ende: Gesellschaft und Gewalt 1944/45.* Quellen und Darstellungen zur Zeitgeschichte 97. Munich: Oldenbourg.

Keller, Sven. 2014a. 'Elite am Ende: Die Waffen-SS in der letzten Phase des Krieges 1945.' In *Die Waffen-SS: Neue Forschungen*, edited by Jan E. Schulte, Peter Lieb, and Bernd Wegner, 354–373. Krieg in der Geschichte 74. Paderborn: Schöningh.

Keller, Sven. 2014b. 'Volksgemeinschaft and Violence: Some Reflections on Interdependencies.' In *Visions of Community in Nazi Germany: Social Engineering and Private Lives*, edited by Martina Bernhard Steber and Gotto, 226–239. Oxford: Oxford University Press.

Kershaw, Ian. 2011. *The End: The Defiance and Destruction of Hitler's Germany, 1944–1945.* New York: Penguin.

Krakowski, Shmuel. 1984. 'The Death Marches in the Period of the Evacuation of Camps.' In *The Nazi Concentration Camps: Structure and Aims, the Image of the Prisoners, the Jews in the Camps: Proceedings of the Fourth Yad Vashem International Historical Conference, Jerusalem January 1980*, edited by Israel Gutmann and Avital Saf, 475–489. Jerusalem: Yad Vashem.

Kraus, Herbert. 1995. 'Karl Dönitz und das Ende des Dritten Reiches.' In *Ende des Dritten Reiches – Ende des Zweiten Weltkriegs: Eine perspektivische* Rückschau, edited by Hans-Eric Volkmann, 1–23. Munich: Piper.

Kunz, Andreas. 2005. *Wehrmacht und Niederlage: Die bewaffnete Macht in der Endphase der nationalsozialistischen Herrschaft 1944 bis 1945.* Beiträge zur Militärgeschichte 64. Munich: Oldenbourg.

Longerich, Peter. 1987. 'Joseph Goebbels und der Totale Krieg: Eine unbekannte Denkschrift des Propagandaministers vom 18. Juli 1944.' *Vierteljahrshefte für Zeitgeschichte* 35, 289–314.

Messerschmidt, Manfred. 1995. 'Die Wehrmacht: Vom Realitätsverlust zum Selbstbetrug.' In *Ende des Dritten Reiches – Ende des Zweiten Weltkriegs: Eine perspektivische* Rückschau, edited by Hans-Eric Volkmann, 223–257. Munich: Piper.

Mommsen, Hans. 1971. 'Nationalsozialismus.' In *Sowjetsystem und demokratische Gesellschaft: Eine vergleichende Enzyklopädie*, vol. 4, col. 695–713. Freiburg: Herder.

Mommsen, Hans. 1976. 'Der Nationalsozialismus: Kumulative Radikalisierung und Selbstzerstörung des Regimes.' In *Meyers Enzyklopädisches Lexikon*, vol. 16, 785–790. Mannheim: Meyers.

Mommsen, Hans. 1999. 'Die Rückkehr zu den Ursprüngen: Betrachtungen zur inneren Auflösung des Dritten Reiches nach der Niederlage von Stalingrad.' In *Von Weimar nach Auschwitz: Zur Geschichte Deutschlands in der Weltkriegsepoche. Ausgewählte Aufsätze*, edited by Hans Mommsen, 309–324. Stuttgart: DVA.

Mommsen, Hans, ed. 2001. *The Third Reich Between Vision and Reality: New Perspectives on German History 1918–1945.* German Historical Perspectives Series 12. Oxford: Berg.

Müller, Rolf-Dieter. 2002. '1945: Der Tiefpunkt in der deutschen Geschichte: Gedanken zu Problemen und Perspektiven der historischen Forschung.' In *Kriegsende 1945 in Deutschland.* Beiträge zur Militärgeschichte 55, edited by Jörg Hillmann and Jörg John Zimmermann 2002, 319–329. Munich: Oldenbourg.

Müller, Rolf-Dieter. 2008. 'Der Zusammenbruch des Wirtschaftslebens und die Anfänge des Wiederaufbaus.' In *Das Deutsche Reich und der Zweite Weltkrieg, vol. 10/part 2: Der Zusammenbruch des Deutschen Reiches: Die Folgen des Zweiten Weltkrieges*, 55–198. Munich: DVA.

Münkler, Herfried. 2005. *Machtzerfall: Die letzten Tage des Dritten Reiches dargestellt am Beispiel der hessischen Kreisstadt Friedberg.* Hamburg: Europ. Verl.-Anst. First published 1995.

Nolzen, Armin. 2008. 'The NSDAP, the War, and German Society.' In *Germany and the Second World War, vol. IX/part 1: German Wartime Society 1939–1945: Politicization,*

Disintegration, and the Struggle for Survival, edited by Jörg Echternkamp, 111–206. Oxford; New York: Clarendon Press; Oxford University Press.

Orth, Karin. 2002. *Das System der nationalsozialistischen Konzentrationslager: Eine politische Organisationsgeschichte*. Zurich: Pendo.

Paul, Gerhard. 2000. "Diese Erschießungen haben mich innerlich gar nicht mehr berührt": Die Kriegsendphasenverbrechen der Gestapo.' In *Die Gestapo im zweiten Weltkrieg: 'Heimatfront' und besetztes Europa*, edited by Gerhard Paul and Klaus-Michael Mallmann, 543–568. Darmstadt: Wiss. Buchges.

Rebentisch, Dieter. 1989. *Führerstaat und Verwaltung im Zweiten Weltkrieg: Verfassungsentwicklung und Verwaltungspolitik 1939–1945*. Frankfurter historische Abhandlungen 29. Stuttgart: Steiner-Verl.-Wiesbaden.

Rusinek, Bernd-A. 1989a. *Gesellschaft in der Katastrophe: Terror, Illegalität, Widerstand - Köln 1944/45*. Essen: Klartext.

Rusinek, Bernd-A. 1989b. "Maskenlose Zeit": Der Zerfall der Gesellschaft im Krieg.' In *ÜberLeben im Krieg: Kriegserfahrungen in einer Industrieregion 1939–1945*, edited by Ulrich Borsdorf and Mathilde Jamin, 180–194. Reinbek bei Hamburg: Rowohlt-Taschenbuch.

Scherner, Johannes and Streb, Jochen. 2006. 'Das Ende eines Mythos? Albert Speer und das so genannte Rüstungswunder.' *Vierteljahrschrift für Sozial- und Wirtschaftsgeschichte* 93, 172–196.

Schmid, Hans-Dieter. 2000. 'Die Geheime Staatspolizei in der Endphase des Krieges.' *Geschichte in Wissenschaft und Unterricht* 51, 528–539.

Schwendemann, Heinrich. 1999. 'Strategie der Selbstvernichtung: Die Wehrmachtführung im "Endkampf" um das Dritte Reich.' In *Die Wehrmacht: Mythos und Realität*, edited by Rolf-Dieter Müller and Hans-Erich Volkmann, 224–244. Munich: Oldenbourg.

Schwendemann, Heinrich. 2002. '"Deutsche Menschen vor der Vernichtung durch den Bolschewismus zu retten": Das Programm der Regierung Dönitz und der Beginn einer Legendenbildung.' In *Kriegsende 1945 in Deutschland*. Beiträge zur Militärgeschichte 55, edited by Jörg Hillmann and John Zimmermann, 9–33. Munich: Oldenbourg.

Schwendemann, Heinrich. 2003. '"Drastic Measures to Defend the Reich at the Oder and the Rhein": A Forgotten Memorandum of Albert Speer of 18th March 1945.' *Journal of Contemporary History* 38, 597–614.

Stargardt, Nicholas. 2010. 'The Troubled Patriot: German Innerlichkeit in World War II.' *German History* 28, 326–342.

Stephenson, Jill. 2006. *Hitler's Home Front: Württemberg Under the Nazis*. London: Hambledon Continuum.

Strzelecki, Andrzej. 1995. *Endphase des KL Auschwitz: Evakuierung Liquidierung und Befreiung des Lagers*. Oswiecim: Verl. Staatl. Museum Auschwitz.

Teppe, Karl. 1986. 'Der Reichsverteidigungskommissar: Organisation und Praxis in Westfalen.' In *Verwaltung contra Menschenführung im Staat Hitlers*, edited by Dieter Rebentisch and Karl Teppe, 278–301. Göttingen: Vandenhoeck & Ruprecht.

Teppe, Karl. 1995. 'Trümmergesellschaft im Wiederaufbau.' *Aus Politik und Zeitgeschichte*, B 18–19, 22–33.

Trevor-Roper, Hugh. 1947. *The Last Days of Hitler*. London and New York: Macmillan.

Volkmann, Hans-Erich, ed. 1995. *Ende des Dritten Reiches – Ende des Zweiten Weltkriegs: Eine perspektivische Rückschau*. Munich: Piper.

Wachsmann, Nikolaus. 2004. *Hitler's Prisons: Legal Terror in Nazi Germany*. New Haven, CT: Yale University Press.

Wegner, Bernd. 1999. 'Defensive ohne Strategie: Die Wehrmacht und das Jahr 1943.' In *Die Wehrmacht: Mythos und Realität*, edited by Rolf-Dieter Müller and Hans-Erich Volkmann, 197–209. Munich: Oldenbourg.

Wegner, Bernd. 2000. 'Hitler, der Zweite Weltkrieg und die Choreographie des Unterganges.' *Geschichte und Gesellschaft* 26, 493–518.

Wolfrum, Edgar, Arendes, Cord, and Zedler, Jörg, eds. 2006. *Terror nach innen: Verbrechen am Ende des Zweiten Weltkrieges*. Dachauer Symposien zur Zeitgeschichte 6. Göttingen: Wallstein.

Yelton, David K. 2002. *Hitler's Volkssturm: The Nazi Militia and the Fall of Germany 1944–1945*. Lawrence: University Press of Kansas.

Zámečník, Stanislav. 1985. '"Kein Häftling darf lebend in die Hände des Feindes fallen": Zur Existenz des Himmler-Befehls vom 14./18. April 1945.' *Dachauer Hefte* 1, 219–231.

Zimmermann, John. 2009. *Pflicht zum Untergang: Die deutsche Kriegführung im Westen des Reiches 1944/45*. Paderborn: Schöningh.

Zimmermann, John. 2012. 'German Soldiers and Surrender, 1945.' In *How Fighting Ends: A History of Surrender*, edited by Holger Afflerbach and Hew Strachan, 369–381. Oxford: Oxford University Press.

Further Reading

Bessel, Richard. 2010. *Germany 1945: From War to Peace*. New York: Simon & Schuster.

Blatman, Daniel. 2011. *Die Todesmärsche 1944/45: Das letzte Kapitel des nationalsozialistischen Massenmords*. Reinbek bei Hamburg: Rowohlt.

Echternkamp, Jörg. 2008. 'At War, Abroad and at Home: The Essential Features of German Society in the Second World War.' In *Germany and the Second World War, vol. IX/part 1: German Wartime Society 1939–1945: Politicization, Disintegration, and the Struggle for Survival*, edited by Jörg Echternkamp, 1–101. Oxford; New York: Clarendon Press; Oxford University Press.

Geyer, Michael. 2006. 'Endkampf 1918 and 1945: German Nationalism, Annihilation, and Self-Destruction.' In *No Man's Land of Violence: Extreme Wars in the 20th Century*, edited by Alf Lüdtke and Bernd Weisbrod, 35–68. Göttinger Gespräche zur Geschichtswissenschaft 24. Göttingen: Wallstein.

Hillmann, Jörg and Zimmermann, John, eds. 2002. *Kriegsende 1945 in Deutschland*. Beiträge zur Militärgeschichte 55. Munich: Oldenbourg.

Keller, Sven. 2013. *Volksgemeinschaft am Ende: Gesellschaft und Gewalt 1944/45*. Quellen und Darstellungen zur Zeitgeschichte 97. Munich: Oldenbourg.

Keller, Sven. 2014. 'Volksgemeinschaft and Violence: Some Reflections on Interdependencies.' In *Visions of Community in Nazi Germany: Social Engineering and Private Lives*, edited by Martina Bernhard Steber and Gotto, 226–239. Oxford: Oxford University Press.

Kershaw, Ian. 2011. *The End: The Defiance and Destruction of Hitler's Germany, 1944–1945*. New York: Penguin.

Kunz, Andreas. 2005. *Wehrmacht und Niederlage: Die bewaffnete Macht in der Endphase der nationalsozialistischen Herrschaft 1944 bis 1945*. Beiträge zur Militärgeschichte 64. Munich: Oldenbourg.

Mommsen, Hans, ed. 2001. *The Third Reich Between Vision and Reality: New Perspectives on German History 1918–1945*. German Historical Perspectives Series 12. Oxford: Berg.

PART III

Economy and Culture

CHAPTER SIXTEEN

The Nazi Economy

STEPHEN G. GROSS

The Nazi economy has been a topic of intense debate since the moment Hitler seized power. The left initially saw National Socialism as a tool of monopoly capitalism, while the right denied any structural links between capitalism and the Nazis. Between these two extremes, scholars have described the Third Reich as a vampire economy, as crisis capitalism with a cudgel, or as heterodox socialism. Today assessments still run the entire gamut, from a 'pristinely' capitalist state (Anievas 2014, 169) to one that was fundamentally anti-capitalist (Tismaneanu 2014).

Remarkably, in analysing the Nazi economy contemporaries anticipated many questions that still animate research today. To give one example, in 1942 the legal scholar Franz Neumann suggested how imperialism tied various groups together under the regime; he underscored how crises in trade and raw materials allowed the state to extend control over industry; he asked how a regime with pretensions to forging a command economy could preserve competition, profit, and entrepreneurial initiative; and he pointed out how 'Aryanization' – the forced removal of Jews from the economy – belonged to a larger process of racial enslavement (Neumann 1963). After 1989, when the opening of new archives revived interest in the Nazi economy, many of Neumann's themes returned to centre stage.

This essay explores how the four issues above – imperialism; crises and foreign trade; state guidance of private industry; and 'Aryanization' – shaped economic development under the Third Reich, and how understanding their mutual interaction can clarify the sources of Germany's recovery from the Great Depression, the readiness of its business elite to collaborate with the Nazis, and Hitler's decision to embark on a war of conquest. Upon gaining power the Nazis drew on existing traditions from the Wilhelmine Empire and the Weimar Republic to overcome the Depression of 1929–1933, yet they also created new institutions and practices

A Companion to Nazi Germany, First Edition. Edited by Shelley Baranowski, Armin Nolzen, and Claus-Christian W. Szejnmann.

that began to delink Germany – historically reliant on foreign trade for growth – from the global market and prepare their nation for war. In doing so, the Nazis created a heavily *dirigiste* – at times coercively so – capitalist economy, which was riddled with cronyism and geared towards imperial expansion, military production, and the despoliation of Jews. The Nazis preserved competition and profit-making as incentives. At the same time, however, they made private property conditional on their broader racial agenda and they transformed prices and wages. Much of this system collapsed with Germany's defeat, yet key legacies survived the war to shape West Germany's economic growth after 1945.

16.1   Imperialism

Between 1914 and 1945 European empires reached their zenith of influence and global territorial control. The Nazis came to power in this competitive environment and saw themselves very much as empire builders (Mazower 2008). The drive for imperial markets formed one of the key bonds between the Nazi regime and German industry, since many of the latter believed some form of imperialism could solve their economic problems.

Indeed, Adam Tooze has convincingly argued that Hitler's quest for empire in Eastern Europe should be understood as 'a response to the tensions stirred up by the uneven development of global capitalism' (Tooze 2006, xxiv). Tooze illustrates how inter-war Germany was in many ways a semi-peripheral economy: the standard of living high but below that of the global leaders such as Britain and the United States; the economy divided between a modern industrial complex and a backward agricultural sector. Contemporary Germans saw their nation in this light, and during the 1920s and 1930s 'living standards became an everyday element of the struggle among great powers for global leadership' (De Grazia 2005, 76). What struck Hitler and others about America was the vast size of its domestic market and the raw materials it commanded within its own borders, which enabled it to become the world's first mass production nation. To compete as a global power, Hitler believed Germany needed a continent of its own – *Lebensraum* – which would provide the space, resources, and markets to sustain its development into a mass production economy.

Both Marxian and liberal scholars have used these concepts of imperialism and semi-periphery to link inter-war conditions to Germany's drive for territorial expansion, as well as to the imperial projects of Japan and Italy. On the left, recent accounts have explained the global conflicts of the twentieth century as a result of capitalism's 'terrible convulsions and drastic changes' (Trotsky cited in Anievas 2014, 47), which generated vastly uneven rates of growth between and within nations, and where radical transitions in one country forced destabilizing change on other regions. Alexander Anievas uses this framework to show how global overproduction following the First World War, alongside the collapse of trade during the Depression, led business elites across Europe to support their governments' efforts to build large economic blocs. *Lebensraum* was just the most radical of these projects that stemmed from the 'intensified intercapitalist competition in a world of contracting markets' (Anievas 2014, 155, 168; Riley 2014). Liberal scholars have found the unifying structural element of the inter-war period to be international indebtedness. Semi-peripheral nations like Germany borrowed heavily on foreign markets to modernize. With the Depression, the cost of fulfilling these international obligations proved so onerous that the liberal elites who had endorsed debt in the first place were discredited. During the Depression, 'an entire stratum of the global social structure – the middle class of nations, neither rich nor grindingly poor' – repudiated their debt, disavowed participation in global markets, and turned towards economic nationalism and imperialism (Frieden 2006, 196).

Both Marxian and liberal approaches stress the primacy of international political economy and identify structural factors common to Germany, Italy, and Japan. But they lose the specificity of the Nazi case and they overlook the utter centrality of racial ideology in Hitler's imperial agenda. As Tooze emphasizes, the Nazis saw the looming competition between empires as an existential struggle the German race must fight, literally with its military, against what they believed was a global Jewish conspiracy stretching from Washington to Moscow. And they drew on a tradition of German contempt for Slavs to justify why Eastern Europe should be the centre of their empire.

Nazi imperialism, in other words, cannot be understood by economics alone. Yet economics does illuminate how imperialism united business elites with the regime, particularly if the concept of empire is disaggregated into informal and formal varieties. In the 1890s, liberal thinkers such as Ernst Jäckh had argued that Germany could best secure its exports and power by commercially penetrating its neighbours rather than through direct colonization (van Laak 2005). In the 1930s, when the Depression disrupted the trade circuits Germany had historically relied upon for growth, various elites began to fear that global markets were now too volatile. They rehabilitated the Wilhelmine vision of commercial penetration of places like Southeastern and Southern Europe, and they advocated a middle path between global trade and autarchy – an informal trading empire through which Germans would gain preferential treatment without the need for political control (Sachse 2010).

This mental reorientation away from global and towards continental markets began before the Nazis seized power, when conservatives in the Foreign Office and the Economics Ministry began shifting trade towards Germany's small neighbours. The banking crises in 1931 and the collapse in world trade provided the ready-made instruments these officials used, most importantly the pairing of debt-clearing agreements with bilateral treaties (Banken 2006). After 1933, Nazi Germany drew on these tools but also added new ones to redirect trade to the continent. During the Spanish Civil War the Nazis formed HISMA-ROWAK, an import–export monopoly that controlled armament shipments to the Franco regime. Before 1937, Franco could only pay for imports by running up debt to Germany, debt that HISMA-ROWAK transformed into direct investment by acquiring ownership of Spanish mining, farming, and transportation businesses (Barbieri 2015). In Southeastern Europe the Mitteleuropäische Wirtschaftstag – an association of export-oriented businessmen – established development programmes that invested in mining and cash crops to remould these nations into better suppliers of raw materials (Gross 2015).

Hjalmar Schacht, German economics minister and central bank director during the mid-1930s, epitomized this path of informal empire. Schacht understood Germany needed trade to thrive yet he wanted to avoid the volatility of global markets. He believed political empire in Europe was too expensive to be worthwhile; questions of political sovereignty should be left in local hands. Instead, he wanted to acquire power over the monetary and economic policies of countries like Yugoslavia or Spain. Schacht proved perfectly willing to collaborate with the Nazis because he believed the regime would use unorthodox economic techniques to stabilize trade and exert political influence abroad (Barbieri 2015; 173–176).

The Nazis used trade in the manner suggested by Schacht and his allies, but only up to a point. Bilateral trade with Spain and Southeastern Europe could secure commodities needed for rearmament without spending precious foreign currency. Yet Hitler never thought Germany could base its power on trade over the long term. 'World trade, world economy,' he maintained, 'are transient means for securing a nation's sustenance.' He believed German power must ultimately be anchored in a formal territorial empire, not an informal economic sphere (quotation in Weinberg 2003, ch. 2).

16.2   Crises

If the Nazis and their business allies aspired to create a relationship between Germany and its neighbours that was imperial in nature, their efforts simultaneously changed the domestic economy by provoking a string of crises that the regime exploited to extend state control over the economy. This process of crises generating government regulation over the economy had begun in the late Weimar Republic, when banking and foreign exchange crises led the state to monitor the financial system and foreign currency. Yet after 1933 this process assumed a new dynamic on account of three factors. First, the Depression discredited the laissez-faire policies associated with the gold standard and created the intellectual space for new, heterodox policies (Jannsen 2000, 290–301). Second, the Depression changed the international environment: as one effort at international cooperation failed after another, and as other Great Powers implemented their own protectionist measures, the Nazis disengaged from global networks by imposing controls over their own economy. Third and most importantly, Hitler's relentless rearmament drive strained Germany's raw material and foreign currency supplies and created macroeconomic imbalances. Rearming meant importing large quantities of goods Germany did not produce itself, such as oil and high-grade iron ore, which exacerbated Germany's tendency to run a trade deficit.

Thus, under National Socialism a dialectic evolved: rearmament-induced crises – most tellingly in foreign trade – enabled the state to expand its regulatory power, thereby generating further crises and creating space for still more regulation. The first crisis erupted in 1934 when Schacht, in response to a growing trade deficit, suspended payment of Germany's international debts and tightened control over foreign currency. The New Plan, as his policy was called, created 25 supervisory agencies that distributed foreign currency to importers according to how they met national priorities, meaning rearmament (Ebi 2004). The New Plan lasted two years before another trade and currency crisis hit in 1936, when both the military and the agricultural sector began demanding more imports. As the trade deficit widened, Germany lost currency reserves. To resolve this crisis Hitler inaugurated the Four Year Plan, which aimed to save foreign currency by producing synthetic goods that could replace imports, by nationalizing certain coal deposits, and by more vigorously controlling imports and exports (Volkmann 1990, 273–316). While these measures vastly expanded the state's role in the economy, they only temporarily staved off problems. By the end of 1938, demand for military imports was growing, exports stagnating, currency reserves falling, and rearmament again precipitated a crisis.

Some historians, most famously Tim Mason, have suggested the economic crises of 1938–1939 explain why Hitler went to war when he did. 'One of the functions of the war of aggression,' he argued, was 'to clear the way to a "solution" of this backlog of economic and social problems' and allow the regime to impose sacrifices on the population that it could not do in peacetime (Mason 1995a, 122). Other scholars have criticized this crisis narrative. Richard Overy claims this framework was really the product of British wishful thinking in the 1930s and conservative resistors to the Nazis, who disliked Hitler's economic controls. By the late 1930s, Overy argues, Germany had already surmounted its greatest crises and was merely experiencing the frictional problems common to all advanced capitalist countries (Overy 1987). Diplomatic historians, moreover, largely avoid reference to economic crisis in explaining the outbreak of war.

The line from crisis to war may not be as straight as Mason thought. Nevertheless, if one focuses on trade this narrative has staying power. David Kaiser has pointed out how there was 'an element of self-fulfilling prophecy in Hitler's economic thought. The rearmament which he undertook … to free Germany from dependence upon the world market in itself made it harder and harder for Germany to draw sustenance from the world market, and impelled him to begin the conquest of *Lebensraum* sooner than he had anticipated' (Kaiser, Mason, and Overy 1989). In 1939, Germany depended as heavily as ever on imports yet it was losing the means to pay for them. Export orders had fallen to a decade low, currency reserves were exhausted, trade with Southeastern Europe and Spain had reached its limits, and consequently munitions production was slumping (Kaiser, Mason, and Overy 1989, 205; Volkmann 1990, 364–365). Key figures in the party thought territorial expansion could solve these bottlenecks. That was one lesson from the annexation of Austria and Czechoslovakia, which brought in valuable ore and currency reserves (Tooze 2006, 309–16).

16.3 Capitalism under the Nazis

Under National Socialism, crises and rearmament changed the face of Germany's economy, but did they change its nature? Was Germany moving towards a command economy similar to that of the Soviet Union? Was it developing its own 'unique and distinctive economic system' (Barkai 1990)? Or was it merely anticipating the Keynesian policies adopted by much of the West after 1945?

The latter characterization – Nazi economy as proto-Keynesianism – gained a certain pre-eminence early on. Before the war, British commentators remarked how 'Hitler had found a cure against unemployment before Keynes was finished explaining it' (cited in Garvy 1975, 403). The economic miracle that National Socialism seemed to achieve by 1936, putting some five million men back to work, suggested the Nazis had an understanding of counter-cyclical spending as well as a distinct plan to implement such policies. This continues to be the view of many historians today, who point out how the Nazis advocated credit-financed job programmes already in 1932, how they implemented such work schemes in the construction and motor industries, how public investment grew to three times the size of private investment after 1933, how the marriage loan programme spurred consumption by 'Aryan' couples, and how the regime improved the business climate. Construction of the autobahn and the creation of Volkswagen are often highlighted as evidence of demand management and the regime's intent to spur consumption in new sectors (Abelshauser 1998; Overy 1996). Most importantly, these scholars stress the novelty of how Hitler financed these programmes, through deficit spending and new central bank money (Barkai 1990).

Yet this Keynesian view needs modification. Using machine tool orders, stock market indices, and business surveys, Christopher Buchheim has illustrated how the Nazis benefited from an upswing in private investment that was already underway in late 1932. If the Nazis changed the business climate, moreover, they did so less by demand management than by utterly destroying the power of unions. The new regime inherited deficit-financed work programmes from the last Weimar administration, it did not invent them (Buchheim 2008). Most importantly, military expenditure dominated public spending already in 1934. By that year, the government was devoting three times as much money to military as to civilian projects. Meanwhile, spending on the autobahn only accelerated in 1936, after Germany had already achieved full employment. Indeed, before the Four Year Plan, Germany does not stand out from other advanced economies in its government deficits or its monetary expansion. Through 1937 the Reichsbank kept money creation in line with GDP (gross domestic product) growth; until 1936 fiscal deficits were not large (countries in the gold bloc and Italy had higher ones); before 1936 the debt-to-GDP ratio stayed basically stable at a 50% (Almunia et al. 2010; Tooze 2006, 62–65; Ritschl 2002). The Third Reich, in other words, was hardly more Keynesian than other Western countries. Germany recovered more quickly from the Depression because it militarized its economy before Britain or the United States (Herbst 1993).

If the Third Reich was not the first Keynesian regime, some argue it should be seen as a command economy in gestation, where rearmament was eroding the fundamentals of the market. Recent business case studies have illustrated how private property under the Third Reich was conditional on its use, not a fundamental right. The state used coercion to impress on firms that their freedom was circumscribed, and that their corporate strategies must dovetail with the Nazi agenda. In 1933, for example, the regime forcibly expropriated Germany's largest aircraft manufacturer, Hugo Junkers' factory in Dessau. And in 1937 they seized the Salzgitter ore fields from private industry to create the Reichswerk Hermann

Göring, a vast state-owned enterprise. Peter Hayes notes how these coercive moves set a precedent industry could not ignore. As the chairman of Mannesmann steel remarked in 1938, 'if we give the state cause to call our performance unsatisfactory, an expropriation will not be avoidable' (cited in Hayes 2009, 35). The Nazis also used crises to control the allocation of critical inputs such as foreign currency, raw materials, and capital. State agencies, moreover, became the largest customer for Germany's most advanced industries (Spoerer 2005). Some scholars argue the regime eliminated the fundamental informational signalling power of the market, wages and prices, when it froze the former in 1933 and the latter in 1936 (Temin 1991).

Yet, to have a command economy someone has to actually be in command. In Germany, it is not clear who that was between Schacht's resignation in 1937 and the organizational reforms associated with Albert Speer in 1942. Indeed, the economy is one of the best examples of Nazi polycracy, as the Army, Navy, Air Force, Four Year Plan, Economics Ministry, Finance Ministry, Labour Ministry, and Agricultural Ministry all pursued their own objectives, frequently at cross-purposes with each other. In this context, many firms retained autonomy by playing one administration against another.

The regime, moreover, valued enterprise and tried to incentivize industry to produce, using the carrot as well as the stick. One tool was pricing policy. There were countless exceptions to the price freeze of 1936, and the state used pricing to prioritize rearmament. Firms that won public contracts often received a guaranteed profit margin above cost, plus a liberal allowance for capital depreciation. They also benefited from generous calculations for wage rates, which allowed them to work around the wage freeze and attract skilled workers. Through such contracts the state assumed the risk of investment, and thereby unleashed a private investment boom alongside the public one. During the war the regime changed this pricing system to one where it generally paid a fixed cost for a given product, allowing firms to compete for orders and reap large profits if they kept costs under the target price (Steiner 2008; Mason 1995b). In both frameworks, competition and profits remained important motivating forces. Corporate profits rose dramatically after 1933, so much so that many firms were able to invest using retained earnings instead of relying on the heavily regulated capital markets (Spoerer 1996).

Some scholars have even argued the Third Reich basically retained a market economy by respecting freedom of contract, at least for 'Aryan' firms. Jonas Scherner and Christopher Buchheim (2006) use the textile industry to show how 'entrepreneurs retained a good deal of their autonomy' regarding investment and production mixtures. Here, the regime hoped to replace imported cotton with synthetic fibre to save foreign currency. In early 1934 the state rationed textile inputs, and later set a minimum level of artificial fibres that firms must use. Yet these command measures did not curb imports and in 1936 the regime changed tactics, adopting an incentive system that gave firms extra raw material rations if they produced for export or for the military. Firms responded by competing for these orders, and by substituting synthetic fibres for cotton in domestic production to a much higher degree than state leaders anticipated. Meanwhile, the regime created new, state-subsidized enterprises to compete with private firms. The latter reacted by shifting investment to 'research-intensive high-value artificial fibers', which they believed held promise for a post-war future. Such examples illustrate how managers thought the armament boom would eventually end, and were able to steer investment towards projects they believed had long-term potential after the war (Ziegler 2013; quotations from Buchheim and Scherner 2006, 394, 399).

The debate over corporate freedom illustrates the difficulty of generalizing about the Nazi economy. Those who stress coercion underestimate the sophisticated way the regime incentivized firms to produce what they wanted. Yet, given the implicit and explicit threats firms faced, the opposite side overemphasizes the latitude enjoyed by private industry. Even the advocates of corporate freedom concede that industry was not an equal partner with the regime (Buchheim and Scherner 2006). The best descriptions combine these two views and portray the 'Nazi economy as a hybrid of market mechanisms and state directives, a mix of incentives and instructions, rewards and reprisals, opportunities and obstructions' (Hayes 2009, 31), in which businessmen operated from a complex blend of 'greed and survival' (Nicosia and Huener 2004, 5).

To a certain extent, however, the debate over corporate freedom reifies the distinction between state and economy. In fact, Nazi Germany illustrates the inseparability of these two spheres. Many technocrats acquired their government positions from corporate jobs through personal connections, and they protected the interests of their firms once in government. Corporations, moreover, often won public contracts because of their party contacts. Frank Bajohr has convincingly argued that corruption and cronyism became a 'constitutive element of National Socialist rule' (Bajohr 2005, 132). A prime example is Friedrich Flick's conglomerate, which excelled precisely because it saw the state as a 'literally resourceful partner rather than as an opponent best kept at arm's length' (Priemel 2012, 759). Flick and his manger cultivated ties with leading Nazis to obtain military orders. Through these nepotistic connections Flick participated in numerous 'Aryanizations', expropriating Jewish-owned mines to become one of Germany's leading coal producers (Bähr 2013).

16.4 'Aryanization'

If imperialism and rearmament united German business with the Nazi regime, a third bridge was 'Aryanization', a topic that witnessed an explosion of interest during the restitution court cases of the 1990s (Goschler and Ther 2007). Recent research has shown how the despoliation of Jews was an essential step in the Nazi campaign to purify German society: National Socialists saw 'Aryanization' as a redemptive process that returned to the national community property 'plundered' by Jews. In Europe, where private property was closely associated with civil rights and personal freedom, robbing Jews of property also robbed them of their dignity, placed them outside the national community, and furthered the process of dehumanization that led to genocide (Goschler 2013).

'Aryanization' was not just about purification; the Nazis also used it to acquire assets. Yet before 1938 they had no master plan, and 'Aryanization' remained a decentralized affair with initiative coming from below. Under laws that allowed the

NSDAP (*Nationalsozialistische Deutsche Arbeiterpartei*, Nazi Party) to confiscate property from political opponents, local party bosses began seizing Jewish businesses, placing them under trustees, and selling them to friends or patrons at a fraction of cost. Local municipalities excluded Jews from the public contracts rolling in under Hitler's government spending (Bajohr 2001). In 1935 the central government began trying to manage these local initiatives, to channel assets to Berlin and to avoid unwanted international publicity. Here a major goal was centralizing control over Jewish foreign currency in order to mitigate Germany's trade crises. One of the first legal mechanisms used by the regime, for example, was the 'Law for Revocation of Naturalization and the Annulment of German Citizenship (July 1933)', through which the Nazis prevented emigrating Jews from taking currency out of the country. After 1936 the Nazis radicalized these measures and turned Germany's new currency offices into instruments for liquidating Jewish wealth. The regime, however, still did not follow a standardized procedure and 'Aryanization' varied by region. While most Jewish firms in the countryside were 'Aryanized' before 1938, the Nazis left many Jewish businesses intact in cities like Hamburg precisely because they earned foreign currency and had close ties with traders in Western Europe (Dean 2008; Bajohr 2001).

Only in 1938 did Berlin finally develop a systematic plan for plundering Jews, one linked to the challenges of trade and rearmament. The precedent for this came from Austria. Following the *Anschluss*, the Nazis registered all Austrian Jewish property, blocked all Austrian Jewish bank accounts, and formally subjected the sale of all Austrian Jewish businesses to central government approval. Hermann Göring, in charge of both the Four Year Plan and 'Aryanization' policy, subsequently applied these techniques to the rest of Germany. That November, *Kristallnacht* led to the further centralization of 'Aryanization' when Göring decreed that all Jewish securities be placed in banks, labelled as Jewish, and monitored by the Economics Ministry. He also levied a punitive tax on Jewish wealth over 5000 Reichsmarks, which brought in 1.1 billion Reichsmarks over the next 15 months. Göring was clearly motivated by the belief that 'Aryanization' would ease Germany's mounting public debt and trade deficit. (Dean 2008, 13). Götz Aly has argued that 'Aryanization' vastly reduced the financial burden on the German people, so much so that before 1942/1943 they hardly bore the costs of rearmament or war. While the numbers do not support Aly's main argument – under the Third Reich Germans remained some of the most heavily taxed people in the world – his secondary claim holds true: Göring's 1 billion Reichsmarks levy came at a critical juncture, augmenting state revenue on the margin just as Berlin was facing its last pre-war financial crisis (Aly 2007).

Thus, by 1938, 'organized state thievery' had become 'business as usual', and Germany's commercial elite did not hesitate to take advantage of this new setting. Initial arguments against 'Aryanization' had already faded by 1934 (Feldman 2003, 6). Banks quickly began working as brokers managing the sale of Jewish assets (James 2001). German businessmen readily exploited political contacts to purchase Jewish firms, and the prices they paid declined over time as Jews found ever fewer options of negotiating with counterparties in good faith (Köhler 2013).

Two decades ago, Michael Geyer argued that Nazi Germany was an 'unabashedly acquisitive society', driven by both the 'scramble for benefits from the exclusion of others' and 'the violent production of space' through conquest. This surely extends from the consumers to which he was referring to Germany's business community. The many case studies of 'Aryanization' illustrate how, in general, managers operated with a truly amoral pragmatism and elevated their professional drive for efficiency and profitability over any concern for humanity. More broadly, 'Aryanization' under the Third Reich demonstrates the utter malleability of capitalism and its ability to thrive under nearly any set of circumstances or institutions, however perverse they might be (Geyer 1992, 98).

16.5   The Second World War and the Legacy of the Third Reich

In 1939 Germany embarked on the violent creation of a formal empire and began ruling over non-German nationalities en masse. For Hitler, the annexation of territory in Eastern Europe would simultaneously realize his vision for *Lebensraum* and solve Germany's economic crises in a way that an informal trading empire had failed to do. This violent, imperial war changed German capitalism and left a bitter legacy that clouds European politics to this day.

In the short term, formal empire paid. As Peter Liberman concludes in his comparison of modern occupations, 'ruthless conquerors – but only ruthless ones – can make defeated modern societies pay a large share of their economic surplus in tribute' (Liberman 1996, 5). German occupation usually began with a wave of plunder as the Wehrmacht confiscated moveable property belonging to foreign governments. In Eastern Europe the occupying forces also stripped local factories to send equipment back to the Third Reich. Germany then offloaded occupation costs by forcing the central banks of conquered states to print local money to redeem IOUs issued by the Wehrmacht. In doing so, Germany contained inflation at home by exporting it to the rest of Europe (Aly 2007). After 1939 Germany ran up massive trade deficits with its subject states, importing more than it exported and paying for this by accruing debt in its clearing accounts. By 1945 Germany owed Europe over 20 billion Reichsmarks, representing real assets confiscated and never repaid after the war despite the London Debt Agreements of 1953. These forced loans took centre stage during the Euro crisis of 2014–2015, when some Greek leaders demanded reparations for the Nazi wartime occupation of their country (Boelcke 1985, 111).

Yet arguments for the economic success of Nazi occupation fall flat once one moves towards a longer term perspective. The policy of exporting inflation led to the collapse of local currencies across Europe. As money lost its value, peasant producers retreated from the marketplace and famines erupted in Greece, Serbia, and elsewhere. Eastern Europe yielded precious few resources because of the sheer destruction wrought by the Nazis. Tellingly, France provided Germany with more food and industrial materials than did all of the occupied Soviet Union. By most estimates, the Nazi empire covered just 25% of Germany's war costs, 35% if one counts foreign slave labour (Klemann and Kudryashov 2012).

Conquest, moreover, revealed a tension in German policy between the objective of plundering assets versus the alternative of keeping them in situ and using them to produce. Hans Umbreit has framed this as the question of whether to kill the cow or milk it, and ultimately the Nazis never settled on a clear policy (Umbreit 2003). In Eastern Europe they preferred plunder. In Western Europe, local Nazi governors wanted to maintain local production to avoid problems associated with labour requisitioning, and until 1942 industry in Belgium, France, the Netherlands, and Bohemia fulfilled substantial military orders. Others, by contrast, wanted to requisition assets for use in the Third Reich. After 1942, when Hitler appointed Fritz Sauckel to hunt for labour across Europe, Sauckel's coercive requisitioning brought foreign workers to Germany. But in the process, it caused many to flee their local workplaces and contributed to the rapid decline in the output of Western Europe (Klemann and Kudryashov 2012).

War also further dismantled the barrier between state and economy. On the one hand, Nazi officials expanded the role of state-owned enterprises. After 1939 Göring used direct investment by the state to take over foreign corporations and ensure the economies of Europe served the Nazi racial agenda (Overy 1994, 323). This scramble for foreign assets led to corruption on a grand scale. In one of the most notorious cases, Belgrade party leader Franz Neuhausen used ties with Göring to become the director of local enterprises and run the Serbian economy like his personal satrapy. Neuhausen's corruption was outrageous even by Nazi standards, and in 1944 he wound up in a concentration camp (Gross 2015). On the other hand, the regime incorporated industrial leaders into the state's economic management as never before. In the drive to rationalize industry after 1942, Albert Speer created a new hierarchy of committees to allocate resources. His slogan was the 'self-responsibility' of industry: he would set targets and prices and allow private industry to meet these goals as it saw fit. By 1943, over 200 such government committees existed, chaired in many instances by the directors of Germany's largest firms (Tooze 2006, 566–574).

Twelve years of Nazi rule and six years of war transformed German society and contributed, in part, to West Germany's economic development after 1945. Some scholars question the importance of economic continuities, arguing that West Germany's economic miracle resulted instead from the rupture with the Nazi past imposed by American occupation. The campaign to break German elites of their penchant for empire, to transplant American notions of consumerism and free trade, and to replace corporatist bargaining with a stronger parliament all belong to this narrative of the 'Americanization' of West Germany (Berghahn 1986).

Recent scholarship, however, has highlighted the problems of seeing 1945 as a *Stunde Null* ('hour zero', beginning of the new Germany), since many initiatives begun by the Third Reich contributed to West German economic success. The Nazis, for instance, provided the automotive sector with a mass production foundation that turned it into a globally competitive industry by the 1950s. Volkswagen and its Beetle – an icon of post-war Germany – would never have existed had Hitler not underwritten the enormous financial risks involved in developing VW's automated factory (Rieger 2013). The Nazis also advanced Germany's corporatist economic institutions. Speer's system of committees solidified the communication channels between state and industry and strengthened the ability of industrial associations to coordinate their member firms. The Nazis also expanded Germany's system of vocational apprenticeships. After 1945, close collaboration between state and business and highly skilled vocational labour became hallmarks of West Germany's distinctive style of coordinated capitalism (Abelshauser 1999; Gillingham 1986).

More work remains to be done in this quarter, to better understand economic continuities between the Third Reich and West Germany. In a second area, recent research on economic incentives and institutions under the Third Reich has opened space for future studies to pursue a more sustained comparison of Nazi political economy with that of other industrial societies, not just across space but also across time. Does nepotism under the Nazis differ qualitatively from the clientelism found in other capitalist systems, such as the developmentalist regimes of Latin America or even the United States today? How do German techniques of informal imperialism in Spain and Southeastern Europe compare with those of other nations trying to transition from regional to global powers, such as China with its direct investment in Africa? Exploring such issues would not only provide a clearer picture of Nazi Germany, it would also help us understand how capitalism adapts – or fails to adapt – to different circumstances, ideologies, and institutions.

References

Abelshauser, Werner. 1998. 'Germany: Guns, Butter, and Economic Miracles.' In *The Economics of World War II: Six Great Powers in Comparison*, edited by Mark Harrison, 122–176. New York: Cambridge University Press.

Abelshauser, Werner. 1999. 'Kriegswirtschaft und Wirtschaftswunder. Deutschlands wirtschaftliche Mobilisierung für den Zweiten Weltkrieg und die Folgen für die Nachkriegszeit.' *Vierteljahrshefte für Zeitgeschichte* 47(4), 503–538.

Almunia, Miguel et al. 2010. 'From Great Depression to Great Credit Crisis: Similarities, Differences and Lessons.' *Economic Policy* 25(62), 219–265.

Aly, Götz. 2007. *Hitler's Beneficiaries: Plunder, Racial War, and the Nazi Welfare State.* New York: Metropolitan Books.

Anievas, Alexander. 2014. *Capital, The State, and War: Class Conflict and Politics in the Thirty Years Crisis, 1914–1945.* Ann Arbor: University of Michigan Press.

Bähr, Johannes. 2013. 'The Personal Factor in Business under National Socialism: Paul Reusch and Friedrich Flick.' In *Business in the Age of Extremes*, edited by Hartmut Berghoff, Jürgen Kocka, and Dieter Ziegler, 153–171. New York: Cambridge University Press.

Bajohr, Frank. 2001. *'Aryanisation' in Hamburg: The Economic Exclusion of Jews and the Confiscation of their Property in Nazi Germany.* New York: Berghahn Books.

Bajohr, Frank. 2005. 'The Holocaust and Corruption.' In *Networks of Nazi Persecution: Bureaucracy, Business and the Organization of the Holocaust*, edited by Gerald Feldman and Wolfgang Seibel, 118–140. New York: Berghahn Books.

Banken, Ralf. 2006. 'Das nationalsozialistische Devisenrecht als Steuerungs- und Diskriminierungsinstrument 1933–1945.' In *Wirtschaftssteuerung durch Recht in Nationalsozialismus*, edited by Johannes Bähr and Ralf Banken, 121–236. Frankfurt am Main: Vittorio Klostermann.

Barbieri, Pierpaolo. 2015. *Hitler's Shadow Empire: Nazi Economics and the Spanish Civil War.* Cambridge, MA: Harvard University Press.

Barkai, Avraham. 1990. *Nazi Economics: Ideology, Theory and Policy*. New Haven, CT: Yale University Press.

Berghahn, Volker. 1986. *The Americanisation of West German Industry, 1945–1973*. Cambridge: Cambridge University Press.

Boelcke, Willi. 1985. *Die Kosten von Hitlers Krieg: Kriegsfinanzierung*. Paderborn: Schöningh.

Buchheim, Christoph and Scherner, Jonas. 2006. 'The Role of Private Property in the Nazi Economy: The Case of Industry.' *Journal of Economic History* 66(2), 390–416.

Buchheim, Christoph. 2008. 'Das NS-Regime und die Überwindung der Weltwirtschaftskrise in Deutschland.' *Vierteljahrshefte für Zeitgeschichte* 56(3/8), 381–414.

Dean, Martin. 2008. *Robbing the Jews: The Confiscation of Jewish Property in the Holocaust, 1933–1945*. New York: Cambridge University Press.

De Grazia, Victoria. 2005. *Irresistible Empire: America's Advance through Twentieth Century Europe*. Cambridge, MA: Harvard University Press.

Ebi, Michael. 2004. *Export um jeden Preis: die Deutsche Exportförderung von 1932–1938*. Stuttgart: Steiner.

Feldman, Gerald D. 2003. 'Confiscation of Jewish Assets and the Holocaust.' In *Confiscation of Jewish Property in Europe, 1933–1945*, 1–8. Washington, DC: US Holocaust Museum.

Frieden, Jeffry. 2006. *Global Capitalism: Its Fall and Rise in the Twentieth Century*. New York: W.W. Norton.

Garvy, George. 1975. 'Keynes and the Economic Activists of Pre-Hitler Germany.' *Journal of Political Economy* 83, 391–405.

Geyer, Michael. 1992. 'The Stigma of Violence, Nationalism, and War in Twentieth-Century Germany.' *German Studies Review* 15, 75–110.

Gillingham, John. 1986. '"Deproletarianization" of German Society: Vocational Training in the Third Reich.' *Journal of Social History* 19(3), 423–432.

Goschler, Constantin. 2013. 'The Dispossession of the Jews and the Europeanization of the Holocaust.' In *Business in the Age of Extremes*, edited by Hartmut Berghoff, Jürgen Kocka, and Dieter Ziegler, 189–203. New York: Cambridge University Press.

Goschler, Constantin and Ther, Philipp. 2007. 'A History without Boundaries: The Robbery and Restitution of Jewish Property in Europe.' In *Robbery and Restitution. The Conflict over Jewish Property in Europe*, edited by Martin Dean, Constantin Goschler, and Philipp Ther, 3–20. New York: Berghahn Books.

Gross, Stephen G. 2015. *Export Empire: German Soft Power in Southeastern Europe, 1890–1945*. Cambridge: Cambridge University Press.

Hayes, Peter. 2009. 'Corporate Freedom of Action in Nazi Germany.' *Bulletin of the GHI* 45, 29–42.

Herbst, Ludolf. 1993. 'Die nationalsozialistische Wirtschaftspolitik im internationalen Vergleich.' In *Der Nationalsozialismus: Studien zur Ideologie und Herrschaft*, edited by Wolfgang Benz and Hans Mommsen, 153–176. Frankfurt am Main: Fischer.

James, Harold. 2001. *The Deutsche Bank and the Nazi Economic War Against the Jews*. Princeton, NJ: Princeton University Press.

Jannsen, Hauke. 2000. *Nationalökonomie und Nationalsozialismus: Die deutsche Volkswirtschaftslehre in den dreissiger Jahren*. Marburg: Metropolis.

Kaiser, David, Mason, Tim, and Overy, Richard. 1989. 'Debate: Germany, 'Domestic Crisis' and War in 1939.' *Past and Present* 122, 200–240.

Klemann, Hein, and Kudryashov, Sergei. 2012. *Occupied Economies: An Economic History of Nazi-Occupied Europe, 1939–1945*. London: Berg.

Köhler, Ingo. 2013. 'Business as Usual? Aryanization in Practice, 1933–1938.' In *Business in the Age of Extremes*, edited by Hartmut Berghoff, Jürgen Kocka, and Dieter Ziegler, 172–188. New York: Cambridge University Press.

Liberman, Peter. 1996. *Does Conquest Pay? The Exploitation of Occupied Industrial Societies.* Princeton, NJ: Princeton University Press.

Mason, Tim. 1995a. 'Internal Crisis and War of Aggression, 1938–1939.' In *Nazism, Fascism, and the Working Class: Essays by Tim Mason.* Edited by Jane Caplan, 104–131. Cambridge: Cambridge University Press.

Mason, Tim. 1995b. 'The Primacy of Politics: Politics and Economics in National Socialist Germany.' In *Nazism, Fascism and the Working Class: Essays by Tim Mason.* Edited by Jane Caplan, 53–76. Cambridge: Cambridge University Press.

Mazower, Mark. 2008. *Hitler's Empire: Nazi Rule in Occupied Europe.* New York: Penguin.

Neumann, Franz. 1963. *Behemoth: The Structure and Practice of National Socialism: 1933–1944.* New York: Octagon. First published 1942.

Nicosia, Francis R. and Huener, Jonathan. 2004. 'Introduction: Business and Industry in Nazi Germany in Historiographical Context.' In *Business and Industry in Nazi Germany*, edited by Francis R. Nicosia and Jonathan Huener, 1–14. New York: Berghahn Books.

Overy, Richard. 1987. '"Domestic Crisis" and War in 1939.' *Past and Present* 116, August, 138–168.

Overy, Richard. 1994. *War and Economy in the Third Reich.* New York. Cambridge University Press.

Overy, Richard. 1996. *The Nazi Economic Recovery, 1932–1938.* Cambridge: Cambridge University Press.

Priemel, Kim Christian. 2012. 'Twentieth Century Flick: Business in the Age of Extremes.' *Journal of Contemporary History* 47(4), 174–172.

Rieger, Bernhard. 2013. *The People's Car: A Global History of the Volkswagen Beetle.* Cambridge, MA: Harvard University Press.

Riley, Dylan. 2014. 'The Third Reich as Rogue Regime: Adam Tooze's Wages of Destruction.' *Historical Materialism* 22(3–4), 330–350.

Ritschl, Albrecht. 2002. 'Deficit Spending in the Nazi Recovery, 1933–1938: A Critical Reassessment.' *Journal of the Japanese and International Economies* 16, 559–582.

Sachse, Carola, ed. 2010. *'Mitteleuropa' und 'Südosteuropa' als Planungsraum. Wirtschafts- und kulturpolitische Expertisen im Zeitalter der Weltkriege.* Göttingen: Wallstein.

Spoerer, Mark. 1996. *Von Scheingewinn zum Rüstungsboom: die Eigenkapitalrentabilität der deutschen Industrieaktiengesellschaften, 1925–1941.* Stuttgart: Steiner.

Spoerer, Mark. 2005. 'Demontage eines Mythos? Zu der Kontroverse über das nationalso-zialistische "Wirtschaftswunder".' *Geschichte und Gesellschaft* 31(3), 415–438.

Steiner, André. 2008. 'Industry and Administrative Price Regulation 1933–1938/39.' In *German Industry in the Nazi Period*, edited by Christoph Buchheim, 85–97. Stuttgart: Steiner.

Temin, Peter. 1991. 'Soviet and Nazi Economic Planning in the 1930s.' *Economic History Review* 44(4), 573–593.

Tismaneanu, Vladimir. 2014. *The Devil in History.* Berkeley: University of California Press.

Tooze, Adam. 2006. *Wages of Destruction: The Making and Breaking of the Nazi Economy.* New York: Allen Lane.

Umbreit, Hans. 2003. 'German Rule in the Occupied Territories 1942–1945.' In *Germany and the Second World War*, vol. 5, edited by Bernhard Kroener et al., 5–292. Oxford: Clarendon Press.

Van Laak, Dirk. 2005. *Über alles in der Welt: deutscher Imperialismus im 19. und 20. Jahrhundert.* Munich: C.H. Beck.

Volkmann, Hans-Erich. 1990. 'The National Socialist Economy in Preparation for War.' In *Germany and the Second World War*, vol. 1, edited by Wilhelm Diest et al. Oxford: Clarendon Press.

Weinberg, Gerhard. 2003. *Hitler's Second Book: The Unpublished Sequel to Mein Kampf.* New York: Enigma Books.

Ziegler, Dieter. 2013. '"A Regulated Market Economy": New Perspectives on the Nature of the Economic Order of the Third Reich, 1933–1939.' In *Business in the Age of Extremes*, edited by Hartmut Berghoff, Jürgen Kocka, and Dieter Ziegler, 139–152. New York: Cambridge University Press.

Further Reading

Barkai, Avraham. 1990. *Nazi Economics: Ideology, Theory and Policy.* New Haven, CT: Yale University Press.

Dean, Martin. 2008. *Robbing the Jews: The Confiscation of Jewish Property in the Holocaust, 1933–1945.* New York: Cambridge University Press.

Gross, Stephen G. 2015. *Export Empire: German Soft Power in Southeastern Europe, 1890–1945.* Cambridge: Cambridge University Press.

Kershaw, Ian. 1993. 'Politics and Economics in the Nazi State.' In *The Nazi Dictatorship: Problems and Perspectives of Interpretation.* New York: Routledge.

Klemann, Hein, and Kudryashov, Sergei. 2012. *Occupied Economies: An Economic History of Nazi-Occupied Europe, 1939–1945.* London: Berg.

Overy, Richard. 1996. *The Nazi Economic Recovery, 1932–1938.* Cambridge: Cambridge University Press.

Tooze, Adam. 2006. *Wages of Destruction: The Making and Breaking of the Nazi Economy.* New York: Allen Lane.

CHAPTER SEVENTEEN

National Socialism and German Business

KIM CHRISTIAN PRIEMEL

17.1 Historiography

The debate on the relations between business and National Socialism precedes the Third Reich. As early as 1932, German agitprop artist John Heartfield published a now famous montage depicting Hitler as the puppet of big business. And in 1935, the Third International endorsed a formula which spelt out that fascism was the most imperialist and terroristic articulation of capitalism and its spearhead, international finance (Caplan 1995). In contrast, economist Friedrich von Hayek found in 1933 that National Socialism essentially was socialism. The Third Reich and the Soviet Union, with their subordination of the economy to the interests of the state and its ruling party, were two of the same kind even if they discounted any likeness. Their common denominator, Hayek asserted, was collectivism (Caldwell 2007, 5–9). Both interpretations failed to convince those who cared to look at the empirical side. An unorthodox Marxist such as Franz Neumann (1944) conceived of Nazi rule as a coalition of the Nazi Party, the military, the civil service's higher echelons, and big business. The Third Reich's policies essentially resulted from a compromise between these four groups, whose interests were not easily balanced and their internal relations subject to shifts. In the economic field, conflict was largely avoided because monopolistic corporations (though not the multitude of smaller firms) pursued interests compatible with those of the regime – expansion, plunder, exploitation – rendering any coercion unnecessary. Neumann would go so far as to detect a process of amalgamation between regime and business elites. Otto Nathan (1944), who wrote another influential early study of the Nazi economy, spoke of a system sui generis, a

A Companion to Nazi Germany, First Edition. Edited by Shelley Baranowski,
Armin Nolzen, and Claus-Christian W. Szejnmann.
© 2018 John Wiley & Sons Ltd. Published 2018 by John Wiley & Sons Ltd.

'curious amalgam' of self-regulation and government regimentation, unlike either Western capitalism or Soviet-style central planning.

Significantly, even these studies, despite trying to avoid crude dichotomies or conspiracy theories, relied on a heuristic paradigm which still asked who was occupying the Third Reich's driving seat(s). The same pattern has characterized virtually the entire debate on the political economy of National Socialism over the past seven decades, although its results have frequently fallen short of the nuance and complexity of the likes of Neumann. Notably, against the backdrop of the Cold War many interpretations regressed to the front lines of the 1930s. West German businessmen, politicians, economists, and historians subscribed to a one-dimensional understanding of totalitarianism while their peers on the other side of the Wall indulged in doctrinaire Marxism-Leninism. Whereas the former came down to an apologetic cant of 'it wasn't us, it was Hitler', the latter clung to Heartfield's iconography (Frei and Schanetzky 2010).

It was only in the 1960s that Tim Mason (1995) revived a sterile debate by suggesting a different terminology to reconcile the seemingly opposed notions of totalitarian dictatorship and monopolistic stage management. His concept of a primacy of politics mirrored Neumann's earlier findings, and the British historian agreed on the continued existence of powerful capitalist interests in Nazi Germany and corporate elites' close cooperation with the regime. However, Mason also maintained that the general direction of war and occupation, mass murder and exploitation, had been determined by ideological creed and political opportunism, not by profits and property. Mason's arguments were bitterly opposed by GDR (German Democratic Republic) historians who retorted that the primacy had been entirely economic (Caplan 1995). The discussion soon turned stale but Mason's interpretation was largely, if sometimes implicitly, endorsed by the mainstream of FRG (Federal Republic of Germany) historiography (Frei and Schanetzky 2010, 9–24), endorsing dualistic sets such as politics/economics, state regulation/private enterprise, or ideology/economic rationality. Subsequent generations of historians would continue along the same lines but with an inclination to interpret the primacy of economics as the theoretical basis for the Nazi 'command economy'. At times this came close to Hayekian terms (Temin 1991) or, more elegantly, in Peter Hayes's conclusion that '"indirect socialization" … became a scarcely contested reality under Nazism' after 1936 (Hayes 2004, 114).

Whatever the merit of such arguments, they often suffered from the lack of reliable empirical studies. With much of the output of German business history falling into the hagiographic Festschriften genre, it was only the discipline's theoretical overhaul in the 1990s, greatly helped by the material support from companies under pressure to face their Nazi-era past, that led to a veritable boom. This surge would continue for roughly two decades and has resulted in a rich (if not wholly balanced) corpus of histories of individual companies and industries. Idiosyncratic as these are, their general drift has been to credit German firms with significant scope of action, depending on their respective size and military significance, as well as with substantial willingness to contribute to the regime's criminal policies. Notably, Christoph Buchheim and Jonas Scherner (2009) vehemently rejected the command-economy concept by showing how both private property and the freedom of contract were upheld in direct negotiations with the state (cf. the criticism by Hayes 2009 for their alleged ignorance of the general coercive atmosphere in Nazi Germany). Remarkably reminiscent of the primacy debate, the argument was still about who was more powerful: the regime which could intimidate and expropriate at will, or the captains of big business who knew how indispensable their capital and know-how were to the Nazi project? If, as Adam Tooze (2006) suggested, authority is understood as 'the capacity to get things done', business continued to exercise power in the Third Reich.

With Tooze trying to avoid the pitfalls of the primacy debate altogether, Werner Plumpe (2004) has come to the concept's rescue. In his system-theory inspired perspective, the regime used various 'media' to direct private business, notably financial incentives, legal regulation, propaganda, and public pressure. But as complex systems cannot be run from outside, the Nazi economy was bound to fail. Divested of its abstract terminology, Plumpe's paradigm essentially reiterates the primacy-of-politics argument with politicians instructing corporate decision making. This overlooks, however, that private enterprise's rationales were inscribed into the decisions of the Third Reich's authorities, too. Even the apparent application of coercion could be the result of private initiative (Middendorf and Priemel 2013).

17.2   Neither Theory nor Blueprint

According to Neumann (1944, 228), there was 'no National Socialist economic theory' and the only identifiable rationale was that of war preparation. This diagnosis has been largely confirmed by subsequent generations of researchers (Barkai 1988; Ambrosius 1990). Economics was never central to Nazi ideology and the 'serving' role it was assigned was unequivocal. Still, several of its key tropes, such as living space and autarky, were manifestly economic in character, suggesting that a Nazi system might be deduced from its policies. Such empiricist analyses have pointed to the high degree of centralization, the massive surge in administrative regulation, and the replacement of markets by government contacts. Without denying the inconsistency of much of Nazi economic policy, some researchers have thus concluded that it amounted to a 'steered economy' which built on nationalist-*étatiste* traditions predating the Third Reich (Ambrosius 2003; Gosewinkel 2005, x–lix).

Alternatively, the regime's blatant disregard for what little 'theory' it had had before 1933, the lack of an ultimate economic goal, its repeated shifts and turnarounds, its literally opportunistic crisis management, and the penchant for ad hoc solutions have been taken as evidence that at the core was improvisation. Claims that Nazi economic policy was essentially Keynesian deficit-spending policy have also been rebuked. Likewise, efforts to interpret the establishment of public or party corporations – the *Reichswerke Hermann Göring*, the sprawling empire of the German Labour Front (*Deutsche Arbeitsfront*, DAF), or the creation of SS enterprises – as evidence of 'Nazi socialism' overlook the fact that most of these undertakings were run along capitalist principles. Nor do parallel privatizations fit the picture (Bel 2010; Buchheim and Scherner 2006).

The fragmentation of the Third Reich's economic history further complicates the search for a coherent paradigm or at least consistent policies. Too short, and with too many protagonists, the economic record does not lend itself to systematization beyond the obvious: expediency and patchiness. Yet 'pragmatism' (Ambrosius 2003, 56), with its connotations of rationality and matter-of-factness, is not an adequate epithet. A combination of ideological tenets, political opportunism, and managerial 'tunnel vision' (Hayes 2004, 18) appears more apposite. Nazi economics ventured to render possible the impossible by radicalizing the instruments of exploitation: from robbery to plunder and from coercion to extermination.

17.3   Winning over Business

Heartfield's artwork had made a strong case: how else was the dramatic rise to power of an obscure Austrian agitator, a crank among Germany's political elite, to be explained if not by his manipulation at the hands of big business? The fact that representatives of German heavy industry, conspicuous for its reactionary stand against the Weimar democracy, had spoken out for National Socialism came in handy. The names of Emil Kirdorf and Fritz Thyssen were often invoked, in fact so persistently that the absence of other businessmen of national standing became rather palpable. Historical research has long established that the majority of Germany's corporate elite did not back the Nazi movement to any significant degree before January 1933. Thyssen's vocal endorsement of Hitler met with indifference on the part of his peers, and the scion of a famous Ruhr dynasty would remain the odd man out for the remainder of his career – ironically also in his subsequent break with the regime (Brakelmann 2010; Turner 1985). What financial support the NSDAP (*Nationalsozialistische Deutsche Arbeiterpartei*, Nazi Party) garnered before 1933 came from its members and a number of smaller and medium-sized enterprises (SME) whose proprietors sympathized with National Socialism. Ideological proclivities were sometimes reinforced by other motives. Hugo Boss's straggling apparel company was saved by uniforms deliveries to several Nazi branches; the hopes of cigarette-paper manufacturer Fritz Kiehn to boost his social status in a conservative Swabian town came true when the NSDAP swept the city council in 1933; and Lübeck-based Heinrich Dräger entertained ambitions to conceptualize Nazi economic policy (Lorentz 2001; Köster 2011; Berghoff and Rauh 2015).

But none of these ranked among the giants of German industry who had been reticent in their support of Hitler, usually backing the conservative right of Weimar's political parties, keeping their distance from the social rabble of the NSDAP, and remaining distrustful of any socialist aspirations. Yet distance and distrust were not the same as disagreement. On key issues there was substantial overlap between the tenets of nationalist conservatives and National Socialists. Notably, heavy industry contributed to the decomposition of Weimar's economic and political fabric, and figures like Paul Reusch were willing to compromise with Hitler in order to defeat the loathed democratic forces. The influential steel industrialist never subscribed to National Socialism (and would retire under official pressure in 1942), yet many of his convictions tied in with those of the new regime: the hostility to social democracy and the welfare state; the goal of overcoming Versailles; the authoritarian spirit (Marx 2013; Bähr, Banken, and Flemming 2008). Another case was Carl Duisberg, founding father of the world's biggest chemical concern, *IG Farbenindustrie*. Hardly an ardent Nazi, Duisberg had vented *völkische* inclinations in the mid-1920s. With Hitler in office the manager repeatedly praised the leadership principle which mirrored the claims to *Führertum* so ubiquitous in German industry, i.e. the idea of complete managerial prerogative over the workforce (Kühlem 2012).

Such attitudes prepared the common ground on which big business performed an impressive turnaround in February 1933. Summoned by Hitler, Goering, and Schacht, several prominent companies agreed to back the party in the upcoming March elections; that these were advertised as the last ever was a boon, not a problem. IG Farben led the list of donors and the collection of monies was organized by Gustav Krupp von Bohlen und Halbach, head of the German Industrial Association (*Reichsverband der deutschen Industrie*, RDI) and himself a late convert to the Nazi cause. An old-school conservative moulded in the Wilhelmine age, Krupp shed his doubts as to the new regime's reliability and realigned his company's political outlook. That Hitler had promised to end parliamentary democracy and destroy the political left while remaining rather silent on antisemitism and war helped to win over an audience which was not fussed about the latter aspects either. But reservations persisted. It remained to be seen what the new government would do about foreign trade, capital flows, and international cartelization, spheres in which significant strata of German business inclined towards economic liberalism, however narrowly defined (Tooze 2006).

If businessmen were asking themselves whether or not Hitler would deliver, they were soon reassured. The dissolution of the Reich's democratic structure was plain for everyone to see, and so was the reconfiguration of the industrial relations system. The trade unions were disbanded and – in what amounted to a precedent of how the regime treated its enemies' property rights – their assets confiscated and taken over by the DAF (Hachtmann 2012); collective bargaining and codetermination were abolished. Management authority was stipulated by the 1934 National Labour Law with its hierarchy of leaders and a disenfranchised workforce. Any ambition within the Nazi Party to replace trade unions with a workers' representation of their own was thwarted by the DAF's claim to exclusive authority over labour affairs (Hachtmann 1989; Barkai 1988). From an executive board vantage point, the abandonment of any effective workers' representation not only reasserted management rule on a level not known since Bismarck's days but also served as a break on wage inflation when demand for labour began rising again. That was also the Treasury's intention, further underpinned by a wage freeze which severed the link between prices and incomes, ensuring low production costs (Tooze 2006).

When, subsequently, the regime tried to enforce greater price stability, this would be to the detriment mostly of the middlemen who suffered from shrinking profit margins. Pressure on the old middle classes would further increase with rationing, rationalization, and recruitment to military service, all of which hit SMEs disproportionately, belying the regime's alleged support for the *Mittelstand*

(Swatek 1972). Likewise the legal reforms of German corporate-governance provisions in the 1930s – drafted with the assistance of corporate lawyers – paid only lip service to *mittelständische* paroles. True, the minimum capital of joint stock companies was raised, and tax benefits were offered to partnerships rather than to anonymous corporations. But this was about entrepreneurial visibility, not about corporate size. Meanwhile transformation of giant concerns into individually- or family-held assets was simplified and squeeze-outs of small shareholders were actively promoted; shareholders' leverage against executive boards was severely curtailed. These legal provisions expressed a clear preference for large companies, their alleged efficiency, and the belief that success breeds success, mirroring the accelerated concentration of industrial assets at the expense of those businessmen who had considered themselves National Socialism's very clientele (Swatek 1972; Spoerer 1996; Bähr 2003).

The trend towards concentration cannot have been wholly surprising to those who witnessed the rapidity with which the proponents of a policy favouring SMEs were marginalized in the early years of Nazi rule. The supporters of antiquated 'Estate' ideas suffered the same fate, and the purported reorganization of German business associations proved to be a case of repackaging. Although the pertinent 1934 law employed the *ständische* vocabulary, very little changed in the structure, composition, and actual workings of most industrial associations, with the notable exception of agriculture. Given the symbolic significance of farming in Nazi ideology, the Reich Food Estate (*Reichsnährstand*, RNSt) turned into a key player which set out to restructure farming and eliminate market-driven pricing altogether. However, despite its massive apparatus, the *Reichsnährstand* failed to guarantee the degree of self-sufficiency which was so badly required by the strains of Germany's recurrent balance-of-payments crises (Freise 1994; Schanetzky 2015). In contrast, manufacturing, wholesale, and retailing organizations were marked by great continuity. The RDI briefly became a *Reichsstand* but was soon rechristened *Reichsgruppe*. Continuity of personnel was safeguarded by Krupp's remaining at the helm until 1934 when he was succeeded by Ewald Hecker, another representative of heavy industry, though with stronger ties to the NSDAP. The fact that the RDI managing director was forced to quit on account of his reputation as a political liberal might tell a different story. But the functionary had been the object of attacks from within his own constituency well before 1933 so that his departure appeared an acceptable loss (Barkai 1988; Turner 1985; Priemel 2007).

To some observers such moves seemed an ominous warning, aggravated by the pressure which was brought on the *Reemtsma* and *Quandt* concerns which had to bribe their way out of open conflict with the new regime. Yet the very fact that this was possible was a hopeful sign: this was a language many industrialists could understand. It has been estimated that official corporate funding of the party, its divisions, and of Hitler personally, amounted to 700 million Reichsmarks. The case of Hugo Junkers, one of Germany's handful of aviation pioneers, who was de facto expropriated in order to speed up the construction of the Luftwaffe, was a crass exception which vindicated the rule of mostly smooth relations between regime and corporate elite, a partnership greased by corruption (Budraß 1998; Jacobs 2008; Scholtyseck 2011; Schanetzky 2015).

17.4   The Politics of Regulation

Regulation in the Third Reich, no different from Weimar and the FRG, was a double-edged sword. The regime issued laws and decrees on virtually everything related to business. However, much of this legislation was influenced – frequently co-authored – by business representatives or flexibly adapted, making 'coercion' a misleading label. Legislation on compulsory cartelization was a case in question. The Reich was widely known as the epicentre of cartels in the inter-war period, and German companies rarely required so much as a nudge to enter into market-rigging agreements. The 1933 decree, whose rationale was to control pricing and restrict inopportune investments (to channel scarce capital into specific industries or product lines), would be seldom used: the private protagonists mostly moved on their own initiative (Freise 1994; Tooze 2006). Far more interventionist, and again motivated by concerns about limited domestic capital, was the introduction of dividend ceilings in 1934. Dividends above a threshold of 6% or 8% were to be paid into a public fund out of which communal investments would be financed. Albeit unparalleled, this measure was not so much about seizing private funds as an incentive to save profits in hidden assets. Rather than being distributed, profits were to be accumulated for further investments. The ceilings helped the state to monopolize the money market but threatened to render the stock market fairly obsolete. Although severe, the intervention hit shareholders far harder than companies. While the stockholders' property rights were curtailed, the managers' financial scope of action was actually enhanced (Bähr and Banken 2006, 35–69).

Meanwhile, the trend towards industrial self-financing deprived banks of a traditional line of business and called for closer relations with state and party agencies. Exploring new fields of activities, banks would participate in the 'Aryanization' (*Arisierung*) of Jewish companies and, later, in territorial expansion. This is not to say that German bankers would have preferred to steer clear of the regime's racist policies; the actual record suggests otherwise. 'Aryan' businessmen not only were reticent in protesting against the violent anti-Jewish boycott just three months into Hitler's reign; corporate headquarters also showed remarkable willingness to accommodate (and often anticipate) calls for purges of their management. In the interest of both the company and of other managers awaiting promotion, Deutsche Bank, Dresdner Bank, and Commerzbank got rid of their Jewish executive board members in 1933. That some managers were retained for a few more years, or the *Berliner Handelsgesellschaft*'s non-compliance (though at the cost of falling behind its competitors), showed that alternative roads were available (James 2001; Ziegler 2006). The same was true for the 'Aryanization' of Jewish property. Pressure was also brought on foreign-owned companies to 'Germanize' their management. If they complied, these firms were usually safe from further molesting as the regime respected foreign property rights, mindful of German assets abroad (Bertrams, Coupain, and Homburg 2013; Wubs 2008; Rauh 2008). No German company was ever forced to take over another firm but many chose to exploit the plight of Jewish businessmen. Nazi entrepreneurs such as Kiehn took advantage of their political offices to grab Jewish property; others lobbied for the authorities' endorsement of their claims (Berghoff and Rauh 2015; Priemel 2007). Banks benefited from both actively 'Aryanizing' and financing others' acquisitions. And while there were cases of friendly takeovers in which businessmen agreed to buy at fair prices or serve as guardians until the Nazi terror was over, the average case of both petty and large-scale 'Aryanization' saw opportunism, greed, and antisemitic prejudice add up to a lethal combination which sought maximum gain at minimum cost and drew on the full arsenal of government coercion (Herbst and Weihe 2004; James 2001; Ziegler 2006).

Insurance companies participated in 'Aryanization' as they, too, found their standard options increasingly limited. With government regulation channelling the capital flow into rearmament, private insurers were forced to sign state bonds, thereby again fuelling military investments. Still, this did not make insurance companies mere objects of government policy. Instead, private firms were able to circumvent regulations by buying and financing real estate projects or by employing new laws to fend off competition from public and DAF companies. Generally, the Reich administration was agreed that restrictions on private finance deserved compensation by guaranteeing decent returns; the logic of profitable investment was never seriously put in doubt. By the end of the war, it was not private insurers that struggled to survive but their party-controlled competitors *Volksfürsorge*, due to a major stake in the life insurance business, and *Deutscher Ring* which had insured wartime risks no private company would have been willing to cover (Middendorf and Priemel 2013; Hachtmann 2012).

Much of the regime's early regulation continued strategies from Weimar's dying days rather than starting fresh. Efforts to use capital market regulation as a means of stabilizing pensions and raising funds for job creation schemes dated back to the Depression (Bähr and Banken 2006, 35–69). So did foreign-exchange controls and the bilateralization of international trade. Both policies reflected the turn to beggar-thy-neighbour policies which proliferated across Europe during the slump. Capital and foreign exchange controls which had been introduced in 1931–1932 were continued and systematized, in particular by Schacht who used bilateral trade as a cornerstone of preserving foreign currency reserves which were desperately needed for essential imports. For companies with vested interests in paying off their foreign debts in order to resume business relations abroad, this was highly inconvenient. To others, willing to forego such prospects, the restrictive foreign exchange regime proved a godsend in putting pressure on their creditors to grant more favourable terms. That foreign-exchange controls would also prove a convenient thumbscrew in the expropriation of Jewish businessmen was instantly realized by the *Reichsfinanzverwaltung*'s clerks and the private profiteers of 'Aryanization' (Tooze 2006; Bähr and Banken 2006, 35–69; Priemel 2007).

Restrictions on foreign trade and cross-border capital flows particularly hit import-intensive industries. In 1934 the purchase of raw textiles was effectively prohibited in order to boost the use of synthetic fibre and free foreign currency. However, synthetic fibres led to declining quality while requiring costly investments in new production sites. Whether or not textile companies were willing to undertake such investments depended on the long-term prospects of the synthetics market – and neither the quality issues nor the expected post-war return to imports suggested a huge demand. Accordingly, it was not only among large firms that the call for autarky and import substitution met with opposition; smaller regional producers also chose not to comply with the regime's demands. Ultimately only those textile mills which had planned a commitment to the synthetic-fibre sector in any case readily invested, whereas subsidies, tax incentives, and so forth were required to create additional capacities elsewhere (Scherner 2008b).

17.5 Recovery and Rearmament

'Civilian' industries like textiles, but also their suppliers of machinery, did not belong to the Nazi economy's front-runners. Yet they, too, participated in the Reich's remarkable recovery in the 1930s. Unemployment was virtually overcome within the first four years of Hitler's rule. Certain strata of skilled labour became scarce even before that which made many employers bypass the wage freeze, notably by disguising pay rises as social benefits. Pre-taxation profits were taking a steep upward trajectory from 1933 onwards and returns on equity soared notably in construction, steel, chemical, and other basic industries. This trend owed something to the ingenuity of producers in undermining the regime's efforts at price control by shifting to higher qualities, changing quantities, or simply adopting new labels. But it was also greatly helped by low costs for labour and raw materials, moderate interest rates, and by economies of scale when surplus production capacities were revived which had been lying dormant since 1929. New investment, however, trailed behind the profit rise during the first years as many companies were wary of building new production sites which would not sustain themselves in the long run. Yet when the exploding armaments demand extended the recovery-driven growth, an investment boom set in which had no precedent in German industrial history (Tooze 2006; Steiner 2006; Hensler 2008).

There are good reasons for dating the shift to a wartime mode to the 1936 Four Year Plan. Hitler's directive that the German economy was to be ready for war in four years' time changed gear from reconstruction and rearmament to autarky and preparation for aggressive war. In 1936 the military budget amounted to 11% of GDP (gross domestic product); three years later, roughly a quarter of national wealth would be fed into the war effort; and a staggering 75% in 1944. Still, much of the earlier, apparently civilian outlay was significant in military terms; directly or indirectly, military spending had a major influence on iron and steel production, non-ferrous-metal mining and processing, machinery, and vehicle construction. In a broader sense, pre-1936 investments prepared the ground for the greatly accelerated armaments production of the decade's latter half: key decisions such as the massive expansion of airplane production were implemented as early as 1933 (Fremdling and Staeglin 2014; Harrison 1998; Budraß 1998).

German corporations were quick to appreciate the opportunities which the regime's armaments drive offered to their plants, many of which were then running at low capacity. Within weeks of Hitler's taking office, machine builders, steel magnates, and chemical companies tried to secure military orders. Lobbying was not limited to the likes of IG Farben or Vereinigte Stahlwerke, Europe's biggest steel combine; smaller companies were also pushing into the military sector (Lorentz 2001). But the top names of German industry also assisted in the clandestine financing of the rearmaments programme. A private consortium which included Krupp, Gutehoffnungshütte, Vereinigte Stahlwerke, and Siemens, but was actually run by Germany's Central Bank, guaranteed credits for armaments orders, thus camouflaging the Reich's rapidly growing debt. In return for their cooperation, these companies could reasonably expect a fair share of the ensuing demand (Overy 1994; Bähr, Banken, and Flemming 2008).

There was no denying that military contracts were highly profitable. Between 1936 and 1940, industrial corporations' nominal returns-on-equity averaged 15%, with the armaments industry registering particularly high incomes. These were, however, safely hidden in the remoter places of the balance sheets, to escape appropriation according to the dividend ceilings. The actual extent of profits was illustrated when a 1941 decree allowed for the liquidation of hidden assets at greatly reduced taxes. A third of all corporations seized the opportunity to increase their capital by more than 50% on average, amounting to 3.2 billion Reichsmarks. Of these, 2.8 billion Reichsmarks had been hidden assets (Spoerer 1996, 88–89, 118–120, 169; Fremdling and Staeglin 2014, 383). These figures suggest that price control had been (and would remain) far from effective. Whereas consumer goods prices were fixed with at least some success, those of capital goods proved hard to regiment. This was partly due to the persistence of a cost-plus system which guaranteed a margin of profit in addition to the producers' expenditures. However, to what extent this system, a clear disincentive to rationalization, actually operated is a matter of debate. Studies of aircraft manufacturing show the massive gains made through cost-plus prices but research on other industries has found a predominance of fixed prices and a keen interest of state agencies to enforce cost-efficient production (Budraß 1998; Scherner 2008a).

Göring, as Four Year Plan plenipotentiary, tried to impose a general stop of inflation in late 1936, intending to direct industrial prices as comprehensively as those for agricultural produce. But such declarations of intent met with practical obstacles, notably the massive information asymmetry. To civilian and military controllers, it proved well-nigh impossible to supervise industrial pricing systematically; the sheer diversity of products and the technical expertise in telling one variant from the other would have been enough to vex any auditor. But most of all it was the intricate pattern of highly integrated combines which proved a major difficulty: the vertical chain from raw material production to various stages of refining and manufacturing meant that the possibilities to manipulate costs were virtually endless. This and the long tradition of intense cooperation of state and corporate bureaucracies meant that prices were usually negotiated with rather than imposed on industries and enterprises. At least big business had a major say in which prices were 'forced' upon them (Middendorf and Priemel 2013).

The short-term profitability of government contracts did not mean that companies implemented the armament programme unfailingly or as efficiently as the regime would have liked them to. More often than not, corporate interests determined which projects were taken on and how these were executed. Few managers lost sight of competition and long-term prospects in their decision making. Thus, firms applied for raw materials in excess of their actual demands rather than allocating materials to competitors, with obvious consequences for the notoriously malfunctioning rationing system and, given the ineffective sanctioning mechanisms, usually with impunity. Companies continued civilian product lines with an eye to maintaining a stake in post-war markets; they tried to keep up exports although their products were needed domestically; they carefully avoided investments which were of uncertain long-term use; and they tried to maximize subsidies while minimizing government checks (Buchheim and Scherner 2006; Hensler 2008). In contrast, Gerald Ambrosius (2003) and Peter Hayes (2009) insist that property rights were severely curtailed after 1933.

There was a major gulf between the professed intentions and direct orders of the Reich's economic authorities and corporate interests. The question if and how these conflicting objectives were sorted out stands at the heart of the debate on state–business relations in the Third Reich. Outwardly the situation could not have been clearer: the Four Year Plan set out to gear the economy to war at all costs. Headed by one of the regime's most powerful men who had already proved that he entertained no scruples in applying force, it looked as if business would indeed be tightly regimented along the lines of autarky and unlimited armament: where and when to invest, what to produce, and whom to supply. Recent research, however, has shown that negotiations between state and private protagonists differed greatly from this 'command economy' (*Kommandowirtschaft*). With few exceptions state agencies respected private property rights (apart from Jewish ownership) as well as their opposite numbers' profit motive. Rather than simply issuing orders, contracts were negotiated and mostly with results that reflected corporate interests. Different types of contracts allowed for agreements which were tailored to the needs of varying projects and in accordance with corporate demands: how the projected plants were to be financed; if and what kind of subsidies were to be provided; what checks Wehrmacht and civilian offices had at their disposal; which risks would be covered by the state; if and how public assets were to be privatized. Iron and steel producers were able to decline orders even from the Wehrmacht well into the war, underscoring the continued (negative) freedom of contract they enjoyed (Buchheim and Scherner 2006). When it came to investments, German companies picked the contract type which was best suited to their needs, carefully weighing profitability expectations against government supervision, as IG Farben did in three successive rounds of negotiations over the creation of synthetic-rubber plants (Scherner 2008a).

More blatant cases of coercion seem to have been the establishment of Brabag, an undertaking for the production of petrol through lignite-based hydrogenation, and the *Reichswerke Hermann Göring*, a steel combine designed to exploit Germany's low-concentrated iron ores. Both have long been regarded as prime examples of how the Nazi regime enforced investment and disregarded property rights (Overy 1994, 93–118; Tooze 2006, 235–238). However, alternative interpretations hold that these conflicts displayed the limitations of government power rather than its effective use. In the Brabag case, compulsion to sign shares proved to be the authorities' last resort. And the Reichswerke were founded as a second-best option only after Göring's office had been unable to either induce or coerce German industrialists into an unviable investment. Piling up sky-high deficits over the next years, the concern's performance would all but vindicate private business's reticence (Buchheim and Scherner 2006).

17.6 War

The distinction between the Third Reich's peacetime and wartime economies is tenuous at best. Many of the features distinctive to warring economies – rationing, fixed prices, restrictions on the freedom of labour and capital, the expansion of government bureaucracy – were in place before the first shot was fired. Still, the run-up to the attack on Poland in 1939 marked an important caesura. The military campaigns which were to follow and the increasing strains placed on the economy could not but affect its protagonists. The volatility of demand grew markedly when strategic shifts – war in Western Europe, the failed invasion of the British Isles, the assault on the USSR, the United States' entering the war – translated into turnabouts in armaments production. Each shift required the reallocation of resources and complicated long-term planning, and threatened to undermine profitability. Concentration and rationalization accounted for much of the growth in output during the war but they also put some companies' products out of the market; licensed goods gave away precious technological know-how. And impressive as they may have been, even these increases were simply insufficient. The eventual multi-front war against a coalition in command of vastly superior resources would carry the Third Reich's economy, despite its control of the occupied countries' resources, to the brink (Harrison 1998; Budraß 1998, 679–682).

That German industry did not crumble until late 1944, despite military retreat and relentless Allied bombing, attested to its effective organization. Under Speer's aegis the integration of private and public offices was further intensified. In the elaborate network of plenipotentiaries, associations, and committees, a vast number of managers assumed official, semi-sovereign functions. This has led some historians to conclude that the war economy was the 'dictatorship of the six thousand managers who were most dynamic … and most loyal to the regime' (Abelshauser 2002, 441). The formula, however, is misleading. While the enormous figure begs the question how many members of the managerial elite were left outside, the administration's double-faced character is lost by the notion of tyranny. Companies which delegated managers into public offices gained access to information and infrastructure; their estimates and priorities informed the regime's determinations. And the difference between what was being done pro patria and pro domo was hardly a valid distinction (Lorentz 2001; Ambrosius 2003; Middendorf and Priemel 2013). However, unrepresented firms, mostly SMEs and those deemed inessential to the war effort, were hit hard by the withdrawal of raw materials, capital, and labour, or by complete shut-down (Swatek 1972; Schneider 2005). All the more irritating seems the dogged continuation of a war already lost or delusional projects such as the private financing of SS factories in the spring of 1945. Here, any economic rationale, let alone rationality, 'is hard to discover' (Feldman 2002, 31).

But economic rationality had already led businessmen deep into complicity in Nazi crimes. War had not only transformed the Reich's economy into a mechanism singularly bent on destruction but had also redefined the means by which that war was fought. Expanding domestic instruments of robbery to the newly occupied territories, German managers were eager to lay hands not only on Jewish property but also on other assets. Strategies differed and included cartel agreements, part-nerships with foreign companies willing to collaborate, or forced takeovers. Nationalized Soviet plants seemed up for grabs anyway, and those interested included the crème de la crème of German heavy industry. At times, the identity of occupation agencies and corporate employees meant that it was almost impossible to decide whether economic exploitation was official policy or a private venture. Mostly, German businessmen were not shy to cooperate with and contribute to regimes of oppression, terror, and extermination (James 2001; Wixforth 2006; Priemel 2007; Bähr, Banken, and Flemming 2008; Marx 2013).

This cooperation was not restricted to the occupied territories. With the massive recruitment of foreign, usually forced, labour the brutal reality of racial policy was plain for everyone to see within the Reich proper. Some 13 million foreigners were brought to 'Greater Germany' where a majority of them toiled under miserable conditions, notably those whose racial status was deemed lowest by the Nazi creed but also in the prejudiced minds of many non-party members. Though worried that these workers would replace the drafted German workforce but inadequately, managers generally showed no moral reservations about drawing on forced labour. While there was no obligation to employ foreign or coerced workers, there is some truth in post-war rationalizations that there was no alternative by 1940, unless one wanted to cut back production. Whether or not this would have provoked repres-sion we do not know because apparently no firm ever tried. As to concentration camp inmates, 'rented out' by the SS in the last years of the war, some companies indeed declined. But the majority of those approached, among them Krupp and IG Farben, did not. Also, just how eagerly the recruitment of forced labourers was undertaken and how these were treated at their workplaces lay by and large in the discretion of their employers. Conditions differed, depending on industry, regional patterns, the nature of the respective enterprises (recently established plants employed nearly exclusively forced labour), and management itself. Quotas varying between 15% and 85% within the same concern were not unusual. But for all the differences, the overall picture was stark: German business did very little to improve the lot of their wards unless they had to. The considerable scope of action compa-nies enjoyed in the treatment of their foreign workforce was generally used not in favour of the men, women, and children but to their detriment. The profitability of forced labour is therefore morally irrelevant and a wholly disingenuous question. But even if we accept economic reasoning for one second, the vital point is not whether extra profits were gained from cheap labour, or if labour costs actually increased, but that factories kept running. Recruiting forced labour allowed them to participate in the wartime economy; it gave them access to resources and a means to hold on to their German workforces as well as to continue production of civilian goods (Rauh-Kühne 2002).

17.7 Conclusion

German business did retain significant scope of action in the Third Reich. Many entrepreneurs and managers agreed with central tenets of National Socialism, and their know-how made them indispensable to the regime's goals. Both aspects helped to avoid fundamental conflict, as did a culture of rampant corruption. But more important was the regime's general respect for private enterprise and its property rights as long as these were not claimed by Jewish businessmen or political opponents. In the politics of plunder which came to be known as 'Aryanization', it was not only the state that disregarded private property rights, but business itself. However, given the disregard for human lives later displayed in the context of forced-labour recruitment or the notorious deliveries of poisonous gas and crematoria to extermination camps, the ease with which avowed capitalists resorted to robbery and blackmail ought to shock no one (Hayes 2004; Schüle 2010).

Strong rhetoric and outright coercion on the part of the authorities did exist, though, notably as a last resort when companies refused to comply with the regime's wishes for lack of profitability; managers were well advised to take the Nazi regime's threats rather more seriously than warnings by Weimar's democrats (Hayes 2009). Standard procedure, however, was a negotiating process in which private firms secured acceptable, usually lucrative, deals for their contribution to autarky and rearmament. Increasingly, such negotiations became 'internal affairs' when prices were established by boards or commissions staffed with managers who had taken on additional responsibilities in the war administration. This chimed in with a general trend of regulation and intervention which, far from being unilaterally decreed by state agencies, was the product of – sometimes taxing, at other times amiable – consultations between private and public protagonists. That, however, was not peculiar to the Third Reich but stood in institutional as well as personal continuity with state–business relations before 1933 and after 1945.

The Third Reich evidently did not operate a liberal, 'free market' economy. But this does not mean that it was not capitalist. Beyond the preparation for war, there was little state direction and central planning; competition continued although it was now rivalry for shares in public spending and access to publicly administered resources rather than for shares in markets. Yet not all companies enjoyed the same scope of action. Size mattered. So did military relevance. Industrial concentration was greatly boosted by Nazi economic policies. Big business enjoyed easier access to the regime's decision-making levels; it dominated the apparatus of 'self-administration' and it received preferential treatment in terms of rationing, labour allocation, and so on. By contrast, Nazi Party affiliation mattered far less. While individual careers such as Kiehn's entered a trajectory out of proportion to their respective companies' significance, enterprises run by less overtly Nazified managers did just as well – or better, if they were essential to the war effort (Berghoff and Rauh 2015; Marx 2013).

Whether Nazi rhetoric and propaganda expressed genuine beliefs or were merely adopted to promote commercial interests is often hard to determine. We are on safer ground if we find that although big business did not bring Hitler to power, it did, through a combination of indifference and support, help the regime consolidate, implement its racist and aggressive policies, and eventually conduct an all-out war. The absence of significant opposition from the ranks of business epitomized a lack of ethics which managers shared with other elites. It is misleading to argue that businessmen did not differ significantly from the average German. The corporate elite, and this included those who ran affiliates of international concerns, had above-the-average responsibilities and far greater opportunities to do either good or bad. It was for the latter that these possibilities were used more often than not. There was no need for any particular kind of business ethics or that obscure German *Kaufmannsmoral* often invoked by businessmen and business historians. Standard moral fibre would have been perfectly sufficient. In fact, the argument is better stood on its head: because there was a peculiar capitalist set of values and norms – at the heart of which were economic considerations and a focus on corporate interests – moral integrity mattered precious little. Business trumped ethics.

References

Abelshauser, Werner. 2002. 'Rüstungsschmiede der Nation? Der Kruppkonzern im Dritten Reich und in der Nachkriegszeit 1933–1951.' In *Krupp im 20. Jahrhundert*, edited by Lothar Gall, 267–472. Berlin: Siedler.

Ambrosius, Gerold. 1990. *Staat und Wirtschaft im 20. Jahrhundert*. Munich: Oldenbourg.

Ambrosius, Gerold. 2003. 'Was war eigentlich "nationalsozialistisch" an den Regierungsansätzen der dreißiger Jahre? In *Wirtschaftsordnung, Staat und Unternehmen: Neue Forschungen zur Wirtschaftsgeschichte des Nationalsozialismus*, edited by Werner Abelshauser et al., 41–60. Essen: Klartext.

Bähr, Johannes. 2003. '"Corporate Governance" im Dritten Reich: Leitungs- und Kontrollstrukturen deutscher Großunternehmen während der nationalsozialistischen Diktatur.' In *Wirtschaftsordnung, Staat und Unternehmen: Neue Forschungen zur Wirtschaftsgeschichte des Nationalsozialismus*, edited by Werner Abelshauser et al., 61–80. Essen: Klartext.

Bähr, Johannes and Banken, Ralf, eds. 2006. *Wirtschaftssteuerung durch Recht im Nationalsozialismus: Studien zur Entwicklung des Wirtschaftsrechts im Interventionsstaat des 'Dritten Reichs'*. Frankfurt am Main: Klostermann.

Bähr, Johannes, Banken, Ralf, and Flemming, Thomas. 2008. *Die MAN: Eine deutsche Industriegeschichte*. Munich: C.H. Beck.

Barkai, Avraham. 1988. *Das Wirtschaftssystem des Nationalsozialismus: Ideologie, Theorie, Politik 1933–1945*. Frankfurt am Main: Fischer.

Bel, Germà. 2010. 'Against the Mainstream. Nazi Privatization in 1930s Germany.' *The Economic History Review* 63, 34–55. doi: 10.1111/j.1468-0289.2009.00473.x.

Berghoff, Hartmut and Rauh, Cornelia. 2015. *The Respectable Career of Fritz K. The Making and Remaking of a Provincial Nazi Leader*. New York: Berghahn Books.

Bertrams, Kenneth, Coupain, Nicolas, and Homburg, Ernst. 2013. *Solvay: History of a Multinational Family Firm*. Cambridge: Cambridge University Press.

Brakelmann, Günter. 2010. *Zwischen Mitschuld und Widerstand: Fritz Thyssen und der Nationalsozialismus*. Essen: Klartext.

Buchheim, Christoph and Scherner, Jonas. 2006. 'The Role of Private Property in the Nazi Economy: The Case of Industry.' *The Journal of Economic History* 66, 390–416. doi: 10.1017/S0022050706000167.

Buchheim, Christoph and Scherner, Jonas. 2009. 'Corporate Freedom of Action in Nazi Germany.' *GHI Bulletin* 45, 43–50. https://www.ghi-dc.org/fileadmin/user_upload/GHI_Washington/Publications/Bulletin45/bu45_043.pdf.

Budraß, Lutz. 1998. *Flugzeugindustrie und Luftrüstung in Deutschland 1918–1945*. Düsseldorf: Droste.

Caldwell, Bruce. 2007. 'Introduction.' In *Friedrich August von Hayek: The Road to Serfdom. Texts and Documents. The Definitive Edition*, edited by Bruce Caldwell, 1–33. Chicago: University of Chicago Press.

Caplan, Jane. 1995. 'Introduction.' In *Nazism, Fascism and the Working Class. Essays by Tim Mason*, edited by Jane Caplan, 1–32. Cambridge: Cambridge University Press.

Feldman, Gerald D. 2002. 'The German Insurance Business in National Socialist Germany.' *GHI Bulletin* 31, 19–33. https://www.ghi-dc.org/fileadmin/user_upload/GHI_Washington/Publications/Bulletin31/19.pdf.

Frei, Norbert and Schanetzky, Tim, eds. 2010. *Unternehmen im Nationalsozialismus: Zur Historisierung einer Forschungskonjunktur*. Göttingen: Wallstein.

Freise, Harald. 1994. *Wettbewerb und Politik in der Rechtsordnung des Nationalsozialismus: Primat der Politik und ständischer Gedanke im Kartell-, Wettbewerbs- und Organisationsrecht 1933–36*. Baden-Baden: Nomos.

Fremdling, Rainer and Staeglin, Reiner. 2014. 'Output, National Income, and Expenditure: An Input–Output Table of Germany in 1936.' *European Review of Economic History* 18, 371–397. doi: 10.1093/ereh/heu017.

Gosewinkel, Dieter. 2005. *Wirtschaftskontrolle und Recht in der nationalsozialistischen Diktatur*. Frankfurt am Main: Klostermann.

Hachtmann. Rüdiger. 1989. *Industriearbeit im 'Dritten Reich': Untersuchungen zu den Lohn- und Arbeitsbedingungen in Deutschland 1933–1945*. Göttingen: Vandenhoeck & Ruprecht.

Hachtmann, Rüdiger. 2012. *Das Wirtschaftsimperium der Deutschen Arbeitsfront 1933–1945*. Göttingen: Wallstein.

Harrison, Mark, ed. 1998. *The Economics of World War II: Six Great Powers in International Comparison*. Cambridge: Cambridge University Press.

Hayes, Peter. 2004. *From Cooperation to Complicity: Degussa in the Third Reich*. Cambridge: Cambridge University Press.

Hayes, Peter. 2009. 'Corporate Freedom of Action in Nazi Germany.' *GHI Bulletin* 45, 29–41. https://www.ghi-dc.org/fileadmin/user_upload/GHI_Washington/Publications/Bulletin45/bu45_029.pdf.

Hensler, Ulrich. 2008. *Die Stahlkontingentierung im Dritten Reich*. Stuttgart: Steiner.

Herbst, Ludolf and Weihe, Thomas, eds. 2004. *Die Commerzbank und die Juden 1933–1945*. Munich: C.H. Beck.

Jacobs, Tino. 2008. *Rauch und Macht: Das Unternehmen Reemtsma 1920 bis 1961*. Göttingen: Wallstein.

James, Harold. 2001. *The Deutsche Bank and the Nazi Economic War Against the Jews: The Expropriation of Jewish-Owned Property*. Cambridge: Cambridge University Press.

Köster, Roman. 2011. *Hugo Boss, 1924–1945: Die Geschichte einer Kleiderfabrik zwischen Weimarer Republik und 'Drittem Reich'*. Munich: C.H. Beck.

Kühlem, Kordula, ed. 2012. *Carl Duisberg (1861–1935): Briefe eines Industriellen*. Munich: Oldenbourg.

Lorentz, Bernhard. 2001. *Industrieelite und Wirtschaftspolitik 1928–1950: Heinrich Dräger und das Drägerwerk*. Paderborn: Schöningh.

Marx, Christian. 2013. *Paul Reusch und die Gutehoffnungshütte: Leitung eines deutschen Großunternehmens*. Göttingen: Wallstein.

Mason, Tim. 1995. 'The Primacy of Politics: Politics and Economics in National Socialist Germany.' In *Nazism, Fascism and the Working Class. Essays by Tim Mason*. Edited by Jane Caplan, 32–76. Cambridge: Cambridge University Press.

Middendorf, Stefanie and Priemel, Kim Christian. 2013. 'Jenseits des Primats: Kontinuitäten der nationalsozialistischen Finanz- und Wirtschaftspolitik.' In *Kontinuitäten und Diskontinuitäten: Der Nationalsozialismus in der Geschichte des 20. Jahrhunderts*, edited by Birthe Kundrus and Sybille Steinbacher, 94–120. Göttingen: Wallstein.

Nathan, Otto. 1944. *The Nazi Economic System: Germany's Mobilization for War*. Durham, NC: Duke University Press.

Neumann, Franz. 1944. *Behemoth: The Structure and Practice of National Socialism, 1933–1944*, Oxford: Oxford University Press.

Overy, Richard J. 1994. *War and Economy in the Third Reich*. Oxford: Clarendon Press.

Plumpe, Werner. 2004. 'Die Wirtschafts- und Unternehmensgeschichte des Nationalsozialismus: Überlegungen aus systemtheoretischer Perspektive.' *Jahrbuch für Wirtschaftsgeschichte* 2, 241–244.

Priemel, Kim Christian. 2007. *Flick: Eine Konzerngeschichte vom Kaiserreich bis zur Bundesrepublik*. Göttingen: Wallstein.

Rauh, Cornelia. 2008. *Schweizer Aluminium für Hitlers Krieg? Zur Geschichte der 'Alusuisse' 1918–1950*. Munich: C.H. Beck.

Rauh-Kühne, Cornelia. 2002. 'Hitlers Hehler? Unternehmerprofite und Zwangsarbeiterlöhne.' *Historische Zeitschrift* 275: 1–56. doi: 10.1524/hzhz.2002.275.jg.1.

Schanetzky, Tim. 2015. *'Kanonen statt Butter': Wirtschaft und Konsum im Dritten Reich*. Munich: C.H. Beck.

Scherner, Jonas. 2008a. 'The Beginnings of Nazi Autarky Policy: The "National Pulp Programme" and the Origin of Regional Staple Fibre Plants.' *The Economic History Review* 61, 867–895. doi: 10.1111/j.1468-0289.2008.00425.x.

Scherner, Jonas. 2008b. *Die Logik der Industriepolitik im Dritten Reich*. Stuttgart: Steiner.

Schneider, Michael C. 2005. *Unternehmensstrategien zwischen Weltwirtschaftskrise und Kriegswirtschaft: Chemnitzer Maschinenbauindustrie in der NS-Zeit 1933–1945*. Essen: Klartext.

Scholtyseck, Joachim. 2011. *Der Aufstieg der Quandts: Eine deutsche Unternehmerdynastie*. Munich: C.H. Beck.

Schüle, Annegret. 2010. *Industrie und Holocaust: Topf & Söhne – Die Ofenbauer von Auschwitz*. Göttingen: Wallstein.

Spoerer, Mark. 1996. *Von Scheingewinnen zum Rüstungsboom: Die Eigenkapitalrentabilität der deutschen Industrieaktiengesellschaften 1925–1941*. Stuttgart: Steiner.

Steiner, André. 2006. *Preispolitik und Lebensstandard: Nationalsozialismus, DDR und Bundesrepublik im Vergleich*. Cologne, Weimar, and Vienna: Böhlau.

Swatek, Dieter. 1972. *Unternehmenskonzentration als Ergebnis und Mittel nationalsozialistischer Wirtschaftspolitik*. Berlin: Duncker & Humblot.

Temin, Peter. 1991. 'Soviet and Nazi Economic Planning in the 1930s.' *The Economic History Review* 44, 573–953. doi: 10.1111/j.1468-0289.1991.tb01281.x.

Tooze, Adam. 2006. *The Wages of Destruction: The Making and Breaking of the Nazi Economy*. London: Allen Lane.

Turner, Henry A. 1985. *German Big Business and the Rise of Hitler*. Oxford: Oxford University Press.

Wixforth, Harald. 2006. *Die Expansion der Dresdner Bank in Europa*. Munich: Oldenbourg.

Wubs, Ben. 2008. *International Business and National War Interests: Unilever between Reich and Empire*. Abingdon: Routledge.

Ziegler, Dieter. 2006. *Die Dresdner Bank und die deutschen Juden*. Munich: Oldenbourg.

Further Reading

Buchheim, Christoph and Scherner, Jonas. 2006. 'The Role of Private Property in the Nazi Economy: The Case of Industry.' *The Journal of Economic History* 66. 390–416. doi: 10.1017/S0022050706000167.
A short but insightful piece which has helped to reverse the old 'command responsibility' interpretation over the past decade.

Schanetzky, Tim. 2015.'*Kanonen statt Butter': Wirtschaft und Konsum im Dritten Reich.*
  Munich: C.H. Beck.
The most up-to-date analysis of economic life in the Third Reich, equally precise and concise.
Spoerer, Mark and Streb, Jochen. 2013. *Neue deutsche Wirtschaftsgeschichte des 20. Jahrhunderts.* Munich: Oldenbourg.
An authoritative textbook which situates the Third Reich within the course of German economic history; relies strongly on quantitative methods.
Tooze, Adam. 2006. *Wages of Destruction: The Making and Breaking of the Nazi Economy.*
  London: Allen Lane.
A broad, widely read analysis of the Third Reich's economic policies, including a good chapter on pre-war business strategies.

Chapter Eighteen

Individual Consumers and Consumption in Nazi Germany

Pamela E. Swett

Germans were living in an increasingly cosmopolitan society before 1933. The expansion of film and photographic reporting during the previous decades meant that Germans knew more about, and had more contact with, their European neighbours and their American counterparts across the Atlantic than ever before. The fact that Germans were trailing behind other Western European countries, particularly the First World War's victor nations, Britain and France, in terms of wages and durable goods consumption was not lost on many, particularly those who still rued the outcome of the conflict. While many Germans may have looked somewhat enviously towards their western neighbours in the 1920s, it was the Americans who jumped the furthest ahead in these years in the enjoyment of new products designed purely for the consumer market. Always very conscious of public opinion and international reputation, the Nazi regime made promises to close the gap in living standards after 1933. Recent analysis of the economic data has made it clear that the regime failed to do so, given the prioritization of rearmament and war (Tooze 2006). And yet questions still remain. Were claims by the regime that it cared about raising living standards simply part of the vast illusion created by the movement's leaders to rally support, or was the goal of developing a consumer culture consistent with National Socialism? Did the Nazi era serve as a break in long-term German or broader European trends towards a mass consumer society? Did the ideology's emphasis on community undermine or shape individual consumers' desires or behaviours?

This chapter demonstrates that while state policy had significant impact on who could participate in the retail/consumer marketplace and what goods were available, the government also permitted and even encouraged Germans to imagine themselves as consumers, continuing transnational trends in this way. This

A Companion to Nazi Germany, First Edition. Edited by Shelley Baranowski, Armin Nolzen, and Claus-Christian W. Szejnmann.

tendency did not run counter to the ideology, which professed a commitment to the well-being of the racial community over individual satisfaction. Rather, it sat comfortably within it, albeit dependent on racist presumptions about the worthiness of so-called Aryan Germans to lead prosperous, comfortable lives and to discern between kitsch and class. As Moritz Föllmer (2013, 113–115) has argued, 'Individuality and community were compatible' within National Socialist ideology, because 'personal regeneration' was deemed essential to 'national regeneration'. At the meeting point of these two lines of thinking – individuality and community – race was critical to differentiating between legitimate and illegitimate consumers. And even among those deemed to be 'legitimate' members of the *Volk*, class and gender continued to shape behaviour in old and new ways.

The chapter also illustrates the ways private sector consumer goods firms and retailers continued along a path charted before 1933, as they sought to woo consumers and maintain profits under conditions that increasingly favoured heavy industry. This path was one that led towards the consumer culture that would emerge in post-war West Germany. Readers should be encouraged, therefore, not to view Nazi-era society as an anomaly in the context of German developments or broader European trends with regard to consumption. While the onset of war brought new challenges to consumers, the Four Year Plan's introduction had forced adaptation to war-like conditions years earlier. Even as conditions worsened from 1942 on, however, we can't really speak of a levelling of society. Race was no longer the most pressing determining factor, as the vast majority of Germany's Jews had been deported by this time. Among the 'Aryans' who remained, however, wealth and connections continued to privilege some consumers over others.

18.1   The Nazi Party and State-Sanctioned Consumption

The early Nazi Party (NSDAP) was not particularly concerned with consumers or consumer goods. The party's populist rhetoric spoke of helping small businessmen against the 'Jewish' chain stores and department stores, but beyond this attempt to woo retailers as voters, topics related to the consumer goods sector were not of interest. Similarly, despite the party's romantic idealization of the domestic sphere and motherhood, female consumers were not seen as an important political or economic category until later (Sneeringer 2004; Lerner 2006). The party's prioritization of production and producers over consumption and consumers suited the electorate just fine in the late 1920s and early 1930s. Coming to power in the depths of the Depression meant that the mandate handed to Hitler's first cabinet was to get people back to work.

Buoyed by international developments, make-work projects, and clandestine rearmament, German unemployment began a steady decline heading towards the mid-1930s. While scholars agree that the German economy did see dramatic growth by 1937, there has been debate about the extent to which men and women felt this boom in their own lives. Industrial wages, for example, did not regain 1929 levels (the last pre-Depression year) until 1938 at the earliest. Even then, compulsory deductions and 'voluntary' dues and fees to public associations meant that real weekly net wages did not reach the 1929 level until the early part of the war (Baten and Wagner 2002, 10–11; Hachtmann 1989, 158–159). High employ-ment rates thanks to rearmament, however, meant that more family members were enjoying a pay check than had been the case since before the economic crisis, so real total household income was in many cases slightly higher by the end of 1937 than at the outset of the Depression. In addition, secure employment convinced many that the economy had finally turned the corner. This confidence was key to growing aspirations around consumer items (Steiner 1996, 82–85; Overy 1996, 31). Perhaps people could not afford to purchase many extras, but as Hartmut Berghoff (2005) has argued, there was a ripe market for 'virtual consumption'.

The regime did not ignore these desires. Nazi leaders were motivated by the need to grow and maintain popular support for their rule. Germans, particularly in the cities, were well aware of new technologies and the consumer goods that were beginning to become commonplace in homes in the United States. In addition, many officials believed Germans, as a superior race, deserved a standard of living that reflected the nation's position among the world's races (Torp 2012, 61). If the 'mongrel' Americans had comfortable homes and new technologies at their disposal, Germans too should have access to these goods (Gassert 1997). While there were strong reasons, then, to support the expansion of consumer goods industries, there were also reasons to hold back. The regime's first priority was to enable the country to go to war. And preparation meant resources should be diverted towards heavy industry.

Virtual consumption, therefore, played an important role in the propaganda efforts of the Nazi regime. German consumers were encouraged to dream of an abundance that, while not yet available to the vast majority of citizens, was prom-ised to be just over the horizon. Advocates of National Socialist rule opined in the mid-1930s that just as the government had conquered unemployment, it would soon deliver on its promises to provide every household with the labour-saving devices and leisure time opportunities enjoyed increasingly by the middle classes in other Western nations. Proof of this claim could be found in some of the regime's and party's flagship programmes (Schanetzky 2015, 101–114). The most famous of these were the People's Products (*Volksprodukte*) and the party's 'Strength through Joy' (KdF) leisure programme. The most attainable *Volksprodukt* was the *Volksempfänger*, or People's Wireless. Goebbels backed this initiative as early as August 1933. The basic set was on offer for just 76 Reichsmarks (though cheaper radios existed in Europe), and individual ownership and access to radios at public and work sites increased dramatically in the years that followed. Many arguments have been made about the *Volksempfänger*. While some have noted that the sets were designed in order to make it difficult to pick up foreign broadcasts, indoctri-nating Germans with carefully crafted news coverage and patriotic high culture was not the only goal. Entertainment was critical, and over time the percentage of broadcasts devoted to popular music and theatre increased (Ross 2010). Peter Fritzsche (2008, 66–68) has also discussed the integrative value of having Germans participating remotely in the historic events orchestrated by the regime before the onset of war: the 1936 Olympics, the remilitarization of the Rhineland, and the annexation of Austria are key examples. These community-building strategies aside, it should not be forgotten that the 'people's radio' came in a series of differently priced models. And some who could afford to chose to purchase the far fancier consoles available from private firms, while the poorest Germans continued to listen in public places. Class distinctions were even more apparent in other *Volksprodukte* campaigns. People's refrigerators and washing machines, for example, never spread beyond the households of the wealthy and upper middle classes (Nolan 1994, 207).

A similar point can be made about the most famous of all People's Products, the Volkswagen. While Hitler's call to the German car industry, at the 1934 Reich auto show, to produce an affordable vehicle (the target price was 1000 Reichsmarks) was popular with the citizenry, manufacturers believed it near impossible. At the time, inexpensive models had sticker prices about twice as high (Rieger 2015, 60). Ferdinand Porsche's prototype of the Beetle was unveiled in 1937 with much fanfare, even though the modern, sturdy design could not be produced for anywhere near the cost demanded by the Führer. Still, Germans anticipated the day when the small car would hit the market, and more than 300 000 Germans made deposits of 5 Reichsmarks per week into dedicated savings accounts. Each time a deposit was made, the account holder received a stamp to paste into a specially designed booklet to chart his progress towards ownership. While these hopeful consumers waited, for none received a car during the Third Reich, the wealthy purchased automobiles from a variety of private manufacturers (Rieger 2009). Overall, the auto market did expand in Germany throughout the pre-war years. In 1937, automobile registrations hit the one million mark for the first time, and the overall rate of ownership increased from 1 in 135 to 1 in 61 persons between 1932 and 1937. However, the number of car-owning Germans still trailed dramatically rates in comparator societies. Bernhard Rieger (2015) notes that the rate of car ownership in France and Great Britain had reached the 1937 German level about a decade earlier. Despite the hype and the attractions of virtual consumption, the purchasing power of the average German consumer remained too low and taxes on imported fuel too high to make mass car ownership a reality in Germany until the 1950s (König 2004).

Restrictions on imports and a shift towards heavy industry in preparation for war meant that the German consumer goods market was shrinking overall in the mid-1930s, but the regime also purported to respond to citizens' desires by offering new experiences. 'Strength through Joy' also offered an array of travel opportunities, such as regional bus tours through Germany's idyllic countryside or train rides to the coastal resorts of the North and Baltic seas. The organization also offered the more adventurous trips abroad by ocean steamer to foreign ports, including towns and cities in Italy, Portugal, Norway, and even North Africa. Here again, the message to Germany's workers was that the regime provided all members of the nation with opportunities once reserved for the rich. Domestic travel reminded tourists of the beauty of the country's landscape, and the foreign excursions, always destined for poorer parts of Europe, affirmed German status in the pantheon of nations. The point was for the community to have new shared experiences for which they could thank the German Labour Front, which administered 'Strength through Joy', and by extension the NSDAP which controlled the Labour Front. Overall the travel programme was extremely popular, with 80% of 'Strength through Joy' income coming from its office for Travel, Hiking, and Vacations (Baranowski 2004, 122). Across the country in the last full year of peace, 8.5 million people enjoyed KdF trips – many of whom were repeat customers (Baranowski 2004, 55).

Here, too, however, Shelley Baranowski's research into KdF travel found that class boundaries did not disappear. On the one hand, prices were kept low to make it possible for workers and the lower middle classes to participate. On the other hand, even at such low costs, manual workers remained under-represented on the longer holidays and foreign excursions that were largely filled by white collar and salaried employees (Baranowski 2004, 68). Moreover, after initially scheduling KdF tours to visit some of Germany's most popular resort towns, which had historically been the playgrounds of the upper classes, subsidized travellers were increasingly steered clear of the prestigious sites by the propaganda ministry's Reich Tourism Association. Baranowski (2004, 132–133) concludes, 'whereas at the beginning 60 percent of KdF's tours went to the established spas and natural wonders, only 5 percent went to them by the outbreak of war'. Among those who did travel, there are a number of reasons workers remained under-represented reasons that existed in previous eras. Although Germany did see progress towards acceptance of vacation time within wage agreements, fewer than 25% of workers received more than 12 days, making a lengthy trip impossible. Working-class wages also remained in many cases too low to afford travel. In the mid-1930s, gains in household income were often achieved by longer working hours, making it less likely, not more, that workers would have the time or energy to participate. Finally, cultural barriers remained. Even when the money existed to pay for travel, some workers saw a cruise as a luxury not worth the investment (Baranowski 2004, 68–70).

Those who did participate in 'Strength through Joy' travel were encouraged to see themselves as members of the national community, and while some welcomed the sense of national cohesion and pride engendered by the new opportunity, at times the prejudices and habits of class (as well as regional and religious discord) remained evident. This point aligns well with what Neil Gregor has found about symphonic concert-going in the Third Reich, concluding that 'the social composition and degree of stratification of audiences remained largely unaltered during the National Socialist era' (Gregor forthcoming). Just as the concert hall remained a space in which certain forms of 'sociability and display took place', the same was true at vacation sites, leading to conflict and resentment. 'Private' guests at some resorts and their hosts complained about the perceived rowdiness of the mass tours. SD (*Sicherheitsdienst*) and Gestapo spies reported that regional differences at times undermined sociability, and Catholic residents in towns visited by the KdF sometimes refrained from opportunities to greet warmly groups of party-supporting Protestant visitors (Baranowski 2004, 165–175).

Nonetheless, most tourists had a good time on KdF excursions, and many were grateful for the new experiences. Ultimately, the high-profile state-sponsored campaigns to respond to consumer desires for new leisure activities and goods had mixed results. The most sought-after People's Products, particularly the Volkswagen, remained items that Germans aspired to but did not enjoy until well after the Third Reich had been destroyed. Travel too – certainly lengthy and international tourism – continued to be beyond the reaches of most members of the *Volk*. However, while the 'quarrelsome racial community' remained just that, rather than the unified harmonious ideal propagandists used to sell these programmes, the regime benefited overall at home and abroad by the steps taken.

18.2   Individual Consumers, the Private Sector, and the Four Year Plan

By 1933 half of all Germans lived in cities and towns with more than 10 000 inhabitants (Hoffmann 1965, 178), and while scholarly attention has focused on the state-sanctioned consumer programmes, the vast majority of Germans purchased all their goods and services from privately owned businesses. Sometimes personal relationships were forged between loyal customers and the owners and staff of local shops. In other cases, powerful emotions developed towards transnational corporate brands. There was a consensus that goods, both everyday and luxury items, conveyed meanings. Sophisticated communications systems, including print, film, and radio advertisements broadcast these meanings to individual shoppers and those dreaming of participation. The state also recognized consumers as economic actors, as was seen in the last section, and in the material that follows. Despite all this, historians do not consider Nazi-era Germany a mass-consumer society (Brewer 1997, 51–74). Only a small minority made durable goods purchases, and expenditures on leisure pursuits was also limited, if expanding slightly owing to initiatives like KdF tourism. Historians have also emphasized the prioritization of preparations for war and the accompanying autarchic policies, which seem to belie the significance of individual consumption. And yet looking at one measure of Germany's emerging consumer culture – the existence of communications systems to promote the circulation of ideas about products between buyers and sellers – we can gain insight into the role of individual consumption in the dictatorship and the relationships that existed between the regime, the private sector, and consumers. This communication includes private sector ads, as well as market research, and official propaganda geared towards consumers.

Particularly after the stabilization of the economy in the mid-1920s, advertising grew substantially. Large companies that sold brand name products had developed in-house advertising teams by this time, and a few agencies had opened their doors – the biggest being outposts of larger American and British firms (De Grazia 2005). By the time the National Socialists came to power, networking between German advertisers and their counterparts elsewhere in Europe and in North America meant the field was changing rapidly, but was also open to attack as 'foreign' and 'decadent' amid the Depression and nationalist fervour that accompanied it. In particular, advertisers were blamed for misleading consumers with false promises about the value or efficacy of products (Swett 2014). While similar charges appeared in other countries, in National Socialist Germany such criticism was overtly linked to antisemitic prejudices about unfair business practices that had 'infested' the German economy, particularly the retail sector (Swett, forthcoming).

And, yet, in the years that followed, the Nazi state sought to 'reform' advertising rather than root it out, which is significant for a number of reasons. First, in seeking to fashion an advertising that fitted the 'new Germany', the state was signalling its recognition of individual consumption as a major economic factor and valuable social activity. Joseph Goebbels, who had ultimate authority over the advertising industry, defended the sector as a way to communicate and educate consumers as well as bring people together around common aspirations and values. Given this sort of language, one might expect that his ministry worked tirelessly to shape the messages consumers received through ads. However, most changes related to the business side of the industry (pricing and sizing standardization) and to the purging of Jews and political opponents of the regime. The overall look of ads and the messages that appeared after 1933 did not change substantially until well into the war.

What we do not see in German advertisements during the 1930s is a rejection of class difference. Expensive brands continued to be sold and consumed, albeit by a very small fraction of the population. Luxury travel, jewellery, automobiles, evening wear, musical instruments, and household appliances remained available through this period, and they were advertised explicitly as luxury items. The very wealthy had the 'class' and 'distinction' necessary to appreciate (and afford) a Mercedes Benz or a Steinway grand piano. Blue- and white-collar workers also appeared clearly identified as such in the advertisements of this period. Certain products were promoted explicitly as fitting the needs and budgets of these groups, from balms and lotions to soothe the tired hands and feet of manual labourers to the practical Salamander brand shoes of the white-collar office staff. How do we reconcile class-based imagery in advertisements with National Socialist ideology? Ultimately, those who sought to promote the regime's integrative aims, including most advertisers, hoped to appeal to harmony between classes, if not the eradication of socio-economic difference. Recognizing the potential contributions to national goals made by labourers, farmers, office staff, soldiers, and housewives was a more realistic aim for 1930s Germany than portraying consumers as a homogeneous middle class. It allowed advertisers to speak to more potential customers and echoed the Nazi romanticization of rural Germany and other communal slogans such as the partnership between physical and intellectual labour (*Arbeiter der Faust* and *Arbeiter der Stirn*).

In other ways, too, product promotions presented to consumers in Germany were not that dissimilar from those running in newspapers and magazines, billboards, and film strips in other Western countries. Women were recognized as the chief consumers, and most ads were geared towards an audience of female shoppers. Although numerous staples were still sold 'anonymously' – without a brand name – companies that had branded their products (and the retailers who sold them) touted their higher quality and consistency. As elsewhere in Western Europe and North America, advertisements also included increasing amounts of text in the inter-war period, as companies sought to convince shoppers of the efficacy and desirability of their products through scientific evidence or compelling narratives. And some brands used very similar campaigns in Germany as in democratic societies, including the United States, through the 1930s (Ross 2007).

One reason for the lengthening of copy was that companies were increasingly seeking to build relationships with consumers, realizing the power of brand loyalty and word-of-mouth support. If a shopper believed that she had learned something from the advertisement or felt connected personally to the narrative offered, she was more likely to try the product, return to it, and recommend it to others. While one could argue that consumers were being manipulated by business owners, these 'teaching advertisements' also took consumers' needs and wants more seriously than ever before. As was often quoted, two thirds of the entire German *Volkseinkommen* (national income) passed through housewives' hands (Peikow 1937; Siemens 1936).

That consumers were increasingly recognized as important actors in society was demonstrated by the forced dissolution of the consumer cooperatives that had grown so popular, particularly among workers in the previous decades (Kurzer 1997). Unorganized shoppers suited the dictatorship, but they were still recognized as vital actors in the domestic economy. In order to study their needs and desires the first consumer research institutes, which received support from the state and private firms, were founded in the early 1930s to interview shoppers about their preferences (Wiesen 2011, ch. 4). Market research had its start in the United States, but the large German firms that could afford such studies also hoped that the information gathered would help them better target consumer demands in an era of increasing incomes and decreasing choice. At the same time, however, this attention to consumers may have instilled a level of confidence in housewives that made it more difficult for the regime starting in 1936, when greater efforts to direct women's purchasing and use of commercial goods were first launched.

The extensive deprivation of the First World War was still fresh in many Germans' memories, and most consumers knew what to expect if should war return. In fact, a number of items like coffee and cocoa, textiles and rubber products were already in short supply sporadically throughout the 1930s. The government (and the Social Democratic Party in exile) monitored closely the periodic hoarding of such products when rationing or rumours thereof percolated through the population (Sopade 1934, 104–105). Although the first examples of rationing were implemented in 1934, a fundamental shift in the consumer sector arrived with the enactment of the Four Year Plan in 1936. Drastically curtailing the importation of raw materials needed for the manufacture of consumer items and finished products destined for store shelves, consumers were forced to alter their buying habits. Germans, particularly women, who controlled household consumption, were also asked to conserve and reuse commonplace items. As Nancy Reagin has explained, 'It was in the household – in the erratic shortages of meats, fats, imported foods, fabrics, toys, and through the introduction of inferior ersatz products – that ordinary Germans first felt the pinch of the Four Year Plan' (Reagin 2007, 150).

Always anxious to retain the allegiance of the public, the state sought ways to manage the impact on individuals and families. Female shoppers were the linchpin in these efforts. The regime needed to convince women of three things: that cutting back on consumption was in the best interest of the nation; that the alternatives to products in short demand were satisfactory replacements; and that all Germans, regardless of class or region, were being asked to sacrifice equally. This was a heavy order, and many officials still believed that German defeat in 1918 had been caused by the inability of the monarchy to provision its people during the blockade, leading to widespread suffering and the radicalization of workers (Gerhard 2015). Avoiding a repeat 'stab in the back' in the future was a job of the utmost importance. So, while the consumer economy took a back seat to rearmament from 1936 on, the consumer was showered with ever more attention by the state and party.

The Nazi *Frauenwerk* and *Frauenschaft* (Women's Bureau and Women's Association) and other offices related to food and home economics were coordinated in 1936 under the authority of the new *Reichsausschuss für Volkswirtschaftliche Aufklärung* or Reich Committee for Popular Economic Enlightenment (RVA). The RVA, which answered to the Nazi Ad Council, and ultimately to the propaganda ministry, attempted to teach women how to handle the changes. In the last years of peace there were hundreds of individual posters, articles, brochures, films, workshops, and lectures geared towards convincing women to cook with more plentiful local products like fish and whole grains and do without products that had become scarce like coffee, meat, and butter. Claudius Torp has referred to these campaigns as an effort to 'nationalise taste' (Torp 2012, 69). Similarly, women were provided with face-to-face lessons and tutorials in booklets and film strips about conserving soaps and detergents, guarding against wastefulness in the kitchen and pantry, and maintaining and mending linens and clothing. The private sector joined in these campaigns by producing advertisements for their products that directed consumers to conserve or make do with substitutes (Swett 2009). Advertisements paid for by private companies in print media and in film helped the regime get across its messages of frugality, while also presenting their brands as loyal to the regime and its goal of military preparedness. In addition to demonstrating implicit support for Nazi aims, reminding consumers to use items in short supply sparingly had an added benefit for owners of popular brands. If the reminders and tips worked, their products would remain in homes and on store shelves as long as possible.

While bureaucrats and party activists worked tirelessly to retrain female consumers, they were consistently disappointed by their pupils. Organizers in the *Frauenschaft* and *Frauenwerk* reported frequently that their charges were stubborn in their loyalty to certain products and practices and were uninterested in change (Reagin 2007; De Grazia 1993). Germans did not want to replace meat with fish. They insisted that the Persil laundry detergent became less effective as its fat content dwindled. They still wanted to buy new clothes rather than mend the old. What bureaucrats underestimated in their attempts to forge a more unified *Volksgemeinschaft* was the strength of the regional and class divisions which segmented this mass market – and perhaps personal taste as well! While they sought to convince women of the necessity of replacing variation with autarchically minded homogeneity in both the selection of goods available, and how they were used, women remained suspicious of these challenges to their know-how.

18.3   The War Years

One benefit of the Four Year Plan, and the accompanying shortages, was that the start of the war had less of an immediate impact on consumers than it would have had otherwise. Food rationing was implemented a few days before the invasion of Poland. Although the system of ration cards was comprehensive, differentiating by age and occupation and persecuting Jewish Germans from the start, it still required the purchase of permissible goods, and so those with more money, including soldiers' families, were better fed, leading to inevitable resentments as the war dragged on (Gerhard 2015, 55–56). Consumer products' firms and retailers quickly scaled back their marketing and advertising divisions. Indeed, some Germans called for the immediate cessation of all advertising of consumer goods, in recognition of the new circumstances. Consumer goods manufacturers, retailers, and consumers themselves largely rejected this option, arguing instead that open lines of communication between the commercial sector and consumers had cultural and educational value, particularly in wartime. For example, private sector advertisements for products used by women serving in jobs traditionally held by men would help the population come to terms with such alterations to the pre-war status quo.

Debate among historians about conditions on the home front has been lively in recent years. Some historians have stressed eyewitness accounts of the well-fed Germans encountered in 1945, as Allied troops crossed into German territory (Grossmann 2007, 30–32). Others have recalled the extent to which the German military requisitioned vast quantities of luxury and daily use items in occupied Western Europe, and permitted individual Wehrmacht soldiers to send unlimited packages and return on leave with whatever they could carry (Aly 2006, 94–107). 'Aryan' Germans not only benefited from the theft of goods from outside their borders, they also refilled their larders and linen closets with items belonging to their own countrymen. Once the Reich began deporting Jewish Germans to the nascent death camp network in the East in autumn 1941, local party officials were quick to auction off the 'resettled' families' goods to their former neighbours (Fritzsche 2008, 257–259). This practice became more common as the intensification of the bombing of German cities drastically increased the demand for furnishings, clothes, and household items.

While recognizing the crimes committed in the occupied territories to the benefit of the Wehrmacht's coffers and individual Germans' supplies of food and other goods, Christoph Buchheim (2010, 314–315), among others, has raised important reservations about overstating the comfort in which Germans lived during the war. While it is true that incomes grew during the war, the cost of living went up in tandem and, more importantly, the availability of non-essential consumer goods dried up. While soldiers were able to purchase goods abroad, they also consumed some of those purchases on site. The packages that did come home were not always essential items that affected basic living standards. He also reminds us that the permission to carry or send home anything and everything was rescinded in 1943, as the Wehrmacht sought more control over remaining supplies in the occupied territories. This shift in policy reflected the shrinking size of the empire, and the declining opportunities to purchase or steal goods.

Communication between the commercial sector and consumers also had contracted markedly by the end of 1941. Paper shortages and the decision to cease promotion of unavailable products meant that advertising shrank dramatically and became mainly limited to small classifieds in which brand name manufacturers simply put forward the values of their firms, as a reminder of a trusted past and hoped-for future. The task of training female consumers to alter behaviour to meet the demands of wartime and the growing scarcity of common items also fell by the wayside. Challenging women's expertise in the domestic realm had always been a point of contention for women who felt harangued and misled by the instructions provided by the women's organizations. By 1944, the lack of resources and the futility of marketing ersatz products to resistant consumers halted most programmes.

Conditions never reached the nadir of the First World War. However, by 1943 many basic items were no longer available. Shoes and new clothes were distributed only to children and adults with specific work-related needs. Food rations were being cut back on a regular basis. Those in rural Germany who grew their own food and workers' families with children managed the best. In the latter case, extra rations for war industry workers and children could be pooled and shared among all family members. Civil servants and other white-collar workers, especially those on their own or without children, did not receive enough calories to cover their bodies' needs. In some cases, these groups could supplement their rations through the black market. Party officials and those with connections to neutral countries continued to find ways around the restrictions to stay well fed (Buchheim 2010, 319–323).

In the last year of the war, life for consumers became very difficult. Ironically, many families had plenty of money, as all able-bodied adults were hard at work keeping the war economy humming. Even some foreign labourers were found to have bundles of cash hidden in their barracks or kept in their pockets for fear of theft (BA-Berlin, NS 6/723, *Ostarbeiter*). Depositing this 'surplus money' in the nation's savings banks was what the regime asked of its citizens. It had become a 'national duty' during the war, because the government used the deposits to finance the war (Tooze 2006, 353–355). We should not overlook the fact, however, that advocates for saving, such as Reich economics minister Walter Funk, continued also to use the language of individual consumption late into the war to motivate Germans to stop 'hoarding cash' and instead add to their savings accounts. As the headline covering Funk's speech to mark the 100th anniversary of the Berlin Savings Bank on 28 June 1943 announced, making deposits now would enable, in the future, 'The Ability to Buy Better, Cheaper and More' (BA-Berlin, NS 6/664, Funk speech *Besser, billiger und mehr*). Similarly, among its final tasks the RVA also planned to convince German consumers in 1944 that war production had made possible the development of new 'standardization methods [that when applied] to consumer products manufacturing would lead to a less expensive and faster rebuilding process; hence it is worthwhile to save during the war for the time after victory' (BA-Berlin, R5002/45, 'RVA Spar Aktion' report).

The problem Funk and his colleagues were sidestepping, however, was that there was simply nothing to buy at present. Provisioning citizens with even the most basic necessities was not only made difficult because of the prioritization of war materiel, it was also severely hampered by the Allied bombing campaign. One report on the economic situation in the central German city of Kassel noted in March 1944 that 98% of the city's retail trade had disappeared during recent attacks. Lost in the fires was an estimated 7.38 million Reichsmarks worth of consumer goods, including almost 2 million Reichsmarks of food stocks and roughly 2.5 million Reichsmarks worth of textiles (BA-Berlin, R 3101/13013, Lagebericht Kassel). While local and national officials worked to re-establish distribution points for goods after such events, many consumers left urban areas and many others turned increasingly to the black market, which had grown throughout the war. At first it had been the easiest way to attain imported goods, specialty foods, and those items that were rationed, like soap. By the closing months of the war, the black market had expanded immensely, despite the fact that such trade was prosecuted severely (Niemann 2012, 107). One employer in Swinemünde complained in February 1945 that the workers at his shipbuilding firm were paying 'fantastical prices' for goods: '10 RM per cigarette and 60 RM for bread' (BA-Berlin, NS 6/391, Burmester to Oberregierungsrat). Even coffins were bought and sold at hyper-inflated prices on the black market (Black 2010). The increasingly public presence of black market activities was an obvious sign to everyone that the regime was losing legitimacy among its own people (Zierenberg 2008). The situation would only worsen after the surrender. Richard Bessel (2009, 372) estimates that in 1947 as much as 95% of the population was active in some fashion in black market trade.

What then of the *Volksgemeinschaft*, or the *Schicksalsgemeinschaft* ('community of fate') during the war, that emblazoned the regime's propaganda? When it came to consumers and individual consumption, was it all just a 'virtual' mirage? The answer is a qualified 'no'. While big-ticket items remained beyond the reach of most families in the pre-war period, inexpensive brand-name consumer items with their promises of quality and even life-altering effects were becoming more common. This development was not put in motion by the dictatorship. Rather it followed a trend begun already at the turn of the century throughout Western Europe and North America. The growing presence of such items meant that the relationships Germans had with consumer goods manufacturers and the retailers of those products was intensifying. More importantly, it meant that consumers were increasingly identifying themselves in this way – as individuals with certain types of expertise related to their role as consumers, and as participants in lifestyles defined in part by consumer goods. As the work of Shelley Baranowski and others attests, even though there were limits placed on consumable goods, the regime did deliver some new experiences for men and women to consume. There are two points, however, to note about the unifying intentions of these new offerings to consumers. First, there has not been enough attention given to the fact that the regime itself accepted different levels of 'taste', which roughly aligned with class difference. Second, even when the state hoped to undermine class or regional differences through homogenizing efforts, individual consumers (increasingly self-assured in their identity as such) did not in many cases relinquish their pre-existing practices or attitudes which reaffirmed social and cultural divisions within German society. In these ways, pre-existing social structures and international trends laying the groundwork for a German consumer culture were at least as strong as the communal attractions of the *Volksgemeinschaft*.

References

BA-Berlin, NS 6/391, Letter from Ernst Burmester company in Swinemünde to the Oberregierungsrat, 1945.

BA-Berlin, NS 6/664, Walter Funk speech 'Besser, billiger und mehr kaufen können', 28 June 1943.

BA-Berlin, NS 6/723, Concerns to party headquarters about money held by *Ostarbeiter*. Bericht der Gauleitung Wartheland, 2 February 1942.

BA-Berlin, R 3101/13013, Lagebericht Kassel, 7 March 1944.

BA-Berlin, R5002/45, 'RVA Spar Aktion' report, 26 July 1944.

Aly, Götz. 2006. *Hitler's Beneficiaries*. New York: Metropolitan.

Baranowski, Shelley. 2004. *Strength through Joy: Consumerism and Mass Tourism in the Third Reich*. Cambridge: Cambridge University Press.

Baten, J. and Wagner, A. 2002. 'Autarchy, Market Disintegration, and Health: The Mortality and Nutritional Crisis in Nazi Germany, 1933–1937.' *Economics and Human Biology* 1, 1–28.

Berghoff, Hartmut. 2005. 'Methoden der Verbrauchslenkung im Nationalsozialismus.' In *Wirtschaftskontrolle und Recht in der nationalsozialistische Diktatur*, edited by Dieter Gossewinkel. 281–316. Frankfurt am Main: Klostermann.

Bessel, Richard. 2009. *Germany 1945: From War to Peace*. New York: Harper.

Black, Monica. 2010. *Death in Berlin: From Weimar to Divided Germany*. New York: Cambridge University Press.

Brewer, John. 1997. 'Was können wir aus der Geschichte der frühen Neuzeit für die modern Konsumgesellschaft lernen?' In *Europäische Konsumgeschichte*, edited by Hannes Siegrist, Hartmut Kaelble, and Jürgen Kocka, 51–74. Frankfurt am Main: Campus.

Buchheim, Christoph. 2010. '"Der Mythos vom 'Wohlleben": Der Lebensstandard der deutschen Zivilbevölkerung im Zweiten Weltkrieg.' *Vierteljahrshefte für Zeitgeschichte* 58, 299–328.

De Grazia, Victoria. 1993. *How Fascism Ruled Women: Italy, 1922–1945*. Berkeley: University of California Press.

De Grazia, Victoria. 2005. *Irresistible Empire: America's Advance through Twentieth Century Europe*. Cambridge. MA: Belknap Press.

Föllmer, Moritz. 2013. *Individuality and Modernity in Berlin: Self and Society from Weimar to the Wall*. Cambridge: Cambridge University Press.

Fritzsche, Peter. 2008. *Life and Death in Nazi Germany*. Cambridge, MA: Belknap Press.

Gassert, Philipp. 1997. *Amerika im Dritten Reich: Ideologie, Propaganda und Volksmeinung, 1933–1945*. Stuttgart: Steiner.

Gerhard, Gerhard. 2015. *Nazi Hunger Politics*. London: Rowman & Littlefield.

Gregor, Neil. Forthcoming. 'Listening as a Practice of Everyday Life: The Munich Philharmonic Orchestra and Its Audiences in the Second World War.' In *Oxford Handbook for the History of Music Listening in the 19th and 20th Centuries*, edited by Christian Thorau and Hansjakob Ziemer. New York: Oxford University Press.

Grossmann, Atina. 2007. *Jews, Germans and Allies: Close Encounters in Occupied Germany*. Princeton, NJ: Princeton University Press.

Hachtmann, Rüdiger. 1989. *Industriearbeit im Dritten Reich: Untersuchungen zu den Lohn- und Arbeitsbedigungen in Deutschland 1933–1945.* Göttingen: Vandenhoeck & Ruprecht.

Hoffmann, Walther G. 1965. *Das Wachstum der deutschen Wirtschaft seit der Mitte des neunzehnten Jahrhunderts.* Berlin: Springer.

König, Wolfgang. 2004. 'Adolf Hitler vs Henry Ford: The Volkswagen, the Role of America as a Model, and the Failure of a Nazi Consumer Society.' *German Studies Review* 27, 249–268.

Kurzer, Ulrich. 1997. *Nationalsozialismus und Konsumgenossenschaften: Gleichschaltung, Sanierung, und Teilliquidation zwischen 1933 und 1936.* Pfaffenweiler: Centaurus.

Lerner, Paul. 2006. 'Consuming Pathologies: Kleptomania, *Magazinitis,* and the Problem of Female Consumption in Wilhelmine and Weimar Germany.' *WerkstattGeschichte* 42, 45–56.

Niemann, Hans-Werner. 2012. '"Volksgemeinschaft" als Konsumgemeinschaft?' In *'Volksgemeinschaft': Mythos, wirkungsmächtige soziale Verheißung oder soziale Realität im 'Dritten Reich?' Zwischenbilanz einer kontroversen Debatte,* edited by Detlef Schmiechen-Ackermann, 87–110. Padeborn: Schöningh.

Nolan, Mary. 1994. *Visions of Modernity: American Business and the Modernization of Germany.* New York: Oxford University Press.

Overy, Richard. 1996. *The Nazi Economic Recovery.* Cambridge: Cambridge University Press.

Peikow, Richard. 1937. 'Die soziale und wirtschaftliche Stellung der deutschen Frau in der Gegenwart', dissertation, Friedrich-Wilhelms Universität, Berlin.

Reagin, Nancy R. 2007. *Sweeping the German Nation: Domesticity and National Identity in Germany, 1870–1945.* Cambridge: Cambridge University Press.

Rieger, Bernhard. 2009. 'The "Good German" Goes Global: The Volkswagen Beetle as an Icon in the Federal Republic.' *History Workshop Journal* 68, 3–26.

Rieger, Bernhard. 2015. *The People's Car.* Cambridge, MA: Harvard University Press.

Ross, Corey. 2007. 'The Americanization of Advertising in Interwar Germany.' In *Selling Modernity: Advertising in Twentieth Century Germany,* edited by Pamela E. Swett, S. Jonathan Wiesen, and Jonathan R. Zatlin, 52–77. Durham, NC: Duke University Press.

Ross, Corey. 2010. *Media and the Making of Modern Germany: Mass Communications, Society, and Politics from the Empire to the Third Reich.* Oxford: Oxford University Press.

Schanetzky, Tim. 2015. *'Kanonen statt Butter': Wirtschaft und Konsum im Dritten Reich.* Munich: C.H. Beck.

Siemens Corporate Archiv, 37/Ls510, 1936. *Der Anschluss: Hausmitteilungen der Siemens-Schuckertwerke AG für Elektro-Fachgeschäfte* 7, no. 11.

Sneeringer, Julia. 2004. 'The Shopper as Voter: Women, Advertising and Politics in Post-Inflation Germany.' *German Studies Review* 27, 476–501.

Sopade. 1934. *Berichte aus Deutschland I* (May/June), 104–105.

Steiner, André. 1996. 'Von der Preisüberwachung zur staatlichen Preisbildung.' In *Preispolitik und Lebensstandard,* edited by André Steiner, 23–86. Cologne: Böhlau.

Swett, Pamela E. 2009. 'Preparing for Victory: Heinrich Hunke, the Nazi *Werberat,* and West German Prosperity.' *Central European History* 42, 675–707.

Swett, Pamela E. 2014. *Selling under the Swastika: Advertising and Commercial Culture in Nazi Germany.* Stanford, CA: Stanford University Press.

Swett, Pamela E. Forthcoming. 'Salesmen, Salesmanship, and Dispossession in the Retail Context.' In *Dispossession: Plundering German Jewry, 1933–1953,* edited by Jonathan R. Zatlin and Christoph Kreutzmüller. Ann Arbor: University of Michigan Press.

Tooze, Adam. 2006. *Wages of Destruction: The Making and Breaking of the Nazi Economy.* New York: Viking.

Torp, Claudius. 2012. *Wachstum, Sicherheit, Moral: Politische Legitimationen des Konsums im 20. Jahrhundert.* Göttingen: Wallenstein.

Wiesen, S. Jonathan. 2011. *Creating a Nazi Marketplace.* Cambridge: Cambridge University Press.

Zierenberg, Malte. 2008. *Stadt der Schieber: Der Berliner Schwarzmarkt, 1939–1950.* Göttingen: Vandenhoeck & Ruprecht.

CHAPTER NINETEEN

Gender

ELIZABETH HARVEY

Opponents of Nazism, including feminists and left-wingers who had actively cam-
paigned before 1933 to defend and uphold women's rights in the face of the looming threat from the radical right, had some idea of what to expect in the case of a
Nazi takeover. NSDAP (Nazi Party) propaganda before 1933 about gender often
repeated well-worn conservative clichés about the 'natural' gender order, the
polarity and complementarity of gendered spheres within political, economic, and
cultural life, and the need to restore a secure and stable home and family life based
on male breadwinners and female homemakers. But above and beyond that, before
1933 the NSDAP had taken up within the spectrum of German right-wing nationalist politics the most extreme anti-feminist position in its outright rejection of
female politicians (Sneeringer 2002, 231–259; Boak 2004). After the Nazi takeover, the sound and sight of marching columns of Stormtroopers dominating the
streets, preserved and amplified through film and photographs, signalled the triumph of fascist hyper-masculinity – a spectacle that Italy had witnessed a decade
earlier. Engelbert Huber's propaganda tract *Das ist Nationalsozialismus* proclaimed
the National Socialist 'uprising' to be a 'male event' and summarily dismissed the
idea of a political role for women (Huber 1933, 122). The new government's
onslaught against the left and against the Jews was accompanied by the destruction
of homosexual rights organizations and a rising homophobia (Micheler 2005,
287–293). Similarly under attack were organizations advocating women's political
and civic rights and professional advancement. Liberal feminist organizations virtually all dissolved themselves in spring 1933 under pressure to exclude their Jewish
activists and members (Evans 1976; Greven-Aschoff 1981); one feminist organization that sought, through compromise, to continue its work was the organization
of academic women (Oertzen 2012, 181–231). Women students wondered – in

A Companion to Nazi Germany, First Edition. Edited by Shelley Baranowski,
Armin Nolzen, and Claus-Christian W. Szejnmann.
© 2018 John Wiley & Sons Ltd. Published 2018 by John Wiley & Sons Ltd.

light of talk of limits on women entering universities – if they would be able to continue their courses (Weyrather 1977). Some sacked Jewish women judges were unsure whether they were being dismissed for being Jews or being women (Röwekamp 2011, 643–659). Measures to dismiss married women civil servants and to incentivize female employees in the private sector to give up their jobs on marriage conveyed in the first months of the regime the impression of a regime setting out to prioritize jobs for men (Winkler 1977, 42–43; Stephenson 2001, 50–52; Stibbe 2003, 84).

If gender is defined as a comprehensive, 'normative symbolic system of difference and power' (Caplan 2010, 84), grasping National Socialism as a variant of fascist anti-feminism offers important insights into its gender politics. The signals given in 1933 continued to reverberate in the regime's gender politics in subsequent years, even if the indications of straightforward reaction were not all sustained in the longer term. Staging a revolution as a 'stag affair' (Waldeck 1944, 14) with marching columns, masculinist demonstrations of unfettered violence against defeated enemies, drives to 'clean up the streets', and threats to push women back into the home was one thing. Governing a highly industrialized society with a large service sector and modern mass media, marshalling its resources and gearing it towards war, coaxing those included in the 'people's community' (*Volksgemeinschaft*) into positive affirmations of support – all these undertakings favoured a more differentiated set of policies regarding the labour market, education, and the role of women in public life as role models and transmitters of regime ideology (Winkler 1977; Stephenson 2001; Stibbe 2003).

And yet, as Gisela Bock forcefully argued in the 1980s, it only takes us so far if we understand the gender politics of National Socialism primarily as an anti-feminist backlash which was followed by certain adaptations in face of the complexities of marshalling and mobilizing German society in preparation for war. Tracing these adaptations, and the opportunities these created for women together with their limitations, has been a crucial dimension of research on gender and National Socialism. However, this approach, if adopted too narrowly, can produce an oversimplifying 'ideology versus reality' interpretation. Hence it is vital to stress that the National Socialist gender order was inseparable from its racism (Bock 1984, 137–138). If there were, indeed, conventionally conservative and bourgeois elements in pre-1933 Nazi propaganda to women, the more radical racialized thinking on gender that the Nazi movement set out to realize was more vividly evident in *Mein Kampf,* which contained little that was conventionally conservative in its scattered pronouncements on women, men, sexuality, reproduction, marriage, and the family and offered instead a vision of endangered 'blood'. The family as an institution rated scarcely a mention and Hitler offered no positive prescriptions regarding German women's place in a future society. His focus was instead on the dangers to German manhood: the spectre of 'un-women' – diseased prostitutes – and 'feminized' men, and on the need for masculine regeneration in the guise of young bodies training for combat (Hartmann et al. 2016 vol. 1, 218–219, 657, 667, 671, 729; vol. 2, 1042, 1045, 1047).

As Bock argued, establishing the primacy of the masculine within a concept of gender polarity and complementarity was not an end in itself for Nazi ideologues: it was a means to secure the racial identity and status of the biologically defined nation. The correct model of gender relations, emphasizing gender difference and male authority in the state and public life, was imagined as a distinguishing characteristic of the elevated and privileged *Volk*. Conversely, the future reproduction of the racially selective community of Germans depended on securing these correct gender roles and gender hierarchy. Gradations of gender difference were, according to racial theorists, a marker of position within a hierarchy of European and non-European peoples: 'lower races' were supposedly characterized by an 'attenuation' (*Applanation*) of sexual difference (Bock 1984, 135–136; Bock 1993, 281–282). This logic, applied by the National Socialists to presumed enemies, 'aliens', and the 'unfit' within and beyond the borders of Germany, dictated far-reaching and potentially lethal consequences. First, those excluded from the *Volksgemeinschaft* were considered inherently devoid of, or destined to be deprived of, the 'privilege' of marked gender identities and gender distinctions. Second, men and women who were judged to deviate in their appearance and actions from prescribed and demarcated gender roles and patterns of sexual behaviour were stigmatized as non-German and unworthy to belong to the 'people's community'.

While Bock's hypotheses were the theoretical point of departure for her detailed study of Nazi sterilization policies, her argument is a general one. But how systematically have historians examined the interdependence between the regime's enforcement of racial privilege, selection, exclusion, and repression, on the one hand, and the gender order, on the other? Since the 1980s, it has become virtually axiomatic to regard the category of 'race' as central to the study of National Socialism (Kershaw 2014, 29). Considerations of how racial ideology structured the policies and practices of the regime have underpinned explorations of the stigmatization and persecution of the Jews and other minorities, of the exclusionary and inclusive practices associated with the idea of *Volksgemeinschaft*, and of Nazi conquest, occupation, colonization, forced labour, and genocide. Meanwhile, it is also increasingly the case that gender is considered by historians as a structuring principle of the policies and practices of the regime across the board. Histories of policies towards women and of women's experiences and agency first laid the basis for a gendered history of National Socialism (Lanwerd and Stoehr 2007; Stibbe 2012). More recently, studies of men and masculinity under National Socialism (Kühne 2006, 2010, 32–54; Dietrich and Heise, 2013) have started to overcome the problem that the 'unmarked male' tends to be less visible as a gendered being to the historian's gaze (Caplan 2010, 84).

Examining how gender was implicated in the regime's racially defined order of exclusion and inclusion, subordination and privilege nevertheless still remains a work in progress. The following discussion focuses on insights from research on gender in relation to three themes: (i) practices of persecution and exclusion in Germany after 1933; (ii) models of activism and comradeship within the Nazi movement, and (iii) conquest and territorial expansion in the Second World War.

19.1   Convergence and Difference: Gender, Exclusion, and Persecution after 1933

There were different ways in which the regime's persecution of political opponents, 'racial others', and social deviants have been interpreted as being bound up with gendered norms and practices. One focus of recent research has been the way in which the penal practices of the regime entailed the disavowal and denial of conventional gender identities and expectations. Isabel Richter's study of treason trials before the People's Court in the years before 1939 concludes that gender-specific evidence was much less likely to be admitted in mitigation than in comparable trials of political suspects in the Weimar courts before 1933. Women accused who had children could expect no quarter on the basis of their maternal role, something that had been routinely brought into consideration in pre-1933 trials. Even when the People's Court after 1933 made the patronizing assumption that women on trial had committed acts of political treason only under the influence of their male partner or husband, this did not necessarily lead to a reduced sentence. Based on this evidence Richter suggests that the Nazi judicial system was opening up a discursive space beyond the *Volksgemeinschaft* in which gender differences were largely disregarded and where racial difference and stereotypes of the enemy loomed much larger. To that extent, she concludes, 'Under National Socialism, the *Other* had no gender' – 'Das *Andere* hatte im Nationalsozialismus kein Geschlecht' (Richter 2003).

Denial and disavowal of specific gender identities also took place within punishment regimes: as recent studies of male inmates in prison camps and concentration camps after 1933 have shown, the attack on inmates' masculine identity was a dimension of disempowering and dehumanizing them. Analysing the memoirs of German Jewish men who survived incarceration in German concentration camps before 1939 – who as Jews were consistently singled out for harsher punishments and worse humiliations compared to their non-Jewish fellow inmates – Kim Wünschmann (2013) has elucidated the challenge to their masculinity that incarceration signified. Traits coded 'masculine', such as the exercise of willpower, risk-taking, and assertiveness, were not merely muted, as they would be in any prison environment, but eradicated by the absolute and arbitrary authority of the SS guards. Wünschmann also traces the different ways in which these inmates retrospectively reasserted their identity as (German) men. With Jewish male bodies caricatured and ridiculed in Nazi propaganda portrayals as weak and hunched, some reconstructed their masculine identities as political combatants by emphasizing their strength and toughness in the face of beatings and torture; educated bourgeois men reacted to their humiliations as camp inmates by presenting the guards as stupid, brutish, perverted, and sometimes homosexual; Jewish veterans recalled their imprisonment as a 'battlefield' (Wünschmann 2013).

With the political enemy defined in the first instance in 1933 as male, the perfecting of the dehumanizing system of the camps was developed first to control male inmates. As Jane Caplan has argued, conditions in Moringen, the earliest concentration camp for women, were more like those of a harsh workhouse than the 'total' environment evolved in the 'Dachau model'. To that extent, a gendered difference of approach made for a markedly different regime in the years after 1933 for the majority of concentration camp inmates (men) and the small minority who were women. Only with the opening of the Ravensbrück camp in 1939, the creation of women's sections of the wartime camps in occupied Poland, and the proliferation of women's sub-camps across the Reich did the dehumanizing and de-sexing camp universe more fully encompass women (Caplan 2010). A trend towards convergence did not mean the erasure of important distinctions between the conditions for male and female prisoners: a comparison of 'like for like' sub-camps for men and women undertaking construction and rubble-clearing work in the wartime *Altreich* ('old Reich', meaning the pre-1938 territories of Germany) shows a markedly lower mortality rate in the women's camps (Buggeln 2014, 114–117). Some developments towards convergence were also evident inside women's prisons, where the majority of incarcerated women in the pre-war period were to be found. During wartime, women prisoners as a proportion of the total prison population increased markedly from 9% in summer 1939 to 23% in 1943 (Wachsmann 2004, 241). Conditions in female prisons/wings worsened as they became overcrowded, and female prisoner labour, which before the war had focused either on manual domestic labour within the prison or work in textiles, was increasingly channelled into the arms industry (Wachsmann 2004, 231).

The reverse of the National Socialist logic that those excluded from the *Volksgemeinschaft* should be stripped of the sense of selfhood associated with a particular gender identity was that persons whose behaviour was judged to fall outside conventional norms of gender would be branded 'asocial'. Here, the consequences of outcast status might be similar or different for men and women, but sex-specific norms provided the yardstick by which individual behaviour was judged. Health and welfare bureaucracies, which had already developed before 1933 punitive and disciplinary measures targeting socially marginal groups, seized upon the new powers bestowed on them by the Nazi regime in order to subject 'deficient men' such as beggars, vagrants, and alcoholics (who fell short of the male norm of hard and regular work) and 'wayward women', such as mothers of multiple illegitimate children or prostitutes (who fell short of the moral standards applied to women) to forms of confinement ranging from the workhouse to the concentration camp, and to sterilization on the grounds of supposed hereditary defects such as the conveniently catch-all diagnosis of feeble-mindedness (KZ-Gedenkstätte Neuengamme, 2009; Hörath 2014; Bock 1984).

The persecution of male homosexuals demonstrates how sexual deviance from the heterosexual norm was persecuted on a sex-specific basis: homosexual men were regarded as a danger to the security of the state, the safety of youngsters, and the reproduction of the 'race' in a way that lesbians were not (Micheler 2005, 286). The regime's drive against homosexual men and their subculture began immediately after the Nazi takeover, but escalated substantially after the murder of SA (*Sturmabteilung*, Stormtroopers) leader Ernst Röhm at the end of June 1934 and the amendment to the criminal code of summer 1935, which enabled the prosecution of a much wider spectrum of sex acts between men. This resulted in around 100 000 homosexual men spending time in prisons or penitentiaries during the years following, a substantially higher figure than the estimated

10 000–15 000 sent to concentration camps (Wachsmann 2004, 144). Criminalizing lesbians was repeatedly considered as an option: however, although the existing law criminalizing homosexual women in Austria remained in place after its annexation in 1938, it was not extended to the rest of the Greater German Reich (Schoppmann 2012).

19.2   Sworn Comrades: the Gender Order and Nazi Activism

The vision of the *Volksgemeinschaft* as a racially exclusive political order was intended to represent the antithesis of both liberal democracy and Bolshevik dictatorship, both of which, according to Nazi ideology, were 'Jewish' political formations. Consequently, Nazism rejected both the application of liberal individualism and communist egalitarianism to gender politics and claimed instead to restore a 'German' gender order based on the complementarity of the sexes and a hierarchy that ascribed primacy in political affairs to men. That still left, as many historians have pointed out, much room for friction and dispute over the exact place of men and women in the new political order, their relative status, and the division of labour within society and the economy (Stephenson 1981; Koonz 1987; Ziege 1997). The homosocial bonds of male camaraderie continued to be cultivated within the National Socialist movement and in other settings designed to train and harden their participants (Kühne 2010, 42–54). At the same time, the idea of comradeship was promoted to girls and women as a model for their participation both in single-sex formations and within the *Volksgemeinschaft* as a whole (Reese 2007; Kühne 2006, 91–97). It suggested a particular brand of womanly politics, combining militancy against enemies and 'aliens' with disciplined service to the 'race'.

The common vocabulary of comradeship spanning the sexes ('Volksgenossen und Volksgenossinnen!') ran up against the continuing bedrock of the male claim on public space and male-dominated spectacles of Nazi power. Studies of the Nuremberg party congresses (*Reichsparteitage*) from a perspective of gender help illuminate this tension and the failure to resolve it. From the Weimar period through to the final party congress held in 1938, the congresses were a celebration of male bonding: each was a week-long, militaristic encampment in which the official programme of parades, processions, speeches, competitive events, and mock military manoeuvres were supplemented by visits to the bars and brothels of Nuremberg (Zelnhefer 1991, 250–252). Initially the party congresses focused on demonstrating the 'faith' of party members and functionaries and renewing their bond to Hitler. Over time, they were refashioned to represent the nation as a whole, with the unity of party and state displayed through the presence of institutions such as the Reich Labour Service and the Wehrmacht (Urban 2007, 63–65). But the enduringly masculine aura of the event continued to be reflected in slogans such as that from Hitler's speech at the 1936 Congress to party functionaries: 'Being a National Socialist means being a man!' ('Nationalsozialist sein, heißt Mann sein!') (Zelnhefer 1991, 112).

That said, some shifts took place to build in women as privileged comrades of the dominant men. The crass attempt in 1933 to exclude women altogether from the party congress, eliciting protest from a long-time female activist, was not repeated (Koonz 1987, 156–157). From 1934 onwards, by contrast, and in order to highlight Gertrud Scholtz-Klink's appointment that year as Reich Women's Leader, a women's event was organized in the Congress Hall, addressed by Scholtz-Klink, Hitler, and the head of the National Socialist Welfare Organization, Erich Hilgenfeldt (Taschka and Schmidt 1999, 217). The 1938 rally included a gigantic choreographed display by 5000 girls from the newly founded 'Faith and Beauty' ('Glaube und Schönheit') section of the League of German Girls (*Bund Deutscher Mädel*, BDM). In 1939, the publicity for the rally even acquired a feminine touch: the official poster for what was billed as the 'rally of peace' featured an image of a mother and child. In the event, the 'rally of peace' never took place, overtaken by the outbreak of war (Taschka and Schmidt 1999, 219–222).

The begrudging inclusion of women as a visible presence at party rallies may have reflected the growing ranks of organized girls and women and a perception of them by the Nazi leadership as a resource to be harnessed. By the start of the war the *NS-Frauenschaft*, with 1.4 million members, was larger than the SA, and the *Deutsches Frauenwerk*, founded in 1934 as the umbrella organization for the mass of German women, had become the largest of all the 'sponsored organizations', with 6.3 million members (Kramer 2011, 48–49). Even before the war, women served as a kind of labour pool for the party and were occasionally appointed to official positions in smaller local party branches (Nolzen 2004, 119). The explicit inclusion of women at the party congress also bolstered Scholtz-Klink's international propaganda offensive (Harvey 2012; Gottlieb and Stibbe 2017), in which she boasted to foreign guests and the world at large about the allegedly peaceful, socially beneficial, and constructive work of the 'world's largest women's organization'.

In Nuremberg, the choreographed presentation of massed ranks of militarized male formations drove home the message that the 'man's world' of the state and the military was about the exercise of power, whereas that of the *Volksgenossinnen* was separate, subordinate, and focused on the mobilization of female energies in diverse forms of 'service'. This representation of the division of labour in the political sphere between men and women corresponded to the male monopoly on the use of violence against presumed enemies and miscreants and the taboo on women's direct involvement in fighting, whether on the street or the battlefield. Correspondingly, the street fighting of the SA before 1933 and the public attacks on Jews after 1933 confirmed masculine violence as a symbolic realization of the new racial order, with a corresponding cult of the 'fallen' (Bessel 1984; Reichardt 2002). Tellingly, the cult did not extend to two female Nazis who died in street violence before 1933, for whom commemorations were muted (Taschka and Schmidt 1999, 220; Willmot 2007, 102). The masculine coding of antisemitic violence was particularly evident in the ritualized attacks on 'mixed' Jewish–'Aryan' couples, where typically attacks by local SA and Hitler Youth members in the name of 'racial honour' would 'de-sex' the delinquents through public humiliation, including instances of head-shaving for women (Wildt 2007, 251). As Michael Wildt has shown, however, female Nazis could and did claim a role as comrades in antisemitic campaigns, for instance in boycotts of Jewish businesses before and after 1933: some Jewish eyewitness reports noted that BDM groups as well as male Hitler Youths were involved in such 'actions' (Wildt 2002, 212). Photographs show women grinning and applauding where Jews were being publicly shamed and ridiculed (Wildt 2002, 236–237). If women were generally not part of the roving gangs attacking Jewish homes, businesses, and synagogues during the November 1938 pogrom, Anette Michel cites the case of a deputy district women's leader of the *NS-Frauenschaft* in Mannheim who accompanied the SA on its trawl of the streets, pointing out sites to target (Michel 2007, 127). Women were more in evidence among the crowds after the pogrom carrying off items of plunder (Steinweis 2009, 61, 79).

19.3   'Boundless Expansion' and Boundaries of Gender and Race: Conquest, Genocide, and Forced Labour

If it once seemed irrelevant or even trivializing to bring a perspective of gender to bear on Nazi conquest, occupation, and genocidal violence in the course of the Second World War, historians are now more frequently engaging with these questions. There is an established literature focusing on gender-specific experiences of persecuted Jews in the ghettos and camps of occupied Europe (Ofer and Weitzman 1998; Pine 2004; Hájková 2013) and an emerging body of research on the experiences of female labour deportees from the conquered countries (Frankenberger 1997; Hauch 2001; Harvey 2016). A number of newer studies have explored the actions of Germans as 'conquerors' and 'masters' in the occupied territories in terms of gendered norms and patterns of sexual behaviour. Among those focusing on occupied eastern Europe, several have focused on male occupiers ranging from ordinary soldiers to SS men, civilian administrators to Nazi bosses (Mühlhäuser 2010; Römer 2011; Werner 2013; Tomberger 2013; Röger 2015), while others have examined the place of German women as wives, including SS wives, or employees ranging from kindergarten teachers and Wehrmacht auxiliaries to camp guards at Majdanek (Schwarz 1997, 2003; Harvey 2003; Maubach 2009; Mailänder Koslov 2015; Mühlenberg 2011, 297–302, 325–40; Lower 2013). So far, less has been written about how far the regime's exploitation and persecution of conquered peoples, Jews and non-Jews, was influenced by perceptions of gender-specific work capacities or the gender balance within a particular population, though Gerlach offers some pointers from his study of occupied Belorussia (Gerlach 1999, 455–456). In discussing territorial expansion, the focus in the following is on eastern Europe: the particular intensity of the ideological drive associated with the occupation of eastern Europe and its consequent exterminatory violence arose from the regime's drive for *Lebensraum* ('living space') and its quest from 1941 to destroy 'Judaeo-Bolshevism'.

The sense of power and entitlement on the part of the occupiers that accompanies any military conquest was heightened in the case of the German civilian and military personnel occupying Poland and the Soviet territories by the construction of the 'East' and its population as primitive and inferior. Propaganda conjured up the image of a Nazi mission to subjugate and purge the territory of alien influence as a historic task worthy to be carried out only by an elite vanguard of dedicated

National Socialists fit for the frontier world of the 'new East' (Lehnstaedt 2010, 244–253). The authority exercised by the German occupiers – many of whom in fact sought or were given posts in the 'East' because of past professional and personal lapses – and their corresponding style of 'mastery' were underpinned by a ruthless system of terror, while common bonds were forged among the German ruling caste through residential proximity, patterns of sociability, 'German houses', canteens and leisure facilities, and the strict rules on segregation from the subject population – which did not, of course, rule out visits to official brothels or illicit consensual relationships with local women (Röger 2015). Whether in the annexed territories of Poland, the General Government, or the occupied territories of the Soviet Union, German civilian administrators found scope for self-enrichment and life in the grand style (Lehnstaedt 2010; Roth 2009).

The freebooting style of the Reich German 'masters' in the occupied territories underlined the character of the 'occupation society' as above all a society of men. However, it was not exclusively a man's world. While civilian administrators were often posted east on their own (giving them opportunities to strike up an 'eastern marriage' in addition to the one back home), some brought their wives. Numerous SS wives accompanied their menfolk to the occupied territories of eastern Europe (Schwarz 1997; Lower 2013). German women worked in the occupied territories for the Wehrmacht, the SS, for party organizations, the civilian administration, and the Red Cross. Auxiliaries recruited by the Red Cross ran 'Soldatenheime' where troops rested, socialized, ate, and drank (Paulus and Röwekamp 2015). Moreover, German women from the Reich were drawn into a range of tasks considered vital for Himmler's overall goal of 'strengthening Germandom' in the annexed territories of western Poland and in parts of the General Government and Ukraine, supporting and monitoring incoming 'ethnic German' families who were settled on Polish farms after the deportation of their Polish owners as well as monitoring those among the resident population who had been classified as German or Germanizable, ensuring they conformed to regime expectations of German behaviour (Harvey 2003).

The presence of women within the 'occupation society' in eastern Europe did not inhibit the endemic culture of violence and impunity. The model of 'sworn comrades' continued: men planned and perpetrated the violence, and women typically restricted their involvement in the policies of deportation and murder to the processing of expropriated property (Harvey 2003). That said, there were women who wanted to get involved in violence, and some wives and girlfriends became direct accomplices and perpetrators in physical attacks on Jews (Schwarz 1997; Lower 2013).

Officially, women's contribution to the work of 'construction' in the East lay in the sphere of the domestic writ large. Blueprints of a German order arising out of the 'chaos' of occupied eastern Europe set great store by the layout of model villages and homes to be populated by German families. The role of Nazi women in the emergence of this order was imagined as a form of homemaking: 'cleaning up' and making homely the supposedly featureless alien spaces (Harvey 2003). The East was, in the eyes of some, also to be a laboratory of Nazi gender relations: the BDM's agricultural expert outlined in 1942 her fantasy for the East as a renewed and reformed German peasant culture in which the farmer's wife would assert herself as the proper comrade of her husband, devoting herself to the cultivation of the home as her rightful sphere and no longer undertaking drudgery in the fields (Essig 1942). Here again, the accentuation of gender difference and complementarity was presented as the marker of racial superiority and privilege for the self-anointed elite.

What was brought about through Nazi occupation was of course not 'order' in eastern Europe but the killing of millions: the systematic genocide of Jewish men, women, and children, the mass death of Soviet prisoners of war through deliberate neglect, and the mass killing of non-Jewish civilians across the occupied territories through starvation, deportation, and anti-partisan massacres. The policy of 'no quarter' to women of 'inferior races' manifested itself in countless instances, and was a matter of boasting for Himmler in his Posen speech of 4 October 1943 when he insisted on his indifference if 'ten thousand Russian women' were to perish in digging a tank ditch (Himmler and Wildt 2014, 315). Further chilling evidence of how in the longer term a Nazi empire in eastern Europe would have sought to destroy the biological substance of enemy peoples was contained in Erhard Wetzel's notorious commentary on *Generalplan Ost* ('General Plan East'), in which his destructive fantasy imagined the effects of mass abortions and anti-natalist propaganda in a future defeated Russia (Madajczyk 1994, 73–75; Bock 1984, 440–441).

Conquest, occupation, and forced labour deportations accentuated the hierarchies of gender and race within the *Altreich*. As the wave of initial German victories gave way to stalemate, efforts to manage morale included promoting the dyad of the front-line soldier and the home front mother/wife/female comrade as the indissoluble basis of the German 'fighting community' (*kämpfende Volksgemeinschaft*) (Kramer 2011). Regime efforts to bridge the growing gulf between front and home included the massive 'field post' operation and the promise (often not realized) of 'home leave'. To secure the morale of men at the front, the morals of women on the home front were all the more sharply policed in the face of the enormous influx of foreign men. By September 1944, the number of foreign civilian workers in the Reich had reached 5.97 million, two thirds of them men (Herbert 1985, 272). Vigilante activism to keep foreigners in their place offered male and female party activists, the latter regarding themselves as particular experts on 'racial issues', an outlet for malice and aggression (Gellately 1990, 232–244; Stephenson 2006, 265–290). Punishments for women who had affairs with foreign workers or prisoners of war including head-shaving (a measure later dropped) and confinement in a prison or concentration camp (Kundrus 2002). For the foreign men concerned, their fate depended on their nationality and their 'racial quality' in the eyes of SS racial experts: Poles and men of other eastern European nationalities (Ukrainians, Serbs, Russians) were subject to the death penalty for sexual relations with German women unless they were judged racially 'Germanizable' (Heinemann 2003, 488–498).

Foreign workers kept in their subordinate place propped up not only the war economy but also the existing gender order. Insoluble conflicts arose for the regime leadership in wartime between equalizing burdens between women on the home front, on the one hand, and preserving, on the other, the 'German home' as the foundation of the *Volksgemeinschaft*, a bulwark against Bolshevism and the source of German men's comfort (Winkler 1977, 102–121, 134–153; Kundrus 1995; Harvey 2015). Contradictory policies sought to stabilize existing levels of German women's employment while supporting the 'German home' and the morale of husbands by postponing the all-out labour conscription of non-employed, typically middle-class, women. The arrival of female labour deportees from the occupied Soviet territories into German industry under Fritz Sauckel's forced recruitment programme, from 1942 onwards, helped square this circle in terms of plugging shortages overall and enabling employers to reorganize production and control absenteeism by giving German women workers lighter work and shorter shifts (Winkler 1977; Hachtmann 1993; Siegel 1991). In contrast to German women workers, who were covered by the new Maternity Protection Law of 1942 (Sachse 1990, 47–53), pregnant Polish and Soviet women workers (the latter known as *Ostarbeiterinnen* or 'eastern workers') were frequently compelled to have abortions; babies that were born were typically removed and many died through deliberate neglect (Czarnowski 2004; Hauch 2001, 422–424). For Hitler, the female 'eastern worker' served as the symbolic antithesis to the 'valuable' but more fragile German woman, as he declared at a meeting in May 1943:

> We are subject to the hard law of war; this law demands that we obtain food and labour from Ukraine ... When we insist on forced labour in Ukraine: remember that our German women must also work, even though they possess on average a far weaker constitution. When we require a certain quota of people: we cannot wait until the Ukrainian women come of their own free will, for our production needs are urgent and cannot be delayed. The Ukrainian women must work. (Baum 2011, 272)

19.4 Conclusion

In the 1970s, Tim Mason noted that the Nazi regime's attitude towards women was unusually self-conscious and well defined, perhaps more so 'than any other modern government'. The anti-feminist aspects of Nazi ideology, he further suggested, had 'probably been under-rated' until that point (Mason 1995, 149, 154). Since then, many studies have underscored the anti-feminism and the gender hierarchy that was intrinsic to the 'people's community', but have extended this to explore more systematically the relationship between gender and racism. If 'race set the limits within which gender was a meaningful category', as Jane Caplan has summed up Bock's argument (Caplan 2010, 100), this still leaves open many questions about where and how gender operated to structure policies and experiences under National Socialist rule, some of which have been outlined here.

Gender difference remained relevant in the Third Reich's persecution of 'enemies' and 'aliens' and in the pursuit of deviance, not least in defining sex-specific norms of behaviour and the labelling of 'deviant' men and women as posing different levels of 'social danger'. That said, the fate of men and women persecuted by the regime shared features in common (sterilization, incarceration, suppression of gender identity), even if there was no complete convergence of treatment. Stigmatized men were denied the markers of masculine identity and privilege, and women who were defined as enemies, aliens, or defectives were granted diminished consideration, or no quarter at all, on grounds of their sex.

Thinking about gender relations within the community of 'valuable Germans', the propagation of a 'German' gender order based on gender difference and complementarity left much unanswered about the exact place of men and women in public life. The notion of 'comradeship' offered itself as an appealing model of membership in the *Volksgemeinschaft* to Nazi activists of both sexes. However, for many 'old fighters', the National Socialist revolution was an endorsement of virility, with women in the movement seen as existing mainly to support and admire men in their struggle. Visions of the *Volksgemeinschaft* as a community encompassing and mobilizing both sexes consequently remained in tension with the male-bonded structures of the Nazi movement forged in the 'time of struggle' before 1933.

The blaringly masculine self-presentation of the party and the state in the annual rituals of the party congresses gave way, over time, to more inclusive gestures towards organized party women. Nazi women organizers made particular efforts to counter the obvious impression to outside onlookers that they were simply a manoeuvrable mass at the command of a masculinist state. Generally steering clear of direct and public participation in physical violence against 'enemies', women Nazis nevertheless proved themselves loyal 'sworn comrades' of party men, applauding male antisemitic actions.

After 1939, war, conquest and the expanding boundaries of the Reich in the 'new East' gave rise to a caste of German occupiers who ruled over the defeated populations through untrammelled terror. The conditions of occupation fostered a new spirit of 'frontier combat' that some men welcomed as a return to the heady days of the pre-1933 'time of struggle' and freebooting male impunity. Women as wives and employed personnel were present in this climate of violence, and some actively entered into the ideologically fuelled drive to repress and destroy 'alien' life and culture in the occupied territories. Meanwhile, the proponents of 'womanly work' in the conquered territories claimed to be laying the foundations of future German homelands and domestic order based on the gender norms and privileges of the master race (*Herrenrasse*). The wholesale destruction of life and fantasies of a future strategy to destroy the capacity of the nationalities of eastern Europe to reproduce once again confirmed the rule that where 'inferior' peoples were concerned, considerations of sex had no place.

Finally, considering the impact of the presence of millions of foreign workers – male and female, prisoners of war and civilians, with the largest contingents being deportees and prisoners from occupied eastern Europe – on the hierarchies of gender and race within the wartime Reich, it emerges that the presence of 'alien' men sparked draconian forms of crackdown and retribution in the name of preserving the moral and sexual order. The presence of foreign women workers, meanwhile, was an opportunity for the regime to ease some of the insoluble difficulties posed by mobilizing German women's labour for the war effort while preserving the idea and reality of the 'German home'. Female foreign workers from eastern Europe, whether in agriculture, industry, or domestic service, were regarded as infinitely flexible 'hands' whose status at the bottom of the racial hierarchy rendered their sex immaterial. The exploitation of foreign women as forced labourers helped maintain the gendered order within the *Volksgemeinschaft*.

References

Baum, Herwig. 2011. '"Für die Stadt Kiew wird eine 'Fangaktion' vorbereitet …": Akteure und Praxis der Zwangsarbeiterrekrutierungen in der Ukraine während des Zweiten Weltkriegs.' In *Arbeitskräfte als Kriegsbeute: Der Fall Ost- und Südosteuropa 1939–1945*, edited by Karsten Linne and Florian Dierl, 270–302. Berlin: Metropol.

Bessel, Richard. 1984. *Political Violence and the Rise of Nazism: The Stormtroopers in Eastern Germany, 1925–1934*. New Haven, CT: Yale University Press.

Boak, Helen. 2004. 'Mobilizing Women for Hitler: The Female Nazi Voter.' In *Working Towards the Führer: Essays in Honour of Sir Ian Kershaw*, edited by Tim Kirk and Anthony McElligott, 68–92. Manchester: Manchester University Press.

Bock, Gisela. 1984. *Zwangssterilisation im Nationalsozialismus: Studien zur Rassenpolitik und Frauenpolitik*. Opladen: Westdeutscher Verlag.

Bock, Gisela. 1993. 'Gleichheit und Differenz in der nationalsozialistischen Rassenpolitik.' *Geschichte und Gesellschaft* 19, 277–310.

Buggeln, Marc. 2014. *Slave Labor in Nazi Concentration Camps*. Oxford: Oxford University Press.

Caplan, Jane. 2010. 'Gender and the Concentration Camps.' In *Concentration Camps in Nazi Germany: The New Histories*, edited by Jane Caplan and Nikolaus Wachsmann, 82–107. London and New York: Routledge.

Czarnowski, Gabriele. 2004. 'Vom "reichen Material … einer wissenschaftlichen Arbeitsstätte": Zum Problem missbräuchlicher medizinischer Praktiken an der Grazer Universitäts-Frauenklinik in der Zeit des Nationalsozialismus.' In *NS-Wissenschaft als Vernichtungsinstrument: Rassenhygiene, Zwangssterilisation, Menschenversuche und NS-Euthanasie in der Steiermark*, edited by Wolfgang Freidl and Werner Sauer, 225–273. Vienna: Facultas.

Dietrich, Anette and Heise, Ljiljana, eds. 2013. *Männlichkeitskonstruktionen im Nationalsozialismus*. Frankfurt am Main: Peter Lang.

Essig, Luise. 1942. 'Unsere Ziele für die Mädchen und Frauen des Landvolks.' In *Landvolk im Werden: Material zum ländlichen Aufbau in den neuen Ostgebieten und zur Gestaltung des dörflichen Lebens*, edited by Konrad Meyer, 139–160. Berlin: Deutsche Landbuchhandlung.

Evans, Richard J. 1976. *The German Feminist Movement 1894–1933*. London: Sage.

Frankenberger, Tamara. 1997. *Wir waren wie Vieh: Lebensgeschichtliche Erinnerungen ehemaliger sowjetischer Zwangsarbeiterinnen*. Münster: Westfälisches Dampfboot.

Gellately, Robert. 1990. *The Gestapo and German Society: Enforcing Racial Policy 1933–1945*. Oxford: Oxford University Press.

Gerlach, Christian. 1999. *Kalkulierte Morde: Die deutsche Wirtschafts- und Vernichtungspolitik in Weißrußland 1941 bis 1944*. Hamburg: Hamburger Edition.

Gottlieb, Julie V. and Stibbe, Matthew. 2017. 'Peace at any Price: The Visit of Nazi Women's Leader Gertrud Scholtz-Klink to London in March 1939 and the Response of British Women Activists.' *Women's History Review* 26, 173–194.

Greven-Aschoff, Barbara. 1981. *Die bürgerliche Frauenbewegung in Deutschland 1894–1933*. Göttingen: Vandenhoeck & Ruprecht.

Hachtmann, Rüdiger. 1993. 'Industriearbeiterinnen in der deutschen Kriegswirtschaft 1936 bis 1944/45.' *Geschichte und Gesellschaft* 19, 332–366.

Hájková, Anna. 2013. 'Sexual Barter in Times of Genocide: Negotiating the Sexual Economy of the Theresienstadt Ghetto.' *Signs: A Journal of Women and Society* 38, 503–533.

Hartmann, Christian et al., eds. 2016. *Hitler, Mein Kampf. Eine kritische Edition.* 2 vols. Munich: Institut für Zeitgeschichte Munich-Berlin.

Harvey, Elizabeth. 2003. *Women and the Nazi East: Agents and Witnesses of Germanization.* New Haven, CT and London: Yale University Press.

Harvey, Elizabeth. 2012. 'International Networks and Cross-Border Cooperation: National Socialist Women and the Vision of a "New Order" in Europe.' *Politics, Religion & Ideology* 13, 141–158.

Harvey, Elizabeth. 2015. 'Housework, Domestic Privacy and the "German Home": Paradoxes of Private Life during the Second World War.' In *Detlev Peukert und die NS-Forschung*, edited by Rüdiger Hachtmann and Sven Reichardt, 115–131. Göttingen: Wallstein.

Harvey, Elizabeth. 2016. 'Last Resort or Key Resource? Women Workers from the Nazi-occupied Soviet Territories, the Reich Labour Administration and the German War Effort.' *Transactions of the Royal Historical Society* 26, 149–173.

Hauch, Gabriella. 2001. 'Zwangsarbeiterinnen und ihre Kinder. Zum Geschlecht der Zwangsarbeit.' In *NS-Zwangsarbeit: Der Standort Linz der 'Reichswerke Hermann Göring AG Berlin' 1938–1945*, edited by Oliver Rathkolb, vol. 1, 355–448. Cologne: Böhlau.

Heinemann, Isabel. 2003. *Rasse, Siedlung, 'deutsches Blut': Das Rasse- & Siedlungshauptamt der SS und die rassenpolitische Neuordnung Europas.* Göttingen: Wallstein.

Herbert, Ulrich. 1985. Fremdarbeiter Politek and Praxis des "Ausländer-Einsatzes" in der Kriegswirtschaft des Dritten Reiches. Berlin and Bonn: Dietz.

Himmler, Katrin and Wildt, Michael, eds. 2014. *Himmler privat: Briefe eines Massenmörders.* Plön: Piper.

Hörath, Julia. 2014. '"Arbeitsscheue Volksgenossen": Leistungsbereitschaft als Kriterium der Inklusion und Exklusion.' In *Arbeit im Nationalsozialismus*, edited by Marc Buggeln and Michael Wildt, 309–328. Munich: Oldenbourg De Gruyter.

Huber, Engelbert. 1933. *Das ist Nationalsozialismus: Organisation und Weltanschauung der NSDAP.* Stuttgart: Union Deutsche Verlagsgesellschaft.

Kershaw, Ian. 2014. '*Volksgemeinschaft*: Potential and Limitations of the Concept.' In *Visions of Community in Nazi Germany: Social Engineering and Private Lives*, edited by Martina Steber and Bernhard Gotto, 29–42. Oxford: Oxford University Press.

Koonz, Claudia. 1987. *Mothers in the Fatherland: Women, the Family and Nazi Politics.* London: Jonathan Cape.

Kramer, Nicole. 2011. *Volksgenossinnen an der Heimatfront: Mobilisierung, Verhalten, Erinnerung.* Göttingen: Vandenhoeck & Ruprecht.

Kühne, Thomas. 2006. *Kameradschaft: Die Soldaten des nationalsozialistischen Krieges und das 20. Jahrhundert.* Göttingen: Vandenhoeck & Ruprecht.

Kühne, Thomas. 2010. *Belonging and Genocide. Hitler's Community, 1918–1945.* New Haven, CT and London: Yale University Press.

Kundrus, Birthe. 1995. *Kriegerfrauen: Familienpolitik und Geschlechterverhältnisse im Ersten und Zweiten Weltkrieg.* Hamburg: Christians.

Kundrus, Birthe. 2002. 'Forbidden Company: Romantic Relationships between Germans and Foreigners, 1939 to 1945.' *Journal of the History of Sexuality* 11, 201–222.

KZ-Gedenkstätte Neuengamme, ed. 2009. *Ausgegrenzt. 'Asoziale' und 'Kriminelle' im nationalsozialistischen Lagersystem.* Beiträge zur Geschichte der nationalsozialistischen Verfolgung in Norddeutschland, vol. 11. Bremen: Edition Temmen.

Lanwerd, Susanne, and Stoehr, Irene. 2007. 'Frauen- und Geschlechterforschung zum Nationalsozialismus seit den 1970er Jahren. Forschungsstand, Veränderungen, Perspektiven.' In *Frauen- und Geschlechtergeschichte des Nationalsozialismus.*

Fragestellungen, Perspektiven, neue Forschungen, edited by Johanna Gehmacher and Gabriella Hauch, 22–67. Vienna: StudienVerlag.

Lehnstaedt, Stephan. 2010. *Okkupation im Osten. Besatzeralltag in Warschau und Minsk 1939–1944*. Munich: Oldenbourg.

Lower, Wendy. 2013. *Hitler's Furies: German Women in the Nazi Killing Fields*. London: Chatto & Windus.

Madajczyk, Czesław, ed. 1994. *Vom Generalplan Ost zum Generalsiedlungsplan*. Munich: Saur.

Mailänder Koslov, Elissa. 2015. *Female SS Guards and Workaday Violence: The Majdanek Concentration Camp, 1942–44*. East Lansing: Michigan State University Press.

Mason, Tim. 1995. 'Women in Germany 1925–1940. Family, Welfare and Work.' In *Nazism, Fascism and the Working Class. Essays by Tim Mason*, edited by Jane Caplan, 132–211. Cambridge: Cambridge University Press.

Maubach, Franka. 2009. *Die Stellung halten: Kriegserfahrungen und Lebensgeschichten von Wehrmachthelferinnen*. Göttingen: Vandenhoeck & Ruprecht.

Michel, Anette. 2007. '"Führerinnen" im Dritten Reich.' In *Volksgenossinnen: Frauen der NS-Volksgemeinschaft*, edited by Sybille Steinbacher, 115–137. Göttingen: Wallstein.

Micheler, Stefan. 2005. *Selbstbilder und Fremdbilder der 'Anderen': Männer begehrende Männer in der Weimarer Republik und der NS-Zeit*. Konstanz: UVK Verlagsgesellschaft.

Mühlenberg, Jutta. 2011. *Das SS-Helferinnenkorps: Ausbildung, Einsatz und Entnazifizierung der weiblichen Angehörigen der Waffen-SS 1942–49*. Hamburg: Hamburger Edition.

Mühlhäuser, Regina. 2010. *Eroberungen: Sexuelle Gewalttaten und intime Beziehungen deutscher Soldaten in der Sowjetunion 1941–45*. Hamburg: Hamburger Edition.

Nolzen, Armin. 2004. 'Die NSDAP, der Krieg und die deutsche Gesellschaft.' In *Das Deutsche Reich und der Zweite Weltkrieg, Volume 9: Die deutsche Kriegsgesellschaft 1939 bis 1945, Erster Halbband: Politisierung, Vernichtung, Überleben*, edited by Jörg Echternkamp, 99–193. Munich: Deutsche Verlags-Anstalt.

Oertzen, Christine von. 2012. *Strategie Verständigung: Zur transnationalen Vernetzung von Akademikerinnen 1917–1955*. Göttingen: Wallstein.

Ofer, Dalia and Weitzman, Lenore, eds. 1998. *Women in the Holocaust*. New Haven, CT: Yale University Press.

Paulus, Julia and Röwekamp, Marion, eds. 2015. *Eine Soldatenheimschwester an der Ostfront: Briefwechsel von Annette Schücking mit ihrer Familie (1941–1943)*. Paderborn: Schöningh.

Pine, Lisa. 2004. 'Gender and the Family.' In *The Historiography of the Holocaust*, edited by Dan Stone, 364–382. London: Palgrave Macmillan.

Reese, Dagmar. 2007. 'Kamerad unter Kameraden: Weiblichkeitskonstruktionen im Bund Deutscher Mädel während des Krieges dargestellt am Beispiel von Schulungsmaterialien.' In *Die BDM-Generation: Weibliche Jugendliche in Deutschland und Österreich im Nationalsozialismus*, edited by Dagmar Reese, 215–253. Berlin: Verlag für Berlin-Brandenburg.

Reichardt, Sven. 2002. *Faschistische Kampfbünde: Gewalt und Gemeinschaft im italienischen Squadrismus und in der deutschen SA*. Cologne: Böhlau.

Richter, Isabel. 2003. 'Das *Andere* hat kein Geschlecht. Politische Gerichtsprozesse in der Weimarer Republik und im Nationalsozialismus.' In *'Bestien' und 'Befehlsempfänger': Frauen und Männer in NS-Prozessen nach 1945*, edited by Ulrike Weckel and Edgar Wolfrum, 175–193. Göttingen: Vandenhoeck & Ruprecht.

Röger, Maren. 2015. *Kriegsbeziehungen: Intimität, Gewalt und Prostitution im besetzten Polen 1939 bis 1945*. Frankfurt am Main: Fischer.

Römer, Felix. 2011. 'Gewaltsame Geschlechterordnung: Wehrmacht und "Flintenweiber" an der Ostfront.' In *Soldatinnen: Gewalt und Geschlecht im Krieg vom Mittelalter bis heute*, edited by Klaus Latzel, Franka Maubach, and Silke Satjukow, 331–351. Paderborn: Schöningh.

Röwekamp, Marion. 2011. *Die ersten deutschen Juristinnen: Eine Geschichte ihrer Professionalisierung und Emanzipation (1900–1945)*. Cologne: Böhlau.

Roth, Markus. 2009. *Herrenmenschen: Die deutschen Kreishauptleute im besetzten Polen – Karrierewege, Herrschaftspraxis und Nachgeschichte*. Göttingen: Wallstein.

Sachse, Carola. 1990. *Siemens, der Nationalsozialismus und die moderne Familie: Eine Untersuchung zur sozialen Rationalisierung in Deutschland im 20. Jahrhundert*. Hamburg: Rasch & Röhring.

Schoppmann, Claudia. 2012. 'Zwischen strafrechtlicher Verfolgung und gesellschaftlicher Ächtung. Lesbische Frauen im 'Dritten Reich.' In *Homophobie und Devianz: Weibliche und männliche Homosexualität im Nationalsozialismus*, edited by Insa Eschebach, 35–51. Berlin: Metropol.

Schwarz, Gudrun. 1997. *Eine Frau an seiner Seite: Ehefrauen in der 'SS-Sippengemeinschaft'*. Hamburg: Hamburger Edition.

Schwarz, Gudrun. 2003. '"During Total War, We Girls Want to Be Where We Can Really Accomplish Something": What Women Do in Wartime.' In *Crimes of War: Guilt and Denial in the Twentieth Century*, edited by Omer Bartov, Atina Grossmann, and Mary Nolan, 121–137. New York: New Press.

Siegel, Tilla. 1991. 'Die doppelte Rationalisierung des "Ausländereinsatzes" bei Siemens.' *Internationale Wissenschaftliche Korrespondenz zur Geschichte der Arbeiterbewegung* 27, 12–24.

Sneeringer, Julia 2002. *Winning Women's Votes: Propaganda and Politics in Weimar Germany*. Chapel Hill and London: University of North Carolina Press.

Steinweis, Alan. 2009. *Kristallnacht 1938*. Cambridge, MA: Harvard University Press.

Stephenson, Jill. 1981. *The Nazi Organisation of Women*. London: Croom Helm.

Stephenson, Jill. 2001. *Women in Nazi Germany*. London: Pearson.

Stephenson, Jill. 2006. *Hitler's Home Front: Württemberg under the Nazis*. London: Hambledon.

Stibbe, Matthew. 2003. *Women in the Third Reich*. London: Arnold.

Stibbe, Matthew. 2012. 'In and Beyond the Racial State: Gender and National Socialism, 1933–1955.' *Politics, Religion & Ideology* 13, 159–178.

Taschka, Sylvia and Schmidt, Alexander. 1999. 'Mutterfrau und "Helferin im Kampfe des Mannes": Frauen auf den Nürnberger Parteitagen.' In *Am Anfang war Sigena: Ein Nürnberger Frauengeschichtsbuch*, edited by Nadia Bennewitz and Gaby Franger. Cadolzburg: Ars Vivendi.

Tomberger, Corinna. 2013. 'Männlichkeiten ins Bild gesetzt: Geschlechteranalytische Überlegungen zu einem Amateurfoto aus dem Polenfeldzug.' In *Männlichkeitskonstruktionen im Nationalsozialismus*, edited by Anette Dietrich and Ljiljana Heise, 141–164. Frankfurt am Main: Peter Lang.

Urban, Markus. 2007. *Die Konsensfabrik. Funktion und Wahrnehmung der NS-Reichsparteitage 1933–1941*. Göttingen: Vandenhoeck & Ruprecht.

Wachsmann, Nikolaus. 2004. *Hitler's Prisons: Legal Terror in Nazi Germany*. New Haven, CT and London: Yale University Press.

Waldeck, Countess. 1944. 'The Girls Did Well by Hitler.' *The Saturday Evening Post*, 11 July.

Werner, Frank. 2013. '"Noch härter, noch kälter, noch mitleidloser": Soldatische Männlichkeit im deutschen Vernichtungskrieg 1941–44.' In *Männlichkeitskonstruktionen im Nationalsozialismus*, edited by Anette Dietrich and Ljiljana Heise, 45–63. Frankfurt am Main: Peter Lang.

Weyrather, Irmgard. 1977. 'Numerus Clausus für Frauen – Studentinnen im Nationalsozialismus.' In *Mutterkreuz und Arbeitsbuch: Zur Geschichte der Frauen in der Weimarer Republik und im Nationalsozialismus*, 131–162. Frankfurt am Main: Fischer.

Wildt, Michael. 2007. *Volksgemeinschaft als Selbstermächtigung: Gewalt gegen Juden in der deutschen Provinz 1919 bis 1939*. Hamburg: Hamburger Edition.

Willmot, Louise. 2007. 'Zur Geschichte des Bundes Deutscher Mädel.' In *Die BDM-Generation: Weibliche Jugendliche in Deutschland und Österreich im Nationalsozialismus*, edited by Dagmar Reese, 89–157. Berlin: Verlag für Berlin-Brandenburg.

Winkler, Dörte. 1977. *Frauenarbeit im 'Dritten Reich'*. Hamburg: Hoffmann und Campe.

Wünschmann, Kim. 2013. 'Männlichkeitskonstruktionen jüdischer Häftlinge in NS-Konzentrationslagern.' In *Männlichkeitskonstruktionen im Nationalsozialismus*, edited by Anette Dietrich and Ljiljana Heise, 201–219. Frankfurt am Main: Peter Lang.

Zelnhefer, Siegfried. 1991. *Die Reichsparteitage der NSDAP: Geschichte, Struktur und Bedeutung der grössten Propagandafeste im nationalsozialistischen Feierjahr*. Nuremberg: Stadtarchiv.

Ziege, Eva-Maria. 1997. 'Sophie Rogge-Börner – Wegbereiterin der Nazidiktatur und völkische Sektiererin im Abseits.' In *Zwischen Karriere und Verfolgung. Handlungsräume von Frauen im nationalsozialistischen Deutschland*, edited by Kirsten Heinsohn, Barbara Vogel, and Ulrike Weckel, 44–77. Frankfurt am Main: Campus.

CHAPTER TWENTY

Religion*

MANFRED GAILUS

20.1 Introduction

Religion did matter during the Third Reich. This is particularly true for the first years of the Hitler era, which many contemporaries considered not only a political turn but also a religious revival and a reversal from the unpopular 'ungodly republic of Weimar'. The dramatic rise in the numbers of people leaving the church, particularly in bigger cities, suddenly stopped and more and more people returned. The large established confessions[1] of Protestants and Catholics underwent changes in direction and personnel, but considerable changes were also in motion in the so-called Free Churches and the *völkisch* and national-religious movements on the edge of the large churches. Religious demonstrations and pamphlets, creeds and memoranda, new journals and books sprang up like mushrooms and invigorated the religious discourse. In a nutshell: faith and religiosity were trendy in 1933 and with good reason contemporaries were talking about a revival of religion. It was no coincidence that one of the most forceful manifestations of symbolic politics marking the path into the Third Reich, the nationally celebrated 'Day of Potsdam' – a state ceremony on the occasion of the opening of the newly elected Nazi-dominated Reichstag with Reich President Paul von Hindenburg and Reich Chancellor Adolf Hitler – took part in the tradition-rich Prussian Garrison Church of Potsdam. Faith, confession, and religion remained contested topics throughout the entire Third Reich and affected the majority of Germans to a greater extent than ever before, or after, in the course of the twentieth century (Gailus and Nolzen 2011; Puschner and Vollnhals 2012; Vondung 2013).

It did not require any force by the Hitler movement in 1933 to bring the churches in line: the Protestant churches, which accounted for two thirds of the German population, eagerly welcomed the rising National Socialism and the Nazi 'ideas of 1933'. The political change was hailed at all levels, in all factions and

---

* Translated by Christine Brocks.

A Companion to Nazi Germany, First Edition. Edited by Shelley Baranowski, Armin Nolzen, and Claus-Christian W. Szejnmann.
© 2018 John Wiley & Sons Ltd. Published 2018 by John Wiley & Sons Ltd.

groups of the Protestant milieu and raised high expectations of a historical reversal, of re-Christianization and growing importance of the churches. The 'national awakening' was seen as a longed-for turning point – as a reversal from the secular culture of the Weimar Republic and as a spiritual relief from the traumatic experiences and the deep humiliation caused by the defeat in 1918. A Berlin pastor summarized this new feeling paradigmatically at New Year's Eve 1933: a 'year of greatness' was drawing to a close; Germany, previously a 'nation of lesser rights', had risen again to become a state with respect, and instead of suicidal class struggle Germany had achieved the miracle of a new people's unity. For him as a pastor, however, the most important result of the year 1933 was a new spirit heralded by the 'innermost experience', by the religious realm. The turning point of 1933 had shown that Germans were not broken spiritually despite their 'enslavement' by the Treaty of Versailles and its consequences, and were moving towards a revival of their faith (Marquardt 1933; in response, Gailus 2002, 2003).

20.2   Protestants: Battle Between Brothers in Their Own House

'One people – one empire – one faith' – this was one of the slogans of the Protestant mass movement of German Christians (*Deutsche Christen*, DC), who aimed at unifying the 28 regional Protestant churches in the German single states into a tightly centralized Reich Church headed by an autocratically ruling Reich bishop according to the 'leadership principle'. Part of the programme of this *völkisch* Protestantism was an 'Aryanized' and Germanized Christ, the belief in Adolf Hitler as the 'Führer' sent by God, the historical mission of the 'German race' engendered by God, and the supposedly Christian obligation to maintain it 'pure' as part of the 'divine order of all creation'. In 1933/1934 such a movement could win over the leadership of several regional churches and deeply penetrate the core of the milieu until it provoked substantial inner-ecclesiastical opposition. This counter-movement emerged in the course of 1934 under the name Confessing Church (*Bekennende Kirche*, BK). From then on, most of the 28 regional churches wore themselves out in a self-destructive struggle, known as *Kirchenkampf* ('church struggle'). This term first and foremost refers to a brotherly struggle about the realignment of theology, cult, and congregational practice – revealing a serious identity problem of Protestantism, which was highly impressed with National Socialism.

Considerable numbers of pastors gave crucial impetus to the *völkisch* restructuring process. Their efforts aimed at a new ecclesiastical cult, a German Christian liturgy of mass. An excessive flag cult became prevalent in the churches: German Christian flags unified the Christian cross with the swastika and were ceremoniously consecrated at the altar, in many churches. Also, the traditional liturgy was Germanized, Hebrew terms were erased from the ecclesiastical language, and Jewish symbols removed from the interior of churches. German Christian sermons annunciated a 'Christianity appropriate to the German race' that was closely related to Nazi ideology: a heroic image of Jesus as stimulus for a 'Christianity of action'. In these sermons the Hitler movement, and Hitler himself, appeared as divine will made manifest, as salvation of the Germans who had suffered so long due to defeat and post-war crises. Theologies of a divine order of creation allowed the religious appreciation of people and family, race, blood, and soil as holy dimensions or divine orders that were to be maintained 'pure' at any cost. This reasoning justified the exclusion of 'non-Aryan' Protestants from ecclesiastical functions and ultimately the racial population policy of the Nazi government. The following features were characteristic of the group profile of DC pastors: The majority were relatively young, and unlike BK pastors many of them originated from non-academic families below the middle classes. Their inner-ecclesiastical insurgence seemed somewhat rebellious: their religious movement epitomized the insurrection of the young against the conservative ecclesiastic establishment, against the traditional conservative church of dignitaries. Fighting in the Great War had been a key experience in their lives. The war had turned them into men in uniform and they wanted to stay this way even after the war – both spiritually and in appearance. German Christian pastors adored marching, flags and party, fight and victory, heroism and sacrifice – those and similar phrases and values constituted the German Christian world of ideas and transformed the religious (Ericksen 1985; Lächele 1994; Bergen 1996; Gailus 2001; Arnhold 2010; Buss 2011).

To state it clearly: without German Christians there would have been no Confessing Church. Wherever the German Christians remained less influential, the ecclesiastic opposition of the Confessing Church was also weak. The latter was not – as still widely held – a resistance movement against National Socialism, but rather an inner-ecclesiastical faction against the advancing *völkisch* Protestantism within the Church. Crucial for the development of Confessing Church congregations were brave and theologically inspired clerics. Apart from church services, Bible studies were at the core of the Confessing Church's identity. Church services were held according to tradition with markedly biblical sermons and only a few concealed and slightly critical time references. Involving male and female laymen to a greater degree in the liturgical service was characteristic for the Confessing Church. Their main concerns included neither human and political rights in general nor democracy; rather they were geared to protect their own religious and ecclesiastic freedom in the context of their milieu and advocated taking Christian values and commandments into greater consideration with regard to the political everyday life of the Nazi regime.

More often than the theologically simple German Christian pastors, clerics of the Confessing Church had a more educated background. Theologians from pastors' families were more prone to opt for the Confessing Church than the German Christians. Although both Confessing and German Christian pastors shared the same mindset of a national Protestantism, the former did not take the step of reshaping these ideas towards National Socialism. 'First Christ, then Germany' was the value order of the Confessing Church, whereas German Christians merged 'Christ and Germany' into two equal statements of faith. With regard to the mass followers of the two *Kirchenkampf* fractions, the German Christians brought the lower social strata, 'ordinary people' and petty bourgeoisie, along with them. Yet gender differences among the two groups of followers were even more striking: to put it bluntly, whereas German Christians were a national religious male movement, the Confessing Church was headed by male clergymen and had disproportionately more women as followers. The German Christians intended to masculinize the old church, which they saw as marginalized and feminized. The German worker, who had been seduced by Marxism, and the 'comrade of the Great War' should return to the church. Faith, theology, and ecclesiastic cult were to be reshaped into something more masculine and heroic (Gailus 2001; Retter 2009; Heymel 2011).

German Protestantism during the Hitler era was an extremely heterogeneous body without strong leadership and consisting of 28 independent regional churches highly oriented to tradition. For this reason, it is a difficult task to write an integrated history of German Protestantism from 1933 to 1945. An overview of these ecclesiastic regions should differentiate between three typical forms or directions of regional Protestant cultures during the Third Reich (in general, see Gailus and Krogel 2006). First, there were those regions with German Christian church leadership and large numbers of the pastors practising a *völkisch* Protestantism, particularly in Thuringia, Mecklenburg, and some other small German states. Second, other regional churches such as in Hanover, Bavaria, and Wurttemberg, with dominant bishops influencing the churches' direction, chose adaptation. Third, there were regions with a highly polarized ecclesiastic landscape. Here, a duplication of institutional structures was characteristic: the ruling German Christian church found itself in sharp conflict with the Council of Brethren of the Confessing Church characterized by a rudimentarily independent organization and leadership and advocating highly oppositional objectives ('Dahlemites'). This constellation was typical for most provinces of the large Prussian church, particularly in the church province of Mark Brandenburg including Berlin.

20.3   Catholics

Compared with German Protestantism – particularly prone to the National Socialist ideology – the picture is different when it comes to German Catholics. As a large confessional minority, they constituted a third of the population of the Reich (Hummel and Kißener 2009). As a result of the annexation of Austria in March 1938 and the Sudeten area in late September 1938, the 'Greater German Reich' became more Catholic; by the beginning of the war, the proportion of Catholics had increased to 40%. As a centralized organization and part of a world church oriented towards Rome, German Catholicism was less prone to the national and *völkisch* temptations of the time, even though the 'Reich theology' and theologians close to the Nazi regime such as Karl Adam and church historian Joseph Lortz provided intersections with the new, 'brown' *Zeitgeist* (Scherzberg 2001). In German Catholicism there was no inner-ecclesiastical movement parallel to the Nazi Party such as that of the German Christians – and this is the most important difference between Catholicism and Protestantism in the Third Reich. The Nazi regime regarded German Catholicism, being part of a world church, as one of the most dangerous 'supranational powers', and propagandists around Heinrich Himmler, Alfred Rosenberg, and Joseph Goebbels fought it more fiercely than the denominationally and regionally divided Protestantism. Overall, the Catholic milieu focused on religious core issues. There were, nevertheless, mass protests against anti-church and other measures of the regime in some regions, for instance in the context of pilgrimages and processions, which recent research has described as a 'demonstration Catholicism'. However, Catholics clearly did not form a unified 'Christian opposition' to the Nazi regime. Most German Catholics, like their Protestant fellow Christians, could easily reconcile their faith with National Socialism, as has been shown in purely Catholic areas such as Southern Bavaria and some parts of the Rhineland, and for other predominantly Catholic regions where Catholics were also Nazi rulers (Blaschke 2014). Moreover, Catholic Munich, as the 'capital of the movement', had proven fertile ground for the Nazi Party in its early years around 1920. Recent research has shown that there were in fact 'brown priests' among the Catholic clergy who were party members or had close ideological ties to the Nazis. However, there still is a striking difference from Protestant pastors. Whereas on average 15–20% of Protestant pastors were members of the NSDAP (*Nationalsozialistische Deutsche Arbeiterpartei*, Nazi Party), there were very few 'brown priests' – according to the present state of research, not more than 150 clergymen (or less than 1%) (Spicer 2008; Forstner 2013).

20.4   Christian Solidarity with Persecuted Jews?

Neither confession displayed much Christian solidarity with Jews persecuted by Nazi racial politics. To a certain extent, and in regard to political measures designed to repress Jewish influence in several areas of administration, culture, and society, both Christian confessions even welcomed Nazi 'Jewish policy'. The influential statement by Gerhard Kittel in 1933, a recognized Tübingen theologian of the New Testament, is an example of how Christians responded to the 'Jewish question' (Kittel 1933; see Junginger 2011). This is to be distinguished from attitudes towards Jewish converts or descendants of mixed marriages, so called non-Aryan Christians, within the churches. Due to their antisemitic attitude and their direct contribution to exclude 'non-Aryans', considerable parts of the Protestant churches were clearly ecclesiastic co-perpetrators. Thus, both churches did more than just fail to render assistance, as was suggested after the war in self-critical reflections. In German Christian dominated regional churches it was the objective to create a 'racially pure' church by excluding all Christians of Jewish origin. In their sermons, at their meetings, in their journals and other publications, a blatant antisemitism came to light. 'Non-Aryan' pastors and other employees were expelled. Jews were no longer to be baptized to prevent conversions. Measures based on the Nuremberg racial laws from September 1935 were welcomed. Some German Christian theologians even met the pogroms of November 1938 with approval. In some radical German Christian parishes, 'non-Aryan' Christians were not allowed to attend church from September 1941. In early May 1939, an initiative of German Christian theologians founded the 'Institute for the Study and Eradication of Jewish Influence on German Church Life' in Eisenach at Wartburg Castle, where Martin Luther had translated the New Testament into German, centuries before. During the war this institute, funded by the church, compiled a 'de-Judaized' version of the New Testament, a *völkisch* hymnbook for church service, and so forth (Heschel 2008; Arnhold 2010). All regional churches were indirectly involved in issuing 'German blood certificates' (*Ariernachweise*) by providing millions of excerpts from church registers. In Berlin, Schwerin (Protestant church of Mecklenburg), Hanover, and elsewhere, pastors and church employees founded ecclesiastical ancestry offices to contribute and push forward the separation of the population into people with 'German blood' and those with 'foreign blood'. The capital 'church register Old-Berlin', headed by Nazi pastor Karl Themel, cooperated closely with the Reich Office for Family Research at the Ministry of the Interior and provided state and party authorities with their 'findings' (Gailus 2008).

Among the 'intact' churches from the ecclesio-political centre, which had adapted to the regime, and even among firm oppositionists, there is evidence of *völkisch* thinking, antisemitism, and exclusion. In general, the Confessing Church rejected the application of the 'Aryan paragraph' (*Arierparagraph*) within the church ('Law for the Restoration of the Professional Civil Service', 7 April 1933, excluding 'non-Aryans' from civil service). In September 1933, the *Pfarrernotbund* (Pastors' Emergency League), the predecessor organization of the Confessing Church, which emerged in the course of the year 1934, was founded in opposition to the introduction of the 'Aryan paragraph'. However, not all factions sustained this opposition. Even in the 'intact' regional churches of Hanover and Bavaria, which considered themselves part of the Confessing Church, 'non-Aryan' pastors were dismissed (Lindemann 1998; Töllner 2007). A committee of theologians of the radical ecclesiastic opposition around Martin Niemöller discussed the 'Jewish question' for years without tangible results. It was only after the pogrom in November 1938 that the Berlin 'Office Grüber' emerged from this initiative, with branches throughout Germany: a church institution that provided legal aid for threatened 'non-Aryans' to emigrate until it was closed in late 1940. Even firm members of the Confessing Church could not bring themselves to announce a public statement until the beginning of the war. Time and again, it took forceful reminders by dedicated figures, such as the Berlin historian and pedagogue Elisabeth Schmitz, to discuss this hushed-up topic. Schmitz, who was a student of Adolf von Harnack, a prominent Protestant theologian and church historian, wrote – on her own initiative and, of course, anonymously – a memorandum in 1935, 'On the Situation of the German Non-Aryans', which she offered to several groups of the ecclesiastic opposition for public use. This was ultimately to little avail, since even the Confessing Church did not dare to publicly express words of solidarity with the persecuted people (Gerlach 2000; Ludwig 2009; Gailus 2010, 2017). The history of Protestantism in the Third Reich, we have to conclude, was characterized by a 'policy of silence' and, to a considerably degree, by perpetration and complicity.

By historical comparison, the Catholic Church of the years between 1933 and 1945 was less burdened with guilt than the Protestant Church because there was no church mass movement such as the *völkisch* German Christians. Also, the number of 'brown priests' was extremely small compared to the considerable number of Protestant NSDAP pastors, as stated above. Nevertheless, traditional and religiously motivated anti-Judaism was hardly less widespread among German Catholics than among Protestants; in some respects it was even stronger than among the often unchurched and more secularized Protestants. Catholics had pronounced anti-Jewish attitudes that, in some cases, clearly included many elements of a 'very "normal" post-emancipatory everyday life anti-Semitism' (Blaschke 2014). The belief in a Jewish world conspiracy, in an exuberant Jewish financial power and the supposed 'Jewification' of the press, in the 'subversion' and 'demoralization' of Christian society caused by the Jews, and so forth were views held by many German Catholics. The article on antisemitism in the official Catholic *Lexikon für Theologie und Kirche* (Lexicon for Theology and Church) insisted on distinguishing between a (bad) racially motivated and another, quite acceptable, antisemitism justified by 'state policy'. The first, it said, was un-Christian; the second version of antisemitism, however, was allowed for Catholic Christians. Just like Protestant parishes, Catholics made their church registers available to Nazi population politics. The encyclical 'With Burning Concern' (*Mit brennender Sorge*) from March 1937 deplored, first and foremost, the suppression of Catholic influence on public affairs. Although the encyclical condemned the National Socialist 'idolization' of race, people, and state, it did not defend the persecuted Jews. As with Protestants, it was only a few critical Catholics acting as individuals who left the Catholic mainstream of the Hitler era and admonished their church to show solidarity and provide practical aid for people persecuted on 'racial' grounds – people such as Edith Stein, Margarete Sommer, Gertrud Luckner, and the Berlin cathedral dean, Bernhard Lichtenberg (Leichsenring 2007; Blaschke 2014, 163–181, 223–230).

20.5   Small Religious Bodies

Apart from the two large Christian confessions, which consistently accounted for around 95% of the Reich population, there were many other smaller (Protestant) religious bodies ('Free Churches') with often no more than a few thousand or hundred thousand (at most) members. In many cases, they were the German branches of international religious bodies located in the United States, such as Methodists, Mennonites and Mormons, Baptists, Seventh Day Adventists, Quakers, Pentecostalists, and Jehovah's Witnesses, to name but a few. The current state of research on these churches and their relation to the Nazi regime is still far from satisfactory. By no means all of them were suppressed or suffered persecution 'as Christians' (Voigt 2005; Heinz 2011; Thull 2014). Strikingly, in many cases they achieved more freedom under the religious policy of the Third Reich – for instance, when they were granted or promised the status of a corporate body that they did not have before. Obedience to the authoritarian state, national enthusiasm, and illusory expectations on an even more extensive acknowledgement of the state caused many of these religious bodies to adapt and comply. Their deeply rooted biblical and theological anti-Judaism – partially in line with or with cautious sympathy for Nazi antisemitism – was essential for this attitude. The often fundamentalist Free Churches saw the persecution of the Jews by the Nazis as an act of divine retribution not to be interfered with. In general, silence prevailed. In some cases, the Free Churches took part in persecuting and excluding their 'non-Aryan' members. Jehovah's Witnesses ('Bible students') were an exception. They regarded the official churches and the state as 'kingdoms of the devil' and refused any form of participation: they did not vote and they refused the Hitler salute, conscription and, from 1939, military service during the war. Roughly 2000 Jehovah's Witnesses were sent to the concentration camps during the Nazi dictatorship and 250 members were executed as conscientious objectors. Another exception was the very small group of Quakers, with only a few hundred members, who showed a strong sense of solidarity with, and offered practical help to, persecuted Jews. Many German Quakers, both men and women, were willing to hide those persecuted 'on racial grounds' and to take part in the life-saving resistance movement.

20.6 'German Believers' and 'Believers in God'

The strong nationalist religious feelings of 1933 finally found expression in the Associated German Religious Movement (*Arbeitsgemeinschaft Deutsche Glaubensbewegung*), renamed the German Faith Movement (*Deutsche Glaubensbewegung*; DG) in 1934, initiated by several *völkisch*-religious bodies, groups, leagues, and comradeships. Their leaders hoped the new state would acknowledge them as religious bodies regulated by public law, equal to the two Christian churches. Referring to themselves as the 'third confession', they considered the DG the new *völkisch* church of the Third Reich. 'German Believers' (*Deutschgläubige*) got together in local organizations and networked with like-minded groups. Their 'Leadership Council' (*Führerrat*) headed by the Tübingen professor of religious studies Jakob Wilhelm Hauer and the Potsdam publicist Ernst Graf zu Reventlow, consisted mainly of previously Protestant professors well known for their affiliation to the *völkisch* movement before 1933. Their intention to organize the religious of the Third Reich independently from and outside of the Nazi Party – both a claim and an offer – did not find much favour among the party leadership. The organized 'German Believers' reached their peak in the early years of the regime, but membership figures hardly exceeded 30 000 even at their peak in 1935. They were under strict surveillance of the SS Security Service, but temporarily enjoyed quite extensive freedom, since the Nazi leadership used the 'German Believers', hostile to Christianity, as a spectre against the two large Christian confessions. From 1935, the SS pursued an approach of infiltration and liquidation towards the 'German Believers'. According to the statistics of religious confessions of 1939, only 86 000 people, or 0.1% of the Reich population, were members of these 'new pagan' religious groups, including the independent Ludendorff movement named League for the German Understanding of God (*Bund für deutsche Gotterkenntnis*).

We have to differentiate between 'German Believers' and 'Believers in God'. Whereas the former founded their own religious groups and were represented by *völkisch* spokesmen outside the NSDAP, the later were fanatical Nazis and saw the party and the SS as their new church. According to the statistics of religious confessions of 1939, 2 750 000 people (3.5%) of the 'Greater German Reich' were registered members of this 'confession', which was in fact no more than a statistical category used by staunch Nazis, who had left the church, when filling in forms. The name originated from the terminology of the *völkisch* movement and was officially mentioned in a decree by Minister of the Interior Wilhelm Frick from November 1936. It was the new 'brown' dissidents of the Nazi era, considering themselves 'religious' beyond and outside the Christian confessions and fending off labels such as 'with no religion', 'atheists', 'new pagans', or 'godless people', who referred to themselves as 'Believers in God'. SS leader Reinhard Heydrich called it a confession of 'the church free German religiosity'. It was a group of people leaving the churches from 1937 onwards inspired by National Socialism, in effect more a statistical figure than an independent group with an explicit religious programme and separate organizational structures. 'Believers in God' were predominantly quite young, higher ranking party officials of the NSDAP, who had left their original Christian confession due to their political faith: members of the SS, party functionaries, civil servants, two thirds of them male. They represented certain effects of the 'new faith' on the landscape of old confessions and were strong in regions such as Thuringia and Saxony, and generally in Protestant and in industrial areas. In 1939, around 440 000 people were registered as 'Believers in God' in the capital, Berlin – 10% of the inhabitants. In the extremely brown Thuringian university town of Jena, they accounted for a remarkable 15.8% of the inhabitants (Nanko 1993; Poewe 2006; Gailus 2007).

20.7 The Nazi Regime – a 'Political Religion'?

The Hitler movement – its charismatic leader, its ideology, its party politics, and even more so the 'brown cult' of their staged mass events – showed, to a certain extent, a religious dimension and thus was part of the religious revival of the inter-war period. Unlike the Communist Party of the Soviet Union and the Marxist-Leninist Communist Party of Germany, the NSDAP was not an atheist party declaring a radical 'God is dead' policy, and the 12-year Nazi period did not cause a sharp increase in secularization. The dynamic of the Nazi movement can hardly be explained without taking into account its fanatical, racial, and excessively religious 'German Belief'. This has recently been discussed by referring to the term 'political religion'. An entirely different matter is the religious policy of the NSDAP towards the traditional Christian confessions: it remained strikingly vague, inconsistent, and multi-pronged. In point 24 of its 1920 party manifesto, the NSDAP declared itself to be committed to a 'positive Christianity', a very vague wording originating from the terminology of the *völkisch* movement, which could be interpreted in several different ways. The religious confessions, as the manifesto additionally stated, were allowed freedom up to the point where they jeopardized the existence of the state 'or violated the moral sense of the Germanic race'. Until his accession to power in 1933, Hitler's religious policy remained deliberately vague. It was not very likely to win over political power in a society with more than 90% of people accounting for the Christian confessions by attacking the churches head on. The vague commitment to a 'positive Christianity' – nobody knew exactly what that would be – proved to be rather useful to win over majorities during the 'time of struggle'. By the time the Nazi regime established its power, this vague religious political position had changed: the ideology of the NSDAP with its non-Christian 'German Belief' was meant to gradually replace traditions of Christian faith. From about 1935, Nazi religious policy based on slogans such as 'deconfessionalization of public life' considerably limited the traditional scope of action of the two large

Christian confessions. However, this process slowed down with the beginning of the war in September 1939 and came to standstill during the later war years (Conway 1968; Siegele-Wenschkewitz 1974; Dierker 2002).

The so-called religious question was anything but solved within the National Socialist movement. According to Nazi self-conception, its world-view (*Weltanschauung*) as a modern, comprehensive interpretation of the world allegedly based on science was supposed to include the religious. Yet this visionary expectation was never met in the everyday life of the regime. Matters of faith were and remained a hardly controllable disturbing factor within the party: they were open, contested, difficult, and often they were silenced; they also caused religious political U-turns and a confusing diversity of opinions. There was no clear religious political party strategy of how to deal with the two large Christian churches regarding issues of confession and religion and of what role the tradition of Christian faith should play within the total Nazi ideology. On this issue, the seemingly almighty NSDAP was uncertain, disunited, and sometimes at a loss. The question of religion remained, divided party members, and formed different factions who self-evidently could not discuss this matter in the open without jeopardizing the image of the omniscient unity party leading a homogeneous 'people's community' through divisive debates on confession.

In terms of confessional sociology, the NSDAP was a 'Christian party', even in the later years of the regime: more than two thirds of its members were registered with a Christian church, and in December 1938, 74% of Himmler's SS were also members of a Christian church. We can distinguish at least three factions with different dispositions and attitudes towards religion and faith within the NSDAP. The ideological rigorists in strategically top-ranking positions (Himmler, Heydrich, Martin Bormann, and Rosenberg), with their radical religious political plans for the future – in the sense of a 'final solution of the religious question' – were predominant and gained influence in the course of the regime years. They drove forward the break with the traditional religious historical mindset, triggering cultural revolutionary consequences, although their eagerness was curbed time and again. They saw themselves as anti-ecclesiastic, ultimately anti-Christian, and referred to themselves as 'Believers in God' or 'German Believers'. They were juxtaposed with the more traditional 'Christian National Socialists' advocating consistency and moderation, who thought Germanized Christianity and National Socialism compatible and regarded a synthesis of both as 'true' National Socialism. Under-represented in leading positions, they had numerous followers at the middle and lower level of the party. Reich Minister of Church Affairs Hanns Kerrl, Bavarian Minister of Cultural Affairs Hans Schemm, the highest party judge Walter Buch, for instance, were representatives of this faction. The idea of 'Christian National Socialism' was one of the key factors engendering the loyalty and allegiance of the Christian population to Nazi society. Third, there was the group of party political centrists around Hitler and Goebbels, political virtuosi of the balance of power, whose religious convictions diverged from Christianity between 1920 and 1940 against the backdrop of staggering gains in political power. Their interventions against the forays of the 'ideological rigorists' were predominantly due to political considerations of the balance of power. For them,

the division of the 'people's community' into a Christian and a non-Christian part
was to be avoided at all costs (Steigmann-Gall 2003; Gailus 2007; Nolzen 2011,
151–159).

In the last two decades, historical research has revived the concept of 'political
religion' to describe and analyse Italian fascism and German National Socialism.
This term was introduced by Eric Voegelin and Raymond Aron in the 1930s and
1940s. The discussions on this concept have also in some cases rekindled the debate
on totalitarianism (Maier 1996; Maier and Schäfer 1997). Numerous publications
have affirmed that National Socialism cannot be comprehended without taking
into account its relevant genuine forms of religiosity. The seeming religious belief
in Hitler, who was worshipped as a saviour sent by God; the 'brown cult' of public
mass events such as the annual celebration in commemoration of the Nazi martyrs
of the Munich putsch on 9 November 1923 and the liturgical staging of the
Nuremberg rallies; and finally the National Socialist 'celebrations of life'
(*Lebensfeiern*) as a substitute for ecclesiastical ceremonies, as well as numerous professions of faith by Nazi ideologists, writers, and poets – all this and more shows an
extensive sacralization of public life in the Third Reich. According to protagonists
of the NSDAP, the post-Christian and total claim of Nazi ideology on the souls of
all Germans was supposed to satisfy still existing religious needs and to not leave
them to the competing traditional churches (Behrenbeck 1996; Vondung 2013).
It is – and will remain – debatable whether or not this overall religious character of
public and social life is sufficient to subsume the entire Nazi period under the concept of a 'political religion' (critical of this approach are Schreiner 1998; Hardtwig
2001). The historian Hans Günter Hockerts (2003), in his thorough study on this
question, has argued that we should understand 'political religion' as an important
aspect – but nevertheless only one aspect among others – for investigating National
Socialism. As a general term, it is too narrow and less useful than other approaches,
such as the concept of racism (*Rassismus-Konzept*) and the theory of charismatic
leadership.

20.8   Religious Historical Changes During the War, 1939–1945

Given the fact that the nearly six years of the Second World War accounted for
almost half of the Nazi period, it is fair to say that religion is a rather neglected
aspect of the historiography of the German war society. The religious political strategy of the NSDAP changed with the beginning of the war in 1939, though not
consistently and not always unambiguously. Conflicts with the churches over faith,
ideology, and Christianity were to be avoided under the exceptional circumstances
of a nation at war. The 'final solution of the religious question' was postponed until
after the victory. At the same time, the anti-Christian religious dystopia of important party leaders such as Hitler, Goebbels, Himmler, Rosenberg, and Bormann
became more radical. Their opinions initially remained unpublished and were only
revealed on the basis of several source collections from the post-war period (Picker
1989; Fröhlich 1993–1996, 1997–2006; Matthäus and Bajohr 2015). In May
1942, for instance, Goebbels noted in his diary that during the course of the last
war winter Hitler's decision had become 'implacable' to

destroy the Christian churches after the victory. They have behaved in such a rotten and devious way, they betrayed the fighting nation in its darkest hour cowardly and infamously and stabbed it in the back so that reconciliation is out of the question ... The Fuehrer sees a major ideological crisis looming that can only be compared with the end of antiquity. (Fröhlich 1993–1996, vol. 4, 360)

By 1942, in the middle of the war, a turning point in religious politics was in the offing: the number of people who since 1937 had increasingly left the churches as 'Believers in God' inspired by National Socialism rapidly dropped again. As early as two or three years before the military capitulation the 'new faith' started to degrade. Its founders' objective to establish a popular practice of the new German 'Belief in God' by implementing several alternative 'celebrations of life' ceased. Probably as a result not least of mass killings on the battlefields as well as on the home front, the Christian-religious endowment of life with meaning and ecclesiastical ceremonies prevailed. Goebbels confirmed this in a diary entry from October 1942, describing how over the course of the prolonged war the people again leaned towards the churches:

> Due to the spiritual helplessness of the current war situation the people seek for a way out and, since we ourselves have rather little to offer in terms of otherworldly values, seek refuge in the traditional churches, even German Believers. Our religious ideas are not rooted deep enough yet that they can offer comfort and support to the people suffering in this war. (Fröhlich 1993–1996, vol. 6, 131)

During the war the conflict between competing Protestant groups lost its virulence. The moderates of both German Christians and the Confessing Church gained influence and tended to agree more with the growing centre of the Protestant Church. Disintegration and fragmentation in the faction of the German Christians, divisions among the Confessing Church, and general exhaustion in both camps contributed to this development. A 'religious truce', as was announced by party and state officials, was, however, a rather inappropriate term to describe the relationship between the state and the churches during the war. This is true for both large confessions, which still faced numerous restrictions, intimidation, and other violent measures. Even though the war was not as welcome as it had been between 1914 and 1918 by and within the church, it loyally aligned itself with the Nazi war society and theologically and religiously justified Hitler's war through sermons and pastoral care. A somewhat 'antagonistic cooperation' between regime and churches emerged despite political and ideological differences (Süß 2007). As in previous wars, both confessions offered military pastoral care and made efforts to gain more pastoral influence, but met increasing opposition: against the backdrop of the religious rivalry between the 'old' and the 'new faith' the Nazi rulers gradually enforced the 'deconfessionalization' of the Wehrmacht and considerably restricted the traditional scope of action of military pastoral care. Protestant and Catholic army chaplains, with their Christian devotional and consolatory pamphlets, lost influence and were replaced by martial war pamphlets, given out to soldiers in millions, describing the 'new belief in Hitler'(among others, see Ziegler 1939; in general, see Pöpping 2011).

There is no doubt that resistance to Nazi rule also came from the Christian churches. However, in the overall context of political resistance against the Hitler regime, Christian resistance remained rather weak. Neither Protestant nor Catholic church bodies, as ecclesiastical institutions, could bring themselves to join the political resistance against National Socialism. A considerable portion of Protestants represented by the German Christians even acted as theological and practical accomplices. During wartime there was no lack of war-enthusiastic sermons from Protestant pastors and other forms of active participation of the church in Hitler's war. Otherwise, obedient participation in line with the traditional belief in ecclesiastical authorities prevailed with both Protestants and Catholics. Resistance motivated by Christian faith remained the exception and depended on the initiative of individuals. Dietrich Bonhoeffer is the most prominent example among Protestants. Equally important was the quiet resistance of brave women in and around the Confessing Church who helped persecuted 'non-Aryans' to escape by relying on resistance networks. Among Catholics there were figures such as the Bishop of Münster, Clemens August Graf von Galen, who protested in his sermons from July to August 1941 against euthanasia measures, and the Catholic dean Bernhard Lichtenberg, who after the 'Crystal Night' in November 1938 stood up for persecuted Jews in his church services in the Berlin Hedwig Cathedral. He was denunciated in autumn 1941 and died during his arrest in November 1943 (Bethge 1967; Barnett 1992; Spicer 2004; Gailus and Vollnhals 2013).

20.9   Conclusion

A wide range of different religious fractions quarrelled with each other during the Third Reich: several Protestant groups who referred to themselves as 'German Christians'; opposed to them, the Confessing Church, the Catholic Church reduced to its core milieu, 'Christian National Socialists', and anti-Christian 'Believers in God' within the NSDAP; also 'German Believers' outside the Nazi Party claiming to be the 'third confession'; and finally, a plethora of smaller Christian religious communities and *völkisch* 'new pagan' groups. All these groups fought for their religious existence, their identity and legitimacy, for dominance, recognition, or sufferance. In view of the strong religious revival beginning in 1933, there was a newly unleashed religious pluralism and a fierce rivalry in matters of faith, in particular in the religiously heated atmosphere of the early years of the regime shaped by an uncontrolled growth of religious statements and avowals as well as the foundation of several religious groups and organizations. It is fair to assume that, in the medium and long run, totalitarian Nazi ideology would never have tolerated any other Gods (religious orientations, confessions, churches). Its objective was to equalize political rule and religious salvation. Thus the NSDAP itself was heading to become the church of a 'new faith' of all Germans. The need for the religious endowment of meaning for future generations was to be met exclusively by referring to its totalitarian *Weltanschauung*. National Socialism, as Goebbels wrote in December 1941, was not yet a religion but could well emerge as one as a result of 'very strong feelings among the people' (Fröhlich 1993–1996, vol. 2, 500). The new rulers could easily instrumentalize, ban, or even destroy smaller religious communities. The situation was different when it came to the two large Christian confessions accounting for more than 90% of the population. Due to their size it was impossible to ban them. After the attempt of German Christian Protestants to enforce a centralized *völkisch*-Christian Reich church 'for the Fuehrer' had failed and ended in fragmentation and chaos, the party leadership left Protestantism to destroy itself. The more solid and compact Catholic Church seemed to be a more substantial religious obstacle to establishing the Nazi church, which is indirectly shown by sharper persecution and more intensive efforts to 'study the enemy' on the part of the Gestapo and the SS Security Service. The regime effectively focused on the religious political strategy of 'deconfessionalizing public life': by playing off traditional confessional antagonisms between Protestants and Catholics, to a certain extent by intimidation and terror, and finally by total rule over youth education. Not least regarding the 'final solution of the religious question', the leadership believed in war as the ultimate cure: facing the foreign 'enemy', the German population was forced into allegiance with the Nazi rulers and the initial military victories strengthened the leadership's charisma.

Regarding the twentieth century as a whole, the Nazi period was, overall, not a time of accelerated secularization, as has often been argued after 1945. The emphatic and quasi-religious experiences of the year 1933 and the often religious impetus of this turning point indicate, rather, a period of intensified religious feelings and newly founded religious groups and associations. The latest process of secularization that had started around 1900 and accelerated during the Weimar Republic reversed. In the religious historical context of the twentieth century the Nazi era represents both turning point and counter-time. This change in trend was, however, not characterized by the re-Christianization or re-churching that Protestantism and Catholicism had longed for at the beginning of the Third Reich. The churches' wish for a conservative-authoritarian, anti-Western, and fiercely anti-socialist 'Christian state' did not come about. The objective of a 'Christian National Socialism', favoured by many Germans, also proved to be a delusion. National Socialism, a temporary ally of the churches against the culture of the Enlightenment, the 'ideas of 1789', liberalism, democracy, and the much-hated 'godless' Republic of Weimar was in the end – after having consolidated its dictatorship – an existentially dangerous rival in the religious fight for the souls of the German people.

Note

1   Translator's note: the German word *Konfession* has been translated as 'confession' in this chapter to distinguish between different groups within Christianity. 'Denomination', the common and frequently used translation, rather refers to different religious groups within Protestantism and is therefore too narrow in this context.

References

Arnhold, Oliver. 2010. '*Entjudung*' – *Kirche im Abgrund: Die Thüringer Kirchenbewegung Deutsche Christen 1928–1939 und das 'Institut zur Erforschung und Beseitigung des jüdischen Einflusses auf das deutsche kirchliche Leben' 1939–1945*. Berlin: Institut Kirche und Judentum.

Barnett, Victoria. 1992. *For the Soul of the People: Protestant Protest against Hitler*. Oxford: Oxford University Press.

Behrenbeck, Sabine. 1996. *Der Kult um die toten Helden: Nationalsozialistische Mythen, Riten und Symbole 1932 bis 1945*. Vierow bei Greifswald: SH–Verlag.

Bergen, Doris L. 1996. *Twisted Cross: The German Christian Movement in the Third Reich*. Chapel Hill: University of North Carolina Press.

Bethge, Eberhard. 1967. *Dietrich Bonhoeffer: Eine Biographie*. Gütersloh: Gütersloher Verlagshaus.

Blaschke, Olaf. 2014. *Die Kirchen und der Nationalsozialismus*. Stuttgart: Reclam.

Buss, Hansjörg 2011. '*Entjudete' Kirche: Die Lübecker Landeskirche zwischen christlichem Antijudaismus und völkischem Antisemitismus (1918–1950)*. Paderborn: Schöningh.

Conway, John. 1968. *The Nazi Persecution of the Churches*. London: Weidenfeld & Nicolson.

Dierker, Wolfgang. 2002. *Himmlers Glaubenskrieger: Der Sicherheitsdienst der SS und seine Religionspolitik 1933–1941*. Paderborn: Schöningh.

Ericksen, Robert P. 1985. *Theologians under Hitler: Gerhard Kittel, Paul Althaus and Emanuel Hirsch*. New Haven, CT: Yale University Press.

Forstner, Thomas. 2013. *Priester in Zeiten des Umbruchs: Identität und Lebenswelt des katholischen Pfarrklerus in Oberbayern 1918 bis 1945*. Göttingen: Vandenhoeck & Ruprecht.

Fröhlich, Elke, ed. 1997–2006. *Die Tagebücher von Joseph Goebbels. Volume 1: Aufzeichnungen 1923–1941*. 14 vols. Munich: Saur.

Fröhlich, Elke, ed. 1993–1996. *Die Tagebücher von Joseph Goebbels. Volume 2: Diktate 1941–1945*. 15 vols. Munich: Saur.

Gailus, Manfred. 2001. *Protestantismus und Nationalsozialismus: Studien zur nationalsozialistischen Durchdringung des protestantischen Sozialmilieus in Berlin*. Cologne, Weimar, and Vienna: Böhlau.

Gailus, Manfred. 2002. 'Overwhelmed by their own fascination with the "Ideas of 1933": Berlin's Protestant Social Milieu in the Third Reich.' *German History* 20, 462–493. doi: 10.1191/0266355402gh267oa.

Gailus, Manfred. 2003. '1933 als protestantisches Erlebnis: Emphatische Selbsttransformation und Spaltung.' *Geschichte und Gesellschaft* 29, 481–511.

Gailus, Manfred. 2007. '"Ein Volk – ein Reich – ein Glaube"? Religiöse Pluralisierungen in der NS–Weltanschauungsdiktatur.' In *Religion und Gesellschaft. Europa im 20. Jahrhundert*, edited by Friedrich Wilhelm Graf and Klaus Große Kracht, 247–268. Cologne, Weimar, and Vienna: Böhlau.

Gailus, Manfred ed. 2008. *Kirchliche Amtshilfe: Die Kirche und die Judenverfolgung im 'Dritten Reich'*. Göttingen: Vandenhoeck & Ruprecht.

Gailus, Manfred. 2010. '*Mir aber zerriss es das Herz': Der stille Widerstand der Elisabeth Schmitz*. Göttingen: Vandenhoeck & Ruprecht.

Gailus, Manfred. 2017. *Friedrich Weißler: Ein Jurist und bekennender Christ im Widerstand gegen Hitler*. Göttingen: Vandenhoeck & Ruprecht.

Gailus, Manfred and Krogel, Wolfgang, eds. 2006. *Von der babylonischen Gefangenschaft der Kirche im Nationalen: Regionalstudien zu Protestantismus, Nationalsozialismus und Nachkriegsgeschichte 1930 bis 2000*. Berlin: Wichern Verlag.

Gailus, Manfred and Nolzen, Armin, eds. 2011. *Zerstrittene 'Volksgemeinschaft': Glaube, Konfession und Religion im Nationalsozialismus*. Göttingen: Vandenhoeck & Ruprecht.

Gailus, Manfred and Vollnhals, Clemens, eds. 2013. *Mit Herz und Verstand – Protestantische Frauen im Widerstand gegen die NS–Rassenpolitik*. Göttingen: Vandenhoeck & Ruprecht.

Gerlach, Wolfgang. 2000. *And the Witnesses Were Silent: The Confessing Church and the Persecution of the Jews*. Lincoln: University of Nebraska Press.

348MANFRED GAILUS

Hardtwig, Wolfgang. 2001. 'Political Religion in Modern Germany. Reflections on Nationalism, Socialism, and National Socialism.' *Bulletin of the German Historical Institute* 28, 3–27.

Heinz, Daniel, ed. 2011. *Freikirchen und Juden im 'Dritten Reich': Instrumentalisierte Heilsgeschichte, antisemitische Vorurteile und verdrängte Schuld.* Göttingen: Vandenhoeck & Ruprecht.

Heschel, Susannah. 2008. *The Aryan Jesus: Christian Theologians and the Bible in Nazi Germany.* Princeton, NJ: Princeton University Press.

Heymel, Michael, ed. 2011. *Martin Niemöller: Dahlemer Predigten. Kritische Ausgabe.* Gütersloh: Gütersloher Verlagshaus.

Hockerts, Hans Günter. 2003. 'War der Nationalsozialismus eine politische Religion? Über Chancen und Grenzen eines Erklärungsmodells.' In *Zwischen Politik und Religion: Studien zur Entstehung, Existenz und Wirkung des Totalitarismus*, edited by Klaus Hildebrand, 45–71. Munich: Oldenbourg.

Hummel, Karl-Joseph and Kißener, Michael, eds. 2009. *Die Katholiken und das Dritte Reich: Kontroversen und Debatten.* Paderborn: Schöningh.

Junginger, Horst. 2011. *Die Verwissenschaftlichung der 'Judenfrage' im Nationalsozialismus.* Darmstadt: WBG.

Kittel, Gerhard. 1933. *Die Judenfrage.* Stuttgart: Kohlhammer.

Lächele, Rainer. 1994. *Ein Volk, ein Reich, ein Glaube: Die 'Deutschen Christen' in Württemberg 1925–1960.* Stuttgart: Calwer.

Leichsenring, Jana. 2007. *Die Katholische Kirche und 'ihre Juden': Das 'Hilfswerk beim Bischöflichen Ordinariat Berlin' 1938–1945.* Berlin: Metropol.

Lindemann, Gerhard. 1998. *'Typisch jüdisch': Die Stellung der Evangelisch–lutherischen Landeskirche Hannovers zu Antijudaismus, Judenfeindschaft und Antisemitismus 1919–1949.* Berlin: Duncker & Humblot.

Ludwig, Hartmut. 2009. *An der Seite der Entrechteten und Schwachen: Zur Geschichte des 'Büro Pfarrer Grüber' (1938 bis 1940) und der Ev. Hilfsstelle für ehemals Rasseverfolgte nach 1945.* Berlin: Logos.

Maier, Hans, ed. 1996. *Politische Religionen: Die totalitären Regime und das Christentum.* Paderborn: Schöningh.

Maier, Hans and Schäfer, Michael, eds. 1997. *'Totalitarismus' und 'Politische Religionen': Konzepte des Diktaturvergleichs.* Paderborn: Schöningh.

Marquardt, Bruno. 1933. 'Ein Jahr der Größe: Silvestergedanken 1933.' *Evangelium im Dritten Reich* 2 (53).

Matthäus, Jürgen and Bajohr, Frank. 2015. *Alfred Rosenberg, Die Tagebücher von 1934 bis 1944.* Frankfurt am Main: Fischer.

Nanko, Ulrich. 1993. *Die deutsche Glaubensbewegung: Eine historische und soziologische Untersuchung.* Marburg: diagonal.

Nolzen, Armin. 2011. 'Nationalsozialismus und Christentum: Konfessionsgeschichtliche Befunde zur NSDAP.' In *Zerstrittene 'Volksgemeinschaft': Glaube, Konfession und Religion im Nationalsozialismus*, edited by Manfred Gailus and Armin Nolzen, 151–179. Göttingen: Vandenhoeck & Ruprecht.

Picker, Henry. 1989. *Hitlers Tischgespräche im Führerhauptquartier.* Frankfurt am Main and Berlin: Ullstein.

Poewe, Karla. 2006. *New Religions and the Nazis.* Oxford: Routledge.

Pöpping, Dagmar. 2011. 'Die Wehrmachtseelsorge im Zweiten Weltkrieg. Rolle und Selbstverständnis von Kriegs- und Wehrmachtpfarrern im Ostkrieg 1941–1945.' In *Zerstrittene 'Volksgemeinschaft': Glaube, Konfession und Religion im Nationalsozialismus*, edited by Manfred Gailus and Armin Nolzen, 257–286. Göttingen: Vandenhoeck & Ruprecht.

Puschner, Uwe and Vollnhals, Clemens, eds. 2012. *Die völkisch–religiöse Bewegung im Nationalsozialismus. Eine Beziehungs- und Konfliktgeschichte.* Göttingen: Vandenhoeck & Ruprecht.

Retter, Ralf. 2009. *Zwischen Protest und Propaganda: Die Zeitschrift 'Junge Kirche' im Dritten Reich.* Munich: Allitera.

Scherzberg, Lucia. 2001. *Kirchenreform mit Hilfe des Nationalsozialismus: Karl Adam als kontextueller Theologe.* Darmstadt: WBG.

Schreiner, Klaus. 1998, '"Wann kommt der Retter Deutschlands?" Formen und Funktionen von politischem Messianismus in der Weimarer Republik.' *Saeculum* 49, 107–160. doi: 10.7788/saeculum.1998.49.1.107.

Siegele-Wenschkewitz, Leonore. 1974. *Nationalsozialismus und Kirchen: Religionspolitik von Partei und Staat bis 1935.* Düsseldorf: Droste.

Spicer, Kevin P. 2004. *Resisting the Third Reich: The Catholic Clergy in Hitler's Berlin.* De Kalb: Northern Illinois University Press.

Spicer, Kevin P. 2008. *Hitler's Priests: Catholic Clergy and National Socialism.* De Kalb: Northern Illinois University Press.

Steigmann-Gall, Richard. 2003. *The Holy Reich: Nazi Conceptions of Christianity, 1919–1945.* Cambridge and New York: Cambridge University Press.

Süß, Winfried. 2007. 'Antagonistische Kooperationen: Katholische Kirche und nationalsozialistisches Gesundheitswesen in den Kriegsjahren 1939–1945.' In *Kirchen im Krieg. Europa 1939–1945*, edited by Karl–Joseph Hummel and Christoph Kösters, 317–341. Paderborn: Schöningh.

Thull, Philipp, ed. 2014. *Christen im Dritten Reich.* Darmstadt: WBG.

Töllner, Axel. 2007. *Eine Frage der Rasse? Die Evangelisch–Lutherische Kirche in Bayern, der Arierparagraf und die bayerischen Pfarrfamilien mit jüdischen Vorfahren im 'Dritten Reich'.* Stuttgart: Kohlhammer.

Voigt, Karl Heinz. 2005. *Schuld und Versagen der Freikirchen im 'Dritten Reich': Aufarbeitungsprozesse seit 1945.* Frankfurt am Main: Lembeck.

Vondung, Klaus. 2013. *Deutsche Wege zur Erlösung: Formen des Religiösen im Nationalsozialismus.* Munich: Fink.

Ziegler, Matthes. 1939. *Soldatenglaube – Soldatenehre: Ein deutsches Brevier für Hitler-Soldaten.* Berlin: Nordland Verlag.

Further Reading

Bergen, Doris L. 1996. *Twisted Cross: The German Christian Movement in the Third Reich.* Chapel Hill: University of North Carolina Press.
The first modern and compact study on the *völkisch* and strongly antisemitic religious mass movement within the Protestant churches.

Blaschke, Olaf. 2014. *Die Kirchen und der Nationalsozialismus.* Stuttgart: Reclam.
A new, unconventional, and critical approach on the role of Protestantism and Catholicism during the Third Reich.

Ericksen, Robert P. *Theologians under Hitler: Gerhard Kittel, Paul Althaus and Emanuel Hirsch.* New Haven, CT: Yale University Press.
A ground-breaking study of three prestigious university theologians and their intellectual complicities with and close relationships to the Nazi regime.

Forstner, Thomas. 2013. *Priester in Zeiten des Umbruchs: Identität und Lebenswelt des katholischen Pfarrklerus in Oberbayern 1918 bis 1945.* Göttingen: Vandenhoeck & Ruprecht.
The best modern case study of a regional Catholic priesthood and its behaviour under the Nazi government.

Gailus, Manfred. 2001. *Protestantismus und Nationalsozialismus: Studien zur nationalsozialistischen Durchdringung des protestantischen Sozialmilieus in Berlin.* Cologne, Weimar, and Vienna: Böhlau.
A social historical and collective biographical study on Protestant pastors and their congregations in the German capital.
Vondung, Klaus. 2013. *Deutsche Wege zur Erlösung: Formen des Religiösen im Nationalsozialismus.* Munich: Fink.
A short but very concise and convincing study of the Nazi movement and its *Weltanschauung* as a form of political religion.

CHAPTER TWENTY-ONE

Family and Private Life

LISA PINE

The history of the family and private life is fundamental to our understanding of societies past and present. It is a history of 'multi-layered complexities', through which a complicated 'interaction between self, identity and society can be approached and understood' (Davidoff et al. 1999, 14). As Paul Ginsborg notes, 'not only the form of the family, but also its place in any given society' are significant concerns for historical research (Ginsborg 2003, 174). The history of the family is one of an institution that has changed and evolved in time and place. The emotional contexts and socialization functions of the family have varied throughout history. At times, the family has provided a private place or haven; at other times, the involvement and intrusion of the state into the family has been heavy. The Nazi regime arguably provides one of the strongest cases of the latter state of affairs in modern European history. This chapter discusses the state of research and writing on the subject of National Socialism, the family, and private life. It briefly contextualizes the Nazi era, by examining the family in the Weimar Republic, before moving on to analyse the policies towards the family implemented by the Nazi regime. The chapter examines the attempts of the National Socialist government to redress both the 'crisis of the family' and the decline in the nation's birth rate. It considers Nazi welfare policies directed at families, especially the work of the *Hilfswerk 'Mutter und Kind'*. It then looks at 'inferior' families, excluded from positive population policies and from the 'national community', examining sterilization policy and the impact of the Nazi regime upon 'asocial' and Jewish families. The chapter then traces the impact of the Second World War on German family life, as well as examining the legacy of the National Socialist regime for the family in the post-1945 era.

The historiography of the Third Reich developed in the 1980s to examine the subject of women in a variety of contexts, such as at work and in the Nazi organizations, and it has continued to grow. From the 1990s, research on the related area of the family has been published. Lisa Pine's book *Nazi Family Policy, 1933–1945* was

A Companion to Nazi Germany, First Edition. Edited by Shelley Baranowski,
Armin Nolzen, and Claus-Christian W. Szejnmann.
© 2018 John Wiley & Sons Ltd. Published 2018 by John Wiley & Sons Ltd.

the first major study of the subject in English (Pine 1997). The book explores the nature of Nazi family ideology and policy, as well as the dissemination of Nazi family ideals through education and socialization. It examines the model *kinderreich* families, which defined the Nazi ideal, and the 'asocial' and Jewish families that represented the 'socially unfit' and 'racially inferior' categories. Subsequently, Michelle Mouton's book, *From Nurturing the Nation to Purifying the Volk: Weimar and Nazi Family Policy, 1918–1945*, was the first on the subject to treat both the Weimar and Nazi eras (2007). Mouton shows that both Weimar and Nazi policymakers used legislation directed at families to increase the birth rate and to improve public health. However, the Nazi regime brought about a drastic change to family policy, with its racial ideology and its attempts to directly intervene in family life. The Weimar Republic was characterized by a plethora of organizations and associations – not only state organizations, but also charitable, church, and private groups – that provided assistance and advice to families. In contrast, the Nazi regime used a monolithic, racially based family policy and more forceful measures. Nazi family policy, Mouton argues, represented a radical departure from that of the Weimar Republic. She discusses marriage, divorce, the promotion of motherhood, and welfare, all of which are essential to a book on this subject and have been well established as such in the secondary literature. Mouton shows that many German women 'found ample opportunities to challenge, negotiate, manipulate, or most frequently, evade Nazi policy altogether' (Mouton 2007, 281) and that Nazi family policy was 'applied inconsistently' (279).

In 2010, Hester Vaizey published a well-researched and interesting book on family life in Germany, which covers the wartime period and the immediate postwar years (2010). In particular, she examines the impact of the war upon family relationships and analyses how men, women, and children experienced wartime separation and subsequent peacetime reunion. Her book builds on Pine's and Mouton's work, examining the impact of the Nazi regime on 'intra-familial relationships'. Vaizey speaks of the 'extraordinary resilience of the nuclear family and the emotional ties that bound its members together' in Nazi Germany (Vaizey 2010, 2). Her discussion of family life under Nazism before the wartime period shows how the NSDAP (*Nationalsozialistische Deutsche Arbeiterpartei*, Nazi Party) aimed to undermine family loyalty and intervene in the private realm.

Paul Ginsborg also notes the importance of 'the relationship between the state and the family' in a regime of this nature (Ginsborg 2003, 174). His most recent book addresses the family not only in the Hitler state, but also in other dictatorial regimes of the twentieth century, including those of Stalin, Franco, and Mussolini (Ginsborg 2014). He examines the relationship between individuals, families, civil society, and the state. He highlights the significance of families as 'actors in the historical process' (Ginsborg 2003, 174). His work on the Hitler regime adds important insights into the family and private life under National Socialism.

21.1   The Family in the Weimar Republic

The Weimar Republic brought a variety of experiences to the German family. In the early years, German families still suffered from the impact of the First World War and its aftermath. The traumatic experiences of the First World War left millions of German families in mourning for fathers, brothers, husbands, and sons. Grief for family members who had died in battle as well as the burden of many men who returned home from the front crippled or psychologically damaged took a harsh toll on family life. During the inter-war period, the German population consisted of about two million more women than men (Ginsborg 2014, 329). The mid-1920s became years of relative stability for the German family, as people searched for a sense of peace and security after the traumas of the war (Sieder 1987, 213). Weimar policymakers tried to strike a balance between upholding traditional values and adapting to the changes engendered by modernity. The Weimar era brought about some important changes in society that affected the family. The Association for Sexual Hygiene and Life Reform and the National Union for Birth Control and Hygiene, established in 1923 and 1928 respectively, introduced new educational initiatives on sexual hygiene and birth control (Frevert 1989, 189). But such changes met an unfavourable response from German conservatives, who considered sexual promiscuity, rising divorce and abortion rates, and higher numbers of working married women to signify the decline and demise of the family. In the 1920s, the birth rate dropped faster than at any other point in German history. This decline was regarded as a 'national catastrophe' in traditional and conservative circles. The traditional relationship between family and state came to be called into question during this period that was characterized by a moral panic about the future of the German family.

The position of the family waned with the effects of the Great Depression engendered by the Wall Street Crash of 1929, as families faced enormous financial difficulties. In particular, the economic crisis eroded the material foundations of middle-class family life, as savings were lost, and of working-class family life as mass unemployment deprived workers of their jobs and incomes (Pine 1997, 7). This placed a considerable strain upon mothers to maintain the cohesion of their families, as well as to search for cheap provisions. Young unemployed family members left home, wandering across the country, and sometimes even beyond its borders, in order to relieve the burden on the family of 'unnecessary eaters' (Sieder 1987, 225). The economic crisis of the early 1930s created many social rifts, for example, between the employed and the unemployed, and between generations. Intergenerational conflict had grown as parents had lost their status and prestige through unemployment and impoverishment. Many parents were no longer able to provide their children with protection and security. Hence, when the Nazis came to power, they sought to redress both the 'crisis of the family' and the decline in the nation's birth rate. They capitalized on the conservative backlash against the changes in sexuality and family life during the Weimar years and claimed that they would restore traditional models of the family. In particular, they sought to reverse the trend of 'one-child families' and to replace it with a trend for 'large families' comprising four or more children. This trend in family life was especially evident in Berlin, where the average household size had dropped to 2.7 by 1933, and where 35% of married couples were childless. Indeed, Berlin had the lowest birth rate not only in Germany, but in the world (Ginsborg 2014, 344–345).

21.2   Nazi Family Policies

Point 21 of the NSDAP's Programme stated: 'The state has to care for the raising of the nation's health through the protection of mother and child.' A woman's 'most glorious duty', according to Joseph Goebbels, Minister for Propaganda and Popular Enlightenment, was 'to present her people and her country with a child' (Figure 21.1). Once in power, the National Socialist regime introduced a whole series of measures and incentives to achieve its goal of increasing the birth rate. Indeed, Ginsborg notes the 'extraordinary combination of strategies' that the Hitler government directed at German families (Ginsborg 2003, 175). In June 1933, the Marriage Loan Scheme was set up to promote marriages between healthy 'Aryan' partners. A loan of 1000 Reichsmarks was made to a German couple in the form of vouchers for the purchase of furniture and household equipment. The loans were given to a couple only if the wife agreed to give up her job. In addition, the loan was only made if the political affiliation and 'way of life' of the couple were considered to be acceptable. It was denied to couples if either or both partners had connections with the German Communist Party (KPD), or had had such connections in the past, and it was denied to prostitutes and the 'workshy'. The repayment of the loan was reduced by one quarter for each child born, and was completely cancelled out with the birth of the fourth child. Between August 1933 and January 1937, some 700 000 marriages were assisted by marriage loans (Pine 1997, 18). In 1937, the prerequisite that women had to give up paid employment was revoked and this instigated a large increase in applications. In 1939, 42% of all marriages

Figure 21.1   A Nazi family, 1930s. Photo: The Wiener Library.

were loan-assisted (Pine 1997, 18). However, couples granted a marriage loan had, on average, only one child.

The Nazi regime also attempted to raise the status of motherhood. A classic example of a symbolic tribute to mothers with large families was the Cross of Honour of the German Mother (Figures 21.2 and 21.3). This was awarded to prolific mothers, in bronze, silver, and gold, for four, six, and eight children respectively. There was a slight increase in the nation's birth rate in the period 1934–1939 as compared with the years 1930–1933, but this was not necessarily attributable to Nazi incentives to promote procreation. Many couples felt more secure about getting married and having children because the economic climate had improved. Hence, the number of marriages increased, but the number of children per marriage did not. In addition, Nazi incentives and propaganda were not sufficient on their own to redress the long-term trend in low birth rates.

A new divorce law was introduced in 1938 that allowed for a divorce if a couple had lived apart for three years or more, and if the marriage had effectively broken down. On the surface, this appeared quite liberal. However, the reasoning behind it lay more in benefits to the state than in benefits to private individuals. The objective was to dissolve marriages that were of no value to the 'national community'. The National Socialists believed that once a divorce had been granted, the two partners involved might then remarry and provide the nation with more children. Premature infertility became a ground for divorce, as did either partner's refusal to have a child (Pine 1997, 18).

Many other measures were taken to encourage marriages between healthy 'Aryan' partners that would result in large families and increase the nation's birth

Figure 21.2 Family mealtime. Nazi propaganda picture of a German mother surrounded by her happy children. Photo: The Wiener Library.

Figure 21.3   The Third Reich 'Honour Cross of the German Mother' (*Mutterkreuz*) of 1938. Photo: The Wiener Library.

rate. Contraceptives were banned and family planning centres were dissolved. In 1941, Himmler's Public Ordinance prohibited the production and distribution of contraceptives (Ginsborg 2014, 380). In addition, the abortion laws were tightened up by the reintroduction of Paragraphs 219 and 220 of the Criminal Code, which made provisions for harsher punishments for abortion (Pine 1997, 20). Eventually, in 1943, the death penalty was introduced for anyone performing an abortion to terminate a 'valuable' pregnancy, as this was considered to be an act of 'racial sabotage' during the crisis of the war (Stephenson 1975, 69).

21.3   The *Hilfswerk 'Mutter und Kind'*

The *Hilfswerk 'Mutter und Kind'* (Mother and Child Relief Agency) was a special agency of the *Nationalsozialistische Volkswohlfahrt* (NSV or National Socialist People's Welfare), established on 28 February 1934. The agency's central concern was with the health of mothers and children, in order to preserve 'the immortality of the nation'. Three of the most significant aspects of its work were welfare for mothers, recuperation for mothers, and advice centres for mothers. The Nazi regime utilized welfare as an instrument to educate the German nation in the spirit of National Socialism. Welfare, understood in population policy terms, was directed at the promotion of the 'racially pure' and 'fit'. Instructors, social workers, and staff in the advice centres and in the recuperation homes were trained in the Nazi *Weltanschauung* ('world-view') so that they could provide German women not only with material, practical, and educational support, but also with ideological guidance.

Welfare for mothers who had recently given birth had existed in Germany since the end of the First World War. However, it was only in the Third Reich that this sphere of welfare became a central element of state policy. Self-mobilization of the family through Nazi social work benefited millions of families. Welfare for mothers entailed help in the home. However, this did not usually take the form of direct financial aid. It consisted of material help, such as the provision of beds, linen, children's clothes, or food allowances. In addition, home helps were assigned to pregnant women or those who had recently given birth to assist with household chores. Welfare workers and/or nurses made home visits to pregnant women in order to help prevent miscarriage, premature birth, and illness. They educated and cared for expectant mothers. After the birth of the child, regular visits continued and welfare workers gave advice on breastfeeding and childcare. They also observed the general behaviour of the family. It is to be noted that welfare visits to 'hereditarily ill' or 'abnormal' children were restricted 'to a minimum' (Pine 1997, 24).

The *Hilfswerk 'Mutter und Kind'* helped single mothers, too, as long as they were 'racially valuable' and 'hereditarily healthy'. Hence, a distinction was not made on the basis of marital status, as all German children were 'valuable' to the nation, but on eugenic and racial grounds. The *Hilfswerk 'Mutter und Kind'* was involved in the organization of foster care and adoptions and in the struggle against abortion. The agency helped single mothers by trying to procure their marriages to their babies' fathers or to seek other solutions if this was not successful or possible, including the recommendation of single mothers to *Lebensborn* homes to give birth discreetly and then give up the baby for adoption.

Welfare for mothers also took the form of recuperation measures. Whilst there had been some moves towards recuperation for mothers during the Weimar era, under National Socialism mother recuperation became ideologically motivated and fundamental to state family policy. Recuperation for mothers took a variety of forms, such as going to stay with relatives, visiting local convalescence centres, or being sent away to recuperation homes. The homes were located in the mountains or by the sea, or at natural springs and spas (Figure 21.4). The average stay was for 26 days. The type of recuperation for each mother was determined by her medical condition, 'state of mind', and social status. The practice of ascertaining the 'hereditary-biological' worth of each mother was a dominant feature of this area of work. Recuperation or convalescence was not made available to the 'hereditarily inferior'. For example, in the period up to the end of October 1941, one third of applications for entry to recuperation homes in the Hamburg area were rejected on the grounds that the women were 'hereditarily inferior' or behaved in a manner that was 'adverse to the community' (Pine 1997, 27).

Other than 'hereditary health', the main prerequisite for convalescence was that a mother did not have sufficient financial means of her own for this purpose. Mothers weakened through childbirth, those with two or more children, and those whose husbands had been long-term unemployed were given priority for

Figure 21.4 Women in a 'Recuperation Home for Mothers' run by the 'National
Socialist People's Welfare', c.1938. Photo: The Wiener Library.

recuperation measures. During a mother's absence from home, a relative, neighbour, or household help stepped in. Mothers received a 50% reduction on train
travel to and from the recuperation homes. Official NSV statistics stated that
40 340 women went to the recuperation homes in 1934, the number rising to
77 723 in 1938 (Pine 1997, 27).

The homes had a strong educational aspect to them. Copies of the educational
pamphlet *Guidelines for the Practical Housewife* were made accessible to mothers.
Along with recuperation in the form of good wholesome food, rest, and exercise,
mothers learned about Nazi ideology, their place in the Nazi world-view and their
role in the 'national community'. Indeed, the aim of mothers' rest care was 'to
toughen up German women for their tasks in the house and family'. Staff observed

the mothers carefully and made reports about their conduct and attitudes. If they behaved in a 'cantankerous' or 'contrary' way, they were required to leave. The work of the recuperation homes ensured that mothers returned home with renewed vigour and spirit in order to undertake their familial tasks and duties. If, on their return home, mothers were still not quite ready to undertake all their household duties, home helps were sent to assist them for up to four weeks.

Letters from mothers expressing their gratitude to the NSV and the Führer were proudly used by the *Hilfswerk 'Mutter und Kind'* to demonstrate the success of its work. 'We live as in fairy tales … It is overwhelmingly beautiful here. I cannot put it into words … This trip, this experience will certainly count as the most beautiful memory of my life' (Pine 1997, 28). Another stated: 'I would like to thank the Führer heartily with the assurance that I am aware as a German woman and mother of my responsibility to look after my children … and to educate them into fit, useful people.' Men also wrote letters to the organization on behalf of their wives: 'She has put on 14 pounds, and the strength she was lacking before her trip has considerably come back again … March forward, NSV, flourish, prosper, and the nation will be healthy' (Pine 1997, 28).

Many women, exhausted physically by the demands of motherhood, enjoyed their time away. Others, though, were reluctant to go to recuperation homes or even outright refused to go because they had no desire to have a 'strange woman' run their household and 'snoop'; because they would not leave their children; or in rural areas because they refused to leave their land. Hence, the impact of Nazi welfare policies on women was not uniform. Furthermore, despite the intentions of the regime, the ideological atmosphere in the homes did not always meet the requirements of inspectors, where staff in recuperation homes either did not introduce politics into rest care or did not pressurize mothers to participate in ideological training if they preferred to sit in a garden chair and relax.

A network of help and advice centres was established throughout Germany to offer advice to mothers, and 25 552 centres had been set up by 1935. This number increased to 28 936 in 1941 (Pine 1997, 34). These were an important focus of *Hilfswerk 'Mutter und Kind'* work. However, reports about the advice centres in the city of Hamburg showed that in the first six months of their existence, they were mainly visited by men seeking financial support. The public perception of the centres changed over time and they came to be used for their intended purpose. They offered advice about all aspects of household management, nutrition, health, and baby- and childcare. The medical profession approved of the work of the advice centres as valuable aspects of state welfare. Educational work was of paramount significance in the advice centres as the staff had direct contact with members of the population. This point illustrates that National Socialist welfare measures were, as Mouton argues 'from the outset … intended to be interventionist' (Mouton 2007, 170). 'Beyond the material, financial and medical advice offered at advice centers, the Nazis also viewed the centers as agents for inculcating Nazi ideology and infused racial hygienic thought into all aspects of clinic life' (Mouton 2007, 171). They advocated *kinderreich* ('child-rich') families, of four or more children, claiming that children did not thrive in 'small families' with no or too few siblings.

21.4 'Inferior' Families

'More happiness, more relaxation, healthier mothers and children – that is the aim!' The *Hilfswerk 'Mutter und Kind'* emphasized its welfare work for mothers and children very strongly. However, as we have seen, welfare was applicable only to those mothers and children who were deemed to be 'hereditarily healthy' and racially pure, and those whose behaviour and lifestyles accorded with the dictates of the regime. Ginsborg rightly notes that: 'The Nazis laboriously developed the most systematic typology, from the early legislation against the "hereditarily unfit", to the discrimination against "asocial families", to the gathering crescendo against all members of racially inferior families' (Ginsborg 2003, 181). At the same time as the positive population policies directed towards fit members of the 'national community' occurred, the more blatantly sinister side of Nazi population policy was taking place. Legal measures were introduced to prevent marriages between Jews and 'Aryans' (Nuremberg Laws, September 1935); and to prevent marriages between healthy 'Aryans' and those deemed 'unfit' for marriage due to physical or mental illness (Marriage Health Law, October 1935). In order to marry, it was necessary to undergo a medical examination first. On passing this, the local health authorities issued a 'certificate of fitness to marry'. The regime was very strict about the implementation of these laws, for the children from 'undesirable' marriages would be 'inferior'. Sterilization was the principal method used by the Nazi regime to prevent people it considered 'undesirable' from having children. On 1 January 1934, a compulsory sterilization edict, the Law for the Prevention of Hereditarily Diseased Offspring, came into effect. It called for the mandatory sterilization of anyone that suffered from 'congenital feeble-mindedness, schizophrenia, manic depression, hereditary epilepsy, Huntington's chorea, hereditary blindness, hereditary deafness, serious physical deformities' and 'chronic alcoholism'. Between January 1934 and September 1939, approximately 320 000 people (0.5% of the population), were forcibly sterilized under the terms of this law (Pine 1997, 13). The majority of them were of German ethnicity, but were considered to be 'hereditarily ill' or simply 'feeble-minded' by the regime and its eugenic experts. The 'feeble-minded' made up two thirds of all those sterilized, of which about two thirds of these were women. Sterilized women became the objects of sexual abuse, especially in the cities, where soldiers or factory workers asked their colleagues on Mondays: 'Did you not find a sterilized woman for the weekend?' (Bock 1994, 238).

Nazi discrimination against 'asocials' spanned a whole course of actions, from the symbolic, such as excluding the mothers of 'asocial' families from the Cross of Honour of the German Mother, through compulsory sterilization, compulsory accommodation in 'asocial colonies', to internment in concentration camps, forced labour, and physical annihilation. The social policy of the regime reacted against all kinds of non-conformist behaviour, by the implementation of force and terror, and in many cases, ultimately, death. What was new in the Nazi state was the penetrating biological argument that proposed the 'elimination' of 'asocials' for the future. In this respect, the families of 'asocials' were directly affected, for, in 'asocial clans', negative traits of every kind – from speech defects to the suicide of distant relatives – were used to demonstrate that 'asociality' was hereditary. This was justification enough for members of 'asocial' families to be institutionalized and sterilized for 'congenital feeble-mindedness' or 'annihilated' just for existing at all. 'Gypsy' clans were doubly excoriated by the Nazi regime on account of their 'asociality' and their 'racial inferiority'. Germany's 'gypsy' population experienced wide-ranging discrimination and harassment during the Nazi era, culminating in their annihilation during the war. These families were considered not to belong to the German nation and were therefore expendable.

Germany's Jews were excluded from the 'national community' and were categorized as 'racially alien' and 'racially inferior'. Jewish families were subjected to a wide array of discriminatory policies throughout the Nazi period, culminating in the 'Final Solution'. There is no clear-cut correlation between the effects of persecution upon Jewish families and their responses to it in the period up to 1939 (Pine 1997, 178). In many cases, there is evidence to suggest that families pulled together, and that, in particular, the Jewish home provided a shelter against the discrimination and growing problems that individual family members had to face outside it. Yet, in other cases, the Jewish home seemed unable to shield its members from the situation, and tensions between spouses and between parents and children arose. Parents often felt unable to maintain their position as protectors of and providers for their offspring, and children sometimes experienced a loss of respect for their parents for not fulfilling this role. Such feelings presented themselves even more strikingly in the transit camps, concentration camps, and death camps, where children saw their parents in a different light imposed by the abnormal circumstances and by those in charge (Pine 1997, 178).

21.5 The Impact of the Second World War on Family Life

As Ginsborg notes, 'even for German Aryan families', the Nazi regime 'entailed their gradual splitting-up and maiming' (Ginsborg 2003, 179). The Second World War had profound implications and consequences for the German family. As fathers and sons were conscripted into the armed services, women were encouraged back into the workforce to replace them. The war created almost impossible circumstances for intimate and stable family life to be conducted. Many women who were accustomed to their husbands making decisions and dealing with family finances had to manage unaided. In rural areas, women had to cope with both their sources of livelihood and their families on their own, as farmers and male farm labourers were conscripted. In urban and industrial areas, women had to bear the strain of industrial work and maintain their families single-handedly. Female relatives, neighbours, and friends helped each other, providing mutual support and relief. Food rationing, bombings, and the destruction of gas and water supplies were among the difficulties experienced in daily life. Air raids disrupted life and many families were made homeless and dispossessed. Many women and children were evacuated from the cities to the countryside, and families became separated in the process. Almost four million German men had died in battle by the end of the war and many millions more were prisoners of war in 1945. Hence, the ultimate legacy of the Nazi regime and of the war to German family life was disastrous.

Vaizey's discussion of the wartime period examines the ways in which family members communicated with each other during periods of lengthy separation. She uses letters and diaries to show how families stayed in touch. Letters helped to bridge the gap of enforced separation in wartime. Of course, it was in the interests of the Nazi regime to maintain popular morale and so it did facilitate letter exchanges, although this process was subjected to heavy censorship. Vaizey maintains that despite the obstacles that confronted family members, they did maintain communication, which was 'crucial to family cohesion' (Vaizey 2010, 61). Through letter writing, spouses could convey to each other their own separate experiences of the war. Soldiers on the front gained comfort from the letters of their wives. Vaizey argues that even if emotional intensity in letters was not necessarily to be replicated in person, couples that communicated by letter 'had good reason to feel optimistic and committed to working on their marriage post-reunion' (Vaizey 2010, 59).

Moreover, in 1944, the *Reichsbund Deutsche Familie* (RDF or National Association of the German Family) established Letter Centres for the purpose of introducing young men and women. These were set up to counteract the decrease in the number of marriages taking place by this stage in the war. Their aim was to bring together 'racially and biologically perfect' young people in accordance with National Socialist principles and values. The first Letter Centre in Dresden received 26 000 letters within three months and appeared to correspond to a genuine need (Pine 1997, 97). As a result, Letter Centres were established in many large German cities to arrange correspondence between prospective marital partners. This was part of the organization's (and the regime's) aim to create new families and to persevere in population policy endeavours.

Despite such measures, Ginsborg notes how 'service to the state engulfed and destroyed families' in the war years (Ginsborg 2003, 196). Spouses worried about how their loved ones were faring under the conditions of the war: women feared for the lives of their husbands on the front; men were concerned about how their wives were managing at home without them, especially as they faced food shortages and air raids. Long periods of separation and scanty communication inevitably meant that some husbands and wives questioned each other's fidelity or were unfaithful. Others were looking forward to a time when they could be together again. Wartime letters show how couples were able to keep their relationships alive and give us an insight into the private world of their marriages. Whilst many letters were nostalgic about the past and painted a rosy picture of the future, some couples were very realistic about their situation. Vaizey notes that, 'As people learned to cope with less, they adjusted their outlooks accordingly' (Vaizey 2010, 92).

Without their men, women had to make decisions and engage in all sorts of different types of work and activities than previously. Their independence impacted upon their subsequent reunions with their husbands. The concept of women 'standing alone' on the home front during the war and the 'Hour of the Woman' after the war meant a new situation for married couples once men returned from the front. Despite the prevalent image in the historical literature of strong women, who dealt with the realities of war and subsequently cleared up the rubble, many women did feel vulnerable or were physically exhausted by the strains of life. Vaizey argues that ultimately they 'wanted to return to a sense of normality' (Vaizey 2010, 109). In the end, she maintains, changes in gender roles engendered by the circumstances of the war were not permanent ones, and power dynamics between spouses adjusted back to how they were previously.

Years of separation took their toll on family life. Both men and women were confronted with changes in the physical appearance of their partners. Feelings of reserve and alienation made it hard for many married couples to communicate with each other. In addition, it was difficult for them to recount painful experiences to each other. Other problems also contributed to the destabilization of families, such as sexual distance between spouses and difficulties in the relationships between children and their recently returned fathers. Many children were unable to recognize their fathers on their return home. Younger children, in particular, had often had no knowledge of their fathers, in some cases having only seen photographs of them. Elder sons, in the absence of their fathers, had become the confidants of their mothers and ersatz fathers to their siblings. With the homecoming of their fathers, there inevitably ensued a conflict about the recognition and maintenance of this status. Many fathers were unwilling to accept it and many sons were unwilling to give it up. Older children, in general, resented their fathers for treating them still as children, when they had been forced to grow up faster as a consequence of the war. They rebelled against and felt alienated from their fathers, which put mothers in the difficult position of trying to maintain some element of harmony and balance within the family.

21.6 Private Life

The subject of private life is always harder for historical investigation and this theme has so far not been adequately addressed in the literature on the Third Reich. Private life between 1933 and 1945 remains relatively unexplored. An inquiry into this area would develop our knowledge of life under National Socialism by looking at the relationship between people's lifestyles and the requirements of the Nazi government. To what extent did Nazism penetrate into the private life and choices of German citizens, in their family and social settings? How far did Nazi ideology invade the private realm of the family?

Encounters between private and public are difficult to ascertain from the documents historians have thus far used, that is, archival records from the National Socialist period. It is only possible to investigate this space through the use of alternative sources. National Socialism promised personal happiness to members of its 'national community' – those who fitted in. But how did that fit with state control? How were distinctions made between private and public?

It was difficult to maintain privacy and personal autonomy under the Nazi dictatorship. The negotiation of the separation of aspects of daily life that were private as opposed to public was difficult terrain. For example, radio listening had formerly been a private activity, yet under National Socialism it was one that was encouraged to be public. There was also a tension between other spare time or leisure activities that in normal times were private but, under National Socialism, became public, for example, attending art exhibitions. Currently, a large research project is underway at the Institute for Contemporary History in Munich, which covers a wide range of different themes pertaining to private life. These include 'mother happiness' and biopolitics – pregnant women and young mothers in the National Socialist dictatorship; and 'home leave' – soldiers between front, family, and the Nazi regime. These topics respectively examine the threshold between the private, domestic sphere and the state, and the threshold between the military and civil society.

Moritz Föllmer, in his work on individuality in Germany, has also made some inroads into analysis of the private life of the individual in the Nazi state. His research focuses on metropolitan life in Berlin. He contends that for most (non-Jewish) Berliners, 'Nazism was compatible with their respective self-interpretations, interests and desires – in short, with their identity as individuals' (Föllmer 2013, 101). Nevertheless, the relationship between the individual and the state was complex. Whilst Föllmer notes that the consequences of the Nazi dictatorship for the private realm were 'severe and ubiquitous', at the same time many Berliners believed that they enjoyed 'new options' under National Socialism (131, 107). In regard to private life, Föllmer concludes that 'ordinary domesticity' was 'widely desired but notoriously elusive' (179).

21.7   Conclusion

Whilst Nazi welfare measures were comparable to those introduced in other countries at around the same time, they differed in terms of their application within German society, as certain sections of the population were excluded from welfare measures on racial or eugenic grounds. As Ginsborg notes, the starting point for Nazi family policy was 'a profound distinction between approved and non-approved families' (Ginsborg 2014, 354). The goal was not, as Goebbels put it, 'children at any cost', but 'racially worthy, physically and mentally children of German families' (Ginsborg 2014, 359). Nazi policies spanned an array of initiatives from positive population policies, such as incentives aimed at encouraging early marriages between 'healthy' German couples, to the sterilization of the 'unfit' and the extermination of the 'undesirable'. Gisela Bock has shown that 'with respect to the "inferior", National Socialism pursued a policy not of family welfare but of family destruction' (Bock 1994, 247).

The Nazis' aims of an increased birth rate, racial homogeneity, and a regimented social life invaded the private domain of the family deeply. As Mary Nolan has argued: 'Few regimes have made as extensive an effort to penetrate, politicize and restructure the private, be it in terms of sociability, reproductive behavior, family life, or attitudes toward the relationship of individual to state and society' (Nolan 1997, 337). Hence, the home was not a safe haven insulated from National Socialism. In the end, the Nazis' recognition of the importance of the family was as a vehicle for their own aims, not as a social unit per se. Marriage and childbirth became racial duties, instead of personal decisions, as the Nazi regime systematically reduced the functions of the family to the single task of reproduction. As Ingeborg Weber-Kellermann has noted: 'In the name of restoring tradition, the Nazi state did more than any other regime to break down parental autonomy and to make the family simply a vehicle of state policy' (Weber-Kellermann 1991, 517). Quite contrary to their rhetoric about the restoration of the family, the National Socialists atomized family units, allowing for intrusion and intervention in everyday life. The Nazi regime undermined the family in an unprecedented way. Privacy, intimacy, and leisure were greatly threatened by the intervention of the Nazi regime into family life. The family under National Socialism became an institution for breeding and rearing children, with its relationships largely emptied of their emotional content. The regime subjected the family to intervention and control, reduced its socialization function, attempted to remove its capacity to shelter emotionally its members, and subjected it to racial ideology. The undermining of the family through racial policies and the policing of the family's daily life ultimately destroyed the private sphere, not only in physical and practical terms, but also morally and spiritually.

The legacy of the Second World War and of the Nazi regime meant that it was only in the 1950s that everyday family life began to regain any true sense of unity and concord. In 1953, the German Federal Republic set up a Ministry for Family Concerns, reflecting the family's status as a source of renewal and stability. The concept of the family as a place of refuge from the outside world came into being. The Second World War and its immediate aftermath had posed an exceptional threat to the family, but by the early 1950s, the family had regenerated, stabilized, and strengthened itself. Once again, it became a source of emotional support to its members, something it had not been permitted to be under the Hitler dictatorship.

References

Bock, Gisela. 1994. 'Antinatalism, Maternity and Paternity in National Socialist Racism.' In *Maternity and Gender Policies: Women and the Rise of the European Welfare States 1880s–1950s*, edited by Gisela Bock and Pat Thane, 233–255. London: Routledge.

Davidoff, Lenore, Doolittle, Megan, Fink, Janet, and Holden, Katherine. 1999. *The Family Story: Blood, Contract and Intimacy 1830–1960*. New York and London: Longman.

Föllmer, Moritz. 2013. *Individuality and Modernity in Berlin: Self and Society from Weimar to the Wall*. Cambridge: Cambridge University Press.

Frevert, Ute. 1989. *Women in German History: From Bourgeois Emancipation to Sexual Liberation*. Oxford and New York: Berg.

Ginsborg, Paul. 2003. 'The Family Politics of the Great Dictators.' In *Family Life in the Twentieth Century*, edited by David Kertzer and Marzio Barbagli, 174–197. New Haven, CT and London: Yale University Press.

Ginsborg, Paul. 2014. *Family Politics: Domestic Life, Devastation and Survival 1900 to 1950*. New Haven, CT and London: Yale University Press.

Mouton, Michelle. 2007. *From Nurturing the Nation to Purifying the Volk: Weimar and Nazi Family Policy, 1918–1945*. Cambridge and New York: Cambridge University Press.

Nolan, Mary. 1997. 'Work, Gender and Everyday Life: Reflections on Continuity, Normality and Agency in Twentieth-century Germany.' In *Stalinism and Nazism: Dictatorships in Comparison*, edited by Ian Kershaw and Moshe Lewin, 311–342. Cambridge: Cambridge University Press.

Pine, Lisa. 1997. *Nazi Family Policy, 1933–1945*. Oxford and New York: Berg.

Sieder, Reinhard. 1987. *Sozialgeschichte der Familie*. Frankfurt am Main: Suhrkamp.
Stephenson, Jill. 1975. *Women in Nazi Society*. London: Croom Helm.
Vaizey, Hester. 2010. *Surviving Hitler's War: Family Life in Germany, 1939–48*. Basingstoke, UK: Palgrave Macmillan.
Weber-Kellermann, Ingeborg. 1991. 'The German Family between Private Life and Politics.' In *A History of Private Life, Volume 5: Riddles of Identity in Modern Times*, edited by Antoine Prost and Gerard Vincent, 503–537. Cambridge, MA: Harvard University Press.

Further Reading

Davidoff, Lenore, Doolittle, Megan, Fink, Janet, and Holden, Katherine. 1999. *The Family Story: Blood, Contract and Intimacy 1830–1960*. New York and London: Longman.
This book gives a very useful introduction to the history and conceptualization of the family.
Ginsborg, Paul. 2014. *Family Politics: Domestic Life, Devastation and Survival 1900 to 1950*. New Haven, CTand London: Yale University Press.
This is a wide-ranging, comparative study of the history of the family in the main European dictatorships of the twentieth century.
Kertzer, David and Barbagli, Marzio, eds. 2003. *Family Life in the Twentieth Century*. New Haven, CT and London: Yale University Press.
This is a really useful overview of the history of the family in the twentieth century, with chapters provided by experts writing on experiences in different countries.
Mouton, Michelle. 2007. *From Nurturing the Nation to Purifying the Volk: Weimar and Nazi Family Policy, 1918–1945*. Cambridge and New York: Cambridge University Press.
This is a fine book, which treats Weimar and Nazi family policies in a single volume.
Pine, Lisa. 1997. *Nazi Family Policy, 1933–1945*. Oxford and New York: Berg.
This was the first major monograph on the history of the family in Nazi Germany published in English.
Sieder, Reinhard. 1987. *Sozialgeschichte der Familie*. Frankfurt am Main: Suhrkamp.
This is an important German book that treats the social history of the family in Germany.
Steber, Martina and Gotto, Bernhard, eds. 2014. *Visions of Community in Nazi Germany: Social Engineering and Private Lives*. Oxford: Oxford University Press.
This is a useful and cutting-edge edited volume, with important historical essays on society and life in the Third Reich.
Vaizey, Hester. 2010. *Surviving Hitler's War: Family Life in Germany, 1939–48*. Basingstoke, UK: Palgrave Macmillan.
This book provides a wealth of material on the history of the German family during the Second World War.
Weber-Kellermann, Ingeborg. 1974. *Die deutsche Familie: Versuch einer Sozialgeschichte*. Frankfurt am Main: Suhrkamp.
This book provides an important social history of the German family.
Weber-Kellermann, Ingeborg. 1991. 'The German Family between Private Life and Politics'. In *A History of Private Life, Volume 5: Riddles of Identity in Modern Times*, edited by Antoine Prost and Gerard Vincent, 503–537. Cambridge, MA: Harvard University Press.
This chapter ably examines the family within the context of National Socialism.

CHAPTER TWENTY-TWO

Sports

FRANK BECKER

22.1 Introduction: Sports and *Volksgemeinschaft*

The defining argument used by National Socialism to describe the German community was the concept of *Volksgemeinschaft*. This compound word combines the terms *Volk* (people) and *Gemeinschaft* (community), each of which served a different purpose: *Volk* addressed the inclusion or exclusion from the collective, *Gemeinschaft* signified the desired kind of communion with the group. *Volk* included all those who could claim the same descent as Germans, Nordic people, or 'Aryans'. Choosing a biological approach to race radicalized the traditional concept of nation, while at the same time extending and blurring it. The call for a community implied a disassociation from the concept of society, which was criticized as being one-sidedly rational, even mechanical. Instead, the collective experience of people was to be marked by a deeply felt togetherness. Knowing one was bound to a common destiny led to a fundamental equalization and equality of treatment, which – in the perception of the National Socialists – harmonized with the 'leadership principle' (*Führerprinzip*) in so far as anyone's authority in decision making was linked to their full responsibility for the welfare of the followers.

Recent research emphasizes the importance of the concept of *Volksgemeinschaft*, stating that the years from 1933 to 1945 cannot be understood without taking this principle into account, because it structured both National Socialists' ideas and actions (von Reeken and Thießen 2013). Since it is difficult to find a more adequate analytical concept, the term *Volksgemeinschaft* is also used as a concept in research. While this practice is understandable, it also requires extraordinary diligence in keeping the source language separate from the analytical language. In this chapter, the history of athletics in the National Socialist era[1] is examined using the

A Companion to Nazi Germany, First Edition. Edited by Shelley Baranowski,
Armin Nolzen, and Claus-Christian W. Szejnmann.
© 2018 John Wiley & Sons Ltd. Published 2018 by John Wiley & Sons Ltd.

perspective of the concept of *Volksgemeinschaft*. What role do sports play within this concept, and which functions were assigned to them? Compared to the assumptions found in previous studies, the present analysis reveals a significantly deeper impact of sports on National Socialism, making clear that sports had to fulfil a variety of functions required by the National Socialist state. Listing these functions according to their importance turns out to be as difficult as clearly setting them off from one another – many aspects are deeply entwined. Hence, the order in which these functions are presented may appear to be rather random. In the end, we are dealing with a field of forces, in which every particle acts on to the others depending on its charge, so that it could be described from the perspective of any single particle.

22.2   The Concept of the Human

In principle, the meaning of sports is open to interpretation. Consequently, National Socialists were able to construe it in their own interest. In doing so, they set off the *vita active*, which seemed to be represented by sports, from a more contemplative concept of life. In sports, the National Socialists' guiding image (*Leitbild*) of a decisive person of action came across vividly and was realized in practice. In the eyes of the National Socialists, athletes differed from rational persons whose excessive reflection got in the way of decisive action, and made them stumble over themselves. By contrast, an athlete was, in principle, always ready to act. Quick action is one of the main virtues in sports, since decisions must be taken within microseconds. In order to take quick action, willpower is needed. An athlete, existing entirely in the here and now, needs courage as well as assertiveness.

Since competition demands constant comparison with the opponent, sports embody a model of competition that can be related to social Darwinism. Wherever there is competition, everybody must constantly work on their performance, or else they will succumb to their competitors. Persons who have been drilled for competition in sports internalize a life principle which they will encounter in all spheres of existence. This applies at an individual as well as a collective level: individuals need to prevail in environments defined by struggle, much like organizations and institutions – even whole nations, peoples, and races – which need to assert themselves and compete for life chances.

National Socialism's equal emphasis on the individual and the group necessitated an important decision regarding the politics of sports, shortly after the party's rise to power in 1933. For decades, sports in Germany had been defined by a 'fraternal struggle' between two different kinds of physical culture: between gymnastics, which went back to the Wars of Liberation in the early nineteenth century, and 'Sport', which had been imported from England only recently, at the end of the nineteenth century. Ever since its beginnings, gymnastics had been deeply rooted within German national culture, so that leading officials in gymnastics, such as Edmund Neuendorff, hoped for special privileges after Hitler was elected chancellor. The disappointment ensuing from the National Socialist regime's predilection for 'Sport' was considerable. The decision was certainly related to the fact that 'Sport' valued personal initiative – and therefore every single athlete – just as highly as it valued accomplishments attained by a team, while the focus in gymnastics lay one-sidedly on team spirit. In addition, the popularity of sports had already been proven during the Weimar Republic, by an enormous increase in participation, which the new rulers were keen to exploit.

22.3 Forming the Body

The National Socialists transformed 'maintenance of the race' (*Rassenpflege*) and 'race-based eugenics' (*Rassenhygiene*) into a duty of the *Volksgemeinschaft*. This meant that everybody had to be aware of physically belonging to the *Volkskörper* ('people's body'), and that the latter could only be healthy, strong, and beautiful as long as every single body had these same attributes. As a result, the pursuit of sports was transformed from an individually chosen activity into a moral obligation to the community. Thus, the National Socialists employed the political concept of a physical education: taking care of the population's physical make-up was a pre-eminent political issue, since a weakened or 'degenerate race' (*degenerierte Rasse*) would not be able to prevail in the competition between peoples.

While other measures of the National Socialist regime were meant to influence the genetic pool itself – for instance, euthanasia and eugenics, even the entire policy of racial segregation – sports were to make an impact on the phenotype: shaping those bodies already existent. Herein, health, strength, and beauty formed an indissoluble unity. Without health there could be no strength, and only a healthy and strong body could in turn be beautiful (Wildmann 1998). For anyone to be included in the *Volksgemeinschaft*, they had to strive to fulfil these criteria, while exclusion from it was justified by declaring a failure to conform to them. Antisemitic propaganda always relied on depicting Jews as being physically weak, deformed, and ugly. Jews, as well as other enemies of the regime, were wilfully disfigured so as to symbolically exclude them from the *Volksgemeinschaft* – one need only to think of the concentration camp prisoners, who by malnutrition were reduced to decrepit figures, and whose hair was shaven off to further worsen their appearance.

In contrast, the health, strength, and beauty of those belonging to the *Volksgemeinschaft* were paraded on a large scale. Every organization within the Nazi regime hosted sports events on a regular basis, intended to show off the results of their particular physical education institution. A particular favourite was crowds of people performing *tableaux vivants* – performances displaying a large number of athletes in concerted action. This was a form of representation with a long tradition in the history of gymnastics and sports. During the nineteenth century, their purpose had been to portray the concept of the nation; during the Weimar Republic, they had been performed on Constitution Day, in order to promote democracy (Rossol 2010). National Socialism reinterpreted them as exhibitions of the *Volksgemeinschaft*'s performance. The synchronized masses of bodies symbolized what the people were able to achieve when united by a common purpose and following a single leader.

Sports provided key images not only in order to have a normative effect on the population. In addition, they offered the opportunity to make an empirical survey of the physical condition of the population. A number of performance tests provided statistical material that served as a basis for new interventions. The Stormtroopers (*Sturmabteilung*, SA) sports badge became one of the main level indicators. Around three million men underwent this performance test between 1933 and 1945, making it possible to create graphs analysing the performance of those who were tested. The results of the analysis provided true values as well as the opportunity to work towards 'normal values' that would reflect the desired average performance (Felsch 2001, 8, 11, 23–26).

22.4   Bodily Experience and 'Racial Identity'

The National Socialist understanding of playing sports includes yet another dimension related to race and the body: personal experience. Any kind of physical enhancement through training (*Leibesertüchtigung*) was meant to add a sense of racial identity to physical experience. After all, the basis for classifying someone as belonging to a racial community was the body with its 'blood characteristics' and the genetic programming that defined the racial community to which a person belonged. It was when playing sports that a person became most intensely aware of their body – and thereby of the substantial racial-biological basis of their being. In consequence, at least in extreme cases, sports could even acquire a cultic and quasi-religious quality (Wedemeyer-Kolwe 2012, 459–472). Thus, it was even more important that only those of the same 'race' get together to play sports; 'strangers to the race' (*Rassenfremde*) would only interfere with rituals in which the *Volksgemeinschaft* conjured their common ancestry.

22.5   Antisemitism

The Jews were the *Rassenfremde* excluded in this manner. Their exclusion was carried out in several steps. Soon after the NSDAP (*Nationalsozialistische Deutsche Arbeiterpartei*, Nazi Party) was granted power in January of 1933, many sports clubs and associations adopted 'Aryan clauses' that banned Jews from their midst. The German Gymnastics Federation (*Deutsche Turnerschaft*) excluded Jews as early as April 1933 (Peiffer 2011, 218). The initiative for these measures was taken by the organizations themselves, in anticipatory obedience: at this time there existed no directive from the state that would have forced them to act as they did. The fact that some sports clubs and associations were able to evade anti-Jewish restrictions for a prolonged period of time is proof that alternatives were in fact possible.

Antisemitism was widespread in the German gymnastics and sports movement, even before 1933. This is true not only for the ordinary rank-and-file members, but also for many top-level administrators. The private writings of some of the actors clearly show their antisemitism, even though they often refrained from articulating it openly in order to protect their careers: officially, antisemitism was frowned upon during the Kaiserreich and the Weimar Republic. Nevertheless, we must differentiate between Wilhelmine antisemitism motivated by socio-cultural arguments, and the deterministic antisemitism of the National Socialists, rooted in racial biology. While the first permitted the acceptance of assimilated Jews, the latter's image of the enemy (*Feindbild*) also included them, because for the National Socialists, alleged racial characteristics remained in place regardless of the kind of life chosen by the individual. Carl Diem, for instance, general secretary of the umbrella association for German sports during the Weimar Republic, the German Reich Commission for Physical Exercise (*Deutscher Reichsausschuss für Leibesübungen*, DRA), and organizer of the 1936 Summer Olympics, was antisemitic in the Wilhelmine sense, and did not embrace the antisemitism of the National Socialists (Becker 2009a, 148–150, 2011, 94–95, 248; Schäfer 2011a, 254, 258–261, 355–357, 2011b, 254–258).

The Aryan clauses (*Arierparagraphen*) caused massive shifts within German Jewish sports. While the majority of German Jews who engaged in sports during the Kaiserreich and the Weimar Republic were affiliated to clubs of the sports and gymnastics movement of the time, and only a minority to Jewish clubs, after 1933 the latter practically became a catchment basin for Jewish German athletes. Thus an alternative world was created, in which the athletes contradicted the National Socialist propaganda cliché of the physically weak Jew by their very participation in sports. An analysis of the Jewish press reveals that the sports movement constantly grew in significance within the spectrum of German Jewish cultural activities. German Jews drew belief in their own power and future from sports activities and preoccupation with sports.

Jewish sports functionaries employed the knowledge about organizations they had acquired in the gymnastics and sports movement as they extended their own sports clubs and even set up their own competitions. Until 1936, Jewish and 'Aryan' clubs could compete against each other. After the Summer Olympics in Berlin, however, these competitions were forbidden, since there was no longer any need to consider repercussions abroad. Even more severe was the cut inflicted by the pogrom on 9 November 1938, following which German Jews were deprived of the last of their possibilities to train and compete. The final blow was the official prohibition of activities at the end of 1938/beginning of 1939 (Wahlig 2015, 211).

There is even a sports history aspect to the history of the persecution and murder of the Jews during the Second World War. Concentration camp guards employed a form of physical harassment of concentration camp prisoners which demands special attention, since it took the interaction of sports, antisemitism, and exclusion to the extreme. In order to decide whether the inmates were still able to work, the Protective Squads (*Schutzstaffeln*, SS) tested them in sports: if they were not able to perform a certain number of push-ups or sit-ups in a given amount of time, it was practically a death sentence. To fail physically meant not to be fit for work, which in turn meant that those who failed the tests were sent to the gas chambers (Springmann 2014, 244–245.). Concentration camp guards cynically used the ability to perform athletically (a criterion for inclusion into the *Volksgemeinschaft*) as a measure of their victims' right to live.

22.6 Education

In accordance with their demand for a 'New Man', National Socialists strove for the transformation of education. They held that previous pedagogy had focused too much on mental abilities. Their argument ran as follows: anyone who understood that character traits were the immediate outcome of a person's physical strengths and weaknesses, while at the same time considering that intellectually endowed persons who lacked physical strength and determination were unable to assert themselves, would inevitably reach the conclusion that people had to be educated by way of their body. Only a strong body combined with an iron will would procure the resilience which enabled a person of action to make quick decisions. Only on this basis could a sharp intellect come into its own. Consequently, sports assumed a high priority for National Socialist pedagogy. The National Socialists wanted sports to step out of the shadow existence they had led alongside the humanistic school subjects, and be recognized as their equals in the schools. Sports were also to be taught more often: since 1935, boys' secondary schools had prescribed three hours of physical training per week; for the school year 1937/1938, training was supposed to take place daily. It is uncertain whether daily classes were in fact implemented, as many schools lacked competent teachers, sports equipment, and playing fields. The prescription itself, however, clearly demonstrates the importance of this goal.

The regime's elite schools, the Adolf Hitler Schools (*Adolf-Hitler-Schulen*, AHS) and National Political Institutes of Education (*Nationalpolitische Erziehungsanstalten*, Napola), which had outstanding equipment, provided more possibilities. Here, an additional focus was laid on the idea that physical training had to be linked to training valour, an idea which had already been upheld by the early gymnastics movement. Apart from its positive impact on health, the connection of sports to valour should never be lost from sight: practice and competitions always include the danger of pain, injury, and physical damage. The pedagogical perception was that by not evading this danger, people who practised sports tempered their character. At both AHS and Napola, regular sports classes were supplemented by exercises that resembled rituals which were meant to prove toughness and courage. One example of such an exercise was, in winter, swimming in ice holes of frozen lakes.[2]

Universities were places where the danger of a one-sided mental attitude towards life seemed most likely. If, however, future academics became weaklings, they would not be able to fulfil their tasks in life and – contrary to the idea of the *Volksgemeinschaft* – their physical appearance would divide them from other social strata. If, instead, they practised sports, they would develop the same habitus as all their fellow *Volksgenossen*, who also underwent schooling in physical education. The National Socialist state implemented the obligatory practice of sports during the first three semesters at universities, in 1934. By doing this, they were continuing a development which had already been started during the Weimar Republic. A nationalistic – increasingly also National Socialist – student body prepared themselves for civil war or war through a self-organized sports programme. At the same time, many Reich territories had promoted the creation of institutes for physical activities at their universities, where sports were taught as a science and were studied as a regular subject. Those institutes already had the coaches needed for the students' obligatory sports practice during the National Socialist period. Especially in 1933/1934, these trainers were supported by representatives of the SA Offices of Higher Education (Bach 1991, 57–71).

Sports were part of the education of both boys and girls. Previous research was based on the premise that girls and women were urged to practise sports in order to improve their 'capacity for giving birth': if a woman was seen merely as house-wife and mother, it seemed to fit that physical education should prepare her for her role. Recent research has considerably altered and corrected this perception. The part assigned to women in National Socialist Ideology was threefold: women had to fulfil the biological task of reproduction as well as take on the responsibilities identified with the social role of a 'mother': welfare and health care, education and counselling. But they had also to be able to deal with a possible war situation on the home front and perform as needed at work and in providing for families – something that women had already been required to do during the First World War. The 'fighting *Volksgemeinschaft*' included the female part of the population. Consequently, the objective of physical education for girls and women was to promote the characteristics needed for a broad range of life tasks. Toughness, determination, and decision making were considered as indispensable for the education of girls as they were for the education of boys.

22.7 Organized Popular Sports

Prior to 1933, all sports organized in clubs and associations were split into various factions. Middle-class sports were represented by the DRA, and stood in opposition to the workers' sports movement, while the confessional division of the country was expressed by the rivalry of the Catholic association German Youth Power (*Deutsche Jugendkraft*, DJK), and the Protestant Oak Cross Bearers (*Eichenkreuzler*, EK). Whoever wanted to practise a certain kind of sport could choose to do this either in a middle-class, a proletarian, a Catholic, or a Protestant association. In addition, they could select from the offers made by the *Deutsche Turnerschaft*, which in practice had long been opened up for popular sports. Under these circumstances, sports officials in the Weimar Republic had been constantly challenged in their efforts to organize games and contests. Spectators had to accept the fact that Germany could not have 'the one' champion team or 'the one' record holder, but only the champion of middle-class sports or the top rankings of workers' sports.

When the National Socialists, in 1933, claimed to bridge any chasm within German society, and, by attaining unity, to unfold a maximum of national strength, the disruptions in sports must have seemed like a thorn in their sides. They installed a unitary administration led first by a Sports Commissioner of the Reich (*Reichssportkommissar*) and later by a Sports Leader of the Reich (*Reichssportführer*), the man elected to the post being Hans von Tschammer und Osten. Under his direction, all previous sports associations split by their ideological preferences were gathered into unitary management departments. Henceforth, the maxim was that any kind of sports could only be practised in *one* association, that is, in the corresponding management department within the so-called *Deutscher Reichsbund für Leibesübungen* (DRL), which was the name of the new unitary association.[3]

This policy of unification applied in particular to the workers' sports movement. Other organizations were either prohibited – in their previous political orientation – or integrated into new structures. Workers' associations that were willing to comply with the system could, in a practical sense, continue working with the same personnel, but within a different ideological framework. Each successful transfer strengthened the NSDAP, which claimed to be the one, true workers' party. To irrupt into the workers' sport milieu meant to irrupt into the whole of the socialist milieu.[4] It was one of the regime's main objectives during the phase of coordination to estrange the workers' sport milieu from the workers' parties (SPD and KPD), and to win them over for the project of the *Volksgemeinschaft*.

Another incision in the history of German sports clubs was made in 1938. In this year, the DRL was declared a sponsored organization (*betreuter Verband*) of the NSDAP, and was renamed the National Socialist Reich League for Physical Exercise (*Nationalsozialistischer Reichsbund für Leibesübungen*, NSRL).[5] Researchers have explained this step by referring to the DRL's need to seek protection under the umbrella of the party. This need arose in view of the heavy competition represented by National Socialist mass organizations which sustained their own sports organizations. The association was possible since the SS's sports apparatus itself needed assistance in their disputes with the SA. However, the NSRL had to pay a price for its new positioning within the structures of power of the National Socialist state. It had to hand over to SS officials several of the leading positions in the different management departments (Bahro 2013, 266–269).

The head of the NSRL changed twice during the war. The first reappointment became necessary when Tschammer died, in March 1943. Even though the SS tried to launch their own candidate, the post went to Tschammer's deputy, Arno Breitmeyer. Breitmeyer, however, stayed in the position only until he reported back to the Wehrmacht, in September 1944. He was succeeded by Karl Ritter von Halt, former decathlete and track and field functionary, who was a member of the NSDAP, the SA, and the Circle of Friends of the Reichsführer SS (*Freundeskreis Reichsführer SS*). Given the significant decrease of sports management activities, the tasks of the *Reichssportführer* shrank considerably towards the final phase of the war.

There were a large number of DRL/NSRL management departments. This chapter will focus only on soccer, since it has received particular attention in recent research[6] that has led to a powerful controversy. On the one hand, researchers hold the view that soccer fully supported National Socialist ideology (Heinrich 2000, 122–162). According to this view, soccer, as a highly physical team sport, had already been turned into a symbol for the struggle for survival of the *Volksgemeinschaft* in the Weimar Republic (Oswald 2008, 65–91). On the other hand, other historians have explained the cooperation of the soccer players with the National Socialist state differently: not as a perfect ideological fit, but as the result of the responsible leaders' opportunistic search for admission wherever there seemed to be a promise of money and prestige (Havemann 2005).

After 1933, a substantial sports business set up by the mass organizations of the National Socialist state came to exist alongside the traditional sports clubs and associations. While the dominant focus of the SA lay in defensive sports,[7] the interest of the SS and the Hitler Youth (*Hitlerjugend*, HJ) also encompassed competitive sports. After the 1936 Summer Olympics, both organizations made the resolution to send their own contestants to future Olympic Games. Grassroots sport was promoted as well: any member of the SS had to practise some sort of sport and, if given the opportunity, to regularly acquire the sports badge of the Reich (*Reichssportabzeichen*). Himmler himself led by example, although it seems that his results may have been favourably altered (Bahro 2013, 105–106).

The SS focused mainly on three sports: motorsports, fencing, and equitation. While motorsports were associated with the bourgeois elite, fencing and riding related to aristocratic traditions. All three of them expressed elite consciousness. Dominating figures were, in fencing, Reinhard Heydrich, who headed the Reich Main Security Office (*Reichssicherheitshauptamt*, RSHA) until his death in June 1942; in riding, Hermann Fegelein, who during the final weeks of war belonged to Hitler's entourage in Berlin. Both Heydrich and Fegelein were top officials and active athletes who excelled in their achievements, and seemingly lived up to the National Socialist model of 'leadership by the best'. Fegelein especially was regarded as the SS man par excellence, given the pairing of his achievements in sports with military awards. He wanted the riding associations of the SS to play a significant role: while the time of the cavalry had seemed to be over since the end of the First World War, Fegelein assigned them the task of fighting partisans on impassable grounds. The SS riders perpetrated numerous war crimes on these assignments (Fahnenbruck 2013, 294–312), but were hardly ever prosecuted after the war. Whenever they mentioned that they had been members of the riding SS, they were regarded as mere athletes who had not been active in any relevant area within the National Socialist rule – a striking example of how the meaning of sports for National Socialism has long been underestimated or downplayed in order to protect particular interests.

Athletics were an integral part of the education programme of the Hitler Youth. The activities covered a broad spectrum, from Olympic disciplines to outdoor games that overstepped the boundaries of the paramilitary (Buddrus 2003, 224–249). The sports practised in the League of German Girls (*Bund Deutscher Mädel*, BDM) also included some that require a lot of strength, like rowing. In addition, the BDM offered disciplines like fencing with a floret and shooting with small calibre weapons which prepared girls for the use of weapons (Sauer-Burghard 2008, 39–42). Women were not actually considered for direct combat. Still, the handling of fencing weapons and rifles did alter the female habitus: aggression was now permitted and physical confrontation enjoyed. HJ and BDM championships took place in regular intervals, which helped to root sports deeply in the consciousness of their members (Becker 2009b, 208–209).

National Socialist propaganda laid much emphasis on the opportunities which the HJ and the BDM – along with other National Socialist mass organizations – offered its members. As members of these organizations they were able to perform 'expensive' kinds of sports which would not have been accessible to them in a middle-class life: all necessary equipment and installations were available to anyone affiliated to the organizations. Class differences within the *Volksgemeinschaft* were to be eradicated even in regard to preferred sport activities. For example, young people whose parents were not well situated could now dedicate themselves to an activity like gliding, if they became members of the Flying HJ (*Flieger-HJ*). In reality, however, these offers remained very rare because of their cost.

From August 1936, boys and girls between the ages of 10 and 14 were no longer allowed to play sports in the traditional clubs, but were either integrated into the *Jungvolk* (boys) or the *Jungmädelbund* (girls). Older youths and members of the HJ and the BDM were generally not interested in becoming members of an additional club, since they already enjoyed an attractive range of athletic activities. In consequence, the divisions for youths in the sports clubs suffered a heavy loss of members. The fact that the DRL started to look for associates in the competition with other 'sports providers', in the late 1930s, was in part due to this experience.

22.8   Work and Leisure

Athletics is evidently linked to the military; however, its close relation to other social areas must be kept in mind. In connection to the National Socialist era, research had previously been inclined to describe sports as totally married to war. However, this perspective fails to recognize how sports in those times also played an important role in relation to work, productivity, and regeneration. Sports and work science had already been collaborating during the Weimar Republic. Both disciplines studied similar problems. How could motion be optimized? How could fatigue be minimized? How could nutrition help achieve maximum performance? Preoccupation with the *Volkskörper* also meant a focus on the worker's body. On the one hand, the body of a worker had to be able to perform at the highest possible level; on the other hand, in order to prevent premature deterioration the body could not be overstressed, therefore all effort needed to be counterbalanced with sufficient time for regeneration. Every National Socialist organization dedicated to issues concerning either work or leisure somehow involved sports. The German Labour Front (*Deutsche Arbeitsfront*, DAF) promoted sports activities within companies; the department for Beauty of Labour (*Schönheit der Arbeit*) built sports facilities directly on the companies' grounds; so-called *Sportappelle* took the employees out into the fresh air for physical activities (Luh 1998, 208–337). Planning joint sports activities was meant to transform groups of co-workers into working communities. The time that persons of different hierarchic levels spent together promoted the ideology of a 'workers' front' built in communion. Work accidents lessened, since sports improve mental presence and quick reaction. Altogether, the engagement of the workforce in physical activities refined their skills, improved their health, and helped them to recover their freshness for work.

The organization of leisure time came to stand alongside the National Socialist regulation and control of work life. Italian fascism set the example: their free time organization was named Opera Nazionale Dopolavoro. After work, when companies' doors were closed for the night, no individual was to be left to him- or herself. Instead, anyone could partake in a leisure programme designed to reconnect them with their fellow workers and to showcase the *Volksgemeinschaft*. The name chosen for the German counterpart to Dopolavoro represented the programme itself: 'Strength through Joy' (*Kraft durch Freude*, KdF). It conveyed the idea that a joyfully experienced free time would help people return to their workplaces with renewed strength. Aside from after-work evening activities, the organizations offered opportunities for travel. Also, sports activities played an important role. The expectations, however, were kept low, there was no pressure to perform; instead, the intention was to have joyful get-togethers where the *Volksgemeinschaft* could be united and enjoy play and sports. It goes without saying that the resulting improvement in both health and capacity for work was a desired side effect. The enormous quantity of coaches required by KdF provided jobs and incomes for many sports graduates (with diplomas or state exams) who would have hardly had a chance for employment during the later Weimar Republic.[8]

22.9 Performative Aspects: the Self-Representation of the *Volksgemeinschaft*

The *Volksgemeinschaft* was an idea and had to be made palpable. As a concept that was constantly conjured, a concept that was to constantly guide action, it had to be perceived by the senses at least every now and then. The outstanding role of the Nuremberg Nazi Party rallies (*Reichsparteitage*) has often been pointed out in this context. However, the aspect of sports involved has not received the same attention, even though athletic performances were a standard within the festivities' programme in Nuremberg. There existed plans for a gigantic stadium on the National Socialist Party's rally grounds, designed to accommodate 400 000 spectators (Teichler 1991, 292).

The National Socialist regime used the 1936 Olympic Games, first the Winter Games in Garmisch-Partenkirchen, later the Summer Games in Berlin, as a means to showcase the *Volksgemeinschaft*. All Germany was to partake of its symbolism during the Olympics. In order to achieve this, considerable efforts were made to broadcast the sporting events in all available media. Radio was broadcasting them live via the new ultra-short wave. In Berlin, they could even be heard in public spaces, where loudspeakers had been installed for this very purpose (Becker 2009b, 136). There also were other means to anchor the sporting event in people's everyday lives: visitors to the Olympics from abroad were accommodated by German host families. Every member of the *Volksgemeinschaft*, the so-called *Volksgenosse*, could contribute to some extent, even if only by cheering on the German athletes with whom the people were supposed to identify: their athletic achievements were the achievements of the German *Volk*.

Many countries – foremost the United States of America – started to boycott the Nazi Games directly after the NSDAP was granted the power. Aside from wanting to set an example against the discrimination of Jews in Germany, their intention was to prevent giving National Socialist propaganda opportunities inside and outside the country which the sporting event would amply provide. The Germans countered this movement early, in May 1933. At the IOC (International Olympics Committee) Congress in Vienna, they promised not to ban Jews on principle from participating in the games. This declaration, however, allowed the possibility of disqualifying Jews in the case of unsatisfactory performances, and in this regard, the ever-worsening training conditions for Jewish athletes in Germany helped the regime. The boycott movement failed when, by the end of 1935, the Americans decided to participate in the Olympics. It would not have needed to fail, had not the IOC been extremely ready to cooperate with Germany. The IOC's examination of the situation of the Jewish athletes was merely a means for saving face: in the end, it was deemed satisfactory to have single 'alibi Jew' Helene Mayer on the German Olympic team (Large 2007, 69–109).

22.10   Culture of the Masses

Fascist states were searching for new artistic expressions that would break with middle-class traditions and live up to the image of the 'New Man'. No longer was it to be individuals, expressing their subjective views of the world and their unique set of emotions, who would stand in the centre of attention. The focus now lay on the community, which dealt with the challenges of its time. The culture in demand was no longer a culture of interiority and passivity, the so-called *Stubenhocker*-culture ('couch potato' culture) of the nineteenth century, but a culture which was active, related to the present, and which united all social strata. A connection to the masses could be established via the new technical media, radio and film. Just as important were the masses co-present at big party and sporting events: mass event performances on fields and in stadiums were considered an art form in their own right, and the interaction between leaders and masses was showcased like a ritual (Lissinna 1997). National Socialism regarded its mass events (including sports events), as total works of art (*Gesamtkunstwerke*), and practically any participant could consider themselves an artist.

22.11   External Effect

On the one hand, sport had an internal effect as it fulfilled certain functions for the *Volksgemeinschaft*. On the other hand, it had an external effect as it conveyed to the world a specific image of the Germans and their ability to perform. The latter task fell mainly to competitive sports, which were in the hand of the DRL, respectively the NSR, even though over time the SS started to develop their own ambitions in this area. Demonstrating the performance of the 'Nordic race' meant, first of all, great athletic achievements. The German victory, in the evaluation of the nations in the 1936 Summer Olympics, corresponded almost perfectly with this objective. There were, however, other competitions in which the athletes of the host country had to accept sensible defeats – even totalitarian dictatorships cannot control the outcomes of competitions at will. So, the demonstration of the attitude of the 'master race' (*Herrenmenschentum*) on the sports grounds always remained subject to risk.

It was safer to bet on the 'good impression' that German athletes were able to make abroad, when they presented themselves as sanguine, friendly, and disciplined. As such they were meant to serve as ambassadors of the Third Reich. This form of image advertising was valuable during the time of peace from 1933 to 1939, but became even more important during the war, in situations when they needed to influence the public in neutral countries. For example, every so often teams were sent to Sweden in order to preserve the good will of this important source of raw materials towards Hitler's state (Teichler 1991, 271–273, 295–300). Equally important were the sports-related connections to Finland. While Finland actually belonged to the group of friendly powers, it had been affronted by the Hitler–Stalin Pact, which had led to its being attacked by the Soviet Union in the winter of 1939/1940. However, a competition between the three countries, Germany, Finland, and Sweden, held in September 1940 in Helsinki, aided the rapprochement (Becker 2009b, 207–208). Yet another effect of propaganda consisted in Germany's display of strength as it continued to fulfil its athletic engagements. After all, a country that was fighting a world war and could still spare people for athletics had to have enormous resources (Becker 2009b, 236).

22.12   Disposition to Fight

It is evident that people who played sports increased their physical strength and were thereby more apt for military tasks. The same applies to the transformation of habitus which was intended by promoting sports, that is, to improve quick action, speed, and decision making. In addition, modern warfare almost always implied the handling of machines, which was helped by motor sports and aviation. It was now possible to experience dynamics and speed in a way that, especially under the circumstances of war, referenced the fascist topos of a dangerous life – which was to be preferred to middle-class security. The concept behind the blitzkrieg consisted in transferring this model to the general strategy of warfare. The fact that public talk and analysis of the events of the war were often conveyed using sports metaphors is not surprising when seen in this context. Even the letters from soldiers and ordinary sports club members often draw parallels between war and sports (Cachay, Bahlke, and Mehl 2000, 222–353, esp. 239–242). Prominent athletes who fought in the war demonstrated in a practical way the closeness between these two realities, as did world boxing champion Max Schmeling when he participated in the spectacular attack of the German paratroopers on Crete in May 1941. In 1941, Carl Diem proposed setting up sport regiments that would be able to follow advancing tanks in endurance runs (Becker 2009b, 206). Conversely, soldiers like undersea divers developed abilities in specialized areas that allowed them to perceive themselves as top athletes. It was generally true that the armed forces profited from the findings provided by sports science. The science of the body and its performance, a young science at the time, resolved questions about strain, fatigue, and nutrition and helped in the rehabilitation of the wounded and maimed.[9]

The Second World War had an impact on the sports politics of the National Socialist regime. During the first phase of the war, attempts were made to extract profit from Germany's temporary power position. In 1940, the IOC was to be brought under control; in 1942, a European Sports Conference was to be held. Both attempts were intended to increase German influence on international sports (Teichler 1991, 291–295, 328–331) and both came to nothing. The IOC ceased its activities until the end of the war, and the European Sports Conference failed.

The failure was due on the one hand to quarrels among the heads of the National Socialist regime and on the other, to rivalry with Germany's Axis partner Italy (Becker 2009b, 236–237).

There has been very little research on the sports administration of the zones either annexed or ruled by the Germans, or occupied by the German military. The available studies indicate that the National Socialist state built different structures depending on each case and the kind of interests connected to the area in question. After the annexation of Alsace-Lorraine, in 1940, there followed a complete transfer of the sports system of the German Reich to the new regional districts (*Gaue*) (Schäfer 2014, 156–158). An entirely different strategy was applied in the case of the Protectorate of Bohemia and Moravia. Here, in order to suggest normality to the Czechs, the domestic sports organization was to remain unaltered. The only restriction consisted in limiting international encounters to meeting German teams, so as not to give occasion for anti-German demonstrations in the event of protectorate teams competing in other countries. In February 1940, however, competitions between German and Czech teams were forbidden as well. Far from suggesting an amiable relationship between the peoples, as the National Socialist regime had wished, the meetings had repeatedly provoked violent outbreaks among the spectators. The first massive intervention in the protectorate's domestic sports organization took place in April 1941, when the traditional gymnastics and sports association Sokol was forbidden. Sokol combined Czech nationalism with pan-Slavic ideas and sheltered one out of ten Czechs. The prohibition was motivated by the German campaign in Yugoslavia. In this situation, Hitler deemed it advisable to cut off all activities of pro-Slavic organizations (Teichler 1991, 217–254).

22.13   Conclusion

The various aspects of athletics in the Third Reich have been analytically separated in this discussion. However, in reality, they were bound together, overlapped, and acted on one another in multiple ways. Sports were simultaneously leisure, means to health, and an instrument of war. Each could easily be converted into one of the others. This finding shows how little sense it makes to differentiate those elements of National Socialist rule which aimed at the enjoyment of life and welfare from their politics of violence. In fact, both domains stand in an indivisible horizon of experience and function. The multiple uses of athletics for the National Socialist project of *Volksgemeinschaft* led to a promotion of physical education which was unique in German history. The regime invested unprecedented resources in an area which had previously had to beg for public funding. Hand in hand with this came the attempt at the full political and ideological assimilation of the domains to National Socialism. Previously, sports in Germany had been characterized by their pluralism. An analysis of this subject must keep in mind that the requirements and objectives of the regime were not always implemented on a one-to-one basis. Rather, they took place in complicated processes of negotiation that took into account the interests and attitudes of specific actors.[10] Conversely, it is also the case that actors who subjectively regarded themselves as non-conformist, by their actions often served a functional context constructed by the National Socialist state.

The question arises whether the linkage of athletics and National Socialism has to be completely rethought within the frame of the *Volksgemeinschaft*. Previous research implied that the two phenomena were initially independent of each other. In consequence, the main question had been whether sport was lured or pressured to participate in National Socialism. Against this interpretation, the above findings suggest an inversion of the perspective: athletics should be related to National Socialism not merely as an object, but also as a subject. This means that if athletics (and this is crucial) were interpreted and practised in a special way, they became themselves an integral part of National Socialism, and belonged to the fundamental building blocks out of which it was constructed. The tying together of body culture and the idea of the nation, of the individual body and the body of the *Volk*, of schooling in competition and the 'New Man', to give only a few examples, were the matter with which National Socialism worked on the planes of thought, language, and action. It goes without saying that sports only entered this constellation in a specific historical situation. Under other circumstances, interpreted otherwise, athletics could and can have wholly other, even opposite, political implications.

Notes

1 Peiffer (2015) gives a thorough account of the publications on this subject. Due to limited space, this chapter will cite only recent studies; in most cases, references to older studies will be made only if there are no current writings on the same subject.
2 Concerning the AHS, see Buddrus (2003, 874–883, mainly 880); concerning the Napola, see Roche (2013, 181–188).
3 Unlike most organizations, sports clubs had members of all ages and of both sexes. Therefore, they ideally symbolized 'the unitary cooperation of all Germans' and the *Volksgemeinschaft*.
4 See Schmiechen-Ackermann (1998, 461–526) on selected examples in cities.
5 In addition, there followed the 'integration' of Austrian sports into the German sports administration, in 1938. See Marschik (2008) for a fundamental outline; also, regarding the example of mountaineering, see Koll (2012, 124–145).
6 This includes several studies that specialized on single soccer associations. Examples are Goch and Silberbach (2005) and Herzog (2006).
7 However, over time, the SA did broaden the spectrum of sports they offered. An encompassing study on SA sports is still missing.
8 On KdF sports in general, see Hachtmann (2016).
9 On sports science during the Nazi period, see Court (2008).
10 See Marschik (2008, 613–616) for a concise study on Austria.

References

Bach, Hermann. 1991. 'Körperliche Wiederaufrüstung: Die Einführung des Pflichtsports für Studenten.' In *Die Freiburger Universität in der Zeit des Nationalsozialismus*, edited by Eckhard John, Bernd Martin, Marc Mück, and Hugo Ott, 57–71. Freiburg im Breisgau and Würzburg: Ploetz.

Bahro, Berno. 2013. *Der SS-Sport: Organisation – Funktion – Bedeutung*. Paderborn: Schöningh.

Becker, Frank. 2009a. *Den Sport gestalten: Carl Diems Leben (1882–1962), Volume 1: Kaiserreich*. Duisburg: Universitätsverlag Rhein-Ruhr.

Becker, Frank. 2009b. *Den Sport gestalten: Carl Diems Leben (1882–1962), Volume 3: NS-Zeit*. Duisburg: Universitätsverlag Rhein-Ruhr.

Becker, Frank. 2011. *Den Sport gestalten: Carl Diems Leben (1882–1962). Volume 2: Weimar Republic*. Duisburg: Universitätsverlag Rhein-Ruhr.

Buddrus, Michael. 2003. *Totale Erziehung für den Krieg: Hitlerjugend und nationalsozialistische Jugendpolitik*. Munich: Saur.

Cachay, Klaus, Bahlke, Steffen, and Mehl, Hartmut. 2000. *'Echte Sportler' – 'Gute Soldaten': Die Sportsozialisation des Nationalsozialismus im Spiegel von Feldpostbriefen*. Weinheim and Munich: Juventa.

Court, Jürgen. 2008. 'Sportwissenschaft.' In *Kulturwissenschaften und Nationalsozialismus*, edited by Jürgen Elvert and Jürgen Nielsen-Sikora, 781–822. Stuttgart: Steiner.

Fahnenbruck, Nele Maya. 2013. *'...reitet für Deutschland': Pferdesport und Politik im Nationalsozialismus*. Göttingen: Die Werkstatt.

Felsch, Philipp. 2001. 'Volkssport: Zur Ökonomie der körperlichen Leistungsprüfung im Nationalsozialismus.' *Sportzeiten. Sport in Geschichte, Kultur und Gesellschaft* 1/3, 5–30.

Goch, Stefan and Silberbach, Norbert. 2005. *Zwischen Blau und Weiß liegt Grau: Der FC Schalke 04 im Nationalsozialismus*. Essen: Klartext.

Hachtmann, Rüdiger. 2016. '"Bäuche wegmassieren" und "überflüssiges Fett in unserem Volke beseitigen". Der kommunale Breitensport der NS-Gemeinschaft 'Kraft durch Freude.' In *Sport und Nationalsozialismus*, edited by Frank Becker and Ralf Schäfer, 27–65. Göttingen: Wallstein.

Havemann, Nils. 2005. *Fußball unterm Hakenkreuz: Der DFB zwischen Sport, Politik und Kommerz*. Frankfurt am Main and New York: Campus.

Heinrich, Arthur. 2000. *Der Deutsche Fußballbund: Eine politische Geschichte*. Cologne: Papy Rossa.

Herzog, Markwart. 2006. *Der 'Betze' unterm Hakenkreuz: Der 1. FC Kaiserslautern in der Zeit des Nationalsozialismus*, Göttingen: Die Werkstatt.

Koll, Johannes. 2012. 'Aufbau der "Volksgemeinschaft" durch Vereinspolitik: Arthur Seyß-Inquart und der Alpenverein 1938–1945.' *Zeitschrift für Geschichtswissenschaft* 60, 124–145.

Large, David Clay. 2007. *Nazi Games: The Olympics of 1936*. New York and London: Blue Guides.

Lissinna, Hartmut E. 1997. *Nationale Sportfeste im nationalsozialistischen Deutschland*. Mannheim: Palatium.

Luh, Andreas. 1998. *Betriebssport zwischen Arbeitgeberinteressen und Arbeitnehmerbedürfnissen: Eine historische Analyse vom Kaiserreich bis zur Gegenwart*. Aachen: Meyer & Meyer.

Marschik, Matthias. 2008. *Sportdiktatur: Bewegungskulturen im nationalsozialistischen Österreich*. Vienna: Turia & Kant.

Oswald, Rudolf. 2008. *'Fußball-Volksgemeinschaft': Ideologie, Politik und Fanatismus im deutschen Fußball 1919–1964*. Frankfurt am Main and New York: Campus.

Peiffer, Lorenz. 2011. 'Der Ausschluss der Juden 1933 aus deutschen Turn- und Sportvereinen und das Beschweigen nach 1945.' *Zeitschrift für Geschichtswissenschaft* 59, 217–229.

Peiffer, Lorenz. 2015. *Sport im Nationalsozialismus: Zum aktuellen Stand der sporthistorischen Forschung: Eine kommentierte Bibliografie*, 3rd edn. Göttingen: Die Werkstatt.

Roche, Helen. 2013. *Sparta's German Children: The Ideal of Ancient Sparta in the Royal Prussian Cadet-Corps, 1818–1920, and in National-socialist Elite Schools (the Napolas), 1933–1945*. Swansea: Classical Press of Wales.

Rossol, Nadine. 2010. *Performing the Nation in Interwar Germany: Sport, Spectacle and Political Symbolism, 1926–36*. Basingstoke, UK: Palgrave Macmillan.

Sauer-Burghard, Brunhilde. 2008. 'Das Frauenbild des Nationalsozialismus: eine Analyse der Leibeserziehung für Mädchen im BDM.' *Beiträge zur feministischen Theorie und Praxis* 31, 31–44.

Schäfer, Ralf. 2011a. *Militarismus, Nationalismus, Antisemitismus: Carl Diem und die Politisierung des bürgerlichen Sports im Kaiserreich*. Berlin: Metropol.

Schäfer, Ralf. 2011b. 'Carl Diem, der Antisemitismus und das NS-Regime.' *Zeitschrift für Geschichtswissenschaft* 59, 252–263.

Schäfer, Ralf. 2014. 'Verdrängen und erinnern: Probleme im Umgang mit der NS-Vergangenheit des deutschen Sports am Beispiel von Carl Diem.' In *Die Spiele gehen weiter: Profile und Perspektiven der Sportgeschichte*, edited by Ralf Schäfer and Frank Becker, 143–169. Frankfurt am Main and New York: Campus.

Schmiechen-Ackermann, Detlef. 1998. *Nationalsozialismus und Arbeitermilieus: Der nationalsozialistische Angriff auf die proletarischen Wohnquartiere und die Reaktionen in den sozialistischen Vereinen*. Bonn: Dietz.

Springmann, Veronika. 2014. 'Zwischen "Entertainment" und "Punishment": Die Darstellungen von Sport in nationalsozialistischen Lagern.' In *Die Spiele gehen weiter: Profile und Perspektiven der Sportgeschichte*, edited by Frank Becker and Ralf Schäfer, 227–247. Frankfurt am Main and New York: Campus.

Teichler, Hans Joachim. 1991. *Internationale Sportpolitik im Dritten Reich*. Schorndorf: Hofmann.

von Reeken, Dietmar and Thießen, Malte, eds. 2013. *Volksgemeinschaft als soziale Praxis: Neue Forschungen zur NS-Gesellschaft*. Paderborn: Schöningh.

Wahlig, Henry. 2015. *Sport im Abseits: Die Geschichte der jüdischen Sportbewegung im nationalsozialistischen Deutschland*. Göttingen: Wallstein.

Wedemeyer-Kolwe, Bernd. 2012. 'Völkisch-religiöse Runengymnastiker im Nationalsozialismus.' In *Die völkisch-religiöse Bewegung im Nationalsozialismus: Eine Beziehungs- und Konfliktgeschichte*, edited by Uwe Puschner and Clemens Vollnhals, 459–472. Göttingen: Vandenhoeck & Ruprecht.

Wildmann, Daniel. 1998. *Begehrte Körper: Konstruktion und Inszenierung des 'arischen' Männerkörpers im 'Dritten Reich'*. Würzburg: Königshausen & Neumann.

Further Reading

Bahro, Berno. 2013. *Der SS-Sport: Organisation – Funktion – Bedeutung*. Paderborn: Schöningh.
Based on the theory of organizational competition as a main feature of Nazi rule in Germany.

Becker, Frank. 2013. *Den Sport gestalten. Carl Diems Leben (1882–1962)*, 2nd edn. 4 vols. Duisburg: Universitätsverlag Rhein-Ruhr.
The life of the well-known sport organizer and pedagogue is embedded in the general history of sport from the late nineteenth century up to the early 1960s.

Large, David Clay. 2007. *Nazi Games: The Olympics of 1936*. New York and London: Blue Guides.
Enlightening analysis of the Olympics of 1936 combining sport history with political and cultural history.

Marschik, Matthias. 2008. *Sportdiktatur: Bewegungskulturen im nationalsozialistischen Österreich*. Vienna: Turia & Kant.
Unique overview of Nazi sports in Austria 1938–1945.

Wahlig, Henry. 2015. *Sport im Abseits: Die Geschichte der jüdischen Sportbewegung im nationalsozialistischen Deutschland*. Göttingen: Wallstein
The first systematic study on the Jewish sport movement in Nazi Germany.

CHAPTER TWENTY-THREE

Cinema, Art, and Music

DANIEL MÜHLENFELD

23.1 Introduction

This chapter attempts to give a threefold perspective on cinema, art, and music in the Third Reich as they relate to the Nazi regime, the artists, and the recipients. First, the role that cinema, art, and music played for National Socialism before and after 1933 will be discussed. Following that, the various roles artists used to play in the Third Reich will be described and analysed. And third, the question is how Germans adapted to cinema, art, and music until the very end of war will be explored. This chapter ends with some reflections on how the three perspectives described above fit into the available historical research in the field of Nazi cultural policy. This essay argues that the relative stability of the Nazi regime up until the end of the Second World War was the result of Germans being actively engaged in a kind of individual 'mood management' (*Stimmungsmanagement*) – a concept originally developed within media studies (Schenk 2007, 194–195), which nearly two decades ago Kaspar Maase transferred to the historical analysis of European mass society during the nineteenth and twentieth centuries (Maase 1997, 117–119). Adapting this concept to the apparently undisputed field of scholarly research on Nazi Germany's cultural policy brings a new approach to the question of how society in the Third Reich functioned and to which normative principles it adhered.

23.2 Cultural Policy in Nazi Germany

Discussing National Socialist cultural policy is easy and complicated at the same time. One may talk easily about Nazism, the National Socialist party or movement, the Nazi regime, or simply the Third Reich without reflecting upon whom one is

A Companion to Nazi Germany, First Edition. Edited by Shelley Baranowski,
Armin Nolzen, and Claus-Christian W. Szejnmann.
© 2018 John Wiley & Sons Ltd. Published 2018 by John Wiley & Sons Ltd.

really referring to. Historians describing Nazism's idea of culture often refer to programmatic quotations from Hitler himself. Thus, they overlook the problem that National Socialist cultural policy in fact was a polyphonic chorus of rivals literally trying to play their very own note. When the Nazi regime came to power in January 1933, only one thing could have been taken for granted: the rejection of cultural liberalism which Germany's capital, Berlin, had, during the 'roaring twenties', especially reflected (Harvey 2001; Steinweis 1993b). Thereby, culture – no matter how amorphous the term and the phenomena it referred to might have been (Vaughan 2013) – was at the very heart of political debates and discourses in the aftermath of the First World War and during the Weimar Republic. That was even more the case as political or ideological positions found their expressions in specific cultural practices which were essential for defining gaps and boundaries within German society and the electorate: German society was divided into social-moral milieus, as Lepsius classically described it (see Hübinger 2008). There was no clear distinction between culture and politics, and therefore political conflicts were fought out in the arts as well.

But since Nazism itself lacked a binding and coherent cultural canon, it defined the limits of allowance by negation: by stigmatizing everything that seemed incompatible, un-German, degenerate, or simply 'Jewish' in the most pejorative way imaginable, what was left over was acceptable as long as it did not conflict with the regime. But who spoke on behalf of 'the regime' in the field of cultural policy? Joseph Goebbels, Alfred Rosenberg, Hermann Göring, Wilhelm Frick, Robert Ley, Bernhard Rust, Otto Dietrich, and Max Amann were all in some way responsible for important parts of the regime's cultural policy, although who dominated among them changed over the years. Whereas Otto Dietrich and Max Amann played a crucial role in coordinating the formerly free press in Germany, Wilhelm Frick (Neliba 1992, 57–60), Reich Minister of the Interior and former Minister of Education in Thuringia in the early 1930s, soon lost ground to his rivals, Bernhard Rust, the later Reich Minister for Education (Nagel 2012), and Joseph Goebbels, Reich Minister for People's Enlightenment and Propaganda (*Reichsminister für Volksaufklärung und Propaganda*). Göring as head of the Prussian government was in charge of the leading German theatres. Robert Ley, leading figure in the German Labour Front (*Deutsche Arbeitsfront*, DAF), organized cultural leisure programmes for millions of Germans. And finally Alfred Rosenberg, editor-in-chief of the Nazi Party's official newspaper *Völkischer Beobachter*, founder of the Combat League for German Culture (*Kampfbund für deutsche Kultur*, KfdK), and the Führer's commissioner for the monitoring of all intellectual and ideological education of the NSDAP (*Beauftragter des Führers für die Überwachung der gesamten geistigen und weltanschaulichen Schulung und Erziehung der NSDAP*), had at his disposal various instruments to intervene in arts and culture – with fluctuating success (Steinweis 1991; Piper 2005, 259–261, 369–372).

Since none of them except Wilhelm Frick had any governmental experience, the new regime broadly relied on the same civil service staff that had been responsible for cultural policy during the Weimar Republic. That was true for ministries and administrations as well as for professional associations of artists. Genuine National Socialist initiatives in the field of cultural policy – like the burning of books of authors stigmatized for various reasons in May 1933 – were, without question, drastic measures, but they were initiated from within the National Socialist movement rather than from the newly formed government. Moreover, such actions were an exception to the rule, and contemporaries saw them as the harsh but logical continuation of the policy of marginalization against nonconformist forms of cultural expression similar to that of the German Empire and the Weimar Republic's notorious battle versus 'smut and trash' (*Schmutz und Schund*) (Major 2006).

Thus, the notorious process of coordination or alignment (*Gleichschaltung*) of cultural institutions in the spring and summer of 1933 often ended up with little more than the replacement of chairmen and declarations of loyalty to the Führer and his new government (Barbian 2004, 41). Yet what at first looked like a backlash against ideological purists in the long run provoked more radical policies, and not only within the field of culture: on the one hand, the rivalry of diverse protagonists caused what Hans Mommsen classically described as a 'cumulative radicalization' (Mommsen 1997); on the other hand, non-party-affiliated civil service personnel felt obliged to prove their ideological reliability just to secure their own further employment.

Meanwhile, the regime did not create a broadly acceptable style of Nazi art and culture. What all Nazi players in the field of cultural policy shared was a common dichotomous view that divided culture into that which was unworthy and that which was not. 'German' art was 'heroic, Nordic, ecstatic, mystic, soulful, and rooted in blood and soil' (Petsch 2004; my translation). But there was no coherent answer to what kind of art would fill the two categories. In an attempt to conform to the regime's official view, some younger Nazi functionaries declared a 'Nordic modernism', represented, for example, by Emil Nolde (Germer 1990). Nevertheless, National Socialist Germany lacked what fascist Italy had found in the phenomenon of 'futurism' (*Futurismus*) (Schmidt-Bergmann 2009): a specific and more or less original mode of artistic self-expression of at least average quality.

As a consequence, the regime preferred to exploit the classical German cultural heritage – from Goethe to Wagner and Nietzsche to Caspar David Friedrich (Petsch 2004, 246–247; Hinrichs 2011, 179–182) – as the regime's lowest common denominator. Here, too, negation was the preferred method: by idealizing a common German cultural heritage, classical music and literature and figurative painting were characterized as authentically German and set against 'Western attitudes towards reason and rationalist structure' as proof of Germany's superiority (Dennis 2015, 176). Music especially, as an art that touches not only the listener's reason but also emotions, was labelled 'the most German of arts' (Potter 2000, 251–253) – as though people of other cultural or ethnical backgrounds experienced Beethoven or Wagner differently.

The more obvious it became that arts and culture in the Third Reich could not be regulated by content, the more important became the regime's efforts to control German artists by administrative means. Joseph Goebbels established the Reich Chamber of Culture (*Reichskulturkammer*, RKK) in September 1933 to prevent DAF leader Robert Ley from gaining control over cultural professions (Steinweis 1993a, 32–34). Under the umbrella of the RKK, formerly self-administered professional organizations merged into seven, later six, chambers for radio (dissolved in 1939), cinema, music, figurative arts, theatre, literature, and press. Since membership in a chamber was obligatory for artists to work, the chambers became a powerful tool of censorship, although the extent to which the chambers' presidents purged artists differed, especially by racial means. Here, the regime suffered some propagandistic setbacks, since some of the most famous artists appointed as president of a chamber caused public scandals. The composer Richard Strauss, for example, in a private letter that became public, denounced the racial principles of Nazi cultural policy as irrational. But, in general, these conflicts did not prevent the cleansing of Germany's cultural life by racial means, especially after 1938 when anti-Jewish policy turned even more radical (Steinweis 2001).

Another important decision, in November 1936, to guarantee some sort of cultural consistency within the Third Reich was the prohibition of critical reviews of artwork. The regime realized that '[a]rt critics served as extremely important mediators between the regime and the public during the Third Reich. They communicated to a broad audience the ideological precepts manifest in the contemporaneous artworks and played a crucial role in the campaign to generate enthusiasm for these products' (Petropoulos 2000, 111). Therefore, Goebbels ordered that from then on, instead of art criticism there should be an art reporting, which would bring 'less judgement but more description and thereby appreciation' of artists and their work, as the Reich propaganda minister declared (cited after Wulf 1989, 128; my translation).

At about the same time, preparations were begun to organize a Reich exhibition of contemporary German art (*Große Deutsche Kunstausstellung*) in the newly erected House of German art (*Haus der Deutschen Kunst*) in Munich in 1937. According to the regime's dichotomous understanding of art and culture, there was also an exhibition of 'degenerate art'. There, the most famous works of modernist and avant-garde painters were shown publicly for the last time in Germany until the end of the Third Reich (Barron 1992). Both exhibitions were meant to determine what, by now, had become the official consensus as to what art in Nazi Germany should look like. In fact, the exhibition of 'degenerate art' was not new. It followed the medieval logic of putting somebody in the pillory, and, as Christoph Zuschlag (1995) has already documented, there had been numerous prequels on a local or regional level from the very beginning of the Third Reich. In addition to the already mentioned players, there were regional Nazi Party leaders (*Gauleiter*) and mayors, among other local officials, who used the arts and culture to legitimize the new political order at the grass roots (Schmidt 2006). That strategy was not unique to the Nazi regime but applied to other regimes, past and present, as well (Benjamin 1963; Kertzer 1988). Therefore, it was no surprise that in 1938 the concept of a pejorative exhibition was transferred to the field of music: in Düsseldorf, works of 'degenerate music' were played, involving examples of jazz, swing, or atonal music (Kaminiarz 1999, 275–276; Dümling 2002).

The objects presented in these stigmatizing exhibitions had been taken from museums and collections all over the Reich. Cynically, leading figures of the regime like Goebbels, Rosenberg, and especially Göring built up large private collections of artwork that launched one of the largest robberies in history when German art historians and art dealers plundered Nazi-occupied Europe during the war

(Petropoulos 1999; Vries 2000). Pieces of 'degenerate art' were used to acquire foreign currency or to barter for ideologically more convenient artwork. The case of the deceased art collector and dealer Cornelius Gurlitt, revealed in 2012–2013, showed that the complete story of Nazi art plunder has yet to be written: numerous paintings that had disappeared during the war years were recovered from his possession (Frankfurter Allgemeine Zeitung 2015; Hoffmann and Kuhn 2016).

The Nazis' treatment of cinema, however, was slightly different. In the early 1930s, cinema still was a young medium in a state of continuing technical improvement. Apart from the (tabloid) newspaper, cinema was thus the first real mass medium since it reached a steadily growing audience, while the parameters of screening became standardized at least with the appearance of sound films (Ross 2008, 34–37, 156–158). According to Jeffrey Herf's (2003) finding that Nazism's reactionary ideology did not conflict with interest in and exploitation of modern technology, it is no surprise that the Nazi regime, and especially its propaganda minister, made intense use of the new media. For obvious reasons, Felix Moeller's study on National Socialist film policy was entitled *Der Filmminister* (Moeller 1998). Yet Goebbels pushed film production not only for propagandistic reasons. As his diary shows, 'film was important to Goebbels not only as an instrument of public-mood control …, but also as a convenient source of income' (Kater 2000) since his ministry was funded mostly by film-generated revenues and – even more so – by radio licence fees (Mühlenfeld 2006).

Keeping that in mind, Nazi cultural policy sheds a different light on (up to now undisputed) findings of historical research: although the regime's cultural policy depended on the commercial success of its media output, media's content not only satisfied the need for propaganda but also the receptive desires and expectations of German audiences. Therefore, most films produced during the Third Reich were made for entertainment, not for indoctrination. Exceptions such as the notorious 'Wandering Jew' (*Der ewige Jude*) prove the rule (Culbert 2002). In recent years, historians have questioned the artificial distinction between entertainment and indoctrination, arguing that there was less indoctrination than the creation of an artificial normalcy, especially during the war years, that provided diversion and escapism (Rentschler 1996, 1–25; Kundrus 2005).

Finally, one can say that the regime's cultural policy fell victim to its own ideological presumptions. Because it saw cultural output not only as 'l'art pour l'art' but as the concrete expression of unity between regime, culture, and society, its measures to control cultural output undermined that unity and led automatically to a creative paralysis as long as the regime was unwilling to accept even the slightest deviations. Thus artists and recipients, who personally came into conflict, suffered significantly.

23.3   The Artists' Perspective

After January 1933, the regime built up institutions and ministries to control cultural life. What contemporaries witnessed was an apparently smooth or even concerted interaction between rank-and-file members of the Nazi Party (*Nationalsozialistische Deutsche Arbeiterpartei*, NSDAP) and the SA (*Sturmabteilung*) and other regime officials. The takeover of power was the starting point for party members to enforce the cleansing of every public institution, including the arts and cultural life. While ordinary members of the party and SA applied pressure by threatening objectionable cultural figures, such as the Dresden conductor Fritz Busch, with violence, officials used such provocations to prohibit further public appearances of the famous musician because they claimed they would cause public unrest. Busch went into exile and never came back to Germany (Evans 2004, 513–514).

The early initiatives of local Nazi hotspurs soon became the regime's official doctrine: on 7 April 1933, the regime enacted the 'Law for the Restoration of Professional Civil Service' (*Gesetz zur Wiederherstellung des Berufsbeamtentums*, BBG). It paved the way for the removal of undesirable civil service personnel for political or racial reasons (Mommsen 1966, 39–43). For obvious reasons, the law which applied only to the civil service also enabled the cleansing of societies, associations, unions, universities, orchestras, theatre companies, as well as the Prussian academy of arts. Innumerable musicians, actors, and editors lost their jobs even if they had been given no reason to be judged as politically unreliable. Living conditions for those removed were precarious in two ways. First, they faced further repression. Second, having already faced a decline in their living standards during the world economic crisis, they did not know whether they would be able to earn a living again (Steinweis 1995, 25–26). This was especially true for those artists who were unemployed at the end of the Weimar Republic. Some of them joined the NSDAP because the party attributed their unemployment to Jewish and foreign artists. Therefore, the purge of arts and culture in the early days of the regime was similar to that of other professions, a job-creation programme for members and followers of the Nazi Party (Bajohr 2009; Humann 2011). Thus, Nazi cultural policy underscores the materialist dimension of Nazi anti-Jewish policy, as historians have recently recognized (Bajohr 1998). As a consequence, German cultural life suffered a massive loss when artists who were purged went into exile, like the above-mentioned Fritz Busch (Möller 1984). Others, who lacked intercessors abroad or enough money to emigrate, had no chance of evading further repression, especially Jews – for example, the painters Otto Freundlich and Felix Nussbaum who were ultimately murdered (Beyme 2005, 720).

However, stigmatization by the Nazi regime did not automatically mean that an artist opposed Nazism, as the case of Emil Nolde shows. The painter, who already was one of the most important expressionists in Germany before 1933, had been a convinced member of the NSDAP since the early 1920s and kept his faith in Hitler even when he became stigmatized as a degenerate artist (Danker 2001). Even if one concedes that Nolde is an extreme example of loyalty to Nazism, there are others – not just backbenchers – who identified themselves with the regime at least for some time, like the painter Franz Radziwill (Beyme 2005, 729–730). On the other hand, the author Oskar Maria Graf officially urged the regime to burn his book, too, since he declared himself a degenerate und unworthy writer whose books had been forgotten to be burned in May 1933.

As these examples show, the equation of stigmatized artists with opponents of the regime does not hold up; nor does the reverse argument, that artists whose work was not rejected supported the regime. Keeping that in mind might help to analyse the behaviour of those artists who neither came into conflict with the regime nor actively sought its endorsement. After 1945, most defaulted to 'internal emigration' (*innere Emigration*) to justify themselves for not having opposed the regime. Even if one concedes that artists like Käthe Kollwitz or Ernst Barlach remained in Germany because they believed that Nazism was just another episode in a series of short-lived right-wing governments and perceived exile as a betrayal of their fatherland, it has to be kept in mind that everybody living under a regime that demanded political affirmation in everyday life had to make some concessions so that the regime would leave them alone (Beyme 2005, 732–733).

And finally, there were those artists who were ultimately purged for being racially impure – that is Jewish – or politically unreliable but whom the regime protected for a short time because of their extraordinary and irreplaceable artistry (Steinweis 1993a, 112–113). That was the case particularly for Jewish musicians who during the presidency of Richard Strauss were still affiliated with the Reich music chamber and therefore got further engagements (Dahm 1996, 101). Other artists who suffered repression, like the author Erich Kästner, were surreptitiously given a chance to work for the expanding film industry as screenplay writers (Barbian 2010, 402).

Thus, in analysing the relationship between artists and regime, one has to keep in mind that 'the regime' consisted of different spheres of influence. Therefore an artist's chance to come to terms with Nazism depended on the patronage which he or she might have gained. One example often cited in this context is the protection that theatre intendants like Gustav Gründgens received, as well as actors whom Hermann Göring favoured, especially in conflicts with the Goebbels-led Reich theatre administration (Strobl 2009, 207). In any case, artists who stayed in Germany were forced to make concessions to the regime in order to avoid unemployment and repression. Whether these concessions meant they became guilty – morally if not juridically – has to be an individual judgement in each case.

In addition, one has to keep in mind that there were also artists who openly saluted the Nazi regime because they were fervent followers of the NSDAP, or benefited from the new regime, or both. And as the case of Nolde has shown, it is not true that only modestly talented artists clung to the regime for opportunistic reasons – as has been the explanation since 1945 to exculpate German arts and culture from responsibility for what the regime did to those colleagues who were stigmatized, removed, and even murdered.

23.4 Consuming Cinema, Art, and Music in the Third Reich

When discussing arts and culture in the Third Reich, the role of consumers and recipients can hardly be overestimated – focusing on the regime's policymaking and its intentions is merely one side of the same coin. To come to a complete assessment of Nazi cultural policy concerning cinema, art, and music one has to analyse how the public actually responded to the regime's artistic offers. Until recently, the historiography on the Third Reich has not considered this perspective, and thus this chapter aims to convince critics that in fact the Nazi regime itself understood the necessity of examining the reception of its means of communication.

In addition to the SD (the Secret Service), which established a close network of informers who monitored public opinion, the propaganda ministry, too, used its regional branches, the Reich propaganda offices (*Reichspropagandaämter*), to seek information about public opinion related to culture, communication, and propaganda (Mühlenfeld 2010, 186–188). Surveying public opinion was thus common in the Third Reich to gain information that would guide the government in controlling the public mood. At about the same time, the Organisation for Research on Consumption (*Gesellschaft für Konsumforschung*, GfK) was founded. With its reports on ordinary Germans' consumerist behaviour the GfK, too, provided crucial information to the regime (Wiesen 2011, 165–169). As a result, the regime established indirect communication between those who made the media and those who consumed it. That gave the regime and its media makers an opportunity to gauge the reactions of their recipients. Such a form of continuously feedback was crucial not only for the functioning of the Nazi regime but for all modern and differentiated political organizations (Luhmann 2002, 254). In other cases, ordinary Germans reacted actively by sending letters to party officials, radio stations, or even the Reich propaganda ministry (e.g. Connelly 1996). Some pleaded for the fulfilment of individual wishes, but lots of them offered constructive criticism from convinced 'people's comrades' (*Volksgenossen*), who did not criticize the regime as such but sought to improve it. Therefore, such letters often charged that media content did not conform to the ideological roots of Nazism. Thus one can say that it was not only the regime that monitored society's ideological consistency but also rank-and-file Nazis (Luhmann 2010, 321).

Thus those Germans who followed the regime unconditionally were even more important for the stability of the Third Reich during the war. In the pre-war years, even former voters and members of working-class parties came to terms with the regime since the economic recovery relieved the hardships of mass unemployment following the world economic crisis. Thereby, a detailed evaluation of National Socialist economic policy might come to other results. But more important than macroeconomic key data was the perception of Germans. As long as they did not oppose the regime, many Germans experienced the years up to 1939 as a period of recovery, the restabilization of social relationships and therefore normalcy after nearly two decades of turmoil caused by war, inflation, depression, and unemployment (Fritzsche 2008, 56–64; Niethammer 2001, 239–240; Tooze 2008). As long as living conditions improved, most people tended to push aside the thought that others, such as racially stigmatized or unfit people, had to pay the price for their individual well-being.

From the regime's point of view, political stability was of great importance, since there was nothing that Nazism feared more than social unrest such as the revolution and chaos that broke out at the end of the First World War (Mason 1977, 15–41; Aly 2005, 30–35). One strategy was to avoid a setback in public morale by preventing material hardships even during the war – as long as this was possible.

Despite this, several historians some 30 years ago paid attention to the fact that beside the official perspective on everyday life in Nazi Germany, many people themselves adopted 'a split consciousness' (*gespaltenes Bewusstsein*; Schäfer 2009) whereby no contradiction existed between consuming Coca Cola, American movies, foreign newspapers, and literature and being a loyal citizen of the Third Reich. That kind of tacit agreement between regime and people worked as long as the regime did not politicize media and cultural consumption. Here, again, the regime fell into its own trap: since Nazism was trying to create a racially and morally new German man (Fritzsche and Hellbeck 2009) the regime attempted to enforce ideological purity by banning music like jazz and swing, but at the same time it overlooked the popularity of such music to guarantee political stability as long as it did not accompany fundamental opposition to the regime. This paradox became ever more evident during the war. On the same day that Germany invaded Poland, the regime prohibited the reception of foreign radio broadcasts (Hensle 2003, 26–37). Additionally, foreign movies, magazines, and newspapers disappeared from the public sphere. Yet at the same time the regime handled other cultural expressions it disliked, such as jazz, with kid gloves because it preserved the illusion that there was no difference between war and peace for ordinary Germans. Moreover, the military feared unrest among their troops when soldiers were forbidden to listen to their favourite music (Kater 1998, 215–219). This strategy largely corresponded with the regime's decision not to reduce financial support and human resources for arts and culture during the war in general. Theatres and orchestras were kept open, and musicians and actors were released from military service. The regime invited wounded soldiers to the annual Wagner festival in Bayreuth as a special tribute to their sacrifice for the 'people's community' (*Volksgemeinschaft*), thereby once more enacting it for all visitors.

As long as the war effort allowed it, the means of cultural distraction and escapism from wartime realities persisted. As recent historiography has shown, Nazism was defined not only by collectivism but also by individuality. People adapted to the regime more easily if they could retreat in private. Some found relief by going to the theatre, others did so in dance halls, others, as mentioned above, by listening to jazz. As long as the regime did not feel challenged too much, such escapes from everyday life for individuals' mental well-being and morale were accepted as useful to stabilize the social order of the 'people's community'. 'Private interests and desires could thus reinforce rather than undermine loyalty to the Nazi war effort' (Föllmer 2015, 167).

Besides theatres, orchestras, or radio, cinema was the most popular medium in the ensemble of contemporary leisure industry. With a steadily growing number of cinemas in the 1920s and 1930s, the number of visitors in total, as well as the visits per capita and year, grew constantly (Stahr 2001, 175). Especially during the early years of the war, visitors were keen on footage from the front and therefore watched with great interest the newsreels that usually ran before the feature film. As long as the German Newsreel (*Deutsche Wochenschau*) dealt with German victories, visitors often left straight after the newsreel ended and before the movie started (Bartels 2010). At first glance, these findings do not fit with the concept of the 'mood management' (Schenk 2007, 195). If one assumes that media recipients in the Third Reich followed a hedonist strain by looking for content that kept them in a good mood, there was no reason to watch newsreels up to winter 1941 (e.g. Boberach 1984, vol. 4, 1179–1180). What visitors saw until then kept morale high. After the military setbacks accumulated, cinema-goers became more and more interested in those feature films promising escapism, however briefly. What they were looking for was some sort of normalcy that they had now lost in real life (Stahr 2001, 232–233). One can say that media recipients in Nazi Germany (as well as in every other country, anytime and anywhere) made their own media by grasping it in a very individual way which depended on each individual's cognitive preconditions, knowledge, and experience (Berger and Luckmann 2007). People therefore practiced some sort of happy eclecticism (a notion following Berger 2005): they consumed what they wittingly or unwittingly were in need of for the maintenance of their mental and emotional equilibrium.

Therefore, the often-discussed classification of movies as either propaganda or entertainment does not take their reception into account. Whereas there is no clear evidence that watching a film like *Jud Süß* made its audience antisemitic, or at least more antisemitic as it was before (Nolzen 2006), even the dullest buffoonery could, according to the principles of 'mood management' theory, prevent social unrest and achieve the regime's pivotal goal of social stability. In other words: it was successful propaganda in the true sense of the word.

Since the regime realized the connection between entertainment, escapism, and the prevention of social unrest, Joseph Goebbels ceased to cater to the public need for diversion only near the end of the war: at that time, theatres were closed and orchestras were dissolved, whereas cinemas were kept open because they required relatively few personnel. As a consequence of the Allied air war, more and more theatres and concert halls, especially in the cities, had been destroyed. When, finally, all theatres were closed in September 1944, actors and musicians were enlisted for military service (Strobl 2009, 225). That was the moment when the regime tacitly conceded that Germany's strategic situation could hardly become worse. It was no longer a necessity to keep an eye on the public mood in light of the impending total military defeat (Kundrus 2005).

23.5 Still En Route Towards a Social History of the Third Reich

The chosen perspective underlying this chapter refers to an idea that has arisen within the historiography of Nazi Germany during the last decade – especially within Germany itself. Social history, with its classic focus on social stratification and distribution of material goods, has been enriched by perspectives on the circumstances under which people acted – acknowledging that these interactions then reproduced those structures within which the interaction took place. In other words, the younger generation of social historians in Germany has tried to overcome the long-existing dichotomy of structure versus action, or rather, society versus individual (Welskopp 1998). As it has affected the history of Nazi Germany, this methodological debate has become involved in the controversy over the existence or non-existence of the 'people's community'. While some historians have argued that it was nothing more than a fiction since economic data have proved the continuing existence of severe social inequality, others suggested that the way people had experienced their day-to-day life had to be taken into consideration, regardless of whether a 'people's community' existed or not (Mühlenfeld 2013).

This essay's threefold approach to its topic makes clear that any approach to the history of arts and culture in the Third Reich that does not consider the recipients' perspective remains fragmentary and incomplete. The (not yet written) history of society in Nazi Germany would be well advised to follow the classical dictum of Karl Marx in his famous 'Eighteenth Brumaire of Louis Bonaparte': 'Men make their own history, but they do not make it as they please; they do not make it under self-selected circumstances, but under circumstances existing already, given and transmitted from the past' (Marx 1852).

References

Aly, Götz. 2005. *Hitlers Volksstaat: Raub, Rassenkrieg und nationaler Sozialismus*. Frankfurt am Main: Fischer.

Bajohr, Frank. 1998. *'Arisierung' in Hamburg: Die Verdrängung der jüdischen Unternehmer 1933–1945*. Hamburg: Christians.

Bajohr, Frank. 2009. 'Ämter, Pfründe, Korruption: Materielle Aspekte der nationalsozialistischen Machteroberung.' In *Das Jahr 1933: Die nationalsozialistische Machteroberung und die deutsche Gesellschaft*, edited by Andreas Wirsching, 185–199. Göttingen: Wallstein.

Barbian, Jan-Pieter. 2004. 'Die Beherrschung der Musen: Kulturpolitik im "Dritten Reich".' In *Hitlers Künstler: Die Kultur im Dienst des Nationalsozialismus*, edited by Hans Sarkowicz, 40–74. Frankfurt am Main: Insel Verlag.

Barbian, Jan-Pieter. 2010. *Literaturpolitik im NS-Staat: Von der 'Gleichschaltung' bis zum Ruin*. Frankfurt am Main: Fischer.

Barron, Stephanie, ed. 1992. *'Entartete Kunst': Das Schicksal der Avantgarde im Nazi-Deutschland*. Munich: Hirmer.

Bartels, Ulrike. 2010. 'Zwischen Anspruch und Wirklichkeit: Die Wochenschau als Propagandainstrument.' In *Medien im Nationalsozialismus*, edited by Bernd Heidenreich and Sönke Neitzel, 161–202. Paderborn: Schöningh/Wilhelm Fink.

Benjamin, Walter. 1963. 'Das Kunstwerk im Zeitalter seiner technischen Reproduzierbarkeit.' In *Das Kunstwerk im Zeitalter seiner technischen Reproduzierbarkeit: Drei Studien zur Kunstsoziologie*, 9–45. Frankfurt am Main: Suhrkamp.

Berger, Stefan. 2005. 'How Historians Tell Their Tales: Towards a Happy Eclecticism.' *German History* 23, 397–404. doi: 10.1191/0266355405gh350ra.

Berger, Peter L. and Luckmann, Thomas. 2007. *Die gesellschaftliche Konstruktion der Wirklichkeit: Eine Theorie der Wissenssoziologie*, 21st edn. Frankfurt am Main: Fischer.

Beyme, Klaus von. 2005. *Das Zeitalter der Avantgarden: Kunst und Gesellschaft 1905–1955*. Munich: C.H. Beck.

Boberach, Heinz, ed. 1984. *Meldungen aus dem Reich 1938–1945: Die geheimen Lageberichte des Sicherheitsdienstes der SS*. 17 vols. Herrsching: Pawlak.

Connelly, John. 1996. 'The Uses of Volksgemeinschaft: Letters to the NSDAP Kreisleitung Eisenach, 1939–1940.' *Journal of Modern History* 68(4), 899–930. doi: 10.1086/245398.

Culbert, David. 2002. 'The Impact of Anti-Semitic Film Propaganda on German Audiences: Jew Süss and The Wandering Jew (1940).' In *Art, Culture, and Media under the Third Reich*, edited by Richard A. Etlin, 139–157. Chicago, IL: University of Chicago Press.

Dahm, Volker. 1996. 'Kulturelles und geistiges Leben.' In *Die Juden in Deutschland 1933–1945: Leben unter nationalsozialistischer Herrschaft*, edited by Wolfgang Benz, 4th edn, 75–267. Munich: C.H. Beck.

Danker, Uwe. 2001. '"Vorkämpfer des Deutschtums" oder "entarteter Künstler"? Nachdenken über Emil Nolde in der NS-Zeit.' *Demokratische Geschichte* 14, 149–188.

Dennis, David B. 2015. *Inhumanities: Nazi Interpretations of Western Culture*. Cambridge: Cambridge University Press.

Dümling, Albrecht. 2002. 'The Target of Racial Purity: The "Degenerate Music" Exhibition in Düsseldorf, 1938.' In *Art, Culture, and Media under the Third Reich*, edited by Richard A. Etlin, 43–72. Chicago: University of Chicago Press.

Evans, Richard J. 2004. *Das Dritte Reich: Volume 1: Aufstieg*. Munich: DVA.

Föllmer, Moritz. 2015. *Individuality and Modernity in Berlin: Self and Society from Weimar to the Wall*. Cambridge: Cambridge University Press.

Frankfurter Allgemeine Zeitung. 2015. 'Der Fall Gurlitt.' *Frankfurter Allgemeine Zeitung*, 29 September. http://www.faz.net/aktuell/feuilleton/kunst/der-fall-gurlitt/.

Fritzsche, Peter. 2008. *Life and Death in the Third Reich*. Cambridge, MA: Belknap Press of Harvard University Press.

Fritzsche, Peter and Hellbeck, Jochen. 2009. 'The New Man in Stalinist Russia and Nazi Germany.' In *Beyond Totalitarianism: Stalinism and Nazism compared*, edited by Michael Geyer and Sheila Fitzpatrick, 301–341. Cambridge: Cambridge University Press.

Germer, Stefan. 1990. 'Kunst der Nation: Zu einem Versuch, die Avantgarde zu nationalisieren.' In *Kunst auf Befehl? Dreiunddreißig bis Fünfundvierzig*, edited by Bazon Brock and Achim Preiß, 21–40. Munich: Klinkhardt & Biermann.

Harvey, Elizabeth. 2001. 'Culture and Society in Weimar Germany: The Impact of Modernism and Mass Culture.' In *Twentieth-Century Germany: Politics, Culture and Society 1918–1990*, edited by Mary Fulbrook, 58–76. London: Arnold.

Hensle, Michael P. 2003. *Rundfunkverbrechen: Das Hören von 'Feindsendern' im Nationalsozialismus*. Berlin: Metropol.

Herf, Jeffrey. 2003. *Reactionary Modernism: Technology, Culture, and Politics in Weimar and the Third Reich*, 8th edn. Cambridge: Cambridge University Press.

Hinrichs, Nina. 2011. *Caspar David Friedrich – ein deutscher Künstler des Nordens: Analyse der Friedrich-Rezeption im 19. Jahrhundert und im Nationalsozialismus*. Kiel: Ludwig.

Hoffmann, Meike and Kuhn, Nicola. 2016. *Hitlers Kunsthändler Hildebrand Gurlitt, 1895–1956. Die Biographie*. Munich: C.H. Beck.

Hübinger, Gangolf. 2008. '"Sozialmoralisches Milieu". Ein Grundbegriff der deutschen Geschichte.' In *Soziale Konstellation und historische Perspektive: Festschrift M. Rainer Lepsius*, edited by Steffen Siegmund, Gert Albert, Agathe Bienfait, and Mateusz Stachura, 207–227. Wiesbaden: Springer.

Humann, Detlev. 2011. '"Alte Kämpfer" in der neuen Zeit: Die sonderbare Arbeitsvermittlung für NS-Parteigänger nach 1933.' *Vierteljahrschrift für Sozial- und Wirtschaftsgeschichte* 98, 173–194.

Kaminiarz, Irina. 1999. '"Entartete Musik" und Weimar.' In *Das dritte Weimar: Klassik und Kultur im Nationalsozialismus*, edited by Lothar Ehrlich, Jürgen John, and Justus H. Ulbricht, 267–292. Cologne, Weimar, and Vienna: Böhlau.

Kater, Michael H. 1998. *Gewagtes Spiel: Jazz im Nationalsozialismus*. Munich: DTV.

Kater, Michael H. 2000. 'Film as an Object of Reflection in the Goebbels Diaries: Series II (1941–1945).' *Central European History* 33, 391–414. doi:10.1163/156916100746383.

Kertzer, David I. 1988. *Ritual, Politics, and Power*. New Haven, CT: Yale University Press.

Kundrus, Birthe. 2005. 'Totale Unterhaltung? Die kulturelle Kriegführung 1939 bis 1945 in Film, Rundfunk und Theater.' In *Das Deutsche Reich und der Zweite Weltkrieg: Volume 9/2: Die deutsche Kriegsgesellschaft 1939 bis 1945. Ausbeutung, Deutungen, Ausgrenzung*, edited by Jörg Echternkamp, 93–157. Munich: DVA.

Luhmann, Niklas. 2002. *Die Politik der Gesellschaft*. Edited by André Kieserling: Frankfurt am Main: Suhrkamp.

Luhmann, Niklas. 2010. *Politische Soziologie*. Edited by André Kieserling: Berlin: Suhrkamp.

Maase, Kaspar. 1997. *Grenzenloses Vergnügen: Der Aufstieg der Massenkultur 1850–1970*. Frankfurt am Main: Fischer.

Major, Patrick. 2006. '"Smut and Trash": Germany's Culture Wars Against Pulp Fiction.' In *Mass Media, Culture, and Society in Twentieth-century Germany*, edited by Karl C. Führer and Corey Ross, 234–250. New York: Palgrave Macmillan.

Marx, Karl. 1852. 'The Eighteenth Brumaire of Louis Bonaparte.' 1 October, 2015. www.marxists.org/archive/marx/works/1852/18th-brumaire/ch01.htm (accessed 17 November 2017).

Mason, Timothy W. 1977. *Sozialpolitik im Dritten Reich: Arbeiterklasse und Volksgemeinschaft.* Opladen: Westdeutscher Verlag.

Möller, Horst. 1984. *Exodus der Kultur: Schriftsteller, Wissenschaftler und Künstler in der Emigration nach 1933.* Munich: C.H. Beck.

Moeller, Felix. 1998. *Der Filmminister: Goebbels und der Film im Dritten Reich.* Berlin: Henschel.

Mommsen, Hans. 1966. *Beamtentum im Dritten Reich: Mit ausgewählten Quellen zur nationalsozialistischen Beamtenpolitik.* Stuttgart: DVA.

Mommsen, Hans. 1997. 'Cumulative Radicalisation and Progressive Self-destruction as Structural Determinants of the Nazi Dictatorship.' In *Stalinism and Nazism: Dictatorships in Comparison*, edited by Ian Kershaw and Moshe Lewin, 75–87. Cambridge: Cambridge University Press.

Mühlenfeld, Daniel. 2006. 'Joseph Goebbels und die Grundlagen der NS-Rundfunkpolitik.' *Zeitschrift für Geschichtswissenschaft* 54, 442–467.

Mühlenfeld, Daniel. 2010. 'Between State and Party: Position and Function of the Gau Propaganda Leader in National Socialist Leadership.' *German History* 28, 167–192. doi: 10.1093/gerhis/ghq042.

Mühlenfeld, Daniel. 2013. 'Vom Nutzen und Nachteil der "Volksgemeinschaft" für die Zeitgeschichte: Neuere Debatten und Forschungen zur gesellschaftlichen Verfasstheit des "Dritten Reiches".' *Sozialwissenschaftliche Literaturrundschau* 36, 72–105.

Nagel, Anne C. 2012. *Hitlers Bildungsreformer: Das Reichsministerium für Wissenschaft, Erziehung und Volksbildung 1934–1945.* Frankfurt am Main: Fischer.

Neliba, Günter. 1992. *Wilhelm Frick: Der Legalist des Unrechtsstaates. Eine politische Biographie.* Paderborn: Schöningh.

Niethammer, Lutz. 2001. '"Normalization" in the West: Traces of Memory Leading Back into the 1950s.' In *The Miracle Years: A Cultural History of West Germany, 1949–1968*, edited by Hanna Schissler, 237–265. Princeton, NJ: Princeton University Press.

Nolzen, Armin. 2006. '"Hier sieht man den Juden wie er wirklich ist …": Die Rezeption des Films "Jud Süß" in der deutschen Bevölkerung.' In *Jud Süss: Hoffjude, literarische Figur, antisemitisches Zerrbild*, edited by Alexandra Przyrembel and Jörg Schönert, 245–261. Frankfurt am Main and New York: Campus.

Petropoulos, Jonathan. 1999. *Kunstraub und Sammelwahn: Kunst und Politik im Dritten Reich.* Berlin: Propyläen.

Petropoulos, Jonathan. 2000. *The Faustian Bargain: The Art World in Nazi Germany.* London: Penguin.

Petsch, Joachim. 2004. '"Unersetzliche Künstler": Malerei und Plastik im "Dritten Reich".' In *Hitlers Künstler: Die Kultur im Dienst des Nationalsozialismus*, edited by Hans Sarkowicz, 245–277. Frankfurt am Main: Insel.

Piper, Ernst. 2005. *Alfred Rosenberg: Hitlers Chefideologe.* Munich: Blessing.

Potter, Pamela M. 2000. *Die deutscheste der Künste: Musikwissenschaft und Gesellschaft von der Weimarer Republik bis zum Ende des Dritten Reiches.* Stuttgart: Klett-Cotta.

Rentschler, Eric. 1996. *The Ministry of Illusion: Nazi Cinema and Its Afterlife.* Cambridge, MA: Harvard University Press.

Ross, Corey. 2008. *Media and the Making of Modern Germany: Mass Communications, Society, and Politics from the Empire to the Third Reich.* Oxford: Oxford University Press.

Schäfer, Hans D. 2009. 'Das gespaltene Bewußtsein: Alltagskultur im Dritten Reich.' In *Das gespaltene Bewußtsein: Vom Dritten Reich bis zu den langen Fünfziger Jahren*, 9–87. Göttingen: Wallstein.

Schenk, Michael. 2007. *Medienwirkungsforschung*, 3rd edn. Tübingen: Mohr Siebeck.

Schmidt, Christoph. 2006. *Nationalsozialistische Kulturpolitik im Gau Westfalen-Nord: Regionale Strukturen und lokale Milieus (1933–1945)*. Paderborn: Schöningh.

Schmidt-Bergmann, Hansgeorg. 2009. *Futurismus: Geschichte, Ästhetik, Dokumente*. Reinbek bei Hamburg: Rowohlt.

Stahr, Gerhard. 2001. *Volksgemeinschaft vor der Leinwand? Der nationalsozialistische Film und sein Publikum*. Berlin: Verlag Hans Theissen.

Steinweis, Alan E. 1991. 'Weimar Culture and the Rise of National Socialism: The Kampfbund für deutsche Kultur.' *Central European History* 24, 402–423. doi: 10.1017/ S0008938900019233.

Steinweis, Alan E. 1993a. *Art, Ideology, and Economics in Nazi Germany: The Reich Chambers of Music, Theater, and the Visual Arts*. Chapel Hill: University of North Carolina Press.

Steinweis, Alan E. 1993b. 'Conservatism, National Socialism, and the Cultural Crisis of the Weimar Republic.' In *Between Reform, Reaction, and Resistance: Studies in the History of German Conservatism from 1789 to 1945*, edited by Larry E. Jones and James Retallack, 329–346. Providence, RI: Berg.

Steinweis, Alan E. 1995. 'Cultural Eugenics: Social Policy, Economic Reform, and the Purge of Jews from German Cultural Life.' In *National Socialist Cultural Policy*, edited by Glenn R. Cuomo, 23–38. New York: St. Martin's Press.

Steinweis, Alan E. 2001. 'The Nazi Purge of German Artistic and Cultural Life.' In *Social Outsiders in Nazi Germany*, edited by Robert Gellately and Nathan Stoltzfus, 99–116. Princeton, NJ: Princeton University Press.

Strobl, Gerwin. 2009. *The Swastika and the Stage: German Theatre and Society, 1933–1945*. Cambridge: Cambridge University Press.

Tooze, Adam. 2008. 'The Economic History of the Nazi Regime.' In *Nazi Germany*, edited by Jane Caplan, 168–195. The Short Oxford history of Germany. Oxford: Oxford University Press.

Vaughan, Megan. 2013. 'Kultur.' In *Die Neue Geschichte: Eine Einführung in 16 Kapiteln*, edited by Ulinka Rublack, 298–321. Frankfurt am Main: Fischer.

Vries, Willem de. 2000. *Kunstraub im Westen 1940–1945: Alfred Rosenberg und der 'Sonderstab Musik'*. Frankfurt am Main: Fischer.

Welskopp, Thomas. 1998. 'Die Sozialgeschichte der Väter: Grenzen und Perspektiven der Historischen Sozialwissenschaft.' *Geschichte und Gesellschaft* 24, 173–198.

Wiesen, Jonathan S. 2011. *Creating the Nazi Marketplace: Commerce and Consumption in the Third Reich*. Cambridge: Cambridge University Press.

Wulf, Joseph, ed. 1989. *Die bildenden Künste im Dritten Reich: Eine Dokumentation*. Kultur im Dritten Reich. Vol. 3. Frankfurt am Main: Ullstein.

Zuschlag, Christoph. 1995. *'Entartete Kunst': Ausstellungsstrategien im Nazi-Deutschland*. Worms: Werner.

CHAPTER TWENTY-FOUR

Emotions and National Socialism

ALEXANDRA PRZYREMBEL

The history of emotions is a new area of historical research. Back in 1941 the French historian Lucien Febvre, in 'Histoire des Sensibilité', called for a better understanding of emotions in the context of social movements. In this essay Febvre suggested that analysing emotions helps in understanding how our universe turned turned 'into a stinking pit of corpses' (Febvre 1973, 26). Surprisingly, the concept of emotions as analytical category has not really been adapted to the history of National Socialism. This observation is particularly astounding as, at nearly the same time as Febvre, the Frankfurt School for Social Research debated the question why National Socialism appealed to certain groups. According to this analysis, 'suppressed' fear was one of the determining emotions which legitimized total subordination under the new regime (Brockhaus 2014). Interested in patterns of allegiance, the famous contemporary and professor of literature Victor Klemperer (1881–1960) also emphasized the emotional attachment of many Germans to the Third Reich. In his essay 'Gefolgschaft', he observed a submissive obedience to National Socialist political order that to a large extent was caused by the reinterpretation of traditional norms and the creation of a new terminology (Klemperer 2006). In other words: the study of emotional regimes in Nazi Germany refers to a long history which aimed at explaining the fascination that National Socialism held for many Germans. It was the achievement of historians like Ulrich Herbert to stress the *rational* components of National Socialist ideology by analysing its fascination for a young intellectual elite (Herbert 1996).

However, during the last decade, the history of emotions has flourished. In light of this booming interest, diverse models provide an analytic framework for studying emotions (Eustace et al. 2012). The philosopher Martha Nussbaum defines emotions as 'appraisal or value judgment[s], which ascribe to things and

A Companion to Nazi Germany, First Edition. Edited by Shelley Baranowski, Armin Nolzen, and Claus-Christian W. Szejnmann.

persons outside the person's own control flourishing' (Nussbaum 2004, 4). In other words, emotions can be understood as both an affective and cognitive engagement with the world: emotions embrace physical as well as intellectual experiences. Barbara Rosenwein, who contributed an early article to the debate, suggested that we concentrate on 'emotional communities'. According to her analytical model, emotional communities describe 'affective bonds between people that they recognize; and the modes of emotional expression that they expect, encourage, tolerate and deplore' (Rosenwein 2002, 842). The idea of *emotional communities* aims at understanding emotions as individual and social practices which are permanently (re-)negotiated. Thus, emotions are objects of negotiation, as they are bound to specific cultural practices. To give just one example: in 1943 fear had different meanings for the inhabitants of a bunker. During the bombardments in Germany, women and men found very different strategies in order to organize and order their anxieties. Surrounded by chaotic circumstances as the consequence of war, this meant for some men that they fulfilled their duty. A police officer, for example, recalled that he controlled his anxieties by organizing support. Women supposedly reacted more emotionally (Süß 2011, 356).

In this chapter, I argue that integrating the history of emotions into the analysis of National Socialism provides a better understanding of the regime's acceptance by the German population (Gross 2010). By using the term 'spaces of communication' rather than the National Socialist concept of *Volksgemeinschaft* ('people's community'), I focus on the *doing* of emotions in everyday life. Despite its domination as an analytical concept during the last decade, the concept *Volksgemeinschaft* was recently called into question (for a brilliant summary of the debate, see Steuwer 2013). In spite of the appeal of *Volksgemeinschaft* to certain groups, 'the loyalty of large part of the German population to the Third Reich was tied to its success, both military and economic. If success failed to materialize, the regime lost its base of legitimacy' (Herbert 2014, 62). But what kind of emotions were associated with experiences of success and of disillusionment? In order to understand the widespread enthusiasm for the Nazi regime, this chapter analyses 'positive' and 'negative' feelings. I argue that mixed and sometimes contradictory feelings like love for Hitler or revulsion towards Jews structured emotional regimes during the era of National Socialism. As for the question *how* emotions can be analysed at all, this has kept historians occupied for almost a decade now (a good summary of different positions can be found in Eustace et al. 2012), and this chapter concentrates on the *coding* of emotions in written language.

By concentrating on two different case studies, this discussion attempts to disentangle different emotional regimes like women's love for Hitler and the rejection of Jews. Both examples pose fundamental questions regarding the acceptance of National Socialism, specifically in terms of racial politics. The first part of the chapter addresses different definitions of love in pamphlets and personal documents written by women. The analysis of normative texts and personal accounts raises the following questions: How did women describe their attachment to the new German order? Did they refer to different emotional regimes over time? The second section focuses on criminal proceedings against Jews. By concentrating on processes of negotiation in court, the following questions will be discussed: What kind of emotions towards Jews were expressed in court? Did these emotional regimes correspond with other established emotional codes?

24.1 Between Comradeship and Devotion: Women's Love for Hitler

Luise Solmitz belonged to those bourgeois women who had supported Hitler. She worked as a teacher and was married to a converted Jew. The couple enthusiastically welcomed the formation of the National Socialist government in 1933. Solmitz described the inauguration as 'a memorable January, 30th'. According to her notes, three aspects transformed this day into an experience of resurrection: National Socialist 'panache', German national 'rationality', and the 'unpolitical' Stahlhelm: 'Great, unforgettable beautiful day! German resurrection!' Solmitz and her female neighbours shed tears. Mia M.'s tears flowed freely: 'Those who did not burst into tears, did not have a burning heart' (cited by Wildt 2013, 360). Only a few weeks later, in early April 1933, when the Stormtroopers (*Sturmabteilung*, SA) and urban crowds boycotted Jewish shops, her enthusiasm for the new regime waned. A glance at one of the main women's periodicals (*NS-Frauenwarte*) in the Third Reich confirms the moments of awakening which were mobilized in the early years of National Socialism.[1] In a long article about the Nuremberg party rally in 1935 that propagated racial laws that divided Jewish and non-Jewish Germans, the author insinuates an atmosphere of awakening. During Hitler's speech, she experiences a new love towards Germany which she and other attendants have '"never" felt before'. By referring to shared responsibilities and a common destiny as well as future, the author learns a new sense of belonging (von Stieda, 1935/1936, 235). The *NS-Frauenwarte* held on to this shared spirit of community, even after facing the foreseeable breakdown of Nazi Germany in the early 1940s.

The question whether and how women supported National Socialism has occupied historians for decades (Heineman 2002). The image of a young woman falling into ecstasy at the sight of Hitler has even reverberated in leading studies of German modern history. In his *German Social History*, historian Hans Ulrich Wehler graphically described the physical attachment of some women to Germany's chancellor. According to Wehler, this fascination was infused with 'erotic and sexual female longing' for an 'unapproachable' leader (Wehler 2003, 758). The perception of German women seduced by a charismatic politician resonates even in a literature which attempts to locate love in Nazi Germany within a broader political and social context (Geppert 2010, 159). The paradox that German women did not take on roles in National Socialist government, but as voters and activists of women's organizations created a reliable base of Nation Socialism in Germany, has provoked polemical debates among historians during the last decade. I argue that the image of women as devout followers of National Socialism can be traced back to women's self-positioning in Nazi Germany. In other words: love and subordination to the new state was a central trope in women's writing. Further, this self-perception was compatible with strategies of *Vergangenheitsbewältigung* (coming to terms with the past) after 1945.

Despite its explicit anti-feminism, many women decided to join the Nazi Party (*Nationalsozialistische Deutsche Arbeiterpartei*, NSDAP). Whereas membership in the main National Socialist women's organization (*Nationalsozialistische Frauenschaft*) remained steady at around 10% during the Weimar Republic and the Third Reich, National Socialist women's organizations turned its second branch (*Deutches Frauenwerk*) into a visible social movement (Kater 1983). In northern Germany, 15– 20% of all women were registered in National Socialist women's organizations (Kramer 2011, 8). However, the right of women to vote stipulated in the Weimar constitution did not motivate organized National Socialist women's groups. Rather they claimed a separate but independent sphere of political action. Like their male comrades, Nazi women claimed leadership for themselves: in 1938, the National Socialist women's organization even claimed to be one of the world leading women's organizations (Statistical Yearbook of the Reichsfrauenführung, quoted from Kramer 2011, 32).

The case of Guida Diehl is particularly interesting as she belonged to those few women who committed herself to the *völkisch* movement in the early years of the Weimar Republic and who was marginalized in 1933.[2] In her pamphlet *The German Woman and National Socialism* (*Die deutsche Frau und der Nationalsozialismus*) she described National Socialists' empowerment as a semi-religious 'awakening'. Praising the 'dawn of a great new time' in 1933, she referred to the unique role of women in Nazi Germany. According to Diehl, the 'German turnaround' was based on the mother's 'spirit and force' to overcome 'confusion and moral depravity' and to 'achieve sufficient women's work renewal' (Diehl 1933, 4, 6). The empowerment of the new woman in Nazi Germany was based on a joint battle of men and women against internal and external enemies.[3] The 'awakening of the German soul', as she called one of the chapters, is National Socialism's main goal (Diehl 1933, 114–119). In order to highlight female perspectives in the new Germany, Diehl referred to two complementary emotions: mother's love and feminine honour. In accordance with the concept of two separate spheres, female love and honour were subordinated to the domestic sphere, whereas German men defended honour with arms. In contrast to idealized German womanhood in Nazi Germany, the masculinized short-haired woman of former times only deserved 'disgust' (Diehl 1933, 115). These older, democratic times were associated with moral depravity. Although she created a complex ideological programme, Diehl imagined National Socialism's empowerment merely as battle in which both sexes fought independently as warriors defending their separate spheres of political and domestic honour.

Domestic honour, collective warmth, and an intense, almost physical attachment towards Hitler were also invoked in other writings by women. Women also wrote personal letters to him. Those letters indicate that worship became an important facet of political communication. The interrelationship between the staging of male political power by the media and the expression of devotion in private letters can be illustrated by the following example. Gertrude W. addressed her letter to the 'most deeply loved Adolf' (Gertrud W … from April 17, 1943, quoted from Ulshöfer, 1996, 84).

In November 1936, the Italian paper *Corriere della Sera* claimed in the article 'Lettere a Mussolini. Quando si scrive una lettere a Mussolini?' that Mussolini received between 30 000 and 40 000 letters a month, 42 000 in October 1936 alone. The same strategy of confirming positive feelings expressed towards Hitler illustrates the prize competition, published in September 1935, shortly after the party rally in Nuremberg (Geppert 2010, 169). A newspaper in northern Germany raised the question 'What do I owe Hitler?' and published some of the replies. The sheer number of letters written to Hitler that are kept in different archives indicates the popularity of this kind of personal expression. However, the Reich Chancellery did not enforce such adulation, as some of those dedicated female correspondents were punished (Ulshöfer 1996, 81).

Women expressed a broad spectrum of feelings. In their letters they emphasized their loyalty to the political regime, often expressing a semi-religious devotion to Germany's political leader. Some letter writers even addressed Hitler as 'Majesty'. Writing from Prague in 1941, Margarethe explained this form of address: 'I realise, honourable *Reich* Chancellor and *Führer* of the Great German Empire, that Your Majesty has not been formally given the crown; yet, in my inmost heart. I can only address Your Excellency, Your most revered, honourable Reich Chancellor and Führer des Großdeutschen Reiches with the word "Majesty" – and I dare to use this expression in a private letter as an intimate, completely secret – yet, at the same time – completely normal term' (Margarethe to Adolf Hitler, Prague, 22 December 1941, quoted from Geppert 2010, 166). Self-criticism expressed by the correspondent often accompanied the glorification of Germany's political leader. In September 1942, a female writer confessed that she had not yet endured any sacrifices, but was willing to give her love to Hitler (Ulshöfer 1996, 72). Some of those letters clearly indicate the existence of a 'Hitler cult'.

Love and a great deference paid to Hitler also dominated in Traudl Junge's autobiography *Hitler's Last Secretary: A First-hand Account of Life with Hitler*, which was written in 1947 and published in 2002.[4] Both her autobiography as well as the documentary made by a well-known Austrian artist attracted considerable public attention. It was the 'incongruity of Hitler's cruelty in the world and kindness to' his secretary, as the *New York Times* stated, that fascinated the audience in 2002 (Salomon 2002). Her autobiography was widely read in Germany, possibly because she described those last years with Hitler as familiar and intimate. In his book *Anständig geblieben* (2010), Raphael Gross claims that the surprisingly positive response to Junge's first-hand account of her life with Hitler is interwoven with feelings of guilt, and also the denial of guilt.[5] I argue that Junge's autobiography draws attention to something else: the persistence of everyday love and caring as dominant tropes in women's accounts of Nazi Germany. This emotional offer explains the book's broad reception.

We hardly know anything about Junge's earlier life. In the 1920s, her father became associated with a right-wing paramilitary organization, and in 1935 and 1938 respectively Traudl joined the National Socialist girls' and later the young women's organizations (Kramer 2011, 31–102). According to her account she entered the National Socialists' inner circle by chance. Having been employed as a secretary, in November 1942 she was selected to work for Hitler and join his staff of female secretaries. As a result of her new role, Junge belonged to the small group of people who remained faithful to Hitler until the very end. Together with his entourage Hitler had changed his living quarters several times and finally returned to Berlin where he committed suicide. Junge's report documents Hitler's last two years. By omitting details of the correspondence she conducted for Hitler, Traudl Junge obviously downplayed her own responsibility. These 'omissions' concerning individual scope for action belong to essential tropes incorporated into narratives of *Vergangenheitsbewältigung* after 1945. Instead, her autobiography created an atmosphere of familiarity. Emphasizing practices of caring, she imagined life with Hitler as a family idyll. By describing in detail common meals, Hitler's vegetarianism, his joyful playing with the dog, and their everyday conversation at the table, Junge created an atmosphere of normalcy. She mentioned in passing that the inner circle at the bunker was mainly recruited by old members of the NSDAP. Only a few episodes reminded Junge of her previous life. The persecution of the European Jews was alluded to more or less incidentally at the dinner table, when Henriette von Schirach (1913–1992), the wife of Baldur von Schirach, the leader of the Hitler Youth, mentioned the deportation of Jews in Amsterdam: 'It is horrible what these poor people look like, they are certainly poorly treated' (Junge 2002, 101). This dialogue, which is confirmed by other sources, resulted in the couple's exclusion from the social gatherings at the Führerbunker. From her childhood, Henriette von Schirach had been familiar with the *völkisch* and antisemitic goals of the party. This episode barely disturbed the familiarity which existed among Hitler's paladins even in the light of genocide and crimes against humanity (for a discussion of women's participation in Nazi crimes see Przyrembel 2001, 379).

In spite of the political events that occurred in the outside world, Junge's characterization of Hitler as a charismatic – but also sometimes ridiculous – man remained dominant in her narrative. Germany's political leader cared for his intimate followers. Showing a 'great affection and indulgence' towards old members of the NSDAP (Junge 2002, 98), mutual ties between Hitler and his inner circle were confirmed. On his last birthday – on 20 April 1945 – the group swore fidelity to Hitler, and (unsuccessfully) tried to convince him to leave Berlin (Junge 2002, 176). The text created an astounding sense of normalcy and mentioned Goebbels' self-sacrifice and his family's suicide only in passing. By imagining herself as being interwoven in this game of faithfulness, respect, and self-sacrifice, Junge's autobiography insinuates an encompassing caring love for Germany's Reich Chancellor. The concept of caring that is expressed in Junge's autobiography turns out to be compatible with post-war strategies of *Vergangenheitsbewältigung*.

As members of the *Volksgemeinschaft*, most German women participated in the 'community of work and action' ('From the unity to the plurality of tasks', 'Nachrichtendienst der Reichsfrauenführung', 1939, quoted from Kramer 2011, 69). Following established practices of women's social work, National Socialist women's organizations successfully integrated German women into practices of providing aid during the Second World War. As a matter of fact, voluntary work turned into an important instrument of social control. In everyday life, especially in wartime, the act of caring gave women an opportunity to participate in National Socialist political power. Discourses around caring and honour shaped the emotional systems of many women. The *völkisch* writer and active National Socialist Guida Diehl envisioned a gendered version of Nazi ideology in which women proved their activism as loving mothers and defenders of domestic honour. In court, honour also developed into a key category.

24.2   Between Hostility and Honour: 'Race Defilement' and Practices of Antisemitism in Court

Negative emotions towards Jews constituted a decisive element of antisemitism. The private letters of Johanna Bismarck (1824–1894), married to Germany's former Chancellor, and her daughter-in-law Marguerite (1871–1945) demonstrate well the prevalence of antisemitism within the German nobility. In their personal letters and diaries, both women expressed negative emotions towards Jews such as disgust and contempt, which explicitly rejected Jews. Bismarck's women made these condescending remarks irrespective of whether they had to do with tradesmen's deficiencies or German-Jewish political elites (Hopp 2012). Negative emotions towards Jews passed from one generation to the next, thus confirming Lucien Febvre's concept of 'infectious emotions'. According to him, emotions can be 'infectious' as they confirm (pre-)existing expectations. Negative emotions towards Jews which overlapped with racist stereotypes were distributed in private letters, novels, and court decisions long before 1933.

Since the end of the nineteenth century, antisemitic prejudices had radicalized due to racial concepts of pure blood which were distributed in novels or pamphlets. Eugen Dühring's widely read *Die Judenfrage als Frage der Racenschädlichkeit*, first published in 1881, based his racial visions of pure blood by appealing to emotions such as disgust. According to him, any 'pure-minded' German women would feel 'instinctive revulsion' towards having intimate relationships with Jews (Dühring 1881, iii). A few decades later, in 1917, Artur Dinter, who was an early member of the NSDAP, published his novel *Sünde wider das Blut* [Sin Against Blood] (Dinter 1920). Reprinted several times, the novel turned into a page-turner as it combined overt antisemitism with theories of racial purity and pejorative images of Jews (Przyrembel 2003).

In 1935, the National Socialist regime legalized and implemented racial antisemitism. The Nuremberg Laws of September 1935, prohibiting marriage and sexual relationships between Jews and Germans, represented an essential step towards segregation of Jews in Nazi Germany. As a result of the new law, thousands of women and men were persecuted (Przyrembel 2003, 413–425). German courts in Berlin, Leipzig, Cologne, and Nuremberg even imposed the death penalty on the basis of 'race defilement'. However, the implementation of the Nuremberg Laws from 1935 to 1945 rested upon a gradual process of deprivation in court. Court materials provide an insight into everyday life in Nazi Germany. Giving testimony, defendants, lawyers, and police officers were involved in such proceedings. Asserting that emotions inherently shape legal practice, Martha Nussbaum has emphasized the *doing* of emotions in court: 'Appeals to emotion are prominent in the law' (Nussbaum 2004, 21). In the following, I will examine this interaction between traditional norms and social expectations concerning emotions in court using legal cases against Jews in Nazi Germany. The correspondence of Johanna and Marguerite Bismarck indicates that antisemitism was transformed into an accepted cultural practice in Wilhelmine Germany. However, with the writings of Dühring and Dinter negative emotions towards Jews reached new heights. In his essay 'On Disgust', the philosopher Aural Kolnai (1900–1973) defines negative emotions as responses to transgressions of intimacy (Kolnai 2004). It is worth noting that court decisions against Jews merged negative emotions associated with a 'typical' Jewish physical appearance (which had been circulating since the end of the nineteenth century) with new arguments grounded in National Socialism.

The distinction between racial and emotional antisemitism was discussed during a remarkable debate which took place at the German Department of Justice in June 1934. Bernhard Lösener in particular, who was responsible for racial questions at the Ministry of Interior, discussed this issue in detail. In his remarks, which were mostly deleted in the printed edition, Lösener pleads for a clear distinction between racial and other arguments, especially considering the situation of 'half-Jews' in Germany. He makes clear that not an 'emotional', but a 'racial antisemitism' should structure the forthcoming racial law.[6] Hundreds of cases against Jews show that in court such clear-cut distinctions were blurred. They also confirm that emotions shaped arguments in criminal proceedings.

In many cases, negative emotions towards Jews justified court decisions. They referred to a broad spectrum of arguments. On the one hand, negative emotions were associated with a typical 'Jewishness' expressed by a specific physical appearance or (paradoxically) the denial of such classification. On the other hand, this set of stereotypes was further framed by the reference to National Socialist anti-Jewish politics. To give an example: in 1939, the members of Hamburg's district court made a very particular journey. Attempting to prove a couple's racial identity, the German judges travelled to Vienna where the couple used to live. That this couple was not able to verify their claim provided the background to this trip. According to the Nuremberg Laws, proof of racial identity was required up to the third generation (see Reich Citizenship Law of 15 September 1935). In order to 'objectify' this question, the judges fell back upon an established criminal procedure: in some cases a 'visual inspection' (*Inaugenscheinnahme*) replaced evidence. Travelling to Vienna, Hamburg's judges inspected the couple's former living conditions. According to the report, a child's portrait, the woman's Jewish 'manner' of talking, her lively 'gestures' and her husband's peculiar way of speaking confirmed the 'Jewishness' of the couple.[7]

Besides general attributions of an unspecific 'Jewishness', National Socialist arguments of persecution increasingly framed negative emotions towards Jews. One of the early death penalties which was carried out on the basis of 'race defilement' shows this transition of arguments. In 1940, judges in Gdansk concluded that the Jewish merchant Hans Müller behaved like a Jew because he had cheated German authorities by using false identity papers.[8] In criminal proceedings, arguments concerning the 'invisibility' of Jews in Nazi Germany overlapped very often with offences resulting from the strained economic situation. Another capital punishment was assessed against a young man who had survived in Leipzig by dealing in stolen bicycles. He had also used incorrect papers (Przyrembel 2003, 423).

This legal argument, but also a very specific emotional language, justified the legal prosecution of Jews. Oswald Rothaug, who was a committed National Socialist, used a radicalized language to emphasize his decisions. Explaining his view that Jews were no longer allowed to join court proceedings as visitors, Rothaug emphasized that such proceedings belonged to 'one of the oldest' German cultural manifestations. For 'German human beings', it is therefore 'unbearable' to be 'united' with Jews in court. According to Rothaug's world-view, the mere attendance of Jews in court was an act of dishonouring the court as an institution.[9] These final remarks refer to another dimension of emotions which become crucial in criminal proceedings against Jews – the prevalence of honour and dishonour. The fact that Jews did not deserve any civic rights (*bürgerliche Ehrenrechte*) corresponded with discourses of negative emotions towards Jews in court (Przyrembel 2013).

As shown in Guida Diehl's writings, honour was an important category of National Socialist ideology. The Law for the Protection of German Blood and German Honour aimed at implementing racial segregation while at the same time intending to establish national unity based on norms and values attributed to the *Volksgemeinschaft*. As Michael Wildt has shown, discourses of honour and antisemitic violence were deeply intertwined in the 1930s (Wildt 2007, 219– 266). In criminal proceedings, discourses around honour and dishonour became equally significant. The question of whether Jews 'deserved' civic rights at all occupied the attention of many courts in Nazi Germany. As part of court proceedings, civic rights were generally withdrawn in the case of penal servitude. The deprivation of *Ehrenrechte* provoked a variety of consequences. It could entail the revocation of a doctor's degree but also of military honours awarded during the First World War. The deprivation of civic rights on the basis of discourses around honour not only carried symbolic meaning. The Jewish minority had enjoyed full rights as citizens since the nineteenth century in Germany. Therefore, depriving Jews of civic rights in court proceedings was clearly aimed at denying Jewish emancipation. As most Jewish defendants faced these harsher penalties in cases of 'race defilement', discourses of honour shaped many legal proceedings against Jews. This dimension becomes particularly apparent when considering the following correspondence between Germany's Ministry of Justice and Heinrich Himmler, Reichsleader-SS. Himmler demanded that Jews should generally be deprived of *Ehrenrechte*. As in many cases, the Ministry of Justice delegated fundamental decisions to district courts. In May 1942, Frankfurt's judges, in contrast to the established practice, decided in this case not to withdraw civic rights. The court argued that the application of *Ehrenrechte* would suggest that Jews were in possession of 'bourgeois honour'.[10] This process of negotiation between different policy makers illustrates patterns of radicalization. It also emphasizes the meaning of an idea that Febvre expressed decades ago (Hopp 2012, 277). The French historian suggested that emotions were infectious: under certain social conditions they circle from one generation to another or – as we have seen here – become social practice. In court proceedings against Jews, implicit expectations concerning the denial of moral dignity overlapped with the deprivation of civic rights.

Non-Jewish defendants were also threatened with the charge of 'race defilement'. For courts, this question proved to be more challenging than that which asked whether Jews were still in possession of civic rights. In those cases, courts referred to the concept of racial honour (*Rassenehre*). 'Racial honour' carried different implications. Sexual intimacy with a prostitute was subsumed under 'racial dishonour', while relationships between Jewish men and non-Jewish women whose husbands were at war were equally labelled as violations against racial honour (Przyrembel 2003, 409). The following case emphasizes the fluidity of the concept 'racial honor'. Heinrich Kurz, who had raped a Jewish woman, was an early member of both the NSDAP and the SA, and in this case the district judges qualified his conduct as especially 'dishonourable'. The judges of the district court concluded that his 'misbehaviour' situated him outside National Socialist *Volksgemeinschaft*.[11]

In addition to negative emotions and discourses of honour, practices of shaming constituted a third central moment in criminal proceedings. Shaming played a significant role in the cases mentioned above, irrespective of whether Jewish defendants had a typical 'Jewish' appearance or did not look so 'Jewish' as to prevent their admission to the court room. However, practices of shaming were particularly linked to the perception of sexuality, as illustrated in the following example. Elisabeth Meier and Werner Burg had had an intimate and working relationship for years, when the couple was blackmailed. Women serving as witnesses and according to the law were not to be sentenced on the basis of the race defilement. Against this background the police interrogated female witnesses severely and repeatedly, sometimes several times. This is true in the case of Elisabeth Meier. As the records indicate, she was questioned about the quality of their relationship and their sexual practices. In her early statements Meier described her 'love' for Burg, but after several interrogations by the police she finally claimed that 'Jews are swines' (Letter, January 1937, quoted from Schmidt 2003, 73–78).

Analysis of criminal proceedings against Jews has shown that emotions and legal practice were deeply intertwined. Referring to negative emotions which were passed on down the generations, racial antisemitism was based on emotions like disgust, fear, or even hatred. These emotional regimes framed criminal proceedings against Jews on the basis of the Law for the Protection of German Blood and Honour. In addition to the discursive framework, the category honour emerged as a key element in criminal proceedings.

24.3   Mixed Feelings in Nazi Germany

What does the history of emotions add to the history of National Socialism? Generally speaking, the 'history of emotions is a way of *doing* political, social, and cultural history, not something to be added to existing fields' (Plamper 2010, 249, emphasis in original). Taking seriously Wildt's suggestion to reconsider recent debates on *Volksgemeinschaft* and to contribute research findings to a new social history (Wildt 2013, 369), an analysis of emotions can productively add to this project. Despite the intensity of research related to the question of German support for National Socialism and the population's general acceptance of violence, which has been conducted over the last decades, in this chapter I propose two options for how emotions *in praxi* might be included in such an endeavour. First, a detailed analysis of pamphlets and personal accounts of National Socialist women indicates that caring emerged as a dominant emotion in their personal writings. The opportunities that National Socialism provided for many German women found their equivalent in emotions associated with caring and giving. As the close reading of Guida Diehl's *Die deutsche Frau und der Nationalsozialismus* indicated, such emotional regimes were intertwined with racial concepts. However, the analysis of literary or autobiographical texts appears to be the first step towards an understanding of emotions as spaces of communication during National Socialism. To push the observation further – that Nazi women cared for others within a specific community, or at least constructed this as an emotional regime to guide their writing – two questions may be posed in further research: What were the emotional frameworks through which Nazi women justified their action against Jews and other proclaimed outsiders? And what were the emotional frameworks to which women referred that justified their actions after 1945?

In court cases against Jews, emotions proved to be doubly 'infectious'. On the one hand, circulating emotions referred to an implicit knowledge concerning negative emotions towards Jews. This knowledge was passed on from one generation to the next. Negative, even hostile, emotions towards Jews were common long before National Socialists came to power. As Shulamit Volkov suggested decades ago, antisemitism as cultural code circulated in Wilhelmine Germany (Volkov 1978). Emotions like envy and disgust – in some cases also hatred – gave antisemitism its spicy connotations.

On the other hand, emotions were generally (re)negotiated, and particularly so in court (see Nussbaum 2004). The Nuremberg Laws created a legal framework propagating honour as a central category. During court proceedings, attorneys along with judges referred to honour in order to justify the fundamental exclusion of Jews from court. These decisions were not grounded in law. During the course of criminal proceedings, the doing of emotions made possible the continuing exclusion of Jews in court. Due to the fact that court proceedings also negotiated questions of intimacy, discourses of honour were interwoven with practices of shaming. District courts debated intimate questions such as notions of masculinity, sexual practices, or, more generally, bourgeois definitions of faithfulness. It is this melange which illustrates that the doing of emotions generates very specific social practices such as shaming. The analysis of such processes of negotiation can easily be transferred to other spaces of communication like the youth movements, the workplace, or moments of fear at the end of the war. However, one question remains to be answered: How can we conceptualize violence by including emotional practices? In his book *Belonging and Genocide*, Thomas Kühne argued that violence during National Socialism was shaped not only by implementing politics of extermination, but also by creating 'a new sense of national belonging, the knowledge of being part of a grand community of crime'. Despite his dramatic wording, Kühne's idea that emotions of pleasure very often radicalized violence is worth considering (Kühne 2010, 161). Analysing mixed feelings, understood as fluid and negotiable entities, might enable us to understand why and how former worlds might have changed 'into a stinking pit of corpses'. Coming into being 75 years ago, Febvre's plea to include emotions in historical analysis remains a lasting challenge, and not only for historians of National Socialism.

Notes

1 The *NS-Frauenwarte* was the main journal of the National Socialist women's organization and it appeared from 1932 to 1945; in 1938 it was printed with a circulation of
one million.
2 In 1917 Diehl founded the 'Neuland-Bund' which pursued racial concepts as well as
völkisch values; see Kater (1983, 229).
3 The programme of the women's organization and the NSDAP at the end of her book
illustrate her commitment to racial ideas (Diehl 1933, 121–122).
4 The background to Junge's autobiographical notes raises some questions. According to
her account, a businessman who was fascinated by her story suggested she write down
her memories in 1947 (Junge 2002, 17).
5 Raphael Gross discusses at length the absence of moral responsibility in Traudl Junge's
narrative; see Gross (2010, 104–113).
6 BA Berlin, R 22/852, Bl. 75-321, 37, 5 June 1934.
7 See STA HH, Rep. 6186/40, Bd., 1-3, hier Bd. 2, Bl. 323. Report of 10 August 1940.
8 B Arch Berlin, R 30.01, IIIg 22, 1107/40, Bl. 33 f., Death Sentence of Danzig's
Special Court, 29 January 1940.
9 BA Berlin, R 30.02/1 D 622 /1939, decision 10 May 1939.
10 HStAW, Abt. 461, 19048, District court Frankfurt, 18 May 1942. The defendant was
sentenced to eight years.
11 HStAD, RW 58, Urteil Landgericht Kleve of 22 September 1939.

References

Brockhaus, Gudrun. 2014. '"Die Phrase hat Blut getunken und lebt": Zur Aktualität
früherer NS-Analysen.' In *Attraktion der NS-Bewegung*, edited by Gudrun Brockhaus,
95–114. Essen: Klartext-Verl.
Diehl, Guida. 1933. *Die deutsche Frau und der Nationalsozialismus.* Eisenach: Neulandverlag.
Dinter, Artur. 1920. *Die Sünde wider das Blut: Ein Zeitroman.* Leipzig: Matthes & Thost.
Dühring, Eugen Carl. 1881. *Die Judenfrage als Racen-, Sitten- und Culturfrage : mit einer
weltgeschichtlichen Antwort.* Karlsruhe: Reuther.
Eustace, Nicole, Lean, Eugenia, Livingston, Julia, Plamper, Jan, Reddy, Willam M., and
Rosenwein, Barbara H. 2012. 'AHR Conversation: The Historical Study of Emotions.'
American Historical Review 1487–1531.
Febvre, Lucien. 1973. 'Sensibility and History: How to Reconstitute the Emotional Life of
the Past.' In *A New Kind of History: From the Writings of Lucien Febvre.* Edited by Peter
Burke, 12–26. London: Harper & Row.
Geppert, Alexander. 2010. '"Dear Adolf!": Locating Love in Nazi Germany.' In *New
Dangerous Liaisons: Discourses on Europe and Love in the Twentieth Century*, edited by
Luisa Passerini, Liliana Ellena, and Alexander C. T. Geppert, 158. Making Sense of
History 13. New York: Berghahn Books.
Gross, Raphael. 2010. *Anständig geblieben: nationalsozialistische Moral.* Schriftenreihe des
Fritz-Bauer-Instituts, Frankfurt am Main: Frankfurt am Main: Fischer/Fritz Bauer Institut.
Heineman, Elizabeth D. 2002. 'Sexuality and Nazism: The Doubly Unspeakable?' *Journal
of the History of Sexuality* 11(1/2), 22–66.
Herbert, Ulrich. 1996. *Best: Biographische Studien über Radikalismus, Weltanschauung und
Vernunft, 1903–1989.* Bonn: Dietz.
Herbert, Ulrich. 2014. 'Echoes of the Volksgemeinschaft.' In *Visions of Community in Nazi
Germany: Social Engineering and Private Lives*, edited by Martina Steber and Bernhard
Gotto, 60–69. Oxford Oxford University Press.

Hopp, Andrea. 2012. 'Antijüdische Emotionen adeliger Frauen 1824–1945: zwei Fallbeispiele.' *Jahrbuch für Antisemitismusforschung*, 268–293.

Junge, Traudl. 2002. *Bis zur letzten Stunde: Hitlers Sekretärin erzählt ihr Leben*. Munich.

Kater, Michael. 1983. 'Frauen in der NS-Bewegung.' *Vierteljahrshefte für Zeitgeschichte* 31(2), 202–241.

Klemperer, Victor. 2006. *The Language of the Third Reich: LTI, Lingua Tertii Imperii: A Philologist's Notebook*. Translated by Martin Brady. London and New York: Continuum.

Kolnai, Aurel. 2004. *On Disgust*. Chicago, IL: Open Court.

Kramer, Nicole. 2011. *Volksgenossinnen an der Heimatfront: Mobilisierung, Verhalten, Erinnerung*. Göttingen, Oakville, CT: Vandenhoeck & Ruprecht.

Kühne, Thomas. 2010. *Belonging and Genocide: Hitler's Community, 1918–1945*. New Haven, CT and London: Yale University Press.

Nussbaum, Martha Craven. 2004. *Hiding from Humanity: Disgust, Shame, and the Law*. Princeton, NJ: Princeton University Press.

Plamper, Jan. 2010. The History of Emotions: An Interview with William Reddy, Barbara Rosenwein, and Peter Stearns.' *History and Theory* 49, 237–265.

Przyrembel, Alexandra. 2001. 'Transfixed by an Image: Ilse Koch, the "Kommandeuse of Buchenwald".' *German History* 19(3), 369–399.

Przyrembel, Alexandra. 2003. *Rassenschande: Reinheitsmythos und Vernichtungslegitimation im Nationalsozialismus; mit 13 Tabellen sowie einem Dokumentenanhang*. Göttingen: Vandenhoeck & Ruprecht.

Przyrembel, Alexandra. 2013. 'Ambivalente Gefühle: Sexualität und Antisemitismus während des Nationalsozialismus.' *Geschichte und Gesellschaft* 39, 527–554.

Rosenwein, Barbara H. 2002. 'Worrying about Emotions in History.' *American Historical Review* 107, 821–845.

Salomon, Julie. 2002. 'Is a Demon Humanized no longer a Demon?' *New York Times*, 2 February.

Schmidt, Herbert. 2003. *Rassenschande vor Düsseldorfer Gerichten 1935 bis 1944: Eine Dokumentation*. Essen: Klartext.

Steuwer, Janosch. 2013. 'Was meint und nützt das Sprechen von der "Volksgemeinschaft"? Neuere Literatur zur Gesellschaftsgeschichte des Nationalsozialismus.' *Archiv für Sozialgeschichte* 53, 1–49.

Stieda, Renate von. 1935/1936. 'Auf dem Parteitag der Freiheit.' *NS-Frauenwarte*, 8, 233–235.

Süß, Dietmar. 2011. *Tod aus der Luft: Kriegsgesellschaft und Luftkrieg in Deutschland und England*. Munich.

Ulshöfer, Helmut, ed. 1996. *Liebesbriefe an Adolf Hitler – Briefe in den Tod: Unveröffentlichte Dokumente aus der Reichskanzlei*. Frankfurt am Main: Verlag für Akademische Schriften.

Volkov, Shulamit. 1978. 'Antisemitism as a Cultural Code: Reflections on the History and Historiography of Antisemitism in Imperial Germany.' *The Leo Baeck Institute Yearbook* 23(1), 25–46.

Wehler, Hans-Ulrich. 2003. *Deutsche Gesellschaftsgeschichte: 1914–1949*. 5 vols. Munich.

Wildt, Michael. 2007. *Volksgemeinschaft als Selbstermächtigung: Gewalt gegen Juden in der deutschen Provinz 1919 bis 1939*. Hamburg: Hamburger Edition.

Wildt, Michael. 2013. '"Volksgemeinschaft" - eine Zwischenbilanz.' In *'Volksgemeinschaft' als soziale Praxis: neue Forschungen zur NS-Gesellschaft vor Ort*, edited by Dietmar von Reeken and Malte Thiessen, 355–369. Nationalsozialistische Volksgemeinschaft: Studien zu Konstruktion, gesellschaftschaftlicher Wirkungsmacht und Erinnerung. Paderborn: Schöningh.

Further Reading

Despite an increasing interest in the history of emotions, a history of emotions during National Socialism has not yet been written. However, the following publications are recommended.

Eustace, Nicole, Lean, Eugenia, Livingston, Julia, Plamper, Jan, Reddy, Willam M., and Rosenwein, Barbara H. 2012. 'AHR Conversation: The Historical Study of Emotions.' *American Historical Review* 1487–1531.

Gives an overview of the flourishing field and summarizes different historical approaches to analysing emotions across times. In the course of the American Historical Review round table discussion, Barbara Rosenwein and William Reddy, who themselves have contributed ground-breaking books on emotions in European history, explained why they privileged certain methodological approaches, such as the making of emotions through language and the social negotiation of emotions by communities.

Febvre, Lucien. 1973. 'Sensibility and History: How to Reconstitute the Emotional Life of the Past.' In *A New Kind of History: From the Writings of Lucien Febvre*. Edited by Peter Burke, 12–26. London: Harper & Row.

Gives a first introduction to the topic.

For those who are interested in focusing on particular aspects of the impact of emotions on the political and social life in Nazi Germany, I suggest the following two books by Michael Wildt and Thomas Kühne. Both authors are interested in understanding the making of the National Socialist *Volksgemeinschaft* by emphasizing cultures of honour (Wildt) and the experiences of pleasure (Kühne) in moments of violence against Jews.

Kühne, Thomas. 2010. *Belonging and Genocide: Hitler's Community, 1918–1945*. New Haven, CT and London: Yale University Press.
Wildt, Michael. 2012. *Hitler's Volksgemeinschaft and the Dynamics of Racial Exclusion. Violence against Jews in Provincial Germany, 1919–1939*, translated by Bernard Heise. New York and Oxford: Berghahn Books.

CHAPTER TWENTY-FIVE

Environment

CHARLES E. CLOSMANN

The environmental record of Nazi Germany is highly contradictory. On the one hand, the Nazi regime adopted ambitious policies to protect landscapes, forests, and animals. Most famously, the Nazi state decreed the Reich Nature Protection Law in 1935 (*Reichsnaturschutzgesetz, RNG*), one of the most advanced laws to preserve natural areas anywhere in the world at the time (Ditt 2000b, 161–187; Dominick 1987, 508–537). The regime also supported sustainable forestry, decreed progressive animal protection laws, experimented with organic farming policies, and promoted other environmental initiatives (Uekoetter 2006, 44–82). On the other hand, the Nazi state inflicted massive damage to the environment. In order to create arable land, the Labour Service (*Arbeitsdienst*) drained almost two million acres of wetlands and rectified numerous streams, even while critics warned about the danger of erosion, falling water tables, and climate change (Uekoetter 2007, 267–287). Under the Four Year Plan, the regime's 'war for production' led to a partial abandonment of sustainable forestry, while rearmament and industrial activities led to ongoing contamination of Germany's rivers and pollution of the atmosphere (Uekoetter 2006, 44–82, 167–183; Wey 1982, 37–127).

Such a mixed legacy raises important questions about the environmental history of Nazi Germany. First, why did some leaders of a brutal dictatorship support measures to protect picturesque natural monuments, wild animals, and entire forests? Was the Nazi regime pro-environment, and if so, how did Nazi ideology influence ideas about nature and the environment? Second, what explains the Nazi environmental record, and especially the destructive policies that existed simultaneously with measures to preserve forests, fields, and landscapes from degradation? Finally, was Nazi Germany exceptional in its approach to environmental issues, or did its policies reflect more general trends in modern, industrial societies?

A Companion to Nazi Germany, First Edition. Edited by Shelley Baranowski, Armin Nolzen, and Claus-Christian W. Szejnmann.
© 2018 John Wiley & Sons Ltd. Published 2018 by John Wiley & Sons Ltd.

Historians have devoted considerable attention to these questions, especially since the 1990s. In so doing, they have attempted to answer these questions by (i) focusing on the role of key personalities, and especially high-ranking officials in the Nazi regime, (ii) exploring ideological continuities between conservation groups before, during, and after the Third Reich, (iii) scrutinizing details of Nazi legal measures to protect the environment, and (iv) comparing Nazi Germany's environmental record to that of other countries.

Today they have reached a rough consensus on most of these questions, although some disagreement remains. Regarding the role of key personalities, most scholars agree that support existed among some Nazi officials for 'green' ideas, that this support could be decisive, but that it was never consistent or widespread. One early controversy surrounded the role of Richard Walther Darré, Nazi Germany's Minister of Nutrition and Agriculture from 1933 to 1942. According to Anna Bramwell, Darré's encouragement of biodynamic farming (an early form of organic farming) made him a progressive ecologist, with ideas similar to those of Green parties in the 1970s and 1980s (Bramwell 1985, 171–208). Since the 1990s, however, Raymond Dominick and Gesine Gerhard have argued that Darré's backing of organic farming was never wholehearted and only occurred at a time (in 1940) when such agricultural methods had little chance of winning widespread support within the regime. Rather, Darré promoted the interests of German farmers, not because he believed in progressive environmental values, but because he saw the peasantry as the bedrock of a racially pure nation (Dominick 1992, 81–118; Gerhard 2002, 257–272).

Likewise, scholars have discredited Hermann Göring's reputation as an avid supporter of conservation. While acknowledging Göring's decisive role in muscling through the Reich Nature Protection Law, Frank Uekoetter credits the Reich Marshall's backing of this measure to his 'stamp-collector attitude toward titles and tasks' and his enthusiasm for hunting on the large nature preserves created by the law. Göring's inconsistent support for conservation also had environmental consequences, according to Uekoetter. When Göring threw his influence behind the Reich Nature Protection Law, conservation flourished. Yet when Göring's support waned – as it did after 1936 – conservationists were on their own, falling back on bureaucratic routine and pleading desperately for the preservation of rivers, mountains, or heathlands. As Director of the Four Year Plan after 1936, Göring also played a crucial role in many of Germany's most harmful environmental policies, measures designed to increase industrial production and prepare the regime for war. Göring's multiple responsibilities and wavering support for conservation helps explain Nazi Germany's contradictory environmental record, according to Uekoetter (Uekoetter 2006, 44–82, 83–136, 137–166; 2014, 25–58).

Thomas Zeller's work on the *Autobahn* system supports this interpretation of the role played by top officials. In *Driving Germany: The Landscape of the German Autobahn, 1930–1970* (2007), Zeller concentrates on the work of two crucial individuals: Fritz Todt, Inspector General of the German Roadways; and Alwin Seifert, a landscape architect named by Todt as an 'advocate' for aesthetically attractive highway design. According to Zeller, Todt never consistently supported progressive landscape management and rarely specified what kinds of advice he expected from Seifert. In contrast, Seifert enthusiastically advocated policies that reconciled modern industry with the 'soul' of a people, and that 'healed' sick landscapes disturbed by aesthetically unattractive features. Yet Seifert and his team of landscape advocates fought an uphill battle to influence Todt and the engineers who designed Germany's autobahn system. According to Zeller, no reconciliation of nature and technology occurred on the autobahn projects, at least not one that can be attributed to Todt or Seifert (Zeller 2007, 47–78, 79–126, 127–180).

Other work, on lower ranking officials, complicates these conclusions. Peter Staudenmaier, for instance, identifies concerted support for organic farming by members of Darré's staff such as Hans Merkel, Georg Halbe, and other mid-level members of the regime. Together, these men enabled promoters of organic farming 'to publicize their views in the Nazi press and gain notable sympathy and interest from the highest echelons of the Party', at least for a time. Nevertheless, Staudenmaier adds, suspicion by the security services, opposition by other officials in the agricultural administration, and the exigencies of war undermined such efforts (Staudenmaier 2013, 383–411). Likewise, Thomas Lekan explores the role played by conservation officials in the Rhineland in *Imagining the Nation in Nature: Landscape Preservation and German Identity, 1885–1945* (2004). He notes that Nazi officials like Rhenish governor Heinz Haake enthusiastically supported conservation, encouraging development of a comprehensive Rhine Valley landscape plan that was 'conceptually bold for its time and considered a model of landscape planning in Germany', according to Lekan. However, the outbreak of war derailed this ambitious scheme, and thorough protection of the landscape did not occur (Lekan 2004, 153–203, 204–251).

Scholars also point out how some former Nazi conservation officials continued their work in the Federal Republic of Germany and the German Democratic Republic after the end of the Second World War. Gert Gröning and Joachim Wolschke-Bulmahn published extensively on this topic in the 1980s and 1990s, highlighting the role of SS landscape planners like Heinrich Wiepking-Jürgensmann and Konrad Meyer. During the war, Wiepking-Jürgensmann and Meyer developed comprehensive plans to shape landscapes in the 'Annexed East Areas' of Poland and the former Soviet Union. Here, according to Gröning and Wolschke-Bulmahn, the local inhabitants would be removed and German settlers would be transplanted to a harmonious 'German' landscape of farms, village, roads, and woods. Both Meyer and Wiepking-Jürgensmann found employment at the University of Hanover once the war was over (Gröning and Wolschke-Bulmahn 1987, 127–148). More recent work by Jens Ivo Engels, Nils M. Franke, and others highlights these connections, and emphasizes how conservationists who remained active in Germany after 1945 tried to dismiss notions that their work was tainted by National Socialism's racist world-view. These scholars also underscore the importance of uncovering such continuities and the possibility that support for the preservation of 'nature' may conceal politically suspect motives, even under democratic regimes (Franke 2014, 81–96; and Engels 2002, 363–404).

Historians have also explored the ideological overlap between key Nazis and earlier, nature-loving conservation groups. Raymond Dominick argued in 1992 that anti-modern, *völkisch* sentiments among middle-class conservationists in the

1920s made some leaders of this movement vulnerable to the Nazis' appeals to 'blood and soil'. Yet Dominick also pointed out that Nazi promotion of conservation before 1933 was rare, and after 1933 was rarely sincere. In addition, Dominick observed that some conservationists, like Hans Klose, Director of Nazi Germany's Reich Centre for Nature Protection, remained professionally active as government officials after the war, and wilfully oblivious of connections between their former activities and the Nazis' brutal agenda. In 1996, John Alexander Williams offered a more complex theory on the reasons why conservation groups during the 1920s might have been attracted to *völkisch* ideas. In this case, Williams focused in part on the changing meaning of the word *Heimat*. For conservationists in the period from 1900 to the early Weimar era, *Heimat* denoted not only a specific local or regional place, but also the cultural, spiritual, and emotional attachments associated with that place. This rather conservative outlook began to change in the late Weimar years, according to Williams. Increasingly, *Heimat* reflected more modern, popular notions of a German landscape capable of providing stability and national unity during the divisive years of the late 1920s and early 1930s. Consequently, according to Williams, the Nazi regime garnered enthusiastic support from leading conservationists, in part because it appropriated pre-existing popular ideas about the *Heimat* while emphasizing overtly racial motives (Williams 1996, 339–384).

With respect to Nazi Germany's laws, scholars generally see the *RNG* and other decrees as progressive measures that drew heavily from pre-existing ideas. In 2002, Edeltraud Klueting examined the Animal Protection Law of 1933, the Reich Nature Protection Law of 1935, and measures to prevent water pollution. Despite the support of top Nazis such as Hermann Göring, such laws cannot, in her opinion, 'be classified as Nazi laws', reflecting instead previous campaigns, legal drafts, and state laws dating to the Weimar Republic and Wilhelmine Empire. Klueting added that while these laws had enormous potential to protect natural areas, enforcement remained lax, especially after 1936 when demands for industrial production undermined concerns about the landscape (Klueting 2002, 77–106). Karl Ditt has concurred, adding that the *RNG* was 'remarkably free of ideology and contained no racist jargon'. He also asserted that the *RNG* reflected progressive concepts of *Landschaftspflege*, or 'care for the landscape', because it sought not to roll back the clock on economic development, but to shape landscapes which reconciled development, ecological concerns, and aesthetic motives (Ditt 2000, 161–187; Closmann 2005, 18–42). More recent interpretations generally confirm these conclusions, adding that elements of the *RNG* and Animal Protection Laws remained on the books of different states in the Federal Republic of Germany and in the German Democratic Republic well after 1945 (Uekoetter 2006, 184–201).

Some debate remains on the ideological nature of Nazi Germany's animal protection measures. Mahren Möhring asserts that while the Nazis exploited the propaganda potential of the 1933 Animal Protection Law (*Tierschutzgesetz*), the law also reflected Social Darwinian views and 'an integral part of the new ordering of society along *völkisch*-racist foundations'. In other words, the Animal Protection Law of 1933 law was a 'Nazi' law. Accordingly, the law's ban on vivisection, abuse of animals, and ritual slaughter reflected National Socialist views that animals were part of a '*Lebensgemeinschaft*', a living community that excluded races which allegedly treated animals in an instrumental manner (Möhring 2011, 229–244). Stefan Discherl reaches a similar conclusion in *Tier- und Naturschutz im Nationalsozialismus: Gesetzgebung, Ideologie, und Praxis*. He demonstrates that the Nazi state fined and/or sentenced people to prison for abusing animals, and argues that the animal protection law was a progressive regulation which built upon earlier ideas and *did* reflect National Socialist ideology (Discherl 2012, 79–198, 199–206).

Finally, a few historians have compared Nazi Germany's environmental policies with those of other modern states. Karl Ditt, for instance, has noted that conservation policies in Germany, Britain, and the United States during the 1930s reflected romantically inspired concerns about the disappearance of picturesque landscapes as a result of rapid economic development. In each country, conservationists portrayed nature as a source of national identity, although in Germany this was more pronounced, especially after 1933 (Ditt 1996, 499–533). Christof Mauch and Kiran Klaus Patel reach similar conclusions in an essay on Germany and the United States. In Germany, well-known conservationists like Walther Schoenichen looked forward to a 'purification' of the landscape under the Nazis, even while the Nazi state sometimes ignored its own environmental laws in favour of policies that served the regime's expansionist goals. As in the United States, intensive resource extraction coexisted uneasily beside policies to protect the environment (Mauch and Patel 2010, 180–193). Thomas Zeller demonstrates that the construction of scenic parkways in the United States and Nazi Germany helped shape national identity and stimulate the economy, even under very different ideological contexts (Zeller 2012, 1–17).

In fact, Nazi policies dealing with the environment often demonstrated a combination of progressive measures to protect natural resources, professional opportunism, and rhetorical appeals to national identity. Likewise, the relative support for these policies by high-ranking officials often, but not always, proved decisive in their success. Finally, such policies existed in a tenuous relationship to other measures designed to enhance the economic, racial, and power-political goals of a modern industrial state.

Implementation of the Reich Nature Protection Law of 1935 reflected all of these factors. Among other things, the *RNG* owed its quick adoption to Hermann Göring, who now controlled the Reich Forest Office and enjoyed the title of 'Master of the German Forests'. In April of 1935, Göring brusquely intervened in high-level debates over a draft of this law, seizing jurisdiction over conservation from Bernhard Rust's Ministry of Science and Education and putting his own staff to work on a revised draft. On 26 June 1935, Nazi Germany's cabinet proclaimed the *RNG* as law.

An impressive measure by international standards, the *RNG* built upon existing laws at the state level, while also expanding the power of the central government to regulate conservation. It elevated the decades-old Prussian state Agency for Nature Protection to the national level (a largely advisory body of experts), and placed it under the authority of Göring's Ministry of Forests. The law also expanded the number of conservation offices at the regional and district levels, and provided them with enhanced regulatory authority. At the same time, however, the *RNG* left in place the network of unpaid volunteers who identified and recommended protection of natural areas across Germany. Mostly teachers, scientists, and other members of the educated middle class, these men formed the core of Germany's nature and *Heimat* protection associations, groups like the Federation for Heimat Protection, the Bird Protection League, and the Westphalian Nature Protection Association. Members of these groups had long sought passage of such a national law, with its promise of enhanced protection for natural areas and greater recognition of conservation by the state (Uekoetter 2006, 17–43, 44–82).

The *RNG* seemed to fulfil the long-standing dreams of these groups. In addition to enhancing the status of conservation, the law unified the definition of areas worthy of protection for all of Germany, abolishing the welter of state regulations that defined which types of 'natural monuments' or 'nature preserves' could be protected. The *RNG* also went further, in a more progressive direction. Section 5 granted protection to 'other portions of free nature' which 'contribute to the ornamentation and liveliness of the form of the landscape or the animal world, especially with respect to song birds and small game animals …', while Section 19 authorized government officials to issue rules for the widespread protection mentioned in Section 5. Section 20 required government officials to consult with conservation experts on all projects which might alter the landscape. Together, Sections 5, 19, and 20 corresponded to the concept of *Landschaftspflege*, an evolving notion of care for the landscape that sought to reconcile economic development with the preservation of attractive ensembles of countryside, towns, roads, and streams. Finally, Section 24 empowered the government to expropriate land for the protection of nature, with no right of indemnification, while other portions of the law authorized the creation of very large 'Imperial Nature Protection Areas' (*Reichsnaturschutzgebiete*). By any standard, the *RNG* granted more power to conserve natural areas than any previous German law or any laws outside of Germany (Closmann 2005, 18–42; Ditt 1996, 499–534; *Reichsnaturschutzgesetz* 1935, Sections 5, 19, 20).

Why did the Nazi state enact such a draconian measure? In part, the law reflected the spirit of the Nazi motto, that 'The common good takes precedent over the individual good' (*Gemeinnutz vor Eigennutz*), a concept reflected in other Nazi policies of the 1930s. Some conservationists also believed that the new law could 'heal' the German people by creating a healthy organic relationship between people, nature, and 'aesthetically appealing work environments'. In this sense, the law reflected ideas drawn from ecology: that landscapes existed in a holistic relationship with a people. Finally, the *RNG* reflected opportunism, especially on the part of Hermann Göring and the conservationists (mostly middle-class men) who hoped to profit in terms of prestige and careers (Lekan 2004, 153–203; Uekoetter 2006, 44–82).

For a while, the *RNG* enabled German conservationists to achieve their goals. Under the law, conservation authorities designated 800 nature preserves and 50000 natural monuments, for a total protected area of about 50000 acres. This was a considerable achievement, especially compared to the Federal Republic of Germany where only about 3000 acres earned protection from 1945 to 1960.

Moreover, the designation of these areas under the Third Reich undoubtedly protected them in the long run from rampant development under the Federal Republic of Germany. Much of this success was owed to voluntary conservation advisers who cooperated with authorities at all levels to designate and protect natural areas. The advisers' work differed widely from place to place, depending upon the support of the 'nature protection authorities', their own particular interests, and the local geography (Lekan 2004, 204–251; Uekoetter 2006, 137–66).

Germany's *RNG* facilitated these successes, encouraging the creation of new 'nature protection authorities' across the country and giving conservation advocates powerful tools to achieve their goals. For example, in difficult negotiations with landowners, the threat of expropriation of land under Section 24 of the law sometimes proved decisive. This happened in the Ruhr, when nature protection authorities eventually paid a price of 30 000 Reichsmarks to a farmer in order to protect the Westrup Heath. This price was half the market value of the farmer's land, and although mention of Section 24 of the *RNG* never appeared in the administrative files, the threat of expropriation clearly influenced this decision (Uekoetter 2006, 137–166).

Conservation advisers also remained highly active after the war began. Falling back on bureaucratic routine, they scoured the countryside for objects worthy of protection, filled out paperwork, and lobbied high-ranking authorities for the protection of natural areas. Citing one notable example, conservationists attempting to protect Baden's Wutach Gorge from a hydroelectricity project sought, unsuccessfully, to enlist SS leader Heinrich Himmler in their campaign. Although they failed to halt this project under the Nazi regime, conservationists eventually succeeded in the 1960s when the state of Baden mandated protection for the Gorge. In 1942, nature protection authorities even managed to expand the Schorfheide Reich Nature Protection Area from 141 000 to 185 000 acres. A large preserve of woodlands and lakes east of Berlin, the Schorfheide also served as personal fiefdom and hunting ground for Hermann Göring, Master of the German Forests (Uekoetter 2006, 83–136).

In reality, however, much of the conservationists' activity after 1939 'was little more than paperwork', according to Uekoetter. Buried in routine, conservation advisers faced unrelenting demands on their time in addition to conscription into the military. They wrote expert assessments, urged protection from the authorities, and objected when government agencies ignored Section 20 of the *RNG*, which required participation of nature protection experts in decisions that threatened the countryside. In fact, addenda to the *RNG* from 1942 through 1944 required nature protection authorities to limit their activities due to the 'indispensable needs of the war' (quoted in Wettengel 1993, 355–399).

Eventually, conservationists hoped that the conquest of foreign countries would reduce devastation of the environment in Germany and bring new opportunities abroad. They even attempted to extend conservation law into occupied territories, and compiled lists of desirable nature preserves, forests, and other natural wonders. Very little came of this. Heinrich Himmler's SS planning experts also developed a scheme to reshape thousands of square miles of occupied territory along ecological and racial principles in order to create a supposedly 'Germanic' landscape. German settlers would be relocated to Eastern Europe from other parts of the continent, while residents would be forcibly removed. Their 'General Plan East' (*Generalplan Ost*) also envisioned soil and water conservation, pollution control, the planting of hedgerows, and other ecological measures. Not much came of this either, as in-fighting between Nazi officials prevented implementation of such grandiose schemes (Uekoetter 2006, 137–166).

Overall, the reality of Nazi Germany's conservation policies never matched the rhetoric of the regime, its laws, or its ardent supporters. Despite the creation of hundreds of nature preserves and natural monuments, conservationists rarely achieved protection of extensive landscapes. Hitler's ambitious plans to solve Germany's unemployment crisis also devastated the environment. Such schemes entailed putting hundreds of thousands of men to work building dams, straightening waterways, draining wetlands, cultivating moors, and constructing roads. Prominent conservationists like Walther Schoenichen (Director of the Reich Centre for Nature Protection from 1933 to 1938) pleaded with the Labour Service to consider nature and *Heimat* in their decisions, but often to no avail. Yet even Schoenichen conceded that the interests of nature had to be sacrificed in order to rebuild the nation during its time of crisis. Although adoption of the *RNG* in 1935 made conservation a higher priority at most levels, the needs of agriculture and autarky took precedence, especially after the adoption of the Four Year Plan in 1936. By 1941, the Labour Service had drained about 1.8 million acres of swamps and protected just over 650 000 acres from flooding, actions that undoubtedly brought economic and social benefits, but also marred the countryside and reduced biodiversity (Uekoetter 2007, 267–287). Visiting Germany in the mid-1930s, the famous American ecologist Aldo Leopold commented on the appearance of the landscape, noting that, while aspects of the countryside were more attractive than in the past, 'The German marshes are gone' and 'The German heaths are fast going' (Leopold 1936, 102–111).

Rhetoric also exceeded reality in the area of forest policies. In this case, high-ranking Nazis like Hermann Göring shaped the promulgation of forestry decrees, while economic and military factors undermined the original intent of these regulations. Even before the Nazis came to power, Göring proclaimed himself an advocate of *Dauerwald*, a concept of sustainable forestry that encouraged the cultivation of mixed species of indigenous trees, selective cutting of individual specimens, and natural afforestation. Göring probably supported *Dauerwald* because of reverence for German woodlands, enthusiasm for hunting, and a belief that promoting *Dauerwald* would allow him to expand his political power. In any event, *Dauerwald* represented a break from tradition. Under previous methods of 'scientific' forestry, forest owners sought to maximize long-term timber yields through the periodic harvesting of entire stands of the same age and through replanting with fast-growing conifers. Scientific forestry had predominated since at least the late 1700s but it faced increasing criticism by the late 1800s, especially because of the high cost of clear cutting and ecological disadvantages such as soil exhaustion and the vulnerability of monoculture forests to pests. In 1933, Göring appointed Walther von Keudell, a dedicated proponent of *Dauerwald*, to the position of Chief of the Prussian State Forest Office. Shortly thereafter, Nazi Germany's cabinet converted von Keudell's Prussian Ministry to the Reich Forest Office, with Göring as Master of the German Forest and von Keudell as his deputy. In 1934, the Reich Forest Office issued guidelines mandating *Dauerwald* principles for all state and privately owned forests, effectively bypassing local and regional forest offices across Germany (Imort 2005, 43–72).

Aside from the personal role of Hermann Göring and true believers like von Keudell, several other factors explain Nazi Germany's support for *Dauerwald*. Among other things, the economic depression of the early 1930s was suppressing timber prices, making policies that restricted the production of timber and increased prices more appealing. *Dauerwald* also presented the regime with propaganda opportunities. Often called upon to present the regime's ideological positions, German foresters increasingly drew analogies between the organic community of plants in a *Dauerwald* forest and the German people themselves. According to this belief, both a forest and a people were living communities in which individuals of different rank contributed to the health of the collective. Likewise, just as foresters culled weaker trees for timber, so too did the state cull its weaker members in order to create an eternal, living *Volk*. As Michael Imort notes, foresters now praised the 'supposedly natural and eternal bond between forest and *Volk* with never-ending comparisons of silviculture and politics in general, and *Dauerwald* forestry and National Socialism in particular'. Likewise, the Nazi state also inserted such comparisons into education, museum exhibits, film, and other venues (Imort 2005, 43–72).

Yet despite such rhetorical support for *Dauerwald*, the reality was more complicated. In 1935, only one year after Göring mandated *Dauerwald* for all forests, the quickly recovering economy forced Göring to increase timber quotas to 150% of sustainable yield on all publically owned woodlands. A year later he issued a similar decree regarding private land. As head of the Four Year Plan from 1936 onward, Göring now had to 'ramp up the wood output of the German forest at all cost', according to Imort. Göring even replaced the *Dauerwald* advocate Walther von Keudell with the more compliant Friedrich Alpers, a loyal party man more likely to support increased, short-term timber yields. Yet some aspects of *Dauerwald* remained policy, even under the context of autarky and the Four Year Plan. Experts in the Forest Department issued regulations which allowed German landowners more freedom to meet timber quotas so long as they cultivated woodlands of mixed trees, of uneven age. This compromise, known as 'close to nature' forestry (*naturgemäßer Wirtschaftswald*) characterized forestry efforts after 1936, and has remained influential in the Federal Republic of Germany since then. The Reich also initiated a major afforestation campaign in order to put unemployed men back to work, a programme that eventually resulted in a slight expansion of German forest acreage between 1933 and 1945 (Imort 2005, 43–72).

Finally, the Nazis' war of aggression also reduced the pressure on German forests by shifting demands from German to foreign sources of wood. In occupied France, for instance, German officials required a 50% increase in the timber harvest, a harsh demand which slowed France's own economic recovery after the end of the Second World War. Shelling, burning, and other features of military combat also devastated about 1 000 000 acres of French woodlands and burned another

500 000 to the ground. The effects of war and Nazi occupation on forests in other occupied countries have yet to be fully examined (Westing 1980, 51–53; Tucker 2004, 110–141).

Nazi Germany's agricultural policies also reflect a mixed record and a continuation of modern farming practices that pre-dated the Nazi era. As stated above, advocates of biodynamic farming gained some influence under the Nazis, especially among mid-level officials in Richard Walther Darré's Ministry of Nutrition and Agriculture. An idea that dated to the years just after the First World War, biodynamic methods emphasized that the farm was an organic entity linking soil, animals, vegetation, and cosmic forces. Accordingly, biodynamic farmers planted according to astrological signs and promoted the use of natural rather than chemical fertilizers, pesticides, and herbicides. This approach also appealed to some farmers, politicians, and agricultural experts who objected to the industrialization of modern agriculture, especially since the 1920s. One early centre of support formed around Erhard Bartsch, who argued that the Germans had a special love for nature, and that biodynamic methods were most suitable for a race of people with close ties to the soil.

By the mid-1930s, other mid-level figures in the Nazi hierarchy also lobbied for biodynamic methods, including Hans Georg Müller, who as head of the Nazi life reform movement (*Lebensreform*) intervened with the potato growers' guild and the association of grain growers to support biodynamic methods. In 1940, even more influential pockets of support emerged for biodynamic farming. Intrigued by the possibility that biodynamic farming might help preserve soil fertility and increase crop yields, Minister of Nutrition and Agriculture Darré also expressed strong interest, and established semi-private associations to encourage farming along these lines. Once the war began, advocates for what some called 'natural farming' proposed expanding such methods to the occupied eastern territories, where, according to Staudenmaier, 'Biodynamic leaders saw the war as their chance to step forward in support of the German cause and as an auspicious occasion to reshape eastern lands along organic lines.' The SS even established organic plantations in some of its concentration camps (Staudenmaier 2013, 383–411).

Yet biodynamic farming never gained widespread support. Some high-ranking officials viewed biodynamic farming advocates with suspicion, especially because of their alleged support for the occult. After 1936, Nazi Germany's 'war for production' also mandated continued use of mechanized farming techniques and artificial fertilizers, an approach that existed well before the Nazis gained power, and which continued to dominate farming in Germany long after the war. Farms in the United States and other parts of the industrial world also used modern, mechanized farming for most of the twentieth century. Today, of course, an increasing number of people support agricultural methods that emphasize small-scale technology, natural fertilizers, and other features of organic farming (Staudenmaier 2013, 383–411).

The environmental history of water and air pollution control under the Nazis also demonstrates strong continuities with previous and subsequent regimes. As in other areas of environmental policy, the shifting priorities of the regime and conflict between government ministries also undermined effective pollution control, especially after 1936.

By the early 1930s, politicians, scientists, and urban planners were clearly worried about the state of German waterways. Under the Weimar Republic, water quality had declined, due in part to a temporary increase in economic activity, the development of new industrial processes, and the production of a wide range of new chemicals. Municipal governments had made progress in the construction of advanced methods of sewage treatment, but budget shortfalls prevented progress in the treatment of new forms of water pollution (Wey 1982, 33–104).

Advocates for enhanced pollution control believed that the Nazi seizure of power presented an opportunity to further their cause. First, legal experts hoped the Nazi regime would adopt a national water law, one that would unify the confusing maze of regulations, permissions, and other procedures that existed from state to state. In addition, engineers hoped to address the problem of water pollution and unemployment at the same time, through the construction of new wastewater treatment plants in German cities. Some, such as J. Brix, also hoped that the recycling of municipal sewage on crops by means of large 'sewage farms' (*Rieselfelder*) would also improve farm productivity and make Germany independent of foreign sources of fertilizer (Seeger 1999, 51–56; Brix 1934, iii–viii).

Ultimately, supporters of a national water law (*Reichswassergesetz*) made little progress, although their draft law offered the potential for more progressive management of Germany's water resources. In 1936, a committee of the German Academy of Law presented a draft *Reichswasssergesetz* to other government ministries, a measure that would have systematically controlled the release of wastes by government and industry, and imposed tough fines for violations. Nevertheless, the proposed law became bogged down due to resistance from industry and some water utilities, especially after 1941 (Wey 1982, 45–47).

Meanwhile, some cities planned to construct new wastewater treatment plants. In Hamburg, for example, engineers designed a major advanced treatment facility in 1934, one whose construction would employ several thousand workers and reduce the horrific contamination of the River Elbe. Two years later, the Ministry of Nutrition and Agriculture put its own stamp on the plan, and demanded the construction of a giant sewage farm, a project that would also have created jobs, reduced pollution, and provided valuable fertilizer for agriculture. In addition, the project reflected Richard Walther Darré's support for German farmers as the racial bedrock of the German state, a peasantry bound by ties of 'blood and soil' to the land. As designed, the Hamburg plan would have been the largest wastewater treatment facility in the world, one that would handle the sewage of over 1 million people by sprinkling it on 124 000 acres of land beside the river. City workers broke ground on the project in 1937 but suspended construction once the war began (Voigt 1963, 41–64; Struve and Brunotte 1934). The war forced cancellation of similar plans elsewhere in Germany, in part because the Nazi state diverted badly needed building materials to military projects. In fact, while the regime planned to connect some 30 million people to new sewage farms, it only reached a figure of about 8 million people by the end of the Second World War. Overall, water quality continued to decline under the Nazis (Münch 1993, 98–109).

The war also imperilled water quality in other ways. After 1941, Allied bombs devastated underground water distribution systems, pumping stations, sewer lines, and treatment plants. In Hamburg, the air raids destroyed crucial parts of the water supply and sewer system, increasing the level of E. coli bacteria in the city's drinking water during 1944 and 1945, and forcing residents to obtain their drinking water from springs, broken mains, and water trucks (Meng 1993, 291–297; Hamburger Stadtentwässerung 2002, 47–55). Allied raids inflicted similar damage all across Germany, with comparable impacts on drinking water and sewer systems (Diefendorf 2009, 171–192).

The history of air pollution control under the Nazis is similar to that of water pollution measures. Once again, the needs of the economy generally took precedence over thoroughgoing policies to limit pollution of the atmosphere. While bureaucratic measures to reduce the worst abuses continued, the overall trend was probably one of increasingly polluted skies, especially once the war began. In this case, as in others, the economy continued to modernize and industrialize, and the environment continued to degrade (Uekoetter 2006, 167–183).

A final area worth mentioning concerns Nazi Germany's salvage measures, policies we now refer to as 'recycling'. In fact, saving old rags, kitchen scraps, and other materials was a crucial feature of the regime's drive for self-sufficiency in raw materials, especially after 1936. German officials portrayed the collection of wastes as a valuable service to the nation, a civic responsibility for all members of the *Volk*. Women bore the brunt of these demands: as housewives, they were expected to sort, save, and repurpose all manner of old scraps and refuse. Indeed, the salvaging and reuse of 'worthless' material became a deeply ingrained practice among many Germans during the war, a daily activity that built upon years of privation before the Nazis came to power. The Nazi state also linked such systematic policies to its own racial measures, expropriating Jewish scrap dealers who had served for years as middlemen in the salvage and resale of old materials. Finally, the Nazi state also provided a model for salvage programmes in occupied or allied countries once the war began. In France, for instance, the Vichy state implemented comprehensive salvage drives, while also expropriating Jewish-owned scrap businesses. Of course, the Allies also adopted systematic programmes to save metal, leather, fats, and other materials during the war, although under different political and ideological contexts. After the war, such practices of saving and reuse remained more common in Germany than in other countries, a topic that scholars have yet to fully explore. Moreover, such 'sensible' habits of saving and reusing old materials did not re-emerge as environmentally sensitive 'recycling' until sometime in the 1960s or 1970s, in Germany or elsewhere (Oldenziel and Weber 2013, 347–370; Weber 2013, 371–397).

The example of wartime salvaging suggests important areas for future research on the environmental history of Nazi Germany. Scholars need to more fully explore the environmental history of war, not just the effects of combat on landscapes and resources, but also the indirect effects of warfare on resources such as forests, game, and minerals in countries occupied by the Nazis. Likewise, a focus on gender is lacking, as is work that explicitly compares policies in Germany with those of other countries. Finally, and most importantly, relatively little work examines the tangible impact of conservation policies 'on the ground', and especially at the local and regional level in Germany. While difficult to recover, such histories will inevitably produce a more nuanced picture of the environmental history of Nazi Germany.

In summary, the environmental history of Nazi Germany remains contradictory. Despite impressive new laws that reflected modern ideas about ecology and sustainability (although few people would have used these words), the Nazi state inflicted major damage on its natural landscapes, atmosphere, and waterways. As in the United States and Great Britain, resource exploitation was more important than measures intended to 'heal' degraded landscapes and clean up polluted rivers. Some environmental policies – such as those implemented under the *RNG* – have provided long-term benefits. Likewise, the environmental record of Nazi Germany was probably not substantially worse than that of the Weimar Republic, and no worse than that of the Federal Republic of Germany during the 1950s. In the end, Nazi Germany was a state in which some high-ranking officials supported progressive environmental measures, with varying degrees of sincerity. It is this troubled history that has inspired, and will continue to inspire, research in future years.

References

Bramwell, Anna. 1985. *Blood and Soil: Richard Walther Darré and Hitler's 'Green Party'.* Abbotsbrook, UK: The Kensal Press.

Brix, J. 1934. 'Vorwort.' In *Die Stadtentwässerung in Deutschland,* edited by J. Brix, Karl Imhoff, and R. Weldert, iii–viii. Jena: Fischer.

Closmann, Charles E. 2005. 'Legalizing a *Volksgemeinschaft*: Nazi Germany's Imperial Nature Protection Law of 1935.' In *How Green Were the Nazis?: Nature, Environment, and Nation in the Third Reich,* edited by Franz-Josef Brüggemeier, Mark Cioc, and Thomas Zeller, 18–42. Athens, OH: Ohio University Press.

Diefendorf, Jeffry M. 2009. 'Wartime Destruction and the Postwar Cityscape.' In *War and the Environment: Military Destruction in the Modern Age,* edited by Charles E. Closmann, 171–192. College Station, TX: Texas A&M University Press.

Discherl, Stefan. 2012. *Tier- und Naturschutz im Nationalsozialismus: Gesetzgebung, Ideologie und Praxis.* Göttingen, V&R unipress.

Ditt, Karl. 1996. 'Naturschutz zwischen Zivilizationskritik, Tourismusförderung und Umweltschutz. USA, England and Deutschland 1860–1970.' In *Politische Zäsuren und Gesellschaftlicher Wandel im 20. Jahrhundert,* edited by Matthias Frese und Michael Prinz, 499–534. Paderborn: Schöningh.

Ditt, Karl. 2000. 'The Perception and Conservation of Nature in the Third Reich.' *Planning Perspectives* 15, 161–187.

Dominick, Raymond H. III. 1987. 'The Nazis and the Nature Conservationists.' *The Historian* 49, 508–537.

Dominick, Raymond H. III. 1992. *The Environmental Movement in Germany: Prophets and Pioneers, 1871–1971.* Bloomington: Indiana University Press.

Engels, Jens Ivo. 2002. '"Hohe Zeit" und "dicker Strich": Vergangenheitsdeutung und – bewahrung im westdeutschen Naturschutz nach dem Zweiten Weltkrieg.' In *Naturschutz und Nationalsozialismus,* edited by Joachim Radkau and Frank Uekoetter, 363–404. Frankfurt: Campus.

Franke, Nils M. 2014. '"Keine Überspitzung der Demokratie zulassen". Kontinuitäten von Personen und Netzwerken im Naturschutz zwischen 1933 und 1970.' In *Kontinuitäten im Naturschutz,* edited by Nils M. Franke and Uwe Pfennig, 81–96. Baden-Baden: Nomos.

Gerhard, Gesine. 2002. 'Richard Walther Darré – Naturschutzer oder "Rassenzuchter"? In *Naturschutz und Nationalsozialismus*, edited by Joachim Radkau and Frank Uekoetter, 257–272. Frankfurt: Campus.

Gröning, Gert and Wolschke-Bulmahn, Joachim. 1987. 'Politics, Planning and the Protection of Nature: Political Abuse of Early Ecological Ideas in Germany, 1933–1945.' *Planning Perspectives* 2, 127–148.

Hamburger Stadtentwässerung. 2002. *Vom Hasenmoor zum Transportsiel: 160 Jahre Hamburger Stadtentwässerung*. Hamburg: Hamburger Stadtentwässerung.

Imort, Michael. 2005. '"Eternal Forest – Eternal Volk": The Rhetoric and Reality of National Socialist Forest Policy.' In *How Green Were the Nazis?: Nature, Environment, and Nation in the Third Reich*, edited by Franz-Josef Brüggemeier, Mark Cioc, and Thomas Zeller, 43–72. Athens, OH: Ohio University Press.

Klueting, Edeltraud. 2002. 'Die Gesetzlichen Regelungen der nationalsozialistischen Reichsregierung für den Tierschutz, den Naturschutz und den Umweltschutz.' In *Naturschutz und Nationalsozialismus*, edited by Joachim Radkau and Frank Uekoetter, 77–106, esp. 104. Frankfurt: Campus.

Lekan, Thomas M. 2004. *Imagining the Nation in Nature: Landscape Preservation and German Identity, 1885–1945*. Cambridge, MA: Harvard University Press.

Leopold, Aldo. 1936. 'Naturschutz in Germany.' *Bird Lore* 38, 102–111.

Mauch, Christof and Patel, Kiran Klaus. 2010. 'Environment: Conservation versus Exploitation.' In *The United States and Germany during the Twentieth Century*, edited by Christof Mauch and Kiran Klaus Patel, 180–193. Washington, DC: Cambridge University Press.

Meng, Alfred. 1993. *Geschichte Der Hamburger Wasserversorgung*. Hamburg: Medien-Verlag Schubert.

Möhring, Mahren. 2011. '"Herrentiere" und "Untermenschen".' *Historische Anthropologie* 2, 229–244.

Münch, Peter. 1993. *Stadthygiene im 19. und 20. Jahrhundert: Die Wasserversorgung, Abwasser und Abfallbeseitigung unter besonderer Berücksichtigung Münchens*. Göttingen: Vandenhoeck & Ruprecht.

Oldenziel, Ruth and Weber, Heike. 2013. 'Introduction: Reconsidering Recycling.' *Contemporary European History* 22, 347–370. doi: 10.1017/S0960777313000192.

Reichsnaturschutzgesetz. 1935. In *Reichsgesetzblatt*, Part 1, No. 68.

Seeger, Hendrik. 1999. 'The History of German Waste Water Treatment.' *European Water Management* 2, 51–56.

Staudenmaier, Peter. 2013. 'Organic Farming in Nazi Germany: The Politics of Biodynamic Farming Agriculture, 1933–1945.' *Environmental History* 18, 383–411. doi: 10.1093/envhis/ems154.

Struve and Brunotte. 1934. 'Behoerde für Technik und Arbeit: Nachstehende Abschrift nebst. Anl.wird.' Medizinalkollegium II 0 28, Vol. I; Staatsarchiv Hamburg; no. 11a.

Richard P. Tucker. 2004. 'The World Wars and the Globalization of Timber.' In *Natural Enemy, Natural Ally: Towards an Environmental History of War*, edited by Edmund Russell and Richard P. Tucker, 110–141. Portland: Oregon State University Press.

Uekoetter, Frank. 2006. *The Green & the Brown: A History of Conservation in Germany*. Cambridge: Cambridge University Press.

Uekoetter, Frank. 2007. 'Green Nazis? Reassessing the Environmental History of Nazi Germany.' *German Studies Review* 30, 267–287.

Uekoetter, Frank. 2014. *The Greenest Nation? A New History of German Environmentalism*. Cambridge, MA: MIT Press.

Voigt, Wilfried. 1963. *Geschichtliche Entwicklung der hamburgischen Stadtentwässerung*. Technical Exam Project. Staatsarchiv Hamburg, Hygienisches Staatsinstitut, A 457/215, Kapsel 1.

Weber, Heike. 2013. 'Towards "Total" Recycling: Women, Waste and Food Waste Recovery in Germany, 1914–1939.' *Contemporary European History* 22, 371–397. doi: 10.1017/S0960777313000209.

Westing, Arthur H. 1980. *Warfare in a Fragile World: Military Impact on the Human Environment*. London: Taylor & Francis.

Wettengel, Michael. 1993. 'Staat und Naturschutz, 1906–1945: Zur Geschichte der Staatlichen Stelle für Naturdenkmalpflege in Preußen unter der Reichsstelle für Naturschutz.' *Historische Zeitschrift* 257, 355–399.

Wey, Klaus Georg. 1982. *Umweltpolitik in Deutschland: Kurze Geschichte des Umweltschutzes in Deutschland seit 1900*. Opladen: Westdeutscher Verlag.

Williams, John Alexander. 1996. '"The Chords of the German Soul are Tuned to Nature".' *Central European History* 29, 339–384.

Zeller, Thomas. 2007. *Driving Germany: The Landscape of the German Autobahn, 1930–1970*. New York: Berghahn Books.

Zeller, Thomas. 2012. 'Staging the Driving Experience: Parkways in Germany and the United States.' *Flusser Studies* 14, 1–17.

Further Reading

Blackbourn, David. 2006. *The Conquest of Nature: Water, Landscape, and the Making of Modern Germany*. New York: W.W. Norton.

Blackbourn provides an engaging and wide-ranging perspective on attempts to control water in German history since the eighteenth century.

Discherl, Stefan. 2012. *Tier-und Naturschutz im Nationalsozialismus: Gesetzgebung, Ideologie und Praxis*. Göttingen: V&R unipress.

This monograph represents a recent, provocative work on the Nazis' animal protection policies.

Franke, Nils M. and Pfennig, Uwe, eds. 2014. *Kontinuitäten im Naturschutz*. Baden-Baden: Nomos Verlagsgesellschaft.

A very recent and innovative work, this edited collection explores personal continuities among environmental advocates and subsequent German regimes.

Gerhard, Gesine. 2005. 'Breeding Pigs and People for the Third Reich: Richard Walther Darré's Agrarian Ideology.' In *How Green Were the Nazis? Nature, Environment, and Nation in the Third Reich*, edited by Fran-Josef Brüggemeier, Mark Cioc, and Thomas Zeller, 129–146. Athens, OH: Ohio University Press.

This chapter demonstrates how and why Darré was no 'green' Nazi.

Lekan, Thomas M. 2004. *Imagining the Nation in Nature: Landscape Preservation and German Identity, 1885–1945*. Cambridge, MA: Harvard University Press.

This book provides a well-documented and revealing perspective on the influence of Nazi conservation policies at the regional level.

Stokes, Raymond G., Köster, Roman, and Sambrook, Stephen C. 2013. *The Business of Waste: Great Britain and Germany, 1945 to the Present*. New York: Cambridge University Press.

Despite its title, this book also covers recycling and solid waste policies in Nazi Germany. It is one of the few books to do so.

Uekoetter, Frank. 2006. *The Green & the Brown: A History of Conservation in Nazi Germany*. New York: Cambridge University Press.

This book remains the single best overall work on the history of conservation in Nazi Germany.

Uekotter, Frank. 2009. *The Age of Smoke: Environmental Policy in Germany and the United States, 1880–1970*. Pittsburgh, PA: University of Pittsburgh Press.
This work represents a welcome comparative history of air pollution policies in Germany and the United States.
Weber, Heike. 2013. 'Towards "Total" Recycling: Women, Waste and Food Waste Recovery in Germany, 1914–1939.' *Contemporary European History* 22, 371–397.
An insightful perspective on the effects of recycling under the Nazis, this article suggests additional avenues of research on issues of gender in the Third Reich.
Zeller, Thomas. 2007. *Driving Germany: The Landscape of the German Autobahn, 1930–1970*. New York: Berghahn Books.
This monograph is the most important introduction to the role of landscape advocates like Alwin Seifert and the myth that the autobahn reconciled technology and nature.

PART IV

Race, Imperialism, and Genocide

CHAPTER TWENTY-SIX

Terror

DIETER POHL

26.1 Introduction

The Nazi dictatorship brought 12 years of terror: terror in the streets in 1933, terror in the camps inside the Reich, terror in occupied Eastern and Southeastern Europe from 1939 on, and finally, during the last months of the war, terror again in Germany. The term 'terror' was applied to Nazi violence from the very beginning (Comité 1933; Reinowski 1933), and was commonly used to describe political violence during the French and Russian Revolutions, though less so for fascist Italy. Nevertheless, it is questionable how appropriate and how useful the term is for depicting and analysing German violence between 1933 and 1945. In general terms, terror is the systematic spread of fear by applying direct force or by threatening violence intended to subdue political opposition. Although all forms of Nazi violence can be considered political, not all of them targeted political opponents. On the contrary, the major complexes of Nazi crimes affected groups which the Nazis considered as 'racial' enemies or 'racially unworthy', such as Jews, Roma, mentally ill or disabled persons, and 'asocials'. The perpetrators intimidated all of these groups, but terror did not lie at the core of violence.

Thus, this chapter will limit its focus to Nazi violence against alleged or real political enemies. Literature on the Nazi period for a long time dealt predominantly with political enemies as victims of Nazi crimes and neglected most forms of 'racial' persecution. Of course, Jewish authors from the very beginning emphasized the specificity of the fate of Jews under Nazism, but after a brief wave of publications from Europe, research on the Jewish experience arose primarily from Jewish institutions, especially in Israel. In Europe, however, publications

A Companion to Nazi Germany, First Edition. Edited by Shelley Baranowski,
Armin Nolzen, and Claus-Christian W. Szejnmann.
© 2018 John Wiley & Sons Ltd. Published 2018 by John Wiley & Sons Ltd.

from the late 1940s onward tended to consider political enemies of the Nazis as the main victims of the regime, especially members of the resistance. In the Eastern bloc, communists were portrayed as the only force that resisted Hitler, thus being heavily persecuted. In France, on the other hand, the broader term 'déportés' dominated the discourse on Nazi victims until the 1980s, for a long time neglecting deported Jews and forced labourers (Wolikow 2006). After important publications during the 1960s, it was only during the 1980s that Jewish victims came to the forefront of public awareness, first those from Western and Central Europe, and then, in the last two decades, the Jewish communities of Eastern and East Central Europe. Other victims of Nazism, like Roma, Soviet prisoners of war (POWs), inmates of psychiatric institutions, and homosexuals received more attention.

Paradoxically, compared to the early post-war decades, recent historiography emphasizes 'racial' over 'political' persecution. Thus there is almost no newer research on the persecution and murder of communists, and only scattered attention given to the 1933/1934 terror wave, the killing of Polish elites, and (non-Jewish) civilian victims of German anti-partisan massacres. Historiography on concentration camps (Drobisch and Wieland 1993; Orth 1999; Wachsmann 2015), however, is quite developed, although only a few of the major camps have been analysed in a comprehensive way. Knowledge of the institutions of violence, political denunciations, and the victims of the Nazi justice and prison systems has improved significantly during the last decades (Wachsmann 2004). Robert Gellately (2002) published one of the few efforts to synthesize the fields of persecution of the German Reich, focusing not so much on the violence itself, but more on the reactions of the German population.

26.2   The Archaeology of Nazi Violence

Nazi terror did not begin in 1933, but had existed in Germany and Austria since the 1920s. It is necessary to include all right-wing extremist murders into an archaeology of Nazi violence, since the milieus and organizations of the right merged into the Nazi movement before 1933. Unlike other countries, Germany did not have a tradition of political terrorism prior to 1918. But the early post-war period after 1918 marked the heyday of political murder in democratic Germany and abroad. Civil war violence, White terror, and political assassinations until 1924, against liberal or left-wing politicians, so-called *Fememorde* (political assassinations), against alleged traitors killed hundreds. During the global economic crisis after 1929, when the Nazi Party (*Nationalsozialistische Deutsche Arbeiterpartei*, NSDAP) sought to incite a civil war, at least 300 persons died in both left- and right-wing violence in the years 1930–1932. In Austria, political murder rose after 1927, including the near civil war in 1934 and hundreds of bomb attacks by Nazi supporters. All in all, close to 1000 people died from right-wing attacks in both countries prior to the Nazi takeover. This figure does not include the killings by German *Freikorps* members, many of whom later joined the Nazis, during the civil war in the Baltic states and in Bavaria in 1919/1920 (Reichardt 2002, 53–99). This prehistory of Nazi terror is important since its patterns continued into the

Third Reich: the preponderance of militant action over formal procedures, the creation of (civil) war-like conditions, the leniency or absence of judicial restraint against Nazi perpetrators, and the implicit sympathy for violence against the left in some bourgeois circles. At the beginning of Nazi rule, on 21 March 1933, the new government issued an amnesty for all right-wing criminal violence committed during the Weimar Republic (Reichsministerium des Innern 1933, 134).

26.3   The Reichstag Fire as Nazi Terror's Starting Point

With some exceptions, the new Nazi terror started, after a 'delay' of four weeks, in early March 1933, after the Reichstag Fire and the infamous 'Reichstag Fire Decree' (*Verordnung zum Schutz von Volk und Staat*) on 28 February 1933, which lifted all individual rights guaranteed by the Weimar Constitution (Reichsministerium des Innern 1933, 83). Nazi governments took over the police in most German states, democratic police cadres were released from office, and the Nazi Stormtroopers (*Sturmabteilung*, SA) and Protection Squads (*Schutzstaffel*, SS) were installed as auxiliary police. Thus, the SA and SS, and other Nazi Party organizations began to terrorize all political opponents, especially Communists and Social Democrats, but also outspoken Catholic and liberal anti-Nazis. Some opponents of the regime were even murdered outside Germany by Nazi perpetrators, like the philosopher Theodor Lessing, who was assassinated in August 1933 in Czechoslovakia. Known opponents of Nazism were arrested and taken either to SA clubs or to improvised camps. In the small Thuringian town of Nohra, the SA established the very first Nazi concentration camp, on 3 March 1933. It existed for only six weeks, after which the inmates were taken to a different camp (Benz and Distel 2005, 174–176). In 1933, a number of 'early camps' arose, most of them in abandoned business enterprises or army facilities. In addition to the SA and SS, the justice ministries of the states, and even local activists, erected camps (Wachsmann and Steinbacher 2014).

All in all, during 1933 and early 1934, approximately 100 000 persons, almost all of them male, were taken into custody. There the SA and SS, but also average Nazis, could take their revenge on the Weimar 'system'. Prisoners were humiliated, beaten, and kept in inhumane conditions. However, most of them were released after a few weeks or months and silenced for the remainder of the Third Reich. Immediately after their release, thousands left the country with their families. It is unclear how many prisoners died in 1933/1934 – probably several hundred, but perhaps as many as a thousand. The Nazi regime did not invent camps. They emerged during colonial wars, under the Bolsheviks during the Russian Civil War, and were extended during the Stalinist collectivization from 1930 on. The importance of the camps in early Nazi Germany lay in the creation of extra-legal spaces within a modern society. Open violence in the highly developed German public sphere was to be avoided, and therefore it was restricted to closed spaces. On the other hand, the Nazis considered rumours about the cruelties within the camps to be useful – they demonstrated to the broader public that opponents of the regime were in constant danger of arrest and extra-legal confinement (Richardi 1990; Moore 2018, forthcoming).

26.4   Institutionalizing Terror, 1934 to 1937/1938

During the second half of 1934, Nazi rule stabilized and terror was in decline. The SA suffered a heavy blow in the 'Night of the Long Knives' on 30 June, when part of its leadership was arrested and executed, together with dozens of opponents of Nazism, like former Reich chancellor Kurt von Schleicher. From then until 1937, open violence was not considered appropriate to persecute and intimidate political opponents. The motives behind this new strategy lay both in domestic and foreign policy deliberations. The Nazi leadership now sought to integrate the majority of Germans into a new 'people's community' (*Volksgemeinschaft*), attractive to the bourgeois that had less sympathy for 'plebeian' features of Nazism and the unorganized parts of the working class. In addition, negative foreign perceptions of a terrorist Germany would compromise the regime's primary goal of revising the Versailles Treaty. This concern became most obvious after the assassination of the Nazi Party leader in Switzerland, Wilhelm Gustloff, by a young Jew in early 1936. Unlike November 1938 when a Jewish assassin in Paris shot the German diplomat Ernst vom Rath, the attack in Davos did not become a pretext for launching a major pogrom. This would have caused a major international uproar before the Olympic Winter games in Garmisch-Partenkirchen in February 1936. However, neither persecution nor violence stopped altogether between mid-1934 and 1937. Political opponents were tried, thousands of Communists were sentenced to imprisonment, and even critical clerics went to jail under the pretext of sexual misconduct or violations of the foreign currency regulations. The number of prison inmates in the regular justice system rose to 122 000 at the beginning of 1937, probably 50 000 of them sentenced for political reasons (Wachsmann 2004, 71).

Violence in the cities and countryside, which included murders, continued at the local level. The leadership encouraged individual actions against Jews, especially in order to claim initiatives from below which supported central projects. This was the case in July 1935, when the SA systematically attacked Jews in Berlin's favourite shopping mile, the Kurfürstendamm (Wildt 2007, 176–184).

The face of the concentration camp system changed completely between 1934 and 1937. Most early camps were closed by 1934 or 1935. The number of prisoners shrank after the release of 3000 inmates by the end of 1934. Even the infamous Emsland camps (*Moorlager*) near the Dutch border were restructured from 1934 on, transferred from the realm of the SS to the German justice system. There was even debate whether the camp system as a whole should be dissolved and the inmates transferred to prisons. The SS leadership, however, had started to centralize the camp structure in 1934, when it installed an Inspection of the Concentration Camps in Oranienburg, north of Berlin, and insisted on retaining the camps as detention facilities (Tuchel 1991). Dachau concentration camp was the only one which had remained functional since 1933.

In 1936, the SS leadership began to construct 'modern' concentration camps, which had unified topographical and architectural structures built on vast territories near to larger cities. They were included in the recently merged SS-Police structures, with a common reservoir of personnel and parallel administrative organizations. The older Oranienburg camp was closed in 1936 and its inmates transferred to the new Sachsenhausen camp in the same town. In Dachau, a transformation took place. Completely new were the concentration camps Buchenwald (1937, erected near Weimar), Flossenbürg (1938, in Eastern Bavaria), and Mauthausen (1938, near Linz, Austria). Female prisoners from the former Lichtenburg camp were deported to Ravensbrück (1939, near Fürstenberg in Brandenburg). The creation of these new camps was meant to underline the SS's responsibility for 'penal' policies, but also to create a workforce pool for the construction of the new Nazi architectural centres in German and Austrian cities. Finally, the SS considered them necessary for the 'A-Fall', the internment of potential internal enemies in case of war.

In addition to the alterations in the concentration camp system from 1936/1937 on, the policies of persecution also changed. During the first years of National Socialist rule, political opponents were the main target of violence. But even in 1933, the racist and social component of persecution became visible. In autumn 1933, tens of thousands of alleged 'asocials', predominantly beggars, the homeless, and others, were put in prisons or workhouses. The persecution of Sinti and Roma, which had a long administrative tradition before 1933, became radicalized in 1935/1936, when some city administrations installed 'gypsy camps' (*Zigeunerlager*) at the outskirts of their jurisdictions. And from 1934 a policy of forced mass sterilizations was under way, affecting especially the handicapped, specific groups of prison inmates, 'asocials,' and the Sinti/Roma. Up until 1940, at least 350 000 persons were sterilized against their will, often under brutal circumstances. Estimates of the number of victims who died during the procedure, especially women, run to 5000 (Ayaß 1995, 20–40; Bock 1986).

In the mid-1930s, the Gestapo and the Security Service of the SS (*Sicherheitsdienst*, SD) developed a more racist overall strategy for police action. The Political Police was not restricted to the persecution of political enemies, but would become a preventive organ for the protection of a German racial community against Jews, and the Sinti and Roma but also against people at the margins of society. This turn occurred when political opposition was destroyed, infiltrated, or intimidated, and, especially from 1937 on, when the preparations for imminent war started (Herbert 1996, 188–194).

26.5 Military Expansion and the Escalation of Terror

In 1938, open terror returned in full force. After the annexation of Austria in March, Austrian Nazis terrorized especially Viennese Jews, but also Communists and oppositional functionaries of the authoritarian *Ständestaat*. Thousands were arrested and deported to Dachau concentration camp. From late 1937, the SS leadership planned systematic raids against so-called 'asocials'. Mass arrests against men with a criminal record or those who had allegedly refused work started at the end of April. In May more groups were targeted, including beggars, prostitutes, alcoholics, as well as Jews, Sinti, and Roma. All in all, about 9000 men and some women were deported to the newly erected concentration camps in what was labelled the *Aktion Arbeitsscheu Reich* ('Operation Work-Shy Reich'; see Ayaß 1995, 139–164; Faludi 2013). In some cities, anti-Jewish riots accompanied these measures, like those in Berlin. Both the new policies of 'racial prevention' and the aggravating labour shortage in German industry paved the way for this new wave of persecution.

The nationwide pogrom of the *Reichskristallnacht* ('Crystal Night') eclipsed the actions described above. The Nazi leadership's determination to accelerate emigration and to completely take over Jewish businesses motivated its attack on German and Austrian Jewry. Under the pretext of the assassination of a German diplomat in Paris, the Nazi Party leadership and regional party organs systematically hunted down Jews, beginning on 7 November 1938 and culminating in the events of 8 and 9 November. The police and the Nazi Party orchestrated the pogrom, with destruction of synagogues and Jewish shops, looting of Jewish homes and ill-treatment of the inhabitants. The dimensions of the huge pogrom stood out, as did public violence that drew a large audience, although reactions to the violence were mixed (Obst 1991; Hesse and Springer 2002). Approximately 28 000 Jewish men were taken to concentration camps, where 400 of them died after weeks of extraordinarily brutal punishment. Hundreds of Jews in Germany committed suicide (Steinweis 2009). For a while, more than 60 000 persons were imprisoned in the extremely crowded concentration camps. Both the Jews and the 'A socials', now marked with distinctive signs on their prisoners' clothes, were treated especially badly. Most of the Jews, however, were released after they signed declarations that they would immediately leave Germany. Thus, the number of prisoners declined to 20 000 at the beginning of the war.

At the same time, political and anti-Jewish persecution was extended to the Sudeten region annexed by Germany in October 1938, and Bohemia and Moravia, which were occupied in March 1939. Sudeten German militias, now fully Nazified and armed by German authorities, attacked representatives of the Czechoslovak Republic, killed dozens of them, and plundered shops belonging to Czechs and Jews (Röhr 2008; Hruška 2013). After the occupation of the Sudeten areas and Bohemia, the Gestapo arrested thousands of alleged political enemies, and again after students' riots in Prague in November 1939 (Brandes 1969, 89–95).

During the pre-war years, a diverse picture of Nazi terror evolved. Terror was openly visible in 1933 and again in 1938/1939, but it was confined to the camps. The establishment of the concentration camp was the key to the policies of violence before the war. Large parts of German society accepted them as detention spaces for communists, criminals, and social outsiders, especially in the context of a larger pro-Nazi consensus which emerged from the mid-1930s onward. The camps kept away the violence from the German public sphere, and the release of prisoners gave the impression that a reintegration into the national community was possible, as long as they were not 'racially alien'. On the other hand, probably over 5000 individuals fell victim to the Nazi terror prior to the war, predominantly in 1933–1934 and in 1938–1939, including 2000–3000 Jews who died in concentration camps (Wünschmann 2015, 235).

26.6   From Individual Terror to Mass Murder

The German attack on Poland in September 1939 meant a decisive break in the German policies of terror. In enemy territory, with a Slav population and a large Jewish minority, nearly all inhibitions fell, and mass murder for the first time was considered as an appropriate means for occupation rule. Out of partisan hysteria, both Wehrmacht and police units massacred thousands of POWs and civilians as reprisal for alleged attacks, although even now it is not possible to detect any *non-military* Polish resistance during the war (Böhler 2006). Special forces of the Security Police, called *Einsatzgruppen,* systematically searched for Polish intelligentsia or members of anti-German organizations. The SS installed 'ethnic German' (*volksdeutsche*) militias in Western Poland, and together with the *Einsatzgruppen,* they hunted all Poles whom they considered anti-German, often relying on denunciations. Until the following spring, these units killed tens of thousands of Poles in the Polish areas that had been annexed to the German Reich. While most of these crimes were committed in secrecy in forests, one case stands out. In retaliation for the murder of 360 'ethnic Germans' in Bydgoszcz (*Bromberger Blutsonntag*), up to 3000 Poles were shot during the first weeks of German rule in that region. In April 1940, these killings were extended to occupied Central Poland, now called the General Government. There already had been mass arrests of professors of the Cracow and Lublin universities in late 1939; in spring 1940 some 3000 'suspects', especially from Warsaw, were shot in the 'Extraordinary Pacification Operation' (*Außerordentliche Befriedungsaktion*). Estimates run to as many as 60 000 victims in 1939–1940 (Wardzyńska 2009).

It is not clear why the German campaign against, and occupation of, Poland was so violent from the onset. Until 1938, both countries had been quite close. Germany considered Poland anti-Bolshevik, antisemitic, and authoritarian, similar to the regimes in Hungary or Romania. Hitler himself had considered Poland as a second-rate ally for his war against the Soviet Union. During the German–Polish diplomatic conflict from late 1938, this perception changed completely. The old tradition of German–Polish ethnic violence and Polonophobia after the First World War resurfaced. Poland was now meant to be the experimental ground for Hitler's policies of 'living space' (*Lebensraum*), a mixture of complete subjugation, total economic exploitation, and demographic restructuring, including settlement of Germans. That is why the Polish population was completely outlawed in a lawless space. Hitler pardoned all German crimes in Poland in October 1939, and exempted the SS and police from regular justice, long before the attack on the Soviet Union.

The beginning of the war also meant a radicalization of Nazi crimes within Germany, most prominent in the systematic killing of people with mental disabilities. From the end of 1939, groups of psychiatric inmates were selected and sent to killing centres. During the centralized murder programme up to August 1941, more than 70 000 persons were murdered. Later operations killed 140 000 others, including 60 000 in the occupied territories (Hohendorf 2016). This was, however, not a part of Nazi *terror* strategy; rather, the perpetrators tried to keep their crimes secret.

During the first half of the war, the whole universe of Nazi camps came into being (Benz and Distel 2004–2009; Pilichowski 1979): *Polenlager* for deported Poles in occupied territories, 'Work Education Camps' (*Arbeitserziehungslager*), predominantly for foreign forced labourers who had been criminalized, and also camps for Polish farmers who failed to deliver their quota. There were even camps for juveniles – for boys in Moringen (1940) and for girls in the Uckermark (1942) – euphemistically called 'Youth Protection Camps' (*Jugendschutzlager*). The Criminal Police arrested most of the prisoners for minor offences or for sexual misconduct. The worst of these camps came into being in 1942, the *Polen-Jugendverwahrlager Litzmannstadt* in Lodz, a de facto concentration camp for children. Similar camps in 1943 were established in occupied central Russia.

With the war, the concentration camp system was expanded. New camps were erected in Neuengamme (near Hamburg) and Groß-Rosen (Lower Silesia) in 1940, and later extended to the occupied territories: in May 1940 in Oswiecim near Katowice (KL Auschwitz), and in May 1941 the Natzweiler camp in Alsace. The constituency of the prisoner society again changed, to include more and more foreigners, primarily Poles, and to a lesser degree Czechs, and Northern and Western Europeans. Even Spanish citizens, who had fought for the Republic during the Spanish Civil War, then escaped to France and ended up in internment, now were transferred to German concentration camps. By the end of 1940, the number of all camp inmates rose to 53 000. Living conditions, which already had been very bad since 1938, declined even further, with death rates rising from 20% a year in some camps, to 30% in Mauthausen, designated by the SS administration as a category III camp, one with the harshest conditions.

From the beginning of the war, the camps became sites of mass murder. In September 1939, the chief of the Security Police, Reinhard Heydrich, issued an order to use the camps as sites for extrajudicial killings under the camouflage term of 'Special Treatment' (*Sonderbehandlung*). In some camps, specific groups of inmates were systematically killed, especially Jews. From April 1941, the camps were integrated into the 'euthanasia' killings. Teams of physicians from the 'euthanasia' programme visited the camps, choosing weakened and 'undesirable' prisoners, among them many Jews, whom they sent to the killing centres. At least 15 000 prisoners fell victim to this murder operation (Wachsmann 2015, 225–227).

During the first one and a half years of Hitler's rule in continental Europe, resistance was very limited, not only within the Reich, but also in occupied Europe. German terror was first and foremost directed against the Jews in Poland. While all Jews under German hegemony suffered from discrimination, expropriation, pauperization, and isolation, only the Jews in Poland (and in the camps) faced the risk of violent death. In some ghettos, like those in Warsaw and Lodz, the death rates from malnutrition and unbearable living conditions reached genocidal proportions prior to the fateful summer of 1941. All Jews in Poland were at constant risk as targets of German violence. Germans randomly killed Jews, especially in ghettos and forced labour camps. Those Jews who committed minor offences against occupation rules faced the death penalty by extraordinary courts (*Sondergerichte*), as did lots of non-Jewish Poles (Löw 2006, 89).

26.7   The Fateful Year 1941 and the War against the Soviet Union

After September 1939, the next escalation of German terror policies occurred in spring 1941, before the attack on the Soviet Union. During the German invasion of Greece, the Wehrmacht met the fiercest military resistance on the island of

Crete. Both British troops and armed Greek civilians fought the Germans. On the pretext of retaliation, German forces killed the male inhabitants of several villages in May 1941 (Xylander 1989, 28–33). New research by Heinz A. Richter (2011) indicates that the Greek irregulars were probably not acting within the frame of international law. At the same time, the new rule in Yugoslavia escalated into mass killing. Two forces were responsible for this radicalization. The German military administration reacted to the first signs of resistance by former Yugoslav soldiers, which formed guerrilla units named Chetniks, by publicly claiming that for each German soldier killed by irregulars, 100 local civilians would be shot (Vojnoistorijski Institut Jugoslovenske Armije 1949, 333). Actually, this dimension of violence was only realized from October 1941 on, although German units had already committed smaller executions in late spring.

Yugoslavia was the first killing ground of German anti-partisan warfare, and up until spring 1942 the horrible results had similar dimensions to those in the Soviet Union. In Serbia, approximately 30 000 civilians were killed by the end of 1941 (Manoschek 1993; Shepherd 2012). There the murderous German strategy at first seemed successful, although the partisan units escaped to Croatia. The Independent State of Croatia, however, though it was controlled by the terrorist Ustasha government, was considered an ally of the 'Axis' powers, which is why extreme German reprisals were not applicable. Nevertheless, even there the population suffered from extreme violence, especially in western Bosnia, because of the German occupation and the widespread civil war between the Chetniks and Ustasha. Thus, all sides engaged in retaliatory violence, aided by the resources of the German occupation forces (Tomasevich 2001; Hoare 2006). More than anywhere else, the Wehrmacht was responsible for the terrorist anti-partisan warfare in Serbia and Bosnia. Even Italian and Bulgarian troops joined this strategy of unlimited reprisals. Elsewhere the German military and the SS/Police units dominated, the latter more brutally than the Wehrmacht. In Eastern Ukraine, however, the Hungarian army contributed, shooting around 19 000 inhabitants in partisan areas.

The second force which unleashed unrestricted terror was the right-wing extremist Ustasha, a minor political group which assumed control over Croatia and Bosnia in April 1941. Right away, it organized militias in the countryside to terrorize the Serb minority. On 17/18 April 1941, a Ustasha unit massacred Serbian men in a village in Slavonia (Goldstein 2013; Korb 2013). This was only the beginning of a campaign of systematic mass extermination in order to establish Ustasha rule and to force the Serbian population to flee. While the Italian occupation power criticized and restricted Ustasha violence, the German authorities were divided: Hitler and the German envoy to Zagreb supported full-scale violence, while the military feared the destabilization of Croatia.

Thus, the discourse and practice of terrorist mass violence was already under way *before* the attack on the Soviet Union on 22 June 1941. Yet the German political and military leadership developed a strategy of mass violence for the first time when planning Operation Barbarossa. While the Wehrmacht was ordered to kill all captured political officers of the Red Army, the *Einsatzgruppen* were entrusted to undertake mass killings of all inhabitants who might 'endanger' the German occupation, namely communist functionaries and able-bodied Jewish men. The most important part of the planning, however, was the complete lifting of international law for enemy POWs and civilians in the 'Decree on Military Judiciary' (*Kriegsgerichtsbarkeitserlass*). Executive power, rather than military courts, would deal with future opposition. Although there were no precise orders on reprisal killings, ratios like the execution of 30 civilians for one German soldier killed by civilians were discussed (Pohl 2008, 71).

The German leadership (and society) considered Bolshevism an extremely dangerous enemy of mankind, allegedly organized by Soviet Jews, which justified skirting international law. On the other hand, the German military expected to conquer enormous spaces without relying on proper forces for 'securing' the rear areas. This was even more problematic, since German economic planners issued schemes to radically exploit Soviet agriculture, which might lead to hunger revolts. Therefore, the military, economic, and 'security' planning imposed a rule of terror to deter the population from any resistance. There was a broad consensus among German soldiers that terror was necessary and appropriate in this war. Thus, the German invasion forces, right from the outset, launched 'strategic' violence against certain groups of POWs, Jewish men, and communist activists. The local indigenous administrations were forced to compile lists of suspect persons. Some came forward voluntarily to seek revenge for Stalinism, others were coerced into cooperation. Nowhere else in Europe did the German terror dissolve social ties as extensively as in these regions. Some families were torn apart when one brother joined the auxiliary police and another joined the partisans.

When the first acts of civilian or guerrilla resistance surfaced in July 1941, the Germans retaliated with utmost violence. The victims were not so much average citizens, but primarily Jews and Russians in Ukraine and Belarus. The military applied the same selective violence against resistance as in other occupied countries. In Serbia, Jewish men were the main target of hostage killings; in France, Jews were deported to Auschwitz as reprisal for assassinations by the resistance movement. This genocidal retaliation against resistance became the missing link in the onset of the 'Final Solution', the systematic murder of European Jewry.

Though the scattered Soviet resistance groups were ineffective until spring 1942, German units probably killed more than 60 000 civilians under the pretext of partisan warfare (Pohl 2008, 168). Only from spring 1942 was the Stalinist regime able to organize a partisan movement, especially near Leningrad, in Belorussia, Northeast Ukraine, and in the Bryansk region. There, German police and Wehrmacht terrorized whole regions, often by hanging every suspect. When German units tried to encircle and destroy partisan areas without major results, they wiped out whole villages. Large anti-partisan operations (*Bandenunternehmen*) led to the murder of thousands of peasants, including women and children. Only 10% of those killed actually carried arms and were counted among the partisans. If ghettos still existed in a region, as in Western Belorussia, anti-partisan warfare served as pretext for murdering all the remaining Jews (Gerlach 1998, 860–1035; on the Ukraine, see Soldatenko 2013).

This strategy of terror and mass murder was by and large ineffective because it drove many into the arms of the partisans. Younger men and women also faced recruitment as forced labour in Germany, and thus they joined the underground.

After early 1943, German policy was slightly altered: all able-bodied individuals who were apprehended during anti-partisan raids were either sent to forced labour camps or were shot. The population in some areas were either killed or deported, which created 'dead zones' (*tote Zonen*). Nevertheless, large parts of rural Belorussia and Russia fell out of German control by the end of 1943, before the major offensives of the Red Army started. The Germans left behind vast zones of destroyed villages and highly traumatized societies. Approximately half a million inhabitants fell victim to anti-partisan warfare, although only a small minority of them actually belonged to the partisans.

26.8 Terror after the Military Defeat in Stalingrad, 1942–1943

At the turn of 1942/1943, the murderous anti-partisan tactics spilled over to other occupied countries, Poland being the first. It is necessary to underline the fact that nearly all of Poland suffered extreme violence from late 1941 onwards: the Jews in Poland were killed not only in extermination centres, but also during the violent raids on the ghettos, which were visible to the whole population. In autumn 1942, more than 20 000 Jews per day were herded together in the ghettos, driven to railway stations, and deported to places of mass murder. Thousands died on the way, and corpses lay in the streets after the 'ghetto clearances'. From April to May 1943, a war of Jewish resisters against German SS and Police arose in the centre of the Polish capital, the Warsaw Ghetto Uprising.

The main force of the Polish resistance, the Home Army (*Armia Krajowa*), did not provoke clashes with the occupation forces as it wanted to avoid reprisals against the population. However, when the Germans started to deport Poles on a large scale from south of Lublin, in autumn 1942, to make room for a German settlement area, left-wing forces started armed attacks, to which the SS and Police forces responded with massacres against civilians. In the Kielce region, a second partisan area evolved (Brewing 2016; Madajczyk 1965).

In the occupied Czech lands, the Protectorate of Bohemia and Moravia, mass executions remained an exception, though mass arrests were frequent from autumn 1941. After the assassination of Deputy Reich Protector Heydrich, the population of two towns, Lidice and Ležáky (Ueberschär 2003, 126–135), was murdered or deported. Even more affected were other countries: the German practice of mass murder as retaliation for partisan attacks in 1943 was extended to occupied Greece, where an underground movement was active, but divided between communist and Western-oriented partisans. As in Yugoslavia, Greek partisans fought each other and the Germans. When Italian dictator Benito Mussolini was toppled and the Wehrmacht invaded Italy in September 1943, Germany launched a new terror in Italian territory that it occupied. The German military and SS Police units massacred civilians after attacks by the Italian *Resistenza*, not only in northern Italy, where the underground had its stronghold, but also in other regions during Germany's retreat across the peninsula (Gentile 2012).

While the mass murder of non-Jews was restricted to certain regions and places, the general terror in the occupied countries was omnipresent – early on in Eastern Europe, but also in the West during the last year of the war. There was the constant fear of arrest, especially after underground uprisings. Men and women with communist affiliations, or former state officials, and sometimes also POWs who had been released and returned, were constantly at risk. Prisons in all occupied countries were filled with political prisoners, though from 1942/1943 on, the occupation authorities preferred to transfer the latter to prisons or camps inside Germany. From late 1941, the Wehrmacht applied its 'Night and Fog' (*Nacht und Nebel*), a procedure during which the occupation authorities made suspects 'disappear'. They were secretly arrested and deported without trace to German prisons or camps (Gruchmann 1981).

The occupation courts represented one of the main institutions of German repression, with more military justice in the West and more civilian 'Special Courts' in the East. They dealt only with minor political offences against the occupation order, but devoted more attention to 'economic crime'. Especially in occupied Poland, German courts sentenced thousands of Poles to death for violations of the special laws against Poles (*Polenstrafverordnung*). In 1943, the occupation power installed special Executive Courts (*Standgerichte*) – actually, organs of the Security Police – which decided exclusively on acquittal or the death penalty. In Warsaw, between October 1943 and July 1944, more than 2700 Poles were publicly executed after those decisions, the names published widely on placards (Jacobmeyer 1977, 681; Becker 2014). The constant fear extended to the younger generation, whom the occupation's recruitment campaigns sought for forced labour in Germany. From 1942, especially in Poland and the occupied Soviet territories, violent manhunts became a day-to-day practice, as were the mass arrests of persons leaving a cinema or a church service (Müller 1995).

Mass arrests and the mass deportation of Jews became the basis for the last expansion of the German camp system. Between early 1942 and early 1945, the prisoner numbers of the concentration camps rose almost tenfold, from 80 000 to 718 000. German and Austrian inmates constituted a minority, at less than 5%, although they often held higher positions within the prison society. Two new trends were significant in the camp system: integration into the German war economy and mass murder. The SS leadership had to abandon its schemes to use prison labour to rebuild German cities, Nazi style, or to erect German settlements in occupied Eastern Europe. Thus, from 1942 on, many prisoners worked for German armament businesses. Since the latter were not willing to establish their enterprises within the main camps, branches were installed near existing factories. Overall, approximately 1000 branch camps were established in the Reich and annexed territories. The 'economization' had a twofold effect on the prisoners: the able-bodied were treated somewhat better, while the weak were killed right away. Not until spring 1943 did the death rate among prisoners start to decline among those whose labour spared them from the mass murders.

Until summer 1941, mass killings were not a typical feature of concentration camps. Rather, specific groups of prisoners were sent elsewhere to be killed. This pattern changed with the arrival of Soviet POWs in the concentration camps in July 1941. The latter had been selected as especially 'dangerous' and sent to the camp system. There, the SS and Gestapo organized mass killings, first in Sachsenhausen and Dachau, and later in Auschwitz. The installation of mass killing facilities and especially the gas chambers was connected to these crimes, but expanded with the evolving 'Final Solution of the Jewish Question', especially in Auschwitz and Lublin-Majdanek. Other groups were also killed there: prisoners too weak to work, Sinti and Roma, deportees from the Zamość resettlement areas, and others. By 1944 and 1945, most of the concentration camps in Germany had mass killing facilities.

The Allied offensives of June/July 1944 marked a new occasion for the Nazi regime to intensify its terror. Parts of the Polish resistance perceived the Soviet summer offensive as the right moment to launch an all-out attack on German occupation in Poland, the Warsaw Uprising in 1944. But the revolt was successful for only a few days; then the Wehrmacht and SS troops retook control and waged a merciless campaign of mass destruction. From 5–12 August, nearly all inhabitants from two Warsaw quarters, Wola and Ochota, were dragged to the streets and shot. Until the final defeat of the uprising in early October, approximately 160 000 Poles lost their lives by fighting or by execution (Krannhals 1962; Hanson 1982). A similar fate met the Slovak National Uprising, which started in late August 1944. The German army and SS immediately occupied Slovakia and began, together with Slovak collaboration units, its anti-partisan war. Approximately 3000 civilians were shot and another 30 000 deported to German concentration camps (Šindelárová 2013).

To some degree, these violent forms of combating resistance were applied in Western and Northern Europe. After attacks by the French resistance, Waffen-SS units murdered parts of the population in the towns of Oradour-sur-Glane and Tulle in June 1944, and in Vassieux-en-Vercors in July. In October 1944, following an underground attack, all the men from the Dutch town of Putten were deported to a concentration camp, where most of them died (Lieb 2007, 360–362). Nevertheless, in general the German occupation refrained from committing massacres in areas considered 'civilized' or 'Germanic', instead pursuing terror through mass or individual arrests. The same applies within the German and Austrian territories of 1937. There, mass murders occurred in the concentration camps or the 'euthanasia' killing centres. Nevertheless, the pressure on average Germans intensified as the war dragged on. This is clearly visible in the increase in death sentences in political trials. In 1940, 250 persons were sentenced to death. In 1943, however, 5336 were executed. More and more people were criminalized for minor offences (Pohl 2003, 118).

When Allied troops approached from the west and the east in January and February 1945, terror became omnipresent in the areas near the fronts. The weakest victims of this final period were again the camp and prison inmates. In eastern Germany, SS and Police massacred prisoners who were considered unfit for evacuation or who could no longer be evacuated, such as the Uckermark camp or in Hohenstein (eastern Brandenburg). Evacuation of concentration camps started by July 1944 but accelerated from January 1945 on a much larger scale. Both the railway transport and the 'death marches' (*Todesmärsche*) proved to be murderous. Prisoners locked in trains were not fed for days or weeks, and those who were too weak to walk to the next camp were shot on the roads, often fully visible to the German population. Camps which served as collection points were overcrowded, like Bergen-Belsen in 1945, creating little more than a space for death. According to estimates, every third camp inmate died during the last months and weeks of the war (Blatman 2011). But others were subdued by terror, such as the Eastern European forced labourers inside the Reich. Wehrmacht courts sentenced thousands of soldiers to death for desertion or defeatism. Units of all Nazi organizations hunted 'defeatists', who were tried by 'Executive Courts' or killed right away. The nearer the front, the more escalated the random violence (Keller 2013, 217–219). Only the Allied occupation stopped the killings.

26.9 Conclusion

The political terror of the Nazi state developed in several steps. Terror was a means to the Nazi rise to power from the 1920s on, and it was fully unleashed in 1933 and early 1934 when the first camp system was established. While this early wave of persecution targeted political opposition, the second wave in 1938/1939 attacked Nazism's 'racial enemies'. Terror was the central German strategy to secure occupation in Poland and to support the German war against the Soviet Union. From mid-1941, German rule faced resistance in occupied Yugoslavia and the Soviet territories, from 1943 in Poland, Greece, Italy, and finally, in 1944, in France. German rule resorted not only to mass arrests but also to massacres in all of these areas. Meanwhile, a universe of German camps evolved during the war, with the concentration camp system at its heart. This structure expanded significantly from 1942 on, incorporating hundreds of thousands of deported opponents, Jews and Roma. While terror prevailed during the entire existence of the camps, they became, after 1942, a major resource for the German war economy and sites of unprecedented mass murder. Finally, in 1945, terror returned to Germany itself, with repression of German citizens and a final apocalypse for all prisoners.

Nazi and German terror at home and abroad drew, first and foremost, from racial discourses. Jews, Russians, Poles, and Serbs were considered inferior, and their (potential) resistance was met with utmost violence. Imperialist schemes, especially those to restructure Eastern Europe, exacerbated the violence. A major precondition for mass violence lay in the abolishment of the law-abiding state in Germany, then the creation of lawless spaces, beginning in Poland, Yugoslavia, and the occupied Soviet territories. The real resistance against German rule, which started regionally in 1941 and expanded in late 1942, only accelerated the violence. German terror was preventative, structural, and only later reactive.

In retrospective, it is hard to distinguish between victims of political terror and those of systematic racial violence. The two were intertwined. Nevertheless, Nazi German terror was part of a specific strategy of mass murder, although it also partially resembled violence in other authoritarian and totalitarian regimes, among them Germany's allies, Italy, Bulgaria, Romania, Hungary, and Slovakia, and the extremely violent Croatian Ustasha. The persecution and killing of political enemies was a common practice of many modern dictatorships, and some applied extreme mass violence in the fight against armed resistance – as did the Soviet Union, Franco's Spain, Chiang Kai Shek's China, or the Japanese occupation forces in China (Valentino 2004, 668; Gerlach 2010, 177–234; in general, see

Bloxham and Gerwarth 2011). The same can be said about the camp systems, which until 1941 were much more extensive under Stalinism, or after 1950 in Mao's China. But only in the German case were certain camps used as sites of mass murder, predominantly those in occupied Poland and the Soviet Union, and exclusively in the 'Aktion Reinhardt' camps and Kulmhof near Lodz. The specificity of Nazi German terror lies in its dimensions, especially in large parts of Eastern Europe, and in its close entanglement with racial mass murder. The Holocaust and the extermination of the Sinti and Roma found no parallel in other regimes.

References

Ayaß, Wolfgang. 1995. *'Asoziale' im Nationalsozialismus.* Stuttgart: Klett-Cotta.

Becker, Maximilian. 2014. *Mitstreiter im Volkstumskampf: Deutsche Justiz in den eingegliederten Ostgebieten 1939–1945.* Munich and Berlin: De Gruyter Oldenbourg.

Benz, Wolfgang and Barbara Distel, eds. 2005. *Der Ort des Terrors, Volume 2: Frühe Lager, Dachau, Emslandlager.* Munich: C.H. Beck.

Benz, Wolfgang and Distel, Barbara, eds. 2004–2009: *Der Ort des Terrors.* 9 vols. Munich: C.H. Beck.

Blatman, Daniel. 2011. *The Death Marches: The Final Phase of Nazi Genocide.* Cambridge, MA: Belknap Press of Harvard University Press.

Bloxham, Donald and Gerwarth Robert, eds. 2011. *Political Violence in Twentieth-Century Europe.* Cambridge: Cambridge University Press.

Bock, Gisela. 1986. *Zwangssterilisation im Nationalsozialismus: Studien zur Rassenpolitik und Frauenpolitik.* Opladen: Westdeutscher Verlag.

Böhler, Jochen. 2006. *Auftakt zum Vernichtungskrieg: Die Wehrmacht in Polen 1939.* Frankfurt am Main: Fischer.

Brandes, Detlef. 1969. *Die Tschechen unter deutschem Protektorat.* Vol. 1. Munich and Vienna: Oldenbourg.

Brewing, Daniel. 2016. *Im Schatten von Auschwitz: Deutsche Massaker an polnischen Zivilisten 1939–1945.* Darmstadt: Wissenschaftliche Buchgesellschaft.

Comité international d'aide aux victimes du fascisme hitlérien, ed. 1933. *Livre Brun sur l'incendie du Reichstag et le terreur hitlérienne.* Paris: Edition Carrefour.

Drobisch, Klaus and Wieland, Günther. 1993. *System der NS-Konzentrationslager 1933–1939.* Berlin: Akademie Verlag.

Faludi, Christian, ed. 2013. *Die 'Juni-Aktion' 1938: Eine Dokumentation zur Radikalisierung der Judenverfolgung.* Frankfurt am Main and New York: Campus.

Gellately, Robert. 2002. *Backing Hitler: Consent and Coercion in Nazi Germany.* Oxford: Oxford University Press.

Gentile, Carlo. 2012. *Wehrmacht, Waffen-SS und Polizei im Kampf gegen Partisanen und Zivilbevölkerung in Italien 1943–1945.* Paderborn: Schoeningh.

Gerlach, Christian. 1998. *Kalkulierte Morde: Die deutsche Wirtschafts- und Vernichtungspolitik in Weißrußland 1941 bis 1944.* Hamburg: Hamburger Edition.

Gerlach, Christian. 2010. *Extremely Violent Societies: Mass Violence in the Twentieth-Century World.* New York: Cambridge University Press.

Goldstein Slavko. 2013. *1941: The Year That Keeps Returning.* New York: New York Review of Books.

Gruchmann, Lothar. 1981. '"Nacht- und Nebel"-Justiz: Die Mitwirkung der Strafgerichte an der Bekämpfung des Widerstandes in den besetzten westeuropäischen Ländern 1942–1944.' *Vierteljahrshefte für Zeitgeschichte* 29, 342–396.

Hanson, Joanna K.M. 1982. *The Civilian Population and the Warsaw Uprising of 1944*. Cambridge and New York: Cambridge University Press.

Herbert, Ulrich. 1996. *Best: Biographische Studien über Radikalismus, Weltanschauung und Vernunft 1903–1989*. Bonn: Dietz.

Hesse, Klaus and Springer, Philipp. 2002. *Vor aller Augen: Fotodokumente des nationalsozialistischen Terrors in der Provinz*. Essen: Klartext.

Hoare, Marko Attila. 2006. *Genocide and Resistance in Hitler's Bosnia: The Partisans and the Chetniks 1941–1943*. Oxford: Oxford University Press.

Hohendorf, Gerrit. 2016. 'Die Vernichtung von psychisch kranken und geistig behinderten Menschen unter nationalsozialistischer Herrschaft.' In *Online Encyclopedia of Mass Violence*. http://www.sciencespo.fr/mass-violence-war-massacre-resistance/en/document/die-vernichtung-von-psychisch-kranken-und-geistig-behinderten-menschen-unter-nationalsozial (accessed 22 November 2017).

Hruška, Emil. 2013. *Boj o pohraničí: Sudetoněmecký Freikorps v roce 1938*. Prague: Epocha.

Jacobmeyer, Wolfgang. 1977. 'Die polnische Widerstandsbewegung im Generalgouvernement und ihre Beurteilung durch deutsche Dienststellen.' *Vierteljahrshefte für Zeitgeschichte* 25, 658–681.

Keller, Sven. 2013. *Volksgemeinschaft am Ende: Gesellschaft und Gewalt 1944/45*. Munich: Oldenbourg.

Korb, Alexander. 2013. *Im Schatten des Weltkriegs: Massengewalt der Ustaša gegen Serben, Juden und Roma in Kroatien 1941–1945*. Hamburg: Hamburger Edition.

Krannhals, Hanns von. 1962. *Der Warschauer Aufstand 1944*. Frankfurt am Main: Bernard & Graefe.

Lieb, Peter. 2007. *Konventioneller Krieg oder NS-Weltanschauungskrieg? Kriegführung und Partisanenbekämpfung in Frankreich 1943/44*. Munich: Oldenbourg.

Löw, Andrea. 2006. *Juden im Getto Litzmannstadt: Lebensbedingungen, Selbstwahrnehmung, Verhalten*. Göttingen: Wallstein.

Madajczyk, Czesław, ed. 1965. *Hitlerowski terror na wsi polskiej, 1939–1945: Zestawienie większych akcji represyjnych*. Warsaw: Państwowe Wydawnyctwo Naukowe.

Manoschek, Walter. 1993. *'Serbien ist judenfrei!': Militärische Besatzungspolitik und Judenvernichtung in Serbien 1941/42*. Munich: Oldenbourg.

Moore, Paul. 2014. '"Noch nicht mal zu Bismarcks Zeiten": Deutsche Populärmeinung und der Terror gegen die Linke.' In *Die Linke im Visier: Zur Errichtung der Konzentrationslager 1933*, edited by Nikolaus Wachsmann and Sybille Steinbacher, 168–190. Göttingen: Wallstein.

Moore, Paul. Forthcoming. *The View from Outside: The Nazi Concentration Camps and the German Public, 1933–1945*. Oxford: Oxford University Press.

Müller, Rolf-Dieter. 1995. 'Menschenjagd. Die Rekrutierung von Zwangsarbeitern in der besetzten Sowjetunion.' In *Vernichtungskrieg: Verbrechen der Wehrmacht 1941–1944*, edited by Hannes Heer and Klaus Naumann, 92–103. Hamburg: Hamburger Edition.

Obst, Dieter. 1991. *'Reichskristallnacht': Ursachen und Verlauf des antisemitischen Pogroms vom November 1938*. Frankfurt am Main: Peter Lang.

Orth, Karin. 1999. *Das System der nationalsozialistischen Konzentrationslager: Eine politische Organisationsgeschichte*. Hamburg: Hamburger Edition.

Pilichowski, Czesław, ed. 1979. *Obozy hitlerowskie na ziemiach polskich 1939–1945: Informator encyklopedyczny*. Warsaw: Państwowe Wydawnictwo Naukowe.

Pohl, Dieter. 2003. *Verfolgung und Massenmord in der NS-Zeit 1933–1945*. Darmstadt: Wissenschaftliche Buchgesellschaft.

Pohl, Dieter. 2008. *Die Herrschaft der Wehrmacht: Deutsche Militärbesatzung und einheimische Bevölkerung in der Sowjetunion 1941–1944*. Munich: Oldenbourg.

Reichardt, Sven. 2002. *Faschistische Kampfbünde: Gewalt und Gemeinschaft im italienischen Squadrismus und in der deutschen SA.* Cologne, Weimar, and Vienna: Böhlau.

Reichsministerium des Innern, ed. 1933. *Reichsgesetzblatt I.* Berlin: Reichsdruckerei.

Reinowski, Hans Johann. 1933. *Terror in Braunschweig: Aus dem ersten Quartal der Hitlerherrschaft.* Zürich: Verlag Sozialistische Arbeiter-Internationale.

Richardi, Hans-Günter. 1990. *Schule der Gewalt: Die Anfänge des Konzentrationslagers Dachau 1933–1934.* Munich: C.H. Beck.

Richter, Heinz A. 2011. *Operation Merkur: Die Eroberung der Insel Kreta im Mai 1941.* Ruhpolding: Rutzen.

Röhr, Werner. 2008. *September 1938: Die Sudetendeutsche Partei und ihr Freikorps.* Berlin: Edition Organon.

Shepherd, Ben. 2012. *Terror in the Balkans: German Armies and Partisan Warfare.* Cambridge, MA: Harvard University Press.

Šindelárová, Lenka. 2013. *Finale der Vernichtung: Die Einsatzgruppe H in der Slowakei 1944/1945.* Darmstadt: Wissenschaftliche Buchgesellschaft.

Soldatenko, V.F., ed. 2013. *Sozhzhennye sela: Ukraina pod natsistskoi okkupatsiei, 1941–1944 gg.* Moscow: Fond 'istoricheskaia pamiat'.

Steinweis, Alan. 2009. *Kristallnacht 1938.* Cambridge, MA: Harvard University Press.

Tomasevich, Jozo. 2001. *War and Revolution in Yugoslavia, 1941–1945: Occupation and Collaboration.* Stanford, CA: Stanford University Press.

Tuchel, Johannes. 1991. *Konzentrationslager: Organisationsgeschichte und Funktion der 'Inspektion der Konzentrationslager' 1934–1938.* Boppard am Rhein: Boldt.

Ueberschär, Gerd R., ed. 2003. *Orte des Grauens: Verbrechen im Zweiten Weltkrieg.* Darmstadt: Primus.

Valentino, Benjamin A. 2004. *Final Solutions: Mass Killing and Genocide in the Twentieth Century.* Ithaca, NY: Cornell University Press.

Vojnoistorijski Institut Jugoslvenske Armije, ed. 1949. *Zbornik dokumenata i podataka o narodnooslobodilachkom ratu jugoslovenskih naroda, Volume 1: Borbe u Srbji 1941 god.* Belgrade: Vojnoistorijski institut.

Wachsmann, Nikolaus. 2004. *Hitler's Prisons: Legal Terror in Nazi Germany.* New Haven, CT: Yale University Press.

Wachsmann, Nikolaus. 2015. *KL. A History of the Nazi Concentration Camps.* New York and London: Macmillan.

Wachsmann, Nikolaus and Steinbacher, Sybille, eds. 2014. *Die Linke im Visier: Zur Errichtung der Konzentrationslager 1933.* Göttingen: Wallstein.

Wardzyńska, Maria. 2009. *Był rok 1939: Operacja niemieckiej policji bezpieczeństwa w Polsce 'Intelligenzaktion'.* Warsaaw: Instytut Pamięci Narodowej.

Wildt, Michael. 2007. *Volksgemeinschaft als Selbstermächtigung: Gewalt gegen Juden in der deutschen Provinz 1919 bis 1939.* Hamburg: Hamburger Edition.

Wolikow, Serge. 2006. *Les combats de la memoire: La FNDIRP de 1945 a nos jours.* Paris: Cherche-Midi.

Wünschmann, Kim. 2015. *Before Auschwitz: Jewish Prisoners in the Prewar Concentration Camps.* Cambridge, MA and London: Harvard University Press.

Xylander, Marlen von. 1989. *Die deutsche Besatzungsherrschaft auf Kreta 1941–1945.* Freiburg im Breisgau: Rombach.

Further Reading

Gellately, Robert. 2002. *Backing Hitler: Consent and Coercion in Nazi Germany.* Oxford: Oxford University Press.
This book offers an integrated history of the reaction of German society to Nazi violence inside Germany and also a narrative of these crimes.

Mazower, Mark. 2008. *Hitler's Empire: Nazi Rule in Occupied Europe*. London: Allen Lane.
The only English-language up-to-date overall history of German occupation in Europe, including the terrorist violence.
Wachsmann, Nikolaus. 2015. *KL: A History of the Nazi Concentration Camps*. New York and London: Macmillan.
Up-to-date comprehensive history of the central camp system of Nazism, the concentration camps, integrating both perpetrator and prisoner perspectives.

CHAPTER TWENTY-SEVEN

Flight and Exile

DEBÓRAH DWORK

27.1 Current Scholarship

Much of the scholarly literature about Nazi-era refugees is geographically framed, focusing on emigration from one particular country, or on the refugee community where émigrés landed. German scholars have developed a rich literature on refugees from Nazi Germany, British scholars on émigrés in Britain, and American scholars on the impact of refugees on American culture. Few studies widen the lens to show the patterns that emerge by tracking the whole web of refugees fleeing from countries across Nazi Europe to countries all over the globe. Then too, the nation-centric refugee literature largely comprises memoirs or collections of oral histories. Lacking a historical framework, the personal is unmoored from the political.

Government policies with regard to asylum and immigration have also claimed considerable scholarly interest, again structured by geography: most particularly, Canada, France, Great Britain, the United States. Few, however, locate those policies within the context of post-First World War population shifts, or the context of international legal principles with regard to inter-state travel and transit.

Oddly, the refugee experience typically falls beyond the scope of histories of the Holocaust. And indeed, if the Holocaust is understood as the history of people murdered by the Germans and their allies, the refugees hold a minor role. Most émigrés escaped that fate. One might argue a wholly different position, however (Dwork and van Pelt 2009). All European Jews who came under the control of Germany and its allies were targeted for death. Some six million were killed. The remaining three million survived camps, endured life in hiding, 'passed' as a Gentile, fled to safety, or experienced some combination of these. All were victims

A Companion to Nazi Germany, First Edition. Edited by Shelley Baranowski, Armin Nolzen, and Claus-Christian W. Szejnmann.
© 2018 Debórah Dwork. Published 2018 by John Wiley & Sons Ltd.

of the Holocaust. Had Jews not hidden or passed, they too would have been deported. Had they not sought asylum elsewhere, they too would have been caught in the machinery of death.

Fleeing does not write refugees out of Holocaust history, it simply takes that history elsewhere. Indeed: it takes it everywhere. The history of refugee Jews during and after the Nazi era is literally centrifugal: to flee the centre. That centre comprised Germany; then Greater Germany, which included Austria, Sudetenland, Bohemia, and Moravia; and finally, all of German-ruled Europe. The sites of flight grew ever more distant from the countries adjacent to Germany to all the peopled continents.

Perhaps a sequela of the dominant perspective is that historical studies of Jewish refugees from Nazism focus on the pre-war period, assuming that too few managed to flee after the outbreak of war to be significant. Yet hundreds of thousands of Jews continued to flee Nazi-held land from 1939 right through 1942–1943, the peak of the Holocaust. Some fled to another country where they got caught later. Others fled and were turned back at the frontier. And still others managed to reach safe shores. The history of flight and exile encompasses all of them.

27.2   European Diasporas and 'Homecomings' after the First World War

When the Nazis came to power in 1933, Europe faced a refugee problem with which it had struggled since the First World War. After borders closed in 1914, long-dormant passport laws were reactivated and new wartime passport and visa requirements soon became standard (Torpey 2001). Intended to be temporary, these passport and visa requirements were not abolished when hostilities ended. Economic crisis, massive unemployment as a result of troop demobilization, fear of revolution, displaced populations, and an influenza pandemic strengthened the xenophobia born in 1914. States feared beggars, vagabonds, refugees, spies, political agitators, and currency speculators.

Many supported the maintenance of tight control over the movement of strangers for a very different reason: the practical benefits that accompanied citizenship. In most places, the right to employment became a corollary of citizenship. And with the rise of the welfare state and the introduction of education, unemployment, health, and old-age benefits for citizens, the gap widened between national and foreigner. To make matters worse, the United States and the British dominions, sites of mass immigration at the turn of the century, slashed the total number allowed to enter and delimited the countries whence they came.

Yet nine to ten million people sought asylum in 1920s and 1930s Europe. In the reconfiguration of state borders, minority groups fled to countries where they were 'nationally' attached. Some 800 000 Germans moved to Germany from areas accorded to Poland; 1.3 million Greeks to Greece from Turkey; 250 000 Bulgarians to Bulgaria from Turkey, Greece, and Rumania; 750 000 Turks to Turkey from Bulgaria and Greece; and 400 000 Armenians to the Soviet Republic of Armenia from Turkey. These millions of refugees belonged somewhere, and expected to be absorbed into their 'national homes' (Simpson 1938).

A different type of refugee, however, those who fled genocide (Armenians) or revolution (Russians), posed an intractable problem. The slaughter of Armenians by Turks under cover of the First World War sent more than 200 000 Armenians surging into Syria and France. And the Russian Revolution led 700 000 people to flee. These refugees carried the burden of statelessness, which deprived them of the rights, privileges, and protections accorded to citizens (Weis 1956).

Previously a minor problem, statelessness ballooned in the 1920s. Millions of citizens of the former Austro-Hungarian empire found themselves stateless due to the new citizenship rules of the successor states. In post-war reconfigured Europe, ethnic Hungarians, for instance, now lived in Czechoslovakia. But stateless people such as they had their homes and livelihood. They could not travel. Yet, for the most part, they could remain quietly where they were and hope for naturalization in due course.

Not so Russians and Armenians. The Soviet government unrolled the largest denationalization in history with a decree on 15 December 1921 stripping citizenship from nationals who had lived outside Russia for five years and had not got new passports from the Soviet Union; those who had left the country after 7 November 1917 without permission; and those 'who have voluntarily served in armies fighting against the Soviet authority, or who have in any way participated in counterrevolutionary organizations'. Some 863 000 Russians thus suddenly found themselves stateless refugees. Turkey proved equally ruthless. The government confiscated all the property in Turkey of Armenians living abroad (1923), stripped them of their nationality (1927), expelled those who had returned, and forbade those who wished to return from doing so (Flournoy and Hudson 1929). These decrees affected as many as 200 000 to 900 000 Armenians.

The Soviet Union and Turkey denationalized citizens they saw as impediments to their revolutionary vision. Belgium, France, and Italy adopted similar decrees to denationalize anyone the government perceived as a threat to public order or state interests. The League of Nations stepped into this legal vacuum. Accepting responsibility to protect stateless refugees, the League asked the famous Norwegian explorer Fridtjof Nansen to serve as High Commissioner to deal with this problem. It fell to him to create and assign a new identity document, which was popularly called the Nansen passport. Valid for one year, the Nansen passport did not grant the privilege of residence citizens enjoyed, or the right to seek employment. But it looked like a passport, was called a passport, carried the most respected name of its day, and it worked (Hieronymi 2003). Indeed, it accrued additional rights: limited diplomatic protection; legal assistance; eased labour restrictions; limitations on expulsion. By the time Nansen died in 1930, refugees with passports in his name enjoyed many of the same benefits as nationals (Holborn 1975).

27.3 Nazi-era Refugee Movement before the Second World War

The Nansen passport reached its zenith just when a new problem overwhelmed its scope: a wave of refugees from Nazi Germany. Hitler came to power on 30 January 1933, and, within a month, dragnet operations to arrest dissidents triggered their flight. The regime did not cancel passports in the first instance and, as most of the intellectuals and political activists who sought to flee had been abroad before, they had documents in hand now that danger loured.

Jews were especially marked for persecution, however, as the 1 April state-sponsored boycott of all Jewish professionals and businesses proved. Jews experienced the boycott as a caesura, and they were correct. Within weeks, they were disenfranchised, stripped of their rights and privileges as citizens. Fired and without prospects for employment, adult Jews began to consider life elsewhere. Dismissed from school and barred from educational opportunities, younger Jews looked abroad too.

It was the Depression era, and no country wanted immigrants who would take jobs. Nevertheless, the 40 000 Jewish Germans and 10 000 Gentile Germans who fled in 1933 found asylum. Threat of arrest and fear of penury shaped that first wave of emigration – primarily renowned men with international contacts to help them leave. Most planned to secure a place for their families, and imagined the relocation would be short-lived (Bentwich 1936). Surrounding countries opened their doors even though, due to the currency restrictions that applied to all German travellers abroad and the Weimar-legislated Reich Flight Tax that applied to émigrés, they came with little. The host nations, too, thought it was a temporary, emergency measure.

The exodus of 1933 slowed as the regime appeared to pursue a more pragmatic policy. Then too, doors that had opened to Jewish refugees in 1933 began to close a year later. Thus the number of Jews who left dropped to 23 000 in 1934. Planned emigration overtook panicked flight. Jews looked to sell their property and ship their possessions, and they looked for a country that offered the prospect of employment.

In 1934, 37% of German Jews went to Palestine, 37% to European countries, and 26% to countries overseas. The number of Jewish refugees fell again in 1935, to 21 000. The percentage destined for Palestine remained about the same, while European countries received fewer (28%), and those leaving for overseas increased (36%) (Rosenstock 1956). Emigrants sold their assets far below their real value. The proceeds were subjected to the Reich Flight Tax, which creamed off a quarter. The remaining sums went into blocked accounts, which could be sold only to foreign importers of German goods and at 40% (1934) to 20% (1936) of the official value. The regime and those in business with Germany profited handsomely from the Jews' departure (Strauss 1980, 1981). Still, the figures suggest that most Jews felt that if they accommodated sufficiently, they might remain in their native land.

The Nuremburg Laws (September 1935) ended that notion. The Law for the Protection of German Blood and German Honour prohibited marriages and sexual relations between Jews and 'citizens of German or kindred blood'. And the Reich Citizenship Law restricted citizenship only to subjects 'of German or kindred blood'. As to who was a Jew, Nazi lawyers soon introduced a formulary.

Shocked by the legislation, the leaders of the *Jüdischer Centralverein* (Central Jewish Association, the community's official organization) turned to emigration. Many Jews were eager to leave and now set their sights on countries overseas. In 1933 refugees had wished to stay near Germany to be able to return when the regime toppled; by autumn 1935 few thought the Nazis would be booted out so soon. Then too, the worst of the Depression had passed and opportunities abroad opened. Jews assessed their prospects everywhere as liquidation of their community through emigration became a de facto goal of the regime. In 1936, overseas countries absorbed 43% of the Jews leaving Germany; in 1937, that figure reached 60%, while Palestine dropped to 15%, and Europe to 25% (Rosenstock 1956).

Riding high by then, Hitler turned to scoring a foreign policy success and to keep his promise of '*Ein Reich, Ein Volk, Ein Führer*' (One Empire, One People, One Leader): to bring all the Germanic peoples 'home' to the Reich by creating a Greater Germany. The first territory to be claimed for that empire was Austria. The German army marched triumphantly into Vienna on 13 March 1938. Popular euphoria for Hitler, National Socialism, and unification with Germany was matched by hatred for and violence against the Jews.

By the time Berlin annexed Austria, 120 000 of the 500 000 Jews in Germany had left the Reich. The *Anschluss*, however, brought Austria's 200 000 Jews into the now Greater Reich. The Nazis' solution: forced emigration. The mastermind of the new strategy was Adolf Eichmann, the SS 'expert' on Jewish matters. Within days of the *Anschluss*, Eichmann turned up in Vienna to organize the emigration of Jews. His headquarters in a palace stolen from the Rothschild family became the Central Office for Jewish Emigration. Emigration no longer depended upon the initiative of individual Jews. It was an operation supervised by the SD (*Sicherheitsdienst*, or Security Service) and involved officials of the finance ministry, the police, the currency control office, and representatives of the Jewish community. Eichmann compared his system to a conveyor belt. 'The initial application and all the rest of the required papers are put in at one end, and the passport falls off at the other end,' he explained when interrogated for trial in 1962. He did not mention that the conveyor belt swallowed up the Jews' rights as well as their money, and that the passport they received allowing them to leave was valid for a mere 14 days. Nor did he explain that the system was financed with money taken from the Jews themselves. What he did report was that his Central Office for Jewish Emigration had forced 50 000 Jews to leave within six months (von Lang and Sibyll 1983).

For Eichmann, the Central Office for Jewish Emigration was a conveyor belt. For Austria's Jews, it was a nightmare. How were those 'required papers' to be obtained? The Nazis wanted the Jews to leave. The Jews, humiliated, abused, and terrorized, sought to escape. But, as their co-religionists in Germany had learned over five years, emigration was a desperate search for sponsors abroad, tax clearance forms, entry visas, train tickets, and ship berths. As civil society disintegrated, kinship networks emerged as key escape routes. Jews contacted relatives who had settled abroad years before, and depended upon those who had emigrated. And they acquired skills to support their applications for immigration. Young and middle-aged people took classes in all manner of skilled labour.

The Jewish communal organizations of Greater Germany focused on schemes to help children and young adults. Concerned as they were about the entire community, they were especially anxious about the young. In Germany itself, some 83% of Jews under the age of 24 managed to escape by 1939 (Kaplan 1996). The Austrian Jewish community in 1938, and the Czech community a year later, quickly adopted their co-religionists' aims and achieved similar results. The figures bespeak success; they do not reveal the toil and foreboding of Jewish communal workers as they sought to respond responsibly to the catastrophe they faced.

The November pogrom (1938) swelled the number of Jews seeking asylum. The physical demolition of Jews' property, from the destruction of nearly every synagogue to the attacks on businesses owned by Jews on 9 November, left no place for Jewish religious or economic life. The imprisonment of 30 000 Jewish men swept out of their homes the next day (10 November) into concentration camps left no place for Jews at all. The sole escape lay in emigration and all hope for release from concentration camps lay in an exit visa.

Where to go? American immigration policies barred the door to most Jews. Refugees held no status in the American system; they fell in the ordinary immigration system, and responsibility for their maintenance shifted to family and friends in America who were called upon to provide an affidavit, a sworn assurance of financial means to care for the would-be immigrant. As the State Department intended, this proved a major obstacle for Jews desperate to leave Greater Germany.

Britain never envisioned itself as a country of immigration. The United States kept Jews out as immigrants; Britain stopped them at the door as refugees. Britain's refugee policy was a means of enriching the country's intellectual, cultural, and business capital. Thus Sigmund Freud received a warm welcome, while only 50 Jews were admitted with permission to practise medicine.

Yet exceptions obtained. Whitehall opened the door to Jewish women willing to work as domestic servants. British middle-class women pressed the government to ease the labour market in this arena. Their Gentile German and Austrian servants no longer needed work now that rearmament generated full employment at home. And Jews in Greater Germany offered a new pool of potential domestics. Whitehall relaxed some of its regulations (autumn 1938), allowing married couples to obtain domestic permits, and lowering the age limit for women from 18 to 16. With the whole operation under the administrative umbrella of the Central Office of Refugees in London, a streamlined system developed to send refugees to Britain as domestic servants (Kushner 1991).

At the same time, newspaper reports describing the violence of the November pogrom prompted public sympathy and government action in Britain especially, but also in the Netherlands and Sweden. The plight of children struck an especially resonant chord and aid organizations in Greater Germany organized *Kindertransports*, special trains laid on to send endangered children west to safety. The children on board these trains left their parents and other family members at the railway stations of Prague, Vienna, Frankfurt, Berlin, Leipzig, the free city of Danzig, and the Polish city of Zbonszyn, and were sent to the homes of people from all walks of life who volunteered to care for them (Presland 1944). Few were reunited at war's end.

27.4   Destination Palestine

If Britain cracked its doors open for some 10 000 unaccompanied minors and 14 000 young women, it closed the gates to Palestine. The League of Nations Mandate (1922) through which Britain governed Palestine included Foreign

Secretary Lord Balfour's declaration of 1917 affirming that 'H.M. Government views with favour the establishment in Palestine of a national home for the Jewish people' (Jewish Agency for Palestine 1947). With the promise of 'a Jewish national home', Palestine had emerged as a real option for Europe's Jews. In the 1920s, desperately poor young Polish Jews embraced the political solution Zionism offered and flocked to its youth movements. German Jews, comfortable in Weimar Germany, contributed financially but had little wish to participate in person. When Hitler came to power, only 20 000 German Jews (4%) belonged to Zionist organizations and German Jews comprised only 1% of the *yishuv* (Jewish settlement in Palestine) population (Poppel 1977).

Anticipating pressure to admit refugees to Palestine, the British government set up a cabinet committee to consider the matter. 'The number of Jewish refugees who could be allowed to enter is strictly conditioned by what the country can absorb,' the committee reported on 7 April 1933. 'There is no reason to suppose that room could be found in Palestine in the near future for any appreciable number of German Jewish refugees' (Cabinet Committee on Aliens Restrictions 1933). The Zionist leadership agreed with the British authority's rationale and its measures. Then too, it was German Jews, who had shown little interest in the project of Palestine before, who needed asylum now. They had few friends among the Zionist leaders who faced the conflict between their long-range plan for steady and stable growth and the crisis of Jews in Germany.

German Zionists therefore parleyed with the Nazis who, for their part, were willing to negotiate. Nazis and Zionists agreed that Jews had no place in the diaspora: Nazis believed that Jews had harmed Western civilization; Zionists that 2000 years of European antisemitism was more than enough. Both saw Palestine as the solution. The *Ha'avara* (Transfer) Agreement they hammered out allowed German Jews the sum required by Britain for unrestricted entry into Palestine. It also permitted transfer of capital in the form of German products or commodities.

Between August 1933 and early 1937 only 12 000 German Jews used the ha'avara agreement to transfer a portion of their assets to Palestine. Even so, this influx of money stimulated such economic growth that it allowed another 20 000 young German Jews without resources to immigrate to Palestine. The ha'avara agreement also opened up places in Palestine for the besieged Jews in an ever more antisemitic Poland. Thus the number of Jews in the yishuv doubled from 200 000 to 400 000 (or close to 30% of the territory's population of 1.3 million) during the first years of Nazi rule (Black 1984).

Permission to emigrate was one thing, earning a living upon arrival was another. Most German Jews lacked the skills required for the kinds of work available. If, in Central and Western Europe and the Americas, German Jews had considered themselves and their bourgeois culture superior, they found an inverted social hierarchy in Palestine (Schlör 2003). 'The wheel has turned,' Henrietta Szold, the founder of Hadassah, the women's Zionist organization, observed. 'Palestinian Mayflower Jewry is East European!' Szold went to Palestine in 1920; when Hitler came to power she was 72, and now she had a new job to do: settle German Jews (Rosenthal 1942).

Training her sights on the young, Szold embarked upon the greatest initiative of her very accomplished life: the Youth Aliyah movement, the project to send teenagers to Palestine, powered by Recha Freier, a teacher and ardent Zionist in Berlin, and Szold. Freier had the vision; Szold had the skills and connections to establish the infrastructure in Palestine (Amkraut 2006). And, by March 1939, the movement brought some 3262 youngsters from Germany, 1000 from Austria, and 400 from Czechoslovakia (60% boys and 40% girls) to Palestine (Heim 2004).

The influx of Jews suggested that they would soon gain a majority share of the population. The new immigrants fostered an expanding economy, which set a higher absorptive capacity, and thus increased immigration. The German Foreign Office had never imagined that the Jews would be so successful in Palestine, and they dropped their advocacy of the Zionist cause. 'The formation of a Jewish state … is not in Germany's interest,' the foreign office wrote to its embassy in London and consulate-general in Palestine (Nicosia 1985).

The Arab population also saw these developments with increasing alarm. Riots in the streets of Jerusalem escalated in April 1936 into a full-scale rebellion. The British crushed the Arab revolt ruthlessly. But, as of 1937, they also limited the annual immigration of Jews to 12 000 each year for the next five years.

The British regulations spurred a turn to clandestine entry. 'We must wage a battle not *for* aliyah, but *through* Aliyah,' David Ben-Gurion (the future prime minister of Israel) declared in November 1938. Nine months later, more than 30 ships had brought over 6000 illegal immigrants to Palestine's shores. 'We may ask why it is that history did not choose free, wealthy and well-behaved Jews to be the bearers of its mission, but preferred instead the Jewish refugees, the most wretched of all humankind, cast adrift on the seas,' Zionist leader Berl Katznelson mused. 'But this is a fact we cannot change. This is what history determined, and it is left to us to accept its choice and to follow the refugee' (Ofer 1990).

27.5   From the November Pogrom Through the War Years

Desperate to flee Greater Germany, Jews without prospects for any immigration visa looked to Shanghai. Opened to foreign residence and trade as a result of the 'Opium War' (1840–1843), Shanghai allowed Europeans and Americans to establish extraterritorial 'concession areas' or settlements. By the 1930s, the so-called International Settlement and the French Concession were home to 1.5 million people, of whom 60 000 were foreigners who enjoyed extraterritorial status (Miller 1937).

Chinese officials allowed Americans and Europeans to settle in Shanghai so long as they paid a set fee. When Japan occupied northeast China in 1937, it too respected the extraterritorial integrity of the International Settlement and the French Concession, notwithstanding the harsh regime the Japanese imposed. Shanghai was thus a city in the middle of a country at war. Panic-stricken Jews were not deterred. By September 1939, 17 000 had arrived in the city, without a future, but safe from the Nazis (Armbrüster, Kohlstruck, and Mühlberger 2000).

The German invasion of Poland halted ship transport from Greater Germany to the Far East. At the same time, it triggered the flight of hundreds of thousands of

Jews to Europe's east. Few Jews had sought asylum in the Soviet Union before the outbreak of war. The Soviets gave them little reason to do so. Furious that the League of Nations had protected White Russians with its Nansen passport, the Soviets refused to recognize these documents. Except for officially invited visitors, the USSR admitted no one.

War and the German and Soviet division of Poland changed the situation on the ground. Some 300 000 Jewish refugees from western and central Poland fled east to Soviet-occupied Poland (Pinchuk 1978). Forced flight swelled the refugee stream. Once the German–Soviet demarcation line was established, Berlin tried to push 500 000 Jews into Russian territory.

With so many uprooted people on their hands, the Soviets sought to put the refugees to work to regulate the situation and stabilize the economy. Adopting an official policy of Ukrainization and Belorussification, the Soviets offered employment in Ukraine and Belorussia to refugee doctors, nurses, pharmacists, and teachers who spoke Ukrainian or Belorussian. The introduction of communism also brought bureaucracy, which opened opportunities for clerks, accountants, and economists. Few Jews knew these languages, however.

Intent upon absolute control of everyone within their borders, the Soviets offered the refugees citizenship. At a time when no other country offered citizenship to émigrés, the Soviet Union adopted a policy of mass naturalization. They envisioned it as an effective framework of Sovietization and they saw their offer as a gift. For Jewish refugees, it posed a cruel dilemma. They wanted to regularize their situation but, hoping for family reunification and repatriation to western and central Poland, they were loath to take a new nationality. To accept Soviet citizenship meant to give up on the idea of return to home and family, or emigration abroad.

Still, the Soviets needed the newcomers' labour and, xenophobic to the core, they were highly suspicious of those who refused citizenship. Newspapers referred to such refugees as 'garbage to be swept out', and action soon followed propaganda. Deportation of refugees started in June 1940, and those caught were not unduly alarmed. They believed (correctly, as it happened) that this relocation would be temporary. They imagined working deep in the Soviet Union and waiting for the collapse of the Third Reich. Some refugees actively sought transport to the east. Experienced in deporting large populations, the Soviets picked up and packed off over 200 000 refugees in a few days. They landed in the Arctic region of European Russia, Siberia, or the Soviet republics of central Asia where work of strategic importance to the Soviet war effort lay. Most were detailed to internment camps and collective farms (Levin 1995).

The intense cold without proper clothing or heating, hunger, body lice and bedbugs inside and biting flies and bloodthirsty mosquitoes outside, and the backbreaking, unending Soviet labour quotas shaped inmates' lives. Many died. Many more suffered from scurvy and lost their teeth. Even greater numbers endured typhoid, tuberculosis, dysentery, malaria, and accidents on the job. At the same time, these were not like the Nazi camps. The inmates were not beaten, nor were there gas chambers or crematoria. Harsh as these camps were, they offered a possibility of survival.

While the outbreak of war sent hundreds of thousands of Polish Jews east, the German occupation of Western Europe prompted tens of thousands of Jews in France, Belgium, and the Netherlands to try to flee to neutral Switzerland and Spain. Indeed, flight both east and west continued even as the Germans and their allies pursued the total annihilation of the Jews. For Western European Jews, and Jews from Greater Germany who had fled west during the pre-war years, German-speaking Switzerland seemed a place where they could establish a foothold. But Switzerland had worried about *Überfremdung* ('overrun by foreigners') for some time. The government established a special police department, the *Fremdenpolizei* (Aliens' Police) to keep Switzerland for the Swiss. Strict policing during the 1920s and 1930s ensured that refugees of all stripes got only a short respite in their 'onward migration' to a country of permanent asylum.

The *Überfremdung* discourse initially pertained to all foreigners. Influenced by Nazism, however, antisemitic rhetoric linked the perceived problems of *Überfremdung* and *Überjudung* ('too many Jews'). As Heinrich Rothmund, head of the *Fremdenpolizei* and Chief of the Police Department in the Ministry of Justice and Police, put it (April 1937), 'the Jewish Question', was a pure ' *Überfremdungs* problem' (Roschewski 1997).

The Swiss policy of serving as a transit station worked well until 1938. All but 100 of the nearly 6000 Jews who had arrived since 1933 had moved on. With the *Anschluss*, however, trains filled with Jewish refugees crossed the border. In less than three weeks, 4000 Jews poured into Switzerland (Ferro 1999). In addition, over 1000 people had slipped in clandestinely in a single month. Departure for other countries was impossible. The federal council ordered (August 1938) the reinforcement of border patrols and the return of all illegal immigrants to Germany (Nationale Kommission für die Veröffentlichung Diplomatischer Dokumente der Schweiz 1984–1994, vol. 12, 813, 833ff.).

Rothmund dispatched military units to help seal the frontier. That solved the 'green border' problem, but it did not address the legal entry of refugees from Greater Germany, nearly all of whom were Jews. Rothmund met with German envoy Otto Köcher in Berne to discuss the matter in early September. What if the German government marked the passports of German and Austrian Jews identifying them as Jews? Köcher asked. The conversation continued into October. Perhaps a stamp in the top left corner of the first page of a large letter 'J' surrounded by a circle 2 centimetres wide? The Swiss government agreed. And the German government promptly declared all passports held by Jews invalid (5 October 1938). Jews had to turn in their passports for revalidation 'with a symbol designated by the Reich Minister of the Interior, which will mark the holder as a Jew' (Ludwig 1966).

The Swiss took further measures to seal the border when war began. The federal council issued a decree (17 October 1939) to expel illegal refugees. Still, Jews continued to slip into the country and, in the midst of the Holocaust round-ups, Swiss army intelligence reported (16 July 1942) increasing numbers of Jewish refugees stealing into Switzerland.

Alarmed by the numbers and the 'character' of infiltration – 'more and more organized' and 'coordinated by professional "*passeurs*"' – the government demanded action. Rothmund promptly called (4 August) for the strict enforcement of the 1939 decree (Unabhängige Expertenkommission Schweiz – Zweiter

Weltkrieg 2001). But hurling refugees back into the Germans' hands was too much for some, and protests ensued. Walking back his policy, Rothmund instructed (early September) police to admit elderly refugees and family members of earlier asylum seekers. On 26 September, he added ill people, pregnant women, unaccompanied children under the age of 16, and parents with their own children.

Rothmund's September hardship allowances prompted initiatives to spirit Jews to safety. Swiss officials noticed a new pattern in illicit crossing in early 1943: groups of children. Believing that the French Red Cross was responsible, the Swiss government contacted their representative in Vichy, Walter Stucki. The French Foreign Office had looked into the matter, he responded (28 May), but the best they could offer was that there was some evidence that an organization named OSE was involved. Unfortunately, Stucki concluded, neither the French Foreign Office nor he knew anything about OSE (Unabhängige Expertenkommission Schweiz – Zweiter Weltkrieg 2001).

That they did not was sheer luck for everyone in the OSE operation. The officials had no reason for ignorance. OSE (*Oeuvre de Secours aux Enfants* or Children's Aid Organization), a legal philanthropic organization, had operated in France for a decade by that point. Responding to the desperate situation, the OSE directorate decided (16 January 1943) to send children under its care into hiding. Those who could not go underground (due to religious practice, inability to speak French, or too 'Jewish' an appearance) would be smuggled over the border, primarily into Switzerland but also into Spain (Dwork 1990).

OSE was but one of the Jewish organizations to develop clandestine routes to Switzerland and Spain. The *Eclaireurs* (Jewish scouts) and a broad-band Zionist organization, the *Mouvement de Jeunesse Sionist* (MJS), in conjunction with the Jewish armed resistance movement *L'Organisation de Combat*, for example, ran active clandestine operations. At war's end, the MJS reported that 2000 children and many hundreds of families had crossed into Switzerland through their networks, and that they had organized a route to Spain for hundreds of young people to join the Allies. The Eclaireurs reckoned that its routes had served about 500 in all. OSE, for its part, had smuggled more than 2000 children into Switzerland, as well as a number into Spain (Dwork and van Pelt 2009).

We know about these routes because they were developed by organizations that wished to tell their history and the history of the people they had served. We know little about the 'professional' *passeurs*, who had smuggled goods before the war, people during the Occupation, and went back to contraband after the surrender. It is probable that most Jews did not flee through an organized underground. They sought their way on their own and, if they found trustworthy people to help them, and luck, fortuitous circumstance, and timing were with them, they succeeded (Dwork 2010).

27.6 The Challenges of Émigré Life

A small elite group of artists and intellectuals brought their culture with them to their host countries and had a great impact on science, medicine, literature, philosophy, and film. Famous and influential, they loom deceptively large in popular perceptions of the refugee experience (Heilbut 1997). Most émigrés did not fall into that category. The great majority suffered from isolation, marginalization, and loss of esteem in the public realm. For a small number, the bewilderment of their uprooted and déclassé existence in a new land proved too great (Arendt 1943). Fragmentary evidence suggests that age proved a factor in the decision to commit suicide. For elderly refugees, the future even in a safe land was too frightening. They simply did not have the material or emotional resources to brave the challenges.

Nearly all refugees faced great difficulties. Downward mobility and social isolation framed their lives. Only a tiny fraction of refugee professionals such as physicians, lawyers, and dentists found employment in their field. This was not due solely or even primarily to the political agenda of government officials. On the contrary: the restrictions on posts reflected the wishes of the refugees' professional colleagues. The rejection operated on a social level; they were spurned by their professional peers whose attitude was: I didn't want you to come here to practice; I will not accord you recognition as a colleague (who alas is not permitted to work by government regulation); you are just about lucky enough to be my butler.

Menial jobs were the rule, not the exception. People took whatever work they could find to gain a toehold. And they hoped that their employment would lead to security and further opportunities. This philosophy prevailed among refugees who had escaped occupied Europe and settled in countries across the globe.

In Palestine, however, Zionist ideology valorized manual labour. Contrary to social values elsewhere, the culture that prevailed in Palestine honoured those who built up the Jewish homeland with their hands. Not everyone found fulfilment in manual labour, not even all the youngsters of the Youth Aliyah movement. Still, Zionist ideology helped them: their work did not represent shameful downward mobility.

Ideology proved powerful for young refugees elsewhere as well, helping them cope with their new lives and manage their longing for and worries about family. Young Austria, the youth arm of the Free Austrian Movement, was established in England in 1939 on the first anniversary of the *Anschluss*. Officially, it had no specific political affiliation. In fact, it was a Communist organization that aimed to attract adolescent refugees. By the middle of the war, Young Austria counted 1300 members who frequented 15 different centres in Great Britain (1988). The declared ideological line held that Austria remained the true national home of the émigrés, that Austria fell as Hitler's first victim, and that another Austria, which resisted Hitler, existed. The organization proved a bulwark against the social isolation that a great many émigrés experienced. And it gave them a goal: to bring communism to Austria.

If they dreamed about a communist Austria, the 300 000 Jews who had fled to the Soviet Union lived in a fully communist state. Their experience reveals that ideology served merely as fuel to propel a refugee forward or as glue to cement a group together. Young Austria's communist ideology provided a rationale for cohesion, but it was that cohesion rather than the ideology that helped the refugees. The Soviet communist ideology that the refugees lived in the USSR did not protect them from the harsh conditions of daily life, despair, isolation, and loneliness. They coped. But they did not belong. Indeed, no one did, no matter where she or he had managed to alight.

References

Amkraut, Brian. 2006. *Between Home and Homeland: Youth Aliyah from Nazi Germany*. Tuscaloosa: University of Alabama Press.

Arendt, Hannah. 1943. 'We Refugees.' *The Menorah Journal* 31, 69–77.

Armbrüster, Georg, Kohlstruck, Michael, and Mühlberger, Sonja eds. 2000. *Exil Shanghai 1938–1947: Jüdisches Leben in der Emigration*. Teetz: Hentrich & Hentrich.

Bentwich, Norman. 1936. *The Refugees from Germany*. London: Allen & Unwin.

Black, Edwin. 1984. *The Transfer Agreement: The Dramatic Story of the Pact Between the Third Reich and Jewish Palestine*. New York: Macmillan.

Cabinet Committee on Aliens Restrictions. 1933. *Report*. 7 April 1933. The National Archives (United Kingdom). CAB 27/549.

Dwork, Debórah. 1990. *Children With A Star: Jewish Youth in Nazi Europe*. New Haven, CT: Yale University Press.

Dwork, Debórah and van Pelt, Robert. 2009. *Flight from the Reich: Refugee Jews, 1933–1946*. New York: W.W. Norton.

Dwork, Debórah. 2010. 'Refugee Jews and the Holocaust: Luck, Fortuitous Circumstances, and Timing.' In *Jewish Perspectives on the 'Forced Emigration' Period (1938/39 to 1941) until Deportation and Ghettoization*, edited by Susanne Heim, Beate Meyer, and Francis Nicosia. Göttingen: Wallstein.

Ferro, Shaul. 1999. 'Switzerland and the Refugees Fleeing Nazism: Documents on the German Jews Turned Back at the Basel Border in 1938–1939', *Yad Vashem Studies* 27, 213.

Flournoy, Richard and Hudson, Manley. 1929. *A Collection of Nationality Laws of Various Countries as Contained in Constitutions, Statues and Treaties*. New York: Oxford University Press.

Heilbut, Anthony. 1997. *Exiled in Paradise: German Refugee Artists and Intellectuals in America from the 1930s to the Present*. Berkeley: University of California Press.

Heim, Susanne. 2004. 'Immigration Policy and Forced Emigration from Germany.' In *Children and the Holocaust*, edited by the Center for Advanced Holocaust Studies, 1–18. Washington, DC: USHMM.

Hieronymi, Otto. 2003. 'The Nansen Passport: A Tool of Freedom of Movement and Protection.' *Refugee Survey Quarterly* 22, 36–47.

Holborn, Louise, with the assistance of Philip Chartrand and Rita Chartrand. 1975. *Refugees: A Problem of Our Times*. Metuchen, NJ: Scarecrow Press.

Jewish Agency for Palestine. 1947. *Book of Documents*. New York: The Jewish Agency for Palestine.

Kaplan, Marion. 1996. *Between Dignity and Despair: Jewish Life in Nazi Germany*. New York: Oxford University Press.

Kushner, Tony. 1991. 'An Alien Occupation – Jewish Refugees and Domestic Service in Britain, 1933–1948.' In *Second Chance: Two Centuries of German-speaking Jews in the United Kingdom*, edited by Werner E. Mosse. Tübingen: J.C.B. Mohr.

Levin, Dov. 1995. *The Lesser of Two Evils: Eastern European Jewry Under Soviet Rule, 1939–1941*, translated by Naftali Greenwood. Philadelphia: Jewish Publication Society.

Ludwig, Carl. 1966. *Die Flüchtlingspolitik der Schweiz seit 1933 bis zur Gegenwart (1957)*. Bern: Verlag Herbert Lang & Cie.

Miller, G.E. 1937. *Shanghai: Paradise of Adventurers*. New York: Orsay Publishing House.

Nationale Kommission für die Veröffentlichung Diplomatischer Dokumente der Schweiz. 1984–1994. *Diplomatische Dokumente der Schweiz, 1848–1945*. Berne: Benteli.

Nicosia, Francis. 1985. *The Third Reich and the Palestine Question*. Austin: University of Texas Press.

Ofer, Dalia. 1990. *Escaping the Holocaust: Illegal Immigration to the Land of Israel, 1939–1944.* New York: Oxford University Press.

Pinchuk, Ben-Cion. 1978. 'Jewish Refugees in Soviet Poland, 1939–1941.' *Jewish Social Studies* 40, 141–158.

Poppel, Stephen. 1977. *Zionism in Germany, 1897–1933.* Philadelphia: The Jewish Publication Society of America.

Presland, John (Gladys Bendit). 1944. *A Great Adventure: The Story of the Refugee Children's Movement.* London: Bloomsbury House.

Roschewski, Heinz. 1997. *Rothmund und die Juden: Eine historische Fallstudie des Antisemitismus in der schweizerischen Flüchtlingspolitik 1933–1957.* Basle and Frankfurt am Main: Schweizerischer Israelitischer Gemeindebund / Helbing & Lichtenhahn.

Rosenstock, Werner. 1956. 'Exodus 1933–1939: Jewish Emigration from Germany.' *Leo Baeck Institute Yearbook* 1, 337–390.

Rosenthal, Marvin. 1942. *Henriette Szold, Life and Letters.* New York: Viking.

Schlör, Joachim. 2003. *Endlich im Gelobten Land? Deutsche Juden unterwegs in eine neue Heimat.* Berlin: Aufbau-Verlag.

Simpson, John Hope. 1938. *The Refugee Problem: Report of a Survey.* London: Royal Institute of International Affairs.

Strauss, Herbert. 1980. 'Jewish Emigration from Germany: Nazi Policies and Jewish Responses (1).' *Leo Baeck Institute Year Book* 25, 313–397.

Strauss, Herbert. 1981. 'Jewish Emigration from Germany: Nazi Policies and Jewish Responses (2).' *Leo Baeck Institute Year Book*, 26: 343–409.

Torpey, John. 2001. 'The Great War and the Birth of the Modern Passport System.' In *Documenting Individual Identity*, edited by Jane Caplan and John Torpey, 256–270. Princeton, NJ: Princeton University Press.

Unabhängige Expertenkommission Schweiz – Zweiter Weltkrieg. 2001. *Die Schweiz und die Flüchtlinge zur Zeit des Nationalsozialismus.* Zurich: Chronos Verlag.

von Lang, Jochen with Sibyll, Claus, eds. 1983. *Eichmann Interrogated: Transcripts from the Archives of the Israeli Police.* New York: Farrar, Straus and Giroux.

Weis, Paul. 1956. *Nationality and Statelessness in International Law.* London: Stevens & Sons.

Young Austria.1988. *Young Austria in Grossbritannien: Wiedersehenstreffen anläßlich des 50. Jahrestages der Besetzung Österreichs.* Vienna: Verein Wiedersehenstreffen 1938–1988 Young Austria.

Further Reading

Benz, Wolfgang and Neiss, Marion, eds. 1994. *Deutsch-jüdisches Exil: das Ende der Assimilation?* Berlin: Metropole.
An especially important work in the very large German literature on refugees from Nazi Germany, both Jewish and Gentile.

Caron, Vicki. 1999. *Uneasy Asylum: France and the Jewish Refugee Crisis, 1933–1942.* Stanford, CA: Stanford University Press.
A key study of French refugee policy, illuminating continuities as well as fractures, as successive governments took power.

Kaplan, Marion. 2008. *Dominican Haven: The Jewish Refugee Settlement in Sosua, 1940–1945.* New York: Museum of Jewish Heritage.
Provides a nuanced and thoughtful account of a history many reference but about which little was known: the asylum offered to European Jews by Rafael Trujillo, dictator of the Dominican Republic.

Kushner, Tony and Knox, Katherine. 1999. *Refugees in an Age of Genocide: Global, National and Local Perspectives During the Twentieth Century.* London: Frank Cass.
A key starting point for any study of refugees in the 1930s and 1940s.
Marrus, Michael. 1985. *The Unwanted: European Refugees in the Twentieth Century.* New York: Oxford University Press.
A foundational work in this field.
Palmier, Jean-Michel. 2006. *Weimar in Exile: The Antifascist Emigration in Europe and America.* London: Verso.
Offers a cogent account of the flight of anti-Nazi (not anti-fascist) artists, intellectuals, and political opponents.
Spitzer, Leo. 1998. *Hotel Bolivia: The Culture of Memory in a Refuge from Nazism.* New York: Hill & Wang.
Brimming with insights, this work sits at the intersection of history and memory.
Tartakower, Arieh and Grossman, Kurt R. 1944. *The Jewish Refugee.* New York: Institute of Jewish Affairs.
A useful general study from that period that focuses on refugee Jews.
Wyman, David. 1984. *The Abandonment of the Jews.* New York: Pantheon.
Among the many studies of government asylum and immigration policies, Wyman's account is especially arresting.

CHAPTER TWENTY-EIGHT

Germany and the Outside World*

LARS LÜDICKE

28.1 Introduction

The war unleashed by Germany in 1939 was by no means an inevitable, but a possible, consequence of the First World War. Several different traditions and tendencies proved to be a heavy political burden; some contemporaries even used the term 'second Thirty Years War' to stress the internal coherence between the First World War, the inter-war period, and the Second World War. And yet, despite all continuities, the end of the First World War was not simply the beginning of the antecedents of the Second. The year 1933, when Adolf Hitler was appointed Reich Chancellor, marked the turning point of a history shaped by multiple continuities with the past, but it was not the predetermined consequence of the years before. Hitler aimed at something completely new: he wanted to replace politics by war and to instigate a revolution against the political and moral values of the modern age based on the vision of global racial domination and the end of history. The structural problems of the European post-war order were a crucial precondition to achieve these goals – and this was the reason for the continuities from the First World War to the Second.

The Paris Treaties of 1919/1920 did not simply divide Europe into victorious and revisionist states, the former pressing for maintaining the status quo, the latter desirous of winning back their lost territories. Instead several divergent interests existed that resulted in conflicts that seemed to be inevitable. The victorious power Italy, for instance, was not satisfied with the status quo and strove for territorial gains. Under the slogan of the 'mutilated victory', a political movement gained popularity that promoted the imperialist vision of establishing an *Imperium Romanum* around the Mediterranean. Still in 1918, a military conflict escalated in

---

* Translated by Christine Brocks.

A Companion to Nazi Germany, First Edition. Edited by Shelley Baranowski,
Armin Nolzen, and Claus-Christian W. Szejnmann.
© 2018 John Wiley & Sons Ltd. Published 2018 by John Wiley & Sons Ltd.

Eastern Europe that led to the Polish–Soviet War (1918/19–1921): the newly founded Polish state wanted to re-establish the borders of 'Great Poland' from 1772. Soviet Russia, where the civil war between Bolsheviks and White Guards ended only in November 1920, considered Eastern Central Europe its sphere of influence. The conflict ended with a peace treaty that allowed the Polish republic considerable territorial gains – and became its eastern neighbour's main target of revision.

The post-war order created in Paris aggravated border and nationalities problems. Czechoslovakia, for instance, which had emerged from the multi-ethnic state Austria-Hungary, was not a national but a 'nationalities' state. A relative majority of 43% Czechs faced a non-Czech majority consisting of five larger ethnicities, of which the Sudeten Germans located in the Bohemian–Moravian–Silesian border region were the biggest.

Divergent peace concepts added to the problems. While it was France's objective to considerably weaken Germany, the United States and the United Kingdom sought to maintain a balance of power on the European continent and prevent French hegemony. France's ideas of peace in Europe therefore manifested in demands of significant territorial cessions from Germany, drastic limitation of arms and armaments, and immense reparation payments. In addition, Paris strove for strengthening France's security by entering into cooperation with Eastern and Southeastern European states. The 'cordon sanitaire', a protective buffer consisting of newly founded sovereign Central Eastern states, ran from the Baltic to the Adriatic and the Black Sea. It was supposed to serve as a bulwark against Soviet Russia and as a threat of a two-front war against Germany. Whereas France insisted mainly on a security doctrine based on military, economic, and geostrategic superiority, Great Britain followed the concept of integration aiming at Germany's incorporation into the newly established organizations of collective security. US president Woodrow Wilson in particular hoped for a continuous peace by creating the League of Nations as the main and future-oriented idea of the peace conference.

With the signing of the Peace Treaty of Versailles on 28 June 1919, Germany lost one tenth of its population and one seventh of its territory (mainly to Poland), in addition to all of its colonies. As well as these territorial cessions, which also meant the loss of one third of its coal and three quarters of its ore deposits, Germany was forced to agree to reparation payments, which were not yet quantified in total. In the meantime, a considerable amount of goods in kind was requested. The reparation demands were based on Article 231 that stated Germany's and its allies' sole war guilt. This reproach of an exclusive responsibility caused huge indignation in Germany as well as the (temporary) occupation of the Ruhr area by Allied troops, and the same was true of the drastic disarmament regulations. Conscription was proscribed, the army was to be limited to 100 000, the navy to 15 000 men. In addition, the air force, tanks, artillery, and submarines were banned. From the moment the treaty came into effect, a cross-party consensus existed in Germany that this 'disgraceful dictate' was to be revised. The only differences were on the question of how and with what end it had to be revised.

28.2 'Seizure of Power': Reactions

In the evening of 3 February 1933, Hitler developed the basic principles of his policy before Reich Foreign Minister Constantin Freiherr von Neurath and the chiefs of the army and navy. According to this speech, the 'sole aim of the general policy' was the 'regaining of political power', the 'extermination of Marxism root and branch', and the 'removal of the cancer of democracy' in favour of the 'tightest authoritarian state leadership', also 'strengthening of the will to fight with all means' and the spreading of the 'idea that only a struggle can save us'. 'Building up of the armed forces' was the 'most important prerequisite for achieving the goal of regaining political power', which was supposed to be used for 'the conquest of new living space in the East and its ruthless Germanization' (Vogelsang 1954, 434–435; my translation).

The foreign minister had always championed Great Power politics based on military strength. This was the reason why Reich President Paul von Hindenburg had appointed him head of the foreign ministry in mid-1932, where he remained under Hitler. As supporter of Imperial Germany and the monarchy, Neurath opposed the republican-democratic system of Weimar from its beginning. He offered his service to the foreign office in order to contribute to the re-establishment of the Reich as a military great and hegemonic power – in this sense, he wanted to instrumentalize National Socialism. Neurath's first civil servant, Undersecretary Bernhard Wilhelm von Bülow, represented a foreign policy that was supposed to make Germany the economic hegemonic power in Europe (orientated on the *Mitteleuropa* plan of the nineteenth century that aimed to achieve an economic and cultural hegemony over Central Europe by the Reich). Even though Bülow disapproved of National Socialism, he stayed in office as a dutiful Prussian and civil servant on the grounds that 'One does not desert one's country only because it has a bad government' (Hahn and Krüger 1972, 410). Only one senior diplomat, the German ambassador in Washington, Friedrich von Prittwitz und Gaffron, quit the service in the wake of the Nazi seizure of power on political grounds. All others shared the conviction, albeit in different versions, that even Hitler could not steer a course against the diplomats.

Foreign countries reacted with increasing anxiety to developments in the Reich, since Germany was potentially the strongest revisionist power on the continent. As early as the beginning of 1932, the German ambassador in Paris reported a 'war-in-sight-mood in France'[1] caused by the accelerated revisionist policy of the Weimar presidential cabinets. One year later, in March 1933, the ambassador cautioned against a French–Polish pre-emptive action against the Reich. The Polish marshal Józef Piłsudski did in fact order several military security and threatening measures – and confidentially explored France's willingness to conduct a police operation against Germany. Berlin assumed that the city of Gdansk – under Prussian rule until it became the partly sovereign, independent Free City of Gdansk under the auspices of the League of Nations in 1919 – would be the target of a Polish military intervention and the bargaining chip of territorial politics.

At the same time, relations with the Soviet Union deteriorated. Up to this point, Germany's anti-Polish eastern policy had nearly exclusively focused on the USSR.

Due to the German anti-Bolshevist propaganda in general and the violent attacks on German communists and Soviet institutions in particular, the Soviet dictator Josef Stalin increasingly changed his political course towards the West. As early as November 1932, and on grounds of the unpredictable foreign policy of the Weimar presidential cabinets, Moscow entered into a non-aggression pact with Paris. It was supposed to secure the Soviet Union towards the West. Since the Japanese attack on Manchuria in autumn 1931, the Soviet Union felt threatened from the East and wanted to secure itself against the West. With this pact, the German–Soviet cooperation as defined in the Treaty of Rapallo (1922) came to an end. The Third Reich was now dangerously isolated towards both the East and the West. And even in the north, towards Great Britain, it had 'lost ground during the last weeks',[2] as the German ambassador in London reported. Only Italy signalled approval, because Benito Mussolini hoped for closer cooperation and as a result a strengthening of his policy.

28.3   'Peace Politics' and Rearmament

In order to counteract the dangerous isolation, the German Foreign Office worked towards a strategy to avert the political pressure. One of its measures was the ratification of the protocol of prolongation of the Berlin Treaty (signed in April 1926) on 5 May 1933 that reaffirmed the Rapallo Pact (signed in April 1922). The signing of the protocol of prolongation was supposed to signify the continuation of the traditional German policy towards the East. After negotiations between Vice Chancellor von Papen and the Vatican's Secretary of State Cardinal Eugenio Pacelli in Rome, a concordat with the Vatican was signed on 20 July 1933. This contract enhanced Hitler's and the Third Reich's diplomatic prestige considerably. Also in July 1933, and initiated by Mussolini, Germany, Italy, France, and Britain concluded the Four Power Pact, a consultative and cooperation agreement without tangible meaning that, tellingly, never came into effect because only Britain and France ratified it. It was significant mainly due to the fact that it came into being at all: the Third Reich presented itself before the world as a power allegedly prepared to negotiate and – according to the pact – committed to cooperate with all powers and to maintain peace. All these treaties demonstrated the new regime's alleged readiness for peace. Hitler's 'peace speech' in the Reichstag on 17 May 1933, eagerly awaited at home and abroad, underlined this political course.

Hitler's Reichstag speech, which was initiated by Neurath, represented a tactical course correction. From 3 February 1933, the second meeting of the Geneva disarmament conference that had started a year before was held. The German delegation and Foreign Minister Neurath continued the policy they had pursued from summer 1932. The Treaty of Versailles stated that German disarmament would be the start of a general demilitarization process to maintain continuous peace. However, disarmament negotiations had repeatedly been postponed, mainly because France, which had been involved in wars against Germany in 1870 and 1914, was reluctant to agree to concessions on disarmament. During the negotiations from February 1933 onwards, the German delegation tried to 'force the French to admit that they are not willing to concede equality'. Should the conference 'break down as a result', the 'world would be' mainly 'on our side', so Neurath believed.[3]

Without involving the new chancellor, diplomats and military men tried to sabotage the conference with the objective to achieve agreement on Germany's armaments policy. Hitler, on the other hand, advocated flexibility and was in favour of concluding the treaty even though it did not meet all Germany's wishes since he feared France would start a pre-emptive war against Germany. The German foreign and defence ministers, however, were not willing to accept diplomatic compromises and concessions on disarmament. In March, a draft of the treaty was submitted providing for an arms freeze of the highly armed powers, a gradual reduction of troop levels to 200 000 men each, and the armament of the Reichswehr to these levels. However, the German delegation was dilatory to such an extent that they ended up in complete self-isolation. In order to ease the stalemate, Hitler had to play his part with the 'peace speech' – resulting in his foreign policy breakthrough. From this time on, the Reich's policy was increasingly shaped by Hitler.

This is true, for instance, of Germany's exit from the League of Nations and withdrawal from the disarmament conference on 14 October 1933. By spring 1932, the Reichswehr had already drawn up plans for an armaments programme providing for the establishment of an army of 21 divisions by spring 1938. This programme was adopted in December 1933 in a modified version stating an army of 300 000 men. When the German delegation in Geneva still entered into negotiations on arms limitation and control, they only followed the agenda in order to protract the negotiations and to drive their own armaments plans forwards. Unexpectedly, these plans were foiled by a British initiative, because the control system that had been suggested in early October threatened to reveal the extent of German armaments. Frantically, Berlin decided on withdrawal. Hitler justified Germany's exit from international institutions of collective security as being a response to the continuous humiliation of and discrimination against the Reich, combined with the declamatory confession of his alleged desire for peace. England and France, the major European powers to guarantee the status quo, reacted in accordance with their traditional political course: London strove to continue its policy of appeasement, whereas Paris insisted more than ever on maintaining the status quo.

For that purpose, Paris pursued an offensive policy of containment in the form of a system of interdependent treaties, which was supposed to complement France's superiority in armaments (for instance, the French–Soviet Treaty of Mutual Assistance in 1934). It was only under Foreign Minister Pierre Laval, successor of Louis Barthou who had been assassinated on 9 October 1934, that French foreign policy joined the British course of appeasement, which prevailed until 1938/1939. From November 1934 onwards British and Germans were negotiating a bilateral naval treaty along these lines – which also concealed Hitler's next coup. On 9 March 1935, the German government confirmed the existence of a German air force, which could have been kept a secret no longer in any case. The official exposure of the Luftwaffe served as a litmus test for the next step: a week later, the German government announced the reintroduction of conscription, as a response to France's extension of military service which was adopted by the French government on 12 March 1935.

28.4   Strategies and Treaties

On 26 January 1934, Poland and the German Reich signed a non-aggression pact initiated by Hitler that was scheduled to last 10 years. This treaty seemed to defuse a key European crisis and the international community considered it a significant contribution to peacekeeping. In particular, Great Britain regarded the Polish–German agreement as the first statesmanlike act by the chancellor who had come into office only one year earlier. Hitler was in fact the driving force behind the negotiations that were supported by the traditionally anti-Polish Foreign Office for a number of reasons. First, the new pro-Polish and anti-Soviet foreign policy that replaced the former anti-Polish and pro-Soviet *Ostpolitik* averted the danger of a pre-emptive attack and put an end to the French–Polish threat of a war on two fronts. Second, this policy towards the East thwarted Germany's isolation, since the pact marked the beginning of a closer cooperation. Third, Hitler's step towards an agreement with Poland appeared to prove his alleged statesmanlike reason and was seemingly evidence of his wish for rapprochement, because it put an end to the enmity between Poland and Germany and to a European hotspot: the issue of the Polish 'corridor' that divided the German core country from East Prussia. Poland, too, seemed to benefit from the treaty, because the French–Soviet rapprochement had fuelled scepticism at the Vistula. Also, Mussolini's Four Power Pact seemingly involved the danger of institutionalizing a revisionist policy coordinated between Germany, Italy, France, and Britain.

However, in the autumn of 1938, this partnership based on reasons of tactical expedience came to a close in the course of the German expansion policy. The German government had tried to marginalize its Polish neighbour – provided they had been serious about their attempted rapprochement in the first place – which in the end (that is, after almost a year and for a number of different reasons) had the opposite effect. Thus Hitler could expect neither a backup in case of a German attack on France nor a deployment area for the war against the Soviet Union.

Against this backdrop, the German–Soviet Nonaggression Pact (signed on 23 August 1939) came into being according to which both partners, for the duration of 10 years, were obliged to avoid all aggression against one another, or to support a third power or a group of allied powers ranged against the partner of the treaty. A secret additional protocol determined a line along the rivers Pissa, Narew, Vistula, and San, separating a German sphere of influence in the West from a Soviet counterpart in the East. This turned the German–Soviet Nonaggression Pact de facto into a coordinated aggression agreement against Poland.

For the Soviet dictator Josef Stalin, the advantages of a pact with Hitler outweighed the alternative – an anti-German alliance with the Western powers and Poland – by far. It offered the chance of keeping war away from Soviet territory, shifting the defence line to the West, and responding to the Japanese threat in the East. It also opened up an opportunity to expand Soviet influence in Eastern and Southeastern Europe. At the same time, it bought time to drive forward the armament of the Red Army. Finally, Stalin assumed that, in so doing, he would instigate a war among the capitalist powers against each other and prevent a joint anti-Soviet front – a threat that in reality was less dangerous than Stalin believed. Hitler's motivation was based on his ideology, even though he seemingly abandoned his long-term objective of a racial war on *Lebensraum* ('living space') against the Soviet Union with the non-aggression pact between the two dictatorships. Yet under the circumstances of the year 1939, only this agreement offered him the chance to unleash a war according to his 'mission' (Soviet Union) by realizing his long-term plans (against France) and adapting to the new situation (with Poland). Hitler's decision in favour of the pact with the Soviet Union thus was in line with his ideological core view. As he described it himself: he agreed on a 'pact with Satan' to drive out 'the devil' (Jacobsen 1962–1964, vol. 1, 38).

In June 1934, Hitler and Mussolini met in Venice for the first time. In contrast to the widespread opinion, this journey was by no means a 'failure' but a success as planned and prepared for by German diplomats. Hitler stuck to the line of argumentation that was agreed on and insisted that the annexation of Austria, which Mussolini wanted to prevent at all costs, was neither a pressing matter nor feasible in the foreseeable future. Even though Hitler's demeanour appeared to be inexperienced and tense compared to Mussolini's condescending behaviour, the visit in Italy left an 'unconditionally favourable' impression and could have been the beginning of a 'bond of trust'.[4] And yet, only one month later, all cautious attempts at rapprochement were undone when the Austrian National Socialists staged a coup and killed Federal Chancellor Engelbert Dollfuß, who had tried to secure Austria's independence with Italy's support. Mussolini considered the existence of a buffer state between Italy and Germany to be indispensable to guarantee the new post-war boundary after the annexation of South Tyrol in the wake of the First World War. Immediately after the coup he deployed five divisions ready to intervene at the Brenner Pass, to emphasize his role as Austria's protector.

It was only in the course of his war against the East African empire of Abyssinia (1935/1936) that Mussolini sided with Hitler who had offered to support Italy. Double-crossing the war parties by delivering German weapons to both countries was part of Hitler's agenda that paid off in the end: he wanted to prolong the war that strengthened Germany since it weakened Italy, because the economically weak Apennine peninsula became increasingly dependent on German imports of weapons and other products due to sanctions imposed by the League of Nations. The Spanish Civil War (1936–1939) provided an additional boost to German–Italian cooperation, because Mussolini, seeking to expand the Italian sphere of influence in the western Mediterranean, agreed to a military involvement (at Hitler's side). Italy, already destabilized by the war against Abyssinia, was soon overstretched. In this situation, Mussolini arrived in Germany in the autumn of 1937 for a state visit, and declared that for him, the 'axis Rome–Berlin is not just a phrase but a firm resolution according to his conviction. No future event would change his mind to cooperate with Germany ... All attempts to separate Italy from Germany would fail.'[5]

However, the 'axis' did not connect two equal partners since Germany – all the more so after the successes of its foreign and revision policies (armament, occupation of the Rhine area, etc.) – had risen to become a continental European hegemonic power. Il Duce's profession of faith indicates the predicament in which Italy had found itself due to its imperial policy of war: economically weak and politically isolated, Mussolini sought to compensate for Italy's unfavourable situation by cooperating with Germany. Unavoidably, he had to abandon his role as protector of Austria and agreed on a formally independent Austrian state that in fact was nothing more than a satellite state of Germany.

Since Mussolini could not maintain Austria's independence against Hitler after 1936/1937, he tried to secure the existence of this buffer state in league with Germany. Yet as early as March 1938 this approach proved to be a failure that indicated the asymmetrical balance of power between Italy and Germany, since Austria was annexed without consideration for the Mediterranean partner state. In late May 1939, Italy and Germany signed an official treaty, the so-called Pact of Steel, committing both countries to mutual military assistance in case of war, regardless whether the ally was attacked or was the attacker. Mussolini had a double agenda when he agreed to the military alliance which he had long balked at signing: on the one hand, he expected the Western powers to be intimidated by the Pact of Steel and thus to be more willing to compromise and seek rapprochement; on the other, he wanted German politics, in which he expected to gain influence, to commit to a long period of peace. And yet the assumption that Hitler – who during the Steel Pact negotiations kept stressing Germany would not be ready for war before 1942 – would not start a war without his ally proved to be wrong. Hitler sought the war – even against Britain; that had been at the core of his plans for alliances.

In June 1935, a German delegation signed the Anglo-German Naval Agreement in London that Hitler had discussed at a meeting in Berlin with the British foreign secretary (Henke 1973). The subject matter of the agreement was the limitation of naval arms: Germany committed itself to not exceeding the 35:100 tonnage ratio. It also agreed to consider a submarine tonnage of 45% even though parity had been agreed on. The Naval Agreement resulted from complex interest-driven politics: as a consequence of its domestic and foreign politics (withdrawal from the League of Nations, armament, persecution of the Jews) the Third Reich was almost completely isolated. When Berlin admitted the existence of a German air force (March 1935) and shortly afterwards declared the re-establishment of conscription (both prohibited by the Treaty of Versailles), Britain, France, and Italy formed the 'Stresa Front', accompanied by the five-year Franco-Soviet Treaty of Mutual Assistance from May 1935 and the Czechoslovak-Soviet Treaty of Alliance. However, this isolation was still far away from being a complete encirclement – and the Stresa Front should not be misunderstood as a war alliance since the interests and approaches of the signatories differed too much.

Incited by Hitler's 'successes', Mussolini sought Italy's salvation in imperial expansion – which implied a violation of international law and war. Thus, in Stresa he advocated for a mild punishment to be accorded to the breach of treaty on the part of Germany, precisely because Italy had already planned its own breach. France's position differed fundamentally from Italy's stance. Paris had made a U-turn and abandoned its previous offensive policy of containment and the threat of military invention, not least due to domestic turbulence, such as mass strikes, frequent changes of government, and formation of a 'people's front' (*Volksfront*) by socialists and radicals. It became more and more evident that France was following Britain, which maintained its traditional appeasement policy until 1938/1939.

The British were willing to accept peaceful change within the context of contractual agreements in order to maintain peace and the status quo of the post-war order in Europe – and to focus on the periphery of the British Empire. Stretched by the challenges of the Empire that were beyond its economic and military potential, London had agreed to sign the Anglo-German Naval Agreement. Although this treaty sanctioned Germany's repeated violations of several treaties, it addressed, at the same time, British security needs: first, the British government believed that the agreement would prevent a naval arms race, which had shaped the Tirpitz era before 1914 and increased the risk of a great war; second, it secured the supremacy of the Royal Navy in the North Sea; and third, the bilateral agreement provided an opportunity to limit and control German armaments, maybe even a way back to the system of collective security.

Hitler, on the other hand, who called the day of the signing of the treaty 'the happiest day of his life' (Ribbentrop 1953, 64), evaluated the Anglo-German Naval Agreement along the lines of his ideological and political premises. It put an end to Germany's isolation and, at the same time, sanctioned German armament as well as Hitler's policy of violating treaty agreements. But, first and foremost, Hitler sought the chance to form an alliance with Britain as already outlined in *Mein Kampf* (Lüdicke 2016). However, Hitler's 'programme' fundamentally differed from the British appeasement policy: whilst he strove for a war alliance, Britain wanted to maintain peace. Thus, there was simply no chance at all of achieving a political alliance with Britain based on shared ideological beliefs. Gradually Hitler realized this and corrected his political course. From now on, closer ties to Japan were supposed to serve as an addition to the agreement with Britain *and* as leverage to demand compliance.

In 1931, Japan conquered Manchuria, and in February 1932 the Japanese puppet state 'Empire of Manchukuo' was established. In 1937, China was invaded, resulting in the Japanese–Chinese War (1937–1945). Japan's expansion, aiming for a new power balance in Asia, was aided by seeking a supporting counterbalance. That is why a rapprochement between Japan and Germany became possible that put the Soviet Union under pressure on two fronts. At Japan's instigation, Tokyo and Berlin concluded the so-called Anti-Comintern Pact directed against the Communist International in late November 1936. It contained a secret additional agreement that committed both powers to not conclude any contracts with the Soviet Union, which would be contrary to the Anti-Comintern Pact, and to maintain mutual benevolent neutrality in case of a Soviet attack.

However, the anti-communist cooperation between Germany and Japan, later joined by Italy (November 1937) and other states, was of little factual importance – but it had great ideological impact. According to Hitler's world-view, which directed all his strategic considerations, the agreement with Japan was supposed to be an addition to the division of spheres of influence that Germany had tried to negotiate with Britain and Italy – and to make the war against the Soviet Union possible. In so doing – and without completely excluding the 'desired alliance' with London as already described in his 'second book' (*Zweites Buch*) from 1928 – Hitler developed a 'plan B' to realize his 'mission': no longer *with* Britain, but if possible not *against* it.

28.5   The Personnel of Foreign Policy: Structure and Development

Hitler left no doubt that he considered a war of conquest and extermination as the core of his historical mission as outlined in his early speeches and writings. He never lost sight of this objective, even though he sometimes detoured when it was tactically or situationally advisable in order not to jeopardize the final outcome. Therefore, it would be a mistake to differentiate two phases of Nazi foreign politics: a rather peaceful, traditional revisionist period until 1937 and a phase of expansion and preparation for war from 1938 to 1939. Yet it is true that there was a 'partial identity of goals' (Messerschmidt 1969, 1) that explains the support of the 'old diplomatic elites'. It was precisely because of this partial congruency that Nazi racial policy only gradually overlapped with average nationalist desires for revision and Great Powers policy. That is why the transition from Weimar to Nazi Germany was marked by a high level of continuity in terms of both personnel and politics. Authorized by Hindenburg, Foreign Minister Neurath started restructuring personnel as early as summer 1932, which mainly favoured representatives of a national Great Power policy. This personnel policy was continued beyond 30 January 1933, since German foreign politics relied on the experienced, polyglot, and professional German diplomats in the Berlin Central of the Foreign Ministry as well as in the German representations in London, Paris, Moscow, and so on. The reasons for keeping the foreign office personnel were as various as the different types of diplomats: some of them were proud elitists with an attitude of calculated optimism, some were submissive civil servants, others career-driven opportunists. A number of them were National Socialists or sympathizers. Apart from individual motives, inflated political expectations also played a role, such as the hope on a forced revisions policy and on the rise of Germany to a great and hegemonic power. Vice versa, the wish to protect the fatherland from a hazardous foreign policy was also a vital motive.

Given this backdrop, continuities prevailed during a time of continuous change. Also, civil service regulations were as effective as the personnel planning of the Reich government budget. Thus, 1933 saw only one change in personnel within the group of 17 senior diplomats (including minister, ambassadors, undersecretaries, and heads of ministry departments). Neither was the higher grade of civil service marked by radical personnel change: there were only 28 incoming and 53 outgoing employees (including regular retirements and recruitments of young people) out of the 558 members of the higher grade civil servants of the diplomatic service. Until 1939, the number of incoming personnel increased to 566 (324 civil servants and 242 employees), whereas 254 people left (192 civil servants and 62 employees) – out of a total of 702 members of the diplomatic service in 1939 (606 civil servants and 96 employees). Thus, until 1939 inclusive, more higher grade civil servants were newly employed than had been working in the higher foreign service in 1933 altogether, and almost half of the personnel in 1933 were no longer working for the foreign service six years later. In short, with every year and in the wake of the flow of incomings and outgoings of personnel in total with tendency to rise, the ratio shifted in favour of higher grade civil servants employed after 1933 (Kröger 2014, 6–9).

This merely quantitative description already indicates a Nazification of the diplomatic service as a consequence of the fluctuation of personnel. This becomes even more evident from a qualitative perspective. As early as 1933, 10 members of the higher grade foreign service were dismissed on 'racial' grounds and eight for political reasons; one person had to quit because of their sexual orientation. The legal basis for the dismissals was primarily the 'Law for the Restoration of the Professional Civil Service' (*Gesetz zur Wiederherstellung des Berufsbeamtentums*) that came into force on 7 April 1933. It affected three groups of people: (i) the 'membership book officials', that is, those who entered the civil service after 1918 without possessing the required training or qualifications; (ii) those of 'non-Aryan descent', as long as they had not already been employed before August 1914 or had fought or had fathers or sons who were killed during the First World War – an exemption clause initiated by Hindenburg; and (iii) those civil servants whose 'former political activity affords no guarantee that they will act in the interest of the national state at all times and without reservation'. The heads of the Foreign Office accepted the law because it offered the opportunity to dismiss unpopular civil servants. The Nazi alignment (*Gleichschaltung*) of the civil service and the disenfranchisement of Jewish citizens did not meet opposition, particularly because only very few Jews worked as civil servants in the diplomatic service and those considered patriotic were protected by the 'frontline fighters' privilege' (*Frontkämpferprivileg*).

At the same time, the political development had an increasing impact on recruitment and promotion decisions. It was in this context that the lateral entrant Vicco von Bülow-Schwante was appointed. Both the Foreign Office and the Nazi Party considered him a trustworthy man. He took charge of the newly established or re-established department 'Germany', which coordinated cooperation with the security authorities, and was therefore responsible for surveilling German emigrants, the expatriation of German citizens, and the 'Jewish question'. Bülow-Schwante, who headed the department until 1938, was an exception in so far as his deputies were not lateral entrants. Also, the three senior civil servants of the Foreign Office responsible for the 'Jewish question', Emil Schumburg (1933–1940), Franz Rademacher (1940–1943), and Eberhard von Thadden (1943–1945), had been members of the Foreign Office under Minister Neurath, when they were appointed as attachés or moved to the foreign service from an administration position.

Until the death of Secretary Bülow in 1936 it was mostly civil servants (from the senior civil servant to the head of division to the state secretary and the minister) who dealt with the 'Jewish question' – and these men were not members of the Nazi Party (*Nationalsozialistische Deutsche Arbeiterpartei*, NSDAP) or another Nazi organization. Bülow-Schwante joined the NSDAP only in mid-1936; Schumburg, who joined the SS in October 1936, was without party affiliation until mid-1938. This example leads one to the conclusion that guilt and responsibility cannot be measured by membership in a Nazi organization. Indeed, only a case-by-case review can cope with the complexity of the history – as, for example, the case of Georg Ferdinand Duckwitz shows. Duckwitz joined the NSDAP as early as November 1932. On the one hand, therefore, he represents an 'old fighter', because he already belonged to the Nazi Party before Hitler came into power. On the other hand, he broke with the regime, in mid-1934 at the latest. The fact that he made a contribution to save the Jews of Denmark in 1943, when he worked for the German embassy in Copenhagen, was honoured by the Holocaust memorial Yad Vashem in 1971, which awarded him the title 'Righteous among the Nations'.

In other words, the quickly increasing number of party members among civil servants and employees of the higher grade foreign service – namely from 1% (1933) to 12% (1934) to 22% (1935) to 32% (1936) to 41% (1937) to 55% (1938) to 62% per cent (1939) – illustrates most of all how quickly and forcefully the dictatorship was established, because professional careers increasingly depended on loyalty towards the regime being proved by party membership. In fact, due to a Hitler decree from September 1935, Rudolf Hess, the Deputy Führer (*Stellvertreter des Führers*), had to approve all promotions of diplomats – and from early 1939 he did so only when the applicant to a higher grade position within the diplomatic service was a member of the Nazi Party. Even for the recruitment of young employees and civil servants party membership was of growing importance: for example, out of all newly appointed attachés of 1937 there was only one man who was not a member of the NSDAP nor the SA nor the SS. However, in this climate of peer pressure and a mentality focused on career opportunities, the driving force behind the decision to join the party varied from person to person, and in whether it was opportunism or true political belief.

Neurath did not take issue with this 'formal' Nazification of the Foreign Office. His diplomats were explicitly free to decide for themselves; indeed, joining the NSDAP was recommended only indirectly. Nor did he oppose taking into account party political aspects when recruiting young personnel, even though the high number of attachés trained by the Nazi state drove forward the 'forcible coordination' from below, which also served as a control mechanism towards the top. The guiding principle of Neurath's actions remained the same: he wanted to prevent politically motivated lateral entries and, in so doing, the de-professionalization of the diplomatic service by exhibiting a policy of self-alignment (*Selbstgleichschaltung*). He expected that professionalism would have a depoliticizing impact. It was only under Neurath's successor Joachim von Ribbentrop, who took over the Foreign Office in February 1938, that political and ideological loyalty became more important than professional qualifications and expertise.

Ribbentrop joined the NSDAP only in May 1932, but he was able to quickly establish himself within Hitler's entourage. As his foreign political adviser and special commissioner, he set up his own department similar to the NSDAP Office of Foreign Affairs under Alfred Rosenberg and the NSDAP Foreign Organization (*Auslandsorganisation*, AO) under Ernst Wilhelm Bohle and developed his own foreign policy strategies and approaches. Other members of the cabinet, such as Hjalmar Schacht and Hermann Göring, also tried to influence foreign policy, but all these politicians and institutions and their divergent concepts were rather marginal compared to Hitler's ideology. Scholarly discussions on the much-debated question of the polycracy of the Third Reich and the pluralism of foreign political concepts have primarily favoured the by now widely accepted view that these competing institutions did not have substantial influence on foreign policy matters, which were increasingly and decisively determined by Hitler himself.

Thus, Ribbentrop's objective was not to replace but to take over the Foreign Office followed by the faithful and devoted staff of his department. Neurath tried to prevent this development by pursuing the 'pre-emptive coordination' of the Foreign Office and by involving his rival. In mid-1934, Ribbentrop was appointed Special Commissioner for Disarmament and in this function was assigned to Neurath; in mid-1935 he became Reich Ambassador Plenipotentiary at Large; in mid-1936 he was appointed ambassador in London, where Neurath expected him to fail. But due to his close ties to the centre of power, Ribbentrop was able to reinterpret his highhandedness and failures in his favour. Neurath responded by implementing another step of 'forcible coordination' and drove forward the cooperation with the protagonists of the Nazi regime. Appointing Bohle as state secretary was the first step in expanding his position of power. As the former leader of the NSDAP/AO, Bohle was the head of all 'party comrades' living abroad. After being appointed at the Foreign Office he could expand his sphere of influence, since all party members of the Foreign Office both within and outside Germany were subsumed in the Local Group Foreign Office of the AO. Also, Bohle's influence on human resources policy became more and more apparent: at his instigation a number of diplomats were discharged or relocated; several staff members of his Foreign Organization were able to enter the foreign service due to his patronage, and, finally, Munich party headquarters approved of promoting only those diplomats who had been recommended by Bohle.

At the same time, Bohle is a good example of the entangled loyalties that marked the Nazi state. As state secretary of the Foreign Office he was directly and personally assigned to Neurath, as director of the AO he still reported to the highest party office, the *Stellvertreter des Führers*. As a member of the SS, Bohle was also part of the Personal Staff *Reichsführer SS* and directly subordinate to Himmler, who purposely enforced the entanglement of SS and diplomatic corps. In September 1937, for example, Neurath was admitted to the SS in the rank of a *Gruppenführer* (a rank equivalent to lieutenant general); one and a half months later the state secretary became *Oberführer* (a rank between colonel and brigadier general). Ribbentrop had joined the SS already, in May 1933, in the rank of a *Standartenführer* (colonel). In 1935 he was promoted twice, and in 1936 he became finally *Gruppenführer*. These promotions quickly following one another were clearly coinciding with Ribbentrop's swift rise in the Foreign Office, although he was not promoted when he became minister. Obviously, a further promotion was not necessary in order to commit Ribbentrop to Himmler or to protect him in the Foreign Office.

Even after Ribbentrop's entry into office, several long-serving careerist diplomats still held the majority of senior posts abroad. Unless their political loyalty was doubtful, they could still have stellar careers during Ribbentrop's term in office, because without their contribution the technocratic efficiency of the apparatus could not have been guaranteed. At the same time, the Foreign Office was increasingly permeated by careerists leaning towards the ideal of a *Führerstaat*, some of them coming from the *Dienststelle Ribbentrop* (Ribbentrop's office in the NSDAP) to the Foreign Office. Gradually they were promoted or appointed to senior positions. However, since the Foreign Office was neither inundated with (Nazi) outsiders and nor were its key positions infiltrated by them, the intersection of traditional revision and Great Power policy, on the one hand, and Nazi ideology, on the other, played a pivotal role.

28.6 Expansion and War Preparations

Against this backdrop, some decisive events took place. On 13 January 1935 the population of the Territory of the Saar Basin was called to the polls, since the 15-year period of being a mandate territory of the League of Nations stipulated by the Treaty of Versailles ended. Ninety per cent of the electorate voted for reunification with Germany. A success similarly prestigious for the Nazi regime was the reoccupation of the demilitarized Rhineland – a violation of both the Treaty of Versailles and the Locarno Pacts from 1925. Even more important was probably its strategic significance in the context of the *Westwall*, a fortification line 600 kilometres long to secure Germany's western border, which was planned from 1936 and started to be built in 1938.

Without British support, France – paralysed by permanent government crises and internal tensions – was reluctant to take the risk of a military operation. Britain considered Hitler's recent breach of contract primarily as the militarization of German territory – thus a defensive action – and strove to avoid military conflict. However, as a result of this political line the danger of a 'Great' war increased. The Rhineland no longer served as a security and deployment zone for France; moreover, the economically important Ruhr area was out of reach; and it had become completely impossible to use the Rhineland as a political pledge similar to the occupation of the Ruhr in 1923. A military intervention against further German violations of international treaties would have to face heavy losses given the increasingly strengthening German Wehrmacht and the fortified borders. For Hitler, this defensive advantage also had an offensive benefit. The chance to protect the western border by deploying only marginal military forces was the prerequisite of an attack in the East. At the same time, a new military possibility opened up in the West: by occupying the formerly demilitarized security zone of the Rhineland, Hitler was able to circumvent the most strongly fortified part of the Maginot line in the north.

Under these circumstances the balance of power shifted significantly. Because the Central, Eastern, and Southeastern European states could no longer count on the support of the Western powers, Poland, Austria, Romania, Yugoslavia, Hungary, and Bulgaria sought the backing of Germany, which turned into some kind of gravitational centre. As early as 11 July 1936, Austria signed an Austro-German agreement of friendship and alliance that recognized the sovereignty of the Alpine republic. The unofficial part of this 'gentleman's agreement', however, coordinated Austrian with German politics and in a way pre-empted the *Anschluss*. One and a half years later, Austrian Chancellor Kurt Schuschnigg was pressured into giving up Austria's independence by being threatened with a military invasion. On 13 March 1938, it followed Austria's *Anschluss* to the Reich by a law giving Germany the possibility to tap into Austrian raw material and armaments resources as well as its foreign currencies and human capital for the Reich's war preparations. Accordingly, it was no coincidence that Göring – who from May 1935 was in command of the Luftwaffe – played a decisive role in the preparations for the *Anschluss*. In April 1936, Hitler had appointed him commissioner for raw materials and foreign currencies, and, half a year later, in October 1936, plenipotentiary of the Four Year Plan. As the core sentences of a Hitler decree show, the Four Year Plan had two main objectives: 'I. The German army has to be fully operational within four years. II. The German economy has to be ready for war within four years' (Treue 1955, 210). The target of Göring's task was clear: by systematically controlling the economic resources and production to be mobilized for armament, the German economy could be converted to a war economy and the Reich would be on a war footing. This rapid development from 1936 onwards brought the German economy to its limits (shortage of raw materials and workforce, enormous national debt, and an overheating of the economy). The only way out of this self-made dead end was expansion by war and the plundering of the conquered territories – or economic implosion. Against this backdrop Hitler announced, at a meeting on 5 November 1937, that he wanted to solve 'the German question of living space in 1943/45 at the latest'.[6] Werner von Blomberg, the Reich War Minister, and Werner von Fritsch, commander in chief of the German army, protested; even Foreign Minister Neurath remained doubtful. In early 1938 Hitler got rid of these critics, who had been loyal to the regime so far, when he reshuffled his cabinet and army command. To camouflage this personnel change, several posts of the Foreign Office and the Wehrmacht were shuffled and the army restructured: Hitler now took over as Supreme Commander of the Wehrmacht with a High Command of the Armed Forces, formed from the Reich War Ministry and directly subordinate to him.

Shortly afterwards, in late March 1938, he initiated a foreign crisis that was supposed to cover the domestic crisis. At the end of the Sudeten crisis, France, Great Britain, and Italy signed the 'Munich Agreement', on the night of 29–30 September, allowing the annexation of the territory that was mostly inhabited by Germans. The Munich Agreement had prevented a war – yet at a cost. Hitler had achieved substantial changes in his favour. The Wehrmacht marched into the Sudetenland and occupied parts of the 'Czechoslovak Wall', disabling the fortification system along the border between Germany and Czechoslovakia. France lost its two-front alliance against Germany (*Zangenbündnis*), which had been a main pillar of its security policy.

Neville Chamberlain's optimistic prognosis of 'peace in our time', as he pronounced on his return to London, soon proved to be an unrealistic misjudgement. In fact, shortly afterwards Hitler seemed to be annoyed that he had lost this opportunity to unleash war. Only three weeks after signing the Munich Agreement, he gave the order to 'terminate the rump of Czechoslovakia' by military means. When German troops occupied Czechoslovak territory on 15/16 March 1939 – after Hitler had forced the separation from Slovakia and threatened to bombard Prague – the rump of Czechoslovakia was effectively annexed. The Reich was no longer a nation-state, which shows that Hitler's objectives were not confined to a merely revisionist policy.

In strategic and war economic terms, the Third Reich benefited profoundly from the annexation of the Czech territories, which became the Reich protectorate of Bohemia and Moravia. Czech military equipment as well as the entire engineering and armaments industry came under German control, and the same was true for new deposits of mineral resources and raw materials. The countries along the Danube and the Balkans – Hungary and Romania had concluded bilateral economic agreements with Germany only in March – increasingly came under German influence and could be made accessible economically. Also, the German military border was significantly shorter and Poland's southern flank threatened, because Germany forced Slovakia to provide military bases and airports.

Only after Hitler had breached the agreement he had signed himself, and clearly contravened the right of self-determination of the peoples that he had repeatedly claimed for himself, did the Western powers change their course of action. By guaranteeing the independence of Poland (31 March/6 April 1939), Greece and Romania (13 April 1939), and coordinating preparations for war, they signified that they would no longer tolerate any more one-sided border changes without a fight. In a small-group meeting, Hitler indicated that for him it was not about border changes. He stated that 'never ever again' would there be 'a German who enjoyed the confidence of his people to such an extent; only he is capable of war'. For the sake of 'rule over Europe' and 'world dominance for centuries', he claimed, war soon would be inevitable 'because of the armament of the others' (Krausnick 1970, 167). The 'next fight' would be 'purely a war of *Weltanschauungen*, that is totally a people's war, a racial war' (Thies 1976, 115–116).

Europe was on a trajectory towards that war. Between October 1938 and March 1939, Poland received offers that in effect would have turned it into a German satellite state. Since Warsaw did not accept the German offers, Hitler ordered war preparations so that an attack would be possible at any time from 1 September 1939 onwards. In the early hours of 1 September 1939, the Wehrmacht attacked Poland and started a war, which turned into the most widespread military conflict in human history. More than 60 countries were directly or indirectly involved and more than 60 million people lost their lives. It is undisputable that Hitler was responsible for unleashing this war, even though the other powers facilitated this development in different ways and for different reasons. Thus, there was no war guilt question in 1945 as there had been after 1918.

Notes

1 Leopold von Hoesch to AA, 22 January 1932, Politisches Archiv des Auswärtigen Amtes (PA AA) Berlin, R 28252.
2 Hoesch to AA, 12 April 1933, PA AA, R 76982.
3 Neurath to Rudolf Nadolny, 15 February 1933, PA AA, R 29461.
4 Ulrich von Hassell to AA, 21 June 1934, PA AA, R 695a Pol 2a1.
5 Record of von Bülow-Schwante, 25 September 1937, on the conversation between Hitler and Mussolini, PA AA, BA 61140.

6 Record of Friedrich Hoßbach, 10 November 1937, in *Documents on German Foreign Policy 1918–1945, series D (1937–1945), vol. 1: From Neurath to Ribbentrop (September 1937–September 1938*, 29–39. London: Her Majesty's Stationery Office, 1949.

References

Hahn, Erich J.C. and Krüger, Peter. 1972. 'Der Loyalitätskonflikt des Staatssekretärs Bernhard Wilhelm von Bülow im Frühjahr 1933.' *Vierteljahrshefte für Zeitgeschichte* 20, 376–410.

Henke, Josef. 1973. *England in Hitlers politischem Kalkül 1935–1939*. Boppard am Rhein: Boldt.

Jacobsen, Hans Adolf, ed. 1962–1964. *Franz Halder. Kriegstagebuch. Tägliche Aufzeichnungen des Chefs des Generalstabs des Heeres 1939–1942*. 3 vols. Stuttgart: Kohlhammer.

Krausnick, Helmuth, ed. 1970. *Helmuth Groscurth: Tagebücher eines Abwehroffiziers 1938–1940*. Stuttgart: DVA.

Kröger, Martin. 2014. 'Aspekte der Personalentwicklung im Auswärtigen Amt – der höhere Dienst 1933–1945.' In *Das Auswärtige Amt in der NS-Diktatur*, edited by Johannes Hürter and Michael Mayer, 3–20. Berlin, Munich, and Boston: Oldenbourg.

Lüdicke, Lars. 2016. *Hitlers Weltanschauung: Von 'Mein Kampf' bis zum 'Nero-Befehl'*. Paderborn: Schöningh.

Messerschmidt, Manfred. 1969. *Die Wehrmacht im NS-Staat: Zeit der Indoktrination*. Hamburg: R. von Decker.

Ribbentrop, Joachim von. 1953. *Zwischen London und Moskau: Erinnerungen und letzte Aufzeichnungen*. Leoni: Druffel.

Thies, Jochen. 1976. *Architekt der Weltherrschaft. Die 'Endziele' Hitlers*. Düsseldorf: Droste.

Treue, Wilhelm. 1955. 'Hitlers Denkschrift zum Vierjahresplan.' *Vierteljahrshefte für Zeitgeschichte* 3, 184–210.

Vogelsang, Thilo. 1954. 'Neue Dokumente zur Geschichte der Reichswehr 1930–1933.' *Vierteljahrshefte für Zeitgeschichte* 2, 397–436.

Further Reading

Hildebrand, Klaus. 1999. *Das vergangene Reich: Deutsche Außenpolitik von Bismarck bis Hitler*. Berlin: Ullstein.
This book represents the first comprehensive analysis of the foreign policy of the Third Reich. Written by a recognized expert, this comprehensive standard work focuses on diplomacy history.

Hildebrand, Klaus. 2008. *Deutsche Außenpolitik 1871–1918*, 3rd edn. Munich: Oldenbourg.
This compendium provides a brief treatise of German foreign policy as well as an overview of the development of the research regarding this field.

Hillgruber, Andreas. 1984. *Die gescheiterte Großmacht: Eine Skizze des Deutschen Reiches 1871–1945*. Düsseldorf: Droste.
This highly concentrated outline, which was pioneering for the research, summarizes the central developments and strategies of the foreign policy of the Third Reich.

Lüdicke, Lars. 2009. *Griff nach der Weltherrschaft: Die Außenpolitik des Dritten Reiches 1933–1945*. Berlin: be.bra Verlag.
This brief analysis summarizes the entire foreign policy of the Third Reich by examining the different internal and external factors of peace and war.

Lüdicke, Lars. 2014. *Constantin Freiherr von Neurath: Eine politische Biographie.* Paderborn: Schöningh.
This dissertation about the last foreign minister of the Weimar Republic, who was also Hitler's first foreign minister, is an attempt to explain German foreign policy by analysing the different factors, processes, and decision making that had an impact. Concentrated on ideological, strategic, political, social, and diplomatic developments in Germany, it incorporates these results into a history of interactions between the powers.
Lüdicke, Lars. 2014. 'Die Personalpolitik der Minister Neurath und Ribbentrop.' In *Das Auswärtige Amt in der NS-Diktatur*, edited by Johannes Hürter and Michael Mayer, 37–57. Berlin, Munich, and Boston: Oldenbourg.
This article provides a brief history of the personnel of the Foreign Office.
Schmidt, Rainer F. 2002. *Die Außenpolitik des Dritten Reiches 1933–1939.* Stuttgart: Klett-Cotta.
This book is a description of the foreign policy and very suitable as an introduction to this theme.
Schöllgen, Gregor. 2013. *Deutsche Außenpolitik von 1815 bis 1945.* Munich: C.H. Beck.
This work, written by a highly respected expert, is a vivid overview of the history of German foreign policy from the Congress of Vienna to the present. Published in two volumes, these books nevertheless contain a highly concentrated overall history from Metternich to Merkel.

CHAPTER TWENTY-NINE

Social Militarization and Preparation for War, 1933–1939

Jörg Echternkamp

29.1   Introduction

Today, people are astonished by the good impression that Hitler's first foreign policy speech made on many of his contemporaries. When addressing the Reichstag in the Kroll Opera House on 17 May 1933, did not the new Reich Chancellor present himself much more moderately than expected – even as peace-loving – to the global public? 'By clinging to our own folklore in boundless love and loyalty,' announced Hitler, 'we respect the national rights also of other peoples … and wish from our innermost heart to live with them in peace and friendship.' And what is more, 'Germany stands ready to renounce offensive weapons if the rest of the world does the same. Germany is prepared to join any formal non-aggression pact, because Germany is not thinking of any acts of aggression but only of its security' (Domarus 1962/1963, 272, 277; my translation). Secretly, however, Hitler had already instructed the military to carry out rearmament. In contrast to the 1930s peace rhetoric intended to make an opposite impression on the public, the aggressive course of the National Socialist (NS) regime's domestic and foreign policies had been laid down from the outset. Hitler made no secret of the fact towards the Reichswehr leadership that he intended by all means to push ahead with making the Germans 'ready to defend themselves'. While blustering about peace, Hitler wanted to prepare the *Volksgemeinschaft* ('people's community') for the next war.

Such mental preparation for war is referred to in historical science as 'social militarization', a term that accentuates not only the social dimension but also the dynamics of a process aimed at imparting military values to civil society. It has less to do with foreign policy manoeuvring than with 'domestic preparation for war' in

A Companion to Nazi Germany, First Edition. Edited by Shelley Baranowski, Armin Nolzen, and Claus-Christian W. Szejnmann.
© 2018 John Wiley & Sons Ltd. Published 2018 by John Wiley & Sons Ltd.

the relationship between state and society. The expression also indicates a rejection of the older, essentialist acceptance that saw a characteristic trait of the Germans in Prusso-German militarism, presumed a continuity from Imperial Germany to at least 1945 in that respect, and alluded to a 'special direction' (*Sonderweg*) taken by the Germans. But the thesis of there being deeply rooted convictions held by large parts of the population fails to explain why the NS regime achieved such a high degree of mobilization within six years. More recent research sees radicalization as a reason: building upon the bellicism of the Weimar Republic, the widespread consensus about rearmament, the NS regime mobilized society in various social fields towards war. This chapter explores, first of all, the relationship between the military, state, and politics; then the role of the ruling party and its structures for military socialization; and, finally, the key concept of the 'people's community' being ready to defend itself. What attitude did the military have towards the NS regime? How did the NSDAP (*Nationalsozialistische Deutsche Arbeiterpartei*, Nazi Party) go forward with the militarization of the civilian population? How can the ideological essence of militarization be described?

29.2   The Military as the Driving Force for Militarization in the Nazi State

The affinity of the military leadership with National Socialism can hardly be underestimated where the militarization in the NS regime is concerned. What are the reasons for the Reichswehr leadership's readiness to accept the domestic and foreign policy ideas of the Hitler movement and so eventually place the largest instrument of power at the disposal of the Führer for a war of annihilation? Counterfactually speaking, the military machinery could also have taken a confrontational course from the outset and made renewed preparations for war. Because, like any armed force, the Reichswehr was a hierarchically structured fighting force based on the principle of command and obedience, the question of the relationship between National Socialism and the military concerns first and foremost the senior officer corps and how it had developed since the end of the First World War.

The historical lesson which the military leadership drew from the disaster was to avoid any repeat of the to slaughter under any circumstances. It was hoped, however, there would be a new war to take vengeance for the humiliation Germany had suffered and revise the status quo. This meant, specifically, making up for territorial losses, namely regaining Alsace and Lorraine, the colonies, and the Prussian eastern provinces. It was clear that military force would most probably have to be used against France, Great Britain, and newly created Poland to do so. The military was not alone in this way of thinking. The generals and officers could be sure of approval from the major part of the population, including most democrats and liberals. There was also general agreement on the question of under what conditions a future war could be won if acting alone. It was, firstly, necessary to rebuild, expand, and modernize the military machinery itself. Society would, secondly, have to be completely behind fighting a war and provide all available resources; it would be unacceptable for the German home front (*Heimatfront*) to collapse a second time.

The officer corps played an important role in these deliberations. Even though some 25% belonged to the nobility (in 1914 the share was 30%), it had a relatively modern elite of senior officers. These highly qualified majors, lieutenant colonels, and colonels were well versed in war-fighting techniques and had gained experience of their own during the First World War. The commander-in-chief of the army from 1920 to 1926, Hans von Seeckt, who preferred planning to fighting, attached great importance to this type of senior officer. These field-grade officers had a different image of themselves and of the army to the one cultivated under Prusso-German militarism in the last third of the nineteenth century. In their eyes, the military stood neither alongside nor above society, but was interconnected with the civilian population, on whose unconditional support it relied in the event of war. Hundreds of thousands of civilians had long been organized paramilitarily. After 1918, between 305 000 and 400 000 men had got together in a corps of volunteers (*Freikorps*), and up to one million had formed armed citizens' militias (*Einwohnerwehren*). In addition, there was the shadow army or Black Reichswehr (*Schwarze Reichswehr*), and mass organizations such as *Stahlhelm, Bund der Frontsoldaten*, a military association close to the German National People's Party (*Deutschnationale Volkspartei*, DNVP), and the Stormtroopers (*Sturmabteilung*, SA) which had been formed by the NSDAP in 1921 and had grown to four million members by 1934. While the republic had only a 100 000-strong army and 15 000-strong navy officially, there were de facto up to 10 times as many men under arms in Germany who literally were equipped for a future war.

In this mental and military climate, the concept of 'total war', propagated by no less than the former chief of the failed 3rd Supreme Army Command, Erich von Ludendorff, met with great approval. In a booklet dated 1935, he explained his ideas of a war in the future in which all means – not just military but also social, economic, and psychological – would be used. Only through such total mobilization – which had been neglected in 1914–1918 – could the next war be won. This objective was evidently not achievable under a parliamentary, democratic system of government.

Adolf Hitler, who shared the experiences of the world war as well as the lessons that the military drew from them, seemed – as the charismatic leader of a mass movement – to be the ideal person to translate these ideas and plans into deeds. He did not mince his words where the revision of the Treaty of Versailles, rearmament, and the mobilization of the whole of society, which he sought to unite as a 'people's community', were concerned – all demands to which most members of the Reichswehr would have subscribed immediately. It was particularly this impression – that a leading politician was keen to harness the whole of society for the war effort and give backing to the military – that won them over to Hitler. Besides these three areas where interests overlapped, there was a fourth: the programme of an authoritarian state system that left no room for left-wing elements and democrats. This political perception was completely consistent with the world-view of generals and officers who expected, and were used to having, a leading figure: first, the emperor, and then the 'substitute emperor' (*Ersatzkaiser*) Paul von Hindenburg. And, fifth, they also shared common enemies. Like the National Socialists, they, too, were firmly convinced that 'Jewish Bolshevism' (*jüdischer Bolschewismus*) represented the greatest danger. The traditional antisemitism of the officer corps and hatred of the Soviet Union went hand in hand. As early as December 1933, well before the anti-Jewish legislation of February 1934, the Reichswehr leadership had demanded, in a spirit of anticipatory obedience, that the Aryan paragraph (*Arierparagraph*) of 7 March 1933 be taken into consideration when appointing aspiring officers, and that Jews be dismissed. Nor did it come as any surprise that the 'hereditary enemy' (*Erbfeind*), France, and the new hate figure, Poland, were regarded on both sides as potential targets.

In any case, in 1934/1935 the Reichswehr leadership willingly became the second pillar of the Nazi state – alongside the Nazi Party and its armed organizations. Manfred Messerschmidt (2006, 67) saw in this altered political constellation from 1933 onward the cause of 'militarism being given its "new face"'. The destruction of pluralism, the adoption of ideological goals, and the acceptance of friend/foe thinking: these developments led to those dynamics and pooling of forces which resolved ideologically defined problems by military means – and to the perseverance mentality in the spring of 1945. Through the paramilitary forces and the military itself supporting the National Socialist Führer state (*Führerstaat*) as pillars and helping the nation to rearm mentally and materially, the separation of state and society, and of the military and civilian sphere on which the idea of militarism was conditional, was removed. Hitler made no secret of his political objectives towards the military functional elite. Hardly having taken up office, the new Reich Chancellor made it clear at a secret meeting with the commanders-in-chief of the Reichswehr (army) and Reichsmarine (navy) on 3 February 1933 that, where foreign policy was concerned, he sought to change the borders drawn up by the Treaty of Versailles and, domestically, to strengthen the 'military will' and eradicate pacifism which, in his opinion, was on a level with Marxism. Lieutenant General Curt Liebmann noted:

> Build-up of the Wehrmacht is the most important prerequisite to achieve this objective: regaining of political power. Universal conscription must be reintroduced. But before that the state leadership must ensure that the conscripts are not poisoned by pacifism, Marxism, Bolshevism before entering service or succumb to that poison after their term of service. How shall political power be used when obtained? Not yet possible to say. Perhaps winning new export opportunities, maybe – and probably better – conquest of new Lebensraum in the east and its ruthless Germanization. ... The Wehrmacht is most important and most socialist institution of the state. (Michalka 1985, 23–24; my translation)

Which general or admiral could still have any doubt about the aim of militarizing the whole of society and of preparing for a new war? What the Reichswehr leadership had striven for became the government programme under Hitler – even though official assurances of peace were intended to obscure that at first. Hitler with his military policy and not – as before the First World War – the general staff now defined the objectives of the military. And he laid down the time frame in which to achieve them. The early understanding reached between the military and political leadership on the matter of militarization has to be seen as essential for the war of aggression that began six years later and in which Hitler ultimately presented himself as an ingenious commander (Pyta 2015).

Although the Reichswehr was rid of its strongest military rival with the murder of the SA leadership in 1934 (officially referred to as the 'Röhm putsch'), the military could not, however, be completely sure of its monopoly to bear arms, since the SS combat support force – the precursor of the future Waffen-SS – emerged as a new rival in the military field. Against this backdrop, the military endeavoured time and again to score points with Hitler. It can be read as a declaration of loyalty therefore that, at the instigation of the Reich Defence Minister, General Werner von Blomberg, and not through any order by the Nazi leadership, the oath of allegiance was sworn to Hitler as the new commander-in-chief from August 1934 onward. From that time on, the wording of the oath was: 'I swear to God this holy oath, that I will offer unconditional obedience to the *Führer* of the German Reich and People, Adolf Hitler, the Supreme Commander of the Armed Forces, and that I am prepared as a brave soldier, to lay down my life at any time for this oath.' This commitment to the person of Hitler replaced the oath of allegiance to the Reich constitution.

To further blur the dividing lines between politics and the military in terms of militarizing the regime, Hitler continued to interfere with the structures of the military constitution: the introduction of universal conscription, the establishment of a Military High Command (*Oberkommando der Wehrmacht*, OKW) directly subordinate to him, and the opening-up of the officer corps to other social groups spurred on the militarization. On 16 March 1935, Hitler introduced universal conscription. The Reichswehr was renamed as a result of the *Gesetz über den Aufbau der Wehrmacht* ('Act Regulating the Establishment of the Wehrmacht'). The Defence Law of 21 May 1935 prescribed military service for one year for males aged 18–45, before it was extended to two years in August 1936. (When the *Volkssturm* national militia was introduced in 1944, all men aged 16–60 were liable to do military service.) The first conscripts were recruited from the 1914 age group. The Wehrmacht was to comprise 105 divisions, totalling 3.6 million soldiers, and be ready for war by 1939. The Treaty of Versailles had permitted only long-serving regular and professional soldiers and abolished the universal conscription introduced in Prussia in 1813. Without it, the mass armies of the nineteenth and twentieth centuries would not have been possible. Military service was also regarded as a means of education and as honourable, making the defence of the fatherland a matter for all (male) Germans.

This delighted the *Volksgemeinschaft*. Hitler had further fuelled the idea of a militarized 'people's community' by violating the disarmament provisions of the Treaty of Versailles and proclaiming 'military sovereignty'. The protests of the League of Nations and victorious powers proved fruitless. The Stresa Agreement concluded by France, Italy, and Great Britain in April 1935 in response to the unilateral termination of the Treaty provisions proved ineffective. Instead, the Anglo-German Naval Agreement of 18 June 1935 provided a diplomatic framework that officially facilitated the further rearming of the German navy which had begun in secret long before. The flip side of the militarization of society was the ideologization of the military through conscription. The recruits and new aspiring officers were subjected to increasingly frequent National Socialist indoctrination as a result of their socialization in the Nazi state. This younger generation encountered older regulars imbued with older military ideals and values. There were also, of course, older soldiers who had taken part in the First World War and later joined the NSDAP before being reactivated in 1935.

Hitler used the so-called Blomberg-Fritsch crisis to replace the Ministry of War with the OKW. It was headed by the compliant Wilhelm Keitel and was directly subordinate to the Führer. Hitler personally assumed supreme command of the armed forces. In addition, 16 older generals were retired and 44 reassigned. By this move, Hitler had turned the still relatively autonomous Wehrmacht into a largely spineless tool of his Führer dictatorship. When the cabinet met for the last time on 5 March 1938, Hitler also replaced conservative Foreign Minister Konstantin von Neurath with a staunch supporter, Joachim von Ribbentrop. He was thus able, solely on his own initiative, to send the military in the direction of Austria, Czechoslovakia, and Lithuania in the months thereafter.

The accelerated pace of rearmament heightened the Wehrmacht's need for suitable officers. Between 1936 and 1940, the officer corps grew from 3750 to 89 087 posts. This was equivalent to a 28-fold increase. Shortly thereafter, in the summer of 1941, the number jumped to 145 609 posts. These were mostly new additions where the officers were concerned. At the same time, reservists were reactivated and officers recalled from leave to their units. Because the pace of promotion increased and more and more men moved up from the lower officer ranks of second lieutenant, first lieutenant, and captain, the officer profession grew in attractiveness. In the 1930s, as Bernhard R. Kroener (1988) expressed it, the army was on the way to becoming a 'National Socialist people's army'. On account of the lack of personnel resources and the 'people's community' ideology, its officer corps was, by far, no longer as homogeneous as during the period of the Weimar Republic when the military nobility had held the key leadership positions for the last time. For many *Volksgenossen* or 'people's comrades', opening up this elite group of the armed forces was a means of social advancement. Might there not be a possibility to become one of them? That was likely a question many asked themselves. On the one hand, the social permeability of this people's army led to greater political approval of the regime it served; and on the other, the opening-up of the officer corps to other social groups proved conducive to the militarization of society as a whole.

The Wehrmacht allowed itself to be integrated into the Nazi dictatorship institutionally and ideologically, a point on which military historians would tend to agree. They even allowed the murder of comrades from their own ranks and of the SA leaders to go unchallenged, not to mention the antisemitic racial policy. Walther von Brauchitsch, commander-in-chief of the army (1938–1941), expressed his expectations of the officer corps a year before the start of the war: 'The officer corps must not allow itself to be surpassed by anyone in the purity and genuineness of National Socialist ideology.' The colonel general considered it as 'perfectly natural that officers in any situation act according to the conceptions of the Third Reich'. International borders and humanitarian convictions were to prove immaterial, as the war waged in Eastern and Southeastern Europe later demonstrated.

The militarization of the 1930s was peacetime preparation for total war, which was waged as a 'war of ideology' and found its expression in the systematic murder of self-created enemies, including women and children, through the army's cooperation with the *Einsatzgruppen* (murder squads) of the SS. In the Führer state, orders given by the Führer to soldiers who since 1934 had sworn an oath to that very Führer were intended to release them from any responsibility. There could be no talk of the Wehrmacht remaining 'apolitical and non-partisan', as Hitler had assured the commanders on 3 February 1933.

Hitler also dictated the course of the rearmament process. Since assuming power in 1933, at the latest since leaving the League of Nations, he had pushed ahead with rearmament, which had already been initiated in secret during the Weimar period. On 9 March, Hermann Göring announced the expansion of the German air force (*Luftwaffe*) which the Reich should not have possessed at all under the provisions of the Versailles Treaty. The Reichswehr had circumvented the restrictions of the Versailles Treaty as early as the 1920s through secret armaments activities. These included, for instance, the testing of aircraft and tanks in the Soviet Union. Full employment was also achieved thanks to the rapid pace of rearmament, thus adding to Hitler's charisma.

29.3   The NSDAP and Its Organizations as Militarization Agencies

While the Reichswehr was primarily responsible for implementing the armaments programme, the NSDAP, which from 14 July 1933 onward was the only party allowed to exist, took on the task of preparing the nation mentally. The party, its officials, and events indicated their paramilitary character and military-like propensity to violence through martial forms of expression, as Wolfram Wette illustrates (2008, 166–169). The NSDAP, organized internally along military/hierarchical lines, already had a military appearance about it prior to 1933. The right-wing, violence-prone members of the SA, who originally had been meant to serve as protection for party gatherings and as bodyguards, were among the paramilitary organizations of the Weimar Republic that, on the one hand, terrified political opponents yet, on the other, impressed those who were fascinated by marching columns of uniformed personnel and enthused about a militarized totalitarian state. By the beginning of the 1930s, the SA had grown into a veritable army, numbering 4.5 million members in 1934 (in 1938: 1.2 million). The NSDAP, by having the SA at its disposal, made it clear that it was ready to use violence in the political debate.

This also applied to the Protective Squads (*Schutzstaffeln*, SS), which formed the paramilitary structure of the NSDAP after the SA were deprived of power. The SS set up by Heinrich Himmler had been part of the party since 1925. Their visual appearance became a symbol of terror: the death's head badges on their peaked caps or steel helmets and their black uniforms gave the SS, recruited from former *Freikorps* fighters and veterans of the movement as well as from the nobility and educated classes, its uniform look. During the war, it also acted formally as a military formation with its own combat units, the Waffen-SS, under the supreme command of the Wehrmacht. Other mass organizations such as the German Labour

Front (*Deutsche Arbeitsfront*, DAF) which in 1933 had 7–8 million members, and in 1935 16 million, also had a paramilitary appearance.

The military appearance of the National Socialist leadership must also be understood as a similar signal. Nazi officials as well as Hitler himself indicated a readiness to use violence by appearing in a brown shirt, belt, and high boots. After 1933, Hitler wore a uniform which had military features but was not identical to any uniform type of the Nazi organizations. This manner of self-presentation was reflected in his visual appearance during the war. As the commander, the Führer wore the grey uniform of the Wehrmacht in most public appearances (and in most photographs). The swastika armlet and the decorations Hitler had received in the First World War replaced the otherwise customary rank insignia.

The major events of the NSDAP counted among the main forms of self-presentation in the Nazi festival calendar. It was no coincidence that the annual Nazi Party rallies as well as countless other rallies had elements characteristic of military ceremonies. This included the parading of uniformed formations (in particular the SA), the ritual entry of flags and banners, lining up in rank and file, and the presentation of the swastika flag and various guidons. Party meetings also sounded like military ceremonies because of the repeated drumrolls, marching music, and battle songs. This was matched by the tone of the orators. Nazi jargon was full of military expressions, comparisons, and figures of speech. Philologist Victor Klemperer (1996, 14, 25), who had submitted an initial critique of National Socialist language in 1946, observed among other things the increasingly frequent mention of heroism, for example. He also criticized the semantic limitation of the heroic 'ever more exclusively to military bravery and to bold, death-defying conduct in whatever military action'. The adjective *kämpferisch* (combative) became one of the favourite words of the National Socialists. Klemperer suspected they found the term *kriegerisch* (warlike, belligerent) too limited, as it expressly alluded to war and was probably 'too revealing, betraying an aggressive disposition and a yearning to conquer'. The military impregnation of everyday language can also be considered a sign of the militarization between 1933 and 1939.

It is one thing for historians to emphasize the break with tradition by the National Socialist movement; it is another to show how very keen the National Socialist leadership was to create the opposite impression. The creation of all kinds of traditions was intended to give the National Socialist course – and, not least, the militarization of policy – additional legitimacy through the appearance of historical continuity. National Socialist propaganda depicted the Hitler regime as being in continuity with Imperial Germany, if not Prusso-German militarism. This was reflected, for instance, in close personal ties with Prussian nobility such as August Wilhelm von Preussen (a son of the last emperor, Wilhelm II), who had been a member of the NSDAP since 1930, or the over 80-year-old General Field Marshal August von Mackensen who, after the death of Hindenburg, was the most senior serving officer of the erstwhile Prussian army. The supposed historical connectivity of National Socialism was meant to strengthen the militarization of society as a whole, not just in the eyes of Prussian national conservative elites. Nothing illustrated this calculation better than the 'Day of Potsdam' or, more precisely, its staging and mythification by Nazi propaganda. On 21 March 1933, the Reichswehr, SA, SS, and the *Stahlhelm* paraded together in front of the Potsdam Garrison Church where Hitler bowed before Hindenburg. The venerable hero of the First World War, born in 1847, appeared in uniform with a marshal's baton and *Pickelhaube* (spiked helmet).

The military socialization of boys and girls also played a key role in the militarization of National Socialist society. The term 'military socialization' applies not only to the wide-ranging socialization in the armed forces and what is actually experienced in the military (and is the primary focus of military sociologists), but also, in a normative sense, to the socialization processes in civilian society that are aimed at nurturing a pro-military mindset and bolstering the 'fighting spirit'. In what phase of life does which socialization institution – family, school, military – impart the readiness and ability to fight, and by what means? Unlike in Imperial Germany, in Hitler's Germany the paramilitary education of children and teenagers as military preparation was not in the hands of former officers but of National Socialist officials. In the Hitler Youth (*Hitlerjugend*, IIJ), its *Jungvolk* (young male association), and in the Reich Labour Service (*Reichsarbeitsdienst*, RAD) after 1935, as well as in the League of German Girls (*Bund Deutscher Mädel*, BDM) after 1936, the imparting of military thought processes and the practising of military behaviour at an early age played a key role in preparing for war. Hitler had also given notice of this to the commanders-in-chief of the army and navy in the aforementioned speech in February 1933: 'accustom youth and the entire nation to the thought that only fighting can save us, and that everything has to be subordinate to that thought ... training of youth and strengthening of the fighting spirit by all means' (Michalka 1985, 23–24; my translation). In the *Jungvolk* and the Hitler Youth, which built on older forms of youth movement, children and teenagers, boys and girls, not only received paramilitary training according to their age but were also prepared emotionally for waging war and the willingness to make sacrifices. 'Comradeship' was fostered, basic military skills were imparted, and a fascination for modern technology was generated through social evenings, trips, and camping. The *Flieger-HJ* (Aviation Hitler Youth) was designed to meet the growing manpower needs of the new *Luftwaffe* (air force). In 1938 it had a membership of some 80 000 plus around 20 000 members of the German *Jungvolk* who were prepared in model airplane workgroups for later service in the *Luftwaffe*. Young boys, also referred to as *Pimpfe*, were already to be groomed for military air warfare (Buddrus 2003, 190).

The Wehrmacht particularly targeted secondary schools in recruiting for the officer corps – for example, for careers as engineers in the air force and navy. Brochures provided information about the range of tasks and career opportunities, while experiential reports in the form of books gave vivid accounts of how exciting life as an aspiring officer and junior officer would be. In addition to printed media, the recruitment campaign relied on posters. Wehrmacht recruitment posters hung in school corridors and in rooms used by the Hitler Youth. A well-known poster in circulation in 1940 advertised *Offiziere von morgen* ('Tomorrow's officers'). It depicts, on the right in the foreground, a beaming Hitler Youth in uniform, while behind him to the left a Wehrmacht lieutenant with a Knight's Cross on his chest is marching in the background. The analogous body posture and facial expression underline the harmony of the young man and of the child, who can apparently grow seamlessly into his role as a soldier – or so the poster suggests. A recruitment postcard (*Auch Du* – 'You, too') used later by the SS to attract young people for direct entry from the Hitler Youth into the Waffen-SS employed quite similar imagery.

The legal framework for conscripting women in the event of war was also created for the first time. According to the Military Service Act of 1935, 'In war, apart from compulsory military service, every German man and every German woman is obliged to serve the Fatherland.' The mobilization of the female portion of society, consistent with the ideal of total war, stood in opposition to the traditional image of women which, until well into the war, prevented the systematic recruitment of females for labour or war service (as so-called *Wehrmachthelferinnen* – female Wehrmacht helpers).

One component of militarization was (civil) air raid protection, allowed, according to international law, since 1926. The new law of June 1935 gave Göring the possibility to draw on men and women for air raid protection. The problems of mobilizing for air raid protection between 1933 and 1939 made it quite clear how difficult it was to transform the civilian population into a soldierly community fighting on a voluntary basis (Lemke 2005). This held particularly true for women. Propaganda and special protection exercises for the household should prepare them for war. However, the police criticized their lack of interest and military thinking. Drilling the use of gas masks, for instance, or special air raid protection courses for women raised women's resistance rather than enthusiasm for war. In general, they were not convinced by the ideological rather than rational interpretation of protection as a national duty or sign of loyalty to the Führer. Nor did they feel like heroines, as the propaganda tried to suggest. During the war, more than half a million women served as attendants or helpers for air raid protection. By the end of 1932, about 200 000 women were organized in the Reich Labour service for Female Youths. Hitler centralized this *Reichsarbeitsdienst für die weibliche Jugend* (RADwJ) after 1933, but did not make it compulsory until the war. On average, 40 000 'maids' (*Maiden*) joined this paramilitary organization per year. At the same time, the Nazi Women's Organization (*NS-Frauenschaft*) run by Gertrud Scholtz-Klink conveyed a new gender role to women as mothers and wives who also earned money in offices, factories, or in the military if necessary.

The public campaigns supported the recruitment efforts and helped to increase the social prestige of the officer's profession in the mid-1930s. More and more young men were able to imagine themselves as officers in the Wehrmacht. The senior officers served as role models for many. Military socialization was meant to increase the acceptance of military thought processes and behaviour and prepare young people mentally as well as practically for war service. Whether these dispositions were actually conducive to any lasting war enthusiasm during the war, or instead led to disillusionment and disappointment as a result of the sharp contrast between indoctrination and reality, is a much-discussed question.

29.4   Image of War

Among the historical-ideological facets of the Second World War was an image of war that (not only in Germany) originated in the nineteenth century. It glorified death on the battlefield, declared the fallen as sacrifices for the fatherland and as heroes, and elevated world war to a racial struggle for existence. With its racial ideological construction of a National Socialist 'people's community', radical nationalism formed a central element of National Socialism's ideological mixture. The idea of an ongoing struggle between the *Volksgenossen* and their enemies within and beyond the borders of the Reich was able to build on familiar interpretive patterns. Among the 'enemies of the nation' were, in particular, Jews, social democrats, and communists. 'Jewish Bolshevism' was a key enemy image in the war on the Eastern Front. Domestically, this conception of the world led to a central element of Nazi ideology: the cult of the fallen soldier. The Nazi movement owed its rise not least to the tribute it paid to the veterans of 1914–1918 and the 'comrades' who had fallen in the First World War. The National Socialist War Victims' Welfare (*Nationalsozialistische Kriegsopferversorgung*, NSKOV) played an important role in the integration of the victims who had survived the war. The massive number of soldiers' deaths was no longer a reason for demonstrations of mourning but for events at which the fallen of the world war – as well as 'party comrades' who had died in the 'period of struggle' (*Kampfzeit*) before 1933 – were celebrated as heroes. In the new practice of commemoration which picked up on older traditions, the 'fallen heroes' were considered by the living as role models, because they had proven their readiness to give – or 'sacrifice' – their lives for the 'people's community'.

The hero cult of the Third Reich was reflected in mythical narratives, rites, and architecture. In 1934, what previously had been Remembrance Day was rededicated as 'Heroes' Day'. Hitler, in 1939, had this *Volkstrauertag* shifted to 16 March, the anniversary of when universal conscription was reintroduced in 1935, and thus separated it from the church year. After the takeover of power, the hero cult had become a pseudo-religious mass phenomenon: films, theatre plays, and *Thingspiele* (interactive events) celebrated the dead. A military myth that had been well known since the First World War – the myth of Langemarck – was of major importance in the 1930s. The (failed) use of a reserve corps comprising young volunteers and older reservists near Ypres in 1914 had been promptly reinterpreted as a success and as an example of how young Germans sacrificed themselves for their nation. School lessons in the Third Reich were unimaginable without reference to 'Langemarck'. The mythification of the heroes of Langemarck served to teach children and teenagers at an early age to see war as a necessary sacrifice for the nation. This was consistent with the principle of National Socialist educational theory that pupils 'blindly' obey their teachers and youth leaders in the same way as soldiers had to automatically carry out the orders of their commanders. In that respect, military education resembled the civilian variant. Early familiarization with the principle of command and obedience as well as the emotional internalization of notions of honour, loyalty, and willingness to make sacrifices contributed to social militarization and served to prepare young people for self-sacrifice.

A sideways glance at the universities shows how military and civilian areas overlapped in the 1930s. In Halle (Saale), for instance, where in 1933 the university was renamed at the urging of the senate to Martin Luther-Universität Halle-Wittenberg (MLU), the rector, in opening the university's Reformation celebrations, also welcomed 'with genuine pleasure the gentlemen officers of the Reichswehr who have appeared with us here today for the first time in their field-grey dress of honour again' (Hallische Universitätsreden 1933, 3). Two years later, the invitation to the ceremonial act in the main lecture hall on Luther Memorial Day included the following dress code: 'tailcoat/uniform' for the academic staff and 'dark suit/uniform' for guests. The ceremonial address was followed by 'words of commemoration by the rector for the fallen soldiers of Langemarck' before it was the turn of the organist of St Ulrich Church to make his musical contribution.[1] Senior military figures were eventually invited to MLU to give guest lectures. In 1938, for example, the senators were delighted to gain General von Cochenhausen, a veteran of the First World War, as a speaker. Paramilitary training became, conversely, a prerequisite for postdoctoral qualification.

What is more, the 1930s saw a boom in war literature. The 1914–1918 world war had triggered a flood of war novels, accounts of experiences at the front, and war memoirs, making books about the world war a successful literary genre. According to the Institute for Reader and Literature Studies (*Institut für Leser- und Schrifttumkunde*) in Leipzig, world war topics found increasing interest among the public from the late 1920s onward. Bestsellers by Edwin Erich Dwinger, Werner Beumelburg, and Ernst Jünger prompted this 'boom in war books' (Adam 2010, 135–137.) Fiction presenting war as a necessity and reducing it to an adventure for real men were grist to the mills of the social militarization striven for by the National Socialists. The war novel *Gruppe Bosemüller* (1930), which was one of Beumelburg's most successful books at 164 000 copies, is only one example of how the idea of a heroic front generation was meant to inspire the new generation with confidence and make them aware of their duties by calling to mind the sacrifices made. Works critical of war, such as *All Quiet on the Western Front* by Erich Maria Remarque (1928/1929), were a thorn in their side, however, with Joseph Goebbels prohibiting their screen adaptation. Preoccupation with the war and its consequences formed the golden thread extending through the best-selling literature of the Third Reich. When the Wehrmacht then intervened in the Spanish Civil War in 1936, the retrospective view of the world war was augmented by reports from the front and coverage of the current operational theatre. On 13 June 1939, for instance, the propaganda journal *Der Adler* ('The Eagle'), co-edited by the Reich Ministry of Aviation, brought out a special edition entitled *Neue Erlebnisse unserer Spanienkämpfer* ('New experiences of our fighters in Spain'). The cover showed a German soldier with a swastika-emblazoned red-and-white national flag alongside his Spanish and Italian comrades who, for their part, were holding up national flags – denoting the first deployment of German soldiers abroad and a first example of their victorious fight after the humiliation of 1918.

The militarization of society as a whole, in particular of young (male) people, aimed at the acceptance of the social Darwinist idea that the German people had a future only through armed struggle. Reflected in the nationalistic foundation for this militarization was the ontologization of the national collective, which was typical of the *Volksgemeinschaft* ideology. Radical militarization required the German people as a historical subject. Its collective 'readiness to defend itself' was the other side of the idea of the *Volkstumkampf* (struggle between ethnically defined national communities). The standards that were to be internalized in the Wehrmacht conflicted less and less with the values imparted to young people in civilian life during socialization in their childhood and youth. For that reason, under National Socialism, military socialization was *not* in opposition to civilian society. Instead, military service – to use Michel Foucault's argumentation – served as preparation for the society of the Third Reich. Both sides of the civil–military relationship interconnected in the 'militarized people's community'. Civilian and military socialization was interlinked. The *Gehorsamsproduktion* ('production of obedience') (Bröckling 1997) in the Wehrmacht and in paramilitary institutions was linked to social development as part of preparing for war.

29.5 Summary

Since the time of Imperial Germany, 'militarism' had been a tendentious term that denoted civilian society being permeated by military ambitions and thus requiring the separation of civilian and military spheres. This division of state and social order no longer existed under the Nazi regime. The National Socialists integrated older forms and content of militarism into their ideology. They made 'the once strongest exponent of militarism – "armed power" – the functionary of its objectives and methods of realization' (Messerschmidt 2006, 68). The lesson that the German military and parts of society had drawn from the world war overlooked their own failings. They sought to revise the Peace Treaty of Versailles, correct the borders, and reconstruct a Reichswehr with heavy weapons. The military leadership, in point of fact, developed ideas of nationalizing future war.

Because military conflicts of the future were likely to involve 'total war', the preparations for war from 1933 to 1939 had to mobilize as extensive a part of society as possible. The peace rhetoric was intended to obscure that. In a secret speech held before representatives of the German press in Munich on 10 November 1938, Hitler frankly admitted in retrospect that 'circumstances had forced [him] to speak almost solely of peace for decades. Only by a continued emphasis upon the German will for peace and peaceful intentions was it possible for me to win, step by step, freedom for the German people and to give them the armament which, again and again, proved to be the prerequisite for the next step' (Domarus 1962/1963, 974; my translation).

The Wehrmacht benefited, where the increase in its manpower resources was concerned, not only from the introduction of universal conscription but also from the paramilitary practices in the organizations of the NSDAP, namely the Hitler Youth. At the beginning of the war, the Wehrmacht mobilized some 4 556 000 men following the almost unchecked build-up and expansion of the army, navy, and air force. Of those, 750 000 made up the active force (22 600 officers and some 150 000 NCOs) and 3.8 million their replacements (Kroener 2000). The mobilization of personnel, material rearmament, as well as ideologically making the nation 'ready to defend itself' were militarization factors which led, by 1939, to 'such a high level of military build-up that (Germany) could be considered the strongest modernly [*sic*] equipped military power' (Wette 2008, 180). The 100000-strong army of the Weimar Republic was history, the 'people's community' having become a 'military community'. The Wehrmacht numbered some 10 million conscripts in total among the 18 million German soldiers who fought in the Second World War. Up to 39% of any conscription age group were killed between 1939 and 1945.

Note

1   Universitätsarchiv Halle-Wittenberg (UAH), Rep. 4, No. 2098.

References

Adam, Christian. 2010. *Lesen unter Hitler: Autoren, Bestseller, Leser im Dritten Reich.* Berlin: Galiani.

Bröckling, Ulrich. 1997. *Disziplin. Soziologie und Geschichte militärischer Gehorsamsproduktion,* Munich: Fink.

Buddrus, Michael. 2003. *Totale Erziehung für den totalen Krieg: Hitlerjugend und nationalsozialistische Jugendpolitik.* 2 vols. Munich: Saur.

Domarus, Max. 1962/1963. *Hitler Reden und Proklamationen 1932–1945: Kommentiert von einem deutschen Zeitgenossen.* Würzburg: Author.

Hallische Universitätsreden No. 60. 1933. Halle (Saale): Max Niemeyer.

Klemperer, Victor. 1996. *LTI: Notizbuch eines Philologen,* 16th edn. Leipzig: Reclam.

Kroener, Bernhard R. 1988. 'Auf dem Weg zu einer "nationalsozialistischen Volksarme". Die soziale Öffnung des Heeresoffizierkorps im Zweiten Weltkrieg.' In *Von Stalingrad zur Währungsreform: Zur Sozialgeschichte des Umbruchs in Deutschland,* edited by Martin Broszat, Klaus-Dietmar Henke, and Hans Woller, 651–682. Munich: Oldenbourg.

Kroener, Bernhard R. 2000. 'The Manpower Resources of the Third Reich in the Area of Conflict between Wehrmacht, Bureaucracy, and War Economy, 1939–1942.' In *Germany and the Second World War, Volume 1, Part 1: Organization and Mobilization of the German Sphere of Power: Wartime Administration, Economy, and Manpower Resources 1939–1941,* edited by the Militärgeschichtliches Forschungsamt Potsdam, Germany. Translation editor Ewald Osers, 787–1154. Oxford: Clarendon Press.

Lemke, Bernd. 2005. *Luftschutz in Großbritannien und Deutschland 1923 bis 1939: Zivile Kriegsvorbereitungen als Ausdruck der staats- und gesellschaftspolitischen Grundlagen von Demokratie und Diktatur.* Munich: Oldenbourg.

Messerschmidt, Manfred. 2006. 'Das neue Gesicht des Militarismus in der Zeit des Nationalsozialismus.' In *Manfred Messerschmidt: Militarismus, Vernichtungskrieg, Geschichtspolitik. Zur deutschen Militär- und Rechtsgeschichte,* edited by Hans Ehlert, Arnim Lang, and Bernd Wegner, 63–72. Paderborn: Schöningh.

Michalka, Wolfgang, ed. 1985. *Das Dritte Reich: Dokumente zur Innen- und Außenpolitik.* Vol. 1. Munich: dtv.

Pyta, Wolfram. 2015. *Hitler: Der Künstler als Politiker und Feldherr. Eine Herrschaftsanalyse.* Munich: Siedler.

Wette, Wolfram. 2008. *Militarismus in Deutschland: Geschichte einer kriegerischen Kultur.* Darmstadt: WBG.

Further Reading

Behrenbeck, Sabine. 1996. *Der Kult um die toten Helden: Nationalsozialistische Mythen, Riten und Symbole*. Vierow: SH-Verlag.
Underlines the religious aspect of interpreting the loss of one's life in war or in the struggle for Nazism as a national sacrifice.
Berghahn, Volker R. 1984. *Militarism: The History of an International Debate, 1861–1979*. Cambridge: Cambridge University Press.
Pays particular attention to the use of the term 'militarism' in propaganda.
Borggräfe, Henning. 2010. *Schützenvereine im Nationalsozialismus: Pflege der 'Volksgemeinschaft' und Vorbereitung auf den Krieg (1933–1945)*. Münster: Ardey.
Takes the example of traditional Westphalian shooting associations to show how ordinary Germans integrated themselves into the Nazi regime.
Förster, Jürgen. 2007. *Die Wehrmacht im NS-Staat: Eine strukturgeschichtliche Analyse*. Munich: Oldenbourg.
Provides an accessible overview of the German army in the Third Reich.
Frevert, Ute, 2004. *A Nation in Barracks: Modern Germany, Military Conscription and Civil Society*. Oxford and New York: Bloomsbury.
Puts the mass mobilization after 1933 in the context of the history of conscription as a means to instil the will to fight.
Geyer, Michael. 1989. 'The Militarization of Europe, 1914–1945.' In *The Militarization of the Western World*, edited by John R. Gillis, 65–102. New Brunswick and London: Rutgers.
Offers a systematic overview of militarization as a historical process in Europe.
Messerschmidt, Manfred. 1969. *Die Wehrmacht im NS-Staat: Zeit der Indoktrination*. Hamburg: R. v. Decker.
This pioneering work on the interlinking of the German army and Nazism is unrivalled.
Wette, Wolfram. 2008. *Militarismus in Deutschland: Geschichte einer kriegerischen Kultur*, Darmstadt: WBG.
Offers a synthesis of research on the impact of veterans' associations, folklore militarism, parades, the support by German intellectuals, but also the criticism of pacifists such as Ludwig Quidde or Bertha von Suttner.

CHAPTER THIRTY

Race

ISABEL HEINEMANN

30.1   Introduction

When Adolf Hitler wrote his political manifesto *Mein Kampf* in 1925/1926, he based his reasoning on the assumption that contemporary culture and civilization were the products of only one race, the 'Aryan' one. As natural evolution consisted in the survival of the fittest, the members of the 'Aryan' race had the absolute duty to avoid 'racial mixing' (*Rassenmischung*) which would inevitably lead to decadence and finally decay: 'Any human being which ignores and violates the race laws, absolutely deprives himself of the happiness destined for him. He precludes the victory of the superior race as well as the preconditions of human progress. Burdened by human sensitivity, he is trapped like a helpless lamenting animal' (Hartmann et al. 2016, 753, 755). Hitler thus amalgamated elements of evolution theory and social Darwinism with crude antisemitism and anthropological racism, creating an aggressive and highly selective world-view based on seemingly objective 'biological facts': absolute racial superiority of the Aryan that provided him with the historical mission to govern over all other people and purge the Aryan race of any alien influence, above all the Jews. The programme of the NSDAP (*Nationalsozialistische Deutsche Arbeiterpartei*, Nazi Party), proclaimed on 24 February 1920 by Adolf Hitler in Munich, had already affirmed the party's belief in race theory – without even naming it: Article 4 read: 'Each citizen needs to be a People's comrade (*Volksgenosse*). A People's comrade needs to be of German blood .... No Jew, thus, can be a People's comrade' (Tyrell 1969, 23).

   'Race' was the key word of the National Socialist state, also termed the 'racial state' (Burleigh and Wippermann 1991). It served as the guiding principle of not

A Companion to Nazi Germany, First Edition. Edited by Shelley Baranowski,
Armin Nolzen, and Claus-Christian W. Szejnmann.
© 2018 John Wiley & Sons Ltd. Published 2018 by John Wiley & Sons Ltd.

only science and politics but also everyday life. Referring to the concept of 'race' meant 'an attempt to emphasize a physiological dimension in the inequalities of mankind' (Geulen 2014, 14). On the one hand, racism consisted in 'a belief that race is the primary determinant of human traits and capacities and that racial differences produce an inherent superiority of a particular race' (Merriam-Webster 2017) and, on the other hand, in 'an attempt to legitimize or enforce traditional or new boundaries of social affiliation' through the mobilization of specific knowledge and mostly exclusionary practices (Geulen 2014, 11–2).

In National Socialism, anthropology and racial hygiene were considered key sciences that provided methodology and legitimization for the racist policies of the Nazi state, ranging from forced sterilization and euthanasia to the ethnic restructuring of Eastern Europe and genocide. A deep-rooted ideology of racial worth and non-worth structured politics and life in the Third Reich, finding its most tangible expression in an aggressive antisemitism and a host of exclusionary measures targeting German Jews. Also, the brutal 'war of extermination' against the Soviet Union referred to racist premises (the destruction of Slavic 'sub-humans'), as did the practices of expulsion and resettlement in the name of the Germanization (*Germanisierung*) of occupied Eastern Europe. Why did racist thinking develop such a suggestive force in Nazi Germany? The path to the racial state was by no means inevitable, to the contrary.

30.2   New Frontiers? International Race Theories and Racial Policies

Race theories and eugenic ideas held strong currency in all Western countries during the first third of the twentieth century. Drawing on Francis Galton's use of the term 'eugenics' (Galton 1883, 1902) and a comprehensive understanding of social Darwinism, scientists in Western Europe and the United States readily embraced the idea that social ills could be linked to biological developments and that society could be ameliorated by improving its genetic substance. Also, leading eugenicists and race scientists established international contacts and collaborations, especially in the framework of three major international conferences on eugenics: 1912 in London, 1921 and 1932 in New York. At the first conference, a Permanent International Eugenics Committee was founded, which transformed into the International Federation of Eugenic Organizations (IFEO) in 1925 when the famous US American eugenicist Charles Benedict Davenport took over as first president.

In the United States, eugenic ideas proved most influential as immigration laws based on racist thinking and state-run sterilization programmes evolved well before the Second World War. No less than three major eugenic societies propagated eugenic ideas through the publication of journals, exhibitions, and events directed at the American population such as the notorious Fitter Family Contests. The Eugenic Record Office (ERO) was founded by Charles Benedict Davenport in 1910 as the nation's first eugenic research institution. Part of the famous Cold Spring Harbor Laboratory in the state of New York (later the scientific home of Nobel Prize winner James Watson), the ERO received funding from the Carnegie

Institution in Washington, DC. Under its director Harry H. Laughlin, the institute collected data on the heredity of American families, investigated inheritance of mental traits and hereditary diseases, and finally advocated forced sterilizations of people considered mentally handicapped (Black 2004; Kevles 2001; Wilson 2002). Laughlin, who also served on the governmental Committee on Immigration and Naturalization, recommended that the Immigration Act of 1924 comprise a race-based quota system – based on his observations as head of the ERO. German race scientists in particular drew heavily on his publications on eugenic sterilization and immigration control, expressing their esteem by according him an honorary doctorate of Heidelberg University in 1936.

The American Eugenics Society, still existent today under the name 'Society for Biodemography and Social Biology', was founded in 1922, following the success of the second International Congress on Eugenics, on the initiative of American race scholars such as Madison Grant, Harry H. Laughlin, Irving Fisher, and Henry F. Osborn. During the 1920s, the institution sponsored the Fitter Families Contests held in the framework of Agricultural Fairs in the Midwest where families of superior genetic heritage received medals and certificates – after thorough medical examination and establishment of their family pedigree. These widely popular events served to popularize eugenic thinking and in particular addressed the rural population, who were considered to be especially fertile. The most popular handbook on eugenics – Paul B. Popenoe and Roswell H. Johnson's *Applied Eugenics* (1918), comparable to Baur, Fischer, and Lenz's (1921) work in Germany – defined eugenics as the following: '(1) that a larger proportion of superior persons will have children than at present, (2) that the average number of offspring of each superior person will be greater than at present, (3) that the most inferior persons will have no children, and finally that (4) other inferior persons will have fewer children than now' (Popenoe and Johnson 1918, v–vi). In emphasizing sterilization of people suffering from mental disabilities and hereditary diseases Johnson and Popenoe explicitly referred to California. In 1909, the state had set up the first national sterilization programme for inmates of state institutions and hospitals, thus legitimizing the sterilization of more than 6000 individuals by 1929. The Human Betterment Foundation in Pasadena, California was founded in 1928 by Ezray S. Gosney to monitor the results. An ensuing publication by Paul B. Popenoe and Ezra S. Gosney (*Sterilization for Human Betterment*, 1929) received broad international attention, especially from the National Socialist government in Germany (for the German translation, see Popenoe and Gosney 1930). Paul B. Popenoe, in return, praised the Nazi sterilization law of 1933 as 'first example in modern times of an administration based frankly and determinedly on the principle of eugenics' (Popenoe 1934; Kühl 1994). In 1927, a landmark decision of the Supreme Court had underscored the legitimacy of forced sterilizations of those considered mentally handicapped: in the *Buck vs. Bell* ruling the court justified the coerced sterilization of a young single mother from a 'socially degenerate' background in the state of Virginia, declaring 'three generations of imbeciles are enough' (Lombardo 2003, 216) Clearly, this decision further enhanced eugenic population policies in the United States, which gradually turned into racial policies directed against ethnic minorities like African Americans and Mexican Americans

(Kline 2001; Schoen 2005; Stern 2005; Kluchin 2011). Unlike Nazi Germany, however, sterilization laws and programmes in the United States existed only on the state level, receiving support from individual experts like Popenoe and privately financed eugenic organizations like the American Eugenics Society. Despite the Supreme Court's pro-sterilization ruling of 1927, the central state refrained from any coordinated policy making in this field of population policy.

In Great Britain, Francis Galton had been the first to draw a connection between 'social' and 'genetic' worth and to suggest 'negative eugenics' to curb the reproduction of lower-class individuals while stimulating that of the upper classes (Galton 1902). Galton's perception of eugenics as a means to enhance the quality of both the human race and the British population – who nevertheless were more tied to class than race – proved tremendously influential: soon, the Eugenic Record Office at the University of London under Karl Pearson started to collect data on families struck by hereditary diseases. In 1907, the Eugenics Education Society was called into being in London to promote 'eugenic teaching and understanding in the home, the school and elsewhere', with Galton serving as its first president. In 1926 it was transformed into the British Eugenics Society (today, the Galton Society). The institution could count on such prominent members as economist John Maynard Keynes, biologist Julian Huxley, and birth control pioneer Marie Stopes. For nearly 60 years it edited the most prominent journal in the field, *The Eugenics Review* (1909–1968). Unlike the United States and Germany, no forced sterilizations were effected in Great Britain (Schneider 1982, 290), but the Mental Deficiency Act of 1913 allowed for the hospitalization of those labelled feeble-minded. As it did not provide any reliable definition of 'feeble-mindedness', girls of 'morally questionable' behaviour (in particular) were incarcerated (Bland and Hall 2010).

In France, a French Eugenic Society existed from 1912, dedicated to the 'research and application of knowledge useful to the reproduction, preservation and improvement of the species' (Founding Statutes of the organization; see Schneider 1982, 276; in general, Schneider 1990), placing more emphasis on the 'influence of the environment' than on 'heredity'. Following an explicit neo-Lamarckian tradition, the French eugenicists took a different stance from their German, British, or American counterparts. As the losses of the First World War dramatically increased the fear of population decline, eugenicists of the inter-war years placed greater emphasis on enhancing the quantity of French people. This led to a peculiar twist: whereas the government of the Third Republic as well as the collaborationist regime of Maréchal Philippe Pétain resorted to positive eugenics by advocating large families and an increase in the national birth rate, negative eugenics and birth control were advocated in particular by French anarchists – to enhance the freedom of the individual (Sonn 2005). In France, as in Great Britain, negative eugenics never became the official guideline of the regime and did not materialize as concrete population policies (Fogarty and Osborne 2010). During the first third of the twentieth century, eugenic movements existed nearly all over Europe and even in the Soviet Union, but no other country experienced an eruption of racism leading to mass murder and genocide comparable to that in Germany. Consequently, the following sections of this chapter examine historical constellations 'old fighter', because he already belonged to the Nazi Party before Hitler came into power. On the other hand, he broke with the regime, in mid-1934 at the latest. The fact that he made a contribution to save the Jews of Denmark in 1943, when he worked for the German embassy in Copenhagen, was honoured by the Holocaust memorial Yad Vashem in 1971, which awarded him the title 'Righteous among the Nations'.

In other words, the quickly increasing number of party members among civil servants and employees of the higher grade foreign service – namely from 1% (1933) to 12% (1934) to 22% (1935) to 32% (1936) to 41% (1937) to 55% (1938) to 62% per cent (1939) – illustrates most of all how quickly and forcefully the dictatorship was established, because professional careers increasingly depended on loyalty towards the regime being proved by party membership. In fact, due to a Hitler decree from September 1935, Rudolf Hess, the Deputy Führer (*Stellvertreter des Führers*), had to approve all promotions of diplomats – and from early 1939 he did so only when the applicant to a higher grade position within the diplomatic service was a member of the Nazi Party. Even for the recruitment of young employees and civil servants party membership was of growing importance: for example, out of all newly appointed attachés of 1937 there was only one man who was not a member of the NSDAP nor the SA nor the SS. However, in this climate of peer pressure and a mentality focused on career opportunities, the driving force behind the decision to join the party varied from person to person, and in whether it was opportunism or true political belief.

Neurath did not take issue with this 'formal' Nazification of the Foreign Office. His diplomats were explicitly free to decide for themselves; indeed, joining the NSDAP was recommended only indirectly. Nor did he oppose taking into account party political aspects when recruiting young personnel, even though the high number of attachés trained by the Nazi state drove forward the 'forcible coordination' from below, which also served as a control mechanism towards the top. The guiding principle of Neurath's actions remained the same: he wanted to prevent politically motivated lateral entries and, in so doing, the de-professionalization of the diplomatic service by exhibiting a policy of self-alignment (*Selbstgleichschaltung*). He expected that professionalism would have a depoliticizing impact. It was only under Neurath's successor Joachim von Ribbentrop, who took over the Foreign Office in February 1938, that political and ideological loyalty became more important than professional qualifications and expertise.

Ribbentrop joined the NSDAP only in May 1932, but he was able to quickly establish himself within Hitler's entourage. As his foreign political adviser and special commissioner, he set up his own department similar to the NSDAP Office of Foreign Affairs under Alfred Rosenberg and the NSDAP Foreign Organization (*Auslandsorganisation*, AO) under Ernst Wilhelm Bohle and developed his own foreign policy strategies and approaches. Other members of the cabinet, such as Hjalmar Schacht and Hermann Göring, also tried to influence foreign policy, but all these politicians and institutions and their divergent concepts were rather marginal compared to Hitler's ideology. Scholarly discussions on the much-debated question of the polycracy of the Third Reich and the pluralism of foreign political concepts have primarily favoured the by now widely accepted view that these

This merely quantitative description already indicates a Nazification of the diplomatic service as a consequence of the fluctuation of personnel. This becomes even more evident from a qualitative perspective. As early as 1933, 10 members of the higher grade foreign service were dismissed on 'racial' grounds and eight for political reasons; one person had to quit because of their sexual orientation. The legal basis for the dismissals was primarily the 'Law for the Restoration of the Professional Civil Service' (*Gesetz zur Wiederherstellung des Berufsbeamtentums*) that came into force on 7 April 1933. It affected three groups of people: (i) the 'membership book officials', that is, those who entered the civil service after 1918 without possessing the required training or qualifications; (ii) those of 'non-Aryan descent', as long as they had not already been employed before August 1914 or had fought or had fathers or sons who were killed during the First World War – an exemption clause initiated by Hindenburg; and (iii) those civil servants whose 'former political activity affords no guarantee that they will act in the interest of the national state at all times and without reservation'. The heads of the Foreign Office accepted the law because it offered the opportunity to dismiss unpopular civil servants. The Nazi alignment (*Gleichschaltung*) of the civil service and the disenfranchisement of Jewish citizens did not meet opposition, particularly because only very few Jews worked as civil servants in the diplomatic service and those considered patriotic were protected by the 'frontline fighters' privilege' (*Frontkämpferprivileg*).

At the same time, the political development had an increasing impact on recruitment and promotion decisions. It was in this context that the lateral entrant Vicco von Bülow-Schwante was appointed. Both the Foreign Office and the Nazi Party considered him a trustworthy man. He took charge of the newly established or re-established department 'Germany', which coordinated cooperation with the security authorities, and was therefore responsible for surveilling German emigrants, the expatriation of German citizens, and the 'Jewish question'. Bülow-Schwante, who headed the department until 1938, was an exception in so far as his deputies were not lateral entrants. Also, the three senior civil servants of the Foreign Office responsible for the 'Jewish question', Emil Schumburg (1933–1940), Franz Rademacher (1940–1943), and Eberhard von Thadden (1943–1945), had been members of the Foreign Office under Minister Neurath, when they were appointed as attachés or moved to the foreign service from an administration position.

Until the death of Secretary Bülow in 1936 it was mostly civil servants (from the senior civil servant to the head of division to the state secretary and the minister) who dealt with the 'Jewish question' – and these men were not members of the Nazi Party (*Nationalsozialistische Deutsche Arbeiterpartei*, NSDAP) or another Nazi organization. Bülow-Schwante joined the NSDAP only in mid-1936; Schumburg, who joined the SS in October 1936, was without party affiliation until mid-1938. This example leads one to the conclusion that guilt and responsibility cannot be measured by membership in a Nazi organization. Indeed, only a case-by-case review can cope with the complexity of the history – as, for example, the case of Georg Ferdinand Duckwitz shows. Duckwitz joined the NSDAP as early as November 1932. On the one hand, therefore, he represents an that made German racism so distinct and German race scholars so ready to embrace ultimate means in order to purify the population.

30.3 Race Theories: Scientific and Popular Racism since the Nineteenth Century

The history of racial science needs to be understood as a thoroughly international endeavour, leading to distinctly national concepts, that gained momentum in the second half of the nineteenth century. At this time, two strands of racist thinking can be distinguished: cultural and anthropological racism on one side, naturalist and biologist racism on the other. One of the most eminent representatives of cultural and anthropological (albeit not yet biological) racism was the French diplomat and philosopher Arthur Compte de Gobineau. In his four-volume treatise *Essay sur l'inégalité des races humaines* ('Essay on the Inequality of Human Races'), originally published 1853–1855, Gobineau argued that mankind could be divided into three major races: white, yellow, and black. For him, 'any civilization originated within the white race' – which he already termed 'Aryan' (Gobineau 1898, 280, 285). Gobineau identified 'racial mixture' as the motor of both cultural progress (the white race serving the uplift of others) and the decay of civilizations (due to the impact of the non-white races), thus linking history and biology in an unstoppable, yet still God-given flow. Roughly 40 years later, Houston Stewart Chamberlain added a fierce antisemitism to Gobineau's reflections on 'racial mixture'. In his bestseller *Die Grundlagen des 19. Jahrhunderts* ('The Foundations of the 19th Century'), he argued that German culture had to be purged of 'alien influence' and the effects of 'miscegenation' caused by racial mixing of Aryans and Jews (Chamberlain 1899). Thus, the son-in-law of Richard Wagner not only helped to lay the theoretical foundations of race antisemitism, but greatly inspired major National Socialists like Hitler and Alfred Rosenberg.

On the other side of the argument, Charles Darwin explained that the reproduction of plants, animals, and human beings alike resulted from what he called 'natural selection' and 'the survival of the fittest' (Darwin 1859, 1871). Thus, he demonstrated that any 'species' was the product of a complex process of evolution. Darwin's path-breaking approach to evolution theory opened the door to attempts to 'improve' the human race through interventions in the reproductive cycle, as conceived by his cousin, Francis Galton. Galton first coined the term 'eugenics' for the 'science of improving stock, which … takes cognisance of all influences that tend … to give the more suitable races or strains of blood a better chance of prevailing speedily over the less suitable than they otherwise would have had' (Galton 1883, 24). Thus, Galton was among the first to introduce the idea that improvement of the biological substance of populations through marriage incentives for the 'wanted' and restrictions for the 'unwanted' was not only desirable, but also feasible. This was addressed by the new field of 'racial hygiene' that boomed, especially in Germany.

Drawing on Gobineau, Darwin, Galton, and social Darwinists like the German zoologist and anatomist Ernst Haeckel, German race scientists of the late nineteenth century started to establish 'racial hygiene' as a scientific discipline. While physician Alfred Ploetz, the later founder of Germany's first eugenic journal (*Archiv für Rassen- und Gesellschaftsbiologie*) defined races as 'entities of human beings living through generations, united in their physical and intellectual qualities' (Ploetz 1895), physician William Schallmayer (1903) made the case for a 'conscious improvement of human breeding' through race research and a physical classification of all German citizens. In 1905, Ploetz also founded Germany's most eminent racial-anthropological society, the German Society for Racial Hygiene (*Deutsche Gesellschaft für Rassenhygiene*). Until 1916, the institution was called *Internationale Gesellschaft für Rassenhygiene*, emphasizing the international orientation of Germany's most eminent racist pre-thinkers well into the First World War. Members comprised psychologist Ernst Rüdin, biologist Erwin Baur, anthropologist Eugen Fischer, as well as Haeckel and Schallmayer. In its statutes (*Leitsätze der Deutschen Gesellschaft für Rassenhygiene*), issued in 1922, the society declared 'racial degeneration' (*Entartung*) the main danger. As potential remedies, it proposed pro-natalist measures targeting the racially valuable and enhancing race education at universities and schools as well as health certificates for marriage candidates (*Leitsätze* 1922, 372–373). Although the study of race had begun as a special interest of physicians and biologists, mostly private scholars, it soon developed into a well-established science under the name of 'racial hygiene' (*Rassenhygiene*) in Germany. This process gained huge momentum after the First World War.

Although the losses of the First World War served as an argument to stimulate eugenic movements in all Western countries, the question arises why Germany in particular developed such a fierce racial hygienicist and eugenic movement. One aspect of the answer is that the nation had to cope with a devastating defeat and severe territorial losses, a peace treaty that was perceived as humiliating, and with an unwanted democracy in the midst of economic turmoil. For example, publicist Edgar Julius Jung (1927) coined the term 'reign of the unworthy' (*Herrschaft der Minderwertigen*) for the racial and moral decay he observed in 1920s Germany. Many contemporaries called for eugenics to enhance the biological substance of the *Volk*, the so-called *Aufnordnung*, and for a return to an authoritarian regime to resolve the perceived crisis of modernity (Peukert 1987; Raphael 2001). Another, equally important aspect is that the young republic channelled funds into groundwork research on race and population studies to prevent the feared demographic disaster. Money came from the national funding agency, the *Notgemeinschaft der Deutschen Wissenschaft*, later the German Science Foundation (Cottebrune 2008). Together with the activism of human scientists interested in race research – for instance, resulting in the publication of the standard work on heredity and eugenics, the *Grundriß der menschlichen Erblichkeitslehre und Eugenik* by Erwin Baur, Eugen Fischer, and Fritz Lenz in 1921 – this greatly facilitated the foundation of race hygiene as an academic discipline (Baur, Fischer, and Lenz 1921; Fangerau 2001). In 1923, hygienist Fritz Lenz became the first chair in the new field at Munich University, and in 1927 the influential Kaiser Wilhelm Institute for Human Heredity Sciences and Eugenics in Berlin (*Kaiser Wilhelm Institut für Anthropologie, menschliche Erblehre und Eugenik*, KWI-A) was founded which quickly developed into another key institution of academic race science.

At the same time, racial anthropologist Hans Friedrich Karl Günther fiercely advocated the alleged superiority of the 'Nordic race' through a couple of bestsellers, soon to be found in almost every household: the *Rassenkunde des deutschen Volkes* (1922) and *Kleine Rassenkunde des deutschen Volkes* (1928) argued that the value of the 'Nordic race' consisted in the outward appearance, genetic predisposition, and mental qualities of its members (Günther 1927, 1929, 1930, 1933). This strand of 'Nordic racism' was readily embraced by Heinrich Himmler, since 1929 chief of the Protective Squads (*Schutzstaffeln*, SS), originally the Nazi Party's security forces, and adapted for the purposes of his 'Nordic order'. In his crucial marriage order, the *Verlobungs- und Heiratsbefehl der SS, SS-Befehl A Nr. 65* of December 31, 1931, Himmler declared the SS 'an association of predominantly Nordic men', selected in a specific procedure (Heinemann 2003, 50–62). SS members not only had to trace back their ancestry well into the eighteenth century (back to the year 1750 for SS officers, to the year 1800 for the rank and file) to prove their 'Aryan' descent, but also needed to apply for a marriage licence when wanting to marry. Permission depended on the results of racial examinations for both groom and bride, issued by the Race Office of the SS, part of the later Race and Settlement Main Office (*Rasse- und Siedlungshauptamt*, RuSHA). Thus, by tying the idea of the SS as an elitist order to a precise racial selection procedure, Himmler conceived of the SS as a model for the attempted reconstruction of German society during the 1930s and of the occupied territories during the Second World War.

30.4   Everyday Life: Assessing the Social Through Biological Categories

When the National Socialists rose to political power in 1933, they immediately started to access and transform the social sphere with the help of biological categories, understood as the 'biologization of the social' (*Biologisierung des Gesellschaftlichen*) through a series of race laws (Herbert 1990). Thus, the race paradigm – envisioned by Hitler in *Mein Kampf* and scientifically elaborated by the scholars of the KWI-A (Eugen Fischer, Fritz Lenz, and Otmar Freiherr von Verschuer) as well as a group of race scientists from the University of Jena (the notorious Hans F. K. Günther, geneticist Karl Astel, and biologists Viktor Franz and Gerhard Herberer) – became the official guideline of politics, understood as an ostensibly modern blend of current trends in racial biology, anthropology, genetics, and eugenics (Schmuhl and Hagner 2003; Hossfeld 2005). Scholars enthusiastically welcomed the new research possibilities and funding options offered by the new regime, which made racial sciences one of its top funding priorities and eagerly contributed to the fundamental race laws passed during the formative phase of the Nazi state. For example, psychiatrist and eugenicist Ernst Rüdin of the Kaiser Wilhelm Institute for Psychiatry in Munich, and since 1932 also president of the International Federation of Eugenic Organizations (Kühl 2013), helped to draft the Eugenic Law of 14 July 1933 (*Gesetz zur Verhütung erbkranken Nachwuchses*). This core document of Nazi race theory was based on a draft model law concerning the 'voluntary sterilization' of the 'hereditarily unfit' from 1932. It declared that patients suffering from various psychological and bodily defects considered hereditary (such as 'feeble-mindedness, schizophrenia, and epilepsy' as well as inherited deafness or blindness, and 'bodily deformation'), but also socio-pathologies (such as 'severe alcoholism'), could be sterilized not only on request of the patients themselves, but also of doctors, clinic directors, and legal guardians. It thus legitimized the forced sterilization of about 400 000 people during the Third Reich.

Other laws, like the 'Law for the Restoration of the Professional Civil Service' (*Gesetz zur Wiederherstellung des Berufsbeamtentums*) of 7 April 1933 or the 'Land Heritage Law' (*Reichserbhofgesetz*) of 29 September 1933, explicitly tied an acid antisemitism to the promise of enhancing the well-being of 'Aryan' farmers and civil servants. While the first law entailed mass lay-offs and repression of people of 'non-Aryan' descent in the public sector, the second declared the peasantry to be the German people's 'blood source'. It requested an extended race certificate (*Ariernachweis*) from German farmers while their estates were transformed into privileged *Erbhöfe* (for the underlying theory of the connection between blood and soil, see Darré 1930).

When Hitler signed into law the notorious Nuremberg Laws on 15 September 1935, the *Reichsbürgergesetz* and especially the *Gesetz zum Schutze des deutschen Blutes und der deutschen Ehre* served to legitimize the complete exclusion of Jews from the German *Volksgemeinschaft* ('people's community'). The *Erste Verordnung zum Reichsbürgergesetz* of 14 November 1935, finally provided a definition of the term 'Jew'. 'Jews' were either 'the descendants of at least three racially Jewish grandparents' or the 'mixed-bloods descending of two Jewish grandparents'. Thus, while referring to the concept of 'race', the law relied on religious affiliation in the first place when defining who counted as Jew. Although the laws had been drafted mainly by state officials from the Reich Ministries of Justice, Health, and the Interior, the scholars from the KWI-A, as well as individual scholars and party institutions, either publicly approved the discriminatory legislation, or else assisted by issuing the requested racial-biological hereditary certificates (Essner 2002). Taken together, the Nuremberg Laws established antisemitic race theory as the official guideline of the regime and laid the normative groundwork for the expulsion and annihilation of German Jewry in the years to come.

30.5   Racial Policies: Euthanasia, Ethnic Cleansing, Holocaust

After the formative phase of National Socialism had brought about a wealth of race legislation in the years 1933 and 1934, the consolidation period from 1935 to 1938 mainly centred on the segregation and exclusion of the Jews from the German ethnic community. Also, in 1935 the 'Law for the Protection of the Hereditary Health of the German People' (*Gesetz zum Schutz der Erbgesundheit des deutschen Volkes*) was passed, ordering marriage bans for individuals suffering from hereditary defects and mental illnesses (an intentionally vague definition that covered a vast number of people). At the same time, the pressure on individuals considered sick or socially 'abnormal' was heightened through official propaganda, the practice of forced sterilizations (since 1933), and legalized abortions on 'eugenic grounds' (since 1935: *Gesetz zur Änderung des Gesetzes zur Verhütung erbkranken*

Nachwuchses). Official discourse linked the aspects of 'racial purity' and public finances to the detriment of those considered 'unwanted'. Particularly, the standard argument of Nazi eugenics balanced the high cost of care for the infirm and sick with their allegedly non-existent economic performance, and denounced the 'sentimental humanism' that had characterized Weimar social policies.

Current research has argued that there was no inevitable link from Nazi eugenics to euthanasia – the mass killing of the mentally handicapped and infirm that took place from 1939 under the code name *Aktion T4* (Schmuhl 1987; Roelcke 2010). Nevertheless, many eugenicists readily embraced the killing of the 'unworthy' as the ultimate step of population control under the conditions of war. Also, they considered it a crucial element of racial policies. Starting with the registration of handicapped children and the 'children's euthanasia' (*Kindereuthanasie*), the government-ordered killing of institution inmates developed in summer 1939. The next crucial step was Hitler's informal order to Philipp Bouhler, head of the Chancellery of the Führer (*Kanzlei des Führers*), and his chief physician, Dr Karl Brandt, in October 1939. The letter, which Hitler dated back to 1 September 1939, authorized Bouhler and Brandt to oversee the killing of 'the terminally ill', cynically termed 'mercy death'. Since 1940, the central administration of the euthanasia killings was located in Tiergartenstraße 4, Berlin, thus earning the code name *Aktion T4* (Aly 1987). During the years 1940 and 1941, about 70 000 patients were sent to six major killing centres (Grafeneck, Brandenburg, Bernburg, Hartheim, Sonnenstein, Hadamar) and killed in gas chambers with the help of carbon monoxide. In August 1941, escalating unrest in the German population due to protests by family members and the representatives of the churches enforced a formal stop of the *Aktion T4*. Nevertheless, killings continued in a decentralized way, either through hunger and neglect or injections of lethal drugs. About 30 000 patients fell prey to so-called wild euthanasia. Also, the murder of infirm concentration camp prisoners (*Aktion 14f13*) was continued until the end of the war, with a death toll of about 20 000 (Süß 2003; Rotzoll et al. 2010; Schmuhl 2010; Aly 2013).

Once the war began, the prospect of a more comprehensive 'racial purification' – first of the German people and then the occupied countries – arose. In October 1939 Hitler had announced, in a crucial speech in the Reichstag, a 'reordering of ethnographical conditions' in Eastern Europe, which he placed in the hands of Himmler. The first and central element of the planned wide-ranging Germanization of the occupied territories was the complete exclusion of the Jews – first through deportation (plans ranging from 'reservations' in Nisko or Madagaskar and the use of central Poland as a 'dumping ground' for the unwanted to deportation to Siberia) and finally through annihilation (mass killings started in summer 1941, mass murder in gas wagons and extermination camps at the end of 1941). Although the genocide developed as a continuous radicalization process in the course of the war in the East (Longerich 2010; Browning 2004), Hitler and Himmler could count on a vast range of German scholars willing to elaborate the theoretical foundations of such an endeavour – among them, many race scientists. For example, Otto Reche, anthropologist and ethnologist at Leipzig University, was the director of the Institute for Race Research and Ethnology (*Institut für Rassen- und*

Völkerkunde) and member of the SS. At the end of September 1939, just after the defeat of Poland, Reche proposed 'Guidelines for the Ethno-political Reconstruction of the East' (*Leitsätze zur bevölkerungspolitischen Sicherung des deutschen Ostens*) that relied heavily on the category of race: He argued that the majority of the inhabitants of the newly annexed territories were 'racially' (as well as according to their character, intellect, and physical capacity) completely unsuitable for assimilation into the German *Volk* and 'people's body' (*Volkskörper*). According to the race scholar, it was the task of the racial anthropologist to decide which persons would make a favourable addition to the population. Reche continued: 'Above all, the Jews and Jewish mixed breeds [*Judenmischlinge*] ... need to be removed as soon as possible' (Reche 1939). This statement highlights how the discursive connection between 'racial value' and 'expulsion of the unwanted' had already become currency in academic circles.

As Reche had foreseen, the annihilation of the European Jews figured as the cornerstone of the diverse Germanization plans for occupied Europe elaborated by the SS Planning Office under agrarian scientist and Berlin university professor Konrad Meyer, thus adding momentum to the radicalization of mass murder. Starting with the 'Guidelines for the Reconstruction of the New German Eastern Territories' (*Planungsgrundlagen für den Aufbau der neuen Ostgebiete*) of 1940, all such plans had to be considered fundamentally racialized concepts. The crucial General Plan East (*Generalplan Ost*) of 1942, and fragments of the General Settlement Plan (*Generalsiedlungsplan*) for Eastern Europe and some territories of the West of 1942/1943 displayed a blunt racism when proposing the reduction of the Slavic population of Eastern Europe by millions – without even mentioning Eastern European Jewry, whose fate seemed sealed in any case (Heinemann 2003; Strippel 2011; Fiebrandt 2014).

However, the creation of a 'greater Europe under German command', as Himmler put it, meant more than just killing Jews and Slavs; it also claimed a 'positive' side: the incorporation of carefully selected 'racially valuable' ethnic Germans and non-Germans into the ethnic community. Since the outset of the war, academically trained race experts of the RuSHA worked out a racial selection procedure for ethnic Germans and non-German civilians modelled after the SS selection proper, thus fragmenting entire populations into groups of different 'racial value'. Here, one of Reche's students, the anthropologist Bruno Kurt Schultz, played a key role. As chief of the RuSHA's Race Office, Schultz coordinated the racial screenings and trained the racial examiners involved, thus further enhancing the position of biological racism in SS-directed population policies. In total, the RuSHA oversaw the racial screening of at least 1.2 million ethnic Germans and another 1.5 million non-Germans during the war – besides 1 million members of the SS and the Waffen SS and about 240 000 SS brides (Heinemann 2003).

When Reinhard Heydrich and Adolf Eichmann discussed the 'Final Solution' with high-ranking government officials and representatives of the SS, police, and occupation bureaucracies during the Wannsee Conference of 21 January 1942, the participants (among them RuSHA chief, Otto Hofmann) were also concerned with the question of 'racial purity'. Besides demonstrating their principal consent to mass murder and outdoing themselves on where to start the killing, they also debated the need for a 'final solution of the question of Jewish mixed-breeds' (*Endlösung der Judenmischlingsfrage*). Diverse suggestions for the treatment of *Mischlinge* came up, ranging from forced sterilization to racial screening and 'voluntary' sterilization to deportation. The willingness to eradicate (or assimilate after racial examination) even those considered of mixed ancestry again highlights the radical character of official Nazi racism that sought for an all-encompassing 'final solution of the Jewish problem'.

In the course of the war, the idea of a coherent Germanization and occupation policy based on the premises of race was challenged in many ways: party institutions like the Racial Office of the Nazi Party (*Rassenpolitisches Amt*), Himmler's SS, and the district chiefs (*Gauleiter*) of the occupied regions debated diverging definitions of race, especially regarding the registration of ethnic Germans into the German People's List (*Deutsche Volksliste*) (Szejnmann and Umbach 2012; Wolf 2012). German soldiers engaged in relationships with Slavic women, thus directly violating orders that sought to preserve the purity of German blood (Mühlhäuser 2010). These practices nevertheless did not challenge the racist paradigm of the Nazi state in general. On the contrary, the contingencies of racism served as an argument for the continuous radicalization of racial policies directed against those deemed 'racially unwanted', underscored by the mass murder of the European Jewry, the mass violence directed at the civilian population in the East, and the treatment of forced labourers.

The exploitation of about 10 million civilians and prisoners of war as forced labourers in the Reich and the occupied countries primarily served the economic benefit and war effort of the Reich (Herbert 2013). But it also followed a deeply racialist rationale: due to National Socialist ideology, people of 'Germanic origin' (*Germanen*) were considered superior to those of 'alien blood' (*Fremdvölkische*) and thus were accorded better treatment and remuneration for their work. Poles especially (having to wear a purple 'P' on their clothing) and slave labourers from the Soviet Union (declared *Ostarbeiter*, having to wear the blue 'OST'), faced dire working and living conditions and received little or no compensation for their work. Fraternization or sexual relations with Germans were strictly forbidden for racist reasons and severely punished – usually with the killing of the male 'delinquent' and imprisonment of the German woman. Only when SS race experts testified that the forced labourer and the German woman involved (most cases reported referred to pregnancies of German women) qualified as 'wanted population addition', due to their 'racial value', was persecution stopped (Herbert 1997; Spoerer 2001). Recent studies have pointed out the crucial entanglement of racism and utilitarian motives in the whole system of forced labour and have hinted at the European-wide dimensions of the phenomenon which are still largely unexplored (Wagner 2014; Pohl and Sebta 2013).

30.6 Conclusion: An Extremely Racist Society

Unlike their European counterparts that weighed the benefits of interventionist population policies comprising eugenics and forced sterilizations of the 'unwanted' and pro-natalist measures for the 'wanted' in the first half of the twentieth century,

National Socialist Germany must be considered an extremely racist society. Five factors underscore this claim. First, a fierce biological racism was propagated as official ideology of the ruling party and quickly implemented by a host of discriminatory legislation in the formative phase of the regime. No other country saw such a speedy and comprehensive reordering of its social sphere due to biological categories of 'racial worth' and 'unworth' that permeated even the daily routines of the population. Interestingly, it was not only the ruling elite around Hitler, Himmler, and others that subscribed to this paradigm shift, but also large parts of the German population who were ready to find their place in the new 'ethnic community' under creation. The enthusiasm of young university-educated academics, born around the year 1900 and having experienced the dire effects of the 1919 defeat, greatly helped to establish race science at German universities and to conceive of new, previously 'unthinkable' applications that broke with traditional morals.

Second, an aggressive antisemitism helped to single out one narrowly defined group as definitely 'other', the Jews. Experts sought to trace them with the help of modern race science, statistics, and early forms of computer technology. This seemingly rational, scientific, modern antisemitism incorporated older strands of cultural and religious antisemitism, which made it attractive even to a broader public. Although the definition of who should be considered a 'Jew', in the course of the Nuremberg Laws, had to draw on the religious affiliation of the grandparents as a central reference category, the explicit intent was racialist – the 'protection of German blood'.

Third, when eugenic ideals became political guidelines, this had an integrative effect on the creation of a German 'ethnic community'. While the right (or duty) to reproduce depended on the successful proof of racial fitness, hereditary health, and proper conduct, this also emphasized a positive sense of belonging to the chosen 'people's community'. At the same time, it also instilled a feeling of vulnerability and insecurity among Germans not (yet) targeted by the negative measures that further reduced the chance of outright opposition or critique.

Fourth, as recent scholarship has shown, 'race' did not stand in opposition to other basic tenets of the regime like 'economic exploitation of the occupied countries', 'territorial expansion', and the quest for 'total dominance'. On the contrary, the different discursive fields could be smoothly integrated and linked by referring to the concepts of 'racial worth' and 'racial purity': People of the occupied countries, slave labourers, and even the inhabitants of a greater Europe destined for German domination were classified into race groups and treated differently according to their ascribed racial value.

Finally, when Germany decided to start a ruthless war of expansion, this was presented as a legitimate fight for racial purity and more living space from the outset. Obviously, the war situation facilitated the use of extreme violence towards non-combatants and seemed to create the need for even more radical 'solutions'. Also, euthanasia, mass killings, and finally genocide only became conceivable and feasible under the conditions of war. But if one wants to explain why millions of Germans – decision makers, soldiers, policemen, doctors, civilians, bystanders, eyewitnesses – readily renounced the basic human principles of human dignity and equal rights vis-à-vis the killing of handicapped children, the mass starvation of Soviet 'subhumans', and, of course, the mass murder of the European Jews, one cannot escape the pervasive effects of the 'race' paradigm. Because of its modern, all-encompassing, and relatively flexible character, 'race' needs to be considered one of the central integrating principles of the National Socialist state – if not *the* guiding concept.

References

Aly, Götz, ed. 1987. *Aktion T4: 1939–1945: Die 'Euthanasie'-Zentrale in der Tiergartenstraße.* Berlin: Edition Hentrich.

Aly, Götz. 2013. *Die Belasteten. 'Euthanasie' 1939–1945: Eine Gesellschaftsgeschichte.* Frankfurt am Main: Fischer.

Baur, Erwin, Fischer, Eugen, and Lenz, Fritz. 1921. *Grundriss der menschlichen Erblichkeitslehre und Rassenhygiene.* 2 vols. Munich: Lehmann.

Black, Edwin. 2004. *War Against the Weak: Eugenics and America's Campaign to Create a Master Race.* New York: Thunder's Mouth Press.

Bland, Lucy and Hall, Lesley A. 2010. 'Eugenics in Britain: The View from the Metropole.' In *Oxford Handbook of the History of Eugenics,* edited by Alison Bashford and Philippa Levine, 213–227. Oxford: Oxford University Press.

Browning, Christopher. 2004. *The Origins of the Final Solution: The Evolution of Nazi Jewish Policy, September 1939 – March 1942.* Lincoln: University of Nebraska Press.

Burleigh, Michael and Wippermann, Wolfgang, eds. 1991. *The Racial State: Germany 1933–1945.* Cambridge: Cambridge University Press.

Chamberlain, Houston Stewart. 1899. *Die Grundlagen des 19. Jahrhunderts.* 2 vols. Munich: Bruckmann.

Cottebrune, Anne. 2008. *Der planbare Mensch: Die Deutsche Forschungsgemeinschaft und die menschliche Vererbungswissenschaft, 1920–1970.* Stuttgart: Steiner.

Darré, Richard Walther. 1930. *Neuadel aus Blut und Boden.* Munich: Lehmann.

Darwin, Charles. 1859. *On the Origin of Species by Means of Natural Selection, or the Preservation of Favoured Races in the Struggle for Life.* London: John Murray.

Darwin, Charles. 1871. *Descent of Man, and Selection in Relation to Sex.* London: John Murray.

Essner, Cornelia. 2002. *Die 'Nürnberger Gesetze' oder die Verwaltung des Rassenwahns 1933–1945.* Paderborn: Schöningh.

Fangerau, Heiner. 2001. *Etablierung eines rassenhygienischen Standardwerkes 1921–1941: Der Baur-Fischer-Lenz im Spiegel der zeitgenössischen Rezensionsliteratur.* Frankfurt am Main: Peter Lang.

Fiebrandt, Maria. 2014. *Auslese für die Siedlergesellschaft: Die Einbeziehung Volksdeutscher in die NS-Erbgesundheitspolitik im Kontext der Umsiedlungen, 1939–1945.* Göttingen: Vandenhoeck & Ruprecht.

Fogarty, Richard and Osborne, Michael A. 2010. 'Eugenics in France and the Colonies.' In *Oxford Handbook of the History of Eugenics,* edited by Alison Bashford and Philippa Levine, 332–346. Oxford: Oxford University Press.

Galton, Francis. 1883. *Inquiries into Human Faculty and Its Development.* London: Macmillan and Co.

Galton, Francis. 1902. 'The Possible Improvement of the Human Breed under the Existing Conditions of Law and Sentiment, Huxley Lecture at the Royal Anthropological Institute 1901.' In *Annual Report of the Board of Regents of the Smithsonian Institution,* 523–538. Washington, DC: Government Printing Office.

Geulen, Christian. 2014. *Geschichte des Rassismus*, 2nd, rev. edn. Munich: C.H. Beck.

Gobineau, Arthur Compte de. 1898. *Versuch über die Ungleichheit der Menschenracen*. Stuttgart: Fr. Frommans Verlag (*Essay sur l'inégalité des races humaines*, 1st edn 1853–1855).

Gosney, Ezra Seymour and Popenoe, Paul B. 1929. *Sterilization for Human Betterment: A Summary of Results of 6,000 Operations in California, 1909–1929*. New York: Macmillan.

Günther, Hans F.K. 1927. *Der nordische Gedanke unter den Deutschen*. Munich: Lehmann. First published 1925.

Günther, Hans F.K. 1929. *Kleine Rassenkunde des deutschen Volkes*. Munich: Lehmann. First published 1928.

Günther, Hans F.K. 1930. *Rassenkunde des jüdischen Volkes*. Munich: Lehmann.

Günther, Hans F.K. 1933. *Rassenkunde des deutschen Volkes*. Munich: Lehmann. First published 1922.

Hartmann, Christian et al., eds. 2016. *Hitler, Mein Kampf. Eine kritische Edition*. 2 vols. Munich: Oldenbourg.

Heinemann, Isabel. 2003. *'Rasse, Siedlung, deutsches Blut': Das Rasse- und Siedlungshauptamt der SS und die rassenpolitische Neuordnung Europas*. Göttingen: Wallstein.

Herbert, Ulrich. 1990. 'Traditionen des Rassismus.' In *Bürgerliche Gesellschaft in Deutschland: Historische Einblicke, Fragen, Perspektiven*, edited by Lutz Niethammer, 472–488. Frankfurt am Main: Fischer.

Herbert, Ulrich. 1997. *Hitler's Foreign Workers: Enforced Foreign Labour in Germany Under the Third Reich*. Cambridge: Cambridge University Press.

Herbert, Ulrich. 2013. 'Zwangsarbeit im 20. Jahrhundert: Begriffe, Entwicklung, Definitionen.' In *Zwangsarbeit in Hitlers Europa: Besatzung – Arbeit – Folge*, edited by Dieter Pohl and Tanja Sebta, 23–36. Berlin: Metropol.

Hossfeld, Uwe. 2005. *Geschichte der biologischen Anthropologie in Deutschland: Von den Anfängen bis in die Nachkriegszeit*. Stuttgart: Steiner.

Jung, Edgar Julius. 1927. *Die Herrschaft der Minderwertigen: Ihr Zerfall und ihre Ablösung*. Berlin: Deutsche Rundschau.

Kevles, Daniel J. 2001. *In the Name of Eugenics: Genetics and the Uses of Human Heredity*. Cambridge, MA: Harvard University Press.

Kline, Wendy. 2001. *Building a Better Race: Gender, Sexuality, and Eugenics from the Turn of the Century to the Baby Boom*. Berkeley: University of California Press.

Kluchin, Rebecca. 2011. *Fit to Be Tied: Sterilization and Reproductive Rights in America, 1950–1980*. New Brunswick and London: Rutgers.

Kühl, Stefan. 1994. *The Nazi Connection: Eugenics, American Racism, and National Socialism*. New York: Oxford University Press.

Kühl, Stefan. 2013. *For the Betterment of the Race: The Rise and Fall of the International Movement for Eugenics and Racial Hygiene*. New York: Palgrave Macmillan.

'Leitsätze der Deutschen Gesellschaft für Rassenhygiene'. 1922. *Archiv für Rassen- und Gesellschaftsbiologie* 14, 372–375.

Lombardo, Paul A. 2003. 'Taking Eugenics Seriously: Three Generations of Imbeciles Are Enough.' *Florida State University Law Review* 30, 191–218.

Longerich, Peter. 2010. *Holocaust: The Nazi Persecution and Murder of the Jews*. Oxford: Oxford University Press.

Merriam-Webster. 2017. 'Racism.' http://www.merriam-webster.com/dictionary/racism (accessed 24 November 2017).

Mühlhäuser, Regina. 2010. *Eroberungen: Sexuelle Gewalttaten und intime Beziehungen deutscher Soldaten in der Sowjetunion, 1941–1945*. Hamburg: Hamburger Edition.

Peukert, Detlef. 1987. *Weimarer Republik: Krisenjahre der Klassischen Moderne*. Frankfurt am Main: Suhrkamp.

Ploetz, Alfred. 1895. *Die Tüchtigkeit unserer Rasse und der Schutz der Schwachen: Ein Versuch über Rassenhygiene und ihr Verhältnis zu den humanen Idealen, besonders zum Socialismus.* Berlin: Fischer.

Pohl, Dieter and Sebta, Tanja, eds. 2013. *Zwangsarbeit in Hitlers Europa: Besatzung – Arbeit – Folge.* Berlin: Metropol.

Popenoe, Paul B. 1934. 'The German Sterilization Law.' *Journal of Heredity* 25, 257–260.

Popenoe, Paul B. and Gosney, Ezra Seymour. 1930. *Sterilisierung zum Zwecke der Aufbesserung des Menschengeschlechts.* Berlin: A. Marcus & E. Weber's Verlag.

Popenoe, Paul B. and Johnson, Roswell Hill. 1918. *Applied Eugenics.* New York: The Macmillan Company.

Raphael, Lutz. 2001. 'Radikales Ordnungsdenken und die Organisation totalitärer Herrschaft: Weltanschauungseliten und Humanwissenschaftler im NS-Regime.' In *Geschichte und Gesellschaft* 27, 5–40.

Reche, Otto. 1939. 'Leitsätze zu bevölkerungspolitischen Sicherung des deutschen Ostens.' In *Der 'Generalplan Ost': Leitlinien der nationalsozialistischen der nationalsozialistischen Planungs- und Vernichtungspolitik,* edited by Mechthild Rössler and Sabine Schleiermacher, 351–355. Berlin: Akademie-Verlag.

Roelcke, Volker. 2010. 'Deutscher Sonderweg? Die eugenische Bewegung in europäischer Perspektive bis in die 1930er Jahre.' In *Die nationalsozialistische 'Euthanasie'-Aktion 'T4' und ihre Opfer: Geschichte und ethische Konsequenzen für die Gegenwart,* edited by Maike Rotzoll et al., 47–55. Paderborn: Schöningh.

Rotzoll, Maike et al., eds. 2010. *Die nationalsozialistische 'Euthanasie'-Aktion 'T4' und ihre Opfer: Geschichte und ethische Konsequenzen für die Gegenwart.* Paderborn: Schöningh.

Schallmayer, Wilhelm. 1903. *Vererbung und Auslese im Lebenslauf der Völker.* Jena: Fischer.

Schmuhl, Hans-Walther. 1987. *Rassenhygiene, Nationalsozialismus, Euthanasie: Von der Verhütung zur Vernichtung „lebensunwerten Lebens", 1890–1945.* Göttingen: Vandenhoeck & Ruprecht.

Schmuhl, Hans-Walter. 2010. 'Die Genesis der "Euthanasie": Interpretationsansätze.' In *Die nationalsozialistische 'Euthanasie'-Aktion 'T4' und ihre Opfer: Geschichte und ethische Konsequenzen für die Gegenwart,* edited by Maike Rotzoll et al., 66–73. Paderborn: Schöningh.

Schmuhl, Hans-Walter and Hagner, Michael, eds. 2003. *Rassenforschung an Kaiser-Wilhelm-Instituten vor und nach 1933.* Göttingen: Wallstein.

Schneider, William. 1982. 'Toward the Improvement of the Human Race: The History of Eugenics in France.' *Journal of Modern History* 54, 268–291. doi: 10.1086/244134.

Schneider, William. 1990. *Quality and Quantity: The Quest for Biological Regeneration in Twentieth-Century France.* Cambridge: Cambridge University Press.

Schoen, Johanna. 2005. *Choice and Coercion: Birth Control, Sterilization and Abortion in Public Health and Welfare.* Chapel Hill: University of North Carolina Press.

Sonn, Richard. 2005. '"Your Body is Yours": Anarchism, Birth Control and Eugenics in Interwar France.' *Journal of the History of Sexuality* 14, 415–432. doi: 10.1353/sex.2006.0045.

Spoerer, Mark. 2001. *Zwangsarbeit unter dem Hakenkreuz: Ausländische Zivilarbeiter, Kriegsgefangene und Häftlinge im Deutschen Reich und im besetzten Europa 1939–1945.* Munich: DVA.

Stern, Alexandra Minna. 2005. *Eugenic Nation: Faults and Frontiers of Better Breeding in Modern America.* Berkeley: University of California Press.

Strippel, Andreas. 2011. *NS-Volkstumspolitik und die Neuordnung Europas: Rassenpolitische Selektion der Einwandererzentralstelle des Chefs der Sicherheitspolizei und des SD, 1939–1945.* Paderborn: Schöningh.

Süß, Winfried. 2003. *Der 'Volkskörper' im Krieg: Gesundheitspolitik, Gesundheitsverhältnisse und Krankenmord im nationalsozialistischen Deutschland, 1939–1945.* Munich: Oldenbourg.

Szejnmann, Claus-Christian W. and Umbach, Maiken. 2012. *Heimat, Region, and Empire: Spatial Identities under National Socialism.* Basingstoke, UK: Palgrave McMillan.

Tyrell, Albrecht. 1969. *Führer befiehl … Selbstzeugnisse aus der 'Kampfzeit' der NSDAP.* Düsseldorf: Droste.

Wagner, Jens-Christian. 2014. 'Arbeit und Vernichtung im Nationalsozialismus: Ökonomische Sachzwänge und das ideologische Projekt des Massenmords.' *Einsicht* 12, 20–27.

Wilson, Philip K. 2002. 'Harry Laughlin's Eugenic Crusade to Control the "Socially Inadequate" in Progressive Era America.' *Patterns of Prejudice* 36, 49–67. doi: 10.1080/0031322202128811367.

Wolf, Gerhard. 2012. *Ideologie und Herrschaftsrationalität: nationalsozialistische Germanisierungspolitik in Polen.* Hamburg: Hamburger Edition.

Further Reading

Bancel, Nicolas, David, Thomas, and Thomas, Dominic, eds. 2014. *The Invention of Race: Scientific and Popular Representations.* New York: Routledge.
This volume provides an indispensable overview of the international roots of modern racism, recounting the history of racial classification since the eighteenth century as well as the institutionalization of racial anthropology during the nineteenth century and the development of anthropological exhibitions in the early twentieth century.

Etzemüller, Thomas. 2015. *Auf der Suche nach dem Nordischen Menschen: Die deutsche Rassenanthropologie in der modernen Welt.* Bielefeld: transcript.
This recent study recounts the origins of German racial anthropology, concentrating on the new science's main protagonists and the techniques employed.

Friedländer, Saul. 1997–2007. *Nazi Germany and the Jews, Volume 1: The Years of Persecution, 1933–1939, Volume 2: The Years of Extermination: Nazi Germany and the Jews, 1939–1945.* New York: HarperCollins.
Friedländer's masterful works give a perfect example of how racism permeated everyday life in Nazi Germany. He uses a wealth of sources and especially focuses on the victims' perspective.

Geulen, Christian. 2004. *Wahlverwandte: Rassendiskurs und Nationalismus im späten 19. Jahrhundert.* Hamburg: Hamburger Edition.
Standard work on the nineteenth-century roots of contemporary racist movements.

Hannaford, Ivan. 1996. *Race: The History of an Idea in the West.* Baltimore, MD: Johns Hopkins University Press.
This volume offers a thorough study of the origins of racial thinking in the nineteenth century.

Harten, Hans-Christian, Neirich, Uwe, and Schwerendt, Matthias, eds. 2006. *Rassenhygiene als Erziehungsideologie des Dritten Reiches: Bio-bibliographisches Handbuch.* Berlin: Akademie Verlag.
State-of-the art overview of the Third Reich's racial hygienicist movement; also contains biographical sketches of the leading protagonists.

Oxford Handbook of the History of Eugenics. 2010. Edited by Alison Bashford and Philippa Levine. Oxford: Oxford University Press.
This compendium provides an indispensable overview on the eugenic movements of the twentieth century in international comparison.

Schmuhl, Hans-Walther. 1987. *Rassenhygiene, Nationalsozialismus, Euthanasie: Von der Verhütung zur Vernichtung „lebensunwerten Lebens', 1890–1945.* Göttingen: Vandenhoeck & Ruprecht.
This monograph is an absolute standard work on the history of racial science and policies in Germany by one of the most eminent specialists in the field.
Weindling, Paul. 1989. *Health, Race and German Politics between National Unification and Nazism, 1870–1945.* Cambridge: Cambridge University Press.
Focusing roughly on the same time frame as Schmuhl, this book by another doyen of the history of racism and Nazi medicine provides indispensable information on the transformation of racism into Nazi racial policies and its consequences.
Weiss-Wendt, Anton and Yeomans, Rory, eds. 2013. *Racial Science in Hitler's New Europe 1938–1945.* Lincoln: Nebraska University Press.
This volume focuses on the European dimensions of racial science and scientific racism – a valuable addition to the abovementioned literature that mostly focuses on Germany alone.

CHAPTER THIRTY-ONE

Unfree and Forced Labour*

MARC BUGGELN

31.1 Forced Labour Until 1933: German Practices and International Debates

In the nineteenth century, a labour society based on free and market-related gainful employment gradually emerged as a mass phenomenon. Liberals in particular considered labour a contribution of all free citizens to the betterment of the nation. They saw all negative outcomes as transitional and expected them to disappear as society progressed (Conze 1972). Ironically, this optimistic concept of labour produced its opposite concept, forced labour. Although socialists and communists were more ambivalent about free wage labour, along with liberals they opposed most forms of coercion. Some conservative critics of the emerging liberal labour relations, on the other hand, considered forced labour useful. They believed in a hierarchical natural or divine order according to which the lower classes had to do hard manual work because they lacked other skills and, where necessary, could be forced to do so. Although in a *völkisch* community forced labour supposedly no longer existed since all labour was regarded as 'honourable service for the people', for many conservatives, forced labour was still an option for inhabitants of defeated countries.

During the First World War these theoretical considerations gained practical significance. Almost all belligerent nations used prisoners of war (POWs) as forced labourers even though most of them complied with international law. In Germany, around 1.4 out of 1.6 million POWs carried out forced labour. Moreover, since the beginning of the war the government of the German Reich had prevented 300 000 Polish seasonal workers from returning to their home country and extended their contracts by force. In addition, the civil administration of German-occupied Poland

---

* Translated by Christine Brocks.

A Companion to Nazi Germany, First Edition. Edited by Shelley Baranowski, Armin Nolzen, and Claus-Christian W. Szejnmann.
© 2018 John Wiley & Sons Ltd. Published 2018 by John Wiley & Sons Ltd.

recruited 120 000 Poles to work in Germany and prohibited their return. Because more and more of these workers fled Germany, in 1916 the government expanded the free movement of labour and allowed home leave. They also recruited a work-force in Western Europe. Until October 1916, 30 000 Belgians were mobilized to work in Germany. After October 1916, authorities implemented forced labour in Western Europe because of Germany's substantial labour shortage. About 61 000 Belgians were brought to Germany as forced labourers, and at least 900 of them died due to atrocious living and working conditions, which caused a wave of indignation in the Allied media and confirmed the image of Germans as barbarians. The media's coverage brought efforts to transport more civilian forced labourers to Germany to a halt. However, the local populations of the occupied territories were often, violently, forced to work in their home countries.

Recent research agrees that the Nazis predominantly built on the German experience from the First World War rather than on colonial forced labour. Whereas the international media strongly criticized German politics in this respect, only left-wing parties in Germany expressed moral concerns. The right wing assessed forced labour overall as an economic failure, but only because it had not been comprehensive enough. General Ludendorff, in particular, argued along these lines in his memoirs, which Adolf Hitler praised as an important source of inspiration. Thus, the essential lesson the Nazis drew from the use of forced labour during the First World War was to be more ruthless and violent in the next war (Thiel and Westerhoff 2014).

Because of the First World War, the advocates of forced labour were criticized. In the 1920s, the liberal concept of freedom of work became an international legal standard. The deportation of Belgian workers to Germany was declared a war crime in the Peace Treaty of Paris. On the international level, the establishment of the League of Nations and the International Labour Organization (ILO) banned all forms of coerced labour. Reports of colonial incidents contributed to a stronger focus within the ILO on banning forced labour, and finally to the adoption of the Forced Labour Convention (Miers 2003, 134).

Thus, the notion of forced labour found its way into the international legal sphere through this convention, which it defined as involuntary labour or labour extracted through the threat of punishment. Although it provided for exceptions for colonial states, the convention stipulated a maximum period of two months a year and wages paid according to local custom. Forced labour in coal mining and underground and as collective punishment was banned under all circumstances. Thus, international law accepted that the local population of a colony or an occupied territory was forced to work even though it included more and more restrictions during the inter-war period. The ILO did not accept the deportation of civilians and foreign nationals into the occupying country as forced labourers.

The Convention Relative to the Treatment of Prisoners of War, issued on 27 July 1929 in Geneva, regulated some aspects of forced labour in wartime. According to this agreement, it was legal to use POWs as forced labourers as long as the detaining power provided proper maintenance, medical treatment, and payment. It did not allow the employment of POWs in the production and transport of arms. Also, 'conditions of work shall not be rendered more arduous by disciplinary measures'. The duration of the workday should 'in no case exceed that permitted for civil workers', and a day of rest was to be provided. POWs were entitled to a payment according to local rates and costs for board and lodging could be deducted (Convention 1929; Segesser 2010, 282–294). Thus, employment of POWs was unfree labour, yet considered compulsory rather than forced labour. The term 'forced labour' applies only when the regulations of the abovementioned convention are no longer followed.

31.2   Unfree Work in Germany, 1933–1939

In 1933 when the Nazis assumed power, unemployment was high in Germany (Buggeln 2014b). Thus, extended compulsory work programmes for the German population – in particular the expansion of the Reich Labour Service – initially aimed to decrease the unemployment rate. The fact that these compulsory services were not abolished but expanded after a drop in unemployment shows that the Nazis considered them not just as an emergency measure (Humann 2011). Instead, they were to train the German youth in the spirit of manual work for the community, the counter-image of Jewish 'individualistic' work. Also, the Nazis restricted the working conditions of German employees in many other ways even before the beginning of the war, for instance by implementing the workbook (*Arbeitsbuch*), which made job changes difficult.

Forced labour relations first occurred in concentration camps. Initially, work in the camps was primarily intended to terrorize the inmates. However, gradually economic motives came to the fore, which mainly aimed at expanding the concentration camp system at low cost by using inmates as forced labourers. After full employment in Germany was achieved, the inmates' workforce gained more importance. In 1938, the SS (*Schutzstaffel*) covenanted to deliver stones for Albert Speer, the General Building Inspector of the Reich Capital (*Generalbauinspekteur für die Reichshauptstadt*), and his gigantic architectural plans. As a result, new concentration camps were established in the vicinity of quarries, and brick factories were built in several camps. This was the first step in economizing the forced labour of inmates (Buggeln 2014a, 12–14; Wachsmann 2015, 157–170).

From 1936, unemployed Jews could be obliged to do unpaid work. The decree of the Institute for Labour Exchange and Unemployment Insurance of 20 December 1938 on the 'deployment of unemployed Jews, segregated from non-Jewish workers', did not mention any applicable measures, but was more a threat to force emigration than to ensure a significant contribution to the German economy (Gruner 2006, 3–8). Only when the war had started did the German authorities begin to press a larger number of Jewish people into forced labour.

31.3   Unfree and Forced Labour in the German Reich, 1939–1945

The closer the war came, the more the political leadership and Supreme Command of the Armed Forces became convinced that remedying labour shortages required state control. At the war's outset, a decree restricted job changes and allowed compulsory work. Labour exchange offices put 1.3 million people temporarily into compulsory work during the first few months of the war. However, this and other regulations such as pay cuts and lengthening the workday created substantial popular resentment. For this reason, and because the bottlenecks eased, the authorities retracted these measures to a large extent. From then on, they rarely took coercive action against German labourers. They were equally cautious when it came to German women, abstaining from compulsory measures to increase an already large female workforce (Kroener 2000, 846–940).

Instead, German authorities recruited foreign workers in order to reduce labour shortages. Before the outbreak of war, they drafted Italian workers who staffed newly established industries. Polish migrant workers still played a significant role for Germany's agriculture. Despite Polish POWs being deported to Germany as forced labourers, representatives of industry and agriculture demanded the recruitment of Polish civilian workers. Yet, the Reich Security Main Office (*Reichssicherheitshauptamt*, RSHA) in particular aimed to outsource low-skilled work to the occupied territories and to restrict the number of Polish workers entering the Reich. By the end of 1939, the RSHA had withdrawn its resistance, but introduced special racial legislation for Polish workers in March 1940: Poles were required to wear a special badge; they were no longer allowed to use public transport and frequent pubs or inns; and sexual relationships with German women would incur the death penalty. In May 1940, around 1.2 million POWs and foreign civilian workers were deployed in the German Reich, 700 000 of whom worked in agriculture. After military victories in the west, approximately 1.2 million French POWs followed, by late 1940. Like the Polish prisoners, many of whom were released and deployed as civilian labourers, the French POWs mainly worked in agriculture (54% by the end of 1940), but also in the industrial and construction industry (23%). Until the attack on the Soviet Union, the Nazi regime of forced labour in Europe was predominantly characterized by ad hoc initiatives, despite three million foreign nationals who worked in the German Reich. These foreign labourers mainly had jobs in the agriculture and construction sectors which required hard physical labour and were shunned by German workers (Herbert 1997, 61–135).

The attack on the Soviet Union was the key caesura of German labour politics during the war. Only in the autumn of 1941, when the blitzkrieg stalled, did labour shortages become a constant severe problem for the German economy. Until November 1941, Nazi authorities had planned to deploy Soviets as workers in the German Reich instead of releasing German soldiers from the front to work in the armaments industry. The entire organization of the war economy was to be centralized under the recently established Reich Ministry for Armaments and War Production, headed by Albert Speer, and the likewise newly appointed Fritz Sauckel (*Gauleiter* of Thuringia) as General Plenipotentiary for Labour Deployment (*Generalbevollmächtigter für den Arbeitseinsatz*, GBA). Sauckel's stated objective was to recruit masses of foreign workers for the German armaments industry within a very short time. Initially, foreign workers were supposed to come to Germany voluntarily, but the coercive methods of the recruiting staff dramatically reduced the number of volunteers. Thus, the Germans began forced recruitment. Sauckel's staff brought 2.7 million workers into the Reich during the first eight months of his campaign. Most of them were from the occupied territories of the Soviet Union, who as 'Eastern workers' (*Ostarbeiter*) faced even tighter racial regulations than Polish forced labourers (Herbert 1997, 137–204).

The foreign civilian workers made the most significant contribution to German war production. Apart from them, Soviet POWs were also brought into the Reich (in general, see Streit 1978). In the prisoner-of-war camps in the Reich, the SS selected all detainees who were supposed to be 'intolerable elements' – roughly 40 000 of them were killed by the SS in one camp. An even larger number of prisoners was transferred to a concentration camp as a result of escape or sabotage, without being directly killed (Keller 2008). Yet even they, who were not 'selected' by the SS, suffered terrible conditions. On Reich territory, 227 000 Soviet POWs died between mid-July 1941 and mid-April 1942: that was roughly half of the prisoners who were brought into the Reich up to that point (Keller 2011, 436). However, in the course of 1942 it became necessary to adapt to economic necessities. As a consequence, the Supreme Command of the Wehrmacht gradually improved the food supplies of Soviet POWs from March 1942 which, albeit very slowly, reduced the mortality rate.

Moreover, in March 1942 Speer and Himmler agreed that henceforth concentration camp inmates should be deployed in the armaments industry. Initially they planned to relocate industrial facilities inside the main camps, but in September 1942 Hitler decided, after a conversation with Speer, that the SS should establish sub-camps near production facilities. As a result, a network of more than 1000 sub-camps emerged and the SS increased the number of inmates from nearly 100 000 in 1942 to more than 700 000 by January 1945. At the same meeting in September 1942, Sauckel assured Hitler that the influx of civilian workers would remain high and thus German Jews were not needed as workers in the armaments industry. This was the death sentence for a large majority of German Jews who had worked in the armaments industry since the beginning of the war. During the next six months, they were deported to extermination camps (Buggeln 2014a, 18–21).

By 1940, another camp system was being developed in order to improve workplace discipline. The first *Arbeitserziehungslager* (re-education work camps) were built under the cooperation of Gestapo, local authorities, and industries. The objective of these camps was to discipline reluctant or defiant workers through hard forced labour, low food provision, and violence. In contrast to concentration camps, the detention period was limited to eight weeks, so that the often wrecked and haggard people could return to their previous workplace. Thus, they would again be available as workers for their employers while simultaneously having been served a warning (Lotfi 2000).

In so doing, the key coordinates of the forced labour system in the Reich were established by late summer 1942. Given the difficult military situation and the need to expand armaments production, the authorities involved were predominantly concerned with maintaining the influx of forced labourers. Initially they succeeded: between May 1942 and May 1943, two million forced labourers were brought to Germany. To a much larger extent than before (from 745 000 to 1.2 million) these workers were brought to Germany from Western European countries. Yet the majority of forced labourers still came from the occupied territories of the Soviet Union. Their number increased during the same period of time from 1.1 million to 1.8 million (Herbert 1997, 273–282). Whereas Italy's capitulation came as a shock to the German leadership, it was an lucky strike for the Sauckel office since 600 000 Italian POWs were deported to Germany, which nearly met the economy's demand for workers.

After spring 1944, the opportunity to bring more forced labourers into Germany decreased significantly due to the Wehrmacht's retreat from all fronts. Also, from summer 1944, more and more forced labourers fled and tried to survive on their own in the bombed cities. In the Reich, reports of lootings increased and resulted in a drastic tightening of repression. From early November 1944, the RSHA allowed the Gestapo to execute 'Eastern workers' and Poles at their own discretion. This decree was extended to Western European forced workers in spring 1945. As a result, the Gestapo increasingly conducted mass executions of forced labourers on site. Even some ordinary Germans took the law in their own hands by killing apprehended forced workers. In many places, the violence of the Gestapo during the last days before Germany was conquered turned into a killing spree against forced labourers, which only Allied troops could prevent by occupying German territory (Herbert 1997, 359–381). When the German forced labour system reached its peak in late 1944, 6 million foreign civilians (Table 31.1), about 2.2 million POWs, and 700, 000 concentration camp inmates contributed as forced labourers to the German war economy, alongside 23 million German workers. Thus roughly 30% of the workforce consisted of foreign nationals. Germany not only took possession of a large resource worth approximately 27 billion Reichsmark, but was also responsible for the forced displacement of masses of foreign workers into the German Reich, which was one of the most destructive aspects of the war for their home countries (Klemann and Kudryashov 2012, 162).

Table 31.1 Foreign civilian workers in the German Reich 1939–1945 according to countries of origin.

	Number on 30 Sept 1944	Thereof women in %	Total number 1939–1945	Survivors mid-1945
Belgium	199 437	14.7	375 000	365 000
France	646 421	6.6	1 050 000	1 015 000
Italy	287 347	7.8	960 000	940 000
Netherlands	254,544	8.2	475 000	465 000
Poland	1 375 817	34.4	1 600 000	1 470 000
Soviet Union	2 461 163	49.3	2 775 000	2 525 000
Czechoslovakia	276 340	16.1	355 000	330 000
Others	475 604	–	845 000	835 000
Total	5 976 673	16.5	8 435 000	7 945 000

Source: Spoerer (2001, 222). © 2001, Deutsche Verlags-Anstalt, in der Verlagsgruppe Random House GmbH, Munich.

31.4   Unfree Labour and Different Chances of Survival: Forced Labourers in Germany

Mark Spoerer has pointed out that the common classification of forced labourers into three main groups (foreign civilian workers, POWs, and inmates) has to be differentiated further because there were substantial differences within these three groups. He defines 'exit, voice and probability of survival' as criteria (Spoerer 2001, 15–16). Following Mark Spoerer and Jochen Fleischhacker (2002), I distinguish different groups of workers in the German Reich since the beginning of the war according to their living and working conditions (Table 31.2). Spoerer and

Table 31.2   Situation of different groups of workers in the German Reich, 1939–1945.

	Free		Unfree		
		Compulsory work	Forced work		
			Forced work	Slave work	Slave work with high mortality rate
Germans					
German wage earner	X				
DP, LH, PJ, AD		X			
prison inmates			X		
German-Jewish forced labour				X	
Foreign civilian workers					
Slovakia & Croatia	X				
Italy	X			X (since Sept. 1943)	
Western Europe	X		X (since 1941/1942)		
Serbia & Baltic States			X		
Poland & Soviet Union				X	
Prisoners of war					
France		X			
Great Britain & USA		X			
Serbia		X			
Poland				X	
Italy				X	
Soviet Union				X (since 1944)	X
Inmates					
Concentration camps					X
AEL inmates					X

Note: DP = *Dienstpflicht* (compulsory service); LH = *Landhilfe* (rural support); PJ = *Pflichtjahr* (mandatory year); AD = *Arbeitsdienst* (Reich Labour Service); AEL = *Arbeitserziehungslager* (re-education work camps).

Fleischhacker have calculated that foreign nationals in the first three columns had a 1–2% probability of dying due to their labour deployment in Germany. For slave labourers, in comparison, this figure amounted to 10%, and for slave labourers with a high mortality rate, to 60% (2002, 196).

In what follows I will only discuss the situation of the forced and slave labourers, pointing out the reasons for the substantial differences in living conditions between forced labourers from Western and Eastern Europe. This was already apparent in the way they were accommodated. Whereas forced labourers from Western European countries were accommodated in private households, Soviet forced labourers exclusively lived in camps, which initially were surrounded by fencing and watched by armed guards. However, due to the negative effects on the labourers' will to work, these measures were soon abandoned. Still the authorities crowded Eastern Europeans into less space than Western Europeans. Also, food rations for Eastern European workers were initially much smaller. Only when this affected their work performance were portions gradually adjusted. However, the amount of food rations for Eastern European workers depended on their performance.

Western European forced labourers were paid the same as German workers. Thanks to a separation allowance, they could in some cases earn more than their equally ranked German colleagues. Workers from Eastern Europe, on the other hand, paid a special tax deducted from their wages, even though authorities had more leeway by the end of the war. Whereas Western Europeans were allowed to visit cultural events, Eastern Europeans had no opportunity to participate in cultural life apart from some themed nights in the camps specially arranged for them. All in all, forced labourers from Western Europe, as long as they were not suspected of escape, shirking, or sabotage, could live their lives without being in acute danger and with some humble cultural entertainment, despite repression and harassment. Eastern European forced labourers did not have this opportunity (Spoerer 2001, 116–143). Particularly in 1942, the life of a Soviet forced labourer resembled that of a slave who was hardly allowed the basic necessities. Towards the end of the war, the conditions of Eastern European forced labourers improved slowly, but they never approached those of the workers from Western Europe. The Nazi leadership maintained the racially segregated work society that it had created up to the end of the war.

31.5 German Companies and German Population

Companies and employers had considerable leeway regarding the deployment of forced labourers. The Nazi regime determined the outlines, but within this framework German business was marked by huge differences. In some companies the percentage of foreign nationals was 10%, in others it was more than 50%. Also, employers had a certain amount of choice; there were many Soviet POWs working in the Ruhr mining industry, for example, because they were thought capable of hard work and were less likely to escape than civilian forced labourers because the military watched them (Seidel 2010, 397). The aviation industry, on the other hand, deployed concentration camp inmates early on (from Heinkel and

Oranienburg camps), because they were the most inexpensive, unfree workers and seemed able to meet the low requirements of assembly line work.

In general, companies submitted their requests for all sorts of forced labourers directly to the authorities. They did so because there was a shortage of German workers and because they wanted to maintain or expand their production capacity. Since low capacity equalled losses and almost every expansion resulted in additional profits, given the high demand on commodities during the war, the deployment of forced labourers was always profitable. It is, however, controversial whether it was more profitable than the deployment of German workers. Recent research predominantly holds the view that this was often not the case, because gross wages paid to forced labourers were only a little less than those paid to German workers and the difference was usually levelled by a lower productivity (for a seminal discussion, see Spoerer 2001, 183–189).

Regulations regarding the treatment of foreign forced workers laid down by German companies were usually general in nature and left considerable scope for action for the middle and lower management. Thus, working conditions could vary between different departments of the same company depending on whether or not the workshop master was a racist, a disciplinarian, or a performance fanatic. In this respect, the companies mirrored German society, since various courses of action were open. In some places, militias watched and abused foreign forced labourers, and in others the relationship between foreigners and Germans was based on a mutual give and take. Friendships could even develop. It is difficult to systematize the different types of action due to their diversity and the heterogeneous source material. Even though Nazi security authorities considered friendly contact between Germans and foreigners a potential risk, there was never a realistic security threat. There is hardly any evidence of protests against the harsh treatment of forced labourers and only very few resistance groups that had Germans and foreigners working together. Thus, it was mostly no more than a friendly attitude and presents given by a few Germans that remained the only positive memory of the foreigners. On the other side of the spectrum were those Germans who had internalized the Nazi concept of the 'master race' (*Herrenrasse*) and thought all foreigners inferior. Very often, fierce protests by the local Nazi Party leadership attacked forced labourers – even those from Western Europe – for attending bars, cinemas, or swimming pools and talking in their native language. By the end of the war racism had become even more hysterical and culminated, in some places, in incidents where ordinary Germans participated in mass violence and mass killings of foreigners (Plato, Leh, and Thonfeld 2010; Lemmes 2010a, 407–412).

31.6   The Situation in the Occupied Territories

The current advanced state of data and research allows us to define and differentiate the conditions for the almost 30 million workers in the German Reich in detail. However, this does not apply to the occupied territories. Karl Heinz Roth and Jan-Peter Abraham assume that roughly 36 million people had to work as unfree labourers in the German occupied territories (2011, 455). In the occupied the Soviet Union alone, more than 22 million Soviet citizens worked for the German occupiers, because as early as in August 1941 the Reich Minister for the Occupied Eastern Territories introduced a 'labour obligation' (*Arbeitspflicht*) for all inhabitants between 18 and 45 years old and a 'labour compulsion' (*Arbeitszwang*) for Jews aged 14 to 60 (Penter 2004, 66).

In general, it is necessary to examine labour deployment in connection with the occupation policy that served as its framework (Binner 2011; Lemmes 2010a, 444). German occupation policy was based on how Nazi racial ideology ranked the population of the respective country. In terms of a very rough geographical classification, Northern Europeans were likely to be treated less badly than those from Western Europe. The situation was far worse for Southeastern Europeans, whereas Eastern Europeans ranked at the bottom of the Nazi hierarchy. A second important factor determining Nazi policy in the occupied territories was the economic significance of the respective country. The more crucial a territory's resources to the war effort, the more directly did the Germans interfere, even though they were, at the same time, reluctant to reorganize the existing economic structures for fear of weakening production. There is hardly any comparative research on how this framework affected the people in the occupied territories. Investigating labour deployment policies would be a promising field of research, since almost everyone in the occupied territories was faced with the consequences of Nazi labour politics. However, even though working conditions are a good way to explore the history of everyday life, we should recognize that forced labour was not always the greatest danger for Eastern Europeans (Binner 2011, 73). Rather, they feared hunger and starvation, prohibitive rules, harsh exemplary punishments, and mass murder. In what follows, I will first examine labour deployment in Western Europe, using France as an example, and compare this with deployment in the occupied territories of the Soviet Union.

31.7 Unfree Labour in Occupied Western Europe

Similar to the occupied territories of the Soviet Union, a general labour obligation was introduced in almost all those in Western and Northern Europe, albeit not before 1942. The historiography focuses almost exclusively on the potential of the labour obligation for the recruitment of forced civilian workers for Germany, but often ignored the possibilities of control it offered in the occupied territories (Lemmes 2010b, 236). In Northern and Western Europe, labour obligation resembled that in Germany and often had similar effects. Average wages and food supplies were similar to those of the pre-war period. The coercive enforcement of the labour obligation remained an exception until 1943, but increased significantly from that date, especially in France. There were also considerable differences between Western European countries. Natalie Piquet (2008) has shown that the working conditions of Belgian labourers improved compared to their colleagues in France, because French entrepreneurs collaborated with the German occupiers on a larger scale. The status of the Soviet and Serb POWs was completely different, as well as that of Ukrainian civilian workers, 15 000 in total, who were deported from Germany to the collieries in northern France and Belgium. They received lower wages and food rations than similar workers deployed in the Reich, but because they were more likely to be supported by Belgian and French miners they were sometimes better off than their fellows in Germany (Piquet 2008).

Construction workers for the Todt Organization (*Organisation Todt*, OT) suffered far worse conditions than the miners in France. Fabian Lemmes shows that although the OT could mobilize some voluntary French workers between 1940 and 1942 by offering high wages, this changed at the turn of the year 1942/1943. Wages were reduced and more and more workers were recruited by force. Additionally, the military commander in November 1942 prohibited French construction workers from leaving the sites on the coast, which would prevent them from attempting to escape (Lemmes 2010b, 237). To counteract the increasing number of escape attempts, the OT started to place the workers in camps fenced with barbed wire and heavily guarded. However, French workers still received local pay rates and received adequate food. These conditions mainly applied to French employees, who in 1944 accounted for less than a third of the workers deployed at the OT in France. The workforce of 300 000 labourers comprised 15 000 Germans, 85 000 French, 25 000 people from the French colonies, and 165 000 foreign civilian workers (Lemmes 2010b, 227).

Yet working conditions got worse from spring 1943, not only in the construction industry. More and more forced deportations to Germany, and constantly decreasing real wages due to inflation, resulted in strikes, absenteeism, and other forms of resistance. The German occupiers and the Vichy regime responded by tightening working conditions, which from 1944 became increasingly compulsory, not just in the construction industry but in other industries as well (Zielinski 1995, 176–190).

31.8   Unfree Labour in Occupied Eastern Europe

In Eastern Europe, the situation for the local population who were deployed to work was far worse right from the outset. Apart from concentration and re-education work camps, which were also known in Germany, there was also slave labour in ghettos and camps with civilian Jewish forced labourers – for instance, the Schmelt Organization (Hensel and Lehnstaedt 2013; Gruner 2006). The Nazis also established camps for Soviet POWs with even more dreadful conditions than in camps on Reich territory (Plath 2012, 346–368). The term 'slave labour with high mortality' is arguably appropriate to characterize these camps and ghettos.

However, I want to discuss the working conditions of the majority of the non-Jewish Eastern European civilians. Rainer Karlsch has investigated the employees of the Carpathian Oil Company (Karpathen-Öl AG), who were comparatively privileged, and has concluded that working conditions there should be characterized as 'unfree labour under a brutal occupation regime' instead of 'forced labor' (2004, 12). Also privileged – even though not to the same extent as the Galician oil workers – were the miners of the Donets Basin. In both cases, the labourers' relatively good situation was because the German occupiers were in dire need of workers for the production of indispensable resources. Therefore, they received wages above the national average and were comparatively well provided with food, even though workers in the Ukraine were considerably worse off than those in Poland

528   MARC BUGGELN

(Penter 2010). Both groups can be seen as positive exceptions, with clearly better working and living conditions than the majority of the population (for the General Government, see Linne 2013).

Different again were in the steelworks in the Ukraine operated by the Flick group and the *Reichswerke Hermann Göring*. Since skilled workers had been evacuated by the Soviet army, there was a shortage of suitable workers from the outset. The problems were aggravated when during the winter of 1941/1942 large numbers from the cities fled for the countryside for lack of food. When, in 1942, the plants were to be rebooted, the recruitment of workers competed with the Sauckel department. Thus, the steelworks prioritized force and violence instead of high wages from the beginning (Priemel 2007, 499–502).

The construction industry was even more prone to forced labour than the steel sector. The OT paved the way for the deployment of forced labour on a large scale in the Baltic states (Dieckmann 2011, 678–679) and Belarus. The organization established fenced labour and punishing labour camps with particularly harsh conditions. It deployed both prisoners and Soviet POWs. In one OT plant, 3000 persons 'suspected of partisan activities', including old men, children, and women, were forced to work under the watch of the *Sonderkommando* 7b. Given these findings, Christian Gerlach concludes: 'The men of the OT turned into true experts of forced labour deployment' (Gerlach 1999, 418).

The majority of people in the occupied Soviet Union were deployed neither in production nor construction industries, but in agriculture. In the Reichskommissariat Ukraine, 6.1 million (81%) out of 7.5 million employees worked in agriculture (Penter 2004, 71). Karel C. Berkhoff has shown that Ukrainian farmers had more food available during the German occupation than in the Soviet period (Berkhoff 1998, 93–143). If they did not reach their target, they had to face the same severe punishment as urban 'shirkers', but since the occupiers were more present in the cities, the level of repression remained lower (Penter 2004, 79).

On the other hand, Roth and Abraham (2011) have shown that in the Crimean this lenient practice was by no means true everywhere. They emphasize that at the beginning of the occupation the starvation policy of the Wehrmacht and German administration was radically enforced, so that soon people died from hunger. This course of action, however, aimed at a state of chronic malnutrition that allowed survival instead of starvation. The occupiers used the threat of starvation to enforce their labour deployment policy. Receiving ration cards was made conditional on reporting to the employment office, which effectively registered almost the entire potential workforce. In addition, the military police, albeit sparsely manned, hunted down those who did not report to the authorities or refused to work. In autumn 1942, this procedure reached its limit. The deportation of large numbers of the population to Germany as forced labourers caused a substantial worker shortage in Crimea. More and more Crimeans escaped and hid in the countryside, making the shortage of workers even worse. The German administration tried to solve the problem by giving out wages in kind instead of money. Because of inflation, wages were no longer sufficient to buy food, so employers increased the attractiveness of the jobs they offered and the will to work by handing out sumptuous meals (Roth and Abraham 2011, 177–194).

Roth and Abraham thus conclude that in the Crimea the occupiers' measures, such as 'the general obligation of residency and registration, the linkage of the immediate survival to the readiness to work, abolishing the freedom of movement, compulsory job placement and the ban on associations', plus harsh exemplary punishment, added up so that 'all fundamental criteria of the definition of "forced labour" are fulfilled' (Roth and Abraham 2011, 359).

31.9   Analytical Categories and Individual Assessment

Not only according to the criteria Roth and Abraham have mentioned but also based on the Forced Labour Convention which applied at the time, working conditions in Crimea predominantly have to be seen as forced labour. The same is true for the vast majority of workers in the occupied Eastern and Southeastern European countries. In France, on the other hand, forced labour was in place only in some areas and not before the final phase of the war. And yet, for two reasons, there are some scholars who do not regard working conditions in Eastern and Southeastern Europe as forced labour. First, rather than basing their studies on the Forced Labour Convention, some researchers adopt the wording of the German reparations debate that uses the term 'forced labour' only in cases when the people involved were recruited by force, barracked, and constantly watched at their workplace (Pohl 2010, 203). In so doing, many civilian forced workers in the occupied territories were denied compensation after the reparation negotiations. Second, some scholars following the approaches of Oral History and the History of Everyday Life draw on self-definitions and descriptions of the people involved. Accordingly, forced labour is only applicable if the interviewees themselves use that term. Tanja Penter, for instance, emphasizes that the miners from Donbass did not consider themselves as forced labourers under German occupation, not least because their working conditions resembled those during Soviet times so that the term 'forced labour' does not apply (Penter 2010, 227–9).

However, this makes little sense for a general assessment. It would mean that working conditions in France had to be called 'forced labour', because the majority of French workers were accustomed to free labour conditions and considered their new status as coercive. Conditions in the occupied Soviet Union, on the other hand, were not regarded as such even though they were far worse than in Western Europe, only because Soviets did not share the same prior experiences as French people did. Having said this, the self-descriptions of those involved are far from irrelevant for the historiography. Quite the contrary, the self-perception of the protagonists was crucial for their course of action.

31.10   Desiderata

Research on forced labour is by now quite advanced. A substantial number of local studies and single companies in the German Reich have been published. There are research gaps mainly on some basic questions and some economic areas. Thus, research is needed predominantly on the construction industry and housekeeping. Also, research has focused less on female forced workers who, in contrast to the

First World War, were brought to Germany in high numbers – therefore, gender relations have gained in importance. Despite a plethora of studies on individual companies, there is still little data on wage groups, special wage payments, and the labour productivity of different groups of forced labourers. Much has happened since 10 years ago when unfree working conditions in the occupied territories still were a terra incognita. Despite these pioneer studies, there is still further need for research on almost all occupied countries.

References

Binner, Jens. 2011. 'NS-Besatzungspolitik und Zwangsarbeit: Ideologie und Herrschaftspraxis.' *Zeitschrift für Weltgeschichte* 12, 67–90. doi: 10.3726/84534_67.

Berkhoff, Karel C. 1998. 'Hitler's Clean State: Everday life in the Reichskommisariat Ukraine 1941–44'. PhD thesis, Toronto.

Buggeln, Marc. 2014a. *Slave Labor in Nazi Concentration Camps.* Oxford: Oxford University Press.

Buggeln, Marc. 2014b. 'Unfreie Arbeit im Nationalsozialismus.' In *Arbeit im Nationalsozialismus,* edited by Marc Buggeln and Michael Wildt, 231–252. Munich: Oldenbourg.

Convention Relative to the Treatment of Prisoners of War. 1929. www.icrc.org/ihl.nsf/52 d68d14de6160e0c12563da005fdb1b/eb1571b00daec90ec125641e00402aa6 (accessed 25 November 2017).

Conze, Werner. 1972. 'Arbeit.' In *Geschichtliche Grundbegriffe*, edited by Otto Brunner, Werner Conze, and Reinhart Koselleck, Vol. 1, 154–215 Stuttgart: Klett-Cotta.

Dieckmann, Christoph. 2011. *Deutsche Besatzungspolitik in Litauen 1941–1944.* 2 vols. Göttingen: Wallstein.

Gerlach, Christian. 1999. *Kalkulierte Morde: Die deutsche Wirtschafts- und Vernichtungspolitik in Weißrußland 1941 bis 1944.* Hamburg: Hamburger Edition.

Gruner, Wolf. 2006. *Jewish Forced Labour Under the Nazis: Economic Needs and Racial Aims, 1938–1944.* Cambridge: Cambridge University Press.

Hensel, Jürgen and Lehnstaedt, Stephan, eds. 2013. *Arbeit in den nationalsozialistischen Ghettos.* Oldenburg: fibre.

Herbert, Ulrich. 1997. *Hitler's Foreign Workers: Enforced Foreign Labour in Germany Under the Third Reich.* Cambridge: Cambridge University Press.

Humann, Detlev. 2011. *'Arbeitsschlacht': Arbeitsbeschaffung und Propaganda in der NS-Zeit 1933–1939.* Göttingen: Wallstein.

Karlsch, Rainer. 2004. 'Ein vergessenes Großunternehmen: Die Geschichte der Karpaten Öl AG.' *Jahrbuch für Wirtschaftsgeschichte* 1, 95–138.

Keller, Rolf. 2008. 'Sowjetische Kriegsgefangene in Konzentrationslagern der SS.' In *Einvernehmliche Zusammenarbeit? Wehrmacht, Gestapo, SS und sowjetische Kriegsgefangene,* edited by Johannes Ibel, 15–43. Berlin: Metropol.

Keller, Rolf. 2011. *Sowjetische Kriegsgefangene im Deutschen Reich 1941/42: Behandlung und Arbeitseinsatz zwischen Vernichtungspolitik und kriegswirtschaftlichen Zwängen.* Göttingen: Wallstein.

Klemann, Hein and Kudryashov, Sergei. 2012. *Occupied Economies: An Economic History of Nazi-Occupied Europe, 1939–1945.* London: Berg.

Kroener, Bernhard R. 2000. 'The Manpower Resources of the Third Reich in the Area of Conflict between Wehrmacht, Bureaucracy, and War Economy, 1939–1942.' In *Germany and the Second World War,* vol. V, pt. I, edited by the Militärgeschichtliches Forschungsamt, 787–1154. Oxford: Clarendon Press.

Lemmes, Fabian. 2010a. '"Ausländereinsatz" und Zwangsarbeit im Ersten und Zweiten Weltkrieg: neuere Forschungen und Ansätze.' *Archiv für Sozialgeschichte* 50, 395–444.

Lemmes, Fabian. 2010b. 'Zwangsarbeit im besetzten Europa: Die Organisation Todt in Frankreich und Italien, 1940–1945.' In *Rüstung, Kriegswirtschaft und Zwangsarbeit im 'Dritten Reich'*, edited by Andreas Heusler, Mark Spoerer, and Helmut Trischler, 219–252. Munich: Oldenbourg.

Linne, Karsten. 2013. '"Sklavenjagden" im Arbeiterreservoir – das Beispiel Generalgouvernement.' In *Pflicht, Zwang und Gewalt. Arbeitsverwaltungen und Arbeitskräftepolitik im deutsch besetzten Polen und Serbien 1939–1944*, edited by Florian Dierl, Zoran Janjetovic, and Karsten Linne, 171–316. Essen: Klartext.

Lotfi, Gabriele. 2000. *KZ der Gestapo: Arbeitserziehungslager im Dritten Reich*. Stuttgart: DVA.

Miers, Suzanne. 2003. *Slavery in the Twentieth Century: The Evolution of a Global Problem*. Walnut Creek, CA: AltaMira.

Penter, Tanja. 2004. 'Arbeiten für den Feind in der Heimat – der Arbeitseinsatz in der besetzten Ukraine 1941–1944.' *Jahrbuch für Wirtschaftsgeschichte* 1, 65–94.

Penter, Tanja. 2010. *Kohle für Stalin und Hitler: Arbeit und Leben im Donbass 1929 bis 1953*. Essen: Klartext.

Piquet, Natalie. 2008. *Charbon – Travail forcé – Collaboration: Der nordfranzösische und belgische Bergbau unter deutscher Besatzung, 1940 bis 1944*. Essen: Klartext.

Plath, Tilman. 2012. *Zwischen Schonung und Menschenjagden: Arbeitseinsatzpolitik in den baltischen Generalbezirken des Reichskommissariats Ostland 1941–1944*. Essen: Klartext.

Plato, Alexander von, Leh, Almut, and Thonfeld, Christoph, eds. 2010. *Hitler's Slaves: Life Stories of Forced Labourers in Nazi-Occupied Europe*. New York: Berghahn Books.

Pohl, Dieter. 2010. 'Zwangsarbeit im besetzten Osteuropa – ein Forschungsüberblick.' In *Zwangsarbeit: Die Deutschen, Die Zwangsarbeiter und der Krieg*, edited by Volkhard Knigge, 202–207. Weimar: Stiftung Gedenkstätten Buchenwald.

Priemel, Kim Christian. 2007. *Flick: Eine Konzerngeschichte vom Kaiserreich bis zur Bundesrepublik*. Göttingen: Wallstein.

Roth, Karl Heinz and Abraham, Jan-Peter. 2011. *Reemtsma auf der Krim: Tabakproduktion und Zwangsarbeit unter der deutschen Besatzungsherrschaft 1941–1944*. Hamburg: Nautilus.

Segesser, Daniel Marc. 2010. *Recht statt Rache oder Rache durch Recht? Die Ahndung von Kriegsverbrechen in der internationalen fachwissenschaftlichen Debatte 1872–1945*. Paderborn: Schöningh.

Seidel, Hans-Christoph. 2010. *Der Ruhrbergbau im Zweiten Weltkrieg*. Essen: Klartext.

Spoerer, Mark. 2001. *Zwangsarbeit unter dem Hakenkreuz: ausländische Zivilarbeiter, Kriegsgefangene und Häftlinge im Deutschen Reich und im besetzten Europa 1939–1945*. Stuttgart: DVA.

Spoerer, Mark and Fleischhacker, Jochen. 2002. 'Forced Laborers in Nazi Germany: Categories, Numbers, and Survivors.' *Journal of Interdisciplinary History* 33, 169–204.

Streit, Christian. 1978. *Keine Kameraden: Die Wehrmacht und die sowjetischen Kriegsgefangenen 1941–1945*. Stuttgart: DVA.

Thiel, Jens and Westerhoff, Christian. 2014. 'Forced Labour.' In *1914–1918-online. International Encyclopedia of the First World War*, edited by Ute Daniel et al., issued by FU Berlin, Berlin 2014-10-08. doi: 10.15463/ie1418.10380.

Wachsmann, Nikolaus. 2015. *KL: A History of the Nazi Concentration Camps*. New York: Farrar, Straus and Giroux.

Zielinski, Bernd. 1995. *Staatskollaboration: Vichy und der Arbeitskräfteeinsatz im Dritten Reich*. Münster: Westfälisches Dampfboot.

Further Reading

Buggeln, Marc. 2014. *Slave Labor in Nazi Concentration Camps.* Oxford: Oxford University Press.
The main study on forced labour in concentration camps.

Buggeln, Marc and Wildt, Michael, eds. 2014. *Arbeit im Nationalsozialismus.* Munich: Oldenbourg.
A collection of essays concerning labour in Nazi Germany, the last part of it on forced labour.

Gruner, Wolf. 2006. *Jewish Forced Labour Under the Nazis: Economic Needs and Racial Aims, 1938–1944.* Cambridge: Cambridge University Press.
The main study on Jewish forced labour.

Herbert, Ulrich. 1997. *Hitler's Foreign Workers: Enforced Foreign Labour in Germany Under the Third Reich.* Cambridge: Cambridge University Press.
The ground-breaking work on foreign forced labour in Germany, originally published as a PhD in German in 1985.

Lotfi, Gabriele. 2000. *KZ der Gestapo: Arbeitserziehungslager im Dritten Reich.* Stuttgart: DVA.
The main study on work education camps.

Militärgeschichtliches Forschungsamt, ed. 2000/2003. *Germany and the Second World War, Volume V: Organization and Mobilization of the German Sphere of Power* (2 parts). Oxford: Clarendon Press.
The articles of Bernhard R. Kroener are the best overview on the manpower resources of the Third Reich.

Pohl, Dieter and Sebta, Tanja, eds. 2013. *Zwangsarbeit in Hitlers Europa: Besatzung – Arbeit – Folgen.* Berlin: Metropol.
The most valuable collection of articles concerning forced labour in Nazi occupied Europe.

Spoerer, Mark. 2001. *Zwangsarbeit unter dem Hakenkreuz: ausländische Zivilarbeiter, Kriegsgefangene und Häftlinge im Deutschen Reich und im besetzten Europa 1939–1945.* Stuttgart: DVA.
The best overview on forced labour, mostly dealing with the conditions within the German Reich.

Wachsmann, Nikolaus. 2015. *Kl: A History of the Nazi Concentration Camps.* New York: Farrar, Straus and Giroux.
The best overview on the concentration camp system including an extensive discussion on camp labour.

CHAPTER THIRTY-TWO

'Ethnic Germans'

ALEXA STILLER

32.1 Introduction: The Invention of 'Ethnic Germans' (*Volksdeutsche*)

The architects of German nationalism had already coined the terms *volksdeutsch* (Ernst Moritz Arndt), *völkisch* (Johann Gottlieb Fichte), *Volksgemeinschaft* (Friedrich Schleiermacher), and German *Volkstum* (the essence of being German; Friedrich Ludwig Jahn) in the early nineteenth century.[1] Nevertheless, after the foundation of the German national state in 1871, right-wing and *völkisch* circles were still concerned with pan-German or *auslandsdeutsche* (Germans abroad) ideas, some of them in explicit opposition to the Prussian Lesser German Empire (*kleindeutsches Reich*; see Petzinna 2000, Chickering 1984). Simultaneously, there were many political and religious (Catholic and Lutheran) organizations concerned with the conservation of the German language and cultural traditions among German *Kolonisten* (which was understood by contemporaries to mean 'free farmers'), traders, and expatriates (*Auswanderer*) in the Russian Empire, the German colonies, the Americas, and beyond (O'Donnell, Bridenthal, and Reagin 2005), or, more specifically, with supporting German-speaking groups in the Habsburg Empire and the territories of East Prussia in the German Empire. The most important of these was the Association for Germandom Abroad (*Verein für das Deutschtum im Ausland*, VDA; see Weidenfeller 1976). Though all of these diverse interests in Germans abroad had existed before 1914, they had not been on the agenda of the German government. That changed with the annexations and resettlement plans of the First World War (Liulevicius 2000).

However, 'the moment of Auslandsdeutsche' (Krekeler 1973), or, better, the invention of *Volksdeutsche*, took place after the First World War, when millions of

A Companion to Nazi Germany, First Edition. Edited by Shelley Baranowski, Armin Nolzen, and Claus-Christian W. Szejnmann.
© 2018 John Wiley & Sons Ltd. Published 2018 by John Wiley & Sons Ltd.

German speakers were scattered across Europe in newly founded states. The government's policies for European German minorities changed after 1919 with the signing of the treaties of Versailles and Saint-Germain-en-Laye. The decisive factors were the independence of Austria (and, therefore, the failure of a union with Germany), the territorial losses (and the expulsions and emigrations that followed), and the subsequent plebiscites with all their struggles (which were stylized as *Abwehrkampf* or cultural defence), which reinforced the ideology of a common German *Volkstum* or *Deutschtum* from Masuria to Carinthia. Because of these changes in borders, many native German speakers migrated to Germany and Austria after November 1918, but millions stayed in the new countries (Oltmer 2005; Sammartino 2010). As a result, the German expatriates of the nineteenth century who went to the Americas fell into oblivion. German organizations no longer showed any interest in those overseas communities. In the 1920s, the *auslandsdeutsche* organizations gained political influence through the approximately six million 'ethnic Germans' living in Poland, Czechoslovakia, Hungary, Romania, Yugoslavia, Estonia, Latvia, and Lithuania (Scheuermann 2000) and the further approximately three million in Italy, France (mainly in Alsace), Belgium, Denmark, and the Soviet Union. However, it was particularly the German minorities in Central and Southeast Europe who were referred to as *Volksdeutsche* from the mid-1920s onwards.[2] The agrarian 'ethnic Germans' in the Soviet Union (the so-called Russian Germans or 'colonists') did not come into view for the German *Volkstum* organizations before the famines in the early 1930s (Mukhina 2007).

As these facts suggest, the 'ethnic Germans' were not a homogeneous group. In fact, they were not a homogeneous group even within a single country. In Poland, for example, there were more or less three different regional groups: the *Volksdeutsche* in the areas of Poland that were formerly part of Prussia; the 'ethnic Germans' in the cities of Łódź and Warsaw, who were not always considered to be real *Volksdeutsche* but, rather German-Polish or German-Jewish; and the former Russian Germans in Volhynia whom the *Volksdeutsche* of Western Poland 'orientalized' (Chu 2012, 140). The 'ethnic Germans' in Romania were also regionally differentiated. And there were class distinctions within these German minority groups, most obviously in Estonia and Latvia, where there was a German nobility, an urban middle class, and peasant labourers (most of whom were twentieth-century immigrants from Volhynia and other rural parts of Russia). The 1920s saw not only a nationalistic mobilization of the German minorities in accord with the concept of Germandom (*Deutschtum*) but also a socialist mobilization of 'ethnic German' workers, especially in Poland and Czechoslovakia. In addition to regional, political, and class distinctions, native German speakers were historically divided into Catholics and Protestants. The majority of 'ethnic Germans' in Europe were Lutheran, but among these Protestants were small groups of Methodists, Baptists, Mennonites, and so on. Thus, one may conclude that it is most likely not the case that the most important category of self-identification for all, or even most, of the estimated nine million native German speakers in Europe living outside of Germany and Austria was 'ethnic German'. Rather, German, Austrian, and *Volkstum* organizations with *völkisch*, nationalistic, and revisionist agendas invented the idea of a homogeneous European *Volksdeutsche* community through an ethnicizing process that started in the mid-1920s.

The notion of a German diaspora or a German nation or ethnic group that extended beyond the borders of Germany was already in place when the Nazis gained power. The Nazi bureaucracy only added legal definitions of *volksdeutsch* and *auslandsdeutsch*. According to their definition, the *Volksdeutsche* were all German descendants by blood and native German speakers who belonged to German minorities in Central, Southeastern, and Eastern Europe and did not have German or Austrian citizenship (Bergen 1994, 1999). *Auslandsdeutsche* were German citizens (i.e. passport holders) living abroad. Neither the term *Volksdeutsche* nor the politics of German *Volkstum* abroad were new when the Nazis came to power, but the new regime turned both into policies guiding its actions.

32.2   1933–1939: *Gleichschaltung* and Early Annexations

In 1933, all of the networks of political, cultural, scientific, and administrative organizations supporting the *Volksdeutsche* were already established; the Nazis had only to bring them into line (Krekeler 1973; Komjathy and Stockwell 1980; Grams 2001; Haar and Fahlbusch 2008). First of all, they imposed political conformity on *Auslandsdeutsche* and other *Volkstum* organizations in Germany (Jacobsen 1968, Lumans 1993). At the same time, they instituted the coordination (*Gleichschaltung*) of the European German-minority organizations beyond Germany's borders. In Poland, the *Gleichschaltung* of the leading 'ethnic German' political organizations was complete in 1933 (Chu 2012), but in Romania not before the beginning of 1939 (Milata 2007). Again, it is important to note that not all of the groups one today considers to have been German minorities were ethnically homogeneous at the time. All of them were multilingual, many were multi-religious, and some were multi-ethnic with a considerable number of intermarriages. Nor was every self-avowed German politically mobilized. Rather, what the Nazi regime did was support those political organizations within the various German minorities whose ideologies and political interests were close to their own. The large German minorities in Czechoslovakia and Poland were fragmented into several political parties. In the so-called Sudetenland, which was important to the Nazis because of the sheer number of native German speakers there (around three million), Konrad Henlein and his Sudeten-German Party (*Sudetendeutsche Partei*, SdP) attracted the assistance of the Nazi regime and maintained it from 1935 onwards (Smelser 1975; Vierling 2014). In Poland, Nazi organizations supported the aggressively anti-Polish and anti-Jewish Young German Party (*Jungdeutsche Partei*, JdP), which became the most influential German-speaking political group in Poland (Blanke 1993; Chu 2012). But Germany's incorporation of Austria was the first big test of whether the ideologies of *Volksgemeinschaft* ('people's community') and *Volkstum* would be attractive to a society not composed of only radicalized and Nazified groups.

The seizure and incorporation of territory before the outbreak of the Second World War went smoothly for the Nazi regime, and large proportions of the populations, or at least of the German minorities, in the relevant territories backed annexation. With the *Anschluss*, the whole Austrian population – except Jews – immediately acquired German citizenship. Political opponents were arrested after the invasion. In April 1938, a plebiscite on the unification resulted in over 99% of the vote being in favour of Adolf Hitler (Bukey 2000). The incorporation of the Sudetenland as a result of the Munich Agreement set up a new model: a contractually agreed upon population transfer with 'ethnic Germans' moving west and Czechs and others moving east into what was left of Czechoslovakia. However, only people with Czech, Slovakian, or Jewish backgrounds could resettle in eastern Czechoslovakia; German anti-fascists living in the Sudetenland, for example, were not allowed to leave. The Nazis initiated a political 'cleansing' policy in the Sudetenland, imprisoning thousands of social democratic and communist Sudeten Germans in concentration camps. And, as in Austria, they began to institute anti-Jewish measures. In November 1938, the Nazi pogrom against Jews occurred in both of the incorporated territories as well. One month later, in elections in the Sudetenland over 97% voted for the Nazi Party. The 'ethnic Germans' were then granted German citizenship (Zimmermann 1999). With the German invasion of the remainder of Czechoslovakia in March 1939, the majority of Czechs and other inhabitants came under Nazi rule. Despite the fact that only around 3% of the inhabitants were considered to be 'ethnic German' (Brandes 1969), Nazi propaganda spoke of the 'reintegration' (*Rückgliederung*) of Bohemia and Moravia into the German Reich. In the same month, Germany annexed the Klaipėda Region/Memel Territory (a former region of East Prussia which belonged to Lithuania at that time). On this occasion, the propaganda proclaimed the 'homecoming' (*Heimkehr*) of the Memel Territory.[3] In contrast to the population of the Protectorate of Bohemia and Moravia, over 41% of the population of the Memel territory were native German speakers (Eberhardt and Owsínski 2003). The German invasion of Prague and the subsequent occupation of the remainder of Czechoslovakia made clear that the Nazis' goals went beyond revising the treaties of Versailles and Saint-Germain-en-Laye and annexing border regions where a majority of the population was German. The German invasion of Poland in September 1939 finally made that conclusion unavoidable.

32.3   1939–1945: Population Transfers, Expulsions, Settlement, and Mass Murder

The German invasion of Poland was a new high point of mass violence. The incidents in Bydgoszcz (a Pomeranian town with a sizable German minority) on 3 and 4 September 1939, in which Polish soldiers and civilians killed between 100 and 300 *Volksdeutsche*, added to the violent dynamic. In the wake of so-called Bloody Sunday (*Blutsonntag*), the *Wehrmacht*, the *Einsatzgruppen*, and the *Volksdeutsche Selbstschutz*, a local militia, shot thousands of Polish and Jewish civilians in and around Bydgoszcz. In other regions of western Poland, the Germans persecuted and murdered Polish political opponents, hostages, Jews, and other civilians between September and December, but nowhere as many murders were committed as in Bydgoszcz. The Nazi Propaganda Ministry spun the facts, proclaiming the murder of 54 000 *Volksdeutsche* (Jansen and Weckbecker 1992; Wildt 2002;

Böhler 2006; Krzoska 2012; Stiller 2012a). Until the end of the occupation of Poland, the German authorities cited this Bloody Sunday in justifying mass violence against the Poles. Furthermore, the Nazi regime appropriated the alleged nationality conflict (*Volkstumskampf*) between the German minority and the Polish government, which had occurred in the inter-war period, and the German Reich struck back. It was clear from the outset of the subsequent relocation of 'ethnic Germans' that Poles and Jews would be expelled from annexed Poland to make room for *Volksdeutsche* (Aly 1995; Rutherford 2007: Stiller 2009).

The German and Soviet regimes arranged an exchange of populations in secret supplementary articles of the German–Soviet Treaty of Friendship, Cooperation and Demarcation, signed on 28 September 1939. In a secret protocol, the Hitler–Stalin Pact, signed on 23 August 1939, had already determined the German and Soviet 'spheres of influence', namely, the division of Poland between them, the assignment of Estonia and Latvia to the Soviet Union, and the Soviet occupation of Bessarabia. It was only at the end of the military campaign that both powers defined precise demarcation lines. Hitler had decided to relocate German minority groups only a few days before the final negotiations of the so-called Friendship Treaty in September (Kershaw 1999). The German minorities in Estonia and Latvia were the first groups permitted to immigrate to Germany. According to Erhard Kroeger, who was the leader of the *Deutsche Volksgruppe* (the politically organized and Nazified *Volksdeutsche*) in Latvia at the time, it was he who had suggested to Himmler that the entire 'ethnic German' population of both countries be relocated. Himmler, again according to Kroeger, then convinced Hitler that such resettlement was imperative; otherwise, the Baltic Germans could face deportation to Siberia (Kroeger 1967; Aly 1995). A couple of days later, the people concerned learned of the arrangement from Hitler's notorious speech on 6 October 1939.

In that speech, Hitler rationalized the German aggression against Poland as a revision of the Treaty of Versailles. However, he said, the aim of the Nazi programme was to re-establish not only the old borders but also, 'The order of the whole living space by nationalities, i.e. a solution to those minority questions that do not pertain only to this space [Poland] but also to almost all Southern and Southeastern European states.'[4] Hitler's 'new ordering' (*Neuordnung*) of populations along *völkisch* and racial lines explicitly targeted 'ethnic Germans' and Jews. He openly said that through relocations – though that also meant displacements and deportations – 'minority conflicts' would come to an end. The next day, 7 October 1939, Hitler charged Himmler, the Reichsführer-SS and Leader of the German Police, with implementing the programme for the 'strengthening of Germandom'. The decree consisted of three components: first, the removal of *Volksdeutsche* from the Soviet 'sphere of influence'; second, the 'elimination of the harmful influence of such alien parts of the population that may constitute a danger to the Reich and the *Volksgemeinschaft*'; and, third, the settlement of Germans in the 'new living space' (*Lebensraum*).[5] Henceforth, Himmler, now the Reich Commissioner for the Strengthening of Germandom (*Reichskommissar für die Festigung deutschen Volkstums*, RKF), considered himself and his apparatus, which included several independent SS agencies, to be responsible for the 'ethnic Germans' of Europe.

Most historians see this decision at the end of September 1939 to resettle German minority groups as a caesura in the German policy towards *Volksdeutsche*. However, plans for the integration of 'ethnic Germans' into the German labour force had been advanced, and already put into practice, before the outbreak of the Second World War. German economic and governmental organizations and Nazi Party organizations had explicit racial concerns about the recruitment of foreign workers. After the annexations of Austria and the Sudetenland, from where the greatest number of native German-speaking seasonal labourers in Germany before 1938 had come, Nazi authorities began secretly recruiting *Volksdeutsche* from Poland and Danzig. The SS Bureau of the *Vierjahresplan* (Four Year Plan), which SS-*Oberführer* Ulrich Greifelt headed, took the leading role in that venture. Himmler made the agency responsible for the relocation of the South Tyrolians from summer 1939 on and for the resettlement of the *Volksdeutsche* in the Greater German Reich (Germany and Austria) from October 1939 on. It was Greifelt who had first, in April 1938, raised the idea with Himmler of resettling 'ethnic German' workers to Germany. During the war, however, *Volksdeutsche* were at a premium not only as labourers but also as settlers and soldiers (Koehl 1957; Stiller 2008).

All of the German minority groups in Europe knew of Hitler's speech soon after 6 October 1939. Even though eastern Poland was the only territory occupied by the Soviet Union at that time, the relocation of 'ethnic Germans' from Latvia and Estonia had already begun by mid-October (Bosse 2001). Furthermore, the leaders of the German *Volksgruppen* in Bessarabia, Bukovina, and Dobruja proposed to Berlin the relocation of the total 'ethnic German' population from these regions (of what was at that time Romania). On the one hand, the German minority groups were anxious about the threat of Soviet annexation; on the other, each of the leaders of those groups, and many of the ordinary *Volksdeutsche*, were loyal to the Nazi regime and most were eager to emigrate to the Greater German Reich (Jachomowski 1984). Though the leaders of the *Volksdeutsche* and the RKF apparatus had no idea how to resettle half a million 'ethnic Germans' in time of war, they still did not expect the variety of problems that followed.

Hence, planning for how and where to settle the relocated *Volksdeutsche* started only when the Baltic Germans began to arrive in Danzig-West Prussia in mid-October 1939. According to Himmler's vision, they would find a new homeland in annexed western Poland, primarily in the Wartheland in the 'incorporated Eastern Territories' (*eingegliederte Ostgebiete*). This settlement was intended to constitute the first step in Germanizing the region. From the beginning, it was clear to the RKF apparatus, as well as the regional authorities, that Poles and Jews would be made to give way for the settlement of 'ethnic Germans'. But the conflicting interests of the different SS offices under the umbrella of the RKF, and of other competing agencies, and practical constraints complicated the settlement process for the RFK. In particular, more and more 'ethnic Germans' continued to show up on the doorstep of the Greater German Reich, while the authorities in the incorporated Eastern Territories were running short of housing.

Historian Götz Aly has made an important contribution to this area of research in his book *Final Solution*, where he has shown that the Nazis' destruction of European Jewry was in part the result of their broader agenda of Germanization through deportation and resettlement. Spatial planning and the transformation of Europe's population mixture, both of which Nazi scholars advocated, were certainly driving forces in the origin of the 'Final Solution' (*Endlösung*). But Aly claims that it was the early failure of the various plans for deportation and resettlement that caused the mass murder of Jews (Aly 1995). Undoubtedly, the resettlement of *Volksdeutsche* affected the dynamics of the annihilation policy. But my conclusions are that these effects were confined, more or less, to the overall ideology of German supremacy and the planning for a German 'new living space', and mass murder was not an inherent necessity of the resettlement of 'ethnic Germans'.

The RKF apparatus carried out 71% of its settlement activity in the Wartheland. By spring 1940, the Nazis had given some 62 000 Baltic Germans the former homes of Poles and Jews and also provided them jobs. Thereafter, a rural settlement programme for the 'ethnic Germans' from Volhynia and Galicia began in the Wartheland. The expulsions that followed (the so-called '2nd *Nahplan*') almost exclusively targeted Polish farming families, since the prime reason for this second wave of deportations was to 'make room' for these 'ethnic German' peasants. Between September 1939 and March 1941, the RKF apparatus expelled approximately 400 000 Poles and Jews from annexed western Poland to the General Government. By the end of 1943, the Nazis had displaced a further 200 000 Poles from the Wartheland as part of the task of settling *Volksdeutsche* from Bessarabia, Bukovina, and Dobruja there (in the course of the '3rd *Nahplan*' and '3rd extended *Nahplan*'). By the summer of 1944, the Nazis had settled about 400 000 'ethnic Germans', 320 000 of these in the Wartheland alone.

After the annexation of western Poland, Nazi Germany, following its invasion of Western Europe, annexed small border regions of Belgium, the whole of Luxembourg, and the regions of Lorraine and Alsace. The Nazis implemented there the same policy of cleansing, namely, internment or expulsion of 'undesired' individuals and groups, on the one hand, and Germanization and settlement programmes, on the other. They did the same in the annexed territory of Slovenia after the invasion of Yugoslavia in April 1941. But all of this was on a smaller scale than in western Poland. In addition, 'ethnic Germans' in occupied France could register for emigration to Germany, and the German minority in Croatian-occupied Bosnia was relocated to Germany. *Volksdeutsche* from Lithuania were the last 'ethnic German' group resettled by the RKF apparatus before the German invasion of the Soviet Union (Stiller 2009).

A new dimension of mass violence emerged with the invasion of the USSR. The *Einsatzgruppen* and other German units shot hundreds of thousands of Jews, political commissars, and Roma. Simultaneously, they had the task of registering 'ethnic Germans' and taking care of them before the Ethnic German Liaison Office (*Volksdeutsche Mittelstelle*, VoMi), an SS agency within the RKF apparatus, arrived. Persecution and mass killing of the 'undesired' and fostering of the 'desired' were two antagonistic sides of Nazi race and population policies. The *Einsatzgruppen* of the Security Police and the Security Service (*Sicherheitsdienst*, SD) had killed 535 000 people, mostly Jews, in the occupied Soviet territory by the spring of 1942 (Mallmann et al. 2011, 7–8). The total number of Jews murdered on Soviet soil by German *Einsatzgruppen* and army, police, and paramilitary units ranges from 1.38 million (Dawidowicz 1986, 403) to 2.1 million (Robel 1991, 560).[6] The death toll among the Soviet civilian population during the Second World War is estimated to be around 15.2 million, half of whom fell victim to Nazi mass violence, intentional starvation, and counter-insurgency measures (Hartmann 2011, 115–116). Simultaneously with the Nazis' annihilation policy, the VoMi looked after over 350 000 'ethnic Germans' in the occupied regions of the USSR,[7] over 400 000 when the Baltic countries are included (for Ukraine and Transnistria, see Angrick 2003; Lower 2005; Steinhart 2015; for the Crimea, see Kunz 2005; for Lithuania, see Stossun 1993; Dieckmann 2011.)

However, the Nazis never incorporated the majority of Russian Germans into their resettlement scheme because, following the German invasion, the Supreme Soviet declared that all 'ethnic Germans' were collaborators and abolished the Volga German Autonomous Soviet Socialist Republic on 28 August 1941. Approximately 700 000 'ethnic Germans' were deported to the Kazakh SSR and Siberia (Pinkus and Fleischhauer 1987, 311–112), including around 33 500 'ethnic German' soldiers from the Red Army (Mukhina 2007). As with Bloody Sunday in Poland, the Nazis used the violence against 'ethnic Germans' to rationalize their mass violence against Soviet civilians. Western European Jews also became caught up in these events. A couple of days before the Soviets actually deported the 'ethnic Germans', Alfred Rosenberg had asked Hitler to allow the radio broadcast of propaganda bluntly promising that if the Soviets deported the Volga Germans east, then the Nazis would deport Western European Jews to 'their' east, namely, the occupied Soviet territories (Gerlach 1999, 749), which they in fact did. The systematic deportation of Jews from Germany and Austria to the ghettos in the east began in mid-October 1941. During the Second World War, the Nazis murdered around 6 million Jews.

By the end of the war, the number of 'ethnic Germans' relocated to the Greater German Reich had reached one million, more than one third of whom were Russian German evacuees from the Soviet Union, who had begun arriving in the autumn of 1943 (Strippel 2011). The RKF apparatus and local agencies were barely able to settle these later evacuees from Southern Ukraine, Transnistria, Himmler's Hegewald settlement project, Lithuania, and the General Government. They were housed in temporary camps, mostly in the Wartheland, Danzig-West Prussia, and East Prussia.

32.4   1940–1945: Recruitment of Soldiers and Manpower

The RKF apparatus placed about 10% of the relocated *Volksdeutsche* in the 'Old Reich' (*Altreich*).[8] The reason was not settlement problems in the annexed territories but economic interest. Certain professions were desperately needed in 'Greater Germany'. In addition, some *volksdeutsche* resettlers (*Umsiedler*) were not permitted to settle in the annexed territories because they did not make it through the racial-ethnic selection process. Therefore, they had to remain in Germany permanently working as farm or industrial labourers, at first without restitution. These 'ethnic Germans' were made second-class citizens (Leniger 2006; Strippel 2011). The RKF apparatus also imposed a work obligation on all of the 'ethnic German' resettlers who were waiting in the camps of the VoMi for their settlement. Additionally, some 'ethnic German' immigrants from North and South America and the former German colonies were integrated into the labour market, settlement projects, and the army (Lumans 1993).

Those 'ethnic Germans' living in other Axis countries and Axis client states (Bulgaria, Hungary, Romania, Slovakia, and Croatia), or German-occupied Serbia were not relocated to the Greater German Reich. Altogether, around 1.26 million 'ethnic Germans' were living in Southeastern European countries. From 1944 on, they were called *Auslandsvolksdeutsche* ('ethnic Germans' abroad) to differentiate them from the *Volksdeutsche* living inside the Greater German Reich (Stiller 2006, 109). The *Auslandsvolksdeutsche* were recruited to fight in the Waffen-SS. Voluntary recruitment started in 1940 in Romania. In 1941, Himmler created the 7th SS Volunteer Mountain Division *Prinz Eugen*, which, in its early days, around 22 500 'ethnic Germans', mainly from the Banat region, joined (Lumans 1993; Wittmann 2002; Casagrande 2003). In 1942, about 18 500 'ethnic Germans' from the occupied regions of Hungary (Bačka, Northern Transylvania, and the Satu Mare region) volunteered for the Waffen-SS.[9] Altogether, around 63 000 *Volksdeutsche* from Romania served in the Waffen-SS in the Second World War (Milata 2007). Between 1940 and 1945, a total of 310 000 *Volksdeutsche* were members of the Waffen-SS (34% of the force), according to the former SS general Paul Hausser (Wegner 1982). Further 'ethnic Germans' were conscripted into the Wehrmacht or voluntarily joined police units.

Together with the 'ethnic Germans' from the territories annexed or occupied by Germany, hundreds of thousands of people without German citizenship (not only foreigners but also so-called 'Germanizables'), at least not before 1938, served in the Wehrmacht, the Waffen-SS, *Einsatzgruppen*, the police, and militias. For example, around 134 000 men from Alsace and Lorraine were conscripted into the Wehrmacht (Vonau 2003). After the war, these men were referred to as *Malgré-nous* (against our will). Already during the war, Soviet propaganda labelled the 'ethnic German' soldiers as *Beutedeutsche* (which referred to inhabitants of annexed or occupied regions who had fallen prey, as spoils of war, to the Nazis and been classified as German).[10] In both wartime and post-war discourses about the 'ethnic Germans', the terms *Beutedeutsche*, *Malgré-nous*, and *fünfte Kolonne* ('fifth column') revealed the spectrum of conditions, from compulsion to voluntary participation, under which 'ethnic Germans' served. Like 'fifth column', *Volksdeutsche* became a pejorative term, meaning collaborator, in Central and Eastern European countries after 1945 (Kochanowski and Sach 2006).

32.5   1939–1945: Citizenship

The Nazi regime granted most 'ethnic Germans' citizenship. However, the process was actually a selection procedure which led to a system of graded integration into the *Volksgemeinschaft*. *Volksdeutsche* resettlers; 'ethnic Germans' in annexed or occupied territories; and *Volksdeutsche* volunteers in the army, Waffen-SS, or police units could acquire either full citizenship or a revocable (*auf Widerruf*) citizenship, with fewer rights, granted for 10 years as probational for full citizenship. However, some 'ethnic Germans' neither originally had nor received German citizenship during the war, for the regime did not grant citizenship unless racial experts determined that the applicant was 'Germanizable' (*eindeutschungsfähig*).

The criteria for inclusion in the *Volksgemeinschaft* varied; in fact, they were fluid. They depended on the occupation or satellite status of the region where the 'ethnic German' applicant lived, the history and social background of his minority group, and which agency was in charge of the relevant Germanization programme. Broadly speaking, there were three different approaches to selecting new members of the *Volksgemeinschaft*. The guiding principle for the Reich Ministry of Interior was its commitment to Germandom, in a political and ethnocultural sense. The Nazi Party and the regional *Gauleiter* in the annexed territories promoted people as fit for classification as German if they had been supporters of the party before the war. And the decisive criteria for the SS's race experts were a combination of a person's phenotypical characteristics, personality, and supposed potential for efficiency – in short, her alleged racial affiliation (Heinemann 2003; Stiller 2012b). However, there was one criterion that the German bureaucracy, the Nazi Party, and Himmler's RKF apparatus agreed on: German ancestry. In all of the different procedures for selecting 'ethnic Germans' that emerged during the Second World War, German origin or 'blood' usually played the decisive role.

In the Wartheland, for example, a '*Deutsche Volksliste*' (list of people belonging to the German *Volksgemeinschaft*) was established as early as October 1939. Initially, the list included only two groups, though eventually there were four. Group 1 consisted of resident *Volksdeutsche* who had already demonstrated their political commitment to Germandom (*Deutschtum*) during the inter-war period. Group 2 were all of the resident *Volksdeutsche* who had both preserved their 'Germanness' (*Deutschsein*) and had three or four German grandparents. Resident 'ethnic Germans' with fewer German grandparents (*deutschstämmig*, in contrast to *volksdeutsch*) were placed in Group 3. The Nazis also registered all 'mixed cases and cases in doubt' (*Misch- und Zweifelsfälle*) in this group. A further set of people to fall into this group were the so-called *Zwischenschicht*, a *völkisch* term for those whose alleged ethnicity lay somewhere between German and Polish. Finally, Group 4 was created for resident *Volksdeutsche* who had been active in Polish national organizations or otherwise struck the Nazis as 'hostile to Germandom'. The Security Police and the SD kept these 'renegades' under surveillance and later sent some of them to concentration camps as 'security risks'. By January 1944, a total of 2 760 000 people from all of the incorporated Eastern Territories had been registered on the *Deutsche Volksliste*. Sixty per cent were placed in Group 3 and acquired only revocable citizenship (Brandes and Stiller 2010; Wolf 2012; Frackowiak 2013).

But how could the authorities ascertain a person's partial German descent (*Deutschstämmigkeit*) when that person and his family had not been members of the *Volksdeutsche* community before 1939? The *Volkstum* and race experts verified German origin through either surname and religious affiliation or racial-ideologically determined features such as physical appearance, behaviour, and the tidiness of one's family and home (Stiller 2009; for the importance of tidiness in Nazi Germanization policy, see Harvey 2003). The general criteria for registration in Group 3 were not, however, identical in all of the four regions of the incorporated Eastern Territories. In Danzig-West Prussia, for example, the *Gauleiter*, Albert

Forster, set down his own rules for Germanization: residents with only one German grandparent qualified for the *Deutsche Volksliste* in the region he controlled. But the RKF's race and ethnicity experts were against this practice in the incorporated Eastern Territories. However, an agency of the RKF, the Central Immigration Office (*Einwandererzentralstelle*, EWZ), would register such people as 'German' (the so-called *Deutschstämmigenaktion*) in the General Government.

As the war changed course in 1942, the Nazis needed more German manpower, and this led to two sorts of modification in the Germanization process: a widened eligibility for German citizenship and an intensified search across Europe for 'good blood'. They pursued this second project with such vehemence that compulsory race assessment replaced voluntary enrolment in some places. In order to recruit more soldiers, the Reich authorities, in the first modification, granted citizenship to all of the young male population in the annexed territories of France and Slovenia. They were also supposed to grant citizenship to the *Auslandsvolksdeutsche* who were conscripted into the Wehrmacht, Waffen-SS, or police force. Hitler signed a decree to this effect in May 1943, but it took the RKF apparatus and the Reich Ministry of Interior a year to devise the necessary rules, issued in May 1944, which demanded racial examinations (Stiller 2006). By the end of the war, the EWZ had registered only 10 000–12 000 of these men but estimated that the total number exceeded 100 000.[11]

Compulsory racial selection was the second programme; it targeted people of supposedly 'good blood' for whom there was no evidence of German origin at all (i.e. no German surname and no identifiable German ancestors). The 're-Germanization procedure' (*Wiedereindeutschungsverfahren*), which had already begun in 1940, was exclusively controlled by the RKF apparatus, more precisely, by the SS Race and Settlement Main Office (*Rasse- und Siedlungshauptamt*, RuSHA). The procedure consisted mainly in racial examinations among expelled Polish families and individuals. Those families (and, less often, individuals) judged to be 'racially valuable' were sent to the *Altreich* for Germanization and put to work as farm labourers. Himmler had already expounded on this programme for the Germanization of Poles who had 'good blood' to high party officials and *Gauleiters* at the beginning of 1940, when it was established. Those Poles who 'qualified for Germanization' would be, in Himmler's words, 'absorbed and digested … after ten years' in Germany.[12] After 1942, the Nazis expanded this programme to include Slovenians, Estonians, and Latvians. In the course of these 're-Germanization' efforts, the RKF apparatus sent 30 000–35 000 bearers of 'qualified for Germanization' certificates to Germany and Austria (Heinemann 2003; Stiller 2012b). But citizenship and the (full or diminished) rights it involved are only one facet of the integration of 'ethnic Germans' into the Nazi *Volksgemeinschaft*. A second marker is *Volksdeutsche* relations to Nazi mass violence.

32.6 Conclusion: Agency and Complicity

Speaking generally, 'ethnic Germans' had less capacity to act than Germans and Austrians from the *Altreich*, but more capacity than the 'undesired' and other people marginalized by the Nazis. However, the agency of individuals in the constructed 'ethnic German' group was very diverse. According to Nazi doctrine, the *Volksdeutsche* and *Deutschstämmige* included the same sorts of 'undesired' people as the German and Austrian populations: 'work-shy people', 'asocial elements', 'hereditarily diseased', homosexuals, Jewish *Mischlinge* and 'mixed marriages', political opponents, communists, and so on. Whether *reichsdeutsch* or *volksdeutsch*, such persons were persecuted by the Nazi regime. They could end up in concentration camps or ghettos or in the programme of forced euthanasia. Furthermore, the German authorities sent people classified as *Volksdeutsche* to concentration camps when they resisted Germanization or rejected German citizenship (Stiller 2006; for the murder of 'ethnic Germans' during Action T4, see Fiebrandt 2014).

At the same time, 'ethnic Germans' were accomplices to Nazi mass violence, they instigated it, and they profited from it. *Volksdeutsch* militia participated in the persecution and mass murder of the Polish intelligentsia in 1939 (Jansen and Weckbecker 1992) and of Jews in southern Ukraine later (Angrick 2003; Steinhart 2015). 'Ethnic German' members of the *Einsatzgruppen*, Waffen-SS, Wehrmacht, and police units took part in mass shootings of Jews in the occupied Eastern Territories; two out of sixteen *Einsatzkommandos* were even led by Baltic Germans (Schröder 2001). 'Ethnic Germans' were also members of the staff of concentration camps (Stiller 2006). Numerous cases are reported in the literature of *Volksdeutsch* guards meeting their old Jewish neighbours in concentration and extermination camps (Bergen 2003; Milata 2007). And 'ethnic Germans' profited from 'Aryanization' (*Arisierung*), expulsions, and ghettoization, for the RKF apparatus and regional and Reich authorities distributed the expropriated property of Jews, Poles, Slovenes, and others among the 'ethnic Germans' (Stiller 2012a; Zakić 2014). The Nazis' support of the 'ethnic Germans' was the other side of their persecution and annihilation of Jews and other 'undesired' populations.

Notes

1   For the terms *volksdeutsch*, *völkisch*, and *Volksgemeinschaft*, see *Deutsches Wörterbuch*, 'Volk': http://woerterbuchnetz.de/DWB/?sigle=DWB&mode=Vernetzung&lemid=GV09940#XGV09940 (13.8.2015); for *Volkstum*, see Emmerich (1971, 48).

2   In 1925, the VDA named its journal *Der Volksdeutsche*. See *Der Volksdeutsche: das Blatt des Volksbundes für das Deutschtum im Ausland*, Berlin 1925–1944.

3   'Memelland kehrt heim', *Deutschtum im Ausland*, 22 (1939), 4, 146–153; 'Sieg des völkischen Gedankens', *Deutschtum im Ausland*, 22 (1939), 4, 154–178.

4   Hitlers Reichstagsrede, 6 October 1939, cited in Domarus (1973, 2/1, 1377–1393), here p. 1391. I would like to thank Greg Michael Sax for his proper translation.

5   Decree of Hitler, 7 October 1939, 686-PS (Exhibit USA-305), *IMT*, vol. 26, 255–257.

6   Both figures, and the contemporary one for *Einsatzgruppen*, include Jewish victims in the Baltic countries.

7   The EWZ (*Einwandererzentralstelle*) reported that 385 000 persons were evacuated from the Soviet Union in January 1945. See state of the *Durchschleusung*, 15 January 1945, EWZ, Bundesarchiv (BArch) Berlin, R 186/1.

8 After the annexations of Austria and the Sudetenland, the term *Altreich* designated Germany with its 1937 borders. However, the definition changed after the annexation of additional territories. Over the course of the war and Germany's territorial expansion, the *Altreich* came to include Austria and the Sudetenland.

9 RLD [*Reichsleiterdienst*], Folge 42, 28.12.1943, Volksdeutsche in der Waffen-SS, National Archives and Records Administration (NARA), RG 238, NO-2015.

10 'An die "Beutedeutschen" des 4. SS-Panzerkorps' ('To the "Beutedeutsche" of the IVth SS Panzer Corps'), Soviet leaflet, 20 September 1944, by RIO 7, Division PU I OF, Staatsbibliothek zu Berlin.

11 Report of the EWZ, 30 January 1945, BArch, R 186/2; Memo of the EWZ, 31 January 1945, BArch, R 186/1.

12 Heinrich Himmler, Speech before *Gauleiters* and higher party functionaries, 29 February 1940; Smith and Peterson (1974, 115–144), here p. 143.

References

Aly, Götz. 1995. *'Endlösung': Völkerverschiebung und der Mord an den europäischen Juden*. Frankfurt am Main: Fischer.

Angrick, Andrej. 2003. *Besatzungspolitik und Massenmord: Die Einsatzgruppe D in der südlichen Sowjetunion 1941–1943*. Hamburg: Hamburger Edition.

Bergen, Doris L. 1994. 'The Nazi Concept of "Volksdeutsche" and the Exacerbation of Anti-Semitism in Eastern Europe, 1939–1945.' *Journal of Contemporary History* 29(4), 569–582.

Bergen, Doris L. 1999. 'The "Volksdeutsche" of Eastern Europe, World War II, and the Holocaust: Constructed Ethnicity, Real Genocide.' In *Germany and Eastern Europe: Cultural Identities and Cultural Differences*, edited by Keith Bullivant, Geoffrey Giles, and Walter Pape, 70–93. Amsterdam: Rodopi.

Bergen, Doris L. 2003. 'The Volksdeutsche of Eastern Europe and the Collapse of the Nazi Empire, 1944–1945.' In *The Impact of Nazism: New Perspectives on the Third Reich and Its Legacy*, edited by Alan E. Steinweis and Daniel E. Rogers, 100–128. Lincoln: University of Nebraska Press.

Blanke, Richard. 1993. *Orphans of Versailles: The Germans in Western Poland 1918–1939*. Lexington: The University Press of Kentucky.

Böhler, Jochen. 2006. *Auftakt zum Vernichtungskrieg: die Wehrmacht in Polen 1939*. Frankfurt am Main: Fischer.

Bosse, Lars. 2001. 'Vom Baltikum in den Reichsgau Wartheland.' In *Deutschbalten, Weimarer Republik und Drittes Reich*, vol. 1, edited by Michael Garleff, 297–387. Cologne, Weimar, and Vienna: Böhlau.

Brandes, Detlef. 1969. *Die Tschechen unter deutschem Protektorat*. Vol. 1. Munich: Oldenbourg.

Brandes, Detlef and Stiller, Alexa. 2010. 'Deutsche Volksliste.' In *Lexikon der Vertreibungen: Deportation, Zwangsaussiedlung und ethnische Säuberung im Europa des 20. Jahrhunderts*, edited by Detlef Brandes, Holm Sundhaussen, and Stefan Troebst, 186–189. Cologne, Weimar, and Vienna: Böhlau.

Bukey, Evan Burr. 2000. *Hitler's Austria: Popular Sentiment in the Nazi Era, 1938–1945*. Chapel Hill: University of North Carolina Press.

Casagrande, Thomas. 2003. *Die volksdeutsche SS-Division 'Prinz Eugen': Die Banater Schwaben und die nationalsozialistischen Kriegsverbrechen*. Frankfurt am Main and New York: Campus.

Chickering, Roger. 1984. *We Men Who Feel Most German: A Cultural Study of the Pan-German League, 1886–1914.* Boston, MA: George Allen and Unwin.

Chu, Winson. 2012. *The German Minority in Interwar Poland.* Cambridge: Cambridge University Press.

Dawidowicz, Lucy S. 1986. *The War against the Jews, 1933–1945.* New York: Bantam.

Dieckmann, Christoph. 2011. *Deutsche Besatzungspolitik in Litauen 1941–1944.* 2 vols. Göttingen: Wallstein.

Domarus, Max. 1973. *Hitler, Reden und Proklamationen 1932–1945, Volume 2: Untergang. Erster Halbband 1939–1940,* 4th edn. Wiesbaden: Löwit.

Eberhardt, Piotr and Owsínski, Jan, eds. 2003. *Ethnic Groups and Population Changes in Twentieth-century Central-Eastern Europe: History, Data and Analysis.* London: M.E. Sharpe.

Emmerich, Wolfgang. 1971. *Zur Kritik der Volkstumsideologie.* Frankfurt am Main: Suhrkamp.

Fiebrandt, Maria. 2014. *Auslese für die Siedlergesellschaft: Die Einbeziehung Volksdeutscher in die NS-Erbgesundheitspolitik im Kontext der Umsiedlungen 1939–1945.* Göttingen: Vandenhoeck & Ruprecht.

Frackowiak, Johannes. 2013. 'Die "Deutsche Volksliste" als Instrument der nationalsozialistischen Germanisierungspolitik in den annektierten Gebieten Polens 1939–1945.' In *Nationalistische Politik und Ressentiments: Deutsche und Polen von 1871 bis zur Gegenwart,* edited by Johannes Frackowiak, 181–220. Göttingen: Vandenhoeck & Ruprecht.

Gerlach, Christian. 1999. *Kalkulierte Morde. Die deutsche Wirtschafts- und Vernichtungspolitik in Weißrußland 1941–1944.* Hamburg: Hamburger Edition.

Grams, Grant. 2001. *German Emigration to Canada and the Support of Its Deutschtum During the Weimar Republic: The Role of the Deutsches Auslands-Institut, Verein für das Deutschtum im Ausland and German-Canadian Organizations.* Frankfurt am Main: Peter Lang.

Haar, Ingo and Fahlbusch, Michael, eds. 2008. *Handbuch der völkischen Wissenschaften: Personen, Institutionen, Forschungsprogramme, Stiftungen.* Munich: Saur.

Hartmann, Christian. 2011. *Unternehmen Barbarossa: Der deutsche Krieg im Osten 1941–1945.* Munich: C.H. Beck.

Harvey, Elizabeth. 2003. *Women and the Nazi East: Agents and Witnesses of Germanization.* New Haven, CT: Yale University Press.

Heinemann, Isabel. 2003. *'Rasse, Siedlung, deutsches Blut': Das Rasse- und Siedlungshauptamt der SS und die rassenpolitische Neuordnung Europas.* Göttingen: Wallstein.

Jachomowski, Dirk. 1984. *Die Umsiedlung der Bessarabien-, Bukowina- und Dobrudschadeutschen: Von der Volksgruppe in Rumänien zur 'Siedlungsbrücke' an der Reichsgrenze.* Munich: Oldenbourg.

Jacobsen, Hans-Adolf. 1968. *Nationalsozialistische Außenpolitik 1933–1938.* Frankfurt am Main: Metzner.

Jansen, Christian and Weckbecker, Arno. 1992. *Der 'Volksdeutsche Selbstschutz' in Polen 1939/40.* Munich: Oldenbourg.

Kershaw, Ian. 1999. *Hitler 1889–1936: Hubris.* New York: W.W. Norton.

Kochanowski, Jerzy and Sach, Maike, eds. 2006. *Die 'Volksdeutschen' in Polen, Frankreich, Ungarn und der Tschechoslowakei: Mythos und Realität.* Osnabrück: fibre.

Koehl, Robert Lewis. 1957. *RKFDV. German Resettlement and Population Policy 1939–1945: A History of the Reich Commission for the Strengthening of Germandom.* Cambridge: Cambridge University Press.

Komjathy, Anthony T. and Stockwell, Rebecca. 1980. *German Minorities and the Third Reich: Ethnic Germans of East Central Europe Between the Wars.* New York: Holmes & Meier.

Krekeler, Norbert. 1973. *Revisionsanspruch und geheime Ostpolitik der Weimarer Republik: die Subventionierung der deutschen Minderheit in Polen*. Stuttgart: DVA.

Kroeger, Erhard. 1967. *Der Auszug aus der alten Heimat: Die Umsiedlung der Baltendeutschen*. Tübingen: Deutsche Hochschullehrer-Zeitung.

Krzoska, Markus. 2012. 'Der "Bromberger Blutsonntag" 1939.' *Vierteljahrshefte für Zeitgeschichte* 60, 237–248. doi: 10.1524/vfzg.2012.0012.

Kunz, Norbert. 2005. *Die Krim unter deutscher Herrschaft (1941–1944): Germanisierungsutopie und Besatzungsrealität*. Darmstadt: WBG.

Leniger, Markus. 2006. *Nationalsozialistische 'Volkstumsarbeit' und Umsiedlungspolitik 1939–1945: Von der Minderheitenbetreuung zur Siedlerauslese*. Berlin: Frank & Timme.

Liulevicius, Vejas Gabriel. 2000. *War Land on the Eastern Front: Culture, National Identity, and German Occupation in World War I*. Cambridge: Cambridge University Press.

Lower, Wendy. 2005. *Nazi-Empire Building and the Holocaust in Ukraine*. Chapel Hill: University of North Carolina Press.

Lumans, Valdis O. 1993. *Himmler's Auxiliaries: The Volksdeutsche Mittelstelle and the German National Minorities of Europe 1933–45*. Chapel Hill: University of North Carolina Press.

Mallmann, Klaus-Michael, Angrick, André, Matthäus, Jürgen, and Cüppers, Martin, eds. 2011. *Die 'Ereignismeldungen UdSSR' 1941: Dokumente der Einsatzgruppen in der Sowjetunion*. Darmstadt: WBG.

Milata, Paul. 2007. *Zwischen Hitler, Stalin und Antonescu: Rumäniendeutsche in der Waffen-SS*. Cologne, Weimar, and Vienna: Böhlau.

Mukhina, Irina. 2007. *The Germans of the Soviet Union*. London: Routledge.

O'Donnell, Krista, Bridenthal, Renate, and Reagin, Nancy, eds. 2005. *The Heimat Abroad: The Boundaries of Germanness*. Ann Arbor: University of Michigan Press.

Oltmer, Jochen. 2005. *Migration und Politik in der Weimarer Republik*. Göttingen: Vandenhoeck & Ruprecht.

Petzinna, Berthold. 2000. *Erziehung zum deutschen Lebensstil: Ursprung und Entwicklung des jung-konservativen 'Ring'-Kreises, 1918–1933*. Berlin: Akademie-Verlag.

Pinkus, Benjamin and Fleischhauer, Ingeborg. 1987. *Die Deutschen in der Sowjetunion: Geschichte einer nationalen Minderheit im 20. Jahrhundert*. Baden-Baden: Nomos.

Robel, Gert. 1991. 'Sowjetunion.' In *Dimension des Völkermords: Die Zahl der jüdischen Opfer des Nationalsozialismus*, edited by Wolfgang Benz, 499–560. Munich: Oldenbourg.

Rutherford, Phillip T. 2007. *Prelude to the Final Solution: The Nazi Program for Deporting Ethnic Poles 1939–1941*. Lawrence: University Press of Kansas.

Sammartino, Annemarie H. 2010. *The Impossible Border: Germany and the East, 1914–1922*. Ithaca, NY: Cornell University Press.

Scheuermann, Manfred. 2000. *Minderheitenschutz contra Konfliktverhütung? Die Minderheitenpolitik des Völkerbundes in den zwanziger Jahren*. Marburg: Verlag Herder-Institut.

Schröder, Matthias. 2001. *Deutschbaltische SS-Führer und Andrej Vlasov 1942–1945: 'Rußland kann nur von Russen besiegt werden'. Erhard Kroeger, Friedrich Buchardt und die 'Russische Befreiungsarmee'*. Paderborn: Schöningh.

Smelser, Ronald. 1975. *The Sudeten Problem, 1933–1938: Volkstumspolitik and the Formulation of Nazi Foreign Policy*. Middletown, CT: Wesleyan University Press.

Smith, Bradley F. and Peterson, Agnes F., eds. 1974. *Heinrich Himmler, Geheimreden 1933 bis 1945 und andere Ansprachen*. Berlin: Propyläen.

Steinhart, Eric C. 2015. *The Holocaust and the Germanization of Ukraine*. New York: Cambridge University Press.

Stiller, Alexa. 2006. 'Zwischen Zwangsgermanisierung und "Fünfter Kolonne": "Volksdeutsche" als Häftlinge und Bewacher in den Konzentrationslagern.' In *Nationalsozialistische Lager: Neue Beiträge zur NS-Verfolgungs- und Vernichtungspolitik und zur Gedenkstättenpädagogik*, edited by Akim Jah, Christoph Kopke, Alexander Korb, and Alexa Stiller, 104–124. Münster: Klemm & Oelschläger.

Stiller, Alexa. 2008. 'Reichskommissar für die Festigung deutschen Volkstums.' In *Handbuch der völkischen Wissenschaften: Personen, Institutionen, Forschungsprogramme, Stiftungen*, edited by Ingo Haar and Michael Fahlbusch, 531–540. Munich: Saur.

Stiller, Alexa. 2009. 'Grenzen des "Deutschen": Nationalsozialistische Volkstumspolitik in Polen, Frankreich und Slowenien während des Zweiten Weltkrieges.' In *Deutschsein als Grenzerfahrung. Minderheitenpolitik in Europa zwischen 1914 und 1950*, edited by Mathias Beer, Dietrich Beyrau, and Cornelia Rauh, 61–84. Essen: Klartext.

Stiller, Alexa. 2012a. 'Gewalt und Alltag der Volkstumspolitik: Der Apparat des Reichskommissars für die Festigung deutschen Volkstums und andere gesellschaftliche Akteure der veralltäglichten Gewalt.' In *Gewalt und Alltag im besetzten Polen 1939–1945*, edited by Jochen Böhler and Stephan Lehnstaedt, 45–66. Osnabrück: fibre.

Stiller, Alexa. 2012b. 'On the Margins of Volksgemeinschaft: Criteria for Belonging to the Volk within the Nazi Germanization Policy in the Annexed Territories, 1939–1945.' In *Heimat, Region and Empire: New Approaches to Spatial Identities in National Socialist Germany*, edited by Claus-Christian W. Szejnmann and Maiken Umbach, 239–255. Basingstoke, UK: Palgrave Macmillan.

Stossun, Harry. 1993. *Die Umsiedlung der Deutschen aus Litauen während des Zweiten Weltkrieges: Untersuchungen zum Schicksal einer deutschen Volksgruppe im Osten*. Marburg: Verlag Herder-Institut.

Strippel, Andreas. 2011. *NS-Volkstumspolitik und die Neuordnung Europas: Rassenpolitische Selektion der Einwandererzentralstelle des Chefs der Sicherheitspolizei und des SD (1939–1945)*. Paderborn: Schöningh.

Vierling, Birgit. 2014. *Kommunikation als Mittel politischer Mobilisierung: die Sudetendeutsche Partei (SdP) auf ihrem Weg zur Einheitsbewegung in der Ersten Tschechoslowakischen Republik (1933–1938)*. Marburg: Verlag Herder-Institut.

Vonau, Jean-Laurent. 2003. *Le procès de Bordeaux: les Malgré-Nous et le drame d'Oradour*. Strasbourg: Editions du Rhin.

Wegner, Bernd. 1982. *Hitlers politische Soldaten: Die Waffen-SS 1933–1945*. Paderborn: Schöningh.

Weidenfeller, Gerhard. 1976. *VDA, Verein für das Deutschtum im Ausland, Allgemeiner Deutscher Schulverein (1881–1918): Ein Beitrag zur Geschichte des deutschen Nationalismus und Imperialismus im Kaiserreich*. Frankfurt am Main, New York, and Bern: Peter Lang.

Wildt, Michael. 2002. *Generation des Unbedingten: Das Führungskorps des Reichssicherheitshauptamt*. Hamburg: Hamburger Edition.

Wittmann, Anna M. 2002. 'Mutiny in the Balkans: Croat Volksdeutsche, the Waffen-SS and Motherhood.' *East European Quarterly* 36, 255–279.

Wolf, Gerhard. 2012. *Ideologie und Herrschaftsrationalität: Nationalsozialistische Germanisierungspolitik in Polen*. Hamburg: Hamburger Edition.

Zakić, Mirna. 2014. 'The Price of Belonging to the Volk: Volksdeutsche, Land Redistribution and Aryanization in the Serbian Banat, 1941–1944.' *Journal of Contemporary History* 29, 320–340. doi: 10.1177/0022009413515539.

Zimmermann, Volker. 1999. *Die Sudetendeutschen im NS-Staat: Politik und Stimmung der Bevölkerung im Reichsgau Sudetenland (1938–1945)*. Essen: Klartext.

Further Reading

Beer, Mathias, Beyrau, Dietrich, and Rauh, Cornelia, eds. 2009. *Deutschsein als Grenzerfahrung: Minderheitenpolitik in Europa zwischen 1914 und 1950*. Essen: Klartext. This collection of articles provides a good overview.

Chu, Winson. 2012. *The German Minority in Interwar Poland*. Cambridge: Cambridge University Press. Chu's is an exhaustive study on the 'ethnic Germans' of Łódź.

Epstein, Catherine. 2010. *Model Nazi: Arthur Greiser and the Occupation of Western Poland*. Oxford: Oxford University Press. Epstein provides a detailed study of Nazi policy in the Wartheland.

Fahlbusch, Michael, Haar, Ingo, and Pinwinkler, Alexander, eds. 2017. *Handbuch der völkischen Wissenschaften. 2 Vols. 2nd, fundamentally expanded and revised edition*. Berlin: De Gruyter Oldenbourg. This handbook is an important compendium of the organizations and protagonists that pursued Nazi race, space, and *Volk* theory.

Fielitz, Wilhelm. 2000. *Das Stereotyp des wolhyniendeutschen Umsiedlers: Popularisierungen zwischen Sprachinselforschung und nationalsozialistischer Propaganda*. Marburg: Elwert. This is a theoretically and empirically excellent study of Nazi propaganda regarding the *Volksdeutsche* from Volhynia.

Harvey, Elizabeth. 2003. *Women and the Nazi East: Agents and Witnesses of Germanization*. New Haven, CT: Yale University Press. Harvey describes the participation of German women in Nazi resettlement and ethnicity policy.

Krekeler, Norbert. 1973. *Revisionsanspruch und geheime Ostpolitik der Weimarer Republik: die Subventionierung der deutschen Minderheit in Polen*. Stuttgart: DVA. Krekeler's is still the best study of German governmental politics regarding 'ethnic Germans' in Poland during the Weimar Republic.

Münz, Rainer and Ohliger, Rainer, eds. 2003. *Diasporas and Ethnic Migrants: Germany, Israel and Post-Soviet Successor States in Comparative Perspective*. London: Routledge. This collection of comparative essays focuses on the period after 1945.

Strippel, Andreas. 2011. *NS-Volkstumspolitik und die Neuordnung Europas: Rassenpolitische Selektion der Einwandererzentralstelle des Chefs der Sicherheitspolizei und des SD (1939–1945)*. Paderborn: Schöningh. Strippel's book is an in-depth study of the Nazis' selection procedure for 'ethnic German' immigration to Germany.

Tilse, Mark. 2011. *Transnationalism in the Prussian East: From National Conflict to Synthesis, 1871–1914*. Basingstoke, UK: Palgrave Macmillan. Tilse provides a new perspective on and approach to the analysis of German–Polish social coexistence.

Weidenfeller, Gerhard. 1976. *VDA, Verein für das Deutschtum im Ausland, Allgemeiner Deutscher Schulverein (1881–1918): Ein Beitrag zur Geschichte des deutschen Nationalismus und Imperialismus im Kaiserreich*. Frankfurt am Main, New York, and Bern: Peter Lang. Weidenfeller is still the best study of the VDA, though, unfortunately, only until 1918.

CHAPTER THIRTY-THREE

Ghettos

ANDREA LÖW

33.1 History of Ghettos in Nazi-Occupied Europe

The majority of Jews persecuted by the Nazis shared the experience of being forced to live in a ghetto for a certain period. Some of these ghettos existed for several years, others only for a few weeks or even days. While several ghettos were hermetically sealed and surrounded by a wall or a fence, others remained open and were only defined by designating certain streets. According to recent research conducted by the United States Holocaust Memorial Museum (USHMM), there were more than 1100 ghettos in occupied Eastern Europe, among them about 600 on former Polish territory, 130 in the Baltic States and about 250 in the pre-war territories of the Soviet Union. To these numbers one can add the ghettos in Romanian-controlled Transnistria and those established in Hungary in 1944 (Dean 2012). Yad Vashem in its encyclopaedia offers slightly different numbers (Miron and Shulhani 2009). The difficulties in determining the exact number refer to different definitions of a ghetto and the problem of missing sources from and about many places. This chapter will focus on the ghettos in occupied Poland, as many of them existed long enough to allow the development of social structures and the creation of documents. However, this does not mean that other regions will be left out of consideration.

As there was no centralized policy of ghettoization, there was no consistent typology of the ghetto. Instead, there were significant local differences and differences concerning the aims and means of ghettoization throughout the war. Where and when a ghetto was established had great influence on living conditions, the duration of its existence, and ultimately the fate of its inmates. We can differentiate two important periods: between September 1939 and summer 1941 ghettos were set up

A Companion to Nazi Germany, First Edition. Edited by Shelley Baranowski, Armin Nolzen, and Claus-Christian W. Szejnmann.
© 2018 John Wiley & Sons Ltd. Published 2018 by John Wiley & Sons Ltd.

in German-occupied Poland at different times and for different reasons. They were intended as a means to temporarily concentrate Jews before their ultimate displacement. However, many ghettos existed longer than the occupiers expected. The second period started with the German attack on the Soviet Union in summer 1941. Ghettos which were established in the newly occupied territories were immediately connected to the implementation of the 'Final Solution'.

There were closed ghettos which were sealed off, so-called open ghettos without borders, as well as work ghettos and destruction ghettos, where Jews were only concentrated for a short period of time before they were killed. Since there was and is no clear definition of what constituted a ghetto, it is not easy to define whether there was a ghetto or not in a particular location. Some ghettos were huge like the ones in Warsaw or Lodz, but there were also small ghettos with only a few dozen inhabitants. Living conditions differed tremendously. In some cities, more than one ghetto was established, sometimes due to lack of space in one designated area, sometimes in order to separate the workers from those unfit to work, and sometimes in order to separate the local inhabitants from Jews deported from Germany.

The official contemporary terminology also differed, with terms such as *Wohngebiet der Juden*, *Jüdisches Wohnviertel*, or *Jüdischer Wohnbezirk* as well as *Ghetto* being used. There was no overarching order from Berlin for the creation of ghettos, rather the emergence of ghettos instead depended on local initiatives and developments (Michman 2009).

33.2   Ghettos in Occupied Poland 1939–1941

About two million Polish Jews came under German rule when the Second World War started. Whereas in 1933 the Nazi government counted about 500 000 German Jews, it now faced a much larger Jewish population under its control. There were no plans for ghettoization, as the occupiers hoped to get rid of all the Jews in their sphere of control. Reinhard Heydrich's infamous *Schnellbrief* of 21 September 1939 (English translation in *Documents on the Holocaust* 1981, doc. no. 73) shows that he did not intend stable ghettoization. His goal was to ensure the concentration of Jewish communities in well-connected cities to control them and to make their future deportation easier. Heydrich also ordered the establishment of Jewish Councils as the central organ designated to fulfil German orders and organize Jewish life. It depended on the local administration as to whether, when, and under what circumstances ghettos were established. In the Radom District of the General Government, the Germans separated the Jewish population soon after occupation started. The *Landräte* had been assigned to regulate local conditions which they did by ordering the establishment of special Jewish quarters in Piotrkow Trybunalski (October 1939) and Radomsko (December 1939) (Młynarczyk 2007; Silberklang 2013).

The two largest ghettos were the ones in Warsaw and Lodz (the city was part of the *Reichsgau Wartheland*). They were closed ghettos: the one in Lodz was sealed off with a fence, the one in Warsaw with a wall. Preparations for the Lodz ghetto had already started in late 1939, and on 30 April 1940 the ghetto was closed. In this case, the ghetto was clearly meant as a transitory means of concentration until it was possible to expel all Jews from the city, which was supposed to be 'Germanized'. After a while, it became clear that the Jews would not be expelled in the near future and local officials had to accept the ghetto's long-term existence. It then became the first ghetto where the Germans exploited Jewish labour on a large scale: the Wehrmacht, but also many German companies, benefited from cheap Jewish labour. In the end, the ghetto in Lodz turned out to be the ghetto in occupied Poland that existed for the longest period. Throughout 1940 and 1941 most of the smaller communities in the Wartheland were ghettoized as well (Trunk 2006; Löw 2006; Klein 2009).

The ghetto in Warsaw was established in November 1940. In Lodz and Warsaw, just as in many other places, the act of moving the Jews to the designated area was quite complicated as far too many people had to find housing in an area that was almost always too small. The Jewish Councils had to organize this difficult task. A new wave of ghettoization in spring 1941 can partly be explained by the preparations for the attack on the Soviet Union: already earlier, lack of housing had been one possible reason for the establishment of ghettos; now German soldiers were supposed to be accommodated in apartments or houses formerly owned by Jews. In March, ghettos were established in Cracow and Lublin, and one month later in Kielce, Radom, and Czestochowa; ghettoization was ordered throughout many communities in the Cracow and Radom districts. In the smaller towns, this tended to result in open ghettos. Sometimes ghettoization was limited to ordering Jews not to leave the limits of their villages.

However, even after this period, ghettos had not yet been established throughout the General Government. Until the summer of 1941 in the Lublin district, most of the Jews were still not living in a ghetto. Also in the Cracow district, most ghettos were not established before 1941 and 1942 (Silberklang 2013). The motives for ghettoization varied during this first period: Jews were supposed to be isolated from the rest of the population and concentrated to make their future resettlement easier. A reason frequently cited by German officials was the alleged danger of diseases spread by Jews. Ghettoization also was a comfortable means of enrichment: Jews were forced to leave many of their belongings behind when they had to move to the designated area within a very short time and had to sell everything they could below its actual value. In occupied Poland, some ghettos were only established much later, in 1942, when deportations to the annihilation centres had already started, in order to serve as assembly points for future victims. There were also differences concerning the policy towards the Jews within the ghettos: there were German officials who wanted to take advantage of the available cheap workforce for German production, while others sought to annihilate the Jewish population by letting them starve to death or die of epidemic diseases (Browning 2004). In spite of all these differences, the ghettos established in occupied Poland before the summer of 1941 were quite distinct in character from those installed after 22 June 1941. As of this time, ghettos were clearly connected to mass murder.

In occupied Western or Northern Europe, no ghettos were created. There were discussions about the setting up of a ghetto in Amsterdam, but these ended by the end of November 1941. Only in the Protectorate of Bohemia and Moravia, in the German-occupied Czech Lands, was a ghetto established in Theresienstadt

(Terezín) by the end of 1941. To clear the protectorate of Jews, that seemed to be the appropriate interim solution. There has been a scholarly debate about the question whether Theresienstadt was a ghetto or rather a concentration camp, as German sources refer to Theresienstadt as both a 'ghetto' and a 'camp'. There is good reason to define it as a ghetto, however: some aspects to be mentioned in this regard are the Jewish administration (Council of Elders) and the social and cultural life that was still possible here. Also, family members, even after separate housing for women and men was introduced, were still able to meet freely after work hours. In particular, Czech, Austrian, and German Jews were sent to Theresienstadt. For many Jews, it was only a stopover on their way to the sites of mass murder further east. The Germans also used it as a ghetto for elderly and privileged Jews and as a 'model ghetto' for propaganda purposes. Theresienstadt was liberated by the Red Army in May 1945 (Adler 2005; Klein 2005).

33.3   Organization of Life Within the Ghettos

In the larger ghettos, which existed for a longer period, social structures developed and many Jews tried to organize their lives under these new conditions. This organization was achieved through both the already mentioned Jewish Councils or Councils of Elders and the many initiatives from within the community to structure life and to resist physical and psychological destruction. People tried to live life as 'normally' as they could. In some ghettos a rich cultural and social life developed, with schools, concerts, and theatres. In contrast to concentration camps, families continued to live together in the ghettos, even if they now existed under totally changed circumstances. Thus family and private life still existed there, which is quite well documented for some of the ghettos.

In his *Schnellbrief* of 21 September 1939, Heydrich ordered the establishment of Jewish Councils of Elders (*Ältestenräte*) or Jewish Councils (*Judenräte*) as the central organ to disseminate and fulfil German orders and organize Jewish life. They were supposed to have up to 24 members, depending on the size of the respective Jewish community. In many cases, the pre-war leaders of the communities had fled eastwards and German officials appointed the chairmen of the new Councils. Some Councils were already established under military administration, but General Governor Hans Frank issued a central decree by the end of November 1939. About 400 Jewish Councils were established in occupied Poland. A variety of chairmen represented these Councils and there were also huge differences concerning their ways of dealing with difficult conditions. The attitude the average Jewish population exhibited towards their officials also differed, ranging from respect to hatred and contempt.

In the larger ghettos, a large and sophisticated Jewish administration was created. These Councils organized the food supply, work, medical care, culture, education, and other aspects of life in the ghettos. To maintain order and to combat smuggling there was also a Jewish police, the Order Service (*Ordnungsdienst*). The Jewish administration's situation was desperate: with only a few resources at their disposal, they tried to take care of the ghetto population. They also had to engage in a permanent struggle with the German authorities. Many of the chairmen, such as Mordechai Chaim Rumkowski in Lodz or Ephraim Barasz in Bialystok, saw working for the German economy as the only way of saving the Jewish population; they thus created factories and workshops in the ghettos. Many conflicts between these officials and the Jewish population arose. In order to prevent further exacerbating the situation, many Jewish functionaries advocated that cooperation was necessary.

33.4 Daily Life

It is not possible to give a single framework of daily life in the ghettos that would describe the experience of every ghetto inhabitant. The circumstances described here applied to many ghettos, especially the larger and closed ones, but not necessarily to all and certainly not to the very small ghettos. Constant problems in many ghettos were the massive overcrowding as well as the lack of food which resulted in constant hunger and epidemics. Ghettos normally were established in torn down and neglected areas without sufficient space, into which thousands of people were now concentrated. For many Jews, the first problem was to find housing. Strangers, often refugees with hardly any belongings, had to move in together, and rooms with six, eight, or even more inhabitants were not infrequent. German authorities even downsized some of the ghettos as time went on. Typhus and typhoid fever were rampant, and death rates were extremely high: in Lodz and Warsaw, almost one quarter of the total population died due to illnesses, weakness, and malnutrition. After mass murder and deportations started, daily life in the ghettos was largely influenced by the constant fear of deportation and of the next round-up; the majority of the inhabitants spent their time trying to avoid this by having a work pass. In those ghettos that were established after the attack on the Soviet Union, this fear dominated life from the very beginning. Many of the aspects of daily life in the ghettos described here do not apply to those ghettos in the Soviet territory that existed only for a very short period.

On reading diaries and memoirs, it becomes clear that the worst problem of all for most people in the ghettos was constant hunger. In April 1941 Dawid Sierakowiak, a teenager in the Lodz ghetto, wrote in a pessimistic but realistic manner in his diary: 'The inevitability of death by starvation grows more evident' (Sierakowiak 1996, 82). Hardly any documents neglect to mention the constant hunger and the permanent lack of food. It was necessary for people in the ghettos to find work in order to be able to buy food, but also because the factories or other workplaces provided them with a bowl of soup. Beggars populated the ghetto streets, trying to get some food in order to be saved for one more day. Little children with rags instead of clothes cried for a piece of bread. The streets were crowded with all these poor people roaming around or selling their last belongings. Diaries and memoirs testify to the smell and the noise in the courtyards and the streets, the narrowness and the tight crowds. Especially in the Warsaw ghetto, documents show that after a while people got used to the sight of dead corpses lying in the street. There were periods with 5000 deaths a month. Conditions tended to be better in the smaller ghettos and in those that were closer to the countryside.

Smuggling became an important means of survival in many ghettos. Under the constant threat of death, ghetto inhabitants brought food and medicine into the ghetto. Smuggling could take place on an individual scale with persons, mainly children, trying to provide for their own families (Engelking and Leociak 2009). For most Jews, ghettoization meant radical impoverishment and social downgrading. The longer the occupation continued, the more Jews were living in extreme poverty. Yet the situation was not equally bad for everybody. A complex social hierarchy developed in the ghettos. For a minority in the larger ghettos, it was possible to make a limited fortune by smuggling on a large and organized scale or by becoming an informer to German officials, especially the Gestapo. A new elite emerged under these new circumstances. Many conflicts arose under the conditions in the ghettos about how to react and how to behave. Corruption too played an important role in the ghettos: knowing the right persons in the Jewish administration could help in finding a better job or getting more and better provisions.

There were also far-reaching changes in family life and structures as well as changes in gender roles. There was hardly any privacy, a phenomenon that had a huge impact on family life and sexuality. Women had to work; in many families, the children became engaged in smuggling, often becoming the main bread-earners. Husbands often lost their source of income, and many men had fled eastwards at the beginning of the occupation or had been sent to labour camps. In the ghettos established in the former Soviet Union, the situation was even worse, as in many cases mass killings were conducted before ghettos were established, so that most families had already experienced the loss of family members.

The arrival of refugees and deportees in some of the already overcrowded ghettos brought new problems: housing and supplies had to be guaranteed for new ghetto inhabitants who did not have any connections, had no work, and in many cases hardly any belongings. They were dependent on public aid from the Jewish Councils or the self-help organizations. Particularly when German Jews came to the Eastern European ghettos, such as Lodz and Warsaw, groups that had hardly anything in common except for falling under the Nazi definition of being a 'Jew' were forced to live together. For these German or Austrian Jews, daily life in the ghettos was an absolute shock. They were in no way prepared for the reality of the ghettos and many of them did not live long enough to get used to the situation.

33.5 Organizing Life and Culture

When the ghettos were established, the local population had to get used to radical new conditions. Ripped out of their former normal lives, bereft of almost everything, in many cases unemployed, the new ghetto inhabitants had to organize their lives anew. They had to find a way to maintain their physical and mental health. At least in the larger ghettos where these structures could develop, both the official Jewish administrations and general members of society started organizing help for the poor and the ill, but also an educational and cultural life. Many inhabitants tried not to resign themselves to their fate, but instead attempted to remain active and build a society in which people cared for and helped each other. These activities were an important means of self-assertion. Many sources document the strong will of ghetto inhabitants to retain some sort of 'normal' daily routine that was connected with their lives before the war – be it a normal family life, normal surroundings for children in an orphanage or school, or a normal evening in a theatre.

Public kitchens were set up so that poor people were able to get a bowl of soup for a few pennies or even without paying – this often constituted their only meal each day. Doctors and nurses tried to help the sick in the hospitals as well as was possible under these dire circumstances: in some cases, hospitals had to move to within the new ghetto borders where their new premises were unsuitable for the needs of a hospital. Medical drugs were lacking and the constant scarcity of food made the patients even weaker. Often two or more patients had to share a bed. Diaries and memoirs testify to how shocking the sight of hungry, sick, and suffering children, wrapped in rags, was for the ghetto inhabitants and how important they all thought it was to help them. Many orphanages moved to the ghettos or were founded there. The most famous was the one run by Janusz Korczak in Warsaw, but there were many more.

Ghetto dwellers perceived the youth as the future of the Jewish community. It thus seemed important to people in the ghettos not only to feed but also to educate their children, to ensure that they learnt about other realities than just the one in the ghetto, the reality of hunger, suffering, and death. There were both clandestine and official schools where the children were taught and prepared for a life after the war. In schools and orphanages, children also staged plays or sang in a chorus, sometimes even performing in public. In some ghettos, like in Warsaw, Lodz, or Wilno, there were cultural performances of a very high level as many actors and musicians were locked up inside the ghettos. They founded professional theatres and symphony orchestras. There were also many groups of amateur actors or musicians who got together to play. Often these performances were accompanied by social commitments: part of the revenue was used to support orphanages, hospitals, or soup kitchens, as all public welfare activities suffered from lack of funding. In cafes and restaurants, artists performed concerts or cabaret as well.

We do not know enough about the situation in small ghettos, but probably there were similar activities on a less extensive level, like private readings or music circles. For many Jews who were forced to live in a ghetto for a certain period, it was a necessity to create an intellectual *Gegenwelt* to the destructive reality of the ghetto where they had to confront hunger, pain, and death every day. A very important cultural reaction to persecution in the ghettos was documentation. Jews in the ghettos in Nazi-occupied Europe documented what was happening to them in many ways: they wrote diaries, poems, short stories, and chronicles; they painted and took photographs. They did not want to let the perpetrators determine how their fate and their suffering would be remembered. Emanuel Ringelblum, who initiated the famous Underground Archive of the Warsaw Ghetto, wrote in a letter to his friend Adolf Berman: 'If none of us survives, at least let that remain' (Kassow 2007, 2). As Jakub Poznański put it in his diary written in the Lodz ghetto in July 1943: 'Above all I am writing so that the future chronicler can not only make use of official documents, but also of private sources' (Poznański 2011, 130; Garbarini 2006; Löw 2015).

33.6   Ghettos and the 'Final Solution'

In the occupied Soviet territories, there was even less of a uniform policy of ghettoization than in occupied Poland. It strongly depended on the timing and logistics of the mass murder of the Jews. In many cases, conflicts arouse between the SS (*Schutzstaffel*) and police forces and the newly installed civil administration, which sought to use Jewish labour for their purposes. Sometimes there were mass shootings which resulted in the annihilation of complete Jewish communities without the setting up of any ghettos at all, as was the case in the Babi Yar shooting in Kiev. Often there were mass killings before the rest of the Jewish population was concentrated in a ghetto. The survivors, in many cases, were workers with their families. For them, the ghetto was a place where they had a chance of survival by working for the Germans. However, even these survivors of the first massacres were by no means safe, because there were constant 'selections' and further 'reductions' of the population.

In Wilno (Vilnius) mass murder in nearby Ponary started in July 1941, when about 5000 Jews were killed; another 14 000 were murdered during the first days of September, before two ghettos were established for the remaining approximately 40 000 Jews. There were more selections and shootings of those unfit to work in November and December. Afterwards, the situation stabilized, as most of the ghetto inhabitants worked for the German war economy. Before the ghetto was liquidated in September 1943, about half of the remaining Jews were taken to labour camps. A similar development occurred in other large cities in the region, such as in nearby Kaunas (Dieckmann 2011). Ghettos were also set up in the areas where the *Einsatzgruppen* carried out the first mass shootings in summer 1941, but then moved on further east, such as in the Bialystok district and the *Generalkommissariat Wolhynien und Podolien* in the Ukraine. Here the ghettos which were established after the first wave of killings, such as the Bialystok ghetto, existed for quite a while afterwards (Bender 2008).

Eastern Galicia was incorporated into the General Government. After a first wave of killings in summer 1941, two ghettos were established in Tarnopol and Stanislawow in the autumn; in Stanislawow, about 10 000 Jews were killed in October, as the area designated for the ghetto was considered too small to hold them all. During 1942, the majority of Jews in Eastern Galicia was killed, mainly in the Belzec extermination camp. Most of the ghettos in this region were only established in 1942, shortly before the local population was transported to Belzec. Mass deportations from Lwow took place in August 1942. Only afterwards was a ghetto established. Jews still alive in Eastern Galicia by the end of 1942 lived either in labour camps or in one of the 'work ghettos' (Pohl 1996; Sandkühler 1996).

The ghettos in Minsk (Belarus) and Riga (Latvia) were special cases, as German Jews were deported there in late 1941 and early 1942. The SS and police killed thousands of local Jews because they wanted to make space for the new arrivals. The ghetto in Minsk had already been established in July 1941 under military administration. At its peak, about 80 000 Jews were held here. After several mass murder operations, thousands of Jews lived in this ghetto, working for the

German war effort, until October 1943 (Angrick and Klein 2009; Epstein 2008; Rentrop 2011). Relatively few ghettos in the occupied Soviet territories existed long enough to develop social structures like those in the larger Polish ghettos. Wilno, Kaunas, Riga, and Bialystok could be mentioned as examples, as they lasted until 1943.

The escalation of anti-Jewish violence developed into genocidal killings during the attack on the Soviet Union in the summer of 1941. This was accompanied by a process of decision making in the German leadership that eventually led to the inclusion of all Jews in the German sphere of influence into a programme of total extermination. The large Jewish population in the ghettos in occupied Poland would soon become the target of mass murder by gassing. The Lodz ghetto was the first major ghetto from which Jews were deported en masse to their deaths. Mass murder by gassing in the Chelmno (Kulmhof) extermination centre had started in December 1941. At the same time, the German administration ordered Mordechai Chaim Rumkowski to choose 20 000 Jews to be deported – supposedly to villages and small towns to improve the overcrowded situation in the ghetto. In January 1942, deportations from Lodz to Chelmno started. By the end of May, more than 55 000 Jews had been deported. Rumkowski argued that he had to choose those marked for deportation himself, together with his administration, in order to limit the losses (Löw 2006).

The capabilities of the *Judenräte* to exert influence were extremely limited. When the Nazis called on Adam Czerniakow to organize the deportation of the Jews of Warsaw to the Treblinka extermination camp on 22 July 1942, he took his own life. This did not change the fact that the population was sent to their deaths (Engelking and Leociak 2009; Gutman 1982).

In Cracow the first head of the *Judenrat*, Marek Bieberstein, a respected personality, had already tried to intervene in favour of the Jewish population in 1940, which resulted in his arrest that summer. The *Stadthauptmann* of Cracow selected his successor, the lawyer Artur Rosenzweig, in autumn 1940. As he was not sufficiently cooperative during the deportations to the Belzec extermination camp, he was himself deported and murdered in June 1942. His successor, Dawid Gutter, obviously implemented German orders satisfactorily. According to the investigations of Aharon Weiss, this was a typical pattern: he distinguishes among first, second, and third *Judenräte*. The latter are almost universally rated negatively by the survivors (Weiss 1977; Löw and Roth 2011).

If the Jewish administration and the Jewish police did not fulfil the orders quickly enough, the Germans came into the ghettos anyway. They did so, for example, in September 1942 in Lodz, when they selected more than 15 000 sick persons, children under 10, and people older than 65 years for death. Just under 90 000 Jews remained in the Lodz ghetto, which by then was the only ghetto that remained in the Wartheland. It had turned into a working ghetto and existed until summer 1944. Most Jews in the ghettos in the General Government were murdered in the camps of the *Aktion Reinhardt*. Starting in March 1942, the Nazis killed Jews from the Lublin and Galicia districts in Belzec. To make the mass murder more efficient, two more killing centres with gas chambers were constructed in Sobibor and Treblinka. At the latter, more than 260 000 Jews from the Warsaw ghetto were murdered from the end of July until 22 September, while several thousand were shot in the ghetto during the raids. Only a few ghettos remained in the General Government after the mass murder campaign of 1942. Examples of these ghettos are Warsaw, Radom, Kielce, Częstochowa, and Cracow. They were all liquidated during the course of 1943 together with the last remaining ghettos in the Galicia district.

After the completion of *Aktion Reinhardt* in the General Government, the Jews in the neighbouring region of Upper Silesia experienced similar decimation by deportations to Auschwitz in 1943, whereas the actions reached the Bialystok region in late 1942. In the occupied Soviet territories, most of the still existing ghettos were either completely dissolved in 1942 – usually by mass shootings in the Ukraine and in the *Generalkommissariat Weißruthenien*, with some major exceptions in 1943 (Minsk, Vilnius, Kaunas, Siauliai) – or transformed into labour camps.

33.7   Jewish Reactions to Deportation and Death

Jews responded in different ways to the deportations and later on to the liquidations of the ghettos. Even if they knew about the deportees' fate, they did not necessarily believe that the Germans were planning a total annihilation. Many of them hoped until the very end that their work for the German war production would ensure their families' survival. Many of the Jewish Councils tried to ensure Jewish survival by organizing work and were against armed resistance. Some Jews were so overwhelmed by their pain and suffering that only agony and despair was left for them. Many were, after years of living under these terrible conditions, too exhausted to resist their deportation. They just went to the assembly points, especially if the Germans told them that they would get a loaf of bread for their journey.

Escape from the ghettos required help from the non-Jewish local population, who also lived under great pressure and under the threat of capital punishment for hiding and aiding Jews. The atmosphere of expected reprisals and the social dynamics of fear had great impact on people's willingness to help Jews and sometimes turned rescuers into traitors or even murderers. At the same time, the Germans rewarded locals for providing information on hidden Jews. In addition, it was very hard to procure rations for those in hiding under wartime conditions imposed by the occupier. Going to the 'Aryan' side required good contacts and financial means, and several non-Jews were necessary to help a single Jew to survive in hiding. The non-Jews' reactions were hard to predict, roles could change, and friends could turn into traitors. It was extremely hard for Jews to interpret the situation and know where to turn to for help (Paulsson 2002; Grabowski 2013).

The specific conditions under which Jews lived made resistance very difficult for the isolated, weak, and diverse Jewish population in the ghettos. The attitude of the local population played an important role; often they were hostile and did not support Jewish efforts. Ghetto underground groups needed time to organize themselves, to overcome mistrust between different political groups, and to smuggle weapons. Due to the superior armed power of the Germans and to the fact that an armed revolt put whole communities in danger of collective punishment, most activists decided to wait until the final liquidations of the ghettos. The first underground organization, the *Fareynigte Partisaner Organisatsie* (FPO), was formed in Wilno in January 1942. In Warsaw, a unified resistance movement only came into being after the deportations to Treblinka in summer 1942. Here German troops met organized armed resistance for the first time during the deportation 'action' in January 1943. When they wanted to liquidate the ghetto completely in April 1943, the famous uprising started. SS troops killed or deported all Jews found inside the ghetto and destroyed the whole area.

Similar uprisings, on a much smaller scale, followed in other locations. Altogether, in at least in 60 ghettos, we find attempted revolts or mass escapes, and resistance was widespread in eastern Poland, Lithuania, and Belarus. Here, some Jews hid in forested areas and became partisans. Due to systematic hunts by the occupying forces and hostile actions of other partisan groups, many of these groups were detected, and some Jews even went back into still existing ghettos because the situation was too difficult in the forests (Arad 1980; Krakowski 1984; Dieckmann 2011; Ainsztein 1974).

33.8   Conclusion

The majority of Jews persecuted by the Nazis shared the experience of having to live in a ghetto for a certain period. Nevertheless, historians did not give the ghettos much attention for quite some time, although research began as early as 1943 when the last ghettos still existed. Most of the early works were written by survivors (Jockusch 2012), and later works dealt with the Jewish Councils and the Jewish resistance (Trunk 1972; Ainsztein 1974, Gutman and Haft 1979; Arad 1980; Krakowski 1984; Bauer 2001; Unger 2004), two topics closely linked to the history of the ghettos. Starting in the 1990s, the ghettos generated a broader interest and we now have more works on them, especially those in the Polish cities. On the smaller ghettos, however, we still do not have much historiographical work (Pohl 2010; Lehnstaedt 2012). The finding that Jews in the ghettos strived to find work has been a major issue over the last few years in Germany: in June 2002, the German Bundestag approved the ZRBG – the *Gesetz zur Zahlbarmachung von Renten aus Beschäftigungen in einem Ghetto* ('Law Regarding the Conditions for Making Pensions Payable from an Employment in a Ghetto') – which stipulated that work carried out in ghettos could, under certain conditions, be grounds for entitlement to a pension. Numerous historical testimonials were produced describing the working conditions in each of the ghettos and districts – in some cases, for the very first time. For this purpose alone, a detailed survey has been conducted. Our knowledge of work in the ghettos, which constituted an important role in the reality of human life, has now been increased (Hensel and Lehnstaedt 2013).

What we still do not have is a comprehensive general history of the ghettos. In most cases, the historiography has dealt with single places or regions and has not provided a comparative analysis of the ghettos. The two extensive encyclopaedias mentioned at the beginning of this chapter offer important information about many of the ghettos in occupied Europe and are important starting points for further research.

References

Adler, H.G. 2005. *Theresienstadt 1941–1945: Das Antlitz einer Zwangsgemeinschaft.* Göttingen: Wallstein.

Ainsztein, Reuben 1974. *Jewish Resistance in Nazi–Occupied Europe. With a historical survey of the Jew as fighter and soldier in the Diaspora.* New York: Barnes & Noble.

Angrick, Andrej and Klein, Peter. 2009. *The 'Final Solution' in Riga: Exploitation and Annihilation, 1941–1944.* New York and Oxford: Berghahn Books.

Arad, Yitzhak. 1980. *Ghetto in Flames: The Struggle and Destruction of the Jews in Vilna in the Holocaust.* Jerusalem: Yad Vashem.

Bauer, Yehuda. 2001. *Rethinking the Holocaust.* New Haven, CT: Yale University Press.

Bender, Sara. 2008. *The Jews of Białystok During World War II and the Holocaust.* Waltham, MA: Brandeis University Press.

Browning, Christopher (with Jürgen Matthäus). 2004. *The Origins of the Final Solution: The Evolution of Nazi Jewish Policy, September 1939–March 1942.* Lincoln: University of Nebraska Press.

Dean, Martin, ed. 2012. *Encyclopedia of Camps and Ghettos 1933–1945, Volume 2: Ghettos in German-Occupied Eastern Europe.* Bloomington: Indiana University Press in association with the United States Holocaust Memorial Museum.

Dieckmann, Christoph. 2011. *Deutsche Besatzungspolitik in Litauen 1941–1944.* Göttingen: Wallstein.

Documents on the Holocaust. Selected Sources on the Destruction of the Jews of Germany and Austria, Poland and the Soviet Union. 1981. Jerusalem: Yad Vashem.

Engelking, Barbara and Leociak, Jacek. 2009. *The Warsaw Ghetto: A Guide to the Perished City.* New Haven and London: Yale University Press.

Epstein, Barbara Leslie. 2008. *The Minsk Ghetto 1941–1943: Jewish Resistance and Soviet Internationalism.* Berkeley: University of California Press.

Garbarini, Alexandra. 2006. *Numbered Days: Diaries and the Holocaust.* New Haven, CT: Yale University Press.

Grabowski, Jan. 2013. *Hunt for the Jews: Betrayal and Murder in German–Occupied Poland.* Bloomington and Indianapolis: Indiana University Press.

Gutman, Israel and Haft, Cyntia J., eds. 1979. *Patterns of Jewish Leadership in Nazi Europe 1933/45.* Jerusalem: Yad Vashem.

Gutman, Yisrael. 1982. *The Jews of Warsaw, 1939–1943: Ghetto, Underground, Revolt.* Brighton, UK: Harvester Press.

Hensel, Jürgen and Lehnstaedt, Stephan, eds. 2013. *Arbeit in den nationalsozialistischen Ghettos.* Osnabrück: fibre.

Jockusch, Laura. 2012. *Collect and Record! Jewish Holocaust Documentation in Early Postwar Europe.* Oxford: Oxford University Press.

Kassow, Samuel. 2007. *Who will Write Our History? Emanuel Ringelblum, the Warsaw Ghetto, and the Oyneg Shabes Archive.* Bloomington: Indiana University Press.

Klein, Peter. 2005. 'Theresienstadt: Ghetto oder Konzentrationslager?' In *Theresienstädter Studien und Dokumente,* edited by Jaroslava Milotová and Michael Wögerbauer, 111–123. Prague: Sefer.

Klein, Peter. 2009. *Die 'Gettoverwaltung Litzmannstadt' 1940 bis 1944: Eine Dienststelle im Spannungsgfeld von Kommunalbürokratie und staatlicher Verfolgungspolitik.* Hamburg: Hamburger Edition.

Krakowski, Shmuel. 1984. *The War of the Doomed: Jewish Armed Resistance in Poland, 1942–1944.* New York: Holmes & Meier.

Lehnstaedt, Stephan. 2012. 'Kleine Ghettos: Plädoyer für eine Perspektiverweiterung.' *Zeitschrift für Genozidforschung* 13, 12–28.

Löw, Andrea. 2006. *Juden im Getto Litzmannstadt: Lebensbedingungen, Selbstwahrnehmung, Verhalten*. Göttingen: Wallstein.

Löw, Andrea. 2015. 'Documenting as a "Passion and Obsession": Photographs from the Lodz (Litzmannstadt) Ghetto.' *Central European History* 38, 387–404. doi: 10.1017/S0008938915000801.

Löw, Andrea and Roth, Markus. 2011. *Juden in Krakau unter deutscher Besatzung 1939–1945*. Göttingen: Wallstein.

Michman, Dan. 2009. 'The Jewish Ghettos under the Nazis and Their Allies: The Reasons Behind Their Emergence.' In *The Yad Vashem Encyclopedia of the Ghettos During the Holocaust*, edited by Guy Miron and Shlomit Shulani, xiii–xxxi. Jerusalem: Yad Vashem.

Miron, Guy and Shulhani, Shlomit, eds. 2009. *The Yad Vashem Encyclopedia of the Ghettos during the Holocaust*. Jerusalem: Yad Vashem.

Młynarczyk, Jacek. 2007. *Judenmord in Zentralpolen: Der Distrikt Radom des Generalgouvernements 1939–1945*. Darmstadt: WBG.

Paulsson, Gunnar S. 2002. *Secret City: The Hidden Jews of Warsaw, 1940–1945*. New Haven, CT: Yale University Press.

Pohl, Dieter. 1996. *Nationalsozialistische Judenverfolgung in Ostgalizien 1941–1944: Organisation und Durchführung eines staatlichen Massenverbrechens*. Munich: Oldenbourg.

Pohl, Dieter. 2010. 'Ghettos im Holocaust: Zum Stand der historischen Forschung.' In *Ghettorenten: Entschädigungspolitik, Rechtsprechung und historische Forschung*, edited by Jürgen Zarusky, 39–50. Munich: Oldenbourg.

Poznański, Jakub. 2011. *Tagebuch aus dem Ghetto Litzmannstadt*. Edited by Ingo Loose. Berlin: Metropol.

Rentrop, Petra. 2011. *Tatorte der 'Endlösung': Das Ghetto Minsk und die Vernichtungsstätte von Maly Trostinez*. Berlin: Metropol.

Sandkühler, Thomas. 1996. *'Endlösung' in Galizien: Der Judenmord in Ostpolen und die Rettungsinitiativen von Berthold Beitz 1941–1944*. Bonn: Dietz.

Sierakowiak, Dawid. 1996. *The Diary of Dawid Sierakowiak: Five Notebooks from the Łódź Ghetto*. New York: Oxford University Press.

Silberklang, David. 2013. *Gates of Tears: The Holocaust in the Lublin District*. Jerusalem: Yad Vashem.

Trunk, Isaiah. 1972. *Judenrat: The Jewish Councils in Eastern Europe Under Nazi Occupation*. New York: Macmillan.

Trunk, Isaiah. 2006. *Łódź Ghetto: A History*. Edited by Robert M. Shapiro. Bloomington: Indiana University Press.

Unger, Michal. 2004. *Reassessment of the Image of Mordechai Chaim Rumkowski*. Jerusalem: Yad Vashem.

Weiss, Aharon. 1977. 'Jewish Leadership in Occupied Poland – Postures and Attitudes.' *Yad Vashem Studies* 12, 335–365.

Further Reading

There is a lot of research on the ghettos in Polish and Hebrew, but I am concentrating here and in the references on English and German publications.

Corni, Gustavo. 2002. *Hitler's Ghettos: Voices From a Beleaguered Society, 1939–1944*. London: Oxford University Press.

Provides a livelily and profound account on life in the ghettos based on ghetto dwellers' diaries and memoirs.

Dean, Martin, ed. 2012. *Encyclopedia of Camps and Ghettos 1933–1945, Volume 2: Ghettos in German-Occupied Eastern Europe*. Bloomington: Indiana University Press in association with the United States Holocaust Memorial Museum.
Articles on every ghetto the researchers can find information on, with information on sources and further reading for all the places and regions.
Dieckmann, Christoph and Quinkert, Babette, eds. 2009. *Im Ghetto 1939–1945: Neue Forschungen zu Alltag und Umfeld*. Göttingen: Wallstein.
New works on different ghettos and different aspects of ghetto life.
Engelking, Barbara and Leociak, Jacek. 2009. *The Warsaw Ghetto: A Guide to the Perished City*. New Haven, CT and London: Yale University Press.
A detailed and thoughtful study on all aspects of life in the Warsaw ghetto.
Feuchert, Sascha, Leibfried, Erwin, and Riecke, Jörg, eds. 2007. *Die Chronik des Gettos Lodz/Litzmannstadt*. 5 vols. Göttingen: Wallstein.
The first complete edition of the Chronicle of the Lodz Ghetto, in the German language.
Hansen, Imke, Steffen, Katrin, and Tauber, Joachim, eds. 2013. *Lebenswelt Ghetto: Alltag und soziales Umfeld während der nationalsozialistischen Verfolgung*. Wiesbaden: Harrassowitz.
Provides new research on different aspects of ghetto life for different regions, in German and English.
Jewish Historical Institute Warsaw, ed. 1997–. *Archiwum Ringelbluma*. Warsaw: Wydawnictwo Uniwersytetu Warszawskiego.
Documents of the Underground Archive of the Warsaw Ghetto; 20 volumes have already been published so far, all in Polish.
Lehnstaedt, Stephan and Platt, Kristin, eds. 2012. *Alltag im Ghetto: Strukturen, Ordnungen, Lebenswelt(en) im Blick neuer Forschung*. Paderborn: Fink/Schöningh.
New research on everyday life in the ghettos in German and English.
Miron, Guy and Shulhani, Shlomit, eds. 2009. *The Yad Vashem Encyclopedia of the Ghettos during the Holocaust*. Jerusalem: Yad Vashem.
General articles on ghettoization and entries on single places and ghettos.
Sakowska, Ruta. 1999. *Menschen im Ghetto: Die jüdische Bevölkerung im besetzten Warschau 1939–1943*. Osnabrück: fibre.
A relatively early account that concentrates on the Jewish ghetto population and is based on documents of the Warsaw ghetto's Underground Archive.

CHAPTER THIRTY-FOUR

Holocaust Studies: The Spatial Turn

WENDY LOWER

In early 1947 the Chief Counsel of the United States Nuremberg Military Tribunals, Brigadier General Telford Taylor, prepared indictments against the second-tier Nazis. By then, the liberation of the concentration camps and the research, testimony, and publicity surrounding the international trial against the Nazi leadership had revealed the horror and extent of the regime's war crimes and crimes against humanity. An adviser to the US prosecution team, Raphael Lemkin, lobbied for the inclusion of a new crime, what he called 'genocide'. With this growing awareness of the Holocaust, Taylor sounded out his legal team about the possibility of holding a trial that focused exclusively on the Nazi extermination of six million European Jews, stressing 'that this is by far the most important and sinister item in the entire Nazi history' (Taylor 1947, 380). Though such a trial did not occur, it is striking that Taylor and others who first sifted through tons of captured German records (Eckert 2014), conducted interrogations of perpetrators, and recorded witness testimony from victims and bystanders realized that the 'Final Solution' held an outstanding place in the history of the Third Reich.

The UN Convention to Prevent and Punish Genocide was passed in 1948, yet it would take decades for the popular and academic recognition of the Holocaust as a major event to be memorialized, studied, and taught. There were exceptions – for example, local initiatives to collect testimony and memorial *Yizkor* books. In the 1950s, survivor-historian Phillip Friedman published an extensive list-to-do of Holocaust research. However, nearly all of the items on his agenda remained untouched until the 1980s. There was no field of Holocaust Studies then – rather, research focused on Nazi Germany as a totalitarian or fascist dictatorship. Now, Holocaust Studies have dominated interpretations of Nazi Germany, and in many ways of modern Germany itself.

Holocaust Studies originated outside of Germany, mostly in North America, Britain, Israel, Australia, and in other places where Jews emigrated after the war.

A Companion to Nazi Germany, First Edition. Edited by Shelley Baranowski,
Armin Nolzen, and Claus-Christian W. Szejnmann.

But in the 1990s, it emerged in Germany itself with a new generation of graduate students (Dieter Pohl, Christian Gerlach, Andrej Angrick, Wolf Gruner, Christoph Dieckmann, Frank Bajohr, Andrea Löw, among others) who completed their doctoral dissertations on regional studies about the implementation of the 'Final Solution' in Eastern Europe and on Nazi antisemitic practices in Germany and the annexed territories (Herbert 2000). At the same time, camp memorials and former euthanasia killing centres such as Hadamar expanded their exhibits. Today, more German scholars are engaged in the topic than ever before but the history of the Holocaust has lost its centre in Germany and has become a subject of European history, and especially of Eastern European history.

The recent trend is towards both a broader geographical scope of the 'Final Solution' and a deeper examination of local events and diverse actors. Paralleling the rise of social history, perpetrator studies turned to biographies of the ordinary killers, mostly men, and of the killing itself and mostly outside of the camp system. A cumulative effect of these research trends – of regional studies in Eastern Europe and imperial biographies – has been the Europeanization of Holocaust history; the regional studies took Nazi Germany specialists beyond Germany's wartime borders, as did the biographies that traversed Axis-dominated Europe.

The European view has also shifted the chronology to the war period when Axis forces dominated the continent and when the mass murder phase came to its climax. The pre-war stages of persecution in Germany (anti-Jewish legislation, boycotts, racial laws) are not questioned; they are generally accepted as foundational or as mere background to the more compelling and pressing problem of the mass complicity and violence across Europe. Research revolving around the killing phase actually started with the earlier debate on decision making and now has proliferated into micro-histories of the crimes – the 'who, what, where' – and the different crimes that constituted the Holocaust: theft, torture, slave labour, ghettoization, sexual violence. Post-war testimonies are more widely used and cited than Nazi documentation. The contrast between Raul Hilberg's magisterial work on the destruction of European Jews (1961) and Saul Friedländer's two volumes on German Jews and on the years of extermination (1997, 2007) provides a clear example of the historiographical shift away from an emphasis on the behemoth of the Nazi bureaucracy as a Berlin-centred machine to a stress on the diverse experiences of the Jews and the details of their mass murder across Europe. Bookending the historiography in this way, of course, does not account for all the published volumes in between. Taken together, the voluminous library of case studies and grand narratives reveals how the Holocaust happened, but not why. No single explanation, be it antisemitism, Nazi colonialism, Nazi culture, Hitler, or working towards the Führer, suffices. There were many causes, which are still being identified, explained, and compared.

In this chapter, I argue that the Europeanization of Holocaust Studies, above all its 'spatial turn', has been the most important recent development in the field, and that it is important because it challenges scholars of Nazi Germany to become transnational comparativists, which entails paradigm shifts and acquiring additional languages and interdisciplinary methodological approaches. It also forces a rethinking of the distribution of power in the Nazi system, the imperial dynamic of the centre and periphery, as well as the relations between the occupier and occupied. The categories of victims and perpetrators have also expanded to include non-Jews and non-Germans. I focus here on four features of the current Holocaust historiography that pertain to the Europeanizing trends: (i) decision making and proximity, (ii) biography, (iii) collaboration, and (iv) sources. In my conclusion, I assess advances and lacunae in the historiography, and suggest future research directions.

34.1 Decision Making and Proximity

In September 1942, Reich Führer of the SS Police Heinrich Himmler assembled the top brass at his field headquarters in Ukraine. At one point in his long lecture, he urged his SS and police commanders to 'make decisions in the field' (Lower 2002, 1–22). About one year later in Poland, Himmler gathered his men again, this time speaking about the 'Jewish question', remarking: 'Most of you know what it means to see a hundred corpses lying together, five hundred, or a thousand.' By then, more than 80% of the Jews who were murdered in the Holocaust were dead, as well as millions of Soviet prisoners of war, and other victim groups. In the 1990s, the origins debate branched out into studies of regional decision making, locating the centre in the periphery and tracing the dynamics of policy formulation and implementation vertically from the bottom up and top down, and horizontally across German agencies, including those that dealt with non-German Axis leaders in Slovakia, Hungary, Croatia, and Romania. As a result, the evolution and implementation of the Nazi 'Final Solution' as a state policy has been recast as a series of radicalizing, incremental decisions that occurred chronologically, and in different key regional centres (e.g. Pretzsch, Lublin, Minsk, Mogilev, Warsaw, and Zhytomyr). Is the lack of one Hitler order as important as the existence of hundreds, perhaps thousands of orders issued by regional commanders in the SS police and the Wehrmacht, and by their indigenous helpers in their native languages? A document such as the Wannsee Protocol, which had long been misunderstood as evidence of a fundamental decision, has been deconstructed into its parts: each of the agencies and persona represented at that infamous meeting has been covered in biographies, and many of the countries listed as genocidal targets have been researched as regional histories (Roseman 2003).

While there is still no consensus about a single order or decision made by Hitler, there is general agreement about the stages of implementation, and that the mass murder of innocent civilians commenced with the outbreak of the war in September 1939, and expanded most aggressively against the Jews with the unleashing of Operation Barbarossa in late June 1941. While mass murder operations against Jews can no longer been seen in isolation from the campaigns against the Nazis' other targeted victims – the mentally and physically disabled, Polish intellectuals, the Roma, and Soviet prisoners of war – an integrated history of all victim perspectives (Jewish and non-Jewish) and perpetrator motivations (German and non-German) is still lacking. Saul Friedländer came closest in his synthesis of

German and Jewish history (1997, 2007). Timothy Snyder's focus on Poland and Eastern Europe (2010), placing the Holocaust in the Nazi–Soviet vice, is geographically narrower but historically more inclusive of political and social actors who were perpetrators, victims, rescuers, collaborators, and bystanders. Christian Gerlach's study (2016) grapples with the European context in a comparative manner that is geographically more expansive, and thematically selective. He teases out specific topics such as antisemitic legislation in under-studied countries, arguing in this case that anti-Jewish attitudes based on race, economy, and xenophobia coexisted in 'different strands' and 'were everywhere enmeshed' (Gerlach, 2016, 314). Although an impressive synthesis, Gerlach's pioneering comparative study of various national histories has not closed the gap between the historiography of Eastern and Western Europe. In other words, while the history has become more European, a European history of the Holocaust has not yet been written.

The spatial turn has operated at a macro and micro level, and pivoted to the East's mass murder sites. The collapse of the Soviet Union opened up the archives as well as the killing fields to researchers, encouraging analysis that combines micro history, forensic anthropology, and testimony collection. The Soviet Extraordinary Commission records, former KGB investigations, and post-war trials centre on the crime scenes and local witnesses, and often contain details about the exhumation of mass graves (Lutz et al. 2015; David-Fox, Holquist, and Martin 2014). Soviet memorials to the victims of fascism provide scholars with additional signposts for identifying the sites of mass murder, and the victims. Karel Berkhoff studied the Soviet obliteration and dispersal of ashes at Babi Yar as the history of the Communist Party's suppression of the history there and the continuity of antisemitism. With digital mapping software, historians can more easily plot and visualize the paths of deportees or the layout of a ghetto, thereby corroborating and combining testimonies (Berkhoff 2016).

A proponent of the Geographical Informational System (GIS), historian Waitman Beorn (2014) applies spatial concepts to his analysis of Wehrmacht complicity. After retracing the steps of Jews who were marched to the mass shooting site in the Skrydlevo Forest in Belarus, he argued that 'this journey impressed upon me the value of actually visiting these sites of killing and of thinking of the killing as a spatial problem, for this is how the perpetrators themselves viewed their task in the East and … the task of murdering Jews in general … Thinking spatially means more than merely investigating the landscape; it means questioning the importance of such historical concepts' (2014, 293).

Beorn re-examines key documents of the Holocaust with a new emphasis on the meaning of topography and distance. After the Mogilev conference of September 1941, where the killing of Jews was sanctioned by generals in the Wehrmacht and Waffen-SS as an acceptable form of 'anti-partisan' warfare, local army commanders (such as those attached to the 707th Infantry Division in Belarus) were empowered to execute or ghettoize Jews in the countryside. The killing sites that they selected (often with the help of local collaborators) varied significantly (ravines, Jewish cemeteries, wells, peat bogs, shell craters) but they were not random. They were selected for physical, spatial, and ideological reasons (e.g. ease of excavation, concealment, and access). Beorn questioned whether these spatial decisions reveal the attitudes of ordinary soldiers on the ground who became complicit, and he discovered that 'one attribute all soldiers had concerning their participation in a variety of killings across the Soviet Union was that of position'. Soldiers were routinely tasked with encirclement operations. They formed a cordon around a village to prevent Jews from escaping deportations or shooting sites. Soldiers could decide on the spot whether they remained at the edge of the operation, blocked Jews who beseeched them to open up the circle to allow escape, or moved closer to the centre of the action. These choices of position reflected attitudes and shaped peer relationships and individual reputations. Those who opted to stand outside the cordon were deemed weaker characters. Post-war memoirs and testimonies of soldiers continued to draw on spatial references. When questioned about massacres, a former soldier gave a vivid account, which proved his proximity, but then claimed that he was hundreds of metres from the violence – amounting to a proximity version of self-exculpatory testimony and a form of psychological distancing. Beorn concludes that 'the overlaying of a mental (moral) map on the physical position of individuals may be a useful approach' (Beorn 2014, 302–303). It applied to his analysis of complicit German soldiers, and Beorn suggests that it might also help to explain wartime attitudes and memories of victims and collaborators.

In both studies of Germans who stayed close to home in Germany and of the millions who experienced Nazi-occupied Europe, the theme of proximity is significant. The nearness of historical actors to the crimes, their response and choices, and the impact on their lives have become questions of historical inquiry. Proximity is also a vexing methodological matter that combines elements of time and space. The Holocaust is recent history, and contemporary history. It is being written from private archives, interviews with direct witnesses including survivors and perpetrators, and in former camps and crime scenes where bones, ashes, and personal effects are uncovered. Proximity also relates to the emotional impact – how closely one directly experienced the violence. A Jewish-Lithuanian philosopher of this era, Emanuel Levinas, described the act of violence as an ontological event that changes the lives of all involved: victims, survivors, perpetrators, collaborators, witnesses, and their descendants. Historians interact with those involved and with their descendants. They mine personal photographs, diaries, letters, and recollections. These opportunities to get closer to the past in a more intimate, personal way also challenge historians to maintain their distance, and to avoid bias and moralizing.

The European Holocaust as geography is also taking shape in the form of cartography. The plotting of Nazi detention sites is now so extensive that they virtually blanket the continent. According researchers at the United States Holocaust Memorial Museum, there were more than 40 000 sites. The historical implications of this astounding number are significant. Who managed these sites? Who were the prisoners? What were the functions of these sites, and what were the mortality rates of prisoners who suffered there? How were these sites connected to local communities and persons who staffed and supplied the camps with guards and material? Deborah Dwork, Robert Jan van Pelt, and Sybille Steinbacher wrote histories of the town of Auschwitz and region, placing the killing centre in its historical setting (Dwork and van Pelt 1996; Steinbacher 2005).

Auschwitz-Birkenau remains at the centre of our imagined European landscape and history of the Holocaust. Yet, new work by Nicholas Wachsmann (2015) places it within a total and 'distinct system of domination'. The concentration camps, he finds,

> came to reflect the burning obsessions of the Nazi leadership, such as the creation of a uniform national community through the removal of political, social, and racial outsiders; the sacrifice of the individual on the altar of racial hygiene and murderous science; the harnessing of forced labor for the glory of the fatherland; the mastery over Europe, enslaving foreign nations, and colonizing living space; the deliverance of Germany from its worst enemies through mass extermination; and finally the determination to go down in flames rather than surrender. (5–6)

In his comprehensive analysis, Wachsmann depicts the evolution of the system as Nazi Germany's rise and fall in Europe, not as a collection of discrete camp histories somewhat detached from Hitler's imperial, racial ambitions and military conquests across Europe. Wachsmann offers an explanation, not a plotting. Outside the gassing factories of death, some 1.7 million men, women, and children lost their lives in the system of SS-run concentration camps. A system of this magnitude could not be remote, neither in an ordinary German's imagination nor in everyday experiences. In short, micro histories of these camps can no longer be seen in isolation from the regional economies and local power structures. This fact raises questions about the daily decisions and choices made by ordinary Germans, and how they intentionally or unwittingly contributed to a total system of domination. To what extent was the Holocaust the sum of these many closely moving parts?

34.2 Biography

For scholars of Nazi Germany and the Holocaust in Europe, one way to deal with the *Transfergeschichte* of porous regional borders and overlapping cultures is through biography. High-ranking and ordinary German occupiers, be they policemen, regional governors, plunderers, technocrats, or women in various supportive roles, appear in a new light, not in the shadow of Berlin but as everyday agents in an openly genocidal system that expanded across Europe. Individual patriotism, zeal, motives, and ethical dilemmas are being studied, thus giving us a greater understanding of the diverse generational cohorts of German men and women who operated the machinery of destruction of both the war and the Holocaust as intertwined endeavours. The biographical trend stresses the inter-war period as the formative years, or as a stage of development that is then, in wartime, put to the test of adaptation, complicity, or resistance, and all the grey areas of behaviour in between. Catherine Epstein's work on Wartheland *Gauleiter* Arthur Greiser (2012), Martin Cueppers' on gas van expert Walther Rauff (2013), and various collections of biographies such as *Die Taeter der Shoah* paint a more nuanced picture of individual agency and character development (Paul 2002). In Mary Fulbrook's *A Small Town Near Auschwitz: Ordinary Nazis and the Holocaust* (2012), the main subject is Udo Klausner, a county administrator sent to Bedzin to govern the area around Auschwitz. Klausner is close to an epicentre of the mass murder and is forced to confront the depths of his antisemitism, at first being indifferent to the Jews and then, in the face of the genocide, struggling with his conscience and humanity. Rather than condemn or judge Klausner as 'a perpetrator', Fulbrook reconstructs the complex pressures and changing circumstances that he navigated. Intertwining multiple biographies of ordinary Germans is also the threading technique found in the larger syntheses by Richard Evans and Nicholas Stargardt, made possible by the diary, letter writing, memoir, and testimony boom of the twentieth and twenty-first centuries. Based largely on *Feldpostbriefe*, Stargardt's *The German War: A Nation Under Arms, 1939–1945* (2015) offers a group portrait of Germans as both reluctant warriors and violent conquerors acting to defend the fatherland. They did not blindly follow Hitler on a quest for global domination, but could hardly fathom the genocidal war in the East that they unleashed.

The biography boom (fuelled by vast testimonial sources) has also placed the Nazi era in a twentieth-century narrative of German history. The question of continuity in German history is no longer about tracing the peculiar development of Germany's special path to Nazism, but rather about charting the Reich's radical turning points during the war, and tracing how this catastrophe reverberated into the post-war era. Holocaust history has also been pushing the chronology of Nazi Germany forward into aftermath studies. As historians David Blackbourn (2013) and Helmut Walser Smith observed, 'Once the big question was, how did we get to 1933, now the question is "how was the Holocaust possible?" 1941, not 1933 has become the "vanishing point".' The continuity questions pivot on the war period and zero hour of 1945. The deep causes – structural ones that extend backwards into the nineteenth century (and earlier) – are treated lightly, if at all. While the chronology contracts around the Holocaust, the space of action of actors expands beyond Germany's shifting borders. Most ordinary Germans in the twentieth century left their home towns, willingly or not – or if they did not leave, the spaces in which they lived changed dramatically from regime, to occupation, to reunification, as the German question and the criminal legacy of the Third Reich became central to European history.

34.3   Collaboration

Before the rise in Holocaust Studies in the 1990s, 'collaboration' was defined mainly by its occurrence in France and Norway – in its crudest depictions, as sexual or 'horizontal' female collaboration and as political or quisling betrayal. Holocaust researchers discovered that the voluminous trial records in former communist archives identified 'traitors to the homeland' as those who committed war crimes related to the mass murder of Jews, communists, and other victim groups. In fact, most individuals who were convicted of crimes related to the Holocaust were not Germans but Poles, Lithuanians, Ukrainians, Latvians, and Belarusians. The political implications of this proved incendiary. Jan Gross's *Neighbors* (2001), in which he describes how roughly half the population of Poles in the town of Jedwabne slaughtered and burned alive the other half of the town's population of Jews, set off a firestorm in Poland epitomizing how individual nations have been coming to terms with complicity in the Holocaust, expanding Hitler's shadow beyond Germany and the Germans, and illuminating the depths of violent antisemitism across Eastern Europe. Complicity was more than a local affair, as in Jedwabne, or in Vilnius or Kiev. Timothy Snyder's comparative study, *Bloodlands: Europe Between Hitler and Stalin* (2010), argues, in a manner reminiscent of the totalitarian theorists decades earlier, that Hitler and Stalin had much in common with one another – and in particular their shared desire to destroy Poland and exploit Eastern Europe as empire builders and ideological foes. The entanglement of the Hitler and Stalin regimes had a lethal force of its own. However, taking Doris Bergen's critique of *Bloodlands* further (2012), the mass shootings of Polish and Ukrainian Jews and the inter-war history of Stalin's terror do not fully explain the actual and planned Nazi deportation of Jews from the Netherlands, Greece, North Africa, and Ireland. Also, there were other important regional leaders whose biographies intersected and shaped history, not just Hitler and Stalin, for example, the Axis leaders Mussolini, Tito, Antonescu, Pétain, Horthy, Franco, Kvaternick, and the Grand Mufti.

As a history both of collaboration and of Nazi occupation in the East, historian Christoph Dieckmann's case study of Lithuania (2011) is an outstanding achievement, largely owing to his command of German, Lithuanian, Russian, English, Yiddish, and Hebrew sources. He demonstrates that while Nazi colonization in theory entailed doing away with the 'useless eaters' and 'inferior Slavs', in practice German rulers also needed the local population to help implement their plans. The occupied consisted of those who suffered immediate death (Jews, communists, the disabled) and those who benefited in the interim. Lithuanian patriots were eager to maintain their independent nationhood in a state purged of communists and minorities, which dovetailed with the Nazi aims. Shared antisemitism, anti-communism, as well as opportunism and greed, forged unlikely alliances – mostly fleeting ones but deadly and destructive nonetheless. Rivalries and internecine struggles, long a theme in polycratic theories of the dynamism of power and terror in Hitler's Germany, were not the overriding force in the German occupation administrations where military, civilian, and private sector agencies collaborated in waging the war, defending the fatherland and colonizing Europe. Studies of Germans at war, in the Holocaust and in the Nazi empire in the East, stress the unifying forces of nationalism and antisemitism in the *Heimat*, and in the imperial borderlands. Nazi leaders at Wannsee and elsewhere spoke of a European solution to the 'Jewish question'. The anti-communism of the Nazi campaign also united Europeans, especially as Hitler was portrayed as the liberator of Europe, leading Axis forces in the anti-Bolshevik crusade.

The radicalization and escalation narrative is no longer restricted to studies of German rank and file, but narrated as Polish, Ukrainians, Lithuanian, French, and Dutch history. Jan Grabowski's regional case study of the Polish Blue Police (2013) is exemplary in this regard. Polish police wishing to avoid harsh reprisals from Nazi leaders secretly killed Jews they uncovered in hiding. Local Poles assisted by turning over Jews because they feared that the discovery of Jews would lead to more violence against them and their families residing in or near the hidden Jews. Rather than judge and condemn collaborators, historians are teasing out the myriad motives and local factors. But more could be done to show how the biographies of local collaborators intersected with German ones, producing a negative synergy that expanded the number of Jews murdered across Nazi-occupied Europe.

34.4   Sources

Arguably, the Europeanization of the Holocaust could not have occurred without the collapse of the Soviet Union. As long as the Iron Curtain divided scholarship between East and West and blocked access to archives, there scarcely existed an opening for the many topics referenced here: spatiality, imperialism and colonialism, Eastern Europe's killing fields, and the biographies and forms of individual and group collaboration. Research has increased as a result of major declassification efforts and a rise in oral history and memoir writing, and many collections (digital and in print) provide excellent samplings of the powerful material, which consists of tens of millions of pages and tens of thousands of hours of videotaped testimony. No single scholar could watch all the footage in her lifetime (Greenspan 2010). The International Tracing Service archives and restitution records are already moving the field into new directions that will represent the experiences of millions of non-Jewish forced labourers and displaced persons. While some historians bemoan the continued ethnic approach to the past (i.e. reifying national differences and assuming stable, definable ethnonational identities), this approach is unavoidable in Holocaust Studies since the Nazi era was a crisis of ethnonationalism and statelessness, and a near-triumph of the evils of racism. Whether or not one believed oneself to be German, Jewish, Polish, French, Slavic, or Nordic, these labels determined one's destiny in Nazi-dominated Europe. And they influenced the source material and how historians interpret it. For example, a large proportion of German Jews survived through emigration, and there exists more survivor testimony from Western European Jews who survived Auschwitz-Birkenau than Jews who were deported to gassing centres in Poland or who were shot in Ukraine. Thus, German Jews are over-represented in the testimony, and the narrative of pre-war Jewish life focuses on Hitler's Germany. We know less about pre-war Jewish life in other countries.

Historians have relied on judicial records and witness testimonies for centuries, but the situation in Holocaust Studies is unusual because the records are being used almost exclusively to reconstruct the histories of crimes as social, political, cultural, and environmental history. Holocaust historian-detectives, writing in this 'era of the witness', have introduced a narrative discourse and methodology that is historiographically unprecedented. A subfield of trial histories in European comparison has grown up (Frei 2006; Matthäus and Heberer 2008). Historians are finding the legalese morally problematic and imprecise yet difficult to avoid in their narrative explanations. Scholars have become uncomfortably aware of this, and many have been critical of Hilberg's categorizing of perpetrators, victims, and bystanders (1993) as too rigid and judgemental. Testimony as a source base and concept has been problematized (Scholars' Forum 2014).

The voluminous archival material and the challenge of reading its many languages have led to a diffusion and imbalance of historical topics and disciplinary approaches. Some thematic approaches lend themselves to transnational analyses, such as the trials and studies of pogroms, or of diaries and diary writing, or of the theft of Jewish property and restitution. Yet scholars of the Holocaust working on national or regional cases, such as Diana Dumitru's excellent work on Moldova (2016), and Natalia Aleksiun's (2016) study of Jewish families hiding in bunkers in western Ukraine, demonstrate that it is possible to write histories of the Holocaust with little or no mention of Germans. For Holocaust specialists working in Poland, France, and elsewhere outside of Germany, the lack of expertise on German history, the Nazi Party, and pre-war events – and an inability to read German sources – may lead to a provincializing and not Europeanizing of Holocaust history. More translations of monographs, and exchange of scholarship between those specializing in Nazi Germany and German history more generally and those who are working on Holocaust history outside of Germany, could correct these imbalances and encourage the writing of a truly integrated, European history.

34.5 Future Directions

The overall growth in Holocaust Studies is impressive but fractured. There are few of the central questions and binding themes found in earlier studies on antisemitism, the origins of the 'Final Solution', perpetrator motivations, resistance of victims, and responses of bystanders. The stress on multi-causality has added the necessary nuance but diverted attention from core issues that engulfed all of Europe, and could be applied to genocide studies more broadly. At present there are few debates driving the field.

As for narrative histories centred on Germany, Richard Evans' three volumes are probably the most comprehensive (2003, 2005, 2008). But the intersections between the historiography of the Holocaust and Nazi Germany are not as clear and logical as one might assume. Whereas study of everyday history – *Alltagsgeschichte* – is well established, it is just beginning to be applied to the occupied territories of Europe (Bergerson and Schmieding 2016). Perhaps this is in part because survivors rarely speak about the everyday. Perhaps they don't remember the mundane, or perhaps they don't wish to recount it for fear of trivializing or normalizing the history. During the Holocaust their lives were in crisis mode and they struggled for a sense of normalcy, and perhaps survivors anticipate that listeners would rather hear about the ruptures in their lives.

Economic histories of the Reich, especially during the war, have looked at various macro and micro developments in financing the war, armaments productions, and the use of labour, consumption patterns, and spoliation. However, few have analysed the economy as a field of social interaction where integration or alienation took place among Germans and Jews. Rather than focus on the relationship between 'economic constraints and ideological imperatives in Nazi genocidal policy' or calculate whether genocide is profitable, research into economic crimes as well as the overall financial system created by the Germans could open up new areas of understanding social, cultural, and political history (Bartov 2015). Did the war economy, including its local German and non-German profiteers, developers, and entrepreneurs, in some way produce relationships and conditions that contributed to the erosion of human rights and the violence of the genocide? How does the history of theft and consumption relate to the motivations of perpetrators and collaborators across socio-economic classes who bartered the most personal Jewish belongings during and after the war?

Saul Friedländer, in *The Years of Extermination* (2007), aimed for an integrated history and called on other historians to follow his lead. What does this mean, exactly? Can the perspectives and experiences of the victims, perpetrators, and bystanders all be represented in a comprehensive way, especially with the inherent imbalances of source material? Friedländer, and recently Omer Bartov, railed against Holocaust history writing that omitted or muted the voices of the victims. Syntheses such as Friedländer's strike a better balance thanks to the increasing availability of survivor testimonies. Yet the diversity of Jewish experiences – religious and secular, age groups, gender, etc. – has not been represented as a total history of Jewish experiences (victims and survivors). Calls for integration are not calls for artificially balancing out stories so that all can be represented. The argument is for a heightened sensitivity to the real diversity of prisoner populations and more rigour in recording events from multiple perspectives. Studies that integrate victim experiences – for example, showing the interaction of prisoner populations across categories – are rare (Langbein 2004).

The Jewish question and Nazi antisemitism were at the centre of Nazi ideology and are accepted among historians as a core story and legacy of the Third Reich, as Telford Taylor observed, yet the interactions of the different genocidal programmes and among the victims themselves have not been adequately analysed. What were relations among prisoners, across categories inside and outside the camps? Why does there seem to have been little solidarity? Likewise, how did German officials discuss and compare Nazi policies of mass murder? Henry Friedlander's work is among the few to demonstrate the connections between the euthanasia campaign and the 'Final Solution'. Recent work on the *Rasse- und SiedlungsHauptamt* has focused on the causal connections and, to some extent, the perceptions of the regional German officials working on resettlement operations. The work implicitly seeks to contextualize the Holocaust of the Jews, sometimes diminishing it as a function or byproduct of Nazi Germanization or Himmler's the General Plan East. Here the spatial turn most clearly takes its cue from Celia Applegate's (1990) work on the mediating forces and influences bridging the provincial and national. The expansionist drive was a defining feature of Nazism, keeping the idea of *Heimat* in flux as Germany's borders changed rapidly during the war, and as German leaders undertook social engineering campaigns constantly reshaping and testing the idea of a 'native Germany' and racially pure German (Szejnmann and Umbach 2012). For German historians, this change forced a re-examination of agency in an imperial context where Germans (and *Volksdeutschen*) held power but were a minority that depended on indigenous helpers.

On the perpetrator side, the forms and scale of participation are being delineated along the lines of direct killing, indirect contribution, and active and passive bystanding. But the fact that people slipped in and out of roles along this scale, and that they changed while navigating the everyday in extremes, is under-represented. This understanding should steer scholars away from the moralizing trap of lumping together individual action and response into legalistic categories of victims, accomplices, perpetrators, and bystanders. While it is possible to estimate the number of victims, to tabulate death tolls and come up with rough estimates (knowing that in many communities, especially in Eastern Europe, Jews were annihilated without any trace of documentation), a similar attempt to quantify perpetrators falls short – especially as the forms of involvement become more elastic, such as the stealing of property, acts of denunciation, extortion of those in hiding, sexual transgressions, and forms of exploitation and persecution. In addition, by definition genocide is a collective crime – ergo there is a division of labour in the abuse and annihilation, a spreading of complicity into grey areas that the courts could not prosecute and historians are better able to describe and interpret. Instead of condemning behaviour or judging entire institutions – such as the Catholic or Protestant (Evangelical) churches – work by Martina Cucchiara (2016) and Jonathan Huener (2014), for example, focuses on the regional differences manifested in a particular diocese, religious-run school or orphanage, and other local variations. These discoveries, driven by bottom-up approaches as textured social histories, illuminate how the social informs the political and vice versa, but challenge us to identify the broader patterns of behaviour within Germany and indeed across Europe. The key is not to place individuals into categories, but to trace how they change over time – as individuals and as a generational cohort in particular settings, circumstances, administrative cultures, occupations, and so on.

How can the history of the Holocaust be written as German and European history, considering the great diversity of state institutions, people, and ideas set in a tumultuous era of revolutionary change and continental war? Even integration as a historical form needs to be problematized as such. Integration operates on many planes; thus one must consider not only the historical subjects – the people who interact and shape each other's destinies, seeing where power is held and how it is abused and experienced by men and women of different ages – but also the multiple forces or causes: the ideology, the political, social, economic, and cultural traditions and institutions. The overarching challenge will be to reconstruct the past along these varied axes, not only to be more comprehensible and careful in considering all possible causes and influences, but to be able to determine their imbalances, and changing configurations across time and space. This may not be achievable. And it may not be the right goal in the end, because when one reads the sources closely and listens to individual testimonies, one discovers new factors and phenomena that defy explanation and comparison. Telford Taylor and his team of prosecutors at Nuremberg were correct in suggesting that the 'Final Solution' would be the main legacy of the Third Reich, but they could not have imagined this fertile, expanding field of Holocaust Studies.

References

Aleksiun, Natalia. 2016. 'Daily Survival: Social History of Jews in Family Bunkers in Eastern Galicia.' In *Lessons and Legacies XII: New Directions in Holocaust Research and Education*, edited by Wendy Lower and Lauren Faulkner Rossi. Evanston, IL: Northwestern University Press.

Applegate, Celia. 1990. *A Nation of Provincials: The German Idea of Heimat*. Berkeley: University of California Press.

Bartov, Omer. 2015. 'Genocide and the Holocaust: Arguments over History and Politics.' In *Lessons and Legacies XI: Expanding Perspectives on the Holocaust in a Changing World*, edited by Hilary Earl and Karl Schleunes, 5–28. Evanston, IL: Northwestern University Press.

Beorn, Waitman Wade. 2014. 'Walking in the Footsteps of the Vanished: Using Physical Landscapes to Understand Wehrmacht Participation in Einsatzgruppen Killings in Belarus.' In *Lessons and Legacies XI: Expanding Perspectives in a Changing World*, edited by Hilary Earl and Karl Schleunes. Bloomington: Indiana University Press.

Bergen, Doris. 2012. '"The Loneliness of the Dying": General and Particular Victimization in Timothy Snyder's *Bloodlands: Europe Between Hitler and Stalin*." *Journal of Modern Russian History and Historiography* 4(1), 206–222.

Bergerson, Andrew and Schmieding, Leonard, eds. 2016. *Ruptures in the Everyday*. New York: Berghahn Books.

Berkhoff, Karel. 2016. 'The Dispersal and Oblivion of Ashes and Bones of Babi Yar.' In *Lessons and Legacies XII: New Directions in Holocaust Research and Education*, edited by Wendy Lower and Lauren Faulkner Rossi. Evanston, IL: Northwestern University Press.

Blackbourn, David. 2013. "Honey, I Shrunk German History." GSA address. *German Studies Association Newsletter* 38(2).

Cucchiara, Martina. 2016. 'Jewish Girls in Catholic Schools in Nazi Germany, 1933–1938.' In *Lessons and Legacies XII: New Directions in Holocaust Research and Education*, edited by Wendy Lower and Lauren Faulkner Rossi. Evanston, IL: Northwestern University Press.

Cueppers, Martin. 2013. *Walther Rauff, in deutschen Diensten, Marine, Massenmorde und Exil*. Stuttgart: Wissenschaftliche Buchgesellschaft.

David-Fox, Michael, Holquist, Peter and Martin, Alexander M., eds. 2014. *The Holocaust in the East: Local Perpetrators and Soviet Responses*. Pittsburgh, PA: University of Pittsburg Press.

Dieckmann, Christoph. 2011. *Deutsche Besatzungspolitik in Litauen 1941–1944*. Wallstein.

Dumitru, Diana. 2016. *The State, Antisemitism and Collaboration in the Holocaust: The Borderlands of Romania and the Soviet Union*. New York: Cambridge University Press.

Dwork, Debórah and Jan van Pelt, Robert. 1996. *Auschwitz, 1270 to the Present*. New York: W.W. Norton.

Eckert, Astrid. 2014. *The Struggle for the Files: The Western Allies and the Return of German Archives after the Second World War*. Cambridge: Cambridge University Press.

Epstein, Catherine. 2012. *Model Nazi: Arthur Greiser and the Occupation of Western Poland*. New York: Oxford University Press.

Evans, Richard. 2003. *The Coming of the Third Reich*. New York: Penguin.

Evans, Richard. 2005. *The Third Reich in Power*. New York: Penguin.

Evans, Richard. 2008. *The Third Reich at War*. New York: Penguin.

Frei, Norbert, ed. 2006. *Transnationale Vergangenheitspolitik: Der Umgang mit deutschen Kriegsverbrechern in Europa nach dem Zweiten Weltkrieg*. Wallstein.

Friedländer, Saul. 1997. *Nazi Germany and the Jews, Volume 1: The Years of Persecution, 1933–1939*. New York: HarperCollins.

Friedländer, Saul. 2007. *Nazi Germany and the Jews, Volume 2: The Years of Extermination, 1939–1945*. New York: HarperCollins.

Fulbrook, Mary. 2012. *A Small Town Near Auschwitz: Ordinary Nazis and the Holocaust*. Oxford: Oxford University Press.

Gerlach, Christian. 2016. *The Extermination of the European Jews*. Cambridge: Cambridge University Press.

Grabowski, Jan. 2013. *Hunt for the Jews: Betrayal and Murder in Occupied Poland.* Bloomington: Indiana University Press.

Greenspan, Henry. 2010. 'Survivors' Accounts.' In *The Oxford Handbook of Holocaust Studies*, edited by Peter Hayes and John K. Roth, 414–427. New York: Oxford University Press.

Gross, Jan. 2001. *Neighbors: The Destruction of the Jewish Community in Jedwabne, Poland.* Princeton, NJ: Princeton University Press.

Herbert, Ulrich, ed. 2000. *Nazi Socialist Extermination Policies: Contemporary German Perspectives and Controversies.* New York: Berghahn Books.

Hilberg, Raul. 1961. *The Destruction of the European Jews.* New Haven, CT: Yale University Press.

Hilberg, Raul. 1993. *Perpetrators, Victims, Bystanders: The Jewish Catastrophe, 1933–1945.* New York: Harper Perennial.

Huener, Jonathan. 2014. 'Nazi Kirchenpolitik and Polish Catholicism in the Reichsgau Wartheland, 1939–1945.' *Central European History* 47(1), 105–137.

Langbein, Hermann. 2004. *People in Auschwitz.* Chapel Hill: University of North Carolina Press.

Lower, Wendy. 2002. '"Anticipatory Obedience" and the Nazi Implementation of the Holocaust in the Ukraine: A Case Study of Central and Peripheral Forces in the Generalbezirk Zhytomyr, 1941–1944.' *Holocaust and Genocide Studies* 16(1), 1–22.

Lutz, Thomas, Silberklang, David, Trojański, Piotr, Wetzel, Juliane, and Bistrovic, Miriam, eds. 2015. *Killing Sites: Research and Remembrance.* Berlin: Metropol.

Matthäus, Jürgen and Heberer, Patricia, eds. 2008. *Atrocities on Trial: Historical Perspective on the Politics of Prosecuting War Crimes.* Lincoln: University of Nebraska Press.

Paul, Gerhard. 2002. *Die Taeter der Shoah: Fanatische Nationalsozialisten or ganz normale Deutsche.* Wallstein.

Roseman, Mark. 2003. *The Wannsee Conference and the Final Solution: A Reconsideration.* New York: Picador.

Scholars' Forum. 2014. 'Testimony and Trauma: Engaging Survivors: Assessing "Testimony" and "Trauma" as Foundational Concepts.' *Dapim: Studies on the Holocaust* 28(3), 190–226.

Snyder, Timothy. 2010. *Bloodlands: Europe Between Hitler and Stalin.* New York: Basic Books.

Stargardt, Nicholas. 2015. *The German War: A Nation Under Arms, 1939–1945.* New York: Basic Books.

Steinbacher, Sybille. 2005. *Auschwitz: A History*, translated by Shaun Whiteside. Munich: C.H. Beck.

Szejnmann, Claus-Christian W. and Umbach, Maiken, eds. 2012. *Heimat, Region, and Empire: Spatial Identities under National Socialism.* Basingstoke, UK: Palgrave Macmillan.

Taylor, Telford. 1947. 'Memorandum of Taylor to Ervin, 6 February 1947.' In *Papers of Paul Gantt, Former Prosecutor.* Towson University Library: Archival Collections, File 'Genocide.'

Wachsmann, Nicholas. 2015. *KL: A History of the Nazi Concentration Camps.* New York: Farrar, Straus and Giroux.

Further Reading

Bajohr, Frank and Lowe, Andrea, eds. 2015. *Der Holocaust: Ergebnisse und Neue Fragen der Forschung.* Frankfurt am Main: Fischer Vrlag.

Baranowski, Shelley. 2011. *Nazi Empire: German Colonialism and Imperialism from Bismarck to Hitler.* New York: Cambridge University Press.

Confino. Alon. 2015. *A World Without Jews: The Nazi Imagination from Persecution to Genocide*. New Haven, CT: Yale University Press.

Cueppers, Martin, Matthaeus, Juergen, and Angrick, Andrej, eds. 2014. *Naziverbrechen: Taeter, Taten, Bewaeltigungsversuche*. Stuttgart: Forschungsstelle Ludwigsburg der Universitaet Stuttgart.

Dumitru, Diana. 2016. *The State, Antisemitism and Collaboration in the Holocaust: The Borderlands of Romania and the Soviet Union*. New York: Cambridge University Press.

Jockusch, Laura. 2012. *Collect and Record! Jewish Holocaust Documentation in Early Postwar Europe*. New York: Oxford University Press.

Kuehne, Thomas. 2010. *Belonging and Genocide: Hitler's Community, 1918–1945*. New Haven, CT: Yale University Press.

PART V

Legacies of Nazism

CHAPTER THIRTY-FIVE

Memories of Nazi Germany in the Federal Republic of Germany

ALEIDA ASSMANN

When investigating memories of the Nazi past in post-war Germany, it is important to start with a few general observations. The first point is that we have to be aware of an ambivalence in the meaning of 'memories' with respect to the Nazi past. While it took decades before a memory of the Holocaust was built up in Germany, clearly there was, after 1945, an abundance of personal and collective memories relating to involvement or non-involvement in the National Socialist (NS) regime, the Second World War, and its consequences. Saul Friedlander (1994, 257) drew attention to this important difference when he wrote: 'What was traumatic for the one group was obviously not traumatic for the other.' While the Jewish trauma emanated from the Holocaust, the German trauma was focused on the national defeat and expulsion, combined with feelings of shame and guilt. A second point is that the term 'memory' is slippery. It requires a constant shifting between the individual, social, cultural, and political levels. As memories are embodied, mediated, and embedded in larger contexts, it is a methodological premise to combine private and official, individual and collective perspectives. And a third point must be added: memory is a cover term for the dynamics of remembering *and* forgetting. Memory is always selective and involves strategies and practices of ignoring, distancing, silencing, denial, and erasure that require special attention.

In West Germany, the memory of the Nazi past has changed considerably over the last 70 years. The periodization of the 'return' of this memory in the post-war and post-unification years evolved over various phases, which provide the chronological structure for this chapter. The division into chunks of 20 years

A Companion to Nazi Germany, First Edition. Edited by Shelley Baranowski,
Armin Nolzen, and Claus-Christian W. Szejnmann.
© 2018 John Wiley & Sons Ltd. Published 2018 by John Wiley & Sons Ltd.

may seem at first somewhat arbitrary but it happens to be supported by seminal and iconic events:

1. The period of transition following the end of the war (1945–1949)
2. The Adenauer era: drawing a final line and starting over (1949–1965)
3. First attempts at a moral engagement with the past (1965–1985)
4. The rise of a new memory culture (1985–2005)
5. New developments, discontents, challenges (2005 onwards)

35.1   The Period of Transition Following the End of the War (1945–1949)

The end of the Second World War initiated a period of transition in which the Allies created measures and new institutions channelling the transformation of the political system from a dictatorship into a Western democracy. The most important measures deployed by the Allies to mark a fundamental break with the former regime were demilitarization, deindustrialization, denazification, re-education, and the Nuremberg trials. The trials, which were the most conspicuous of these measures, implemented transitional justice by convicting and executing leading functionaries of the Third Reich as war criminals. Enforcing for the first time the new law of 'crimes against humanity', these public and publicized trials performed a retrospective trans-valuation of the Nazi era, but they were not yet part of a system of public commemoration. The majority of Germans did not immediately endorse the new value system but assumed a passive stance to the past and dismissed the trials as 'victor's justice'.[1] In 1947, former judge and later president Gustav Heinemann (2005) even argued that the trials may have had the opposite effect of what had been intended: 'Instead of isolating those who had been really responsible for the functioning of the Third Reich, a new (German) solidarity was created (against the allies) which can only be adequately termed as "renazification".'

After the unconditional surrender on 8 and 9 May 1945, and the re-education enforced through the occupation of Germany by Allied forces, new cultural values and memorial frameworks were installed together with the two German states in 1949 that mirrored the political polarization of the Cold War. In both German states, they involved a radical forgetting of the official memory of the Nazi state which had been centred around the First World War, the 'shameful' Treaty of Versailles, and the 'heroes of the movement' (the Kapp-Putsch in Munich in 1923), commemorated on 9 November. In search of a new, usable past in the Cold War, West Germany accepted the political role of the successor state of the NS regime and opted for a (Western) European identity in the NATO (North Atlantic Treaty Organization) alliance, while the East German state (GDR) established a heroic national narrative of communist resistance and became a strong partner within the Soviet bloc. Sociologist Rainer Mario Lespsius coined the terms 'externalization' and 'internalization' to describe a basic law of repression in memory policies. 'Externalization' means that a shameful and burdened legacy of crimes and violence is warded off by attaching it to other historical agents;

'internalization' refers to the much rarer case of a state acknowledging a negative past and integrating it into the public self-image. The GDR, establishing a heroic anti-fascist resistor narrative, 'externalized' the guilty past on to West Germany, while the West German society 'externalized' it on to Hitler and a small clique of criminals (Lepsius 1989; Padover 1946).

While it was easy to overwrite the politicized commemoration calendar of the NS regime with new official dates and rites, it was not so easy to abandon and forget personal biographical memories that no longer fitted into the new political framework. While it is impossible to intentionally erase biographical memories, they can be effectively neutralized by silencing them or circulating them only in small groups, thus withdrawing them from public attention. In his memoir, Uwe Timm (2005, 78) describes the atmosphere of obsessive but hushed-up conversations of former German soldiers: 'The battles were fought over and over again, commands were corrected, incapable generals were dismissed, and Hitler was deprived of his military command. It is unimaginable today that these were themes for long nights among this generation.'

While some struggled with the difficulty of shedding their entrenched illusions and adapting to the new reality, other groups in society arrogantly resisted the new values of re-education, sternly maintaining their former opinions, pride, traditions, and values, continuing to sing the same songs, reading the same books, and admiring the same heroes. But it soon became obvious that these practices had to disappear from public sight. The new political framework imposed a form of self-censorship on society that enforced political correctness and compliance with the new public conventions and values. Eventually, it was adapting to the new rules of conduct rather than a moral conversion that ushered in the new democracy, maintaining a split between a public and a private stance that became a characteristic feature of post-war German memory.

While German memories of the Nazi past and its aftermath abounded, there remained a blind spot, a non-memory of the Holocaust. With the liberation of the concentration camps in the early months of 1945, the unfathomable crimes of the Nazi regime had been immediately and utterly exposed to the eyes of the world. The public images of the liberation of Bergen-Belsen put an abrupt end to a period of secrecy, repression, and looking away. There was a brief period of enforced visual exposure when posters of the liberation of the death camps multiplied and the documentary film *Todesmühlen* was screened in German cities, forcing the population to look at what it had chosen not to see and not to know. This visual policy radically transformed former secrets into public knowledge, but it did not succeed in creating a lasting memory in the German people. To shield themselves against this bitter and shameful truth, many engaged in a discourse of reckoning German against Allied war crimes. Nor was there as yet a public language available for clearly expressing what had happened. Despite explicit statements from survivors, Germans continued rendering the horrendous events in a vague mystic language or shrouding them in silence. Emotions of shame and guilt shattered the collective self-image of the German people, mobilizing various mechanisms of self-defence in order to keep the recent past at bay. While the NS state had pushed pride and collective narcissism, declaring the superiority of the German race, Germans had now to face the negative reputation of being – as Thomas Mann predicted – the 'pariah among the nations'. Sober retrospection and introspection, accompanied by feelings of guilt, empathy, and remorse, were not on the public or private agenda after the catastrophic collapse of Hitler's 'Third Reich'. It took decades before the society as a whole was ready and able to face the past, to create symbols for it and to shape a common narrative that paved the way for new forms of collective commemoration.

35.2   The Adenauer Era – Drawing a Final Line and Starting Over (1949–1965)

In retrospect, philosopher Hermann Lübbe offered a technical term for the decades of German self-censorship after the war, referring to it as 'communicative silence' (*kommunikatives Beschweigen*).[2] When he first presented his description of a 'pact of silence' in 1983, he met with harsh moral criticism by opponents who preferred to label this strategy as post-war politics of repression. In the meantime, Lübbe's theory of a communicative silence has been more or less accepted as a necessary step in the long-term process of a mental and emotional transformation of German society. While change of a political system can be imposed from above by restructuring political institutions, the internal transformation of the society is a process that takes time and evolves over two and more generations. According to Lübbe (1983, 334), silence was an important transformative medium in this long-term process: 'This silence of sorts was the medium that was socially, psychologically and politically necessary to transform our post-war population into the civic society of the Federal Republic of Germany.'

The transformation of the German state has to be qualified as both rupture and continuity. There was an hour zero for the political framework and its institutions, but not for the people who functioned within this framework and its institutions. It turned out that silence, non-communication, and an amnesia of sorts helped people to establish and adapt to the new democratic system.

West Germany's first chancellor, Konrad Adenauer, was the incarnation of this attitude. A resistor against the Nazi regime himself, he had lived in hiding until he was arrested, together with his wife, in the crackdown raids which followed 20 July 1944.[3] Adenauer, who had never chosen to publicize, let alone make political use of his own personal history, felt entitled to a policy of forgetting and forgiving. His political endeavour was oriented towards national and transnational integration and the creation of a common future for all Germans. In his strong determination to let bygones be bygones he even put all considerations of the past behind when recruiting Hans Globke, a jurist and former commentator of the Nazi race laws, as a high-ranking functionary in his administration.

The key terms of the Adenauer political era (1949–1963) were *Aufbruch* ('energetic beginning'), *Schlussstrich* ('closure or drawing a final line under the past'), *Vergangenheitsbewältigung* ('mastering the past'), and *Wiedergutmachung* ('restitution, reparation'). Adenauer was also the architect of the reparations policy with Israel. He hoped to pay off a huge debt, but had no understanding whatsoever for the Jewish culture of remembrance (Blasius 2009). Drawing a final line under the past and putting it to rest was also Adenauer's motive for creating a first central national monument commemorating the Second World War and its consequences in Friedland near Göttingen. Because of its monumental shape it is also known as 'Adenauer's Stonehenge'. This location was symbolic because it was the site of a transit camp for returning German refugees and soldiers after the war, whom Adenauer's political negotiations with Moscow had helped to bring back from Russian captivity. Friedland was designed as a monument to German refugees and returning soldiers, exclusively focusing on the message of German suffering documented in long lists of numbers. Except for a vague reference to 50 million war dead, there is a conspicuous absence of non-German victims of the war and the NS regime, mirroring the self-enclosing preoccupation with German suffering in the 1950s (Schwelling 2008). While Adenauer's politics relating to refugees, integration, and the bringing home of soldiers had been very successful, his monument was not. Nor did he live to see it opened to the public in 1967, when it was already outdated with its anonymous pathos, its vague phrases, and its total elision of questions of cause and effect or guilt and responsibility. In spite of its monumental scope, it is today virtually unknown in Germany.

The central idea behind his policy of forgetting was that the past could and should be left behind in order to embrace a new future (Lübbe 2007). Looking forward was the general exhortation of the 'modern-time regime', and looking backward was considered dangerous and counterproductive. This was not only a post-Nazi German perspective culminating in the restorative spirit of Adenauer, but also a much wider European perspective, which made it all the more consensual, convincing, and compelling. 'We must all turn our backs upon the horrors of the past. We must look to the future,' argued Winston Churchill in 1946 when addressing the youth of Switzerland in Zurich. His view of the past was purely negative, compromising the great promise of a new European future. No wonder that he argued for forgetting rather than remembering:

> We cannot afford to drag forward across the years that are to come the hatreds and revenges which have sprung from the injuries of the past. If Europe is to be saved from infinite misery, and indeed from final doom, there must be an act of faith in the European family and an act of oblivion against all the crimes and follies of the past. (Churchill 1948, 200)

35.3 First Moral Engagements with the Past (1965–1985)

Before and during the Adenauer regime, there were also important and influential German voices that pleaded for remembering as a form of facing and reworking the past. Political scientist and writer Dolf Sternberger, for instance, edited a journal with the telling name 'Transformation' (*Die Wandlung*, 1945–1949) in which he edited essays of anti-Nazi writers in the hope of stirring a movement of self-reflection among the educated population. His hope for a transformation was not fulfilled. Sternberger declared his experiment a failure and ended it in 1949 when two German states were founded with polarized ideologies. It is important to emphasize that Germans after the war had no shortage of information about the system of concentration camps and the experience of the victims of the Nazi regime (such as Eugen Kogon's *The SS State*) but, except for iconic exceptions (such as *The Diary of Anne Frank* in the 1950s), they showed little interest in a discourse on these topics, mystifying Auschwitz and keeping it at by as the apex of shame and guilt.

In the 1950s and 1960s, Frankfurt became an intellectual centre where inclusive and self-critical reflections on the Nazi past and the war crimes were initiated in various institutions: at the university through the writings and teaching of the Jewish remigrant professors Theodor Adorno and Max Horkheimer, also known as the 'Frankfurt School'; at the newly refounded Sigmund Freud Institute with its first director Alexander Mitscherlich; and at the Assize Court with Fritz Bauer, State Attorney General and Jewish remigrant who led the prosecution at the Auschwitz trials (1963–1965). The works of Adorno did much to re-educate the young post-war generation, also known as the 'generation of '68'; psychoanalysis later became an important tool for working through the past, and the Auschwitz trials contributed to building a more democratic legal system. In terms of engaging the public, however, the Auschwitz trials could in no way compare with the Eichmann trial in Jerusalem (1961). On the contrary, the German media reporting on the trials 'externalized' the perpetrators as monsters, separating them neatly from the normal German mainstream. Bauer received valuable support from historians of the new Institute of Contemporary History in Munich, but he also met with much animosity and resistance. He confessed to his friends that he lived 'in the German legal system as in exile', fully aware of his hostile environment: 'When I leave my office, I enter alien territory.' Even after the Fritz Bauer Institute was founded in Frankfurt in 1995 for the research, teaching, and memory of the Holocaust, his name remained unknown to most Germans until feature films presented his person and his work to a larger public in 2015. Back in the 1960s, the social frame of 'communicative silence' still worked as a protective shield that proved difficult to pierce. Alexander Mitscherlich and his wife Margarete had coined the influential formula of the Germans' 'inability to mourn' (Mitscherlich and Mitscherlich 1967). They psychoanalysed the German society like a patient on the couch, noticing that the 'collective occupational therapy' of clearing the rubble and building a new state had caused the freezing of memory and the emotions (M. Mitscherlich, 1987). The Mitscherlichs corroborated what Sternberger had already remarked in 1949: that there was no moment of collective catharsis, and that it was difficult to stir German interest, emotions, memories, and conscience regarding the topic of the Nazi past: 'In Germany after 1945 it was the quick reconstruction of the national economy and not taking responsibility for millions of people meaninglessly murdered that pushed the society forward' (A. Mitscherlich, 1965, 11).

German memories were mainly focused on German suffering, relating to four events: the bombing of German cities, the period of hunger and lack of infrastructure after the capitulation in May 1945, the loss and return of soldiers of the Wehrmacht, and the trauma of German refugees from Eastern territories. Another topic, however, remained largely excluded from public memory: the rape of German women by (mainly Russian) soldiers of the occupation troops. It has remained a taboo topic, even after later attempts to deal with it.[4] In the early post-war years, much attention was focused on German refugees (*Heimat-Vertriebene*) who had to flee before and after the end of the war from Eastern European territories. Some of them held revisionist opinions that undermined the validity of the post-war national borders. In the 1950s and 1960s, they were supported by the right-wing party, the Christian Democratic Union (CDU), in the hope of gaining their votes.[5]

Next to communicative silence, the embrace of German suffering had a collectivizing effect, supplying emotional ties that bound the society of the Federal Republic together. While suffering connected, resistance split the society and proved divisive. It was extremely difficult to anchor the courage and suffering of dissidents and active opponents of the Third Reich in German post-war memory. Their status was considered to be dubious. An important first success in reshaping German memory was achieved by Fritz Bauer with his verdict in 1952 against Otto Ernst Remer, a right-wing politician who had publicly denigrated the resistance fighters against Hitler and referred to their attempted assassinations as 'high treason'.

Even during the 1950s, however, there were also isolated voices and initiatives that deviated from the social norm of communicative silence and pleaded for 'internalizing' rather than 'externalizing' German guilt (Lepsius 1989). One of those voices was that of Lothar Kreyssig (1898–1986), a judge, Protestant, and member of the Confessing Church who had openly protested during the NS regime against the euthanasia murders and the unrestrained violence in concentration camps. He founded *Aktion Sühnezeichen* in 1958, an organization that sends young German volunteers for social work into countries that had particularly suffered under German occupation. The Christian emphasis on expiation (*Sühne*) was another manifestation of the desire for 'reconciliation' (*Versöhnung*) between victims and perpetrators. While the perpetrators can offer expiation, it is the exclusive prerogative of the victims to offer reconciliation. But nobody is authorized to provide absolution for six million murdered victims.[6]

Religious overtones linger in the language of the Holocaust. Many Germans were mesmerized when President von Weizsäcker quoted in his commemoration speech in 1985 a Chassidic phrase by Baal Shem Tov: 'the secret of salvation is remembering'. Although acts of remembering and commemorating the traumatic history have largely replaced the Christian emphasis on expiation and reconciliation, notions like salvation, purification, and decontamination remain powerful for the second and third post-war generations of Germans who long for liberation from their negative legacy.

The purely intellectual and discursive process did little to change the memories of the Nazi regime and to stimulate empathy for the Jewish victims among the general public in the 1960s and 1970s. It was an American product of commercial culture that changed this situation and – to put it in the words of Franz Kafka – became the axe that broke the ice inside the Germans. In January 1979, the broadcasting of the mini TV series *Holocaust* managed to speak directly to the emotions of Germans of all generations. The individual story of the Weiss family in the progressive stages of discrimination, persecution, and murder reached up to 15 million German viewers. The film offered individual faces and a narrative for what had remained without a language or had been covered up under the abstract name of Auschwitz, triggering an emotional catharsis. The emotional impact of this media event spilled over to those who had no share in the historical experience of the Nazi past but were able to join a new media memory community on the basis of empathy. It was perhaps no coincidence that in 1979 the statute of limitations for the prosecution of Nazi criminals was lifted in the German parliament, initiating a new phase of legally confronting the past.

35.4   The Rise of a New Memory Culture (1985–2005)

The term 'memory culture' was first introduced in the 1990s, replacing the term *Vergangenheitsbewältigung* ('mastering the past') of the 1960s. This new shift was propelled by two factors. The first was demographic and consisted in the gradual taking over of responsibility by the generation of '68; the second was symbolic and related to a series of commemoration dates and other historical events. To start with the generational shift. The members of the war generation retired from influential positions and became increasingly marginalized, ceding their influence in the state and their hold on public opinion. During the chancellorship of Helmut Kohl (1982–1998), who signalled the new era of a generation profiting from the 'mercy of a later birth' (*die Gnade der späten Geburt*), the theme of 'personal guilt' was more and more translated into the theme of 'historical responsibility'. It is true that the post-war generation of '68 had already violently confronted their parents in the 1960s and 1970s, accusing them of being Nazis and perpetrators, hiding seminal episodes of their shameful biographies, or remaining unreformed in their values and attitudes. These family confrontations had torn family ties and caused deep rifts in society. They had been richly documented since the 1970s in the very personal literary genre of 'father-novels' (*Väterliteratur*) and since the 1990s in the genre of 'family novels' (*Familienromane*).[7]

The emotional eruptions and vocal proclamations of the young '68 generation, however, radical and expressive as they were, had not automatically ushered in a German memory culture. This evolved less from emotions of anger and hate when confronting the parents than from emotions of concern and empathy with individual Jewish victims. It started not with the youth of '68, their provocative signs and politicized proclamations, but with the mature members of '68, and their local practices such as inviting surviving Jewish family members to German cities and marking places of their former existence. These activities grew out of a new mindset. It was no longer directed at abolishing the state but oriented towards recovering the history and memory that the state had shed when it came into being. It required serious historical interest and minute archival work to find out the names and biographies of former German citizens who had been expelled or deported and murdered. This new personal contact with the families of murdered and surviving Jewish victims laid the foundation for a new era of German memory that is visually continued to this day in the memorial practice of *Stolpersteine* ('stumbling stones'; small brass plaques laid into the pavement that are inscribed with the names of local Jewish victims).

In addition to these generational shifts and changes, the new memory culture was also propelled by symbolic events. The 1980s and 1990s saw a number of commemoration dates with the cumulative effect of linking the 1930s and 1940s to the present. The date 8 May 1985 had a particular impact, because it is connected with two rival memories, one of Chancellor Helmut Kohl and the other of President Richard von Weizsäcker. Chancellor Kohl had already created his specific profile in matters of memorial policy a year before. Together with French president Francois Mitterrand, Kohl had celebrated reconciliation on 22 September 1984 in French and German war cemeteries, 70 years after the battle of Verdun in which both Mitterrand's and Kohl's fathers had fought.[8] It was this style of reconciliation that Kohl had in mind when he invited President Reagan to the soldiers' cemetery in Bitburg for a commemorative event on the occasion of Reagan's visit to Germany 40 years after the end of the Second World War. What Kohl had not considered in his plans was that the commemoration practices of the First World War were in many ways different from those of the Second World War, and that the Bitburg Cemetery contained not only graves of American and German soldiers but also graves of members of the Waffen-SS. All this became evident at the ceremony on 5 May 1985 at Bitburg, an event that triggered a heated controversy in Germany and the United States (Hartman 1986). Another unintended sequel of the Bitburg ceremony was the beginning of 'wild diggings' carried out in the centre of Berlin by young people on the territory of the headquarters of the Gestapo. By this public performance, the younger generation of Germans reclaimed a past that the older generation of Germans had wished to see disappear by tearing down buildings and clearing the rubble. These diggings laid bare the foundations of the *Reichssicherheitshauptamt*, a site of memory that can be visited today under the name 'Topography of Terror'.

It was against the background of this turmoil that president Richard von Weizsäcker gave his commemoration speech in the German parliament in Bonn three days later. This speech has since been proclaimed, time and again, as a historic event and is considered as a first manifestation of the new German memory culture that was to develop in the 1990s. There were three reasons in particular for its unexpected and unanimous resonance. The first reason was that von Weizsäcker explicitly addressed all Germans, male and female, of all generations, from different backgrounds with their different personal experiences, placing considerable emphasis on German suffering. This had a liberating, unifying, and integrating effect, helping the Germans to imagine themselves as a nation. The second reason was his clear message: von Weizsäcker taught the Germans to no longer think of 8 May 1945 in terms of defeat and catastrophe but in terms of liberation, thus paving the way for a transnational (Western) European memory. The third reason for the breakthrough and lasting success of his speech was that von Weizsäcker did not argue for reconciliation but for memory. Memory was the central theme of his speech, introducing references to biblical practices and Chassidic sources to emphasize the religious valance of remembrance. His ambition was to transform German memory by connecting the memory of German suffering with a new memory of historical responsibility towards Jewish and other victims of the NS period. Forty years after the Holocaust, at a moment when personal responsibility for the crimes was waning, a new emphasis on memory was introduced which was passed on to the succeeding generations. The speech was the turning point that replaced the concept of *Vergangenheitsbewältigung* (mastering the past) with *Vergangenheitsbewahrung* (remembering the past).

Von Weizsäcker's speech would perhaps have been forgotten by today had it not been consistently reaffirmed by a series of memory events that followed. One of them, in 1986, was the so-called *Historikerstreit* ('historians' controversy'), an academic but public media debate about the appropriate treatment of the Holocaust in historiography. This media debate had a normative drive: it established the singularity and the ongoing impact of the Holocaust as an 'unmasterable past'. The new interpretation of the Holocaust evolved around the thesis that this event was not about to recede into history and therefore had to be treated differently. Influential new descriptions were coined in the course of this discourse, such as 'anamnetic solidarity' (Johann Baptist Metz) and 'solidary remembrance of what can never be restituted' (Jürgen Habermas).

The fall of the Wall in 1989 and German reunification in 1990 brought about unexpected and radical political and social changes, but they did not mark a turning point in the rise of the new German memory culture.[9] We may speak, on the contrary, of a continuous crescendo of Holocaust memory from the 1980s and 1990s into the new millennium. It is true that German unification created a new political context for German memory; it placed a new emphasis on responsibility and on the material preservation and maintenance of concentration camps, which were recognized in the unification treaty as national sites of memory in East and West Germany. This development helped to consolidate processes that had already been on the way and did not change their course.

Three commemoration events in the 1990s are worth mentioning here. In 1992, Helmut Kohl, the chancellor of unification and a great supporter of 'normalization', made a last attempt at shaping German memory in the tradition of Adenauer's symbolism of closure (*Schlussstrich*). He recreated the *Neue Wache* in Berlin, a central memorial of the GDR, by dedicating it 'To all victims of War and Tyranny', a vague formula that was to cover the 'two dictatorships' and to level all differences in order to reaffirm the self-image of the German nation as a victimized collective.

Kohl's emphasis on German victimhood was crossed by an exhibition that opened in Hamburg in 1995 under the title 'War of Annihilation – Crimes of the Armed Forces 1941–1944'. It presented photos, mainly from private albums, showing German soldiers in Eastern and Southern Europe engaged in mass killings of civilians and other atrocities.[10] The exhibition was a huge provocation because it broke a taboo in challenging the myth of the 'clean Armed Forces' by showing that they had worked together with the SS (*Schutzstaffel*), Hitler's special unit. Presenting these images in public had an explosive effect: on the one hand, it undermined the neat separation been war crimes and the Holocaust, and, on the other, it confronted every former German soldier with the question of what he had done in the war. This meant that a neat barrier between 'good guys' and 'bad guys', between Germans and Nazis, could no longer be maintained. The show caused scandals in many German and Austrian cities and was accompanied by local protest and heated media debates. While many members of the older generation furiously rejected its message, it was accepted by members of the younger generation and 'internalized' as 'our guilt'.

In June 1999, Kohl's monument in Berlin was complemented by another one when the German parliament voted for a memorial in Berlin to be dedicated to the murdered European Jews, realized in 2005 by Peter Eisenman. German memory of the Holocaust was not only anchored in space but also in time. In 1996 President Roman Herzog established 27 January 1945, the liberation of Auschwitz, as a new annual German commemoration day, including all victims of Nazi Germany such as Jews and other minorities, resistors, and victims of euthanasia. This date was taken over by the International Holocaust Remembrance Alliance (IHRA) that was formed in Stockholm in January 2000, bringing together political leaders from various countries with the common commitment of forming a long-term transnational and perhaps even global memory of the Holocaust. While the IHRA narrowed the focus of this memory down to Jewish victims, it radically multiplied the members of this memory community. There are voices like that of Peter Reichel who has argued that Germans are not entitled to this commemoration date with its strong focus on the Jewish victims. He proposed 9 November 1938 instead as a more appropriate German commemoration date because it is linked to public acts of German violence against Jewish neighbours in German cities. Such a memory, Reichel argues, could also alert German society to contemporary problems of racism, drawing attention to discrimination and exclusion as early stages of genocidal violence.[11]

35.5 New Developments, Discontents, Challenges (2005 onwards)

National memory in the nineteenth century was created in a heroic spirit. The nation was endowed with a sacred aura and built on the pride and strength of the collective. After the fall of the Berlin Wall, new nations came into being in Europe that chose the experience of victimhood and collective suffering as their unifying bond. The German case of embracing a 'negative memory' (Koselleck 2002) by internalizing the guilt of historic crimes and accepting responsibility for the previous political regime as a national legacy is not only different, it is *unique in history*. Many political analysts have expressed their scepticism about it, have called it masochistic and argued that this is an impossible option. Others have praised it as 'the German model' that is introducing an important turn into the evaluation and construction of the past. So far, constructions of national memory had been monologic, self-aggrandizing, and self-serving; there is now a new model that can make them more dialogic and self-critical. This turn from a monologic to a more dialogic memory is evident in the long list of heads of state who, since the 1990s, have apologized publicly to the victims of slavery, colonialism, and the state terror of dictatorships for crimes against humanity committed in the past of their countries.

This new development may be due to the fact that, from the beginning of the millennium, memory cultures in general are evolving in a European and transnational context, presenting themselves in a global arena (Assmann and Conrad 2010). While many countries, and in particular those transitioning from dictatorships to democracies, have engaged historical commissions and adopted self-critical standards vis-à-vis their past, the current resurgence of ethnonationalism in Europe shows that in spite of these new standards, monologic constructions of national memory and identity are again on the advance.

German memory is often praised from an external point of view; if looked at from within, the assessment is much more critical. The universalization of the Holocaust, it is feared, leads to a flattening and vacating of the meaning of the historic event, diverting the attention not only from the perpetrators, but also from the historical and local specificity of the event. This trend is countered by memory projects of the civil society, which recover traces of the Nazi past in their own local milieu and restore personal stories that would otherwise be forgotten. A similar criticism addresses the problem of ritualization. How can a memory of the Holocaust be kept up in Germany without repeating continually the same phrases and confirmations? In a secular society that has disengaged itself from all religious rites and symbols, the yearly official commemoration liturgy strikes many citizens as void and meaningless, lacking life and authenticity. Other voices make the point that the obsession with the past leaves too little space for new developments and diverts attention from the great challenges of the future. These are some of the most frequent critical arguments (Assmann 2013).

More important, however, are the concerns about the necessary transformations of German memory culture. Seventy years after the end of the war, the number of historical witnesses is rapidly dwindling. With the growing historical distance, the past will soon be accessible only through archival sources, historical scholarship, public mediations, and artistic representations. Historical sites and authentic objects will gain in importance, but the stories that will bring their evidence to life will also have to be reconstructed. As family memory and transmission is dissolving, an ethnic interpretation of German memory is losing its grip. German millennials have hardly more contact to the Nazi past than young immigrants, who also bring their own burden of history and memory into the society. Since 2000, Germany has undergone a deep transformation into an immigration society. The growing impact of migration therefore is another great challenge for German memory culture. Immigration is no longer conceived to be a one-way process in which immigrants are absorbed in a society by taking over the country's myths, memories, symbols, and traditions. Integration involves active participation and interaction, which means that German memory has to become more accessible and inclusive for new immigrants, accommodating also their experiences and stories on a local and national level. As immigrants from former German colonies in Africa are becoming German citizens, there is also a demand that Germany extends its past to include its colonial history.

35.6   Conclusion

More than 70 years after the liberation of Auschwitz and the end of the war, we look back not only at the traumatic events themselves, but also at a history of forgetting and remembering that has evolved between ourselves and these events. What becomes visible in retrospect is that the question whether to remember or to forget was not only an individual choice but it defined general attitudes and orientations generated within social and political frames.

Various forms of forgetting played an important role in this development. They started in Nazi Germany with psycho-social forms of repression and the collective training of 'looking away' (Sachsse 2003) which prevented the possibility of a self-critical German memory of this period. Adaptation and defence mechanisms also characterized the post-war communicative silence. Some of the blocked empathy was released in connection with the television series *Holocaust*. Furthermore, emotions that had been withheld by the first generation were re-enacted as 'belated empathy' in films and novels of succeeding generations (Assmann 2015). Media historians have made us aware of the fact that historical TV documentaries or films like Joachim Fest's *Hitler* often unwittingly reproduced the visual regime of the Nazis, reinforcing the self-monumentalization of their propaganda. In stark contrast to these practices, film-artists such as Alexander Kluge and Edgar Reitz explored new strategies to change these visual stereotypes and to open up a new access to the Nazi past. Regaining a new access to this past by 'unlearning' habitualized patterns is indeed the vital contribution of art to German memory. In the memory of pop culture, Hitler occupies a special place as a global icon and has generated a media life of his own.

German post-war memory has evolved over a number of phases due to historical change, the construction of new social frames, the introduction of new values, and the emergence of new actors. In these various phases we may discern a larger pattern of transformation that can be described as a shift from 'mastering the past' to 'preserving the past'. This memorial transformation involves another important shift from a 'finishing line' to a 'dividing line'. The finishing line puts the past behind it in order to provide closure. Through silence and forgetting, the past is supposed to lose its relevance and is dissolved by the sheer passing of time. The 'dividing line' follows a different logic. In order to distance the present from the past, it has to be confronted, discussed, and worked through. It is through remembering rather than through forgetting that a social transformation is effectively achieved in which the past is kept from repeating itself by facing it and adopting this experience as a moral compass for the future.

Notes

1 A detailed account of German opinions around the Nuremberg trials can be found in the memoir of Karl Heinz Bohrer from the point of view of a 13-year-old boy (2014, 118–121).

2 Almost a decade earlier, social scientist Elisabeth Noelle Neumann had coined the term *Schweigespirale* ('spiral of silence') to describe the power of mass media to shape public opinion into a mainstream that isolates and progressively eliminates nonconformist and other counter opinions (Noelle Neumann and Petersen 2004).

3 Both Adenauer and his wife were interned in Brauweiler near Cologne, one of the first concentration camps, and later in a secret police (Gestapo) prison. His wife died of the consequences of this imprisonment (Daners and Wißkirchen 2006, 93–95).

4 New engagements with the topic were the documentary film by Helke Sander, *BeFreier und Befreite* (1992/1992), and the book *Anonyma: Eine Frau in Berlin. Tagebuchaufzeichnungen vom 20. April bis 22. Juni 1945* (2003) which was turned into a film in 2008.

5 When the topic of German post-war refugees finally reappeared on the memory agenda after 2000, it was no longer framed primarily by political motives. New media presentations allowed for a new personal and empathetic involvement in these stories by the younger generations.

6 Kreyssig's organization has been updated and enlarged as *Aktion Sühnezeichen und Friedensdienste* ('action expiation and peace services'). The peace projects of ASF keep the historical memory of the Holocaust alive while at the same time opening a common future for succeeding generations through continuous commitment and social actions. The children and grandchildren of the perpetrators who embrace this memory work perform a belated ethical act: they focus on and take to heart what their parents and grandparents had been eager to overlook and to disremember.

7 While the father-novels featured painful personal confrontations between sons and daughters with their fathers (the mothers were of less interest in this genre because they were neither models nor the bearer of controversial norms), the family novels introduced a more investigative and exploratory style. They also changed the plot and temporal frame from the polarized clash of two generations to a more complex and extended configuration of three generations, which were connected by the ties of memories, blanks of forgetting, and family secrets.

8 A joint French–German statement confirmed 'the shared commemoration of the dead of both world wars', which was meant as 'a sign of Peace and Brotherhood' among both nations. 'For this reason almost 40 years ago the Germans and French have ended the European civil war and started to look into a common future.' 'Ein Zeichen des Friedens im Geist der Brüderlichkeit'. Bulletin No. 108/p. 953 (Bonn, 25 September 1984.)

9 While there was continuity in the development of a new German memory culture centred on the Holocaust, the collapse of the Soviet Union marked a rupture in the configuration of national memories on the European level. During the Cold War, much had to be forgotten as Western European nations were eager to build 'the house of Europe'. This selective forgetting had produced what Tony Judt (1992, 87, 92) has called the 'postwar myth'. According to this myth all European nations had either been the passive victims of Nazi crimes or had opposed them as heroic resisters. The post-war myth crumbled after 1989 when Eastern archives became accessible and some national narratives had to be rewritten, revealing diverse stories of collaboration – in France, Poland, Austria, or Switzerland, for instance.

10 The exhibition was organized by the Hamburger Institut für Sozialforschung and curated by Hannes Heer. It toured German and Austrian cities for five years before it was withdrawn. Critics had discovered that some of the images did not show soldiers of the German Wehrmacht but of the NKWD (the Soviet secret police). After an intermission for reconstructing and redesigning, the exhibition continued to tour from 2001 to 2004.

11 'Der 27. Januar steht uns nicht zu', interview with Peter Reichel, tagesschau.de: www.tagesschau.de/inland/meldung201874.html (accessed 28 November 2017)

References

Assmann, Aleida. 2013. *Das neue Unbehagen an der Erinnerungskultur: Eine Intervention.* Munich: C.H. Beck.

Assmann, Aleida. 2015. 'Looking Away in Nazi Germany.' In *Empathy and Its Limits*, edited by Aleida Assmann and Ines Detmers, 128–148. Basingstoke, UK: Palgrave Macmillan.

Assmann, Aleida and Conrad, Sebastian. 2010. *Memory in a Global Age*. Basingstoke, UK: Palgrave Macmillan.

Blasius, Rainer. 2009. 'Der gute Wille muss auch anerkannt werden': Review of *Adenauers Erinnerungen: Die letzten Lebensjahre 1963–1967.' Frankfurter Allgemeine Zeitung* 12.3, no. 60, L 21.

Bohrer, Karl Heinz. 2014. *Granatsplitter: Erzählung einer Jugend*. Munich: Deutscher Taschenbuch Verlag.

Churchill, Winston S. 1948. 'Post-War Speeches.' In *The Sinews of Peace*. Edited by Randolph S. Churchill. London: Cassell.

Daners, Hermann and Wißkirchen, Josef. 2006. *Was in Brauweiler geschah: Die NS-Zeit und ihre Folgen in der Rheinischen Provinzial-Arbeitsanstalt*. Pulheim: KS-Verlag.

Friedlander, Saul. 1994. 'Trauma, Memory and Transference.' In *Holocaust Remembrance: The Shapes of Memory*, edited by Geoffrey Hartman, 252–263. Oxford and Cambridge, MA: Wiley Blackwell.

Hartman, Geoffrey, ed. 1986. *Bitburg in a Moral and Political Perspective*. Bloomington: Indiana University Press.

Heinemann, Gustav. 2005. 'Eine zweite Chance für Hitlers Helfer.' *Stern*, 22 March. www.stern.de/politik/geschichte/entnazifizierung-eine-zweite-chance-fuer-hitlers-helfer-3545212.html (accessed 28 November 2017).

Judt, Tony. 1992. 'The Past Is Another Country: Myth and Memory in Post-War Europe.' *Daedalus* 121, 83–119.

Kogon, Eugen. 1946. *Der SS-Staat: Das System der deutschen Konzentrationslager*. Munich: Karl Alber.

Koselleck, Reinhart. 2002. 'Formen und Traditionen des negativen Gedächtnisses.' In *Verbrechen erinnern: Die Auseinandersetzung mit Holocaust und Völkermord*, edited by Volkhard Knigge and Norbert Frei. Munich: C.H. Beck.

Lepsius, Mario Rainer. 1989. 'Das Erbe des Nationalsozialismus und die politische Kultur der Nachfolgestaaten des "Großdeutschen Reiches".' In *Kultur und Gesellschaft*, edited by Max Haller et al., 247–262. Frankfurt am Main and New York: Campus.

Lübbe, Hermann. 1983. 'Der Nationalsozialismus im politischen Bewusstsein der Gegenwart.' In *Deutschlands Weg in die Diktatur: Internationale Konferenz zur national-sozialistischen Machtübernahme im Reichstagsgebäude zu Berlin. Referate und Diskussionen. Ein Protokoll*, edited by Martin Broszat, Ulrich Dügger, et al. Berlin: Siedler.

Lübbe, Hermann. 2007. *Vom Parteigenossen zum Bundesbürger: Über beschwiegene und his-torisierte Vergangenheiten*. Munich: Fink.

Mitscherlich, Alexander. 1965. *Die Unwirtlichkeit unserer Städte: Anstiftung zum Unfrieden*. Frankfurt am Main: Suhrkamp.

Mitscherlich, Alexander and Mitscherlich, Margarete. 1967. *Die Unfähigkeit zu trauern*. Frankfurt: Suhrkamp.

Mitscherlich, Margarete. 1987. *Erinnerungsarbeit: Zur Psychoanalyse der Unfähigkeit zu trauern*. Frankfurt: Fischer.

Noelle Neumann, Elisabeth and Petersen, Thomas. 2004. 'The Spiral of Silence and the Social Nature of Man.' In *Handbook of Political Communication*, edited by Lynda Lee Kaid. Mahwah, NJ: Lawrence Erlbaum.

Padover, Samuel. 1946. *Experiment in Germany: The Story of an American Intelligence Officer*. New York: Duell, Sloan and Pearce.

Sachsse, Rolf. 2003. *Die Erziehung zum Wegsehen: Fotografie im NS-Staat*. Dresden: Philo Fine Arts.

Schwelling, Birgit. 2008. 'Gedenken im Nachkrieg. "Die Friedland-Gedächtnisstätte".' *Zeithistorische Forschungen* 2, 189–210.

Timm, Uwe. 2005. *In My Brother's Shadow: A Life and Death in the SS*, translated by A. Bell. New York: Farrar, Straus and Giroux. [First published as *Am Beispiel meines Bruders*, 2003, Cologne: Kiepenhauer & Witsch.]

Further Reading

Assmann, Aleida. 2016. *Shadows of Trauma: Memory and the Politics of Postwar Identity*, translated by Sarah Clift. New York: Fordham.

Herf, Jeffrey. 1997. *Divided Memory: The Nazi Past in the Two Germanys*. Cambridge, MA: Harvard University Press.

Koselleck, Reinhart and Jeismann, Michael, eds. 1994. *Der politische Totenkult: Kriegerdenkmäler in der Moderne*. Munich: Fink.

Moeller, Robert. 2003. *War Stories: The Search for a Usable Past in the Federal Republic of Germany*. Oxford: Oxford University Press.

Müller, Jan Werner, ed. 2002. *Memory and Power in Post-War Europe: Studies in the Presence of the Past*. Cambridge: Cambridge University Press.

CHAPTER THIRTY-SIX

Remembering National Socialism in the German Democratic Republic

DAVID CLARKE

The starting point for any discussion of the ways in which the German Democratic Republic (GDR) came to terms with National Socialism must be an acknowledgement that the vision of German history formulated by the ruling Socialist Unity Party (*Sozialistische Einheitspartei Deutschlands*, or SED) was, although by no means static, always bound up with the party's own claim to power and the legitimacy of its state socialist project. This desire to legitimize the SED's project was not only an internal matter, but also related to the GDR's assertion of moral superiority over its capitalist rival, the Federal Republic of Germany, which was perceived as essential to the GDR's push for international recognition (Wolfrum 2002, 142). The GDR's official view of German history was not limited to a concentration on the years 1933–1945, yet the National Socialist period remained the most important in terms of its prominence in official commemoration, memorialization, historical education, culture, and throughout public life in the GDR in general. As we will see in what follows, the dominance of this official politics of memory did not necessarily amount to a uniform view of National Socialism and the anti-fascist tradition among GDR citizens, or even among those loyal to the regime. However, before considering how individual East Germans might have related to the official politics of memory, it is necessary to trace the development of that politics over time.

36.1 The Genesis of Anti-Fascist Memory

The period between the establishment of the Soviet Zone of Occupation (*Sowjetische Besatzungszone*, or SBZ) in May 1945 and moves towards the creation of a separate state in that zone under SED rule from 1948 is generally regarded as

A Companion to Nazi Germany, First Edition. Edited by Shelley Baranowski, Armin Nolzen, and Claus-Christian W. Szejnmann.

a transitional moment in which it was possible to conceive of broader coalitions between those of various political persuasions who had opposed National Socialism (Meuschel 1992, 103–104). Even before the end of the war, German communists in Soviet exile who had previously decried their rivals in the Social Democratic Party (SPD) as 'social fascists' now expressed a willingness to work with progressive forces to bring about a unified and democratically socialist Germany (Bessel 2009, 304–305). Following the end of the conflict, communists who had been persecuted under National Socialism initially worked together with a range of other victims, including representatives of the 20 July 1944 plot to assassinate Hitler, Jews and Christians, in a prominent association of Victims of Fascism (*Opfer des Faschismus*, or OdF) (Monteath 1999, 101). However, once it became clear around the summer of 1948 that the western zones under Allied occupation were moving towards the creation of a new state, the SED's preparations for a rival communist-run polity were put in place, creating the need for a greater emphasis on the party's leading role in resistance to National Socialism (Naimark 1997, 57–60).

This new political situation, in which the SED and the Soviet Union had nevertheless not yet officially given up on the prospect of German unity, required a recalibration of the definition of the anti-fascist struggle. For example, within the Union of Victims of Fascism (*Vereinigung der Verfolgten des Naziregimes* or VVN), a communist-led yet nevertheless relatively pluralistic organization which emerged in 1947 as a successor to the OdF, the run-up to the founding of the GDR was characterized by a gradual marginalization of non-communist victims (Monteath 1999, 102). From 1949, membership of the VVN, which was coterminous with state recognition of victim status, was only available to those who could demonstrate that their resistance to National Socialism had been the result of their anti-fascist and democratic politics, understood implicitly in terms of their political compatibility with the new regime (Hölscher 2002, 111–112).

The SED's increasing tendency to equate anti-fascism with anti-imperialism and anti-capitalism (Groehler 1995, 26), a move which essentially excluded non-communist resisters and 'racial' victims, was part of the broader effort to establish the leading role of the SED in the emerging GDR state. Here the SED relied on a definition of fascism whose origins can be traced back to Comintern positions of the 1920s, which regarded fascist politics as a last-ditch attempt by the capitalist system to defend itself against the imminent revolution by introducing a new form of barbaric dictatorship (Backes 2009, 11; Vogt 2000, 19). In this context, only the Communist Party (or, later, the SED) could be regarded as legitimately anti-fascist, because also anti-capitalist.

This shift in the definition of anti-fascist resistance can be seen, for example, in Stefan Hermlin's collection of resister biographies written in the early 1950s, *The First Rank* (*Die erste Reihe*). Published in a special edition for the SED's youth wing, the Free German Youth (*Freie Deutsche Jugend*; O'Doherty 1997, 20), Hermlin's book begins by stressing the plurality of resistance, mentioning religious groups, nationalists, and even resisters with a background in the Boy Scout movement. However, the focus of this work is clearly on the leading role of the working class in resistance, and on the power of the workers' movement to give purpose and theoretical clarity to the impulse to resist across a broader spectrum of the population, be that among young Jews initially attracted to Zionism, or even among workers who were at first seduced by National Socialism. In the case of the non-communist White Rose group, Hermlin at first criticizes the anti-Nazi leaflets they distributed for failing to recognize that capitalism was at the root of the problem of National Socialism, before going on to speculate that this failure may have been the result of the interventions of their mentor, Professor Huber, who is accused of waylaying the young resisters from the path to Marxism-Leninism (Hermlin 1951, 176–178). Here and in the cases of other non-communist resisters, these figures can only be incorporated into the pantheon of anti-fascist resistance fighters if they can be portrayed as proto-communist, if not communist in fact.

36.2   Anti-Fascist Memory as Legitimation of SED Rule

Parallel to these developments, the Soviet occupiers were pursuing policies of denazification, both through the (often inconsistent) purging of local and regional administration, and by means of the detention of former National Socialists, as well as suspected resisters to the Soviet occupation and the dominance of SED in the Soviet Zone and emerging GDR. Such policies were driven primarily by the priority of subduing the territory occupied by the Red Army and only secondarily by the desire to stamp out the influence of Nazi ideology (Bessel 2009, 191).

Like the Soviet Union, the SED also fundamentally mistrusted the East German population, which had at the very least failed to resist National Socialism in large numbers (Groehler 1992, 33; Vogt 2000, 37), and whose older generations in particular were so hostile to the SED regime that Mary Fulbrook has described it as arguably the most unpopular German government of all time (Fulbrook 2011, 308). However, given the party's narrow base of committed communists either returning from exile or released from the concentration camps and prisons of Nazi Germany, the SED had to seek to integrate wide sections of that population, including those with important skills and knowledge (Vogt 2000, 47). There was also real internal opposition, particularly among those working with the eastern offices of the western political parties and other anti-communist groups, who initially believed that the GDR would be a short-lived phenomenon. Such opposition needed to be contained and delegitimized.

The number of loyal functionaries on which Ulbricht's government could hope to draw was further diminished by divisions between different factions with divergent experiences of the National Socialist period. Exiles who had fled to countries in the West rather than to the Soviet Union, and former concentration camp inmates and political prisoners, many of whom had been active in their opposition to National Socialism under conspiratorial conditions within Nazi Germany, were regarded as a potential threat to the dominance of those who had survived the purges of Moscow exile, and who could (by reason of that very survival) be regarded as loyal to the Soviet Union (Groehler 1995, 19–22; Hölscher 2002, 201–202). Nevertheless, the survivors of the camps possessed a moral capital which, while potentially dangerous to Ulbricht's faction, was also a potent source of legitimation for the SED regime as a whole.

The ideology of anti-fascism as it emerged from the founding of the GDR to the mid-1950s, and which remained dominant thereafter in terms of the GDR's politics of memory, can be understood as an attempt to address all of these issues. While internal opposition aligned with the West could be framed as inherently fascist, as was the case, for example, in the SED's interpretation of the causes of the workers' uprising of 17 June 1953, the foregrounding of the leading role of communists in resistance to National Socialism did not mean that those who had been active in that resistance were allowed to accrue a moral authority in the GDR which could potentially challenge the current leadership of the SED.

In the course of the Stalinization of the SED after 1947, the party leadership came to view the VVN in particular as an organization from which a challenge to its authority might emerge. Consequently, the VVN was kept under close scrutiny (Pritchard 2000, 179–180) and was eventually disbanded in January 1953, to be replaced with the much less prominent Committee of Anti-Fascist Resistance Fighters (*Kommitee der Antifascistischen Widerstandskämpfer*, or KdAW), run by loyal SED officials. By this time, the regime was more strongly interested in integrating GDR citizens who had no history of supporting the Communist Party before 1945. In this context, an overemphasis on the role of former resistance fighters in the regime was perceived as potentially alienating for those who might be co-opted to the cause, in that it seemed to emphasize active resistance to National Socialism as a prerequisite for integration into the new structures of the state (Danyel 1995, 42; Hölscher 2002, 163–165). There is certainly evidence that some former anti-fascist resisters were increasingly unhappy with the swift pace of the reintegration of members of the NSDAP (*Nationalsozialistische Deutsche Arbeiterpartei*, Nazi Party) by the early 1950s (Danyel 1999, 190).

The SED's appeal to citizens beyond its own pre-1945 ranks extended in particular to former soldiers and officers who had been won over to the National Committee for a Free Germany (*Nationalkommitee Freies Deutschland*) and the League of Germany Officers (*Bund deutscher Offiziere*) while in Soviet captivity (Lapp 2000), as well as *kleine Pgs* (small-time NSDAP members) seeking a new start, many of whom could be integrated into the National Democratic Party of Germany (*Nationaldemokratische Partei Deutschlands*, or NDPD), founded in 1948 as an SED-loyal part of the so-called Democratic Bloc. However, the integration of *kleine Pgs* was not limited to this party. Analysis of the presence of former NSDAP members among SED cadres has shown that they were a significant presence in the GDR regime, (perhaps unsurprisingly) outnumbering those who could lay claim to a background in the anti-fascist resistance (Best and Stalheiser 2006). In this respect, the GDR ran into some rather embarrassing difficulties when journalists from the Federal Republic would periodically highlight the Nazi career of SED officials in the self-proclaimed anti-fascist state, which rather undermined the moral force of the SED's own campaigns against former National Socialists with prominent careers in the West. These included a trial *in absentia* in 1963 of Hans Globke, the lawyer who had been responsible for writing the official commentary on the Nuremburg racial laws of 1935, and who had gone on to work as the head of Konrad Adenauer's Federal Chancellery (Lemke 1995, 70–75).

It is also important to note, following Fulbrook's analysis, that the functionaries of the SED regime in all spheres came to be dominated particularly by a generational cohort which had experienced the catastrophic violence of the end of the Second World War in Germany on the cusp of adulthood and had suffered a total disillusionment with the Nazi values they had assimilated as children (2011, 296). The new SED state with its anti-fascist ideology offered a new form of commitment which, by allowing these individuals to align themselves with the legacy of anti-fascist resistance fighters, could retrospectively exculpate their generation from its implication in the National Socialist regime. Looking back on the early years of the GDR from the perspective of the regime's crisis in the autumn of 1989, a prominent representative of this generation, the author Christa Wolf, described the situation as follows:

> At some indeterminate point in time, and for practical reasons, the small group of antifascists who governed the country transferred their sense of triumphalism onto the whole population. The 'victors of history' ceased to engage with that population's real past, the past of those who, under National Socialism, had been conformists (*Mitläufer*), who had been seduced, or who had believed. (Wolf 1990, 96; my translation)

In essence, the SED under Ulbricht offered a form of anti-fascist identification which relied less on having *been* one of the relatively scarce anti-fascist resistance fighters than on one's willingness to identify with their legacy. Furthermore, this legacy was increasingly portrayed not just as that of the resistance fighters themselves, or even of the SED, but of the German working class in general as the bearers of the progressive heritage (*Erbe*) of German history. Although suspicions within the SED about the ideological correctness of the population remained until the end of the GDR, at least officially the East German population had to be understood as wholeheartedly committed to the anti-fascist tradition in its anti-capitalist guise.

36.3   Remembering Anti-Fascist Resistance Fighters

Despite the prominent place ascribed to them in the GDR's official politics of memory, the image of the anti-fascist resistance fighters (*antifaschistiche Widerstandskämpfer*) as a group had to undergo a process of idealization in order for them to serve as role models for the GDR's populace. In the late 1940s and early 1950s, there were a number of internal investigations into the behaviour of communists in Buchenwald, where they had wielded influence as camp functionaries (*Kapos*). The priority established by the Communist Party within the camp to preserve the lives of its members (Niethammer 1994, 45) led to moral compromises which sat ill with the heroic image which the SED sought to exploit for its own purposes (Niethammer 1994, 46–48). While the various purges and demotions of former camp inmates within the SED need to be seen in the context of the Moscow faction's assertion of its dominance during the early Cold War (Niethammer 1994, 72–79; Oversch 1995, 217–237), and while we also need to be wary of shifting the blame for conditions in the concentration camps from National Socialist perpetrators to their victims, it is nevertheless clear that there was a disjuncture between the complex experience of resistance and suffering in the camps and the idealized vision of the anti-fascist resistance fighter which emerged in the GDR's official memory politics and in GDR culture more widely. These difficulties were epitomized by Bruno Apitz's canonical 1958 anti-fascist novel *Naked Among Wolves* (*Nackt unter Wölfen*), the writing of which was subject to significant scrutiny in order to preserve the preferred image of camp resistance (Niven 2007, 93–103).

At the National Memorial at Buchenwald, which was opened in 1958 and then later integrated into a national memorial complex including the camps at Sachsenhausen and Ravensbrück, the multifaceted reality of camp experience was subsumed under a heroic presentation of communist resistance in the camps, emphasizing the struggle of democratic forces against fascism and the leading role of the Communist Party within that struggle (Niven 2002, 20). Elevated to this abstract, symbolic level (Danyel 1995, 38–39) (as evidenced very much by the statuary commissioned to commemorate the victims at these sites), the image of the anti-fascist resistance fighters could contribute to the legitimation of the state socialist project without the need to explore the contradictions of individual experiences in detail.

One individual whose fate was the focus of considerable commemorative effort was Ernst Thälmann, the murdered pre-1933 Communist Party leader who became the most important figure in the GDR's pantheon of anti-fascist heroes. However, the historical Thälmann was clearly not the infallible and unwavering leader portrayed, for example, in Kurt Maetzig's two-part biopic, *Ernst Thälmann – Son of his Class* (1954) and *Ernst Thälmann – Leader of his Class* (1955). This film, which was very much a Party-driven project (Barck 2000, 153), brings together the key elements of the GDR's anti-fascist reading of the recent German past as established in the 1950s. The film lays responsibility for the National Socialist regime firmly at the door of reactionary military and aristocratic figures, in league with the capitalist class (represented by the United States) and Social Democrats, with the latter only serving to distract the workers from the need to join with the Communist Party to overthrow capitalism and resist its servants, the Nazis. Although the film shows Thälmann's dignified suffering in his cell during his years of incarceration under National Socialism, the second part focuses not on resistance activities within Germany, but rather on communists in exile in the Soviet Union as they prepare for a new Germany and, eventually, fight alongside Red Army troops to drive out German forces, all inspired by Thälmann's example. Thälmann was also the most prominent figure in the GDR education system's rendering of the history of National Socialism (Ring 1996, 60) and, from 1952 the namesake of the GDR's Pioneer organization for primary school-age children. This version of Thälmann, as in Maetzig's film, was one stripped entirely of his errors and his doubts, so that the former Communist Party leader became something like a secular saint in what Bernd Faulenbach has called the 'martyr cult' of anti-fascism (1993, 757).

There was little change in the SED's official conception of the nature of German history and National Socialism's place in that history until the end of Ulbricht's period in office in 1971. His successor, Erich Honecker, shifted the emphasis of anti-fascist memory to the extent that he was willing to pay greater attention to a broader range of anti-fascist resistance fighters who had remained in Germany (Groehler 1995, 30; Leo 1992, 152; Hölscher 2002, 219). This shift led to the building of new local monuments and a reinvigoration of the KdAW. Honecker encouraged new local organizations of the KdAW to commemorate the sacrifices of their comrades, initiating a whole series of local historical displays in 'Anti-Fascist Tradition Cabinets' across the GDR (Kulturamt Prenzlauer Berg and Aktives Museum Berlin 1992), which were often managed by the resistance fighters themselves. Although there is no evidence that these displays diverged from the SED's line, they nevertheless represented Honecker's more relaxed attitude to the internal resistance to National Socialism, doubtless informed by his own experience of 12 years of incarceration under National Socialist rule. Under Honecker, schools were encouraged to take on namesakes from the anti-fascist resistance movement, with pupils researching the lives of the figures whose names their schools were to bear, many of whom had local connections (Plum 2015, 36–37).

Although anti-fascism remained the key element in the GDR's official memory politics in relation to National Socialism under Honecker's rule, its role was also relativized to an extent by a new focus on other aspects of German history which were supposed to underpin a GDR-specific nationalism. As a result of the thawing in Cold War relations between the two German states, which included mutual recognition and the GDR's renunciation of national reunification as a political goal, Honecker sought to mitigate the closer links between the two Germanys by encouraging a stronger territorial identification with the GDR, drawing on those aspects of German history which could (sometimes rather tenuously) be interpreted as 'progressive', including Martin Luther and the Reformation, and Frederick the Great's Prussia. In one sense, this was nothing new. As early as 1952, and as noted above, the SED had begun to reclaim the positively connoted features of German history as part of the historical *Erbe* fulfilled in the GDR (Nothnagle 1993, 102). However, Honecker's emphasis was very much on events which had occurred on what later became the territory of the GDR, rather than on German history as a whole. This shift in the politics of memory can be understood as a tacit acknowledgement that the focus on National Socialism in official, anti-fascist memory alone was inadequate to secure the loyalty which the SED sought from the citizens of the GDR. Indeed, as Jan Pawlowski has argued, the inefficacy of anti-fascist identifications as a means to secure legitimacy both for the GDR as a state and for its political and economic system were arguably already recognized as early as the 1960s, when the regime began to pursue policies to support the cultivation of local cultural activity of various kinds, which were designed to promote a love of *Heimat* or homeland which could increase citizens' commitment to their place in the GDR (2009, 305). Thus, while the SED regime remained committed to anti-fascism as a cornerstone of its memory politics, there are good reasons to doubt even its own belief in its efficacy as an all-purpose legitimation of SED power.

36.4   Remembering the Holocaust

As Joanne Sayner has observed, it is often supposed that the GDR's official focus on anti-fascist resistance to National Socialism meant that the Holocaust was not discussed in the GDR (2013, 23). Such claims are clearly hyperbolic, not least in view of the fact that the portrayal of Jewish suffering under National Socialism was the subject of significant representation in the cultural sphere (Maser 1995, 357). Equally, GDR historians of the National Socialist period began to take a much stronger interest in the subject from the 1970s onwards, gradually adding complexity to the otherwise economically determined interpretation of antisemitism which had been official doctrine in the profession (Jarausch 1991, 90). A more accurate interpretation of the GDR's relationship to the Holocaust would recognize that, while certainly secondary to the narrative of anti-fascist resistance, the persecution and murder of Jewish people by the National Socialist regime was a feature of official memory politics in as far as discussion of the subject could be regarded as bolstering the GDR's claim to legitimacy and, by extension, the SED's claim to power.

The SED's interpretation of National Socialism in primarily economic terms favoured a view of the Holocaust in which antisemitic policies could be interpreted either as further evidence of fascism's exploitation of human beings in the service of capital, for example through the slave labour of Jewish prisoners for major German companies; or as an ideological smoke-screen mobilized by capitalists to distract the working class from the true nature of fascism (Fox 1999, 54). Other victim groups who were still regarded as 'asocial' in the GDR, such as Roma and Sinti or homosexuals (Gilsenbach 2001; Hölscher 2002, 78–79), were ignored entirely, however.

The perception that the GDR failed to address the Holocaust in any way is clearly not only a post-unification phenomenon, given that West German Christian Democrat (CDU) leader (and later Chancellor) Helmut Kohl called upon the GDR government to show the US drama *Holocaust* (1978) on East German television following its notable success in the Federal Republic (Schieber 2007, 10). This was largely a rhetorical point, since the vast majority of GDR citizens could have watched the West German broadcast on their televisions if they had wanted to. However, it also demonstrates Kohl's own ignorance of the GDR's efforts to bring the situation of Jews under National Socialism into the public consciousness, for example through the broadcast some eight years earlier of a four-part television mini-series, *The Pictures of Witness Schattmann* (*Die Bilder des Zeugen Schattmann*) which attracted 26.8% of all GDR viewers in a prime mid-week evening slot (Schieber 2007, 31). This film contains some of the most shockingly direct representations of the physical and mental suffering of German Jews available to GDR audiences at that time. It was also a rarity in post-war German cinema and television more generally for its direct depiction of conditions inside Auschwitz, including the humiliation of innocent victims by brutal Nazi fanatics and the 'selection' of those deemed unfit to continue working who would be sent to the gas chamber (Wolfgram 2006, 70). In the post-war sequences of the film, we see the protagonist, the painter Schattmann, returning to Auschwitz after years of struggling with the painful memories of his experience under National Socialism, which amounts to a very public acknowledgement of the traumatization of Jewish victims.

Nevertheless, it is important to note that, in *The Pictures of Witness Schattmann*, the protagonist's confrontation with antisemitic oppression becomes a catalyst for political engagement in the communist cause, or at least a recognition of the relationship between the capitalist system and the emergence of the National Socialist regime. Schattmann's wife's uncle, who appears in the first episode of the series, and who is himself a German nationalist and member of the bourgeoisie, makes explicit his own failure to recognize that the National Socialists are a product of the rule of his own class, which must be overcome if Nazism is to be defeated. The lesson that Schattmann himself learns on his descent into the hell of the camps is that he must become a communist and work in solidarity with other communists in order to overcome capitalism and fascism, and, eventually, build a better world in the GDR. It should also be noted that the representation of the (non-Jewish) German working class here is consistently positive, as encapsulated in the figure of Frau Müller, the Schattmanns' neighbour, who is always ready to slip them extra food and who is seen contributing to the building of a socialist Germany in the final part of the film. This contrasts starkly with early portrayals of German antisemitism in GDR culture, such as in Elfriede Brüning's 1949 novel ... *so you can live* (... *damit du weiterlebst*; originally published by the VVN) or Maetzig's film *Girls in Gingham* (*Die Buntkarrierten*, 1950), in which the often enthusiastic participation of ordinary Germans in the persecution of Jews is emphasized.

The Pictures of Witness Schattmann is symptomatic of the extent to which the Holocaust could sometimes achieve prominent representation in the GDR, but only in such a fashion that this representation could be made compatible with the ideology of GDR anti-fascism. A particularly noteworthy aspect of the film is its mapping out of a path for Jewish people to overcome their religious and ethnic affiliation in order to identify with the class struggle and the GDR as an anti-fascist state. This reflects the position of a number of high-ranking SED officials and cultural figures, such as Politburo members Hermann Axen and Albert Norden, who, despite their Jewish origins, neither identified with the wider Jewish community nor perceived the Holocaust as relevant to their identity as a phenomenon distinct from the anti-fascist struggle (O'Doherty 1997, 13–14). Where Jewish people were perceived as resistant to giving up their allegiance to Judaism in favour of an anti-fascist identification, however, the SED regarded them with suspicion.

The party leadership, following the Soviets' lead, identified Zionism (and Israel as its representative) with capitalism and imperialism, which provided a helpful narrative against any assumption of GDR responsibility for reparations when the Federal Republic began to develop such policies in the 1950s. In addition, the late Stalinist period from 1948, with its show trials of Jewish communists regarded as fascist agents both within the Soviet Union and in its satellite states, was characterized by an atmosphere of antisemitic hostility which was taken up by the SED. A number of purges of the SED's ranks in the early 1950s disproportionately affected party members of Jewish descent (O'Doherty 1997, 32–43) or those who had associated themselves with the Jewish cause (Herf 1994). In the GDR, although there were no explicitly antisemitic show trials, many religious leaders from the

Jewish community responded to the Slansky trial in Czechoslovakia and announcement of the 'Doctors' Plot' in the Soviet Union by leaving for the Federal Republic in January of 1953, to be followed by around 25% of the GDR's Jewish population, according to some estimates (O'Doherty 1997, 39). From the mid-1950s, however, an individual's Jewish heritage was no longer widely perceived as grounds for exclusion for politically committed socialists. Judaism itself was viewed purely as a religious practice (Fox 1999, 5), which, like other religions, was an anachronism which would be overcome in the development of socialism (O'Doherty 1997, 47). In relation to the National Socialist past, there nevertheless remained a distinct hierarchy, in which Jewish suffering, while acknowledged in the system of 'honorary pensions', received a less substantial compensation than that reserved for those who were deemed to have actively resisted National Socialism (Hölscher 2002, 198).

Although it should also be noted that the GDR state provided significant subsidies to Jewish communities, primarily for the upkeep of synagogues and cemeteries (Maser 1995, 355), it was only in the 1980s, when the GDR was seeking wider international recognition, that it became politically opportune to commemorate Jewish suffering as a historical phenomenon in its own right. Whereas in the 1960s the GDR sought recognition from states such as Iraq, Syria, and Egypt, and had become close to the Palestine Liberation Organization (Burgauer 1993, 194), its desire to build closer ties with the West in the 1980s expressed itself in a new commitment to invest in the commemoration of the 50th anniversary of the *Reichskristallnacht* pogrom of 9 November 1938 (Schmid 2004) and in the reconstruction of the synagogue in Oranienburgerstraße in East Berlin as a cultural centre. By this time, however, practising religious Jews in the GDR numbered only 380 (Burgauer 1993, 145).

36.5   GDR Citizens' Perceptions of National Socialism

The focus of this chapter so far on official memory politics in the GDR tells us little about how the state's narrative on the causes of National Socialism and the nature of the anti-fascist struggle played a role in shaping ordinary citizens' understanding of German history, or of their own role in that history. Clearly, we should be extremely wary of assuming that a top-down memory politics, even one practised by a dictatorship, produces a uniform view of history within the population. It is certainly the case that the anti-fascist narrative was a key feature of the educational system and dominated all kinds of public memorialization and commemoration, but it ultimately only offered one interpretative frame within which individuals could make sense of their own and their family's history against the broader backdrop of the history of National Socialism and the subsequent emergence of the state socialist regime.

The memories of family and friends, as well as later critical assessments of the GDR's understanding of National Socialism and anti-fascist resistance by critical-loyal GDR cultural intellectuals in the 1970s and 1980s, not to mention access to Western media, potentially provided other frames, which the official narrative had to contend with (Sabrow 2000, 13; Plum 2015, 201–207). GDR citizens were also more than capable of interpreting the SED's version of history in light of their own contemporary experience of socialist society (Olsen 2015, 44). Such everyday interactions with the state-driven politics of anti-fascist memory are hard to capture in retrospect, especially since individuals' present-day attitudes to the views they held under SED rule are coloured by their subsequent experience of the regime's collapse (Moller 2003). The archives of work produced by schoolchildren between 1945 and 1949 studied by Benita Blessing give us a sense of how young citizens could draw upon official discourse to discuss their own experiences of war and National Socialism (2006, 128–139). However, these examples originate in a context in which particular normative expectations were in play, and are limited to a snapshot of a particular phase in the development of the anti-fascist narrative. There is clearly more work to be done in this area.

Research carried out in the GDR itself has left behind little material which might give us a sense of how ordinary citizens understood the National Socialist past (Olsen 2015, 133): Lutz Niethammer suggests that this may have been a result of the GDR's suspicion of the population, which was regarded as being bound to some extent to fall behind the progressive position occupied by the SED as the avant-garde of the working class (Niethammer, von Plato, and Wierling 1991, 10). The Central Institute for Youth Research (*Zentralinstitut für Jugendforschung*) in Leipzig did manage to conduct some research in this vein at the very end of the 1980s, when it found that 78% of 15- and 16-year-olds identified positively with anti-fascism (Friedrich and Griese 1991, 132), while expressing a distinct scepticism about the leadership of the SED (135–150) and its view of history (151). Mark Allinson's study of popular opinion in Thuringia from 1948 to 1968 provides similar findings from an earlier period. As he notes, organs of the state did compile reports on popular attitudes to Soviet and SED policy, but these do not allow us to assume a clear link between the public's acknowledgement of the anti-fascist heritage of the SED and any broader acceptance of the political and economic system it created (Allinson 2000, 160–163).

Nevertheless, a case can be made that the GDR's official memory politics did shape a specifically East German view of the Second World War in broad terms. In the first decade after German unification, former GDR citizens still tended to see Hitler's war in the East as the most significant catastrophe of the period 1933–1945, while westerners were more likely to name the Holocaust (Kocka 1998, 104). As noted above, many GDR citizens had a positive view of the anti-fascist tradition, even if this did not translate into faith in the SED. Some researchers argued that this positive view of anti-fascism would have negative consequences in terms of the unwillingness of older citizens of the former GDR to assimilate to the culture of contrition for National Socialist crimes which has come to dominate in the Federal Republic (e.g. Faulenbach, Leo, and Weberskirch 2000, 332–333; Leo 2009). Others have proposed that, because the GDR's anti-fascism was merely *verordnet* (imposed) by the SED, it failed to demand of GDR citizens that they overcome the ideological legacies of Nazism, rather than simply paying lip service to the party's view of history. Prominent instances of xenophobic violence in eastern Germany after unification seemed to add weight to this argument, by apparently providing evidence of a 'failed' anti-fascist socialization in the GDR (Waibel 2014). However, such violence was by no means confined to the former east.

36.6   Coming to Terms with Anti-Fascism

Such criticisms of the GDR's official politics of memory are part of a wider discussion about the potential value of the anti-fascist tradition for the united Germany, which was particularly prominent in the years immediately following the fall of the SED regime. The 1990s saw the development in the united Germany of what Andrew Beattie has called a 'state-mandated' memory, which has sought to install a modified version of the totalitarian paradigm for the interpretation of the 'two German dictatorships' (2011). Referring back to the totalitarianism theory of the 1950s, which equated the National Socialist and Stalinist dictatorships, defenders of the 'totalitarian' paradigm have argued for a comparability of the two regimes, while maintaining a privileged status for National Socialism, determined by the Holocaust. Commentators who have resisted attempts to 'save' anti-fascism as a valid historical identification after the collapse of the GDR have criticized anti-fascist ideology as a delegitimizing strategy aimed at the political and economic system of the Federal Republic, which they claim was mobilized not just by the former SED regime, but also by West Germany's own 'generation of '68' against the post-war capitalist order (Diner 1996; Grunenberg 1993, 162).

As Robert Erlinghagen (1997) shows, a wide range of actors have been involved in this debate, from the left to the far right. However, for those on the 'new right' and their more radical counterparts, the attempt to maintain the notion of anti-fascism, free from the taint of SED ideology, is a dangerous move by the left to preserve the stigma around nationalism and right-wing politics which they had sought unsuccessfully to throw off at the time of the 'historians' debate' of the mid-1980s, when conservative historians attempted to explain National Socialism as a kind of allergic reaction to Soviet communism. Equally, for CDU politicians and the intellectuals close to them, the continued attraction of left-wing politics after the end of the Cold War presents a real political threat, in that the former SED, renamed twice since unification as the Party of Democratic Socialism (*Partei des demokratischen Sozialismus*, or PDS) and (from 2007) DIE LINKE, has shown itself capable of working with the SPD in regional government, essentially blocking out the CDU as 'grand coalition' partner for the SPD (most notably in Berlin from 2001 to 2011). In this context, and from the point of view of the editors of a volume of essays published by the CDU's Konrad Adenauer Foundation in 2002, the PDS/DIE LINKE are regarded as instrumentalizing anti-fascism as a consensual term in order to shift the political centre ground in the Federal Republic to the left (Agethen, Jesse, and Neubert 2002, 16).

Although the debate around anti-fascism has been significantly quieter since the early 2000s, such controversy demonstrates the extent to which the GDR's official memory politics has itself been subject to a process of historical reckoning. Indeed, much of the research which has emerged on GDR memory politics in the 1990s and 2000s can be understood as contributing to that reckoning. Whether the GDR's legacy will actually lead to divergent understandings of the National Socialist past in the long term between East and West seems doubtful, however, given that the historical understanding of younger generations appears to have converged with remarkable speed after unification (von Borries 1995), when the curricula, exhibitions, and many of the memorials which once underpinned the GDR's version of the history of National Socialism were quickly adapted, removed, or fell into neglect (see Zorn 1994 for a highly partisan account of the latter process). As a recent television reworking of Apitz's *Naked Among Wolves* (2015) suggests, however, the legacy of communist resistance to National Socialism, which underpinned the GDR's memory politics, has not entirely disappeared from the scene, and may in fact still be in the process of being assimilated into post-unification cultural memory.

References

Agethen, Manfred, Jesse, Eckhard, and Neubert, Erhardt. 2002. 'Vorwort der Herausgeber.' In *Der missbrauchte Antifaschismus: DDR-Staatsdoktrin und Lebenslüge der deutschen Linken*, 13–18. Freiburg, Basle, and Vienna: Herder.

Allinson, Mark. 2000. *Politics and Popular Opinion in East Germany 1945–1968*. Manchester: Manchester University Press.

Backes, Uwe. 2009. 'Antifaschismus: Anmerkungen zu Begriff und Geschichte.' In *Der Antifaschismus als Staatsdoktrin der DDR*, edited by Stephanie Pasler, 6–15. Bonn: Konrad Adenauer Stiftung.

Barck, Simone. 2000. 'Widerstands-Geschichten und Helden-Berichte: Momentaufnahmen antifaschistischer Diskurse in den fünfziger Jahren.' In *Geschichte als Herrschaftsdiskurs: Der Umgang mit der Vergangenheit in der DDR*, edited by Martin Sabrow, 119–173. Cologne, Weimar, and Vienna: Böhlau.

Beattie, Andrew. 2011. 'The Politics of Remembering the GDR: Official and State-Mandated Memory since 1990.' In *Remembering the German Democratic Republic: Divided Memory in a United Germany*, edited by David Clarke and Ute Wölfel. 23–34. Basingstoke, UK: Palgrave Macmillan.

Bessel Richard. 2009. *Germany, 1945: From War to Peace*. London: Simon & Schuster.

Best, Heinrich and Salheiser, Axel. 2006. 'Shadows of the Past: National Socialist Backgrounds of the GDR's Functional Elites.' *German Studies Review* 29, 589–602.

Blessing, Benita. 2006. *The Antifascist Classroom: Denazification in Soviet-occupied Germany, 1945–1949*. Basingstoke, UK: Palgrave Macmillan.

Burgauer, Erica. 1993. *Zwischen Erinnerung und Verdrängung: Juden in Deutschland nach 1945*. Reinbek bei Hamburg: Rowohlt.

Danyel, Jürgen. 1995. 'Die Opfer- und Verfolgtenperspektive als Grundkonsens? Zum Umgang mit der Schuldfrage in der DDR.' In *Die geteilte Vergangenheit: Zum Umgang mit Nationalsozialismus und Widerstand in beiden deutschen Staaten*, edited by Jürgen Daniel, 31–46. Berlin: Akademie.

Danyel, Jürgen. 1999. 'Die SED und die "kleinen Pgs": Zur politischen Integration der ehemaligen NSDAP-Mitgliedern in der SBZ/DDR.' In *Helden, Täter und Verräter: Studien zum DDR-Antifaschismus*, 177–196. Berlin: Metropol.

Diner, Dan. 1996. 'On the Ideology of Antifascism.' *New German Critique*, Vol. 67: 123–132.

Erlinghagen, Robert. 1997. *Die Diskussion um den Begriff des Antifaschismus seit 1989/1990*. Berlin and Hamburg: Argument.

Faulenbach, Bernd. 1993. 'Zur Funktion des Antifaschismus in der SBZ/DDR.' *Deutschland Archiv* 6, 754–759.

Faulenbach, Bernd, Leo, Annette, and Weberskirch, Klaus. 2000. *Zweierlei Geschichte: Lebensgeschichte und Geschichtsbewusstsein von Arbeitnehmern in Ost- und Westdeutschland*. Essen: Klartext.

Fox, Thomas C. 1999. *Stated Memory: East Germany and the Holocaust*. Rochester, NY: Camden House.

Friedrich, Walter and Griese, Hartmut, eds. 1991. *Jugend und Jugendforschung in der DDR: Gesellschaftspolitische Situation, Sozialisation und Mentalitätsentwicklung in den achtziger Jahren*. Opladen: Leske + Budrich.

Fulbrook, Mary. 2011. *Dissonant Lives: Generations and Violence Through the German Dictatorships*. Oxford: Oxford University Press.

Gilsenbach, Reimar. 2001. 'Sinti und Roma – vergessene Opfer.' In *Vielstimmiges Schweigen: Neue Studien zum DDR-Antifascishismus*, edited by Annette Leo and Peter Reif-Spirek, 67–83. Berlin: Akademie.

Groehler, Olaf. 1992. 'Antifaschismus – Vom Umgang mit einem Begriff.' In *Zweierlei Bewältigung: Vier Beiträge über den Umgang mit der NS-Vergangenheit in den beiden deutschen Staaten*, edited by Ulrich Herbert and Olaf Groehler, 29–40. Hamburg: Ergebnisse.

Groehler, Olaf. 1995. 'Verfolgten- und Opfergruppen im Spannungsfeld der politischen Auseinandersetzungen in der SBZ und DDR.' In *Die geteilte Vergangenheit. Zum Umgang mit Nationalsozialismus und Widerstand in beiden deutschen Staaten*, edited by Jürgen Daniel, 17–30. Berlin: Akademie.

Grunenberg, Antonia. 1993. *Antifaschismus: Ein deutscher Mythos*. Reinbek: rororo.

Herf, Jeffrey. 1994. 'East German Communists and the Jewish Question: The Case of Paul Merker.' *Journal of Contemporary History* 29, 627–661.

Hermlin, Stefan. 1951. *Die erste Reihe*. Berlin: Neues Leben.

Hölscher, Christoph. 2002. *NS-Verfolgte im 'antifaschistischen Staat': Vereinnahmung und Abgrenzung in der ostdeutschen Wiedergutmachung (1945–1989)*. Berlin: Metropol.

Jarausch, Konrad H. 1991. 'The Failure of East German Antifascism: Some Ironies of History as Politics.' *German Studies Review* 14, 85–102.

Kocka, Jürgen. 1998. 'Geteilte Erinnerungen: Zweierlei Geschichtsbewusstsein im vereinten Deutschland.' *Blätter für deutsche und internationale Politik* 1, 104–111.

Kulturamt Prenzlauer Berg and Aktives Museum Berlin. 1992. *Mythos Antifaschismus: Ein Traditionskabinett wird besichtigt*. Berlin: Links.

Lapp, Peter Joachim. 2000. *Ulbrichts Helfer: Wehrmachtsoffiziere im Dienst der DDR*. Bonn: Bernard und Graefe.

Lemke, Michael. 1995. 'Instrumentalisierter Antifaschismus und SED-Kampagnen im deutschen Sonderkonflikt 1960–1968.' In *Die geteilte Vergangenheit: Zum Umgang mit Nationalsozialismus und Widerstand in beiden deutschen Staaten*, edited by Jürgen Daniel, 61–86. Berlin: Akademie.

Leo, Annette. 1992. 'Antifaschismus und Kalter Krieg.' In *Mythos Antifaschismus: Ein Traditionskabinett wird besichtigt*, 143–153. Berlin: Links.

Leo, Annette. 2009. 'Antifaschismus.' In *Erinnerungsorte der DDR*, edited by Martin Sabrow, 30–42. Munich: C.H. Beck.

Maser, Peter. 1995. 'Juden und jüdische Gemeinden in der Innenpolitik der DDR.' In *Schwieriges Erbe: Der Umgang mit Nationalsozialismus und Antisemitismus in Österreich, der DDR und der Bundesrepublik*, edited by Werner Bergmann, Rainer Erb, and Albert Lichtblau, 339–368. Frankfurt am Main: Campus.

Meuschel, Sigrid. 1992. *Legitimation und Parteiherrschaft: Zum Paradoxon von Stabilität und Revolution in der DDR*. Frankfurt am Main: Suhrkamp.

Moller, Sabine. 2003. *Vielfache Vergangenheit: Öffentliche Erinnerungskulturen und Familienerinnerungen an die NS-Zeit in Ostdeutschland*. Tübingen: Diskord

Monteath, Peter. 1999. 'Narratives of fascism in the GDR: Buchenwald and the "Myth of Antifascism".' *The European Legacy: Toward New Paradigms* 4, 99–112.

Naimark, Norman M. 1997. *The Russians in Germany: A History of the Soviet Zone of Occupation, 1945–1949*. Cambridge, MA: Belknap.

Niethammer, Lutz, ed. 1994. *Der 'gesäuberte' Antifaschismus: Die SED und die roten Kapos von Buchenwald*. Berlin: Akademie.

Niethammer, Lutz, von Plato, Alexander, and Wierling, Dorothee. 1991. *Die volkseignene Erfarhung: Eine Archäologie des Lebens in der Industrieprovinz der DDR*. Berlin: Rowohl.

Niven, Bill. 2002. *Facing the Nazi Past: United Germany and the Legacy of the Third Reich*. London and New York: Routledge.

Niven, Bill. 2007. *The Buchenwald Child: Truth, Fiction and Propaganda*. Rochester, NY: Camden House.

Nothnagle, Alan. 1993. 'From Buchenwald to Bismarck: Historical Myth-Building in the German Democratic Republic, 1945–1989.' *Central European History* 26, 91–113.

O'Doherty, Paul. 1997. *The Portrayal of Jews in GDR Prose Fiction*. Amsterdam: Rodopi.

Olsen, John Berndt. 2015. *Tailoring the Truth: Politicizing the Past and Negotiating Memory in East Germany*. New York and Oxford: Berghahn Books.

Oversch, Manfred. 1995. *Buchenwald und die DDR oder die Suche nach Selbstlegitimation*. Göttingen: Vandenhoeck & Ruprecht.

Pawlowski, Jan. 2009. *Inventing a Socialist Nation: Heimat and the Politics of Everyday Life in the GDR, 1945–1990*. Cambridge: Cambridge University Press.

Plum, Catherine. 2015. *Antifascism after Hitler: East German Youth and Socialist Memory, 1949–1989*. London and New York: Routledge.

Pritchard, Gareth. 2000. *The Making of the GDR 1945–1953: From Antifascism to Stalinism*. Manchester: Manchester University Press.

Ring, Florian. 1996. *Die Darstellung des Widerstandes gegen Hitler in der SBZ/DDR – in Bezug auf die Schulbücher sowie in der Publizistik der NVA*. Sinzheim: Pro Universitate.

Sabrow, Martin. 2000. 'Einleitung: Geschichtsdiskurs und Doktringesellschaft.' In *Geschichte als Herrschaftsdiskurs: Der Umgang mit der Vergangenheit in der DDR*, edited by Martin Sabrow, 9–35. Cologne, Weimar, and Vienna: Böhlau.

Sayner, Joanne. 2013. *Reframing Antifascism: Memory, Genre and the Life Writings of Greta Kuckhoff*. Basingstoke, UK: Palgrave Macmillan.

Schieber, Elke. 2007. *Recherche zu einem Fernsehfilm: Die Bilder des Zeugen Schattmann*. Potsdam: Filmmuseum Potsdam.

Schmid, Harald. 2004. *Antifaschismus und Judenverfolgung: Die 'Reichskristallnacht' als politischer Gedenktag in der DDR*. Göttingen: V&R Unipress.

Vogt, Timothy R. 2000. *Denazification in Soviet-Occupied Germany. Brandenburg, 1945–1948*. Cambridge, MA and London: Harvard University Press.

Von Borries, Bodo. 1995. *Das Geschichtsbewusstsein der Jugendlicher: Eine repräsentative Untersuchung über die Vergangenheitsdeutungen, Gegenwartswahrnehmungen und Zukunftserwartungen von Schülerinnen und Schülern in Ost- und Westdeutschland*. Weinheim and Munich: Juventa.

Waibel, Harry. 2014. *Der gescheiterte Antifaschimsus der SED: Rassismus in der DDR*. Frankfurt am Main: Peter Lang.

Wolf, Christa. 1990. *Reden im Herbst*. Berlin: Aufbau.

Wolfgram, Mark A. 2006. 'The Holocaust through the Prism of East German Television: Collective Memory and Audience Perceptions.' *Holocaust and Genocide Studies* 20, 57–79.

Wolfrum, Edgar. 2002. 'Die beiden Deutschland.' In *Verbrechen erinnern: Die Auseinandersetzung mit Holocaust und Völkermord*, edited by Volkhard Knigge and Norbert Frei, 133–149. Munich: C.H. Beck.

Zorn, Monika, ed. 1994. *Hitlers zweimal getötete Opfer: Westdeutsche Endlösung des Antifaschismus auf dem Gebiet der DDR*. Freiburg: Ahrimann.

CHAPTER THIRTY-SEVEN

Presenting and Teaching the Past*

KARL HEINRICH POHL AND ASTRID SCHWABE

37.1 Introduction

After the Second World War, remembrance of the Third Reich was mainly determined by political and military events. The Holocaust and associated issues, on the other hand, were often ignored (Young 1993; Assmus 2002; Lässig 2006, 184–210; Davies and Szejnmann 2007). First and foremost, the victims (non-Jewish as well as Jewish) were left alone with their experiences of suffering. During the Cold War the discourse on the Holocaust was mainly overshadowed by discussions on 'totalitarianism' and 'democracy'. And from the late 1960s onwards, in the context of the Nazi trials in Germany and Israel especially, the international public focused on the perpetrators rather than on the victims. At the same time, the history of 'Fascist everyday life' moved centre stage (Smith 2000; Wandres 1995; Wojak 2001).

In Western Europe, early discourses oscillated predominantly around the question of German responsibility and guilt (Frei 1996; Frei and Steinbacher 2001; Bergmann, Erb, and Lichtblau 1995; Herf 1997; Danyel 1995). These debates were integral to the process of identity formation of the two German states (Möwe 2007) and also contributed to the self-discovery of several (Western) European nations, often by distancing themselves from Germany with its history of severe guilt and by marginalizing their own (potential or joint) responsibility (Uhl 2003; Knigge 2005; Gautschi, Zülsdorf-Kersting, and Ziegler 2013; Flacke 2004; Köhr and Lässig 2007, 235–260).

For some decades, however, European debates have been incorporated into a broader, international discussion on the Holocaust, which is considerably different and takes many different levels into account (Novick 2001). The discourse is still a

* Translated by Christine Brocks.

A Companion to Nazi Germany, First Edition. Edited by Shelley Baranowski, Armin Nolzen, and Claus-Christian W. Szejnmann.
© 2018 John Wiley & Sons Ltd. Published 2018 by John Wiley & Sons Ltd.

'vanishing point of the culture of remembrance in Europe' (Probst 2003, 45–58), but has, in addition, emerged into a global point of reference. It is quite evident that we live in a new era of global commemoration (Morsch 2013, 97).

Social transformation processes in Eastern and Southeastern Europe paved the way for this development after the end of the Cold War in Europe. Often, they were closely linked to the challenge of a historical repositioning (Mihok 2005; Faulenbach and Jelich 2006), which resulted in the development of new tendencies of Holocaust commemoration in the respective countries that up to then had been frequently ignored (David-Fox, Holquist, and Martin 2014; Sachse and Wolfrum 2008).

However, the Stockholm declaration of the 'International Forum on the Holocaust' on 28 January 2000 – according to Welzer and Lenz (2007), the starting point and foundation of a transnational culture of commemoration – was essential for addressing the Holocaust in all its facets. The declaration made the remembrance of the Holocaust worldwide a moral and political imperative (The Stockholm International Forum 2002; Assmann 2013b, 67–78). An international Holocaust Memorial Day on 27 January (in remembrance of the liberation of Auschwitz) was established, which, some have remarked, has increased the rather questionable 'obsession with history' (Assmann and Frevert 1999).

Since then, two tendencies have shaped international commemoration (Diner 2007). On the one hand, the discussion has been universalized and dehistoricized (Levy and Sznaider 2007; Eckel and Moisel 2008; Junker 2001, 122–139; Steininger 1994). The Holocaust is increasingly understood as a general human disaster mirroring 'evil itself' instead of as a very real and specific catastrophe caused at a certain time by German perpetrators, who can be identified through historical investigation. The Holocaust 'as a universal "container" for memories of myriad victims' (Levy and Sznaider 2006, 195) serves as a reference point for discussing genocides, peace, and moral rules in general and to draw universal 'lessons'. Such an approach often ignores the history of the actual victims, which is a worrying development, and not only from their perspective. It overlooks 'illuminating and self-reflective aspects' and neglects addressing the perspective of 'both victims and perpetrators' (Knigge 2005, 457). Instead, discussions have a high moral impetus (Assmann 2013a, 56–58).

At the same time, national narratives have emerged in many countries, even more so during the last years. Some European countries are emphatically 'obsessed' with construing their 'own' Holocaust narrative: in Norway, France, Switzerland, Ukraine, Hungary, and Latvia, for instance, the Holocaust is increasingly (and very controversially) discussed regarding the question whether, or to what extent, their own respective populations had been involved (Altrichter 2006).

Considerable changes in commemorating the Holocaust worldwide in the course of the third millennium are imminent, not least because of the shift from collective to cultural memory (Assmann 2006; Assmann and Frevert 1999; Giesecke and Welzer 2012; Koselleck 1994, 17–132). Given that the last members of the eyewitness generation are passing away, secondary accounts of the history of the Holocaust replace primary narrations nearly everywhere. Instead of eyewitnesses, these secondary accounts will determine how the Holocaust will be addressed and discussed in future, and what will be forgotten, what remembered, and how (Paul and Schoßig 2010). This places an even greater emphasis on the question of how to appropriately represent the Holocaust, the unimaginable.

37.2 'Official' Remembrance: School History Books

Since, at present, remembering the Holocaust effectively falls within the remit of the state, school books still represent a reliable indicator of the officially favoured, most widespread, and probably dominant version of Holocaust remembrance – despite the increasing role of other (digital) media (Fuchs, Pingel, and Radkau 2001; Davies 2000; Lecomte 2001). According to a recently completed global empirical study on the presentation of the Holocaust in school history books and curricula of further education commissioned by UNESCO, roughly 50% of all curricula directly refer to the Holocaust. They show many similarities (Carrier, Fuchs, and Messinger 2015) – for instance, in regard to representational patterns – but also differences in the strategic focus and specific omissions. Some curricula, to give an example, mention only Jews as victims of the Holocaust while ignoring Romani, disabled people, homosexuals, politically persecuted persons, and others. The study found several narrative idiosyncrasies, such as in the usage of the terms 'Shoah', 'Holocaust', 'genocide', 'massacre', and 'extermination', to give one example.

One of the most important tendencies we can identify is a certain domestication (Pettigraw 2009), that is, an emphasis on the local dimension of the Holocaust or on how the Holocaust is interpreted in regard to the people of a certain area. This is particularly true for some Eastern European countries. At the same time, relativization and banalization of the Holocaust take place on a worldwide scale. In many countries not directly involved in the Holocaust, a generalized, 'updated', and 'moralized' account is common, referring to recent or current problems, for instance by using the phrase 'nuclear holocaust' (Schmid 2008, 177). The tendency to highlight comparative studies on different genocides past and present is particularly, but not exclusively, common for countries outside of Europe. Here, the Holocaust is (and will probably be even more so in future) discussed in the context of a general 'peace and human rights' education and various forms of fascination with the Holocaust are analysed, aiming at prevention strategies for the future and the political will to strengthen democracy. This is particularly true for South Africa, Columbia, Chile, Brazil, and Rwanda – that is, for countries with a history of dictatorship or recent genocide.

The study also confirms the assumption that curricula and school books in countries not directly or indirectly involved (such as Angola, Bahrain, New Zealand, Iceland, Mozambique, Ghana, and Bolivia) and without any actual historical memory of the Holocaust, only rarely mention it; and if it is mentioned, then it is often incorporated into different historical frameworks, for instance into the history of the Second World War, such as in China. It is due to this selective approach that there is still a substantial lack of empirical knowledge worldwide (even in Europe) on the 'historical Holocaust', that is, on the actual events. In the curricula of Finland and Zimbabwe, for instance, the historical complexity of the Holocaust is replaced by a dehistoricized universal conception.

In Germany, on the other hand, where the Holocaust is a key topic in school, a certain feeling of 'saturation' is noticeable. Thus there are discussions about whether or not an historical engagement with the Holocaust – a topic apparently deeply rooted in the German culture of remembrance – can foster democratic and civic values. Some argue that the history of National Socialism should be told from the beginning instead from its terrible end (the unimaginable Holocaust and the war of extermination). According to this position, the decisive issue is why and how the Nazis succeeded in winning over the majority of the German population (Giesecke and Welzer 2012), and an analysis of the gradual dissolution of the democratic and constitutional state. This approach is believed to offer better chances to raise awareness of the dangers for a free society – even today – among young people. It remains to be seen if this approach is likely to prevail in school books.

37.3   The Holocaust in the Museum

The seemingly endless new 'Holocaust hype' has also influenced the museum sector, not only in Germany, but throughout Europe (Köhr 2012; Pieper 2006; Engelhardt 2002). Between 2000 and 2011 at least eight key permanent exhibitions on the Holocaust opened in Germany and Israel alone (Köhr 2012, 12; März 2008). As with curricula and school history books, they show considerable similarities and also noticeable differences in terms of design and presentation.

Differences between Holocaust museums – just like between different public discourses – are mainly due to their master narrative. Poland, Lithuania, France, Hungary (Fritz 2008, 29–149; Holocaust Memorial Center Budapest 2006), Germany, the United States, Israel, or Italy – every nation has developed its own approaches and perspectives that are characterized by continuous change. Thus there are not just 'two kinds of Holocaust', but 'several' (Zuckermann 1999). It is striking that even in Germany, Holocaust remembrance and 'guilt discourse' are increasingly seen as separate topics (which only partially applies to Eastern European countries). Instead, there is an emphasis on information, on rational and less emotional aspects and on education to develop civic and democratic values. Thus, apart from national peculiarities, the tendencies of dehistoricization and universalization of remembrance are also reflected in museum exhibitions. Nearly all (new) museums try to create empathy; this corresponds to a global current. Individualization and personification are the main presentational tools. It is noteworthy that the focus is predominantly on the victims: 'victim and survivor narratives are [still] allotted the role of the bearers of remembrance in museum exhibitions' (Köhr 2012, 245).

Furthermore, nearly all museum exhibitions neglect more or less fundamental aspects of history didactics. It appears that exhibiting the Holocaust cannot be done without tapping into emotions and feelings of being overwhelmed, and not without ignoring controversies and an open understanding of history. This, however, involves the risk of turning history into a morality tale. Many exhibition managers and curators respond to this challenge by contextualization, substantiating, and putting lines of action into historical context.

We can distinguish between two main exhibition design concepts: one is predominantly narrative, the other is documentary and argumentative (Knigge 2005, 405). The more distant the Holocaust is in geographic and emotional terms, the more common are exhibitions based on authenticity. The USHMM (United States Holocaust Memorial Museum) in Washington, DC, for instance, offers a clear storyline: coherent, convincing, comprehensible, offering the opportunity to identify with the persecuted persons and to distinguish easily between 'good' and 'evil' (Berenbaum 1993; United States Holocaust Memorial Museum 2001, 2007; Weinberg and Elieli 1995).

The documentary approach, favoured not least in Germany, offers 'scientificity' in reply. The exhibition in the concentration camp memorial at Buchenwald, near Weimar, for instance, is thought- and reflection-provoking and, in so doing, counters potential emotions. It suggests that there is not just 'one' history of the Holocaust.

And yet, the concepts of universalization and individualization are not necessarily mutually exclusive. Universalization aiming at an education for moral, civic, and democratic values has to rely on individualized approaches to reach the audience. Individualization, on the other hand, requires a universal perspective in order to convey history based on examples instead of getting lost in trivia and individual stories, a framework that a universalizing approach can provide (Köhr 2012).

37.4 Snapshots of Germany in 2015: Should Victims Be Trampled On?

'Stumbling Stones' (*Stolpersteine*) is a project initiated by German artist G. Demnig: small brass plaques sunk in the pavement remind passers-by of the fate of individual victims of National Socialism. There are currently (January 2015) 70 000 inserted stones in Germany (6000 in Berlin) and in 18 other European countries. Demnig's 'stumbling stones' can be seen as the largest decentralized memorial worldwide. During recent years they have become the subject of a fierce debate, particularly in Munich, the capital of the Nazi movement, and predominantly amongst Germans of Jewish faith. This controversy is paradigmatic of the fight over the 'right' way of commemorating the victims of the Holocaust in modern times.

Charlotte Knobloch, a leading German representative of the Jewish community, has taken the view that the 'stumbling stones' in fact increase the suffering of the people killed and abused by the Nazis. She has (so far) successfully enforced a ban on implementing the 'stumbling stones' in Munich: 'In my mind's eye I see the people, already on the ground, being trampled on again and again, kicked into the train carriages with heavy boots. People cowering on the ground, wounded, dying or already dead. These stones can be spit at, covered with dirt, filth and soil, smeared with animal excrements and even deliberately desecrated' (Käppner 2015). According to her, the 'stumbling stones' are most inappropriate for the purpose of commemoration. Terry Swartzberg, also a member of the Jewish community in Munich, emphasizes the exact opposite (Käppner 2015). He not only considers the 'stumbling stones' appropriate but also points out their international significance: 'The "stolpersteine" have become well known in American English just as "angst" and "kindergarten". All these words have been adopted into the American language. Just as "schlepp", originally Jiddish, we have now "stolpersteine".' According to Swartzberg, this is important for the global commemoration. His rhetorical question is: 'Who can have any objections against blonde German school girls thoughtfully standing in front of a stumbling stone and covering it with flowers?' In Munich, this fight over the appropriate form of commemoration has now gone to court.

37.5   Audio-Visual Representations of the Holocaust

Even though the impact of films and television shows cannot be measured accurately, the plethora of audio-visual representations of the Holocaust on both the small and big screen (seminal: Schultz 2012; Bruns, Dardan, and Dietrich 2012a; Corell 2009) influenced, and still influences, our memory of the Holocaust (Bruns, Dardan, and Dietrich 2012b; Zülsdorf-Kersting 2007). The facts about the annihilation of the European Jews have become well known at least since the Nuremberg trials. The documentary movie *Nazi Concentration Camps* (G. Stevens, 1945), produced by the American army, on the situation in concentration and death camps after they were liberated by the Allies, showed shocking pictures of corpses and survivors as evidence. This material was also used in many atrocity films shot later. However, they did not emphasize the Jewish victims and their suffering (Bösch 2010, 417–418; Hickethier 2003, 117–118). The silence on the Holocaust during the immediate post-war period and the early 1950s nearly everywhere (Levy and Sznaider 2007, 64) was mirrored by film and TV productions, which tended to focus on the Second World War from a military perspective. Films different from the mainstream remained niche products.

Most Israeli films and TV shows threw the spotlight on living in the new home country (Bösch 2009, 53–54; Novick 2001, 142–164; Shandler 1999, 5–80). Those countries formerly occupied by German troops, such as France, emphasized the subject of heroic resistance (Azouvi 2012, 125–151; Vatter 2009). The German 'rubble film' showed the misery and hardship of senseless wars in general (Kramer 2009; Bösch 2009, 59-60; Deutsches Filminstitut 2001; Claasen 1999). The state-controlled film industry in the German Democratic Republic idealized communist resistance and pointed to the involvement of West German elites in Nazi crimes. Soviet films glorified the resistance and the Red Army; the Holocaust was almost a taboo.

Apart from the Swedish film *Den blodiga tiden* (E. Leiser, 1960), the documentary *Nuit et brouillard* by A. Resnais (1955), which is composed of Nazi propaganda material, scenes from the atrocity films, and contemporary pictures of Majdanek and Auschwitz (Knaap 2006), is regarded as an early milestone in the 'awareness of the Holocaust' (Levy and Sznaider 2007, 17). The television broadcasting of the documentary's gruesome pictures in 1957 and the following viewings in German schools and institutions of political education initiated a different way of dealing with Nazi crimes (Bösch 2009, 55–56).

Media coverage of the Eichmann and the Auschwitz trials (in 1961 and 1963–1964 respectively) worldwide served as a catalyst for a growing and more sophisticated representation of the Holocaust, often as documentaries. From then on, the

Holocaust evolved into a 'major news story' (Shandler 1999, 83). Also, last but not least, television that had become a mass medium in the course of the 1960s contributed to this development: unlike the movie industry, it was independent of economic concerns (Bösch, 2010, 430–432; Bösch 2009, 56–70; Hickethier 2003, 119–131). Still, many productions showed the Holocaust as only one aspect among others. War events, foreign policy, and the 'fascination with Hitler' (Fischer and Lorenz 2007, 211) continued to be at the centre of attention.

The fictional TV series *Holocaust: The Story of the Family Weiss*, which was broadcast in the United States in April 1978 with 120 million viewers (Shandler 1999, 155) and many more in several other countries in the following months, is often considered the turning point in the international history of remembrance (Fischer and Lorenz 2007, 243; Shandler 1999, 155–178; Azouvi 2012, 322–331; Reichel 2004, 249–263: Novick 2001, 269–275). According to Levy and Sznaider (2007, 116–118), it even paved the way for the universalization of the Holocaust. However, in light of the great attention, the high media coverage, and the public debates it triggered in several countries, it is fair to argue that the TV series represented a culmination point rather than a caesura (Paul 2010, 15–18; Baron 2005, 23–63; Fritsche 2003, 182–183; Shandler 1999, 81–82).

The construed, personalized, and dramatized narration of the TV series transferred the (by no means new) debate on an adequate representation of the Holocaust – depending on the respective cultural adaptation – to a public level (Bösch 2010, 420–421; Paul 2010; Shandler 1999, 155–178). It became the – both positive and negative – point of reference in the discourse on visual representations of the indescribable (Reichel, Schmid, and Steinbach 2009, 19). Issues of authenticity, aestheticization, trivialization, and commercialization were under dispute. The fictional images of the gradual process of exclusion and determination were criticized in particular, because they violate the rules of aniconism and the dignity of the victims (Bannasch and Hammer 2004; Köppen and Scherpe 1997). Proponents did not deny the popularization, but considered it inevitable in order to reach a mass audience (Reichel 2004, 259–263; Thiele 2007, 298–398; Doneson 2002, 227; Shandler 1999, 155–178).

The French filmmaker Claude Lanzmann set a clear counterpoint with his documentary *Shoah* of nine hours and twenty-three minutes, even though only reaching a niche audience (Thiele 2007, 378–419; Reichel 2004, 286–301). The film, primarily consisting of interviews, avoided visual representation and did not contain any Nazi source material. In so doing, it addressed another issue of representation: many films included propaganda material produced by the perpetrators implicitly containing Nazi ideology.

Since the 1980s the range of cinematic representations has broadened. An increasing number of rather emotionalizing documentaries and feature films of varying quality focused on individual victims, perpetrators, and onlookers (Baron 2005, 65–134). Many feature films, however, use history only as the background for romantic dramas and heroic stories, in particular the 'German heritage cinema'. From the mid-1990s, 'contemporary witness TV', which disempowered the eyewitnesses, dominated the landscape of documentaries, weaving interview snippets into the narration. Whereas US American TV was predominantly keen on showing the 'survivors' (Shandler 1999, 183–211), the globally highly influential productions of the German TV channel ZDF (G. Knopp) focused on high-ranking Nazi perpetrators and onlookers, who considered themselves as victims of a difficult time, by mixing archive material and current pictures (Fischer and Lorenz 2007, 341–345).

Another – exemplary – global media event (Uhl 2008) was the movie *Schindler's List* (S. Spielberg, 1993) with over 300 million viewers (Corell 2009, 451). It rekindled the debate on fictionalizing the Holocaust (Thiele 2007, 420–471; Berghahn, Fohrmann, and Schneider 2002). Spielberg tells a 'true story' of the Holocaust in Hollywood style by tapping into the visual language of seeming authenticity (Bruns, Dardan, and Dietrich 2012a, 34–36; Fischer and Lorenz 2007, 254–246; Köppen 1997). *Schindler's List* is the most famous of those movies that focus on survival as the main theme and raise hopes by telling the story of rare moral and humane actions. Unlike such films as *Nuit et brouillard* and *Shoah*, *Schindler's List* is 'bearable' for the audience (Rosenfeld 2015, 77–92; Levy and Sznaider 2007, 141–143).

'Holocaust comedies', such as *La vita è bella* (R. Benigni, 1997) and *Train de vie* (R. Mihaileanu, 1998), represent a completely different approach that has caused fierce debates. With more or less aptitude, both films intertwine reflections on the appropriate form of representation with their narrations: assuming that the historical facts are well known, they deliberately do not pursue an authentic portrayal, but fictionalize in a twofold manner without hiding it. Unlike movies such as *Schindler's List*, they do not want the audience to identify with the victims, which is impossible anyway (Reichel 2004, 320–324; Loshitzky 2004; Oster and Uka 2003; Frölich, Loewy, and Steinert 2003).

An even more radical cinematic visualization of National Socialism and the Holocaust is offered in Quentin Tarantino's *Inglorious Basterds* (2009), controversial mainly because of its excessively graphic images (Bruns, Dardan, and Dietrich 2012a, 41; Waldhof 2010). By telling the story of a Jewish victim and a group of American Jewish soldiers assassinating the entire Nazi leadership, the film raises the question of constructing and reconstructing history and therefore 'dehistoricizes history' (Geilert and Voorgang 2015, 216).

Meanwhile, the Holocaust is a common topic in mainstream cinema. Even countries not directly involved in the Holocaust and its consequences such as China, Mexico, or the African states have produced feature films on the extermination of the European Jews (Baron 2005, 25), and every 'taboo on visual representation' is broken (Schultz 2012, 364). The history of the Holocaust has become a globally marketed commodity on commercial television with its focus on ratings. This development has fostered emotionalized narrations and narrative patterns enabling the audience to identify with the victims across borders.

37.6   Fluid and Individualized Memories: World Wide Web and Web 2.0

A climax of the current development is the representation of memories on the Internet that has changed the boundaries between private and public. The worldwide hypermedial network allows unlimited uploading and downloading of digital texts, pictures, sound, moving images, and animations about the Holocaust. Forgetting becomes the exception (Meyer 2009b, 272). Numerous 'old' representations are also to be found – at least in part – accessible for everyone.

Some of the users become producers, actively contributing to the Internet and therefore to the public historiography of the Holocaust. Almost everyone can publicize whatever they want (Schwabe 2012; Pscheida 2009, 258–259; Danker and Schwabe 2007; Hein 2007). Thus we find an unbelievable range of websites on the Holocaust: some are individual, reliable, and humorous, some are abusive, dehumanizing, and degrading, and some even openly deny the Holocaust. All of them are publicly accessible (Pfanzelter 2015). The Internet as a global network that is constantly and rapidly changing refuses to give an overview of 'its' representations of the Holocaust; research on historical content on the Internet, forms of appropriation, and prevalent 'interpersonal negotiation processes' (Burckhardt 2015, 107) regarding history is still in the early stages (Altenkirch 2015; Schwabe 2012; Meyer 2009a; Krameritsch 2007; Erll and Nünning 2004). A systematic coverage of Internet content on the history of the Holocaust, as presented by Dornik (2004), is rather pointless; even an attempt to classify websites in this respect remains rough and temporary (Schwabe 2012, 118–123; Dornik 2010).[1]

Apart from museums, memorials, and educational institutions, numerous private individuals offer Internet content on the Holocaust in all possible ways – ranging from visual snippets created from existing YouTube videos, to Facebook accounts of victims and perpetrators, to images of interviews with eyewitnesses (Burckhardt 2015; Hodel 2013). It is controversial whether or not Web 2.0 is an adequate platform for representing and mediating the history of the Holocaust. The discourse on Henio Zytomirski illustrates this (Pfanzelter 2015, 69–74). In 2009, P. Brozek opened a Facebook account in the name of the Polish Jew who was murdered in Majdanek aged nine, posting original documents and photos as well as fictional letters and diary entries of the boy, until Brozek closed the account in summer 2010. However, the posted material appeared on other 'fan' websites that were less strictly supervised. More and more antisemitic comments and adverts emerged.

In addition to the violation of Zytomirski's personal rights, critics of the project condemned the trivialization, the lack of authenticity and of contextualization, as well as the fact that it was all about entertainment rather than historical understanding. Proponents, on the other hand, welcomed the fact that social media were used to commemorate the Holocaust in order to reach more target groups. An international conference of the USHMM in December 2009 even put the potential of Internet projects on commemoration culture on its agenda. Some of them have been successfully established in the wake of these discussions.

Thus, the virtual Holocaust remembrance is characterized by great arbitrariness, a sense of 'anything goes'. In cyberspace everyone can publicly tell their story and give their opinion (Leggewie 2009; Assmann 2006; Levy and Sznaider 2007). Discussions on authenticity and adequate representation are almost obsolete and taboos no longer exist. Competition for attention and coverage seems to be even more vigorous when it comes to the vastness of the Internet. Websites that do not immediately draw interest, that do not emotionalize information and present it in small bits, that do not present history in a catchy fashion run the risk of being ignored. The manifold 'placeless' presentations of the Holocaust on the Internet, which can be cost-effectively produced and received from almost everywhere in the virtual space without borders, foster the universalization of the Holocaust memory. At the same time, the Web increases the fragmentation of remembrance when users select only presentations that match their own opinion and serve their own identity formation and construction (Pfanzelter 2015, 81; Dornik 2010, 86–88). Thus the history of the Holocaust has become more 'malleable' through (though not exclusively) the Internet. It remains to be seen whether the similarities of remembrance will increase or decrease. By any means, memory seems to be more dependent than ever on media and popular culture: 'In the virtual era the Holocaust remembrance has become a collective project with many active contributors. Historians have lost their monopoly on this history – given they ever had one' (Assmann 2013b, 76).

Note

1 Due to the fluidity of the Internet we do not attempt to provide exemplary links.

References

Altenkirch, Manuel. 2015. 'Situative Erinnerungskultur.' In *Geschichte lernen im digitalen Wandel* edited by Marko Demantowsky, and Christoph Pallaske, 59–76. Berlin: De Gruyter.

Altrichter, Helmut, ed. 2006. *GegenErinnerung – Geschichte als politisches Argument im Transformationsprozeß Ost-, Ostmittel- und Südosteuropas.* Munich: Oldenbourg.

Assmann, Aleida. 2006. *Der lange Schatten der Vergangenheit. Erinnerungskultur und Geschichtspolitik.* Munich: C.H. Beck.

Assmann, Aleida. 2013a. 'Das Crescendo der Holocaust-Erinnerung.' In *Das neue Unbehagen an der Erinnerungskultur: Eine Intervention,* edited by Aleida Assmann, 56–58. Munich: C.H. Beck.

Assmann, Aleida. 2013b. 'Die Erinnerung an den Holocaust: Vergangenheit und Zukunft.' In *Handbuch Nationalsozialismus und Holocaust,* edited by Hanns-Fred Rathenow, Birgit Wenzel, and Norbert H. Weber, 67–78. Schwalbach am Taunus: Wochenschau.

Assmann, Aleida and Frevert, Ute, eds. 1999. *Geschichtsvergessenheit: Vom Umgang mit deutschen Vergangenheiten nach 1945.* Stuttgart: DVA.

Assmus, Burkhardt, ed. 2002. *Holocaust: Der nationalsozialistische Völkermord und die Motive seiner Erinnerung.* Berlin: DHM Minerva.

Azouvi, François. 2012. *Le mythe du grand silence: Auschwitz, les Français, la mémoire.* Paris: Fayard.

Bannasch, Bettina and Hammer, Almuth, eds. 2004. *Verbot der Bilder – Gebot der Erinnerung: Mediale Repräsentationen der Schoah.* Frankfurt am Main: Campus.

Baron, Lawrence. 2005. *Projecting the Holocaust into the Present: The Changing Focus of Contemporary Holocaust Cinema.* New York: Rowman & Littlefield.

Berenbaum, Michael. 1993. *The World Must Know – The History of the Holocaust as told in the United States Holocaust Memorial Museum.* New York: Johns Hopkins University Press.

Berghahn, Klaus L., Fohrmann, Jürgen, and Schneider, Helmut J., eds. 2002. *Kulturelle Repräsentationen des Holocaust in Deutschland und den Vereinigten Staaten.* Frankfurt am Main: Peter Lang.

Bergmann, Werner, Erb, Rainer, and Lichtblau, Albert, eds. 1995. *Schwieriges Erbe: Der Umgang mit Nationalsozialismus und Antisemitismus in Österreich, der DDR und der Bundesrepublik Deutschland*. Frankfurt am Main: Campus.

Bösch, Frank. 2009. 'Der Nationalsozialismus im Dokumentarfilm: Geschichtsschreibung im Fernsehen, 1950–1990.' In *Public History: Öffentliche Darstellungen des Nationalsozialismus jenseits der Geschichtswissenschaft*, edited by Frank Bösch, and Constantin Goschler, 52–76. Frankfurt am Main: Campus.

Bösch, Frank. 2010. 'Entgrenzte Geschichtsbilder? Fernsehen, Film und Holocaust in Europa und den USA 1945–1980.' In *Massenmedien im Europa des 20. Jahrhunderts*, edited by Ute Daniel and Axel Schildt, 413–437. Cologne: Böhlau.

Bruns, Claudia, Dardan, Asal, and Dietrich, Anette, eds. 2012a. *'Welchen der Steine du hebst': Filmische Erinnerung an den Holocaust*. Berlin: Bertz + Fischer.

Bruns, Claudia, Dardan, Asal, and Dietrich, Anette. 2012b. 'Zur filmischen Erinnerung an den Holocaust. Eine Einführung.' In *'Welchen der Steine du hebst': Filmische Erinnerung an den Holocaust*, edited by Claudia Bruns, Asal Dardan, and Anette Dietrich, 17–46. Berlin: Bertz + Fischer.

Burckhardt, Hannes. 2015. 'Geschichte im Social Web: Geschichtsnarrative und Erinnerungsdiskurse auf Facebook und Twitter mit dem kulturwissenschaftlichen Medienbegriff Medium des kollektiven Gedächtnisses' analysieren.' In *Medien machen Geschichte: Neue Anforderungen an den geschichtsdidaktischen Medienbegriff im digitalen Wandel*, edited by Christoph Pallaske, 99–114. Berlin: Logos.

Carrier, Peter, Fuchs, Eckhardt, and Messinger, Torben, eds. 2015. *The International Status of Education about the Holocaust: A Global Mapping of Textbooks and Curricula*. Paris: UNESCO. http://unesdoc.unesco.org/images/0022/002287/228776e.pdf (accessed 29 November 2017).

Classen, Christoph. 1999. *Bilder der Vergangenheit: Die Zeit des Nationalsozialismus im Fernsehen der BRD 1955–1965*. Cologne: Böhlau.

Corell, Catrin, 2009. *Der Holocaust als Herausforderung für den Film: Formen des filmischen Umgangs mit der Shoah seit 1945. Eine Wirkungstypologie*. Bielefeld: transcript.

Danker, Uwe and Schwabe, Astrid. 2007. 'Historisches Lernen im Internet.' *Geschichte in Wissenschaft und Unterricht* 1, 4–19.

Danyel, Jürgen, ed. 1995. *Die geteilte Vergangenheit: Zum Umgang mit Nationalsozialismus und Widerstand in beiden deutschen Staaten*. Berlin: Oldenbourg.

David-Fox, Michael, Holquist, Peter, and Martin, Alexander M., eds. 2014. *The Holocaust in the East: Local Perpetrators and Soviet Responses*. Pittsburgh: University of Pittsburgh Press.

Davies, Ian, ed. 2000. *Teaching the Holocaust: Educational Dimensions, Principles and Practice*. New York: Continuum.

Davies, Martin. L. and Szejnmann, Claus-Christian W., eds. 2007. *How the Holocaust Looks Now: International Perspectives* New York: Palgrave.

Deutsches Filminstitut, ed. 2001. *Cinematographie des Holocaust: Die Vergangenheit in der Gegenwart. Konfrontation mit den Folgen des Holocaust im deutschen Nachkriegsfilm*. Frankfurt am Main: edition text + kritik.

Diner, Dan. 2007. *Gegenläufige Gedächtnisse: Über Geltung und Wirkung des Holocaust*. Göttingen: Vandenhoeck & Ruprecht.

Doneson, Judith E. 2002. *The Holocaust in American Film*, 2nd edn. New York: Syracuse University Press.

Dornik, Wolfram. 2004. *Erinnerungskulturen im Cyberspace: Eine Bestandsaufnahme öster-reichischer Websites zu Nationalsozialismus und Holocaust*. Berlin: Trafo.

Dornik, Wolfram. 2010. 'Internet: Maschine des Vergessens oder globales Gedächtnisspeicher: Der Holocaust in den digitalen Erinnerungskulturen zwischen 1990 und 2010.' In

Öffentliche Erinnerung und Medialisierung des Nationalsozialismus, edited by Gerhard Paul and Bernhard Schoßig, 79–97. Göttingen: Wallstein.

Eckel, Jan and Moisel, Claudia, eds. 2008. *Universalisierung des Holocaust? Erinnerungskultur und Geschichtspolitik in internationaler Perspektive*. Göttingen: Wallstein.

Engelhardt, Isabelle. 2002. *A Topography of Memory: Representations of the Holocaust at Dachau and Buchenwald in Comparison with Auschwitz, Yad Vashem and Washington DC*. Brussels: Peter Lang.

Erll, Astrid and Nünning, Ansgar, eds. 2004. *Medien des kollektiven Gedächtnisses: Konstruktivität – Historizität – Kulturspezifizität*. Berlin: De Gruyter.

Faulenbach, Bernd and Jelich, Franz-Josef, eds. 2006. *'Transformationen' der Erinnerungskulturen in Europa nach 1989*. Essen: Klartext.

Fischer, Torben and Lorenz, Matthias N., eds. 2007. *Lexikon der 'Vergangenheitsbewältigung': Debatten- und Diskursgeschichte des Nationalsozialismus nach 1945*. Bielefeld: transcript.

Flacke, Monika, ed. 2004. *Mythen der Nationen – 1945 – Arena der Erinnerungen: Eine Ausstellung des Deutschen Historischen Museums*. 2 vols. Berlin: Deutsches Historisches Museum.

Frei, Norbert. 1996. *Vergangenheitspolitik: Die Anfänge der Bundesrepublik und die NS-Vergangenheit*. Munich: C.H. Beck.

Frei, Norbert and Steinbacher, Sybille, eds. 2001. *Beschweigen und Bekennen: Die deutsche Nachkriegsgesellschaft und der Holocaust*. Göttingen: Wallstein.

Fritsche, Christiane. 2003. *Vergangenheitsbewältigung im Fernsehen: Westdeutsche Filme über dem Nationalsozialismus in den 1950er und 1960er Jahren*. Munich: Martin Meidenbauer.

Fritz, Regina. 2008. 'Gespaltene Erinnerung: Museale Darstellung des Holocaust in Ungarn.' In *Nationen und ihre Selbstbilder: Postdiktatorische Gesellschaften in Europa*, edited by Regina Fritz, Carola Sachse, and Edgar Wolfrum, 129–149. Göttingen: Wallstein.

Frölich, Margrit, Loewy, Hanno, and Steinert, Heinz, eds. 2003. *Lachen über Hitler – Auschwitz-Gelächter. Filmkomödie, Satire und Holocaust*. Frankfurt am Main: edition text + kritik.

Fuchs, Eduard, Pingel, Falk, and Radkau, Verena, eds. 2001. *Teaching the Holocaust and National Socialism: Approaches and Suggestions*. Vienna: University of Vienna.

Gautschi, Peter, Zülsdorf-Kersting, Meik, and Ziegler, Béatrice, eds. 2013. *Shoa und Schule: Lehren und Lernen im 21. Jahrhundert*. Zürich: Chronos.

Geilert, Sabrina and Voorgang, Juliane. 2015. '"Es war einmal …" historische Authentizität – Tarantinos *Inglourious Basterds* (2009): Eine filmische Absage an die Dominanz des Faktischen? Narrative Geschichtstransformationen durch Märchen und Märchenmotivik.' In *Geschichtstransformationen: Medien, Verfahren und Funktionalisierungen historischer Rezeption*, edited by Sonja Georgi et al., 213–237. Bielefeld: transcript.

Giesecke, Dana and Welzer, Harald, eds. 2012. *Das Menschenmögliche: Zur Renovierung der deutschen Erinnerungskultur*. Hamburg: Edition Körber-Stiftung.

Hein, Dörte. 2007. *Erinnerungskulturen online: Angebote, Kommunikatoren und Nutzer von Websites zu Nationalsozialismus und Holocaust*. Konstanz: UVK.

Herf, Jeffrey. 1997. *Divided Memory: The Nazi Past in the Two Germanies*. Cambridge, MA: Harvard University Press.

Hickethier, Knut. 2003. 'Die Darstellung des Massenmordes an den Juden im Fernsehen der Bundesrepublik von 1960–1980.' In *Die Shoah im Bild*, edited by Sven Kramer, 117–131. Augsburg: edition text + kritik.

Hodel, Jan. 2013. 'Internet: Das Internet und die Zeitgeschichtsdidaktik.' In *Handbuch Zeitgeschichte im Geschichtsunterricht*, edited by Markus Furrer and Kurt Messmer, 352–378. Schwalbach am Taunus: Wochenschau.

Holocaust Memorial Center Budapest, ed. 2006. *From Deprivation of Rights to Genocide – To the Memory of the Victims of the Hungarian Holocaust.* Budapest.

Junker, Detlef. 2001. 'Die Amerikanisierung des Holocaust – über die Möglichkeit, das Böse zu externalisieren und die eigene Mission fortwährend zu erneuern.' In *Die Finkelstein-Debatte,* edited by Petra Steinberger, 122–139. Munich: Piper.

Käppner, Joachim. 2015. 'Gut gemeint.' *Süddeutsche Zeitung* 181, 8–9 August, 3.

Knaap, Eout von der, ed. 2006. *Uncovering the Holocaust: The international Reception of Night and Fog.* London: Wallflower Press.

Knigge, Volkhard. 2005. 'Statt eines Nachworts: Abschied der Erinnerung: Anmerkungen zum notwendigen Wandel der Gedenkkultur in Deutschland.' In *Verbrechen erinnern: Die Auseinandersetzung mit Holocaust und Völkermord,* edited by Volkhard Knigge and Norbert Frei, 443–460. Bonn: BpB.

Köhr, Katja. 2012. *Die vielen Gesichter des Holocaust: Museale Repräsentationen zwischen Individualisierung, Universalisierung und Nationalisierung.* Göttingen: Vandenhoeck & Ruprecht.

Köhr, Katja and Lässig, Simone. 2007. 'Zwischen universellen Fragen und nationalen Deutungen: der Holocaust im Museum.' In *Europa in historisch-didaktischen Perspektiven,* edited by Bernd Schönemann and Hartmut Voith, 235–260. Idstein: Schulz-Kirchner.

Köppen, Manuel. 1997. 'Von Effekten des Authentischen Schindlers Liste: Film und Holocaust.' In *Bilder des Holocaust: Literatur – Film – Bildende Kunst,* edited by Manuel Köppen and Klaus R. Scherpe, 145–170. Cologne: Böhlau.

Köppen, Manuel and Scherpe, Klaus R. 1997. 'Zur Einführung: Der Streit um die Darstellbarkeit des Holocaust.' In *Bilder des Holocaust: Literatur – Film – Bildende Kunst,* edited by Manuel Köppen and Klaus R. Scherpe, 1–12. Cologne: Böhlau.

Koselleck, Reinhart. 1994. 'Nachwort.' In *Das Dritte Reich des Traums,* edited by Charlotte Beradt, 117–132. Frankfurt am Main: Suhrkamp.

Kramer, Sven. 2009. 'Wiederkehr und Verwandlung der Vergangenheit im deutschen Film.' In *Der Nationalsozialismus – die zweite Geschichte: Überwindung – Deutung –Erinnerung,* edited by Peter Reichel, Harald Schmid, and Peter Steinbach, 283–299. Bonn: BpB.

Krameritsch, Jakob. 2007. *Geschichte(n) im Netzwerk: Hypertext und dessen Potentiale für die Produktion, Repräsentation und Rezeption der historischen Erzählung.* Münster: Waxmann.

Lässig, Simone. 2006. 'Vom historischen Fluchtpunkt zur transnationalen Metapher: Holocaust-Erinnerung in Museen zwischen Geschichte und Moral.' In *Museum und Geschichtskultur: Ästhetik – Politik – Wissenschaft,* edited by Olaf Hartung, 184–210. Bielefeld: Verlag für Regionalgeschichte.

Lecomte, J.M. 2001. *Teaching about the Holocaust in the 21st Century.* Strasbourg: Council of Europe.

Leggewie, Claus. 2009. 'Zur Einleitung: Von der Visualisierung zur Virtualisierung des Erinnerns.' In *Erinnerungskultur 2.0: Kommemorative Kommunikation in digitalen Medien,* edited by Erik Meyer, 9–28. Frankfurt am Main: Campus.

Levy, Daniel and Sznaider, Natan. 2007. *Erinnerung im globalen Zeitalter: der Holocaust.* Frankfurt am Main: Suhrkamp. (*The Holocaust and Memory in the Global Age,* Philadelphia, PA: Temple University Press, 2007.)

Loshitzky, Yosefa. 2004: 'Forbidden Laughter? The Politics and Ethics of the Holocaust Film Comedy.' In *Re-Presenting the Shoah for the 21st Century,* edited by Ronit Lentin, 127–137. New York: Berghahn Books.

März, Susanne. 2008. *Die langen Schatten der Besatzungszeit: 'Vergangenheitsbewältigung' in Norwegen als Identitätsdiskurs.* Berlin: Berliner Wissenschafts-Verlag.

Meyer, Erik, ed. 2009a. *Erinnerungskultur 2.0: Kommemorative Kommunikation in digitalen Medien.* Frankfurt am Main: Campus.

Meyer, Erik. 2009b. 'Problematische Popularität? Erinnerungskultur, Medienwandel und Aufmerksamkeitsökonomie.' In *History Goes Pop: Zur Repräsentation von Geschichte in populären Medien und Genres*, edited by Barbara Korte and Sylvia Paletschek, 267–287. Bielefeld: transcript.

Mihok, Brigitte, ed. 2005. *Ungarn und der Holocaust: Kollaboration, Rettung und Trauma*. Berlin: Metropol Verlag.

Morsch, Günter. 2013. 'Entwicklungen, Tendenzen und Probleme einer Erinnerungskultur in Europa.' In *Handbuch Nationalsozialismus und Holocaust*, edited by Hanns-Fred Rathenow, Birgit Wenzel, and Norbert H. Weber, 95–107. Schwalbach am Taunus: Wochenschau.

Möwe, Katja. 2007. *Verarbeitung des Holocaust in der Literatur und im Lehrplan Geschichte in der sowjetischen Besatzungszone und der DDR: Mit einem Abriss über die politische Verarbeitung des Holocaust*. Munich: GRIN.

Novick, Peter, 2001. *Nach dem Holocaust: Der Umgang mit dem Massenmord*. Stuttgart: dva.

Oster, Anja and Uka, Walter. 2003. 'Der Holocaust als Filmkomödie: Komik als Mittel der Darstellung des Undarstellbaren.' In *Die Shoah im Bild*, edited by Sven Kramer, 249–266. Augsburg: edition text + kritik.

Paul, Gerhard. 2010. 'Holocaust – Vom Beschweigen zur Medialisierung: Über Veränderungen im Umgang mit Holocaust und Nationalsozialismus in der Mediengesellschaft.' In *Öffentliche Erinnerung und Medialisierung des Nationalsozialismus: Eine Bilanz der letzten dreißig Jahre*, edited by Gerhard Paul and Bernhard Schoßig, 15–38. Göttingen: Wallstein.

Paul, Gerhard and Schoßig, Bernhard, eds. 2010. *Öffentliche Erinnerung und Medialisierung des Nationalsozialismu: Eine Bilanz der letzten dreißig Jahre*. Göttingen: Wallstein.

Pettigraw, Alice. 2009. *Teaching about the Holocaust in English Secondary Schools: An Empirical Study of National Trends, Perspectives and Practice*. London: Department of Arts and Humanities, Institute of Education, University of London.

Pfanzelter, Eva. 2015. 'Inszenierung – Vernetzung – Performanz: Holocaust-Repräsentationen im Netz.' In *'Holocaust'-Fiktion: Kunst jenseits der Authentizität*, edited by Iris Roebling-Grau and Dirk Rupnow, 63–84. Munich: Fink.

Pieper, Katrin. 2006. *Musealisierung des Holocaust: Das Jüdische Museum in Berlin und das U.S. Holocaust Memorial Museum in Washingon DC – ein Vergleich*. Cologne: Böhlau.

Probst, Lothar. 2003. 'Founding Myths in Europe and the Role of the Holocaust.' *New German Critique* 90, 45–58.

Pscheida, Daniela. 2009. 'Das Internet als Leitmedium der Wissensgesellschaft und dessen Auswirkungen auf die gesellschaftliche Wissenskultur.' In *Leitmedien: Konzepte – Relevanz – Geschichte*, edited by Daniel Müller, Annemone Ligensa, and Peter Gendolla, 247–266. Bielefeld: transcript.

Reichel, Peter. 2004. *Erfundene Erinnerung: Weltkrieg und Judenmord in Film und Theater*. Munich: Hanser.

Reichel, Peter, Schmid, Harald, and Steinbach, Peter. 2009. 'Die zweite Geschichte der Hitler-Diktatur: Zur Einführung.' In *Der Nationalsozialismus – die zweite Geschichte: Überwindung – Deutung –Erinnerung*, edited by Peter Reichel, Harald Schmid, and Peter Steinbach, 7–21. Bonn: BpB.

Rosenfeld, Alvin H. 2015. *Das Ende des Holocaust*. Göttingen: Vandenhoeck & Ruprecht.

Sachse, Carola, Fritz, Regina, and Wolfrum, Edgar, eds. 2008. *Nationen und ihre Selbstbilder: Postdiktatorische Gesellschaften in Europa*. Göttingen: Wallstein.

Schmid, Harald. 2008. 'Europäisierung des Auschwitzgedenkens? Zum Aufstieg des 27. Januar 1945 als "Holocaustgedenktag" in Europa.' In *Universalisierung des Holocaust?*

Erinnerungskultur und Geschichtspolitik in internationaler Perspektive, edited by Jan Eckel and Claudia Moisel, 174–202. Göttingen: Wallstein.

Schultz, Sonja. 2012. *Der Nationalsozialismus im Film: Von Triumph des Willens bis Inglourious Basterds*. Berlin: Bertz + Fischer.

Schwabe, Astrid. 2012. *Historisches Lernen im World Wide Web: Suchen, flanieren oder forschen? Fachdidaktisch-mediale Konzeption, praktische Umsetzung und empirische Evaluation der regionalhistorischen Website Vimu.info*. Göttingen: Vandenhoeck & Ruprecht.

Shandler, Jeffrey. 1999. *While America Watches: Televising the Holocaust*. New York: Oxford University.

Smith, Gary, ed. 2000. *Hanna Arendt Revisited: 'Eichmann in Jerusalem' und die Folgen*. Frankfurt am Main: Suhrkamp.

Steininger, Rolf, ed. 1994. *Der Umgang mit dem Holocaust: Europa–USA–Israel*. Vienna: Böhlau.

The Stockholm International Forum on the Holocaust. 2002. A Conference on Education, Remembrance and Research, Stockholm 26–28 January 2000, Stockholm.

Thiele, Martina, 2007. 'Publizistische Kontroversen über den Holocaust im Film.' Dissertation, University of Göttingen.

Uhl, Heidemarie, ed. 2003. *Zvilisationsbruch und Gedächtniskultur: Das 20. Jahrhundert in der Erinnerung des beginnenden 21. Jahrhunderts*. Innsbruck: Studienverlag.

Uhl, Heidemarie, 2008. 'Medienereignis Holocaust: Nationale und transnationale Dimesionen eines globalen Gedächtnisortes.' In *Medienereignisse der Moderne*, edited by Friedrich Lenger and Ansgar Nünning, 172–191. Darmstadt: WBG.

United States Holocaust Memorial Museum, ed. 2001. *Teaching about the Holocaust: A Ressource Book for Educators*. Washington, DC.

United States Holocaust Memorial Museum, ed. 2007. *You Are My Wittnesses: Selected Quotations*. Washington, DC.

Vatter, Christoph. 2009. *Gedächtnismedium Film: Holocaust und Kollaboration in deutschen und französischen Spielfilmen seit 1945*. Würzburg: Königshausen & Neumann.

Waldhof, Lara. 2010. 'Umerzählen – Umwerten – Umwerfen: Geschichtsschreibung in "Das Leben ist schön" und "Inglourious Basterds".' In *Filme über die Shoah*, edited by Susanne Pedarnig and Lara Waldhof, 185–215. Innsbruck: Studia Universitätsverlag.

Wandres, Thomas, ed. 1995. *Auschwitz vor Gericht: Völkermord und bundesdeutsche Strafjustiz*. Munich: C.H. Beck.

Weinberg, Jeshajahu and Elieli, Rina. 1995. *The Holocaust Museum in Washington*. New York: Rizzoli International.

Welzer, Harald and Lenz, Claudia. 2007. 'Opa in Europa: Erste Befunde einer vergleichenden Tradierungsforschung.' In *Der Krieg der Erinnerung: Holocaust, Kollaboration und Widerstand im europäischen Gedächtnis*, edited by Harald Welzer, 7–40. Frankfurt am Main: Fischer.

Wojak, Irmtrud, ed. 2001. *'Gerichtstag halten über uns selbst …': Geschichte und Wirkung des ersten Frankfurter Auschwitz-Prozesses*. Frankfurt am Main: Campus.

Young, James E. 1993. *The Texture of Memory: Holocaust Memorials and Meaning*. New Haven, CT: Yale University Press.

Zuckermann, Moshe. 1999. *Zweierlei Holocaust: Der Holocaust in den politischen Kulturen Israels und Deutschlands*. Göttingen: Wallstein.

Zülsdorf-Kersting, Meik. 2007. *Sechzig Jahre danach: Jugendliche und Holocaust: Eine Studie zur geschichtskulturellen Sozialisation*. Berlin: Lit.

Further Reading

Bajohr, Frank and Löw, Andrea, eds. 2015. *Der Holocaust: Ergebnisse und neue Fragen der Forschung*, Frankfurt am Main: Fischer.

Brinkmann, Tobias. 2003. 'Amerika und der Holocaust: Die Debatte über die "Amerikanisierung des Holocaust" in den USA und ihre Rezeption in Deutschland.' *NPL* 48, 251–270.

Bromley, Patricia and Russel, Susan G. 2010. 'The Holocaust and Human Rights: A Cross-national Analysis of Holocaust Education in Social Science Textbooks, 1970–2008.' *Prospects. Quarterly Review of Comparative Education* 1, 153–177.

European Union Agency for Fundamental Rights (FRA). 2010. *Excursion to the Past: Teaching for the Future. Handbook for Teachers.* Vienna: FRA.

Fracapane, Karel and Haß, Matthias. 2014. *Holocaust Education in a Global Context.* Paris: UNESCO.

Knigge, Volkhard and Norbert Frei, eds. 2005. *Verbrechen erinnern: Die Auseinandersetzung mit Holocaust und Völkermord.* Bonn: Bpb.

Lentin, Ronit, ed. 2004. *Re-presenting the Shoah for the Twenty-first Century.* New York: Berghahn Books.

Novick, Peter. 1999. *The Holocaust in American Life.* Boston, MA: Houghton Mifflin.

OSCE. 2005. *Education on the Holocaust and on Anti-semitism: An Overview and Analysis of Educational Approaches.* Strasbourg: OSCE.

Pedarnig, Susanne and Waldhof, Lara, eds. 2010. *Filme über die Shoah.* Innsbruck: Studia Universitätsverlag.

Rathenow, Hanns-Fred, Wenzel, Birgit, and Weber, Norbert H., eds. 2013. *Handbuch Nationalsozialismus und Holocaust: Historisch-politisches Lernen, außerschulische Bildung und Lehrerbildung.* Schwalbach am Taunus: Wochenschau.

Segev, Tom. 1995. *Die siebte Million: Der Holocaust und Israels Politik der Erinnerung.* Hamburg: Rowohlt.

Index

A Companion to Nazi Germany, First Edition. Edited by Shelley Baranowski, Armin Nolzen, and Claus-Christian W. Szejnmann.
© 2018 John Wiley & Sons Ltd. Published 2018 by John Wiley & Sons Ltd.